elieved with Meal gratuitously

Monday 22d of J...

| Names | Where From | By Whom Recommended | Quantity Given |
|---|---|---|---|
| Nancy Lowry | Church Street | Revd R. Evans | 2 Stone |
| Anne Lewis | Farm beg | Do | 1/2 |
| Widow Ferguson | Britmacknany | Revd Mr Bryt | 1/2 |
| Cath Roulten | Cushowna | Do | 1/2 |
| Margt Byrne | Elphin St. | Revd Mr Evans | 1/2 |
| Elizabeth Reynolds | Farm beg | Revd R. Evans | 1/2 |
| Widow McConey | Do | Do | 1/2 |
| Widow ..... | Do | Do | 1/2 |
| Widow Flanigan | Do | Do | 1/2 |
| Widow McKeon | Do | Do | 1/2 |
| Widow Kennedy | Do | Do | 1/2 |
| Widow Monaghan | Do | Do | 1/2 |
| Widow Butler | Do | Do | 1/2 |

# ATLAS OF THE GREAT IRISH FAMINE

# THAT THE SCIENCE OF CARTOGRAPHY IS LIMITED

— and not simply by the fact that this shading of
forest cannot show the fragrances of balsam,
the gloom of cypresses
is what I wish to prove.

When you and I were first in love we drove
to the borders of Connacht
and entered a wood there.

Look down you said: this was once a famine road.

I looked down at ivy and the scutch grass
rough-cast stone had
disappeared into as you told me
in the second winter of their ordeal, in

1847, when the crop had failed twice,
Relief Committees gave
the starving Irish such roads to build.

Where they died, there the road ended
and ends still and when I take down
the map of this island, it is never so
I can say here is
the masterful, the apt rendering of

the spherical as flat, nor
an ingenious design which persuades a curve
into a plane,
but to tell myself again that

the line which says woodland and cries hunger
and gives out among sweet pine and cypress,
and finds no horizon

will not be there.

*Eavan Boland*

# ATLAS OF THE GREAT IRISH FAMINE

EDITED BY JOHN CROWLEY, WILLIAM J. SMYTH,
AND MIKE MURPHY

GIS CONSULTANT: CHARLIE ROCHE

NEW YORK UNIVERSITY PRESS
*Washington Square, New York*

First published in the U.S.A in 2012 by
New York University Press
Washington Square
New York, NY 10003
www.nyupress.org

References to Internet websites (URLs) were accurate at the time of writing. Neither the author nor New York University Press is responsible for URLs that may have expired or changed since the manuscript was prepared.

Library of Congress Cataloging-in-Publication Data
Atlas of the great Irish famine / editors, John Crowley, William J. Smyth, and Mike Murphy.
    p. cm.
 Includes bibliographical references and index.
 ISBN 978-0-8147-7148-8 (cl : acid-free paper)
 1.  Ireland--History--Famine, 1845-1852. 2.  Famines--Ireland--History--19th century. 3.  Ireland--Social conditions--19th century. 4.  Irish--Migrations--History--19th century.  I. Crowley, John, 1966- II. Smyth, William J., 1944- III. Murphy, Mike, 1966 Feb. 3.
 DA950.7.A85 2012
 940.5081--dc23                    2012018447

New York University Press books are printed on acid-free paper, and their binding materials are chosen for strength and durability. We strive to use environmentally responsible suppliers and materials to the greatest extent possible in publishing our books.

Typesetting: Cork University Press

Printed in Italy by Printer Trento

This publication has received support from the Heritage Council under the 2012 Publications Scheme

**Mr William (Bill) M. Murphy**
**Douglas Management & Realty Inc.**

**Mr Joseph M. Cassin**
**Cassin & Cassin LLP**

# CONTENTS

# LIST OF CONTRIBUTORS

DAVID BUTLER is the Academic Director of the Irish Ancestry Research Centre in the University of Limerick.

NEIL BUTTIMER is a Senior Lecturer in the Department of Modern Irish, University College Cork.

JULIAN CAMPBELL lectures in the Crawford College of Art and Design, Cork.

LORRAINE CHADWICK is a graduate of the Department of Geography, University College Cork.

PETER CONNELL completed a PhD on the impact of the Famine in County Meath and works in Information Services, Trinity College Dublin.

DAVID DICKSON is Professor in the Department of Modern History, Trinity College Dublin.

LUKE DODD is Director of the Newsroom at *The Guardian* Newspaper and former curator of the Strokestown Famine Museum.

TERENCE DOOLEY is a Senior Lecturer in the Department of History, NUI Maynooth and Coordinator of the Centre for the Study of Irish Historic Houses and Estates.

PATRICK DUFFY is Professor in the Department of Geography, NUI Maynooth.

JOHN FEEHAN is a Senior Lecturer in the School of Biology and Environmental Science, University College Dublin.

CONNELL FOLEY is Director of Strategy, Advocacy and Learning, Concern Worldwide.

KIERAN FOLEY is a teacher and historian based in Malahide, Dublin who completed a PhD on the impact of the Famine in County Kerry.

MARITA FOSTER is a historian and acting Head of the International Education Office, University College Cork.

LAURENCE GEARY is a Senior Lecturer in the Department of History, University College Cork.

JONNY GEBER is a graduate of Stockholm University and Gotland University and is currently undertaking a PhD at Queen's University Belfast.

PETER GRAY is Professor of Modern History and Head of School of History and Anthropology, Queen's University Belfast.

BRIAN GURRIN is a post-doctoral fellow at NUI Maynooth.

JENNIFER HARRISON is a Lecturer in the School of History, Philosophy, Religion and Classics, The University of Queensland, Australia.

HELEN E. HATTON is a Senior Lecturer in the Department of History, University of Toronto, Canada.

ANNETTE HENNESSY is a sculptor who has worked internationally and on public sculpture throughout Ireland.

PATRICK HICKEY is a historian based in Timoleague, County Cork and author of *The Famine in West Cork: the Mizen Peninsula Land and People 1800–1852*.

KEVIN HOURIHAN, Senior Lecturer (retired) in the Department of Geography, University College Cork.

MARION INGOLDSBY is a composer and teacher.

MARY KELLY is a Lecturer, Department of Geography, NUI Maynooth.

THOMAS KENEALLY won the Booker Prize in 1982 for *Schindler's Ark*. He also wrote *The Great Shame: A Story of the Irish in the Old World and the New*.

LIAM KENNEDY is Professor of Economic and Social History at Queen's University Belfast.

CHRISTINE KINEALY is Professor of History at Caspersen Graduate School, Drew University, New Jersey.

JOE LEE is Professor and Director of Glucksman Ireland House, New York University.

GERARD MAC ATASNEY is a historian who has published widely on the Famine.

PIARAS MAC ÉINRÍ is a Lecturer in the Department of Geography, University College Cork.

JIM MACLAUGHLIN, Senior Lecturer (retired), Department of Geography, University College Cork.

CATHERINE MARSHALL is a former collections curator at the Irish Museum of Modern Art (IMMA).

MARK McGOWAN is Professor and Principal, Department of History, St. George's Campus, University of Toronto.

DYMPNA McLOUGHLIN is a Lecturer, Department of History, NUI Maynooth.

KERBY MILLER is Curators' Professor at the Department of History, University of Missouri.

CHRIS MORASH is Professor and Head of the Department of English at NUI Maynooth.

DAVID NALLY is a Lecturer in Geography at Cambridge University.

GRACE NEVILLE is Vice-President for Teaching and Learning and Professor in the Department of French, University College Cork.

MÁIRÉAD NIC CRAITH is Professor of European Culture and Society, School of Languages, Literatures and Cultures, University of Ulster (Magee).

WILLIAM F. NOLAN is Associate Professor at the School of Geography, Planning and Environmental Policy, University College Dublin.

PATRICK NUGENT is a Lecturer in Irish Studies at the University of Liverpool.

JOHN O'CONNELL is a genealogist and local historian living in Donoughmore, County Cork.

CORMAC Ó GRÁDA is Professor in the School of Economics, University College Dublin.

HILARY O'KELLY is a Lecturer in the History of Design at The National College of Art and Design, Dublin.

MICHELLE O'MAHONY is a graduate of the Department of History University College Cork and author of *Famine in Cork City*.

CHARLES E. ORSER, curator of historical archaeology, New York State Museum.

CATHAL PÓIRTÉIR is a broadcaster and producer with RTE and has published widely on the folklore of the Famine.

NATASHA POWERS is Head of Osteology at the Museum of London.

JOHN REID is a former cabinet minister in the British government and former chairman of Glasgow Celtic FC.

CIARÁN REILLY is a research fellow attached to the Centre for the Study of Historic Irish Houses & Estates.

COLIN SAGE is a Senior Lecturer in Geography at University College Cork.

REGINA SEXTON is a food historian, food writer, broadcaster and cook.

JOHN SHEEHAN is a Senior Lecturer in the Department of Archaeology, University College Cork.

ANELISE H. SHROUT is completing a PhD on the Famine and New York at the Department of History, University of New York.

MATTHEW STOUT is a Lecturer in the Department of History, St Patrick's College, Drumcondra.

LIZ THOMAS is an archaeologist at Queen's University Belfast.

CARMEN TUNNEY works in the Institute of Irish Studies, University of Liverpool.

KATHLEEN VILLIERS-TUTHILL is a native of Clifden and the author of five books and numerous articles on the history of west County Galway.

# PREFACE

Writing about and representing the Great Irish Famine, the most tragic event in Irish history has not been straightforward. For many years the event was cloaked in silence, its memory for the most part buried or neglected. The deaths of over one million people and the emigration of a further million had a profound and devastating impact on Irish society. It is only in recent decades that our understanding of what took place has deepened and we have come to know more intimately the suffering and hurt of those who perished – the 'true witnesses' of this central event in the island's history.

Remembering and understanding has been central to the work of the contributors to this monumental publication. This *Atlas* is original and unique in its telling of the story. The mapping of the Famine at parish level provides us with new ways of seeing the Famine which challenge traditional perspectives. By revealing complex local and regional dimensions, it naturally follows that they beg questions about the social conditions which prevailed in different localities and the diverse responses in terms of relief. Visually they are very striking and subvert the notion of a monolithic Famine landscape so clearly evinced in early popular writings. The provincial case studies included here lend weight to the argument that there was indeed a plurality of famines as well as a plurality of responses. Later maps in turn detail the journeys of those who fled the country, in oft-times harrowing conditions, to foreign lands and cities where new lives and new identities had to be forged.

The editors have not relied on maps alone, however, in their rendering of this event. Behind the maps are the stories of individuals and communities and how they fared during this traumatic period. Turning the pages one sees the names of individuals and families on relief lists and further on those whose homes were levelled and, on taking to the road, died in the worst of circumstances. Such human signatures are vital to our understanding of this event. Indeed as if to bring it home, among them is an application for food for a starving family, from a likely relative of my own, a young widow. The mindset of those in power and those who directed relief policy is also revealed in the letters written by key figures such as the Liberal Prime Minister Lord John Russell and Assistant Secretary to the Treasury Sir Charles Trevelyan. They provide powerful testimony in their own right to the political, economic and religious thinking of the day that shaped government policy but which ultimately failed the Irish people. As the Famine crisis worsened across the country, the overriding concerns of government were to reduce the burden of relief on the Treasury and to bring about reforms in the Irish agricultural system. As we now know, the result was a humanitarian disaster.

This *Atlas* commemorates not only those who perished but those whose compassion helped many to survive. While the Famine may have heightened social divisions in some localities with better-off farmers, for example, turning their back on their less well off neighbours, nevertheless there are countless examples of men and women (clergy, doctors, local officials and community leaders) who worked tirelessly to feed the hungry and treat the sick. In this respect one can only admire the fortitude of the Quaker community whose courageous efforts meant that many people would survive the worst of the Famine. Again, the archival record underlines the thoroughness of their approach. A completed questionnaire detailing famine conditions in the barony of Glenahiry in County Waterford reveals their eagerness to elicit information and their determination to send aid to where it was needed most. Surely the willingness of Irish people today to give of themselves so freely in fighting hunger worldwide owes something to the memory of those selfless individuals who helped the stricken people in their time of need. It is also well to remember that Famines can take place not because of a lack of food but, as Amartya Sen explains, as an 'entitlement failure' – a person's inability to access the available food within the state's jurisdiction. In this context it is interesting to note the report on Puck Fair in Killorglin carried in the *Tralee Chronicle*, 14 August 1847, which describes a crowded market with an 'immense quantity of stock' – many for export. Even in 'Black 47', such markets were thriving, as people were starving.

Very few books have been written on the greatest catastrophe in Irish history which encompasses both the diversity of perspectives and the parish-by-parish detail found in this book. This magnificent compilation – a series of essays by over fifty distinguished scholars, combined with the detailed maps, photographs, archival material, paintings and other artistic insights – redresses an imbalance in the literature on the Great Irish Famine. The inclusion of photographs of Famine landscapes, for example, including mass graves and workhouse sites, add to the poignancy of the story being told. Such images invite the reader to contemplate the real human suffering which lies at the heart of the Famine. Remembering is important but it is equally important to remember in ways which challenge our understandings of such tragic events. By its imaginative and accessible approach, the editors have produced a book which will be widely valued and appreciated by both the scholarly community and the general reader.

MARY McALEESE
(PRESIDENT OF IRELAND 1997–2011)

# ACKNOWLEDGEMENTS

In preparation for the one-hundred-fiftieth anniversary of the foundation of Queen's College, Cork and to commemorate the Great Famine of 1845–52, the Department of Geography at University College Cork received an invitation from President Michael Mortell to mount an exhibition entitled *Famines Yesterday and Today: The Irish Experience in a Global Context*. This map-based exhibition was opened by President Mary Robinson in November 1995 and in the following year travelled to Boston. Subsequently, two of the editors were involved with the atlases of Cork (2005) and Iveragh (2009) and the third with research on seventeenth-century Ireland. Building on the earlier exhibition, this specific atlas project began three years ago. We wish to thank Presidents Michael Mortell, Gerard Wrixon and Michael Murphy for their support to the department in initiating, developing and realising the whole Famine project.

The preparation of this book has been a significant financial undertaking and generous support was given by FEXCO Financial Services Centre, the Department of Arts, Heritage and the Gaeltacht and the Heritage Council of Ireland. Funding was also received from the College of Arts, Celtic Studies and Social Sciences (CACSSS), University College Cork and the Department of Geography, UCC. We express our sincere thanks to these for their assistance. We would especially like to thank Mr Brian MacCarthy FEXCO for his deep interest in and earnest support of this project from the very beginning. Special thanks also to Mr William (Bill) M. Murphy, Douglas Management & Realty, Inc. and Mr Joseph M. Cassin, Cassin & Cassin LLP for their generous support. Sincere thanks to Minister Jimmy Deenihan, Chris Flynn and Sara Doyle of the Department of Arts, Heritage and the Gaeltacht as well as Mary Hanafin (Minister for Tourism, Culture and Sport, 2010–11). We would also like to thank the following individuals: Professor Caroline Fennell (Head of College of Arts Celtic Studies and Social Sciences), Professor Donald Lyons (Head of the Department of Geography, UCC), Professor William O'Brien (Head of School of Geography and Archaeology: The Human Environment, UCC), Professor Robert Devoy and Dr Barry Brunt (Department of Geography, UCC) who facilitated us in the preparation of this book. Special thanks also to Mr John Fitzgerald (Librarian, UCC), Dr Jean van Sinderen-Law (Director of Development, UCC), Ms. Virginia Teehan (Director of Cultural Projects and Humanities Research Support, UCC), Professor Grace Neville (Vice-President for Teaching and Learning, UCC) and Mr Trevor Holmes (Vice-President for External Relations, UCC). We would like to thank all our colleagues in the Geography Department as well as all in the Postgraduate Room, notably Gearóid McCarthy and Richard Scriven.

The editors wish to thank those who were directly involved in the production of the book. First and foremost we are most grateful to the many contributors who invariably produced excellent material in a timely fashion. To Charlie and Mary Roche we offer particular thanks for invaluable work on both digitising the maps and data capture from the census. Thanks also to Helen Bradley and Tomás Kelly for all their expertise. Particular thanks to Brendan Dockery who sourced and reproduced innumerable documents and texts; to Noreen McDowell and Agnes O'Leary who provided great assistance in the administration of the project as well as Joan Walsh for her hospitality. Special thanks to Orla O'Sullivan for skilfully deciphering 'certain texts'.

We are greatly indebted to the photographers for their expertise and skill in producing a fine series of images for this publication. We would especially like to thank Frank Coyne who responded to our requests for particular images in a reflective and informed manner. We would also like to thank Gail Edwin-Fielding, Michael Diggin, Denis Minihane, Valerie O'Sullivan, Clare Keogh, Tomás Kelly, Caleb Smith, Tim McCarthy, Piaras Mac Éinrí, Canon Stephen Neill, Michael Gibbons, William Gallagher, Judith Hitchman, Tomás Tyner, A. Laburda, Kevin Egan, Patrick Duffy, Brian Graham, Kelvin Boyes, Therese Kenna, Kevin Kenna, Connell Foley and Nicoleta Coman for their photographic contributions to this publication. We would like to extend out thanks to Anne Kearney, Head of Library Services, *Examiner* Publications (Cork) Ltd for her help in sourcing relevant material. For permission to reproduce other photographs we are most grateful to Maxwell Photography, Sean Sexton Collection, Rev. Michael Johnston, Gerard J. Lyne, Concern Worldwide and the Simon Cumber Media fund which supported Clare Keogh's journey to Ethiopia.

The editors wish to acknowledge the assistance of the following institutions and their staff: National Library of Ireland (special thanks to Honora Faul for all her help and advice); Ordnance Survey Ireland; National Gallery of Ireland (Dr Brendan Rooney); National Archives of Ireland (especially Aideen Ireland); National Museum of Ireland; Irish Architectural Archive; Public Record Office of Northern Ireland; National Museums Northern Ireland; National Portrait Gallery, London; Dublin City Gallery The Hugh Lane; Irish Museum of Modern Art; Crawford Art Gallery, Cork; Boole Library, University College Cork (to all the dedicated staff and particularly Mary Lombard, Peadar Cranitch and Carol Quinn in the Archives Division and Garret Cahill in Interlibrary Loans); Trinity College Dublin Art Collection; Irish Virtual Research Library and Archive, University College Dublin; Delargy Centre for Irish Folklore and the National Folklore Collection, University College Dublin; NUI Maynooth Archive and Research Centre at Castletown, County Kildare (special thanks to archivist Roisín Berry); Library, NUI Maynooth; Friends Historical Library, Dublin; Port of Cork; Bridgeman Art Library London; National Maritime Museum, Greenwich, London; New York City Department of Records and Information Services; The New York Public Library; John J. Burns Library, Boston College: John F. Kennedy Presidential Library and Museum, Boston; Library and Archives Canada; Strokestown Estate Archive, NUI Maynooth Archive and Research Centre; Archives Services, Donegal County Council; Cork City and County Archives; Cork Public Museum, Central Library Letterkenny; Mayo County Library; Local History and Archives Department, Tralee, County Kerry, Limerick Chamber of Commerce; Tipperary Studies Centre at Thurles County Library (especially Mary Guinan-Darmody and John O' Gorman) and Strokestown Park House and Famine Museum. We acknowledge and are indeed grateful for permission to reproduce maps under Ordnance Survey Ireland/Government of Ireland copyright permit no. MP 0005212.

Numerous individuals deserve special recognition for their advice and assistance. These include Tim Vaughan (Editor *Irish Examiner*), Ciarán Ó Murchadha, Rob Goodbody, Daniel O'Connell, Robert O'Neill, Christóir Mac Cárthaigh, Niamh Brennan, Michael Lynch, Aoife McBride, Catherine Giltrap, Brian Magee, Frank J. Conahan, Julie Cochrane, Colum O'Riordan, Gillian O'Leary, Liz Foster, Maria Kelly; Stella Cherry, Trevor McClaughlin, Colette Daly, Una Matthewson, Michelle Ashmore, Emma Butterfield, Victoria Hogarth, Kylie Larmour, Louise Morgan, John O'Driscoll, Noel Cashman, John Sheehan, Nick Hogan, Ray O'Connor, Frank Morrissey, Mary O'Leary and Pat Gunn.

We wish to thank many colleagues for additional help: Willie Nolan, Toby Barnard, Joel Mokyr, Kevin Whelan, Patrick Nugent, Hilary O' Kelly, Julian Campbell, Gearóid Ó Tuathaigh, Neil Buttimer, Matthew Stout, the late Maurice Craig, Mary Kelly, Anngret Simms, Fran Walsh, Kay McKeogh, Niall Ó Cíosáin, Tim O'Neill, Máirín Ní Dhonchada, Ben Kiernan, Gerry Kearns, Edmund Riordan and Michael Farrell. Particular thanks to Mary Daly, David Dickson, David Fitzpatrick and all involved in the National Famine Research Project. Our greatest academic debt is to Cormac Ó Gráda who has been generous in his support to the UCC Famine Research Team since 1995 and most particularly in mentoring the progress of this Atlas. His critical comments are greatly appreciated.

Special thanks to Dr Patricia Noone and the George Moore Society (County Mayo), who in 1995 invited amongst others, artists Basil Blackshaw, Seán McSweeney, Jay Murphy, Tony O'Malley and Charles Tyrell to work on Famine themes. Our thanks to these artists – and to Jane O'Malley – for permission to reproduce their work. Thanks also to Taylor Galleries Dublin. Our particular appreciation of all Peter Murray's assistance as Director of the Crawford Art Gallery. Thanks also to poets Eavan Boland and Michael Coady for permission to include their work.

We want to thank all the people across the island who helped identify famine sites and local records – roads, piers, ridges ('lazy beds'), burial places, fever hospitals, workhouses – including Liam Phelan and Trevor Stanley (Donaghmore Museum), Willie Kirwan (Borris-in-Ossory), Rev. Michael Johnston (Shinrone), John O'Connell (Donoughmore, County Cork), Norma Buckley, Danny and Joe Hegarty and John Healy (Glenville, County Cork),  Ciarán Ó Murchadha (County Clare) Deirdre McQuillan (Belfast), Johanna Dooley (Portlaoise), George Cunningham (Roscrea), Ann MaGee (Glenties), Joe McGowan (Sligo), Tom McHenry (Swinford), Fergal McCabe (Tullamore) and Tom Ryan (Doon).

We would like to express our thanks to our families for their constant encouragement. A sincere thanks to the Crowley family, Jer and Anne (Ciarán and Martin), and Kevin and Margaret (Eoin, Joe and Paul) for all their support and hospitality; special thanks to Vera Ryan for sustained moral and academic support; the Smyth families in Cork, Dublin and Tipperary, especially Mary and Michael for identifying famine sites in the Roscrea district; the Ryan families in Rathdowney, particularly Kathleen Ryan, and the late Caroline Walsh, who honoured and nurtured so many books including this one; the Deering family in Terenure; Nuala Fenton, Maria Huss, Assumpta Duffy, Teresa Nolan and Brendan O'Mahony. Special thanks also to the Murphy family, Ethan, Neil and Aoife and in particular Caliosa for proofreading, general advice and commentary.

Finally the editors wish to thank sincerely the staff of Cork University Press and in particular, Publications Director Mike Collins for commissioning this book. We are especially grateful to Maria O'Donovan, Production Editor, for the care and patience she exercised in the production of this volume. We cannot thank Maria enough given the inordinate challenges involved in completing this project. Thanks also to Mary White-Fitzpatrick and Mary O'Mahony for their hospitality and kindness on our frequent visits to the Press.

# INTRODUCTION

The Great Irish Famine is surrounded by controversy, silence and shame. Scholars, politicians and commentators argue about what happened and who was responsible. The voices of the million men, women and children who died of hunger and disease in cabins, by roadsides, in bogs and ditches, in workhouses and fever hospitals are absent. If each of these people who died because of this Great Famine could write the stories of their experiences and feelings, we could not bear to read these accounts. And it is almost certain that their narratives of the Great Famine would clash with ours. The first great silence relates to the Famine dead.

The record left by the survivors is selective. While we have some stories of those who managed to survive and emigrate, there are thousands and thousands of desperate people who fled this island – losing all faith in their ancestral lands and communities – who were not so successful abroad and whose stories remain untold. Yet the Famine tragedy and its consequences are still remembered amongst the emigrant Irish, particularly in America. The picture is even more complicated for the Irish who survived the Famine and remained at home. Many witnessed and/or committed terrible deeds to carry on. Is that why their children and grandchildren had so little to say about that awful period? One answer is that the best way of handling such a trauma is not to talk about it. We recognise that 'survivors, as well as victims, suffered hunger, lost loved ones and neighbours, suffered the ignominy of the poorhouses and the dangers of fever'.[1] Suffering and pain apart, there is no doubt that both shame and guilt were important determinants of many silences. In a world where empathy and compassion were at a premium, some survived by making small profits out of the misery of the poor, by abandoning spouses and children, by denying food or money to other family members so as to survive themselves, by isolating fever-stricken siblings or neighbours in pigsties and outhouses. Others were willing to collaborate with the landlord in the levelling of the many homes of the evicted and may have facilitated the often stingy administration of all forms of food relief.[2] If the shame and guilt of these actions were denied, compassion was obliterated between people. Stark choices were made; moral ambiguities abound. We have to excavate carefully along these fissures to try to expose the wounds, the memory loss, that which is hidden.

A part of this ensuing silence relates to the rapid retreat of the Irish language and the large number of deaths that occurred in Irish-speaking areas. There is also the mute evidence of so many desolate landscapes where once vibrant households, townlands and village communities were scattered, abandoned or levelled. This silence is, perhaps, partly because of the universal feeling of being ashamed that our ancestors were so poor, hungry and humiliated in the first case; partly, perhaps, because we are the survivors and beneficiaries of the post-Famine adjustment, and also partly because it is impossible to remember or represent the scale, pain and horror of those trauma-laden years.

However, it is not entirely valid to argue that the Famine was hidden or repressed in the people's memory. The Irish Folklore Commission (IFC) contains a rich archive of oral tradition relating to the Great Famine. This includes insightful materials recorded and collected by scholars and diligent IFC collectors from the 1930s and 1940s, significant materials from the schools folklore scheme of 1937–38 and, most particularly, the results of the centenary questionnaire organised by the IFC in 1945–46. This latter survey produced seven volumes of Famine material. Over thousands of pages, the memories, stories and interpretations of the Famine are presented for many localities from the perspective of ordinary, and sometimes illiterate, people. The materials make for harrowing reading – stories of the bodies of young and old found dead along the roads, of fever-stricken families shunned by their fearful neighbours and of the horror of the poorhouse. Memory is selective and in Cathal Póirtéir's *Famine Echoes*, it is noticeable that memories of hunger and starvation are far stronger than those of fatal diseases and that relief institutions of all kinds – deemed good or bad – are well remembered. The greatest odium is reserved in the folk memory for those who acted as agents and estate officials for often heartless landlords and for those who 'grabbed' land. Folk memory is kind to all – landlords included – who were generous to others in those awful times. This folk evidence is highly localised, broken and fragmentary. Yet, as Póirtéir observes, 'the echoes of those silenced voices which we have in folk memory are the nearest we can get to the experience of the poor in the 1840s and 1850s'.[3] However, absent from these IFC volumes are the key decision-makers and administrators in London and Dublin and any sense of the wider structural forces shaping the Great Famine tragedy.[4]

In contrast, the public record of the Famine, as captured in the correspondence, official notices and institutional accounts of those in power, is very detailed. Newspapers and archives also preserve the actions and thoughts of political and administrative elites and intellectuals. We have the almost fanatical adherence to, and promulgation of laissez-faire and poor law ideologies born of a new bourgeois English political economy which described the Irish – especially its poorer classes – as deeply resistant to 'refinement and reformation' along a cherished English model of capitalist (as opposed to 'peasant') agriculture. We have the economist Nassau Senior wondering would a million Irish deaths 'scarcely be enough to do any good'[5] in effecting such a reformation. We have the great untruth of Charles Trevelyan announcing in his book *The Irish Crisis* – written in late 1847[6] – that the Famine was over. We have the records of the voices of quite a number of Government appointees to Ireland, from the Lord Lieutenant to regional and local officials – not to speak of Irish bishops, clergymen, politicians and others – pleading for more food and aid, for more local autonomy and greater understanding from the London administration. We have inherited literally tons of official documentation relating to the Great Famine: committee reports on the operation of the poor laws, commissariat reports, papers relating to the relief of distress, correspondence and reports of the Poor Law Commissioners, police reports on 'outrages', Censuses and so on. There are seven tons of materials alone relating to the activities of the Board of Works in Famine Ireland.[7] There are also thousands of union workhouse volumes housed all across the county libraries, detailing down to the last farthing the money spent on food, clothing, medicine, staff, turf, coffins etc. every week in each workhouse. Yet, until relatively recently, there was a strange reluctance on the part of historians, historical geographers and others to address these vast documentary archives. A further silence relates to the historiography and geography of the Great Famine.

The following graph illustrates the number of books and journal articles published since 1945, dealing directly with the Great Famine. What is striking is the paucity of research and publications on the Famine up until the decade preceding the one-hundred-and-fiftieth commemorations from 1995 onwards. Since then there has been an impressive, but not overwhelming, expansion in studies of the Great Famine. Such an upsurge in research and publications may also mean that the Irish have finally come to terms with the trauma and scale of famine losses. The paucity of such research writing stretches back to the 1850s. The earliest interpretation of the Great Famine came in 1860 with the publication of John Mitchel's *The Last Conquest of Ireland (Perhaps)*.[8] Although often either ignored or heavily criticised by some professional historians, others such as James Donnelly and Cormac Ó Gráda have noted Mitchel's indignation, insights and 'Swiftian outrage at official attitudes' to relief.[9] Mitchel's extreme nationalist position placed far too great an emphasis on deliberate and prior British planning of objectives and policies to be pursued during the Great Famine years, so as to ensure 'the last conquest of Ireland'. Yet Mitchel is insightful on a whole host of issues: for example, his emphasis on the rigid Government policy favouring highly centralised administration and control of the Famine while insisting on the local resourcing of relief; and how the poor had – in his words – been 'slaughtered by stationery'. Mitchel is also alert to the relationship between language and power. He highlights the unquestioned assumptions behind the use of the concept of Ireland's so-called 'surplus populations' in British policy-making circles and the freedom such a damning concept/belief might provide in making crucial decisions with mortal consequences for the Irish poor. Likewise, he is the first to note the concept of the 'pauper' as an English language imposition. The Irish word for a poor person is 'duine bocht', a descriptive term which still recognises their individuality; the 'pauper' was an 'object' of relief in the workhouse, a status confirmed by having to always wear a workhouse uniform. Supported by Canon John O'Rourke's *History of the Great Irish Famine* (1875)[10] – an explicitly Catholic nationalist interpretation – Mitchel's powerful nationalist narrative dominated interpretations of the Great Famine from the 1860s until the mid-twentieth century, up to which point very little research had been initiated on the Famine.

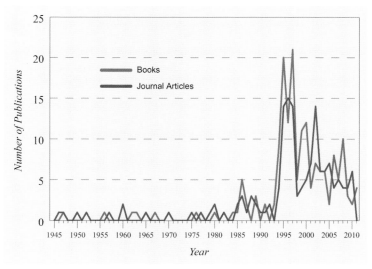

Fig. 1 Number of books and journal articles published since 1945, dealing with the Great Famine.

Early in 1944, An Taoiseach, Eamon de Valera, proposed that the centenary of the Great Famine be commemorated with a historical monograph. Edited by Robert Dudley Edwards and Desmond Williams, a rather delayed *The Great Famine: Studies in Irish History* went on sale in January 1957.[11] Outstanding chapters were provided by younger research workers, now familiar with the archives: Kevin Nowlan writing on the political context; Oliver MacDonagh on emigration and Thomas P. O'Neill on public relief policies. The established scholar, Sir William MacArthur, wrote on the medical history of the Famine. Yet de Valera responded more enthusiastically to *The Great Hunger* (1962),[12] the work of the non-academic woman historian, Cecil Woodham Smith. As Cormac Ó Gráda notes 'the worldwide enduring success of that more evocative study … points to an opportunity lost by professional Irish historians.'[13]

The Dudley Edwards/Williams book reflected the ethos of a new, scientific, objective historiographical approach and generally eschewed a nationalist interpretation. Woodham Smith's livelier, more graphic account and feeling for the period was to reach a far wider audience. While criticised for being too melodramatic and 'emotive' on occasion,[14] two other strengths of Woodham Smith's work are its clarity in locating the Great Famine within a colonial/imperial framework and its highly original integration of evidence from many private papers previously unused, including those of Trevelyan. Perhaps the greatest weakness of *The Great Hunger* is that it overemphasises the terrible famine conditions in the far west and does not provide a representative picture of the famine island-wide. On the other hand, perhaps Cecil Woodham Smith's greatest strength – and here she anticipated future research trends – may have been her ability to merge formal, 'official' history with history as experienced by people on the ground.

Yet neither of these major studies was to stimulate a raft of research publications on the Famine. Amongst geographers, only T.W. Freeman and S.H. Cousens were to interrogate pre-Famine, Famine and post-Famine sources.[15] Christine Kinealy, Cormac Ó Gráda and Kevin Whelan have all commented at length on both this research lacuna and the downgrading of the centrality of the Great Famine in Irish historical accounts over the following decades.[16] In 1982, historian George Boyce was to assert that 'even the scale of the Great Famine was not unique in the context of contemporary European experience'.[17] In Roy Foster's acclaimed *Modern Ireland 1600–1972* (1988),[18] a chapter entitled 'The Famine: Before and After' is overshadowed by much more detailed and comprehensive chapters on, for example, 'The Ascendancy Mind' and 'The 'Politics of Parnellism'. In these years – noticeably while the Northern Troubles raged – there was a distinct tendency in historical literature and commentaries to talk down excess mortality and levels of landlord evictions. 'The implication seems to be,' as Cormac Ó Gráda argues, 'that the lower the death toll, the less the blame.'[19] And if mortality was actually higher, it was argued that no mid-nineteenth-century government could have alleviated such a problem over such a lengthy period.

Overall, there was a noticeable tendency to remove the Great Famine from the central stage of nineteenth-century Irish history. Indeed the arguments that the real watershed in nineteenth-century Irish economic and social history was 1815 (after the Napoleonic wars) rather than 1845 – that such trends as the decline of the Irish language, the shift from tillage to pastoral farming and the strengthening of impartible inheritance patterns began then – won widespread acclaim.[20] Looking back, it is still simply astonishing that the Great Famine period – which witnessed one million excess deaths, when two and a half million people deserted Ireland within ten years and emigration became deeply institutionalised in Irish culture, which saw the elimination of close on 300,000 family farms, the virtual disappearance of the cottier class with less than one acre, not to speak of the social and economic contraction and impoverishing of so many towns – was not seen as a major watershed. In truth, the Great Famine is a great abyss, a great chasm, between pre-Famine and post-Famine Ireland. This was a profoundly revolutionary period, accompanied by immense levels of violence – ecological, physical, psychological and social – only matched in intensities and long-term implications by the Cromwellian conquest and settlement in the mid-seventeenth century.

It took a group of historians and scholars working outside Ireland in the 1970s and 1980s to open up the research vistas that have allowed us to more fully understand what happened and why between 1845 and 1852. Innovative conceptually and sophis-

ticated in its economic methodologies, it was *Why Ireland Starved: An Analytical and Quantitative History of the Irish Economy 1840–1850* (1985)[21] by Chicago-based economic historian Joel Mokyr, which helped revolutionise Famine Studies. Using an array of fresh techniques and concepts, Mokyr carefully estimated the number of excess deaths – at least a million dead – and if averted births were included the number rose to a staggering 1.4 million. Mokyr stressed the unpredictability rather than the inevitability of the Famine disaster. Using careful measures of economic activity and demographic behaviour, he concluded – controversially it is true – that while Ireland was very poor in the pre-Famine decades, it was not overpopulated. His judgements about the British Government's responsibilities were severe: 'The real problem was that Ireland was considered by Britain as an alien and even hostile country' and 'When the chips were down in the frightful summer of 1847, the British simply abandoned the Irish and let them perish'. Mokyr's findings prompted vigorous responses from two other young quantitative economic historians, Peter Solar and Pat McGregor.[22]

Madison-based scholar, James Donnelly, in a series of contributions in *The New History of Ireland* and elsewhere,[23] also provided new insights into our understanding of the Famine. Unburdened by the home-grown assumptions of Irish historiography, Donnelly included writers like Mitchel in his analysis and highlighted the inadequacies of official responses to the Famine catastrophe. He also highlighted the scale of evictions and clearances during the Famine years. Due to his work, along with that W. E. Vaughan and Timothy O'Neill, Mary Daly's figure of 19,000 families evicted between 1846 and 1848 and Roy Foster's 50,000 for the famine period 1847–50 are now deemed serious underestimates. Vaughan, in his wide-ranging book *Landlords and Tenants in Victorian Ireland*, puts the number at 70,000 families for the 1846–54 period as a whole.[24] Armed with his knowledge of both the folkloric evidence and the intricacies of legal procedures, O'Neill has significantly revised these figures upwards, arguing that there may have been 80,000 families evicted in 1846-48 alone and emphasising that the peak of evictions happened in 1847 and 1848 and not in later years.[25] Overall, his figures correspond more closely with Donnelly's estimates. Clearly, the actual numbers evicted may never be known but detailed research for this Atlas supports the thesis that evictions and clearances were a central and devastating element in the Famine tragedy. Also making good use of both detailed local records and national archives, then Liverpool-based Christine Kinealy brought fresh perspectives, not least to the successes and failures of the poor law and workhouse system during the Famine and has further developed these insights since moving to America.[26]

Bringing a range of skills – including his training as an economic historian, his intimate knowledge of Irish language and cultural sources and a sensitivity to both quantitative and qualitative methodologies – Cormac Ó Gráda (UCD) has evaluated many of these new insights in a series of wide-ranging studies of the Great Famine.[27] In conjunction with Mokyr's work, he has challenged both the marginalisation of the Great Famine as the central event in modern Irish history and many of the old nationalist assumptions. In this context, it is interesting that in an interview in 1993, Roy Foster noted '… we are coming back to views of, say the Famine, which the people of the 1960s [and later] would have thought were being replaced. Ó Gráda, Mokyr and others have given us a view of famine administration which is closer to Cecil Woodham Smith than the essays in *The Great Famine* [1956]'. Ó Gráda has asked, and continues to ask, pertinent questions about the capacity of the Irish economy and the well-being of the potato-dependent Irish poor in pre-Famine and Famine times, about the nature of landlord indebtedness before and during the Famine, about the quality of workhouse management then, about the functioning of food and credit markets at retail level, about mortality, medicine and diseases, about the use and integration of folklore evidence and many other imponderables. He has also led the field in providing a firm comparative framework for locating Ireland's Great Famine in the context of other world famines.[28]

Peter Gray has made outstanding contributions in unravelling the very particular political and cultural contexts – including the place of providentialism – within which Famine policies were determined amongst the British political elite. He has also clearly identified the many policy decisions made during the Famine 'which can be connected with unnecessary mortality'.[29] The most recent major contributor to the Famine debate is geographer, David Nally, with his *Human Encumbrances: Political Violence and the Great Famine* (2011).[30] This innovative work enlarges our understanding of the comparative literature on world famines, particularly those that occurred across the British empire. He, therefore, reiterates the need to locate British Government policy on faminestricken Ireland within its imperial and colonial contexts, a feature also of the work of literary critics and scholars who pay close attention to the relationships between language, political narratives and the exercise of power.[31] Nally has unearthed a series of critical voices from the Famine era – particularly in Britain – who challenged the prevailing dominance of laissez-faire and providentialist orthodoxies. His book also brings new theoretical insights to bear on the analysis of the Great Famine, notably in relation to issues of governmentality and the body and the role of structured, legalised violence in this context. One of the most difficult questions arising from Nally's and earlier pioneering interpretations relates to how deliberate and how long in gestation was the British policy drive to eliminate cottiers and smallholders – the 'human encumbrances' and 'surplus populations' – from the agricultural economy, so as to accelerate the creation of a capitalist agricultural system. Unlike the situation in previous, more obviously violent centuries, the argument is advanced that such policies and objectives may have been masked and concealed in the language of relief, reform and 'rescue'. Like the seventeenth-century Irish experience but in the very different nineteenth-century contexts, one could argue that colonialism and modernity were still two sides of the same coin.

This *Atlas of the Great Famine* has been strongly influenced by these new and not so new research insights, emanating from a range of disciplines. Many of the scholars currently working in Famine Studies – both at international and national levels – have made invaluable contributions to the *Atlas*. However, there has been no attempt made to provide an overarching, unifying synthesis. Rather what is recognised in this *Atlas* is the necessity for a great diversity of approaches and perspectives in seeking to illuminate and represent the monstrous reality of the Famine tragedy and its consequences. Hence the importance attached to the work of poets, visual artists, musicians, folklorists, photographers and writers of Irish and English literature as well as the research of other established scholars and the extensive use of archival sources. The generation and interpretation of *c*.200 computerbased maps of population decline, social transformation and other key changes between the census years 1841 and 1851 is naturally central to this *Atlas* exploration. On the one hand, the *Atlas* provides original, island-wide, almost panoptic views of the Famine which, while very helpful, are nevertheless limiting in other respects. We can see every parish from above but we still do not know how the Famine affected individual families and communities on the ground. Hence, the parallel analysis of famine conditions in the provinces, counties, parishes and townlands and in overseas emigrant destinations, so as to try to tell the stories of particular individuals and families caught up in these terrible events. What these maps document is a range of human worlds and conditions never previously published and revealed in Irish Famine studies. While recognising the power and effects of the general political and administrative forces at work and the devastating impacts of the Famine island-wide, the interpretation of these maps and other evidence equally highlights the diversity of local, county, provincial and emigrant conditions and experiences.

The cartographic journey to the *Atlas of the Great Famine* began almost twenty years ago with a discussion in the Department of Geography, University College Cork, on the best way to calculate the shape and size and then map the civil parishes of Ireland. It was decided that the best approach was to computerise/digitise the civil parishes from the Ordnance Survey six-inch County Index Maps and then compute the shape and size, and map the distribution, of the parishes. With the approach of the 150th anniversary of the Famine and in conjunction with the 150th celebration of the foundation of Queen's College Cork, the department accepted the President's invitation to research and mount an exhibition of the Great Famine for 1995. It was then decided to generate a computer database of the 1841 (pre-Famine) and 1851 (post-Famine) censuses. Then, using GIS (Geographical Information Systems) to link the civil parish maps to the Census database, chloropleth (thematic) maps could be produced to visualise changes in population and social structures before, during and after the Famine.

The Famine data maps in this *Atlas* are, therefore, based on comparing the most relevant data classes from the Census of 1841 and the Census of 1851. The Census was collected at townland level. Townlands are the smallest administrative units in the country. All other administrative units and boundaries are based on the original structure of over 60,000 townlands. Townlands build into civil parishes (used in the General Census Report, which the maps are based on) and civil parishes in turn build into baronies. This island-wide, nested, administrative and territorial hierarchy is completed by the counties and provinces. Civil parishes were originally Christian (pre-Reformation) ecclesiastical areas. In the post-Reformation period, they became the established administrative units of the Church of Ireland and acquired civil administrative functions after the Tudor conquest of Ireland. (The modern Catholic parish – created mainly in the eighteenth and early nineteenth centuries – is for the most part, an entirely separate geographical entity.)

The Department of Geography (UCC) then commissioned postgraduate Charlie Roche to digitise the island-wide map of civil parishes. This demanding cartographic project was carried out over a twelve month period. This process was complicated by the fragmentation of parish and town areas and the critical need to ensure that the civil parish maps corresponded with the equivalent listing in the Census. This was followed by the data capture from the Censuses of 1841 and 1851 which went on for almost a further two years.

A total of twenty-one categories were captured including PERSONS (male/female), HOUSES (fourth-class and total number of houses), FAMILIES (residing in first-, second-, third- and fourth-class houses), PURSUITS (agriculture, manufacturing, trade and commerce, other pursuits), MEANS (professional, and vested, the direction of labour, own manual labour and means not specified), EDUCATION of males and females, five years and older (who can read and write, who can read only and who can neither read nor write). From these categories, any number of combinations could be calculated including totals, persons under five years of age and so on. The process was completed for over 3,300 parishes (including separate portions) and 1,400 towns (including separate portions). This *Atlas* contains over seventy such maps, derived from the database. A total of 130 additional maps were drawn for this publication over the past three years. These maps are at the centre of the unravelling, analysis and interpretation provided here of the origins, varying impacts and consequences of the Great Famine for Ireland and for the Irish people, both at home and abroad.

Yet, after all the work, we are left wondering about a whole range of issues. How different would Ireland have been in the second half of the nineteenth century and today if the Great Famine had not occurred or if its deadly effects had been more rapidly contained? The work of Kevin O'Rourke suggests that such an Ireland would be very different indeed.[32] While recognising that the Great Famine broke the back and self-confidence of the nation, we are still left wondering why it took so long to recover from the trauma. Unlike the experiences of peoples after other world famines, why is it that emigration remains so deeply embedded in Irish life and in the Irish psyche? As Maureen Gaffney puts it: 'So many have gone and continue to go, that the sheer energy of their absence acts like a magnetic field.'[33] We are still not sure of the effects of deprivation, malnutrition and indeed trauma on the psychic health of those who survived the Famine. With a rapidly declining population in the second half of the nineteenth century, why was it that more and more people ended up in mental asylums and institutions? We recognise that the consolidation of both farms and impartible inheritance patterns created fewer marriage opportunities. Yet why did the number of nuns in Ireland increase eightfold between 1841 and 1901, even though the Catholic population had halved. Apart from the increasing cultural power of the Catholic Church, was there something about the devastation of family and marital life during the Famine which made more attractive the solace of the convent? This *Atlas* highlights how the Famine affected, not only rural communities, but also towns and cities, leading to the erosion of a more diverse and dynamic urban bourgeoisie and the much greater expansion of urban families now dependent on their own manual labour. How different would Ireland have become with a more diverse and more dynamic urban economy and society? And its associated political and cultural impulses? Questions abound.

Reading the published and unpublished materials on the Great Famine, the dominant feeling evoked is one of sadness – sadness for all that horror and all that suffering and sadness about the failures at all levels to stop that suffering. We honour those who gave generously of themselves to alleviate that suffering and continue to regret the betrayals, failures and inhumanity of those in many positions of authority, especially those with the greatest power and responsibility to shape other people's destinies. This *Atlas* is a study which seeks to more fully understand the Great Famine and its consequences. It is an act of commemoration of the known and unknown dead of the Famine and of the millions who had to flee Ireland. In seeking to establish a greater understanding, this *Atlas* is an attempt to address the wounds and transcend this formative tragedy.

# SECTION I
## IRELAND
## BEFORE AND AFTER
## THE GREAT FAMINE

UNVEILED BY
KAREN GEARON,
DUNNES STORES STRIKERS,
7th MAY 1994.

ERECTED BY AFRI.

Famine memorial, Doolough Valley,
County Mayo. [Photo: Frank Coyne]

# The story of the Great Irish Famine 1845–52: A geographical perspective

## *William J. Smyth*

Over the two centuries or so between 1641 and 1852, Ireland endured three phases of enormous population loss, plague and famine. The experienced observer and pioneer statistician, Sir William Petty (1623–87) estimated that during the years between 1641 and 1653, between 30 to 40% of Ireland's population may have been lost through war, out-migration, famine and disease. Modern estimates would put the mid-seventeenth-century losses at between a quarter and a third of the population. During a continental-wide crisis in food supplies and with a war-induced trade embargo, Ireland's second great famine in the modern era began in 1740 (see David Dickson, below). After seven weeks of the most severe frost in early 1740, almost two years of exceptionally cold and dry weather followed. It is estimated that the population of Ireland was reduced by 12.5% to 16% and that as many as one person in four perished in the southern province of Munster. In relative terms, therefore, the mid seventeenth century, and probably the mid eighteenth century, famines may have been as traumatic and destructive as the Great Famine (see Figs. 1 and 5).[1]

### ABSOLUTE SCALE
The Great Famine of 1845-1852 is naturally remembered as the most devastating in Ireland's history. This is because of its absolute scale. Over

one million excess deaths occurred (c.1.4 million if averted births are included). At least one million and a quarter (possibly as many as 1.35 million) emigrant-refugees fled

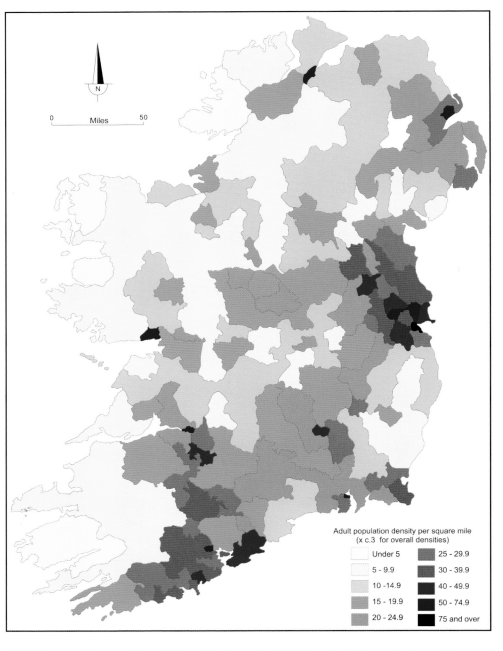

Adult population density per square mile
(x c.3 for overall densities)

| | |
|---|---|
| Under 5 | 25 - 29.9 |
| 5 - 9.9 | 30 - 39.9 |
| 10 -14.9 | 40 - 49.9 |
| 15 - 19.9 | 50 - 74.9 |
| 20 - 24.9 | 75 and over |

Fig. 1 DISTRIBUTION OF ADULT POPULATION IN IRELAND C.1660. This map is based mainly on William Petty's so-called '1659 Census', a highly original population count from the poll-tax records of 1660-61. The mid-seventeenth-century population distribution is dominated by a number of maritime regions, indicated on the map by the darker shadings. The Dublin–Pale region stands out as the zone of highest population density. Between the midland bogs and the hills and woods of the Wicklow/Wexford borderlands, the Liffey and Barrow valleys form a bridgehead into the second region of population concentration along the riverine lowlands of the southeast. Waterford city is the dominant focus here. The power of the Munster province is revealed in the port-dominated regions of Cork and Limerick. An embryonic core region is also beginning to emerge in northeast Ulster. In sharp contrast to these densely populated maritime regions are the relatively lightly populated regions of the southwest, the west and most of the north. By the time of the Great Famine in the mid-nineteenth century, these population density patterns were almost totally reversed with the west and the north registering the greatest concentration of populations and the south and east the least, emphasising the great political, economic and social transformations that had occurred across the island over the previous two centuries (see also Figure 5).

Fig. 2 Lazy beds in Connemara, relic features in the Irish landscape that remain as poignant a reminder as any of the Famine and its impact. [Photo: Michael Gibbons]

the country for other lands. It is also better remembered because it is the most recent and best-documented famine. In short, the Great Famine is remembered because of the terrors of hunger and fever, the many deaths and broken homes and because it led to a revolution in Irish society as deep and as traumatic as the Cromwellian conquest two centuries earlier. As Terry Eagleton has written:

> Part of the horror of the Famine is its atavistic nature – the mind-shattering fact that an event with all the premodern character of a medieval pestilence happened in Ireland with frightening recentness. This deathly origin then shattered space as well as time, unmaking the nation and scattering Irish people and history across the globe.[2]

Young Irelander, James Fintan Lawlor, saw the Famine as a kind of negative revolution, bringing with it 'a deeper social disorganisation than the French Revolution – greater waste of life – wider loss of property – with more of the horrors, with none of the hopes'.[3]

Nobel laureate and economist-philosopher, Amartya Sen has surmised that '[in] no other famine in the world [was] the proportion of people killed … as large as in the Irish famine in the 1840s'.[4] The death toll of the Irish Famine 'was the equivalent of the doubling of normal mortality for a five year period (1846–51)', making for a much more long-term disaster than most other world famines.[5] Joseph Lee has described the Irish Famine as 'the greatest single peace-time tragedy since the [fourteenth-century] Black Death'.[6] It certainly was the greatest social disaster to occur in any one country in nineteenth-century Europe. Commentary on Ireland's 'Great Hunger' or 'Great Starvation' is everywhere in the literature. 'In the world list of famines the Great Irish Famine is perhaps best known of all' is how Cormac Ó Gráda describes it.[7] He goes on to emphasise that the Famine is the main event in modern Irish history, as important to Ireland as, say, the French Revolution to the French and the First Industrial Revolution to the English. As Joel Mokyr observes: 'The vastness with which the Irish potato failure looms over Irish history is not diminished by revisionism.'[8]

FAILURE OF THE POTATO CROP

After the partial failure of the potato crop in 1845, when

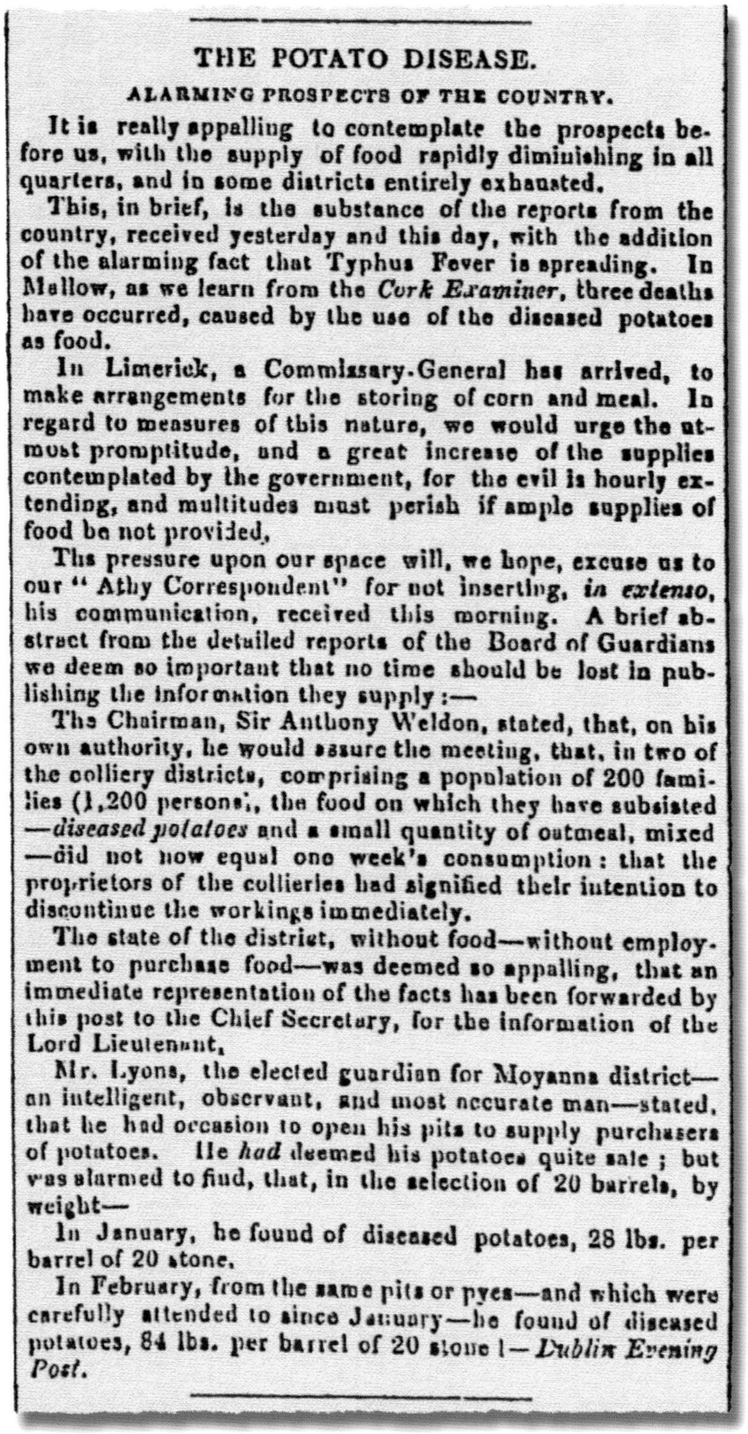

## THE POTATO DISEASE.
### ALARMING PROSPECTS OF THE COUNTRY.

It is really appalling to contemplate the prospects before us, with the supply of food rapidly diminishing in all quarters, and in some districts entirely exhausted.

This, in brief, is the substance of the reports from the country, received yesterday and this day, with the addition of the alarming fact that Typhus Fever is spreading. In Mallow, as we learn from the *Cork Examiner*, three deaths have occurred, caused by the use of the diseased potatoes as food.

In Limerick, a Commissary-General has arrived, to make arrangements for the storing of corn and meal. In regard to measures of this nature, we would urge the utmost promptitude, and a great increase of the supplies contemplated by the government, for the evil is hourly extending, and multitudes must perish if ample supplies of food be not provided.

The pressure upon our space will, we hope, excuse us to our "Athy Correspondent" for not inserting, *in extenso*, his communication, received this morning. A brief abstract from the detailed reports of the Board of Guardians we deem so important that no time should be lost in publishing the information they supply:—

The Chairman, Sir Anthony Weldon, stated, that, on his own authority, he would assure the meeting, that, in two of the colliery districts, comprising a population of 200 families (1,200 persons), the food on which they have subsisted —*diseased potatoes* and a small quantity of oatmeal, mixed —did not now equal one week's consumption: that the proprietors of the collieries had signified their intention to discontinue the workings immediately.

The state of the district, without food—without employment to purchase food—was deemed so appalling, that an immediate representation of the facts has been forwarded by this post to the Chief Secretary, for the information of the Lord Lieutenant.

Mr. Lyons, the elected guardian for Moyanna district— an intelligent, observant, and most accurate man—stated, that he had occasion to open his pits to supply purchasers of potatoes. He *had* deemed his potatoes quite safe; but was alarmed to find, that, in the selection of 20 barrels, by weight—

In January, he found of diseased potatoes, 28 lbs. per barrel of 20 stone.

In February, from the same pits or pyes—and which were carefully attended to since January—he found of diseased potatoes, 84 lbs. per barrel of 20 stone !—*Dublin Evening Post.*

Fig. 3 A report in *The Londonderry Journal* 18 February 1846 warning of the impending calamity resulting from the failure of the potato crop: 'for the evil is hourly extending, and multitudes must perish if ample supplies of food be not provided'. [Source: Central Library, Letterkenny]

close to one-half of the crop was lost, there were high hopes that the new potato crop of 1846 would be a very good one. But, as John O'Connor notes, 'in late July and early August [of that year] disaster struck with unbelievable rapidity'.[9] He quotes the report of Frances Power Cobbe of Newbridge in County Dublin who described the onset of the blight in that part of Ireland:

I happen to recall precisely the day, almost the hour, when the blight fell on the potatoes. A party of us were driving to a seven o'clock dinner at the home of our neighbour, Mrs Evans of Portrane. As we passed a remarkably fine field of potatoes in blossom, the scent came through the open windows of the carriage and we remarked to each other how splendid the crop. Three or four hours later, as we returned home in the dark, a dreadful smell came from the same field and we exclaimed: 'something has happened to these potatoes'.[10]

The subsequent reports made to the English Poor Law Commissioners from 2,000 localities all over the country on the state of the potato confirmed how complete was the devastation of the crop. Many thousands faced starvation and many thousands died in the bitter winter of 1846/47. The greatly reduced acreage of potatoes sown in 1847 yielded a better crop but the disaster continued into 1848, when the whole crop was again practically wiped out. Excess mortalities rose rapidly in 1847/48 and persisted in some areas until 1851 and 1852.

The blight on the potato was the fuse that set off the time-bomb of the Great Famine, the echoes of which still reverberate down to our own times. It began by shattering

Fig. 4 *Two Potatoes* by Basil Blackshaw, mixed media on canvas, 48x36cm. [Courtesy of artist]

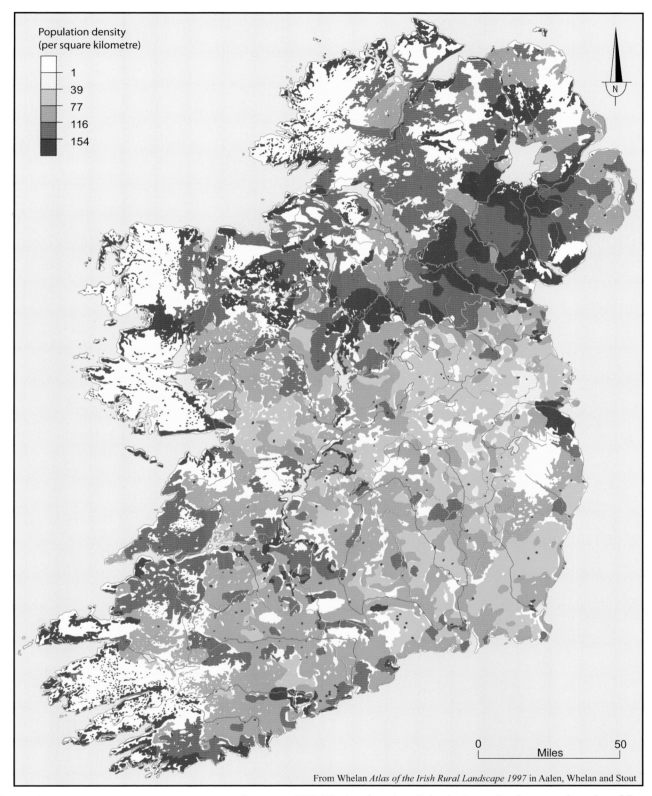

Population density
(per square kilometre)

1
39
77
116
154

0        Miles        50

From Whelan *Atlas of the Irish Rural Landscape 1997* in Aalen, Whelan and Stout

Fig. 5 FREEMAN'S MAP OF THE DISTRIBUTION OF POPULATION IN IRELAND IN 1841. Nineteenth-century Ireland witnessed a phenomenal number of Government reports on social and economic conditions across the island. Among the most significant sources of information were the decennial Census of population reports – none more so than the 1841 Census, which its director, Thomas Larcom, hoped would also be seen as a 'social survey'. This map is based on T.W. Freeman's magnificent work on this Census. Using the first edition Ordnance Survey six-inch maps, he first isolated the unsettled regions, shown in white on this figure. The mountains and uplands of the Wicklows, mid- and southwest Munster, the Burren and Slieve Aughty and those over much of west and north Connacht are distinguished as well as those of Donegal, mid-Ulster and Antrim. Bogland stretches are also indicated in white. Freeman then mapped population densities per parish while still keeping a careful eye on the patterns of housing distributions shown on the Ordnance Survey maps. The great concentrations of population in an extensive belt from the Lough Neagh region on across south Ulster and into north Connacht are emphasised. Also shown are the very high densities of west Clare, the peninsular worlds of southwest Munster, and some of the lowlands of mid-Munster. In sharp contrast are the relatively low population densities of the pastoral zones on the best lands of north Leinster and east Galway as well as pockets in south Leinster. Urban concentrations around Belfast, Cork and particularly Dublin are also emphasised. Above all, this map highlights the very varied population densities, and hints at the great social differences across the island of Ireland in 1841.

and withering the bodies of the poor as they starved in their cabins, in the fields, on the relief roads and in the lanes of towns and cities. The unspeakable had happened. Tadhg Ó Scanaill, a farmer from Cathair Crobh Dearg in Rathmore, County Kerry, tells how his mother – then a child – recalled the Famine of 1848:

She remembered finding a mother and daughter on the path locked in each other's arms, within a few yards of Rian an Daimh, on the cosán (path) going across to Claedach, above the Gleann an Phriacháin Lake. The night was snowy, there was a little snow on their clothes, they were around here the day before.[11]

Miss Mary Kettle of Cohaw, Cootehill, County Cavan, recalled:

My grandfather was going with a cow to the fair of Cootehill, and he saw a girl standing up against a gate that was along the road. The cow moved over to the gate and when my grandfather went over to drive the cow away from it, he got a terrible shock when he found that the girl

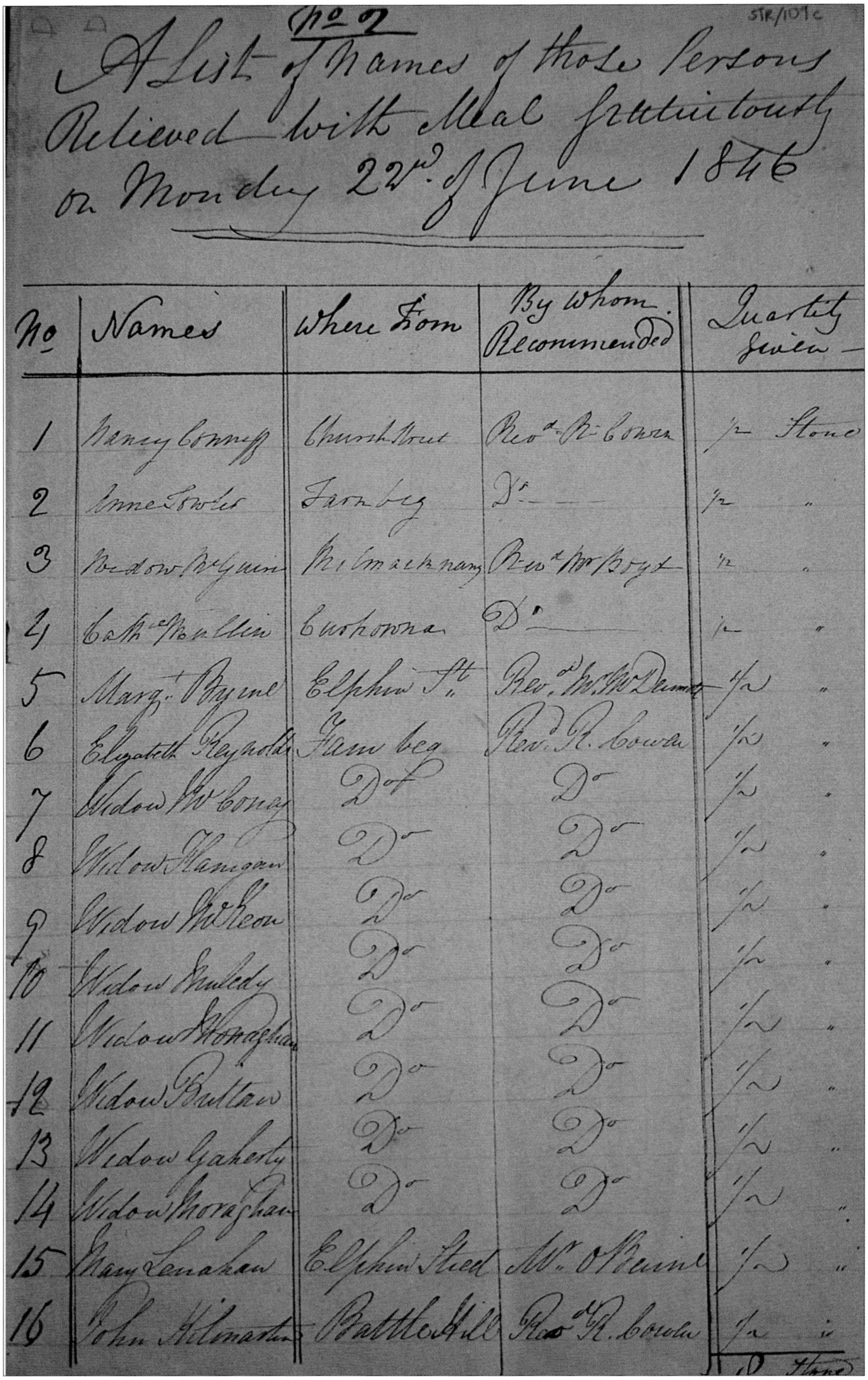

STR/107c

No 2

A List of Names of those Persons Relieved with Meal gratuitously on Monday 22nd of June 1846

| No | Names | Where from | By whom Recommended | Quantity given |
|---|---|---|---|---|
| 1 | Nancy Conniff | Church Street | Revd R. Cowen | 1/2 Stone |
| 2 | Anne Fowler | Farnbeg | Do | 1/2 " |
| 3 | Widow McGuire | Kilmacknany | Revd Mr Boyd | 1/2 " |
| 4 | Cath McMullin | Curhowna | Do | 1/2 " |
| 5 | Margt Byrne | Elphin St | Revd Mr McDermott | 1/2 " |
| 6 | Elizabeth Reynolds | Farnbeg | Revd R. Cowen | 1/2 " |
| 7 | Widow McConey | Do | Do | 1/2 " |
| 8 | Widow Flanagan | Do | Do | 1/2 " |
| 9 | Widow McKeon | Do | Do | 1/2 " |
| 10 | Widow Mulledy | Do | Do | 1/2 " |
| 11 | Widow Monaghan | Do | Do | 1/2 " |
| 12 | Widow Beattan | Do | Do | 1/2 " |
| 13 | Widow Gaherty | Do | Do | 1/2 " |
| 14 | Widow Moraghan | Do | Do | 1/2 " |
| 15 | Mary Lenahan | Elphin Street | Mr O'Beirne | 1/2 " |
| 16 | John Kilmartin | Battle Hill | Revd R. Cowen | 1/2 " |
| | | | | 8 Stone |

Fig. 6 List of individuals relieved with meal gratuitously on Strokestown Estate, County Roscommon, listing names, residence, who recommended them, and quantity given, 22 June 1846. [Source: Strokestown Estate Archive, OPW-NUI Maynooth Archive and Research Centre at Castletown]

was dead. She died from hunger and cold. Her clothes were stiff with the frost.[12]

Of the hundreds of narratives which attempt to describe the desperate situation of the starving during the Famine years, I shall include one by Mr Nicholas Cummins, the well-known Cork magistrate who describes one townland which he visited near Skibbereen on 15 December 1846:

I was surprised to find the wretched hamlet apparently deserted. I entered some of the hovels to ascertain the cause, and the scenes which presented themselves were such that no pen or tongue can convey the slightest idea of. In the first, six famished and ghastly skeletons, to all appearances dead, were huddled in a corner on some filthy straw, their sole covering what seemed a ragged horsecloth, their wretched legs hanging about, naked above the knees. I approached with horror, and found by low moaning they were alive – they were in fever, four children, a woman and what had once been a man. It is impossible to go through the detail. Suffice it to say, that in a few minutes I was surrounded by at least 200 such phantoms, such frightful spectres no words can describe, either from famine or from fever. Their demoniac yells are ringing in my ears, and their horrible images are fixed upon my brain. My heart sickens at the recital, but I must go on.[13]

As blight and death spread everywhere and the potatoes failed in fields and gardens all over the land in 1846 and again in 1848, this same Famine catalyst ripped into and revealed the fragile and often dysfunctional social, cultural, economic and political structures of mid-nineteenth-century Ireland. It tore apart the erstwhile interdependent nature of farmer–labourer relationships. Previously the life-enhancing potato plot had been rented by the farmer in return for the work-inputs of the labourer (and his family); the potato crop was also a vital rotational crop in the cultivation of grain crops. When the potato failed, the labourer wanted a money payment

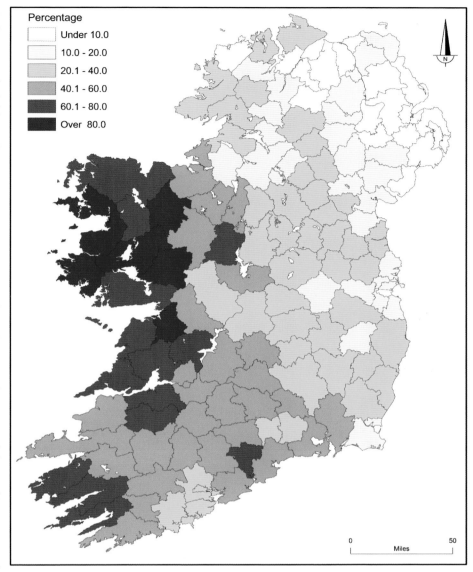

**Percentage**
- Under 10.0
- 10.0 - 20.0
- 20.1 - 40.0
- 40.1 - 60.0
- 60.1 - 80.0
- Over 80.0

0    Miles    50

Fig. 7 PERCENTAGE DISTRIBUTION OF THE MAXIMUM POPULATION RECEIVING FOOD RELIEF UNDER THE TEMPORARY RELIEF (SOUP KITCHEN) ACT. Probably the most successful Government intervention over the years of the Great Famine was the introduction of the soup kitchens in the spring of 1847. The Government had come to recognise that the public relief works were both failing to stem the march of famine and fever and were deemed to be far too costly. Hence the change in policy. Although there were often deadly delays between the closure of public work schemes and the provision of soup kitchens, nevertheless, when established, the food provided saved the lives of thousands of starving people. The relative success of this scheme was a consequence of effective interaction between local relief committees in the parishes/district electoral divisions and central Government. The demand for and provision of food for the starving people varied tremendously across the country: in some northeastern and east coast poor law unions, the proportion falls below 10% whereas in much of Connacht, Clare, west Limerick and peninsular southwest Munster four out of every five persons were often dependent on the soup kitchens. Over the island as a whole, one-third of the population was dependent on these food supplies in the summer of 1847. But the soup kitchens were only part of a Temporary Relief Act – their discontinuation in the autumn of 1847 condemned many to certain death.

from the farmer to purchase food; many farmers, in turn, now wanted payment in cash rather than in kind for the renting of the plot of ground. Their symbiotic relationship was broken.

Elsewhere, the Famine broke up the clustered settlements and neighbourhood–townland networks which had sustained poor, subsistence communities for so long. And as bodies weakened, hunger-induced dysentery, smallpox and typhus fever (and later, even cholera), all wreaked havoc amongst those communities.

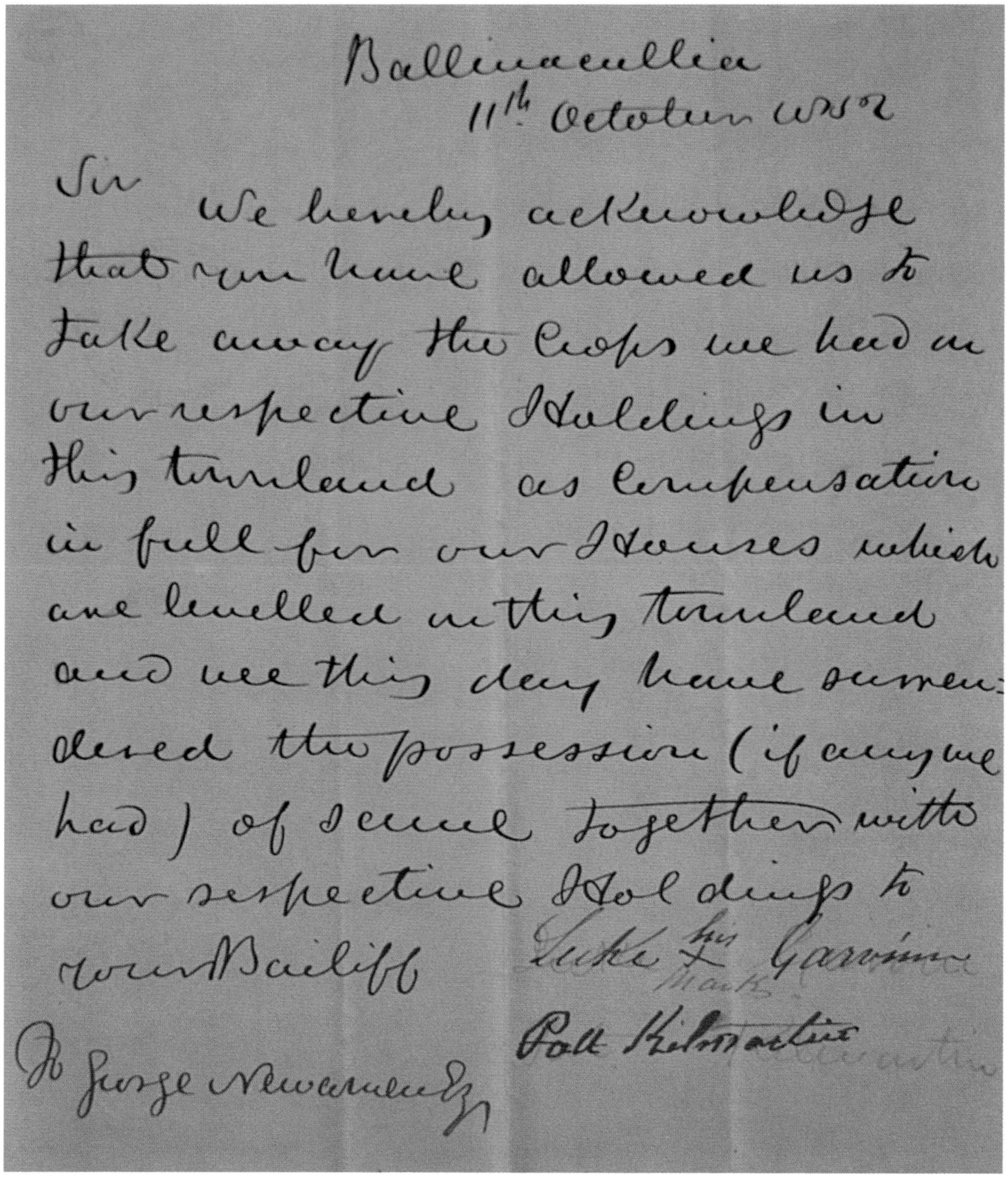

Ballinacullia
11th October 1852

Sir
We hereby acknowledge that you have allowed us to take away the Crops we had on our respective Holdings in this townland as compensation in full for our Houses which are levelled on this townland and we this day have surrendered the possession (if anyone had) of same together with our respective Holdings to your Bailiff

Luke his X mark Garvin
Patt Kilmartin

To George Newcomen Esq

Fig. 8 Evictions and clearances became widespread during the Famine years. Above, a letter addressed to George Newcomen and signed with the marks of Luke Garvin and Pat Kilmartin of Ballinacullia in County Roscommon, stating 'We hereby acknowledge that you have allowed us to take away the crops we had on our respective Holdings in this townland as compensation in full for our Houses which are levelled … and we this day have surrendered the possession … of same together with our respective Holdings to your Bailiff' (11 October 1852). [Source: Strokestown Estate Archive, OPW-NUI Maynooth Archive and Research Centre at Castletown PP/STR/54].

It tore apart some families as parents, children and adult sons and daughters sometimes fought and scrambled for food, or were broken up on entering the workhouse, or scattered via the emigrant ships.[14] However, the folklore tells of heroic efforts by parents to protect their children while the bonds of kinship saw early emigrants assist their brothers and sisters to cross the Atlantic.[15] The public works witnessed violent scenes as starving men insisted on being included and savage struggles occurred as the soup kitchens were first opened in January 1847. In some regions, people were still dying both inside and outside the workhouse as late as 1851-52. As in all famines, it was the poor, the honest, the very young and the old who suffered most.

## Socially selective

While it is true that many of their cousins or brothers in the medical and religious professions laboured heroically in these years and died in disproportionate numbers,[16] the Famine exposed and accentuated the gaps between the resource-rich families of the strong farmer and gentry classes and the increasingly impoverished smallholders and cottiers. Farm families with holdings over twenty acres generally endured. Those beneath this threshold were increasingly exposed and often so desperate as to be involved in robbing corn, turnips, sheep and even cattle from their wealthier neighbours.[17] Most of the better off ruthlessly defended their properties, if necessary hiring armed guards to defend their crops, mills and stores. Food left the market towns under the gaze of the hungry people, defended by a military escort: 'the barges leave Clonmel once a week for Waterford port with the export supplies under convoy, which, last Tuesday [24 April 1846], consisted of two guns, fifty cavalry escorting them on the banks of the Suir as far as Carrick'.[18]

Most tellingly, the Great Famine revealed the cracks and fissures in an already unwieldy and ramshackle property structure. It revealed the continuing exploitative role of both a host of middlemen and an alien and sometimes absentee landlord class, for the most part out of touch and out of sympathy with their tenants. State policy required landlords to bear a significant share of the poor rates and to provide local employment. Perhaps a third of this class endeavoured to meet their obligations to their estate communities (including paying the full rates on holdings valued at less than £4 per annum); however, another one-third were already so indebted (via mortgages and extravagant life-styles) as to be incapable – if they so wished – of rendering any support to their often

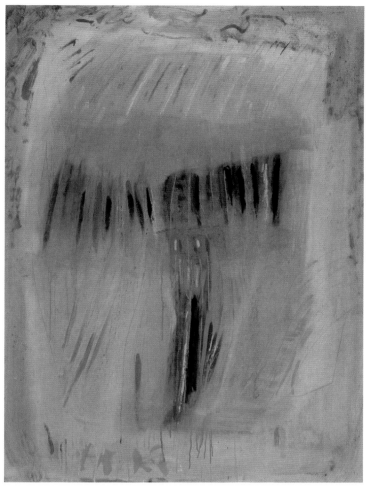

Fig. 9 *Famine Spectre*, by Tony O'Malley, oil on board, 122x91cm. [Courtesy Jane O'Malley]

policy arguments in London's Government, the Famine – under the cloak of a Malthusian-cum-Providentialist interpretation – was seen as a useful instrument for the acceleration of 'proper' economic development and the radical reconstruction of related property structures in a recalcitrant Ireland.

The relative success of the provision of food for close on three million people in July 1847, via the soup kitchens, proved that neither questions of access nor administrative capacity need hinder the provision of necessary relief. As Ó Gráda argues, 'given the political will to spend more money, the relief framework erected could have been marshalled to distribute more aid'.[20] But the shameful retreat by central Government from funding necessary reliefs – and the placing of the primary responsibility on the poor Poor Law unions from mid-1847 – clearly added to mass mortality. The dedicated efforts of local, regional and national officials were frustrated and often crippled by the numerous acts and regulations emanating from a distant London. Deaths in workhouses alone increased from 5,979 in 1845 and 14,662 in 1846 to a massive 66,890 in 1847 and was 64,440 in 1849 and still close to 40,000 over 1851. In truth, this enormous and inhumane policy failure during the Famine meant the beginning of the end for British rule over much of Ireland.

### THE SCATTERING
The Famine was to scatter Irish people across the world.

poor and desperate tenantry: but more than a further one-third ruthlessly rode roughshod over their poor rate obligations and utilised new legislative openings (such as the Gregory Clause, which ruled that any occupier of more than a quarter of an acre of land could not be deemed destitute and so could not receive relief), to get rid of their poor tenantry.[19] Evictions increased dramatically as cabins, people and thousands of smaller holdings were cleared from the land, leaving a human landscape scavenged by famine deaths, deprivation and dispersion. The many sounds of the lively pre-Famine world were replaced by an eerie silence.

### UNION WITH BRITAIN
The cumulative impact of the same time-bomb of the Famine was to shatter any misconceptions many Irish people might have held about the benefits of the union with Britain. They were to discover that the union did not mean parity of esteem or an equal entitlement to sharing in the ample resources of the world's first industrialised country. The devastating effects of the Famine challenged, but did not break, the ideologies of laissez-faire and the pre-eminence of the market. What it did expose was the poverty of a blinkered mindset amongst British decision-makers at the highest levels. For those decision-makers who won the

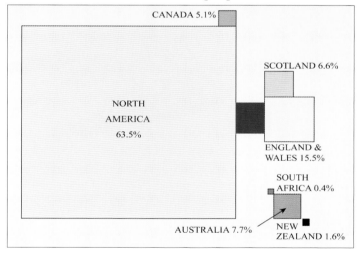

Fig. 11 PERCENTAGE OF IRISH-BORN LIVING ABROAD IN THE LATE NINETEENTH CENTURY. Emigration – both seasonal and permanent – had long been a feature of Irish life. Already about a million people had left the country in the two decades between 1821 and 1841. This annual level of emigration continued up to 1845-46; then, as famine intensified, the exodus from Ireland became an unstoppable flood. Close on a million desperate Irish people emigrated to overseas countries between 1846 and March 1851 with close on a further half million leaving Ireland by the end of 1852. In addition, between a quarter and one-third of a million famine-stricken people ended up in the slums of Liverpool, Glasgow, London and other British cities. By 1891, four out of ten of the total Irish-born population were then living abroad. As this map confirms, the great majority had emigrated to North America, particularly to the United States. Britain had also been a major recipient of Irish emigrants and Australia and New Zealand were becoming other havens. The scattering of the Irish across the English-speaking world was in full flow – southern Africa had also emerged as a possible destination by the late nineteenth century.

independence from Britain intensified.[21] At home, the impact and aftermath of the Famine set in motion a social and economic revolution which, amongst other things consolidated farms, intensified a now almost pathological love of the land, institutionalised late or no marriages, and still populated the workhouses and asylums.

A rejuvenated Catholic Church now reinforced its cultural power with the elaboration of a vast array of buildings, religious orders and functions. The number of Irish men and women who joined the diocesan clergy and the numerous religious orders and institutions increased from 5,000 in 1851 to over 14,000 in 1900.[22] In the countryside, unlike the tillage farmers, the big winners from the Famine catastrophe were the cattlemen graziers and dairymen who substantially increased their stock even during the Famine. In a parallel process, employment in agriculture was progressively reduced.[23] And in the towns, the shopkeepers and traders who survived (and sometimes prospered) during the severe contraction of the economy during the Famine years, were to again prosper as standards of living rose in town and countryside. The commercialisation and modernisation of Irish life

**GOING FOR A LICENCE TO KEEP FIRE-ARMS.**

Fig. 12 Alexander Somerville, a Scot by birth was commissioned by the *Manchester Examiner* to report on conditions in Ireland in the early months of 1847. He spent three months travelling the country. In Dungarvan, Carrick-on-Suir and Clonmel he noted the large increase in the sale of arms: 'most of the farmers have corn in their possession, and all who have it feel uneasy about it. They are purchasing arms and ammunition to defend it, and are doing this the more anxiously and generally that they see the common people, the very poorest, procuring arms' in K. D. M. Snell (ed.) *Letters from Ireland during the Famine* by Alexander Somerville (Dublin, 1994) p. 51 [Source: *Illustrated London News,* 26 August 1848]

As many as two and a half million people had fled the island by 1855, accentuating an exodus which has ebbed and flowed ever since. Apart from crowding into the slums of Britain's major cities, the cities of the English-speaking New World were to be the major recipients of the fleeing Irish – creating what Kevin Whelan has called 'the Green Atlantic' – and a powerful political voice when issues of proceeded apace – and moved smartly away from the ruins and horrors of the Famine landscape. Yet the horrors of the Famine and its long term consequences – if sometimes repressed and driven underground – surfaced regularly to remain still etched on the folk memory of the Irish at home and, more especially, overseas. It remained, like a running sore, 'wherever green was worn'.

# 'Mapping the people': The growth and distribution of the population

*William J. Smyth*

The Census of Ireland from 1841 brings in a population total for Ireland of 8.175 million. The population in 1851 was returned at 6.55 million. The general assumption, therefore, about Ireland's population by mid-1846 – before the Famine intensified – suggests a population of 8.5 million. However, serious doubt has been cast on the accuracy of the Census returns for Ireland in not only 1821 and 1831 but also in 1841. Joseph Lee suggests the returns for 1821 should be increased from 6.8m to 7.2m; that of 1831 from 7.77m to 7.9m and 1841 from 8.175m to 8.4 m.[1] The latter figure takes account of Tucker's highly innovative identification of the failure to include *c.*150,000 very young children in these returns[2] and also suggests that the 1841 Census suffers from adult under-numeration of at least 1%. These amendments require that the assumed figure in the mid-1840s also needs to be reassessed. It is suggested that Ireland's population in mid-1846 is likely to have been *c.*8.75 million and possibly higher.

As a general rule, the parishes of greatest size contain very large populations in 1841. Kilcommon (Erris) and Kilgeever in County Mayo, Ballynakill/Moyrus in County Galway, Offerlane and Clonenagh in Queen's County, Clonfert and Skull in County Cork, Lismore and Mocollop in County Waterford, Inver in County Donegal, Aghamullen, Donaghmoyne and Creggan in County Monaghan and Kilkeel in the 'Mournes', County Down, are clear examples of this feature. The converse also applies – many of the small-sized parishes contain the smallest populations in 1841. Nevertheless, transcending the parish size factor is a very old island-wide distinction between parishes north of a line from Galway Bay to the Cooley peninsula characterised by higher populations and the southern half of the island (with the exception of pockets in west and southwest Munster). Many parishes and regions north of this ancient boundary return populations of 6,000 and over with a significant number containing populations in excess of 12,000. In contrast, the southern half of the island contains many parishes whose populations rarely exceed 6,000. Indeed with the exception of upland and bogland regions, the norm in the southern zone is *c.* 2,500 people per civil parish.

The effect of parish size is eliminated and a much more precise picture emerges when one examines population densities per 100 acres in 1841 (see Figure 1). A quite extraordinary belt of very high densities – of at least 50 and often 100 people per 100 acres (in the latter case indicating a density of one person per every acre!) – encircles Lough Neagh and sweeps in a large crescent southwestwards as far as the borderlands of south Leitrim, north Longford and north Roscommon. There are equally very high densities in a smaller crescent curving between Killala and Clew Bay, along the length of the Shannon estuary and extending eastwards into the Golden Vale, as well as along the coastal parishes of all of County Cork. In contrast, the uplands of Donegal, west Mayo, much of Connemara, south Kerry, the Wicklow mountains and smaller pockets in the 'Pale' region return very low densities per 100 acres.

If one sharpens the lens even further and look at the number of persons per square mile of arable land, parishes in Armagh county emerge as the pivot of the highest densities with over 500 (and sometimes over 1000) per square mile of arable land, with densities of over 400 revealed for many parishes in Counties Cavan, Down, Monaghan and Tyrone, as well as most of the coastal parishes in the western counties (where again some reach 1000 per square mile of arable land). Parts of northern and western Ireland then had population densities of Chinese and southeast Asian proportions. In contrast, the rich lands of County Kildare reveal the lowest densities of 187 per square mile of arable land, followed by Meath (201), Wexford (217), Westmeath (230) and Kilkenny (236). A large transitional belt of 300 to 350 persons per square mile of arable land runs along an axis from Cork and Limerick northwards to County Louth. It is clear, therefore, that there were very striking local and regional variations in population densities and living conditions across Ireland in 1841.

## POPULATION INCREASE

Current estimates show Ireland's population increases by 2–2.5% per annum after 1740-41 to reach 4m by 1790, 5m by 1800, over 7m in 1821, to register *c.*8.7m by mid-1846. Figure 2 seeks to illuminate population changes between 1732 and 1821.[3] There is an issue about the overall reliability of the 1732 returns. Nevertheless, they provide by far the best evidence of population numbers per barony at this time. It should also be remembered that the 1740–41 famine be taken into account in examining this map, especially in relation to the midlands and the province of Munster, the latter losing close to 25% of its population in those two years. Nevertheless, Figure 2 presents a convincing picture.

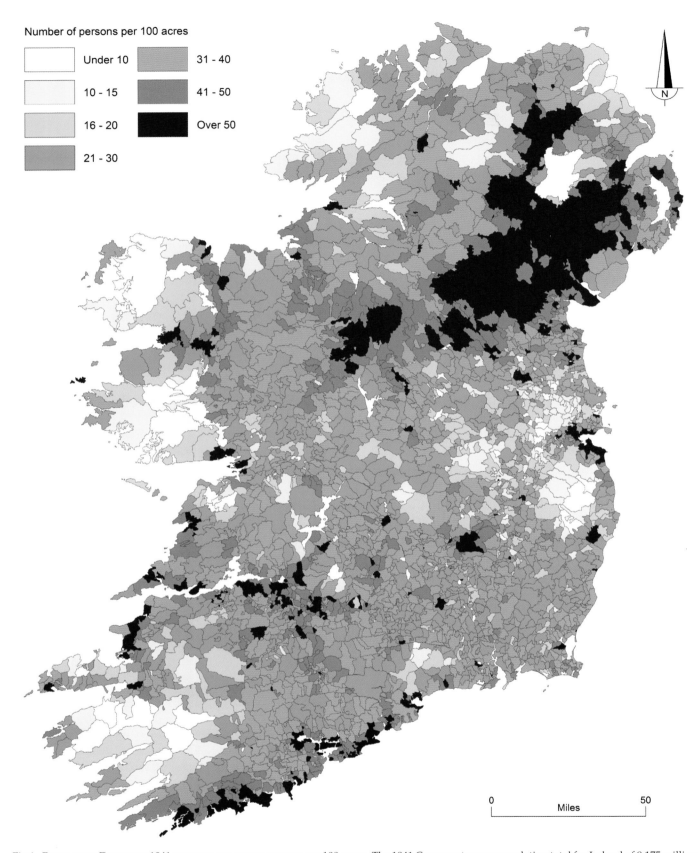

Number of persons per 100 acres

- Under 10
- 10 - 15
- 16 - 20
- 21 - 30
- 31 - 40
- 41 - 50
- Over 50

Miles 0 — 50

Fig 1. POPULATION DENSITY IN 1841 SHOWING NUMBER OF PERSONS PER 100 ACRES. The 1841 Census returns a population total for Ireland of 8.175 million. However, this may well be a significant underestimation; the more likely figure is 8.4 million with the population reaching 8.6/8.7 million by 1846. This map examines population densities per 100 acres as returned in 1841. A quite extraordinary level of very high densities – of at least 50 and often 100 people per 100 acres encircles Lough Neagh and sweeps in a large crescent southwestwards as far as the borders of south Leitrim, north Longford and north Roscommon. In contrast the uplands of Donegal, west Mayo, much of Connemara, south Kerry, Wicklow Mountains and smaller pockets in the east Leinster return very low densities per 100 acres. This map highlights the very varied living conditions across pre-Famine Ireland.

As along many other vectors, there are striking differences between the Ireland lying north and west of the Galway Bay–Cooley axis and the country to the south and east of this line. Apart from pockets of significant population growth such as in Rathdown (County Dublin), Garrycastle (County Offaly), the baronies of mid-Tipperary and the peninsular baronies of west Munster, which saw at least a trebling of population numbers in the ninety years between 1732 and 1821, the most striking feature of the rest of the south and east is the relative stability of population levels. Some baronies in the 'Pale' do not even register a doubling of population. Likewise, it appears that much of the rest of Leinster, in Wexford, and Wicklow and a large swathe of baronies across south Munster see only a doubling of population. All of this suggests a propertied society where late arranged marriages, impartible inheritance and the absence of subdivision were characteristic. These are also regions where significant urban centres with important milling, provisioning, brewing and distilling industries existed, where off-farm opportunities were available and where a commercialised agriculture prevailed – involving intensified tillage cultivation.

In contrast, most of the baronies of the north and west (but excluding Counties Down and Antrim) display dramatic increases in populations. Southwest Clare, west Mayo and much of Donegal lead this list. A number of baronies in east Connacht and south Ulster also belong to this region characterised by sensational population growth. What is particularly striking is the deeply incised cultural boundary between the long-settled stable world of Counties Louth and Meath to the south and the very significant regions of new settlement, colonisation and population growth which stretch north across from south Cavan and Monaghan, continuing into north Longford and north Roscommon and beyond. These more pastoral subcultures where the potato

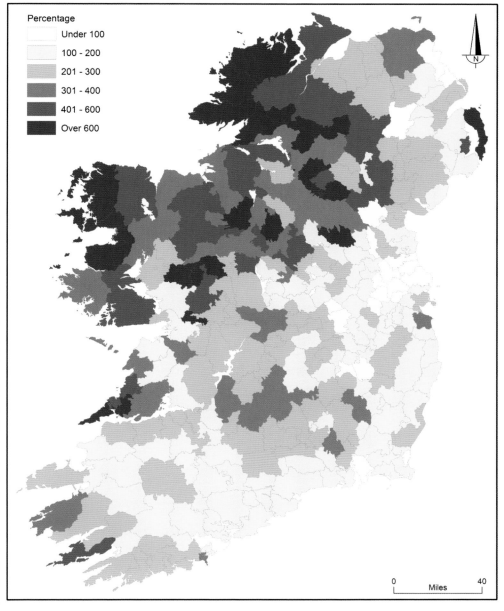

Percentage

Under 100
100 - 200
201 - 300
301 - 400
401 - 600
Over 600

0    Miles    40

Fig. 2 PERCENTAGE CHANGE IN THE DISTRIBUTION OF POPULATION BETWEEN 1732 AND 1821. Overall, Ireland's population increased from c.2.4 million in 1732 to 5m in 1800 and over 7m by 1821. However, this dramatic trebling of the country's population was unevenly distributed across the island. In the Pale and pockets elsewhere, the population had scarcely doubled in these ninety years. Across much of the rest of Leinster and south Munster, populations increased by between 100 and 200%. In contrast, over much of central and west Ulster, Connacht (and Longford) as well as west Clare and parts of peninsular southwest Munster, population numbers rocketed with dramatic increases of between 300 and 600%. North Munster, Kilkenny and much of east Ulster reveal transitional growth patterns with population increases of 200 to 300%. By 1821, there were striking differences in population pressures and living conditions across the island with the poorest lands often witnessing the most dramatic population increases.

flourished reflect the creation of 'new wests' and 'new norths', following on from settlement, and the commercial, communication and domestic industrial expansion which spilled over onto these extensive marginal lands from the late seventeenth century onwards.[4]

East Ulster, however, diverges somewhat surprisingly from this pattern of spectacular population growth. This reflects, perhaps, a more settled, propertied society where the impact of the linen industry was more centralised and more sophisticated. The peninsular baronies of west

Fig. 3 *Return from the Fair*, 1828 by John George Mulvany (c.1766–1838) The interior of a strong farmer's house. The people's clothing, along with the arrangement and quality of the household furniture, is an indication of the wealth and status of a very settled propertied class. (Source: Private collection)

Munster also show signs of significant population growth over these ninety years. However, one might overemphasise the northwest/southeast distinctions across Ireland. It is noticeable that there are significant transitional regions stretching from west Wicklow and the south Midlands and incorporating all of Counties Kilkenny, Tipperary, much of County Limerick and northwest Cork, whose populations have come close to trebling over this ninety-year period.

In the immediate pre-Famine decades of the 1820s and 1830s it appears that the dramatic population increases of the second half of the eighteenth and early nineteenth centuries are slowing down. Population growth of less than c.10% characterises north Leinster and pockets in north Ulster, Connacht and coastal south Munster. Over much of lowland Ireland, the population increase is between 10 and 20%. Population growth had slowed down to between 0.6% and 1.0% per annum in these regions. The intensification of emigration is a significant controlling factor here. About one million people left the country between 1821 and 1841.[5] In

contrast, in both peninsular Connacht and Munster, and along an axis from Kilmaine through the south Mayo/Sligo baronies to Drumahaire in Leitrim, populations come close to a 50% increase over these two decades. Likewise, much of the rest of Connacht, upland and lowland Munster and the upland flanks of south Leinster display middle-level population increases of 20 to 40%. Ireland, on the eve of the Famine, reveals very contrasting population growth patterns and living conditions.

CHECKS AND BALANCES
Overall, this analysis of regional patterns of population growth from 1732 to 1821 and from 1821 to 1841 demonstrates that checks and balances were significant operational features in the rural societies of much of eastern and southeastern Ireland. Here more commercialised farming systems, strict marriage regimes, primogeniture and impartible inheritance patterns prevailed amongst the solid farmer class. Both urban and rural middle-class populations lived relatively comfortable lives in a highly

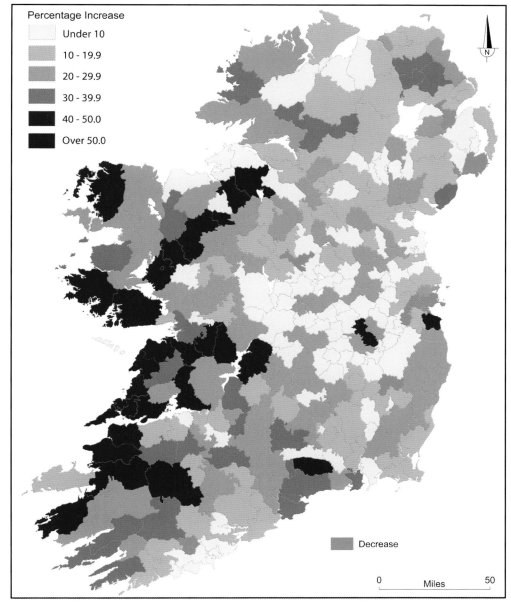

Percentage Increase

Under 10
10 - 19.9
20 - 29.9
30 - 39.9
40 - 50.0
Over 50.0

Decrease

0        Miles        50

Fig. 4 PERCENTAGE CHANGE IN THE DISTRIBUTION OF POPULATION BETWEEN 1821 AND 1841. The two decades between 1821 and 1841 also witnessed contrasting patterns of population growth across the island. Overall, the rate of population increase was reducing, with significant emigration levels also a feature. Population growth is least across north Leinster and pockets in north Ulster, the Sligo region and parts of coastal south Munster with less than a 10% increase. Growth rates of 10 to 30% are unevenly distributed across the island, being most noticeable across the rest of Ulster, south Leinster, Munster and parts of Connacht. However, populations continued to increase dramatically all along the west coast from west Donegal, through west Connacht, much of Clare and southwest Munster. These rates of increase also extended inland in parts of Munster (in Clare, Tipperary and Waterford) and in mid-Connacht. Overall, regional patterns of population growth between 1732 and 1841 demonstrate that the more commercialised rural societies of the east and southeast of the island operated more strict controls over both marriage regimes and inheritance patterns. In contrast, in the lands of the mid-west and northwest, the subdivision of family holdings and early marriage were far more characteristic, facilitated both by the availability of poorer land for colonisation by the potato and the expansion of the domestic textile industry.

stratified world, underpinned by a significant landless and cottier labouring class.

In contrast, in what was still mainly an Irish-speaking Ireland over much of the southwest, west and northwest, partible inheritance systems, lack of parental and landlord control, resultant early marriages and the availability of poorer land for colonisation by the sturdy potato all facilitated rapid population growth. As Kevin Whelan notes: 'the spade and the spud conquered the contours' as

settlement climbed up to 800 feet all across the fragmented uplands in the country.[6] The spread of domestic textile activities throughout rural Ulster and the adjacent counties of Leinster and Connacht was an additional spur to both the proliferation and subdivision of smallholdings and dramatic population surges. The gradual spread of small-pox inoculation was also seen as a critical factor.

In the decades before the Famine, the diet of these smallholding communities and that of landless labourers and cottiers was dominated by potatoes and milk. Nevertheless, as Ó Gráda and Mokyr have argued so cogently, this is not to suggest that Ireland, and particularly these densely settled regions, were overpopulated.[7] Ó Gráda quotes the observations of commentators such as Arthur Young and Adam Smith about the handsome, athletic and robust Irish poor 'as capable of enduring labour as any upon the earth'.[8] These people were nourished on a wholesome and nutritious diet of potatoes and benefited from a plentiful supply of inexpensive domestic fuel in the form of the turf fire. Their relative health and nutritional status has been confirmed by comparative studies which have found that Irishmen's heights were greater than those of equivalent Englishmen in a variety of occupations and situations. The life expectancy of the Irish was then equal to if not greater than most other Europeans except those of Denmark and England. So despite a somewhat superficial literature which overemphasises the very visible signs of the tattered clothing and poorer housing, Ó Gráda has argued that 'the Irish were better fed, better heated and healthier and perhaps happier' than many Europeans and certainly in a better state than these Malthusian interpretations would suggest.[9]

Nevertheless, it appears that the poorer populations were becoming much poorer. A significant minority of the population practically starved in the summer months

Fig. 5 'Spade and spud conquering the contours' – potato ridges, Ballygriffin, County Kerry. [Photo: Frank Coyne]

before the new potatoes became available. Their living standards were falling while urban and rural middle-class consumer patterns reveal a relatively well-to-do section of the population. It was the accident of an unpredictable potato blight in 1845 and the bad luck that the blight would return and intensify in a number of subsequent years which exposed these hardworking, coherent but mainly cashless townland communities (often living in clustered settlements) to hunger, starvation and the spread of fever and disease. Those few who could afford the passage scrambled to reach the nearest port and escape. For the majority of the poor, however, it was not a question of food shortage but their lack of money, their inability to purchase what food was available which defeated so many.

## DECLINE

The population of Ireland declined from *c*.8.5m (8.7m?) in mid-1846 to 6.55m in 1857. It is estimated that close on one million people died as a direct consequence of the Famine. More than one million and a quarter fled the country, with close on two-thirds emigrating to the United States alone. Marriage rates slumped during the Famine years and birth

rates declined by approximately one-third. If averted births (those who would have been born if fertility had not been reduced by the tragedy of the Famine) are included, the direct and indirect effects of the tragedy effectively saw a population decline of *c*.2.5m. In a short few years close on 30% of the people had vanished from the land.

The inset map (Fig. 6) is not, therefore, a map of decline consequent on the number of Famine deaths alone but is a map of population decline which includes population loss arising from both emigration and reduced family size. In the southwest, west and northwest as well as parts of the north Midlands and south and mid-Ulster, the map likely underestimates the absolute population decline in many parishes after 1845, given the rate of population growth of these localities in the years prior to the Famine. Between 1841 and 1851, the recorded population loss for the parish of Schull in County Cork is as high as 7,662 persons, for the parish of Cloone in County Leitrim; 6,559 persons, for the parish of Kilglass in County Roscommon; 5,771 persons, Aghamullen in County Monaghan; 5,636 persons, and Kilgeever in County Mayo, 5,579 persons. In all such parishes, and

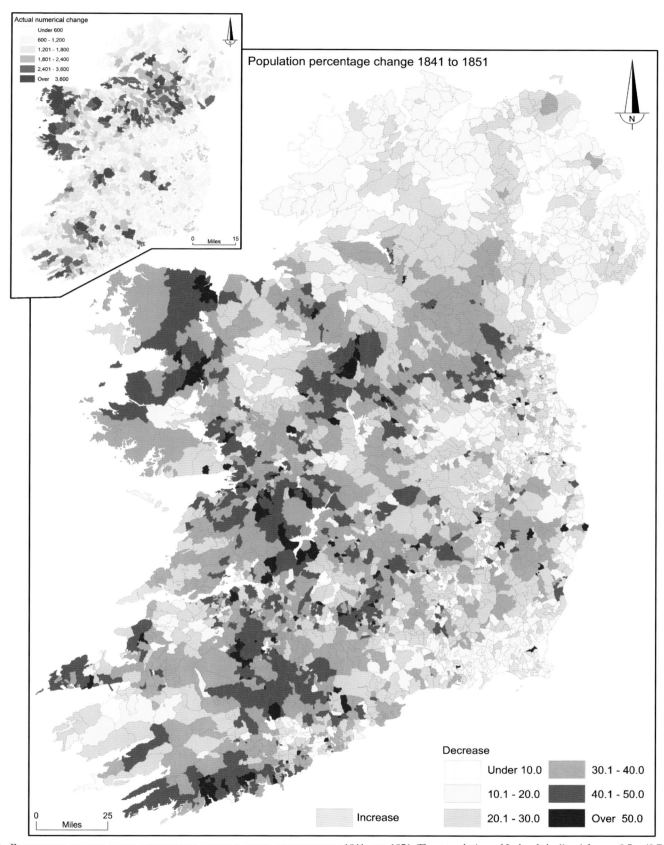

Fig. 6. PERCENTAGE CHANGE IN THE DISTRIBUTION OF RURAL POPULATION BETWEEN 1841 AND 1851. The population of Ireland declined from c.8.5m (8.7m?) in mid-1846 to 6.55m in 1851. In a limited number of parishes around Belfast, Dublin, Waterford and Cork small population increases are recorded, reflecting for the most part immigration into these city regions. Secondly, much of Ulster north of a line from Donegal to Carlingford Lough shows the lowest population decreases – for the most part of 10 to 20%. In contrast, the heavier shading on the map reveals the contrasting fortunes of parishes which lost over 40% and in some cases over 50% (i.e. over half of the population) in this short period. Dramatic population losses are shown from southwest Cork through much of Munster including north and east Clare, as well as the Connacht counties of Galway and Mayo. In some parishes, population losses reflect heavy mortalities, in others a significant emigration level, but in others again both excess mortality and substantial outmigration are major reinforcing agents. This map is central to any analysis of the vulnerabilities that led to so many famine deaths.

Fig. 7 *Collecting the rent at Manor Hamilton, Co. Leitrim, c.1847* by David Frederick Markham (1800–53). The inability to meet rent and rate demands by land-lords and poor law collectors led to eviction and mass outmigration. [Source: Private collection]

many others, the actual population loss after 1845 was likely to have been greater.

Comparing the absolute population distributions in 1841 and 1851 and using the same population categories and shading patterns, the two most striking features of the 1851 map is the persistence of the northwest/southeast contrasts and the emptying of the map of the heavier shades. Population loss is reflected in the darker shading patterns. Whereas the island-wide average for the number of persons per square mile of arable land in 1841 was 386, by 1851 this average has been dramatically reduced by fifty-one to 335 per square mile. It is important to emphasise again that all parts of the island were affected – for example, even the densities in the parishes of County Kildare and County Wexford were reduced on average from 187 to 155 and from 217 to 181 per square mile of arable land. Much of the northeast of Ulster and all of Leinster and east Munster reveal densities in 1851 well below the national average. All the western and southern

Ulster counties return densities well above the national average, although the Census of 1851 exaggerates the reductions in Counties Donegal, Mayo, Galway and Kerry.

Figure 6 illuminates the percentage change in rural population between 1841 and 1851, with dark shading showing the highest decreases and light shading the lowest. In a limited number of parishes around Belfast, Dublin, Waterford and Cork (as well as rural south Wexford), small population increases are recorded, reflecting for the most part immigration close to these city regions. Secondly, much of Ulster, in a line from Donegal Bay to Carlingford Lough, shows the lowest percentage decreases – for the most part of 10–20%. Here the impact of the Famine was most severe in 1847 but populations were recovering by 1851. The 'old Pale' region and south Wexford, as well as pockets in the Suir Valley, the Iveragh Peninsula and in a number of exceptional parishes in the west and northwest (especially in mid-Connacht), also experienced relatively small declines. The various shades of brown on the map reveals

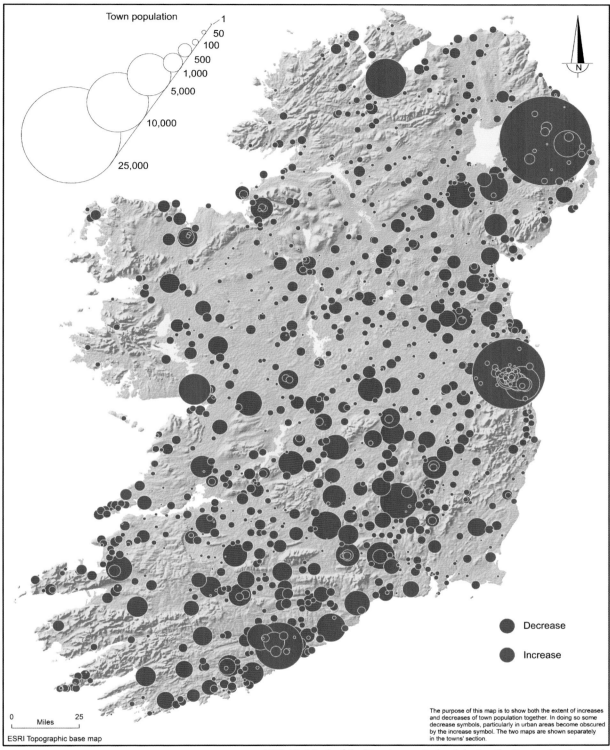

Town population
1
50
100
500
1,000
5,000
10,000
25,000

Decrease

Increase

0    Miles    25

ESRI Topographic base map

The purpose of this map is to show both the extent of increases and decreases of town population together. In doing so some decrease symbols, particularly in urban areas become obscured by the increase symbol. The two maps are shown separately in the towns' section.

Fig. 8 PERCENTAGE CHANGE IN THE DISTRIBUTION OF URBAN POPULATION 1841–51. Much of the literature on Ireland during the Famine has focused on the many tragedies occurring in the Irish countryside. What is less often recognised is that the Great Famine and its consequences were almost equally devastating for both the populations and vitality of Irish towns and cities. This map shows the levels of population increase or decrease in over 1,200 Irish towns between 1841 and 1851. Over this period only one-fourth of Irish towns either managed to maintain or increase their populations. As the map shows, much of these gains were in the port cities and other coastal towns – including ferry ports such as Cobh (Queenstown) and Dún Laoghaire (Kingstown) involved in the business of shipping Irish emigrants overseas. As in the case of Dublin, much of this increase was due to immigrant populations flocking to the port-cities seeking either relief or a passage to America or both. Northeast Ulster is exceptional in its urban growth levels, reflecting the impact of factory-based industrialisation in this region. But what is most striking about this map is that three-quarters of the towns had in many cases sizeable losses of 1,000 to 2,000 people. Only two out of ten regional centres with populations in 1841 of between 10,000 and 25,000 increased their populations while only 10 out of 50 towns in the 3,000–5,000 category gained populations. Towns such as Charleville, Castledermot and Freshford lost almost half their populations and Cashel, Loughrea, Rathkeale and Roscrea were amongst these medium-sized towns which lost c.one-third of their populations. And even more devastating for most of these towns was the loss of numerous craft, industrial and service functions. The emptying of the countryside stripped the towns of many of their functions and led to the collapse of their emerging urban bourgeoisie. Unlike the rest of urbanising Europe where the middle-classes came to play such a powerful role, not just economically but also culturally, this severe weakening of the Irish urban middle class had long-term negative consequences. Many towns would not recover for a hundred years.

the contrasting fortunes of parishes which lost over 40% and in some cases over 50% (i.e. one-half of their total population) in this short period.

Not surprisingly, the ill-fated parishes of southwest Cork centred on Skibbereen suffered heavy losses, but so did many parishes – such as Grenagh and Mogeely – in the ostensibly wealthier zones of mid-Cork, mid-Limerick and mid-Tipperary. East and north Clare saw dramatic population losses as did parishes in east and west Galway, and much of west Mayo. Another region suffering major losses extended north and west of Lough Allen in the upper Shannon basin, including the parishes of Kilglass, Annaduff and Mohill. Finally, there were large swathes of parishes which lost at least a third of their populations, particularly in south Ulster and along the borders with Leinster, in east and west Connacht, south Leinster and all of the west of Munster. In some parishes, population losses reflect heavy mortalities and in others they indicate significant emigration levels, but in others again both excess mortality and substantial outmigration are major reinforcing factors.

Fig. 9 *Skellig Night on the South Mall c.1845* by James Beale. [Source: Crawford Art Gallery] Despite the appearances of a relatively poorer population, travellers' descriptions of pre-Famine Ireland often marvelled at the vitality and gaiety of the communities they observed. In particular, the strength of musical and dancing traditions were noted. This painting vividly portrays the carnival atmosphere on the South Mall in Cork city on Shrove Tuesday night, just before the beginning of the Lenten period when marriages were forbidden. Since it was believed that the monks on Skellig began their observance of Lent several weeks later than the mainland, however, the myth/fiction persisted that recalcitrant bachelors and spinsters could be 'persuaded'/'carried off' to Skellig for 'the nuptials'. Hence, the scenes of riotous behaviour on the streets as suitably unmarried men and women – whose names were printed on broadsheets known as the 'Skellig lists' – are chased and mockingly 'transported' to Skellig. The painting also reminds us that marriage was seen as both normal and inevitable in the pre-Famine world. In the post-Famine world, the music was often silenced and the dancing ceased. The age at marriage increased sharply and many men and women never married. It was a much more sombre world.

# 1740–41 Famine

## David Dickson

Rural Ireland in the 1730s still bore the scars of the revolutionary social changes of the previous century. Control over its productive resources, its grassland, woodlands and rivers, was concentrated in relatively few hands, and they operated in a comparatively unregulated environment. Compared to the situation in neighbouring jurisdictions, little protected the poor or the marginalised from the actions of the powerful, be they big Catholic tenant farmers or 'improving' Protestant landlords. Contemporary critics like Thomas Prior, Jonathan Swift or George Berkeley, themselves drawn from the political establishment, railed against both luxury-loving and myopic gentry, and the rapacious graziers who were their tenants. This pervasive inequality was explained by contemporaries in a variety of ways, but as Louis Cullen pointed out long ago, it is striking that what was represented in the literature as endemic structural poverty only became a matter of intense public debate in the 1720s and 1730s, a time of cyclical depression compounded (in the 1720s) by very bad weather.[1]

Over the previous sixty years wool products, butter and salted beef had become Ireland's major export earners, but the benefits from these trades accrued to the owners of stock and their landlords, not to the majority of rural households. The exception to this rule was the vast trade in flax products, in which Ireland was becoming a leading European producer. Here the benefits of a lively export trade in the finished product, linen, trickled down to the smallholder, the only problem being that linen production was concentrated in the lowlands of east, north and south Ulster. The diffusion of linen manufacture into other regions would only come about later in the century.

Thus by the end of the 1730s signs of economic development were most evident in parts of Ulster and in the burgeoning port cities of the south, conduits for the pastoral exports being shipped out to Europe and the Atlantic. The decade itself had been untypically mild and harvests generally good. But the economy was sluggish, with weak international prices. The return of maritime war in October 1739 (initially between Britain and Spain) depressed economic sentiment even further.

### GREAT FROST

Then came the coldest winter in half a millennium. The Great Frost of 1739–40 affected much of northern Europe, beginning after Christmas with a week of extraordinary Siberian winds; exceptionally low temperatures lasted for over six long weeks in Ireland and longer elswhere.[2] Without

Fig. 1 The Great Frost of 1739/40 impacted on much of northern Europe. A period of exceptionally low temperatures began after Christmas and lasted for over six long weeks in Ireland and longer elsewhere. The inland lakes of Ireland ice up two or three times a century, the tidal estuaries of its rivers even less often, but in those weeks in 1740 every waterway froze. Barfinnihy lake is located six miles from Kenmare in County Kerry. [Photo Frank Coyne, winter 2011]

uneatable. In addition, there was a huge loss of livestock. Cattle, horses and sheep were always wintered in the open; in many areas they were decimated during the frost, with even greater mortality occurring during the spring as fodder supplies became exhausted.

The frost lifted in early February but the abnormal weather had another eighteen months to run: a dry spring became a cold summer drought, and the landscape in some districts turned from green to brick. There was a spate of major fires in many towns. The drought was really only

Fig. 2 *Hugh Boulter* by Francis Bindon, oil on canvas. Francis Bindon was commissioned by the governors of the Dublin Workhouse to paint the portrait of Hugh Boulter, the elderly Church of Ireland archbishop of Armagh (*d.* 1744), surrounded by the Dubl–41'. Boulter had been an active member of the Irish Government since coming to Ireland in 1724, and had taken the lead in organising grain imports to relieve the Ulster famine of 1727–29. More famously he oversaw relief operations in Dublin during and long after the Great Frost, 'wide scattering round whole harvests from his hand'. At its height he was reputed to have spent fifty pounds a day of his own money on food doles. The portrait, executed in 1742, is the sole contemporary image of the crisis and hung for a century in the hall of the Foundling Hospital. [Source: Trinity College Dublin Art Collection: reproduced by kind permission from the Board of Trinity College Dublin]

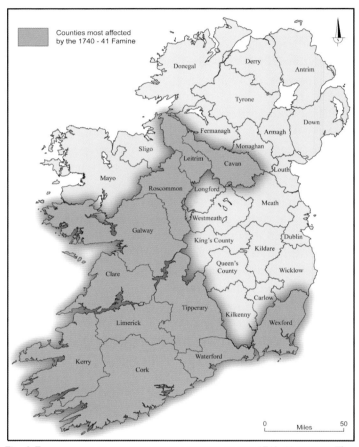

Fig. 3 DISTRIBUTION OF COUNTIES MOST AFFECTED BY THE 1740–41 FAMINE. The Great Frost of the Winter of 1739/40 deeply affected most of northern Europe. And after the frost, came an abnormally dry spring and summer, autumnal floods, heavy winter snow and a very dry spring in 1741. Yet excess human mortality did not coincide with the coldest northern countries of Europe. Rather it was Atlantic Europe, characterised by somewhat less severe weather conditions that witnessed the greatest human suffering and highest mortalities. These regional variations point up deep-seated structural forces shaping patterns of mortality across Europe. Within Ireland, levels of welfare provision and public intervention to deal with such a crisis were both weak generally and varied regionally. Where urban corporations, the parish vestries of the Established Church of Ireland and landowners were active, the impact of the 1740–41 famine was reduced – as in much of Ulster and the Dublin and Kilkenny hinterlands. In contrast, as this map shows, an extensive zone across the middle of Ireland – from Roscommon and Galway southwards to include Clare, Tipperary, Limerick and Cork – especially in the rich Golden Vale of Munster – suffered most from the famine. Here, the commercialisation of sheep and cattle farming had produced a world of great social extremes. Huge pastoral farms and cottier holdings subsisting on the potato had been established here in a world which had seen the elimination of both corn-growing farmers and their village settlements and the creation of great grazier enclosures from at least the mid-seventeenth century. It was these marginalised smallholding and labouring families which were most exposed to the catalogue of disasters – cold, famine, disease and death – which characterised the year known in Irish as *bliain an áir* (the year of the slaughter).

an accurate temperature record we can only speculate as to the depth of the mercury in the few thermometers in the country, but this was unambiguously the coldest event in anyone's memory. Coming after a run of soft winters it caught people quite off-guard. The inland lakes of Ireland ice up two or three times a century, the tidal estuaries of its rivers even less often, but in those weeks in 1740 every waterway froze. Mill-wheels were completely halted, fuel where it could be extracted ran low, and employment came to a standstill. But the most sinister aspect of the frost was the impact it had on the food supplies and the livelihood of rural families. The main winter foodstuff of most country people, the potato, was destroyed within days: stored in the ground where it had been cultivated, it was terribly affected by the extreme frost and vast quantities were deemed

Fig. 4 The 140-foot high Castletown Obelisk, probably designed by Richard Castle, is the iconic symbol of the Great Frost, although the precise circumstances of its construction remain unclear. We know that it was initiated in 1740 by Katherine Conolly (d. 1752), the childless chatelaine of Castletown House near Celbridge, County Kildare, and that it was designed to close the northern vista from the great house. As an employment project the Obelisk would have kept many dozens of workers busy. She followed this with the construction in 1743 of a seventy-foot high conical granary, the 'Wonderful Barn', which closed the eastward vista, and had vast storage capacity to cope with any future food crisis. [Source: Castletown House Archive]

broken in the autumn – by storms and blizzards, then floods in December. A second maverick winter followed with exceptional snowfalls. The spring of 1741 was also very dry, followed by a blazing summer. Normality of sorts only returned in the autumn.

## Impact

In a pan-European study of these anomalous years, John Post has suggested that there was no strong correlation at national level between the extremity of cold in 1739–40 and the rates of excess human mortality in the year or two following, and that it was in Atlantic Europe, where the intensity of the Great Frost was somewhat less, that the greatest human damage was done. He argued that the impact of an extreme natural episode such as this reflected the strengths and weaknesses of social infrastructure, specifically the presence or absence of traditions of welfare provision and public intervention at times of extreme distress.[3] Post's hypothesis is highly plausible (if impossible to prove), but if we examine the differential impact of the Great Frost within Ireland itself, does this hypothesis help

account for regional differences?

Judging from the swings in Dublin wheat prices, the food supply crisis built up to its first peak in June/July 1740.[4] With the great diminution in potato supplies, poorer families switched to oatmeal consumption a season early: thus the scale of the overall food scarcity only became evident some months after the Frost. The drastic losses of cattle, especially of young stock, had by then wiped out the capital of countless small farmers, and during that summer there was the first surge in vagrancy. The depleted cultivation of potatoes and the exceptionally deficient grain yields in that year's harvest meant that there was only a short respite during what was usually a season of abundance. Dublin food prices began to rise again, reaching all-time highs in December 1740. Food riots had occurred in a number of towns in the late spring of 1740 and reappeared – with a vengeance – around Christmas, the direct action of urban artisans attempting to pressurise bakers and dealers to bring their stocks of grain to the market, or to halt the shipments of grain and meal to other Irish destinations.[5]

## Intervention

Compared with later times, the intervention by Dublin Castle in this crisis was miniscule, partly because Government had such a minimalist conception of its role in public welfare, partly because of the very modest resources available to marshall food supplies or to counter a public health crisis. In practice only three types of authority had any capacity to intervene and alleviate the distresses of the poor – urban corporations, parish vestries of the established Church of Ireland, and the gentry. At the time of the Great Frost itself there was a groundswell of local philanthropy, which was generally channelled through the parish officers where they functioned, but as the year went on that kind of haphazard activity gave way to more coordinated action in the cities, and to larger-scale initiatives by some landowners.

In Dublin the acting head of Government in the winter of 1740–41 was the Church of Ireland archbishop Hugh Boulter: he coordinated relief works and doles in the city, and for a number of months several thousand citizens were on daily rations, administered via the city workhouse. The municipal authorities in Cork and Waterford also became active and seem to have been quite effective, not least in organising the importation of American wheat and flour (which only began to arrive in the spring of 1741). In the countryside, relief such as it was seems to have depended on one of two factors: the existence of a sufficiently numerous Church of Ireland population to ensure that parish structures of relief could function; and/or the presence of at least one landowner willing to underwrite relief works on whatever terms. Some of the most eloquent monuments to the crisis include the 140-foot obelisk built as a relief work on the instructions of Katherine Conolly that stands to this day on

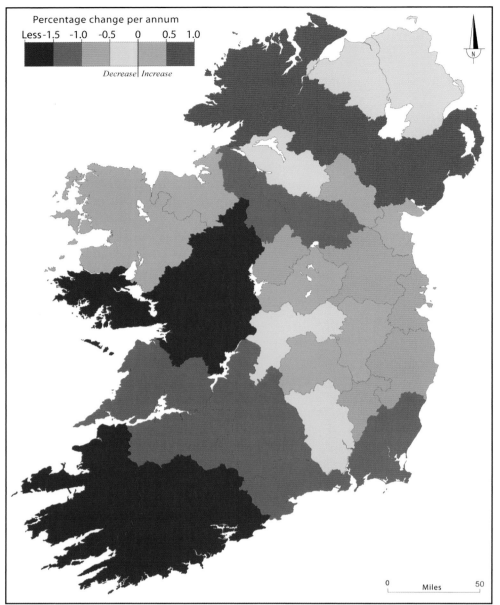

Percentage change per annum

Less -1.5  -1.0  -0.5  0  0.5  1.0

*Decrease* | *Increase*

0 Miles 50

Fig. 5 DISTRIBUTION OF POPULATION CHANGE PER COUNTY 1732–44. Ireland experienced three great famines in the modern period – one in the mid-seventeenth century (after the 1641 rising/rebellion and the Cromwellian conquest), the Great Famine of 1845–52 but it also suffered a major famine between late 1739 and late 1741. This famine began with a great frost in the winter of 1739–40 which destroyed the potato crop, saw drastic cattle losses, and later a lengthy drought which deeply affected the grain crops. This was followed by the spread of infectious diseases – especially typhoid fever – in both town and countryside. The above figure shows the extent of population decline (based on hearth-tax records) between 1732 and 1744. Percentage decrease in populations per annum (often over 1 per cent) were greatest in south Connacht and Munster but were also significant for Cavan south to Wexford. Overall, Ireland's population loss from this famine was of the order of 16% with perhaps one-quarter of the population perishing in the Munster province. Parts of Leinster and most of Ulster were less affected by this famine although excess mortalities were characteristic of some urban populations.

contagious waves. Munster was certainly first and probably worst affected, then much of Leinster and south Connacht. And while the Frost itself had hit the northern counties very hard, the subsequent demographic impact on Ulster in terms of sickness and death seems to have been modest compared to the carnage in the south.[6]

The hardest evidence for Munster comes from Church of Ireland sources. Two burial registers are extant which include all, or certainly a great many, Catholic interments in the parish graveyards: St Mary's in Limerick city and Macroom in mid-County Cork. In both parishes the number of burials in 1740 and 1741 were around four times the annual rate of the previous three years, with the worst months being between December 1740 and March 1741 in Macroom, and February to July 1741 in the Limerick case. Only one attempt at actual measurement of the crisis is recorded: a Church of Ireland minister for the Golden Vale parish of Cullen claimed that 252 of the 666 inhabitants in his parish had by the late summer of 1741 died of 'distempers' associated with the calamity. Such an extreme collapse, if true, was untypical even of County Tipperary; some of his lost neighbours may have fled their homes and gone a-begging. There was of course no mass emigration at this time – perhaps some increase in the seasonal traffic to England, but for most their wanderings were within the compass of the country.[7]

Cullen parish epitomised a wider aspect of the crisis. It was excellent sheep country, home of the first Dexter cattle, had superb soils and good communications. This was a perfect setting for the extreme social inequalities driven by commercial growth which contemporaries like Berkeley had found so disturbing. Whether there was a functioning Church of Ireland vestry here is not clear, but probably not. But we can assume that there were very large numbers of labouring families with very limited reserves and only too vulnerable to the catalogue of disasters visited upon them in 1740.

the edge of the Castletown demesne, and the more modest Killiney Hill obelisk, constructed together with extensive parkland walls on the Mapas estate.

## HUMAN TRAGEDY

Such actions, in the towns and on a small number of estates, modified what by the end of 1740 was an all-encompassing human tragedy. The classic diseases of malnutrition and vagrancy – dysentery, succeeded by the 'violent fevers' associated with typhus – struck country districts in

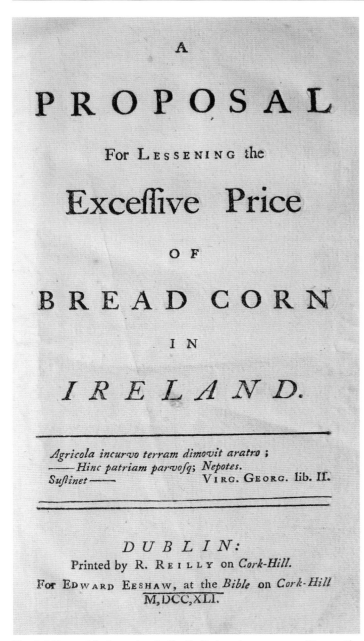

A

# PROPOSAL

For Lessening the

## Excessive Price

O F

## BREAD CORN

I N

## IRELAND.

*Agricola incurvo terram dimovit aratro ;*
*——— Hinc patriam parvosq; Nepotes.*
*Sustinet ———* Virg. Georg. lib. II.

DUBLIN:
Printed by R. Reilly on *Cork-Hill*.
For Edward Eeshaw, at the *Bible* on *Cork-Hill*
M,DCC,XLI.

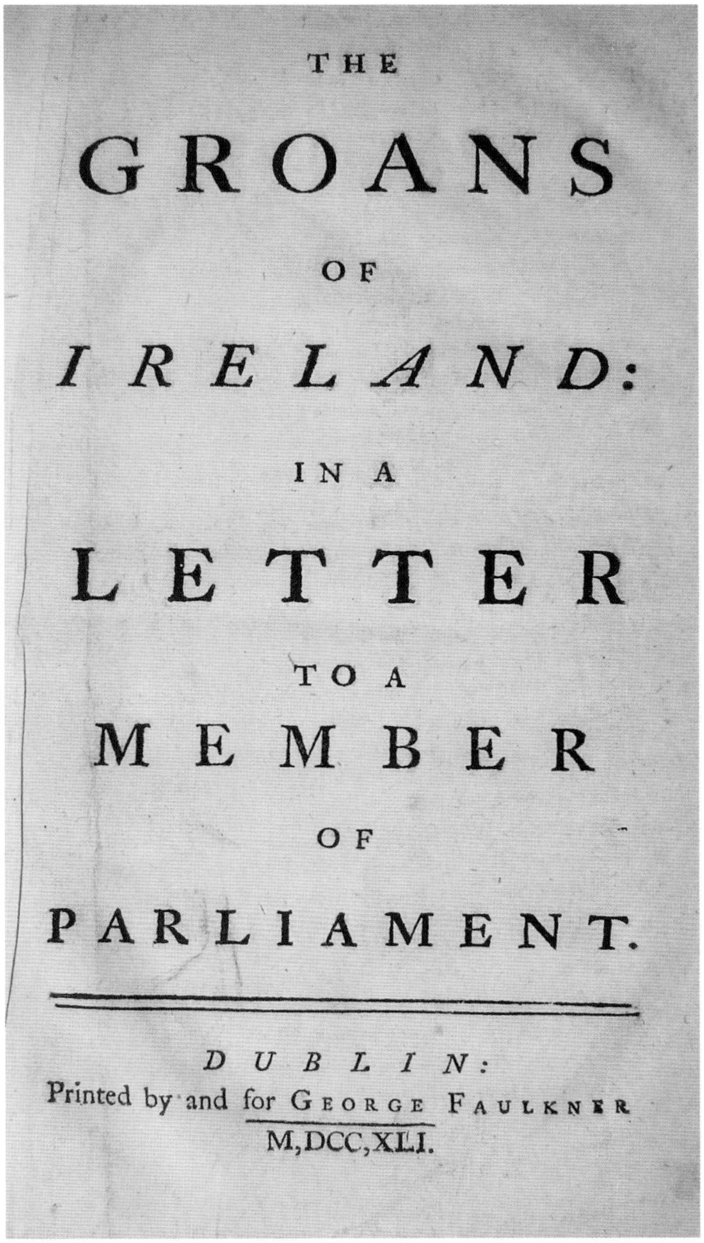

T H E

# GROANS

O F

## IRELAND:

I N A

## LETTER

T O A

## MEMBER

O F

## PARLIAMENT.

DUBLIN:
Printed by and for George Faulkner
M,DCC,XLI.

Fig. 6 *A Proposal for Lessening*. In the limited contemporary writing on the Great Frost, most of the attention was focused – as in this essay - on the unprecedented food prices, the absence of public granaries, the decay of cereal farming and the dangers of Ireland's dependence on external supplies of corn. These were all urban concerns and there was very little printed comment on the food crisis in the countryside, on the devastating effects of the loss of livestock or on the fever pandemic. [Source: Private Collection]

Fig. 7 *Groans of Ireland*. This short essay, published just after the crisis in November 1741, was probably the most widely read piece among the eight or nine pamphlets published in reaction to it. The anonymous author graphically describes the impact of the Frost, before concentrating on a series of economic prescriptions that strongly echo George Berkeley's *Querist*. [Source: Private Collection]

## EPIDEMICS

The killer epidemics that were being fanned by the wandering poor were no respecter of persons. A number of high-status fatalities in 1741, including the Lord Chief Justice Sir John Rogerson, helped reinforce the fear of the rich that a well-fed stomach was no protection when typhus was rampant. Vigorous attempts were made in 1741 to exclude or corral beggars from the towns, at a time when jails and other institutions of close confinement were becoming charnal houses. Insofar as there were any positive consequence of the crisis, one can see in the renewed enthusiasm for establishing voluntary hospitals in Irish towns during the 1740s that some lessons were being learnt. But the development of urban asylums for the industrious poor really only took off in the 1770s, and the emergence of a comprehensive Poor Law was almost a century away.

In terms of lessons learnt more generally, the search for more robust strains of potato continued, while the practice of leaving the mature tubers in their cultivation ridges was replaced by the general practice of storing them in deeper clamps. In the era of the potato's dominance in Ireland no other exceptional winter (and there were several) was ever as remotely destructive as the Great Frost. The next potato catastrophe had a quite different catalyst.

# The potato: root of the Famine

## *John Feehan*

Potatoes all belong to a single species, *Solanum tuberosum*, a member of the nightshade family (*Solanaceae*) which also contains many other important food plants. There are no fewer than 235 species of potatoes, very widely distributed throughout South America, up through Central America and into the southwestern United States. The two main centres of diversity are in the High Andes from Peru to northwest Argentina, and in central Mexico.

This wide range is a reflection of the ecological diversity of potatoes: between them they show great adaptation to such ecological variables as temperature and humidity. Some of the species have a very wide distribution, whereas others are restricted to specific ecological situations. For instance, some species can live under hot, dry, semi-desert conditions, while others can tolerate sub-zero temperatures. The majority, however, are forest or woodland species, but potatoes have colonised nearly every natural habitat and many man-made habitats in South America. Some species are weeds of cultivated fields; one potato is an epiphyte, growing on the mossy branches of oak trees. Wild potatoes look like miniature versions of crop potatoes, but they are very seldom eaten by man. They also exhibit a wide range of variation when it comes to resistance to diseases and pests of all kinds. This great diversity enhances their potential economic importance because of what they might contribute to the genomes of the cultivated species.

In the foothills of the Andes several species of wild potatoes had featured in the diet of people for thousands of years before they began to cultivate them as a central part of a system of farming that involved more species of edible roots and tubers than on any other continent; there is evidence from southern Chile that wild potatoes were being eaten as far back as 13,000 years ago. In the course of time thousands of cultivars were developed from seven or eight wild ancestors, suited to every variation in altitude and climate, resistant to varying degrees to the pests and diseases to which potatoes, like every plant, are subject. They come in a bewildering variety of shapes and sizes, flavours and colours after millennia of selection and breeding, each variety adapted for a different set of conditions, a particular corner of the landscape. They are still the foundation of traditional farming over large areas of the Andes. Upwards of 4,000 varieties are still grown in smallholdings on the vast Andean altiplano around 1,200m above sea level and on the precipitous slopes of the cordillera, often in spectacular terraced fields banked with dressed stone; a single farm may have as many as fifty varieties under cultivation. On these small upland farms every scrap of land is carefully used and conserved in a system of agriculture 'of extraordinary craftsmanship and ecological intelligence'; as in an earlier Ireland each little field has its own name, 'known with the intimacy of the lifetime not just of individuals but of families – a knowledge centuries old'.[1]

Potatoes were the very foundation upon which the successive waves of pre-Columbian civilisations in the west of South America were built, culminating in the sophisticated empire of the Incas. Under the Incas an elaborate system of aqueducts supplied water from the Andes to the lands bordering the Pacific, where maize could thrive, while guano from the coast was transported to the upland potato fields along a network of highways that connected them with the maize-growing lands bordering the Pacific. And just as before the introduction of the potato the cow and her produce were at the centre of life in Ireland, the potato was the measure of all things in Peru: it was the unit of measurement, and it pervaded language and culture.[2]

### THE POTATO IN IRELAND

The potato very quickly came to the notice of the invading Spaniards in the sixteenth century. In their New World empire they were quick to note the way a large population of healthy soldiers or conscripted labourers could be supported by potatoes, and they adopted the Inca system to their own ends and had hopes of applying it back home. By 1567 the potato was in the Canaries; from Spain it spread to Portugal and later to Italy, and within fifty to sixty years had made its way across Europe (in spite of Spanish efforts to maintain a monopoly). The potatoes brought to Europe were varieties of the *andigena* sub-species, which (with 3,000 cultivars) was and continues to be the most widely-farmed, both in South America and worldwide. The potato probably arrived in Ireland in 1586, at a time of great crisis, when the population was coming to terms with the social and political changes that followed the devastation of the sixteenth century, and it changed the direction, and perhaps the course, of Irish history.

For its first century in Ireland the potato was largely confined to the south and southeast where it played a subsidiary and balanced role in the diet except when other

The principal varieties of potato in pre-Famine Ireland were the Black Potato, the Cup, the Apple and the Lumper. The latter is an old variety and was first recorded in 1808. Initially it was used primarily as an animal feed. However by the 1840s it accounted for over ninety per cent of the potato crop and was pivotal to the diet and survival of the small farmer, cottier and labourer. The nutritional value of the potato is considerably reduced by removing the skin, however the knobbly Lumper is unpeelable and was eaten whole, thereby improving its quality and flavour.

Fig. 1 [Adapted from James Choiseul, Gerry Doherty and Gabriel Roe, *Potato Varieties of Historical Interest in Ireland*, Dublin, 2008]

food was scarce. The mild and frost-free climate proved ideal for early varieties, abundant seaweed proved an ideal fertiliser, and disease was of little consequence in these first decades. But it was beginning to exert a wider dominance before the end of the seventeenth century, replacing whitemeats in Munster and a diet hitherto rich in cereals and pulses in Leinster. In his *Journal* (1689), John Stevens wrote how 'None but the best sort or the inhabitants of great towns eat wheat or bread baked in an oven or ground in a mill; the meaner people content themselves with little bread, but instead thereof eat potatoes which with sour milk is the chief article of food.'

Potatoes are scarcely mentioned in agricultural pamphlets written as late as the first quarter of the eighteenth century. They are never mentioned in the rotations practised by progressive farmers at this period: wheat, barley, oats, rye, clover, peas and beans, turnips, sainfoin, lucerne, buckwheat, tares, lentils, hops and fallow occur over and over in endless permutations – but never potatoes. But the fact that they were absent from the agricultural treatises does not mean that they were not grown: it merely emphasises the extent to which their cultivation was confined to the poor who managed to survive because of them on marginal lands. John Keogh's

*General Irish Herbal* of 1735 described potatoes as 'a healthy nourishing food (as is evidenced by the robust constitutions of a vast number of the natives who are almost entirely supported by them)'.

## INCREASING DEPENDENCE

By the middle of the eighteenth century the potato had become part of the diet at every level of society over most of the country, and poorer people became increasingly dependent on it. Between 1750 and 1810 it reached its zenith, as the potato fields crept further and further up the hillsides of the west. It became the staple food of labourers and cottiers, and milk and oats disappeared altogether from the tables of the poorest. At the time of Arthur Young's visits to Ireland (1776, 1779), potatoes with milk were the food of the people for at least nine months of the year everywhere he went – except for parts of Ulster, where most people still had oat bread and some meat.

Two parliamentary measures may have contributed to the spread of potato culture in Ireland and were particularly instrumental in bringing about an increase of potato cultivation. The first (1742) was the Act to Encourage the Reclaiming of Unprofitable Bogs, which made it lawful 'for every Papist, or person professing the Popish religion' to lease fifty acres, plantation measure, of such bog, and one half acre of arable land thereunto adjoining, 'as a site for a house, or for the purpose of delving for gravel or limestone for manure'. To qualify as 'unprofitable', the bog had to be at least four feet deep after reclamation, and a minimum of ten acres had to be reclaimed. The bog had to be at least a mile from the nearest town, and half of the reclamation work had to be completed within twenty-one years. In return, the tenant would be free from 'all titles, cesses, or applotment' for the first seven years after the bog was reclaimed.

The second Act was the Catholic Relief Act of 1793, which gave the elective franchise to Catholics who were 'forty-shilling freeholders'. At this time the population was somewhere over four million, and three million of these were Catholics. Because the number of votes in the landlord's control was an important political asset, it suited them to maximise the number of such freeholders they had on their land. As a result, landlords were quite happy to lease bits of marginal land to people desperate for land of any kind. The forty-shilling voting threshold was withdrawn by the Relief Bill of 1829, but the tenants kept their land, though with less enthusiastic landlord support. The extensive bog reclamation that took place between the late seventeenth and mid-nineteenth century as a result of these acts would not have been possible without the potato.[3]

The depression that followed the ending of the Napoleonic wars in 1815 further exacerbated dependence on the potato. Agricultural prices soared, cottage spinning

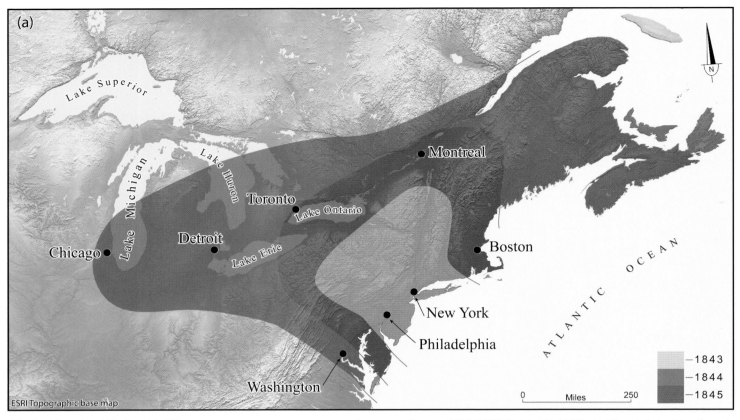

Fig. 2a (above) and 2b (on right) THE SPREAD OF THE POTATO BLIGHT FROM AMERICA TO EUROPE (1843–1845). Potato blight (*Phytophthora infestans*) is a fungal infection which thrives in damp, mild weather conditions. This fungus firstly damages the leaves and stalks above ground before penetrating beneath the surface soil to destroy the potato tubers. It was a new disease which was first noticed on the eastern seaboard of the United States in 1843 (see Fig. 2a), spreading rapidly from a New York–Philadelphia axis northwards and westwards to reach both the Maritime Provinces and the Great Lakes area by 1845. By June 1845 it had spread to Flanders, the rest of Belgium, the southern Netherlands and adjacent parts of the German Rhineland (Fig. 2b). By late August, the disease had expanded rapidly over much of northern and western Europe including all of England and Wales and eastern Ireland. Its initial expansion was linked to the development of an international trade in seed potatoes but, once established, the blight spread extremely rapidly in the particularly damp summer of 1845. By the start of September the blight had reached all parts of Ireland and Scotland. However, some areas escaped the full impact of the disease in the first year – it was the more prosperous eastern regions of Ireland which were initially most deeply affected. However, almost the whole crop failed in 1846.

declined as factories spread throughout the northeast; the weather was wet, and what oats were still grown had to be sold to meet the rent.[4] By the 1830s one-third of the population depended on the potato –mainly, on one variety of potato – for more than 90% of their food requirements. On the eve of the Famine 'a sup of sweet milk among the poor in Ireland [was] as much a rarity and a luxury as a slice of plum pudding in a farmhouse in America'.[5]

**THE GREAT FAMINE**

The hegemony of the potato was broken by the Great Famine. In 1845 there were one-quarter of a million acres under potatoes in County Cork alone, much more than the total under all crops combined on the island of Ireland today. After the late failure of 1845, 25% less land was sown with potatoes; potato land that was abandoned in 1845 was mainly sown with oats (where it was not allowed to lie fallow or revert to grass). This would have meant a shortfall in 1846 even without blight. The almost total failure of 1846 meant that few had seed tubers to plant the following year. In those fortunate areas that did manage to plant, a round-the-clock vigil was often maintained to prevent the precious

tubers from being dug out and stolen in the night.

The potato acreage planted in 1847 was only one-seventh what it had been the previous year, but the yield was good because the weather that summer did not favour the spread of blight. This raised people's hopes, and the acreage was three times as high in 1848. But blight struck again that year, though less virulently than in previous years, leading to a reduction again in 1849. Between 1846 and 1859 there was a reduction of up to 40% in the acreage grown; between 1845 and 1859 it was over 50%. Yields also fell, from a pre-Famine figure of more than six tons to less than four tons. There was a gradual rise to a plateau of a million acres or so up to 1871, after which there was a slow but steady decline that, apart from wartime increases, has continued to the present day.[6]

After the Famine wheaten bread became much more important in the diet of those who could afford it and cheap Indian meal was now available as a fall-back when the potato was scarce. It is an indication of how the status of the potato in the Irish diet was changing that although the failure of 1879 (which followed two years of scarcity) was comparable in intensity to 1846 and there was widespread

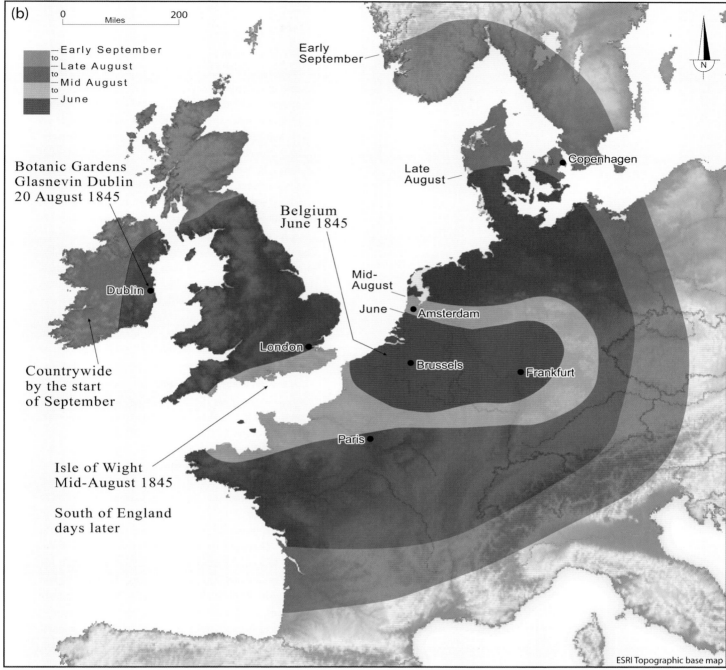

(b)

0 Miles 200

Early September
to
Late August
to
Mid August
to
June

Early September

Botanic Gardens
Glasnevin Dublin
20 August 1845

Belgium
June 1845

Late
August

Copenhagen

Dublin

Mid-
August

June

Amsterdam

Countrywide
by the start
of September

London

Brussels

Frankfurt

Paris

Isle of Wight
Mid-August 1845

South of England
days later

ESRI Topographic base map

and severe distress, there was little starvation. The area in which the decline of the potato was greatest was in the southeast corner, the very area from which the potato had launched its conquest of Ireland two-and-a-half centuries earlier, and the centre of cultivation began to retreat northward, coming to rest in the northeast, where it remains today.

But behind these figures of declining acreages and shifting centres of cultivation there are two other important changes that became increasingly prevalent in the twentieth century. One is the way in which potatoes were increasingly substituted in the diet not by other crops cultivated within the same district or even on the island of Ireland, but by imports. The second is the way in which, especially in recent decades, the genetic base has again constricted –

much as it was allowed to do two centuries ago – to a small range of varieties, chosen for such qualities as ease of peeling, floury texture, and 'chippability'.

The establishment of the Department of Agriculture and Technical Instruction for Ireland in 1899 saw a great rise in attention to crop diversity and awareness of the importance of education. At the newly-established Albert College in Glasnevin up to 130 varieties were planted out and assessed for yield and resistance in the early years of the last century, most of them varieties long forgotten. The 1935 Potato Handbook of the Department of Agriculture lists over 200 varieties for the consideration of the grower. Today, at most, we can expect to encounter a handful of varieties of potatoes. Even at Scariff, the home of the Irish Seed Savers

Table 1. Extent of potato crop in Ireland in selected years

| Year | Acreage statute acres 000 | Yield tons per acre | Estimated produce 000 tons |
|------|---------------------------|---------------------|----------------------------|
| 1844 | 2,378 | (6.25) | (14,862) |
| 1845 | 2,516 | (4.0) | (10,063) |
| 1846 | 1,999 | (1.5) | (2,999) |
| 1847 | 284 | 7.2 | 2,046 |
| 1848 | 810 | 3.8 | 3,077 |
| 1849 | 719 | 5.6 | 4,024 |
| 1855 | 982 | 6.4 | 6,287 |
| 1856 | 1,105 | 4.0 | 4,419 |
| 1859 | 1,200 | 3.6 | 4,321 |
| 1872 | 992 | 1.8 | 1,785 |
| 1879 | 843 | 1.3 | 1,095 |
| 1897 | 677 | 2.2 | 1,490 |
| 1951 | 466 | 8.5 | 3,963 |

Association, no more than fifty varieties are grown.

POTATO VARIETIES

A large number of new varieties were developed in Britain and Ireland during the course of the eighteenth and nineteenth centuries. Each period can be characterised by its own handful of favoured varieties (fifteen were grown extensively in Kilkenny, for example, at the end of the eighteenth century), but one or two generally stood out because of their better keeping quality, flavour or yield. The five most outstanding potatoes of the eighteenth century were the Black, Apple, Cluster, Manly and Ox Noble varieties – in that order over time. In the 1730s the Black – so called from its skin colour – was preferred to any other; it would keep right through the year until the potatoes came again, and could be ten centimetres in diameter. The Irish Apple was the outstanding variety of the later eighteenth and early nineteenth centuries, famous not only because it was the best in terms of quality, but because 'it stood its ground the longest'. The 'king of potatoes' in its heyday, the Apple was beginning to degenerate by the 1830s and did not survive the blight attack of 1846.

The Lumper made its appearance towards the end of the eighteenth century, and because of its amazing productivity ousted all other varieties in the diet of the poorest: 'so charged with vitality that it would grow without manure in any soil, of large size, and producing 160 barrels to the acre, but of a quality more fit for cattle than for man'.[7] The variety had many advantages. It gave

Fig. 3 (right) This article from *The Northern Standard*, 18 October 1845 underlines the fear and panic surrounding the spread of disease in the potato crop. The immediacy of the crisis is registered by the correspondent from Aughnacloy, County Tyrone who 'writes in great terror' and says 'that one-half the crop within a diameter of ten miles round him is lost, and suggests the purchase, by the landlord, of the corn on their estates, in order to prevent a famine'. [Source: Monaghan County Library]

THE POTATOE DISEASE.

We have various and contending accounts from different parts of the country, respecting the fearful disease in the potato crop. A Clones correspondent says, from observation, he thinks the rot has ceased and that not more than those already affected will be lost— and this assertion is very generally rumored through the country. We cannot say how true it may be, but it is needless to say how much we wish it may turn out correct. Another respectable farmer correspondent writes to us to say, that it is our duty to tell the landlords that they should ask little or no rent this year, in consequence of the loss of the potato crop. Another writer says that potatoes. if properly attended to, should not sell at more than 4d. a stone all through the year, as there will not be 15 per cent less than an average crop. An intelligent correspondent from Aughnacloy, writes in great terror, and says, that one-half the crop within a diameter of ten miles round him is lost, and suggests the purchase, by the landlord, of the corn on their estates, in order to prevent a famine. This, tho' an exaggerated, is not an unwise view :— There is at the present moment a fearful trade driving upon the panic. Men are jobbing upon the terrors, and misfortunes of the people. Markets are made to rise and fall, by the monopolist capitalists, to suit their purchases. No one can calculate the prices of the corn markets. To-day meal will be raised to a fearful price, and the peasantry rush in to-morrow to sell their oats. There is a glut, and the buyers fall the prices, purchase low, and next day, again, rise them. There should be something done to prevent this. We would suggest, that benevolent societies should be formed for the purchase of grain at fair prices, to be kept in store until time reveals whether there will, or will not be, a dearth. Under all circumstances it can be sold without a loss, while a small profit, which would realise a sufficient per centage, properly remunerative to those societies, would keep the markets at such an average that the poor could be fed. If the proprietors of property met together in each county, and subscribed sums equal to one third or one fourth their rentals, and purchased grain now, they could sell it again the ensuing summer at a fair price, realise a profit equal to the legal interest of their money, and do a great good to their tenantry, and to the country generally. This may at first be thought impossible, but it is not so—it would be a mere mercantile speculation, based upon a feeling of humanity—it would keep the community from a state, that if it reaches the height apprehended, will eventually fall upon the landlords by giving them a ruined and starving tenantry.

32

a higher yield than any other, and it did very well on poorer land and where many varieties lost their vigour over time, the Lumper did not. It was immune to wart disease and leaf roll, but it had no resistance to late blight. This Achilles' heel was invisible, however, because blight was unknown before 1845. It kept its vitality down to the 1840s, but was almost wiped out in the Famine years. By the 1840s a third of the population, especially in Munster, Connacht and west Leinster, grew nothing but Lumper potatoes. Almost all the potatoes grown on the eve of the Famine were either Red Cups or Lumpers. Cups were to the rich what the Lumper was to the poor between 1810 and 1846, but they too were practically eliminated by the blight.

A variety called the Rock took over from the Lumper and the Cup after the Famine, and remained the most popular potato variety until the arrival of the Champion in 1876. The failure of the potato crop in 1879 was possibly worse than in 1846, but the Champion was unaffected and retained its remarkable resistance to blight for a decade or so, after which it began to deteriorate. During that time it

was the most universally popular variety ever grown in Ireland, with superb cooking qualities.

### EARLIER FAMINES

The blight epidemic of 1845–47 was the culmination of a long series of crop failures. There had been thirty famines of greater or lesser severity over the previous hundred years or so. Between 1720 and 1740 there were twelve years when harvests were bad, and several years of famine, but the famine of 1739–41 was particularly severe. The winter of 1739–40 was the coldest on record; it is usually remembered because all the great rivers of the country froze over for months on end. It had devastating effects on plant and animal life, and its most disastrous impact was that it killed the potato tubers which still lay in the beds in which they had been grown: the custom of storing them in protective pits was not in use at that time.

The famine continued through 1740 and 1741, causing ever-increasing misery. As many as half a million may have lost their lives through famine or as a result of the fever and

Fig. 4 Potato ridges in Mulranny, County Mayo. The potatoes were grown in long ridges (lazy beds), adapted from those ridges that had been a characteristic feature of Irish farming since the beginning. It was a highly labour-intensive system, but three times as productive as horse-ploughed drill culture and labour was the one resource the poor could afford. The potato acreage reached its apogee between 1830 and 1835, and declined in the face of a rising tide of pasture in the decade that followed; with the wholesale abandonment of the potato fields that took place after 1846 that tide became a flood. On marginal land the sod was never turned again, and the ridges were frozen in time, one of the most widespread and poignant relics of those awful years. [Photo: Frank Coyne]

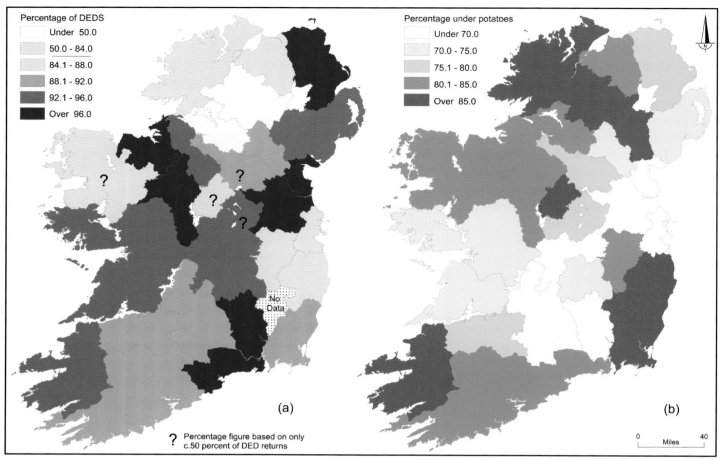

**Percentage of DEDS**
- Under 50.0
- 50.0 - 84.0
- 84.1 - 88.0
- 88.1 - 92.0
- 92.1 - 96.0
- Over 96.0

**Percentage under potatoes**
- Under 70.0
- 70.0 - 75.0
- 75.1 - 80.0
- 80.1 - 85.0
- Over 85.0

(a)

(b)

? Percentage figure based on only c.50 percent of DED returns

0    Miles    40

Fig. 5a PERCENTAGE OF DEDS (DISTRICT ELECTORAL DIVISIONS) WHERE AT LEAST THREE-TENTHS OF THE POTATO CROP WAS LOST IN 1845. FIG. 5B PERCENTAGE OF AREA PER COUNTY PLANTED UNDER POTATOES IN 1846 VIS-À-VIS 1845. The official returns show that in 42.6% of DEDs island-wide at least half of the potato crop was lost in 1845 (a further 30% of DEDs had lost at least four-tenths of the crop). In counties Antrim and Monaghan the proportions of DEDs losing at least half the crop were 70.5% and 65.6%; in County Clare 72.2% and 85.7% in County Waterford; 81.8% in County Louth and 73.5% in Kilkenny. Roscommon was most affected in Connacht with 55.8% of DEDs showing at least half of the crop lost – Leitrim had the least at 31.5%. This map illustrates where three-tenths (30%) or more of the potato crop was lost. Eastern and north-eastern counties from Meath to County Antrim, were clearly greatly affected as were Counties Sligo, Kilkenny and Waterford. An extensive part of the island from Armagh through the midlands, south Connacht and all of Munster were also deeply affected by losses. East Leinster – Counties Dublin, Kildare, Wicklow and Wexford – were somewhat less affected but the counties showing the least damage to the potato crop lay in the northwest, centred on Fermanagh and Tyrone but also including Donegal and, one assumes, Mayo. There is a striking correlation between Figs 5a and 5b, the latter showing the percentage area planted with potatoes in 1846 vis-à-vis 1845. This correlation is most noticeable in the southeastern and northwestern counties, those least affected by crop losses in 1845 and characterised by the highest percentage of potato acreage in 1846. Likewise, east Ulster and much of north Leinster and Munster display more moderate levels of crop losses in 1845 and a somewhat reduced acreage in 1846. However, some counties, like Armagh and Kerry, still manage higher than expected levels of potato planting in 1846.

dysentery that followed in its wake out of a population of around 1.5–2.0 million. Rich as well as poor were affected. The roads were spread with dead and dying bodies, 'mankind of the colour of the docks and nettles they fed on'. It was from this time on that the potato became really popular, in spite of the famine of 1741 – and indeed, in some ways because of it – and it began to feature in rotations. This was more from necessity than choice. Tenant farmers had very little land to support their families, and no other crop could compete for productivity. Acre for acre, the potato could provide four times as much food as any other crop.

The potatoes failed again in 1821, once again because of the weather, plunging a great part of the south and west into starvation. What harvest there was had to remain in the ridges, so wet was the autumn. In many areas, fields of potatoes were simply washed out of the ground by the floods. The wet weather continued into the spring of 1822, making work in the fields very difficult. There was also a

great shortage of seed potatoes, and there were many cases of planted sets being dug by starving people for food. In the counties of Limerick, Clare, Cork, Kerry, Mayo and Galway there was famine. The price of potatoes rose from the usual penny or two pence to eight pence a stone. The grain harvest was abundant, but corn and oatmeal were beyond the means of many. In parts of the west 'the living were unable to bury the dead, more especially on Achill, where, in many cases, the famine-stricken people were found dead on the roadside'.[8] Most of these crop failures were of local occurrence: the famine of 1784 affected Ulster mainly, whereas the great failure of 1821 in which thousands died of starvation or hunger-related disease, was largely confined to the west and southwest. In the years between 1824 and 1849 the crop failed at least eight times.

### THE BLIGHT

Like every other species of plant and animal, the potato has its peculiar pests, parasites and pathogens, which are kept at bay by the genetic variability of the species as a whole, different varieties having varying levels of resistance to different enemies. Modern crops are particularly susceptible to attack, because they consist of very large numbers of individuals of a standard clone. If one plant succumbs to attack, the likelihood is that all the others will also succumb, over the entire field – indeed, throughout the district or country. This is less likely to happen in traditional agriculture, where the crop consists of a number of different strains (clones or genotypes) of a crop.

Most of the important diseases of the potato (twenty or so) were recognised by the early nineteenth century, but these could be kept under some measure of control by good husbandry: proper crop rotations, hygienic storage, using clean seed, boiling diseased tubers before feeding them to animals; but the majority of poor tenant farmers did not have the resources to do this. Without careful husbandry, disease could spread rapidly and virulently through an entire crop that consisted of a single variety with virtually no genetic variability, as uncontrollably as wildfire burning its way through brushwood.

Blight arrived in Europe in 1845, with a shipment of seed potatoes sent to Belgium from the United States. It made its first effective appearance in Ireland in the first half of September 1845, but its impact was limited by its late arrival; the early varieties were long out of the ground by then, and apparently a fair proportion of the maincrop varieties escaped attack. The Lumper, however, matures very late. It was a very different story the following year, when the now-established fungus almost totally destroyed the potato crop. It struck at almost the same time everywhere, at the beginning of August. Captain Mann, R.N., described how at the end of July he inspected thirty-two miles studded with potato-fields in full bloom; when he re-visited the area a week later 'the face of the whole country was changed; the stalk remained bright green, but the leaves were all scorched black. It was the work of a night'.[9] Panic in the early months gave way to despair and hopelessness.

The blight continued to strike at regular intervals in the second half of the century, though with less calamitous results because at least the danger was now known, if only barely kept at bay with careful management and chemical control.

## THE POTATO AND THE FUTURE

In nutritional terms the potato is almost a complete food in itself. It can produce four times as much complex carbohydrate as grain, is high in vitamin C, complex B vitamins and trace elements; a kilogram provides half the daily protein requirement. It is easy to grow and easier to prepare and it can be stored where it grows as long as the soil is pest-free. It is now the fourth most important food

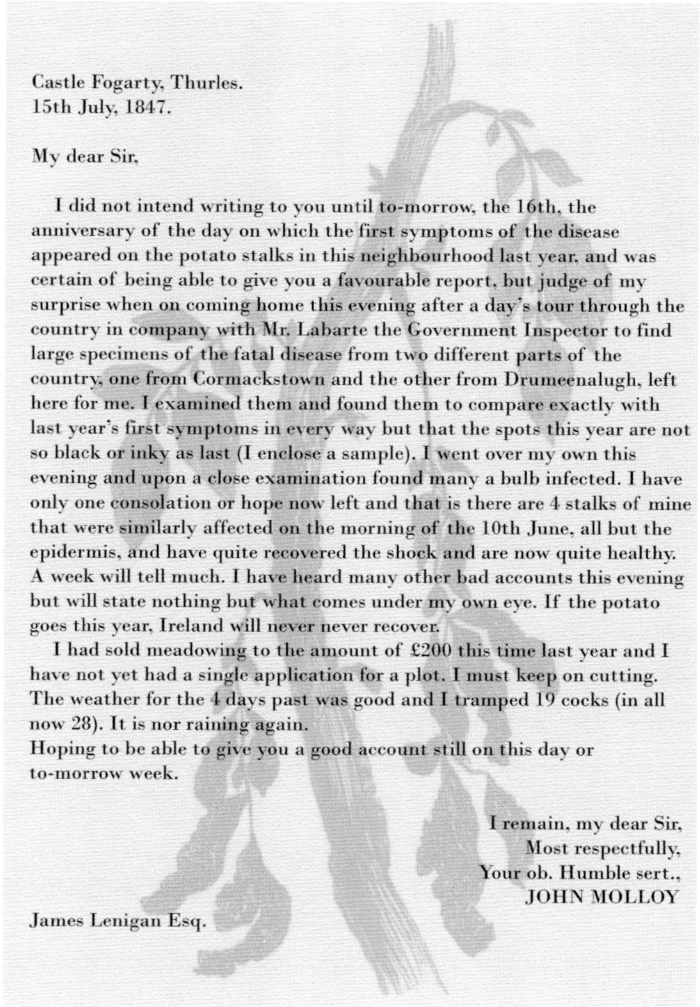

Castle Fogarty, Thurles.
15th July, 1847.

My dear Sir,

I did not intend writing to you until to-morrow, the 16th, the anniversary of the day on which the first symptoms of the disease appeared on the potato stalks in this neighbourhood last year, and was certain of being able to give you a favourable report, but judge of my surprise when on coming home this evening after a day's tour through the country in company with Mr. Labarte the Government Inspector to find large specimens of the fatal disease from two different parts of the country, one from Cormackstown and the other from Drumeenalugh, left here for me. I examined them and found them to compare exactly with last year's first symptoms in every way but that the spots this year are not so black or inky as last (I enclose a sample). I went over my own this evening and upon a close examination found many a bulb infected. I have only one consolation or hope now left and that is there are 4 stalks of mine that were similarly affected on the morning of the 10th June, all but the epidermis, and have quite recovered the shock and are now quite healthy. A week will tell much. I have heard many other bad accounts this evening but will state nothing but what comes under my own eye. If the potato goes this year, Ireland will never never recover.

I had sold meadowing to the amount of £200 this time last year and I have not yet had a single application for a plot. I must keep on cutting. The weather for the 4 days past was good and I tramped 19 cocks (in all now 28). It is nor raining again.

Hoping to be able to give you a good account still on this day or to-morrow week.

I remain, my dear Sir,
Most respectfully,
Your ob. Humble sert.,
JOHN MOLLOY

James Lenigan Esq.

Fig. 6 John Molloy was an experienced farmer, and a tenant of James Lenigan of Castle Fogarty, who was visiting England at the time. He had been charged with the task of keeping a close eye on the potato crop in his employer's absence, and in this letter he describes the recurrence of blight in 1847. The first signs of the blight were brown spots on the leaves, soon spreading to affect the whole stem. It often appeared noticeably in one particular part of a field first, under high hedges or trees, 'and I have sometimes observed the very first symptoms of the disease opposite an open gateway, as if a blighting wind had rushed in, making for some distance a sort of avenue of discoloured leaves and stalks, about the width of the gateway at first, but becoming wider onwards', but it quickly spread to the entire field. As it spread through the plant, a dreadful smell was produced, which was perceptible a long way off (See Baunreagh pp. 38–40). [Adapted from UCD Archives, IE UCDA P146]

crop in the world, surpassed in importance only by wheat, maize and rice, and it is the most important root crop. It is almost unsurpassed for yield. The average worldwide is 16 tonnes per hectare, which is equivalent to 3.7 tonnes of dry matter, compared to 3.2 for rice, and it has a similar yield advantage over wheat and maize.

Potatoes are grown today in nearly 170 countries, most of them in Africa. Consumption in Asia has increased from 10% of world production in the 1960s to more than a third today; China is now the world's leading producer and India produces twice as much as the United States. Rising living standards across Europe in recent decades have seen a decline in the role of the potato here, but there has been a great increase in North America, where two-thirds of the

Fig. 7 Farmers and dealers inspect new potatoes at Macroom show, County Cork, in August 1929. [Photo: *Irish Examiner*]

produce go into the manufacture of chips, crisps and other pre-packaged foods. The potato is likely to play an increasingly important role as this century advances; food supplies must increase 75% to feed an extra three to four billion people in the world by 2050.

The great weakness of the potato is its susceptibility to blight. This can be controlled by regular spraying – it is more dependent on chemical sprays than any other crop – but this is a short-term solution and may be harmful to the environment. It is also expensive and beyond the means of farmers in developing countries in particular. Genetic resistance has much more to offer, and potato scientists have been working over the last century to incorporate the resistance to late blight of primitive South American land-races and wild species through cross-breeding into cultivated potatoes. This is a slow and uncertain process; potatoes are a notoriously difficult crop to breed because of their atypically complex genetics.

The sword of blight still hangs over mankind by a slender thread of defence. The strain of blight that invaded Europe in the 1840s and has plagued us ever since is the same A1 strain that originated in Mexico: this is one 'gender' of the fungus. But in 1976 there was a shortage of potatoes in Europe because of the drought of that year, and potatoes were imported from Mexico. With them came the other (A2) 'gender', which swept through potato fields in

Europe, Asia and Latin America in the 1980s. This strain is extremely virulent, and mating between the two strains has boosted the genetic diversity of the fungus and makes control even more challenging. In 1992 a still more virulent strain (US8) was discovered in Mexico and within a year or two had moved up into the United States. This overpowers the resistance genes that have been bred into potatoes, and is able to withstand conventional fungicides.

Because of this, and with more and more people in developing countries increasingly dependent on the potato, a twenty-first century version of the Great Famine is a real possibility. Efforts to exploit the enormous potential of the potato are now concentrated on two fronts. One of these is the conservation of the diversity that thousands of years of farming have provided us with. There are important potato germplasm collections in several countries, among them the German–Dutch collection at Braunschweig, Germany; the Potato Introduction Station at Sturgeon Bay, Wisconsin, in the United States, and, most importantly, the International Potato Center (CIP) in Lima, Peru, where some 5,000 cultivar genotypes are housed, together with large collections of wild species. Modern trends in farming have brought this diversity under threat, but in a recent CIP initiative Andean farmers are now paid to maintain this crucial diversity in their fields.

The other front lies in the genetic revolution – still only

Fig. 8 Potatoes being grown on the Dingle Peninsula, County Kerry. The number of potatoes produced in Ireland has declined in recent years (from 436,028 tons in 2010 to 375,774 tons in 2011). The principal variety being planted is the Rooster. [Photo: Michael Diggin]

gathering momentum – which holds a promise in this regard that could hardly have been dreamed of hitherto. In 2009 the Potato Genome Sequencing Consortium (PGSC) announced that the first draft sequence of the potato genome had been produced. This will allow potato breeders to reduce the ten to twelve years currently needed to breed new varieties and this makes the prospect of developing blight-resistant potatoes of optimum nutritional quality, suited to every sort of climate, a real possibility in the future.

# Baunreagh, County Laois: The failure of the potato

## John Feehan

The potato made possible the reclamation for agriculture of extensive areas of upland that would otherwise have remained unproductive in farming terms except as rough summer grazing. Much of this reclamation was piecemeal, the work of tenant families extending the reach of cultivation as the burgeoning population pushed the arable front-line further and further up the hills. Not all upland reclamation was of this nature however; some of it was on a more intensive scale, and for commercial gain rather than mere subsistence.[1]

William Steuart Trench was one of the most efficient and progressive land agents of his day. He also managed land in his own right, and in the early 1840s he took a lease on lands at Baunreagh, in the foothills of the Slieve Bloom mountains in County Laois, where, in an extraordinary demonstration of what could be done with such land, he successfully converted some 180 acres of deep peat to highly productive arable.[2] A number of factors underpinned his success. Firstly there was his own skill and experience: the methods he used were based on several years of painstaking experimentation; secondly, there was no shortage of cheap labour: he had 200 full-time labourers at work draining, levelling, liming, then sowing and harvesting the enormous quantities of potatoes; thirdly, he applied liberal quantities not only of lime, but of that most crucial nutrient lacking in peat – phosphate in the form of guano– which was just at that time beginning to be imported from Chile.[3]

This was Trench's process:

1. Lime was first spread broadcast over the land at a rate of fifty barrels to the statute acre (one barrel was thirty-two gallons).
2. Five-foot-wide lazy beds were prepared, and the potatoes were planted on the ridges.
3. Guano was scattered on top of the ridges, six cwt. to an acre.
4. Finally, clay was dug up from the furrows and spread on top of the guano, and the beds were levelled off.

Excellent crops were produced in this way, and when they were harvested, 'the act of digging mixed the lime, manure, and the several soils together into an even texture, leaving the land which had hitherto been scarcely worth one shilling per acre, in excellent order for sowing corn crops or grass seeds, and permanently worth at least one

pound per acre'.[2] Apart from this enormous increase in the value of the land, the costs of reclamation were repaid by the sale of the first year's crop of potatoes, at that time worth about £30 an acre, which was 3d a stone.[3]

Trench's mountain farm was a tremendous achievement. Lord Devon and all the members of his Commission visited Baunreagh, and were greatly impressed. From deep blanket peat he had carved out a farm of some 150 acres, which in 1843 produced 515 tons of potatoes, 240 barrels of oats and 90 tons of hay. Steuart Trench was awarded both the silver and gold medals offered by the Royal Agricultural Society of Ireland for the best report on the largest quantity of waste land reclaimed in Ireland. 'A more cheering sight it was scarcely possible to conceive than to witness these numerous labourers, employed at good wages themselves, collected from all quarters where labour was abundant, producing food for

Fig. 1 William Steuart Trench (1808–72). (Source: The late Mrs Leonora Powell, Trench's great-granddaughter).

thousands of people while reclaiming one of the wastes of Ireland.'[4]

In spite of the labour-intensive nature of the enterprise, mechanical assistance was not neglected. He installed a huge water wheel eighteen feet in diameter and three feet wide, mounted on strong oak posts, and which could be moved as required. Employing the principle of the windlass, this could draw sledge-loads of dung or stones for making drains up to four tons in weight right up a slope so steep 'as to ascend about 3000 feet perpendicular in a distance of 400 yards, and up which a horse can scarcely carry a man upon his back, much less draw a loaded car; and so powerful is the machine that it will do this over the roughest land, covered with heath and tussocks, and independent of road or railroad.' There was a second water wheel attached to the barn on his home farm, fourteen feet in diameter, which he used for threshing and operating various other machines as required. His cattle sheds were of particular interest; they were circular and thatched with rushes 'which form an excellent roof,' and used to house young cattle over the winter (one hundred cattle to each shed), fed with oaten straw and hay, and littered down with heather and sedge from the mountain.

In 1846 Steuart Trench planted 162 statute acres of potatoes in Baunreagh; his account of the total failure of the crop – which in July was 'for its extent and luxuriance ... the wonder of everyone who saw it' – is one of the most vivid eyewitness accounts of the arrival of the potato blight. In 1846 the blight reached the Irish Midlands towards the end of July, and by early August it was in Slieve Bloom.

For some years I had not less than two hundred labourers, employed constantly at those works, draining, levelling, liming, and the heavy work of sowing and digging out again enormous quantities of potatoes. A more cheering sight it was scarcely possible to conceive than to witness these numerous labourers, employed at good wages themselves, collected from all quarters where labour was abundant, producing food for thousands of people while reclaiming one of the wastes of Ireland. But all this passed away like a dream on the sudden failure of the potato, and 'the happy valley', as the sloping sides of my mountain property of Baunreigh, with a clear trout stream running in the hollow, was frequently called by those who visited the works, was by that fearful calamity turned into a valley of woe.

On 1 August of that calamitous year, 1846, I was startled by hearing a sudden and strange rumour that all the potato fields in the district were blighted; and that a stench had arisen emanating from their decaying stalks. I immediately rode up to visit my crop; but I found it as luxuriant as ever,

in full blossom, the stalks matted across each other with richness, and promising a splendid produce, without any unpleasant smell whatever. On coming down from the mountain, I rode into the lowland country, and there I found the report to be but too true. The leaves of the potatoes on many fields I passed were quite withered, and a strange stench, such as I had never smelt before, but which became a well-known feature in 'the blight' for years after, filling the atmosphere adjoining each field of potatoes. The next day I made further enquiries, and I found the disease was fast extending, and on rooting up some of the potato bulbs under the withered stalks, I found that decay had set in, and that the potato was rapidly blackening and melting away. In fields having a luxuriant crop, the stench was generally the first indication of disease, and the withered leaf followed in a day or two afterwards. Much alarm now prevailed in the country; people looked blank enough, as they asked each other if they had seen this new and formidable disease. Those, like me, who had staked a large amount of capital on the crop, hitherto almost a certainty, and at least as sure as the crop of wheat or turnips or any other agricultural produce, became extremely uneasy; whilst the poorer farmers looked on helplessly and with feelings of dire dismay at the total disappearance of all they had counted on for food.

Each day, from the time I first heard of the disease, I went regularly to visit my splendid mountain crop, and each day saw it apparently further advanced in course of arriving at a healthy and abundant maturity.

On August 6, 1846 – I shall not readily forget the day – I rode up as usual to my mountain property, and my feelings may be imagined when before I saw the crop, I smelt the fearful stench, now so well known and recognised as the death-sign of each field of potatoes. I was dismayed indeed, but I rode on; and as I wound down the newly engineered road, running through the heart of the farm, and which forms the regular approach to the steward's house, I could scarcely bear the fearful and strange smell, which came up so rank from the luxuriant crop then growing all round; no perceptible change, except the smell, had as yet come upon the apparent prosperity of the deceitfully luxuriant stalks, but the experience of the past few days taught me that all was gone, and the crop was utterly worthless.[5]

After the Famine the slopes of Baunreagh reverted to grass. In 1911 the Forestry Branch of the Department of

Figs 2a, b and c  Surviving farm buildings, potato ridges and drainage culvert from Baunreagh. In the early 1840s, William Steuart Trench took a lease of lands at Baunreagh in the foothills of the Slieve Bloom mountains and reclaimed 180 acres of deep bogland for cultivation. In 1846, 162 acres of potatoes there were struck by the blight. Figure 2a shows firstly the Steuart Trench home farm on Baunreagh with the mountain lands on the horizon. The steward's house is long since gone but some of the farm buildings still survive. Some of the grass covered potato ridges also still survive since that awful day on 6 August 1846 when the death-knell of the potato crop was signalled by a fearful stench. Shown here are surviving 'lazy beds' on the borders of Baunreagh and Castleconor (Fig. 2b). Also shown here is a drainage culvert, part of the impressive engineering of stone-based drains, walls, gate entrances and roads established by this reforming landlord in a most difficult environment (Fig. 2c). [Photos: William J. Smyth]

Agriculture and Technical Instruction for Ireland acquired 2,000 acres in Baunreagh, which were planted, mainly with Sitka spruce. This has now been clear-felled, allowing the open character of Baunreagh to be seen once again. On some of the higher slopes here and there the last of the grass-covered potato ridges from one of the most remarkable agricultural ventures of pre-Famine Ireland can still be traced, and the fine stonework of the bridges and drainage culverts constructed as part of the Famine relief reclamation works of which Steuart Trench was put in charge in 1846 (and which became the basis of the Land Improvement Act), crumble further into ruin with each passing year.

# Diet in pre-Famine Ireland

## Regina Sexton

The diet of the rural poor in pre-Famine Ireland was predominantly potatoes and a liquid accompaniment.[1] Additional supplements or 'kitchen' brought relish to an otherwise bland and repetitive pattern of consumption. These accompaniments/additions may be classed as flavour enhancers – salt, pepper, salted herring, shore foods like shellfish and seaweed – or texture improvers – liquids like skimmed milk, buttermilk and sowans (sour liquid of fermented oat husk and chaff). This broad pattern of consumption saw slight regional variation. In the oatmeal zones of the north, northeast and areas in south and north

Leinster,[2] for instance, the potato diet was balanced with oatmeal foods like porridge, stirabout, flummery and oatcakes.[3] In these oatmeal regions, 'the poorer classes had at least an oatmeal breakfast in place of the full potato diet of their counterparts in most of Ireland';[4] although the oatmeal element to the diet may have been more pronounced when old potatoes were poor and between-season stocks scarce.[5]

In coastal areas, seaweed, especially dulse, could be gathered and used as a dressing with boiled potatoes. After his visit to Aran Island in 1845, Foster details its use and preparation: 'They gather ... a kind of sea-weed called "dillisk"

Fig. 1 *The Potato Market*, c.1800 Nathaniel Grogan (1740–1807) [Source: Crawford Art Gallery]. In the early decades of the nineteenth century the potato became dominant in the diet of the poorer classes. The overall atmosphere conveyed by the artist in this painting is sombre which is reinforced by the dark figures in the background. In times of great scarcity Cork Corporation distributed potatoes to the poor at this market place. The connection with poverty and dearth may explain the melancholy mood.

which they dry, and boil as "kitchen" with their potatoes. It boils down to a kind of gluten with the potatoes, the salt in it … makes the potatoes more palatable.'[6] Cheap and flavoursome foods like herrings with their high salt and oil content were commonplace and often replaced milk.[7] When the shoals were good, herrings, fresh and salted, were frequently used and valued for the relish they imparted to the otherwise bland potato. The Halls note the use of herring and its rudimentary preparation: 'Generally they contrived to have a salt herring with their dinners; this is placed in a bowl or dish, water poured over it, and the potato, dipped in it, obtained a relish.'[8]

## VOLUMES CONSUMED

In the normal pattern, the monotony of the full potato diet was offset by the volumes consumed – 14lbs daily for the adult male, with downward adjustment for women and children.[9] Diminishing stocks in late spring and summer saw restriction in the volume of potatoes consumed and a corresponding reduction in the number of daily meals.[10] Cooking methods were basic and directed by a meagre range of cooking utensils. Typically, potatoes were boiled in an iron pot or simply ember roasted. The practice of half-boiling potatoes is referred to in a number of accounts[11] and the potato-eating ritual was one of communal eating centred around a basket of cooked potatoes, which were eaten from the hand. Travelling toward Ballygawley, Country Tyrone, Reid describes the scene as encountered in the early 1820s:

> The repast consisted of dry potatoes only, which were contained in a basket set upon the pot in which they had been boiled; this was placed on the floor in the middle of the cabin. The father was sitting on a stool, and the mother on a kreel of turf; one of the children had a straw boss; the youngest was sprawling on the floor, and five others were standing around the potato-basket … I took a potato, which not being enough, I put down, and took up another, and another, but all were equally hard. The man instantly put one onto the hot turf-ashes to have it better cooked for me. He said, 'We always have our praties hard, they stick to our ribs, and we can fast longer that way.'[12]

Meat, butter and eggs were infrequent items in the diet and therefore took on luxury status, making them the choice foods of festive and holy days.[13] In the service of the farmer, the labourer's diet may also have seen periodic improvement with the addition of meat or butter for the duration of his employment.[14]

As the diet contracted to a single foodstuff, the pattern of consumption was easily susceptible to further deterioration. Bad weather or a bad harvest, for instance, impinged on not only post-harvest food supply but also jeopardised seed crop and food security for the following

year. Similarly, access to milk varied with season and market conditions. Foster, in his 1845 letter from Donegal, for example, says that 'if the tenant lives near a town where he can sell his milk he sells that also, and the common drink with their potatoes is then an infusion of pepper – pepper and water, being as more tasty than water.'[15] When milk was difficult to procure, Reid saw sowans (also called 'bull's milk') used as a substitute liquid accompaniment.[16]

The diet was most vulnerable to seasonal collapse in the months of July and August. These were the 'waiting months'[17] between the exhaustion of the old stocks and the harvesting of the new potato crop. The remaining old season potatoes were at their worst at this time and this coincided with a slump in agricultural activity,[18] thus forcing the poor to resort to unsound measures of negative agricultural, economic and nutritional consequence. Premature and undersized potatoes were dug for food, attempts were made to buy potatoes at high prices or on credit and, by necessity, substitution foods like cabbage, nettles, wild mustard/charlock, entered the diet.[19] Oatmeal and Indian meal/maize served as cheap potato replacements.[20] In the late 1820s, Humphrey O'Sullivan records of Callan, County Kilkenny, that cheap maize at the July and August market was sustaining the poor and 'keeping them from stark famine'.[21] This annual cycle of distress saw restrictions in the number of potato meals taken from three to two or one in the day. The seasonal period of elevated distress served to weaken the people in the most vulnerable groups – widows, the aged and the infirm – leading to an increase in vagrancy and a resort to field and shore gleaning, which brought poor food returns relative to the expenditure of time and energy given.

## INSTABILITY

The instability of the pattern in the waiting months was exacerbated by the increased displacement of other foods in the decades leading to the Great Famine. As summer-ripening crops like barley, rye, beans, peas, vetches and other esculent garden vegetables were abandoned to increased potato cultivation, the hungry gap remained unfilled.[22] Additionally, the adoption and reliance on potato varieties of inferior or late-maturing varieties delayed the harvest of new potatoes to a period between September and November. A considerable number of potato varieties were known and grown in pre-Famine Ireland.[23] The cultivation of early varieties like the Kidney was often the preserve of the gentleman farmer[24] and while these came to market during the summer months, their price put them beyond the reach of the poor. Of the maincrop varieties, the Irish Apple, the Cup and the Lumper were most prevalent in the foodways of the poor and impoverished.[25] Variously criticised as ill tasting, wet or difficult to digest, these varieties were chosen for their lasting/storing qualities (as in the Irish Apple), their

which traverse the country, added to its cheapness, has rendered it an article of general use. Tea is used at least once a day by farmers, and is no longer looked on as a luxury by them.[27]

For others, particularly those close to centres of commercial activity and with a strong market-gardening enterprise, a variety of foods were on offer, especially for those of means. Food retailers, specialist suppliers and markets provided everything from staple items to luxury, indeed, exotic goods. In particular, from the late eighteenth century, the benefits of horticultural improvement augmented the range and availability of vegetables and fruits.[28] Interest in horticulture

Fig. 2 *In a Fishermen's Hut*, 1844 by Alfred Downing Fripp (1822–95). This painting shows the interior of a cabin in the Claddagh, Galway. The empty *sciob* (used in the straining of potatoes) in the foreground is pointedly used by the artist to convey the poverty of the household. Fripp was one of a number of artists who visited the Claddagh to paint the lives of the local people. [Source: National Library of Ireland]

productive returns (Cups/Lumpers) or low manuring requirements (Lumper).[26] Essentially, the potato of the poor in pre-Famine Ireland was one suited to precarious, near subsistence existence.

By the 1830s, the diet was debased and characterised by little if any variety, low quality and lack of security. The poor were limited to the foods surplus to market requirements and the attempts to enliven the diet were confined to the residue of producing market goods – skimmed milk, buttermilk, sowans, and, in distress, that which could be gleaned and gathered for free.

### COMFORTABLE FARMERS

While the pre-Famine diet of the rural poor and impoverished was potato-dominated, comfortable farmers also enjoyed a diet with a strong potato profile but nonetheless one that was secure and varied relative to the potato and milk regime. In the Grange of Ballywater, County Antrim, Doyle, in 1838, describes a northern dietary pattern of substance with instances of relative luxury:

With the farmers the consumption of animal food is daily. Salt meat, either fried with eggs or boiled, milk, butter, oatmeal made into porridge and large thin cakes called 'farls' [mashed potato and flour bread] with potatoes constitute their food. Broth made with leeks, cabbage, groats and some beef is in general use. The consumption of baker's bread is daily increasing. The facility of procuring it, either from the bread carts,

and gardening was no longer the prerogative of wealthy demesne owners with their sometimes-vast walled gardens. Town houses also had gardens and market gardeners supplied centres of population. Commercial nurserymen and seedsmen facilitated these changing tastes and trends.[29] Individual and local growers of note also supplied to market, as in the case of the eminent Kilkenny nurseryman and pomologist, J. Robertson:

The market of Kilkenny is well supplied with every article, with sea fish in plenty from Dungarvan, and with all kinds of garden stuff and fruit in season; even peaches, melons, grapes, pineapples; as the produce of several gardens are sold besides that of Mr. Robertson's hot houses and nursery: the cultivation of vegetables by market gardeners has increased [*sic*] three or four fold, within these twenty years.[30]

The diet and foodways of the landed elite and demesne owners were elaborate and highly structured. Estate records, in particular household accounts and recipe collections, reveal a food economy that was balanced between the internal production of raw ingredients and commercial supplies of high-quality goods. One representative illustration of extravagance at this level is the culinary treatment of the potato in recipes for potato puddings. Here the potato is but one ingredient amongst many and its identity almost disguised as it acts as a base filler and flavour carrier for butter, cream, eggs, sugar, spice, lemon, candied fruit, ground nuts and fortified spirits.

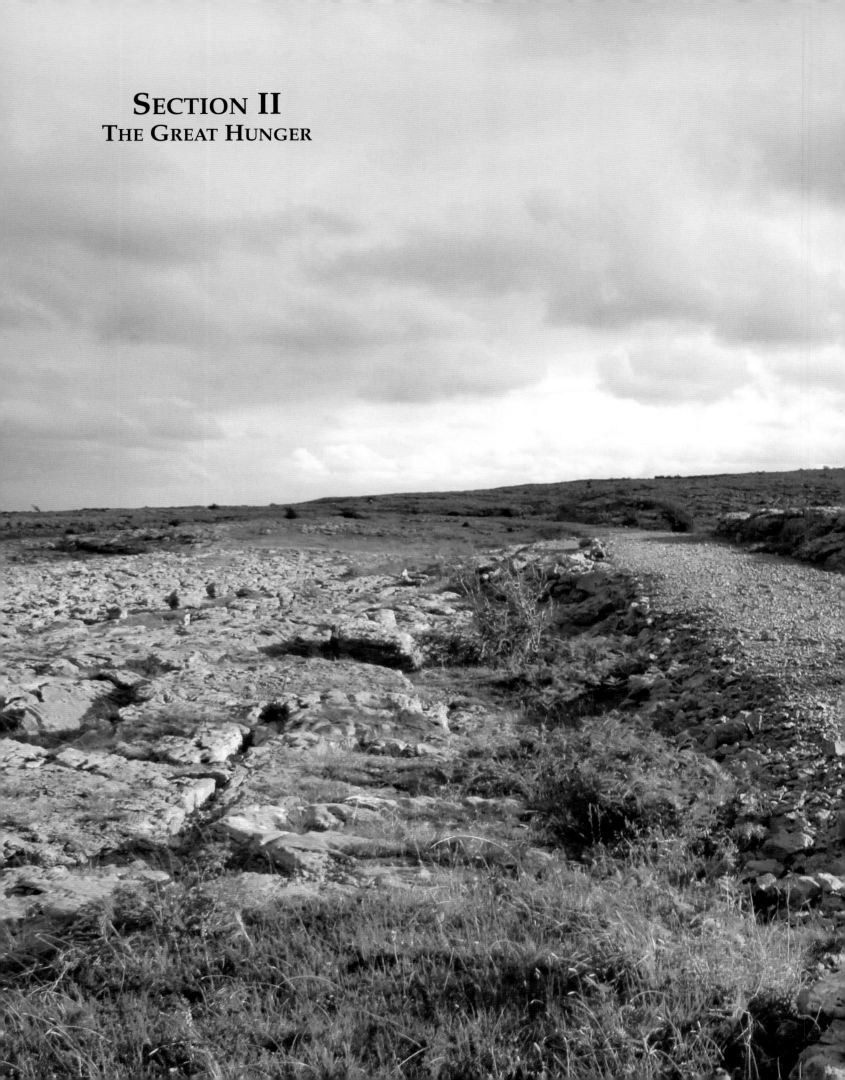

# SECTION II
## THE GREAT HUNGER

Famine relief road, Burren, County
Clare. [Photo: Frank Coyne]

# The *longue durée* – imperial Britain and colonial Ireland

## William J. Smyth

The proper geographical and political unit for the analysis of the Great Famine is Britain and Ireland. Since the Act of Union in January 1801 which put an end to the Irish Parliament, all legislative power was openly vested in Westminster. All the most crucial decisions and legislative acts relating to the handling of the Famine crisis were made at Whitehall and the Westminster Parliament respectively. These decisions and associated regulations acted as the crucial parameters within which the tragic drama of the Famine was played out. Hence, while acknowledging that there were many other powerful actors and institutions involved in this tragedy, primary responsibility for the successes and failures in dealing with the Famine catastrophe rested with the London administration. Mary Daly is correct in arguing that responsibility does not lie solely with the Government; that landlords, farmers, clergy, grain traders and Irish politicians could have been more pro-active.[1] Clearly, oscillating hierarchies of power, exploitation and suffering characterised the Famine years. But in the final analysis it was the London Government which had the most responsibility, the most freedom and the greatest number of options in determining the ground rules (if not always the conditions) under which other groups, organisations and individuals had to adapt to, work with, survive or die.

### RESPONSIBILITY

The extent to which the London administration was responsible for succeeding or failing to meet its obligations to the Famine-stricken Irish, the extent to which it was responsible or not for famine deaths and for prolonging and intensifying Famine miseries, is still a contested domain.[2]

Fig. 1 *The House of Commons* (1833) by Sir George Hayter, oil on canvas. Decisions made in the House of Commons and Whitehall had disastrous consequences for Ireland. It was never the case that Whitehall mandarins were uninterested in the plight of the starving. A cursory examination of the parliamentary papers for the period provides evidence that conditions in Ireland did occupy the minds of civil servants and Government ministers alike. In any case dispatches from various parts of the country, including the most devastated (like Skibbereen), kept the Government well informed of the growing crisis. Yet, even such reports of starvation and death in Ireland, when held up in the light of contemporary economics, did not move the Government enough to deal with the Famine on a long-term basis. Policy-makers were adamant that prolonged Government intervention was not the cure for Ireland's ills. By the end of 1847 – with the phasing out of the soup kitchens – it had become all too clear that the Government had accepted the principle that wise and good governance entailed leaving the Famine run its course. [Source: National Portrait Gallery, London]

of the state of the Coast population my Annual Inspections of the Coast Guard force on the Coast of Ireland, *for nearly 30 years* giving me facilities in that respect which probably no other Person possesses in an equal degree

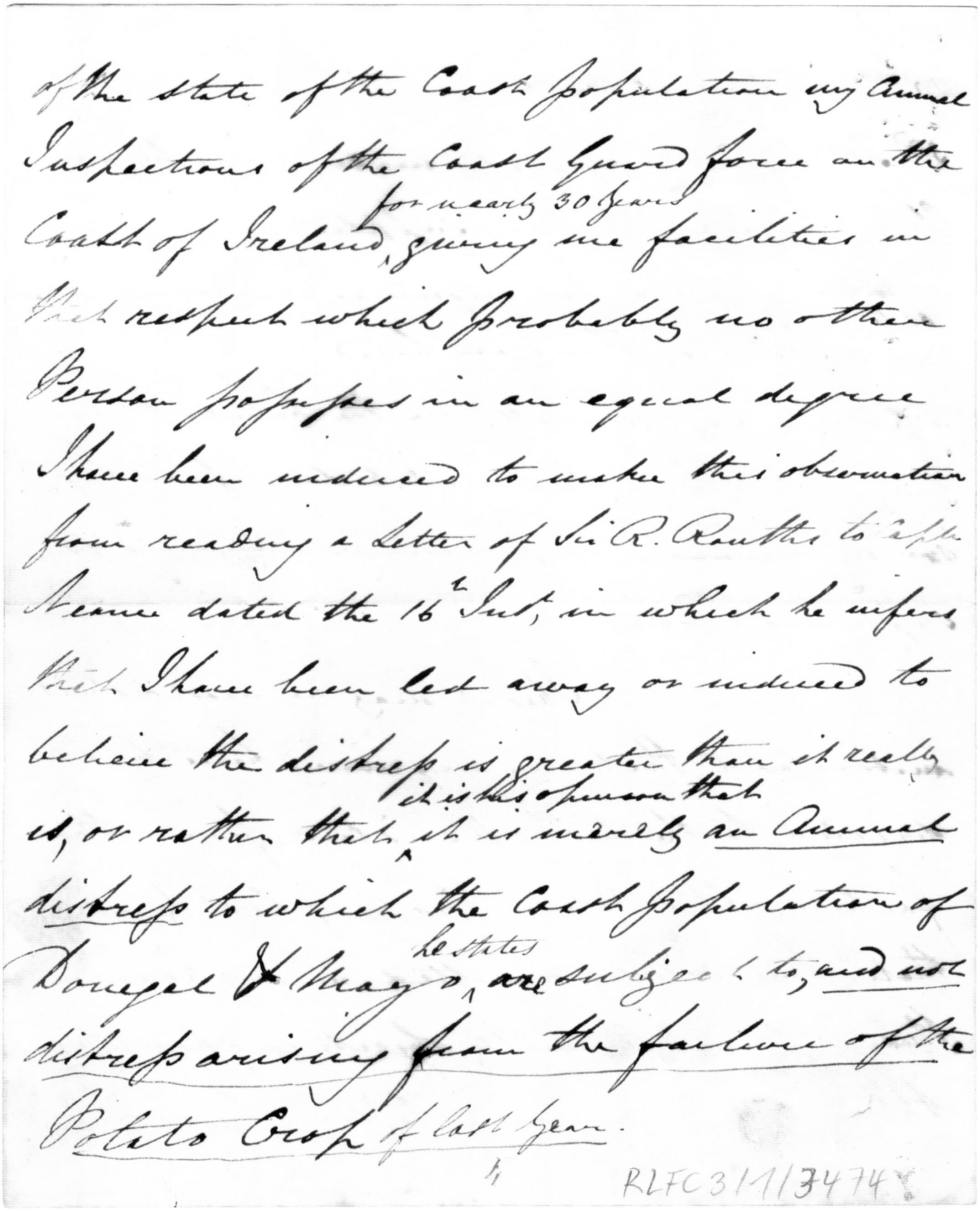

I have been induced to make this observation from reading a Letter of Sir R. Rouths to Capt Keane dated the 16th Int, in which he infers that I have been led away or induced to believe the distress is greater than it really is, or rather that, *it is his opinion that* it is merely an Annual distress to which the Coast population of Donegal & Mayo, *he states* are subject to, and not distress arising from the failure of the Potato Crop of last Year.

4

RLFC 3/1/3474

Fig. 2 The extent of the distress caused by the failure of the potato was a matter of debate within the Central Relief Commission. Sir James Dombrain, Inspector General of the Coastguard, took exception to the assertion of Chairman of the Commission, Sir Randolph Routh, that he was exaggerating the levels of distress in the coastal districts of County Donegal and County Mayo. Writing from Galway on 21 June 1846, Dombrain was adamant that what was occurring in these districts was substantially more than the annual cycle of distress. He was convinced that intense suffering was an inevitable outcome unless the Commission took urgent action to deliver supplies or provide public works so that food could be procured. [Source: Relief Commission Papers, 3/1/3474, National Archives of Ireland]

Given these contexts, it may be useful to set out a brief summary of the actions of successive governments in dealing with the Famine crisis.

As the first reports of potato failure in the summer of 1845 were confirmed, Sir Robert Peel, Tory Prime Minister, acted promptly by secretly purchasing 100,000 tons of Indian corn (maize) in the United States to meet the food needs of the starving poor. Peel chose the previously untraded Indian corn so as not to interfere with the existing trade in cereals. Despite much suffering in the first half of 1846, the relief measures put in place by Peel helped to avert many deaths. A Central Relief Commission had been established to raise subscriptions to purchase more food and establish food depots in the most affected areas. It should also be noted that the coastguard opened up seventy-six food depots for the poor along the west coast under Peel's administration. The related policy of seeking to persuade landlords to increase employment was, for the most part, unsuccessful even though landlords were initially generous with their subscriptions for the relief of distress.[3] Public works were then commenced – under the jurisdiction of the Board of Works – to increase employment and provide the starving poor with monies to purchase food. Peel's Government fell in late June 1846 after bitter opposition to the repeal of the Corn Laws – enacted by the Parliament so as to enable grain to be imported freely.

Prime Minister Sir John Russell's Liberal (Whig) Government adopted a more stringent policy in relation to the Famine crisis. Charles Trevelyan – who had previously served in India and would do so again later – remained as head of the Treasury.[4] All expenditure, all recommendations and all correspondence relating to Famine relief in Ireland came under his direct gaze. Described as 'a capable official of strong character, he became virtual director of Famine relief efforts'.[5] In this context, Chancellor of the Exchequer, Charles Wood – himself a strong advocate of laissez-faire (the non-interference of the Government in the market) and very much opposed to any measures involving new expenditure or new taxes – became an even more emphatic supporter of Trevelyan's strict policy controls and views. In this, they were supported by the Home Secretary, Sir George Grey. These three constituted the dominant 'moralistic' group in Russell's Government even though the Prime Minister himself was more sympathetic, it appears, to a more active intervention in the Irish crisis. But unlike the partial failure of the potato which Peel's administration had to handle, Russell's Government now had to face up to an almost complete failure of the potato crop as the despairing poor everywhere faced the bitter winter of 1846–47 without food. Millions could starve; the Government was faced with an enormous task.

## SHIFTING THE BURDEN OF RELIEF

The Whig Government moved immediately to shift the burden of relief onto local rates. Treasury monies were advanced to continue to fund the public works scheme designed to provide employment and wages so the starving poor could buy food. But these monies were to be repaid out of local rates over a ten-year period. Despite inordinate delays, influenced profoundly by the bureaucratic paper demands for the stringent approval of relief projects, methods of surveying, overseeing, and above all strict accounting, employment on the public works increased from c.150,000 in October 1846 to over 700,000 in March 1847.[6] Even with these numbers, not all the destitute poor could get work on the relief roads and other public work schemes. For those who could, now often poorly dressed and weak from hunger, the piece-rates offered per day – 8d

Fig. 3 *John Russell*, 1st Earl Russell (1853) by Sir Francis Grant, oil on canvas. [Source: © National Portrait Gallery, London]

to one shilling – were hardly sufficient to pay for one meal per day for the family. And food prices continued to soar. Without coin to purchase food, many people either starved or died of famine-related diseases. Corruption, favouritism and intimidation were features of the public works scheme, and far more people suffered rather than gained from the whole operation.

Having advanced £5m to fund the public work scheme and finding it ineffectual, the Government introduced the Temporary Relief or Soup Kitchen Act in late January 1847. It should be noted that this Act was a prelude to a further trimming of Treasury costs as it was planned to transfer all responsibility for the distressed to the Irish Poor Law Unions and the Irish rate-payers. 'Irish property must pay for Irish poverty'[7] was the maxim employed. As noted already, the provision of soup kitchens, where the people queued for the cooked food, represented a relatively successful interweaving of union and parish-cum-district electoral division relief committees and central Government. Over three million people availed of these food rations in the summer of 1847 at a cost of £1.75m.[8] For some the soup kitchens came too late and for others, they were closed too abruptly; most kitchens were phased out between August and October 1847. In the place of the soup kitchens, all relief was now to be administered by the local Poor Law Union. As few as twenty-two of the 130 unions were classified as 'distressed' and would receive assistance with their costs from 'the imperial Treasury'.[9] In two striking changes, the able-bodied were now to get relief within the workhouse while outdoor relief was to be introduced for the first time. The non-able-bodied – the widows, the old and the infirm – could now get relief outside the workhouse and retain their homes. Attempts were made to keep the number of people on outdoor lists down to the minimum.[10] There were sharp revisions downwards in these lists in the winter months of

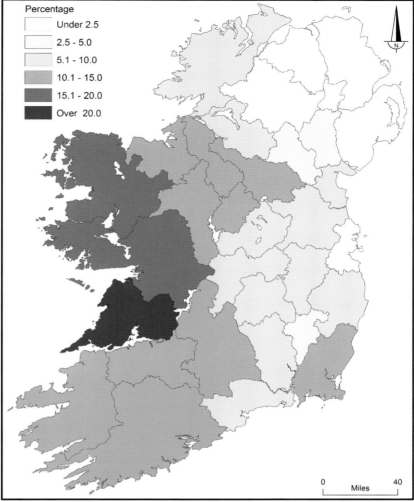

Fig. 4 PERCENTAGE DISTRIBUTION OF POPULATION SUPPORTED BY THE PUBLIC WORKS IN EARLY 1847. This map shows the percentage of the 1841 adult population employed on public works in the spring of 1847. County Clare had more than one-fifth of its population employed on these relief schemes, while counties Galway and Mayo were almost equally heavily involved with 15 to 18% of their population so engaged. The remaining counties in Connacht and Munster (excluding Waterford) as well as Ulster's County Cavan and Leinster's County Longford and County Wexford employed 10–14% of their 1841 population on the public works. The remaining counties of Ulster and Leinster employed less than 10%. Carlow, Dublin, Antrim, Down, Londonderry and Tyrone saw fewer than 5% employed on these schemes. The distribution of public works was therefore concentrated in these regions which had consistently shown high levels of vulnerability. However, the public works were abandoned because mortality had reached such alarming proportions. The poorest areas in the west and south – which had depended largely on these works for relief – lost heavily in population in the spring of 1847. Even before the beginning of 1847, sickness and weakness arising from the want of food meant that many families were unable to provide an able-bodied member who could go to work on the roads. Long journeys to works on foot, aggravated by a severe winter and lack of clothing, were further major handicaps to a weakened population. Food prices rose and public works wages were insufficient to support a large family. Death from starvation and/or fever resulted.

1847 but by February 1848,[11] nearly half a million people were on outdoor relief lists and others were clamouring to be so included by the local relieving officers. The now infamous Gregory (or quarter-acre) clause was part of this Act. This clause 'denied relief to tenants holding more than a quarter of an acre of land which turned the act into a charter for land clearance and consolidation'.[12] In this context, it is not clear why so few Irish members of Parliament opposed the passing of this infamous clause, which was now releasing its deadly charges. Landlords swept landscapes clear of the poorer tenants as other

families starved to death in their homes rather than relinquish their ancestral holdings. Troops and police were regularly used to enforce the payment of the rising rates, especially in the poorer unions.

Then and now, the actions of the United Kingdom Government in relation to the Irish Famine have been severely criticised. As the potato crop failed all over the land in the autumn of 1846 and while relief committees were reporting that the imminent closure of the food depots would produce 'the extremist misery', that the people were 'not far from starvation' and even *The Times* was finding it inexplicable that the food depots were being closed at the moment of total potato failure, Archbishop John MacHale (Tuam) remonstrated with Sir John Russell: 'you might as well issue an edict of general starvation as stop the supplies'.[13] From the period November 1846 to April 1847, the Roman Catholic clergy of the diocese of Derry under the leadership of their bishop, Dr Maginn, compiled a list for each parish register of all the deaths attributable to starvation. As Christine Kinealy reports, they placed this list in black crepe in the diocesan archive on 1 May 1847, with the following inscription:

> The records of the murders of the Irish Peasantry, perpetuated in A.D. 1846-47, in the 9 and 10 Vic., under the name of economy during the administration of a professedly, liberal, whig Government, of which Lord John Russell was premier.[14]

### RAGE

Local newspapers also raged against the premature closure of the public works before the whole apparatus surrounding the introduction of the soup kitchens had been properly put in place:

> For it is nothing short of a deliberate mockery, and betrayal of the entire nation – an act of suicidal folly, for which no excuse can be given, and one of its hideous features, next to the blind adherence to political economy in the transactions of the Executive. Men in power appear to imagine that starvation is a farce; that there is no real woe, or want, or misery in the land, or if these things do exist, then progress is to be met, not by rapid appliances of a sanatary [sic] policy, but by the slow, lingering, excruciating process of protocols – little dreaming how many lives depend on a day's delay or a day's action.[15]

But it is not the criticism of Irish politicians, journalists and clergy, which is most striking. It is the voices of the British officers working in Famine-struck Ireland – including those of successive Lord Lieutenants – which are most eloquent on the situation and British failures. The leading member of the first Relief Commission for Ireland (approved in November 1845), the very experienced Sir Randolph Routh – who had served in Canada and was previously a senior officer in the Commissariat department which supplied food for the British Army – begged Trevelyan to allow further purchases of Indian corn to supplement Peel's imports.[16] Trevelyan refused. And it was Routh (and not the radical Young Irelander, John Mitchel),

when pressing Trevelyan to import more food at once in August 1846, who said: 'you cannot answer the cry of want by a quotation from political economy'.[17] Once again Trevelyan refused.

Because of dwindling supplies, the food depots remained closed until December 1846. Trevelyan later relented and ordered supplies of corn from the United States but by then the supply season had closed and would not resume until the spring of 1847. Too little, too late, was a common feature of this administration. As Cormac Ó Gráda observes: 'Timing was crucial: a given sum spent on food in late 1846, before fever became universal would have saved more lives than the same sum six months later.'[18] For example, soup kitchens could have been started earlier and have lasted longer. Figure 7 shows the additional unions created by 1850.[19] They highlight the

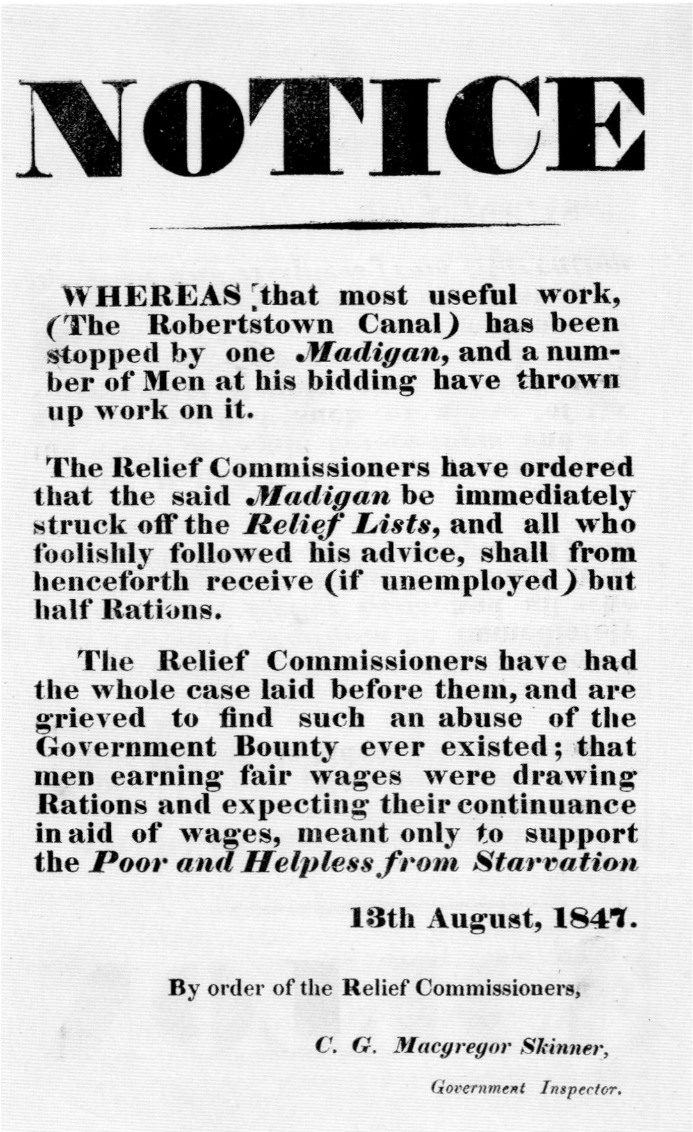

# NOTICE

**WHEREAS** that most useful work, (The Robertstown Canal) has been stopped by one *Madigan*, and a number of Men at his bidding have thrown up work on it.

The Relief Commissioners have ordered that the said *Madigan* be immediately struck off the *Relief Lists*, and all who foolishly followed his advice, shall from henceforth receive (if unemployed) but half Rations.

The Relief Commissioners have had the whole case laid before them, and are grieved to find such an abuse of the Government Bounty ever existed; that men earning fair wages were drawing Rations and expecting their continuance in aid of wages, meant only to support the *Poor and Helpless from Starvation*

### 13th August, 1847.

By order of the Relief Commissioners,

*C. G. Macgregor Skinner,*

*Government Inspector.*

Fig. 5 Accusations of jobbery and fraud were frequently used to strike off workers from relief lists. In the case of the Robertstown Canal (County Kildare) the Relief Commissioners were adamant that such 'an abuse of Government bounty' would not be tolerated. The scale of such abuses across the country was often exaggerated, a fact acknowledged in the report of the Commissioners for Public Works (1847). [Source: National Library of Ireland] areas most distant from existing workhouses – Belmullet was fifty miles from Ballina yet still part of the original union. Such areas had already suffered much deprivation. Many of these workhouses did not open until 1852. Again, it was too little, too late.

Commissariat officers, such as the very able Edward Pine Coffin, were of the view that the English knew as little about Irish conditions as those in West Africa and possibly less.[20] There was a profound failure to recognise that Ireland was not England – that poverty levels in Ireland were of a completely different order, that the concept of a 'wage' took on a different meaning, that food markets were few and far between in the most distressed regions of the west, that prosperous merchants and grocers were not evenly distributed across the landscape and that grain crops were produced specifically to pay the rent and not for home consumption. The March 1847 closure of the public works produced terror in the people (with cries 'the hunger is upon us'), as the provision of soup kitchens had hardly begun.

Major faultlines between the ending of one scheme and the beginning of another proved fatal for many people. Sir Lucius O'Brien, lord of Dromoland Castle in Clare, wrote to the Lord Lieutenant that March stating: 'I am going out to meet hungry and excited mobs. What am I to say to them. Is the population to be left to starve? Are you going to abandon us?'[21] By then the epidemic of typhus fever – which the Government had been warned would follow back in the Autumn of 1846 – had been spreading for up to three months. (Unlike food shortages, typhus fever did not distinguish the rich from the poor.) The new Irish Fever Act was not introduced until late April 1847; the Government sometimes seemed to be in denial about the depth of the health crisis. However, a central Board of Health was established in March 1846 and the implementation of the Fever Act brought good results.[22] Yet with three million starving in the middle of 1847 and only sustained by the soup kitchens, the Irish Poor Law Extension bill, in which the distressed persons were now to be classified as paupers and where outdoor relief was legalised, was passed in June 1847.

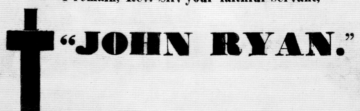

# IMPORTANT CIRCULAR
## FROM THE
# CATHOLIC BISHOP.

The following circular was read from every altar in the diocese of Limerick on Sunday last, by directions of the Right Reverend Dr. RYAN:—

"Limerick, December 24th 1846.

"Rev. Sir,

"You will be pleased to announce to your congregation on SUNDAY next, the 27th instant, that, in consequence of the unprecedented state of destitution so universally existing in this county, we consider ourselves warranted **in hereby declaring that the obligation of abstaining from servile works, and observing the usual religious services on holy days, ceases with regard to all persons employed on the public works** during the continuance of this awful visitation; and that this exemption likewise extends to tradesmen and operatives depending for support on daily wages.

It should, however, be remarked that artisans having continual employment and fair wages should not avail themselves of this indulgence, unless the wants of their families will imperatively demand it. The present may be a favorable opportunity of inculcating the duties of patience and moderation, and of avoiding all undue and factious opposition to those holding situations in the public works. As persons of every degree and denomination have corresponding duties to perform, the affluent, the influential, and the educated, should be admonished to assist, encourage, and console the destitute, while a reciprocity of gratitude and dutiful submission should be expected from the humbler classes. *Thus, by a combination of Christian efforts on the part of all, let us still hope that, through God's mercy, this country may be rescued from the horrors of famine, and enabled to surmount the fearful calamities by which she is at present surrounded.*

I remain, Rev. Sir, your faithful servant,

✝ "JOHN RYAN."

Fig. 6  As a consequence of this 'awful visitation' the Bishop of Limerick gives notice (Christmas Eve, 1846) to those on public work schemes that obligations as regards 'observance of the usual religious services on holy days' ceases. The fact that many distressed people were refused places on such schemes resulted in local tensions and conflict which in part explains the bishop's advice to members of his flock to avoid 'all undue and factious opposition to those holding situations in the public works'. [Source: National Library of Ireland]

The burden of the distressed and destitute was now the responsibility of the Irish Poor Law and the funding of such a burden was to fall almost entirely on Irish rate-payers.[23] Yet, when the Poor Law was first introduced in Ireland back in the late 1830s, the Government was then advised that outdoor relief was impossible in the Irish situation since it would swamp property owners and other rate-payers. Now

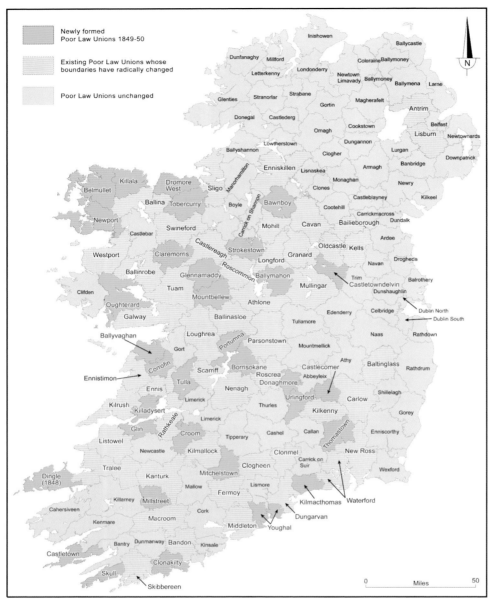

Legend:
- Newly formed Poor Law Unions 1849-50
- Existing Poor Law Unions whose boundaries have radically changed
- Poor Law Unions unchanged

0 — Miles — 50

Fig. 7 DISTRIBUTION OF BOTH THE ORIGINAL POOR LAW UNIONS AND NEWLY FORMED POOR LAW UNIONS. The creation of the original 130 Poor Law unions was an extraordinary feat in applied geography. It needs to be emphasised that these administrative units were entirely new creations, as were the thousands of district electoral divisions which underpinned – both spatially and financially – these new territories. Decisions had to be made in a relatively short time about which towns to select as union centres, what size populations they should serve and what shape their union territories should take. A key decision-maker here was Thomas Larcom, then assistant director of the Ordnance Survey in Ireland. Under his guidance, this new territorial framework emerged, overriding and displacing the historic network of counties, baronies and civil parishes. Many of the union centres and territories seem eminently sensible. However, as one moves westwards across the country – where, as we have seen, the greatest population numbers and densities existed in 1841 – the size and extent of the union territories becomes unwieldy. Unions such as Ballina, Westport, Galway and Tralee were far too extreme in size and shape and were responsible for serving far too great a union population. The original 130 unions incorporated far greater populations and more extensive areas than their English equivalents. Major gaps emerged when all of famine relief was devolved on those Poor Law unions in 1847. For example, Ballina was supposed to serve the starving population of Belmullet more than 50 miles away. Much deprivation, hardship and excess mortalities resulted. In the middle of the Famine, a Government committee was established to recommend the creation of a number of new unions. This committee did not report until 1850 and the majority of these new union workhouses (Dingle is an exception – built in 1848) were not built and open to the poor until 1851 or 1852. This map shows the distribution of these new unions – pointing up the areas of greatest need during the Famine years.

at the height of the Famine crisis, it was to be introduced. By then, however, it seems the British Government had decided that its responsibility towards the starving Irish must come to an end. As Cecil Woodham-Smith observes:

'From this point onwards, good intentions on the part of the British Government become increasingly difficult to discern.'[24]

Both British Government appointees and other independent agencies working in Ireland were also finding it difficult to discern any such good will. The very able Richard Griffith was very doubtful if the Poor Law Unions could bear the burdens being placed upon them. The Society of Friends (Quakers), who had been such a stalwart force in alleviating distress and who had initiated soup kitchen support as early as 1846, refused to participate in the new system. They did not think the Poor Law Unions could alone alleviate the desperate conditions of the populations in many parts of the south and west, where often no workhouse existed for thirty to forty miles. The Central Relief Committee of the Society took the view that only central Government funding and Government measures could alleviate the level of distress and save the people.[25]

TWISTLETON'S RESIGNATION

London-born Edward Twistleton, Irish Poor Law Commissioner from before the Famine, was increasingly highly critical and frustrated by Trevelyan's policies and style. Twistleton bitterly resented both the introduction of the Gregory quarter-acre clause and Trevelyan's and Grey's emphasis on a ruthless economy where nothing was to be advanced out of public funds and where there was to be no interference in the market. The dominant Government view was that the free market could achieve more than any Government agency.[26] Twistleton resigned his office with the introduction of the rate-in-aid scheme. The introduction of the rate-in-aid levy in February 1849 forced the better off unions *in Ireland* to subsidise the most distressed unions by adding an additional 6d in the pound, with the Treasury advancing a

Fig. 8 George William Frederick Villiers, 4th Earl of Clarendon (1860s), probably by John Watkins, albumen print. [Source: © National Portrait Gallery, London]

further £50,000 to the most distressed unions.[27] Not surprisingly, the Ulster unions were furious with the new manoeuvre. Catholic Irish and Protestant Irish met in Fermanagh in February, pointedly raising the question, since Ireland, after the Union, was an integral part of the empire, should not 'the Imperial Exchequer' (and the English Poor Law Unions?) also contribute to such a scheme. Twistleton resigned on 12 March 1849, thinking 'that the destitution here [in Ireland] is so horrible and the indifference of the House of Commons so manifest', that he found himself 'to be an imperfect agent of a policy which must be one of extermination'. Twistleton felt that as Chief Poor Law Commissioner he had been placed in a position 'which no man of honour or humanity could endure'.[28]

It was the Lord Lieutenant, William Frederick Villiers, Earl of Clarendon, who informed Prime Minister Russell of Twistleton's resignation. Back in October 1847, Clarendon had warned Chancellor Wood that the detailed reports of the Assistant Poor Law Commissioners confirmed that the

power to pay the rates was absolutely wanting in a number of localities and unions. Yet the relentless imposition and gathering of rates proceeded. On 23 October 1847, Lord Clarendon appealed to the Prime Minister, pointing out:

> Whatever may be the anger of people or Parliament in England, whatever may be the state of trade or credit, Ireland cannot be left to her own resources, they are manifestly insufficient, *we are not to let the people die of starvation* [my italics], we must not believe that rebellion is impossible.[29]

Earlier in October Clarendon observed the great social revolution going on in the country. What he called 'the accumulated evils of misgovernment and mismanagement' was coming to a head. (However, Clarendon was mistaken about the extent of an uprising at the time.) As the cholera epidemic brought further stresses – if that was possible – to the Poor Law Unions and their populations, Clarendon wrote to Sir John Russell in late April 1849, asking for the House of Commons to make an advance of monies to deal with the new situation, stating: 'I don't think there is another legislature in Europe that would disregard such suffering as now exists in the west of Ireland and *coldly persist in a policy of extermination*' [my italics].[30] No advance was granted.

The above analysis of British officials in Ireland seeking to implement British policies to deal with the Famine points up the huge chasm between decisions and laws made in distant London and their often crippling effects on the practice of many officials and the lives of the people in Ireland. It should also be noted that it is British officials in Ireland who have been quoted in relation to the extraordinary chasm between abstract theories of political economy and the stinking biological realities of rotten potatoes and bodies wasted by hunger and disease. The accusation of 'extermination' – which has surfaced in the political and historical literature ever since – was first articulated by people like the Chief Poor Law Commissioner and the Lord Lieutenant of Ireland.

## CULPABLE NEGLECT

It is now generally if not universally agreed that the British Government was deeply irresponsible in abandoning Ireland to the Poor Law Unions in the autumn of 1847. In the language of Trevelyan and others, Ireland was to be left to the working of Malthusian 'natural causes'[31] – 'natural' here really needs to be translated as 'cultural and political causes'. As Peter Gray puts it, 'the charge of culpable neglect of the consequences of policies leading to mass starvation is indisputable'.[32] Commenting on the response (or rather lack of response) to the devastating crop failure of 1848, James Donnelly observes: 'the official responses to

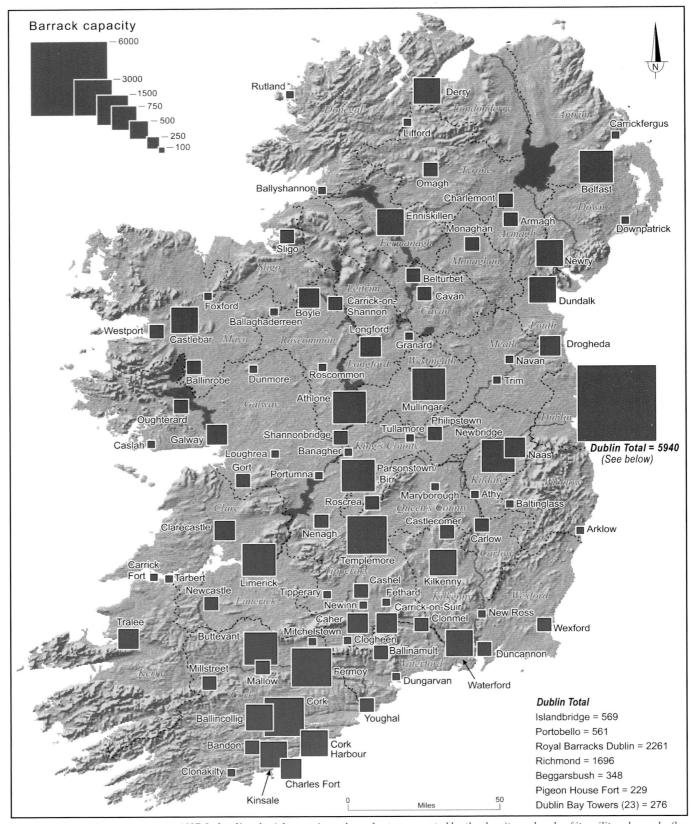

**Barrack capacity**

— 6000
— 3000
— 1500
— 750
— 500
— 250
— 100

Rutland
Derry
*Donegal*
*Londonderry*
*Antrim*
Carrickfergus
Lifford
Omagh
*Tyrone*
Belfast
Ballyshannon
Charlemont
*Down*
Enniskillen
Monaghan
Armagh
*Armagh*
Downpatrick
Sligo
*Fermanagh*
Belturbet
*Monaghan*
Newry
Cavan
*Leitrim*
Carrick-on-Shannon
*Cavan*
Dundalk
Foxford
Boyle
Longford
*Louth*
Westport
Ballaghaderreen
Granard
*Meath*
Drogheda
Castlebar
*Mayo*
*Roscommon*
*Longford*
*Westmeath*
Navan
Ballinrobe
Dunmore
Roscommon
Trim
Oughterard
Athlone
Mullingar
*Dublin*
Caslah
Galway
Shannonbridge
Philipstown
Newbridge
**Dublin Total = 5940**
Loughrea
Banagher
*King's County*
Naas
*(See below)*
Gort
Portumna
Parsonstown/Birr
*Kildare*
*Wicklow*
Maryborough
Athy
Baltinglass
Roscrea
*Queen's County*
*Clare*
Castlecomer
Arklow
Clarecastle
Nenagh
Carlow
Carrick Fort
Templemore
*Carlow*
Tarbert
*Tipperary*
Cashel
Kilkenny
Newcastle
Limerick
Tipperary
Fethard
*Kilkenny*
*Wexford*
*Limerick*
Newinn
Carrick-on-Suir
New Ross
Tralee
Caher
Clonmel
Wexford
Mitchelstown
Buttevant
Clogheen
Duncannon
*Kerry*
Millstreet
Ballinamult
*Waterford*
Mallow
Fermoy
Dungarvan
Waterford
*Cork*
Cork
Ballincollig
Youghal
Bandon
Cork Harbour
Clonakilty
Charles Fort
Kinsale

0        Miles        50

**Dublin Total**
Islandbridge = 569
Portobello = 561
Royal Barracks Dublin = 2261
Richmond = 1696
Beggarsbush = 348
Pigeon House Fort = 229
Dublin Bay Towers (23) = 276

Fig. 9 DISTRIBUTION OF ARMY BARRACKS IN 1837. Ireland's colonial status is, perhaps, best represented by the density and scale of its military barracks (known locally as garrisons) across the island. Because of the social disorganisation and chaos that followed the potato failures and resulting hunger and disease, the number of soldiers garrisoned in Ireland almost doubled from their pre-Famine complement. Figure 9 shows the distribution and capacity of these barrack complexes by 1837. Apart from the coastal cities, the most noticeable feature of this map is the concentration of soldiers and military control in a broad triangle over middle Ireland with its apex in the north Midlands and its base in the more troublesome province of Munster. The enforcing of relief regulations, including the collection of rates; the protection and support of landlords in their often ruthless clearance of the poorer tenantry; the escorting of food/grain convoys bound for export and the control of urban food riots and starving famine crowds – looking for bread and work – all involved the interventions of both army and police. The cost of maintaining this military and policing presence in Famine Ireland was greater than the total monies advanced by Britain for famine relief in Ireland in the years 1846 to 1852. [Source: adapted from Table 20.3 in Jacinta Prunty, 'Military barracks and mapping', in ed. H.B. Clarke et al, *Surveying Ireland's Past*, [Dublin, 2004] pp. 527–28] extreme destitution then were murderous in their consequences though not their intentions'.[33] These policies were born of a belief that Ireland was over-populated and under-developed; that economic development could only be achieved via a reformation of the landowning and landholding system to allow for capitalist farming on the English model. Social engineering – long a central feature of the English/British imperial project in Ireland – took on new forms during the Famine crisis.

Irish landlords were seen as exploitative on the one hand and failing to provide leadership on the other. Such views were favoured in a political climate which stressed laissez-faire policies, free trade and non-interference in the so-called free market for labour, goods and land. These ideas were under-pinned by a Malthusian Providentialism; the belief that the Irish potato blight was a visitation from God to achieve human good – that there was a moral to all this suffering.[34] As we have seen, the 'moralists' in the British administration – particularly Grey, Wood and Trevelyan – came to dominate cabinet thinking in this area as Prime Minister Russell increasingly 'sought to steer a untenable middle course' between the imperatives of state intervention and strict economy 'and in the process presided over the decimation of the Irish people'.[35] Ireland's needs were further exacerbated by a financial crisis in Britain towards the

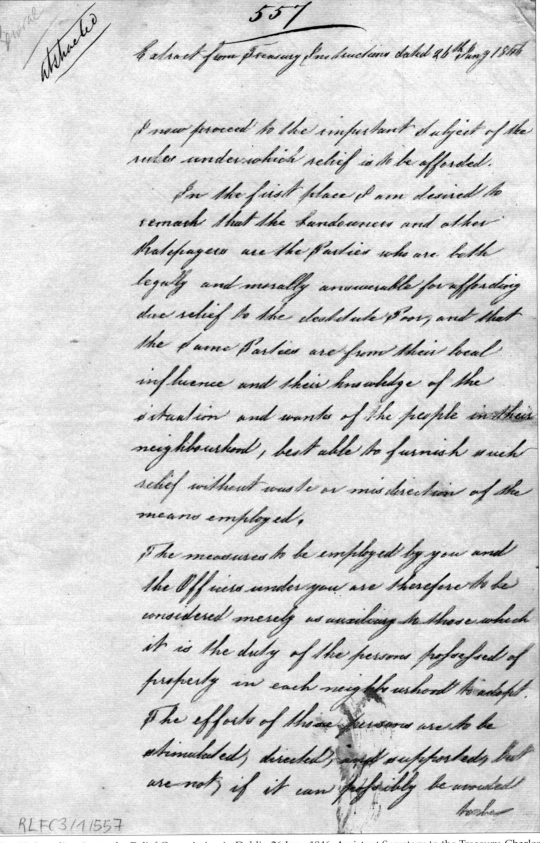

RLFC3/1/557

Fig. 10 In a directive to the Relief Commission in Dublin 26 June 1846, Assistant Secretary to the Treasury, Charles Trevelyan, insists 'that the landlords and other ratepayers are the parties legally and morally answerable for affording due relief to the destitute poor'. The measures to be employed by Sir Randolph Routh and the officers under him are therefore to be considered merely as auxiliary to measures adopted by the landed classes in each neighbourhood. Landed proprietors are not to be superseded by the direct agency of the officers of government. Trevelyan makes clear that waste or the misdirection of funds in the administration of relief would not be tolerated. (Source: Relief Commission Papers 3/1/557, National Archives Ireland) end of 1847 which saw British public opinion – especially that of its liberal middle-class – highly critical of any further state spending and intervention.[36] So-called 'agrarian outrages' – for the most part desperate, hungry people protesting over the lack of work or food – and the attempted rebellion in 1848, all fuelled deep-seated anti-Irish feelings, feelings further intensified by cultural and racial stereotypes promulgated in the British press. Such unsympathetic, antagonistic feelings are also expressed by Trevelyan and particularly Wood, who distrusted the Irish, sometimes his comments even denigrating the character of a whole nation.[37]

This narrative of events, policy conflicts, deep misunderstandings and misreadings of Irish conditions and needs by the ruling power situated on the larger island, of associated profound economic and political inequalities as well as deep ethno-religious divisions, all point to the workings of powerful structural forces much older than the Famine. Extraordinary levels of physical, political and cultural violence characterised Ireland in the early modern period (c.1530–c.1750), expressed in a military, legal and linguistic conquest, a vast programme of property confiscations, the systematic shaping of a colonial economy subservient to the metropolitan imperial power and the related centralisation of political and administrative procedures.[38] In a striking conclusion to his book, *Why Ireland Starved*, Joel Mokyr summarises the British response to the Irish Famine catastrophe: 'The real problem was that Ireland was considered by Britain an alien and even hostile country.'[39] If such a famine had begun in Britain, there is little doubt but that there would have been a different response. Yet, despite the political Union, Ireland and the Irish were, in the end, not considered part of the British community.

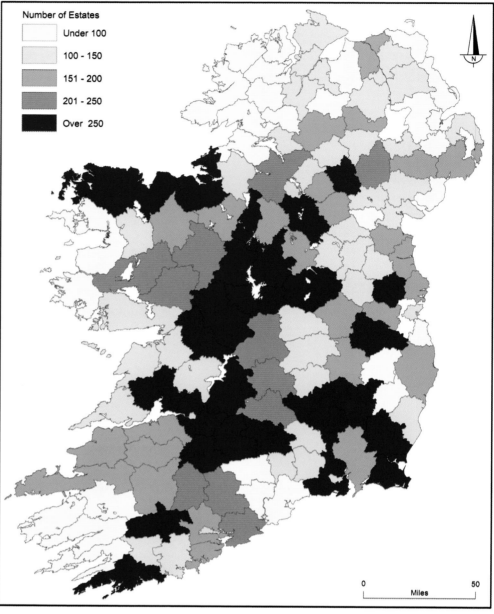

Fig. 11 DISTRIBUTION OF THE NUMBER OF ESTATES PER POOR LAW UNION IN 1847. The landlord estate system was, for the most part, carved out by a process of conquest, confiscation, plantation and colonisation in Ireland's early modern period (c.1530–c.1730). Some older estate units were to survive in pockets in the east and southeast of the island, but overall these landlords' estates constituted new territorial, cultural and administrative entities. The eighteenth century saw some further fragmentation in ownership patterns. By the mid-nineteenth century some 12,600 estate units were valued at £200 or more. The smaller estates valued at less than £200 numbered a further 8,800. This map shows the number of estates per each Poor Law union. Since quite a number of the bigger estates crossed union and county boundaries, the actual number of estates island-wide is, therefore, somewhat exaggerated on this map. Estate numbers range from only 31 in Antrim to 377 in Limerick Poor Law Union. Large estates valued at £1,500 and higher (while technically only comprising 6.8% of the total) actually accounted for close on two-fifths of the total value of all estates, embraced c.8 million acres and controlled c.300,000 tenant holdings in 1847. Medium-sized estates valued at between £500 and £1,500 numbering one-fifth of the total, accounted for one-third of the total value and encompassed a further 7 million acres, involving c.250,000 tenant holdings. Smaller estates valued at less than £500 while comprising close on three-quarters of the total number, accounted for 28% of the total value of all estates, covering a further 5 million acres and c.230,000 tenant holdings. It was a highly uneven patchwork, further complicated by high levels of absenteeism (especially in the poorer, densely populated counties), by complex leasing and subleasing arrangements, and by the level of indebtedness already characteristic of so many estates even before the Famine catastrophe.

## ENFORCING RELIEF REGULATIONS

When reading the vast literature on the British response to the catastrophe, one is struck by the emphasis on law and order throughout, the deep establishment fears of outrage and insurrection: the ruling class's fear of revolution from below. Hence the use of the police, the legal system and the military in enforcing the relief regulations emanating from London. At the height of the Famine, the Irish population – and not only in the poorest and most deprived regions – were being coerced into the payment of heavy rates, were being driven from their farms by landlords because their holdings were valued under £4, or more particularly because of the infamous quarter-acre clause. British imperial rule had ensured a well-garrisoned grip on the country. Military quarters in Ireland comprised close on 4,000 acres – still only one-eighth of the total for military establishment in the two islands. Yet in 1849 the number of troops in army barracks in Ireland comprised close on 29,500 – constituting 82% of the 36,000 stationed in Britain – and almost double the number of soldiers stationed in Ireland before the famine began (15,046 in 1843).[40]

The need for military control was thus intensified during the Famine years. Figure 9 shows the dense distribution of army barracks in 1837 and their designated military populations.[41] Both the literature on local and national histories of the Famine contain references to the use of troops and police in enforcing rate collections, in protecting food crops destined for export, seizing property by force in lieu of rates and other relief operations.[42] Even before the Famine, hundreds of troops supported by the police, were required to collect Poor Law rates in Galway, and in Mayo a warship and two revenue cruisers stood off Clew Bay 'to assist' rate collection in that county.[43] The increasing number of protests by the distressed, desperate poor looking for work on the relief schemes, or admission to the workhouses, or challenging the export of grain products, saw the regular calling out of troops across the south and west of Ireland, from Ballina to Nenagh, Dungarvan, Clonmel and Tralee. The advice given by Charles Wood to Clarendon in enforcing rate collection in late November 1847 was as follows:

> Arrest, remand, do everything you can, send horse, foot and dragoons, all the world [e.g. British public opinion] will applaud you and I should not be at all squeamish as to what I did, to the verge of the law, and a little beyond.[44]

These words echo many similar admonitions over the previous two centuries, and regiments – sometimes reluctantly – were called upon to enforce evictions at the landlord's request. As Tom Bartlett has pointed out, the Government's function in Ireland was to pay, clothe, feed and administer the English military establishment distributed across Ireland – a Government acting as a kind of revenue wing to the army.[45] The British Treasury spent a total of £9.5 million on famine relief; maintaining the military in Ireland over the same period cost over £10 million and the constabulary police a further £4 million.[46]

## ARMY BARRACKS

In Ireland, unlike in Britain, the Irish gentry favoured the dispersal of small-scale army barracks all over the country. Each landlord was anxious to have troops established in their own neighbourhood; they could sell land to the Government for barrack ground, further the local economy thereby and most significantly enhance their own security and enforce estate rules and rent payments.[47] During the Famine crisis, the latter considerations were to the forefront as was the business of clearing the landscape of unwanted tenants. Landlordism had been created in the colonial conquests of the sixteenth and seventeenth centuries, in a process which David Harvey has called 'capital accumulation through dispossession'.[48] A powerful series of processes was thus set in train whereby class and ethnic inequalities and tensions spiralled upwards and downwards in the society and deepened and expanded in an uneven fashion across the island.

Whatever the processes, the social, cultural, economic and political distance between the great majority of smallholders on an estate and the landlord in the Big House was immense. Alien to one another in nationality and religion, these two groups, as Tom Jones Hughes has emphasised, lived side by side 'yet out of touch and out of sympathy with each other.'[49] With some notable exceptions, the Famine exposed this brittle relationship and revealed the incapacity of this imposed land-owning class to provide the sympathetic leadership to their tenants which was so much a feature of the Scottish landlords' role in Scotland's potato famine.[50] However, the duration and intensity of the Irish famine often meant a severe reduction in the rents received and so damaged landlords' incomes severely.

Overall, the landlords' behaviour during the Famine had two major negative characteristics: they failed to provide leadership and they used the Poor Law regulations in a ruthless, often devastating manner. With the establishment of the Encumbered Estates Court in 1849, the Famine also revealed the depth of indebtedness of so many of the landlords (see David Butler, below). The British Government hoped that through these courts a new, modernising, capitalist landlord class would emerge to lead economic development, given what they saw and hoped would be the reduction of perceived surplus populations via famine deaths or emigration. In truth, the fate of landlordism in Ireland had been sealed during the Famine. An Indian summer followed before the Land League saw the farmers (with Gladstone's help) smash landlordism in Ireland – the opposite of what happened in England where the landowning aristocracy destroyed the

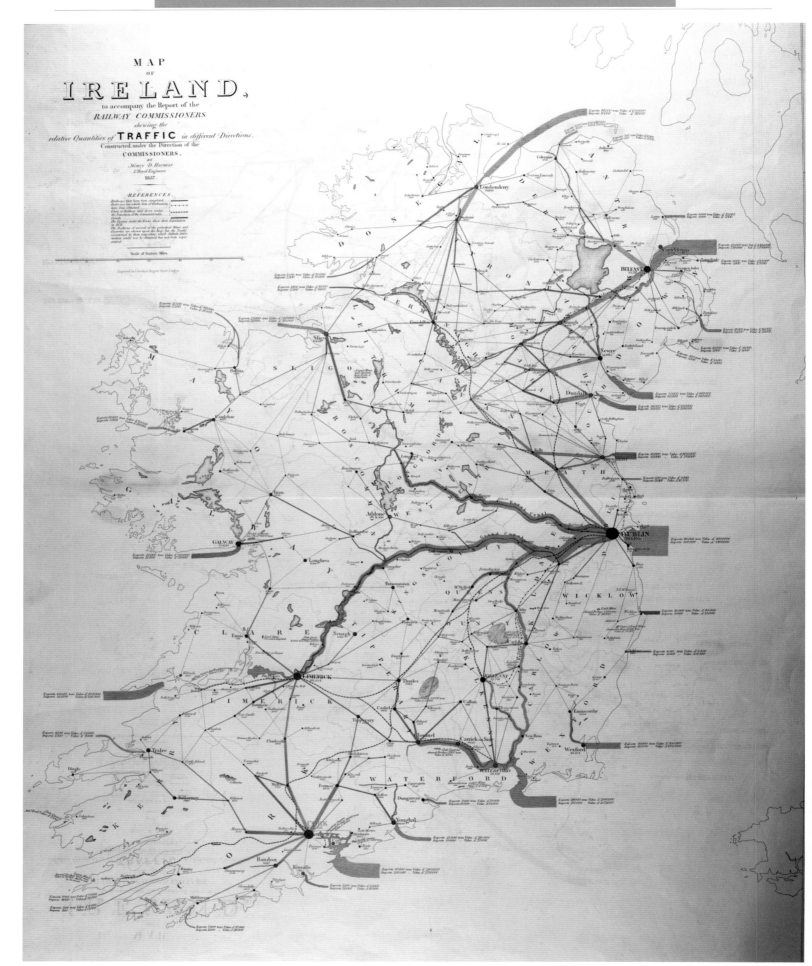

English peasantry via the enclosure movements.[51]

## SUBSERVIENT TO BRITISH NEEDS

Since the conquest of Ireland from the latter half of the sixteenth century and culminating in the Cromwellian and Williamite settlements, the human and economic geography of Ireland had been reconfigured to both face and serve England. Apart from blanketing the country with over a hundred garrisons with their nerve centre at Dublin Castle and apart from the establishment of a loyal landlord class, agents of the imperial state and protected by its military arm, the Irish economy was, for the most part, made subservient to British needs. Typical of any colony, Ireland was not given much autonomy to develop enterprises directly in competition with the imperial power.[52] Irish trade and the Irish economy generally was increasingly focused on Britain and British needs. In 1683, only 38% of Irish exports went to England, while scarcely a century later in 1774, the figure was as high as 74% and higher still in the 1840s.[53] Ireland's primary role in this imperial network was to supply both foodstuffs and labour to Britain's burgeoning industrial-cum-urban economy (and after the 1780s provide soldiers for the British army).[54] The contours of the Irish rural landscapes and their social structures were, therefore, profoundly influenced by economic circuits centred on Irish port cities and especially the colonial capital Dublin, which in turn were linked to complex networks of trade and credit dominated by British merchants. Likewise, the transfer of £3 million of Irish rental incomes, mainly via absentee landlords, helped both building and investment in a number of British cities, most notably in the capital, London.

In the process, the different components of Irish agriculture became much more specialised and focused on particular regions. Paradoxically, as David Nally argues, the commercialisation of Irish agriculture – notably the development of vast grazing farms across the middle of the country, but equally the consolidation of a commercialised tillage and mixed farming world in the southeast – promoted new divisions of labour and facilitated the growth of a flourishing subsistence economy where the potato was to play a vital role.[55] By the early nineteenth century, both these pastoral and tillage worlds relied on cheap manual labour hired from the subsistence sector, thus forming a patchwork quilt of very large farms and very small farms 'intertwined and mutually dependent'. This smallholding/cottier population also played a vital role in the pig and grain trades to Britain. These potato grounds acted in rotation to enhance the subsequent grain crops and also allowed for some pig-rearing. Britain's industrial cities were thus beneficiaries of foodstuffs produced in these patchwork landscapes.[56] However, as we have seen, the potato failure shattered this symbiosis between farmer and cottier/labourer.

Elsewhere the influence of the fat cattle and sheep trade centred on the grasslands of north Leinster, east Connacht and north Munster radiated deep into west Connacht, south Ulster and south Munster, drawing the small farmers into this commercial world to supply calves and yearlings for the trade in the great fairs of Ballinasloe and Templemore which linked the big farmer with these worlds. The intensification of these economic networks – again focused on Britain's food needs – was reflected in a phenomenal expansion of the fair sites all over the country, expanding four-fold between the seventeenth and nineteenth century.[57] Even the far western populations and poorest farming regions of west Ulster, west Connacht and southwest Munster were penetrated by these impulses.

Reflecting the dominance of the English market, the commercialisation and integration of Ireland's regional economies were uneven in their impacts but were present everywhere. Given the buoyant demand for labour and a byzantine hierarchy of grasping middlemen, the potato had facilitated population growth and extreme landholding fragmentation in the far western regions.[58] As T.W. Freeman has emphasised, one of the best indicators of the strength of links between the economies of Ireland (especially in the north and west) during the early nineteenth century is the size of permanent and seasonal emigration flows to Britain.[59] Emigration was already deeply embedded in Irish society as more and more Irish migrated to the industrialised regions of Britain and America. Even in the far west, traditional economies were being eroded as these external forces deepened. As some prospered in this changing world, others became more marginalised, made poorer, pauperised and powerless. As Liz Young points out, 'Malthusian interpretations of poverty constructed such marginal populations as "redundant" – simplistic correlations between population expansion and increasing poverty were understood to reflect "natural" and "inevitable" relations rather than the gradual erosion of rural livelihoods induced by incorporation' into this wider economy.[60] It became fashionable to blame the poor for their poverty – and not to see the wider networks of social and economic relationships which impoverished many and enriched others.

Fig. 12 DISTRIBUTION OF IRELAND'S OVERSEAS TRADE PER EACH PORT IN 1837. By the 1840s, over three-quarters of Ireland's export trade went to Britain. Demonstrated here in the highly original Harness map from the *Second Report of the Railway Commissioners, Ireland 1837* is the proportion of trade in and out of each port by the thickness of the lines as well as accompanying diagram of the volume of exports and imports at each port. The most striking feature of the map is the dominance of east and southeast ports and an almost absolute focus on Irish Sea traffic between Ireland and Britain. Practically all trade routes are focused on the needs (and products) of the large island. Dublin's trade is dominated by imports while Belfast (textiles-industrial) and Cork and Waterford (agro-industrial) are more involved in the export trade.

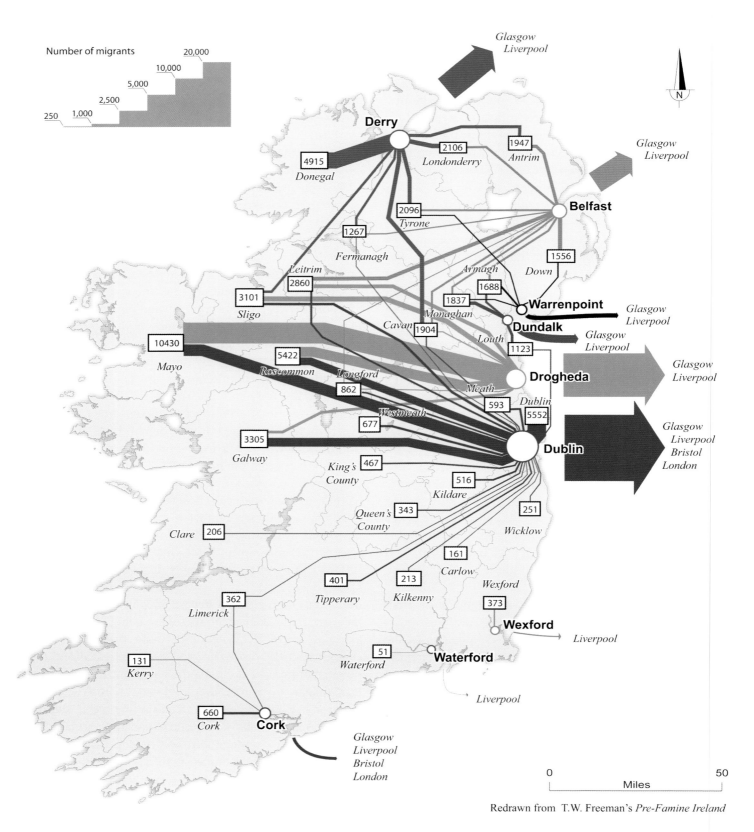

Number of migrants

20,000
10,000
5,000
2,500
1,000
250

Derry
4915 Donegal
2106 Londonderry
1947 Antrim
Glasgow Liverpool

Belfast
Glasgow Liverpool

2096 Tyrone
1267 Fermanagh
Leitrim
2860
3101 Sligo
Armagh
1688
1837
Down
1556
Warrenpoint
Glasgow Liverpool

Cavan
1904
Monaghan
Dundalk
Louth
Glasgow Liverpool

10430 Mayo
5422 Roscommon
862 Longford
Meath
1123
593
Drogheda
Glasgow Liverpool

3305 Galway
677 Westmeath
Dublin
5552
Glasgow Liverpool Bristol London

467 King's County
516 Kildare
343 Queen's County
251 Wicklow
Glasgow Liverpool Bristol London

Clare 206
161 Carlow
401 Tipperary
213 Kilkenny
Wexford

362 Limerick
373 Wexford
Liverpool

131 Kerry
51 Waterford
Waterford
Liverpool

660 Cork
Cork
Glasgow Liverpool Bristol London

0          50
Miles

N

Redrawn from T.W. Freeman's *Pre-Famine Ireland*

Fig. 13 VOLUME OF SEASONAL MIGRATION TO BRITAIN IN 1841. This map, derived from Freeman's book *Pre-Famine Ireland* (1957), is based on the results of the 1841 count carried out at every port by the police. It includes close on 58,000 seasonal migrants bound for Britain but does not include those who joined boats lying off the coast during the busy harvest season. The thickness of the lines on the map are proportional to the number of seasonal migrants using each port. Connacht is recorded as sending over 25,000 and Ulster over 19,000 seasonal migrants to Britain in 1841. There were also over 11,000 from Leinster but many of these – travelling through Dublin or Drogheda ports – were in fact Connacht men who had tramped the 100-odd miles to the east coast and went to Liverpool with migrants from west Leinster. The Ulster stream was focused mainly on Glasgow port and spread out from there. The virtual absence of seasonal migrants in southern Ireland does not mean that spailpíní were not part of the Munster–south Leinster world. Here, however, the seasonal migrants were moving within Ireland from the poorer western and upland areas to the bigger farming lands in the east.

60

This was particularly true of the rural textile industry. Both geographical proximity to a wealthy Britain and the Act of Union had exposed Ireland to the full impact of the former's Industrial Revolution. Britain now had free access to a large market in Ireland for its surplus of manufactured goods. A wide galaxy of rural craftsmen – nailers, coopers, carpenters, boot- and shoe-makers – were being made redundant. But the most dramatic consequence of industrialisation was in the clothing arena. The emergence of the factory-based textile industries saw a relatively swift contraction of the extensive cottage linen industry across the northern half of the island, where women played a major role. Figure 14 shows the distribution of manufacturing in 1821. Already in the 1840s the number working in textiles had fallen by 9%.[61] Between 1821 and 1841, there was an overall 14.5% decline in people employed in industry in Connacht, with Mayo hardest hit with a decline of 20.2%; Leinster saw a 9.5% decline with Wicklow (-28.7%) and Kilkenny city (- 22.6%) badly affected. The retreat of rural industries in Ulster saw an overall decline of 9.4% with Monaghan (- 16.1%) worst hit. Munster, with a lower overall industrial workforce, saw only a 2.9% decline; the hardest hit were Waterford (- 11.5%) and Limerick cities (- 11.2%). The most vulnerable communities were those devoted to the production of coarse linens. These were the first to be exposed to the harsh winds of competition. Such former textile workers were either obliged to emigrate (as many did)[62] or sink down into an already crowded subsistence-cum-marginalised class. Thus they became another very vulnerable group as the potato failed.

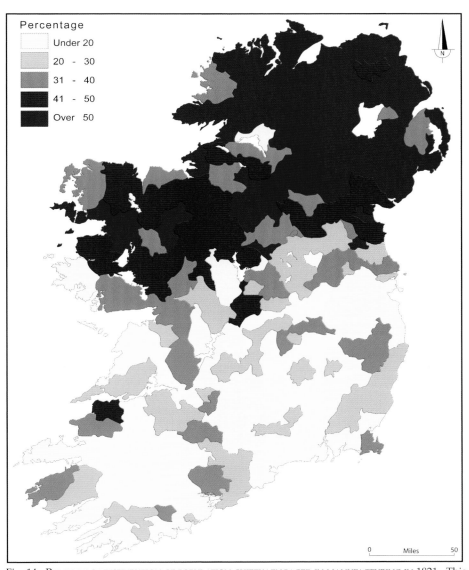

Percentage

Under 20
20 - 30
31 - 40
41 - 50
Over 50

0    Miles    50

Fig. 14. PERCENTAGE DISTRIBUTION OF POPULATION CHIEFLY ENGAGED IN MANUFACTURING IN 1821. This map demonstrates the very high proportion of the population chiefly engaged in manufacturing in 1821. Over 50% of Ulster's workforce is so employed, comprising on the one hand those in factory-based industries in and around the Belfast core and also involving a large number of domestic textile workers in the smaller towns and in the countryside. Equally striking are the many men, women and older children – 30 to 50% of the workforce – employed in industrial activities in the province of Connacht and the bordering counties of Leinster. Many of these workers – especially the females – were involved in the spinning and weaving of coarse linens. Smaller pockets of textile workers were scattered in the mainly agrarian worlds of south Leinster and Munster – as in east Clare, north Kerry and west Cork. However, the rapid expansion of Britain's factory-based textiles and other industries was to undermine the rationale for those intensive, domestic-based textile products. Already in the decades before the Famine, many of these spinning and weaving communities – especially those in Connacht and south Ulster – were suffering from underemployment. Some workers emigrated. Others sank down into an already overcrowded subsistence-cum-marginalised class.

## IMPERIAL/COLONIAL DIALECTIC

Apart from the exercise of military force, the workings of landlordism as a privileged property system and the integration and assimilation of the Irish economy to serve British needs, an outstanding feature of this imperial/colonial dialectic was the exercise of centralised political and administrative control over Ireland and the Irish people – an exercise which increased after the passing of the Union. One of the most staggering features of the Famine years is the immense weight of Parliamentary and other documentation chronicling the workings of Government relief schemes, detailing initiatives, instructions given, correspondence entered into, accounts rendered.[63] Trevelyan came close to exhausting the members of the Statistics department of the Irish Poor Law Commission with his incessant demands for more statistics, more accounts, more tables, more order, more method.[64] This reflects James Donnelly's point that 'economy in public expenditure being one of the gods that Trevelyan worshipped'.[65] If documentation and statistical accounts were sufficient to prevent the spread of famine conditions,

Major Parker to Captain LARCOM.

*Skibbereen, December* 21, 1846.

THE distress of this place is truly deplorable and heart-rending; its mortality is very great and likely to continue so, nine died on Saturday; the greatest number of deaths is in the Union workhouse. An officer of the Commissariat arrived here a few hours before me, and the fact of his having got buried by the police two bodies almost in a state of decomposition, and partially eaten by rats, as also the body of a girl which was left in the streets, will show you in what a wretched condition this place is. It has been recommended by the priests from the altar, that it is better to save for the living instead of being at the expense of coffins for the dead; and, I understand, bodies are taken in coffins to the burial ground, taken out, and the coffins kept for conveying more for burial. A woman with a dead child in her arms was begging in the streets yesterday, and the guard of the mail told me, he saw a man and three dead children lying by the road-side a few miles from this place. To narrate the many sad stories I have heard, would occupy sheets of paper. I cannot ascertain at present, with anything like accuracy, the number of deaths the last few weeks, but I fear I should not overrate them, if I said 200 in this barony. In short, nothing can exceed the miserable state of this place.

The officer of the Commissariat, Mr. Inglis, has brought a sum of money to dispose of as he thinks best, (as a private charity), and has consulted me, and determined on establishing two additional soup kitchens, one being already in operation. The dirt and mud in the streets is very great, and no doubt increases the malady. Mr. Tracey, county surveyor, is here this evening, and agrees with me that *the streets should be cleaned;* he has set on some men for that purpose, having about 30*l.* left out of 50*l.*, which he was authorized to spend in town *improvements*; but this sum will do very little. As the same process is desirable in other towns of this barony, and referring to what Colonel Jones and yourself intimated to me about a sum of money being specially allowed, it might be most advantageously and *productively* employed in this and other towns where the pestilence prevails, in employing those persons who from being crippled and otherwise disabled by infirmities, cannot come to work from a distance.

I have seen Mr. Somerville, the chairman, and other members of the Relief Committee. It is a remarkable fact, that although the flour and biscuit depot has been opened ten days, only 2*l.* 5*s* has been received for sales, the price being 17*l.*, while the retail price in the shops is about 18*l.*; no complaints are made as to quality, but no two persons of this place agree in explaining this circumstance. This matter belongs to the Commissariat, and will no doubt be reported to Sir R. Routh.

I hear of no complaints about irregularity of pay to those employed on his works. I do not hear of any outrages; on the contrary, I hear of acts of the greatest patience and forbearance, and I am sure the people suffering under so dreadful a calamity, deserve any indulgence which can be reasonably afforded.

About 400 men will be out of work in one place near this, after to-morrow, but I trust the arrangements made by Mr. Tracey will prevent any disturbance.

Mr. Allen's flour-mill, at Clonakilty, was accidentally burnt down last night, and about 70 or 80 sacks of best flour destroyed.

On Saturday, notwithstanding all the distress, there was a market plentifully supplied with meat, bread, and fish, in short every thing. Those who have been entirely dependent on potatoes, are of course the greatest sufferers; but as the resources of a rather better class are gradually diminishing, the demand for relief will not decrease, save by death. The poor are almost without clothing, having pawned nearly every thing.

Fig. 15 In a letter dated 21 December 1846 a Major Hugh Parker of the Board of Works describes the wretched scenes he witnessed in the town of Skibbereen, County Cork. He writes about the increasing mortality, the dead bodies lying by the roadside, the coffin less burials, and the widespread pestilence and yet 'on Saturday notwithstanding all the distress, there was a market plentifully supplied with meat, bread, and fish, in short everything. Those who have been entirely dependent on potatoes, are of course the greatest sufferers; but as the resources of a rather better class are gradually diminishing, the demand for relief will not decrease, save by death. The poor are almost without clothing, having pawned nearly everything'. Major Parker later contracted fever and died on 8 March 1847. [Source: Funeral at Old Chapel Lane, Skibbereen, *The Illustrated London News*, 13 February 1847]

the famine would have been very quickly halted. But it is a far cry between order and method and fulfilling what surely is the primary political function of a Government – the defence and protection of its people.

It is clear that Ireland suffered badly because of the unrepresentative nature of its social and political institutions. Given that situation, the great irony is that, as Peter Gray points out, 'the Irish administration was the most advanced and interventionist in Europe, and was staffed by committed and conscientious men of high quality such as Larcom, Griffith and Twistleton. These officers recognised that the crisis of relief after 1847 resolved ultimately into a question of money [and food] skilfully distributed via reformed and efficient structures to specific areas and needs.'[66] But their hands were tied behind their backs by a dogmatic London administration that placed moralistic and economic arguments and policies above the much more profound moral objective of saving human lives. Joel Mokyr's conclusion seems entirely valid: 'most serious of all, when the chips were down in the frightful summer of 1847, the British simply abandoned the Irish and let them perish'.[67] One could never imagine any Irish Government of whatever hue – whether the Confederation Government at Kilkenny in the mid-seventeenth century, or Grattan's late-eighteenth-century Parliament, or Dáil Éireann and the Northern Ireland Assembly today – turning their backs and ignoring 'the cry of want'.

# The colonial dimensions of the Great Irish Famine

## David Nally

> Why, what is this grand question of the 'occupation' of land in Ireland? The 'occupation of land' is a simple-sounding phrase. But what if we say, instead of it, a 'war for land' – land against life – and both against law! – for so, if we call things by their proper names – so it stands – a bloody war, which rages against rich and poor, and against the laws that are insufficient for the defence of either – a mutual war of the stomach against the purse, and vice versa – of desperate passion, on behalf, and for the relief, of inevitable hunger – of the right to live, original and inalienable, against the right to possess, the creation of conventional society.
>
> – *The Times*, 6 February 1844

In his widely praised account of nineteenth-century colonial famines, *Late Victorian Holocausts*, Mike Davis claims that 'devastating drought provided an environmental stage' in which commodity markets, price speculation, and the 'will of the state' shaped vulnerability to famine 'and determined who, in the last instance, died'. Although Davis' specifically excludes the Irish experience from his study – hence the 'late' in his title – he more than hints that Ireland may have been the prototype for the sorts of doctrines that shaped British famine policy, especially in India, from the 1870s onwards.[1]

Surprisingly, the connections suggested by Davis have been ignored in the recent literature on the Great Irish Famine, even though those same associations were emphasised by well-placed Victorian personalities. Writing in 1880, for example, as India was experiencing a series of catastrophic famines, the Assistant Secretary to the Treasury, Charles Trevelyan (1807–86), told readers of *The Times* that the earlier events in Ireland were 'full of instruction on the present occasion'.[2] 'At the commencement of the Irish Famine,' Trevelyan recalled, 'there was the same popular desire to prohibit the exportation of grain, but it was successfully resisted.'[3] Although the clamour for public intercession was pronounced, the Government aligned itself to the 'free trade' movement, which insisted that market mechanisms were the best protection against want and scarcity. Adam Smith's (1723–1790) belief that food crises were prolonged by 'the violence of Government' restricting the freedoms of the market was indicative of the new commercial pressures that placed the administration of economic life in tension with the sovereign prerogative to guarantee the people's subsistence.[4] The ideological message of the new political economy was simple enough: the threat of prolonged scarcity was no longer an acceptable reason to meddle in grain markets.

Trevelyan certainly saw things in this manner. Like other economic liberals he believed in the salvation of humanity through the self-regulating market and applied this faith to the political orchestration of Government relief. The difficulty was, of course, that existing socio-economic conditions did not always lend themselves to the organisation of free trade and where free markets were absent or retarded it was the duty of Government to aid their establishment. Under the auspices of the new political economy the Government's role was to suppress all conduct that might impede the market mechanism and to embrace every opportunity to progress a more commercialised economy.[5] The crises of famine would thus not only test the Government's resolve not to intervene in food markets; it presented the prospect of birthing a radically new kind of society. 'The result in Ireland,' Trevelyan later reflected, 'has been to introduce other better kinds of food, and to raise the people, through much suffering, to a higher standard of subsistence. We shall see how it will be in India.'[6] Refracted through the icy prism of classical political economy, famines became a short cut to modernity.

It is intriguing to consider how one of the most important innovators of modern Government could characterise one of the greatest demographic tragedies of recent times as a success story of prophetic consequence for the future management of India. It is perhaps even more peculiar that scholars of the Irish Famine have been altogether reluctant to pursue the colonial connections latent in Trevelyan's comparison.[7] Indeed, the experiences of other British colonies remain quite marginal to the mainstream historiography of the Famine, a fact that partly reflects the fractious and ongoing debate regarding the applicability of colonial models to Irish history more generally. This chapter attempts to address this oversight by considering the significance of colonialism, first as an organising force shaping rural vulnerability, and secondly as an ideology that advanced violent views about 'regenerating' Irish society.

### FATAL CIRCUMSTANCES

The degree to which Irish society was exceptionally vulnerable to mass famine is still too often overlooked in the literature on the Great Famine. Indeed, most accounts begin their analysis in 1845 – coinciding with the appearance of *Phytophthora infestans*, the potato-killing pathogen – and among the many books now available, very few choose to situate their account within the historical geography of colonisation.[8] This failure to treat historically Irish vulnerability is even more perplexing given the common distinction drawn between 'trigger factors' and the 'underlying causes' of famine. Amrita Rangasami, for example, understands famines as a process, not an event, while David Arnold maintains that they are 'a symptom rather than a cause of social weakness'. Such distinctions have a long genealogy.[9] Writing in 1840s, the Catholic Archbishop, John MacHale, insisted on distinguishing the 'antecedent circumstances and influences' from the 'primary, original causes' of famine, although it was the radical nationalist, John Mitchel, who most memorably captured this difference in his colourful aphorism: 'The Almighty, indeed, sent the potato blight, but the English created the famine.'[10] If the historical antecedents to famine are to be properly examined it is important to consider how colonisation might have generated mass vulnerability.

By colonisation I mean to imply not merely the seizure, occupation and reconstitution of native domestic space, but also the repertoire of cultural images that depict indigenous life as degenerate, thereby underlining the necessity for remedial interventions in the name of improvement. It is next to impossible to sketch the political and economic trajectory of rural society in Ireland without reference to the unprecedented upheaval in landownership, driven by an expansionary English state, in the sixteenth and seventeenth centuries. The Elizabethan conquest of Munster and Ulster, and the replacement of Gaelic lords with loyal English and Scottish planters, helped fortify the power of an elite, loyal and largely Protestant aristocracy. By the time of James II's accession to the throne, the new settlers (though numerically still small), possessed nearly 80% of Irish land. Oliver Cromwell's brutal suppression of another Irish rebellion

prefigured a further wave of dispossession and displacement. By the eighteenth century Irish land ownership had fallen to a mere 5%.[11] According to the geographer William Smyth, the process of property confiscation was matched in 'no other country of the period', forcing him to turn to the 'scale and ruthlessness . . . of Soviet Russia's land appropriations' in the twentieth century for comparative purposes.[12]

These colonial encounters can only be briefly discussed in a chapter-length discussion, but their legacy was significant and long lasting. Plantation policy paved the

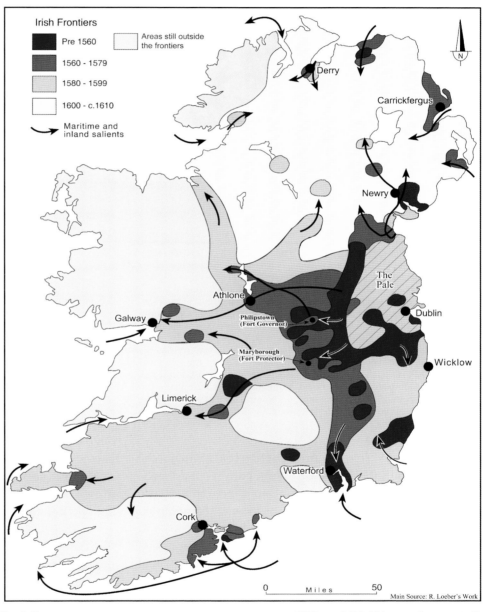

Fig. 1 ENGLISH MILITARY SETTLEMENT AND FRONTIER EXPANSION, C.1530 TO C.1610. This map documents the march of the English military and settlement frontier in sixteenth- and early seventeenth-century Ireland. It pinpoints the step-by-step extension of the old Pale westwards – via a number of new fortifications – in the 1550s and 1560s. It also illustrates the parallel foundation of strategic military fortifications to protect Dublin city and to extend the frontier both southwards along the River Barrow to Waterford city and northwards to front the still hidden world of Gaelic Ulster. By the 1580s, following the crushing of the Desmond Rising/rebellion, most of the lordships of Munster are opened up to formal state plantation. By the early seventeenth century, the power and ritual of the last regional lordship – O'Neill's Ulster – had yielded to the hammer of the centralising state. This is followed by the successful plantation of that province by English and Scottish settlers.

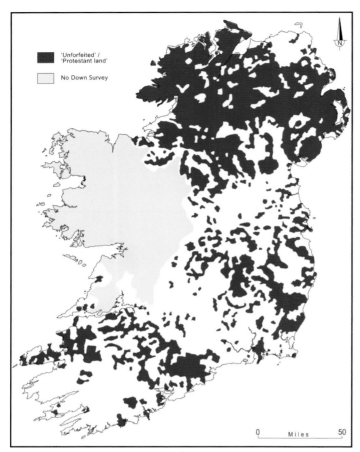

Fig. 2 THE DISTRIBUTION OF 'FORFEITED/PROTESTANT LAND' BY C.1650. Based on the detailed evidence of the Down Survey parish maps which distinguishes 'Protestant land' from the lands of the Catholic Irish landowners, who are, for the most part, to be dispossessed, this map highlights the expansion of English and Scottish settlement between the mid-sixteenth and mid-seventeenth centuries. The foundations for this geographic pattern of land acquisitions were laid by a series of plantations – Laois/Offaly (eastern parts), Munster, Ulster and Carlow, Longford, Laois/Offaly (western parts), Wicklow and north Wexford. However, this map also reflects the piecemeal selling of lands by a number of Gaelic and old English lords who had failed to adapt to the new market and political conditions. It also reflects the insidious expansion of land acquisitions – 'by fair means and foul' – by an aggressive and acquisitive Planter class. Even before the Cromwellian plantation, it is clear that more than half of the island – and certainly more than half of the best land – was now in the hands of this new landlord class.

way for a cultural project of Anglicisation that involved the steady criminalisation of indigenous culture: the Gaelic brehon laws were proscribed, English rules of inheritance replaced local custom, central Government supplanted traditional institutions for regulating services and obligations, and the Catholic religion was suppressed through a complex body of legislation known as the Penal Laws. The field of economic activity was no less circumscribed. The Navigation, Cattle and Wool Acts synchronised Irish industries with England's domestic growth and commercial expansion in the Atlantic world and beyond. By the nineteenth century almost all the major Irish towns were seaports, reflecting Ireland's new role as a subordinate supplier of commodities for a rapidly expanding empire. An official Select Committee, reporting in 1819, recommended establishing an efficient transportation network on the grounds that it would 'insure

to England supplies of grain at moderate prices, which might render it [England] wholly independent of foreign countries for the food of its manufacturing population'.[13] According to Karl Marx, the aim was to transform Ireland into 'an agricultural district of England, marked off by a wide channel from the country to which it yields corn, wool, cattle, industrial and military recruits'.[14]

POTATO CULTURE AND SUBDIVISION

The usurpation of indigenous land was therefore the prelude to the superimposition of an entirely new political, social and economic structure. These transformations had a precipitous effect on traditional livelihoods. As alternative sources of income, Irish 'peasants' resorted to the potato, which had the distinct advantage of being a cheap provider of calories that could be acquired without having to enter the cash economy. The potato, popularly known as the 'staff of life', quickly became the mainstay of the poor. As the potato crop rose in importance, so too did the possession of land. The situation was exacerbated by the fact that the vast majority of Irish people worked the land but did not own it. In the absence of legal restraint, some tenants sublet their land, creating the notorious middleman system and the terminable subdivision of estates into barely viable smallholdings. Given the immense competition for land, and the crippling necessity of planting potato seed, Irish labourers often agreed to the highest possible rents on small slips of land, placing the lowest possible value on their labour. According to one economist, a tenant-labourer might work as many as 250 days to pay for a cabin plus one acre of manured potato ground and might still be expected to provide petty commodities, such as poultry and eggs, or perform services like threshing corn or drawing turf, when requested by his landlord.[15] These exactions significantly 'increased the real, as distinguished from the nominal rent, paid by occupiers' and ensured that less time could be devoted to the nutritional needs of the peasantry.[16] Tawney's classic image of the Chinese peasant 'standing up to his neck in water, so that even a ripple is sufficient to drown him' aptly describes the vulnerability of Irish smallholders but not the strong farmers to exogenous shocks.[17]

Suffice to say that many of the structural weaknesses of the Irish economy in the nineteenth century – including the grossly inequitable land tenure system, the reliance on vulnerable forms of monoculture, the presence of an 'alien' and largely absentee landlord class, intense demographic pressures, and the steady decline of domestic industry – can be thought of as a material legacy of conquest. It is also important to note that the British reaction to Irish problems drew from the wellsprings of this colonial history, both its perceived failures and its professed successes. The persistence of Irish poverty, in particular, continued to puzzle and confound the many commentators who had assumed that political and economic annexation would precede the conversion of Ireland into a smiling and flourishing colony. Passing through Dublin just three years after the Act of Union (1801), an anonymous English writer found 'on every street the most shocking spectacles present themselves . . . I would not have given sixpence for the whole apparel of any man, woman, or child whom we saw all along the road'; in Skibbereen in County Cork another visitor noted 'whole streets, and not very short ones, consisting entirely of the wretched mud cabins of the peasant.'[18] Walter Scott (1771–1832) was totally unprepared for the extremities of hardship he witnessed in Ireland. 'Their poverty is not exaggerated,' he remarked. 'It is on the verge of human misery; their cottages would scarce serve as pigstyes, even in Scotland.'[19] These sorts of descriptions did little to endear Victorian readers to Irish conditions and by the nineteenth century Irish destitution was commonly explained as an obdurate moral failing – the symptom of a far broader culture of domestic degeneracy – that called for swift corrective action. Tellingly, in his *History of the Irish Poor Law*, George Nicholls (1781–1865) suggested that Irish problems stemmed from the fragmented character of English colonisation which had, evidently, failed to teach the Irish the rudiments of civilised behaviour. 'If Cromwell had remained longer in Ireland,' he opined, 'it is probable that he would with his usual vigour have crushed the seeds of many existing evils, and laid the foundation for future quiet; but this was not permitted, and the elements for disorder remained, repressed and weakened it

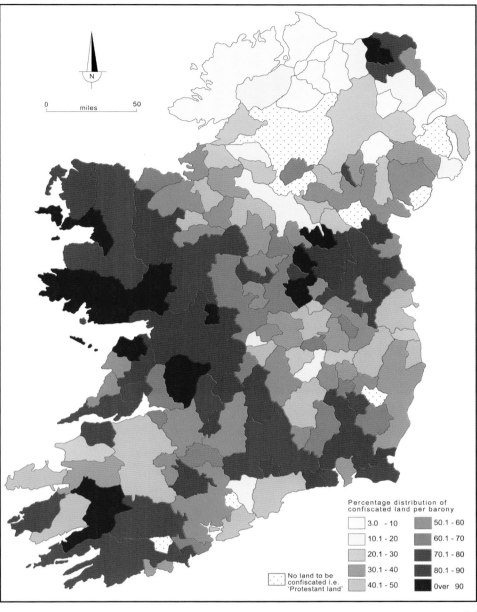

Fig. 3 **DISTRIBUTION OF CONFISCATED LAND AT BARONY SCALE AS PER THE CROMWELLIAN PLANTATION.** Following the Cromwellian conquest, William Petty and his cartographic 'army' mapped most of this island in preparation for the single greatest transfer of property ever seen in Ireland, of *c*.11 million acres. For the most part, this map depicts the confiscation of all the land of Ireland that had as yet not been newly acquired by plantation, purchase and/or intrigue from the mid sixteenth century onwards. It highlights the confiscation of three-quarters of the lands of Meath and Westmeath, formerly held by Catholic Irish landowners. It also highlights the great majority of properties in Munster which had not been confiscated in earlier plantations. For example, the old landowners of County Tipperary saw 77% of the county confiscated in the Cromwellian plantation. This map also depicts the massive confiscation of land in County Clare and over most of Connacht. Because of the depth of the earlier Ulster plantation (1609–10 onwards), that province was least affected by the Cromwellian settlement.

is true, but still ready to burst forth whenever circumstances should give vent to the explosion.'[20] Rendered vulnerable and now derided as backward, the Irish were once again made targets for externally imposed reform.

## INSIDE THE UTILITARIAN LABORATORY

It is worth noting the many competing visions of social improvement. Confirmed Malthusians, such as John Wheatley and Robert Torrens, promoted overseas colonisation to rid Ireland of its 'supernumerary hands.' Others such as John Stuart Mill, William Thornton and James Caird

favoured plans for the 'internal colonization of Ireland', by which they meant the removal and replacement of some 200,000 families on reclaimed wasteland.[21] Archbishop Richard Whateley and the economist Nassau Senior advocated public works and 'assisted emigration,' while Charles Trevelyan and George Nicholls favoured implementing an Irish variant of the English Poor Law. While there are some significant differences between these models of social improvement, I want to insist that there are many more – and *more important* – similarities.

First, they all draw on popular stereotypes about native

Fig. 4 *Sir George Nicholls* (1781–1865) (1834) by Ramsay Richard Reinagle, oil on canvas 1834. [Source: National Portrait Gallery, London]Poor Law reformer and administrator, Nicholls was the principal architect of the Irish Poor Law. On the passing of the Poor Law Relief (Ireland) Act in 1838, Nicholls was given the task of overseeing its introduction and implementation. He viewed the Poor Law as a key instrument in effecting a transition to a more civilised agrarian economy in Ireland.

character – Irish obduracy, mendacity, improvidence, domestic primitivism, agricultural backwardness and habits of lassitude – stereotypes that had been repeated and reinforced over centuries of intercultural contact. To nineteenth-century English eyes, Ireland reflected 'civilisation' precisely by being the site of its absence.[22] Second, they each assume that the proper response to Irish conditions was to stimulate economic development rather than simply aid destitution. As Trevelyan remarked:

> Our object, therefore, ought to be permanently to improve the condition of the poor – to restore them, as far as possible, to self-respect and self-support . . . With this end in view, we must not confine ourselves to treating the symptoms. Instead of merely pumping water out of a sinking ship, we must try to stop the leak. Instead of merely burning the weeds, we must clean the ground to prevent their growing at all.[23]

Thirdly, and following on from this, these visions of social improvement invariably take the historical development of England as the norm to understand social conditions elsewhere.

These ideas crystallised in contemporary opinion regarding the design and implementation of the Irish Poor Law. Modelled on the reformed English system the Irish

Poor Law was conceptualised as a tool for 'dispauperising' Ireland and putting the country on a more commercial footing. The author of the Poor Law, George Nicholls, believed that social development occurred in decisive stages and that the Irish needed to be encouraged to 'transition' to a more civilised agrarian economy. Nicholls clarified:

> By the term 'transition period', I mean to indicate that season of change from the system of small holdings, allotments, and subdivision of land, which now prevails in Ireland, to the better practice of day-labour for wages, and to that dependence on daily labour for support. This transition period is, I believe, generally beset with difficulty and suffering. It was so in England; and it is, and for a time will probably continue to be so, in Ireland.[24]

If the promotion of agrarian capitalism was the obvious panacea to Irish underdevelopment, the aim of Government policy (vis-à-vis the Poor Law) was to stimulate 'great organic changes' and disencumber Irish property of its smallholders.[25] Put simply, Nicholls was advocating the proletarianisation of Irish farming through administrative measures. The fact that the Poor Law was situated within a more expansive discussion on social regeneration is surprisingly overlooked in the Famine literature, which tends to underscore the punitive nature of workhouse life and the appalling treatment of pauper inmates.

Let me offer two brief examples to illustrate just how closely the debates about Irish poor relief were mapped onto designs to encourage agrarian 'transition'. In the third and final Report on the Irish Poor Law, Nicholls details his travels to Belgium and Holland, where with Dr Kay, he was authorised to report on the different systems of institutional relief for the poor. In fact the report devotes the majority of its attention to the condition of smallholders, especially the Belgian small farmers who, in contrast to the Irish, they found to be perfect examples of 'scrupulous economy and cautious foresight':

> There was no tendency to the subdivision of the small holdings; I heard of none under five acres, held by the class of peasant farmers, and six, seven, or eight acres, is the more common size. The provident habits of these small farmers enable them to maintain a high standard of comfort, and are necessarily opposed to such subdivision. Their marriages are not contracted so early as in Ireland, and the consequent struggle for subsistence among their offspring does not exist.[26]

This brand of comparative anthropology convinced Nicholls that Ireland's 'cotter tenantry' were out of sync with modern, rationalised farming and would not therefore

Fig. 5 Portumna workhouse, County Galway, which opened in 1852. Such institutions were central to the implementation of the Irish Poor Law and became a dominant feature in the Irish landscape during the nineteenth century. Having been derelict for a number of years, the building was opened to the public in the summer of 2011 as the Irish Workhouse Centre. [Photo: Frank Coyne]

develop capitalist modes of production without rigorous encouragement. The Irish Poor Law was to be a central pillar in this broader vision of development:

> This [Poor Law] would, in fact, be beginning at the lowest point in the scale – improved management in the small farms would bring increase of capital, and improved habits among the cottier tenants – with the increase of capital will come the desire to extend their holdings, and thus will arise a tendency to consolidate occupancies for the employment of increased capital which the vast extent of now waste, but reclaimable, land in Ireland, will greatly facilitate. An increase of agricultural produce will speedily act upon all the other sources of industry, and thus the demands of the home market for agricultural produce will be augmented, while, for all that is produced above that demand, the markets of England will be open.[27]

It is also little known that Nicholls authored a small agricultural booklet to better publicise his opinions on agrarian improvement. Published in 1841, *The Farmer's Guide: Compiled for the Use of the Small Farmers and Cotter [sic] Tenantry of Ireland*, was designed to be 'a small book of plain instruction, to which you may refer in your agricultural occupations and domestic economy'.[28] The *Guide* is an extraordinary testament to colonial paternalism, offering worldly advice, ironically to a largely illiterate audience, on everything from cropping and livestock breeding to personal cleanliness and appropriate 'domestic arrangements'. The *Guide* underscores the need for formal discipline (what Nicholls termed 'moral training') to improve slovenly habits – the same themes that peppered his Poor Law report. 'Every man in good health may obtain a sufficiency of wholesome food, if he will make due exertion,' Nicholls admonished, 'and when we hear the complaints every year of the want of food, and observe the want of care and industry in making provision against the recurrence of evil one's

commiseration is sometimes weakened by the blame which we cannot but see is too often deserved.'[29] Adopting Malthusian tones, Nicholls urged moral restraint in the formation of 'early and improvident marriages' and made clear his belief that depopulation was a cornerstone in regenerating Ireland:

> We by no means deny, but on the contrary would wish to secure to the poorer classes, all those enjoyments which spring from the exercise of domestic and social feelings; but it must be borne in mind that every one is bound both in a religious and moral sense, to keep his animal impulses under the control of reason; and not to wreck his own happiness, and that of others, by levelling them and himself with the brutes, and disregarding the plainest dictates of prudence.[30]

On the inside cover of the booklet is a note from the Poor Law Commission Office, dated 10 December 1841, which describes the *Guide* as contributing to 'promoting the Improvement in Agricultural Operations'. It also declares Nicholls' intention to form agricultural societies that would comprise 'an area co-extensive with the limits of each Poor Law Union'. In a very practical way *The Farmer's Guide* built on Nicholls' conceptualisation of the Poor Law as the first stage in the 'rapid consolidation of small holdings'.[31] These attempts at social engineering have striking parallels with seventeenth-century colonial practice in which newly planted estates were purposefully designed 'to stimulate a mimetic response' amongst the Irish.

### COLONIAL IMPROVEMENT

Nicholls was aware that his vision to anglicise Ireland ran counter to the *laissez-faire* principles promoted by orthodox political economists. Although he understood that 'danger attends all interference with industrial pursuits, which prosper best when left to their own natural development' he argued that 'the state of Ireland constitutes an exception to

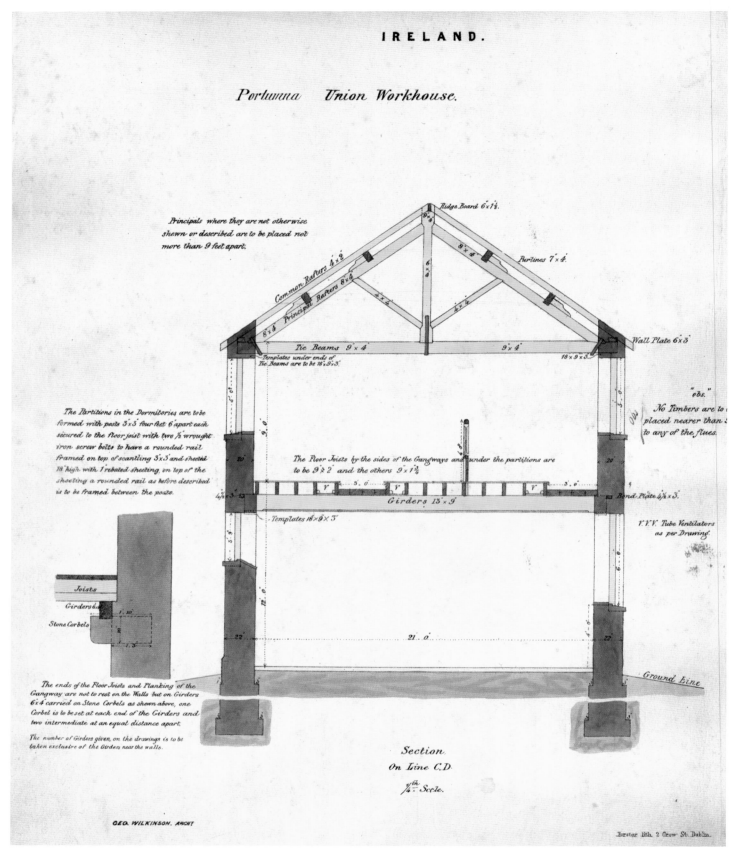

Fig. 6 Plan of dormitories in Portumna workhouse showing gangways and partitions. [Source: Irish Architectural Archive]

the general rule, and that the aid of Government in support of local effort is there absolutely necessary'.[32] Notwithstanding these visionary impulses, Nicholls was a pragmatist who recognised that in Ireland 'the obstructions which arise from fixed habits and social arrangements generally render great organic changes impossible, except in the lapse of years'.[33] Even accepting Government interference, change would be painfully slow because of the recalcitrant nature of the Celt.

These views changed, however, with the appearance of the potato blight in 1845. To many contemporaries it seemed that 'divine providence' might now accomplish what human ingenuity had only fitfully started. In line with the Irish Poor Law, famine policy would be organised according to the utilitarian principle of corrective regulation. Robert Peel's (1788–1850) programme of direct food aid, for example, was openly theorised as a means to stimulate food markets and encourage the dietary regeneration of Ireland. In fact the policy went hand in hand with the Government's turn to *laissez-faire* signalled by the repeal of the Corn Laws (one of the most significant legislative coups in British history and the first defeat of landed aristocracy by the new English industrial class). The appearance of blight handed Peel – a late convert to free-trade – an opportunity to argue that the difficulties in Ireland were the result of a shortfall in cheap grain rather than the more immediate failure of the potato harvest. Through Peel's intercession *Phytophthora infestans* was turned into a 'divine indictment' against economic protectionism.[34] The policy was pursued even when it was felt that the discipline of the market might *increase* the vulnerability of the Irish agricultural sector by *decreasing* the effectiveness of local economies. The Prime Minister himself was aware of such adverse consequences: 'If there be any part of the United Kingdom which is to suffer by the withdrawal of protection, I have always felt that that part . . . is Ireland,' he coldly declared.[35]

Similar logics ran through the public works programmes established by Peel and revamped under Lord John Russell's (1792–1878) administration when Peel eventually lost his ministry. The new Labour-Rate Act substituted the 'task labour' or 'piece work' system for the daily wages previously paid on the public works. In addition to making work less tolerable than ordinary employment, Irish labourers were now only to be paid according to the amount of work they could complete. To reinforce the principle of 'less eligibility,' and as an incentive to independent industry, it was directed that 'task work' be paid below what was normally provided locally. Paying labourers anything more than was necessary to keep them alive risked encouraging unscrupulous conduct. Not only were the public works schemes designed to 'test' destitution (in the same way the Poor Law workhouses were supposed to 'test' for indigence), the financial burden of the programme was placed on the shoulders of land

owners in order to encourage habits of self-reliance – hence the popular nostrum of this period: 'Irish property must pay for Irish poverty.' During the harsh winter of 1846–47, thousands died on the Government's public works.

By early 1847 the Government began to reel somewhat from its previous policies of affording relief. With little in the way of options, the poorest were now pouring onto the works schemes. By March the Government was superintending the employment of over 700,000 persons. Critics such as Nassau Senior described this system of supervised labour as an 'eleemosynary allowance, under the name of wages',

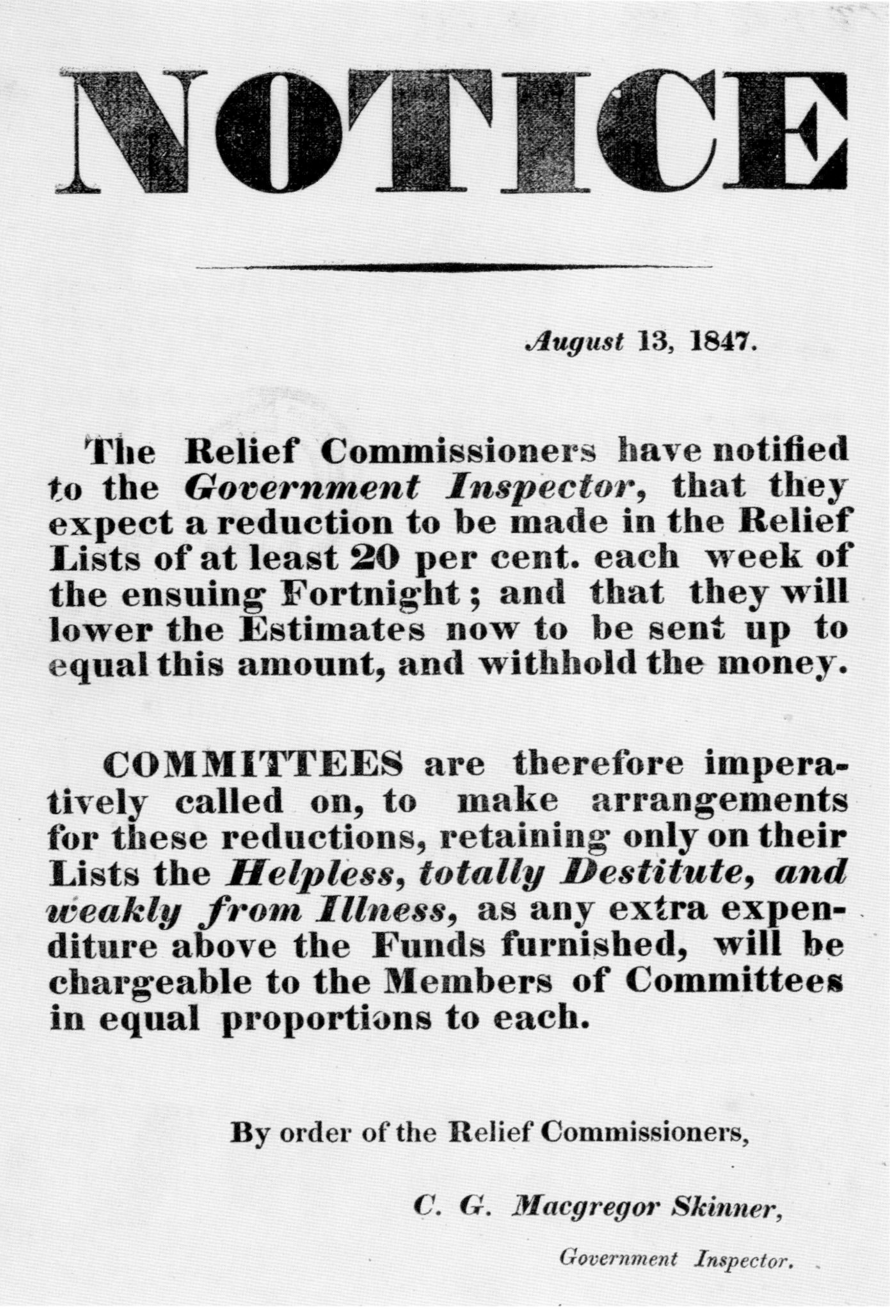

# NOTICE

*August* 13, 1847.

The Relief Commissioners have notified to the *Government Inspector*, that they expect a reduction to be made in the Relief Lists of at least 20 per cent. each week of the ensuing Fortnight; and that they will lower the Estimates now to be sent up to equal this amount, and withhold the money.

COMMITTEES are therefore imperatively called on, to make arrangements for these reductions, retaining only on their Lists the *Helpless, totally Destitute, and weakly from Illness*, as any extra expenditure above the Funds furnished, will be chargeable to the Members of Committees in equal proportions to each.

By order of the Relief Commissioners,

*C. G. Macgregor Skinner,*

*Government Inspector.*

Fig. 7 In Charles Trevelyan's eyes the success of the soup kitchens in getting food directly to the people during the summer months of 1847 had effectively brought an end to the Irish crisis. While the potato crop was largely unaffected by blight, the fact that very little had been sown meant the harvest was small. Despite this small harvest, the instruction to local relief committees was increasingly to lessen expenditure, hence the pressure to reduce the numbers on relief lists. [Source: National Library of Ireland] which merely 'indulged habits of indolence'.[36] In response to such criticisms the Government 'took matters into its own hands' as Trevelyan directed that 20% of persons employed on public works should be summarily 'struck from the [relief] lists'.[37] In the interim soup kitchens would be mobilised under the Temporary Relief Act, but the long-term goal was to make the Poor Law system and workhouse relief the established norm. As part of the revision of the Irish Poor Law, the Government introduced the infamous 'Gregory clause', named after its author William Gregory (1816–1892). The provision precluded tenants holding more than a quarter acre of land from receiving relief without first conceding possession of their property. Under the operations of the old Poor Law paupers were asked to exchange their liberty (by entering the workhouse) and the product of their labour (by consenting to punitive work) in return for state assistance. Now Irish paupers were ordered to relinquish their holdings in exchange for the right to live. Dispossession thus became the latest in a long list of deterrent tests, even though one correspondent for *The Times* acknowledged that a test

'must cease to be a test at all when there is no option but to accept it or die'.[38] In his autobiography Gregory remained defiant: 'though I got an evil reputation in consequence, those who really understood the condition of the country have always regarded this clause as its salvation'.[39] Modern

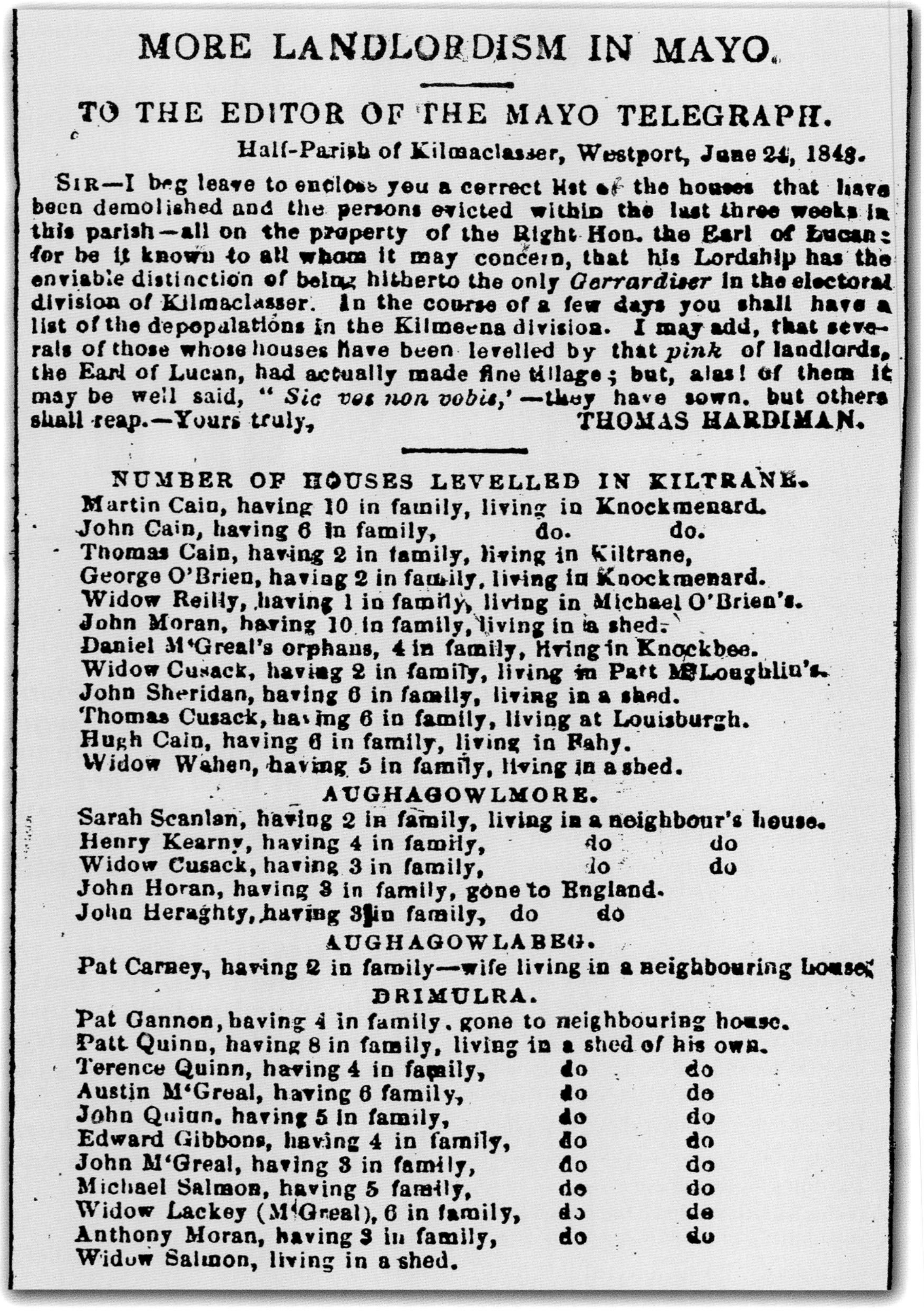

# MORE LANDLORDISM IN MAYO.

## TO THE EDITOR OF THE MAYO TELEGRAPH.

Half-Parish of Kilmaclasser, Westport, June 24, 1848.

SIR—I beg leave to enclose you a correct list of the houses that have been demolished and the persons evicted within the last three weeks in this parish—all on the property of the Right Hon. the Earl of Lucan: for be it known to all whom it may concern, that his Lordship has the enviable distinction of being hitherto the only *Gerrardiser* in the electoral division of Kilmaclasser. In the course of a few days you shall have a list of the depopulations in the Kilmeena division. I may add, that severals of those whose houses have been levelled by that *pink* of landlords, the Earl of Lucan, had actually made fine tillage; but, alas! of them it may be well said, " *Sic vos non vobis*," —they have sown. but others shall reap.—Yours truly, THOMAS HARDIMAN.

### NUMBER OF HOUSES LEVELLED IN KILTRANE.

Martin Cain, having 10 in family, living in Knockmenard.
John Cain, having 6 in family,      do.      do.
Thomas Cain, having 2 in family, living in Kiltrane,
George O'Brien, having 2 in family, living in Knockmenard.
Widow Reilly, having 1 in family, living in Michael O'Brien's.
John Moran, having 10 in family, living in a shed.
Daniel M'Greal's orphans, 4 in family, living in Knockbee.
Widow Cusack, having 2 in family, living in Patt M'Loughlin's.
John Sheridan, having 6 in family, living in a shed.
Thomas Cusack, having 6 in family, living at Louisburgh.
Hugh Cain, having 6 in family, living in Rahy.
Widow Wahen, having 5 in family, living in a shed.

### AUGHAGOWLMORE.

Sarah Scanlan, having 2 in family, living in a neighbour's house.
Henry Kearny, having 4 in family,      do      do
Widow Cusack, having 3 in family,      do      do
John Horan, having 3 in family, gone to England.
John Heraghty, having 3 in family, do      do

### AUGHAGOWLABEG.

Pat Carney, having 2 in family—wife living in a neighbouring house.

### DRIMULRA.

Pat Gannon, having 4 in family, gone to neighbouring house.
Patt Quinn, having 8 in family, living in a shed of his own.
Terence Quinn, having 4 in family,      do      do
Austin M'Greal, having 6 family,      do      do
John Quinn, having 5 in family,      do      do
Edward Gibbons, having 4 in family,      do      do
John M'Greal, having 3 in family,      do      do
Michael Salmon, having 5 family,      do      do
Widow Lackey (M'Greal), 6 in family,      do      do
Anthony Moran, having 3 in family,      do      do
Widow Salmon, living in a shed.

Fig. 8 A ruthless policy of eviction was pursued by many landlords, including the Earl of Lucan in County Mayo. This letter to the editor of the *Connaught Telegraph* (24 June 1848), lists the houses levelled in the half-parish of Kilmaclasser, Westport, within the previous three weeks. [Source: Mayo County Library]

scholars have been less charitable in their assessment, describing the clause as 'a charter for land clearance and consolidation' that was clearly premeditated.[40]

The Gregory clause needs to be discussed alongside another piece of legislative engineering known as the Rate-in-Aid Act. The act made *all* Irish Poor Law Unions taxable for the relief of stricken western regions as well as for the loans dispensed by the Government. Nationalist rancour reached fever pitch: if Ireland was truly an equal partner, why was not the rest of British property proportionately taxed to lighten the Irish burden? 'When calamity falls upon us,' wrote Isaac Butt (1813–1879), 'we then recover our separate existence as a nation, just so far as to disentitle us to the state assistance. If Cornwall had been visited with the scenes that have desolated Cork,' Butt continued, 'would similar arguments have been used?'[41] The Catholic Archbishop, John MacHale, echoed these criticisms. 'If there be a real union between England and Ireland,' he reasoned, 'it should have reciprocal conditions of all such covenants – mutual benefits and mutual burdens.'[42] George Nicholls couldn't but agree that the bill violated the civic principle of 'one part of the empire coming to the assistance of the other', although he believed that the new policy was essential if the Irish were to be encouraged to relinquish their old barbarous ways:

> [T]he repeated failures [of the potato] caused apprehensions as to the perpetuity of the burden, and seemed to point to the necessity of compelling the Irish to abandon the treacherous potato, which it was thought they would hardly do, so long as they could turn to England for help whenever it failed them. The rate-in-aid was *calculated to effect this object* [my emphasis], by casting the consequences of the failure entirely upon Ireland itself, which in such case would be unable to persist in its reliance upon a crop so treacherous and uncertain as the potato.[43]

These policies gave landlords clear *incentives* to turn the poor from their land. According to John Forbes, a keen observer of Irish affairs and an avid supporter of agricultural reorganisation, the very presence of the workhouse system meant that evictors could not be accused of 'knowingly exposing' their tenants to fatal conditions. Irish landowners, he claimed, 'were not merely legally but morally justified in carrying it [clearances] into effect'. 'The existence of the Poor Law system,' Forbes continued, 'with its Union Workhouses in every district, was an essential preliminary, not merely to render such an act justifiable, but to render it possible without incurring the responsibility of a most positive outrage on humanity.'[44]

## SOCIAL ENGINEERING

As the Famine wore on – and the tendency to blame the victims became more entrenched – appeals to social engineering became more common and less controversial. The Foreign Secretary, Lord Palmerston (1784–1865), who engaged in clearances on his own Irish estate, informed the cabinet on 31 March 1848: 'It is useless to disguise the truth that any great improvement in the social system in Ireland must be founded upon an extensive change in the present

state of agrarian occupation, and that this change necessarily implies a long continued and systematic ejectment of Small Holders and of Squatting Cottiers.'[45] The Chancellor of the Exchequer, Charles Wood (1800–1885), wrote, 'Except through a purgatory of misery and starvation, I cannot see how Ireland is to emerge into a state of anything approaching to quiet or prosperity.'[46] Trevelyan viewed the Irish Famine as 'a salutary revolution in the habits of a nation'. Surveying the scene in 1848, he declared, 'Supreme Wisdom has educed permanent good out of transient evil.'[47] The Englishman John Ashworth (1795–1882), who came to Ireland in a bid to resettle his family in 1850, voiced the conviction that the smallholders of Ireland were impeding the modernisation of the Irish economy: 'The small sub-divisions of land which have caused so much misery and moral degradation in Ireland are on all hands condemned, and better were it that the present race of occupants should emi-

Fig. 9 *John MacHale* (1791–1881), Archbishop of Tuam (1855) by Alessandro Capalti, oil on canvas, 1855. [Source: National Gallery of Ireland, Dublin] MacHale was a robust critic of British policy in Ireland during the Famine. He was particularly scathing of Lord John Russell's Liberal Government. Russell had earlier proclaimed that the people would not be allowed to starve and yet as the crisis worsened the overriding concern of his Government was to reduce the burden of relief on the Treasury. This overarching fiscal concern had dire consequences for people on the ground. As MacHale sarcastically remarked: 'How ungrateful of the Catholics of Ireland not to pour forth canticles of gratitude to the ministers who promised that none of them should perish and then suffered 2 million to starve.'

grate and leave the whole country to be re-colonised, than such a scandalous and demoralising system should be continued.'[48] The Times linked destruction with renewal through the colonial image of terra nullis: 'In a few years,' one editorial rejoiced, 'a Celtic Irishman will be as rare in Connemara as a Red Indian on the shores of Manhattan.'[49]

Others openly challenged this rhetoric, showing how the discourse of improvement had been transformed into a violent policy of removal. According to James Fintan Lalor (1807–49), the thinly veiled assumption was 'that the small occupier is a man who ought not to be existing'.[50] The Donegal man, Hugh Dorian, claimed that a 'war upon cottiers was underway. It was, he said, 'eviction on the plea of giving to other men their rights' – which was another way of saying that the rights to property were accorded greater value than the right to food and life.[51] According to Dorian, the word 'ejectment' was the best understood word in the English language, understood by 'young and old who had not a second word of English'.[52] The English MP, G.P. Scrope, charged the Government with a policy of 'extermination' not by direct design, but 'by their deprivation of the means of living, of shelter, clothing, and of sufficiency of food'.[53] John Mitchel claimed that ejectment laws were used 'to clear off the "surplus population"', while Butt condemned them as 'a measure of confiscation'.[54] 'If the rights of property are to be exercised for the extinction of the people,' warned Butt, 'we must wonder if the people begin to think that their only hope of safety lies in the extinction of all rights of property in land.'[55]

## MAKING CRISES MORE PROBABLE

It is clear that the discussion of the Great Irish Famine invites a deeper consideration of the 'stable background factors', including official conduct over an extended period of time, that make crises more probable.[56] In the Irish case, the violence of conquest and plantation settlement, backed by the administrative and legal reorganisation of indigenous society, contributed to acute poverty and rural stagnation and made subsistence crises a recurrent feature of Irish life. A similar example of official wrongdoing can be found in the British Government's attempt to use the Famine as a lever to accelerate socio-economic change. This policy arose from a dogmatic insistence on the laws of political economy and an equally firm belief, fostered through centuries of colonial contact, that the Irish were slovenly, improvident and uncivilised, and therefore in need of external disciplining. This discipline would be delivered in various ways. By enforcing a rigid programme of qualified famine relief, based on a Benthamite system of 'checks' and 'tests' meant to distinguish the 'deserving' from the 'undeserving' poor, Government officials could eliminate imposture, stimulate positive behaviour, and force labour from reluctant bodies. As we have seen, the establishment of free markets was openly theorised as a tool to teach poor cottier farmers the social autonomy and industry neces-

sary to become independent labourers. The shift from a potato diet to cereal foods would, it was felt, force households to abandon subsistence practices and accelerate the 'transition' to a more civilised economy based on commodity production. And, finally, through the implementation of policies like the Rate-in-Aid Act and the Gregory clause, officials felt that they had finally uncovered the 'master key' to unlock industry and disencumber Irish property.

E.M. Wood has shown how in England 'the history of early agrarian capitalism – the process of domestic "colonization", the removal of land from the "waste", its "improvement", enclosure and new conceptions of property rights – was reproduced in the theory and practice of empire.'[57] This insight has yet to be given serious consideration in historical accounts of the Great Irish Famine. Yet there is little doubt that the Famine hastened the transformation of non-market social formations into a capitalist market economy. By the end of the nineteenth century the acreage of potatoes and grain had halved as cattle, sheep and poultry played an increased role in Ireland's agrarian economy.[58] These transformations were part of a larger shift from labour-intensive tillage to pastoral production. It is estimated that one in every four agricultural holdings disappeared in the immediate aftermath of the Famine, most of them being less than fifteen acres.[59] The de-peasantisation of the Irish countryside gratified several officials, including Nassau Senior (1790–1864), who noted that the Famine had 'destroyed much of what was best established in Irish rural economy; above all, it has destroyed three, five acre, or even eight acre farms'.[60]

The link between catastrophe and regeneration found intellectual support in utilitarian political economy, which, in its most stringent form, regarded famines as a natural purge of redundant populations. But it also drew from the wellsprings of colonial thought that had long considered Ireland as a diseased social body that needed to be conquered and restored to sound health. Although the methods of colonisation were constantly adjusted, the project invariably entailed the subversion of existing customs and political arrangements in favour of presumably more advanced forms of social organisation. In the sixteenth and seventeenth centuries, military force and plantations were used as an engine of modernisation. By the nineteenth century a 'milder enlightenment ethos of order, progress and rationality' was considered by many to be the most expedient harbinger of social reform.[61] The tension between coercive reform and political conversion resurfaced again during the Great Irish Famine as expropriation was once more considered to be the sine qua non for improvement. Although the synergies between the state and capital were in continuous motion, they shared the same basis: violence.[62] It is precisely this shared experience of violent upheaval in the name of progress that connects the Irish historical experience to the great famines of the late nineteenth century.

# British relief measures

*Peter Gray*

Two British Governments were confronted with the responsibility of responding to the Famine in Ireland. The first, headed by the Conservative, Sir Robert Peel, had been in power since 1841 and had adopted a confrontational attitude towards Daniel O'Connell's Repeal campaign before opting for a more conciliatory strategy towards 'moderate' Irish Catholics in 1844–45. Peel's administration was credited retrospectively with adopting a relatively generous policy towards the victims of famine, although its reputation unquestionably benefitted from the fact that its tenure of office terminated in June 1846, shortly before the second and much more extensive potato failure threw Ireland into a crisis of much greater intensity. The succeeding Whig administration, headed by Lord John Russell, attracted vituperative denunciation of its policies from many contemporaries and – despite some apologetic efforts by revisionist historians to minimise its responsibility – remains the object of substantial historical criticism for its manifest failures. Paradoxically, the Whigs had as recently as 1841 been popular in much of Ireland for their pro-Catholic reforms. In that year 300,000 people had signed a testimonial, supported by O'Connell and the Catholic clergy, to the outgoing Whig Chief Secretary, Lord Morpeth, and even at the height of the Famine in May 1847 the public funeral in Dublin of the personally popular Lord Lieutenant, Lord Bessborough, was respectfully observed. What the Famine revealed was the severe limitations of the reformist Whig position on Ireland, and the strength of countervailing ideological and political imperatives – a providentialist theodicy and a moralist obsession with self-help, Smithian liberal political economy, and the ascendancy of British middle-class pressures for budgetary restraint and transferring the fiscal and moral responsibility for the Famine back to the Irish countryside.

## SIGNIFICANT DISTRESS

In the wake of the first appearance of blight in autumn 1845, Peel's cabinet mustered sufficient Irish experience to know that an extensive potato failure must lead to significant distress. The Prime Minister was also all too aware, however, of the acute political sensitivities associated with food policy. An Irish subsistence crisis would inevitably draw attention to protectionist restrictions on the import of foodstuffs to the United Kingdom and provoke demands for reciprocity for British tax-payers for any relief expenditure in Ireland. He was also under pressure to be seen to be

acting promptly in the face of noisy agitation for action by the Irish press and the Dublin Mansion House Committee. Mixed in with these calculations was a genuine perception, shared by his evangelical Home Secretary, Sir James Graham, that the blight was a manifestation of divine providence, a 'visitation' issued to expose 'unnatural' and hence unsustainable elements in the economic and social constitutions of both Britain and Ireland.[1]

This combination of political and ideological considerations helps explain the Government's response to the crisis of 1845–46 – a reaction that arguably helped stave off significant starvation in the first year of the Famine, at the expense of splitting the ruling Conservative Party and terminating Peel's political career. As soon as he was persuaded of the extent of the blight, the Prime Minister committed himself to tying relief to the repeal of the UK Corn Laws, and hence drew on himself the ire of the landed interest, including many of his own backbenchers. While facilitating the temporary import of maize and rice as cheap substitutes

Fig. 1 *Sir Robert Peel, 2nd Bt 1838* by John Linnell, oil on panel. [Source: © National Portrait Gallery, London]

for the potato might have been accomplished without repeal, Peel combined an element of free-trade opportunism with a serious concern for what he hoped would be a long-term replacement of peasant potato subsistence with the consumption of imported grain (purchased in the marketplace by proletarianised wage-labourers), and a belief

Fig. 2 Local priest Fr Patrick McManus wrote to the Relief Commissioners from Louisburgh, Westport, County Mayo, on 27 April 1846 expressing his frustration at the specific directions issued by the Commissioners with regard to the formation of local relief committees. Such directions were delaying the process of providing urgent relief 'as the destitution and wretchedness of the people are so very close upon us and have been already felt by many of the people that relief should be given promptly and directly'. A committee composed of 'individuals best qualified to administer to a suffering people' had been formed in the locality. Even though it did not meet the requirements of the commission McManus was unapologetic about its necessity: 'In the absence of the Magistracy, in the absence of the Lieutenant of the county, and with absentee landlords we do not see what else we could do but what we have done. We beg therefore most earnestly of the commissioners not to suffer the people to starve. We seek not alms, we solicit employment. But whatever the mode of relief, we again repeat our hope that the people will not be allowed to starve'. [Source: Relief Commission Papers 3/1/1884, National Archives Ireland; Photo of lazy beds in Mulranny, County Mayo, by Frank Coyne]

Beggars and Peasants assembled for Indian meal —
July 1847

Fig. 3 A sketch of the poor assembled for the distribution of Indian meal in July 1847 [Source: National Library of Ireland]

that the providential warning of the blight could not safely be ignored by the United Kingdom. At the same time he ignored appeals from O'Connell and others for a ban on distillation and a temporary suspension of grain exports from Ireland, a policy his successors would also adhere to religiously.

Peel's relief policy for Ireland was accepted by the opposition radicals and Whigs. It featured a Relief Commission chaired by Sir Randolph Routh, head of the army Commissariat (the supply agency best placed to implement relief logistics), which would co-ordinate the local relief committees and subsidise their voluntary charitable subscriptions. Legislation was passed to finance public relief works, principally on roads and drainage schemes, in collaboration with local landowners and county Grand Juries, and employing those deemed by the committees to be deserving of relief. This was a long-established policy in response to Irish food crises, albeit now undertaken on a larger scale. Peel's other principal measure was more innovative, but intended as a temporary expedient to pump-prime the as yet under-developed grain import trade. In early 1846 the Government secretly purchased £100,000 worth of maize (Indian corn) on the New York market for transhipment to Ireland, where it was parcelled out to depots managed by the Commissariat and the Coast Guard. The purpose was

not to feed the Irish poor directly, but to regulate the market price of grain and to accustom the peasantry to this new staple (the Commissariat distributed numerous handbills to educate the people on the preparation of what was labelled 'Peel's brimstone' by his critics). As growing distress in spring 1846 led to food and employment riots, the relief works and depots were gradually opened.[2]

Peel's measures are generally regarded as having been generally effective in curbing famine mortality in the first season of the crisis. However, the policy was transitional and suffered from a number of flaws. Having intervened once in the international food trade, the Government was evidently reluctant to do so again, and regarded the significant private import of maize to Ireland in summer 1846 as a vindication of this withdrawal from further interference. In line with Conservative social thought, relief policy relied heavily on the voluntary contributions of local landed elites, and offered relatively generous grants and loan terms to support this. Both Dublin administrators and the chief civil servant at the Treasury in London, Charles Trevelyan, grew increasingly critical of what they regarded as the reluctance of these local elites to take a fair share of the relief burden, and their apparent readiness to exploit the relief works to improve their own estates at public expense, and abuse the relief ticket system to favour their

Fig. 4 *Daniel O'Connell* (1775–1847) by George Mulvany, oil on canvas, *c.* 1849. [Source: National Gallery of Ireland] O'Connell, regarded as the 'defender of Ireland' was unflinching in his efforts to convince the British parliament of the 'vastness of the calamity facing the Irish people'. His final speech in the House of Commons on 8 February 1847 was a plea to Government to come to Ireland's aid. Barely audible due to his failing health, O'Connell issued the solemn warning: 'Ireland is in your hands, in your power, if you do not save her, she cannot save herself. I solemnly call on you to recollect that I predict, with the sincerest conviction, that one-fourth of our population will perish unless you come to her relief.' [Source: Patrick M. Geoghegan, *Liberator: The Life and Death of Daniel O'Connell, 1830–1847* (Dublin, 2010), pp. 228–31.

disaster (he predicted two million might perish if not assisted), and recognised that only the British parliament could command the food and logistical resources sufficient to diminish its fatal impact. O'Connell aimed to revive the lobbying tactics that had elicited significant concessions in the 1830s, but his health collapsed from late 1846, his party machine fell apart following his death in May 1847, and appeals for sympathetic treatment of Ireland made limited inroads when confronted by political and ideological imperatives generated from within the British body politic as the famine progressed.[3]

The Russell Government quickly came under pressure to terminate the perceived 'abuses' of Peel's policy. Corn merchants lobbied successfully to ensure that there would be no repeat of the state's purchase of grain on the international markets. Depots with remaining stocks would be retained, but sales would henceforward be at market price. Peel's Relief Commission was stood down, paving the way for stricter and more direct Treasury control of the relief administration. At the same time, Russell announced on 17 August 1846 that his Government would use 'the whole credit of the Treasury and means of the country . . . as it is our bounden duty to use them . . . to avert famine and to maintain the people of Ireland'.[4] The contradictions between these imperatives would soon become more than evident.

Despite doubts expressed by Lord Lieutenant Bessborough, the administration adhered rigorously to its faith in the optimising effects of the laws of supply and demand in the food trade. However, after summer 1846 private maize imports to Ireland dried up, and what was available on the international markets was drawn to countries where demand was most robust. Grain prices escalated steeply in Ireland, peaking in February–March 1847 at more than double the normal average. Nationalists asserted that famine could be averted if Ireland's non-potato food output was retained in the country, and damned the administration for refusing to embargo exports. Claims that the Famine was wholly artificial were driven more by political rhetoric than the reality of a sharp food availability decline – but did give vent to moral outrage at continuing exports from a starvation-racked country (even if this was substantially less than in previous seasons).[5] The export of locally-produced foodstuffs undoubtedly worsened the 'hunger winter' of 1846–47, but acted as a multiplier to the real food shortage produced by the loss of the bulk of the subsistence potato crop. Moreover, retaining higher-cost grain and livestock products in Ireland would have done little for the rural labouring poor without some effective distribution mechanism (and indeed there is evidence that some retained grain was fed to cattle).

own dependants and tenants rather than the truly needy. As the British press began to pick up these criticisms, a perception that Peel's system had been too generous took hold. At the same time, Peel's insistence on pressing a robust coercion bill on Ireland to deal with an upsurge in agrarian unrest provoked opposition from Catholic and nationalist interests in Ireland, and provided the opportunity for his parliamentary opponents to combine to bring down his administration in June 1846.

## RUSSELL'S WHIG ADMINISTRATION

The task of responding to the renewed Irish catastrophe fell to Russell's incoming Whig administration, a weak minority Government dependent on the continuing division of its parliamentary opponents for survival. Daniel O'Connell's initial confidence in the goodwill of this Whig Government was soon to appear woefully misplaced, but in his defence he correctly discerned the true scale of the 1846 ecological

## REVAMPED SCHEME OF PUBLIC WORKS

Russell's Government retained the principle of relief by public works, but revamped it under the 1846 Labour Rate

Fig. 5 Famine Road in Glenville, County Cork. The Liberal Government's strategy for dealing with Irish distress initially favoured public works such as the repair or improvement of existing roads or the construction of new roads. The administration did not believe in handouts. What was perceived as Irish indolence would not be tolerated to any extent hence, in return for their labour, the starving would be given the means of acquiring food. What they received in aid was measured in terms of the work completed. Task work fitted neatly the Liberal agenda. With over 700,000 dependent on such public works in the winter and spring months of 1846–47, the Government decided to phase out such relief works. [Photo: Kevin Egan]

Act. Designed to take a harder line against opportunism by local elites, this measure centralised administration under the Board of Works (itself answerable directly to the Treasury) and made the total cost repayable by the rates levied on the localities. Despite attempts by Dublin Castle officials to soften its impact, the underlying purpose of the new system was to introduce a more penal element to the public works, aimed at landowners and labourers alike. The Treasury sought to veto all useful or 'reproductive' works (thereby obliging landowners to borrow privately to improve their estates and avoid the ultimate costs of state relief works), while moving to impose 'piece work' payments on the labourers – a measure intended to stimulate work discipline and reward effort but which in practice pushed those least able to exert themselves, such as the ill and elderly, below the threshold of subsistence.

Despite its gross limitations, desperation led thousands to throw themselves on the public works relief in the harsh winter of 1846–47. The official headcount soared from 114,000 in late October 1846 to a peak of 714,390 in March 1847, with each labourer typically seeking to support a family of four or five on their meagre earnings. As

numbers escalated the Board of Works bureaucracy struggled to keep up. Works were disrupted by strikes or riots against petty tyrannies, delays in wage payments and the imposition of piece rates, while rising food prices outran the wages deliberately pegged at low levels to encourage labourers to seek a return to agricultural employment. Despite the high costs of the relief works (which would account for some £5 million in 1846–47), the outcome of the system was almost certainly to augment rather than contain excess mortality. Heavy labour, especially in the harsh winter conditions of 1846–47, placed extreme stresses on the bodies of the malnourished, who began to die in large numbers on the works in early 1847.[6] Social upheaval and distress created the ideal condition for contagious fevers such as typhus and relapsing fever, which now also reached epidemic proportions.[7]

By early 1847 Irish and British press reports were replete with eyewitness accounts of mass mortality in western Ireland and increasingly with calls for charitable assistance. The Government was not slow to react to this change in mood, supporting the establishment of the British Association for Relief in London, instigating a 'Queen's Letter' to raise charitable funds at church doors and ultimately endorsing a 'National Day of Fast and Humiliation' on 24 March. In spring 1847 the popular response to these appeals was generous, raising upwards of £435,000 within the UK for distribution by the British Association, in addition to separate funds generated by the Quakers, American philanthropists and the Vatican to meet Irish needs. For most, however, Irish philanthropy was a passing fashion, ebbing from mid-1847 under the combined impacts of the UK industrial recession, anxiety about pauper Irish immigration, political upheaval in Europe and a growing sense in Britain that Irish 'ingratitude' for this largesse should be punished rather than indulged.[8]

RADICAL SHIFT IN POLICY

The sympathetic impulse of early 1847 combined with sev-

eral factors to spur a radical turn in relief policy. Russell's Government, ostensibly 'friendly' towards Ireland, was shamed by public exposures and lobbied by its own officials in Dublin into abandoning the failed public works. In addition, the costs of the system were becoming prohibitive and its consequences evidently demoralising as well as largely ineffective. After debating various options, the Government decided to follow the Quakers' example and offer direct food aid to those most in need, through a network of state-sponsored soup kitchens. The Prime Minister observed that 'the pressing matter at present is to keep the people alive', but other ministers noted other attractions to such a system – a cooked food test of destitution would prevent importunity (ever an obsession despite the evident collapse of much of Irish rural society), while transferring the ultimate repayment costs of the new scheme onto the Poor Law rates

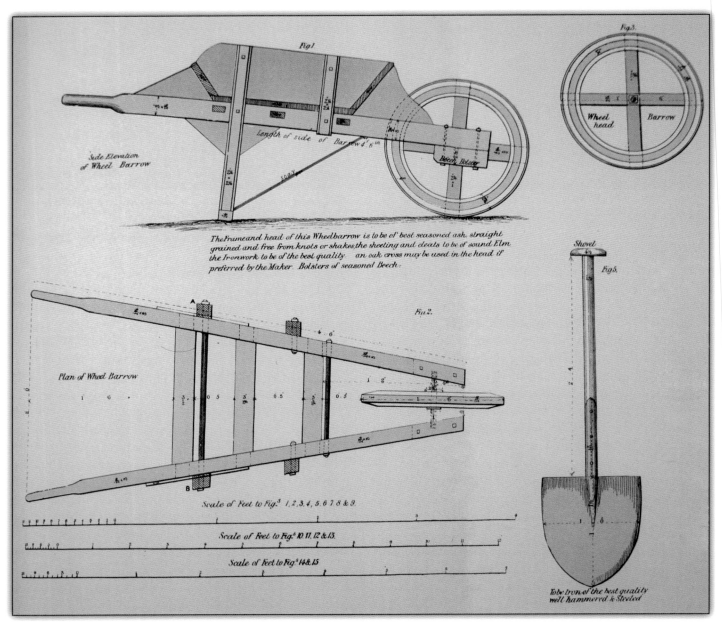

Fig. 6 Plans and description of economic implements used in the execution of public works [Source: Correspondence from July 1846 to January 1847 relating to the measures adopted for the relief of distress. [Board of Works series, *British Parliamentary Papers 1847* (764) p. 217]

80

Fig. 7 The draining of the River Fergus, County Clare, was one of the biggest public works schemes undertaken in Ireland during the Famine. It was started under the Drainage Act of March 1846 and lasted into the mid-1850s. The Ballyhee Cutting, three miles north of Ennis, half a mile long and in places over forty feet deep through limestone rock, is the most impressive surviving aspect of this scheme. In mid-July 1847, when all the local road schemes had been closed down, the Fergus scheme was the only source of relief work and employed 600 labourers. [Source: Ciarán Ó Murchadha, *Sable Wings over the Land: Ennis, County Clare and Its Wider Community during the Great Famine* (Clare, 1998), pp. 259–66; Photo: Frank Coyne]

THE PUPPET-SHOW.    7

" ———— PADDY! WILL YOU NOW,
TAKE ME WHILE I'M IN THE HUMOUR?"

Fig. 8 'Paddy! will you now, take me while I'm in the humour?', *The Puppet-Show*, 9 September 1848. This cartoon satirises Lord John Russell's brief visit to Ireland in September 1848 in an abortive attempt to elicit support for 'remedial measures' following the Young Ireland rising in July. The savage and simianised 'Paddy' is depicted as both ungrateful for previous British aid and contemptuous of Russell's proffered hand.

Fig. 9 *Sir Charles Wood*, Chancellor of Exchequer 1846–52 by Anthony de Brie, oil on canvas. [Source: © National Portrait Gallery, London] The Liberal response to the Famine was largely underpinned by the predominant political, economic and religious beliefs of the period. During the course of 1847–48, Wood was at the heart of the struggle over financial aid for Ireland. While defending the Treasury, it is also clear that his response was shaped by more fundamental beliefs. He viewed the Famine as providential in design; hence it was not wise to disrupt too much God's plan for Ireland's reconstruction: 'Now financially my course is very easy. I have no money and therefore I cannot give it . . . assistance to Ireland means only a further loan, and in the present state of the money market and depression in all our manufacturing towns, this is out of the question. Ireland must keep herself somehow or other; this at least is certain, that the public funds of this country will not . . . Where the people refuse to work or sow, they must starve, as indeed I fear must be the case in many parts. Ellice . . . says that all our difficulties arise from our impious attempt to thwart the dispensation which was sent to cut the Gordion knot in Ireland and I believe this must be the end of it.' (Source: Wood to Lord Clarendon, 15 August 1847 in Peter Gray, *Famine, Land and Politics: British Government and Irish society 1843–50* (Dublin, 1999, p. 292)

would (it was hoped) act as a more direct stimulus to proprietors to offer employment and pave the way for a permanent extension of the Poor Law system. While a Temporary Relief Act was rapidly passed in February 1847, establishing a new relief bureaucracy under Sir John Burgoyne took an inordinate length of time, and staged lay-offs from the public works from March, when few soup kitchens were operational before late May or June, threw thousands into the overcrowded workhouses, or onto the roads, with nothing but the erratic ministrations of private charities and mutual or landlord assistance to support them.

Only when the soup kitchens came fully into operation, distributing free rations of a cheap 'stirabout' porridge of maize, rice and oats, did the appalling mortality rates of 1847 begin to abate. Although far from flawless, the soup kitchen regime, issuing as many as three million daily rations by July, to over 90% of the population of some western unions, demonstrated the capacity of the Victorian state to curb, if not to terminate, the horrors of famine. The initiative also was significantly cheaper than the public works to run, and was aided by a rapid fall in the market price of grain within Ireland in spring and summer. As if in belated vindication of Trevelyan's faith in the free market, massive US shipments of maize began to arrive in Irish ports, bringing down the price by August to half what it had been in February. Maize and rice imports would continue at a high level for the rest of the Famine period, outweighing the continuing grain exports from Ireland. Paradoxically, this sudden influx of cheap grain had several unexpected effects, undermining (in some cases bankrupting) many of the Irish merchants who had profited from the inflated prices of 1846–47, and also reducing the winter feeding costs of 'strong' farmers in a position to shift (with their landlord's encouragement) into the cattle economy in these years.

## EXTENDED POOR LAW

All too quickly, the soup kitchen relief scheme was abandoned from September 1847 and replaced as the principal mode of relief by the extended poor law. Despite strong opposition from Irish landowners and their British Conservative allies, this policy shift fitted with a growing conviction in Britain that 'Irish property must pay for Irish poverty'.[9] The Poor Law Extension Act permitted (for the first time) outdoor relief from the rates for certain classes of paupers, and for the 'able-bodied' poor if the workhouses were full, and required elected boards of guardians to relieve all those classed as destitute. As a concession to landowners, however, the act also contained an amendment restricting relief to those holding more than a quarter acre of land – a provision used by many proprietors to facilitate the permanent clearance of smallholding peasants from their estates.

In essence the extended poor law, while welcomed by many Irish Catholic clergymen as a well-merited punishment for the landed class who had created the social conditions triggering famine, transferred the full costs of relief from the Treasury to the Irish localities. Several developments made this expedient for the state. Growing economic difficulties in Britain made raising loans in the money markets more difficult and stimulated middle-class demands for lower taxation, and the general election of summer 1847 returned a turbulent group of laissez-faire radicals, led by Richard Cobden, who held the parliamentary balance of power. Russell observed that 'we have in the opinion of Great Britain done too

" WHILE THE CROP GROWS IRELAND STARVES."

Fig. 10 'While the crop grows, Ireland starves', *The Puppet-Show*, 13 May 1849. Rival party leaders Lord John Russell and Robert Peel sow rival political schemes that offer little short-term relief to Ireland. Russell's 'rate in aid' angered northern and eastern Irish unions by taxing them for the benefit of the distressed west (and leaving Britain untouched); Peel's 'plantation scheme' for western development drew favourable press commentary but came to nothing.

much for Ireland and have lost elections for doing so'.[10] In addition, the potato did not fail in 1847 (although as few were planted, the crop was meagre). The apparent absence of a renewed 'visitation', along with low food prices and a good grain harvest provided the illusion that the famine was now over.

The latter years of the Famine, from 1848 through to 1850, and in some western and southern districts extending into 1851 and 1852, were marked by a withdrawal of state intervention and expenditure, as the burden of relief was thrown almost exclusively on to the poor law (dealt with separately in this volume). With several 'remedial schemes' of public works or assisted emigration stymied by opposition within the cabinet and parliament, and with British popular resentment at Irish 'ingratitude' stoked by reports of revived agrarian violence and Young Ireland activism, ministers reverted to a fatalistic rhetoric of ineluctable 'natural causes' operating in Ireland. The

Government's last major legislative initiative, the Encumbered Estates Act of 1849, was intended to create a 'free trade in land' by facilitating a summary process of sale of indebted estates. Whig moralists and anti-landlord radicals regarded this measure as a panacea, which would reinvigorate Irish agriculture by encouraging investment by British entrepreneurs. While significant quantities of land were sold under the act, it did next to nothing to alleviate distress, but rather added a further motivation to many landowners to clear their estates of 'surplus' population. In sum, as a later British Prime Minister was to observe, the Government in London 'failed their people through standing by while a crop failure turned into a massive human tragedy'; while not guilty of intentional genocide, the reasons for this failure include adherence to misplaced ideological dogmas and political calculations that placed the interests of Great Britain before those of Ireland.

# Charles Trevelyan

## Peter Gray

Charles Edward Trevelyan's role in the Great Famine remains highly controversial. For twentieth-century followers of his contemporary nationalist critics he remains a 'Victorian Cromwell', the malevolent *eminence grise* of the Famine administration.[1] Taking an opposite tack, a recent detailed study seeks to exonerate him of such charges by stressing his non-political function as a civil servant, and (from a neo-liberal perspective) the reasonableness of the policy adopted in 1846–50.[2] The truth lies somewhere in-between; Government policy was circumscribed by British public opinion, parliamentary arithmetic and a deteriorating fiscal situation following the banking crash of autumn 1847; the cabinet also contained other powerful and vociferous laissez-faire ideologues such as Charles Wood and Earl Grey. At the same time, Trevelyan was never a distant mandarin; closely related by marriage and politics with leading Whig figures such as T.B. Macaulay, his correspondence also reveals him to have been an ideologically-driven workaholic with a clear conviction that the 'social revolution' he believed essential in Ireland was mandated by divine providence.[3]

In the absence of much experience in managing food crises in Ireland, the Government placed heavy reliance on the guidance of Trevelyan who had held the assistant secretaryship at the Treasury since 1840, after a previous spell in the British administration of India. He sought, with significant success to micromanage Irish relief from his offices in Whitehall, to the frequent frustration of officials in Dublin or the localities. Trevelyan strongly believed in the utility of non-interference in the food trade and had suitable extracts from Adam Smith's *Wealth of Nations* circulated to bolster the doubts of relief officials in Ireland on this head. At the same time, he distanced himself from the racist stereotyping of journals like *The Times,* and declared that his own Cornish 'Celtic' ancestry made him confident of the improvability of the Irish character.[4] Personally a devout Anglican evangelical, like most Whigs he avoided anti-Catholic dogma and emphasised instead the social and behavioural roots of Irish agrarian backwardness, reserving particular venom for the moral failings ('demoralisation') of the Irish landed elite. His confidence that he could discern and was working to advance the intentions of divine providence, combined with an intensely held belief that the visitation was sent with a beneficent rather than punitive purpose (Trevelyan blamed famine mortality on the moral failings of selfish landowners and feckless peasants rather than on any inevitable outworkings of a Malthusian population trap), allowed him to distance himself and the state he served from responsibility for what was happening in Ireland.

Trevelyan's apologia, *The Irish Crisis*, published in late 1847 in the *Edinburgh Review* and later as a pamphlet, offered the 'official' view of the meaning of the Famine and the state's response to it. Although approved by ministers, the text was Trevelyan's own. Warning of the need to eliminate the 'canker' of state dependency manifest in the tendency of all Irish classes to 'make a poor mouth', he concluded his triumphalist account of British policy with a liberal-unionist paean to the success of the cultural and social revolution from above that the country required: 'God grant that the generation to which this great opportunity has been offered may rightly perform its part, and that we may not relax our efforts until Ireland fully participates in the social health and physical prosperity of Great Britain, which will be the true consummation of their union!'[5] In 1848 Trevelyan was knighted for his work in Ireland.

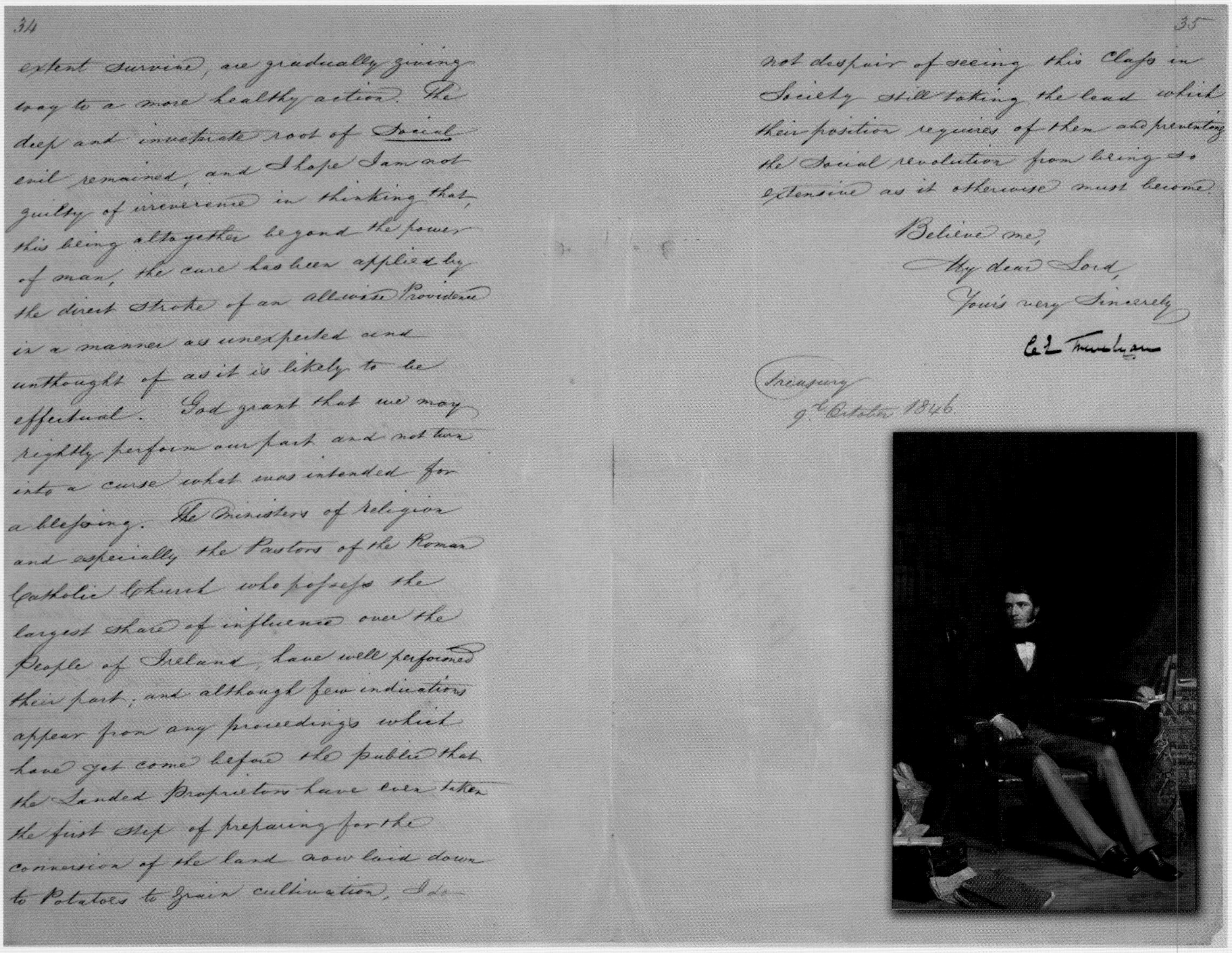

*[Handwritten letter pages 34–35, reading:]* extent survive, are gradually giving way to a more healthy action. The deep and inveterate root of Social evil remained, and I hope I am not guilty of irreverence in thinking that, this being altogether beyond the power of man, the cure had been applied by the direct Stroke of an allwise Providence in a manner as unexpected and unthought of as it is likely to be effectual. God grant that we may rightly perform our part and not turn into a curse what was intended for a blessing. The Ministers of Religion and especially the Pastors of the Roman Catholic Church who possess the largest share of influence over the People of Ireland, have well performed their part; and although few indications appear from any proceedings which have yet come before the public that the Landed Proprietors have ever taken the first step of preparing for the conversion of the land now laid down to Potatoes to Grain cultivation, I do not despair of seeing this Class in Society still taking the lead which their position requires of them and preventing the Social revolution from being so extensive as it otherwise must become

Believe me,
My dear Lord,
Yours very Sincerely
C E Trevelyan

Treasury
9th October 1846.

Fig. 1 *Sir Charles Trevelyan* (1807–86) by Eden Addis. [Portrait: Courtesy of National Trust] In a lengthy thirty-five page letter to Thomas Spring-Rice, 1st Lord Monteagle, dated 9 October 1846, Trevelyan laid bare his thinking in relation to the role of government in terms of relief: 'It forms no part of the functions of government to provide supplies of food or to increase the productive powers of the land.' In his view, the Famine was a heaven-sent opportunity to reform Irish agriculture along capitalist lines, thus ending the over-reliance on the potato: 'and I hope I am not guilty of irreverence in thinking that, this being altogether beyond the power of man, the cure has been applied by the direct stroke of an all-wise Providence in a manner as unexpected and unthought of as it is likely to be effectual. God grant that we may rightly perform our part and not turn into a curse what was intended for a blessing.' He was also clear about the responsibilities of landlords in this transformation: 'few indications appear from any proceedings which have yet come before the public that the landed proprietors have even taken the first step of preparing for the conversion of the land now laid down to potatoes to grain cultivation, I do not despair of seeing this class in society still taking the lead which their position requires of them, and preventing the social revolution from being so extensive as it otherwise must become.' [Source: National Library of Ireland, MS 13,397, Monteagle Papers]

# The operation of the Poor Law during the Famine

## *Christine Kinealy*

In England, Scotland and Wales, state involvement in poor relief dated back to the late sixteenth century. An attempt had been made to extend the English legislation to Ireland in 1640, but it had become subsumed in the political turmoil of the period.[1] At the time of the Act of Union, therefore, Ireland, unlike Britain, had no national Poor Law. By the nineteenth century, especially following the ending of the Napoleonic Wars, rising costs resulted in a re-evaluation of the way in which relief was provided. Some commentators, led by Thomas Malthus, suggested that poverty was the fault of the individual, and resulted from over-population. State intervention, therefore, would exacerbate rather than ease the problem. In England and Wales these opinions resulted in the passing of the harsher Poor Law Amendment Act of 1834, with its emphasis on more stringency and lower costs.

In Ireland, assistance to the poor had been provided in a variety of ways, some voluntary, some church-based, and some through the mechanism of local Government bodies, such as Dublin Corporation. The creation of a unitary parliament based in Westminster in 1801 resulted in more state intervention in Irish affairs, although in areas such as policing, education, voting and poor relief, Ireland was treated differently from other parts of the United Kingdom.[2] However, they each marked a step towards more centralisation and taking power from the hands of the churches and the local gentry to central Government and its representatives. Government-sponsored inquiries were also a feature of the early decades of the Union. One of the largest and most detailed was that of the Irish Poor Inquiry Commission, which sat between 1833 and 1836 and was chaired by the political economist, Richard Whately. Their findings suggested that poverty was even more extensive than had been suspected, with an estimated 2,385,000 people requiring

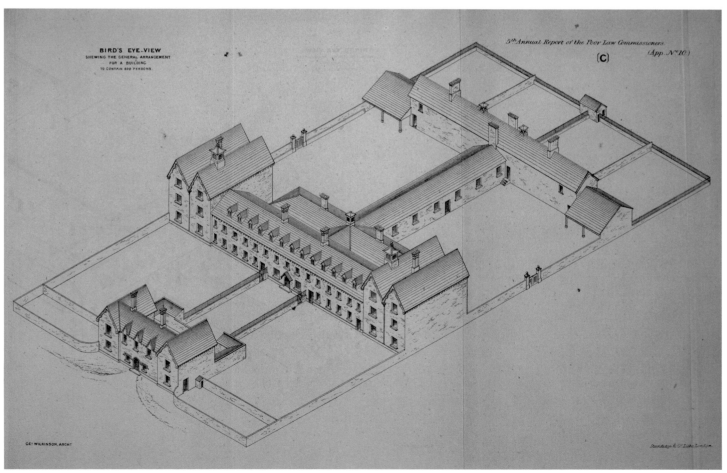

Fig. 1 Bird's eye view showing the general arrangement for a building to contain 800 persons. [Source: *5th Annual Report of the Poor Law Commissioners*, Appendix no. 10]

Fig. 2   The main block of the Roscommon workhouse, which was erected in 1840–42 following the standard design of the Poor Law Commissioners' architect, George Wilkinson. The surviving buildings today form part of the Sacred Heart Hospital. [Photo: William J. Smyth]

assistance, especially during the summer, or 'hungry', months.[3]

### INTRODUCING A POOR LAW TO IRELAND

The Irish Poor Inquiry Commissioners concluded that a poor law should be introduced into Ireland as part of a package of measures. Their recommendations were based on their vision of combining poor relief with a longer-term aim of providing state-sponsored works that would provide employment and help develop the infrastructure of Ireland. They also suggested state-sponsored emigration schemes. Despite the thoroughness of its enquiry and report, the recommendations made by the Commissioners were by-passed. The proposals were both more costly and more encompassing than the ruling Whig Party had envisaged. Moreover, by the time the report was completed, the amended English Poor Law was operative and, from the perspective of the authorities, was believed to be having a 'salutary' effect.[4]

Instead, George Nicholls, an English Poor Law Commissioner, was asked to visit Ireland with the limited remit of judging the suitability of the 'new' English Poor Law to Ireland. Not surprisingly, despite only spending a few weeks in the country, he judged in favour of extending a limited version of the English system to Ireland.

The outcome was the 1838 Poor Relief Act.[5] There were three essential differences between the English and Irish, each of which demonstrated that the Irish poor were to be treated more stringently that those in England: in Ireland,

there was to be no right to relief, outdoor relief was not permitted, and there was no law of settlement. In Ireland also, relief could only be given to those who became inmates of specially-designed institutions known as workhouses, whereas the English system allowed for a combination of both 'outdoor' and 'indoor' relief. The decision not to allow outdoor relief in Ireland, according to the Limerick-born peer, Lord Monteagle, emanated from the belief that, 'all the evils produced in England in 300 years would be produced in Ireland in 10'.[6] The variations in the treatment of the Irish poor suggested that they were regarded as less deserving of assistance than the English poor. Regardless of these substantial differences, standardisation was achieved by the system being controlled from London, although in the first instance George Nicholls was to be based in Ireland. It was not until 1847, in the midst of the Famine, that a separate Poor Law Commission was established for Ireland.

### IMPACT OF THE POOR LAW

The impact of the new Poor Law extended beyond merely providing for the relief of the Irish destitute. The legislation changed the administrative structure and the fiscal and electoral arrangements of the country. It also introduced a new body of language for dealing with the poor – now designated as paupers. In addition to providing a safety net for the destitute, each workhouse had its own infirmary, which meant that the Poor Law provided a national system of medical relief, although they were for the use of paupers, not the public. The latter function was extended with the passing of the Medical Charities Act in 1851.[7] As well as providing a safety net for the destitute, the Poor Law was viewed by British legislators as an engine for change that would allow Ireland to become a more productive society. During the years of the Famine, the desire to bring about radical changes in Irish society underpinned the way in which Poor Law relief was provided.[8]

The new legislation was implemented quickly. The country was divided into 130 Poor Law Unions, which did not conform to any previous administrative boundaries. Each union had its own workhouse and these buildings were the embodiment of the harsh ideology or deterrent principle that permeated the new system. Workhouses were deliberately designed to be unattractive and austere, reflecting life within them, which was to be forbidding and regimented. Dull, repetitive work was a further part of the principle of deterrent, as was a monotonous diet that was to be less substantial than that provided in local prisons. Within the workhouses, families were split up and resided in separate buildings. The day-to-day running of the workhouse was left to salaried officers. Where possible, the Master was to be retired from the army, as a way of ensuring that discipline was imposed. The principle of local responsibility was an essential part of the legislation. A new type of taxation was introduced to finance the workhouses, which made each union responsible for imposing a levy, known as a poor rate. Those who paid taxes over a certain level were entitled to vote annually to elect 'Poor Law Guardians'. Inevitably, landowners and merchants dominated the Boards of Guardians.

Percentage

Under 10.0    30.1 - 40.0

10.0 - 20.0    40.1 - 50.0

20.1 - 30.0    Over 50.0

No data

0    Miles    50

Data input by Tomás Kelly

Fig. 3 PERCENTAGE DIFFERENCE BETWEEN THE PROPORTION OF THE UNION POPULATIONS BENEFITING FROM ALL FORMS OF RELIEF IN SEPTEMBER 1848 AND THE HIGHEST PROPORTION OF THE 1841 POPULATION BENEFITING FROM THE TEMPORARY RELIEF (SOUP KITCHEN) ACT IN THE SUMMER OF 1847. At the peak of the Soup Kitchen Act, 36.8% of the Irish population were receiving food relief: 15.8% in Ulster, 29.8% in Leinster, 50.2% in Munster and 62.4% in Connacht (see Fig 7, Chapter 1). The range across all the Poor Law unions was from Ballinrobe with 93.2% of its population receiving relief via the public soup kitchens, to three unions in Ulster – Antrim, Belfast and Newtownards – which officially did not provide any public relief but did operate private soup kitchens. By September 1848, the national ratio of those receiving relief vis-à-vis the peak in 1847 was 1:7.4 or, put another way, for more than every seven persons receiving relief in mid-1847, only one person was in receipt of relief in September 1848. Even allowing for greater mortalities in the west and south over the period, this map illustrates profound regional and local differences across the unions in the provision of relief as between these two critical time periods. Across the island, the average difference between those on relief in mid-1847 and September 1848 was –31.8%. North and east of an uneven line from the Glenties in Donegal through Athlone and Athy to Enniscorthy, this difference was substantially reduced in unions which were less in need of massive relief in both time periods. In contrast, west and south of this line the gap in the provision of relief between the two periods increased dramatically. In a number of unions in Connacht (Westport, Swinford, Castlebar, Ballinrobe, Tuam and Gort) there is a –75% difference between the two periods, not to speak of –50% difference in Ballina and Clifden. Over many of the Munster unions from Scariff, Nenagh, Rathkeale, Newcastle, Kilmallock, Kanturk, Cahirciveen, Bantry, Dunmanway, Lismore and Clogheen, there is a –50% difference in the number of people receiving relief. These figures for all the unions beg the question: what was the fate of so many of these families and individuals who were in receipt of food relief until the late summer of 1847 and were no longer in receipt of any relief by September 1848? The contrasting fortunes of the populations of north and east Leinster and most of Ulster (some unions in Cavan and Meath excepted) are also emphasised in this map. Overall, this map confirms the utter failure of the policy which placed all forms of relief on the shoulders of the Poor Law unions alone after the summer of 1847.

## THE ONSET OF FAMINE

Within less than ten years of being introduced, the Irish Poor Law was faced with a catastrophe of unforeseen proportions. The appearance of previously-unknown blight on the potato crop in 1845 was initially viewed as nothing more than a temporary difficulty. Although a national network of workhouses was in place, the Government, led by Robert Peel, decided to keep temporary and permanent relief separate. Consequently, a limited system of public works was put in place and a small supply of Indian corn was imported from the United States.[9] These measures were successful and nobody died in the year following the first appearance of blight.

Peel's premiership came to an abrupt end in June 1846, as a result of his support for a repeal of the protectionist Corn Laws. He was succeeded by Lord John Russell. Russell's minority Whig Government was immediately confronted with the reappearance of the blight – but even earlier in the season than in the previous year. Potato disease was not unknown in Ireland, but it generally lasted for no more than one year. The return of blight in 1846 and subsequent years transformed the temporary food shortages into a subsistence crisis of unique range and longevity.

The second and more devastating failure of the potato crop put pressure on the new administration to provide relief on a far larger scale than that of the previous year. Despite the success of Peel's measures, the Whigs decided to keep their intervention in the market place to a minimum and to place more of the financial burden for providing assistance on the localities. As Russell informed the House of Commons, his Government had 'declined to undertake the feeding of the people of Ireland by the importation of provisions from abroad'.[10] Instead, public works were to be the main form of relief, although the conditions governing employment on them were made deliberately harsh and the wages paid were kept artificially low. Regardless of the severe conditions, demand for employment far exceeded supply.

The inadequacies of the public works system put pressure on the workhouses and by the end of 1846 over half of them were full. Because of the rigorous regulations governing relief in Ireland, when an institution became full, the guardians had no ability to grant assistance, even to people who were clearly destitute or infirm. Income from the poor rates, which had generally been set some months in advance, often was insufficient to meet the demands now being placed on it. The reluctance, and increasingly the inability, of guardians to impose high taxes proved to be an ongoing source of annoyance for the British Treasury which, as the Famine progressed, took more control of the distribution of resources to the unions.

It was not only the Poor Law that was struggling to cope with the demands being made on it. The public works too were proving inadequate, both in terms of the level of employment they could provide, and the wages (determined by piece work) that they afforded. The bureaucratic and financial implications of managing such an unwieldy scheme resulted in their being closed prematurely at the beginning of 1847. In their place, soup kitchens were to be opened, initially paid for by the state, but ultimately

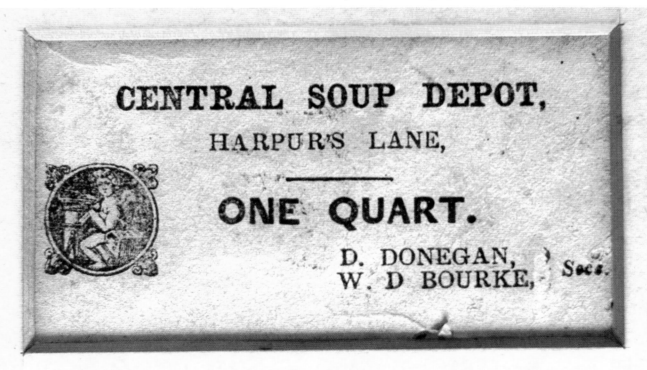

Fig. 4 Ticket for Soup Depot, Harpur's Lane, Cork City. The introduction of the Soup Kitchen Act in January 1847 allowed for the distribution of food directly to the starving. [Source: Cork Archives Institute]

financed from the poor rates. The legislation governing this new provision, the Temporary Relief Act, was so-called because the giving of gratuitous relief, however minimal and necessary, was regarded as ideologically unsound. The soup kitchens, therefore, were to be a short-term measure only. Simultaneously, famine relief was to be put on a more permanent basis through the mechanism of an amended and extended Poor Law, which was to become operative in September.

## THE END OF GOVERNMENT ASSISTANCE

At its peak in July, over three million people were receiving free rations of soup and bread. Despite the relative cheapness and efficacy of the scheme, in early August the Government was urging that all soup kitchens should be closed in readiness for the transfer to Poor Law relief. In preparation for the changeover, all relief

# NOTICE
## TO ALL RECEIVING
# RELIEF.

The **RELIEF COMMISSIONERS** in **DUBLIN**, call upon the *Inspecting Officers* to cease the issue of *FOOD* under the Relief Act on the 15th of August, especially in this fine *Agricultural Union of Rathkeale*.

The Helpless Poor must then be provided for under the New Poor Law Bill.

The Able-Bodied must seek Labour wherever to be obtained.

In the mean time, the supplies of Money, and Food from the Commissariat Stores will be decreased week by week.

All Holders of Land will first be struck off the Lists by the 1st of August, and those above 5 Acres sooner.

The Able-Bodied Labourers will come next, and they are called on to assist Relief Committees to strike off week by week those who can soonest shift for themselves.

By order of the

RELIEF COMMISSIONERS, *Dublin Castle*.

Fig. 5 Notice from the Relief Commissioners in Dublin calling upon the inspecting officers to cease the issue of food. In July 1847 over three million people were collecting rations from the Government's soup kitchens. Under the provisions of the Poor Law Extension Act passed in June 1847, the burden of relief would eventually fall on a Poor Law system, which was singularly ill-equipped to deal with a crisis on the scale of the Famine. The result was a humanitarian disaster. [Source: National Gallery of Ireland]

officials were notified that Government assistance was about to end.[11] The Poor Law Extension Act was passed in June 1847. Under the 1838 legislation, the workhouses had provided accommodation for 110,000 inmates. Following the second appearance of blight, workhouse accommodation had been increased, but now the number and capacity of these institutions had to be greatly expanded. Accordingly, thirty-three new unions were created. More significantly from an ideological perspective, the 1847 legislation permitted a limited form of outdoor relief. The transfer to the Poor Law was symbolic of the fact that assistance from the Government was at an end and that Irish taxpayers were responsible for future relief.

The fact that the crisis was not over was evident from the announcement that twenty-two unions were to be officially labelled as 'distressed' on the grounds that they would require external assistance in the approaching year. The unions so designated were: Ballina, Ballinrobe, Bantry, Cahersiveen, Carrick-on-Shannon, Castlebar, Castlerea, Clifden, Dingle, Ennistymon, Galway, Glenties, Gort, Kenmare, Kilrush, Mohill, Roscommon, Scariff, Sligo, Swinford, Tuam and Westport. Edward Twistleton, the English-born Poor Law Commissioner, who was increasingly disillusioned with the Govern-

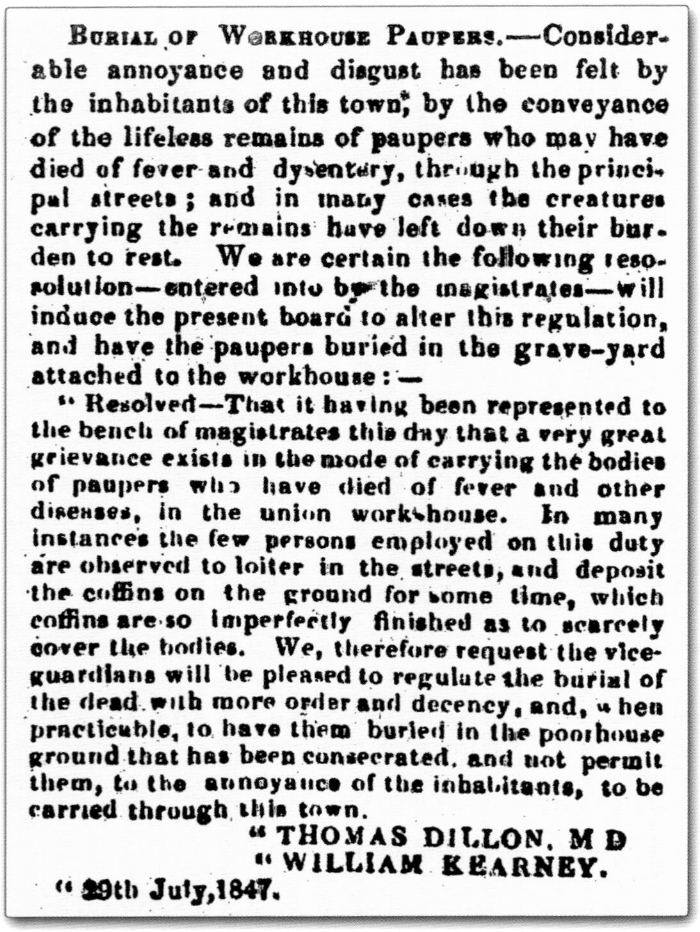

BURIAL OF WORKHOUSE PAUPERS.—Considerable annoyance and disgust has been felt by
the inhabitants of this town, by the conveyance
of the lifeless remains of paupers who may have
died of fever and dysentery, through the principal streets; and in many cases the creatures
carrying the remains have left down their burden to rest. We are certain the following reso-
solution—entered into by the magistrates—will
induce the present board to alter this regulation,
and have the paupers buried in the grave-yard
attached to the workhouse :—
  " Resolved—That it having been represented to
the bench of magistrates this day that a very great
grievance exists in the mode of carrying the bodies
of paupers who have died of fever and other
diseases, in the union workhouse. In many
instances the few persons employed on this duty
are observed to loiter in the streets, and deposit
the coffins on the ground for some time, which
coffins are so imperfectly finished as to scarcely
cover the bodies. We, therefore request the vice-
guardians will be pleased to regulate the burial of
the dead with more order and decency, and, when
practicable, to have them buried in the poorhouse
ground that has been consecrated, and not permit
them, to the annoyance of the inhabitants, to be
carried through this town.
               " THOMAS DILLON, M D
               " WILLIAM KEARNEY.
  " 29th July, 1847.

Fig. 6 Given the increasing rates of mortality during 1847, the burial of the dead became a contentious issue especially in workhouse towns like Castlebar. The report in the *Mayo Constitution*, 3 August 1847, points to the fear of contagion amongst the town's inhabitants. [Source: Mayo County Library]

ment's policies, privately warned Charles Trevelyan at the Treasury, that double the number of unions would need outside intervention.[12] Just as worrying was the fact that under the principle of local taxation, the unions with the highest level of poverty were generally those with the least resources. Charles Wood, the Chancellor of the Exchequer, approved of the harshness of the new system, on the grounds that, 'except through a purgatory of misery and starvation, I cannot see how Ireland is to emerge into anything approaching either quiet or prosperity'.[13] However, the policies pursued by the Government after 1847 were not only criticised by Irish nationalists, but also by some liberal politicians and relief officials. The Marquis of Clanricarde, a Galway landowner who served in Russell's cabinet, regarded the transfer to Poor Law relief as damaging to relationships between Britain and Ireland.[14]

GREGORY CLAUSE

On the suggestion of a conservative Irish landowner, William Gregory, a clause was included in the new Poor Law, the 'quarter-acre clause', which stipulated that any-body who occupied more than a quarter acre of land was not eligible to receive Government relief. Many smallhold-ers who had survived two years of shortages were now faced with a stark choice of either seeking relief or risking starvation. Despite the crisis being no fault of theirs, the famine poor were now being categorised as paupers who were to be subjected to the harsh conditions governing Poor Law relief.

Although the 1847 harvest was relatively blight-free, it was small. Despite some optimistic assertions by some officials in Britain that the worst of the Famine was over, this was far from the case, and in 1848, the Poor Law provid-ed assistance to over one million people through a combina-tion of indoor and outdoor relief. The main financial burden for financing the Poor Law fell on landowners, some of whom were already struggling as a consequence of the fall in income from rent. The unsympathetic attitude evident in the treatment of the poor was also shown to landowners, who were widely held responsible for the backwardness of Irish agriculture. The new Lord Lieutenant, the Earl of Clarendon, saw the benefit of the proposed change: 'It will give the upper classes an interest that they never yet felt in preventing the lower from falling.'[15] Even more optimistical-ly – and insensitively given the number who had already died or emigrated – he referred to the failure of the potato crop and the introduction of a Poor Law as 'the salvation of the country' because, in combination they had 'prevented land being used as it hitherto had been'.[16] However, as George Nicholls, the original champion of the Poor Law had warned, the system was not suitable to deal with large-scale subsistence crises or famines, because the principle of local taxation would place the highest burden on the areas with the fewest resources.[17]

INDEBTEDNESS OF THE UNIONS

As a consequence of the previous two years of shortages, many Poor Law Unions were in bad financial shape, the combined debts of the 130 unions being £250,000.[18] The indebtedness of the unions was frequently attributed by British politicians as arising from the selfishness of the guardians and the rate-payers. Despite the unprecedented demand on their resources, some guardians were accused of turning the poor away rather than increase the level of poor rates. Earl Grey cited the case of the Castlebar Union in County Mayo, which had maintained the same level of rate from September 1845 to March 1847, a policy that resulted in potential inmates being turned away.[19] Blaming the local administrators for the inadequacy of the relief sys-tem became commonplace and, by the end of 1848, thirty-nine boards of guardians had been removed from office and replaced by Government officials.

In 1848, blight returned and destroyed over 50% of the already small potato crop. No new relief measures were introduced and the Poor Law was again to be responsible for relief. By July 1849, the number of people receiving Poor Law relief exceeded one million, and over fifty unions were financially insolvent. Regardless of the widespread suffering, the Prime Minister, Russell, believed that the small and unsuccessful rebellion that had taken place at the end of July had totally vanquished sympathy for the poor of Ireland in Britain.[20] Reluctantly, he asked parliament to agree to a small and final grant of £50,000, to assist the Irish unions. To accompany this money, a further tax was imposed on Ireland. The 'rate in aid', was a famine tax on the whole country that was to be redistributed to the most impoverished Poor Law Unions. It proved to be particularly unpopular amongst northern Protestants who resented paying for poor relief in other parts of the country.

The tax signalled the British Government's determination that the burden for financing relief should fall on Irish taxpayers, and not be shared by British ones. Furthermore, the rate in aid exposed the limits of the political union created in 1800. This point was taken up by the two Englishmen who were most familiar with the Poor Law, Twistleton and Nicholls. Nicholls viewed the tax as an 'alarming response' to the situation within Ireland, which he believed

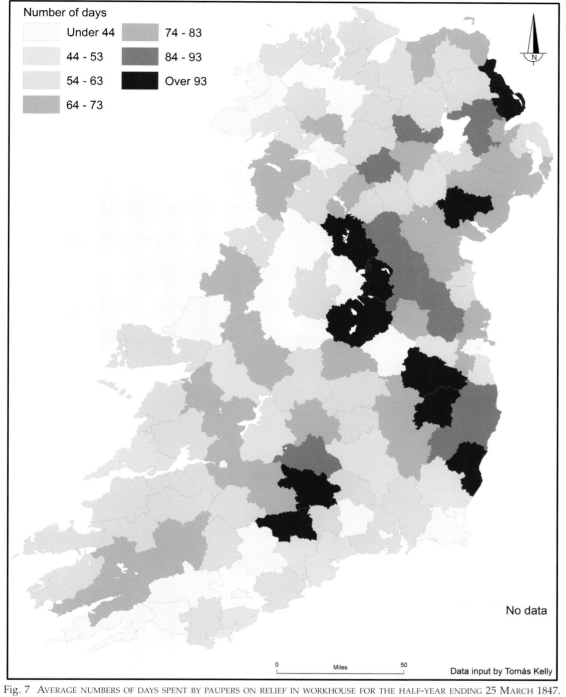

Number of days

Under 44
44 - 53
54 - 63
64 - 73
74 - 83
84 - 93
Over 93

No data

Data input by Tomás Kelly

Fig. 7 AVERAGE NUMBERS OF DAYS SPENT BY PAUPERS ON RELIEF IN WORKHOUSE FOR THE HALF-YEAR ENDING 25 MARCH 1847. Admissions to and deaths in Irish workhouses have naturally received more attention than the routine business of whether paupers remained in, discharged themselves or were discharged from the union workhouse. This map provides some clues to these latter behaviour patterns for the half-year ending 25 March, 1847, i.e. for c.132.5 days. In Baltinglass and Dunmanway unions, the average number of days of relief for each pauper was 127 and 131 respectively, suggesting the great majority of inmates – averaging 715 in Baltinglass and 3,124 in Dunmanway – remained in situ for this half-year. In contrast, the average number of days of relief for each pauper in Tuam workhouse was only 34 – suggesting a much more rapid turnover amongst its 1829 inmates. (It is difficult to establish if this average figure includes deaths as well as discharges.) Other unions characterised by very long stays (over 100 days) amongst their inmates include Cashel, Larne and Oldcastle, while those receiving relief for the half-year in Antrim, Bailieborough, Cavan, Clogheen, Cootehill, Gorey, Kells and Mullingar, Naas, Navan, Newry and Rathdrum did so for over 90 days. At the other end of the spectrum, the average number of days of relief for each pauper in Bantry, Carrick-on-Suir, Donegal, Dungarvan, Enniscorthy, Fermoy, Glenties, Kilkenny, Lowtherstown, Macroom and Nenagh was less than 50. As these lists for unions scattered all over the country and this map confirm, there is no immediately recognisable island-wide logic to these patterns of relief days per inmate, whether in relation to the size of the workhouse population or the relative wealth of the respective Poor Law unions. Clearly the policies of different boards of guardians varied although regional clusters with similar patterns are noticeable. Likewise, there is no striking relationship to regional economies – such as male and female harvest workers from the tillage lands over-wintering in the workhouses. There are strong suggestions that longer stays are more closely related to workhouses with smaller populations and shorter stays characteristic of workhouses operating under greater demographic and mortality pressures. Overall, however, a very varied mosaic of behaviours is revealed.

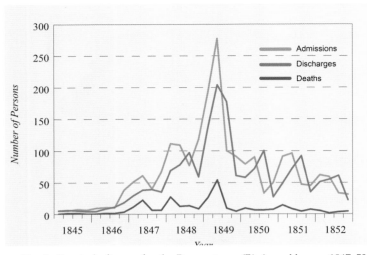

Fig. 8 Quarterly figures for the Parsonstown (Birr) workhouse, 1847–53, showing weekly averages for admissions, discharges and deaths. The TCD/UCD Famine Research Project provides a detailed analysis of the Parsonstown (Birr) workhouse statistics for 1842-55 and particularly 1847–53. After the early intake of paupers in 1842, quarterly admissions and discharges invariably average below 10 in July/Sept 1847. By Oct/December 1846 admissions almost quadrupled to 38 – by Oct/December 1847, 1848 and 1849 admissions averaged 67, 118 and 91 respectively. Admissions peak in April/June 1849 at 277. As the graph shows, substantial discharges of inmates follows closely after peaks in admissions – usually in the harvest months from July and September. For 1847, 1848, 1849 and 1850 discharges in these months rise to averages of 39, 97, 177 and 100 respectively. Eiríksson's analysis of Parsonstown's Indoor Relief Register for 1849 demonstrates that almost two-thirds of those who died in the workhouse did so between the third and sixth week after admission. As Eiríksson suggests: 'rather than being sick on admission most inmates became ill . . . very soon after entering the house' (Eiríksson, 1996). The total workhouse population peaks at 2,509 in April/June 1849. The death rate in the workhouse accelerates from the last quarter in 1846 to as high as 39 per 1,000 inmates in April/June 1849, reaches 25 per 1,000 in Jan/March 1848 and 22 per 1,000 inmates in April/June 1849. Death rates only return to pre-Famine averages in 1852/53.

# ATHY UNION.

**List of Destitute Persons Relieved Out of the Workhouse in the STRADBALLY District, from First Week, ending Saturday, 1st April, to Twenty-first Week, ending Saturday, 19th August, (both included), in the half-year ending 29th September, 1848.**

**STRADBALLY ELECTORAL DIVISION.**

| No. in Family...Name,...Residence. | No. of Weeks, at per week. s. d. | No. of Weeks, at per week. s. d. | No. of Weeks, at per week. s. d. | Total No. of Weeks, and Amount paid. £ s. d. |
|---|---|---|---|---|
| Mary Mason, Stradbally | 21...1 3 | | | 21... 1 6 3 |
| 3 Judith Dowling, do. | 21...2 5 | | | 21... 2 9 10 |
| Mary Foley, do. | 21...1 3 | | | 21.. 1 6 3 |
| Bridget Hanlon, do. | 12...1 0 | | | 12.. 0 12 0 |
| Biddy Dowling, do. | 21...1 3 | | | 21... 1 6 3 |
| Mary M'Cabe, do. | 21...1 3 | | | 21... 1 6 3 |
| Eliza Brenan, do. | 21...1 3 | | | 21... 1 6 3 |
| Eliza Murry, do. | 21...1 3 | | | 21... 1 6 3 |
| Patrick Brophy, do. | 21...1 3 | | | 21... 1 6 3 |
| Catherine Conway, do. | 21...1 3 | | | 21... 1 6 3 |
| Mary M'Evoy, do. | 21...1 3 | | | 21... 1 6 3 |
| 4 CatherineFitzpatrick, do. | 21...3 0 | | | 21... 3 3 0 |
| Margaret Connor, do. | 20...1 3 | | | 20... 1 5 0 |
| Anne Purcell, do. | 21...1 3 | | | 21... 1 6 3 |
| Eliza Quinn, do. | 21.. 1 3 | | | 21... 1 6 3 |
| Martha Gaughen, do. | 5...1 3 | | | 5... 0 6 3 |
| Mary Cody, do. | 21...1 3 | | | 21... 1 6 3 |
| 3 Margaret Lawler, Aughavale | 20...2 9 | | | 20... 2 15 0 |
| Alley Doran, Stradbally, | 21...1 3 | | | 21.. 1 6 3 |
| Margaret Cantwell, do. | 21...1 3 | | | 21 .. 1 6 3 |
| Patrick B——, do. | 21...1 3 | | | 21... 1 6 3 |
| Ellen Carney, do. | 21...1 3 | | | 21.. 1 6 3 |
| 3 Catherine M'Mahon, do. | 21...2 9 | | | 21... 2 17 9 |
| Nancy Brennan, do. | 16...1 3 | | | 16... 1 0 0 |
| Judy Kennedy, do. | 21...1 3 | | | 21... 1 6 3 |
| Mary Butler, do. | 21 .1 3 | | | 21... 1 6 3 |
| 3 Anne Bailey, do. | 21...2 5 | | | 21... 2 9 10 |
| Biddy Moore, do. | 21...1 3 | | | 21... 1 6 3 |
| James Buggy, do. | 21...1 3 | | | 21... 1 6 3 |
| Dennis Holohan, do. | 21...1 3 | | | 21... 1 6 3 |
| Mary Dunne, Stradbally | 21 ..1 3 | | | 21... 1 6 3 |
| Anne Kenna, do. | 21...1 3 | | | 21... 1 6 3 |
| 3 Bridget Redmond, do. | 21...2 6 | | | 21... 2 12 6 |
| Catherine Carroll, do. | 21...1 3 | | | 21... 1 6 3 |
| 4 Rose Brenan, do. | 21...3 0 | | | 21... 3 3 0 |
| 4 Mary Healy, do. | 21...3 0 | | | 21.. 3 3 0 |
| 4 Ellen Dowling do. | 21...3 0 | | | 21... 3 3 0 |
| Judith Cahill, do. | 21...1 3 | | | 21... 1 6 3 |
| John Keeffe, do. | 21...1 3 | | | 21... 1 6 3 |
| Margaret Bond, Garrons | 12...1 3 | | | 12... 0 15 0 |
| Margaret Moore, Stradbally | 21...1 3 | | | 21... 1 6 3 |
| Jane Coffey, do. | 21..1 3 | | | 21... 1 6 3 |
| 4 Ellen Shirley, Garrons | 18 ..3 0 | 2 ..1 6 | | 20 .. 2 17 0 |
| James Broider, Stradbally | 21...1 3 | | | 21... 1 6 3 |
| Margaret Bourke, do. | 21...1 3 | | | 21.. 1 6 3 |
| James Flaherty, do. | 21...1 3 | | | 21... 1 6 3 |
| 4 Jane Cavanagh, Inch | 21...3 0 | | | 21... 3 3 0 |
| 3 Catherine Hyland, ditto | 18.. 2 5 | | | 21.. 2 3 6 |
| Nancy Moore, Stradbally | 21—1 3 | | | 21... 1 6 3 |
| Mary Carey, do. | 21...1 3 | | | 21 . 1 6 3 |
| Matt Moore, do. | 5...1 3 | | | 5... 0 7 6 |
| Betty Lennon, Inch | 21...1 3 | | | 21... 1 6 3 |
| Mary Dempsey, do. | 21.. 1 3 | | | 21... 1 6 3 |
| 4 Biddy Scully, do. | 21...3 0 | | | 21... 3 3 0 |
| 4 Eliza Dunne, do. | 21...3 0 | | | 21.. 3 3 0 |
| Mary Cosker, Garrons | 21...1 3 | | | 21.. 1 6 3 |
| Nancy Doran, Stradbally | 21...1 0 | | | 21.. 1 1 0 |
| 3 Judy Curran, do | ...2 5 | | | ... 1 18 9 |
| Margt. Cavanagh, do. | 21.. 1 3 | | | 21.. 1 6 3 |
| 3 Biddy Whelan, do. | 21...2 4 | | | 21... 2 9 0 |
| 2 Thomas Delany, do. | 20..2 6 | | | 20.. 2 10 0 |
| Biddy Malone, do. | 21 ..1 3 | | | 21.. 1 6 3 |
| 3 James Hayes, Rathmore | 21...2 6 | | | 21... 2 12 6 |
| Catherine Mulhall, do. | 21...1 3 | | | 21... 1 6 3 |
| 5 Sally Reid, Stradbally | 14...3 5 | 2.. 2 0 | | 16... 2 11 10 |
| Mary Purcell, do. | 12.. 1 3 | | | 12... 0 15 0 |
| 2 Richard Meehan, do. | 20 ..2 6 | | | 20... 2 10 0 |
| Betty Kelly, do. | 21...1 3 | | | 21.. 1 6 3 |
| 2 Biddy Dowling, do. | 21...1 6 | | | 21.. 1 11 6 |
| Catherine Conolly, do. | 21...1 3 | | | 21 .. 1 6 3 |
| 7 Henry Byrne, Aughvale | 9...3 6 | 2...3 0 | | 11.. 1 14 6 |
| Judy Leigh, Inch | 21...1 3 | | | 21... 1 6 3 |
| 2 Martin Kehoe, Stradbally | 21...2 6 | | | 21.. 2 12 6 |
| Fanny Byrne, do. | 21...1 3 | | | 21.. 1 6 3 |
| 7 John Neill, do. | 13...4 0 | 8...2 0 | | 21... 3 8 0 |
| 4 Honor Stapleton, Inch | 21...3 0 | | | 21... 3 3 0 |
| Betty Cashen, Garrons | 21...1 3 | | | 21... 1 6 3 |
| Ennis Lag, do | 11...1 0 | | | 11... 0 11 0 |
| Judy Farrell, Aughvale | 21...1 0 | | | 21... 1 1 0 |
| Luke Fennelly, Stradbally | 21...1 3 | | | 21 .. 1 6 3 |
| Essy Scully, Inch | 21...1 0 | | | 21... 1 1 0 |
| 3 James M'Donald, Inch | 11...2 6 | 1...1 6 | | 12... 1 9 0 |
| Sally Carroll, Stradbally | 21...1 3 | | | 21 .. 1 6 3 |
| 2 Mick M'Loughlin, do. | 15.. 2 6 | | | 15... 1 17 6 |
| 6 Patt Flanagan, do. | 15...3 0 | | | 15... 2 5 0 |
| 2 Patt Fingleton, do. | 14...2 0 | | | 14.. 1 8 0 |
| Margaret Conolly, do. | 21 ..1 0 | | | 21... 1 1 0 |
| Maria Whelan, do. | 21...1 3 | | | 21.. 1 6 3 |
| 2 Patrick Minton, do. | 14...2 6 | 7.. 1 3 | | 21.. 2 3 9 |
| William Quinn, do. | 21...1 3 | | | 21.. 1 6 3 |
| William Moore, do. | 4 ..1 3 | | | 4... 0 5 0 |
| 5 John Paisley, do. | 14...3 0 | | | 14.. 2 2 0 |
| Mary Wall, do. | 21..1 0 | | | 21 . 1 1 0 |
| James Egan, do. | 2...1 0 | | | 2... 0 2 0 |
| Thomas Dwyer, do. | 21..1 3 | | | 21.. 1 6 3 |
| 3 Martin Mackessy, do. | 19...1 10 | | | 19... 1 14 10 |
| 4 James Boe, Garrons | 19...2 5 | 1., 3 0 | | 20... 2 8 11 |
| John Maher, do. | 6...1 3 | | | 6... 0 7 6 |
| 4 William Moore, do. | 4..3 0 | | | 4... 0 12 0 |
| Mary Cody, Stradbally | 21...1 3 | | | 21... 1 6 3 |
| Betty Large, do. | 15. .1 0 | | | 15... 0 15 0 |
| Ellen Phillips, do. | 21...1 3 | | | 21... 1 6 3 |
| 3 Betty Donahoe, Inch | 21 ..2 6 | | | 21.. 2 12 6 |
| 5 Barny Gannon, Stradbally | 13...3 0 | | | 13.. 1 19 0 |
| Mary Byrne, do. | 21...1 3 | | | 21.. 1 6 3 |
| Biddy Corcoran, do. | 21...1 3 | | | 21... 1 6 3 |
| Mary, Wall, do. | 21...1 3 | | | 21... 1 6 3 |
| 4 Michael M'Cabe, do. | 3...3 6 | 7...3 0 | 9...2 3 | 19... 2 11 9 |
| William Devoy, do. | 21...1 3 | | | 21.. 1 6 3 |
| 4 Michael Murphy, do. | 13...3 0 | | | 13.. 1 19 0 |
| 3 Edward Goulding, Garrons | 17...2 6 | | | 17... 2 2 6 |
| Mary Doyle, do. | 17.. 1 3 | | | 17 .. 1 1 3 |
| Mary Moore, Stradbally, | 16...1 3 | | | 16 .. 1 0 0 |
| Catherine Chambers, do. | 16,. 1 3 | | | 16... 1 0 0 |
| Edward Lyons, do. | 16...1 0 | | | 16... 0 16 0 |
| Catherine Whelan, do. | 7 ..1 3 | | | 7.. 0 8 9 |
| Catherine Carry, Garrons | 15...1 3 | | | 15... 0 18 9 |
| Anne Carry, do. | 15...1 3 | | | 15... 0 18 9 |
| 3 Ellen Ryan, Stradbally | 14 . 2 5 | | | 14... 1 15 0 |
| Anne Cahill, do. | 5...1 10 | 5.. 1 3 | | 10... 0 15 5 |
| 2 Judy Gannon, Rathmore | 12...1 6 | | | 12... 0 18 0 |
| John Maher, Stradbally | 11...1 3 | | | 11... 0 13 9 |
| 3 Thomas Butler, do. | 11.. 2 0 | | | 11... 1 2 0 |
| Anne Paisley, Stradbally | 11 ..1 3 | | | 11 . 0 13 9 |
| Judy Gorman, do. | 4...1 3 | | | 4... 0 5 0 |
| 3 John Porter, do. | 5...2 6 | | | 5 . 0 12 6 |
| 5 Michael Keating, do. | 6...4 0 | | | 6... 1 4 0 |
| John Scurlock, do. | 6...1 3 | | | 6... 0 7 6 |
| 4 Patt Lawlor, do. | 8...3 0 | | | 8 .. 1 4 0 |
| 3 Alley Carney, Rathmore | 4...2 3 | 4.. 1 3 | | 8 .. 0 14 0 |
| William Whelan, Stradbally | 8..1 0 | | | 8... 0 8 0 |
| Mary Cavanagh, Garrons | 8...1 3 | | | 8... 0 10 0 |
| Patrick Coffey, Stradbally | 4...1 3 | | | 4... 0 5 0 |
| 4 Bryan Kenny, do. | 3...2 6 | 3...2 0 | | 6... 0 13 6 |
| 4 Edward Brennan, do. | 6...2 6 | | | 6 .. 0 15 0 |
| 3 Bridget Crossin, Garrons | 3...2 6 | 3..2 0 | | 6... 0 13 6 |
| 2 David Smith, Stradbally | 4...2 0 | | | 4.. 0 8 0 |
| Richard Green, do. | 3...1 3 | | | 3... 0 3 9 |
| 4 Patt Fitzpatrick, do. | 7..3 0 | | | 7... 1 1 0 |
| Michael Walsh, Garrons, | 7...1 3 | | | 7... 0 8 9 |
| James Paisley, Stradbally | 5...1 0 | | | 5... 0 5 0 |
| 3 Judy Fennelly, do. | 7.. 1 6 | | | 7. . 0 10 6 |
| Biddy Moore, Inch | 5...1 0 | | | 5.. 0 5 0 |
| John Neil, Stradbally | 4...1 3 | | | 4... 0 5 0 |
| Judy Moran, do. | 5...1 3 | | | 5... 0 6 3 |
| 2 Patt Gorman, do. | 5...2 6 | | | 5... 0 12 6 |
| Mary Flanagan, Garrons | 5...1 0 | | | 5... 0 5 0 |
| 6 Patt Byrne, Aughvale | 5 . 4 0 | | | 5 .. 1 0 0 |
| 4 William Carroll, Stradbally | 2 ..3 0 | 1..1 6 | | 3... 0 7 6 |
| 4 John Campion, do. | 4...2 6 | | | 4... 0 10 0 |
| Michael Curran, do. | 3..1 3 | | | 3... 0 3 9 |
| Mary Hyland, Garrons | 2.. 1 3 | | | 2 .. 0 2 6 |
| Edward Carroll, Stradbally | 2...1 3 | | | 0... 0 2 6 |

**MOYANNA ELECTORAL DIVISION.**

| No. in Family...Name...Residence. | No. of Weeks, at per week. s. d. | No. of Weeks, at per week. s. d. | No. of Weeks, at per week. s. d. | Total No. of Weeks, and Amount paid. £ s. d. |
|---|---|---|---|---|
| Mary Lalor, Killeen, | 21...1 3 | | | 21 . 1 6 3 |
| Biddy Regan, do. | 20...1 3 | | | 20 .. 1 5 0 |
| 2 Catherine Bryan, Ballythomas | 14..1 6 | 7...2 0 | | 21... 1 15 0 |
| Mary Neil, Rosnamullin | 21...1 3 | | | 21.. 1 6 3 |
| 4 Mary Mullhall, Ballyrider, | 21.. 3 0 | | | 21 .. 3 3 0 |
| 3 Michael Deegan, do. | 21...2 5 | | | 21... 2 10 9 |
| 4 James Redmond, Tomfarna | 14...3 0 | | | 14... 2 2 0 |
| Margaret Deeran, do. | 4.. 2 0 | 13.. 1 0 | | 17 .. 1 1 0 |
| William Carr, Garrymaddock | 10.. 1 3 | | | 10... 0 12 6 |
| 3 Andrew Roe, do. | 11...2 0 | | | 11... 1 2 0 |
| Catherine Farrell, Mullen | 21...1 3 | | | 21... 1 6 3 |
| 6 Biddy Connor, Vicarstown | 21..3 7 | | | 21... 3 15 3 |
| 2 Mary Whelan, Moyanna | 21.. 1 6 | | | 21... 1 11 6 |
| Biddy Moore, Garrymaddock | 21...1 3 | | | 21... 1 6 3 |
| 3 Mary Bailey, Garrymaddock | 21...2 5 | | | 21... 2 10 9 |
| 2 Harry Casey, Garrymaddock | 21...2 0 | | | 21... 2 12 6 |
| 6 Joseph Gannon, Mullen, | 21 ..3 8 | | | 21... 3 17 0 |
| Betty Bourke, Garrymaddock | 21...1 3 | | | 21... 1 6 3 |
| 4 Biddy Feeney, Mullen | 21...3 0 | | | 21... 3 3 0 |
| Biddy Buggy, do. | 21...1 3 | | | 21... 1 6 3 |
| 3 Margaret Sheppard, Killeen | 20...2 5 | | | 20.. 2 8 4 |
| Margaret Cranny, do. | 21...1 3 | | | 21 .. 1 6 3 |
| 6 Thomas Baillie do. | 19...4 0 | | | 19... 3 16 0 |
| Catherine Whelan, Inch | 21...1 3 | | | 21... 1 6 3 |
| 3 Mick Doran, Ross | 21...3 1 | | | 21... 3 4 9 |
| 3 Margaret Moran, Ballyrider | 21...2 5 | | | 21... 2 10 9 |
| 3 James Connor, Moyanna | 21.. 2 0 | | | 21... 2 2 0 |
| Patt Deegan, do. | 21...1 3 | | | 21... 1 6 3 |
| 4 Michael Lewis, Ballyrider | 17...2 5 | | | 17.. 2 1 1 |
| Denis Mullhall, do. | 19...1 3 | | | 19... 1 3 9 |
| Betty Byrne, do. | 21...1 3 | | | 21... 1 6 9 |
| George Lewis, do. | 21.. 1 3 | | | 21.. 1 6 3 |
| Mary M'Cabe, do. | 21...1 3 | | | 21... 1 6 3 |
| Alley Farrell, do. | 6..1 3 | | | 6 . 0 7 6 |
| Mary White, do | 21..1 3 | | | 21... 1 6 3 |
| 5 Ned Mullowney, Moyanna | 3 ..3 0 | 4.. 2 6 | 2 ..2 0 | 9... 1 5 0 |
| Margaret M'Donald, do. | 21.. 1 3 | | | 21... 1 6 3 |
| Nancy Kelly, Vicarstown | 21..1 0 | | | 21 .. 1 1 0 |
| 5 Laurence Dunne, Mullen, | 18...3 0 | | | 18. . 2 14 0 |

Fig. 9 List of destitute persons relieved out of the workhouse in the Stradbally district (Athy Union), 1 April 1848 to 19 August 1848 (21 weeks). This list provides the number in each family group, names and addresses of families and other adult inmates, their maintenance cost per week and the total cost for the 21 weeks involved. Rather surprisingly, there is very little difference in the size of families headed by a mother/female (3.5) and those headed by a father/male (3.4). Families of all kinds comprised 73.2% of the total inmate population, of which 57.8% were children. Heads of families comprise 36.4% of the total number of adult inmates so close on two-thirds were other individual adults. As many as 74% of this latter group were women. However, judging by the fact that the great majority of these women were resident for all of the 21 weeks, this list does not suggest that many women came and went to and from the workhouse during the sowing and harvesting season as has been suggested elsewhere. The composition of the Moyanna electoral division (part of) reveals the same patterns as Stradbally. Overall, the ancient family names of this locality – the Moores, Dowlings, Byrnes and Cavanaghs – are well represented in this list. However, the dominant pattern is of a diversity of family names, the great majority of which appear to be of Catholic-Irish origin. [Source: National Library of Ireland]

should be treated as an 'imperial calamity'.[21] Twistleton, who had frequently clashed with the Treasury over the parsimonious way in which the latter had released funding, believed that this exclusively-Irish tax was a betrayal of the Act of Union. He resigned in protest at its introduction. In the same year, he made an impassioned plea for the British Government to

> spare itself the deep disgrace of permitting any of our miserable fellow subjects in the Distressed Unions to die of starvation. I wish to leave distinctly on record that, from want of sufficient food, many persons in these Unions are at present dying or wasting away; and, at the same time, it is quite possible for this country to prevent the occurrence there of any death from starvation, by the advance of a few hundred pounds.[22]

Despite the unpopularity of the rate in aid, a second one was introduced in 1850.

After 1850 the pressure on the Poor Law started to ease with the return of better harvests, although pockets of severe distress remained, notably in Kilrush Union in County Clare, which lost an estimated 50% of its people between 1846 and 1851. Although the demand for relief declined, the numbers in the workhouses in the 1850s remained higher than they had been prior to 1845.

In 1837, George Nicholls, the man responsible for introducing the Poor Law to Ireland, had warned of the limitations of having a self-financing relief system during a period of famine, pointing out that, 'where the land has ceased to be reproductive, the necessary means of relief can no longer be obtained from it and a Poor Law will no longer be operative'.[23] At this stage, nobody could have foreseen the tragedy that was to unfold in Ireland only a few years later. After 1845, the Poor Law provided Ireland with an administrative structure and a network for providing assistance, but as Nicholls had pointed out, there were limits on its financial capacity. Yet, this fact was ignored by the British Government as they sought to transfer the responsibility for financing relief to local tax payers, irrespective of the latter's resources. After 1847, financial and ideological concerns, rather than humanitarian ones, shaped the way in which relief was provided.

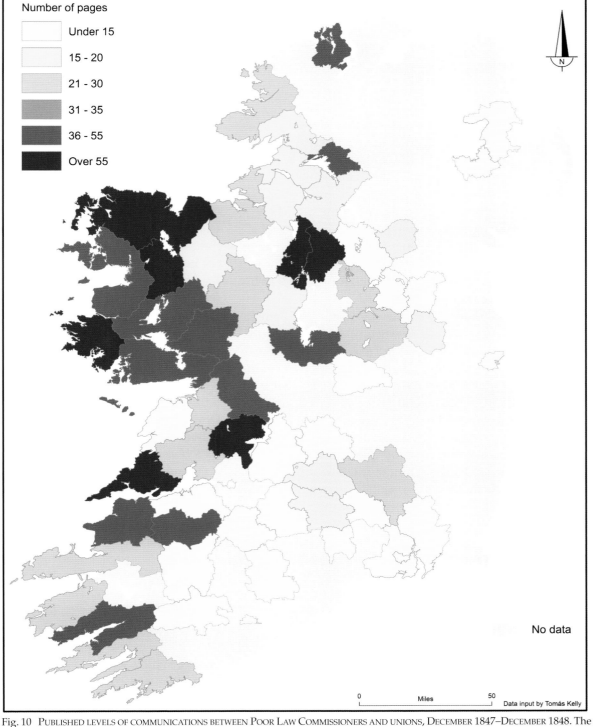

Number of pages

Under 15

15 - 20

21 - 30

31 - 35

36 - 55

Over 55

No data

0    Miles    50

Data input by Tomás Kelly

Fig. 10 PUBLISHED LEVELS OF COMMUNICATIONS BETWEEN POOR LAW COMMISSIONERS AND UNIONS, DECEMBER 1847–DECEMBER 1848. The board of guardians in every Poor Law Union were under the jurisdiction of the Poor Law Commissioner, first directly from London but from Dublin after the establishment of the Irish Poor Law Commissioners in 1847. The level of monitoring and surveillance of the unions by the Poor Law Commissioners – in turn governed by the London's Treasury department and in particular Trevelyan's office – was always immediate but grew in scale and intensity after the legislative changes in the spring/summer of 1847. This map illustrates the scale of communications (as measured in the number of published pages) between the Poor Law Commissioners (PLCs) and the unions from December 1847. Most of the unions of Ulster, Leinster and south Munster seemed to have escaped the often severe critiques – if sometimes encouragement – of the PLC. In contrast, most of the unions in Connacht and the northwest generally, Clare, west Munster and pockets along the Tipperary/Kilkenny borders were under severe scrutiny. In particular, Ballina, Castlebar, Clifden, Carrick-on-Shannon, Mohill, Scariff and Kilrush – characterised by poor rate returns, overcrowding, high mortalities and mismanagement – were involved in a vast correspondence with the PLC. Likewise, Westport, Ballinrobe, Galway, Tuam, Loughrea, Listowel, Newcastlewest and Kenmare all received strictures with regard to a whole range of issues. Overall, the map highlights the regions and localities where unions and workhouses were under most stress from the Famine catastrophe.

The death and emigration of so many people was less due to the failure of the Poor Law than to the failure to treat the Irish poor as deserving of not only a right to relief, but also of a right to life.

# Queen Victoria and the Great Famine

## Christine Kinealy

In Irish popular memory, Queen Victoria is remembered as the 'Famine Queen'. Consequently, her sixty-three-year-long sovereignty is defined by a catastrophe that occurred early in her reign. A number of myths about her alleged parsimony during the Great Famine have arisen also, some of which have roots in popular traditions of the time. Beliefs regarding her lack of compassion were subsequently embellished and politicised by nationalists. In 1880, at the time of another subsistence crisis, Charles Stewart Parnell described Victoria as 'the only sovereign of Europe who gave nothing out of her private purse'.[1]

Even more damning was the sobriquet, 'the Famine Queen', which resulted from an article of this name written by Maud Gonne and published in Ireland in 1900. It was banned by the British authorities, thus giving it more notoriety than it may otherwise have warranted. This view of Victoria as a heartless and indifferent monarch during the Great Hunger has proved to be enduring. During the Irish Republic's sesquicentenary commemoration between 1995 and 1997, the decision to display a statue of the young Queen in University College Cork resulted in bitter controversy.[2] As recently as 2003, the unveiling of a restored fountain to Queen Victoria was picketed on the grounds that

> The people in Dún Laoghaire and beyond are genuinely appalled that a monument that commemorates and celebrates the British monarch who reigned in this country during the time of the Famine, when over a million Irish people starved to death, has been rebuilt in the town.[3]

The memory and controversy surrounding Victoria's role during the Famine rarely point to the complexity of her involvement or the fact that many nationalists of that period were monarchists. At the time, it was suspected by some in Ireland that she had wanted to give more assistance, but had been prevented from doing so by her ministers.[4]

### VICTORIA'S GIFT

When the potato blight first appeared in Ireland in 1845, Victoria was aged twenty-six and had been on the throne for eight years. She had never visited Ireland. The Queen became directly involved with the tragedy in Ireland at the beginning of 1847 when she was named as the first person to donate to the newly-formed British Association for the Relief of Distress in Ireland and Scotland. In fact, her £2,000 gift made her the largest individual contributor to famine relief. In the same year, Victoria issued two official letters to Anglicans asking them to contribute to Irish distress and calling for a day of Fast and Humiliation on 24 March. The first appeal raised almost £172,000. The second appeal, made in October, raised only £30,000. Moreover, the Queen was criticized within Britain, with attacks led by the London *Times,* for helping to perpetuate Irish dependence on the people of Britain.[5]

Victoria visited Ireland for the first time in 1849. Despite the easy crushing of the Young Ireland rebellion in the previous year, the political situation remained unstable. Four leaders of Young Ireland had been sentenced to be hanged but, in advance of the Queen's visit, their sentence was commuted to transportation to Van Diemen's Land. However, habeas corpus remained in place and inflamed sectarian tensions had resulted in the killing of five Catholics by Orangemen in Dolly's Brae, County Down, during their annual commemoration of the Battle of the Boyne.[6] Victoria's visit coincided with the introduction of the 'rate in aid', a famine tax on the whole country that was particularly unpopular amongst northern Protestants who resented paying for relief in other parts of the country.

Victoria's itinerary was confined to the east coast, with visits to Cork, Dublin and Belfast. She travelled to these locations by yacht, not overland. Additional troops and constabulary were deployed to each place she visited.[7] Despite the political tensions and the continuation of famine in many parts of the country, for the most part, Victoria was warmly greeted. Her visit to Cork was marked by the donation to the newly-opened university of a statue of the Queen, which was removed in 1934 and buried in the grounds of the college – the retrieval of the same statue would cause controversy in 1995. The young Queen seemed delighted with her reception, writing to her uncle, King Leopold I of Belgium:

> Everything here has gone beautifully since we arrived in Ireland, and our entrance to Dublin was really a magnificent thing . . . Our visit to Cork was very successful . . . the enthusiasm is immense . . . The entrance at seven o'clock into Kingston Harbour was splendid; we came in with ten steamers, and the whole harbour, wharf and every surrounding place was *covered* with *thousands* of people, who received us with the greatest enthusiasm.[8]

Fig. 1 Queen Victoria visited Ireland for the final time in 1900. To mark the visit the Royal Dublin Society decided to erect a statue in her honour outside its headquarters at Leinster House. The statue was sculpted by John Hughes RHA and unveiled in 1908. Its tenure outside Leinster House (above) lasted until July 1948 when it was removed and placed in storage in the Royal Hospital Kilmainham, its removal very much reflecting the changed political landscape in Ireland. (Part of Leinster House was used by the Free State Government in 1922 for parliamentary purposes. The entire building was acquired in 1924 becoming the seat of the Irish Parliament). The statue was later stored at the disused reformatory school building at Daingean, County Offaly, before finding its present location outside the Queen Victoria Building (QVB) shopping mall in Sydney, Australia. [Photo: National Library of Ireland]

Victoria appeared less impressed with her visit to Belfast. While she had commented on the beauty of the Irish women in Cork and Dublin, she wrote of her visit to the northern town, 'The people are a mixture of nations, and the female beauty has almost disappeared.'[9]

### DIVIDED OPINION

Despite Victoria's warm reception by the Irish people, her visit had divided opinion, especially amongst the hierarchy of the main churches. The Archbishop of Cashel, Michael Slattery, accused her of 'indifference' to the Irish poor, while John MacHale of Tuam refused to sign the welcome address to Dublin. In Belfast, however, she was warmly welcomed by members of the local Catholic Church. In contrast, she was shunned by Dr Drew, leader of the Anglican Church, in protest at the non-denominational character of the new Queen's colleges. Controversially also, the royal party refused an invitation to visit the town's Deaf and Dumb Institute when it was pointed out the school was exclusively Protestant and opposed to inter-denominational education.[10] Following her brief visit in 1849, Victoria never

returned to Belfast, despite the town's overt assertions of loyalty to the monarchy and the Union.

From on board a prison ship in Bermuda, the exiled Young Irelander, John Mitchel, noted Victoria's visit to Ireland in his jail journal. He commented acerbically that, 'Loyalty, you are to know, consists in a willingness to come out into the street and see a pageant pass.' He added:

> After a few years, however, it is understood that her majesty will visit the west. The human inhabitants are expected by that time to have been sufficiently thinned, and the deer and other game to have proportionately multiplied. Prince Albert will then take a hunting lodge in Connemara.[11]

Mitchel's comments were a foretaste of the attitudes of a later generation of 'advanced' nationalists.

Victoria spent eight days in Ireland in 1849. Economic regeneration did not follow the Queen's first visit. High levels of eviction, emigration and excess mortality continued, demonstrating that the Famine was far from over. The death, these competing visions contributed to the partition of Ireland.

## STATUES AND MONUMENTS

In post-independence Ireland, statues of and monuments to British monarchs and war heroes were a reminder of Ireland's colonial past.[14] In the case of Queen Victoria, they symbolised a period of Irish history which encapsulated British misrule – and for which she – rather than her male politicians and civil servants – had become personally responsible. Her gender did not protect her from blame and opprobrium, Gonne opining that

Fig. 2 Queen Victoria statue residing at her present location outside the QVB shopping mall, across from the Sydney Town Hall on Bicentennial Square. [Photo: Kevin Kenna]

in the decrepitude of her eighty-one years, to have decided after an absence of half a century to revisit the country she hates and whose inhabitants are the victims of the criminal policy of her reign, the survivors of sixty years of organised famine, the political necessity must have been terribly strong; for after all she is a woman, and however vile and selfish and pitiless her soul may be, she must sometimes tremble as death approaches when she thinks of the countless mothers who, shelterless under the cloudy Irish sky, watching their little starving ones, have cursed her before they died.[15]

remaining years of Queen Victoria's reign were marked by continued demographic decline, poverty and intermittent food shortages in Ireland. Victoria revisited Ireland in 1853, 1861 and 1901, but in total, she spent less than two months in the country.[12] During the years between her first and final visit, attitudes of nationalists towards the monarchy changed, with even constitutional nationalists questioning the future of a British monarch in an independent Ireland.[13] During Victoria's reign also, unionism became more allied with monarchy and empire. In the decades after Victoria's

Queen Victoria remains a divisive figure in Ireland as the erection and removal of several of her statues has shown. Nationalist opposition to the monarchy has been shaped by a powerful (if not totally accurate) narrative of the Queen's role during the Famine. However, the reality of the role played by the 'Famine Queen' is far more complex than this title would suggest.

# Burying and resurrecting the past:
## the Queen Victoria statue in University College Cork

### John Crowley

The history of the Queen Victoria statue in University College Cork provides an insight into the role of symbolism in Ireland. University College Cork (UCC) or Queen's College, Cork, as it was originally named, was built during the Famine years. The statue of a young Queen Victoria was presented to the college by its principal architect, Sir Thomas Deane, in 1849 and occupied a central position at the university, located on top of the eastern gable of the Aula Maxima. Its chequered history from that date reflects the changing political climate in Ireland. With the emergence of an independent state in 1922 there was little time and space for monuments which reminded the people of their colonial past and in particular a monarch whose reputation as the 'Famine Queen' was already copper fastened in the eyes of nationalists.[1] The statue was removed in 1934 and replaced by a statue of Saint Finbarr, the local patron saint, by a young Cork sculptor, Seamus Murphy. It was a decision very much in keeping with the mood of Catholic triumphalism which prevailed in the newly independent state.[2]

The Victoria statue was put into storage and later buried in the grounds of the President's garden in UCC. As part of the university's sesquicentennial anniversary in 1995, a decision was taken by the governing body to exhume the statue and it was proposed that it would become part of the 'Universitas' exhibition that documented and celebrated the history of the university from its foundation. The decision provoked an angry response from a number of individuals. A series of letters appeared in the local newspaper, the *Cork Examiner*, which condemned the decision based primarily on the fact that Victoria had presided over the most tragic event in Irish history. The college defended the decision on the grounds that the 150th anniversary of the founding of the university was an appropriate time to examine its own past and that the statue was a significant artefact belonging to that history. The college authorities sought to deflect criticism by widening the discussion to include attitudes towards other symbols on the island of Ireland in what was then a burgeoning climate of hope fostered by the Peace Process. Given that important context, people could afford to look at monuments that were previously ignored or neglected in a new light. As a piece of sculpture the statue is not of great artistic merit but its symbolism runs deep. In Irish

folklore Victoria, along with Trevelyan, came to personify official British indifference towards the suffering in Ireland during the Famine years. Even today it is difficult to change that perception.

Fig. 1 Statue of Queen Victoria in University College Cork sculpted by Edward Ambrose. It is now located in the Staff Common room in University College Cork. [Photo: Tomás Tyner]

# The largest amount of good: Quaker relief efforts

*Helen Hatton*

While not the largest relief agency in the field during the Great Famine, the Society of Friends, or Quakers, were the most successful and 165 years on, are still revered by Irish people, who, if asked about the Quakers, invariably answer 'they fed us in the Famine times'. Set up in Dublin on 13 November 1846 to coordinate the work of Quaker auxiliary committees already working in Cork, Clonmel, Waterford and Limerick, the Central Relief Committee of the Society of Friends (CRC) immediately circulated an appeal for funds, food and clothing, with the object of affording 'the largest amount of good with the means at our disposal'.[1] Questionnaires were distributed to those requesting aid, not only to create an accurate record of the dispersal of funds, but to obtain a current and objective picture of Ireland in terms of need and employment. Information in relation to agriculture, specifically the acreage under cultivation, was also collected. Details on cultivation became crucial as the Famine depleted labour and resources.

Quaker investigators travelled throughout Ireland, particularly in the west and south, arranging to work with individuals and local committees where they could be found, and to obtain first-hand information of the true conditions. These reports were immediately published, refuting charges that the distress was exaggerated,[2] and confirming that the failures of

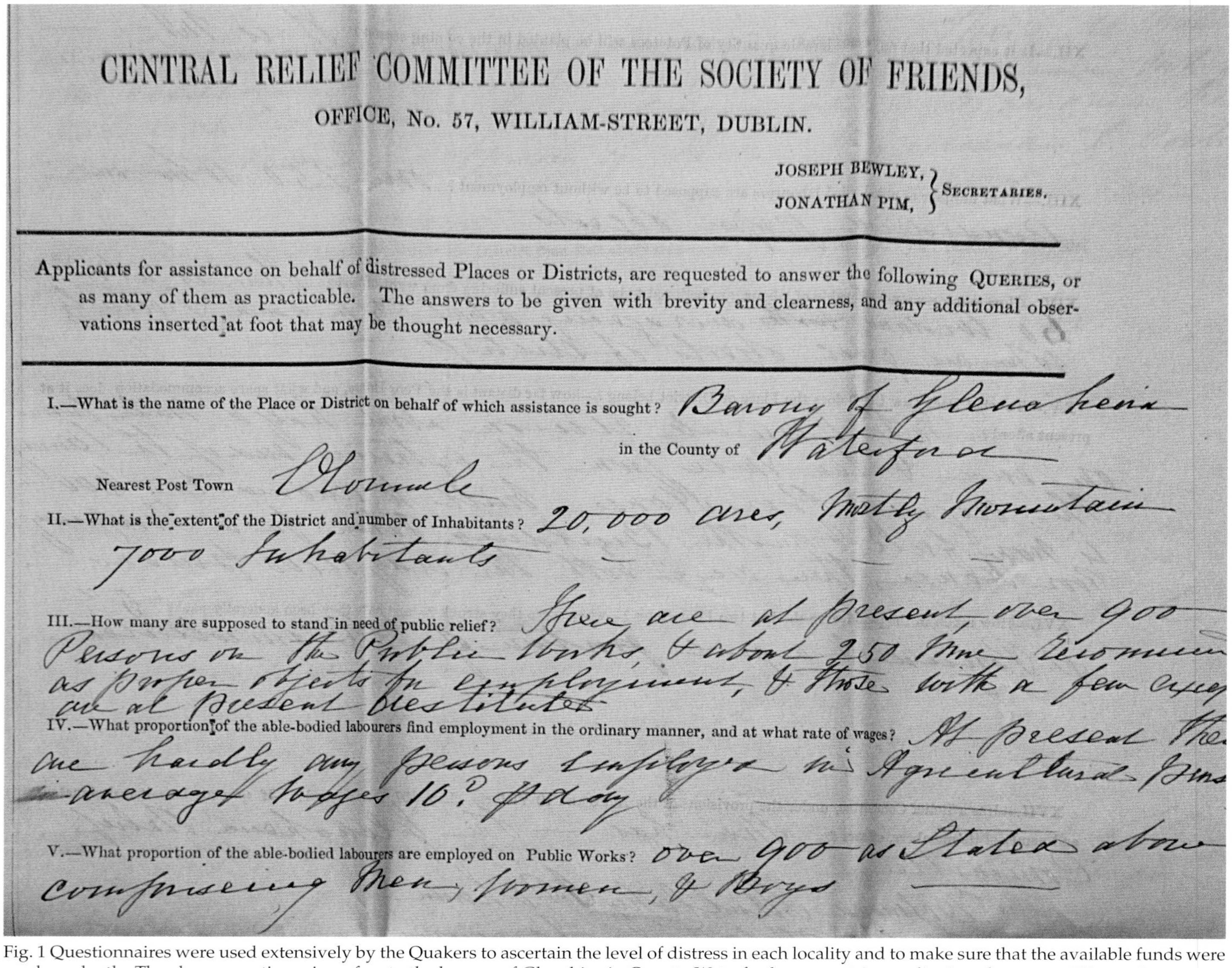
CENTRAL RELIEF COMMITTEE OF THE SOCIETY OF FRIENDS,

OFFICE, No. 57, WILLIAM-STREET, DUBLIN.

JOSEPH BEWLEY, } SECRETARIES.
JONATHAN PIM, }

Applicants for assistance on behalf of distressed Places or Districts, are requested to answer the following QUERIES, or as many of them as practicable. The answers to be given with brevity and clearness, and any additional observations inserted at foot that may be thought necessary.

I.—What is the name of the Place or District on behalf of which assistance is sought? Barony of Glenahiry

in the County of Waterford

Nearest Post Town Clonmel

II.—What is the extent of the District and number of Inhabitants? 20,000 acres, mostly mountain 7000 Inhabitants

III.—How many are supposed to stand in need of public relief? There are at present over 900 Persons on the Public Works, & about 250 more recommended as proper objects for employment, & those with a few exceptions are at present destitute

IV.—What proportion of the able-bodied labourers find employment in the ordinary manner, and at what rate of wages? At present there are hardly any persons employed in Agricultural ... average wages 10d. a day

V.—What proportion of the able-bodied labourers are employed on Public Works? over 900 as stated above comprising Men, Women, & Boys

Fig. 1 Questionnaires were used extensively by the Quakers to ascertain the level of distress in each locality and to make sure that the available funds were used prudently. The above questionnaire refers to the barony of Glenahiry in County Waterford, a mountainous district where over 900 people were on public works, 'comprising men, women and boys.' [Source: Friends Historical Library] the potato crop was a disaster of such proportions that the Quaker appeal was extended to North America. The Quakers are credited with bringing the true state of Ireland to North American attention.[3] A committee of English Quakers in London (London Committee), followed immediately on the organisation of the CRC, to raise funds, coordinate, purchase, and crucially, as the Famine continued, to pressure the Russell Government, whose policies were largely a failure, despite vast sums spent.[4] The Quakers persuaded Russell to release two Admiralty steamers to them to get cargoes into the south and west, and to pay all shipping costs of cargoes consigned to them. Ultimately Russell paid out £33,017 5s 7d on Quaker cargoes,[5] and eventually paid all relief cargo charges.

## QUAKER RELIEF

Quaker relief was distributed in grants of funds, food, clothing and blankets to individuals and committees who could organise relief, but finding individuals in the far west who could manage remained a serious problem. The criteria were complete impartiality in distribution, and return of the Quaker questionnaire. Relief was consistently given to those ineligible for Government measures. No charge of souperism – aid contingent upon attending a Protestant church or school, or even conversion – was ever levelled at the Quakers. Cash grants were:[6]

| | |
|---|---|
| Leinster | £890 12s |
| Connacht | £4,320 5s 11d |
| Ulster | £3,123 14s 5d |
| Munster | £10,062 13s 2d |

As relief supplies poured in from North America (substantial amounts came from Canada as well as the United States of America), as much as possible was given as cooked food, what the Irish people called 'stirabout' and the Friends labelled 'soup'. Huge boilers were distributed, thirty-seven in Leinster, sixty-five in Connacht, thirty-five in Ulster and 137 in Munster. Quaker 'soup' was substantial and sustaining.

RECIPE FOR QUAKER 'SOUP'
100 gallons of water
75 lbs of meat (salt beef or pork)
35 lbs of dried peas
21 lbs each of oatmeal and barley
1½ lbs pepper
14 lbs of salt

This was 'the minimum' requirement for the making of the soup. Other vegetables and grains were added as American supplies arrived, especially rice, beneficial when famine diseases appeared. This was in marked contrast to the highly touted Government 'soup' created by Alexis Soyer, once chef to the Prince Regent, then chef of the Reform Club, at a cost of £1 for 100 gallons, including fuel:

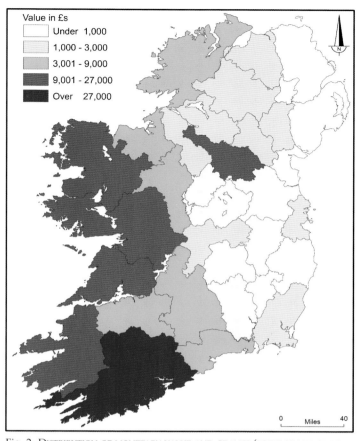

Fig. 2 DISTRIBUTION OF MONETARY VALUE AND GRANTS (TOTAL VALUE OF BOILERS, FOOD AND MONEY) PROVIDED BY THE SOCIETY OF FRIENDS PER COUNTY FROM 11 DECEMBER 1846 TO 1 MAY 1848. This map, showing the total value of specific Quaker relief efforts – whether in the provision of boilers, food and/or monies – both illustrates how well informed the Central Relief Committee of the Society of Friends was about where destitution was greatest during the Famine and its ability to coordinate supplies to the most needy in those areas. Communities in Counties Galway and Mayo in Connacht and Clare, Kerry and especially Cork received the most support from the Quaker relief effort. Interestingly, County Cavan alone in Ulster is singled out for major relief efforts. A middle group of counties from Donegal, through Sligo Roscommon, Tipperary, Limerick and Waterford also received substantial support from the Quakers. In contrast, the remainder of Ulster and much of Leinster were not seen as so critical to Quaker relief efforts. Breaking down these figures it is clear that Munster communities received over half of Quaker cash grants, Connacht almost a quarter, Ulster 17% and Leinster only 5%. Much the same ratios prevailed in the actual provision of food supplies although Leinster improved its share in the provision of huge boilers (to serve the soup kitchens) to 13.5%. It is interesting that Quakers also saw the need to provide clothing grants. Here, Leinster communities received about one-third of this total, Connacht and Munster one-fourth and one-fifth, respectively, and Ulster less than one-fifth of clothing grants. Quaker relief committees were also centrally involved in the provision of seed for green crops and in seeking to revitalise the fisheries along the west and south coast of Ireland. The generosity of the Quakers during the Great Famine is still remembered and honoured by the Irish people.

RECIPE FOR GOVERNMENT 'SOUP'
12½ lbs beef
6¼ lbs dripping
25 lbs each of flour (seconds) and barley
100 onions
1½ lbs brown sugar
9 lbs salt[7]

In weight, food supplies of £148,560 tons were distributed:[8]

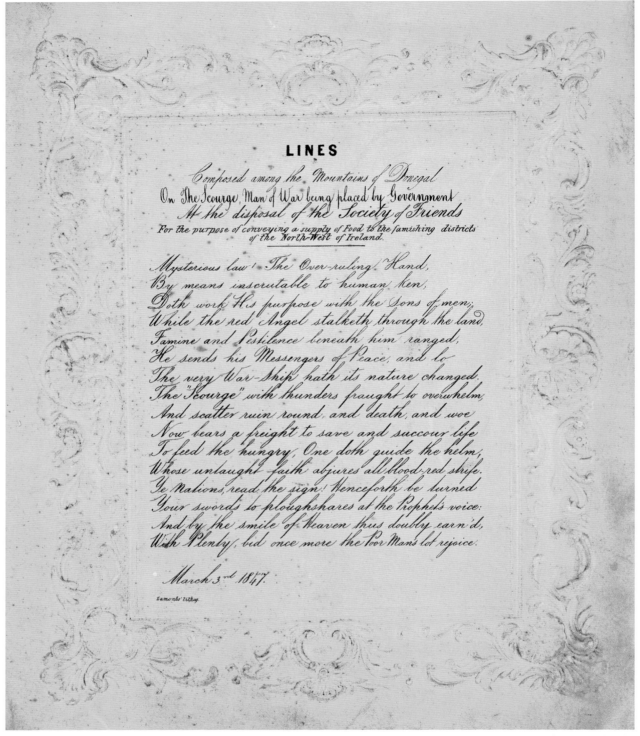

## LINES

Composed among the Mountains of Donegal
On The Scourge, Man of War being placed by Government
At the disposal of the Society of Friends
For the purpose of conveying a supply of Food to the famishing districts
of the North-West of Ireland.

Mysterious law! The Over-ruling Hand,
By means inscrutable to human ken,
Doth work His purpose with the Sons of men;
While the red Angel stalketh through the land,
Famine and Pestilence beneath him ranged,
He sends his Messengers of Peace, and lo
The very War-Ship hath its nature changed.
The "Scourge" with thunders fraught to overwhelm,
And scatter ruin round, and death, and woe
Now bears a freight to save and succour life
To feed the hungry, One doth guide the helm,
Whose untaught faith abjures all blood-red strife.
Ye Nations, read the sign! Henceforth be turned
Your swords to ploughshares at the Prophet's voice:
And by the smile of Heaven thus doubly earn'd,
With Plenty, bid once more the Poor Man's lot rejoice.

March 3rd 1847.

Fig. 3 The Society of Friends was an important agency in getting food to some of the most distressed districts in the west of Ireland. The shipments of food, such as that undertaken by the ship-of-war *The Scourge*, (see praise poem above), which 'was placed by Government at the disposal of the Society of Friends', proved vital in providing relief in counties such as Donegal, which received £8,000 by way of grants of food and money. [Source: National Library of Ireland]

| Leinster | 448 |
|----------|-----|
| Ulster | 1,053 |
| Connacht | 1,849 |
| Munster | 3,852 |

This list does not include hundreds of cargoes for con-signees all over Ireland, shipped to the Quakers because of their reputation for probity, stewardship and lack of bias, which the Quakers delivered. Clothing grants, distributed without charge totalled 668 grants:[9]

| Ulster | 121 |
|--------|-----|
| Munster | 145 |
| Leinster | 224 |
| Connacht | 178 |

In addition, materials were distributed with patterns to provide work for women who were not allowed to participate in the Russell Government's work projects, to make up clothing which was given to the destitute or paid for a penny or two at a time as the recipients earned it. Similarly, hemp was supplied to fisherwomen to make nets for the Quakers' fisheries projects, and shoe leather was supplied to make shoes. Lace-making, spinning, weaving and knitting projects were funded and the London Committee marketed the goods and solicited orders for more. The total expense was £6,333 2s 6d plus a grant of £1,000 to the non-sectarian Ladies Clothing Committee of Ireland,[10] and £500 was granted to the Belfast Ladies Association to establish schools in Connacht to teach women the skills. By 1850, thirty-two schools were operating, earning £1,000 a year, not including the women's wages, amounting to £5,000 a year. The goods produced were in great demand in America, and their work was included in the Great Exhibition of 1851.[11]

## CHALLENGING GOVERNMENT POLICY

In spring 1847 Russell placed the burden of relief on the Irish Poor Law. The CRC continued its policy of subverting the Government strictures that relief could only be given to the totally destitute in the Poor Law Union workhouse, by issuing grants to feed those denied relief. In August 1847, with Government soup kitchens in full operation, the CRC was still spending over £3,083 a week, and continued, with the Union relief in full operation, at over £1,000 a week into April 1848.[12] The Friends refused Russell's request that their resources be given to the unions, because the 1847 Amendment to the Irish Poor Law ordering the union guardians 'to make provision to relieve all the destitute' established the right for support, but with the cost falling on the landholders and not the Government. Government policy had been decreed despite ample advice from Ireland from its own agents as well as Quaker statistics, and the CRC would not ease the Government's responsibility, nor appear to condone the policy by tacitly cooperating.

THE CORK SOCIETY OF FRIENDS' SOUP HOUSE.

Fig. 4 Quaker soup kitchen in Cork city. Quakers were instrumental in establishing soup kitchens across the country, particularly in some of the worst-affected districts. This considerable relief effort was helped substantially by the donation of fifty boilers by the Quaker ironmasters Abraham and Albert Darby. [Source: *The Illustrated London News*, 16 January 1847]

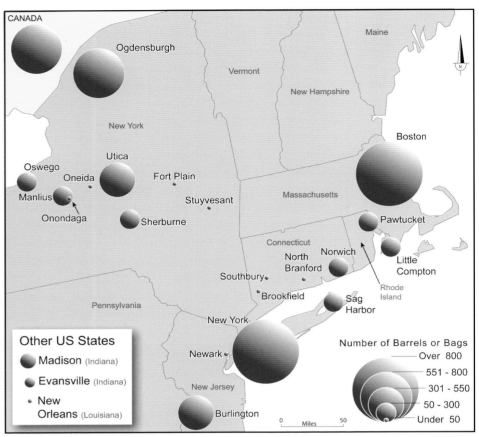

**Other US States**

- Madison (Indiana)
- Evansville (Indiana)
- New Orleans (Louisiana)

Number of Barrels or Bags
- Over 800
- 551 - 800
- 301 - 550
- 50 - 300
- Under 50

Fig. 5 DISTRIBUTION OF CONTRIBUTIONS FROM THE NORTHEASTERN STATES OF NORTH AMERICA FOR QUAKER RELIEF EFFORTS IN IRELAND. Having obtained first-hand information on the true conditions prevailing in Ireland in the autumn of 1846, and having confirmed that the failure of the potato crop was a major disaster for so many of the Irish poor, the Quaker appeal for funds, food and clothing was extended to North America. This map shows some of the originating centres which shipped many barrels of corn, flour and meal (as well as smaller consignments of beans, oats, ryemeal and wheat and some boxes of clothing) to Ireland from the third month (March) to the tenth month (October) of 1847. Cork port received nine of these shipments, Liverpool eight, Dublin two and Limerick one. Boston and New York head the list but Ogdensburgh (upstate New York) on the Canadian border and Utica also made substantial contributions, as did Burlington, New Jersey. Significant contributions also came from the smaller New England states as well as from other centres in upstate New York. Further south (just off the map), Philadelphia became a major receiving centre for contributions. Canadian groups were also generous in their contributions. Not only Quaker communities but also Irish Relief Committees in American cities, Protestant Episcopalian Churches as well as one Reformed Dutch Church entrusted their contributions to the Quaker relief effort. Given their justified reputation for independence, probity and foresight in directing famine relief efforts, overall a large proportion of American contributions were directed to the Quakers.

Quaker James H. Tuke toured the unions compiling statistics on the disease, overcrowding, lack of clothing, bedding, food, and the unworkable sizes of the western unions. For example, in one case a union covered an area of 1,800 square miles with a population of nearly 121,000. Belmullet in Erris was fifty miles from the workhouse. The CRC was well aware that rates could not bear the cost and in any event, could not be collected as almost no crops had been sown or harvested.[13] Instead, the CRC determined to use its resources to invest in Irish development, if the alleviation of Irish poverty was to be more than momentary. Quaker Barclay Fox, investigating cultivation in Mayo and Galway, found seven-eighths of the arable land uncultivated, and thousands without any relief when Russell closed the public works in April 1847.[14]

## DISTRIBUTING SEED

In May 1847 the CRC began the distribution of 35,196 pounds of seed for 'green crops' – peas, beans, turnips, carrots and cabbage, that landlords would not take for rent – which while providing immediate food, would reduce total dependence on the potato. Just under 10,000 acres were sown, producing 193,000 tons of food in 1847. An additional 15,680 pounds were placed in County Mayo directly, in the charge of a naval officer who undertook the distribution. In 1848, 122,872 pounds of seed were distributed in over 143,000 grants in twenty-four counties, excepting only the relatively prosperous area of north-east Ulster at a cost of £6,271 14s 2d.[15] The only requirement was that the recipient have land ready.

The CRC rented 572 acres of farms in Mayo, the bleakest and most destitute area, for diverse food crops, and flax, to establish the linen industry in the west. Loans were given without interest or a guarantee, including £1,600 at Ballina. By 1851, flax as a cash crop in Mayo increased from the 160 acres of the first seed distribution to more than 350, and the linen mill funded by a Quaker loan of £400, employed more than 100.[16] In September 1848, the CRC leased 650 acres (400 Irish acres) at Colmanstown in Galway for a model farm with an instructor hired from the Royal Agricultural Society. The farm included a 'poor man's farm' to teach small landholders how to get the best from few resources. The model farm was the principal source of employment in the area until 1863 (another famine year) when it was sold and the proceeds given to the Hospital for Incurables. Other projects included harvesting seaweed for the seed distribution farms in Mayo, Sligo and Galway. This was an essential dressing on the acidulous reclaimed bog soil, but was less successful because of the lack of roads.[17]

## FISHERIES

From January 1847, grants were made to redeem fishermen's tackle pawned for food, and in June the CRC began massive efforts, assembling detailed statistics, presented in Parliament and to Russell, on the numbers and types of boats, types of fishing, numbers employed and numbers of dependants, ultimately forcing the Government to revise inapplicable regulations dating back to 1805 and based on

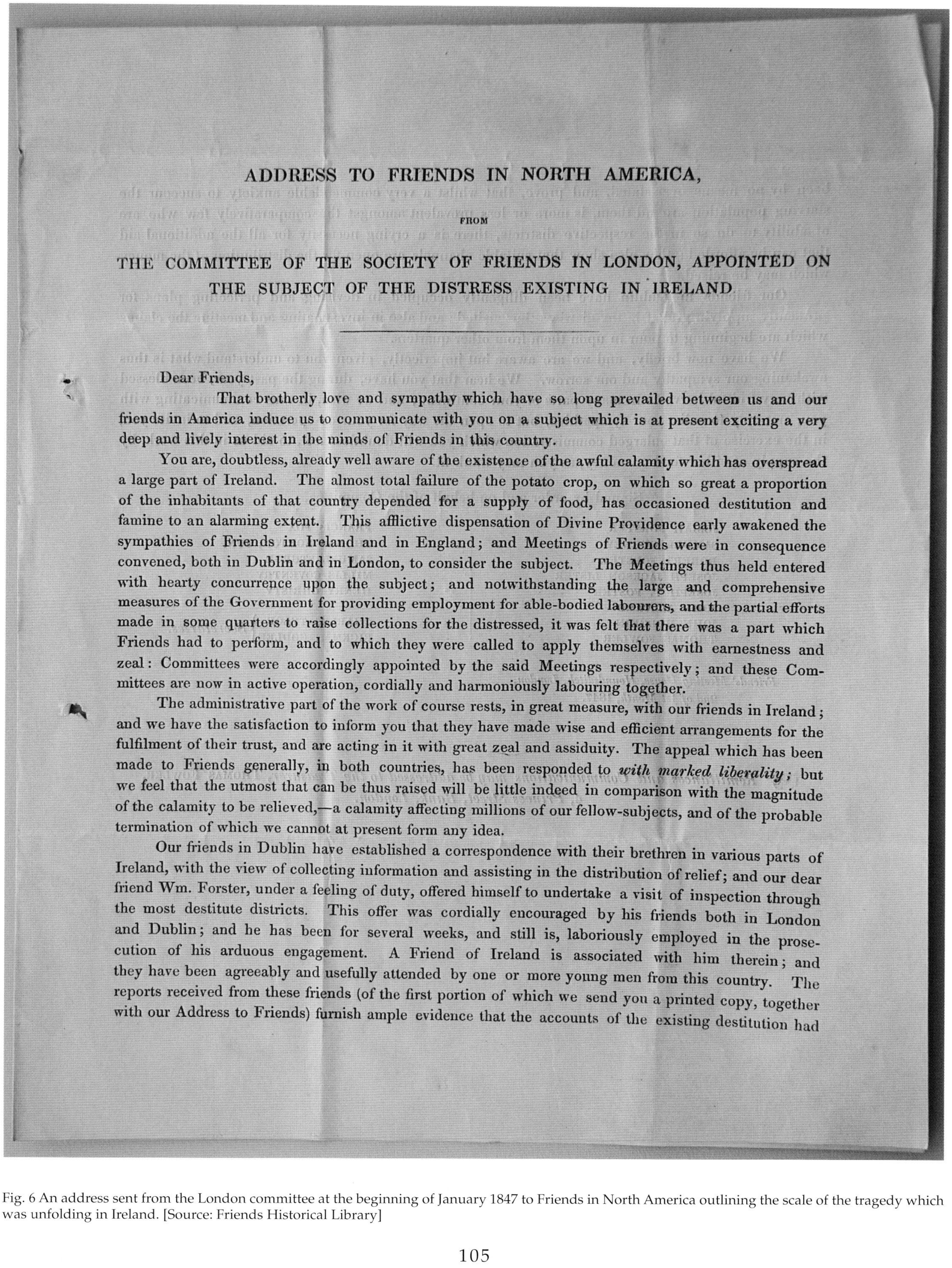

# ADDRESS TO FRIENDS IN NORTH AMERICA,

FROM

## THE COMMITTEE OF THE SOCIETY OF FRIENDS IN LONDON, APPOINTED ON THE SUBJECT OF THE DISTRESS EXISTING IN IRELAND

---

Dear Friends,

That brotherly love and sympathy which have so long prevailed between us and our friends in America induce us to communicate with you on a subject which is at present exciting a very deep and lively interest in the minds of Friends in this country.

You are, doubtless, already well aware of the existence of the awful calamity which has overspread a large part of Ireland. The almost total failure of the potato crop, on which so great a proportion of the inhabitants of that country depended for a supply of food, has occasioned destitution and famine to an alarming extent. This afflictive dispensation of Divine Providence early awakened the sympathies of Friends in Ireland and in England; and Meetings of Friends were in consequence convened, both in Dublin and in London, to consider the subject. The Meetings thus held entered with hearty concurrence upon the subject; and notwithstanding the large and comprehensive measures of the Government for providing employment for able-bodied labourers, and the partial efforts made in some quarters to raise collections for the distressed, it was felt that there was a part which Friends had to perform, and to which they were called to apply themselves with earnestness and zeal: Committees were accordingly appointed by the said Meetings respectively; and these Committees are now in active operation, cordially and harmoniously labouring together.

The administrative part of the work of course rests, in great measure, with our friends in Ireland; and we have the satisfaction to inform you that they have made wise and efficient arrangements for the fulfilment of their trust, and are acting in it with great zeal and assiduity. The appeal which has been made to Friends generally, in both countries, has been responded to *with marked liberality;* but we feel that the utmost that can be thus raised will be little indeed in comparison with the magnitude of the calamity to be relieved,—a calamity affecting millions of our fellow-subjects, and of the probable termination of which we cannot at present form any idea.

Our friends in Dublin have established a correspondence with their brethren in various parts of Ireland, with the view of collecting information and assisting in the distribution of relief; and our dear friend Wm. Forster, under a feeling of duty, offered himself to undertake a visit of inspection through the most destitute districts. This offer was cordially encouraged by his friends both in London and Dublin; and he has been for several weeks, and still is, laboriously employed in the prosecution of his arduous engagement. A Friend of Ireland is associated with him therein; and they have been agreeably and usefully attended by one or more young men from this country. The reports received from these friends (of the first portion of which we send you a printed copy, together with our Address to Friends) furnish ample evidence that the accounts of the existing destitution had

Fig. 6 An address sent from the London committee at the beginning of January 1847 to Friends in North America outlining the scale of the tragedy which was unfolding in Ireland. [Source: Friends Historical Library]

105

We endeavoured at first, to avoip this difficulty by confining our grants to classes who were not the objects of adequate Poor Law relief; by assisting schools, by distributing seeds; and by cultivating ground by spade labour, and at length decided on bringing our system of almsgiving to a final close, and on devoting the balance then remaining to objects which might encourage the industry of the country. In pursuance of this decision we have for the past nine monts expended very lsttle money, except in the completion of some objects previously undertaken, in some operations for the encouragement of the Fisheries, in loans for the cultivation of land by spade labour, and in some considerable loans to encourage the cultivation and improved preparation of flax in tne county of Mayo. We have also appropriated a sum of £12,000, being nearly the whole of our available balance, to the purpose of conducting a model farm and agricultural school in the county of Galway.

About a month since, our Dublin Committee had the opportunity of consulting many of our country friends, who have taken an active part in relief operations, and the question was then again considered, whether the great and increasing distress prevailing in many parts rendered it advisable to make renewed efforts for affording gratuitous relief, and the conclusion adopted was in the negative. We felt that even if we asked for another contribution, the utmost amount we could expect would be utterly insufficient; that even with ample funds we could no longer hope for that active and self-denying co-operation in the distressed districts on which we had formerly relied, and without which we could not work usefully. In short, that our plan of acting was no longer practicable alongside of the Poor Law, and that the relief of destitution on any extended scale must in future be trusted to those arrangements which the Imperial Parliament has provided for that purpose. Seeing that the difficulty was so far beyond the reach of private exertion, and that the only machinery which it was practicable to emply was that under the control of the public authorities, and belieuing that the government alone could raise the funds, or carry out the measures necessary in many districts to save the lives of tke people, we feared, that if we ventured to undertake a work for which our resources were so inadequate, we might through our incompetency, injure the cause of those whom we desired to serve.

Under these circumstances, we are not now in a position to undertake the distribution of charitable relief, and we are truly sorry that it is therefore out of our power to offer ourselves as the distributors of Lord John Russell's bounty to our suffering fellow-countrymen.

Trusting thou wilt excuse this long explanation of our views,

~~I remain,~~

~~Thine very respectfully,~~

(Signed)   JONATHAN PIM.

Fig. 7 Last page of a galley proof of a letter from Jonathan Pim (Secretary of the Central Relief Committee [CRC] to Sir Charles Trevelyan on behalf of the CRC, 6 June 1849, refusing Lord John Russell's offer of £100 if the CRC would undertake a new relief campaign and placing responsibility for relief on the British Government (corrected in Pim's hand). The burden of Quaker relief efforts eventually took their toll. Fifteen Quakers died of famine-related diseases while others such as Pim collapsed from exhaustion.

Norwegian, not Irish, conditions. Generations of subsistence operations left Irish fishermen with primitive equipment and no knowledge of modern methods.

Fishing stations were funded on the west and south coasts at Newport on Achill Sound, Belmullet in Erris, Ballinakill, and Castletown-Berehaven. Interest-free loans recovered equipment, and four trawlers, a decked sailboat and a smaller sailboat were added. Ownership of the boats, tackle and gear was invested in the CRC until the men gradually liquidated the debt. The CRC funded a fishing project run by an Anglican clergyman at Ring, County Waterford, which included a fish curing house that produced a high-quality product the Quakers helped market. Similarly, working with the Dominicans, who maintained a school at

Galway, the Quakers invested in a large trawler and funded a fish curer to work with the Claddagh fishermen. They were taught deep-water fishing (not possible in their small coracles and rowboats), and the curing and marketing of their fish. Refuting the commonly held English argument that the sea was full of fish the Irish were too lazy to gather, the Friends took soundings all around the south and west coasts to prove that while fish passed the coast at particular seasons, the rocky bottom did not produce feeding grounds. Eventually the Admiralty was forced to produce new accurate charts.[18] In all, Friends invested £5,365 1s 1d in the fisheries projects.

The Quakers recognised that their relief and employment work, while crucial in the great crisis, were not a permanent solution. If Ireland was to be lifted from chronic wretchedness and susceptibility to famine, land reform was essential. In 1849, estates whose income was valued at £1,500,000 yearly were held for debt in Chancery and their income lost to Ireland. Led by CRC Secretary, Jonathan Pim, the Friends embarked on a crusade to pass an Encumbered Estates Bill. It was passed in 1849, as the first step. Pim sat as an MP from 1865 to 1874, writing the Landlord and Tenant (Ireland) Bill passed in 1870, and is believed to have written the great Land Act of 1881, which finally gave the Irish tenantry the 'three Fs' of fair rents, fixity of tenure and fair sale.[19]

Fig. 8 Jonathan Pim, Secretary of the Central Relief Committee. A tireless worker during the Famine, Pim continued to campaign for the reform of the Irish land system in the decades after the Famine. He was elected to Parliament in 1865 as a member for Dublin. [Source: Rob Goodbody, *A Suitable Channel: Quaker Relief during the Great Famine* (Bray, 1995), p. 80]

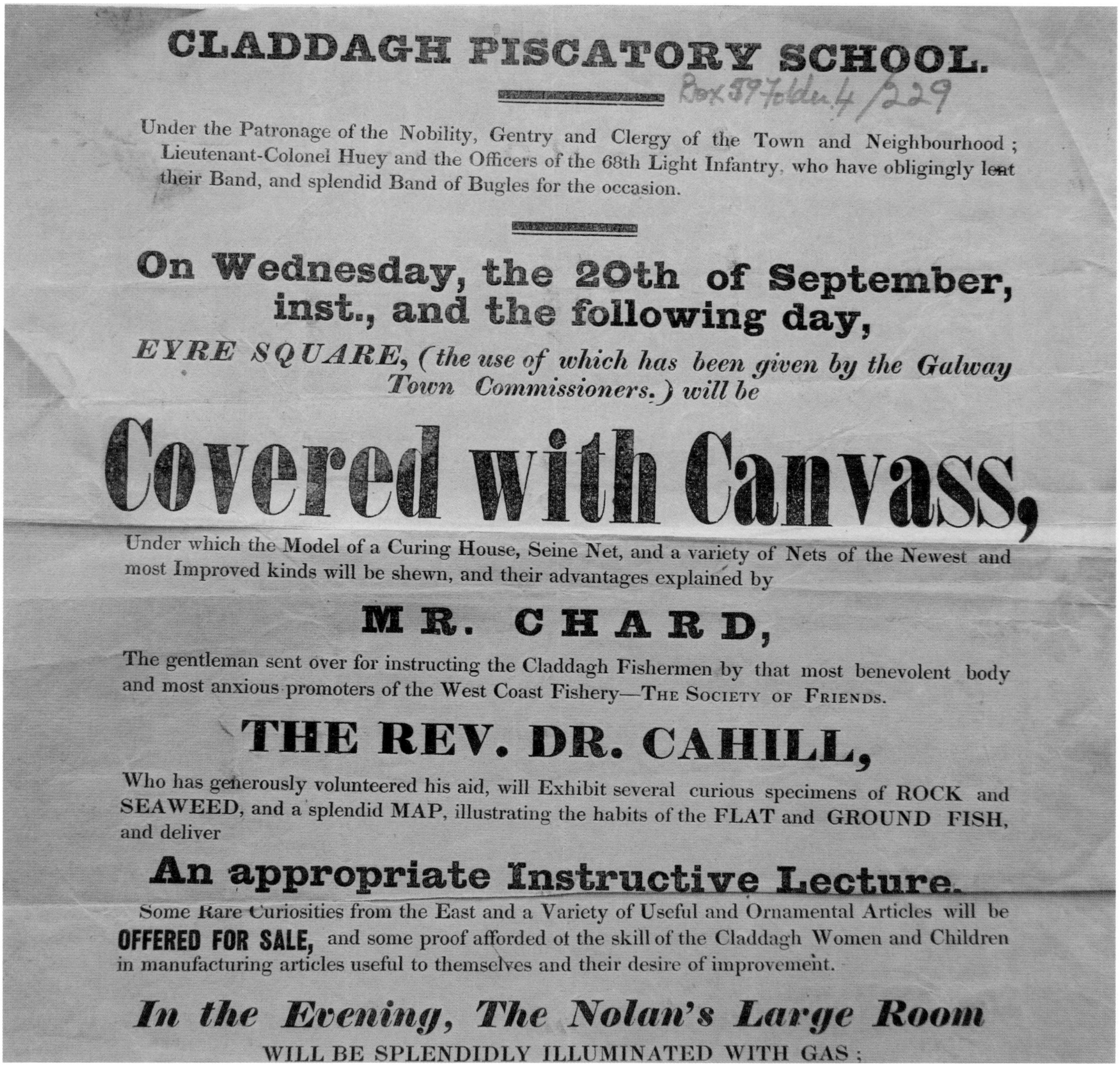

# CLADDAGH PISCATORY SCHOOL.

*Box 59 Folder 4 /229*

Under the Patronage of the Nobility, Gentry and Clergy of the Town and Neighbourhood ;
Lieutenant-Colonel Huey and the Officers of the 68th Light Infantry, who have obligingly lent
their Band, and splendid Band of Bugles for the occasion.

## On Wednesday, the 20th of September, inst., and the following day,

*EYRE SQUARE, (the use of which has been given by the Galway Town Commissioners.) will be*

# Covered with Canvass,

Under which the Model of a Curing House, Seine Net, and a variety of Nets of the Newest and
most Improved kinds will be shewn, and their advantages explained by

# MR. CHARD,

The gentleman sent over for instructing the Claddagh Fishermen by that most benevolent body
and most anxious promoters of the West Coast Fishery—THE SOCIETY OF FRIENDS.

# THE REV. DR. CAHILL,

Who has generously volunteered his aid, will Exhibit several curious specimens of ROCK and
SEAWEED, and a splendid MAP, illustrating the habits of the FLAT and GROUND FISH,
and deliver

# An appropriate Instructive Lecture.

Some Rare Curiosities from the East and a Variety of Useful and Ornamental Articles will be
**OFFERED FOR SALE,** and some proof afforded of the skill of the Claddagh Women and Children
in manufacturing articles useful to themselves and their desire of improvement.

## In the Evening, The Nolan's Large Room
### WILL BE SPLENDIDLY ILLUMINATED WITH GAS ;

Fig. 9 The Quakers viewed the Claddagh fishery in Galway as significant from an early stage. Initial grants were used by the fishermen to redeem their nets and tackle. Later improvements included the establishment of a piscatory school and fish-curing plant and the employment of a Cornish deep-sea fisherman, Captain Arthur Chard, in the spring of 1848 to instruct the fishermen in more modern methods. [Source: Rob Goodbody, *A Suitable Channel: Quaker Relief during the Great Famine* (Bray, 1995), pp. 48–58/Friends Historical Library]

The Quakers based their work on their perception of need over theory. In their relief and in giving unguaranteed loans they rejected the Government's economic thinking and management and said so in their publications and briefs. They did not equate endemic poverty with moral failure or Catholicism, nor did they require total destitution for relief. Crucially, they asserted that while an emergency was one thing, which charity might rightly move to relieve, famine such as stalked Ireland was not a limited single event, and they made their position unmistakable.

If the Government chose to remain deaf to informed advice and declare that its system must be the organ of relief, then Government could not be relieved of its responsibility. The methodology created in their work in Ireland – investigate, develop resources, teach the people how to use them and turn them over to the people (which became the basis of Third World relief and development for many agencies) was incorporated into the Society as the Friends Service Council in 1927.

# 'Born astride of a grave': The geography of the dead

*William J. Smyth*

The Famine catastrophe is first measured by the number of people – men, women and children – who perished because of the Famine. Some literally died of starvation, others of nutritional deficiencies, but the great majority were swept away by infectious diseases – typhus, fever, dysentery and diarrhoea and eventually cholera. Diseases were spread as the hungry people congregated around food depots and soup kitchens or were crowded together in workhouses and other public institutions where conditions were rife for the diffusion of such infectious diseases.[1] 'Famine and fever' spread throughout the land. In Beckett's phrase, subsequent generations 'give birth astride of a grave'[2] – the 'grave' that was Ireland, that received Ireland's dead in these deadly years between 1846 and 1852.

It is agreed by all commentators that the number of excess deaths during the Great Famine was greater than the numbers indicated in the official census returns. The generally agreed number of excess deaths is now put at approximately one million and if averted deaths are taken into account the figure is much higher. It is also agreed that the correct statement of the number of famine deaths could *not* be provided by the Census Commissioners since the estimated number of deaths outside of public institutions was governed by the evidence provided by surviving family members on the census forms.[3] Thus account could *not* be taken of *whole* families who had either emigrated or perished at home in Ireland. Neither was the evidence of emigrants available who had lost other family members during the Famine. Given the overwhelming impact of the Famine, even the records of some public institutions are either incomplete or very seriously deficient. There are some deficiencies in returns for at least a dozen fever hospitals and very serious deficiencies and no returns for the number of the dead in the fever hospitals of Athlone, Caher-

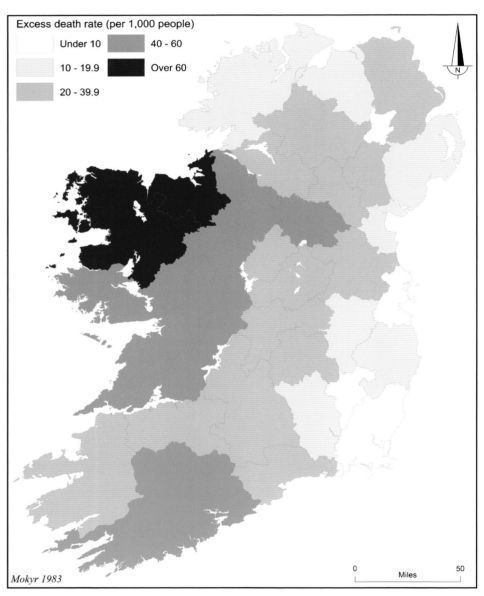

Fig. 1a AVERAGE LOWER BOUND ESTIMATES BY JOEL MOKYR FOR ANNUAL EXCESS DEATH RATES PER 1,000 POPULATION 1846–51. Joel Mokyr's pioneering book *Why Ireland Starved* calculates both upper bound estimates and lower bound estimates (this map) for annual excess death rates per 1,000 population during the years 1846–51. His table of upper bound estimates per county includes averted births while his lower bound estimates do not. Using an elaborate series of calculations which are particularly sensitive to assumptions about regional variations in patterns of emigration during the Famine period, Mokyr locates the highest incidence of famine-induced deaths in all the counties of Connacht and in Counties Cavan, Clare and Cork. The lowest excess death rates are located in much of Ulster and east Leinster. However, it is likely that Mokyr underestimates the levels of excess mortality in Munster while overestimating these for Ulster. Overall his lower bound county estimates strongly suggest that at least one million excess deaths occurred during the Famine period. If averted births are included, the likely figure of excess deaths climbs to 1.3–4 million.

Map legend:
Excess death rate (per 1,000 people)
- Under 10
- 10 - 19.9
- 20 - 39.9
- 40 - 60
- Over 60

*Mokyr 1983*

0   Miles   50

siveen, Castleblayney, Clones, Cootehill, Fermoy, Lismore, Listowel and Mallow.

## REGIONAL VARIATIONS

Figure 1a illustrates Joel Mokyr's estimated regional variations in average annual excess rates between 1846 and 1851.[4] Figure 1b renders S.H. Cousens' mapping of excess mortality between 1846 and 1850 as a percentage of the total population at county level.[5] Mokyr's map of upper bound estimates includes the category of averted births while his lower bound estimates do not. Both maps emphasise the intensification of the Famine crisis and associated excess deaths as one moves from east to west. Mokyr constructed these maps via an elaborate series of assumptions and calculations which, amongst other things, are highly sensitive to his estimates of regional variations in emigration between 1841 and 1851. Clearly emigration was the other major factor making for significant population losses. While constituting an original and brilliant exposition, it seems likely that Mokyr overestimated excess mortality levels in Ulster and, perhaps, underestimated excess mortalities in Munster and south Leinster.

Cousens' map (1b) is based mainly on the totality of information on deaths contained in volume 2 of part V of the *Census of Ireland, 1851*. Cousens also carried out important empirical work on parish baptismal records, burial records and workhouse accounts. It is now recognised that his conclusions, putting the excess deaths at just over 800,000, is probably too low by the order of *c*.200,000 people. Because of his dependence on data from public institutions, it is very likely that he underestimates excess mortalities in Connacht. Otherwise, his regionalisation of variations in excess mortalities across the counties – while relatively similar to Mokyr's estimates – may be more convincing.

My concern here is to try to map more precisely at the Poor Law Union level the *relative location* of these deaths as they piled up across the island. The most reliable series as to the number of deaths that occurred were recorded in public institutions. In particular, the number of deaths that occurred between

1841 and 1851 in the workhouses and fever hospitals can be ascertained.[6] There are also county census figures for the total number of deaths, estimated and otherwise, for the period from 6 June 1841 to 30 March 1851. One can, therefore, map the approximate number of deaths over this whole period which can be allocated to each Poor Law Union by calculating each union's percentage share of institutional deaths (in workhouses and fever hospitals) onto the equivalent percentage share of the total county figure. This allows one to map at Poor Law Union level the *relative* distribution of all deaths while recognising that the absolute

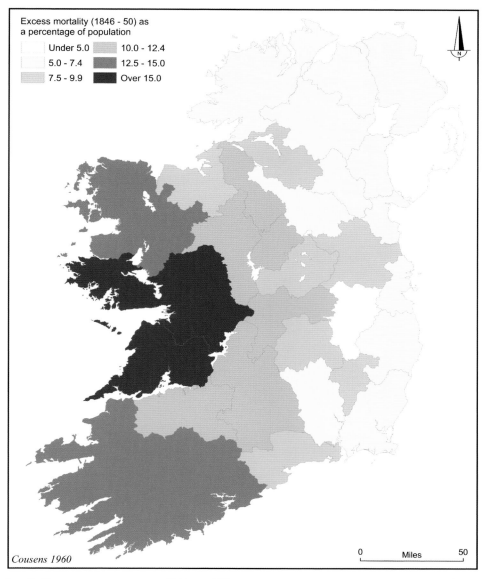

Cousens 1960

Excess mortality (1846 - 50) as a percentage of population

| | |
| --- | --- |
| Under 5.0 | 10.0 - 12.4 |
| 5.0 - 7.4 | 12.5 - 15.0 |
| 7.5 - 9.9 | Over 15.0 |

0    Miles    50

Fig. 1b EXCESS MORTALITY BETWEEN 1846 AND 1850 AS A PERCENTAGE OF THE POPULATION PER COUNTY (as per S.H. Cousens). Historical geographer S.H. Cousens has written extensively on both mortality during the Famine and on Famine and post-Famine emigration. Unlike Mokyr, who calculates annual excess death rates, Cousens maps excess mortality over the whole period 1846 to 1850 as a percentage of each county's 1841 population. Cousens also makes detailed use of the totality of information on deaths contained in the 1851 Census as well as comparative evidence from baptisimal and burial records as well as workhouse accounts. While his estimate of total excess deaths at *c*.800,000 is now considered too low, his regionalisation of famine deaths may be more convincing than that of Mokyr. Cousens shifts the focal region for excess famine deaths to the midwest, to Counties Clare and Galway, recognises greater levels of excess mortality in the Munster province as a whole while modifying Mokyr's figures for excess deaths in Ulster. Nevertheless both sets of estimates are highly instructive and provide very reliable platforms for visualising and understanding the striking regional differences in famine-related deaths between 1846 and 1851.

total of excess deaths was far greater, especially in the most distressed unions of the west and southwest. Hence these unions are specifically designated on Figures 2 and 3 – by a darker underlying shade.

Figure 2 is the first approximation, highlighting the massive regional variations in numbers of deaths recorded in the Census of 1851. A clear and major division emerges between two Irelands – but it is not the familiar north/west versus south/east distinctions that emerge. Rather, Figure 2 shows that north and east of a line from Donegal Bay to Wexford harbour – the numbers dying in the Poor Law Unions were much lower – particularly across the northern half of Ulster and in the north Dublin hinterland. In some of these unions, the total number of the dead falls either under 2,500 or 5,000. In contrast, over much of Connacht and Munster and adjacent areas of southwest Ulster and west and south Leinster, the number of deaths recorded are far greater. In the unions of Belfast, Sligo, Loughrea, Fermoy and Kilkenny over 20,000 deaths are recorded per union and in two Dublin Unions as well as Cork and Limerick, the figures climb over 30,000.

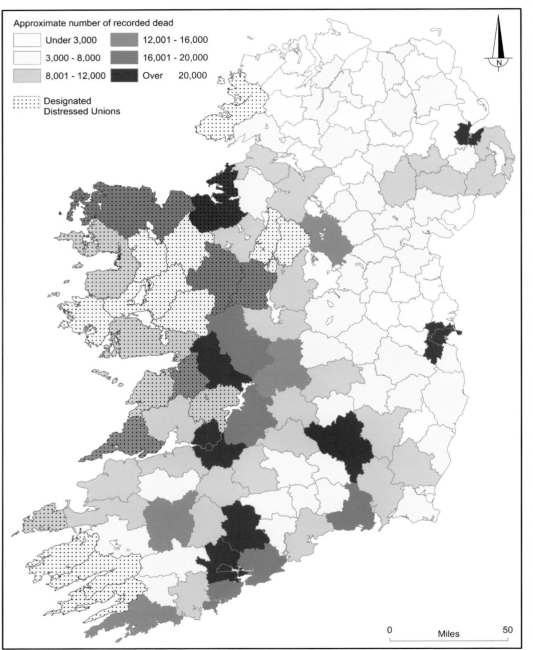

Fig. 2 APPROXIMATE NUMBER OF DEAD AS PER POOR LAW UNION, 6 JUNE 1841 TO 30 MAY 1851. This map seeks to show more precisely at the Poor Law union level the relative location of deaths as they piled up across the island. The most reliable figures for deaths recorded between 1841 and 1851 come from the workhouses and fever hospitals. One can map the approximate *total* number of deaths over this whole period which can be allocated to each poor law union by calculating each union's percentage share of recorded institutional deaths onto the equivalent percentage share of the total number of deaths in the county as reported in the 1851 Census for the period 6 June 1841 to 30 March 1851. Major regional differences emerge. North and east of a line from Donegal Bay to Wexford, the numbers dying in the Poor Law unions are much lower, particularly in north Ulster and the Pale. In contrast, in Connacht and Munster and adjacent areas of southwest Ulster and west and south Leinster respectively, the number of deaths recorded are far greater. Deaths exceed 20,000 per union in Belfast, Sligo, Loughrea, Fermoy and Kilkenny and reach over 30,000 in Dublin, Cork and Limerick cities. One must remember, however, that the Census estimates of deaths are deficient and that the actual number of deaths was far greater.

### A MORE NUANCED AND REALISTIC PICTURE

It is even more instructive to map these very approximate mortality figures per Poor Law Union as a percentage of the union's total population in 1841 to provide a more nuanced and realistic picture. Here the boundary line between the northeast versus the south and west can be drawn more sharply. It runs from west of Sligo southeast to Waterford Harbour. West and south of this line, the number of recorded deaths usually constitute at least 20% of the total population in 1841. Ballyshannon, Loughrea, Ennistymon, Nenagh, Abbeyleix, Clonmel, Kanturk and Mallow constitute eight unions which record mortality levels of 22.5% to 25.0%. Three unions – Castlerea, Fermoy and Midleton – are above 25%. Gort, Scariff and Kinsale register mortalities of at least a third of their 1841 population numbers. It should also be remembered that these proportions refer only to estimated numbers of the dead in the census – in much of the west and south the actual mortality levels were much higher.

North and east of the Sligo–Waterford line, approximate mortality figures fall below 20% although all along the borders of this line – from Sligo south through Mohill, Longford, Parsonstown (Birr) and on to the unions of Carlow, Rathdrum, Gorey, Enniscorthy, New Ross and Wexford – these levels exceed 15%. It is noticeable that *all* the County Wexford Unions record these moderately high levels. In sharp contrast, along the north Ulster coast from Milford in Donegal, through Inishowen, Coleraine, Ballymoney, Ballycastle and Larne, approximate mortality levels are as low as 7 to 8%, levels which are also recorded for Stranorlar, Castlederg, Cookstown, Clogher and Castleblayney. Granard and Edenderry record similar levels in the midlands. In contrast, a cluster of unions in south Ulster – Lisnaskea, Clones, Cavan and Bailieborough (and Kells and Dunshaughlin in County Meath) – record mortality levels of over 15%. The probabilities of dying from famine-related causes increased sharply along an axis from Ballycastle in County Antrim through south Ulster and on through unions west of the Shannon and southwards to Kinsale and Skibbereen. What this map also suggests is that the existing literature may have underestimated somewhat the high levels of mortality in east Munster and related areas of south Leinster.

One can focus the angle of this analysis by examining the recorded distribution of deaths during the Famine years proper, i.e. for the census years 1846 to 1851 (as well as late 1845). At the county level, if one maps the percentage distribu-

tion of all recorded deaths for the decade that occurred between 1846 and 1851, the same east/northeast *versus* west/southwest gradients emerge. Among the eastern and northern coastal counties, 70–72% of the recorded deaths from 1841 to 1851 occurred in these famine years. The gradients then worked their way west/southwestwards with

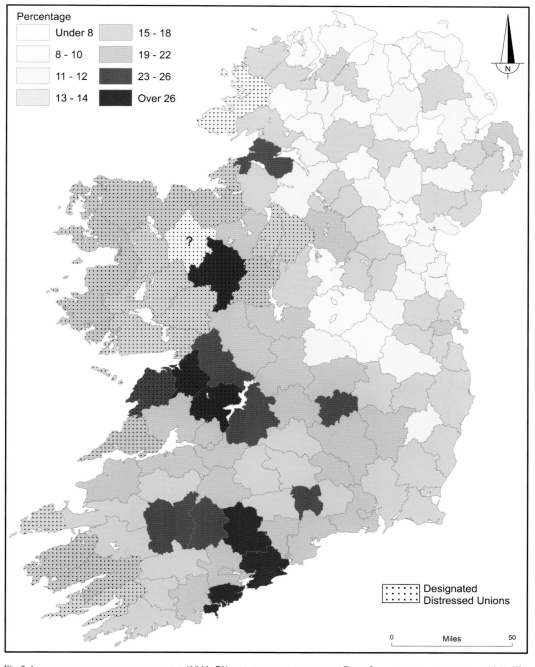

Fig 3 APPROXIMATE DISTRIBUTION OF DEAD (1841–51) AS A PERCENTAGE OF EACH POOR LAW UNION POPULATION IN 1841. This figure maps approximate mortality figures for each Poor Law union as a percentage of the union's total population in 1841 so as to provide a more nuanced and realistic picture. Now a border zone runs from Sligo southeastwards to Waterford harbour. West and south of this line the approximate proportion of recorded deaths per Poor Law union exceeds 20% and in Ballyshannon, Loughrea, Ennistymon, Nenagh, Abbeyleix, Clonmel, Kanturk and Mallow unions reaches up to 25%. Deaths in Gort, Scariff and Kinsale Poor Law unions exceed 30% of the 1841 populations. In a line of unions from Sligo through Mohill, Longford, Birr and Carlow onto all the Wexford unions, recorded death levels exceed 15%. In contrast, over much of Ulster and north Leinster, recorded mortalities are only half this level at 7 to 8% – the exception being the Cavan and north Meath Poor Law unions, which again rise over 15%. This map emphasises the high levels of mortality in east as well as west Munster and in adjacent unions of south Leinster. However these percentages are based on the estimated number of deaths in the unions – in much of the west and south the actual mortality levels were higher again.

the average national percentage of deaths for the famine years centred on the King's County (Offaly) at 77.4% – constituting part of a middle zone with similar values stretching from south Tipperary through Westmeath, Longford, Cavan, Fermanagh and veering westwards to Sligo. On the other hand, with over 80% of all deaths recorded for these famine years, clearly the counties most devastated by the famine stretch from Mayo (81.1%) through Galway (82.8%) to Clare (84.4%), north Tipperary (81.1%) Limerick (81.0%), Kerry (81.7%), west Cork (84.1%) to east Cork (82.8%). Close by the counties of Waterford, Roscommon and Leitrim are in the very high seventies. By using these census-based county proportions, one can refine the analysis of both the absolute and percentage distribution of the recorded dead at the Poor Law Union level strictly for the famine years and *not* for the whole decade (see Figure 8).

County Galway registered 1,029 starvation deaths in

1848 and 1,215 in 1849. County Mayo recorded 885 starvation deaths in 1848 and 984 in 1849 (Figure 9). Yet Charles Trevelyan, the obsessive, moralistic and doctrinaire head of the Treasury in the London administration, wrote a book in 1847 stating that the Famine was over that summer.[7] Issues of outstanding relief could, therefore, fall back on the Poor Law Unions alone. The Census of 1851 – particularly Part V, dealing with the Tables of Deaths – clearly refutes that extraordinary premature interpretation, which, in combination with associated Government policies, had such devastating consequences. As Paul Krugman has argued in relation to more recent events: 'when an ideology backed by immense wealth and great power confronts inconvenient facts . . . the facts lose'.[8]

## STARVATION DEATHS

While it is clear that the great majority of famine deaths

Fig. 4 Mass grave at Abbeystrewery cemetery, Skibbereen, County Cork. More than 9.,000 people were buried here during the Famine: 'Our next visit was to the churchyard; it was the burying place to an ancient abbey, the ruins of which still remained mouldering away in the midst of the surrounding tombs . . . It was a very large graveyard, and most of the graves had evidently long since been made; but in one corner there was about an acre of uneven and freshly-turned earth. This was the portion allotted to the late victims of famine and disease; by these graves, no service had been performed, no friends had stood, no priest had spoken words of hope, and of future consolation in a glorious eternity! The bodies had been daily thrown in, many without a coffin, one over another, the uppermost only hidden from the light of day by a bare three inches of earth, the survivors not even knowing the spot where their most dear to them lay sleeping. In one place the ground had been hollowed out to a depth of two feet, where several coffins were piled up in layers one above another, with but a sprinkling of earth between them, the ends protruding into that part of the shallow trench which still remained unfilled . . . [T]he most fearful anticipations are entertained of a pestilence breaking out, as soon as the hot weather shall set in, from the effluvia that must necessarily arise from bodies decomposing so near the surface, and pestilence once begun, who shall say how far its ravages shall extend?' [Source: Lord Dufferin and The Hon G. F. Boyle, *Narrative of a Journey from Oxford to Skibbereen in the Year of the Irish Famine* (Oxford, 1847)/Photo: Frank Coyne]

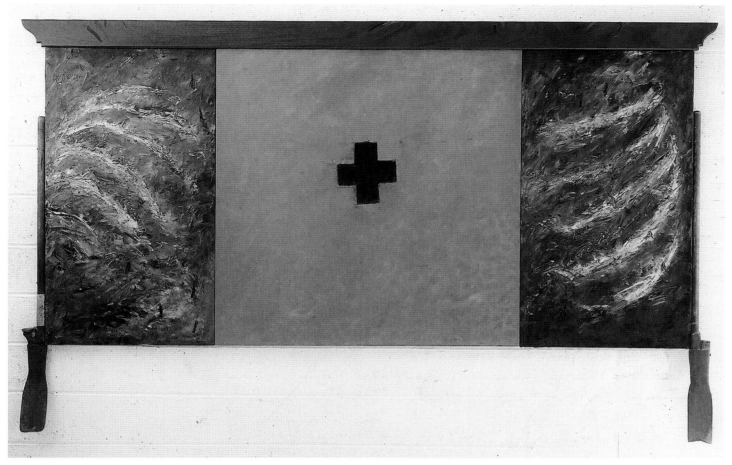

Fig. 5 *A Spade, a Spade* by Charles Tyrrell, oil on canvas, mahogany spades, 190x311cm. [Courtesy of the artist]

were a product of famine-induced fevers and infectious diseases arising from nutritional and other deficiencies, nevertheless it is instructive to examine the timing of deaths which the census reports were due to literal starvation. In examining these deaths due to starvation, one may map the proportion of deaths that occurred during 1847 and the two previous years vis-à-vis the proportion for the years 1848, 1849 and 1850 combined. Island-wide, 'Black '47' saw the greatest number of reported starvation deaths (6,058), 29.7% of the total between 1845 and 1850.[9] However, as Figure 10 shows, in only twelve counties do the number of starvation deaths from 1845 to 1847 outnumber those in the subsequent three years. And apart from Queen's County and County Wicklow, this pattern of deaths is concentrated in the Ulster province and the adjacent north Connacht counties of Leitrim, Sligo and Roscommon. In sharp contrast, less than 20% of starvation deaths in County Clare and King's County occurred during or before 1847. Over the two periods, the national ratio is 42.3% for 1845 to 1847 vis-à-vis 57.7% for 1848 to 1850.

Clearly the years 1848 to 1850 saw more devastating starvation deaths in two-thirds of all the counties. Figure 9 demonstrates even more profound gradients in this distribution – Counties Carlow, Dublin and Wicklow each register less than thirty such deaths and over much of the north and east of the country starvation deaths per county

did not exceed 100 over the whole period. But County Galway reported 3,818 such deaths and Mayo 3,341 with over 1,000 reported from Counties Clare, Kerry, Cork and Roscommon. County Galway registered four times the number of starvation deaths as the whole of the province of Leinster (916) and Mayo three times as many such deaths as the whole of Ulster (1,064). Of the reported starvation deaths 90% occurred in the provinces of Connacht and Munster.

It is also important to recognise significant regional variations in the longevity of high mortality levels over the years of the Great Famine. The Census of 1851 provides a table showing the percentage distribution of all deaths per year, per each county, between 1841 and 1851. At the national level, 9.1% of all deaths in that decade occurred in 1846 as famine deaths began to increase (the annual number of deaths in the years 1842 to 1844 averaged 5.3%). The relative proportions for the counties of Ulster, north Connacht and east Leinster are somewhat above the national average while south Connacht, west Leinster and Munster are much lower. However, it should be remembered that the proportionate distribution of deaths per county is, of course, profoundly influenced by varying levels of mortality in each county for subsequent years. The national average proportion of deaths for 1847 is 18.5% – Fermanagh records a 26.9% figure while the rest of the Ulster counties (and Longford, Leitrim and Roscommon) each average 20–22%. After 1847 the mortality levels decline progressively in the northern province. For example, over the decade in County Down, 20% of all its deaths occurred in 1847 and declined in subsequent years by 13.5%, 12.6%, 11.3% to reach 9.6% in 1851.

## DOMINANT PATTERNS OF MORTALITY

It is striking that the cities of Cork, Kilkenny and Galway all register above average mortality levels in 1847. Cities provided little protection against disease or death. By 1848, what was to become the dominant pattern of mortalities has emerged with higher proportions per county in Connacht and southwest Ulster, extending southwards through Clare and Tipperary to Cork. The national average is 15.4% of deaths in this year – Cavan is as high as 23.7% and the Connacht counties average c.18–19% with

somewhat lower figures (16–17%) further south. Much of Ulster and practically all of Leinster record county proportions well below the national average. These patterns of higher and lower mortality levels are reinforced by 1849. The national average for that year is 17.9% of all deaths in the decade, but from Mayo and Galway into the counties of west Leinster (and also including County Cavan to the north) and stretching southwards to include practically all of the Munster counties, the county averages are in the range of 21 to 23% with Galway recording 26.5% of its deaths in this year. The counties of Ulster and east Leinster record levels 5 to 6% below the national average. North County Tipperary is typical of the Munster pattern in 1849 with 22.5% of its estimated deaths recorded in that year, vis-à-vis 7.5% in 1846, 15.6% in 1847 and 14.2% in 1848. And it is noticeable that the relatively high north Tipperary mortality levels continue into 1850 (16.9%) and 1851

Fig. 6 *Reilig an tSléibhe*, Famine grave in Dungarvan, County Waterford which was opened in order to cope with the ever increasing number of workhouse dead. The impact of the Famine is recalled in the poem *Amhrán na Prátaí Dubha*. In this image, the Famine monument has been juxtaposed with a view of that graveyard. [Photo: William J. Smyth]

*B'iad na prátaí dubha a dhein ár gcomharsan do scaipeadh orainn,*
*Do chuir ins na poorhouse is anonn thar na farraigí;*
*I Reilig a' tSléibhe thá na céadta acu treascartha,*
*Is uaisle na bhFlaitheas go ngabhair a bpáirt.*

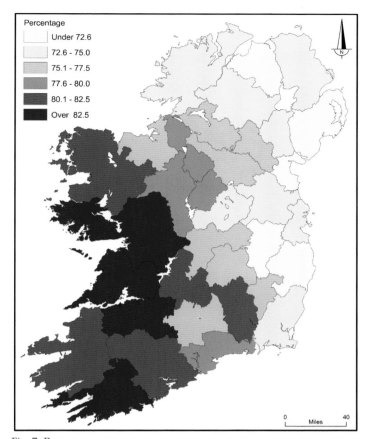

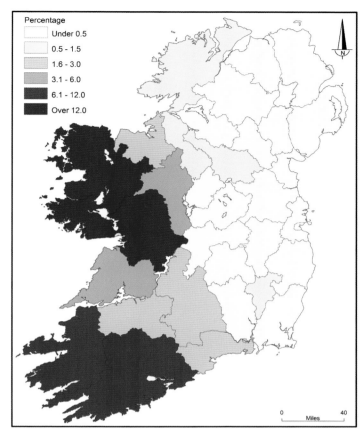

Fig. 7 PERCENTAGE NUMBER OF DEATHS RECORDED FOR EACH COUNTY BETWEEN 1846 AND 1851 AS A PROPORTION OF TOTAL DEATHS RECORDED BETWEEN 1841 AND 1851. The Census of 1851 provides figures for the number who died in each county in each year from 1841 to 1851 – based on the records of public institutions and the returns on the Census forms. It is recognised that these figures are underestimated since they were particularly dependent on families returning information on the deaths of individual members. The Census, therefore, does not take account of whole families who had either died during the Famine or had emigrated. Nevertheless, these county figures – if analysed for the Famine years 1846–51 – do provide a very good indication of the relative distribution of excess deaths – and therefore the intensity of the famine catastrophe – across the island. Obviously, far more people are recorded as dying during the Famine years. Indeed, of the total number of dead recorded for the 1840s decade, the county average for deaths between 1846 and 1851 is 77.3%. But the returns range from 70.7% for Dublin city to 84.4% for County Clare. Along the eastern and northern coastal counties, the percentage of deaths recorded for 1846–51 falls below 73% while the returns for the remaining counties of Ulster and Leinster (Offaly and Longford excepted) fall below the national average. The great boundary line between well above average and below average excess deaths runs from County Leitrim and Longford south through Offaly and north Tipperary to Waterford, all of which return percentage deaths of 78% or more for the latter half of the decade. Mayo, Galway, north Tipperary, Limerick, Kerry and east Cork – as well as the cities of Kilkenny and Limerick – are all above the 80% range. West Cork and County Clare return the most devastating death rates at 84% plus. Galway city has an even more dramatic official death level from 1846 to 1851 of over 86%.

(15.3%). County Clare equally reinforces this distinctive southern pattern of mortality levels. The county is well above the national average (9.1%) at 13.9% in 1846 (a year when Clare saw the greatest number of court-registered evictions of any county). Clare registered 19.3% of its deaths in 1847, 17.6% in 1848, 18.0% in 1849, 17.9% in 1850 and as high as c.23.7% in 1851.

In summary, well over one-third (37.5%) of all estimated Munster deaths occur *in and after* 1849. Leinster

Fig. 8 PERCENTAGE SHARE OF DISTRIBUTION OF RECORDED STARVATION DEATHS FROM 1845 TO 1851. In the Tables of Deaths from the 1851 Census, officially recorded starvation deaths are reported for each county. 'Black 47' recorded the greatest number of reported starvation deaths (6,058), nearly 30% of the total between 1845 and 1850. It is striking that only in twelve counties – in Ulster and adjacent counties in north Connacht – do starvation deaths between 1845 and 1847 outnumber these in the subsequent three years. It is clear that the years 1847 to 1850 were far more devastating in the west and the south. County Galway alone registered 1,029 starvation deaths in 1848 and 1,215 in 1849. County Mayo returned 885 and 984 starvation deaths in 1848 and 1849, respectively. This map highlights the overall concentration of starvation deaths for the whole Famine period in the western and southern counties. The county and city of Cork and County Kerry each return close on 15% of the island-wide recorded starvation deaths while the proportions for Galway and Mayo at 18.7% and 16.4% are even more startling. Nine out of ten of all reported starvation deaths occurred in the provinces of Connacht and Munster.

(34.3%) and Connacht (33.0%) are in the in-between categories while only 27.6% of Ulster deaths are recorded in these later years. It is also relevant to note that of the seventeen 'towns' (with populations in excess of 2,000 in 1841) which 'disappeared' from the list of 'civic districts' in 1851, one was in Connacht, two in Ulster, four in the north Leinster midlands but nine (over half the total) were from Munster.

Over the whole decade (from 6 June 1841 to 30 March 1851), 16% of all recorded deaths in Ireland occurred in civic districts (i.e. towns with a population of 2,000 or more) with 57% occurring in rural districts and 27% in public institutions. In this context, it should be noted that 75 to 77% of all such deaths occurred during the Famine years. Leinster with 23.8% of all civic district deaths heads the list but Dublin city's 47,570 mortalities comprises a massive 56% of

Fig. 9 Famine graveyard, St John's Hospital Sligo. It is estimated that over 2,000 people were buried here during the Famine [Photo: William J. Smyth]

this provincial total. Munster occupies the modal position with 16.4% of civic deaths – and here the three cities of Cork, Limerick and Waterford account for 46% of that total. Ulster, given its significant number of urban/civic districts, is below the average with 13.2%. Here Belfast with 16,814 deaths takes up 41.1%. Connacht with the weakest urban structure only accounts for 6.6% of deaths in civic districts, with close on one-third of these in Galway town. Counties where civic district deaths are above the national average include Dublin County (32.3%), Carlow (17.5%), Wexford (15.2%), south Tipperary (17.0%) and Down (15.1%). Overall, however, the proportion of civic district deaths is a reflection of how developed the urban system was in each county.

Outside of the major cities, every other group of towns lost populations between 1841 and 1851. Of all towns (ninety-five) with a population of between 5,000 and 25,000, over three-quarters (seventy-three towns) lost populations and many suffered serious losses (see Kevin Hourihan below). Outside of Dublin City, even the bigger towns and cities had a strong agrarian character – a factor in such population losses. As the economy shrank

during the Famine, manufacturing and trade also declined. During the Famine years, shops were boarded up, artisan workshops deserted, as many of their owners sought out the emigrant ship. Other shopkeepers – especially those holding contracts with the workhouse and/or other public institutions – prospered. Pawnshops were everywhere as the desperate poor pawned all kinds of goods to purchase food. But as the Famine crisis deepened, all towns and especially the workhouse towns saw a regular stream of desperate people seeking refuge in these centres.

TOWNS AS BATTLEGROUNDS

Towns became battlegrounds on many fronts as the Famine crisis deepened. Crowds of near starving people often swarmed the streets, threatening to plunder the shops and upturn carts of Indian meal. Towns were sites for numerous protests over the lack of public works in their hinterland. Port towns, such as Dungarvan and Youghal – and indeed many more – were the scenes of violent disturbances as desperate crowds sought to prevent the loading of grain on the quays for export. The police, with backup from troops, were

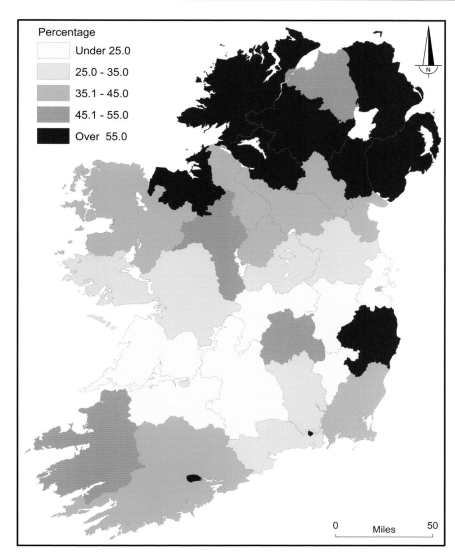

Percentage

| | |
|---|---|
| | Under 25.0 |
| | 25.0 - 35.0 |
| | 35.1 - 45.0 |
| | 45.1 - 55.0 |
| | Over 55.0 |

0    Miles    50

Fig. 10 PERCENTAGE OF STARVATION DEATHS RECORDED FOR EACH COUNTY FOR THE FIRST THREE YEARS OF FAMINE, 1845, 1846 AND 1847 (1851 CENSUS). It should not be assumed that the number of excess deaths remained constant for each county over the five years of the Great Famine. There are significant regional variations in the timing of high mortality levels over the period 1846 to 1851. For example, the percentage of starvation deaths recorded for 1845, 1846 and 1847 display, as in this map, a pronounced northern regional bias with over 50% of deaths for each of seven of the nine Ulster counties (excluding Cavan and Monaghan) occurring in these early Famine years. Communities in Wicklow and Sligo counties also witnessed this pattern of relatively more early starvation deaths. North Connacht and north Leinster Counties and Counties Cork, Kerry and Wexford occupy the middle category. In sharp contrast, a belt of counties from Dublin through the Midlands into Counties Clare, Tipperary and Waterford saw less than 25% of their officially recorded starvation deaths recorded for the early Famine years. Clearly, the impact of famine conditions were cumulative in these latter counties, making for massive famine mortalities from 1848 onwards.

regularly involved in controlling such crowds. Food riots also occurred in some towns – again countered by troop movements. Towns were invariably centres for malnutrition and for the spread of contagious diseases. Following the passing of the Irish Fever Act, great efforts were made to clean the dirty streets and cabins. Similarly during the cholera outbreaks in 1849, labourers on outdoor relief were involved in sweeping streets and whitewashing the houses. However, overall levels of urbanisation were no protection against the Famine catastrophe.[10]

'Funeral at Skibbereen', *The Illustrated London News*, 30 January, 1847.

# SECTION III
## THE WORKHOUSE

View of Birr workhouse.
[Photo: Frank Coyne]

# The creation of the workhouse system

## *William J. Smyth*

After an intensive three-year, island-wide survey (1833–36), the Irish Commission asked to assess the feasibility of establishing a Poor Law system in Ireland recommended a poor relief scheme combined with a whole range of economic development projects – not the Poor Law system on the English model. But the then Home Secretary, Sir John Russell, asked English Poor Law Commissioner, George Nicholls, to reinvestigate the issue; he was able to report after a mere six-week sojourn in Ireland that such a Poor Law system was both feasible and necessary. So the act 'for the more effectual relief of the destitute poor in Ireland' passed into law on 31 July 1838.[1] It was a far-reaching and as it turned out, a fatal decision.

Under George Nicholls' direction and following architect

Fig. 1  Scene at the Gate of an Irish Workhouse, (*c*.1846?) (engraving). [Source: Private Collection/The Bridgeman Art Library]

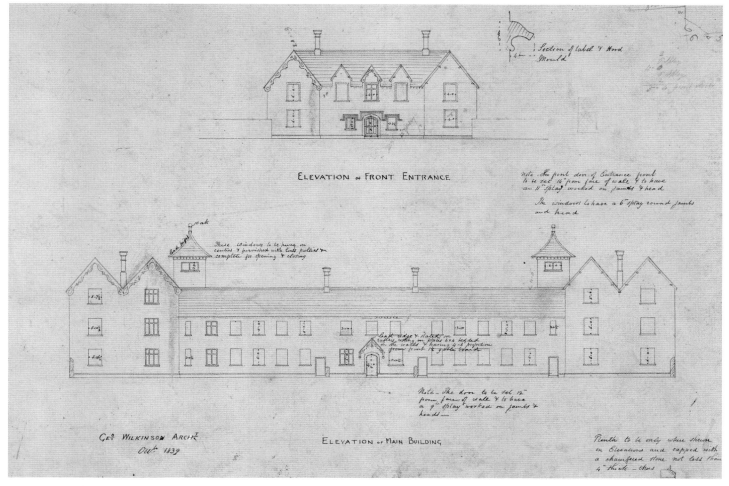

Fig. 2  Original drawing of the elevation of the main building of Lismore Union workhouse. [Source: Irish Architectural Archive]

George Wilkinson's designs, 130 workhouses were deliberately built at speed – almost in haste – in a country where such a Poor Law system had been opposed by almost everyone, by Protestant-Irish, Catholic-Irish, landlords, tenants, smallholders, shopkeepers and industrialists. As Daniel O'Connell was to point out, Ireland was too poor to afford such a Poor Law system.[2] Even in pre-Famine times the burden on ratepayers was severe – when famine struck these burdens increasingly became immense. The workhouse system then buckled under a strain it was never meant to carry.

The function and design of all workhouses reflected a particular ideology born of the ideas of people like Jeremy Bentham. He had worked out a scheme for workhouses in loving detail, calculating the maximum number of people to be housed in dormitories, the hours of sleeping they would be allowed, the kind of food they would be permitted. These ideas were further elaborated upon by key English Poor Law ideologues, such as Nassau Senior and Bentham's former assistant, Sir Edward Chadwick.[3] It reflected a radically new consolidation and centralisation of the British state's infrastructural powers in both islands.

## INSPECTION AND INTERVENTION

A new central authority, the Poor Law Commission, was established with immense powers of inspection and intervention. As Kinealy notes 'overall, both in principle and in underlying ethos, the Irish Poor Law was intended to be more stringent than its English counterpart. Its provisions illustrated an approach to policy that underpinned the government's response to the onset of famine in Ireland only seven years later.'[4] At the local level, an entirely new tier of government administration – the Poor Law Union network – was put in place, and not just uniformity in administration procedures was sought but uniformity in the design of the workhouse building itself. Complete with its guardians' boardroom, officers' quarters and great dormitory blocks, the workhouse was so designed that the poor inside would feel it utterly futile 'to contest the physical and institutional array of awesome power'.[5]

It appears that the original English Poor Law workhouse layout was copied from the design of American prisons. The bleak, forbidding design was clearly geared to *deter* people from entering. Irish workhouses were almost invariably much larger than their English counterparts – 'more ishing new creations in a mainly rural landscape long dominated by a vernacular architecture of relatively simple but effective arrangements of farmhouses, townhouses, churches and mills built on a more human scale.

Both the design and functions of the Irish workhouses were imbued with the prevailing ethos of the modern English welfare state – that of laissez-faire. This involved rules based on the concept of classification, its associated symbolic and disciplinary dimensions and its corollary, geographical or spatial separation. Hence the debates about the layout of the workhouse, the need for the division of the sexes into separate wards and the need for strong internal, walled boundaries. Hence the need for high external walls, nine to eleven feet high, to make a powerful statement – both physical and symbolic – about the world *inside* vis-à-vis the world *outside* the walls. Today, 170 years later – even if every other feature of the workhouse has been eradicated or refurbished – these great enclosing walls survive on practically every workhouse site in Ireland. They were to perpetuate a profoundly disturbing social boundary in the landscape.

Poor Law social policy assumed the existence of discrete social groups who were to be bounded by recognisable territorial limits and governed by specific dietary and other norms and patterns of conduct:

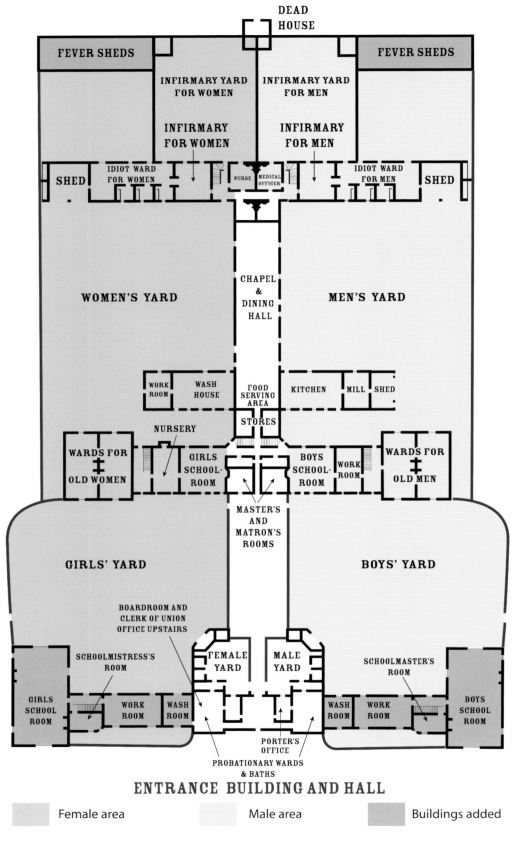

Fig. 3 General workhouse plan: classification, segregation, surveillance and control of inmate activities and movements and a hierarchical management system were central motifs in the design of the workhouse.

When workhouse inmates are spoken to, where they are set to work, where they dress, where they eat, and where they retire for rest, where husbands and wives and children and parents meet, where sickness falls, where the old (and sick) die and the

forbidding and even more gloomy, narrow and repulsive'[6] and they were expected to serve union areas much larger than their English equivalents. The workhouses were aston-

Fig. 4  Workhouse walls which survive on many workhouse sites throughout Ireland. [Photos: William J. Smyth]

young are born, where the House is 'entered' and where it is left – it matters not when and where – the statement [both symbolic and geographical] is forever proclaimed. 'You are a pauper and you ought to know it.[7]

At the centre of this social system was the new 'technology' of classification, used for differentiating and regulating human populations, most particularly the 'means of testing' as to whom were eligible or ineligible for relief. But the Irish Poor Law had one notable omission as compared with the English Poor Law: the absence of a legal or statutory right of the Irish poor to be provided with relief: in England every destitute person had that right. So during the Famine, when a workhouse was deemed full, the Poor Law administrators were under no obligation to fund alternative accommodation for the destitute outside the gates. Like most other Irish workhouses, some of the destitute of Roscrea Union (see below) were to suffer from that discriminatory law.

## A DELIBERATE DETERRENT

The *laissez-faire* ideology of this so-called liberal state was 'to subordinate the activity of the state to the needs of the self-regulating markets', emphasising 'the moral virtues of individual self-exertion, the sanctity of private property and the vices of political centralism'.[8] And yet, as Felix Driver has demonstrated, the so-called 'free market' 'was opened and kept open by an enormous increase in continuous and centrally organised and controlled interventions by the state'.[9] And these workhouses were built to play a powerful role in *protecting* the labour market – not replacing it. The entire strategy of the English 1834 – and the later Irish – Poor Law, was to draw a major line of distinction between the class of independent labourers (outside in the countryside and the towns) and the class of paupers (confined to workhouses). The workhouse system was designed as a deliberate deterrent to repulse the able-bodied population and to ensure that only the truly destitute would seek relief in those heavily regulated institutions. As John O'Connor emphasises, the workhouse regime involved labour, discipline, *confinement* and

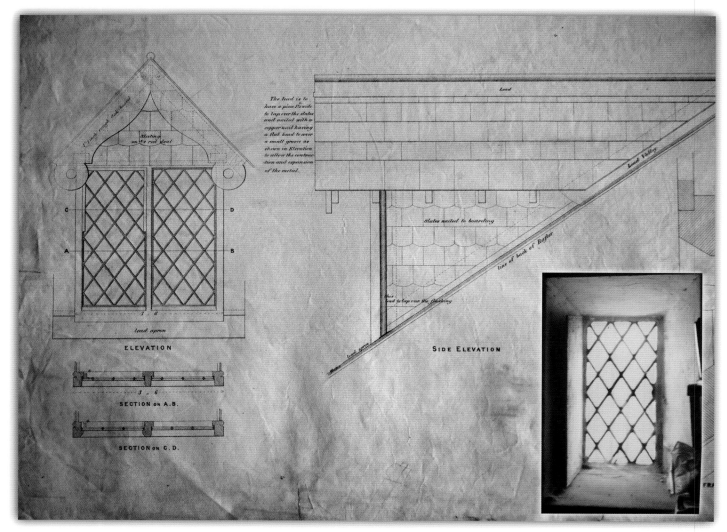

Fig. 5  Detailed plans for the construction of windows at Mallow Union workhouse. The windows with their distinctive diamond-shaped panes of glass were generally small in size, resulting in inadequate ventilation and light. [Source: Irish Architectural Archive]

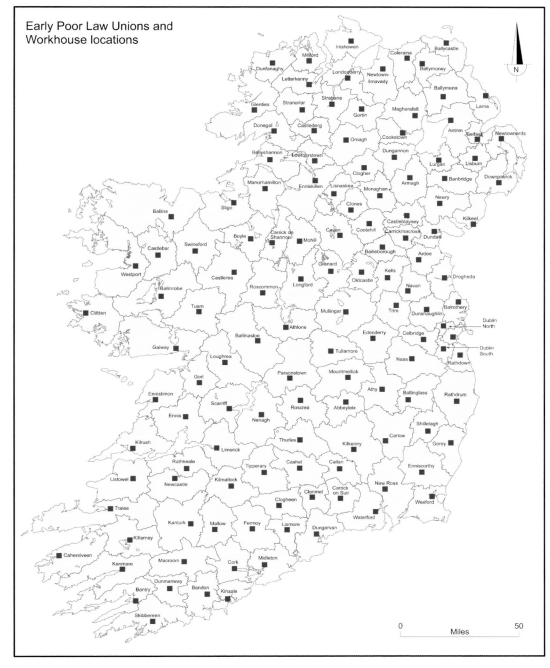

Early Poor Law Unions and Workhouse locations

Fig. 6  POOR LAW UNIONS, 1842–49.

local responsibility; henceforth the striking and payment of the poor rate was to be a central concern of both landlords and other ratepayers.

It is important to realise how revolutionary this new territorial framework of unions – each with its own newly designated central place and workhouse – was in the Irish context. The radical reorganisation of Ireland's administrative system in the second half of the sixteenth century, with its creation of many new counties and baronies, was still built on *older* territorial units.[11] Now in the late 1830s, with the advice of the very able geographer-engineer, Thomas Larcom, a brand-new territorial system is superimposed with great alacrity over the whole country. It was an astonishing achievement. Not for the first time, Ireland was perceived as a *tabula rasa*, 'a blank page in terms of poor relief, upon which the government could impose policies that would have proved unacceptable in England'.[12]

Judgments had to be made about which towns to select as the new union centres and estimates made of the populations in the hinterlands to be served by each centre. However, the trauma of the Famine years revealed gaps in these judgments and estimates; Ballymahon (County Longford), Ballyvaughan (County Clare), Bawnboy (County Cavan), Belmullet (Mayo), Borrisokane (County Tipperary), Castlecomer (County Kilkenny), Castletownbere (County Cork), Castletowndevlin (County Meath), Claremorris (County Mayo), Clonakilty (County Cork), Corofin (County Clare), Croom (County Limerick), Dingle (County Kerry, 1848), Donaghmore (Queen's County), Dromore West (County Sligo), Glenamaddy (County Roscommon), Glin (on the Limerick/Kerry border), Kildysart (County Clare), Killala (County Mayo), Kilmacthomas (County Waterford), Mill-

the deprivation of ordinary living standards.[10] A radically new surveillance and disciplinary regime had been introduced to manage and control the Irish poor. The Poor Law planners saw themselves as *modernisers* – initiating and 'normalising' a programme of social control.

All of the workhouses were part of this extraordinary new territorial network of 130 unions and 2,049 electoral divisions, built upon 65,000 pre-existing townlands. These newly constituted electoral divisions were not only the units for the election of members to the union's board of guardians but also the units for the imposition of a new local tax which came to be known as the poor rate. The maintenance of the workhouse and the union was to be a street and Mitchelstown (County Cork), Mountbellew (County Galway), Newport (County Mayo), Oughterard and Portumna (County Galway), Schull (County Cork), Strokestown (County Roscommon), Thomastown (County Kilkenny), Tubbercurry (County Sligo), Tulla (County Clare), Urlingford (on the Kilkenny/Tipperary border), and Youghal (on the Cork/Waterford border), all had to be added in the early 1850s, highlighting both distant peripheries and in-between areas badly served by the network established in the early 1840s.

Even more striking was the fact that these new territorial units christened 'unions' were not built up from the civil parishes. These had been utilised from at least the early seventeenth century as both units of administration and enumeration – hence the term *civil* parish'. In England, the new Poor Law unions were built upon the older parish networks – the units for Poor Law delivery since Elizabethan times. But Ireland was a very different place. Unique in Western Europe by the mid-nineteenth century, it contained two parish sys-

tems, that of the Church of Ireland (using the medieval/civil parish units) and that of the refurbished and reconstituted parishes of the now resurgent Catholic Church.[13] The civil parish in Ireland had never functioned in any meaningful sense as a unit for helping all the poor, whatever their religious affiliation. The English-born planners of the new Poor Law unions avoided the use of any religious-defined territories. They decided to build up such units from an amalgamation of townlands – the most ancient administrative and landholding units in the country – into new district electoral divisions (DEDs).

These DEDs were the areal units for electing members to the board of guardians and for taxing its rate-payers. Within a period of three years a radically new grid for managing and ruling the populations had been put in place and these union entities and administrations often transcended ancient county boundaries, thus further weakening the power of the county grand juries, the latter essentially committees of landlords or their represen-

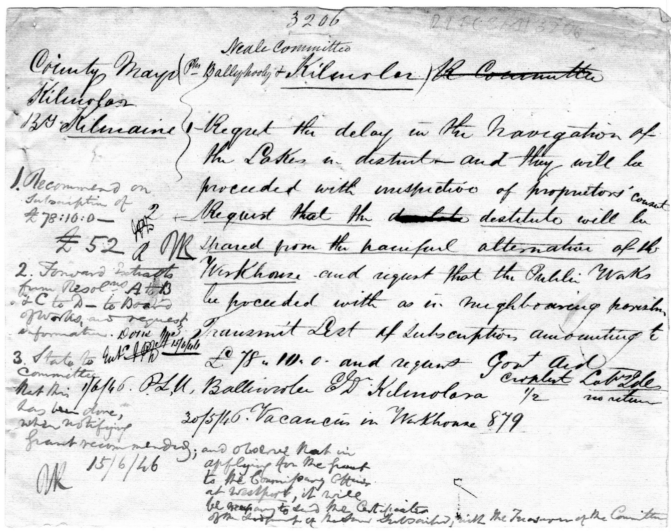

Fig. 7 The workhouse as an institution was feared as evident from the following request. The Kilmolara Relief Committee, County Mayo, 13 June 1846, make known to the relief commissioners their concerns in relation to the delay in the introduction of public works in the parish. They ask specifically that the destitute will 'be spared the painful alternative of the workhouse' and request 'that the public works be proceeded with as in neighbouring parishes'. [Source: Relief Commission Papers, 3/1/3206, National Archives Ireland]

Fig. 9 Dormitory in Birr workhouse. [Photo: David Haslam]

Fig. 8 Some volumes of the Tipperary Poor Law unions in Thurles library. All of the surviving records, from 1839 onwards, of every Poor Law Union in County Tipperary are housed in the 'Tipperary Studies' section of the Tipperary County Library at 'The Source' in Thurles town. This photo is of one of the six bays devoted to these records. Included in the collection are board of guardian minutes, letters to and from the Poor Law Commissioners, rate books, financial statements and some later indoor relief registers as well as communications from the local government board. Very few admission records survive for Tipperary unions during the Famine period, but some do for the later nineteenth century (personal communication: Ms Mary Guinan-Darmody). Given that the volumes shown in this photo comprise less than 1% of the total of union records for the whole country, the reader can more fully appreciate the intense levels of scrutiny and accounting that accompanied the operation of the Poor Law system throughout all of Ireland. [Photo: William J. Smyth]

tatives. For example, Roscrea Union incorporated electoral divisions from three counties – King's, Queen's and Tipperary. All of these changes emphasised the very deliberate 'modernising' thrust that underpinned both the English and Irish Poor Law.

But the union workhouses had never been designed to deal with atrocious famine conditions. It had never been envisaged that the workhouses would have to deal with such large numbers or with so many sick people. 'Death became a way of life in the workhouse.'[14] The average annual number of deaths in the workhouses in pre-Famine years from 1842 to 1845 was 4,944. In 1846 this figure comes to 14,662. But in 1847, the workhouses alone saw 68,890 deaths; in 1848 45,482 deaths; in 1849 64,440 deaths in 1850 46,721 and in 1851 *c*.38,000.[15] Close on one-third of a million people died in the workhouses in the Famine years from 1846 to 1852. Over 50,000 are recorded as dying in the associated fever hospitals in those years. And we have no certain record of the thousands and thousands who died outside these institutions across the island because of the placing of the full burden of famine relief on the 130 Poor Law Unions in 1847.

# Classify, confine, discipline and punish – the Roscrea Union:[1]
# A microgeography of the workhouse system during the Famine

*William J. Smyth*

## INTRODUCTION

The building of Roscrea Union workhouse was completed in April 1842 – and its first admissions were on 3 May of that year. It was built in the townland of Scart to the south

Fig 1. LOCATION MAP, INCLUDING THE CIVIL PARISHES IN ROSCREA POOR LAW UNION. This is a map of the civil parishes (or parts thereof) in the Roscrea Union. They vary greatly in size, a reflection of the long and complicated ecclesiastical and landowning history of their evolution. Early medieval in origin, these civil parishes remained as crucial units of assessment, administration and enumeration until the Poor Law Act established the new territorial entities of district electoral divisions, rate collection districts and unions. However, these parishes were still the basic reporting units in the 1841 and 1851 censuses.

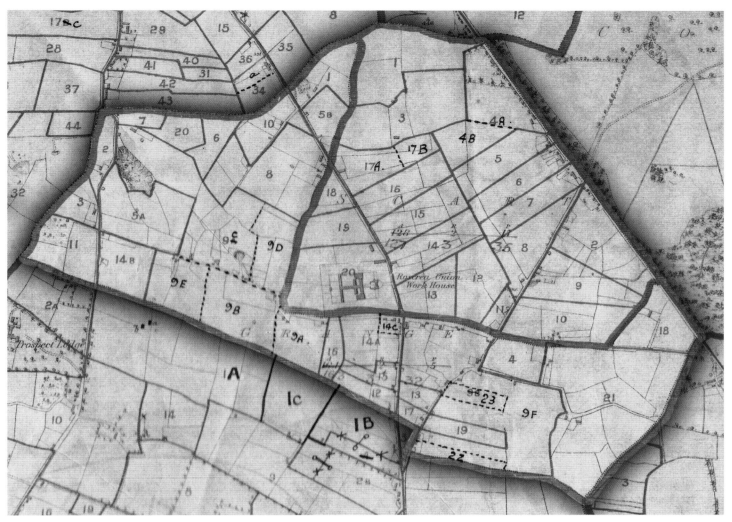

Fig. 2 VALUATION MAP OF LOCATION OF ROSCREA UNION WORKHOUSE. The mapping of Ireland at the six-inch scale by the Ordnance Survey was primarily instituted to facilitate Richard Griffith's valuation of each townland on the island. This early valuation map includes the townland of Scart where the Roscrea workhouse was built in 1842 close to the southern boundary with the townland of Grange. To the northeast are the demesne lands of Corville House while the Roscrea–Templemore Road bisects the map and passes by the workhouse entrance on the east side. The location of the workhouse well away from the town of Roscrea should be noted – it is typical of so many workhouse locations. The landholding unit number twenty defines the territory of the workhouse, comprising the original geometric six acres allocated and also includes extensions to the north and west to comprise an overall unit of eleven acres. The workhouse cemetery extended into the western part. It is also probable that the need for additional cemetery ground led to the acquisition of part of the Grange holding in the general area marked 9D. Apart from the institutional land of the union workhouse, all the other nineteen holdings in Scart and twenty-one others in Grange (like every other holding in every townland in the country) were subject to the annual payment of rates to support the Poor Law system in their union. [Source: Valuation Office, Irish Life Centre, Dublin]

of the town to accommodate 700 poor people at a cost of £6,700. Roscrea, then with a population of 5,275, was a strong market and fair town and contained a woollen mill, two breweries, two tanneries and three flour mills. The fitting out of its workhouse cost a further £1,296. The relatively swift building and opening of the Roscrea workhouse clearly reflected the capacity of the local elite to raise sufficient funds for the building work to begin. In parts of the West of Ireland, the building and opening of workhouses were much slower. Clifden did not do so until 8 March 1847, Westport on 5 November 1845, Swinford on 14 April 1846, Tuam on 4 May 1846, Castlerea on 30 May 1846, Glenties on 24 July 1846, and Cahirciveen on 7 October 1846, Listowel on 13 February 1845 and Letterkenny on 14 March 1845. Dunfanaghy did not open until 24 June 1845. Kenmare opened on 25 October 1845, Killarney on 5 April 1845 and

Lowtherstown on 1 October 1845. Antrim, Ballymena, Ballyshannon, Carlow, Clogher, Clones, Donegal, Dungarvan, Inishowen, Kanturk, Lisnaskea, Macroom, Roscommon, Stranorlar and Tralee did not open their doors to the poor for at least one year and often two years after Roscrea's opening.[2]

Roscrea workhouse cost nearly £1,000 more than that of Thurles (opened on 7 November 1842), built to accommodate 700; £1,500 less than Nenagh (opened on 28 April 1842), built to accommodate 1,000, and just £200 less than Birr (Parsonstown), built to house 800 (and opened on 2 April 1842). Except for Mountmellick (built for 800 at a cost of £6,900 and opened as late as 3 January 1845), all the other workhouses in the midland counties of King's (Offaly), Queen's (Laois) and Tipperary were built and opened between 1841 and the middle of 1842.

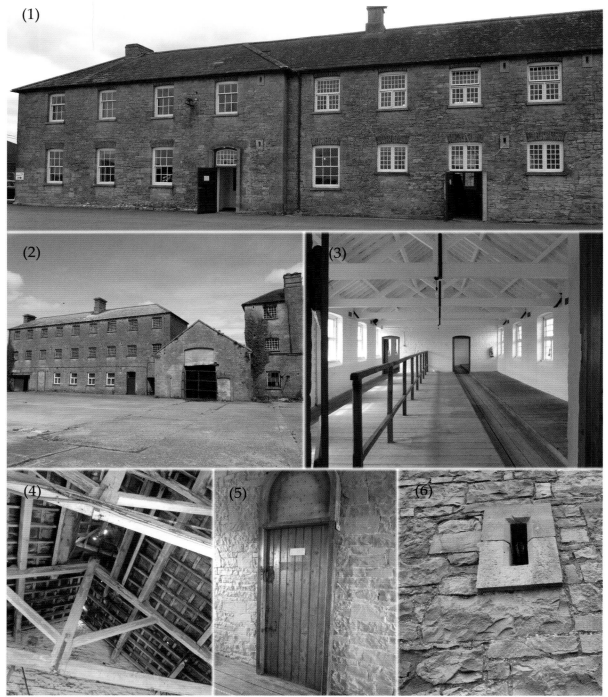

Fig. 3  Donaghmore workhouse. Donaghmore Poor Law Union was established on 7 June 1850, comprising thirteen electoral divisions, twelve of which were separated from Roscrea union and one, Grantstown, from Abbeyleix Union. The specific inclusion of Grantstown points to the political influence of the Fitzpatrick landlord family. The Poor Law Boundary Commission only ranked Donaghmore at number forty-six (out of fifty) of the most urgently required new unions that needed to be established. As it happened, only thirty-three new unions were created: clearly Donaghmore had succeeded in being moved up the priority list. Nearly 600 people from the Donaghmore Union were inmates at Roscrea workhouse in mid-1850, but by December 1853, Donaghmore workhouse – opened earlier in that year – contained only 229 inmates or 2.3% of the union's population. Closed in 1886, it remained underutilised until the Donaghmore Co-operative creamery established its headquarters there in 1927. More recently was been acquired by Laois County Council. It is one of the best preserved workhouses on the island. Its front line of buildings now function as the home of a very worthwhile agricultural and workhouse museum. In the top photo (1) the master's rooms are located to the left. Here he could both observe the poor people waiting for admission and more critically observe the boy's yard from his back window. Between the two doorways on the ground floor was the storeroom – strictly controlled with large lock and key by the master or his deputy. The second door in this photo opens into the rather spacious boys' schoolroom. Above the room were the schoolmaster's room (with fireplace) and the boys' dormitory – the latter as shown in photo 3. Its raised bed platforms recall the extreme spartan conditions that characterised workhouse life for young and old. At the right end of the building was the probationary ward for males. In photo 2, the entrances to the dining hall (cum chapel) are highlighted, emphasising the separate doorways for the men on the left side and the women on the right side of these dormitory buildings. Strict gender segregation was one of the central principles in workhouse design. Originally, a high wall separated the men's yard (to the left) from the women's yard. The ground floor of these dormitory buildings contained workrooms and a day-room on the men's side and the matron's rooms and day-room for the women inmates. Photo 4 emphasises the starkness of the interiors – in this case of the roof – while photos 5 and 6 emphasise the critical importance of ventilation in dormitories, often characterised by overcrowded and congested conditions, so conducive to the spread of infectious diseases. [Photos: William J. Smyth]

Every aspect of Roscrea's workhouse design reflected the classificatory and discriminatory ideology of the Poor Law system, as did the rules governing the lives of both staff and the poor people admitted. Thereafter the latter would be called 'inmates' or 'paupers' in all the records – a classification and standard terminology which matched the specific 'Roscrea Union'-stamped uniforms they would wear after being admitted into the ground hall of the admission or entrance block. Admission beyond this space meant that one's identity was radically transformed and subsumed under the same union uniform, the same rules and discipline that governed every other pauper inside.

Like many other unions in the west and south, Roscrea Union was eventually deemed to be too large and its eastern electoral division in Queen's County (comprising Borris-in-Ossory, Donaghmore, Erke, Kyle and Rathdowney) was combined with one electoral division – Grantstown – from the western part of Abbeyleix Union to create the union of Donaghmore. Constituted in 1850, it opened up its doors to Poor Law applicants in the summer of 1853. Located in the open countryside, it occupied a site located halfway between the town of Rathdowney and the new important railway junction at Ballybrophy.

Back in the summer of 1845 there are few signs of the gathering storm in the Roscrea Union workhouse. With an 'inmate' population of *c.*330, the workhouse – like most workhouses in Ireland – was less than half-full. Before the Famine, most of the Irish poor 'preferred the freedom of their precarious trade for the dismal certainty within [workhouse] walls'.[3] Master O'Malley of the workhouse – Mr George A. O'Malley – notes there are twenty-three paupers in the workhouse for more than three years. The hay on the workhouse land is being sold by auction for £1. The manure of the workhouse is ordered to be sold by auction and is purchased by Mr Smallman for £5. Earlier in January 1845, an advertisement for tenders to flag the potato stores appears. In a vote to elect the union's treasurer, the National Bank defeats the Agricultural and Commercial Bank by seventeen votes to fourteen. Master O'Malley suggests the propriety of taking the shoes off the children as the weather is so fine – and the board of guardians approve. The state of the children's dormitories and nursery is reported as satisfactory.

Three farmers' wives from the parish of Bourney, 'Mrs. Wall', wife of Thomas

Wall, Eliza Cotton, wife of Francis Cotton and Jane Wall, wife of Henry Wall request permission to hire Catherine Curley (orphan, aged fifteen years), Maura Fitzgerald (orphan, aged ten years) and Mary Fitzgerald (orphan, aged fourteen years) respectively as servants 'at 5/- a quarter' to be retained for at least six months. Two of these young girls, resident for a long time in the workhouse, and having outgrown their workhouse clothes, have new suits of clothes ordered for them as they venture into the outside world. The workhouse is populated by very old people (average age of seventy-three) or the very young (average age of seven). Captain W.H. Smith has never been absent from a meeting of the Board of Guardians since its foundation in 1842.

The rules and regulations of the Poor Law are regularly enforced. Paupers Margaret Wallace and Betty Moten appeal to Master O'Malley as to the unsuitability of the infirmary nurse, Johanna Hickey. The chaplain and medical officer are consulted, the case of the nurse is investigated and her resignation is accepted. A complaint of misconduct is brought against some of the female paupers who are brought before the Board of Guardians. It appears that they have acted indecently and three of them are discharged. Peggy Ryan and her family are also discharged for it

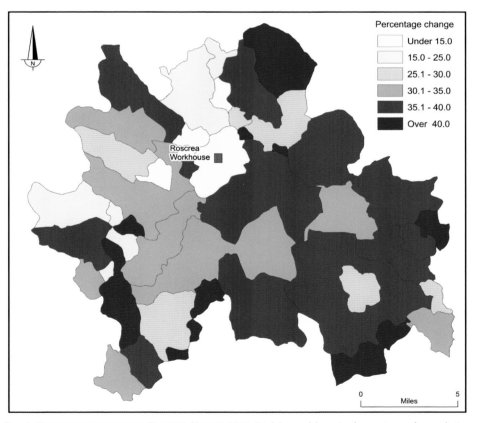

Fig. 4 POPULATION DECLINE IN ROSCREA UNION, 1841–51. Mapped here is the pattern of population decline across these civil parishes in the Famine decade. Declines vary from 4% to over 40% with the heaviest population losses mainly in the eastern half of the union. However, it is also noticeable that the very highest losses (at over 40%) are very much on the periphery (and distant from the union centre at Roscrea) – as at Erke, Kildelig, Roscomroe, Borrisnafarney and the parts of Templemore parish in the Roscrea Union. This map also confirms the highly varied population densities of neighbouring parishes. Hence the difficulties of generalising about Famine conditions locally.

emerges that her husband is at work in Thurles when she had reported he had gone to America.

The turf contractor is called before the board for failing to meet his contract. The tailor is reported to have gone missing and the Clerk of the Union, Edward Wall, is ordered to advertise for another. William Butler is summoned before the magistrates for building a cabin which had taken advantage of the road wall of the workhouse to give it solidity. Betty Mannion is accused of stealing clothes from the laundry and secreting them under beds in the hospital. She is ordered to be put on a half-diet and on four hours confinement for four days. A Christmas dinner is ordered for the paupers. They are to get their special meat and vegetable dinner on Christmas Day and on New Year's Day, 1846, tea and coffee is to be ordered for the paupers.

In January 1845, John Davis is discharged for refusing to work and for stealing potatoes. On 7 November 1845, Master George O'Malley is involved in a discussion with the board as to the quality of the potatoes; as a consequence it is resolved that an additional half pound of potatoes is to be added to the diet of each class of inmate and the Physician Dr Henry Powell and Master O'Malley are to report on same the next Friday meeting of the Board. On 21 February 1846, the Clerk (Edward Wall) notified the guardians by circular on the subject of the potato disease. A letter from the Poor Law Commissioners (PLCs) is received on 27 February 1846 on the question of the status of the potato crop and requesting information from the several members of the board on the subject. The board replies to the Commissioners on 6 March 1846. Over the twelve months in 1845, twenty-six people die in the workhouse – only twelve had died in 1844. No one would have expected this figure to quadru-

Fig. 5 Board of Guardians minute books for Roscrea Union, 1843–48. These sturdy volumes contain the minutes of the Board of Guardians for Roscrea Union and workhouse which were begun in June 1839. Included here is vol. 2 (February 1843–February 1844), vol. 3 (February 1844–January 1845), vol. 4 (January 1845–October 1845), vol. 5 (November 1845–August 1846), vol. 6 (August 1846–July 1847) and vol. 7 (July 1847–January 1848). There are a further eight volumes dealing with the remainder of Famine period up to and including vol. 15 (April 1852-November 1852). As the Famine intensified, the time period covered by each volume is reduced, beginning with volumes dealing with a full year but later on each volume is confined to a half-year of proceedings. Volume 90 is the final minute book dealing with the period January 1923 to September 1923. Also surviving are volumes of letters from the Poor Law Commissioners and local government board running from June 1849 to October 1900 as well as some few rough minute books, union ledgers and indoor relief regulations. All these volumes are classified from BG141/A/1 to BG141/G/4 in the Thurles library. [Photo: William J. Smyth]

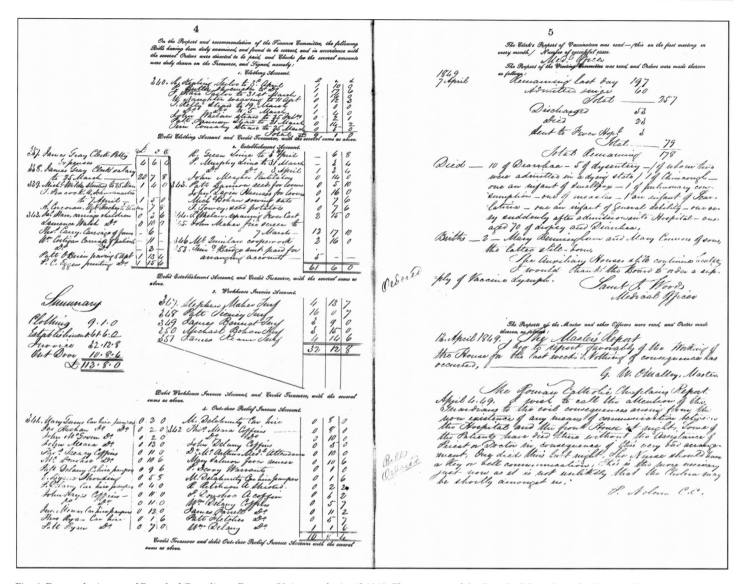

Fig. 6 Pages of minutes of Board of Guardians, Roscrea Union, early April 1849. The minutes of the Board of Guardians for Roscrea Union have survived for the whole period of the Great Famine (1845–52). Here, pages 4 and 5 of these minutes are illustrated, providing an example of the report and recommendations of the finance committee in early April 1849. Included is the workhouse and outdoor relief invoices account, the report of the medical officer, the master and the Roman Catholic chaplain. The finance committee directs payment of the clothing account of £9.1.0 comprising the work of tailors, shoemaker, weaver and others; it also confirms payment of all establishment costs (£61.6.0) of the clerk of the union, James Gray, the steward Michael Wilde, the schoolmaster T. Peacock, and agricultural teacher, A. Corcoran as well as the cost of the carriage of children and patients and the printing cost of P.E. Eggers. The heating and cooking needs of the workhouse requires the payment of bills for turf loads supplied by Stephen Maher, Patrick Tierney, James Bennett, Michael Bohan and James Keane, amounting to £21.12.8. A very informative outdoor relief account details monies paid for car-hire, many coffins, shrouding and attendance by medical doctor and fever nurse. The medical officer, Samuel Woods, details the numbers remaining in the infirmary (178), those discharged (53), those who died (23) in the previous week while three had been sent to the Roscrea fever hospital. The cause of the death of those who died is provided: ten of diarrhoea, five of dysentery (two of the latter had been admitted in a dying state). Chincough (whooping cough), smallpox, consumption, measles, scarlatina, general debility, sudden death (after admission) and dropsy and diarrhoea (of a seventy-year-old) accounted for the other deaths. Two births are recorded but one, a boy, is still-born. The master, G.W. O'Malley, reports favourably on the 'Working of the House' during the previous week noting that 'nothing of consequence' has occurred. The chaplain, P. Nolan C.C. identified the 'evil consequences' of a lack of adequate communication between the hospital and the front house at night. The board orders that the nurse is to be provided with a bell. The chaplain notes that the matter is even more urgent now since 'the cholera may be shortly amongst us'. [Source: Minute Book, BG 141/A/9].

ple to just over 100 in 1846. That close to 700 paupers would die in the workhouse in the following year – 1847 – was then beyond the gloomiest of imaginations. By May 1852 over 3,000 paupers had perished in the Roscrea workhouse since 1845. The relative calm worlds of 1844 and 1845 had vanished. In their stead, came famine, hunger, overcrowding, disease and death, as well as conflict, shame and humiliation.

The objective of this chapter is to explore in detail the microgeography of the Roscrea Union workhouse during the years of the Great Famine. At all times it is hoped to situate these specific experiences and behaviour patterns within an island-wide context. The previous chapter looked at the workhouse system, its design, and its rules and regulations at its inception. This chapter summarises the congestion problems that arose and the building adaptations carried out in the workhouse consequent on the intensification of the Famine crisis. The final part of the chapter documents the enormous death toll that occurred within the workhouse. The chapter concludes with an evaluation of the impact of the Poor Law and particularly the union and its workhouse on the lives of the people of this region as well as island-wide during the years of the Great Famine.

The two main sources for this work are the Minute and Letter Books of the Roscrea Board of Guardians. However, we have to accept that the reality of life inside and outside the workhouse is only partially revealed in these books. There are the inevitable gaps, repressions and partial amnesias that characterise all such official records. Careful attention has also been paid to local newspapers and the work of local historians. In addition, the vast workings of the imperial bureaucracy – as revealed in this case in the voluminous documentation relating to 'proceedings for the relief of distress and state of the unions and workhouses in Ireland' – have received due attention.

## CONGESTION AND BUILDING ADAPTATIONS

As the recognition of the scale of the potato blight deepened in early January 1846, the PLCs forwarded a general circular to all the unions on the best models for extending the workhouse buildings. They noted, in particular, that the wing buildings could be extended by about half their present length in each direction and that a range of single buildings could be created along the side walls of the men's and women's yards, allowing for dormitories of one or two stories high. However, already in 1845, a Lt Col of the Royal Engineers, George Barney – commissioned to make a report on the execution of building contracts for the Irish workhouses – while generally satisfied with the work, had noted a series of defects which were to prove highly problematic during the approaching famine years.[4]

Addressing workhouses like Roscrea, built for accommodating 700 inmates, he noted the inadequate size and poor ventilation of the dayrooms. But in what turned out to be a more deadly defect, he criticised the inadequate size of the nurseries and infirmaries – and if there was no fever hospital attached, as was the case with Roscrea, infirmary accommodation was further compromised. The kitchen and washhouse was also too small, badly lit, and badly ventilated. He noted that the privies in the men's and women's yards were sufficient and well situated to the rear of the buildings whereas those in the boys and girls yards were a nuisance, especially in the summer months. Damp walls were still an issue, given the speed of the building of the workhouses during winter as well as summer months. While the inner boundary walls were adequate, he noted that the outer boundary of ditch and hedge was insufficient – that adequate walling of the whole workhouse grounds was necessary, particularly if the workhouse – like that of Roscrea – was located beside a major public road. He confirmed that these institutions would be totally inadequate if there was either a failure of crops or a severe winter

occurred. Both destinies were on their way.

At the same time as the relief committees in the parishes were endeavouring to address the dreadful increasing misery in the countryside, the first sign of stresses requiring spatial adjustment in the workhouse came in April 1846. Then the smallpox patients were placed in the ward set aside for 'male idiots'. Able-bodied inmates filled in the cellar under the women's wing and a drain was dug to carry off the rising water in the cellar from land springs. On 20 June, there was the necessity of sinking other wells in the yards – the provision of wells and good drinking water had been a weakness from the beginning. In August 1846, following the recommendation of the Medical Officer, Dr Powell, a new partition was erected in the hospital between the women's and men's wards, given the consistently greater number of women patients.

However, the first major crisis of numbers and space occurs in November/December 1846. On 14 November 1846, the *Tipperary Vindicator* reports that:

Fig. 7 George Wilkinson (1814–1890). Wilkinson was born in Witney, Oxfordshire. An architect by profession, he was appointed the Poor Law Commissioners' architect in Ireland in January 1839 with the sole responsibility of designing and erecting 130 Irish workhouses. This vast building programme was complete by 1847. However, the impact of the Famine and the increasing numbers of destitute necessitated an extended building programme, including the construction of a further thirty workhouses. [Source: Irish Architectural Archive]

134

dreadful instances of extreme suffering and destitution have been reported to us . . . The workhouses are everywhere filling even beyond the numbers for which they were built and in more than one locality hundreds have been obliged to go away without admission whilst the Poor Law Commissioners have issued a letter against receiving a far greater number than that for which the Workhouses were originally intended.[5]

The newspaper goes on to observe that in several cases 'landlords are keeping aloof from the performance of their obvious duties . . . literally doing nothing for the people'.[6] It also notes that 'the land is lying idle because . . . the poorer description of farmers cannot possibly pay the labourer, nor could the labourer support himself or the wages which the farmer heretofore was accustomed to give him'.[7]

On 4 December, Master O'Malley referred to the number admitted to the Roscrea workhouse that day – 123 paupers. This meant that the workhouse now accommodated ninety more than the house was built to contain. The Board of Guardians then inspected the sheds and requested permission from the PLCs to build stone walls to enclose the straw sheds for the purposes of converting them into additional wards 'which are now much required'. Given the

great influx of paupers, the board held further emergency meetings. On 12 December 1846, Master O'Malley reported on the crowded state of the nursery, which was only large enough for half the number of children in it. He feared the breaking out of infectious diseases since there were already four cases of smallpox, some of 'chincough' (whooping cough) and the means of keeping the sick separate was very difficult. The need to build an additional nursery was urgent. In addition, it was planned to add a storey to the idiot wards so as to provide additional hospital room. Equally, sleeping platforms needed to be erected on the upper floors of the dormitories. Both Master O'Malley and the Visiting Committee – informing the board of the crowded state of the hospital – recommended that no more be admitted, particularly women and children as all these wards were overcrowded. Accommodation problems were thus exacerbated since women and children then comprised 88% of the total intake.

Carpenter Michael Hall won the contract to erect the sleeping platforms for the contract sum of £93/15/0. He was to find all materials; strong boards to be of the best deal uprights, joins and bearers to be of the best yellow pine, according to the specifications provided by the PLC architect, George Wilkinson. The contractor was not to receive any money until the work was completed and approved.

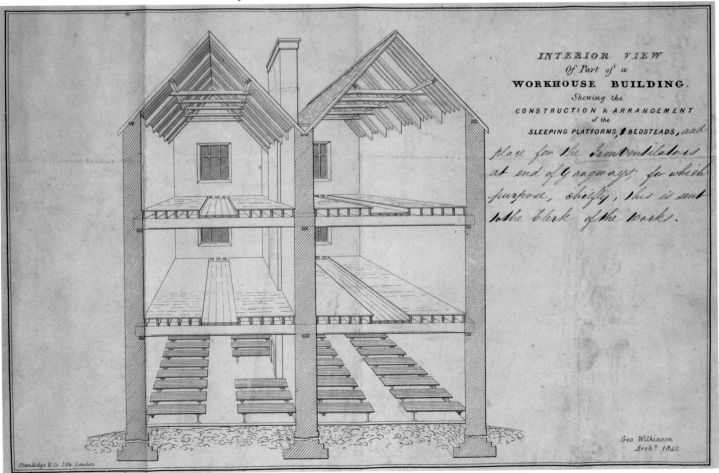

Fig. 8 Wilkinson's construction plans for sleeping quarters and bedsteads. [Source: Irish Architectural Archive]

grounds to serve as probationary and convalescent space for fever patients. The era of the dreaded 'fever sheds' had arrived (more fever sheds were added in 1848). The number in the workhouse had trebled from 339 to 940 between 1 January 1846 and 1 January 1847.

Behind these grim statistics lay 'the truly awful condition of the great mass of the population'.[8] The worst horrors of a famine was seen to threaten everywhere. On 16 December 1846, the *Tipperary Vindicator* observes that 'there is a universal outcry from friend and foe against the policy of the Government . . . Food is becoming scarcer everyday and it has reached an enormous price.'[9] And the newspaper is correct in noting that supplies were not coming into the country. Earlier still on 11 December 1846, this newspaper reported that 'the places in Clare and Tipperary which have not local markets for supplies are the worst off, and in the greatest state of excitement'.[10] In such situations, the newspaper thinks 'the Government is extremely remiss in not forming depots'.[11] As for work on the relief roads, it laments 'how shocking to think of half-clad women and children sitting from dawn till dark breaking stones by the roadside, to procure the price of a meal for themselves!!'[12]

Hunger and fear of starvation also lay behind the unsettled state of the countryside in the winter of 1846/47. The local newspaper reports: 'we have accounts of general outages consequent of the extreme miseries of the people'.[13] Sheep, especially, as well as cattle were regularly stolen and killed for food. Bread, Indian meal and flour carts were attacked and bags and stacks of wheat and barley stolen. Turnip fields were defended and attacked; carriers were assaulted and goods and money stolen.[14] Unable to pay £1/5– yearly at 7d a day to the farmer Martin Brophy for the house and land, Patrick Delaney and his family 'had to go to the Poor House of Roscrea, leaving nothing in the house and 12/- rent due'.[15]

Labourers were intimidated on public relief works because the road cutting might 'injure' a small portion of a farmer's holding. Ancient conflicts and rights to land and rent payments erupted: 'one hundred and fifty persons, all strangers assembled on the land of Carrig Inane, near Roscrea, to prevent the sale of certain effects seized by the Widow Egan for rent'.[16] It is also reported that 'arms have been generally obtained by the peasantry, etc., in the neighbourhood of Roscrea'.[17] Four men, two armed with pistols, robbed John Kirwan, 'an industrious farmer', of £1/10/- acquired for 'the sale of pigs disposed of at the fair of Shinrone, which the poor fellow had to pay his rent with'.[18] On

Fig. 9 Men's dormitory, Donaghmore workhouse. [Photo: William J. Smyth]

Subsequently, the carpenter was urged to employ an increased number of hands so as to expedite the work given the awfully pressing claims for admission. In the meantime, the Medical Officer, Dr. Powell and Master O'Malley recommended no further admissions until these new spaces were made available.

The completion of the sleeping gallery range in the women's dormitory required decisions on modes of ventilation. By the end of January 1847, the sleeping platforms were completed as was the enclosure of the straw sheds. Given congestion in the males' dayroom, a temporary dayhouse is built in the men's yard. By early March 1847, it is agreed to raise the men's ward one storey and to plan for a two-storey nursery dayroom and dormitory over the female ward of the infirmary. Originally built for the guardians' horses, the stable is now converted to enable fifty additional able-bodied males be accommodated. The stable is to be whitewashed, glazed and furnished with 'soil bedsteads'. In June 1847, Master O'Malley recommends to the board the necessity of erecting wooden sheds in the workhouse the same page as this reported robbery, the newspaper records that 'two additional infantry regiments are ordered for Ireland'.[19]

By early January 1847, the local newspaper reports that 'sheep stealing has become so universal that particulars possess no interest' and by 6 March 1847, accounts of the spread of destitution from all parts of the country are reported: 'the means of the people are becoming more and more exhausted every day and the number of these who are reduced to dependence on public works or public charity is rapidly increased'.[20] It is reported that hundreds of paupers have now gone to the workhouses and thousands of families 'are daily received at the Soup Kitchen'.[21] From southwest Cork, it is reported that 'the climax of mortality and misery has arrived. The peasantry are absolutely rotting off the surface of the earth'.[22] As Donnelly observes 'the tardy, frugal, short-sighted and ideologically-based policies adopted by the Whig Administration made inevitable the slide from distress to the national calamity of the Famine'.[23]

## ADAPTATIONS 1847–1850

Meanwhile, on 7 April 1847, the PLCs had accepted Guardian James W. Rolleston's offer of the old Dunkerrin Charter School as a site for the first auxiliary workhouse for Roscrea. On 2 April, Mr. Hancock, Assistant Inspector, confirms its fitness for the purpose with six acres adjoining. The Assistant Architect provides specifications for its adaptation to accommodate 200 boys. The upper floor is to function as dormitories, the ground floor as dayrooms with the rest as offices and the dining hall to be located at the back. Given child mortalities in the main workhouse, repairs are to be hastened

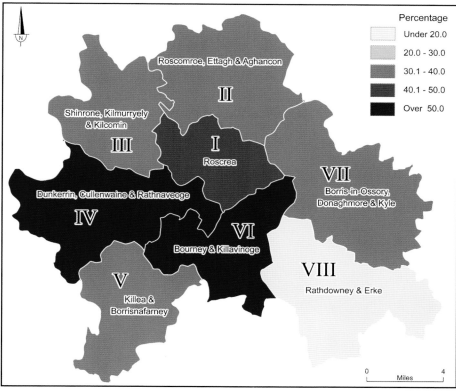

Fig. 10 PERCENTAGE DISTRIBUTION OF THE MAXIMUM NUMBER OF PERSONS SUPPLIED WITH FOOD UNDER THE SOUP KITCHEN ACT (EARLY SUMMER, 1847) PER RATE-COLLECTOR (AND LATER RELIEVING OFFICER) DISTRICTS. At the height of the Famine in mid-1847, over two-fifths of the total population of Roscrea union were in receipt of food relief via the soup kitchens. However, the initiation of this provision of food relief under the Soup Kitchen Act varied between electoral divisions and rate-collector districts. Soup kitchens in Cullenwaine, Dunkerrin and Rathnaveoge (and Aghancon) were put in place by 28 March 1847. The majority were established by mid- to late April 1847, but some, as at Borris-in-Ossory and Donaghmore, Borrisnafarney and Killea, Erke and Rathdowney, and at Bourney were not in place until mid- or late May. Consequently, the period of food relief provision could have varied by up to two months between districts. All soup kitchens were closed down by order between 15 and 29 August 1847. This map shows significant variations in the proportions receiving relief in the different rate-collectors' districts. Only 18.9% of the population of Rathdowney and Erke (opened late) received food relief at the peak of the scheme. In the 30 to 40% range, were Borrisnafarney and Killea (opened late), Borris-in-Ossory and Donaghmore and Kyle (apart from Kyle, opened late), Aghancon, Ellagh, and Roscomroe, Kilmurry, and Shinrone (opened reasonably early). In contrast, it would appear that the population of Roscrea (45.3%) and particularly Cullenwaine, Dunkerrin and Rathnaveoge (58.9%), plus Bourney and Killavenoge (53.8%), all opened quite early – were in the most desperate circumstances. Just over half of those receiving food at the peak were still in receipt of relief as the soup kitchens were sadly closed down – with Roscrea at 27% the seemingly least dependant on such relief by late August 1847. It needs to be stressed that the rate collection and relieving officer districts – underpinned by the newly constructed district electoral divisions – were entirely new territorial creations, bypassing the old civil parish districts (see Figure 1). This map shows that the focus of this new territorial system was Roscrea town, the union centre, with its own rate collection district. Radiating out from the centre were seven other districts, each of which were the responsibility of the local rate-collector (and later, when outdoor relief was introduced, by the local relieving officer). And at the base of this territorial hierarchy were the numerous townlands – each of which had been valued to provide a rate of so much in the £1 in support of the Poor Law system in the union.

and the boys removed there as quickly as possible. The whole building is whitewashed, tables, chairs and forms ordered. New oatmeal and rice orders are made and porridge cans and tin plates purchased. On 8 May 1847, Master O'Malley sends the first eighty-seven boys to the old Charter school. (Later on, workhouse girls are sent to Dunkerrin.) A chaplain for the boys is requested by the local parish priest. By 19 May 1847, an Assistant Matron is appointed and the schoolmaster is also to act as Assistant Master. A former pauper, Peter Kelly, is appointed porter and four

other paupers – two men and two women – are to assist in the supervision of the boys and in cooking respectively. Yet already by May 1847, three fever cases are reported for Dunkerrin. By late March 1848, there are forty-one patients in Dunkerrin in fever sheds and its parish priest refers to an epidemic in the surrounding district: 'Its wards are already dreadfully crowded and far from clean.'[24]

By 1 May 1847, Roscrea workhouse had adopted the following strategies to deal with its accommodation problems arising from the famine crisis: the conversion/adaptation of existing sheds and stables; the hiring of another building;

Fig. 11 Part of the remains of the auxiliary workhouse at Dunkerrin (formerly the site of the old Dunkerrin Charter School). [Photo: William J. Smyth]

the erection of sleeping galleries, and the raising of wards, which it had already begun to do. Across the country on this date and excluding the one-quarter of the workhouses which, as yet, had made no adaptations, over one-quarter of the other workhouses were involved in conversions and adaptations; one-fifth had hired another building; one-fifth had constructed new sheds to accommodate the pressures; 17% had erected sleeping galleries; and 5% were in the business of adding storeys to existing wards.[25] Of the thirty-three workhouses (out of 130), which the evidence suggests had made no alterations or adaptations, twenty-three were in the counties west of the Shannon, plus Counties Kerry and Donegal. The following workhouses were involved: Ballina, Ballinasloe, Ballinrobe, Ballyshannon, Baltinglass, Castlebar, Castleblayney, Castlerea, Celbridge, Clifden, Cootehill, Dunfanaghy, Ennis, Ennistymon, Glenties, Gort, Inishowen, Kenmare, Kilkeel, Killarney, Kilrush, Letterkenny, Longford, Loughrea, Lowtherstown (Irvinestown), Milford, Mohill, Newtown Limavady, Oldcastle, Parsonstown (Birr), Stranorlar, Swinford, Westport and Wexford. And, as we have seen, some of these workhouses – such as Clifden, Glenties and Cahirciveen – were only opened as late as 1846.

These workhouses in the poorest unions did not have the resources to even make these early crucial adaptations.

On the other hand, it is clear that the Roscrea Union's behaviour is much more characteristic of the better-off unions in the eastern half of the island. However, Roscrea workhouse is in a minority (15% of all workhouses) of availing of an existing fever hospital in the vicinity: one-third of the unions already had their own fever hospitals, and close on a further one-fifth were in the process of erecting one. Another one-fifth were appropriating the workhouse infirmary or other existing building for the purpose and/or building fever sheds. The remainder of workhouses (13%) were hiring another house to act as a fever hospital.

In the first half of 1847, the average number in the workhouse is 1,126, the infirmary is crowded with 125 patients, the Roscrea Fever Hospital receives an average of seventy-four paupers weekly and the death rate averages eighteen per week. Workhouse life becomes even more bleak, even more precarious. The Clerk is ordered to advertise the manure (dirty straw bedding, etc.) for sale. There are no takers.

By 31 July 1847, Roscrea Union's workhouse accommodation had been increased from its original 700 to 1,130; the sleeping platforms added 150, Dunkerrin auxiliary 200 and the 'airing' fever sheds for convalescent patients a further eighty places. Yet overcrowding, with all its ill effects, was still a problem in the winter of 1847/48. On a number of occasions, several destitute persons were refused entry for want of room. And only in early May 1848 do we get the occupation of the new buildings over the 'idiot wards' for nursery and hospital needs. In June 1848, a new baker house is constructed with oven and hot plates, so the workhouse can provide its own bread and is no longer dependent on what was sometimes a poor and inferior supply from the town's bakeries. A number of bakers are now added to the payroll. In that same summer, the union hires additional houses in Roscrea town as temporary dormitories for accommodating male paupers applying for relief when there is no room left in the main workhouse. The guardians also consider the building of its own fever hospital on workhouse grounds. Plans are sought from George Wilkinson but peace is restored with the Roscrea Fever Hospital and the workhouse does not build its own until 1850.

In August 1848, as the crowds gather at the workhouse gate, sentry boxes are erected for the nightwatchmen. Plans for the acquisition of another auxiliary workhouse are begun in September and by early December the proposal to rent Mr Edward Stephen Egan's brewery in Abbey Street in Roscrea is agreed at a cost of £180 per annum – to also include the dwelling house (now called Parkmore House), lawn and field. Likewise, agreement is reached with guardian, Mr William Minchin, to have premises at Money-gall for another auxiliary workhouse. These buildings had lately been fitted out for a military barracks with officer quarters, high walls and well-enclosed yard and garden.

So the crisis of accommodation in late 1848/early 1849 was addressed by the creation of two new auxiliary workhouses. A flurry of new activity brings more tables, forms, foodstuffs, fuel and clothing to these buildings, as well as a whole series of building adaptations. For the brewery building 1,000 glass panes and wire lattices are required, roofs have to be repaired and gates and piers erected to the specifications of the Commission's architect. And the architect recommends that the central axis, set aside for chapel and back kitchen, would be better occupied by dormitories. The temporary dormitories in Roscrea town are now discontin-

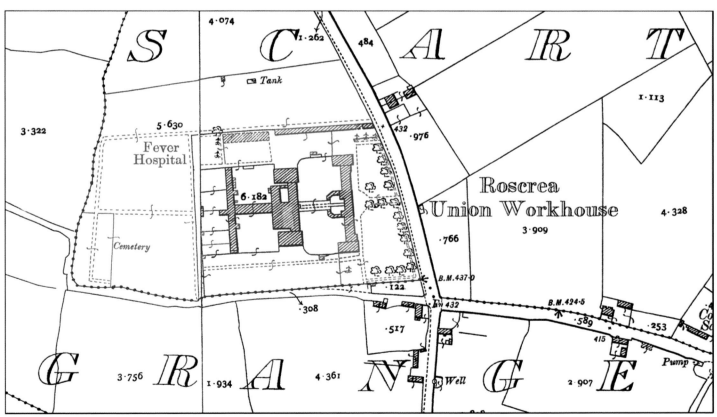

Fig. 12 LAYOUT OF, AND BUILDING ADAPTATIONS TO, THE ROSCREA WORKHOUSE DURING THE FAMINE. Roscrea workhouse – completed in April 1842 at a cost of £6,700 (and £1,296 for fittings) – was built (in the townland of Scart south of the town) to accommodate 700 'inmates'. The original layout – shown in blue – reproduces Wilkinson's design for workhouses of this size. An admission/entrance block leads to the main block with its strictly segregated quarters, dormitories and yards for both men and women and boys and girls on each side of the main axis of the workhouse. Centrally located in this main block were the office and residence of the master and matron and the nearby and closely monitored provision stores, kitchen, wash-house and laundry. Extending lengthwise from this central area was the dining hall (cum chapel) which in turn was linked to the backbuildings and the male and female infirmary wards and yards. Beyond these again on either side were male and female 'idiot' and 'lunatic' cells and yards. Already by December 1846, the great influx of paupers necessitated building adaptations which continued into 1850. Some of these adaptations are shown in red on the map. These included the conversion of strawsheds and stables into additional wards, followed by the erection of fever sheds on the old northern boundary of the workhouse complex of 6.2 acres (a further 5.6 acres was added later to the union grounds). By the summer of 1850, two front wings had been added north and south of the admission block, a fever hospital had been added at the rear and an additional burial ground acquired. However, this map does not show the early building of sleeping galleries nor the raising of the new dormitory wards one storey nor the building of a nursery dayroom and dormitories over the female infirmary and the idiot wards. The second (1901) edition of the O.S. map is embellished by many tree-lined edges and pathways – in sharp contrast to the starkness of the 1840s' representation of the site.

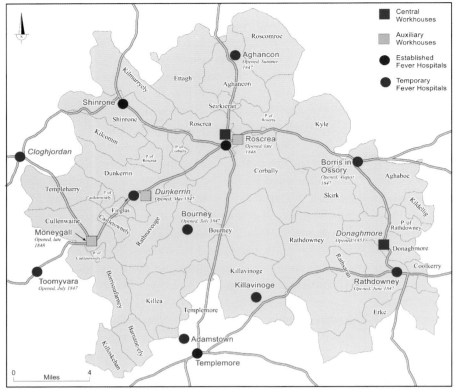

Fig 13 AUXILIARY WORKHOUSES AND HOSPITALS IN THE ROSCREA UNION DURING THE FAMINE. At the beginning of the Famine, the union territory had two hospitals – that of the Roscrea town fever hospital and the Shinrone fever hospital, already established in 1824 and 1826 as private charitable institutions. All through the Famine years, there were serious stand-offs between the workhouse and the Roscrea fever hospital administrations, mainly because of the regular inability of the union to pay the quarterly bills due to the fever hospital for taking care of the many fever patients from the union. As fever spread in the early years of the Famine, temporary fever hospitals were also established or refurbished in the rural districts of Aghancon and Bourney and near the villages of Borris-in-Ossory, Dunkerrin and Rathdowney. These temporary fever hospitals were under the ultimate control of the Central Board of Health, if locally managed by the union administration. By 1848, in a bid to reduce costs, the union attempt to close all temporary fever hospitals was met with resistance both from the affected local communities and the relevant medical officers. However, by 1849–50, all these hospitals are closed down as a large new fever hospital is finally erected by the union at the back of the Roscrea workhouse. (This fever hospital survived until the 1970s.) Meanwhile auxiliary workhouses were established at (i) the old Dunkerrin Charter School (April–May, 1847), (ii) Egan's Brewery in Abbey Street, Roscrea (December 1848) and (iii) the newly erected military barracks at Moneygall (December 1848).

pressure of other work, he has not furnished the plans for the new wings which 'unless they are carefully prepared will only create ultimate delay and difficulties'.[26] These two great wings (which I remember still stood in the 1950s when I, as a boy, passed by going into Roscrea town), were completed by early 1850. A sum of £2,100 is expended on this major initiative (see Figure 16).

Before this venture, accommodation for 2,300 inmates was scattered between the main workhouse (1,070), Dunkerrin (300), Moneygall (230) and the brewery auxiliary (700). With the front wings added, in the summer of 1850 the main workhouse could accommodate 1,650; Dunkerrin and Moneygall auxiliaries were closed; the Brewery held 730 inmates, making a total of just under 2,400 places. It is also at this time, that the decision is made to construct the separate union of Donaghmore (and associated workhouse) encompassing electoral divisions from both the Roscrea and the Abbeyleix Unions. Donaghmore workhouse was opened in the summer of 1853 – from 1850 until then its designated pauper population was still served by Roscrea Union. The latter had trebled its capacity to absorb the destitute, but there were still thousands in the surrounding districts needing and seeking outdoor relief.

### THE DEATH TOLL

The most fatal months in 1850 were from March to June when 257 (53.1%) people died out of an annual death total of 472, as many as eight or nine inmates were dying each week then. In 1851, the worst months were from February to April when 174 (41.6%) out of the yearly total of 418 deaths occurred. The number of workhouse inmates still hovered around 2,000 – there were still around 100 people ill in the hospital every week and thirty to forty sent to the fever hospital. There were still over eight or nine deaths per week.

The Great Famine has had a very long shadow. Its immediate deadly effects did not stop in 1851 but carried on into 1852. February and March released their deadly campaigns in 1852 when 164 (47.1%) out of the annual total of 348 deaths occurred. There were still an average of nine or ten deaths per week in the first half of that year. The year 1852 was a far more deadly year than 1846 in Roscrea Union.

To summarise, over the years from 1845 to 1852, 26 inmates (0.8% of the total) died in 1845, 101 (3.2%) died in 1846, 685 (21.2%) in 1847, 239 (7.6%) in 1848, 867 (27.6%) in 1849, 472 (15.1%) in 1850, 418 (13.3%) in 1851 and 348 (11.1%) in 1852.

ued and the associated bedding, furniture and clothes – after stocktaking by the Visiting Committee – are transferred to the brewery.

By 13 January 1849, total workhouse accommodation in the Union comes to 1,860, comprising the main workhouse (900) and its temporary buildings (120) with 840 paupers now located in three auxiliary workhouses. By March 1849, the board rents a house in Roscrea to act as a cholera hospital as the clerk advertises for more coffins, wire lattices and straw. On 5 May 1849, a tender for the erection of more fever sheds is sought. As the number of inmates escalate, a new clothes shed is added. Another fever convalescent shed is built in the men's yard. By 16 June 1849, there are now 2,197 inmates with 233 in the hospital and a further 5,482 persons on outdoor relief. It is then that the plan for erecting a major addition to the union workhouse is adopted and advertised for tenders in the four local newspapers. Now the strategy is to build two front wings east and west of the entrance block. In August 1849, George Wilkinson reports that due to

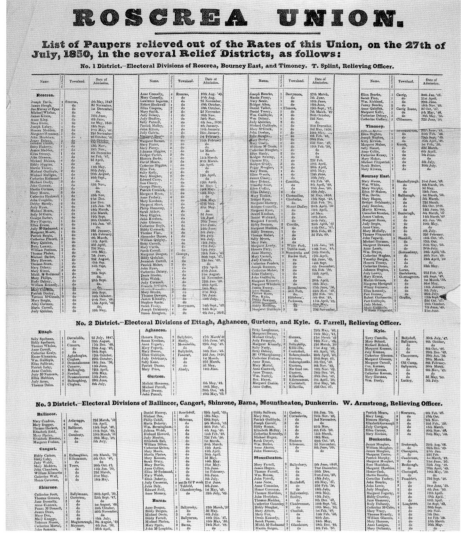

# ROSCREA UNION.

**List of Paupers relieved out of the Rates of this Union, on the 27th of July, 1850, in the several Relief Districts, as follows:**

No. 1 District.—Electoral Divisions of Roscrea, Bourney East, and Timoney.  T. Splint, Relieving Officer.

No. 2 District.—Electoral Divisions of Ettagh, Aghancon, Gurteen, and Kyle.  G. Farrell, Relieving Officer.

No. 3 District.—Electoral Divisions of Ballincor, Cangort, Shinrone, Barna, Mountheaton, Dunkerrin.  W. Armstrong, Relieving Officer.

Fig. 14 List of paupers relieved in Roscrea Union, 27 July 1850. Since no register of inmates in Roscrea workhouse has survived, this very specific list of paupers provides some clues to the composition of these on relief in mid-1850. Of the over 800 adult paupers on the list, 27% came from the Roscrea relief district, only 6% from the Ettagh–Aghancon district, 13.6% from the Shinrone–Dunkerrin area, 17.6% from the Bourney–Rathnaveoge district and 17.0% from the Borrisnafarney–Killea district. As many as 160 (18%) – with no townland address provided – are described as coming from the 'union at large'. Close on 50% of this pauper group as a whole were children and of the adults, just over 70% were females. Dates of admission for the five named districts indicate just over one-half were admitted in the seven months of 1850, 31% in 1849, 5% in 1848, 7% in 1847, 2% in 1846 and just over 1% in 1843. In contrast, the list of adult paupers from the 'union at large' group indicates that we are dealing with a far greater proportion of 'long-stayers'. Only 33% of the latter group were admitted in 1850, whereas about 30% had been admitted between 1843 and 1848, double the proportion admitted in those years for the five districts where townland addresses are provided. And since the month of admission is also provided, one can confirm that between one-fourth and one-fifth of all paupers were admitted in the month of September – suggesting, in part at least, the seasonal entry or return of paupers after the harvest season. In contrast, the busy farming period from May to August sees the smallest number of admissions. Local family names such as the Bergins, Bourkes, Egans, Kennedys, Mahers and Walshes are strongly represented in the list. The majority of the great diversity of family names are of Gaelic origin but names such as Abbott, Blackwell, Davis, Hobbins, Kirkland, Nutley, Price, Welword and Whitford point to the diverse settlement history of the wider region since the late sixteenth century. [Source: National Archives of Ireland]

It was late in the year of 1852 that the first rays of hope and light appeared. For four weeks in October 1852 'no deaths' are recorded. You have to go back to September 1846 for a similar 'no deaths' entry in the records. For six years from October 1846 to October 1852, the Roscrea Union workhouse, like most other workhouses, had no escape from the spectre of numerous deaths and many burials. As many as 3,156 people died in the Roscrea workhouse between 1845 and 1852.

In looking at the distribution of deaths as between different age and gender groups, from 1 July 1845 to the end of 1852, in only two six-month phases does the number of adult deaths exceed those of children aged fifteen or under – in the second half of 1851 (45.7%) and in July to September 1852, when only 36.8% were in the 'children' category. The pattern was very different in 1848 and 1849. From July 1848 to the end of 1849, children aged fifteen and under comprised two-thirds or more of all workhouse deaths, reaching 68.8% in the second half of 1848 (36.8% of these were infant deaths). Children are also major victims in the spring of 1852, contributing 67.9% of the deaths and probably a factor in their low proportion in the second half of that year. Likewise the low proportion of able-bodied women who died in the spring of 1852 may be related to an excess number of deaths in this group in the previous autumn and winter. January 1850 to December 1851 constitutes a kind of transitional phase when child mortality is only 4 to 6% greater than that of adults. A more 'normal' pattern of mortality seems to assert itself in the second half of 1852 when adults constitute the majority of deaths and where the old, especially the oldest women, are now the single largest category.

As for the seasonality of deaths, Roscrea workhouse and North Tipperary public institutions are very much aligned with the national average (shown here in brackets). In North Tipperary, spring deaths account for 32.1% (33%), summer for 27.5% (28%), autumn for 14.7% (14%) and winter for 25.6% (25%). Similar patterns prevailed in the counties surrounding North Tipperary.[27] In 1846, the worst months were May and October. In 1847, the darkest months were from January to July, in 1848 from January to April, in 1849 from February to May with a second peak in August, in 1850 from April to May and in 1851 from February to April. Mortality ran highest in April and May in five of the Famine years, for four years February and March were deadly months and January and October were highly destructive of life for two years. June and July were only deadly in one year. The seasonality of the deaths was matched by the seasonality of burials in the adjacent cemetery.

141

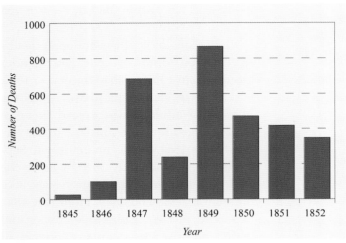

Fig. 15 Number who died in Roscrea workhouse between 1845 and 1852. As illustrated by this graph, Famine deaths in Roscrea workhouse have two clear peaks in 1847 (685) and 1849 (867), with the intervening year (1848) having a significantly lower amount of deaths (239). The lowest number of deaths recorded over this period is in 1845 (26) and there is a steady decline after the absolute peak in 1849 to 348 deaths in 1852. However, it should be noted that the number of deaths in 1852 is very much greater than in 1846 (101), when the Famine began.

By 17 June 1847, a problem had arisen with regard to the interment of bodies of deceased inmates of the workhouse. The PLC strongly recommend to the guardians to 'desist from interment of any more bodies on existing workhouse premises'.[28] The board are therefore encouraged to purchase or hire ground *detached* from the workhouse that could be used as a cemetery. By late June 1847, the close proximity of the graveyard to the workhouse infirmary is also commented upon. As the graveyard is now full, it is agreed by the guardians on the necessity of providing another graveyard at a distance from the workhouse. The board orders the Clerk to advertise for a plot of ground *not exceeding* an acre and not *less* than a half an acre to be within a mile of the workhouse and for the purposes of a burial ground. Tenders are required to state title, purchase money and rental status of the land.

On 12 July 1847, the first effort at acquiring a cemetery is made with the Board paying Mrs Bridget Maher £70 for her interest in an acre of ground to be listed as a cemetery and as a site for a Fever Hospital. Again on 1 January 1848, Master O'Malley calls attention to the crowded state of the burial ground, it being quite inadequate in its present extent to meet the increased mortality of the inmates. Again the PLCs advise the guardians on 13 January 1848 not to delay in purchasing or hiring a piece of land *not exceeding 3 acres* to be used as a cemetery. On 24 March 1848, the guardians of Roscrea acquired 3 acres, 2 roods and 18 perches of land almost adjoining the rear outer wall of the workhouse. These lands, located a quarter of a mile from the workhouse, were acquired at a yearly rent of £5/15/9 from a middleman on three lives (Mr E.S. Egan) who held the land from Lord Portarlington, then landlord of much of Roscrea town. Almost one and a half acres of the land is to act as a burial ground, a quarter acre is a quarry and the remainder,

as yet, unoccupied. It would be occupied by 1852, when the number of the dead to be buried had quadrupled.

## IMPACT OF THE POOR LAW

The Poor Law system, as enacted and implemented via the Poor Law Commission and the Board of Guardians, had enormous power to redefine and redraw the contours of life for so many in Roscrea Union – as did the great majority of Poor Law unions throughout Ireland. The imposed, 'modernising' nature of the Poor Laws saw a whole series of new administrative territories and officers created across the country, transcending the old structures and powers. When the Famine struck, this system was required to handle a crisis of enormous proportions which it was never designed to do. In all of this, one notes the overarching control of the imperial state – exemplified by the fusion of the Poor Law, police, magistrates and military in an attempt to maintain administrative surveillance and control. Numerous examples have been provided of this effort at institutional integration which also involved the Central Board of Health, the National Board of Education and, to a lesser extent, the Grand Juries.

The Poor Law system created a new 'landscape' of unions, electoral divisions, rate collector and relieving officer districts; it swiftly imposed these massive, awesome and ultimately very sad workhouse buildings at the centre of these unions. It imposed so many new social classifications and gatekeepers: 'the workhouse test', the 'deserving poor' and those entitled or not entitled to relief; parish wardens with rights to issue tickets of admission to the workhouse; blue and red tickets for the right to enter the workhouse or fever hospitals; highly segregated categories of human beings separated by high boundary walls *within* the workhouse and by a range of stiff social categories *outside* the workhouse walls. The Famine and the Poor Law drove deep divides between landlords, strong farmers, smallholders and labourers. The violent action of some landlords least sympathetic to the struggling smallholders – taking advantage of the Gregory clause 'which drove the poor from their own homes'[29] – left a bitter legacy which culminated in the Land League battles and the eradication of the estate system. The strong farmers and their cousin shopkeepers emerged as beneficiaries of this turbulent and crisis-laden period. Some died of typhus fever and cholera; most had to tighten their belts. Some were forced to resort to the pawnbroker – previously only the domain of the poor. But their acquisitive and aggressive behaviour towards both smallholders and cottiers often soured and severed social relationships. Many of the latter faced poverty, hunger or emigration. As the Famine intensified, a wide gap opened up between rich and poor in the countryside – a pattern noted by the regional newspapers which criticised some landlords and strong farmers for not contributing to the funding of local relief committees and standing aloof from the general crisis.

The letters and addresses of both doctors and priests to the Board of Guardians in the Roscrea Union highlighted the plight of the disease-stricken people in town and countryside. The Poor Laws drew invidious distinctions between families in townlands, districts and parishes: those whose names were posted or not posted on chapel walls as deserving or not deserving of outdoor relief; those who succeeded in getting their names on the Relieving Officer's books and those who did not; those who could read and know about these reliefs and those who could and did not; landlords whose valuation was above or below £4, and a new punitive distinction – the Gregory clause – between those holding more or less than a quarter acre. Power structures were changing radically in the countryside – not just between landlord, farmer and labourer – but also with the addition of new functionaries such as rate collectors, relieving officers, overseers and stewards of the stone-breakers to the Poor Law payroll.

Roscrea Union occupies a middle position in terms of its quality of administration and the kinds of support and pressures it had to work with during the Famine. For example, 41.8% of its population was receiving relief under the Soup Kitchen Act of 1847 and over 84% of Tuam's, Clifden's and Swinford's populations were in a similar position. Ballinrobe was in an even more desperate state with 93.5% of its population in this category. In contrast, for a number of unions in northeastern Ireland the figure is less than 10% and no such relief is recorded for the unions of Antrim, Belfast and Newtownards.[30] However, many unions, like that of Roscrea, reveal sharp differences in the levels of wealth and poverty as between their constituent district electoral divisions.

In terms of administrative competence, the performance of the Roscrea Board of Guardians was very average, whereas the evidence suggests that the performance of Master O'Malley, the Matron, the medical officers and the chaplains was more than adequate. They carried out their

| | | | | |
|---|---|---|---|---|
| Pat Bohen (22) | Kitty Fitzgerald (10) | Anne Bergin (infant) | Ellen Tierney (infant) | Austin Mullally (infant) |
| Martin Kennedy (infant) | Mary Cashin (60) | Dan Lalor (16) | Margaret Cashin (infant) | John Meehan (36) |
| Margaret Whelan (6 ) | Betty Mangan (60) | Betty Ryan (40) | Margaret Clooney (2) | Mary Bergin (infant) |
| Patrick Meara (8) | Mary Breen (14) | James Farrell (60) | Kitty Parkinson (12) | Eliza Kavanagh (4) |
| John Stapleton (40) | Biddy Dooley (16) | James Flannery (60) | John Matthews (infant) | John Hanrahan (infant) |
| Owney Bergin (5) | Owney Madden (10) | John Gorman (40) | Martin Darcy (infant) | ? Kennedy (93) |
| Daniel Dunne (3) | Susan Orps (6) | William Butler (infant) | Kitty Ryan (infant) | Michael Kelly (28) |
| Biddy Butler (7) | John Carty (35) | Peggy Gready (80) | Catherine Moran (7) | John Sheedy (40) |
| William Philips (?) | Mary Neale (4) | James Smith (3) | Patrick Lambe (10) | James Parkinson (12) |
| John Madden (55) | Pat Delaney (2) | Honor Walsh (50) | Billy Burns (infant) | Margaret Walsh (12) |
| John Deegan (4) | James Guilfoyle (2) | James King (55) | Willie Duggan (infant) | Mary Bergin (?) |
| Judy Whelan (30) | Barney Dunne (60) | John Lyons (infant) | John Rafter (4) | James Fitzpatrick (12) |
| Mary Ryan (5) | Thomas Harte (9) | Pat Quinlan (40) | Margaret Ryan (infant) | Tom Ryan (12) |
| | John Birne (11) | John Connell (12) | Michael Harney (infant) | Margaret Curren (12) |
| | Peter Kelly (11) | Mary Cashin (3) | Patrick Meara (infant) | Stephen Egan (35) |
| | Catherine Bray (infant) | Jane Donnelly (40) | John Lambert (infant) | Ellen Shields (40) |
| | Biddy Carroll (35) | Nancy White (50) | Joseph Moore (36) | James Lawler (infant) |
| | Paddy Bradley (60) | Ellen Butler (40) | Michael Greedy (?) | David Sheilds (14) |
| | Ellen Purcell (12) | Johanna Finn (infant) | Bridget Keenan (12) | Betty Duggan (35) |
| | | May Bohen (18) | Kate Duggan (4) | Michael Doolin (70) |

Fig. 16 Remembering the dead in Roscrea Union workhouse. The names of those who died in Roscrea workhouse have only rarely survived in the existing records. But between the months of March and October 1848, the medical officer does provide the first and second names of some of those who died and the age at which they died. The existence of this record of names allows us to remember each one as an individual and so not lost in the mass of statistics which number the many anonymous dead. However, beginning in November 1848 and consistently from early 1849, the medical report in the minutes notes the number dying and the causes of death but no longer provides the names of those who died. For example, on the week ending 24 February 1849, twenty-one are reported as having died, thirteen of whom were infants and three of whom were aged over forty-five years of age. By 19 November 1849, the medical officer's minute in the medical report is even more brisk: 'the deaths were 19 with the causes carefully detailed in the Report Book'. The 'Report Book' is not included in the minutes. The photo underneath the list of the dead is of first line of buildings of the Roscrea union workhouse facing the Roscrea–Templemore Road. Only the entrance building at the centre of this photo, with its two large chimneys and elaborate doorway with the capstone dated to 1842 belongs to the first phase of the building of this workhouse. The remainder of the building comprising girls' and boys' schoolrooms, the rooms of schoolmistress and schoolmaster and upstairs dormitories was added in 1850. Subsequently renamed St Cronan's Hospital, the last remnants of these buildings were demolished in 1993. The 1842 doorway capstone was salvaged for the nearby Scart Memorial Garden opened in 2004 (see Figure 17). [Photo courtesy of Mr. George Cunningham, Roscrea]

children. The workhouse, with its monotonous food and work regime, was confining, punishing and irksome; inevitably informal power structures emerged amongst such an enclosed and increasingly crowded and diverse 'inmate' population. Food was the gold currency and isolated adults, smaller children and infants occupied the weakest and most vulnerable positions in this complex hierarchy. Even for those that survived, the institutional discipline of the workhouse was deeply traumatic. The workhouse records only provide odd glimpses – the rare haunting image like the woman smashing over 200 windows – which make real the lives of so many people in these grim places.

Overall, the legacy of the workhouse system was and is immense, epitomised today by the high enclosing walls that still survive on so many workhouse sites and the feared memory of having to enter and particularly to die in the dreaded 'poor house'. (Yet many still function – if transformed – as jealously guarded local hospitals and/or old people's homes.) The workhouse system is a legacy of the powerful few – remote both geographically and socially – determining the conditions under which thousands and thousands of people lived and died. Governed as they were by an economic philosophy that placed parsimonious accounting above human life, the iron rules that were introduced and emanated from the Treasury and Parliament in London respectively placed far too great a burden on an already inflexible and increasingly cumbersome workhouse system, never created to handle a catastrophe of this proportion. Beneath the central power base, lay many

Fig. 17 Famine Memorial Garden at Scart, Kennedy Park, Roscrea. In the foreground is the memorial cross designed by Tommy Madden while the focal point of the garden is the cut-stone doorway of the Roscrea workhouse, which was carefully removed from its original site and stored in Thurles while the remaining buildings were being demolished. [Photo: Frank Coyne]

prescribed duties as best they could. However, there were clear deficiencies in the quality of the nursing staff and to a lesser extent amongst the schoolteachers. And, as in other unions, it is clear that the senior staff were either not cognisant of or unable to prevent inequalities developing amongst an increasingly desperate pauper population in both the distribution of food and in the caring for the younger

layers of responsibility, many layers of silence, heroism, guilt, and betrayal. Despite the best efforts of people like the effective if wily Master George O'Malley and the dedicated Medical Officer, Dr Samuel Woods, nearly 3,200 people died in Roscrea workhouse and 370,697 people in workhouses and other public institutions across the island.

# Famine and workhouse clothing

## Hilary O'Kelly

We have come to rely on the photograph as documentary evidence but, although newly invented, photography was not yet adequately established to record the Famine. For images, therefore, we are thrown on verbal descriptions and newspaper engravings, both subject to manipulation by contemporary ideologies. The following account, building on existing research, similarly relies on contemporary written and documentary records from Poor Law inspectors and pawnbrokers, along with workhouse minute books, to provide additional evidence towards an understanding of dress in Ireland during the Famine.

Both the latter sources tend to confirm that dress in pre-Famine Ireland was mainly comfortable and diverse. The Poor Law inspector in Tralee, Mr Lloyd, indicates the condition of dress in his union in 1848–49:

> I cannot from my own knowledge state whether there is a perceptible difference between the manner in which the peasantry used to be dressed on Sundays and the manner in which they are so dressed now; but I learn from persons competent to form an opinion, that the peasantry are much worse clad on Sundays now than they were formerly.
>
> There are six pawnbrokers in this union . . . and I find their stores filled with wearing apparel of every description, home-made clothing materials . . . of a much better quality than can be had by contract.[1]

Judging also by the range of clothing the government intended to issue to the workhouse, the dress of the poor must have been at least decent – as it is well established that 'The governing principle of the workhouse system was that relief given at public expense should be less than that which could be obtained by exertion outside it . . . [I]nmates should be worse clothed, worse lodged and worse fed than independent labourers in the district.'[2] Each workhouse was issued with a clothing ledger arranged in columns printed for specifying each garment to be supplied to the workhouse. These were, for men: coats, waistcoats, trowsers (sic), shirts, shoes, stockings, hats and handkerchiefs. For women the intended clothing was listed as gowns, petticoats, shifts, aprons, handkerchiefs, shoes, stockings, caps and bonnets. The workhouse children were to be similarly attired except that in Ireland no shoes or stockings were actually provided, as the children were unaccustomed to either.[3]

Indeed the gulf between what was originally envisaged

as the poorest dress by the Poor Law Commission and reality during the Famine is reflected in the clothing receipt book of the Roscrea Union. In October 1848 the workhouse store for men amounted to thirty-two coats and only ten trowsers, and it had ninety-three shirts but no hats or handkerchiefs, both being garments worn for public nicety rather than private decorum or utility. The ledger did however have additional hand-written columns for men's flannel

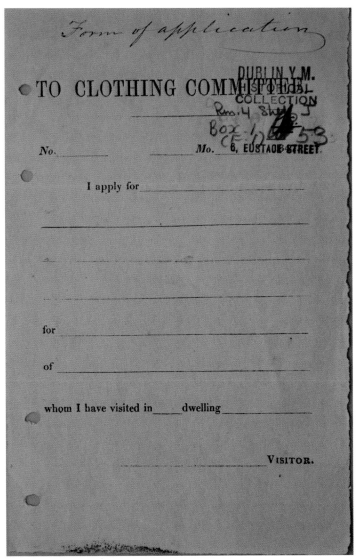

Fig. 1 Application for clothing grants to the Society of Friends. The tendency of the distressed to pawn their clothes in order to buy food resulted in much hardship, particularly during the bad winter of 1846–47. William Foster's reports of suffering in the west of Ireland sparked an immediate response amongst Quaker women in London, which resulted in 'bales of clothing' arriving from communities in England. [Source: Rob Goodbody, *A Suitable Channel: Quaker Relief during the Great Famine* (Bray, 1995), p. 40/Friends Historical Library]

vests and drawers.

For women the intended outfit appears that of a domestic servant, suggesting the workhouse as a place of training and reform. The Roscrea store records its best supply being of aprons, numbering 270; there were, however, no caps or bonnets. The column for bonnets has in fact been hand-written over with 'striped petticoats'; two more opposing garments it is difficult to imagine. The bonnet was the quintessential mark of Victorian femininity while striped cloth, long the mark of servitude and working dress, was becoming established in America, and subsequently in England, as the signifier of criminal identity.[4]

Bonnets were not normally worn by the rural poor in Ireland where a woman's shawl and man's coat were the most prized garments. These were the outer expression of local status and the garments essential for market days or Mass, and the want of which kept people away from such public occasions. Inadequate clothing precluded dignified engagement with the world, and, as the Famine endured, the diminished dress of the poor was widely remarked upon and taken, by many, to account for the reduced numbers attending fairs and religious services, Protestant as well as Roman Catholic.[5]

Worn clothing might be shameful, but in terms of shape and fabric, it normally bore some indication of the garment it once was, at least in the eyes of its owner. This was not the case, however, in the eyes of members of the nineteenth-century establishment, who commonly characterised the appearance of the poor as 'naked' or 'in rags'. As Juliet Ash has shown, however, this has to be seen as the perspective of the propertied classes relative to their own increasing culture of sartorial display. It might be more accurate to see the poor in early-nineteenth-century Ireland as a 'group whose precarious means, living in hard times presented an appearance that might change according to social, economic and regional fluctuations'.[6]

### 'PAWNING THEIR BEST CLOTHES'
It was common practice at the time for people in Ireland (as elewhere in Europe) – especially the towns – to use their clothes as a source of short-term liquidity, pawning their best clothes on Monday morning and redeeming them on Saturday night in readiness for Sunday Mass. The weekly shift in appearance, through pledging and redeeming at the pawnbrokers, had a seasonal counterpart when people could survive without the heavier winter clothes in summer:

> [T]he practice of pledging prevailed to the greatest extent during the months of April, May, June and July and the redemptions principally occur immediately after the harvest. The reason for this appears to be, that during the months from April to July the stock of potatoes is exhausted, and labour very scarce, whilst during the harvest the labourer

can support himself on the potatoes he has himself planted, and apply his wages to the redemption of his clothes from the pawn-office.[7]

When the potato crop failed this fragile system broke down. Many were unable to redeem their warm coats and shawls and as circumstances deteriorated even less good clothes were pawned; feather bedding was sacrificed in order to retain something to wear when venturing out in search of sustenance. By November 1848 the medical inspector, Denis Phelan, was of the view that people were seeking admission to the workhouse as much from a want of clothes and fuel as from a want of food and enquired of the Poor Law inspectors if they concurred.[8]

Inspectors from all over Ireland returned accounts of deteriorating destitution among the poorest inhabitants, but only minor distress was reported from the district of Counties Antrim, Down, parts of Armagh, Tyrone and Londonderry. The neighbouring district reported a similar lack of marked change in the clothing of the adult peasantry of Londonderry and Tyrone, but concurred with Mr Phelan regarding the rest of the district: Sligo, Manorhamilton, Glenties, Milford and Dunfanaghy. From Counties Monaghan, Cavan, Fermanagh, parts of Tyrone, Down, and Louth great misery was reported, but Cavan (and particularly Cootehill) were singled out as being among the most distressed. Queen's County and County Westmeath were generally very bad, but conditions were not as wretched as in Counties Roscommon, Leitrim, Longford, and parts of Cavan, Galway and King's County. Tipperary reported the covering of the peasantry being 'no longer worthy of the appellation clothes'. However, Cashel was not so bad, and nor was Nenagh, where 'Some have, undoubtedly, very wretched clothing; but taken as a whole, paupers here do not present the very miserable and wretched appearance that the same class invariably did in the counties of Donegal and Leitrim.'

Reports from Counties Wexford, Carlow, Kilkenny and Waterford fully coincided with the view of Mr Phelan, but not 'to the same extent . . . as it must be in the western unions', which, from Donegal to Clare, were described as miserable and 'painful to behold'. The poor of Listowel were 'very much in want of clothing . . . but the distress I have observed here, does not bear a shade of comparison with what I daily witnessed in the county of Clare'. Newcastle and Rathkeale Unions were also reportedly less severe and:

> extreme destitution . . . was not obsevable in the Caherciveen Union. Previous to the famine, I think they were the most comfortably dressed peasantry in the west of Ireland; and even now the peasantry in the Killarney and Kenmare Unions are worse off for clothing than in Caherciveen.

However, despite these observations, most respondents could not agree with Mr Phelan that 'many seek the workhouse partly from want of clothes' and were rather more of the view expressed in Ballinrobe, that 'scanty as their raiment is, they would infinitely prefer remaining in it, and upon the out-door relief, to obtaining admission to the Workhouse'.[9]

When by necessity or occasionally by design, people did enter the workhouse, the clothes they wore were removed and the owners were washed and re-clothed in workhouse attire. Their own clothes were bundled, labelled and placed in a clothing store, but often when they came to reclaim it on departure, it had disintegrated or rotted away in the damp conditions of the store.[10] This may partly account for the pawnbroker in Westport claiming (and he was not alone) 'that it is by no means uncommon for parties on their way to the workhouse to leave their best clothes with him in pledge, stating that they were about seeking admission, and thought their clothes would be safer with him than elsewhere'.[11]

The medical inspector further considered 'that several of the in-door paupers of the class that could be placed on out-door relief, are unwilling to accept it, chiefly influenced by [the want of clothes and fuel]'.[12] The Poor Law inspectors were more inclined to agree with him on this count. In the Oldcastle Union 'The greatest difficulty we experienced in turning persons out of the workhouse, is the want of clothing; and on last week the guardians were obliged to clothe a great number with the condemned clothing of the workhouse.'[13] Some inmates took matters into their own hands, resulting in permanent concern about inmates absconding in workhouse dress.[14]

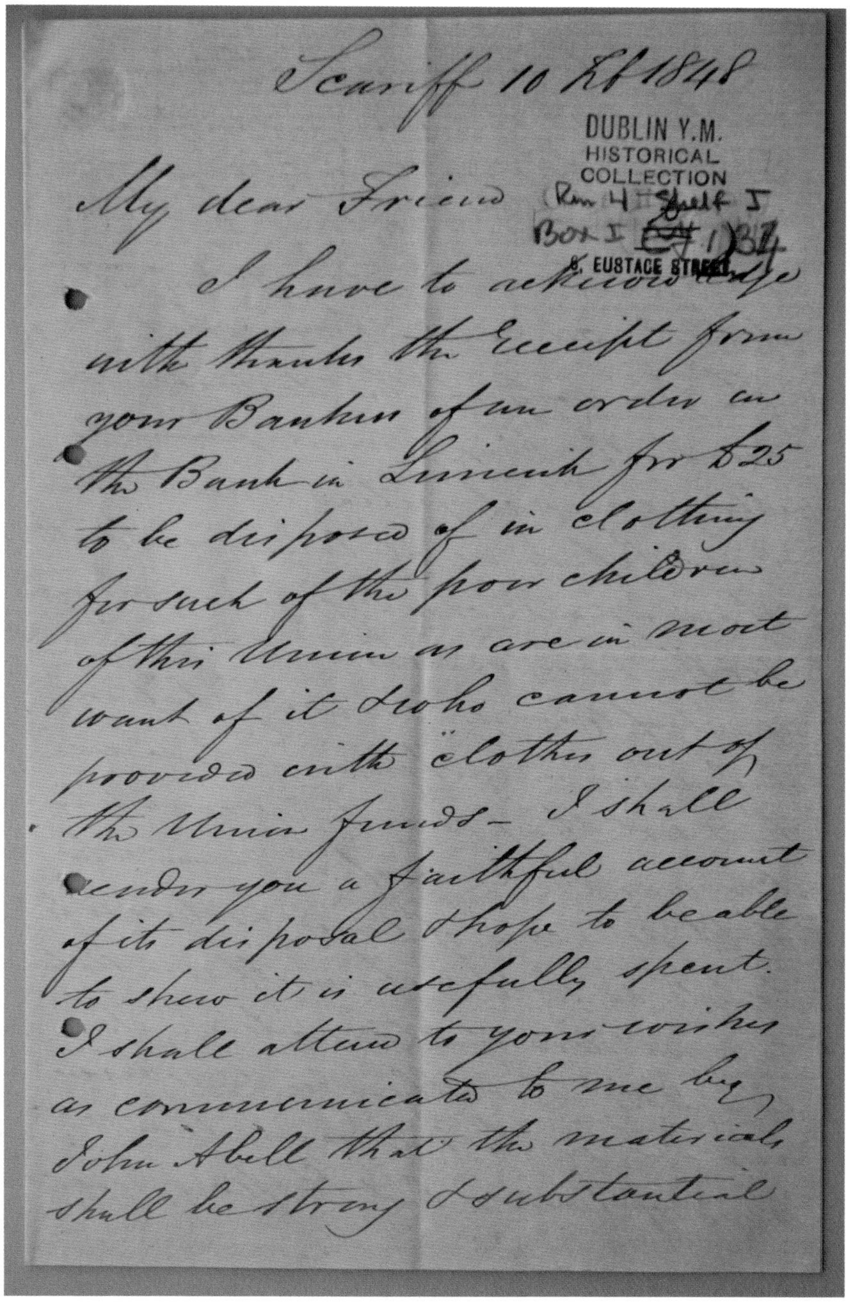

Based on the County Tipperary minute books, Ó Cleirigh records that in some unions, for at least some of the time, the clothing was branded, sometimes with a stamp that could be cut off. But a mark that cannot be eliminated is a stripe woven into the structure of the cloth. Perhaps this

Fig. 2 Quaker John Hodgkin, a London barrister, received a letter from a J.J. Fisher of Limerick who described the miserable situation of the children discharged from the Scariff Union workhouse. Hodgkin responded by making a £25 donation which, as Fisher explained, 'was to be disposed in clothing for such of the poor children of this Union as are in most want of it and who cannot be provided with clothing out of the Union funds'. Fisher promised to attend to Hodgkin's wishes 'as communicated to him by John Abell that the materials shall be strong and substantial'. [Source: Friends Historical Library]

accounts for the prevalence of stripes in descriptions of workhouse dress. The Roscrea Clothing Receipt Book has a printed column for petticoats of which fifty are recorded; however, a separate, hand-written column distinguishes the striped petticoat, suggesting it has a separate function or identity. And of the striped variety the workhouse has more than three times as many. John O'Connor records 'a striped jerkin' as the prescribed dress for women.[15] And Bengal striped fabric, produced by many of the Poor Law unions, was shown at the Great Exhibition of 1853 in Dublin.[16] By 1862 stripes were increasingly a matter of policy in govern-

ment-issued dress when Henry Mayhew records, 'Yes, sir, everything made for the convicts has a red stripe in it – sheets, stockings, towels, flannels, and all.'[17]

Despite inadequate dress, some people may have left the workhouse in search of labour or other support. But if intending to emigrate, contingent arrangements were insufficient and the pawnbrokers reported that almost their only custom came from those emigrating. When the Government or the landlords assisted emigration, almost the only essential cost, apart from the ticket and a few shillings for their arrival, was the provision of 'a slender outfit'.[18] The master

SCENE IN A CHAPEL AT THURLES.

Fig. 3 'Scene at a chapel in Thurles, County Tipperary' (1848). As the Famine took its toll the diminished dress of the poor was widely remarked upon. Prized possessions such as a woman's shawl and a man's coat as depicted in the above sketch were pawned. The inability to redeem them meant further shame, accounting in part for the declining numbers attending religious services. [Source: *The Illustrated London News*, 26 August 1848]

of one ship, escorting tenants of Sir Robert Gore Booth to Canada, wrote to him on arrival with the compliment: 'Sir: . . . Your Thanksful Tennants were Highley respected on being landed.' However, the emigrants from Sligo carried in the third ship, in September 1847, were described on landing as 'a freight of paupers . . . [T]hey did not have enough clothes for decency and the master had bought a quantity of red flannel shirts and blue trousers so that they could land without exposure.'[19]

### Orphan girls

No such exposure was permitted for the 'orphan girls', aged between fourteen and eighteen years, being sent to Australia. From the Roscrea workhouse it appears that sixty girls departed around December 1848. They were supplied with soap, towels, combs, hairbrushes and 'such other articles (such as a few yards of Cotton or Calico) as the Matron may know young females to require'.[20] This discreet reference, presumably to sanitary needs, may account for the supply of 120 yards of 'grey calico' to the Board of Guardians, thus allowing three yards to each girl.

In addition, the girls appear almost lavishly supplied with a 'trousseau' mainly furnished by local shopkeepers Mr O'Brien and Mr Fawcette. For each girl was ordered: six shifts, a cotton gown, a woollen gown, two day wrappers, two night wrappers, two flannel petticoats, two cotton petticoats, a worsted shawl, a cashmere cloak, two pairs of shoes, worsted and cotton stockings, two neck handkerchiefs, three pocket handkerchiefs, two linen collars, a check apron (or two), a pair of stays, calico sheets, calico mitts, two muslin day caps, two calico night caps and a straw bonnet.[21] Government regulations required the girls, destined to populate the colonies, be dressed to suggest the respectable values and lady-like qualities they were carrying with them. Indeed, their regulation dress was very similar to that required for Florence Nightingale's nurses in 1854.[22]

When outlining the clothing for Australia it was stipulated that articles of dress be '*new*, of *good quality*, and *various patterns*',[23] which suggests care in seeing that the girls appeared as civic individuals rather than as an institutional group. This emphasising of *various patterns* suggests a uniformity of pattern was acceptable in regular tenders for supplying the workhouse and this is certainly supported by the rare images – for example, of men working the Perrott wheel in Cork. Their clothing suggests almost the dress of sailors. However women's dress may have been less uniform as Juliet Ash records that 'Women prisoners' uniforms were markedly less regulated than that of men.'[24]

Considering British Government plans for managing the poor were developed alongside the management of the criminal and insane, ideas and images relating to prison uniform may have a bearing on the workhouse. No images have yet come to light of women in the workhouse in the 1840s but other sources give some insight to their appearance; later photographs of workhouse women, for example, usually record them dressed very much alike and Thomas Harrington, who was born in the workhouse, has 'harrowing memories of the prison-like interior . . . and the appalling "uniforms"'.[25] The word uniform, however, seems not to appear in contemporary documents for the Irish workhouse but perhaps, like much of dress history, the material manifestation of cultural change precedes its naming.

Fig. 4 Representatives of Dublin's well-dressed and genteel society are very much to the fore in this lithograph of the model soup kitchen in the South Dublin Union while the recipients of the soup rations are faintly visible in the background. [Source: *The Illustrated London News*, 17 April 1847]

# The Cork workhouse

## Michelle O'Mahony

The workhouses of Ireland were always perceived as the last resort in cases of destitution. The Irish pauper class were very reluctant to enter the workhouse. This reluctance was attributed to the Destitute Rule, which stated that workhouse conditions were to be of a standard greatly inferior to those of the lowest class of pauper outside. Entrance to the workhouse in pre-Famine years affirmed both a person's destitution and his inability to provide for his family. For many of the Famine victims, entering the workhouse was not an affirmation of their destitution but a final attempt at survival. However, the Cork Union workhouse, like all workhouses of the time, did not guarantee survival, for conditions were very much conducive to the generation and spread of disease. These institutions which aimed to improve the lot of the pauper, paradoxically by their very nature often accelerated the incidence of disease and death. In September 1845 the potato blight had 'unequivocally declared itself in Ireland, where will Ireland be in the event of a universal potato rot?'[1] With the successive failures of the potato crop came the flight to the workhouses wherein the starving and destitute hoped to gain some respite. Cork Union workhouse was built to accommodate 2,000 paupers. The first meeting of the Board of Guardians occurred on Tuesday, 4 June 1839, but the house was not completed until 1841. In the interim period the old house of industry located off Douglas Street functioned as the temporary workhouse.

Admission figures for the period 1845–50 are testament to how the Cork Union workhouse alleviated destitution while often contributing to the ill-health and death of inmates. The evidence from the workhouse records points to the differential impact of the Famine according to gender and pauper classification whilst also highlighting its fast-moving progress. The number of admissions in 1845 reflected those of the previous year. The blight did not make any significant impact until 1846. The failure of the potato crop in 1845 was interpreted as being similar to previous crop failures and it was expected that recovery would follow the

Fig. 1 The Poor Law functioned in a highly centralised and bureaucratic manner as evident from the cover of the minute books of the Cork Union. [Source: Cork Archives Institute]

next season. However, with the second crop failure there were increased admissions to the house, most notably from October 1846.

### DISTRESS

The Poor Law Commissioner, Joseph Burke, described the distress which he witnessed in Cork in November 1846 and his fears for the following year, which was to be the worst of the Famine years. He noted Cork to be 'an extensive district, the present condition of the people and judging of their future prospects, afforded me information on the subject which may not be open to or taken advantage of by others – although bad as is the state of the people I dread that it will be worse next year'.[2] Rising admission figures took their toll on the mindset of the guardians, so much so that Captain William Martin, guardian of the Glanmire electoral district, tendered his resignation. He stated that the guardians 'are little acquainted with the mental pressures to which the officers of the house are now subjected and they are more detrimental to their health than any bodily exertion'.[3] His letter also referred to the great number of women entering the workhouse and that there was not enough work for them in the various works departments.

**Table 1.** Admissions 1846, September to December

| Month | Admissions |
|---|---|
| September | 1,137 |
| October | 2,358 |
| November | 2,146 |
| December | 2,040 |

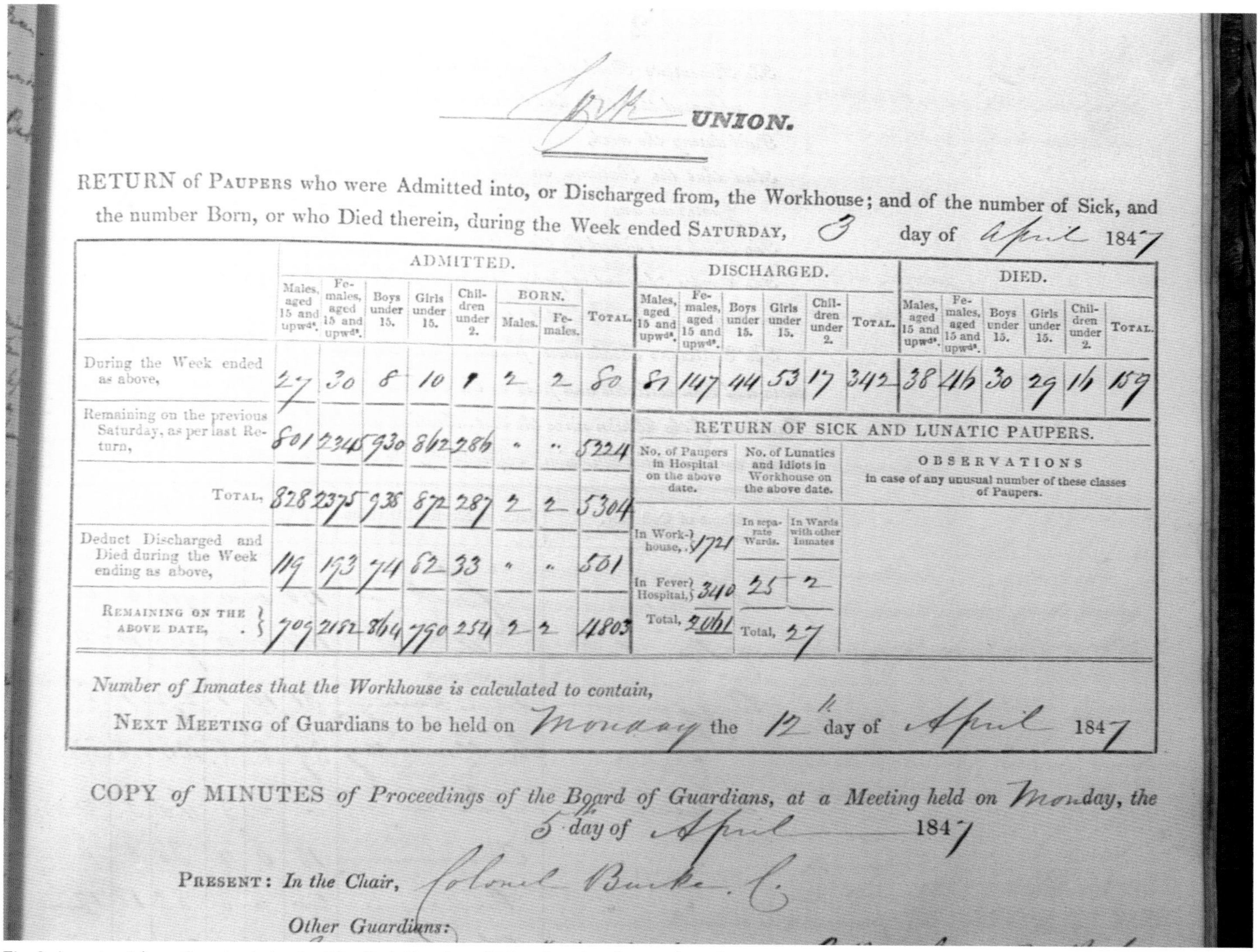

Cork UNION.

RETURN of PAUPERS who were Admitted into, or Discharged from, the Workhouse; and of the number of Sick, and the number Born, or who Died therein, during the Week ended SATURDAY, 3 day of April 1847

| | ADMITTED. | | | | | | | |
|---|---|---|---|---|---|---|---|---|
| | Males, aged 15 and upwds. | Females, aged 15 and upwds. | Boys under 15. | Girls under 15. | Children under 2. | BORN. Males. | BORN. Females. | TOTAL. |
| During the Week ended as above, | 27 | 30 | 8 | 10 | 1 | 2 | 2 | 80 |
| Remaining on the previous Saturday, as per last Return, | 801 | 2345 | 930 | 862 | 286 | " | " | 5224 |
| TOTAL, | 828 | 2375 | 938 | 872 | 287 | 2 | 2 | 5304 |
| Deduct Discharged and Died during the Week ending as above, | 119 | 193 | 74 | 82 | 33 | " | " | 501 |
| REMAINING ON THE ABOVE DATE, | 709 | 2182 | 864 | 790 | 254 | 2 | 2 | 4803 |

| | Males, aged 15 and upwds. | Females, aged 15 and upwds. | Boys under 15. | Girls under 15. | Children under 2. | TOTAL. |
|---|---|---|---|---|---|---|
| DISCHARGED. | 81 | 147 | 44 | 53 | 17 | 342 |
| DIED. | 38 | 46 | 30 | 29 | 16 | 159 |

RETURN OF SICK AND LUNATIC PAUPERS.

| No. of Paupers in Hospital on the above date. | | No. of Lunatics and Idiots in Workhouse on the above date. In separate Wards. | In Wards with other Inmates | OBSERVATIONS in case of any unusual number of these classes of Paupers. |
|---|---|---|---|---|
| In Workhouse, | 1721 | | | |
| In Fever Hospital, | 340 | 25 | 2 | |
| Total, | 2061 | Total, 27 | | |

*Number of Inmates that the Workhouse is calculated to contain,*

NEXT MEETING of Guardians to be held on Monday the 12th day of April 1847

COPY *of* MINUTES *of Proceedings of the Board of Guardians, at a Meeting held on* Monday, *the* 5 *day of* April 1847

PRESENT: *In the Chair,* Colonel Burke. C

*Other Guardians:*

Fig. 2 An extract from the minute book of the Cork Poor Law Union showing the number of inmates in the workhouse on 3 April 1847. 159 individuals had died in the previous week. An enquiry into causes of the high mortality in the workhouse was conducted by Dr Stephens, the Central Board of Health's medical inspector. Its conclusions pointed to the debilitating condition of the poor on admission and the extreme overcrowding being directly responsible for the large number of deaths. [Source: Cork Archives Institute]

In August 1846, women (above fifteen years) constituted 74% of the inmates. The previous year during November–December 1845 following the first crop failure, 65% of all admissions were women. It is evident from the data that at all times there were consistently higher rates of female to male admissions throughout the Famine years. This was attributed to the fact that many women and children were deserted, widowed or their husbands had left to find work abroad and in some instances women falsified desertion to gain admission. Once admitted to the workhouse, families were separated into the male, female, boys and girls sections and were set to work in the various industrial departments such as baking, dressmaking, spinning and carpentry. The public works schemes then in operation were largely directed towards male labour and this was a further reason for the greater volume of female admissions.

### FEVER AND EPIDEMICS

The year 1846 also witnessed an increased incidence of fever and epidemics and associated famine illnesses and diseases. The Fever Act of 1846 extended fever accommodation in the form of wooden sheds, which were usually constructed adjacent to the fever hospitals. Unfortunately, no such sheds were built adjacent to the workhouse. It was some time before the fever victims of the workhouse were sent to isolated sheds nearby. Neither did the number of medical personnel available to deal with the crisis increase sufficiently to help curtail outbreaks and provide assistance in the house.

From 1846 to 1849 two physicians and an apothecary administered relief in the workhouse. This was quite insufficient given that in 1846 according to *Croly's Medical Directory* there were seventy practising physicians in Cork City and only Dr Popham, Dr O'Connor and Apothecary, Dr Gardiner, were affiliated to the workhouse. These physicians were competent and expert and were held in high esteem by their peers. Dr O'Connor lectured at the Cork School of Medicine and had offices in South Mall. By 1849

**Table 2.** Male and Female Admission Figures of those inmates aged 15 and over, January to June 1847

| Admissions | January | February | March | April | May | June | Total |
|---|---|---|---|---|---|---|---|
| Male | 633 | 378 | 420 | 47 | 362 | 107 | 1,947 |
| Female | 1,048 | 658 | 575 | 51 | 414 | 138 | 2,884 |

he was teaching at the medical faculty of the newly established Queen's College Cork. Dr Popham resided at Marlborough Street and was Dr O'Connor's assistant physician. He also tended to patients in the North Infirmary Hospital and held a lectureship in physiology at Queen's College Cork. They contributed articles to contemporary medical journals. Only by 1849 with increased house capacity was Dr Townsend of Old George Street appointed to the medical staff of the workhouse.

The geographical location of the workhouse was also in itself regarded as prejudicial to the health of inmates. Dampness was rampant in the area where the house was situated 'on the verge of the unwholesome, death producing bog of Ballyphehane'.[4] The reluctance of the Commissioners to sanction additional buildings until 1847 other than the fever hospi-

Fig. 3 (right) Given the high mortality rate in the workhouse in 1847 there was an urgent need to acquire extra burial space. This page from the Minute Book of the Cork Poor Law Union relates to the acquisition of burial grounds on the Carrigaline Road (Carr's Hill): 'From the opening of the graveyard on 11 February 1847 to 23 June 1847, 2,216 paupers from the workhouse were buried at the Carr's Hill site'. [Sources: Colman O'Mahony, *Cork's Poor Law Palace: Workhouse life 1838-1890.* (Cork, 2005); Cork Archives Institute]

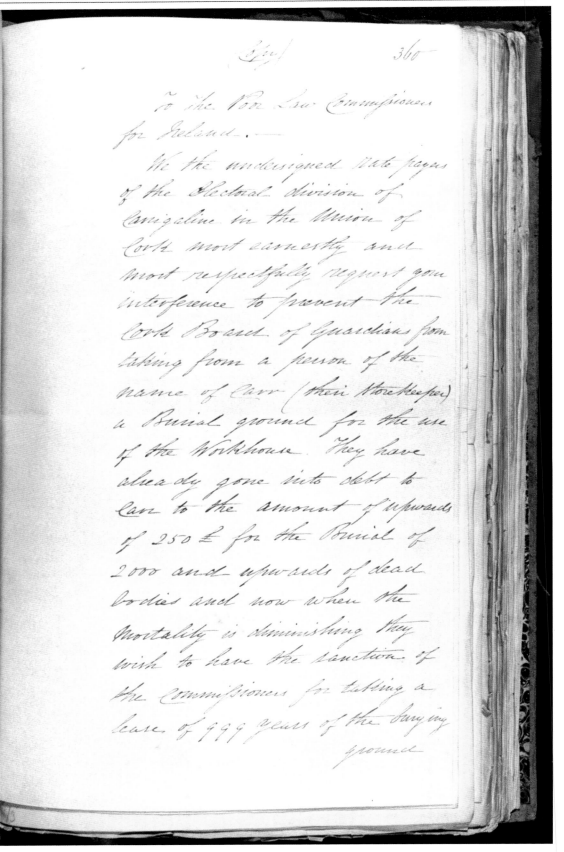

tal emphasised a bureaucratic and ideological inertia.

The year 1847 was particularly devastating. Unfortunately, the evidence for this period in terms of original documentation is fragmentary and the figures compiled relate only to the period January to June 1847. During these months a total of 7,817 persons sought admission to the workhouse, including a record number of admissions, 2,714 for January alone. The average number of inmates resident for that month was 4,345. Joseph Burke, the Assistant Commissioner, noted the excessive overcrowding and after a meeting on 18 January with the Board of Guardians he penned the following:

> Gentlemen, I this day attended a meeting of the guardians of the Cork Union. The number of the inmates in the workhouse and in the two additional wards has now reached 5,310 – 868 of whom were admitted within the last fortnight – the medical officers having given in their report, a copy of which I forward, the propriety of allowing further admissions was discussed, where it was agreed not to exceed the present number in the house and that admissions could only be allowed as discharges occurred . . . [A] resolution was adopted by the guardians that the present state of the poor law was quite inadequate to meet the unprecedented destitution which now prevails. It must certainly be admitted that the poor law was introduced to meet the destitution of an ordinary year – but not to provide against a famine. If the guardians of the Cork Union could procure further accommodation I am certain that the numbers that would avail themselves of workhouse relief would be double or treble what it is now and then would come the question of how funds were to be procured, as adequate means to meet such an extensive system of relief could not be obtained by making heavy rates on an impoverished people.[5]

During 1847 the capacity of the workhouse was extended by 800 to 2,800. However, the numbers of inmates resident usually far exceeded this figure. A higher rate of female admissions was again observed in 1847.

Fig. 4 A plaque commemorating those who died within the Cork workhouse during the Famine years. It is located at a former entrance to the workhouse (now part of the external wall of St Finbarr's Hospital) on the South Douglas Road. [Photo: John Crowley]

These figures were derived from the minute books of the period. In April 1847 the minutes record only ninety-eight adult admissions. This significant reduction can be explained by the fact that the workhouse closed its doors temporarily and engaged in outdoor relief. Additionally, the frequency of discharges of inmates also increased in that particular month. In May the figures reverted back to the pattern of previous months while the usual seasonal decline was also evident. More inmates sought discharge in the summer months as they often emigrated and the improved climatic conditions were an incentive for many to leave the workhouse, even if the situation in Cork outside the house was little better.

## CHOLERA

Natural disasters are predictably accompanied by epi-

**Table 3.** Monthly mortality figures of those inmates aged 15 and over, 1845–1851

| Month | 1845 | 1846 | 1847 | 1849 | 1850 | 1851 |
|---|---|---|---|---|---|---|
| January | 43 | 47 | 178 | | 110 | 130 |
| February | 52 | 64 | 606 | | 120 | 219 |
| March | 55 | 60 | 675 | 164 | 184 | 239 |
| April | 52 | 76 | 523 | 317 | 141 | 176 |
| May | 48 | 88 | 407 | 368 | 156 | 219 |
| June | 42 | 32 | 233 | 255 | 157 | 207 |
| July | 18 | 28 | | 130 | 86 | 110 |
| August | 28 | 42 | | 106 | 64 | 58 |
| September | 28 | 42 | | 90 | 95 | 42 |
| October | 18 | 51 | | 48 | 52 | 48 |
| November | 52 | 113 | | 48 | 54 | 56 |
| December | 50 | 237 | | 83 | 80 | 46 |
| TOTAL | 486 | 880 | 2,622 | 1,609 | 1,319 | 550 |

*Omissions exist where the minute books for particular dates are missing.*

**Table 4.** Yearly Mortality Rates of males and females under 15 years of age

| | 1845 | 1846 | 1847 | 1849 | 1850 | 1851 |
|---|---|---|---|---|---|---|
| Males under 15 | 56 | 91 | 485 | 190 | 162 | |
| Females under 15 | 52 | 48 | 487 | 195 | 209 | 474* |
| Children under 2 | 108 | 245 | 409 | 216 | 214 | 312 |
| TOTAL | 216 | 384 | 1,382 | 701 | 585 | 726 |

demics and disease. Cholera appeared in Cork in the late spring of 1849. Calculations of the figures for 1849 were based on those available from March to December 1849. The earlier evidence was missing. In comparison to the figures for 1847 the admission figures for 1849 increased dramatically. The reason for this was that additional accommodation was eventually sanctioned and the house capacity was extended to provide assistance for 6,300 people. The auxiliary buildings built in 1848 allowed for greater assistance, however, there was no discernible improvement in sanitation and conditions. In fact, conditions were conducive to the spread of cholera. Numbers peaked in June coinciding with the height of the cholera epidemic. In that month alone 3,331 admissions occurred, while the total number of inmates resident in the workhouse was 6,911. House capacity again increased for July and August to 7,100 to deal with the crisis.

Death was never far away in the workhouse. Its acceleration through the house was frequently so great that burials often times were problematical. One commentator, Canon John O'Rourke, reminisced:

> Some idea of the dreadful mortality then prevalent in Cork may be found in the fact that in one day thirty-six bodies were interred in the same grave and from the autumn 1846 to May 1847, 10,000 persons were interred in Father Mathew's cemetery in Cork that he was forced to close it.[6]

Mortality figures for the Cork workhouse have been calculat-

ed from entries in the minute books and they must at best be seen an indicator of the actual number. Given the way in which the figures were written each week into the minute books there were always omissions and some are illegible. If anything, the mortality figures should be higher. We cannot be sure of the exact numbers who died who were resident in the auxiliary buildings and those who were moved from the house to the adjoining fever sheds. The following Tables 3 and 4, which contain information gathered from the available records, indicate mortality figures for adults aged fifteen and upwards and also the mortality figures of those child inmates aged fifteen and under. The figures again highlight the worst months and years of the Famine as it rampaged its way through the Cork workhouse.

The Cork Union workhouse was very much a microcosm of society and as such the administrators of the house performed a diverse range of functions, both bureaucratic and social. These roles included those of judge, jury, lawmaker and enforcer, moral and religious co-ordinator, and on occasions facilitator of assisted passages and grantor of marriage licences. The workhouse was akin to a prison system with a strict penal policy, so much so that 'the prison system seemed to hold more attraction for them and as a result crimes were committed frequently to gain access to prisons, at least there they could be sure of

Fig. 5a Pauper burial site at Carr's Hill Cemetery, Carrigaline Road, Cork. The fifty-foot high lattice-work cross was erected by Jack Sorenson, a Cork taxi owner who maintained it until his death in 1979. [Photo: John Crowley]

Fig. 5b  The cross being put together at Sorenson's, Victoria Road, Cork, in 1958. [Source: *Irish Examiner* Publications]

a bed and of food'.[7]

## ASSISTED EMIGRATION

Assisted passage was another means of escaping the workhouse and Famine conditions. Since female inmates outnumbered male inmates by the ratio two to one, subsidised passages proved financially expedient at a cost of between £3 and £5 per emigrant. Emigration presented a means 'for which the rising generation of workhouse inmates could be permanently provided'.[8] The records state that inmates were assisted in their emigration to such diverse places as 'the Cape of Good Hope',[9] Australia and America, including in one particular instance, to Shawneentown, Illinois. In 1848 Richard Dowden, guardian, was in correspondence with a Mr Flour of Stratford-upon-Avon with a view to sending emigrants from the Cork Union workhouse to Shawneentown. Mr Flour's brother was the contact in Illinois. Dowden received a letter listing those residents in Shawneentown who wished to take emigrants to work as domestic servants. The letter, dated October 1848, stated that they 'will not only be shielded from want and deprivation but will be received with credible families where they will be justly and kindly treated'.[10]

As Famine conditions deteriorated so too was there a corresponding rise in the number of proposals. The Outgoing Letter Book records that in May 1848, 200 names were forwarded to the Poor Law Commissioners for assisted passage to Australia.[11] The minutes for 1848 refer to a demand from the Emigration Commissioners relating to a shortage of women in Australia. This circular was sent to all unions and it enquired as to the number of young orphaned girls aged between fourteen and eighteen years of age who could be candidates for emigration. It advocated that costs would be kept to a minimum and that the only costs the union would incur would be the passage to Plymouth.[12] Perhaps an editorial in the *Cork Examiner*, January 1849, is a fitting assessment of the exodus during the Famine in the Cork area and the rest of the country: 'They fly the land as if a pesthouse and quit the soil of their youth and manhood, as if the demon plague was running riot in the fields.'[13]

The story of the Cork Union workhouse is just one aspect of the history of the Great Famine. Much of what was witnessed in the Cork workhouse was indicative of life in many other workhouses throughout the country. The documents reveal a story of hardship, suffering, fever, death and survival. Perhaps the legacy of what little remains of the original structure – now a well known landmark in the city, St Finbarr's Hospital – is the memory that resides there of all those Famine victims that lived and died within its walls.

# Ulster workhouses – ideological geometry and conflict

## Liz Thomas

George Wilkinson, the architect chosen to design all of the workhouses in Ireland, created a standard plan that enabled the practical implementation of the governing ideologies and policies of the new Irish Poor Act. Adam Smith's *laissez-faire* principle, Thomas Malthus' theory that surplus population resulted in poverty and Jeremy Bentham's ideas on centralisation, classification and 'less-eligibility' to relief were all ideas manifested in the Irish Poor Act (1838). The new Poor Act in Ireland was essentially a system of laws where the key policies were driven by the ideologies of laissez-faire, centralisation, classification, discipline, economy, non-religion and the workhouse test or less eligibility (where the condition within the workhouse was inferior to the condition of the independent labourer). Through the use of uniformity, spatial segregation, ceremony and symbolism, the workhouse plan provided the physical manifestation of the ideological thinking of the Poor Laws. This was the first time that the ideologies of poverty legislation were manifested physically and legislatively. Even though administratively and physically the workhouse system encapsulated the ideologies driving the new Poor Laws, there was often conflict between the Commissioners and the guardians; the conflict between the two was the constant struggle to maintain and enforce the Commissioners' austere ideologies at a pragmatic level in the workhouse.

### INQUIRIES AND IDEOLOGY

There were two key inquiries that highlighted the determination of the Government to enforce their Benthamite and Malthusian ideologies through the policies of the new act. The first of these inquiries was the Royal Commission of Inquiry into the Conditions of the Poorer Classes in Ireland, which was established in September 1833 and chaired by Richard Whately, Archbishop of Dublin. Whately was a radical; his beliefs contradicted the Benthamite and Malthusian ideologies that dominated Government policies on poor relief. Ideologically, Whately was paternalistic and insightful into the Irish character. He had a very strong colonist viewpoint and considered Ireland as being potentially equal to England. In fact, he was more humane than he was policy driven.[1] Whately's relief proposals were dismissed. His detailed and extensive inquiry took three years, but the entire report was met with some indifference and had virtually no impact on the legislation that was eventually introduced.

George Nicholls, known for his Malthusian views, was appointed to investigate further the suitability of a workhouse system in Ireland even before Whately had published the final report of his inquiry. Nicholls' inquiry, or his notorious cyclonic tour of twelve counties over six weeks, produced the pivotal report on which the Poor Law system introduced into Ireland originated.[2] The men who objected to Whately's proposals were the key Poor Law policy makers in England. The ideologies of William Nassau Senior, George Cornwall Lewis and George Nicholls guaranteed the introduction of the workhouse test in Ireland.

### KEY LEGISLATORS

Nassau Senior did not consider the eradication of poverty in the way Whately did. Senior possessed a Malthusian perspective; he believed that poverty emerged from the uncontrolled overpopulation of the poor. His utilitarian proposals were severe and hinted of Benthamite ideologies.[3] Senior opposed any religious influence on any state system that provided for the poor and supported the idea of a central control to direct and guide relief in Ireland, implicitly supporting the workhouse system.

George Cornwall Lewis served on Whately's Commission until 1834, but supported the workhouse system and workhouse test. His beliefs were clearly in line with the Government's ideologies. Lewis considered that the workhouse was the 'keystone' to implementing the objectives of the Poor Law.[4]

George Nicholls was an ardent supporter of Malthus' doctrine and insisted on the moral and social benefits of the workhouse. He believed that the workhouse test was the 'first step, towards effecting an improvement in the character, habits, and social condition of the people'. He believed that 'an excess of population is an evil' and that education, with Malthusian doctrine, would result in the 'improved moral and prudential habits of the community'. As a Benthamite he advocated the 'certainty and efficiency' and 'stability and continuity' of a central control and believed that the workhouse system would work as a Government instrument.[5]

The Poor Law policy of the classification of paupers was physically expressed by spatial segregation throughout the workhouse. In fact, Wilkinson's standard workhouse plan paralleled Bentham's idea of the 'pauper-land'.[6] The workhouse was an efficient and economical way to accommodate and manage all classes of pauper and simultaneously the spatial segregation served as a punitive measure, as an obstacle to moral and physical contagion and as a physical representation of society. The Poor Law Commission was the final authority regarding the administration of relief in Ireland. The Board of Guardians that were elected for each union had no real power; ultimate decisions were vested in the Poor Law Commissioners.

## MORAL GEOMETRY

The geometry or arrangement of the wards portrayed the governing power, discipline and paternal government and reflected a scale ranging from supreme to base morality. The plan shows that the Guardians were at the very top of this scale. The children's wards were nestled around the Master, safe from contamination around them. The pauper adults, being worse in nature, were placed in the extreme wings of the workhouse. The 'idiots' were banished to the extreme end of the workhouse because indifferent to right and wrong they presented the greatest moral threat. The separation of men from women prevented procreation and targeted the problem of excess population. The final purpose of spatial segregation was to maintain the moral

geometry of the workhouse. It was absolutely forbidden for one class of pauper to have contact or communicate with another. A stringent economy was also at the heart of the new act whose primary objective was to relieve destitution of the 'really and unavoidably destitute' in the 'most economical manner'.[7] Wilkinson produced plain elevations and created designs for decorative features, such as the barge boards, gates and ventilation towers that were optional extras. An exact design was not imposed because the guardians were given liberty to choose their own styles. Ideally, the architecture was to be discreet and fitting to the purpose for which the workhouse was built. The pauper's regime and the architectural style of the workhouse were frugal in nature. The location of the building was generally on a hill commanding a domineering view of the nearest town. Conspicuous on the Irish landscape, these structures symbolised a warning against indolence and an expression of power from the Government.

## DISCIPLINE AND PUNISHMENT

Nicholls viewed labour as a means of discipline and deterrence as part of the workhouse test. The same test could not be applied to children and they were trained to 'acquire

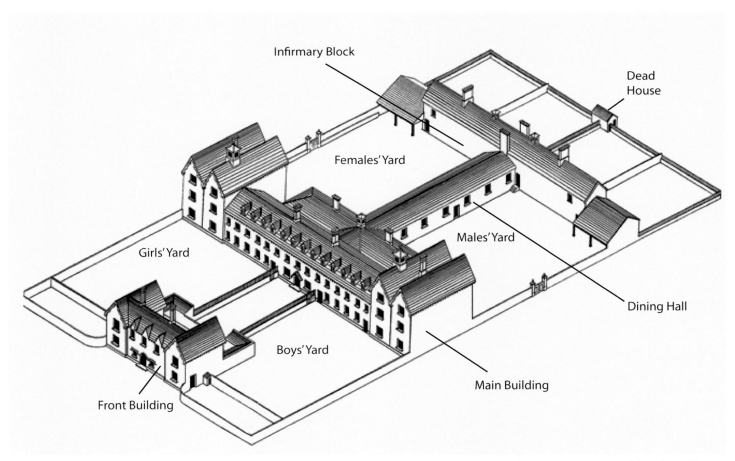

Fig. 1 Wilkinson's Standard Plan. Deviation from the standard plan was almost impossible. On plan each side was a mirror image of the other. All external and internal features maintain perfect symmetry in height and size. This standard plan permitted neither irregularity nor non-conformity within the workhouse. The plan encapsulated the ideologies of the policies of the new law in Ireland. According to George Nicholls, 'It is important to bear in mind, however, that the workhouse constitutes the basis of the whole measure about to be established, and that as on the efficiency of the workhouse all will depend'. (Source: Fifth Annual Report of the Poor Law Commissioners, 1839, 28)

Fig 2 Carrickmacross Union Workhouse. The main building has the ventilation tower, stone barge boards and symmetry common to the workhouses in Ulster. [Photo: Liz Thomas]

habits of industry' and become 'useful members of the community'.[8] Paupers were physically punished, through confinement or whipping, as a means to maintain discipline and order. The boys and elderly inmates managed the piece of land attached to the workhouse while the able-bodied inmates were 'strictly confined' to labour within the workhouse.

The workhouse plan was arranged so that there was no area exclusively set aside for worship; various rooms such as the dining hall and school room were doubled up as areas for worship. Politics and religion were, according to the Commissioners, the two greatest points of contention in Ireland and, therefore, religious ministers could not become guardians. Consequently, politics was forbidden and religion existed just at a pragmatic level in the workhouse.

Pauperism was considered a hereditary disease. Bentham concluded that education would eradicate this disease, but only through an education that befitted them as pauper children. The children were trained according to their rank in society, reinforcing the ideology that indigence and not poverty could be banished.

Through archaeology, architecture and archival material the struggle the guardians had with the austere ideolo-

gies and policies of the Commissioners can be revealed. There are two levels to this struggle: the first was a fundamental disagreement about the policies that the Commissioners wanted to enforce and the second was the difficulty the guardians had to implement those policies on a practical level.

## CLASSIFICATION

The minute books of Boards of Guardians across Ulster reveal difficulties in enforcing the policy of classification. Rigid spatial segregation was especially difficult; workhouses were not meant to be prisons. In 1842 the surrounding walls of the Belfast workhouse were raised to eight feet to prevent both escape and trespass. Even this height was insufficient and by 1849 these walls were capped with broken glass. In 1852 the Belfast guardians allowed, to the Commissioners' astonishment, the workhouse watchman to use a gun, so difficult were confinement, segregation and classification to enforce. The Lisnaskea idiot yard wall was raised by eighteen inches and this change in wall height is still visible in the wall.

Partitions were erected, doors blocked and iron bars and gates installed to enforce spatial segregation and classification, all to little effect. Ballyshannon inmates used a stile to climb from the male yard to the female yard and in 1852 at least two of them made their way to the fever hospital and helped themselves to four bottles of spirits. Consequently, a six-foot-high wall was built.[9] By 1854 the master had exhausted every legitimate physical means to restrain several of the male and female inmates, who were frequent night visitors at the Ballyshannon public houses and returned to the workhouse for a good night's slumber.

Female inmates were impregnated, sometimes even by infirm inmates or workhouse officers. In 1842 the Belfast guardians felt that the penitentiary was a more suitable place for prostitutes than the workhouse and by the early 1850s the Commissioners recommended that prostitutes and 'ill-mannered females' should be separated from the other female inmates. Mothers of only one illegitimate child did not have to be separated from the female inmates because the Commissioners accepted that they were not of bad character but had just made a mistake. However, mothers of more than one illegitimate child were classified with the prostitutes.

The Commissioners and Guardians disagreed on classification. For example, the Belfast guardians and the management of the lunatic asylum exchanged patients when either institution was full, to mutual benefit. This system existed for some time, in spite of the Commissioners' refusal to sanction it and their regular reminders to the guardians that the workhouse was only for the relief of the destitute poor according to the classification system. The Commissioners discovered that the guardians in Lis-

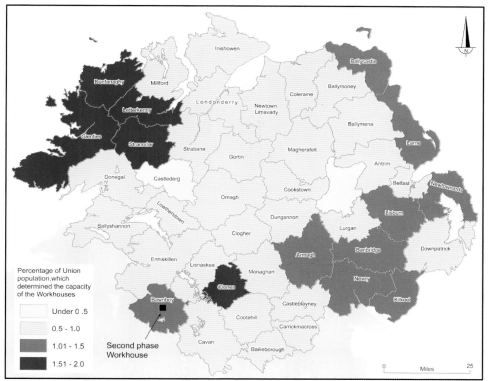

Fig. 3 ULSTER UNIONS AND WORKHOUSE SIZE. The Poor Law Commissioners directed that the workhouses should accommodate only 1% of the population. The guardians chose to build workhouses that provided for more paupers, which clearly shows that the guardians both defied the Commissioners' directions and were more realistic about the nature of poverty in Ireland.

## PRINCIPLE OF ECONOMY

The guardians were generally willing to adhere to the principles of economy; they were indeed emissaries of the union ratepayers. George Wilkinson promised that his standard plan would be cheaper than the average cost of workhouses in England. Wilkinson argued that earthen floors would be a cheaper and viable option to use within the Irish workhouses but already in the early years of many of the workhouses the guardians chose, for sanitary reasons, to have the floors flagged. The washrooms, the laundry rooms, the school rooms and most of the ground floor wards in most union workhouses were eventually flagged or stoned. In May 1848 Wilkinson disapproved of the plan of the fever hospital adopted by the guardians because of the use of timber in the plan. Wilkinson thought that they were 'sacrificing efficiency for the sake of economy'.[11] The Commissioners often criticised the guardians' disregard of economy. In Belfast, in 1843, the Commissioners would not sanction the expense of fireplaces in the accommodation of the assistant officers, the 'subordinates'. The guardians actively monitored costs of workhouse contracts and supplies and sought the cheapest building estimates, even flouting the principle of laissez-faire. In 1843 the Belfast master could supply any other union, with any quantity of potatoes at a rate better than any other 'businessman'.[12]

naskea, Ballyshannon, Belfast, Clogher and Castlederg had permitted their masters' families to live within the workhouse, contrary to regulations. During epidemics and the Great Famine there was a mass convergence of classes. The symmetry of the workhouse was significantly dismantled; training rooms became fever wards, fever sheds were erected in graveyards and auxiliary workhouses were established in other houses or institutions without any adherence to symmetry principles. During these periods of crises able-bodied paupers were even permitted to work on the land outside.

Wilkinson's general plan lacked the necessary provision of certain rooms: storage was insufficient, access between rooms was difficult and the nurseries were not suitably large. In Lisnaskea alterations were made so that the potato store was closer to the kitchen, sheds were converted to sleeping apartments, an infant school was established in the probationary wards (to which the Commissioners objected), and the temporary fever hospital was used for cholera patients. A tailor trained the boys of the workhouse in the women's day room, while a carpenter trained them in the female idiot ward.[10] In a constant endeavour to maintain the principle of uniformity, the Commissioners urged the guardians to maintain symmetry of the buildings, even to the finest detail. For example, in Belfast in 1842 the Commissioners pressed the guardians to render the tops of the yard walls in the probationary wards so that they were uniform with the main building.

## DECORATION

The guardians were economically stringent. For example, the Belfast guardians sought a cheaper estimate by eliminating cut stone, plastering and even ventilation for one of their new buildings on the workhouse grounds. But the guardians also defied the principles of economy and austere architecture through the use of decoration. The front building of the Lisnaskea workhouse displays some of the most flamboyant decoration that is to be found amongst the workhouses in Ulster – architectural additions that would have added expense to the cost of the workhouse. Many of the workhouses also had different coloured cut quoins alternating red to pale stone. Often the keystones on window arches were intentionally coloured bright red. Inverted arches with no functional purposes, like the ones in the Larne and Carrickmacross workhouses, can also be found amongst the workhouses in Ulster.

The Commissioners recommended that the workhous-

Fig. 4 Children's Dormitory. Wilkinson promised a saving in the construction of workhouses in Ireland through the use of earthen floors instead of stone, the elimination of plastering walls and the use of sleeping platforms instead of beds. This dormitory at Carrickmacross Union workhouse slept up to 200 children. This building is presently being preserved and restored. [Photo: Liz Thomas]

es should be located conveniently to the town and in a lofty position. The location of the workhouse, at the discretion of the guardians, was generally dictated by cost and economy. However, the ideology of uniformity overruled that of econ-

omy. In the Ballyshannon Union it appears that the Commissioners pressed the guardians into rejecting the Old Barracks that was offered as a gift so that they could enforce their ideal of a new building that would encapsulate the

principles of the new Poor Laws.[13] The location of the workhouse was dictated by cost but not the orientation. Usually, the workhouses faced towards the towns. However, some, like the Lisnaskea workhouse, faced away from the town while the Clogher workhouse was hidden away in a valley. The guardians' choice of orientation of the workhouse might have been a physical expression of their attitudes towards the workhouse test and their opposition to the forced system.

Labour was a form of discipline. Corn mills and spinning wheels provided labour for the able-bodied inmates. Inmates in the Newtownards workhouse were employed in various tasks, including spade work, working sand and breaking stones, mixing manure, making baskets, cleaning privies, wells and walks, planting vegetables and whitewashing. The Commissioners would not sanction inmates working in a role above their perceived station. However, this restriction was not always practical and inmates were appointed as unpaid nurses, watchmen and assistants in various unions. In 1843 the Belfast master was compelled to appoint a male and female pauper as infirmary and laundry assistants. Their trusted position was not punishment but a divergence from the classification system. The food provided in the Ulster workhouses was used as a means of punishment and an incentive and

was entirely against the Commissioners' directions. Imprisonment, confinement and discharge were the machinery of punishment of the workhouse. Even children were punished through whipping and the withdrawal of meals. In 1842 a thirteen-year-old Belfast boy was discharged for refusing to work.

The Commissioners had the supreme authority over the workhouse system and displayed unyielding control over every aspect of the workhouse, from the diet consumed to the appointment of officers. The guardians of the Ulster unions disagreed with many aspects of the Irish Relief Act, including the 41st article of the regulations, according to which the clerk of the union was not under the control of the board. In 1844 the Belfast guardians complained that this article 'virtually' deprived them of any power over the other officers of the workhouse. The Clogher, Lisnaskea and Londonderry unions, amongst many others, objected by petition to the cost of erecting the workhouses. The Lisnaskea guardians felt that at their 'great expense' the Commissioners had neglected to evaluate the full costs of the workhouse.[14] By February 1849 the Ulster guardians were vehemently opposed to the 'rate in aid'(see Christine Kinealy, above). The Guardians and the Commissioners usually disagreed on the use of buildings, salaries of officers and diet of the inmates. In 1853, the Lis-

Fig. 5 (below) Bawnboy Union Workhouse. During and after the Great Famine there was a second phase of workhouse building. In Ulster there was just one workhouse built, Bawnboy Union Workhouse in 1852. The buildings were designed by Wilkinson according to the same principles of classification. This is the infirmary building, exhibiting the usual principles of uniformity and spatial segregation. [Photo: Marcus Mendenhall]

naskea guardians ventured to ameliorate the condition of the workhouse children by establishing an infant school; the school continued even with the Commissioners' disapproval. In Lisnaskea the Commissioners objected to the guardians' decision to admit the children of a working mother, a servant, who would contribute towards the support of her children in the workhouse. This action was not sanctioned because 'in order to maintain a sound system of relief no principle was of more importance that every able-bodied individual should be supported either wholly by wages or wholly by the Guardians'.[15]

The Great Famine had a massive impact on the workhouse system, a system which was not designed to alleviate mass starvation but which was, inadvertently, on the front line for relief measures during the peak of the Great Famine. In 1837 Nicholls stated that 'The occurrence of a famine, if general, seems to be a contingency altogether above the powers of a poor law to provide for'.[16] Between 1845 and 1852 the Commissioners endeavoured to maintain the principle of the workhouse test. In 1846 they directed the guardians to manufacture flour from diseased potatoes to give food to the poor but more importantly 'as a means of providing suitable employment to the inmates of the workhouse' and to maintain the workhouse's 'proper order and discipline-maintenance and classification'.[17] Throughout the calamity the Commissioners continuously reminded the guardians of the principles of the Poor Law and stated that 'they [the Commissioners] are still strongly of opinion that the workhouse accommodation should be reserved for destitute able-bodied persons and their families'.[18]

The Commissioners were ardent that extra accommodation was made within the workhouses 'so as to avoid the necessity of giving outdoor relief'.[19] Yet, the Commissioners ordered against the financially-pressed Ballyshannon guardians providing extra accommodation and the Belfast guardians apprenticing out their orphan and deserted children. The Commissioners also limited the number of inmates in the Ballyshannon workhouse to 720 and refused financial assistance stating that 'they deeply regret the difficulty which the guardians experience, but – the guardians must rely solely on their own resources'.[20] While some guardians begged for assistance to provide for the masses, many others disagreed with seeking such support. In 1849 the Lisnaskea Guardians declared 'That, it is with indignation, we have, it is recommended by the Majesty's Government to impose a rate in aid on the peaceable, loyal and industrious inhabitants of the North of Ireland for the support of the lazy, vicious and indolent population of the south and west of this Kingdom who neither fear God nor respect the laws of the land.'[21]

Almost every workhouse in Ulster made some form of addition or alteration during the Great Famine. Straw houses and training rooms were converted into dormitories and fever wards, and temporary and dysentery sheds were erected throughout the workhouse grounds. These erratic constructions made during the Great Famine impacted on the uniformity and symmetry of the individual workhouses. The Commissioners' vision of a network of almost identical workhouses throughout Ireland displaying the principles of centrality and uniformity was shattered by the pragmatic needs of the Great Famine. The concept of the mixed workhouse was lost. Premises in the surrounding towns were rented for the accommodation of different classes of paupers. In Belfast the asylums, the Magdalene penitentiary, the Old Barrack's hospital and the House of Correction were obtained for extra accommodation.

The guardians were overwhelmed by the large number of deaths. In 1847, which was one of the worst years of the Great Famine, the Ballyshannon guardians, desperate for space, interred the dead paupers at the rear of the workhouse against the directions of the Commissioners. Dreadful circumstances required that the guardians continued to bury the paupers there until they found another piece of land. In 1847 the Belfast guardians found that the Friars' Bush, Shankill and Belfast Charitable Society's cemeteries were full and on one occasion they were forced to remove coffins to make space for new interments in the workhouse burial ground.

During the Great Famine the strict discipline and order of the workhouse was difficult to maintain and with instances of rebellion a fear of inmate insurrection prevailed. In 1848 the Ballyshannon master was attacked on two occasions by the inmates. An assistant was employed to manage the Belfast male and female inmates to prevent insurrection and a bell pull was erected in the able-bodied wards so 'that in the event of sudden unrest assistance may be immediately afforded'.[22]

## RELIGION

Religion caused disputes between the Commissioners and guardians. At a practical level the masters of many of the Ulster Union workhouses complained that services and holy days disrupted the management of the workhouses. Times were agreed for the services and rooms were set up for them. In Belfast the Protestant services were held in the boys' school, Catholic services in the girls' school and Presbyterians met in the open room/dining hall. Accusations of proselytizing were rampant: at the very least in the Lisnaskea, Belfast, Clogher and Antrim unions. In some instances there were hints of sectarianism amongst the boards of guardians. The Lisnaskea guardians had a very difficult relationship with their Roman Catholic chaplains and refused to provide Catholic religious books to the Catholic inmates, even when ordered to do so by the Commissioners. The Protestant chaplain seemed to hold some authority that was recognised by the guardians. This is evident when in April 1850 the appointment of a new schoolmistress in Lisnaskea could only be confirmed on the recommendation of the Protestant chaplain.[23]

The workhouse system was introduced into Ireland with brutal determination. The key policy makers (Senior, Lewis and Nicholls) enforced their Benthamite and Malthusian ideologies through the policies of the new Poor Law act. These ideologies were reflected in the obdurate standard plan of George Wilkinson. However, the policies proved extremely difficult for the guardians to implement on a pragmatic level – especially during a crisis like the Great Famine – without breaching the principles of the new act and dismantling the symmetry and austere presence of the workhouse building. The constant struggles between the Commissioners, the guardians and even the inmates of the workhouses showed that the workhouse system could not be maintained in accordance with the ideological aspirations of the Irish Poor Act (1838).

Fig. 6  Limavady workhouse, County Derry, now the Roe Valley District Hospital. Newtownlimavady workhouse opened in March 1842. Originally designed to hold 600 inmates, that figure doubled during the worst years of the Famine. [Photo: Brian Graham]

# Lurgan workhouse

## Gerard Mac Atasney

In April 1847 John Dilworth of Killicomaine, Portadown, wrote of an event he experienced whilst helping the destitute of the Lurgan Poor Law Union:

> About the beginning of this month on the old road leading to Portadown, I called on a family named McClean and found the house like a pig-sty. Having fled from the Lurgan Poor House, where fever and dysentery prevailed, they returned home only to encounter greater horrors. Want sent the poor man to bed and I gave him assistance, but he died a few days after. The wife almost immediately after, met the same melancholy fate; and a daughter soon followed her parents to the grave. On the Thursday after, I repeated my visit, and just within the door of the wretched habitation I saw a young man, about 20 years old, sitting before a live coal, about the size of an egg, entirely naked; and another lad, about thirteen, leaning against a post. On turning to the right, I saw a quantity of straw, which had become litter; the rest of the family reclining on this wretched bed, also naked, with an old rug for covering. The boy who stood against the post directed my attention to an object at my feet, which I had not seen before, and over which I nearly stumbled, the place being so dark – and oh! What a spectacle – a young man about fourteen or fifteen, on the cold damp floor, off the rubbish, dead!; without a single vestige of clothing, the eyes sunk, the mouth wide open, the flesh shrivelled up, the bones all visible, so small around the waist that I could span him with my hand. The corpse had been left in that situation for five successive days.

In a follow-up visit the next week Dilworth found three family members, out of a total of eight, still alive and remarked how 'none of these will be any time alive'.

In order to understand why the McClean family, together with many other unnamed families throughout the union, sought their escape from the Lurgan workhouse it is necessary to illustrate the conditions which prevailed in that institution in the early months of 1847.[1]

The most noticeable manifestation of the failure of the potato crop in the Lurgan Poor Law Union was the increase in the numbers of people entering the local workhouse. At the end of September 1846 the number stood at 313 but by the end of December the workhouse was full to capacity with 805 inmates. Again, in common with such institutions throughout the country, the numbers dying in the workhouse showed a marked rise over the same period. Thus, from an average of fourteen deaths per month until November the latter month witnessed thirty-one deaths while December saw fifty-eight. The pages of the various visiting chaplains' notebooks, previously occupied with details of 'divine services' and 'scripture readings' now told a sorry tale of multiple burials, with both the Catholic and Episcopalian chaplains performing interments on a daily basis.

### BLACK '47

The numbers dying in the workhouse increased sharply in the first weeks of 1847 – eighteen in the first week of January, thirty-six in the second and fifty-five in the third. So marked was the increase that the Poor Law Commissioners wrote to the local guardians expressing their regret at the 'great mortality' in the institution and requiring a detailed report from Dr Bell, the medical officer. The doctor's reply stressed that mortality levels were abnormally high as 'it is

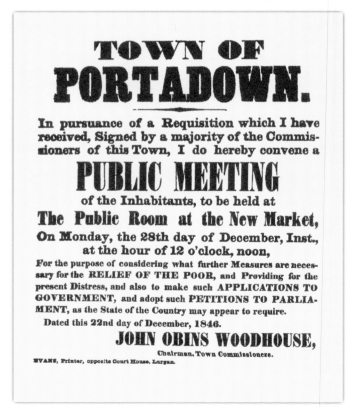

Fig. 1 Poster announcing a public meeting in Portadown on 28 December 1846 to discuss measures necessary for the relief of the poor.

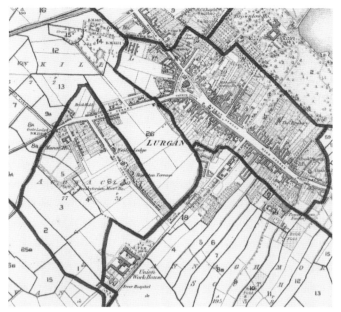

Fig. 2 Location of Lurgan workhouse as shown on an early Griffith's Valuation map which also delineates property boundaries adjacent to Lurgan town.

a well-known fact that many dying persons are sent for admission merely that coffins may be thereby obtained for them at the expense of the Union'. He added that as a consequence of severe overcrowding it had proven impossible to provide dry bedding for inmates and sleeping on damp beds had 'increased fever and bowel complaints which have in many cases proved fatal'.

Explaining the rationale behind the mortality figures was one thing; doing something about them was another. In the weeks that followed the number of those dying, far from abating, actually increased – for the week ending 30 January there were sixty-eight deaths, for 6 February there were ninety-five and for 13 February there were sixty-seven. These figures marked the Lurgan workhouse out as one of the worst in the country for inmate mortality; indeed, for the first six weeks of 1847 the numbers dying in the workhouse were the highest in Ulster.

Obviously, immediate action on the part of the guardians was necessary and on 5 February they announced that the workhouse and fever hospital would refuse any further admissions until the situation had been effectually remedied. However, the Poor Law Commissioners had been monitoring the situation and with the mortality level remaining high they decided to send

Dr Smith from the Central Board of Health to investigate the workhouse. The importance they attached to his opinion can be attested to by the fact that he only visited two other workhouses in the country – those of Bantry and Cork.

## DR SMITH'S INVESTIGATION

Answerable only to the Commissioners, Smith produced a report which was a damning indictment of all those responsible for the poor of the Lurgan Union. In the male and female infirmaries there was an average of two persons per bed, although three and four was not uncommon. The walls and floors of the infirmary were in a 'very discreditable condition' and with the windows closed 'the atmosphere [was] close and foul; the smell upon entering the rooms most offensive'. Walls had not been white-washed, buckets, used as lavatories by patients, were allowed to sit for hours without being emptied, and medicines and drinks were served out on the floor where 'the boards were in a filthy state'. In the idiot department there were no beds and patients simply slept on the wet ground – the wards were described as being in an 'exceedingly foul condition'. Compounding all these problems was the fact that the clothes of those paupers who had died of fever and dysentery were then passed to incoming paupers without prior cleaning and drying.

With regard to burials, Smith ascertained that many paupers had been buried less than four yards from the fever hospital while the well supplying water to the house was situated in the centre of the burial ground. The following observation highlighted the problem:

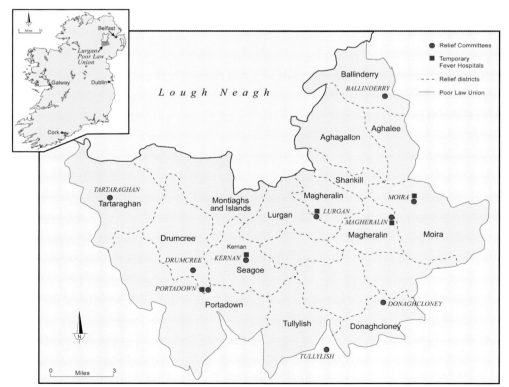

Fig. 3 DISTRIBUTION OF TEMPORARY FEVER HOSPITALS AND RELIEF COMMITTEE DISTRICTS IN LURGAN POOR LAW UNION, 1847.

165

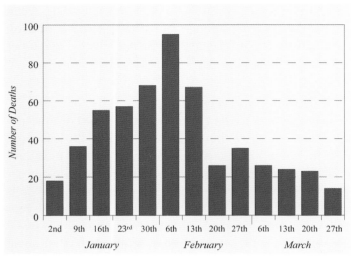

Fig. 4 Deaths per week between January and March 1847 in the Lurgan workhouse.

In the graveyard attached to the house, a large grave is made which fills nearly full of water a short time after it is opened. To its verge are brought the coffins containing the dead bodies – these coffins frequently contain two and three each – they are then put into the grave, in which they usually float. One or two persons then stand on the coffins in the water until the mould is heaped upon them. There are frequently twenty bodies in the one grave.

Consequently, the graves had been dug so close to the well that the water had become unfit for use. Describing the workhouse as 'a picture of neglect and discomfort such as I have never seen in any other charitable institution', Smith pointed to a number of causal factors, primarily amongst the workhouse administrators. He believed that the problems stemmed from the fact that a three-week period was allowed to elapse before a replacement was appointed after the death of John Meason, the workhouse master, in early November.

It was during this hiatus that overcrowding had developed and this, together with the illnesses of various subordinate officers, meant that 'ventilation, whitewashing and cleanliness appear to have been neglected at the very time when the strictest attention to these important means of arresting the spreading of disease were imperatively called for'. While acknowledging the burden on the medical officer, he maintained that what he termed 'a little more activity' on the part of Dr Bell, together with a stricter surveillance by the guardians, would have prevented much of the mortality. In a direct criticism of the latter he commented:

It appeared to me that the Guardians had no knowledge of the state of the infirmary as regard cleanliness, ventilation, etc either from personal observation or otherwise. The reports of the physi-

cians informed them of its overcrowded state and this was the only particular about it which they seem to be acquainted.

Smith concluded that in his opinion 'the chief causes of the evil in question are internal and the result of defective management of the institution'.

### INEFFICIENCY

The ink on Smith's report had hardly dried when a letter to Lord Lurgan from Episcopalian chaplain Rev. Oulton further highlighted the inefficiency of the workhouse administrators. On one of his regular visits to the house, Oulton had noticed that the food appeared sub-standard, prompting the comment that 'it is hardly to be wondered at that so much disease should be in the workhouse if the description of food has for any length of time been such as I saw there today'. He described the meat as being 'of the worst description that could be got in Lurgan Street – more like the flesh of an animal that had died of disease than being killed for food'. In addition, the bread was dark-coloured, insufficiently baked and sour whilst the broth was so bad that many paupers could not use it.

This letter was the catalyst for an internal examination of the principal workhouse officials by the guardians. Ward master, Thomas Lutton, commented how the bread had been bad for more than a week and he believed it 'unfit for human food' – with many sick paupers unable to eat it. Beef used in the paupers' soup had a 'very offensive smell' but was nevertheless sent to patients in the fever hospital. Medical officer, Dr Bell, maintained that the bread had been of poor quality for two months while meat supplied to the house had been 'defective for a long time'. Another workhouse doctor, McVeagh commented how 'from my experience as a medical man I don't know a worse description of food for persons affected with diarrhoea and dysentery than sour bread'.

### 'A VERY FILTHY AND UNCLEAN STATE'

This was not the first occasion on which serious questions had been raised about the administration of the workhouse. In February 1846 a visiting committee from the Poor Law Commissioners had described the house as being in 'a very filthy and unclean state' and a couple of months later, in June, the Fever Commissioners sent a doctor to examine the building in the midst of a fever outbreak. In his observations, this gentleman, Dr Stevens, recommended the building of extra accommodation in order to cater for the increased numbers of patients. However, he stated it as his opinion that the level of fever was much greater than it should have been as Dr Bell had permitted the entry of non-infected children with their ill parents. Consequently, the Fever Commissioners declared Bell to be 'unfit for his present office' and called for his removal 'without delay'.

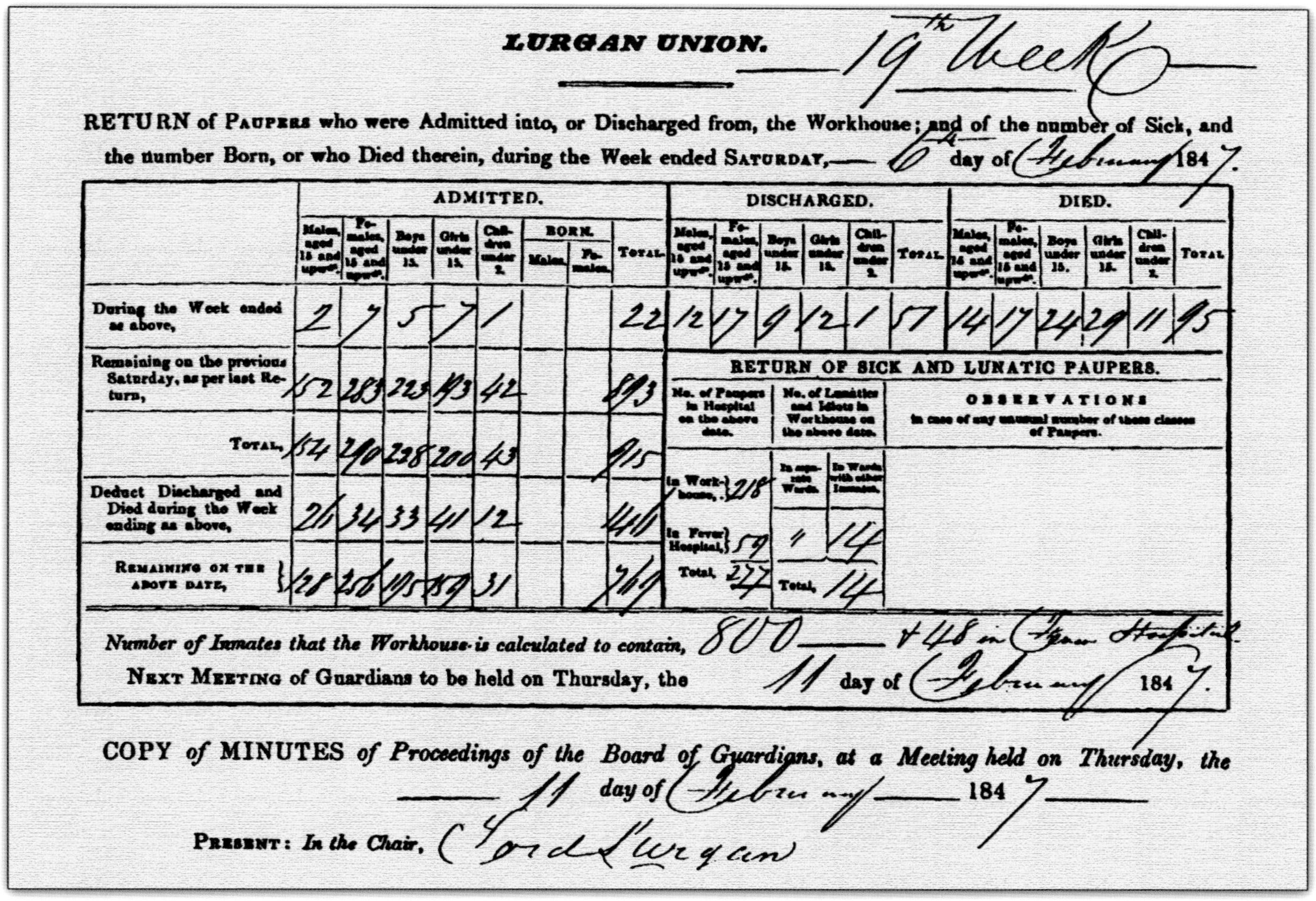

**LURGAN UNION.** _19th Week_

RETURN of PAUPERS who were Admitted into, or Discharged from, the Workhouse; and of the number of Sick, and the number Born, or who Died therein, during the Week ended SATURDAY,— 6 day of February 1847.

| | ADMITTED. | | | | | BORN | | | DISCHARGED. | | | | | | DIED. | | | | | |
|---|---|---|---|---|---|---|---|---|---|---|---|---|---|---|---|---|---|---|---|---|
| | Males aged 15 and upwds. | Females aged 15 and upwds. | Boys under 15. | Girls under 15. | Children under 2. | Males | Females | TOTAL | Males aged 15 and upwds. | Females aged 15 and upwds. | Boys under 15. | Girls under 15. | Children under 2. | TOTAL | Males aged 15 and upwds. | Females aged 15 and upwds. | Boys under 15. | Girls under 15. | Children under 2. | TOTAL |
| During the Week ended as above, | 2 | 7 | 5 | 7 | 1 | | | 22 | 12 | 17 | 9 | 12 | 1 | 57 | 14 | 17 | 24 | 29 | 11 | 95 |
| Remaining on the previous Saturday, as per last Return, | 152 | 283 | 223 | 113 | 42 | | | 813 | | | | | | | | | | | | |
| TOTAL, | 154 | 290 | 228 | 200 | 43 | | | 915 | | | | | | | | | | | | |
| Deduct Discharged and Died during the Week ending as above, | 26 | 34 | 33 | 41 | 12 | | | 146 | | | | | | | | | | | | |
| REMAINING ON THE ABOVE DATE, | 128 | 256 | 195 | 159 | 31 | | | 769 | | | | | | | | | | | | |

RETURN OF SICK AND LUNATIC PAUPERS.

| | No. of Paupers in Hospital on the above date. | No. of Lunatics and Idiots in Workhouse on the above date. | | OBSERVATIONS In case of any unusual number of these classes of Paupers. |
|---|---|---|---|---|
| | | In separate Wards | In Wards with other Inmates | |
| In Workhouse, | 218 | | | |
| In Fever Hospital, | 59 | 4 | 14 | |
| Total, | 277 | Total, | 14 | |

Number of Inmates that the Workhouse is calculated to contain, 800 — + 48 in Fever Hospital.

NEXT MEETING of Guardians to be held on Thursday, the 11 day of February 1847.

COPY of MINUTES of Proceedings of the Board of Guardians, at a Meeting held on Thursday, the 11 day of February 184 7

PRESENT: In the Chair, Lord Lurgan

Fig. 5 Return of paupers, Lurgan Union. In the week ending 6 February 1847, there were ninety-five deaths in the workhouse in Lurgan. This represented slightly less than one-fifth of the province's total mortality for that week (529); the second highest was thirty deaths in Enniskillen workhouse. Nationally, the highest number was in Cork where, with a workhouse population of 5,338, 128 deaths had occurred.

However, far from acquiescing to this request, the Lurgan guardians responded with a strident defence of their medical officer and pronounced their confidence in his 'skill, humanity . . . and great kindness of heart'. Further, they castigated the Commissioners for what they regarded as the inadequate size of the fever hospital, constructed under the latter's guidelines. They also claimed that a request from the medical officer to the Commissioners to supply paid nurses had been refused. For their part, the Commissioners, on re-examining the case, exonerated Bell from the charges made against him while the guardians, obviously delighted with this outcome, resolved unanimously to increase his salary by £20 per annum.

However, now less than a year since this incident, the mistakes made with a workhouse population of 450 became fatal when that number had more than doubled. The reports of 1846 and 1847 pointed to serious maladministration on the part of the Lurgan guardians. Hence, it may have been expected that a number of officers would have been removed while some guardians may have considered their

positions. However, only one member of staff saw fit to resign. In doing so, Dr Bell cited deterioration in his health as a result of overworking as his reason. It appears that, while he may have been able to withstand the criticism consequent upon an internal enquiry, his position became untenable on the publication of Dr Smith's report by the Central Board of Health. Nevertheless, those charged with appointing both the medical and administrative staff and contracting for food – the Lurgan Board of Guardians – did not the feel the need to take similar action and there were no resignations from this body.

The disease and death which permeated the Lurgan workhouse in the early months of 1847 earned it an unenviable reputation throughout Ulster as being little more than a charnel house. This fact was probably best encapsulated in the following comment by Rev. Henry Wynne, Chairman of the Moira Relief Committee, who remarked how 'the mortality in the Poor House of Lurgan is such as would prevent our Guardians from sending any of our poor to the establishment at present'.

SECTION IV
POPULATION DECLINE
AND SOCIAL
TRANSFORMATIONS

Potato ridges on Achill Island.
[Photo: Frank Coyne]

# Mortality and the Great Famine

## Cormac Ó Gráda

The cost of famines in terms of human lives lost is often a controversial issue. There are two quite different reasons for this. The first is that famines are nearly always blamed on somebody, and excess mortality is reckoned to be a measure of guilt. The second is that famines are more likely to occur in economically backward regions and countries, where demographic data are often poor or non-existent, and where non-crisis mortality is not easily separated from famine mortality.

The Great Famine is no exception. At the height of the crisis, Prime Minister Lord John Russell refused to provide an estimate of famine deaths in the House of Commons, rather glibly asserting that measurement was impossible because 'a man found dead in the fields would probably be mentioned in the police returns as having died of starvation'. Opposition leader Lord George Bentinck in turn accused Russell of 'holding the truth down', and predicted a day 'when we shall know what the amount of mortality has been'. Then, argued Bentinck, people could judge 'at its proper value [the Government's] management of affairs in Ireland'. Some nationalists have since talked up the death toll, and some revisionist historians have talked it down.

### MORTALITY

The best scholarly consensus is that about one million died of famine-related causes between 1846 and 1851.[1] Such a number would make the Great Famine exceptional in relative terms, and also Europe's greatest natural disaster of the nineteenth century, albeit modest in absolute terms compared to say, the Great Bengal Famine of 1943–44 or the Chinese Great Leap Forward famine of 1959–61. Since there was no civil registration of births and deaths in Ireland at the time, the estimate of excess mortality is arrived at as a residual. By definition, where $n$ is the annual rate of population change on the eve of the Famine:

$$POP1846 = POP_{1841}(1+n)^5 ] \qquad [1]$$

and:

$$POP1851 = POP_{1846} + B_F + B_{NF}$$
$$- D_F - D_{NF} + M_F + M_{NF} \qquad [2]$$

where $B_i$, $D_i$ and $M_i$ refer to famine-related ($F$) and non-famine ($NF$) births, deaths, and migration.

Only the populations in 1851 (6.65 million) and 1841 (8.125 million) are recorded. Therefore, excess mortality must be calculated as a residual based on assumptions about $n$, $B_{NF}$, $D_{NF}$, and $M_{NF}$. Estimates of all these variables are debatable, if not controversial. Although the 1841 and 1851 Censuses were ahead of their time in the amount

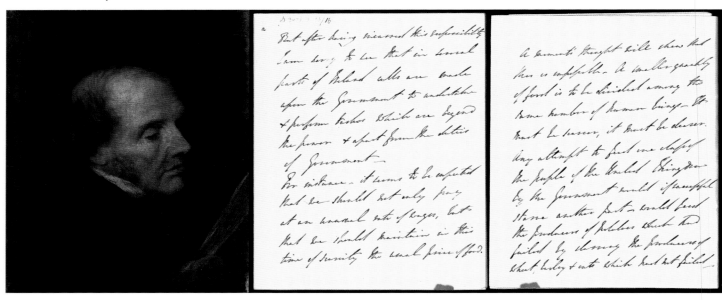

Fig. 1 *Portrait of Lord John Russell, 1st Earl Russell* by George Frederic Watts, oil on canvas, circa 1851. [Source: © National Portrait Gallery, London] A letter from the British Prime Minister Lord John Russell to the leader of the Irish Whigs, the third Duke of Leinster, 17 October 1846, where Russell explains the policies of his government vis-à-vis the Famine. The Whig principle of laissez-faire is very much in evidence: 'in several parts of Ireland calls are made upon the government to undertake and perform tasks which are beyond the power and apart from the duties of government. For instance, it seems to be expected that we should not only pay at an unnatural rate of wages, but that we should maintain in this time of scarcity the usual price of food. A moment's thought will show that this is impossible. A smaller quantity of food is to be divided among the same number of human beings. It must be scarcer, it must be dearer. Any attempt to feed one class of the people of the U[nited] K[ingdom] by the government would if successful, starve another part: would feed the producers of potatoes which had failed, by starving the producers of wheat, barley and oats which had not failed.' [Source: Public Record Office of Northern Ireland, D 3078/3/33/16]

of useful detail they offer, they have their limitations. There are good reasons to believe that the population in 1841 was about 8.4 million.[2] Supposing then that we assume $n = 0.5\%$ (compared to 0.6% in the 1830s), population would have exceeded 8.6 million in 1846. If in the absence of famine population had continued to grow at the same rate, it would have reached 8.83 million by 1851. Then the value of the residual $(B_F - D_F + M_F)$ would equal (6.65 – 8.83), or -2.18 million. A lower counterfactual population growth rate of $n$ = 0.4 would yield a somewhat lower residual (-2.12 million).

A combination of factors led to a reduction in the number of births during the Famine. These included famine amenorrhoea (the hunger-induced absence of menstruation), illness, reduced libido, spousal separation due to migration and death, postponed marriages and social disruption. But by how much did they reduce births? On the basis of a study of a large sample of surviving baptismal registers, Joel Mokyr reckoned the shortfall in births to have been from 0.3 million to 0.4 million between 1846 and 1851. This implies that the combined contribution of excess deaths and excess migration would have been well in excess of two million. Assuming a higher $M_F$ still leaves the traditional estimate of the famine's demographic toll – one million dead and one million lost to emigration – plausible, if not proven.

## THE TABLES OF DEATHS

At first sight, the Tables of Deaths (in two volumes) compiled by William Wilde and his staff as part of the 1851 population census (BPP 1856) seem to offer an inexhaustible treasure of data on famine deaths and on famine demography more generally. Wilde's tables contain extremely detailed cross-tabulations of mortality by cause, by county, by year and by season. Deaths in institutions (fever hospitals, workhouses, prisons) are distinguished from the rest. In reality, the data are seriously flawed, which probably explains why scholars have tended to shun them in the past. They report a total of 985,000 deaths between 1841 and 1851, or only slightly more than half the probable total during the decade. The problem is that the census relied mainly on information given by survivors, but that would have meant the automatic exclusion of deaths in households that had disappeared in the interim. For that reason, underreporting is bound to have varied considerably across the country.

In mitigation, most of the workhouse deaths between 1846 and 1851 – 200,000 of the 250,000 recorded – were famine-related deaths. We may take it that these were recorded and diagnosed accurately by workhouse and medical personnel. A key feature of workhouse mortality is the high proportion of deaths from infectious disease. Not surprisingly, the proportions were highest in workhouses in the worst-affected areas, although the variable quality of workhouse management by local elites also

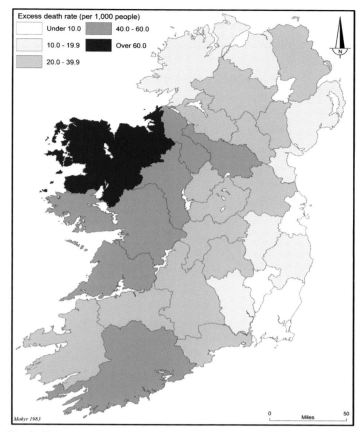

Fig. 2 DISTRIBUTION OF UPPER-BOUND ESTIMATES OF ANNUAL EXCESS DEATH RATES PER COUNTY (after Joel Mokyr). Mokyr based his analysis of annual excess deaths on a series of estimates and assumptions, including the annual level of emigration per county in the Famine years and on established econometric techniques. His upper-bound estimates of excess deaths include 'averted births', i.e. births that would have occurred but for the traumatic social effects of famine conditions. Mokyr estimates that 'averted births' meant a further population loss of 0.3 to 0.4 million. This map identifies a west-to-east pattern in the levels of upper-bound annual excess death rates. County Mayo is identified as the core of the highest excess death rates at over 60 per 1,000 people per annum. The rest of Connacht and Clare, as well as Counties Cork and Cavan, form the second highest level at 41–60 annual excess deaths per 1,000 population. The third major zone stretches from Antrim through central Ulster and north and west Leinster and includes the remaining Munster counties of Kerry, Limerick, Tipperary and Waterford with estimated annual excess death rates of 21–40. Northern and east-coast counties from Donegal, Londonderry and Down to Louth and Wicklow and also including Counties Kildare and Kilkenny are judged to be the second lowest excess death rates at 11–20 per annum. Counties Dublin, Carlow and Wexford are deemed to have the lowest death rates at under 10 per 1,000 per annum. More recent research – as in this chapter – has modified both these estimates and regional generalisations.

played a role.[3]

Wilde's Tables of Deaths corroborate the point that throughout history most famine deaths were due to diseases rather than to starvation per se. Some of those diseases (e.g. dysentery, scurvy) were closely linked to the lack of food, but others (e.g. typhus) less so.[4] However, the proportion of deaths attributed to starvation (2%) in the Tables of Deaths is probably an underestimate, and the deaths attributed to dropsy – hunger oedema in today's language – and marasmus – a form of severe protein-energy malnutrition affecting infants and very young children – should be factored in. In Wilde's tables these accounted for another 2 and 5% of excess deaths, respectively.

Corrected causes of death in Ireland are broadly similar to those reported for roughly contemporaneous famines in India and Russia (see Table 1). Only in the twentieth century, when famines struck relatively developed places such as the western Netherlands and Leningrad and Greece during World War II, is a very different pattern of famine mortality witnessed for the first time.

Karl Marx quipped in *Das Kapital* that the famine killed 'poor devils only'. That is clearly true, although the role of infectious disease meant that the clergy and medical and Poor Law personnel were also at risk. In the Catholic diocese of Cloyne and Ross seventeen priests had died before the end of 1847 'by reason of their attendance on the suffering poor'. Half of the staff of the North Dublin Union were attacked by famine fever, and half of those succumbed, while about two hundred doctors and medical students died, three times the pre-Famine rate.[5] Unequal access to modern medical technologies such as penicillin has made more recent famines more class-specific.

A seemingly universal and striking feature of famine mortality generally is that males are more likely to succumb than females.[6] This seems to have been the case in Ireland in the 1840s too. As English philanthropist Sidney Godolphin Osborne noted on a tour of the west of Ireland in 1849, 'in the same workhouse, in which you will find the girls and women looking well, you will find the men and boys in a state of the lowest physical depression; equal care in every way being bestowed on both sexes'. In the six west Cork parishes investigated by Poor Law inspector J.J. Marshall in late 1847, men were one-third more likely to die than women,[7] although overall the gap was much smaller than that. The female 'advantage' was almost certainly due to physiological rather than cultural causes.

## ACCOUNTING FOR MORTALITY BY REGION

As the accompanying maps amply illustrate, famine mortality varied greatly by region. Although no county or region was untouched, the west and south were much worse hit than the north and east. Mokyr (1985), McGregor (1989) and Ó Gráda (1999) have employed straightforward econometric techniques in seeking to account for the variation in mortality across counties and baronies.[8] Unfortunately, county-level estimates of excess mortality are subject to a wide margin of error, but the percentage population change between 1841 and 1851 (*DPOP*) offers an alternative 'catch-all' measure of the Famine's demographic toll. Table 2 reports the results of a statistical analysis of the variation in *DPOP* at baronial rather than county level. *DPOP* is regressed on a list of plausible explanatory variables. How these variables were constructed is explained in more detail elsewhere.[9] Note, however, that *NUM* is an index of age-heaping based on the 1841 population census. Age-heaping, a commonly employed measure of the lack

Fig. 3  An ill-defined area in the northwest corner of Drumcliff burial ground that contains the remains of many nameless victims of the Famine in Ennis and its environs. [Photo: Frank Coyne].

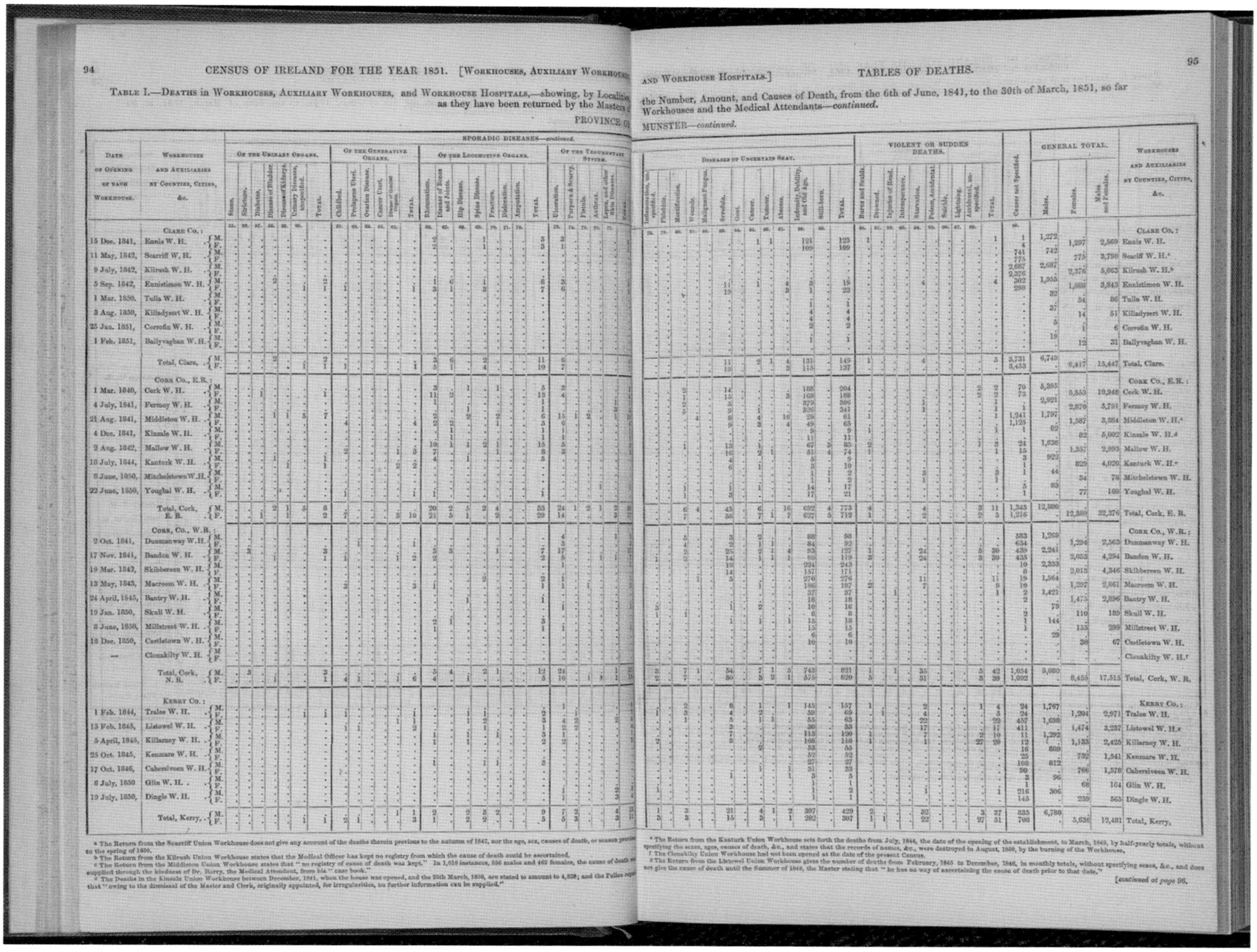

Fig. 4 Page from the Tables of Deaths compiled by William Wilde and his staff as part of the 1851 population census. [Source: British Parliamentary Papers, 1856]

of numeracy, may be seen as a proxy for poor education. Three other variables, the proportions of males and females who could neither read nor write (*MILLIT, FILLIT*) and the percentage of households living in fourth-class housing (*BADHOUSING*), also refer to 1841 Census data. There are data too on the proportion of households with 'vested interests', and the proportions directing labour or reliant on their own labour. *W1834* refers to the relevant county wage in 1834, and the shares of the labour force relying on agriculture and manufacturing (*PCAGR21* and *PCMAN21*) are taken from the 1821 population census. Poor Law valuation per head (*VALPOP*) is also included as a likely measure of living standards.

The results for the most part are predictable and plausible. In non-technical language, they indicate that lower population decline across baronies during the Famine decade was associated with lower illiteracy or a higher ability to both read and write (*MRR* and *FRR*), higher wages, lower numeracy, and higher Poor Law valuation per head. The urban dummy is valued at one for the main urban areas and at zero otherwise, while the coastal dummy is valued at one for baronies next to the sea. Other things being equal, urban and coastal baronies also suffered less. Baronies with lower proportions engaged in agricultural and in manufacturing occupations in 1821 fared relatively better. The link between manufacturing

**Table 1.** Causes of excess deaths in Ireland, Russia and India

| Cause of Death | Ireland 1846–51 | Saratov 1918–22 | Berar 1897 |
|---|---|---|---|
| Diarrhoea, dysentery, gastroenteritis | 24.9 | 19.7 | 30.4 |
| Cholera | 6.8 | 5.1 | 12.1 |
| Fever | 29.2 | 24.1 | 29.0 |
| Respiratory | 4.8 | 9.8 | n/a |
| Starvation/Scurvy | 10.0 | 5.5 | n/a |
| Other, n/a | 24.3 | 35.8 | 28.5 |
| TOTAL | 100 | 100 | 100 |

*n/a = not available*

Source: Mokyr and Ó Gráda, 'Famine disease and famine mortality'.

## INQUEST ON MARY ANN MCDERMOTT

**13 March 1847. Held on view of the body of Mary Ann McDermott, in the townland of Cladone, Parish Clones, Barony of Dartree, Co. Monaghan**

**VERDICT [Special]:** Mary Ann McDermott lived for the past four months (in the village of Killeevan) by begging but refused to go into the poorhouse and charged her children never to do so. She supported herself and her two children by meal which she spent the whole day in collecting. She collected each day about ½ (?) in small quantities, through the country, bringing home at night what she collected during the day and making gruel of it for herself and her two children. She got a few pence also by begging with which she paid her house rent 2 ½ d (per) week and to give herself and her two children two meals on Sunday. On Friday 12th inst. deceased walked from Killeevan to Clones on an errand for which she received a loan of a cupful of meal which she divided amongst herself and children, made into gruel, being a teacupful to each. On Thursday deceased got a quart of soup from the soup kitchen and was told to call each day after it. On Friday deceased's child went for the soup while her mother was in Clones; the two children took a porringer full of it, leaving one for their mother against her return. On deceased's return she became weak and sat down about two miles from Killeevan and close by the house of Bernard Gleeson whose sister went and asked deceased was she ill and would she like any food, who on deceased's saying she would returned to the house and warmed some stirrabout and milk and put it into the mouth of deceased as she would if feeding an infant, but deceased could not swallow it and commenced struggling violently with her arm for about twenty minutes, when she died. It appeared, upon examination of the body, deceased had some greens of a bad quality in her stomach and a small quantity of raw turnips in her bowels insufficient to sustain life. The jury find her death arose from want of proper and nourishing food.

**Coroner William Charles Waddell of Rockcorry**

Fig 5  Inquest on Mary Ann McDermott..[Source: Brian Ó Mórdha, 'The Great Famine in Monaghan: A Coroner's Account', *Clogher Record*, vol. 4, no. 1/2 (1960/61), p. 41]

and mortality is noteworthy, reflecting the strength of manufacturing still in 1821 in many poorer and more peripheral rural areas that would be forced to de-industrialise between then and the famine. These areas would accordingly be hard pressed in the pre-famine decades. More surprisingly, heavily Irish-speaking baronies (*IRISH*) escaped more lightly. The Catholic share of the population was excluded from the results reported here, as it lacked any explanatory power. The coefficients can be interpreted as elasticities, except in the cases of the dummy variables for coastal and mainly urban baronies (*COAST* and *URBAN*) and valuation per head (*VAL*). Thus in Equation [1], a 10% increase in the percentage of males who could neither read nor write (*MILLIT*) was associated with a 1.5% decrease in population.

### CIVIL PARISH RESULTS

Table 3 describes the results of carrying out a similar analysis of the determinants of population change at the civil parish level. Thanks to the labours of the Famine Research Team of the Department of Geography at University College Cork, we have information for 1841 and 1851 on a similar list of variables to that used in Table 2 for nearly 3,000 civil parishes. These include parish size, valuation, literacy, housing quality, and occupational category. The presence of a few

extreme outlying observations prompted the use of robust regression estimation, which increased the explanatory power of our variables considerably. The most extreme outlier was the parish of St Lawrence in the Limerick barony of Clanwilliam, which reported a population increase from twenty-one in 1841 to 720 in 1851. In the worst-affected quintile of parishes the median population loss exceeded a staggering two-fifths, while in the least-affected quintile, the median loss was about 7%.

The outcome of the statistical analysis is broadly similar to that in Table 2. In this case we experimented with two proxies for housing quality, the share of families residing in fourth-class housing (*BADHOUSING*), and the proportion of houses reckoned as fourth-class (*BADHOUSING 2*). In urban areas, in particular, many first- or second-class houses were subdivided into tenement units qualifying as

**Table 2.** Accounting for the variation in population change across baronies, 1841–1851

|  | [1] | [2] | [3] | [4] |
|---|---|---|---|---|
| *MILLIT* | -.150 ** |  |  |  |
| *FILLIT* |  | -.099 |  |  |
| *MRR* |  |  | .150 * |  |
| *FRR* |  |  |  | .289 ** |
| *W1834* | .183 ** | .199 ** | .224 ** | .219 ** |
| *BADHOUSING* | -.181 ** | -.170 ** | -.169 ** | -.161 ** |
| *IRISH* | .115 ** | .106 ** | .103 ** | .100 ** |
| *VAL* | 3.524 ** | 2.098 ** | 1.798 ** | 1.814 ** |
| *NUM* | -.140 | -.155 | -.191 * | -.138 |
| *PCMAN21* | -.148 ** | -.205 ** | -.200 ** | -.136 ** |
| *PCAGR21* | -.399 ** | -.451 ** | -.446 ** | -.382 ** |
| *COAST* | 2.111 | 1.746 ** | 1.766 | 1.687 |
| *URBAN* | 11.385 ** | 11.090 ** | 9.255 ** | 9.216 ** |
| *CONST* | 4.790 | 8.075 | -2.888 | -10.018 |
| N | 293 | 294 | 295 | 294 |
| Prob > F | 0.0000 | 0.0000 | 0.0000 | 0.0000 |

*Note: robust regression estimates.*
*'**' and '*' denote statistical significance at 5 and 1 per cent levels.*

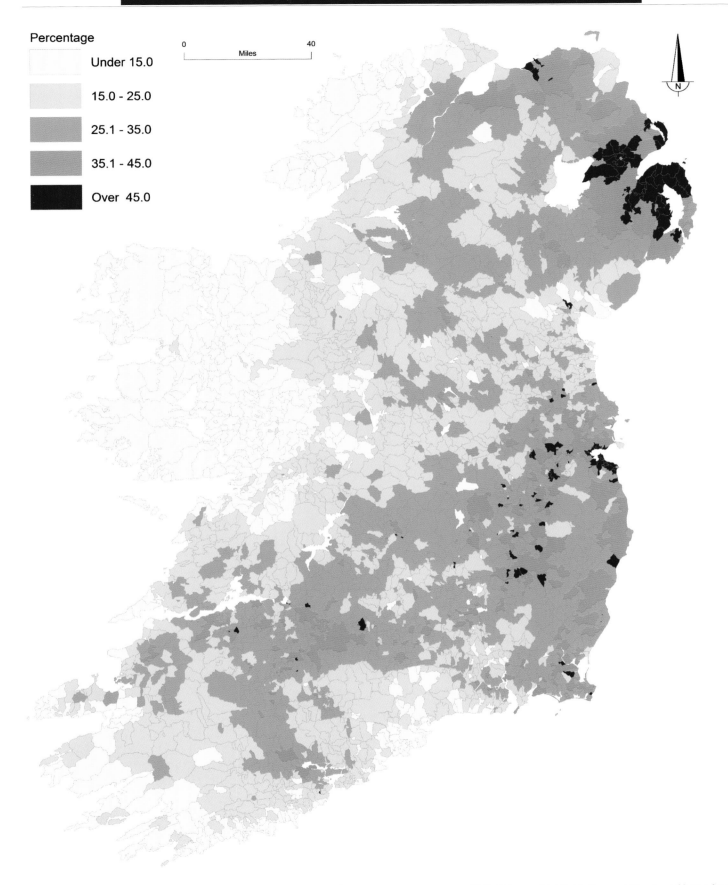

**Percentage**

| | |
|---|---|
| | Under 15.0 |
| | 15.0 - 25.0 |
| | 25.1 - 35.0 |
| | 35.1 - 45.0 |
| | Over 45.0 |

0       Miles       40

Fig. 6 PERCENTAGE DISTRIBUTION OF POPULATION (OVER FIVE YEARS OF AGE) WHO CAN READ AND WRITE IN 1841. This map highlights the most literate and best educated populations in Ireland in 1841. Three regions with over 35% levels of literacy occur: (i) in a significant block in north and east Ulster; (ii) in the Liffey–Barrow valleys and coastlands of east Leinster; and (iii) in a smaller zone in the Golden Vale area of east Limerick. Very significant levels of literacy – where at least a quarter of the population over five years of age can read and write – occur amongst parish communities in much of the rest of Ulster province and in the long-settled, strong farming and urban worlds of Leinster and Munster. As highlighted in the accompanying tables, these areas with high literacy levels were better able to weather the traumas of the Famine years.

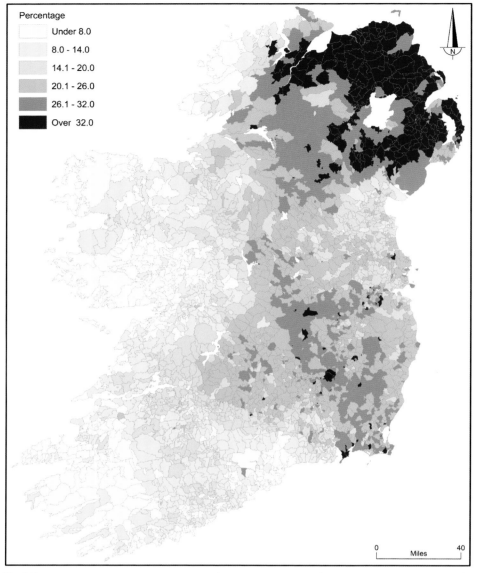

Percentage

| | |
|---|---|
| | Under 8.0 |
| | 8.0 - 14.0 |
| | 14.1 - 20.0 |
| | 20.1 - 26.0 |
| | 26.1 - 32.0 |
| | Over 32.0 |

0        Miles        40

Fig. 7 PERCENTAGE DISTRIBUTION OF POPULATION (OVER FIVE YEARS OF AGE) WHO CAN READ ONLY IN 1841. This map, showing the percentage distribution of the population who can 'read only' in 1841 provides a very distinctive picture. Many members of Protestant communities – for whom Bible-reading was a central religious exercise – are obviously strongly represented in this 'read only' category. That over 30% or 40% of communities in Ulster – and pockets elsewhere in the southern Midlands – were in this 'read only' category is a striking feature of this map. The map also highlights the very strong east–west gradient in advancing literacy levels with one-fifth of the population of counties from east Donegal south along the Shannon to Limerick and curving eastwards to Waterford City revealing a capacity to read – a vital life-saving skill in the Famine years. The 10–20% parishes are transitional bilingual English/Irish-speaking communities while it is clear that the parishes where less than 10% can read are emphatically areas where monoglot Irish speakers are dominant.

higher population loss, in Table 3 the impact of higher proportions in manufacturing in 1841 was the reverse. The manufacturing that survived de-industrialisation was disproportionately urban or northern, and entailed diversification away from an increasingly stretched agricultural sector.

MATERIAL CONSEQUENCES

Our parish-level data also shed some light on the material consequences of the Famine for survivors living in Ireland in 1851. By and large, conditions improved most in parishes where the decline in population was greatest. Table 4 reports the coefficients obtained by running a range of variables on proportionate population change between 1841 and 1851. First, note that the greater the decline in the population during the Famine decade, the fewer relying on their own labour and the more employed in directing others. This reflects the decimation of the agricultural labour force during the Famine. Second, increases in valuation per head and in the share of the labour force in manufacturing, and improvements in housing quality, were associated with population decline. In other words, the more died or emigrated in a typical parish, the better off were those who survived. Third, and more surprisingly, between 1841 and 1851 illiteracy decreased less in areas of heavy population decline.

Taken together, the outcomes of Tables 2, 3, and 4 confirm the link between poverty and land hunger, on the one hand, and vulnerability to the

fourth-class accommodation. We also included the proportion of households with vested interests in the parish (*PCVEST*), and the proportions directing or relying on their own labour (*PCDIR, PCOWN*). Finally, we included occupational shares in 1841 (*PCAGR, PCMAN*), both valuation per head of population (*VALPOP*) and valuation per acre (*VALACRE*), and population density per acre.

Again, the results are broadly as expected, with proxies for poverty and economic backwardness being associated with heightened population loss. Note, however, that whereas in Table 2 higher proportions of the labour force in manufacturing in 1821 were associated with

Great Famine, on the other. The bleak economic context in which the famine struck obviously mattered. The link between the 'improvement' that followed in the wake of the disaster and the price paid in lives lost is also evident in these data at parish level. These outcomes testify to the ineffectiveness of policy-makers and private philanthropy against *Phytophthora infestans*. But they do not let the authorities of the day off the hook: one of the important messages of recent Famine historiography is that the rich and the powerful, both in Westminster and locally, could have done much more than they did to mitigate the ensuing carnage.

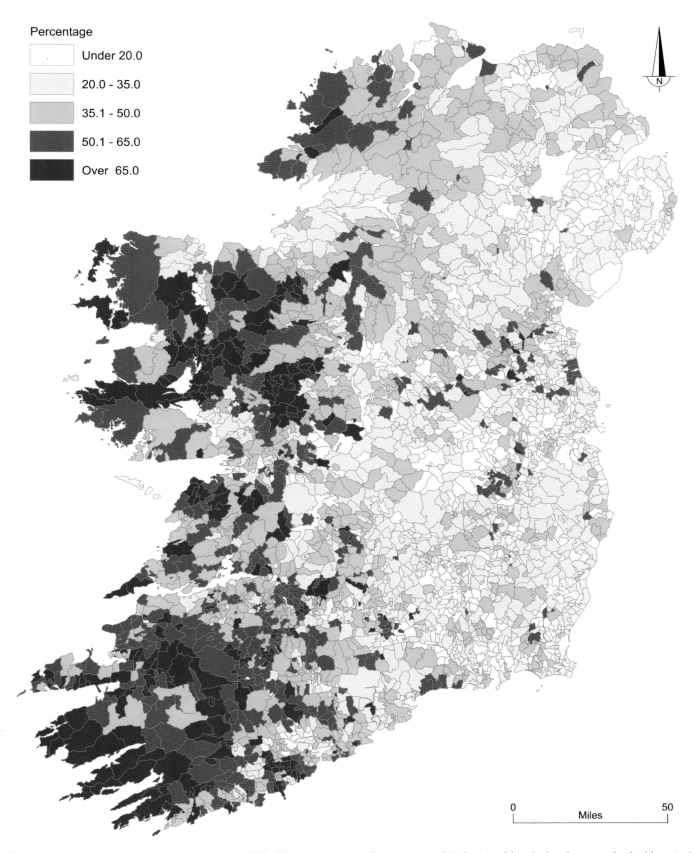

**Percentage**

- Under 20.0
- 20.0 - 35.0
- 35.1 - 50.0
- 50.1 - 65.0
- Over 65.0

0        Miles        50

Fig. 8 PERCENTAGE DISTRIBUTION OF FOURTH-CLASS HOUSES IN 1841. This map measures the percentage distribution of fourth-class houses – the 'bad housing' index used in this chapter. Fourth-class houses consisted of one-roomed, mud-walled cabins and constituted a critical guide to families subsisting in wretched living conditions. Eastern and western Ireland are seen to be very different places and societies. Much of east Ulster, most of Leinster (apart from its Ulster/Connacht borderlands) and the eastern rim of Munster contain housing stock where less than one-third was fourth-class in 1841. In contrast, much of Donegal, practically all of Connacht, Clare and the rest of west and mid-Munster contain parishes where at least one-half and in many cases over two-thirds of the houses were one-roomed, mud-cabins. Not surprisingly, population decline between 1841 and 1851 is powerfully correlated with this critical index of poor living conditions.

**Table 3.** Accounting for the variation in population change across parishes, 1841–1851

|  | [1] | [2] | [3] | [4] |
|---|---|---|---|---|
| *MILLIT* | -.069 ** | -.047 ** |  |  |
| *FILLIT* |  |  | -.054 ** |  |
| *ILLIT* |  |  |  | -.052 ** |
| *BADHOUSING* | -.100 ** |  |  |  |
| *BADHOUSING2* |  | -.110 ** | -.105 ** | -.112 ** |
| *VALPOP* | .019 ** |  | .014 ** | .014 ** |
| *VALACRE* |  | .059 ** |  | -.016 ** |
| *DENSITY* |  | -.338 ** |  | -.213 ** |
| *PCAGR* | -.013 |  |  |  |
| *PCMAN* | .358 ** | .520 ** | .509 ** | .510 ** |
| *PCVEST* | .160 | .238 ** | .363 ** | .393 ** |
| *PCDIR* | .006 |  |  | .030 |
| *PCOWN* | -.033 |  |  |  |
| *CONST* | -.268 ** | -.208 ** | -.260 ** | -.251 ** |
| N | 2,943 | 2,944 | 2,943 | 2,943 |
| Prob > F | 0.0000 | 0.0000 | 0.0000 | 0.0000 |

*Note: robust regression estimates.*
*'**' and '*' denote statistical significance at 5 and 1 per cent levels.*

**Table 4.** Impact of population change 1841–1851 on the change in selected variables: Parish-level data

| | |
|---|---|
| Proportion relying on own manual labour (PCOWN) | .340 |
| Proportion directing labour (PCDIR) | -.184 |
| Proportion with vested interests (PCVEST) | -.055 |
| Proportion Poor Housing (BADHOUSING) | .211 |
| Valuation per head (VALPOP) | -2.210 |
| Male illiteracy (MILLIT) | .051 |
| Female illiteracy (FILLIT) | .054 |
| Share of labour force in manufacturing (PCAGR) | -.009 |
| Share of labour force in agriculture (PCMAN) | .072 |

## FAMINE MIGRATION

Throughout history serious famines have resulted in migrations in search of work and charity. Such movements were usually temporary, with most migrants returning home eventually. The Irish Famine struck at a time when virtually unrestricted mass migration across the Atlantic had already begun. As a result, it gave rise to a larger permanent exodus than any other major famine in history. The Famine forced many hundreds of thousands to emigrate at short notice, often in terrifying conditions. Yet without the safety valve of emigration even more would have succumbed to the crisis at home. Indeed, the assisted emigration of the most destitute would have further reduced the Famine's death toll, though at the cost of increased anti-Irish feeling, already intense, in host countries.

Most of those who emigrated relied on their own

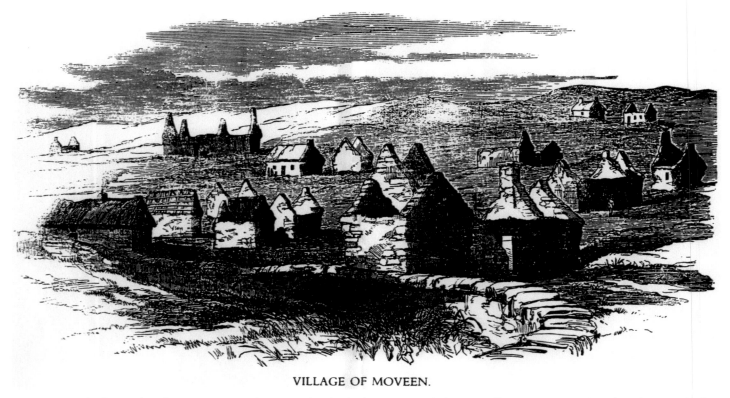

## VILLAGE OF MOVEEN.

Fig. 9 Moveen, *The Illustrated London News*, 22 December 1849: 'The Sketch of Moveen, to which I now call your attention, is that of another ruined village in the Union of Kilrush. It is a specimen of the dilapidation I behold all around. There is nothing but devastation, while the soil is of the finest description, capable of yielding as much as any land in the empire. Here, at Tullig, and other places, the ruthless destroyer, as if he delighted in seeing the monuments of his skill, has left the walls of the houses standing, while he has unroofed them and taken away all shelter from the people. They look like the tombs of a departed race, rather than the recent abodes of a yet living people, and I felt actually relieved at seeing one or two half-clad spectres gliding about, as evidence that I was not in the land of the dead'.

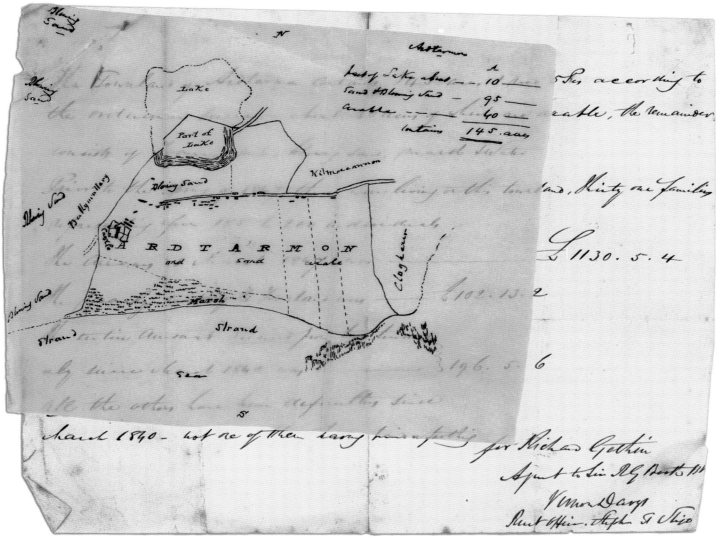

Fig. 10 This map was extracted from the papers of Sir Robert Gore-Booth (who resided at Lissadell) and refers to the townland of Ardtarmon, in his Sligo estate. It reveals the high population density in such townlands. The information was compiled by Vernon Davys, assistant to Richard Gethin, who was agent to Goore-Booth. Both Davys and Gethin were based at the Rent Office, Stephen Street, Sligo. According to the statement accompanying the map, Ardtarmon contained 145 acres, of which only forty were arable, the remainder being sand and marsh: 'Prior to the spring of 1847, there was living on this townland thirty-one families representing from 185 to 200 individuals. The arrears on March 1847 was £1,130 . . . [T]he yearly rent of the townland was £102 . . . [T]he entire amount received from two tenants since March 1840 was £196 . . . All the others have been defaulters since March 1840, not one of them having paid a farthing.' The tenants were given an option 'of either going to the adjacent farm close by the shore and making a village there, giving them sufficient ground for potatoes or emigration'. In June 1848 only three families remained in the townland, the rest having left under the landlord's scheme of emigration. Gore-Booth would use the example of Ardtarmon to justify his system of emigration from his 'over-peopled estate.' [*Great Britain Parliament Committee on Colonization from Ireland,* Report 2 June 1848, p. 270] He was in no doubt that such townlands would be much improved because of the 'remedy applied'. [Source: Public Record Office of Northern Ireland, D4131/H/8]

resources, although the role of landlord-supported migration of cottiers and tenant farmers has perhaps been underestimated in the past.[10] The outflow sometimes resulted in horrific tragedy, particularly at the quarantine station on Grosse Isle near Québec City and on the notorious disease-ridden 'coffin-ships' financed by Major Denis Mahon of Strokestown.[11] However, most of the Famine emigrants survived the Atlantic passage and its immediate aftermath: given the grim conditions they experienced, it is perhaps surprising that the overall death rate was not higher.

Few of the landless poor could afford to leave. Few landlords helped to finance the emigration of landless households and individuals. The exceptions included two absentees – Lord Palmerston and Lord Lansdowne – who shipped hundreds of destitute inhabitants from their estates in Counties Sligo and Kerry, respectively. These emigrants proved highly resilient in face of the hostility and hard conditions they faced in the slums of New York City.[12]

The Irish-born population of Great Britain increased from 415,000 in 1841 to 727,000 in 1851. Those who escaped to England in the 1840s were concentrated in a relatively small number of big cities and towns, where there was already a significant Irish presence. Disease followed migration so that the Famine resulted in excess mortality in Britain too. In Liverpool alone pauper burials, mainly of Irish Catholics, rose by 5,000 in 1847. In Britain as a whole Famine-related mortality may have reached 0.1 million.[13] These deaths might be added to the toll of about one million discussed above.

# 'Variations in vulnerability': understanding where and why the people died

## William J. Smyth

As Joel Mokyr has emphasised, 'the blight responsible for the destruction of the potato crop was wholly *exogenous*' to the Irish environment.[1] In 1846 and 1848, the destruction of that crop was almost total and extended island-wide. The exogenous shock of the potato failure was, therefore, relatively *uniform* across the whole country. Consequently, to understand *regional* variations in the effects of the potato blight requires an examination of living conditions across Ireland in the early 1840s. The Census of 1841 provides a number of useful measures for such an analysis and the 1851 Census points up significant variations in population changes and living conditions as the tragedy of the Great Famine is coming to a close.

### VALUATION OF LAND AND BUILDINGS

To begin with, it is useful to examine the valuation of land and buildings across the island. The Ordnance Survey six-inch mapping of Ireland was accompanied by the Griffith valuation of properties. From 1838 onwards and especially after 1846, this valuation helped determine the specific poor rates which were to be levied on each property and administrative division so as to support the newly created Poor Law unions and their workhouses. The determination of the value of each property, townland and parish involved a careful assessment of soil quality, climatic conditions and, most significantly, accessibility to markets, towns and port cities.[2] The parish map of valuation per statute acre is, therefore, a powerful indicator of the relative distribution of wealth and economic capability around the time of the Great Famine.

The darkest shading on the map (Figure 1) identifies properties very highly valued at over £1 per acre. Three wealthy core regions emerge – in the northeast around Belfast and the Lagan Valley, in the Dublin–Drogheda hinterlands and in east Limerick. A smaller zone of highest land values extends around Cork Harbour. Figure 1 also identifies the relatively highly valued and wealthy regions surrounding these cores – in east and south Ulster (including much of Counties Monaghan and Cavan), and in east Leinster with two vectors extending southwards, one along the coast to Wexford, and one along the Barrow and Nore valleys to reach the Waterford City region. The latter is intimately connected with the wealthy lands of the Suir valley, which in turn extends westwards to include the Golden Vale south from the Limerick core and on into north Cork. West Waterford and coastal south Cork also emerge as regions of good land and relative wealth.

In sharp contrast are the lowly valued and poor economic capacity of the lightly shaded parishes and unions of the southwest, west and northwest (as well as pockets elsewhere in the island). Here, some parishes register a valuation of less than 5p or 10p per acre with the majority achieving valuations of less than 25p per acre – as in much of County Clare, west Cork, west Sligo and Roscommon and the uplands of Wicklow and mid-Tyrone. The parishes of west Donegal, west Mayo, west Galway and southwest Kerry record the poorest land values in the whole island. Under Prime Minister Russell, Chancellor of the Exchequer Charles Wood and particularly Charles Trevelyan – who dominated and directed the administration of Famine relief from London – the British administration's insistence that local property – particularly that of landlords – and the local union must carry the brunt of Famine relief expenses (after the summer of 1847) was, therefore, a devastating policy. The most destitute regions, with the poorest economic base, the highest Poor Law rates and the weakest sources of revenue were, for the most part, expected to pay for their own support.

### NEITHER POOR NOR WEALTHY

Transitional regions in Figure 1 (shaded in light purple with a valuation of 26 to 50p per acre) – not poor and not wealthy – characterise north Kerry, upland Tipperary and Waterford, much of inland Wexford and Wicklow, the Midlands, the lowland corridor of mid-Connacht from Galway to Ballina, much of Leitrim in addition to the upland regions of north and west Ulster. The inset map of valuation in pounds Sterling per parish per family highlights the much greater wealth of the industrialising north and the wealthier families of the Pale and southeastern river valleys and their capacity to offset the worst effects of the potato failure and the Famine. That the rest of Ireland had not so industrialised narrowed the opportunities for survival, given the severity of the conditions during the Famine.

Figure 2 seeks to demonstrate the highly complex numerical relationships between valuation returns and population change between 1841 and 1851. The lightest shading on Figure 2 (Category V) identifies the zones in the far west with the very highest population declines and the lowest valuations. But it also incorporates zones of very high population declines in areas with moderately good land values – as in east Clare, south Leitrim and north Roscommon and mid-Connacht generally. The next category (light green shading) identifies many regions with high

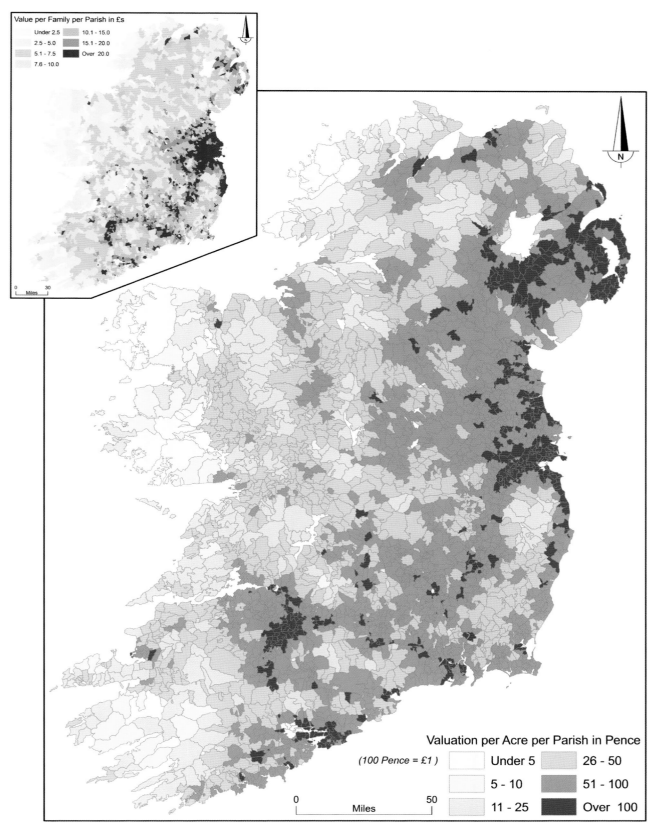

Value per Family per Parish in £s

| Under 2.5 | 10.1 - 15.0 |
| 2.5 - 5.0 | 15.1 - 20.0 |
| 5.1 - 7.5 | Over 20.0 |
| 7.6 - 10.0 | |

0        30
Miles

Valuation per Acre per Parish in Pence

(100 Pence = £1 )

| Under 5 | 26 - 50 |
| 5 - 10 | 51 - 100 |
| 11 - 25 | Over 100 |

0                    50
Miles

Fig. 1 LAND VALUES AS PER GRIFFITH'S VALUATION (INSET: RESOURCES PER FAMILY 1841). The Griffith Valuation of properties in pence per acre – as reported in the 1851 Census – illustrates the relative distribution of wealth during the decade of the Famine. Highly valued lands (over £1 per acre) characterise the Belfast region and Lagan Valley, the immediate Dublin hinterland and also the champion lands of the Golden Vale. Over the eastern and southern half of Ulster, the rest of Leinster (apart from its uplands and boglands), and much of east Munster, lands and buildings are valued at over ten shillings (50p plus) per acre, still indicative of highly commercialised worlds. In contrast, much of west Ulster, practically all of Connacht and County Clare and west Munster reveal lower valuations and poorer economic capacity. The western ends of Donegal, Mayo, Galway and Kerry reveal the lowest valuations (-10p), the poorest lands and most problematic living conditions. The inset map gives some indication of the resource capacity of each family by measuring the population of each parish against its rateable valuation. With some exceptions, a line along the River Bann south along the Ulster–Leinster borders and southwestwards to Limerick and Kinsale reveals more well-to-do families east of this line (shown with darker shadings).

181

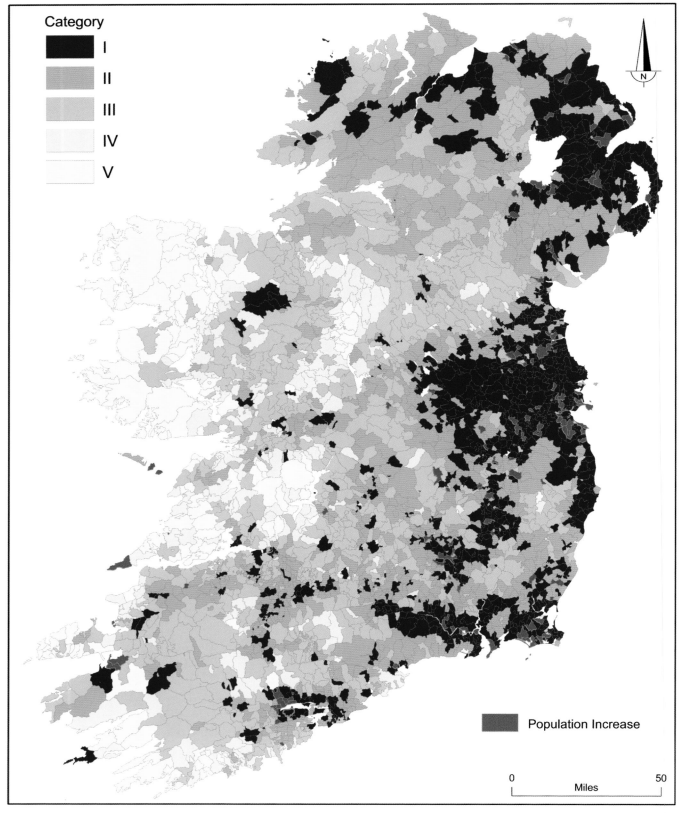

Fig. 2 RELATING LAND VALUES WITH PERCENTAGE POPULATION DECLINE PER CIVIL PARISH. This map attempts to measure the scale of population decline per parish (between 1841 and 1851) vis-à-vis the land valuations. Although much of the pattern is predictable, i.e. the best land is characterised by the lowest population declines and the poorest with the highest losses, this is not always the case. There are many deviations from this pattern e.g. very good lands with high population losses and very poor lands with low population losses (see text). All of this is by way of saying that the forces shaping the distribution of mortality and population change are complex and not amenable to an analysis of simple or single equations.

population declines and very average land values. But Category IV also incorporates regions as in south Ulster (especially in Cavan and Monaghan), north Longford, east

Galway and significant pockets in south Leinster and Munster with both high population losses and relatively high land values. Category III with the darker green shading picks out many parishes in Ulster with low population losses and relatively high land values, whereas it also incorporates as in west Leinster and County Limerick areas of relatively high population declines and relatively high land values.

Finally, the light blue and dark blue shadings (Categories II and I) dramatically illuminate the eastern regions in the north, in east Leinster and a restricted number of parishes in coastal and river valleys of south Leinster and east Munster where the highest land values and wealthiest regions are closely connected with little if any population losses. However, these two shading categories also include regions with low valuations and *low population losses*. County Donegal is the most striking example here – see, for example, the northern parishes of Tulloghbegley, Raymunterdowney, Lettermacaward and Kilteevoge. Likewise, the very exceptional parishes of Kilbeagh, Kilmovee, Castlemore and Kilcolman in east Mayo as well as the parishes of the northern Iveragh Peninsula in Kerry, centred on Glenbehy, are again characterised by low valuations *and* low population losses.

**A COMPLICATED PICTURE**

All of this is by way of saying that understanding variations in the vulnerability of populations and understanding variations in regional and local mortalities is a far more complicated matter than a simple equation between land values and population losses. Pre-Famine Ireland was characterised by enormous variations in levels of dependence on agriculture vis-à-vis other occupations, in the quality of its housing and rural comforts, in income levels, in levels of literacy attainment and in a number of other socio-demographic variables which must be explored if we are to reach a fuller understanding of the reasons why some people died and others survived.

All other things being equal, the greater the extent of a population's dependence on agriculture, the more exposed such a society would be to harvest, in Ireland's case to potato, failure. In 1841, two-thirds of Irish families were classified as 'chiefly employed in agriculture' – 78% of such families in Connacht, 70.6% in Munster vis-à-vis 60.9% and 59.1% in Ulster and Leinster, respectively. Of the enumerated 8.2 million in the population, around three million were classified as agricultural labourers – including those assisting relatives on the family farm. The annual consumption of potatoes by this class constituted *c.*57% of the island's annual human consumption (6.2m in tons) of potatoes in the early 1840s. Cottiers holding 1–5 acres, with a population of *c.*1.4 million, contributed to almost 13% of the human consumption of potatoes; small farmers with 5–20 acres (0.5m) and large farmers with over twenty acres (0.25m) consumed a further 6.5% of the table crop. The remainder of the population (2.9m) of professionals, traders, textile workers, other industrial workers and labourers and those with

vested means accounted for the remaining 23.5% of the potatoes used for human consumption. Overall, every 8.5 out of ten potatoes used for human food were consumed in rural districts. Much of the remainder of the crop (4.4 tons) was fed to the life-enhancing and 'rent-paying' pig and cattle population.[3] Pig numbers halved between 1841 and 1847 as labourers and smallholders consumed and disposed of them but failed to restock.

This is not to suggest, however, that Irish agriculture was not both diversified and deeply commercialised. Potatoes constituted only one-third of the land under tillage – a total of seven million acres was under grain, potatoes and clover in the 1840s. And high yields in Irish grain production were products of intensive systems of cultivation and harvesting, buttressed by a proliferating hard-working labouring class, proficient with spade, reaping hook, and scythe. A quarter of Ireland's exports to Britain was in grain – the cartloads of wheat, flour and oatmeal winding their way to Irish ports were the subject of protests, assaults and police and troop protection as the Famine deepened. In a situation where Britain accounted for three-quarters of all Irish exports and imports, three-quarters of Irish exports were still pastoral in origin – coming from the cattle and sheep-rearing lands of the east and west Midlands or from the cow/dairying regions of the southwest and parts of south Ulster. Expanding everywhere, tillage farming was anchored in the warmer lands of the south and east. The north of the island was characterised by a proto-industrial culture with many subdivided smaller holdings involved in flax production and the linen trade. The far west was dominated by an essentially subsistence economy, but even here both the sale of the oats crop, a few calves or young cattle to the cattlemen from the east or south in its many numerous fairs, kelp-gathering, poteen-making, and the contributions of the *spalpíní* (seasonal labourers) meant that even the most remote regions were exposed to a monetised economy.

Figure 3 shows the percentage distribution of families employed in agriculture in 1841. In terms of absolute numbers in agriculture, once again the boundary line from Galway Bay to Cooley Peninsula emerges. With the exception of coastal east Ulster, north of this line the great majority of parishes contain at least 600 families engaged in agriculture. Parishes in southwest Clare and southwest Munster and a scatter of very large parishes elsewhere also reveal similar figures. Otherwise, parishes with less than 350 farming families was the norm in the southern half of the island.

Far more instructive, however, is the percentage distribution of families engaged in agriculture. In this instance, and of far more relevance in explaining famine conditions and population losses is the geographical division between the parishes west and east of a line from Sheep Haven in Donegal to Waterford Harbour. West of this line, over three-quarters and sometimes as many as 88 to 100% of the families are dependent on both agriculture and potato cultivation.

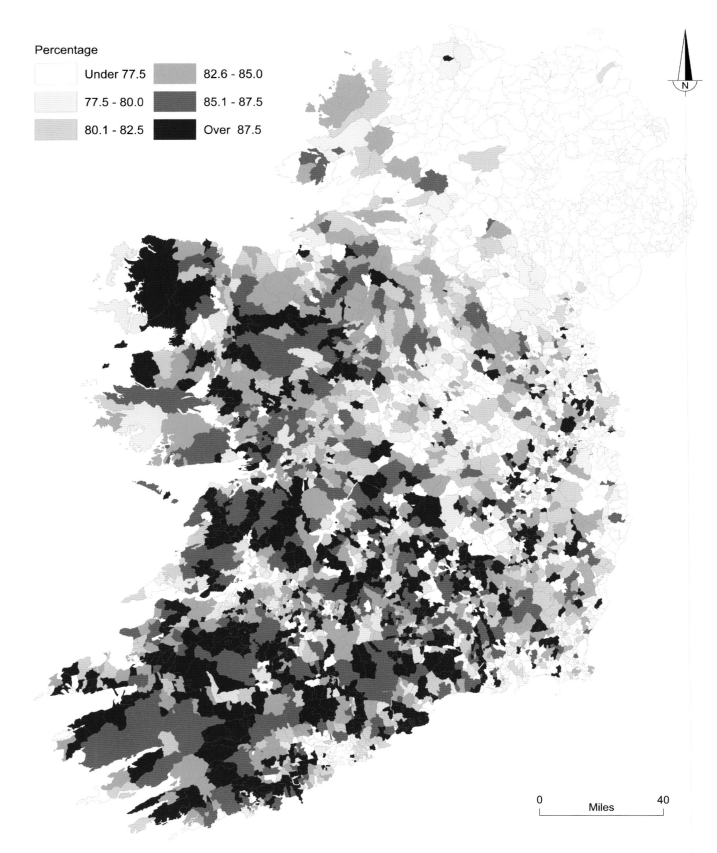

Percentage

| | |
|---|---|
| Under 77.5 | 82.6 - 85.0 |
| 77.5 - 80.0 | 85.1 - 87.5 |
| 80.1 - 82.5 | Over 87.5 |

0    Miles    40

Fig. 3 PERCENTAGE DISTRIBUTION OF FAMILIES EMPLOYED IN AGRICULTURE IN 1841. The greater the proportion of a population engaged in agriculture, the higher their exposure to harvest failure – in Ireland's case, the failure of the potato. This map illuminates significant regional variations in families employed in agriculture (and indirectly measures levels of vulnerability to harvest failures). Dependence on agriculture in making a living is massively pronounced in the western and southern provinces of Connacht and Munster with many parishes reporting 85% and sometimes over 90% of their families engaged in agricultural activities. The northern, western and southern rim of parishes in Leinster also reveals a high dependence on farming. In contrast, the rest of Leinster and most emphatically much of the province of Ulster – especially east of a line from Derry City to Newry – reveal a much lower dependence on agriculture and consequently less vulnerability to harvest failures.

Examples of the latter include the parishes of Kilcommon (Erris), and Kilgeever in Mayo, Oranmore in Galway, close on half of the parishes in County Clare, Cahersiveen, Killinane and Glenbehy in Kerry, Caheragh and a whole series of coastal parishes from the Old Head of Kinsale westwards in County Cork as well as Ardmore and Ballymacart in west Waterford.[4]

## EXPLAINING FAMINE CONDITIONS

The contrast with the eastern and more especially the northern parishes to the east of a line from Donegal Bay to Wexford is further emphasised in Figure 4, which illustrates the percentage of families employed in manufacturing, trade and commerce in 1841. In the northeastern Ulster core comprising much of counties Antrim and Down, north Armagh and east Tyrone at least a quarter, and in parishes all around Lough Neagh at least 35%, of the families are engaged in non-agricultural pursuits. From Connor, Ahoghill, south to Artrea, Arboe and Clonoe on the west side of Lough Neagh, this core of people involved in manufacturing, trade and commerce curves south of Lough Neagh through Tartaraghan, Drumcree, Kilmore and Seagoe and swings back by the Lagan Valley through Magherlin, Moira, Dromore, Hillsborough, Blaris, Magheragall, Ballinderry and Derryaghy to reach Belfast. In all of the rest of the province of Ulster, the adjacent counties of Louth, Longford and parts of Westmeath with pockets elsewhere in east Leinster all the way down to south Wexford, at least a fifth of the families

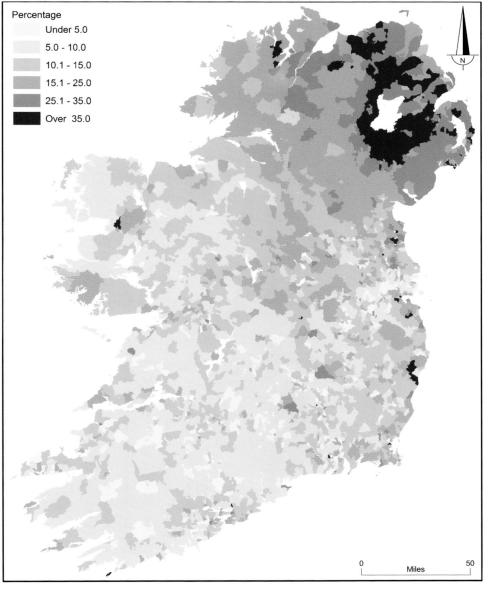

Fig. 4 PERCENTAGE DISTRIBUTION OF FAMILIES IN MANUFACTURING, TRADE AND COMMERCE IN 1841. It has been established that the wealthier, more industrialised and more commercialised communities have a far greater capacity to deal with the threat of famine and associated threats. Fig. 4 is, therefore, almost a mirror image of Fig. 3. It is clear that the parishes of north and particularly east Ulster were best equipped to deal with the threat of famine given the number of parish communities where over 35% of the families were employed in manufacturing, trade and commerce. Over much of the remainder of Ulster and adjacent counties on its southern border – as well as east-coast Leinster and a few pockets elsewhere where c.one-fifth of the population were so employed – a greater proportion of families were in a position to surmount famine conditions. The least industrialised and most exposed communities have been discussed in the previous map – that is, where dependence on agriculture was most emphatic.

are engaged in manufacturing and trade. Such wealthier, more industrialised and more commercialised communities had a far greater capacity and far more flexibility to deal with the threat of famine, disease and death.

All of this is confirmed in Figure 5, which demonstrates the percentage decrease in families employed in agriculture between 1841 and 1851. (The inset figure shows the absolute decline in farming families per parish). Figure 5 closely matches Figure 3 in Chapter 9 – which mapped the approximate distribution of the dead over the same periods. The parishes of Killala in County Mayo, Ballynakill in west Galway, Fohanagh in east Galway, Youghalarra in north Tipper-

ary, Minard on the Dingle Peninsula and Kilshannig in northwest Cork all lost at least two-thirds of the 1841 farming families by 1851. And over large swathes of the south and west, in parishes south of Lough Erne in Fermanagh, and many parishes in Monaghan, Cavan and adjacent difficult farming lands in Longford, Meath and Westmeath either a little over or under a half of all farm families had disappeared. An odd parish scattered through the province of Leinster and east Ulster shows an increase in the number of families engaged in agriculture. Yet even in the wealthiest parishes in northeast Ulster – around Newtownards and Banbridge and over much of County Londonderry – about

185

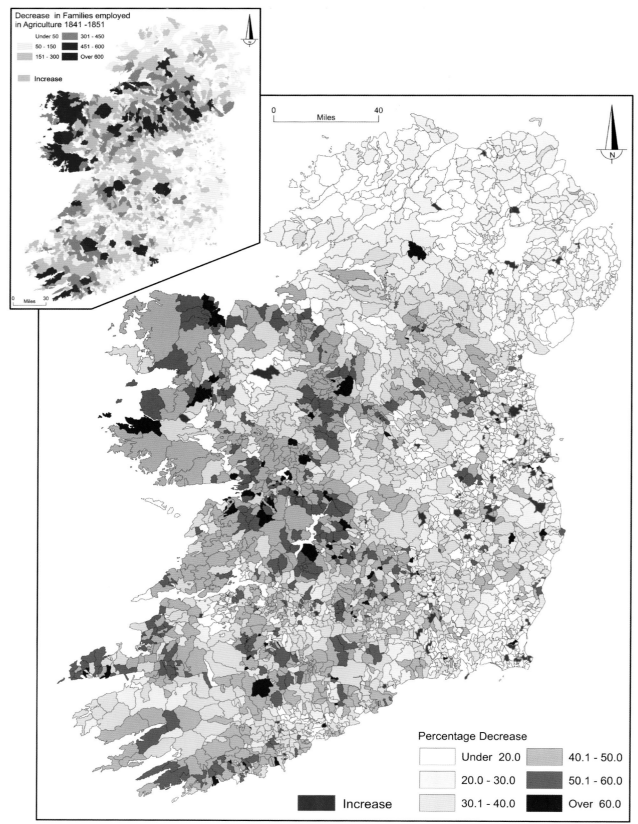

Fig 5 PERCENTAGE DECREASE IN FAMILIES EMPLOYED IN AGRICULTURE 1841–1851 (INSET: ABSOLUTE SCALE OF LOSSES IN AGRICULTURE, 1841–51). This is a very significant map. It highlights on the one hand communities where well over 60% of families engaged in agriculture had died out, been evicted and/or emigrated during the famine. On the other hand some farming communities reveal losses of less than 20%. Apart from farming communities in Fermanagh, Cavan
and Monaghan, the rest of Ulster's agricultural workers and farmers suffered less during the Famine – a destiny shared by agricultural families in the Pale
and parts of south Leinster (as well as a small number of parishes in east Mayo centered on Kilmovee). In contrast, many parishes in Connacht and Munster and other parishes on the west Leinster and south Ulster borderlands suffered devastating losses, often losing half of the families engaged in agriculture. This map can, in many respects, also be seen as a surrogate map of the distribution of excess famine deaths. The inset map, however, is a reminder
of the absolute scale of the losses where in the heavily populated rural worlds of southwest Munster, west Connacht and Connacht/Ulster/Leinster borderland counties, parishes lost over 300 and sometimes over 600 of their agriculturally engaged families between 1841 and 1851.

186

one-fifth of the agricultural families were lost. Despite its western location and small-farming traditions, County Donegal defies the trends and behaves more like the wealthiest counties. And there is that strange anomaly of much smaller losses in central Connacht, pivoting around the parishes of Kilbeagh, Kilmovee and Aghamore.

The overall conclusion – as emphasised in Figure 6 – is the high correlation between the parishes massively dependent on agriculture and high levels of mortality and population loss. The correlation coefficient between the percentage of families in agriculture in 1841 and the percentage population change per parish is 0.88, emphasising an overwhelming interrelationship between the two measures. Figure 6 shows us where the percentage change in those engaged in agriculture was relatively low, population change was low (see overlay of lightest shades with spot symbols). Where there is a middle order percentage change in agriculture families, the percentage of population change is of that order (see light brown shaded areas on map). And where the percentage changes in agricultural families is high or very high, the population losses (emphasised by heavy hatching) is equally devastating.

HOUSING CLASSIFICATIONS

The 1841 Census classification distinguished between four types of houses. Fourth-class houses were defined as 'all mud cabins having only one room'; a third-class house was 'a better description of a cottage, still built of mud but varying from two to four rooms and windows'. 'A good farmhouse, or in towns a house in a small street, having five to nine rooms and windows' comprised the second-class house. First-class houses comprised 'all houses of a better description than previous classes with more than ten rooms and windows'.[5]

According to Joel Mokyr 'housing quality may be viewed as a proxy' or substitute for measuring a family's income. The quality of the house may also provide some indication of family's reserves from past savings and a capacity to weather the bad times. Mokyr acknowledges that the precise relationship between housing and level of wealth remains rather complex.[6] Nevertheless, the quality of a family's housing may reflect strong value preferences for better housing generally. It may also be the case that better housing provided some form of protection against certain diseases. The fourth-class single-roomed mud cabins obviously neither reflected viable incomes and past reserves nor any protection against overcrowding and contagious diseases.

Figures 7, 8, 9 and 10 illustrate the distribution of the families residing in four types of houses. I will return to Figure 10 – showing the percentage living in fourth-class houses in 1841 – which shows the poorest houses massively concentrated west of a line from Lough Foyle and Lough Neagh, then bending west along the Shannon and exiting at Waterford Harbour. The distribution of those living in third-class houses (mud-walled with two to four rooms) may be

a significant indicator of higher population losses in the eastern two-thirds of the country as well as in the Ballyshannon region of Donegal and in the numerous poorer parishes north of Lough Ree and in pockets in east Offaly and Laois and the Murroghs in coastal Wexford.

The distribution of the residents of second-class houses provides a very dramatic picture of well-to-do parishes over much of east Ulster and especially in County Down and secondly in the strong farming lands of the southern belt in Leinster and parts of southeast Munster. The percentage distribution of a small minority of families living in first-class houses – which average between 1 and 5% of the overall total – is even more dramatic. Apart from favoured seaside and riverside vistas everywhere, its distribution for the most part is indicative of the strong farming, urbanised world of the east and south with roots deep in the medieval rather than the early modern era. The Laois–Offaly and Wexford–Wicklow planter regions, however, also emerge with some better housing. However, this region of the best homes need not be free of Famine mortalities – because this is also a zone of many smallholdings, servants, farm labourers and artisans who may have been and often were more exposed to the rigours of famine, fever and disease.

The fourth-class house is seen as one of the great symbols of poverty in pre-Famine Ireland. Island-wide it constituted 37.0% of all houses; third-class comprised 40.1%; second-class 19.9% and first-class houses 3.0%.

Apart from the difficult borderlands from Louth to Longford, in most parishes in Leinster and the eastern fringes of the province of Munster, fourth-class houses were least prevalent in 1841 and well below the national average for that class of house. In contrast, over much of the rest of Munster, in practically all the parishes of County Clare and westwards and south of upland and lowland Tipperary, at least a half and often more than two-thirds of the houses were mud-walled cabins with a single room. In the parishes of the Burren, Loop Head, the Dingle, Beara, Sheepshead and the Mizen peninsulas over 85% of all houses were of this class – revealing desperate living accommodation in those far western lands.

Practically all of Connacht was dominated by fourth-class houses. In a host of parishes from Kilmore and Achill in Atlantic Mayo inland through Crossmolina, Addergoole, Balla, down to Ballinrobe and including Ross, Ballinakill and Omey in west Galway, the proportion of this class of house ranges from 66 to 100%. Western and northern Ulster from the glens of Antrim through to Donegal also contained many parishes with above average numbers of fourth-class houses with over 50% in the northern half of Donegal. County Donegal, therefore, is emphatically western in the low quality of its housing but this does not translate into a major tragedy for the country's population.

The correlation coefficient between the percentage of fourth-class houses and levels of population loss is again very high at 0.81, indicating a massive interconnection

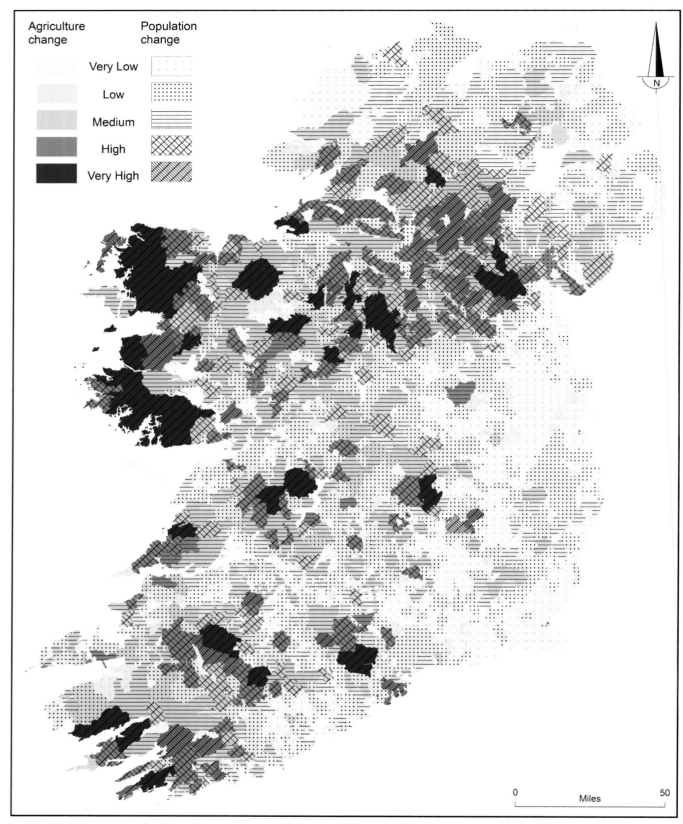

Agriculture change | Population change
--- | ---
Very Low | 
Low | 
Medium | 
High | 
Very High | 

Fig 6 RELATING THE DECLINE IN FAMILIES ENGAGED IN AGRICULTURE WITH OVERALL POPULATION DECLINE. This map confirms the very high correlation between levels of dependence on agriculture and population decline. Generally, as with the light shadings for northern and eastern Ireland, a small decline in agricultural families is matched by low population losses. Conversely, as the darker shadings emphasise, communities massively dependent on agriculture suffered devastating population losses.

between the two conditions. A high percentage of fourth-class houses is strongly paralleled by areas with very significant population losses. But as Donegal and other Ulster

parishes demonstrate, this association was not always consistent. Pre-Famine Ireland was a very varied place.

Joel Mokyr has calculated that for every £1 increase in

188

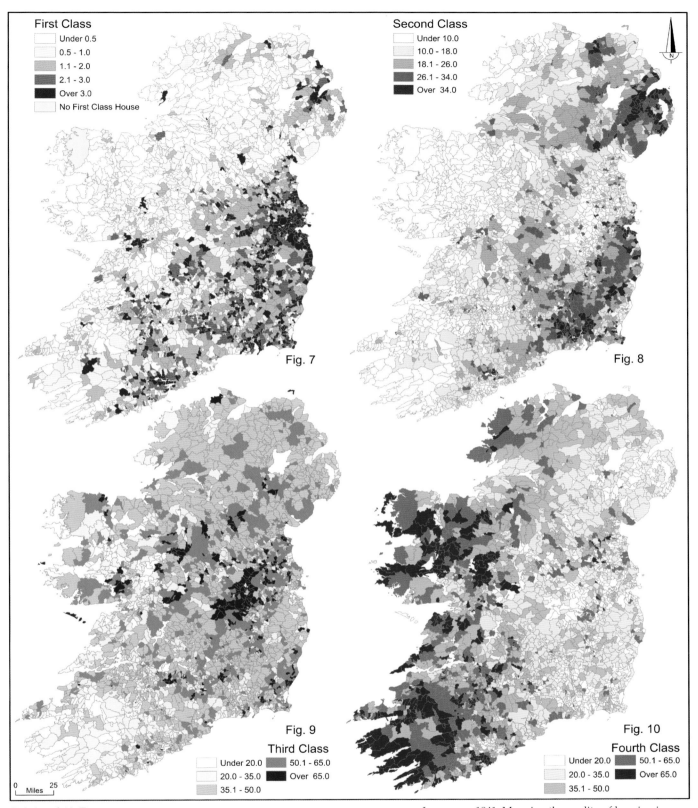

First Class
- Under 0.5
- 0.5 - 1.0
- 1.1 - 2.0
- 2.1 - 3.0
- Over 3.0
- No First Class House

Fig. 7

Second Class
- Under 10.0
- 10.0 - 18.0
- 18.1 - 26.0
- 26.1 - 34.0
- Over 34.0

Fig. 8

Fig. 9
Third Class
- Under 20.0
- 20.0 - 35.0
- 35.1 - 50.0
- 50.1 - 65.0
- Over 65.0

Fig. 10
Fourth Class
- Under 20.0
- 20.0 - 35.0
- 35.1 - 50.0
- 50.1 - 65.0
- Over 65.0

0 — 25 Miles

Figs 7, 8, 9 and 10 THE DISTRIBUTION OF FAMILIES LIVING IN FOUR TYPES OF CLASSES OF HOUSES IN IRELAND IN 1841. Mapping the quality of housing is one way of attempting to map the distribution of family incomes in Ireland in 1841. Fig. 7 details the distribution of families living in the fourth-class mud-walled single-room cabins. Once again sharp contrasts emerge between the eastern and western halves of Ireland. Great concentrations of this class of house – an index to poverty-stricken households – occur in many parishes of central and peninsular Connacht, west Clare and much of west Munster. Families living in the third-class house (Fig. 8) – mud-walled with two to four rooms – are widely distributed over the rest of Ireland and include a number of regions (all along the Shannon, in the Leinster boglands and coastal Wexford) which lost significant populations. In contrast, the distribution of families living in second-class houses (Fig. 9) – with five to nine rooms and windows – confirms the well-to-do farming-cum-industrial communities of east Ulster and the strong farming communities of south Leinster and its borderlands. First-class houses (Fig. 10) – with their families living in residences with over ten rooms and windows – constitute a small minority on the island. Apart from favoured coastal and riverside vistas, they are emphatically eastern and southeastern in distribution, clearly reflecting a medieval heritage of wealthy towns and strong farms as well as planter settlement in the Midlands and wealthy families in the Belfast hinterland.

national income per person, between 63,000 and 125,000 less people would have died of famine-related causes. Since we are using variations in housing quality as a proxy for different incomes, the fourth-class house was a critical indicator of very low incomes. The poverty accompanying living conditions in the mud-walled one-room cabins – once the potato failed – probably 'accounted for at least 600,000 deaths'.[7]

By 1851, the one-roomed mud cabins and many of their occupants had been swept from the land. A total of 271,000 dwelling houses had disappeared, of which 72.4% were in the fourth-class category. The third-class category only increased by 0.16% whereas second and first-class houses increased by 20.7% and 25.2% respectively (Fig. 12). The transformation of Ireland's social structure was mirrored in its rapidly changing housing and settlement patterns. Figure 12 illuminates this dramatic transformation. In cities such as Waterford, Kilkenny, Cork, Derry, Limerick and Belfast from 82 to 84% of the mud-walled, single-roomed cabins had disappeared from the lands and small streets. The counties of Monaghan, Donegal, Clare, Fermanagh,

Mayo and Cavan all registered reductions in the one-roomed mud cabins of between 80 and 75%. The lowest reductions were in the counties of Queen's, Meath and Kildare and in the towns of Drogheda and Galway – ranging from 57% in Queen's to 45% in Galway.

## LEVELS OF LITERACY

Another crucial factor in whether individuals and families lived or died or managed to emigrate was the level of education achieved by these people. The 1841 and 1851 Census details levels of literacy among the population, using the following three criteria: those who could read and write, those who could read only or those who could neither read nor write. Eager for schooling, the Irish literacy rate at 28% in 1841 had been rising from the 1780s. By 1841, it was on a par with Belgium, France and the Austrian Empire and superior to Italy and Spain.[8] Literacy levels are indicative of a wide range of adaptive skills. Firstly, it enabled the literate families to be made aware of the numerous Government and union notices – all written in the English language –

Fig. 11 An example of a fourth-class cabin as painted by the artist William Evans of Eton (1798–1877). *A Cottage near the Shore with Figures, Connemara*, 1838. Watercolour, graphite and glazes on paper [Source: National Gallery Ireland]

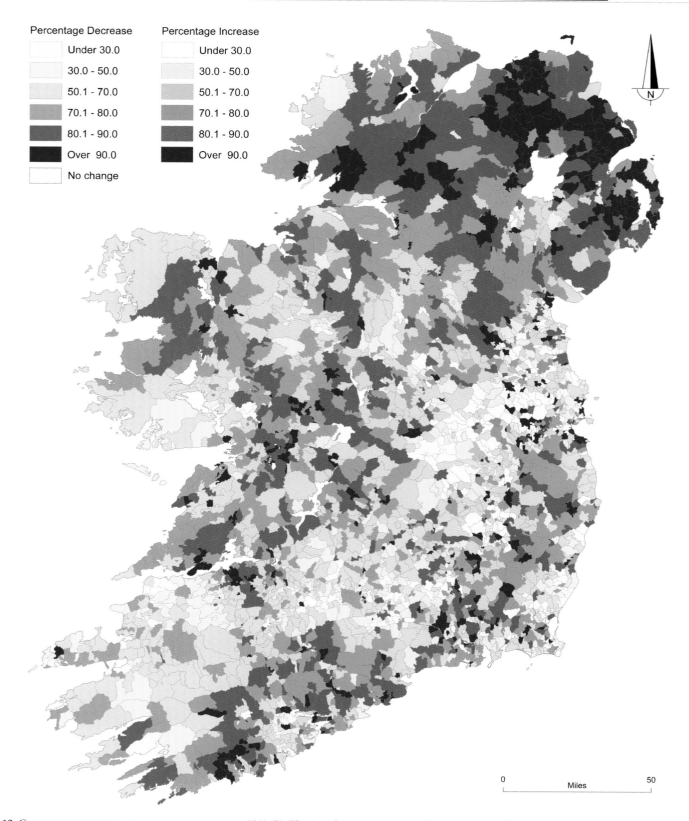

Percentage Decrease

Under 30.0

30.0 - 50.0

50.1 - 70.0

70.1 - 80.0

80.1 - 90.0

Over 90.0

No change

Percentage Increase

Under 30.0

30.0 - 50.0

50.1 - 70.0

70.1 - 80.0

80.1 - 90.0

Over 90.0

0     Miles     50

Fig 12 CHANGING DISTRIBUTION OF FOURTH-CLASS HOUSES 1841–51. This is a dramatic map revealing a number of diverging patterns of change consequent on the Famine. The continued 'modernisation', involving enclosures and small farm consolidation as well as the acceleration of factory-based industrialisation of the north-eastern parishes of Ulster saw an almost total clearing away of fourth-class houses. In sharp contrast, in a number of specific regions in Connacht (see dark brown shadings), Clare, south Munster and upland south Leinster, the disappearance of the one-roomed mud cabin is linked to high levels of mortality under desperate famine conditions. Thirdly, some strong farming zones as in north Kerry, south Tipperary and mid-Wexford retain a significant labourer element still living in fourth-class cabins. Fourthly (shown in light and dark purple shades), are the parishes which saw an increase in the percentage of fourth-class houses during the Famine. These indicate the 'refugee' zones centred on the Pale and highlight how impoverished migrants making their way to the ports of Dublin and Drogheda had settled either along roadsides or on the common lands of towns and villages like Dunboyne and Cloncurry. Smaller 'refugee' pockets emerge around Castledermot, Fethard, Kilmallock and Cork city. Finally, even at this scale, one can glimpse lines of bogland/roadside squatter settlements of one-roomed cabin-dwellers wiped out by the Famine.

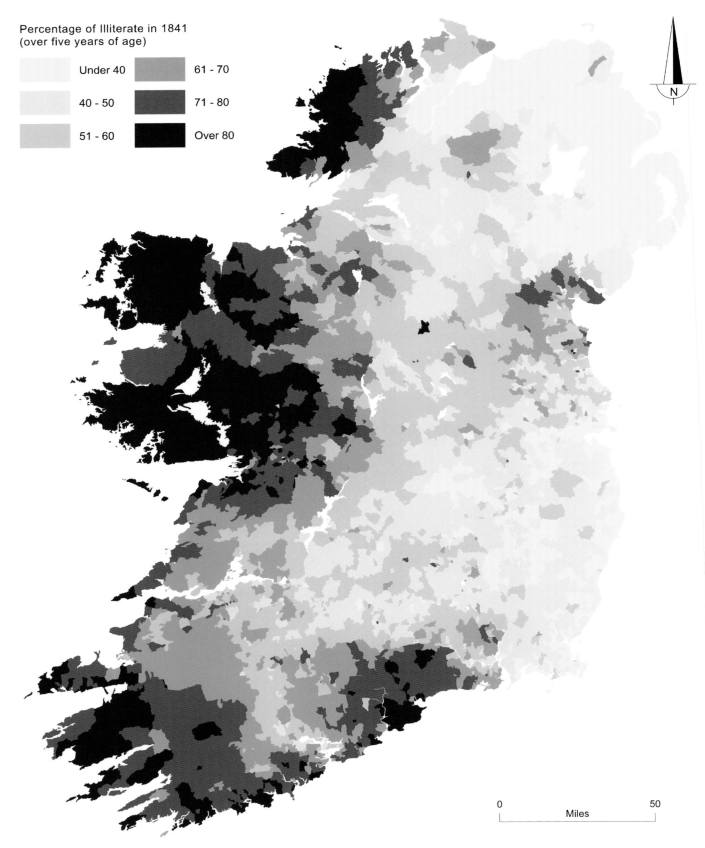

**Percentage of Illiterate in 1841**
**(over five years of age)**

Under 40

40 - 50

51 - 60

61 - 70

71 - 80

Over 80

N

0                  50
Miles

Fig 13 PERCENTAGE DISTRIBUTION OF ILLITERATE IN 1841. This is a dramatic map illustrating the great variations in levels of literacy and illiteracy across Ireland in 1841. Literacy is here seen as a crucial measure of levels of education – and a crucial measure of people's abilities to be made aware of a whole range of information sources which would help them to survive under famine conditions.  High levels of illiteracy militated against the acquisition of many of these life-saving skills and sources of information. The geographical contrasts in these abilities are staggering – between the lightly shaded northeast, and western counties and peninsulas from Donegal to Kerry (and also including Irish-speaking County Waterford and adjacent parishes) where over four-fifths of the population (over five years of age) could not read or write in the English language. It is also a dramatic map insofar as it also pinpoints the areas of English and Irish speechways, with the Irish-speaking areas highlighted in blue.

announcing new relief measures, the location of soup depots or sites for smallpox inoculation and a host of other unobserved factors that made the less informed, illiterate population even more vulnerable.

Literacy also facilitated the awareness of other life-saving opportunities in a locality or region, including vital information about emigration possibilities and shipping opportunities. High literacy levels already indicated greater purchasing power and willingness to allocate scarce resources towards the payment of monies to a teacher to educate younger family members. Levels of education may also have been a factor in issues relating to hygiene, clothing and the preparation of food. The literate population was also more likely to be healthier and better nourished. High levels of illiteracy militated against the acquisition of many of those life-saving skills. It is also certain that the monoglot Irish-speakers were most at risk because of their lack of knowledge and inability to read notices communicated only in the English language.

Figure 13 demonstrates the percentage distribution of the population illiterate in the English language in 1841. To an astounding degree, this also appears like a replica map of the Irish-speaking and English-speaking halves of the island. Outside of Donegal and the Sperrin Mountain region in mid-Tyrone, all of Ulster was characterised by the highest levels of literacy in an essentially English-speaking world. Much of Leinster, south of the Grand Canal, is also highly literate. North Leinster occupies a transitional location between the 40 to 50% levels of illiteracy in the south Ulster parishes and those over 75% in north Louth and the Cooley Peninsula.

Most of the province of Connacht is both essentially Irish-speaking and illiterate in English and this situation continues into north and west Clare. In Munster, much of County Tipperary lies on the extreme western edge of a great belt of a literate, English-speaking world that stretched from Wexford through Dublin to Antrim. Strong axes of expanding literacy extended along the roads from Cork City to Limerick City and southeast Clare as well as the communication lines moving eastwards to Waterford City. The great heartland of both Irish-speech and high levels of illiteracy in English were centred on west Waterford, southwest Cork and peninsular Cork and Kerry. Overall, Leinster and Ulster were the most literate. In contrast, one of the last mainly oral civilisations of northwestern Europe persisted in Connacht and most of Munster.

Figure 14 shows the percentage changes in literacy levels between 1841 and 1851 (the inset figure shows the percentage change in the number of people *unable* to read and write per parish). The correlation coefficient between illiteracy in 1841 and population losses between 1841 and 1851 is as high as 0.83. An intimate relationship existed between illiteracy levels and population change. There is, therefore, no doubt that literacy levels was one of the most critical factors in shaping regional variations in the distribution of the dead. Mokyr has argued that if Ireland's average literacy

rate (i.e. those who could read and write) had been half as high again (say 42% vis-à-vis 28%), the Famine excess death rate might have fallen by, perhaps, half a million.

But as with other key measures, levels of literacy – while powerful indicators – are not always predictive of excess mortalities. The Irish-speaking communities of County Donegal once again buck the trend, as does east-central Mayo. So do some of the Irish-speaking communities in much of the Iveragh Peninsula in Kerry as do some Irish-speaking regions of west Waterford. On the other hand, some of the more literate and English-speaking communities of east Munster and north Leinster reveal far higher levels of excess Famine deaths. Once again, single-vector explanations are not sufficient. But the correlation coefficient between fourth-class housing and illiteracy is a massive 0.89. It was the cumulative impact of a whole range of the poorest living conditions which decimated the population. Vulnerability was a many-sided affair.

## CHILDREN UNDER FIVE YEARS

Figure 16 illustrates the distribution per parish of children under five years of age in 1841. Although there is no direct measure of the distribution of children under five in the Census of 1841 and 1851, their number and distribution can be calculated. By combining the numbers in the population five years of age and upwards who can 'read and write', 'read only' as well as the illiterate and subtracting that composite figure from the total population as returned in each census, one can arrive at the number of children under five years of age. However, it should be remembered that the official returns for both 1841 and 1851 omit the very youngest infants (up to eleven months) and young children aged one year. The *actual* decline in number of children under five is therefore, likely to be much greater. However, the Census figures for 1841 and 1851 are comparable and mapping the relative changes in numbers and distributions remains a valid exercise.

Figure 18 shows the percentage change in the distribution of children under five years of age in each parish as between 1841 and 1851. It is important to remember that what we are comparing here is the distribution of children born between mid-1835 and 30 June 1841 and returned in the 1841 Census, and those born between March 1846 and 31 March 1851 – the latter children born during the most difficult Famine years. This map presents a most dramatic picture and highlights again the enormous variations in life opportunities across the island in the Famine years. It is a profoundly important map since it not only provides a measure of the uneven distribution of child mortalities during the Famine years but also indirectly points to strong regional variations in birth rates, consequent on significant changes in proportions marrying and remaining celibate. In a strange way, the map may also sketch in the shadowy regions of averted births – of those who remained unborn because of the cumulative stresses and horrors of the Famine.

193

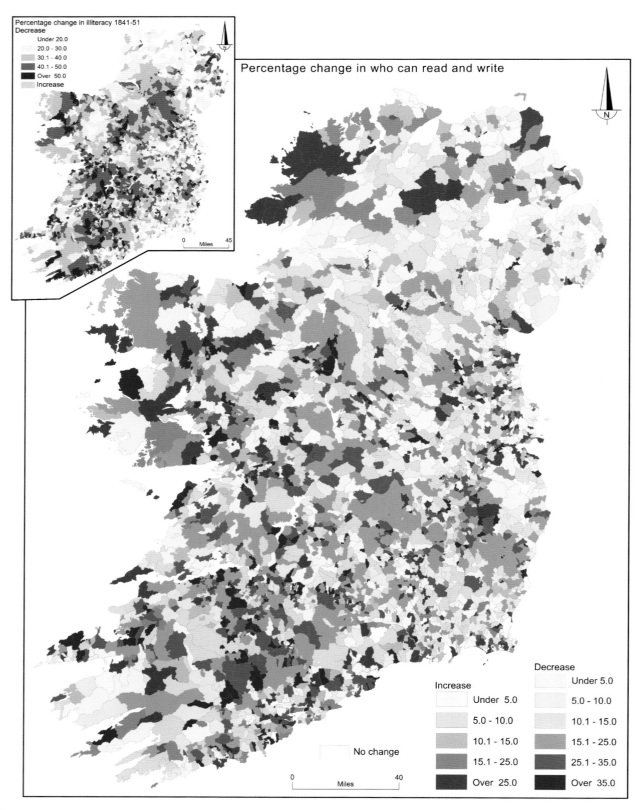

Percentage change in illiteracy 1841-51
Decrease
Under 20.0
20.0 - 30.0
30.1 - 40.0
40.1 - 50.0
Over 50.0
Increase

Percentage change in who can read and write

| Increase | | Decrease | |
|---|---|---|---|
| Under 5.0 | | Under 5.0 | |
| 5.0 - 10.0 | | 5.0 - 10.0 | |
| 10.1 - 15.0 | | 10.1 - 15.0 | |
| 15.1 - 25.0 | | 15.1 - 25.0 | |
| Over 25.0 | | 25.1 - 35.0 | |
| | | Over 35.0 | |

No change

Fig 14 THE CHANGING DISTRIBUTION OF LEVELS OF LITERACY (AND ILLITERACY) 1841–51. Again this map reveals the striking divergent experiences of a highly varied Ireland during the Famine years. Firstly, it is clear that literacy levels continued to expand (see green shadings) in the three core areas already evident in 1841 as characterised by a higher percentage of the population who could read and write: in communities over much of Ulster, in the Pale region of north Leinster, expanding south into the third region of higher literacy in south Leinster and coastal south Munster. Within these patterns, there are also exceptional levels of literacy gains in much of Donegal, the Glens of Antrim, and Tyrone and the Cooley peninsula, all characterised by high levels of Irish speech in 1841. A similar pattern prevails over much of Connacht and west Clare – which may reflect not only significant gains in literacy but more especially the massive clearance of illiterate one-roomed cabin-dwellers. On the other hand, significant decreases in literacy (shown in dark brown) are particularly noticeable in the Castlebar–Westport–Kilgeever parishes in west and Kilglass–Annaduff regions in east Connacht, as well specific parishes in west Clare, the Lough Derg region and mid-Munster. All these parishes suffered devastation both from famine-related mortalities and from evictions. Decreases in literacy in the 10–25% range (shown in light brown) more likely reflect the greater impact of the outmigration of literate families escaping the traumas of the Famine.

194

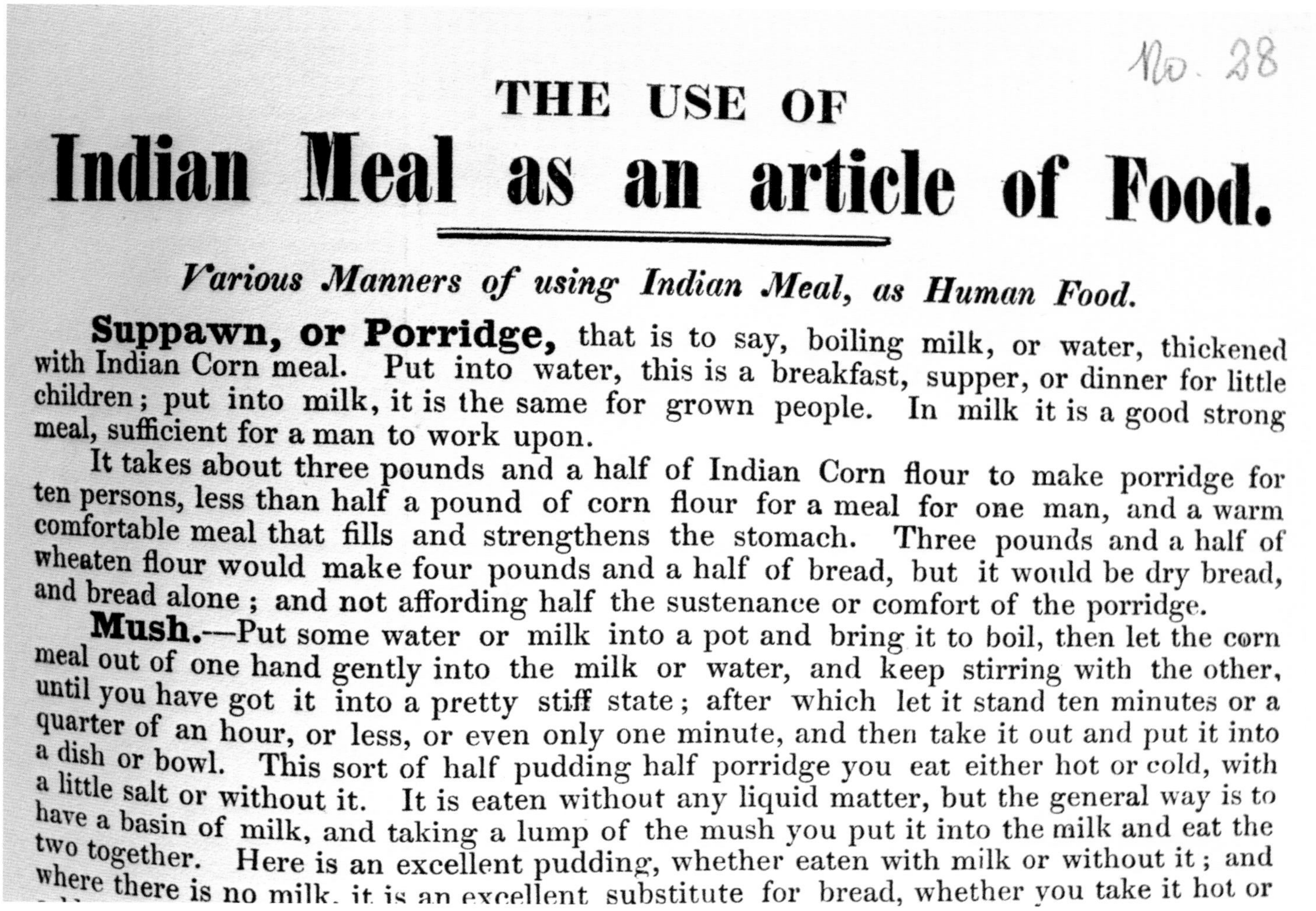

No. 28

# THE USE OF
# Indian Meal as an article of Food.

### *Various Manners of using Indian Meal, as Human Food.*

**Suppawn, or Porridge,** that is to say, boiling milk, or water, thickened with Indian Corn meal. Put into water, this is a breakfast, supper, or dinner for little children; put into milk, it is the same for grown people. In milk it is a good strong meal, sufficient for a man to work upon.

It takes about three pounds and a half of Indian Corn flour to make porridge for ten persons, less than half a pound of corn flour for a meal for one man, and a warm comfortable meal that fills and strengthens the stomach. Three pounds and a half of wheaten flour would make four pounds and a half of bread, but it would be dry bread, and bread alone; and not affording half the sustenance or comfort of the porridge.

**Mush.**—Put some water or milk into a pot and bring it to boil, then let the corn meal out of one hand gently into the milk or water, and keep stirring with the other, until you have got it into a pretty stiff state; after which let it stand ten minutes or a quarter of an hour, or less, or even only one minute, and then take it out and put it into a dish or bowl. This sort of half pudding half porridge you eat either hot or cold, with a little salt or without it. It is eaten without any liquid matter, but the general way is to have a basin of milk, and taking a lump of the mush you put it into the milk and eat the two together. Here is an excellent pudding, whether eaten with milk or without it; and where there is no milk, it is an excellent substitute for bread, whether you take it hot or

Fig. 15 Literacy was a significant factor in determining whether individuals and families lived or died. For example, understanding the ways in which Indian meal could be cooked was critical to survival. The dysentery that ensued from inappropriate or inadequately cooked food was protracted and caused a great amount of suffering. [Source: Cork Archives Institute]

Figure 18 firstly shows in green shading the limited number of parishes where the actual number of children increased and, most likely, where communities were least disturbed by the Famine. In pockets of northeast Ulster, more particularly in parishes along the Liffey Valley in the Dublin region, along the river valleys in the southeast and in the Cork City region, increases are recorded. These patterns most likely reflect the least disturbance to marriage and fertility patterns; they may also reflect some inward immigration by younger families.

In vivid contrast are the parishes where there is at least a 50% – and sometimes an even 65% – reduction in the number of children under five. The parishes of west Connacht, much of north and east Clare and adjacent parishes in south Galway and north Tipperary, from mid-Limerick south to communities encircling the Cork City hinterland and embracing both southwest Cork and west Waterford, show massive declines in their young populations. Likewise, some of the best-endowed parishes in mid- and north Tipperary and adjacent parishes in south Laois as well as outlying pockets in the Shannonside parishes north of Lough Ree, and along the Monaghan/Meath borderlands, reveal dramatic

losses amongst the very young. Parishes registering more than a 65% reduction (shown in dark brown) – that is, where only three to four children remained in 1851 where ten existed in 1841 – include Doonfeeny, Kilfian, Moygawnagh, Lackan, Rathreagh and Ballysakeery in northwest Mayo; Killursa, Shrule, Killeany and Kilcoona east of Lough Corrib, Tomgraney and Ogonolloe in east Clare; Kilcoe and Aghadown in west Cork and Kilglass and Annaduff above Lough Ree. There is little doubt that in these regions child mortality was a major contributor to overall population losses.

But beyond the zones of greatest loss and pain, parishes showing a loss of 45 to 55% of their youngest children occupy vast swathes of the countryside. In south Ulster and the edges of north Leinster, in much of east Connacht apart from that most distinctive region in east-central Mayo, communities lost the potential of half of their very young. Communities of west and south Leinster – especially upland parishes – were deeply affected by these losses as was practically the remainder of the whole province of Munster with the exception of pockets already identified around Waterford and Cork City and smaller zones in the Iveragh Peninsula and the hill country of Tipperary. It is also clear that

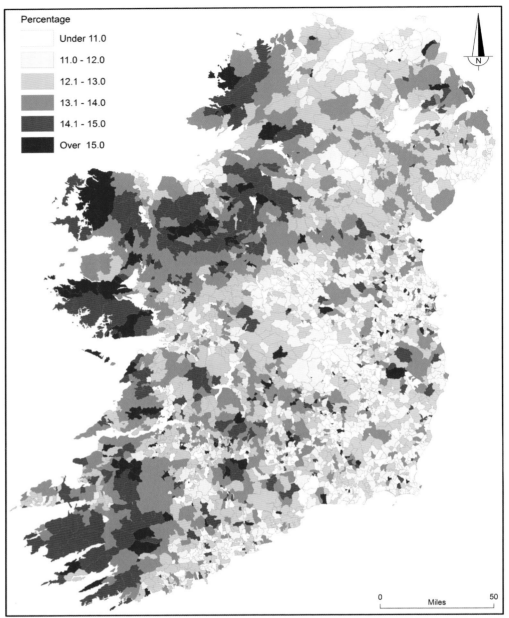

Percentage

Under 11.0

11.0 - 12.0

12.1 - 13.0

13.1 - 14.0

14.1 - 15.0

Over 15.0

0 ——— 50 Miles

Fig. 16 PERCENTAGE DISTRIBUTION OF CHILDREN UNDER FIVE YEARS OF AGE IN 1841. Because of deficiencies in enumerating infants up to eleven months (and young children aged one year), this map underestimates the percentage distribution of the population under five years of age in 1841. Nevertheless it is highly instructive about varied if dynamic pre-Famine population growth patterns across the island. (See also related maps in Chapter 2). Clearly the parishes in the northwest, west and uplands elsewhere where 13% or more of the total population returned are under five years of age, are areas of both continued high population growth and colonisation of available marginal lands. In contrast, parishes with less than 11% in this young age group to the east and especially southeast constitute zones of more stable marriage, farm-holding and population patterns. There are also interesting high levels of very young children in mid-Antrim, south Ulster and lowland Tipperary.

Ulster was the province least affected, registering child population losses of under 35% and in the northeastern and coastal parishes under one-quarter of the equivalent population in 1841. Missed opportunities and painful losses were very unevenly distributed across this Famine landscape.

Yet when one examines the proportion of *total* population change due to the decline of the children under five years of age, a rather different picture emerges. The parishes where over 23% of the total population decline was a product of child losses are mainly concentrated in the upland regions of Antrim, Tyrone, in the Mournes, and

especially in Donegal; in much of County Leitrim, in that puzzling zone in east-central Mayo and in some poorer parishes in west Clare and the Iveragh Peninsula. There are smaller pockets elsewhere, as in the Glen of Aherlow and the Wicklows and in quite a number of parishes scattered throughout 'the Pale' and southeast Ireland. In these latter areas, this pattern of child losses may indicate that the *adult* population may not have been so deeply affected by the Famine itself. There are many and varied factors emerging in this exceptional pattern. Overall, it would appear that the highest proportions are coming from the regions that were still seeing upland colonisation, new family formation and where mortality rates amongst children were still a product of pre-Famine demographic conditions.[9] However, as elsewhere, many mysteries remain.

The correlation coefficient between percentage change in the number of children under five years of age and the percentage change in population per parish between 1841 and 1851 is 0.88. Not surprisingly, the level of geographic correlation between these two variables is simply staggering. If one compares the parishes with an over 30% decrease in population with the parishes with an over 45% decline in the number of children under five years of age, there is an almost 90% correspondence. Beginning with the parishes south of Lough Erne and tracking southeastwards through much of Monaghan, west Armagh and south Cavan, one pattern is a mirror image of the other. The same is true of the parishes of east Sligo and extending along the borderlands of Roscommon and Longford to Lough Ree. Equally, the varying patterns of population decline in west Connacht is replicated in almost identical fashion by the decline of children under five years of age. And the same generalisation applies to west Midland parishes, the parishes of south Wicklow and north Wexford and the Munster parishes.

When one examines parishes with an overall 50% plus decline and an above 65% decline in the number of children

Fig. 17 In many parishes child mortality was a major contributor to overall population loss. *The Irish Famine, 1850* (oil on canvas) by George Frederic Watts (1817–1904) [Source: © Trustees of the Watts Gallery, Compton, Surrey, UK/ The Bridgeman Art Library]

under five, again the patterns practically mirror one another. From Lackan, Killala, Ballysakeery and Templeconry on the western flanks of Killala Bay to Kilmaclasser, Ballintober, Ballyhean and Breaghwy inland from Clew Bay to Kilbecanty in south Galway; Tomgraney, Ogonolloe and Kilseily in east Clare; Kilmeedy, Corcomolude and Tuogh in County Limerick to Kilcoe, Aghadown and Kilmaloda in west Cork; Tullylease, Knocktemple, Mallow and Ballyclogh in north Cork, Mogeely and Kilcockan in east Cork; and Rahelty, Ballysheehan, and Youghalarra in County Tipperary, both patterns of population loss – in short both kinds of experiences – almost replicate each other.

From the evidence of the two Censuses, Figure 18 showing the percentage change in the distribution per civil parish in numbers of children under five years of age may, therefore, be the closest we are ever likely to come to know the overall distribution of the dead (and the unborn) due to the tragedy of the Great Irish Famine.

197

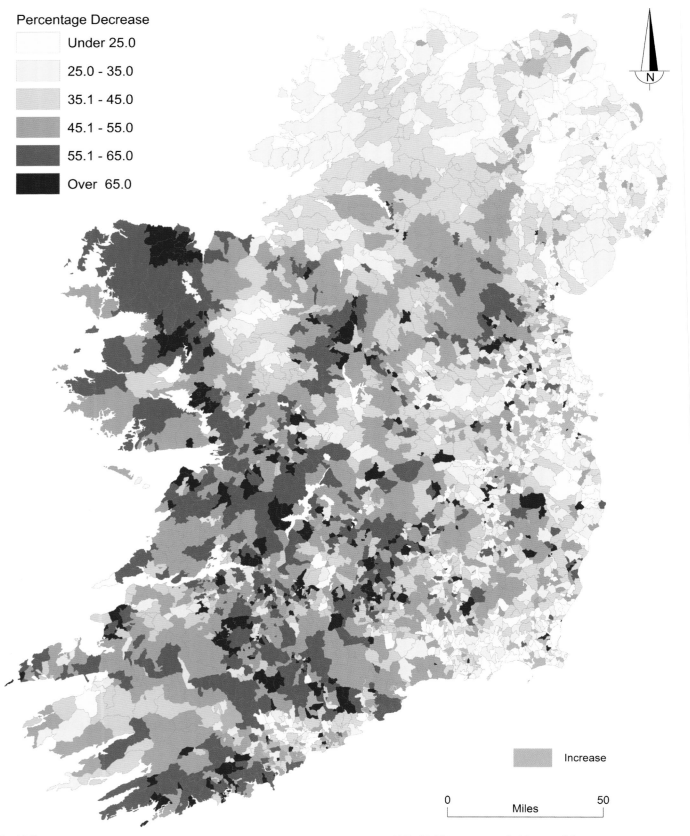

Percentage Decrease

- Under 25.0
- 25.0 - 35.0
- 35.1 - 45.0
- 45.1 - 55.0
- 55.1 - 65.0
- Over 65.0

Increase

0        Miles        50

Fig. 18 PERCENTAGE CHANGE IN THE DISTRIBUTION OF CHILDREN UNDER FIVE YEARS OF AGE 1841–51. This map is probably one of the most poignant maps in the *Atlas*. Young children were major victims of famine conditions, both in their homes and in institutions such as the workhouses. This map may not only provide a picture of the uneven distribution of child mortalities during the Famine but may also indirectly suggest regional variations in birthrates consequent on the relative severity of famine conditions. Apart from some parishes in the Dublin and Cork hinterlands, south Wexford and pockets elsewhere which saw population increases (shown in green), all other parishes lost populations – north Ulster and parts of east Leinster the least. Particular attention should be paid to the parishes characterised by a reduction of 45% or more in this younger age cohort. The detailed correlation with, for example, the map of decline in agricultural families is striking.

# Medical relief and the Great Famine

## Larry Geary

In Ireland in the mid- and late 1840s, death on an unprecedented scale followed on the repeated failures of the potato crop, the staple food of the country's poor. We do not know exactly how many people died during the Great Famine, but Joel Mokyr's pioneering analysis, which appeared in 1983, has won broad acceptance. Mokyr suggested a minimum of 1.1 million excess deaths between 1846 and 1851, which increases to 1.5 million if averted births are included, that is, births that would have occurred had fertility not been checked because of the Famine.[1]

Starvation and dietary deficiency diseases such as scurvy and pellagra accounted for some Famine mortality, but the vast majority of deaths were caused by one or other of a host of contagious or communicable diseases that raged with great malignity during these years: typhus fever, relapsing fever, typhoid or enteric fever, dysentery, diarrhoea, tuberculosis, smallpox, measles among children and Asiatic cholera. The latter, which broke out in late 1848, was not one of the diseases of the Great Famine. Its appearance was entirely coincidental but it did contribute to the overall distress and mortality.

During famine, two factors, often working in tandem, facilitate the occurrence of epidemics. These are the impairment of the individual immune system by starvation and the loss of community resistance to the spread of disease. Several phenomena contribute to the latter, among them increased migration, mendicancy and vagrancy, neglect of personal and domestic hygiene, and overcrowding of public institutions such as hospitals, workhouses and jails.[2] The impact of the prevailing infections was magnified by their occurrence at a time when disease causation and prevention were not properly understood, and before the scientific discoveries in medicine that occurred in the second half of the nineteenth century.

### 'FAMINE FEVER'

The epidemic fever of the late 1840s was variously known in the vernacular as 'famine fever', 'starvation fever', 'the fever', the 'relapse fever of 1847', 'five days' fever', and 'road fever', because of its links with the migratory hordes on the public roads. The term 'fever' embraced two distinct infections, typhus fever and relapsing fever, which have a very similar epidemiology. Both diseases are caused by micro-organisms which are transmitted by head and body lice, and the infections propagate most actively in conditions that favour lice infestation. Subsistence crises and famines create the ideal environment for the generation and dissemination of fevers and other infectious diseases.

During the Great Famine, relapsing fever was the disease that prevailed among the poor, while their social superiors tended to contract the more deadly typhus fever, particularly those who were more exposed to infection, notably clergymen, doctors, members of relief committees, and Poor Law administrators. The mortality rate from typhus was also more pronounced among the middle and upper classes than it was among the poor. Dysentery and diarrhoea were the most frequent and most fatal complications of fever. Chronic dysentery, or 'starvation dysentery' as it was sometimes called, was attributed to the foods substituted for the potato in the diets of the poor, the pickings of field, hedgerow and shoreline, and especially the inadequately ground or partially cooked Indian meal that was consumed by individuals who had neither the knowledge, fuel or restraint to prepare it properly.

At the beginning of March 1846 a committee that had been appointed by the Government to monitor the progress of famine in Ireland informed the Lord Lieutenant that fever was increasing in most parts of the country. Doctors who responded to the 'committee's inquiries commented on the lack of employment, the scarcity, poor quality and high price of food, and the prevalence of gastro-intestinal complaints. Most medical practitioners expected a fever epidemic during the spring and summer of 1846 when food scarcity became more acute, and they were concerned by the inadequacy of the country's existing medical institutions to meet the anticipated outbreak.[3]

The facilities to which they referred were the medical charities that had evolved during the eighteenth and nineteenth centuries to provide free medical aid to the sick poor. There were four categories – voluntary hospitals, mainly in Dublin, county infirmaries, fever hospitals and dispensaries – and more than 800 of these institutions had been established by the time the Great Famine began.[4] In addition, there were fever hospitals in a minority of the country's 130 workhouses.[5] The numerical strength of the medical charities network masked many deficiencies in the system, not least the unequal geographical distribution of dispensaries and fever hospitals, which were the facilities most frequented by the rural poor, as well as the irregular and unsatisfactory financial and managerial arrangements of many of these institutions. The consensus among medical practition-

**RETURNS FROM MEDICAL OFFICERS OF FEVER HOSPITALS.—ULSTER.**

ANTRIM.—Feb. 18, 1846.—Randelstown, H. Neeson, Medical Officer.—Jaundice and diarrhoea exist from unsoundness and insufficiency of food. Breaking out of disease apprehended where destitution exists.

ARMAGH.—Feb. 14, 1846.—Verner's Bridge, Arthur Ardagh, Medical Officer.—Diarrhoea, to a considerable extent, exists in district, produced from constant use of diseased potatoes. If provisions keep high, fever and other diseases are feared to break out. Feb. 16, 1846.—Poyntz Pass, Wm. Moorhead, M.D.—Fever and influenza have increased in the proportion of four to one, within last two months; but not entirely attributable to insufficiency and unsoundness of food. Feb. 16, 1846.—Markethill, Josh. M. Lynn, M.D.—Fever, diarrhoea, and dyspepsia, have increased considerably, and are, in many cases, traceable to the use of unsound potatoes. It is very probable that fever will break out and spread, especially among the lower orders. Would be of the utmost importance for every dispensary to have a small fever hospital attached. District is six miles from the hospital of union workhouse.

CAVAN.—Feb. 23, 1846.—Belturbet, W. M. Wade, M.D., Dyspepsia, diseases of alimentary canal, dysentery and diarrhoea, are caused by unsound food. Cottiers are without even tainted potatoes for food. Many unemployed poor of districts are in a starving condition. Breaking out of disease apprehended with certainty, from destitution arising from scarcity of food; "it cannot be otherwise." Suggests employment, and the erection of a fever hospital, to diminish the probability of disease. Districts is seven Irish miles from Cavan Hospital. Feb. 14, 1846.—Arvagh. Wm. Myles, Medical Officer.—Apprehends breaking out of disease from destitution, arising from want of food, Bowel complaints, painful and violent griping, with other violent symptoms continuing eight or twelve hours; caused by the use of unsound potatoes. Suggests employment of the poor, and formation of store-houses, for oatmeal to be sold, at reasonable prices. Ballyjamesduff, George Nixon, M.D.—Apprehends fever in district; strongly recommends establishment of a fever hospital, and the placing of funds in the hands of the clergy and district medical officers for relief of the poor, who cannot obtain admission into the poor-house. Feb. 18, 1846.—Mullagh, Edward Kellett, M.D.—Five hundred able bodied men, and an equal number of women, besides many small farmers, are seeking employment. Apprehends breaking out of disease, where scarcity exists; the people being unemployed, are unable to purchase food. Outbreak of fever frequent in summer months, and spreads rapidly, for want of an hospital, the want of which is keenly felt by the labouring population. Suggests employment for the poor. Feb. 17, 1846.—Kingscourt, R. Malcolmson, M.D.. and Surgeon.—Three thousand and sixty persons relieved at dispensary, within five months past. Five or six thousand poor unemployed. Breaking out of disease apprehended in the Spring and Summer. Suggests the erection of a fever hospital in a district where destitution is heavily felt, and is the only available means of preventing the spread of contagion. Medical district of officer covers a diameter of 12 miles from his residence. February 18, 1846.—Shercock, James Adams, Medical Officer.—Inflammation of stomach and diarrhoea are frequent, and attributable to the use of bad potatoes. Influenza, now epidemic, but will not say it is so from insufficiency of food. Increase of fever expected in April, or sooner. Suggests that fever hospitals be erected on every three square miles of district. February 16, 1846.—Swadlinbar, Winslow, Finlay, Medical Officer.—Several cases of typhus fever have recently appeared; insufficiency of food the cause, in some instances. Fever will break out to a frightful extent, in the event of scarcity of food. Suggests local fever hospitals to be established for the removal of cases, as they occur.

DONEGAL.—February 17, 1846.—Donaghmore.—R. M. Tagard, M.D.—Influenza, scarletina, small pox, and, much above all, stomach and bowel disease exist, varying to fatal inflammation. Diseased potatoes may be the existing cause. Apprehends the spread of disease, particularly fever; provisions being likely to be dear and scarce, and the supply of fuel scanty. Suggests temporary hospital relief, and that non-contagious medical and surgical cases be admitted to workhouse hospital, without the "workhouse test." Feb. 19, 1846.—Moville.—John Irvine, Surgeon, R.N.—Typhus fever prevails, but not as an epidemic. Apprehends the breaking out of fever, from destitution, arising from failure of potato crop.

Fig. 1 (left) Returns from, medical officers of fever hospitals, in Ulster, *Londonderry Journal*, 25 March 1846. In Markethill, County Armagh, it is reported that 'fever, diarrhoea and dyspepsia, have increased, and are, in many cases traceable to the use of unsound potatoes'. While in Belturbet, County Cavan, it is stated that 'cottiers are without even tainted potatoes for food. Many unemployed poor of districts are in a starving condition. Breaking out of disease apprehended with certainty from destitution arising from scarcity of food; "it cannot be otherwise".' [Source: Central Library, Letterkenny]

ers and other commentators in the spring of 1846 was that the country's medical charities were ill-equipped to meet the impending famine and anticipated disease crisis.[6]

## RESPONDING TO THE CRISIS

The Government's response was to rush emergency fever legislation through the House of Commons, and this became law on 24 March 1846. The preamble to the act stated that it was necessary to make more effectual provision for the treatment of poor persons afflicted with fever and other epidemic diseases in Ireland. To this end, the Government appointed five unpaid Commissioners of Health, collectively the Central Board of Health, with extensive advisory and executive functions, including the power to direct boards of Poor Law guardians to provide fever hospitals and dispensaries in their respective unions for those suffering from fever or any other epidemic disease. The cost of establishing and maintaining these institutions, together with that of patient care and medicines, was borne by the rate payers of the union, while the medical officers' salaries were paid by the Government. The institutions that were established under the act were the responsibility of the boards of guardians, subject to the overall control of the Central Board of Health, and were to continue as long as the board advised and the Lord Lieutenant decreed. The latter was empowered to appoint one or more salaried medical officers to provide professional assistance to the sick poor in each Poor Law Union. The act was to remain in force until 1 September 1847.[7]

On 1 April 1846, a week after the enactment of the temporary fever legislation, the Government appointed the prominent Dublin medical practitioners Dominic John Corrigan and Sir Philip Crampton to the Central Board of Health, along with the distinguished chemist Sir Robert Kane, who was medically qualified but who had almost entirely ceased to practise by the time of the Famine, and two senior civil servants, Sir Randolph Routh, Commissary-general of the army, and Edward Twistleton, who had been sent to Ireland as Poor Law Commissioner in November 1845.[8]

At the first meeting of the board, the members appointed a medical inspector, Dr Robert William Smith of Dublin, to investigate the overcrowded and badly administered Lurgan workhouse in County Armagh. They considered a request for aid from the Tullamore board of guardians in King's County, and a report from John H. Leahy, physician to the Drimoleague dispensary in County Cork. Leahy stated that fever, dysentery and

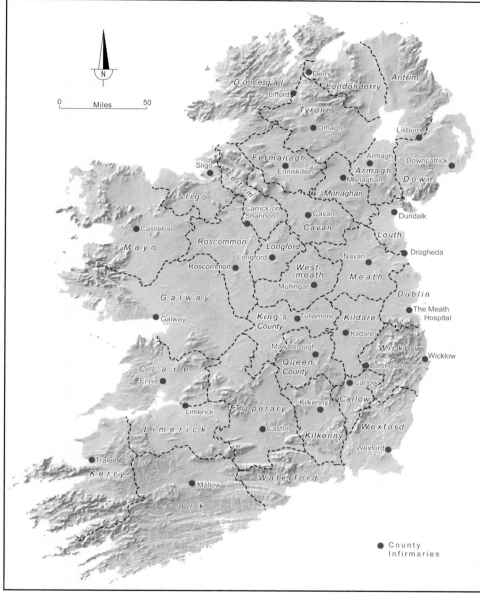

Fig. 2 DISTRIBUTION OF COUNTY INFIRMARIES

been built to accommodate fifty-four patients but now contained 130, and its funds were almost exhausted.[10]

On at least two occasions in the spring of 1847, the Central Board of Health warned the Government that the country was on the verge of a fever epidemic as severe and as widespread as any that had yet occurred, and stressed that current legislation and the existing medical facilities were each inadequate to meet the emergency. The board recommended additional legislation to streamline medical relief at local level, and requested the power to compel boards of guardians to fund the necessary relief to the sick from the poor rates.[11] The Government responded, on 27 April 1847, by amending the temporary fever act that had been introduced in the previous year. Under the new legislation, the Central Board of Health retained overall control of the emergency fever hospitals and dispensaries, but local responsibility passed from the country's 130 boards of guardians to the 700 or so local relief committees that had been established during the spring and summer of 1846, mostly in the south and west of the country. The cost of establishing and maintaining emergency fever hospitals and dispensaries, including the medical officers' salaries, was chargeable to the local relief committees, which derived their funds from voluntary subscriptions and government grants.[12]

dropsy had increased to such an extent throughout his dispensary district that he was unable to cope.[9] (Dropsy means an abnormal accumulation of fluid beneath the skin, or in one or more of the cavities of the body. Oedema, ascites, or anasarca were synonyms for dropsy.) Thereafter, correspondence of a similar nature poured into the office on a daily basis. Communications from many parts of the country referred to the complete absence of medical relief in their respective localities and requested the establishment of temporary fever hospitals. Others commented on the overcrowding and indebtedness of county and district fever hospitals and expressed community fears that these institutions would close due to a lack of funds. A report from Killarney in April 1847 stated that people were 'literally dropping in the streets and perishing in their miserable cabins'. The local workhouse was full, as was the fever hospital, which was the only one in an area of 144 square miles. The hospital had

### EMERGENCY FEVER HOSPITALS

The Central Board of Health recommended the conversion of existing buildings for use as emergency fever hospitals. If this were not feasible, the board supplied plans for the construction of wooden fever sheds and bedsteads, of a simple and economical design, which had been drawn up by the Poor Law Commission's architect.[13] These wooden sheds were preferred by the Central Board of Health to tents belonging to the ordnance department, which were used in some places to accommodate the sick in the spring and early summer of 1847.[14] Three different types of tents were employed – hospital tents, marquees and round tents – which could accommodate fourteen, four, and three patients

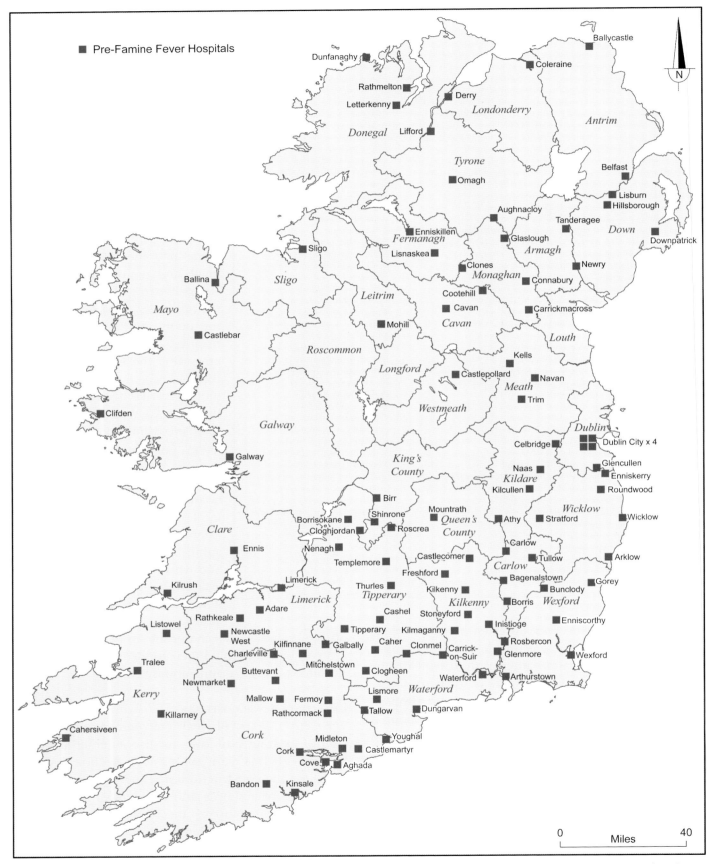

Pre-Famine Fever Hospitals

Fig. 3 PRE-FAMINE FEVER HOSPITALS. The distribution of pre-Famine fever hospitals is highly uneven. In the Munster–south Leinster region, fever hospitals are well represented amongst towns with a population over 1,500 and are also found in some smaller – usually landlord-founded – towns. This reflects the capacity of these urban centres to fund private hospitals as well as the fear of the spread of fever – especially typhus – amongst their middle classes. A second comparable zone in the density of fever hospitals extends from mid- and south Ulster into County Meath. In sharp contrast, practically all of the province of Connacht, the west Midlands, north Clare and peninsular southwest Munster are devoid of such hospitals, emphasising a weaker urban hierarchy and less patronage by local elites.

Fig.4  Fever hospital adjacent to Roscommon Workhouse, built during the Famine. [Photo: William J. Smyth]

respectively, but in the opinion of Dr Dominic Corrigan, the most influential member of the Central Board of Health, only hospital tents were suitable for treating the sick.[15]

The Central Board of Health ordained that the fever hospital's management committee was to provide a separate bedstead for each patient, who, on admission, was to receive a straw bed in sacking, two blankets and two sheets, a pillow, a rug and a nightshirt. The straw, sheets and nightshirts were to be changed weekly, or if soiled,[16] but the regularity envisioned in these ordinances was rarely, if ever, achieved during the Famine.

As far as possible, the emergency medical facilities were staffed by local doctors, who were paid five shillings a day for attending a temporary fever hospital or dispensary and double that for attending a combined fever hospital and dispensary, in addition to any permanent salary they might have.[17] These pay scales were regarded as demeaning and insulting by many members of the medical profession, especially the Dublin-based leadership, who had little or no connection with the medical services provided to the poor. In June 1847 some 1,100 doctors nationwide, including the

leading lights of the profession, signed a petition objecting to the level of payment.[18] The Government, acting on the advice of the Central Board of Health, rejected the petition out of hand. The board cited a number of precedents and reasons to support their contention that the salary offered for emergency work was both just and adequate.[19] The board's stance drew the ire and reprobation of the spokesmen for the profession,[20] which Corrigan and Crampton ignored, and they persevered with their unenviable and unpaid task of coordinating the medical response to the disease emergency. In time, their commitment, diligence and integrity won the support of the doctors who staffed the temporary fever hospitals and dispensaries, and by the closing years of the Famine many rural medical practitioners looked to the Board 'as the natural protectors of their interests'.[21] The Central Board of Health was one administrative body to emerge with credit from the Great Famine, particularly in light of the legislative and financial strictures under which it operated.

OVERCROWDING

The public institutions that existed when the Famine

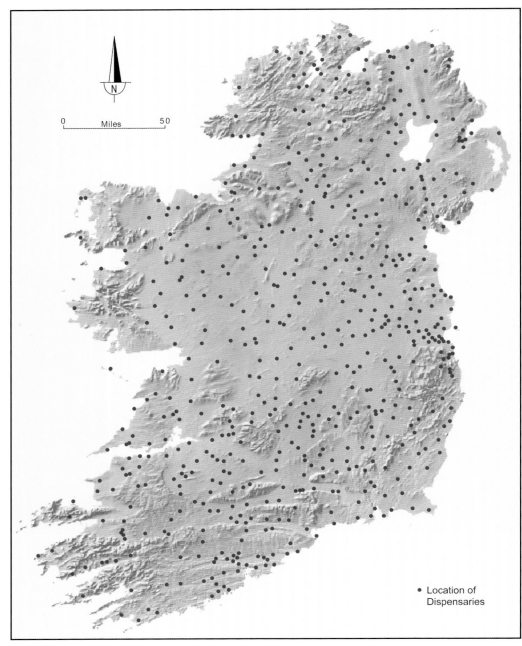

Fig. 5 DISTRIBUTION OF DISPENSARIES IN 1841

affected society differently, that mortality from the disease was considerably greater among the higher social classes than it was among the poor, and self interest, if nothing else, suggested that the socially advantaged should act responsibly.[22]

The Central Board of Health and the Poor Law Commission condemned institutional overcrowding as irresponsible, a stance based on the high levels of mortality in workhouses, fever hospitals and other institutions. However, their position created an appalling dilemma for medical officers and for members of boards of guardians and local relief committees. These individuals were often the arbiters of life and death and were generally loath to exclude the starving, the sick and the dying from relief and shelter. Unquestionably, some of the facilities in which they worked or over which they presided were mismanaged; negligence and parsimony were features of others, and conditions in many were quite appalling. Nonetheless, it would be wrong to attach the entire blame to indifference or ineptitude at local level, to a failure of private initiative and philanthropy. Prevailing doctrines of political economy, providentialism, and moralism notwithstanding, the ultimate responsibility lay with the Government, and its response to the spread of disease and the other challenges posed by the Famine was, at best, indecisive and inadequate.

began were never designed or intended for the emergency that confronted them from the winter of 1846 onwards, and all such bodies came under intense and unprecedented pressure. In response, hospital governors and others entrusted with the relief of the sick and the starving often went to heroic lengths to provide accommodation and assistance. The invariable result was gross overcrowding of facilities, which in turn drew down the wrath of the Central Board of Health and the Poor Law Commission, who were convinced that overcrowding was a major factor in generating disease and as such posed a grave threat to public health. The Central Board of Health argued that fever, once generated, would not be confined to the institution in which it originated, but would spread among all classes and involve the whole population in a common danger if left unchecked. The board emphasised that fever

The legislation governing the temporary fever hospitals and dispensaries expired on 31 August 1850, and the Central Board of Health disbanded. From July 1847 onwards, the board demanded weekly hospital returns, and over the next thirty-eight months 332,462 patients were treated in the temporary hospitals, 173,723 females and 158,739 males. The recorded number of deaths was 34,622, made up of 17,800 males and 16,822 females, a mortality rate of 11.2 and 9.7% respectively.[23] The overall death rate in the temporary fever hospitals was 10.4%.

Like the country's emergency medical facilities, regular or permanent fever hospitals and dispensaries were

204

Fig. 6 Fever hospital in Manorhamilton, County Leitrim, which was built in 1850 as a response to the cholera epidemic of 1832 and the devastating impact of the Great Famine. [Photo: William J. Smyth]

swamped by the sick and dying following the recurrence of potato blight in 1846, and quickly came under severe financial and accommodation pressures. The Government invariably rejected appeals for financial assistance, the standard response being that it had no funds at its disposal to support the country's medical charities.[24] This was a grave mistake, as these institutions should have been the first line of defence against infection, and the Government should have guaranteed their existence.

### DESTITUTION, SICKNESS AND DISEASE

The Government's persistent refusal to sanction emergency funding for the country's permanent fever hospitals and dispensaries placed unsustainable demands on local charity, and communal philanthropy collapsed under the onslaught of destitution, sickness and disease that befell most localities from the winter of 1846 onwards. Many medical charities were driven to bankruptcy and closure. Between 1845 and 1851 the number of fever hospitals that

were supported by subscriptions and grand jury presentments fell from 101 to 41, while the number of fever hospitals based in the workhouses and funded from the poor rates increased from 20 to 148.[25]

By the late 1840s, it was clear that the pre-Famine medical charities' network was in considerable disarray, and government intervention was urgently required to prevent the system from imploding entirely. Ultimately, pressure from doctors attached to permanent dispensaries and fever hospitals, whose institutions and livelihoods were threatened by the combined effects of starvation, disease and a contracting economy, compelled the Government to introduce a medical charities bill to the House of Commons. The bill passed the legislature on 4 August 1851, received the royal assent three days later, and came into force on 1 October 1851.[26]

The 1851 Medical Charities Act, despite its title, applied only to dispensaries and not to the medical charities system as a whole. The Act established a nationwide dispensary network that was funded from the poor rates[27] and administered

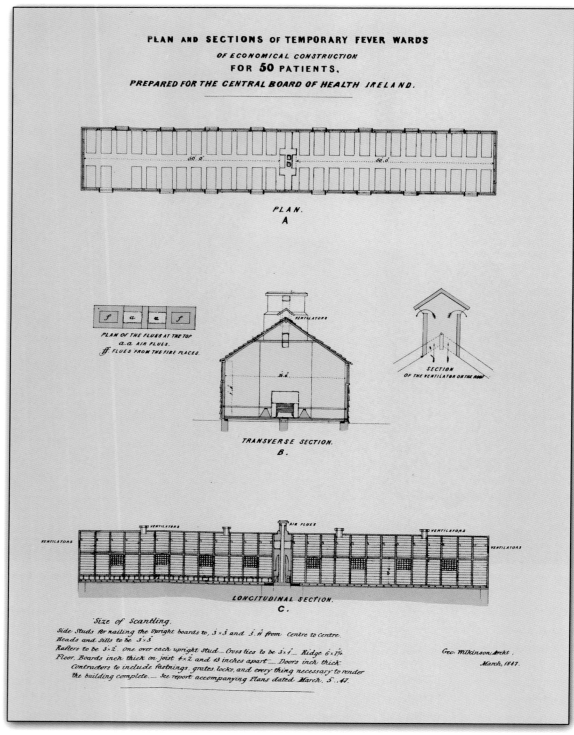

PLAN AND SECTIONS OF TEMPORARY FEVER WARDS

OF ECONOMICAL CONSTRUCTION

FOR 50 PATIENTS,

PREPARED FOR THE CENTRAL BOARD OF HEALTH IRELAND.

PLAN.
A

PLAN OF THE FLUES AT THE TOP.
a.a AIR FLUES.
ff FLUES FROM THE FIRE PLACES.

SECTION
OF THE VENTILATOR ON THE ROOF

TRANSVERSE SECTION.
B.

LONGITUDINAL SECTION.
C.

Size of Scantling,
Side Studs for nailing the Upright boards to, 3 × 3 and 3 ft from Centre to Centre.
Heads and Sills to be 3 × 3.
Rafters to be 3 × 2. one over each upright stud. Cross ties to be 3 × 1. Ridge 6 × 1¼.
Floor, Boards inch thick on joist 4 × 2 and 13 inches apart. Doors inch thick.
Contractors to include fastnings, grates, locks, and every thing necessary to render
the building complete. See report accompanying Plans dated March, 5 .47.

Geo. Wilkinson, Archt.
March, 1847.

Fig. 7 In order to cope with the ever-increasing incidence of fever throughout the country, the Central Board of Health commissioned the architect George Wilkinson to draw up plans for temporary fever wards. Given the extent of the fever epidemics and the significant delays in appointing new medical staff to tend to the fever victims, the impact of such a measure was minimal. [Source: Report of the Commissioners of Health, Ireland, on the epidemics of 1846–50, *British Parliamentary Papers, 1852–53* (1562) XLI]

trict. The 1851 Act entitled 'any poor person' resident in the dispensary district to medicine and advice on presentation of 'a ticket' that could be obtained from any member of the dispensary committee. There were two types of tickets, which were colour-coded. Black tickets entitled holders or their dependants to free medical assistance at the dispensary only, while red ones entitled possessors to free domiciliary treatment, irrespective of distance, provided the patient's home was within the dispensary district.[28]

There were few aspects of Irish life that the Great Famine did not impinge upon. The Poor Law and the country's medical services were particularly challenged. Neither was designed to cope with a catastrophe on the scale that occurred, but, despite their many inadequacies and failings, each managed to alleviate distress and save lives. Starvation and famine-related diseases forced the Government and the Irish administration into a number of emergency measures to plug the more obvious gaps in poor relief and health-care provision. There were more permanent developments also as deficiencies in the originating legislation were exposed.

The 1851 Medical Charities Act, which was a direct consequence of the Great Famine, removed the vestiges of paternalism and philanthropy that were linked to the dispensary network for more than half a century and made these insti-

and supervised by the Poor Law Commission. Under the terms of the Act, the country's Poor Law unions, which had expanded from the original 130 to 163 during the Great Famine, were divided into 723 dispensary districts, with at least one dispensary in each district. Each dispensary was managed by a committee that was elected annually from the Poor Law guardians and wealthier property holders in the dis-

● Temporary or emergency
  fever hospitals

Placenames as rendered in the 1851 Census

Fig. 8 DISTRIBUTION OF TEMPORARY FEVER HOSPITALS DURING THE FAMINE. For the most part, the distribution of temporary fever hospitals – established under the auspices of the Central Board of Health – reflects the varying intensity of desperate conditions during the height of the Famine crisis. The density of temporary fever hospitals in most of Munster and south Leinster – adding to an already strong distribution of pre-Famine fever hospitals – emphasises the depth and extent of famine fever in this stricken region. Noticeable too is the number of temporary fever hospitals that had to be created in Clare and peninsular southwest Munster. Similarly, their dense distribution in mid-Ulster and the Ulster/Leinster/Connacht borderlands reflects high stress levels, although it would appear that the eastern half of this zone was more successful in curtailing deaths due to fever. Almost devoid of pre-Famine fever hospitals, one of the most striking features of this map is the emergence of County Galway as a major zone of temporary fever hospitals to meet the severe conditions existing there. The relative sparsity of such hospitals in County Mayo is somewhat surprising. Not so their distribution in both north Ulster and most of mid-Leinster, two provincial regions less deeply affected by the horrors of famine and fever.

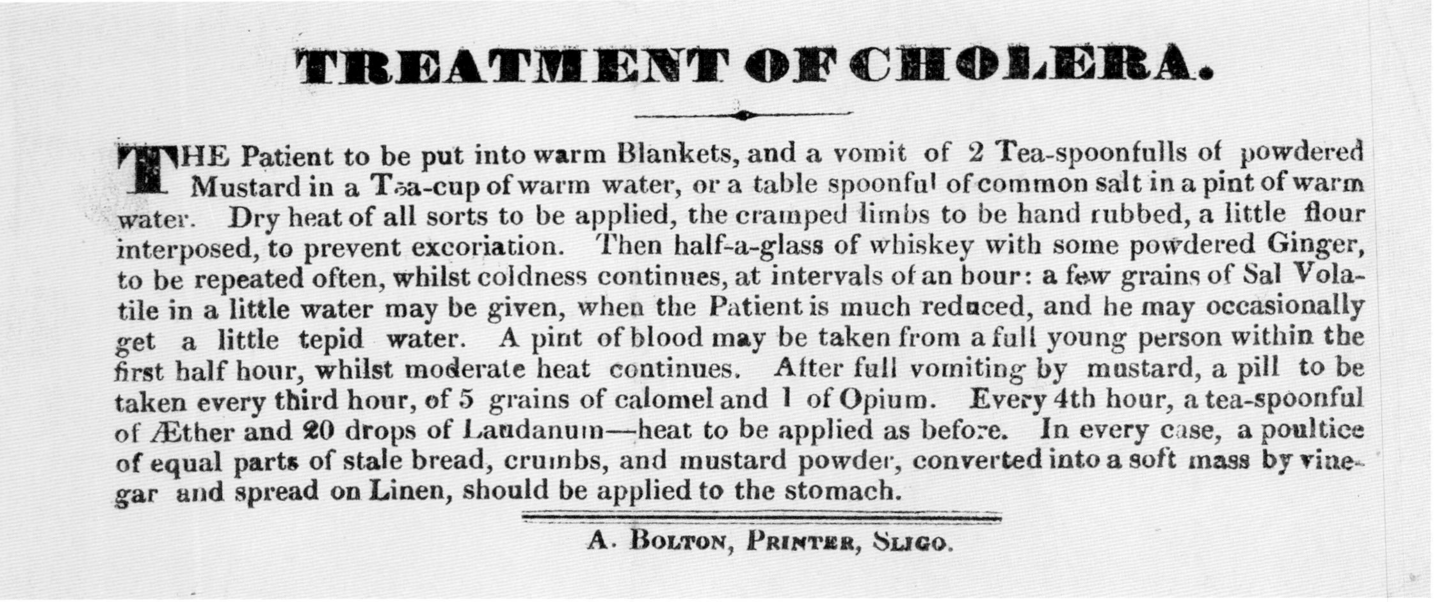

# TREATMENT OF CHOLERA.

THE Patient to be put into warm Blankets, and a vomit of 2 Tea-spoonfulls of powdered Mustard in a Tea-cup of warm water, or a table spoonful of common salt in a pint of warm water. Dry heat of all sorts to be applied, the cramped limbs to be hand rubbed, a little flour interposed, to prevent excoriation. Then half-a-glass of whiskey with some powdered Ginger, to be repeated often, whilst coldness continues, at intervals of an hour: a few grains of Sal Volatile in a little water may be given, when the Patient is much reduced, and he may occasionally get a little tepid water. A pint of blood may be taken from a full young person within the first half hour, whilst moderate heat continues. After full vomiting by mustard, a pill to be taken every third hour, of 5 grains of calomel and 1 of Opium. Every 4th hour, a tea-spoonful of Æther and 20 drops of Laudanum—heat to be applied as before. In every case, a poultice of equal parts of stale bread, crumbs, and mustard powder, converted into a soft mass by vinegar and spread on Linen, should be applied to the stomach.

A. BOLTON, PRINTER, SLIGO.

Fig. 9 Notice issued by the Central Board of Health with regard to the treatment of cholera. A cholera epidemic spread to Ireland in December 1848 and had a particularly devastating impact on some of the most impoverished Poor Law unions, which could not cope with such an outbreak. While not one of the Famine diseases, cholera was an acute, highly contagious and painful disease and it led to mass deaths in many districts. Inmates deserted workhouses on the first sign of cholera, preferring to risk death by starvation outside than to be struck down by the disease in the cramped conditions within. [Source: National Library of Ireland]

Fig. 10 Mass grave in Dromcliff cemetery containing the remains of the victims of cholera in Ennis in 1832. The visitation of cholera to the town during the Famine years also resulted in significant levels of mortality (upwards of 300 deaths) which was spread amongst different social classes. [Source: Ciarán Ó Murchadha, *Sable Wings over the Land: Ennis, County Clare and its wider community during the Great Famine* (Clare, 1998), pp. 199-203; Photo: Frank Coyne]

tutions an integral part of the Poor Law system. The 1838 Poor Law Act, amendments in 1843 and 1847, and the 1851 Medical Charities Act were an acknowledgement of the inadequacy of philanthropy and private initiatives to deal with sickness and poverty in Ireland. They marked both the passing of an old order and the failure of government laissez-faire policies. The 1838 and 1851 acts were part of the process of modernisation. They established nationwide workhouse and dispensary systems that were funded from the poor rates and administered by the Poor Law Commission. For the remaining seventy years of British governance over the entire island of Ireland, the tendency towards greater state involvement and increased centralisation continued.

# 'Report upon the recent epidemic fever in Ireland': the evidence from Cork

## Larry Geary

A period of unexampled distress has passed over this country, the repeated failure of the potato crop having brought among us not only famine and misery but the fatal diseases of epidemic fever and malignant dysentery, which in this country so generally arise from deficient and unwholesome food.[1]

In late August 1848, William Wilde, the editor of the *Dublin Quarterly Journal of Medical Science*, distributed an elaborate questionnaire, containing forty-four separate queries, among Irish medical practitioners. Wilde sought information on what he termed 'the late disastrous epidemic', the deadly famine diseases that had ravaged the country since the first failure of the potato crop in the autumn of 1845. According to Leslie Clarkson and Margaret Crawford, Wilde's survey combined his 'passion for systematic enquiry with acute medical observation'.[2] More than a hundred doctors responded to his request for epidemiological information. Some parts of the country were underrepresented in the returns, especially the west, where, according to Wilde, the epidemic had committed 'fearful ravages', and many doctors had died as a result of disease contracted in the course of their work.[3]

### PRIMARY SOURCE

The medical accounts that were submitted to Wilde run to almost 300 pages of text and constitute one of the most important primary sources for analysing the diseases that prevailed during the first four years of potato failure. These reports provide evidence that two types of disease predominated and that they were largely responsible for excess mortality: fever, a generic term that embraced typhus fever, relapsing fever, and typhoid or enteric fever, infections that had yet to be distinguished scientifically, and the gastrointestinal diseases dysentery and diarrhoea. There were graphic accounts of other infections also, as well as harrowing descriptions of the individual and communal impact of starvation.

Ten reports were returned from Cork, six from the county and four from the city. The former came from Mitchelstown (Dr Phelan), Innishannon (Dr Corbet), Bantry (Dr Tisdall), Schull (Dr Jones Lamprey), and there were two from Cove (later Queenstown/Cobh; Dr Orpen and Dr

Fig. 1 Sir William Wilde (1815–1876). A Victorian polymath, Wilde excelled in diverse fields, including medicine, statistics, folklore and language. His ability as a statistician was recognised by the Irish Census Commissioners when he was given responsibility for classifying and analysing medical matters for the 1841 Census report. His subsequent work as assistant commissioner for the 1851 Census, where he produced tables of deaths and diseases, was widely acclaimed. Wilde believed that the Great Famine was providential in design, a view which effectively cleared the British state of responsibility for the human tragedy which unfolded. 'The overall message was clear; horrific as the Famine may have been, it revealed the best as well as the worst in human nature and gave no grounds for questions of guilt, state responsibility or existential gloom.' He was knighted in 1864 for his contributions to the field of medicine and his work on the Irish census. Peter Gray, 'Accounting for catastrophe: William Wilde, the 1851 Irish census and the Great Famine', in *Power and Popular Culture in Modern Ireland*, ed. Michael De Nie and Sean Farrell (Dublin, 2010), p. 58. [Source: National Library of Ireland]

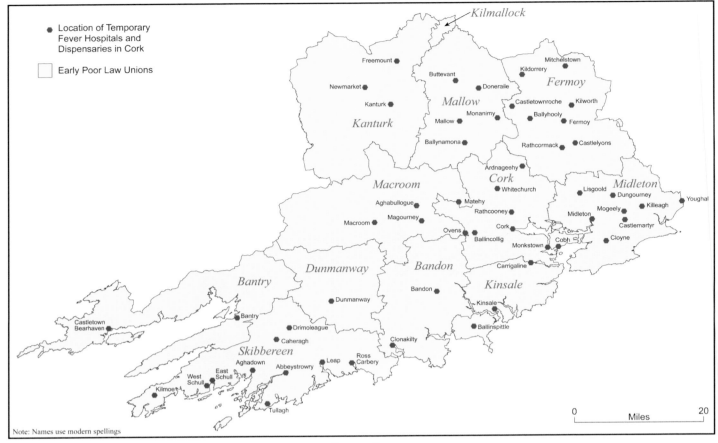

Fig. 2 DISTRIBUTION OF TEMPORARY FEVER HOSPITALS AND DISPENSARIES IN COUNTY CORK

Cronin). There were disparities in the Cove reports, for which, according to Wilde, there were two possible explanations: 'the loose ideas' that existed in relation to demographic analyses and statistics generally, or the possibility that the doctors based their returns on different constituencies – the town population in one case, a combined town and surrounding rural population in the other. Either way, the differences in the reports from one locality provide further evidence of the advisability of maintaining a healthy scepticism in relation to Famine morbidity and mortality statistics. The city reports were submitted by Dr John Popham, who was attached to the North Infirmary, Dr Callanan, Dr Townsend, and conjointly by Drs Armstrong and Flynn.

### SOCIALLY SELECTIVE

The fever epidemic began in Mitchelstown in November 1846, where, according to Dr Phelan, the majority of those attacked lacked the basic necessities of life. At Innishannon, Cove, and Bantry fever appears to have broken out in the following January or February. Most of the Cork respondents agreed that fever was contagious, although two reports from the city acknowledged that the evidence was inconclusive. No one was immune from infection, but there were marked differences in the ways in which the various social classes were affected. Typhus fever was more common and more deadly among the higher classes, while their social

inferiors tended to contract relapsing fever, which was the more prevalent disease throughout the county. In general, dysentery and diarrhoea, which were attributed to the sudden change of diet, appeared in the wake of fever. These diseases preceded fever occasionally but rarely accompanied it, except in Bantry, where dysentery raged uninterruptedly throughout the years covered by the survey.

The duration of the fever attack varied, depending on whether the prevailing disease was typhus or relapsing fever, but convalescence was invariably protracted among survivors, sometimes taking many weeks. Cork medical practitioners, like their colleagues elsewhere in the country, had little faith in the power of medicine to combat the epidemic, and generally relied on wine and other stimulants. For instance, Dr Corbet of Innishannon depended mostly on 'tepid sponging, judicious nourishment, and good nursetenders above all'. There were variations in the mortality returns from the different parts of the county, depending on the nature and severity of the prevailing diseases.[4]

Dr Jones Lamprey submitted a comprehensive report on Schull in the Skibbereen Poor Law Union, where, according to Wilde, 'famine and pestilence raged with probably greater fury than in any other part of Ireland'. Towards the end of March 1847, the Central Board of Health, the body appointed by the Government to coordinate the medical response to the Famine, had sent Lamprey as a temporary medical officer to the Schull district, which, he reported, was remote, extensive and thickly populated by a people dependent on fishing, mining and potatoes for survival. He was informed by local contacts that the complete failure of the potato crop in 1846 had precipitated outbreaks of fever and dysentery, and that by the end of the year some 2,000 people had died from famine and disease in the locality. The situation worsened considerably in the opening months of 1847. At the beginning of February, Stephen Sweetman, a local medical practitioner, estimated that on average thirty-five individuals were dying each day in Schull parish, and that every sector of society was exposed to disease.[5]

Lamprey reported that starving individuals generally contracted a lingering form of fever, 'famine fever', which was 'characterised by great prostration, thirst, a dry, chaffy, hot feel of the skin; a weak, feeble pulse; the intellect generally clear; no cerebral, thoracic, or abdominal complications; nor was it defined by periods, stages, or crisis, and terminated in death from inanition alone'. Lamprey seemed to be describing the physiological impact of starvation rather than developments in cases of either typhus or relapsing fever, observing that the condition responded to the administration of food and did not require medical treatment for its cure.[6] He added that famine fever was frequently followed by anasarca, an abnormal accumulation of fluid in the body and another indicator of nutrition deficiency, and those who were affected 'exhaled a peculiar fetid, septic odour'. This 'famine fever' was associated with the labouring poor; those of a higher social status

tended to contract typhus or typhoid fever.

## INAPPROPRIATE AND INADEQUATELY COOKED FOOD

Lamprey stated that dysentery had been more prevalent than fever in the locality and he attributed its prominence to the seaweed, shellfish and Indian meal that the hungry people had substituted for the blighted potato crops. Indian meal was particularly problematic: Irish people were unaccustomed to it, they did not know how to cook it properly, and in many instances were obliged to eat it raw because of a lack of fuel for cooking. The dysentery that ensued from inappropriate or inadequately cooked food was protracted and caused a great amount of suffering, with patients evincing abdominal pain, distressing and ineffectual attempts to evacuate the bowel or bladder, and great thirst. 'The dejecta mostly consisted of pure blood and mucus', he wrote, and, he added graphically, 'it was easily known if any of the inmates in the cabins of the poor were suffering from this disease, as the ground in such places was usually found marked with clots of blood'.

Lamprey appended to his report Dr Robert Traill's celebrated comment of early February 1847. Traill, the Protestant rector of Schull since 1830, had written in apocalyptic terms to the editor of the *Cork Constitution*:

> Frightful and fearful is the havock (sic) around me . . . The children in particular, he [Dr Stephen Sweetman] remarked, were disappearing with

Fig. 3 Burial place of Dr Robert Traill, the Church of Ireland rector of Schull, who died of famine fever in April 1847 while administering relief to the distressed in the locality. The inscription on the headstone reads: 'Sacred to the memory of Rev. Robert Traill D.D. who for a period of seventeen years that he presided over the parish of Schull as rector with his Blessed Master "went about doing good." "Till at length in full sacrifice to his superhuman efforts in relieving the prevailing distress in the famine years of 1846 and 1847." Interred to his rest April 21 1847'; Sketch of Rev. Traill in Mullins's hut, Schull, *The Illustrated London News*, 20 February 1847. [Photo: John Crowley]

awful rapidity. And to this I may add the aged, who, with the young – neglected, perhaps, amidst the wide-spread destitution – are almost without exception swollen and ripening for the grave.[7]

By the time Lamprey submitted his account to Wilde, Traill, too, had become a casualty of the famine fever that showed no respect for class or creed.[8]

Many famine victims fled the countryside and sought refuge and relief in Cork city. According to Dr John Popham's comprehensive account of his Famine experi-

ences at the North Infirmary, country paupers descending on the city became a problem in the closing months of 1846, and, 'to prevent them from dying in the streets', the doors of the workhouse were thrown open and more than 500 paupers were admitted in a single week. All of these rural refugees were starving and most were afflicted with either fever or malignant dysentery. The fever was commonly termed 'the road fever' as it originated with 'the vast migratory hordes of labourers and their families congregated upon the public roads'. He stated that fever was particularly entrenched in the cheap lodging houses in the city's sub-

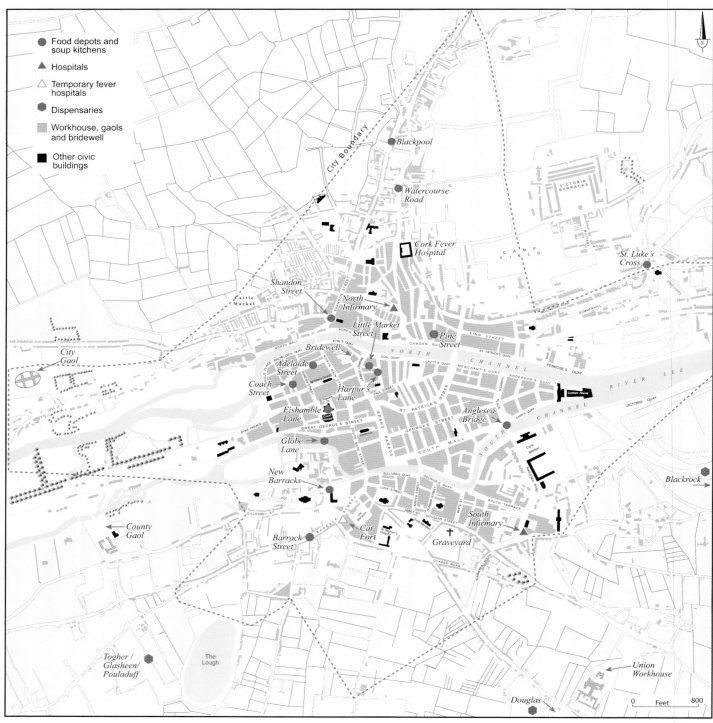

Fig. 4 LOCATION OF MEDICAL AND RELIEF FACILITIES AND BURIAL GROUNDS IN CORK CITY DURING THE FAMINE

urbs, which were generally crowded with pauper migrants en route to England. From these 'nursing places of contagion', fever spread to the homes of the working classes and eventually to those of the city's wealthier citizens. Popham reported that the fever epidemic peaked in the city in July 1847 and was followed by an outbreak of dysentery. The ubiquity and unrelenting nature of distress and disease impacted on the city's medical and relief infrastructure, especially the workhouse, the fever hospital, the North Infirmary, and a number of emergency facilities, and mortality soared in 1847.[9]

### 'INTENSE WANT'

An equally wide-ranging report from Dr Callanan corroborated and complemented Popham's, except that the former traced the fever epidemic in the city to the early months of 1846. But, he added, it was from the beginning of 1847 that the real impact of the Famine was felt and in that year 3,329 deaths were recorded in the Cork workhouse, 757 in the month of March alone. Dr Callanan was unambiguous in his interpretation of the causes of the fever epidemic: 'hunger, cold, impure air, deficient clothing – in short, *intense want* in its most comprehensive and extended meaning, and in its most withering effects both on mind and body'.

There was an implicit political message and concern in Callanan's observation, a concern he shared with many of his medical colleagues who linked illness and disease outbreaks in Ireland to pervasive and intense poverty. Callanan concluded that it was incumbent on the Government, both now and in the future, to create employment for the labouring and agricultural classes in order to prevent a recurrence of the conditions that had made 'the very name of this unhappy country a modern proverb for poverty, disease, and humiliation, in the eyes and on the tongues of the civilised world'.[10]

The analyses offered by the Cork respondents to Wilde's questionnaire shed some empirical and statistical light on the impact of starvation and disease on the city and parts of the county in 1847 and 1848 particularly, on morbidity and mortality in these localities generally, and on medical intervention in the disease crisis. The experiences of these doctors accorded broadly with those of their colleagues elsewhere in Ireland. Fever was the prevailing epidemic and was complicated or exacerbated primarily by dysentery and diarrhoea. The General Board of Health noted in its post-Famine report to the Government that the type of fever varied in different places at different times but in general terms 'the malignity of the disease, and of its complications, seemed mainly to have depended on the lowered state of constitutional strength induced by famine'.[11]

Fig. 5 Many of those who perished in the Macroom area were buried in the mass grave at Carrigastyra, Clondrohid, County Cork. [Photo: Tomas Kelly]

# Emigration to North America in the era of the Great Famine, 1845–55

## Kerby A. Miller

Although perhaps one million Irishmen and women had emigrated to North America between 1815 and 1844, the exodus that occurred during and immediately after the Great Famine was unprecedented in both scale and character. Between 1845 and 1855 almost 1.5 million Irish sailed to the United States, and another 340,000 embarked for British North America, although most (about two-thirds) soon re-migrated to the US. In addition, between 200,000 and 300,000 settled permanently in Great Britain, and at least 50,000 went to Australia, New Zealand and lesser destinations. Altogether, over 2.1 million Irish – about one-fourth of Ireland's pre-Famine inhabitants – left the island; more people emigrated in merely eleven years than during all the two centuries preceding. Between this mass migration and the appalling Famine mortality, an entire generation was virtually swept from the land: only one out of every three Irishmen and Irishwomen born around 1831 died at home of old age – in Munster only one out of four.[1]

### DESPERATE FLIGHT

Irish emigration normally occurred in spring or early summer, and the potato blight made its first appearance in late summer 1845. Nevertheless, that year nearly 75,000 Irish, more than in any previous season, departed for North America. In 1846, when blight destroyed almost the entire potato crop, over 100,000 people left the island, about two-thirds of them bound directly for the United States. Both emigrants and observers now described Ireland as 'doomed and starving', and the exodus assumed the appearance of desperate flight, as thousands risked the perils of winter voyages and embarked without capital or even adequate provisions. In 'Black '47' departures more than doubled: over 214,000 people embarked for North America – 'running away from fever . . . and hunger, with money scarcely sufficient to pay passage for and find food for the voyage'. About 117,000 of the 1847 emigrants sailed directly to the US, but another 100,000 of the very poorest took the cheaper voyage to Canada,

EMIGRANTS ARRIVAL AT CORK.—A SCENE ON THE QUAY.

Fig. 1 'Emigrants arrival at Cork – a scene on the quay', *The Illustrated London News*, 10 May 1851 where their numbers and needs overwhelmed port authorities and local charities. Weakened by malnutrition and disease, at least a third of the Irish who sailed to British North America, and nearly a tenth of those who went directly to the US, perished on the 'coffin ships' or shortly after debarkation, particularly on Grosse Île and Partridge Island, the hastily constructed and pestilential quarantine stations at Quebec and Saint John's, New Brunswick, respectively. As historian Oliver McDonagh wrote, the 1847 exodus was less an emigration than a 'headlong flight of refugees', which 'bore all the marks of panic and hysteria'.[2]

The pace of departures slackened in late 1847 and early 1848, but another total potato-crop failure in summer 1848 produced a second and even greater wave of emigrants, which crested in 1851 and did not subside to pre-Famine levels until 1855. Annual departures overseas rose from 177,000 in 1848 to a peak of 245,000 in 1851, declining slowly thereafter to 134,000 in 1854 and 63,000 in 1855. After 1848, the annual proportion of emigrants going to Canada was merely 10–15% – compared with 45% in 1847 – a sign that the flight overseas of the most destitute had abated. Probably a majority of all the Famine-era emigrants (especially if the poorest migrants to Britain are included) – as well as most of those who perished in Ireland itself – were tenants (particularly sub-tenants) with fewer than ten acres, cottiers, or landless labourers, many of whom (perhaps as many as one million!) had been evicted from their holdings or thrown out of employment by landlords or by strong farmers. In the latter years of the crisis, however, large numbers of formerly 'comfortable' farmers also emigrated, as grain prices collapsed in the aftermath of Parliament's repeal of the Corn Laws (1846) and as the twin burdens of rents and poor-rates – and thus the threats of bankruptcy and eviction – persuaded or forced them to join the exodus. Of these, the more fortunate left with the proceeds of sales of crops, livestock, or tenant-right, but the largest proportion of late Famine emigrants financed departures only with remittances (often prepaid passage tickets), which now poured into Ireland from relatives in North America. Thus, whereas in 1846 clearly identifiable family groups had comprised nearly half of the Irish who arrived in New York, by the early 1850s the largest numbers were the earlier emigrants' siblings, spouses, children, and even aged parents, who had been left behind (often in the poorhouses) when impoverished families had been unable to finance more than one or two initial departures – usually of the strongest male members deemed most likely to survive and find work overseas. 'Dear Pat', begged one Irish mother in County Kilkenny to her emigrant son, 'remember . . . what you promised . . . to take me and little Dickey out' of Ireland; 'for the honour of our lord Jesus Christ and his Blessed Mother hurry', for 'little Dickey longs and

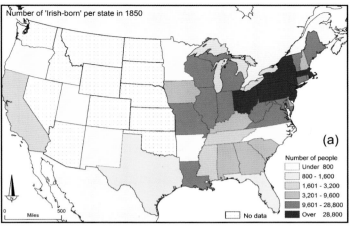

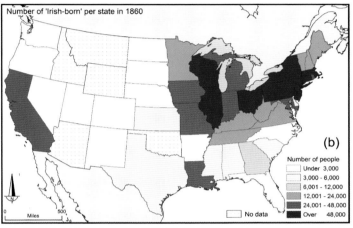

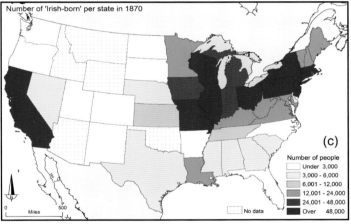

Figs 2a, 2b and 2c. DISTRIBUTION OF IRISH EMIGRANTS ACROSS THE UNITED STATES IN 1850, 1860 AND 1870.

sighs both night and day . . . and says [he] would not be hungry' if he were in America. Responding to such heart-wrenching pleas, in 1850–55 the Irish in the US remitted home an annual average of over £1.2 million, principally to reunite their kindred in the New World.[3]

### EMIGRATION TRENDS

In 1845–55 the broad patterns of pre-Famine emigration could still be discerned. For example, Famine emigration rates were highest in areas – such as de-industrialising south Ulster, north Leinster, and north Connacht, and the commercialised-farming areas of south Leinster, east Munster, and east Connacht – that had witnessed the

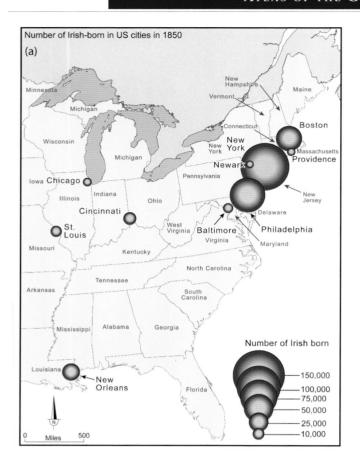

Number of Irish-born in US cities in 1850

(a)

Number of Irish born

150,000
100,000
75,000
50,000
25,000
10,000

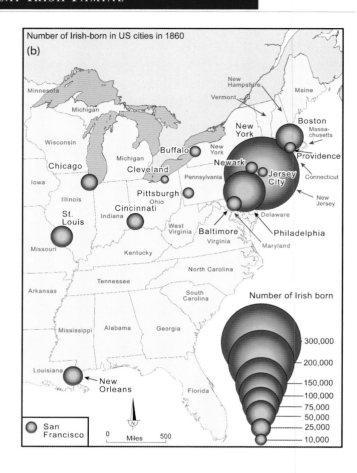

Number of Irish-born in US cities in 1860

(b)

Number of Irish born

300,000
200,000
150,000
100,000
75,000
50,000
25,000
10,000

San Francisco

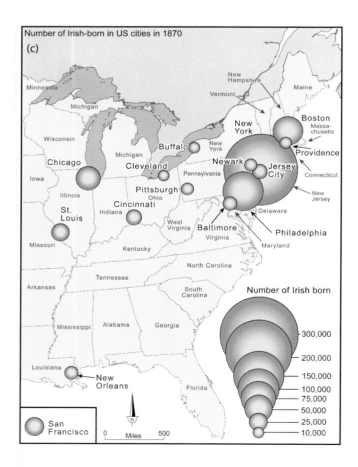

Number of Irish-born in US cities in 1870

(c)

Number of Irish born

300,000
200,000
150,000
100,000
75,000
50,000
25,000
10,000

San Francisco

Figs 3a, 3b and 3c. DISTRIBUTION OF IRISH EMIGRANTS IN AMERICAN CITIES IN 1850, 1860 AND 1870. As both these series of maps show, the Irish Famine immigrants (1850) and those that followed them (1860, 1870) did not tend to follow the rest of the American population as they moved south and west along the frontier. By 1850, the broad parameters of the shape of Irish settlement in the United States had been established and these patterns were consolidated geographically and socially rather than extended during the 1860s and 1870s (Figs 2a, 2b and 2c). Usually poor and unskilled, the Irish concentrated in the most urban and industrialised states in the northeast of the union although as the 1860 pattern shows there was significant if exceptional rural settlement by Irish settlers in the midwestern states of Wisconsin and Minnesota. Apart from settling in the cities of New Orleans, Mobile, Savannah and Charleston, the southern states – more rural and less industrialised – were not so attractive to Irish migrants, whereas California leaped into importance during the 1850s and became a major focus of migration by the 1860s and 1870s. Overall, Irish immigrant settlement was focused on some of America's greatest cities (Figs 3a, 3b and 3c), particularly Boston, New York and Philadelphia – and, by 1870, on Chicago. By 1870, Chicago contained over one-third of the Irish population of the state of Illinois – and by 1900 Chicago's Irish population had risen to two-thirds. Yet Irish migration was highly city selective – Detroit in Michigan, Cleveland in Ohio and, for many years, Wisconsin's Milwaukee were not so favoured. In contrast, by 1870 Irish-born populations constituted more than 20% of the total city populations of Boston, Lawrence, Lowell and Worcester in Massachusetts, New York City and Jersey City, as well as Troy (in upstate New York) and Scranton and Pittsburgh further west. In many other cities and boroughs including Albany, Baltimore, Brooklyn, Buffalo, Cambridge (Mass.), Hartford, Lynn, Newhaven and Providence, Irish immigrant populations constituted at least 15% of total city population while there were many other cities in 1870 – Buffalo, Chicago, Newark, Philadelphia, Rochester, St Louis, Syracuse, Utica and Wilmington – where the Irish contributed more than 10% to each city's total population. And in sharp contrast to many other European immigrant groups, almost half of the Irish immigrants were women.

October the 8th 1850

Dear Patt,

When I receivd your letter on the [8th?] of August last; I wrote you Back an answer hoping that you receivd it with A check of thirty shillings in our greatest of want and [?]    Because Mrs Morrisy got a letter and it said that you wrote me a letter with thirty shillings and that I Did not think [it] worth my while [to] answer it. But, Dear Patt I did write you Back [an] answer thanking you for it as I hope god will Reward you for it    the day that I Receivd your letter last John was 8 weeks without hearing Mass without a stich on him But in Bed And my pett coat And coat of myself was pledged    [I was] out of all without one Bit to eat that morning when [I] Receivd your letter and Shure I could not But thank you then for Getting it. Know Dear Patt we are all without a place to lea our head there that we were lodgding under Jamess Street arch    we were put out of it    And know we are getting for god Sake a few Nights logging up in the Sconce untill I get your letter. And this day we are without a bit to eat and I wood Be Dead long go only for two Nebours that ofen gives me a Bit for god Sake    But little ever I thought that it wood come to my turn to beg No more    I wood Not Beg only for your fathers death But [welcome?] By the will of god for god is good still.

Dear Patt the Morning that James and Mary was  going away I had [not a penny?] And the blankets Bed and Boots of my feet was pledged    And the little things I had in the auction went for very little    And since the day that the[y] left Kilkenny there was never [a] shilling erndd up to this day    Pat I cant let you know whow we are suffring unless you were in sta[r]vation and want without freind or fellow to give you a shilling or a penny    then you wood know what we are suffering    But on my too Bended Neese fresh and fasting I pray to god that you Nor one of you may never know Nor suffer what we are suffering At the present

Dear patt you told me to ask John Nolan of Clara wood he keep John and Joseph for a time And I asked him wood he do that    he said he [would] keep them from the day that I wood go untill whatever time I wood write from America for them    And John wood Be well able to work at coopering if he got it to do. But Dear Patt Mrs Lawlor would not give a penny for gods sake if I died Dead on the street Nor one Belonging to me unless John Nolan of Clara    Mrs Lawlor huspant Died in prison for det    But thanks Bit of god whatever me or his childer thats here is suffering your father died and was Burryd the way that [he] livd thats Respectable and Desant what I hope you and the Rest of his childering will do the same under the Mercyful hand of god

Know Dear Patt what you promised to take me and little dickey out    for the honour of our Lord Jasus Christ and his Blessed Mother hurry and take us out of this hoping that if I was out that I cood do annything for the other two that will Be here after me    Dear Patt you told me that Julia feels to her hart for me But tell her she wood feel ten times wors if she [k]new Rightly the way I am for the Blackest stranger that wood have feelence  wood feel for the way we all are Dear patt i Roat to James this week After I roat to you last And Never got an answer sence from him waht I wonder very mutch of for he promised for to take John and Joseph out the 24th of last June And Never Roat us a letter Sence Send me word in your next letter is he in Provdence atale or how is he going on And send word how Mary is As you Roat to me that she was in good health and in good Sittuwation And I hope she is in that still    Dear patt go to Mary And ask her for the love and honour of god to asist you to Bring me and little dicksy out of this and tell her that poor little Dicksy longs and sighs Both Night And morning untill he sees her and his two little Nieces and Nephews And Julia the poor child says I wood not Be hungary if I was Near them    he says if the letter came in tomorrow for him and his mother that he wood lep in to the shipp Neket as he stands to make haste to see them all

tell Mary that this is the poorest prospect of a winter that ever I had sence I began the world    without house Nor home    fire Nor candlelight    freind Nor fellow Now a Bit of food to eat    So tell her thats my prosspects. Dear Pat if James Be in provvence or whenever you meet him tell him that is is bad to make a game of the aflecked

I [pray] that gods holy Spirit may Be with ye all and send me the letter as Quick as No[vember?]    I Send my love and Best Respects to ye all and gods blessings Be with ye all    Joh[n] Sends his love and Best Respects to Mary and to ye all Joseph Sends his love and Best Respects to ye all    John Nolan of Clara and famely Sends their love and Best Respects to ye all.

Thomas Mackay James Mackay Sends their love and Best Respects to ye all and the [?] [wish?] every turn to [?] your letter

your loving mother untill Death

By John Nolan

Fig. 4 Letter from Mrs Nolan, Clara Upper [parish of Clara, County Kilkenny] to her son Patrick, Providence, Rhode Island, 8 October 1850. [Source: Private collection]

heaviest out-migrations in the 1830s and early 1840s. Indeed, in most parts of the island there appears to have been an inverse relationship between Famine rates of excess mortality and of emigration, with mortality greater than departures in impoverished west Munster and west Connacht, for instance, whereas the opposite was true in the more commercialised eastern and midlands regions.[4] Likewise, although overseas observers often described all Famine emigrants as the dregs of humanity, destitute and unskilled, the latter's wretched appearance on North American docks – often after long, disease-ridden voyages – disguised the presence among them of farmers, craftsmen, and shopkeepers, who possessed capital and skills not inferior to their pre-Famine predecessors. Moreover, although some 50,000 Famine emigrants were 'assisted' to North America (plus c.5,000 to Australia) – that is, given free passages (but usually nothing else) by landlords or poor law officials, in return for peaceably abandoning their homesteads – in general it was true that the most deeply impoverished Irish either perished in Ireland or could afford only to migrate, for a few pence, via cattle boats to Britain, as even the cheapest tickets to Canada still cost between £2 and £5.[5]

Despite certain continuities, however, the Famine exodus across the Atlantic was significantly different from the emigrations of the preceding decades. Statistical evidence confirms contemporary beliefs that the emigrants of 1845–55 *were* generally much poorer and less skilled than those who had embarked before the onset of the potato blight. For example, although the Irish who landed in New York were reportedly much superior in status to those who debarked in Canada, in 1846 about 75% of the former were classified, in their ships' manifests, as labourers and servants – compared with 60% so listed in 1836 – rather than as craftsmen (12%), farmers (9.5%), or businessmen and professionals (2%). Likewise, in the early 1850s Ireland's Emigration Commissioners reported that labourers and servants annually comprised between 80 and 90% of all overseas emigrants; and, as noted earlier, the great majority of these required money from abroad (or other assistance) to pay their passages. In addition, an abnormally large number of Famine emigrants were impaired on arrival overseas, at least initially unable to fend for themselves, either because they were elderly or mere children or suffering from physical or mental debilities – often no doubt the results of severe malnutrition. Many of the latter – like Patrick Coughlin and Mary Murphy, who respectively were 'aged, infirm [and] stone blind' and 'insane, now dead' – perished soon after disembarking; but thousands of spouses and children, who landed in relatively good condition, also suffered severely when, as frequently occurred, partners or parents soon succumbed to disease, overwork or industrial accidents in North America.[6]

In terms of their religious, regional, and cultural backgrounds, Famine emigrants also differed significantly from their predecessors. Roughly half the pre-Famine emigrants to the New World had been Protestants, primarily Presbyterians from Ulster; however, although Protestants comprised about one-fourth of Ireland's population, they may have accounted for no more than a tenth of the Famine emigrants. Moreover, although most pre-Famine Catholic emigrants were from English-speaking or rapidly anglicising districts of northern and eastern Ireland, the Famine exodus had a decidedly Gaelic character. Munster and Connacht, where in 1841 about half the people spoke Irish, contributed at least 50% of the Famine emigrants, and this author estimates that at least a fourth to a third of all those who left Ireland in 1845–55 – perhaps a half-million people – were Irish-speakers, while hundreds of thousands of others were at least familiar with the language. Most native American Protestants, fixated on the newcomers' Catholicism, poverty and drinking customs, usually overlooked the emigrants' linguistic characteristics, and the anglicised members of the Irish–American bourgeoisie often ignored them, at least publicly. However, priests from Ireland regularly, and Irish–American politicians occasionally, testified to the necessity of addressing Famine emigrants in their preferred – and sometimes only – language.[7]

### 'MERE SURVIVAL'

Finally, the motives governing most Famine emigration were qualitatively different from those that had inspired earlier departures. Although neo-liberal historians wrongly impute 'modern' capitalist/individualistic

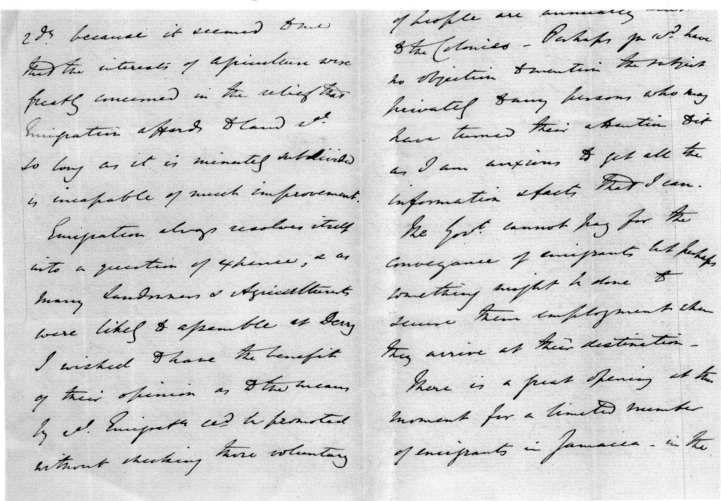

Fig. 5 The Lord Lieutenant of Ireland, Lord Clarendon, writes to the Duke of Leinster on 7 August 1847, convinced of the necessity of promoting emigration as a cure for Ireland's agricultural ills. He wants to elicit the views of Irish landowners and is aware of the duke's influence amongst this landholding elite. The cost of emigration is a key concern: 'Emigration always resolves itself into a question of expense as many landowners and agriculturalists were likely to appreciate . . . I wished to have the benefit of their opinion as to the means by which emigration can be promoted without checking those voluntary exertions by which large numbers of people are annually sent to the colonies . . . The Govt. cannot pay for the conveyance of emigrants but perhaps something might be done to secure them employment when they arrive at their destination. There is a great opening for a limited number of emigrants in Jamaica.' [Source: Public Record Office of Northern Ireland, D3078/3/34/63]

Fig. 6  Erskine Nicol (1825-1904) *An Ejected Family* (1853) oil on canvas [Source: National Gallery of Ireland]

ambitions to pre-Famine Irish emigrants, there is no doubt that the latter's oft-expressed desire to achieve 'independence' in the New World was quite different from the Famine emigrants' typical goal of mere survival.[8] Thus, panicked desperation screams from the letters of would-be emigrants, such as Mary Rush of County Sligo, who begged for assistance to escape the Famine's horrors: 'For God's sake,' she wrote to her father in Canada, 'take us out of poverty, and don't let us die of the hunger.' Likewise, Irish relief workers observed that the peasants' traditional resistance to emigration, particularly strong among western Irish-speakers, had crumbled in the face of mass starvation and epidemic disease; and contemporary ballads sang of death and despair, when 'every hope [was] blighted' along with the potato crops.[9] Although by the early 1850s hunger and fever had abated, evictions continued on a massive scale, and farmers' letters in those years indicate that desperation and demoralisation were even increasing among those who had escaped the worst physical suffering of 1846–48. Ireland 'is abandoned', despaired one woman, Judith Phelan, in Queen's County in 1849–50: 'the landlords sending them away from the cradle to the ditch'. 'We were all ejected in March', she lamented. 'I think [we] will see you in America before long.' Indeed, starvation, disease and the enormous migrations, which already had occurred, so decimated

many areas, socially and culturally, that their disheartened inhabitants often felt little desire to remain in what was now but a sorrowing echo of a once-vibrant society. Thus, the Famine wrought such devastating changes that many emigrants – like Edmund Ronayne, the son of a typhus victim in east County Cork, and William Murphy, a Protestant from County Antrim but also a poor orphan – had lost all that meant 'home' before their departures; and, like Ronayne and Murphy, many no doubt spent the rest of their lives, wandering physically and/or psychologically through North America, searching for something irretrievably lost in the shambles of their own and their people's past.[10]

THE IMPACT OF THE HOST SOCIETY

On one hand, Famine emigration contributed enormously to the societies where the Irish settled as well as to the development of those societies' Irish Catholic communities. In the United States the Famine Irish provided a reserve army of labourers, mostly semi- and unskilled, whose strength and low wages promoted the construction of the American republic's vast urban-industrial and transportation networks (including the northern states' burgeoning railroad system), as well as the rampant exploitation of raw materials, as in mining and lumbering. Likewise, the large proportion of single women among the Famine emigrants promoted the elaboration

Raheen   May 23   1849

My Dear terese   I Recd your Letter on the 20th inst A[nd] am very happy to hear from you   [I] am much fretted to hear of you being alone So far from frend or brother   it grieves me very much to hear of your Brother treating you With So much Coolness   however I hope you are not alone still if you put yourself under the prottection of Jesus mary A[nd] Joseph you Will find Comfort in every thing you do A Company also   I intreat of you to do this A[nd] mind your duty to god   by So doing you will have Success   My Dear terese I must Say we are all alon[e] for what frinds We have at present   I am now nearly as Lonly as you are Since My Poor father died   he departed thus Life in Novembe[r] 26th 1847 he went to bed in good hea[l]th A[nd] at two a Clock he took to Snore more than usual   he had Just got the rights of the Church when he depar[t]ed may the Lord have mercy on his Soul   I fear the ingratitude of his children shorfnd his days A[nd] was A trouble to him for as he often Said Every Man that Rared Children A[nd] Sent them to america had Some Relief from them but him alon[e] moreoever in those Crying times now for the Last three years that ireland is Suffering hunger A[nd] hardship as We have Lost our Crops   you may gess what state we are in Wherin We must buy every bit we eat now nearly four years A[nd] What is Worse no earning no Circulation of money in ireland at present no trade   I must tell you that one ile of our Chapel Would hold our Congration on Sunday at presnt   there is numbers of people dead A[nd] Sick at present With many disorders from the effects of hungar A[nd] bad food as many famlys are now Living on the Wild erribs A[nd] Cannot get that Same   neither Can they go hear Sunday mass as they Were nessissated to Sell A plenge their night A[nd] day Covering to get provision   also there is numbers of our frinds A[nd] Neighbours in the poor house that Were in good Circumst[ances] When you Were yong   We often Say you had good Success to Leave this unfortunate ireland   I often Wished I had gone with you   the person you Recvd the Letter from Buffalo is your Cousin Salley Carrol   she is now Livng With her uncle martin Rohan in buffalo   she mentiond in her Last Letter that she wrote A Letter to st Louise to you but Recvd no answer   I hope you Will Write to her   you may Direct it to Martin Rohan for her   he Lives in Buffalo Eriey County   als[o] I hve to Let you [know] that her mother mary Carrol A[nd] her daughter ellane is dead Last June   also Mrs Hook A[nd] her daughter Ann A Patt   we have not on[e] of the hook  family in Raheen at present   also your uncle James Lalor A Wife Wer both buirred on the one day A her brother Send the children to America   We hav no Letter from Patt or margret Since you Went   We have Reason to believe they have forgot us   matt Berger Sent one but never mentiond there names   he Said they heard of the poverty of

ireland as I Suppose the distress of ireland Would pierce the hard of A stone We Cannot Boast of it piercing our nearest frinds   Were it not for America provision A[nd] money Ireland Would have been Lost before this   the poeple of ireland is So oppressed With poorrate A[nd] taxes that the Landlord has Scarce anny thing to get after   the farmers are all giving up their Land to the Landlord A[nd] Cannot paey the many Cesses that are Levying on evry other day   all by means of the poor houses Suport the poor--

My Dear terese I hope you will pray often for thy Grandfather A[nd] have his nam[e] inserted in the dead List as he never forgot you   he had your name to heart oftener than all the rest of his Children   he often Called Briget terese A[nd] then he Would Say may the Lord be with poor terese Which Caused him to Shed tears freq[u]ently for you   I Would be very happy that you Would Come Back to st Louse or Rather to New york that we might have A better oppertuny of hear[in]g from you   I hope you Will Write freque[n]t[l]y to us as it Would be A great Consolation to us to hear from you   I hope you Will Write as soon as you Receve this A[nd] Let us Know how you are geting on   I Will Write to John on this Week   We have no Letter from him these four months   he Let us Know of Mary death at that time   I Sent h[i]m two Letters Since but Recd no anser   I Would Wish you Would Let me know What William Phelan you mentioned in Your Letter or where he Lived before he went to america   I Will also Write to Sara Carrol to Buffalo A[nd] Let her Know Where you are asit Was her Last promise to me She Would hold A Corrospondence With you when she would Land in America   We are all in good hea[l]th at present thanks be to god for all his goodness   Salley has two Children Bridget A[nd] Patt   they are two very good Children   they are all the Consolation we have   they Buried one A few Days after my father namd Dave   Denny is going on very Well   he is A very industrious man   my mother is very Delicate Since me father Died   I hope You Will Write as Soon as you Receve this   I intract of you to Come nearer to us that We may hav an oppertuny of hearing from you oftener   it [is] useless for me to Say any more to you With Regard to the State of ireland as I Suppose you have it by paper account   I Could not  tell you the many Difficulty occured Since you Left ireland for it would fill Many Newspapers ---

No more at presnt from you affect[ionate] A[nd] Lov[in]g A[un]t Judith Phelan Raheen--

My Moth[er] Sally Denny A[nd] Bridget Desirs to b[e] Rem[ember]ed to you

A Little Patt

Fig. 7 Letter from Judith Phelan, Raheen, Queen's County, to her niece, Teresa Lalor, Memphis, TN, 23 May 1849. [Source: Private collection]

of the American middle class, through the provision of cheap domestic servants, as well as the expansion of low-cost factory production in New England and elsewhere. With respect to the development of Irish–American Catholic society, the Famine emigrants both impelled and contributed to the enormous expansion of the Catholic Church in the US. They also fortified the strength (and locally began to assume leadership) of the Democratic Party in northern US states and cities (otherwise vitiated by sectional conflict and civil war), contributed at least 200,000 bodies to the mass slaughter of 1861–65, played crucial roles in the development of organised labour, and essentially created mass-based Irish–American nationalism. Conversely, with respect to Irish–American Protestants, it is often argued that for them the Famine emigrants served as a sort of foil, or negative reference group, which spurred their communal self-designation as *not* 'Irish' but as 'Scotch–Irish' and hence superior and more acceptable to America's Protestant bourgeoisie.[11]

For all these and other reasons (including the challenge of what its critics called the 'Scotch–Irish myth'), the Famine and its emigrants assumed, and still enjoy, iconic status in Irish–American Catholic history, identity and memory. Yet, in the context of overall Irish Catholic emigration to the United States, this is somewhat para-

doxical. At least a half-million Irish Catholics had already come to the US between the American Revolution and the Famine's eve, and over three million would emigrate to the US between 1856 and 1929, which means that the 1.5 million Famine-era emigrants comprised at best only a third of the five million Irish Catholics who settled in the American republic during the 'long nineteenth century'. By contrast, this author estimates that the Irish Catholics who in 1846–54 settled in Canada comprised between 40 and 45% of all the Irish Catholics who did so between 1815 and 1854, when the overwhelming majority of all nineteenth-century Irish emigration (of Protestants as well as Catholics) to British North America occurred. Ironically, however, middle-class Irish–Canadian Catholics (especially in Ontario), or at least many of their historians, have denigrated the scale and importance of Famine emigration to Canada, emphasising instead the less impoverished and allegedly more 'respectable' Irish Catholics who settled there in the pre-Famine decades.[12]

### EXPLAINING THE FAMINE

This paradox is related in turn to the controversial question of how Irish Catholics, both in Ireland and in their varying 'national' contexts abroad, perceived or

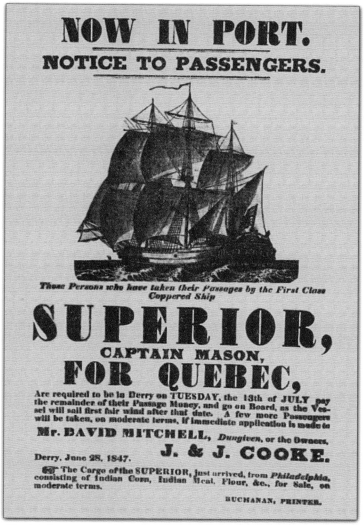

Fig. 8 Advertisement for the *Superior*, an emigrant ship built for J. & J. Cooke, shipping agents of Derry, in 1845 at a cost of £3,200. It was on this particular voyage to Quebec during the late summer of 1847 that 60 of the 360 passengers perished from fever and were buried at sea. The ship subsequently arrived at Grosse-Île with many others sick on board. [Source: Public Record Office of Northern Ireland, T. 1665].

'explained' the Famine and its attendant mass migrations. It has long been argued, for example, that experiences and memories of the Famine engendered 'the savage hatred of England that animate[d] great bodies of Irishmen on either side of the Atlantic', inspiring repeated efforts – beginning with the Fenian movement of 1858–70 – to destroy Irish landlordism and liberate Ireland from British rule.[13] Certainly, many ordinary emigrants' personal letters – as well as the speeches and writings of Irish–American political, nationalist and even religious spokesmen – demonstrate that Irish Americans commonly blamed the British government and Ireland's 'alien' landlord class for the Famine and for their consequent 'exile' overseas, and, in the words of Michael Flanagan, an emigrant in California, prayed and plotted that someday both would receive 'a just reward for their oppression'.[14]

To be sure, some scholars have argued that the Irish in Ireland itself interpreted the Famine, at least initially, in religious terms – as an 'act of God', rather than of British

or even landlord malevolence – and often expressed gratitude for both official and private relief and especially for landlord-assisted emigration during the crisis. However, an unprecedentedly large share of the Famine emigrants were poor country people, from traditional and often Irish-speaking communities, whose customary beliefs and historical memories had long conceived *all* Irish emigration as tantamount to sorrowful 'exile' and, at least since the late 1500s, had attributed it to the tyranny of the *Sasanaigh*, i.e. the Saxons or the English, particularly the Protestant landlord class imposed by past conquests and confiscations. For decades prior to the Famine, Daniel O'Connell and other Irish nationalists had striven with much success to politicise and mobilise these ancient resentments, and it would not be surprising if the horrific events of 1845–55 served to corroborate and intensify them. After all, the wholesale clearances of grieving paupers, carried out under British laws and often enforced by British troops, inevitably linked the Government to the cruellest actions of the Irish landlord class.[15]

## SOCIAL AND CLASS CONFLICTS

Yet it may be equally important, in terms of the Famine's future interpretation, that the crisis not only exposed the hollow and hypocritical nature of the Act of Union, but also the deep social conflicts within the Irish Catholic community itself. For example, an unknown but surely very large proportion of Famine sufferers were not evicted by Protestant landlords but by Catholic strong and middling farmers, who drove off their subtenants and cottiers, and dismissed their labourers and servants, both to save themselves from ruin and to consolidate their own properties. Hundreds of thousands of Catholic (and Protestant) farmers also benefited, directly or indirectly, from their poor neighbours' distress, evictions and deaths, which enabled the former to expand their holdings of both land and livestock. Likewise, Catholic (as well as Protestant) food merchants and money-lenders often profited from their customers' misery. Moreover, subtler psychological processes were also at work in the crisis. As one historian has noted, the disintegrations of personal relationships and the social dislocations (including panic emigration) which occurred after 1845 reflected a widespread 'failure of morale' as well as of the potato crops.[16] As a result, it was perhaps only natural that those who survived the crisis, often at others' expense, or who emerged with more property than they had held before, would feel great personal shame and/or popular resentment for their violations of traditional, communal norms – and that therefore they would seek 'explanations' for what had occurred which would project all blame on 'outsiders', particularly on their community's traditional antagonists.

Thus, although at first both Irish nationalist politicians'

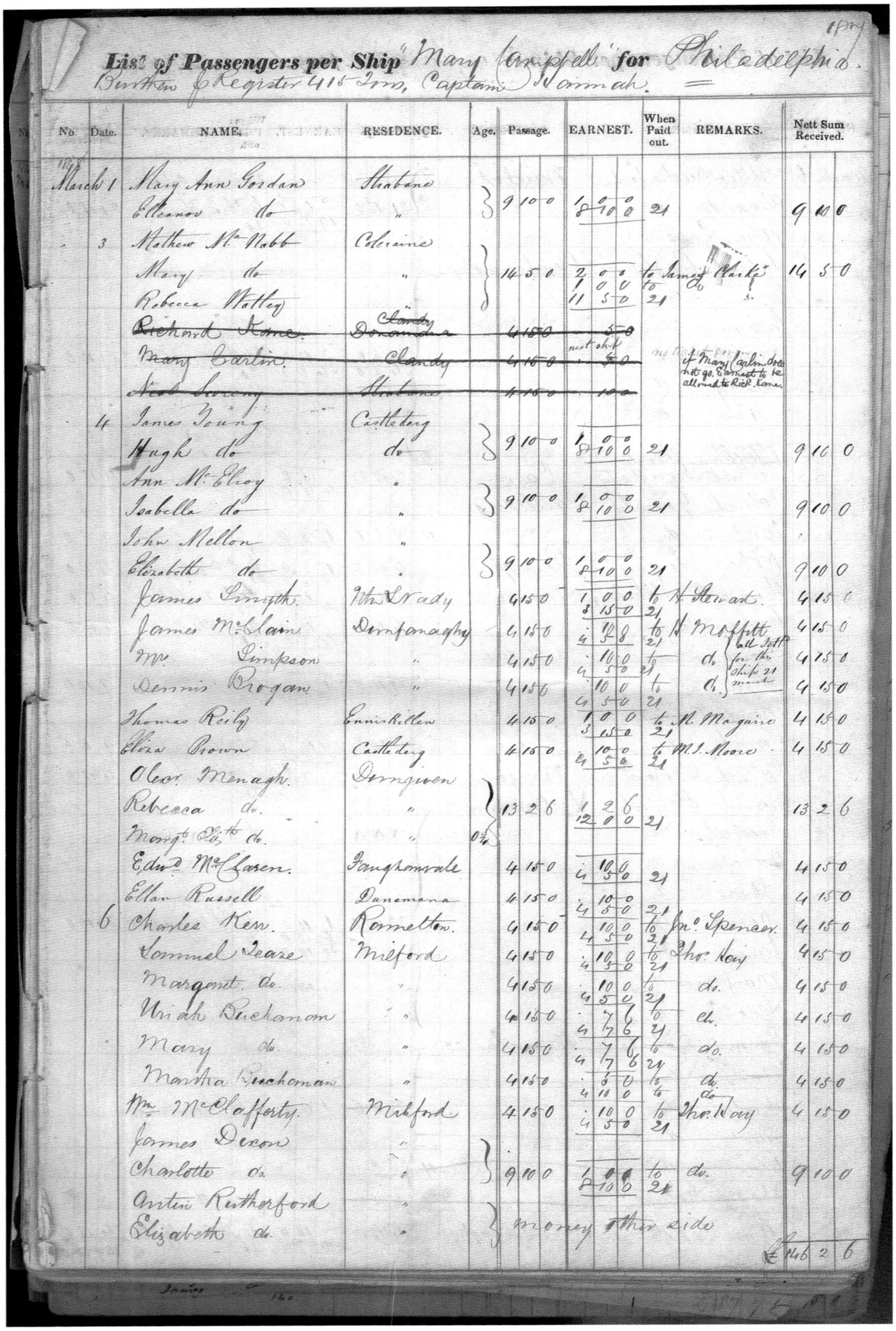

Fig. 9 Page from the passenger list of the *Mary Campbell* bound for Philadelphia (March 1848), a ship belonging to the J. & J. Cooke line operating from the port of Derry. [Source: Public Record Office of Northern Ireland, D2892/1/1]

and Catholic religious leaders' responses to the Famine were hesitant, confused and contradictory, by 1847–48 Catholic clerics and nationalists – including followers of the now-deceased O'Connell as well as the more radical Young Ireland movement – were in full attack on the British government's inadequate relief measures, on the Irish landlord class, and on what they stigmatised as 'forced' emigration or 'exile'. However, as the maverick Young Ireland theorist, James Fintan Lalor, recognised, only a plan of systemic *social* as well as political revolution, involving the destruction of Irish landlordism itself, could eradicate the root causes of rural distress and perhaps inspire the masses to rebellion. Yet, most middle-class Catholic nationalists (wealthy farmers and townsmen), as well as the overwhelming majority of Catholic clergymen, were much too conservative to countenance a peasant assault on Irish property relationships. Hence, it is likely that, aside from John Mitchel and a few other dedicated revolutionaries, the primary function of Catholic leaders' escalating attacks on what they called 'British tyranny' and 'forced emigration' was not to inspire violence or even to halt the exodus, but rather to articulate popular outrage in ways that would reunite the remnants of the fractured Irish Catholic 'nation' behind bourgeois and clerical leadership.

If so, it was ironic that it was Young Ireland's futile but symbolically crucial rebellion of 1848 – vehemently

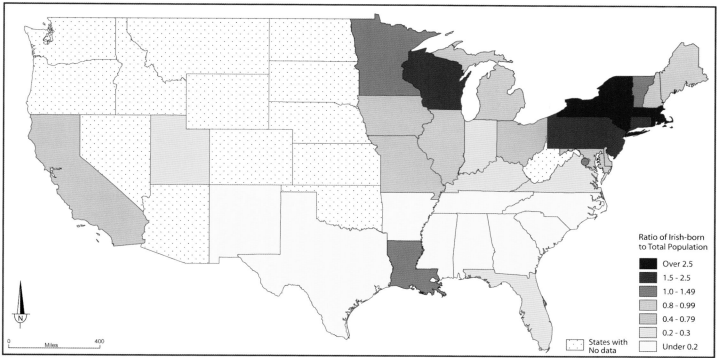

Fig. 10 RELATIVE LOCATION OF IRISH-BORN PEOPLE IN THE UNITED STATES IN 1850. The pattern of Irish settlement in the United States has been very stable since the Famine migrations. Since 1850, at least 60% of the Irish have lived in Massachusetts, New York, Pennsylvania and Illinois. By dividing each state's share of the Irish population with the state's share of the total population in 1850, one can arrive at a figure (called 'the location quotient') which, when above 1.00 signifies that the Irish are overrepresented in that state while a figure below 1.00 signifies that they are underrepresented. As the map shows, Irish immigrants in 1850 are clearly overrepresented in most of the New England states, led by Massachusetts at 2.8. (By 1940, Irish overrepresentation in that state had reached 5.5, i.e. there were five and a half times more Irish in Massachusettes in 1940 than one would expect from the state's total share of the US population as a whole.) In contrast, in 1850 the Irish were underrepresented in the rural states of Maine and New Hampshire. However, it was in the Middle Atlantic states of New York, New Jersey and Pennsylvania that the Irish were most strongly overrepresented and this pattern became even more emphasised in the 20th century. In the midwest in 1850, only Wisconsin had a greater proportion of Irish than the state's share of total population would warrant. Illinois (and Chicago), however, would soon become dominant in the region while Minnesota was briefly overrepresented but this pattern was not sustained. Amongst the southern Atlantic states only Washington, DC, is overrepresented in 1850, but later on Delaware emerges as does Louisiana among the Gulf states. The mountain states of the west must await the mining booms of the later 19th century before the Irish become significant settlers, especially in Nevada and Montana. In 1850, the Irish were still underrepresented in California but this changed rapidly by 1860 and peaked in the 1880s. (Overrepresentation in that state was still sustained until the 1930s.) It is only since the 1960s that the descendants of the Irish have significantly increased their presence in the Sunbelt states, with Florida the leader. [See also Morton D. Winberg's work on 'Irish settlement in the United States, 1850–1980', *Eire–Ireland* (20, 1985), pp. 7–14].

opposed by nearly all Catholic politicians and clergy – that ensured the future credibility of a nationalist interpretation of the Famine and of Famine (and indeed all Irish) emigration. There is evidence, in several Famine emigrants' letters and in contemporary observations, that Young Ireland's politicisation of Famine suffering and emigration influenced at least some of the 1845–55 emigrants before their departures. More certain is that Mitchel's *Jail Journal* and the Young Irelanders' other writings and speeches provided much of the nationalist catechism for later generations on both sides of the ocean. Indeed, it is possible that Young Ireland's greatest ideological influence may have been on the Famine Irish, their descendants and later emigrants in the United States. In part, this was because so many Young Irelanders, such as Mitchel, themselves found refuge in the U.S., where their personal examples and exhortations gave credence to the argument that all Famine emigration was tantamount to political banishment. In part, it was also because that argument provided a traditional and communally binding 'explanation', for the Famine emigrants themselves, of what had happened

to them (and to their dead or abandoned relatives). Equally, it was important that Irish–American nationalists offered possible redemption as well as explanation, arguing that the emigrants' efforts and donations might yet liberate Ireland, destroy landlordism, and – in the words of a popular Fenian ballad – take 'Revenge for Skibbereen'.[17]

## IRISH–AMERICAN NATIONALISM

Finally, Irish–American nationalism, as it developed after 1845, might have been less persuasive and intense if the Famine emigrants' overall experiences in the United States had been less impoverished and embittering. To be sure, the Famine emigrants' condition in the US is a hotly debated subject among historians, partly because later generations of Irish Americans prefer to envision their ancestors' situations as more stable and 'respectable' – and as less isolated and estranged from 'mainstream' America – than contemporaries normally described, and partly because much depends on whether the large numbers of Famine emigrants who, according to the census-takers, held semi-skilled occupations (such as hod-carriers or bricklayers' assistants) should be bracketed with the masses of unskilled Irish day-labourers and domestic servants or with the much smaller minority of truly skilled emigrants (such as carpenters or stone masons).[18]

Indeed, some historians prefer to focus on the even smaller fractions of Famine emigrants who settled on American farms rather than, as did the great majority, in cities, industrial towns, and mining or lumbering camps, primarily in the northeastern and east north Central states. Likewise, some scholars find the Famine emigrants' rates of personal or real property acquisition in 1850–80 'impressive', although they lagged far behind those of native-born Protestants and even of non-Irish immigrants; moreover, such findings are based on the tiny (and perhaps unrepresentative) fraction of Irish men (and, extremely rarely, women) who can be traced, from one census to another, over several decades; and it is still an open question whether the Famine immigrants' remarkable geographical mobility, in search of decent employment and housing, connoted social improvement or chronic instability.[19]

In short, although there is no doubt that the overall mid- and late-nineteenth-century expansion of what was then the world's most dynamic urban-industrial economy generated significant long-term improvements in the socioeconomic status and welfare of Irish America, generally, these varied greatly by region (least in heavily Irish New England, for example) and were of principal advantage to the Famine emigrants' US-born children – and to later Irish emigrants, who, by the late 1800s and early 1900s, could take advantage of well-established kinship and patronage networks, which at mid-century had been rudimentary or impoverished. Most studies of Irish emigrants in 1850–80 – and most emigrants' own letters and memoirs (which of course were penned by literate emigrants, whereas perhaps half the Famine refugees were illiterate) – indicate that in general the Famine emigrants themselves rarely rose far from the bottom of American white society. In large seaport cities, such as Boston and New York, in smaller eastern industrial centres such as Lawrence, Newburyport, and Poughkeepsie, in midwestern towns like South Bend and Milwaukee, even in western frontier cities such as Denver and Sacramento: in all these, the Famine Irish were disproportionately concentrated in the lowest-paid, least-skilled, and most insecure and dangerous jobs. Usually they also experienced the highest rates of transience, substandard housing and sanitation, commitments to prisons and asylums, and excess mortality; indeed, one Irish–American alleged that 'the average

---

Napa City April 14 1877

Dear John

Your letter recalls me and brings to my mind how long it is since I wrote home and how much I am to blame for my neglect in this matter of correspondence. In this busy world one's time is necessarily taken up wiht the performance of his part on the stage of life and in this country where in particular where men are born an die in the midst of haste and hurry, the bare hard facts - the real life, things as they are must recieve a liberal share of attention   in fact just so much as to monopolize a man altogether mentally and physicaly, otherwise body and soul, to the banishment of every vestige of generous sentiment out of his body - nothing remaining but a walking log of wood as it were - anything but what the ideal Christian man should be. Your letter was very welcome, quite refreshing to one's mind after the long drought of home news. The paper which you sent also was a gift not alone to us but also to a little fellow who lives in Napa and who was "raised" in Tandpit  to whome we give those papers after reading ourselves. He is a harness maker by trade, he knew all the people, my Uncle Priest, the widow Burke Dickey Donnelly &c   he devours the news in the home papers with great relish and always enquires after the health of my Uncle Priest and wonders that he is still living and hearty - himself (like more of us) grown a grey old man, when a little sheaver had learned the Catechusm under the guidance of the Priest and had been amused at the oddities of Dicky Donnelly. This is the way the world goes round. The prospect of a good crop of wheat was never better in my time in this country than this season so far but just now there has appeared some indication of rust   this may or may not affect the wheat crop but will not be positivly known untill the beginning of June for good or evil. There is another gorsoon  at Pat's house, no fear of the name dying out anyway even if there be some old "Batchs" in the family.

I am unable at this moment to tell the truth as to the extent of Nicholas's family but I have reason to believe he is by no means behindhand.

You say there was some anxiety felt over there with respect to the beef market beign supplied from this country. I hope you do  not share in the anxiety because if you do I must say I have no sympathy with you - not a leif - in this respect. Who are they who are depending on the price of beed to make money, in Ireland, the rich gluttons who drove the industrious, the useful, part of the population into the Poorhouse or across the Atlantic - the Devils clothed in purple and fine linen who will receive a just reward for their oppression. If it be any solace to any one who is anxious about the future of this matter I can tell you it is my opinion, and there is good and sufficeint evidence to sustain the opinion that if the Texians can ship the beef to England and deliver it there at a price to pay themselves, and compete with the home stock raisers, raising beef at home is virtually at an end. The supply from this country is to use an Americanism "everlasting" and unlimited.

The vast extent of the State of Texas is almost a total stock range. The stock farms there are owned by individuals or two or three in company, the number of cattle owned by each of these vary from 5000 to 200000 head. Out of the increase of the cattle in Texas alone they could supply the United Kingdom with beef, and let them have it eighteen times a week and would scarcly miss what was exported. I hope I m[a]y live to see a good beefsteak within the reach of the poor man who earns it.

A gigantic fraud has been perpetrated in this country, a huge swindle the like of which has not been heard of in the history of the Republic. You know there has been an election for President lately, the man who now occupys that office has not a ghost of a title to it. He has come to be President through corruption and fraud having of course a legal semblance by reason of certain villanous laws which exist in the State of Louisiana. The whole business may be traced directly to a bitter feeling which has existed between the two great political parties since the War and which has been utilised by a crowd of lean hungry Yankees since that time to rob the South

I send you a paper at the same time as this note - I hope you will receive it, and hope all at home will be well     Your brother M. Flanagan

Fig. 11 Letter from Michael Flanagan, Napa City, California, to his brother, John Flanagan, Tubbertoby, Clogherhead, County Louth, 14 April 1877. [Source; Private collection]

length of life of the emigrant after landing here is six years; and many believe it is much less'[20] – probably an exaggeration, but one which reflected the Famine emigrants' alarmingly high mortality rates from disease, harsh climate, industrial accidents and sheer overwork. In addition, Irish Catholic emigrants in the mid-nineteenth-century US often encountered bitter ethno-religious prejudice, which assumed nationwide political dimensions in the Know-Nothing movement of the 1850s, and which often encouraged harsh exploitation by Protestant employers and co-workers. As one outraged emigrant declared, the life of an Irish worker in mid-century America was often 'despicable, humiliating, [and] slavish', for there 'was no love for him – no protection of life – [he] can be shot down, run through, kicked, cuffed, spat on – and no redress, but a response of served the damn son of an Irish b[itch] right, damn him'.[21]

Consequently, the Famine emigrants' harsh experiences in the US often engendered deep disillusion and profound homesickness among those who fondly imagined they had escaped to a land of refuge from poverty and prejudice. 'I have suffered more than I thought I could endure', wrote emigrant Daniel Rowntree, 'in a strange country, far from a friend, necessitated to go on public works from 4:00 of a summer morning until 8:00 at night, enduring the hardships of a burning sun, [and] then by sickness losing what I dearly earned'.[22] According to many observers, such conditions exacerbated 'normal' homesickness for rural Ireland's landscape and close-knit communities and encouraged many Famine emigrants to entertain unrealistic dreams of returning to Ireland. 'So hopelessly irksome do our people find their condition in this country', wrote one Irish–American journalist, 'that hundreds of thousands . . . would ask for no greater boon from Heaven . . . than an opportunity to stake their lives to regain a foothold on their native soil.'[23]

## GAINING RESPECT

Impoverished Irish labourers and servants, who dreamed such dreams and resented poverty and scorn in America, may therefore have been highly susceptible to the appeals of Irish–American nationalists, who characterised emigration as sorrowful 'exile', who blamed it – and the emigrants' plight abroad – on British and landlord oppression, and who promised that, by working and sacrificing to liberate Ireland, they could redeem their sufferings and enjoy at least a vicarious realisation of their longings. Irish–American Catholic clergy, who commonly characterised the Irish as a 'martyr nation', provided religious corroboration of such sentiments. Even personally ambitious or successful emigrants were attuned to nationalist appeals and images, both because they found them useful in mobilizing the Irish-American masses for bourgeois economic or

Fig. 12 James Fintan Lalor (1807–49) monument, sculpted by Rory Breslin, which is located outside the Laois County Council Chambers in Portlaoise. Lalor, a Young Ireland theorist believed in a social as well as a political revolution involving the destruction of Irish landlordism. [Photo: Frank Coyne]

political purposes, but also because they, themselves, had often endured Yankee prejudice, at least by association with their poorer countrymen, and as a result often concluded, like Famine emigrant Patrick Ford, that the Irish in America would never enjoy respect until Ireland itself was free and prosperous.[24]

Thus, Irish–American nationalism – and its recurrent theme that emigration was exile – could serve the social and political interests of Famine emigrants who aspired to full assimilation in bourgeois America at the same time that it could engage the imaginations of the great majority for whom such a goal was far distant or unattainable. Thus as well, Fenianism (like its bitter rival, the Catholic Church) not only mobilised the Irish–American masses for what ultimately became, for most of its leaders, domestic political projects, but also, with its avowed goal of transporting thousands of disaffected, armed emigrants back to Ireland, the movement provided an ideal (if ultimately futile) projection of the aspirations of those Famine emigrants

225

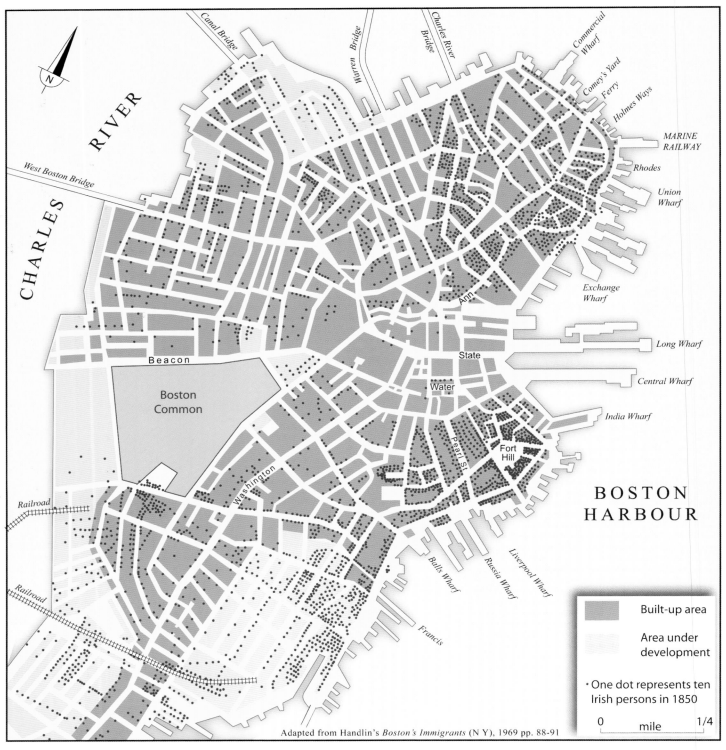

MARINE RAILWAY

BOSTON HARBOUR

Built-up area

Area under development

One dot represents ten Irish persons in 1850

0      mile      1/4

Adapted from Handlin's *Boston's Immigrants* (N Y), 1969 pp. 88-91

Fig. 13 STREET-WIDE DISTRIBUTION OF IRISH IN BOSTON IN 1850. As late as 1845, Boston was a city of small traders, artisans and great merchant princes. The flight of the famine-stricken Irish was to radically transform the population, economy and physical fabric of this city. By 1850, 35,287 Irish comprised 25.8% of the city's 136,881 population. Five years later there were over 46,000 Irish in the city proper and a further 21,000 Irish lived in the greater Boston area, including Cambridge, Charlestown and Roxbury. This map shows the street-wide distribution of the Irish in Boston in 1850. Almost half of the 'labourers' in the city in that year were Irish and 15% of the 'general house servants' were Irish-born. Overall described as 'unskilled, resourceless, perennially unemployed' (Handlin, p. 88), this Irish proletariat were crammed into these streets, financially unable to escape from the teeming, waterlocked peninsula that was the old city. The immigrant Irish concentrated around the commercial heart of the city – the narrow strip of piers and the small area of the city on the peninsula proper pivoting north and south of State Street and extending westwards from the waterfront to Washington Street and from Water Street north to Ann Street. So the poverty-stricken Irish clustered in two logical receiving points – the North End, the most congested zone in the city, and south of Water Street in the Fort Hill and Pearl Street area and also including South Cove. Close to the docks and cheap to rent, these localities were the first homes for Irish immigrants who gravitated towards these quarters in large numbers. As the Irish came to dominate the North End and South Cove, the former inhabitants moved into the West End, including the prestigious Beacon Hill district, north of Boston Common. However, with the advent of horse cars and the railroad, and reduced transportation costs, some Irish by the late 1850s were expanding into the West End, into East Cambridge, Charlestown and south Boston. However, more Irish remained in the tenements of Fort Hill and North End, still struggling with unemployment, disease and crime.

Washington District Co[b]
March 23rd 1852

Dear Brother

The delay of answering your letter must have caused you some uneasiness fearing that all your friends here were not well, or some other unforseen Occurance, it was nothing More than the delay of the money, which I Could not send sooner, I have given nearly all my money to make these people [so very] comfortable, which they are, having the Children going to school. I enclose an order for twenty Dollars which you can get by presenting it to any of the brokers or Bankers, I request of you to see that the graves of our Dear Father & Mother and Brother are preserved, which I have no doubt you have already done, by paying some little you can have them registered untill such time as I Can get a head stone ordered, I am at the Same business still, expecting every day to get an advance My time is limited which leaves me without seeing any of my friends in Phil[a] I expect to do so in July, I have a letter at least english They are all in good health, John is butchering Situated as to when you last herd from Phil[a] Dear La[u] I wish you to give my lov and respects to B[r] James and family and ask him to send me a letter, which would leave me happy to know how they all are, or how he is situated in business, Sister Ellen wishes to give her address to Brother Matt as she supposes he is coming to America this Spring.

N[o] 6 Murrays St. Schuylkill, third, Phil[a] let me know if Margaret is yet in Monaster[?][n] or if she intends remaining so, for my part, I would not advise her in any way I suppose Ellen has said something of the Matter in her letter, it is a serious Consideration, those who have persons to manage their affairs cannot always get along. Therefore her case would be bad, coming here unprotected, all you people in Ireland are deceived, or at least deceive yourselves in your opinion of this Country. I am not going to enter into any particulars, all that I will say is that persons coming here will find as much hardships and difficulty as ever they experienced home, there are some fare well, but that rare case, for myself I am now in a fair way bettering myself, but I will tell you what none of my people here knows, that I have suffered more than I thought I could endure, in a strange Country far from a friend, necessitated to go on public works from four oClock of a Summer Morning until Eight at Night enduring the hardships of a burning Sun, then by Sickness losing what I dearly earned, for my short time in this Country I have experienced a great deal, which may serve me the remainder of my days. this letter I now write at Midnight, which is done in a hurried way, without any form, merely a scrible, which you can easily see and which you will excuse, hoping the receipt of it will meet all my dear friends in the enjoyment of good health I Conclude by Sending you all my love and respects, - expecting an answer without delay.

I remain your

affectionate brother

Dannul Rountree

Fig. 14 letter from Daniel Rowntree, City Hotel, Washington, D.C., to his brother, Laurence Rowntree, Dublin, 23 March 1852.

who truly wished to go 'home'. Likewise, subsequent expressions of Irish-American nationalism, still rooted in transmitted Famine 'histories' (public and private), but shaped by the oft-conflicting strategies of different social groups in an increasingly 'mature' and stratified Irish-American society, could mesh as well with the deeper ideological ambivalence of the US-born Irish, poised uneasily as many of them were between past and present, between an idealised Ireland and the realities of an Irish America, the situation of which generally (albeit haltingly and unevenly) improved in the late nineteenth and early twentieth centuries.[25]

The point is that, even in the early 1900s, for the growing (but largely still insecure) Irish–American bourgeoisie, as well as for what remained the group's working-class majority, Irish–American nationalist rhetoric and activities, still referenced to Famine 'memories' (real or imagined), were not incompatible with personal aspirations or collective advancement. By definition, however, that could not be true in British colonies-cum-Commonwealth nations, whose social hierarchies, political regimes and legal systems mandated (through official press censorship, for instance) 'loyalty' to 'mother country' as the price of individual mobility and group tolerance. In places such as Ontario, especially, or New Zealand, with their large (and often stridently 'Orange') Irish Protestant populations, or in Great Britain itself, especially during its periodic waves of anti-Irish Catholic xenophobia, downplaying the Famine's importance, and ignoring its plausible political 'lessons', were logical expressions of what might be described (before the late 1960s) as 'Ulster [Catholic] models' of ethno-religious adaptation to superior and at least potentially hostile power.[26]

# The cities and towns of Ireland, 1841–51

*Kevin Hourihan*

This chapter is concerned with the cities and towns during the Famine decade. Although there are detailed accounts of many individual towns and the role they played in giving relief to the starving and destitute from the countryside, there is no overall analysis of the experience of the cities and towns at national level. This chapter will first examine the numbers, size and characteristics of the towns in 1841, and then look at the changes they experienced during the decade to 1851.[1] The numbers and profiles of the towns after the Famine will also be examined, and correlation analysis will be used to search for statistical explanations of the changes that occurred.

## THE TOWNS IN 1841

The Census of 1841 identifies 1,257 towns altogether. These include the cities (Dublin, Cork, Limerick, Waterford and Kilkenny), the corporate towns (Belfast, Drogheda and Galway), and all settlements which met the census criterion of twenty occupied houses. Although this may seem very low, it continued in use for all census counts in Ireland until 1971, when a standard of fifty occupied houses was introduced. (Up to 1956, it was not even necessary that the houses be occupied.)

The distribution of towns by size is shown in Table 1. Dublin dominated, with its population of almost 233,000. The primacy of Dublin is still a major issue in Irish life today. Cork (almost 81,000), Belfast (almost 69,000) and Limerick (over 48,000) were the only other substantial centres. There were ten towns with populations between 10,000 and 24,000. These comprise places which have since grown into cities (Waterford, Galway and Derry), and important regional centres like Sligo, Tralee and Armagh. There were thirty-five towns with populations between 5,000 and 9,999. Examples include Newry and Coleraine in Northern Ireland, and Ennis and Tullamore in the Republic. These are still the major shopping and manufacturing centres in their regions today. Fifty towns had populations between 3,000 and 4,999. Their experience since 1841 has been more variable. Some like Mullingar and Athlone have grown, but most, like Skibbereen and Boyle are only of local importance. There were thirty-nine towns with populations between 2,000 and 2,999, and fifty-two between 1,500 and 1,999. A population of 1,500 is the number required by the Central Statistics Office for a settlement to be considered 'urban' today. If we apply this criterion to Ireland in 1841, it means the country had 190 of these settlements. Their distribution across the country is shown in Figure 1. They were most dense in the east and south, and more scattered in Connacht and west Ulster, but every county except Leitrim had at least one town of 2,000 people or more. (Interestingly, Leitrim still remains the least urbanised county in the Republic.)

Adare and Carlingford are examples of the eighty-

**Table 1.** Cities and Towns 1841 Population and Selected Characteristics

| City/Town (population size) | Numbers | Total population | Sex ratio (female per 1,000 males) | 4th class housing % total | % Families in 1st & 2nd class housing | % Families in 3rd & 4th class housing | % Families chiefly employed in agriculture | % Families chiefly employed In manufacturing, trade, etc. | % Families chiefly dependent on vested means, professions & direction of labour | % Families chiefly dependent on their own manual labour | % Adult literacy |
|---|---|---|---|---|---|---|---|---|---|---|---|
| Dublin | 1 | 232,726 | 1,224 | 0.71 | 95.5 | 4.5 | 14.8 | 56.0 | 66.0 | 26.2 | 69.2 |
| Cork, Belfast, Limerick | 3 | 197,722 | 1,232 | 2.28 | 85.9 | 14.1 | 23.4 | 55.5 | 53.9 | 40.1 | 58.7 |
| 10,000–25,000 | 10 | 149,730 | 1,177 | 14.35 | 59.1 | 40.7 | 23.2 | 49.9 | 55.7 | 35.2 | 49.9 |
| 5,000–9,999 | 35 | 242,964 | 1,175 | 16.50 | 55.9 | 44.1 | 24.1 | 49.2 | 52.8 | 39.5 | 49.8 |
| 3,000–4,999 | 50 | 190,385 | 1,128 | 18.38 | 49.8 | 54.8 | 26.8 | 51.6 | 55.5 | 42.3 | 49.0 |
| 2,000–2,999 | 39 | 94,308 | 1,120 | 19.68 | 45.4 | 56.6 | 27.1 | 51.8 | 54.7 | 40.3 | 50.4 |
| 1,500–1,999 | 52 | 88,146 | 1,122 | 23.94 | 44.3 | 57.6 | 32.3 | 47.3 | 52.0 | 43.5 | 49.2 |
| 1,000–1,499 | 89 | 108,309 | 1,134 | 19.89 | 51.7 | 57.0 | 31.6 | 48.6 | 56.1 | 45.8 | 51.1 |
| 500–999 | 233 | 161,831 | 1,129 | 22.77 | 46.5 | 55.3 | 33.8 | 45.2 | 50.7 | 43.8 | 50.6 |
| Less than 500 | 745 | 184,015 | 1,065 | 28.75 | 32.3 | 68.6 | 45.2 | 40.0 | 44.8 | 51.6 | 43.3 |
| | 1,257 | 1,650,136 | | | | | | | | | |

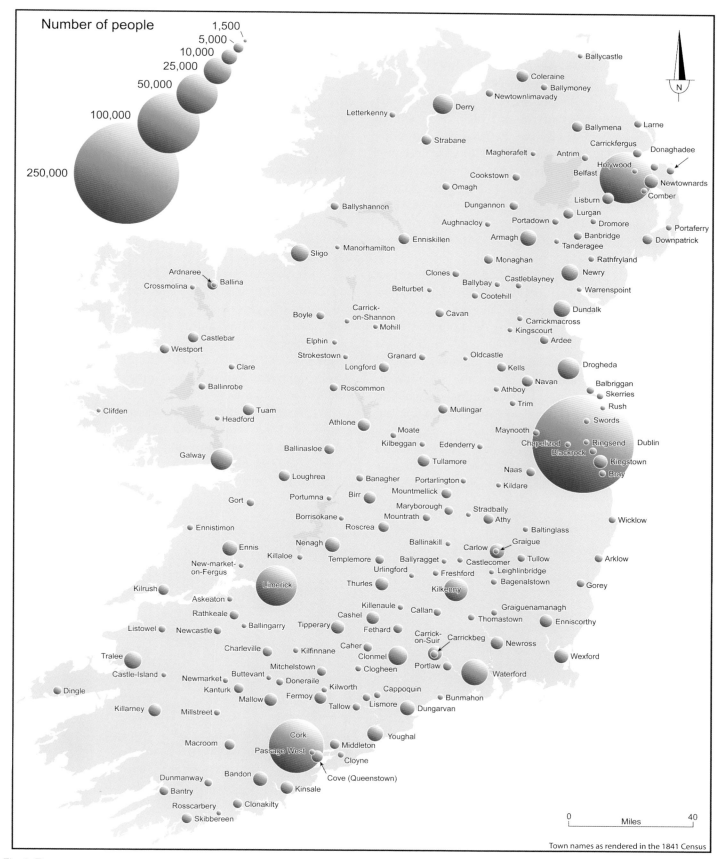

Number of people

1,500
5,000
10,000
25,000
50,000
100,000
250,000

N

0       Miles       40

Town names as rendered in the 1841 Census

Fig. 1 DISTRIBUTION OF TOWNS WITH POPULATION OF 1500 AND GREATER IN 1841. This map shows the distribution of towns with 1,500 plus population – and so would be designated as 'urban' by the Central Statistics Office today. These 190 towns and cities range in size from Dublin's near quarter of a million to fifty-two smaller towns with populations between 1,500 and 2,000. Apart from Dublin's primacy, Belfast, Cork and Limerick can be seen to be dominant regional capitals. Apart from northwest Ulster, Leitrim (with none above 2,000), west and east central Connacht, peninsular southwest Kerry and the uplands of the Wicklow region, there is a reasonable spread of towns of this size throughout the island. Close on 70% of these towns were designated as workhouse and union centres by the Poor Law Act and were eventually asked to bear the brunt of the Famine plague after 1846.

nine towns with populations between 1,000 and 1,499. They all survive, but most have populations similar to 1841; they would now be considered large villages or small towns. The same is true of most of the 233 places with populations between 500 and 999. Some, like Douglas in Cork and Finglas in Dublin, have been incorporated into the cities, but Liscarroll and Lifford are better examples of this group. There were 745 'towns' with populations less than 500. The smallest was Roosky, with just thirty-seven people, and there were eleven more with less than 100 people. Many of these have disappeared since 1841; in fact many were gone by the Census of 1851. These very small settlements were widely distributed across the country; together they accounted for over 184,000 people.

Altogether, the population of the 1,257 towns identified in the census was 1.65 million. This was 20.2% of the national population, considerably below the level of urbanisation of England and Wales but comparable to that of many other European countries. Despite this Irish cities and towns shared some typical characteristics of urbanisation found elsewhere. The ratio of females to males (the 'sex ratio' to demographers) was interesting, with a surplus of females in every size of settlement. This has always been an abiding feature of urbanisation with women migrating to cities in search of employment (and it continues today). It might have been expected in Dublin and the other cities, with jobs in areas like domestic service and shops, but it also applied even to the very smallest category of settlement. Overall though, Ireland's urbanisation was low, with four out of every five people living outside settlements as small as twenty houses.

It might be expected that there were important differences between the towns of different size. Some of these are explored in Table 1. The Census distinguished four categories of housing. First- and second-class houses were solidly built, with several rooms and windows; third-class homes were cottages built of mud, and fourth-class homes were single-room mud cabins. The four cities together had less than 800 fourth-class cabins, less than 1.6% of all their houses. In contrast, every other group of towns had at least 14% of their houses in this very poor category, with the level rising to almost 29% for the smallest settlements. The difference is even more pronounced for family homes. In the four cities less than 9% of families were living in third or fourth-class homes, with over 91% in first- or second-class ones. These ratios disimprove for every other category of settlement. Even in towns of 10,000–25,000 people, over 40% of families lived in third- or fourth-class homes, and this figure rose to almost 69% for the very smallest settlements.

As regards occupations, the Census classified families according to their employment and means. The table shows employment in agriculture, and manufacturing and trade. (A third category labelled 'Other pursuits' is not included.) Less than 15% of Dublin families were employed in agricul-

Fig. 2 View of Skibbereen from Clover Hill, *The Illustrated London News*, 13 February 1847. Skibbereen's population in 1841 was 4,715. By 1851 it had declined to 3,834 resulting in a population loss of 19%. The terrible suffering caused by the Famine in Skibbereen was widely reported in the press, both local and international.

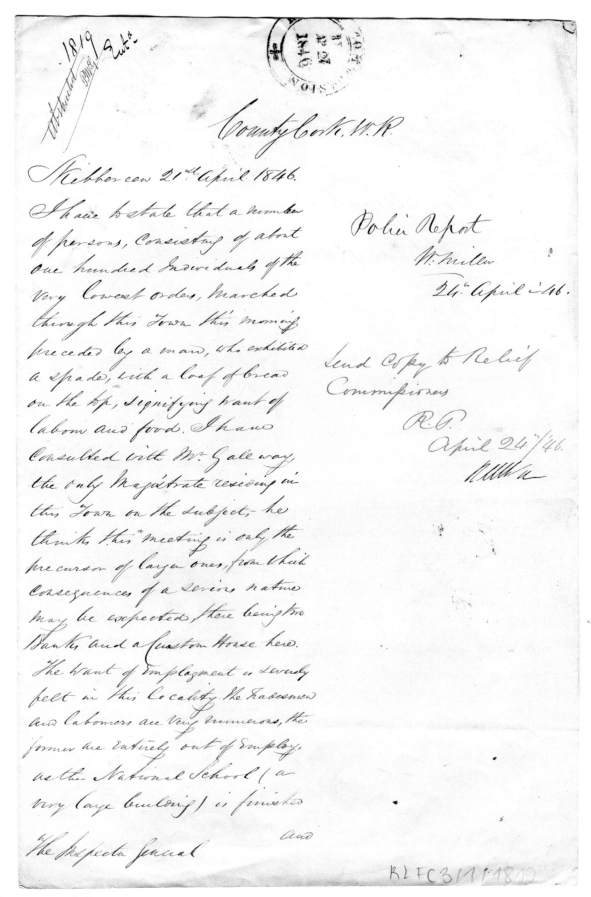

Fig. 3 This police report compiled by Inspector George Minehan states that on 21 April 1846 'about one hundred individuals of the very lowest order marched through this town (Skibbereen) preceded by a man who exhibited a spade, with a loaf of bread on the top, signifying want of labour and food'. The local magistrate believed that such a march this morning was only 'a precursor to larger ones' given the distress in the area. [Source: Relief Commission Papers 3/1/1819, National Archives Ireland]

**Table 2.** Population Change 1841–51

| City/Town (Population Size) | Numbers | Population Increase | Population Decrease | Unchanged | Percent Aggregate Change | Aggregate Change |
|---|---|---|---|---|---|---|
| Dublin | 1 | 1 | - | | 6.0 | 13,953 |
| Cork, Belfast, Limerick | 3 | 3 | - | | 11.9 | 23,536 |
| 10,000–25000 | 10 | 2 | 8 | | -3.6 | -5,334 |
| 5,000–9,999 | 35 | 10 | 25 | | -6.6 | -16,019 |
| 3,000–4,999 | 50 | 10 | 40 | | -13.3 | -25,283 |
| 2,000–2,999 | 39 | 6 | 33 | | -13.4 | -12,617 |
| 1,500–1,999 | 52 | 10 | 42 | | -14.2 | -12,551 |
| 1,000–1,499 | 89 | 20 | 67 | 2 | -9.9 | -10,695 |
| 500–999* | 233 | 84 | 148 | 1 | -6.3 | -10,162 |
| Less than 500* | 745 | 188 | 555 | 2 | -13.7 | -25,249 |
| | 1,257 | 334 | 918 | 5 | -4.9 | -80,421 |

*Estimates only – missing data in 1851 Census*

ture, although the other cities had over 23%. All Irish towns had important agricultural links, with over a quarter of employment in that field, and the percentage rising to over forty-five for the smallest villages. It is tempting to view these villages as simply agricultural hamlets, but the other employment data show this was not the case. Manufacturing and trade provided employment for 56% of Dublin families, but for a very substantial proportion of all the other towns also. Even the smallest villages had 40% of their families dependent on manufacturing and trade, so although they clearly had strong links to the land, there was at least an embryo industrial and commercial element besides. The kind of market economy which was evolving in Ireland in the early nineteenth century was impacting even on the smallest of settlements.

This is reinforced by the other occupational data. Almost two-thirds of Dublin families were 'chiefly dependent on vested means, professions or the direction of labour', and over half of families in towns as low as 500 people were classified the same. Even in those places with less than 500 population, almost 45% of families were in this category. Almost 52% were dependent on 'their own manual labour' in the smallest places. This statistic is lower in every other group of towns, although over 40% in most of them. Only Dublin has a level approaching one-quarter.

The final column on Table 1 shows the levels of adult literacy in the different groups of towns. This was highest in Dublin at over 69%, and lowest in the smallest villages (43%). There was very little variation for the groups in between, with only about half of adults able to read and write.

## CHANGES 1841–51

Table 2 shows population change for the cities and towns during the Famine decade. The population of the four cities grew by almost 37,500, but every other category of towns lost population. It was not just an aggregate loss, but a majority of towns in each size group declined. Of

the ten towns with populations between 10,000 and 25,000 in 1841, only two grew; the other eight had serious population loss. The same pattern applies to every size group; twenty-five of the thirty-five towns in the 5,000–9,999 range lost population, forty-nine of the fifty in the 3,000–4,999 group, and so on. The heaviest losses were in the three groups between 1,500 and 4,999, with aggregate losses of almost 14%. These were the towns which were playing an increasingly important role in marketing and services, and their decline must have had a major impact on local economies. The data for the smallest villages must be treated with caution, because of missing data in the 1851 Census (below), but their overall trend was also one of decline.

The distribution of towns which increased and decreased over the decade is shown in Figures 4 and 6. The cities accounted for the vast majority of population increase; smaller towns which increased were much more scattered, and their increases were mainly very small. In contrast, the towns which lost population were spread over the entire country, and in many cases their losses ran into thousands.

**Table 3.** Bivariate correlations of town characteristics (1841) and population change 1841–51

| Predictor | Pearson's r |
|---|---|
| % Fourth-class housing | -0.13 |
| % Families in first- and second-class housing | 0.24 |
| % Families in third- and fourth-class housing | -0.25 |
| % Families employed in agriculture | -0.19 |
| % Families employed in manufacturing, etc. | 0.07 |
| % Families dependant on vested means, etc. | 0.12 |
| % Families dependant on their own labour | -0.16 |
| % Adult literacy | 0.21 |
| Workhouse numbers | -0.13 |
| Fever Hospital numbers | -0.06 |
| Temporary Hospital numbers | 0.02 |
| Combined workhouse and Hospital numbers | -0.05 |

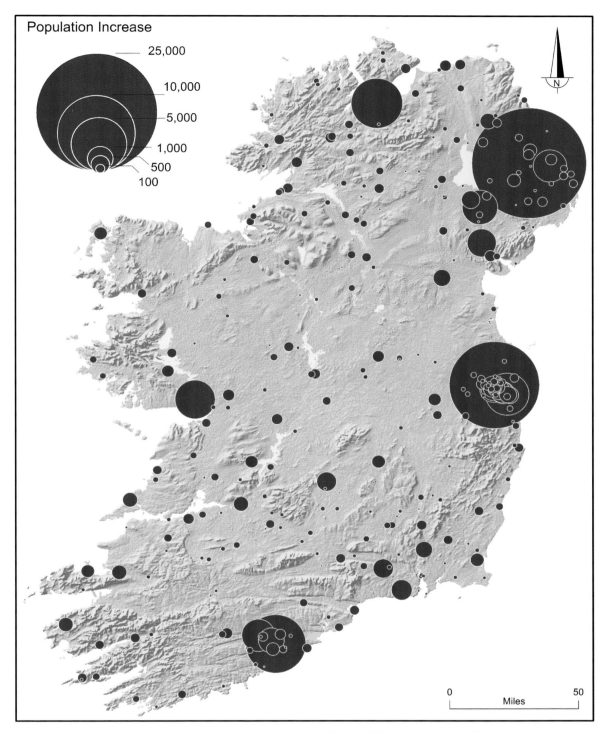

Fig. 4 The distribution of urban population increases between 1841 and 1851. Apart from significant urban growth in the industrialising northeast, in the cities and port-towns and their satellite agglomerations, some 'refugee' towns in the west and along midland routeways to the emigrant ports and isolated new town growth as at Cahirciveen, the most dramatic feature of this map is the lack of growth in the great majority of towns. Only two out of ten grew in the 10,000-24,999 population range, only ten out of thirty-five in the 5,000-9,999 range and only one-fifth (i.e. ten out of fifty-five) expanded in the 3,000-4,999 group. The situation was even more bleak for towns smaller than 3000.

They were spread over the entire country, although there were a few strong clusters. Loop Head in County Clare lost six census towns in close proximity. These also reflect some of the limitations of the census data. Killbalyowne, the parish at the tip of the peninsula, recorded a population increase during the Famine decade, although all the surrounding parishes had large decreases. Killbalyowne's gain was almost certainly because the Census of 1851 recorded the residual town populations as part of the parish. Seven towns disappeared from the western tip of the Beara Peninsula in County Cork. Many of these lost towns have disappeared forever. Some recovered very quickly, like Allihies in Beara, which became an important copper-mining centre before the end of the nineteenth century. Others have reappeared in more recent times, such as Sallybrook near Cork, which was again labelled a census town in the early 1970s.

A total of 165 census towns of 1841 disappeared during the decade. By 1851, their numbers of occupied houses was less than twenty, so they were no longer enumerated as towns. This causes some complications for estimating population change for the smallest places. The vast majority of the disappeared were from the smallest category, although a few had populations over 500 in 1841. The distribution of the missing towns is shown in Figure 9.

Although most towns lost population during the Famine decade, their rates of loss varied considerably, and a minority of towns actually grew. To try to explain these variations, the 1841 characteristics were used as predictors for bivariate correlations with population change over the decade. The results are shown in Table 3.

Most of the relationships are intuitively correct. It

233

ENTRANCE TO CAHIRCIVEEN.

Fig. 5 Entrance to Cahirciveen, *The Illustrated London News*, 1846

would be expected that the stronger towns would survive the Famine better than weaker ones. Population growth correlates positively with families in better-quality houses, higher employment in manufacturing, vested interests and adult literacy, and negatively with fourth-class housing, families in third- and fourth-class housing, employment in agriculture, and manual labour. However, the correlations are all pretty low, so the level of explanation is far from complete.

In addition to the characteristics of the towns, change was also correlated with the numbers of places in the institutions set up to give relief to the destitute and sick: the workhouses, fever hospitals and temporary hospitals. It must be acknowledged that the official number of places in these institutions did not mean very much in light of the scale of the catastrophe that occurred, so it is only a crude indicator of the relief available. Intuitively, it would be expected that towns with these institutions would grow during the decade, or at least that their loss would be lower than would otherwise have been the case. The correlations do not support this; they are mainly negative and also very weak, so they played no role in reducing population loss in the towns where they were located.

## AFTER THE FAMINE: THE TOWNS IN 1851

The 1851 Census of Population maintained the same definitions and categories as ten years earlier, so direct comparisons can be drawn between the two years. Table 4 shows the numbers of towns in the groups used in Table 1. The population loss experienced by many towns meant that many fell out of the group they belonged to in 1841. Every category below 10,000 has fewer towns than the earlier year: twenty-six in the category 5,000–9,999, compared with thirty-five in 1841; forty-four in the 3,000–4,999 group compared with fifty ten years before, and so on. Altogether, the Census identified 1,188 towns in 1851, sixty-nine less than in 1841. As noted above, 165 of the 1841 towns disappeared from the 1851 Census, but others broke through the twenty-houses threshold in 1851 and were counted as census towns. These include places like Ballincollig and Carrigaline near Cork, which are now important, growing towns, but they also include many minor settlements which virtually disappeared later in the nineteenth century. Interestingly, despite the large population loss, the sex ratios for all groups were still showing a surplus of females over males. The aggregate population of the 1,188 towns was 1.57 million, 24% of the national total.

The housing statistics in Table 4 reflect the changes

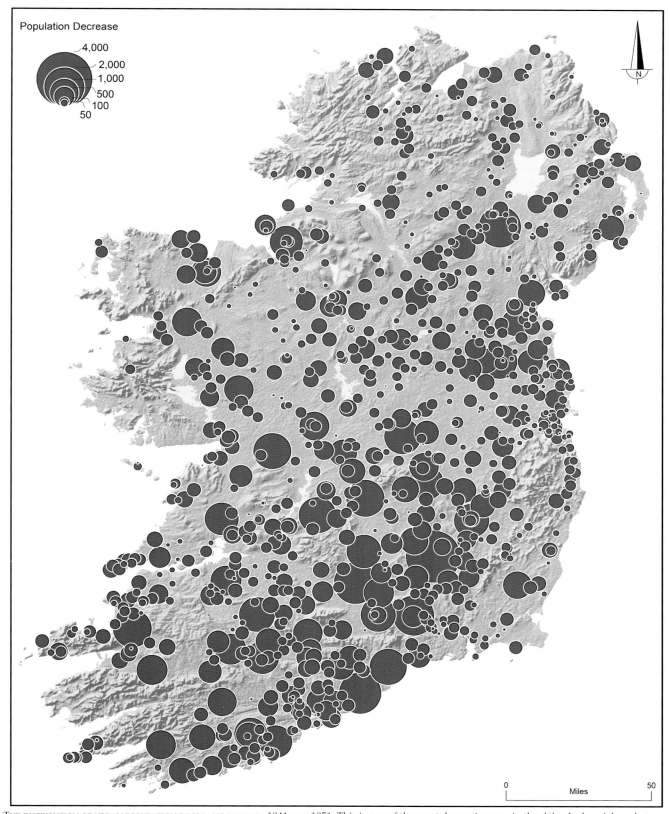

Population Decrease

4,000
2,000
1,000
500
100
50

0       Miles       50

Fig. 6 THE DISTRIBUTION OF URBAN POPULATION DECREASES BETWEEN 1841 AND 1851. This is one of the most dramatic maps in the *Atlas*. It chronicles what can only be described as an island-wide landscape of urban collapse, and migration and desolation. As we have seen, the populations of the major cities – Dublin, Belfast, Cork and Limerick – grew, but a majority of towns in every other category declined. As many as two-thirds of towns ranging from 5,000 to 25,000 had lost significant numbers of people and with them went a whole series of urban functions and social roles. Even heavier losses occurred in the smaller towns with between 1,500 and 5,000 populations, ranging from 80 to 85% of all towns in these groups. In the 2000-plus group, towns such as Doneraile, Millstreet, Freshford, Banagher, Claremorris and Tallow lost over 30% of their 1841 population and towns such as Cloyne, Maynooth, Graiguenamanagh, Thomastown, Granard and Clogheen lost over 20%. And 165 'census' towns disappeared altogether. Limited areas of northeast Ulster excepted, the staggering aspect of this map is its almost universal, island-wide character. The fabric, populations and functions of towns had contracted everywhere. In a Europe which was then experiencing rapid urbanisation at this time, the picture for most of Ireland is, therefore, even more exceptional – not only a country of rural desolation but one also of urban stagnation, decay and very limited and confined urban growth.

235

SKETCHES IN THE WEST OF IRELAND.—BY MR. JAMES MAHONY.

WOODCUT.

SMYTH

BALLYDEHOB, FROM THE SKIBBEREEN ROAD.

Fig. 7 Ballydehob in west Cork as sketched by James Mahony for *The Illustrated London News*, 20 February 1847. Its population declined by 7% in the decade 1841–51.

which occurred during the Famine. The numbers of fourth-class houses collapsed. The four cities together had only 132 of these cabins and even in the smallest villages less than one in eleven houses were listed in this category. First- and second-class homes dominated in Dublin (96%) and the other cities (90%), and were over 50% in every other town

**Table 4.** Cities and Towns 1851 Population and Selected Characteristics

| City/Town (population size) | Numbers | Total popula-tion | Sex ratio (female per 1,000 males) | 4th class housing % total | % Families in 1st & 2nd class housing | % Families in 3rd & 4th class housing | % Families chiefly employed in agricul-ture | % Families chiefly employed in manu-facturing, trade, etc. | % Families chiefly dependent on vested means, professions & direction of labour | % Families chiefly dependent on their own manual labour | % Adult literacy |
|---|---|---|---|---|---|---|---|---|---|---|---|
| Dublin | 1 | 246,679 | 1,181 | 0.18 | 96.4 | 3.6 | 1.1 | 50.4 | 30.4 | 59.0 | 71.0 |
| Cork, Belfast, Limerick | 3 | 221,258 | 1,172 | 0.29 | 89.9 | 10.1 | 3.3 | 60.7 | 26.6 | 65.2 | 62.4 |
| 10,000–25000 | 10 | 151,275 | 1,136 | 4.26 | 67.4 | 32.6 | 11.2 | 52.6 | 22.1 | 67.5 | 53.3 |
| 5,000–9,999 | 26 | 181,738 | 1,180 | 2.69 | 66.0 | 34.0 | 16.1 | 51.4 | 20.3 | 67.3 | 55.3 |
| 3,000–4,999 | 44 | 165,334 | 1,136 | 4.97 | 57.7 | 42.3 | 18.9 | 46.9 | 24.0 | 64.1 | 52.5 |
| 2,000–2,999 | 41 | 100,786 | 1,180 | 6.17 | 56.1 | 45.2 | 19.1 | 47.7 | 23.9 | 66.4 | 55.5 |
| 1,500–1,999 | 39 | 68,091 | 1,158 | 4.54 | 57.4 | 42.4 | 22.5 | 44.1 | 25.2 | 62.9 | 53.5 |
| 1,000–1,499 | 90 | 109,970 | 1,164 | 6.20 | 54.8 | 45.2 | 22.6 | 42.0 | 24.0 | 64.0 | 56.5 |
| 500–999 | 218 | 156,754 | 1,137 | 5.71 | 53.7 | 46.3 | 24.7 | 42.4 | 23.0 | 66.7 | 53.9 |
| Less than 500 | 716 | 167,830 | 1,077 | 8.44 | 46.1 | 53.9 | 32.1 | 37.1 | 24.6 | 65.0 | 50.4 |
| | 1,188 | 1,569,715 | | | | | | | | | |

Fig. 8 DISTRIBUTION OF 'TOWNS' THAT DISAPPEARED BETWEEN 1841 AND 1851. In the 1841 and 1851 Censuses, the category 'town' included all agglomerations that contained twenty or more houses. In 1841, there were 745 'towns' with populations of less than 500. Roosky contained the smallest population with thirty-seven persons but there were eleven of the 'towns' with less than 100 people. In effect, most of the smallest 'towns' were small hamlets or villages where some 40% were involved in trade and manufacturing. But other 'towns' were large farm clusters or roadside streets of labourers' cabins. By 1851, as many as 165 of these 'towns' had disappeared. Some of them – as in the Mizen and Loop Head peninsulas – were farm clusters that had either disappeared or shrunk. The majority were either small hamlets – often parish centres like Dunkerrin in Leinster and Kilcash in Munster – with limited urban functions or roadside squatter settlements (as in east Leinster) whose house numbers had fallen below twenty as both family mortality and out-migration took their toll. It is noticeable that far more census 'towns' disappeared in Munster than in any other province. South Leinster and much of Ulster seem least affected while south Connacht, coastal and northeast Leinster as well as the far northwest also saw quite a number of 'disappearances'. A small number of other places with more than twenty houses had emerged by the 1851 census and some, such as Ballincollig and Carrigaline near Cork city, were to prosper. The great majority were to vanish again in a few decades.

237

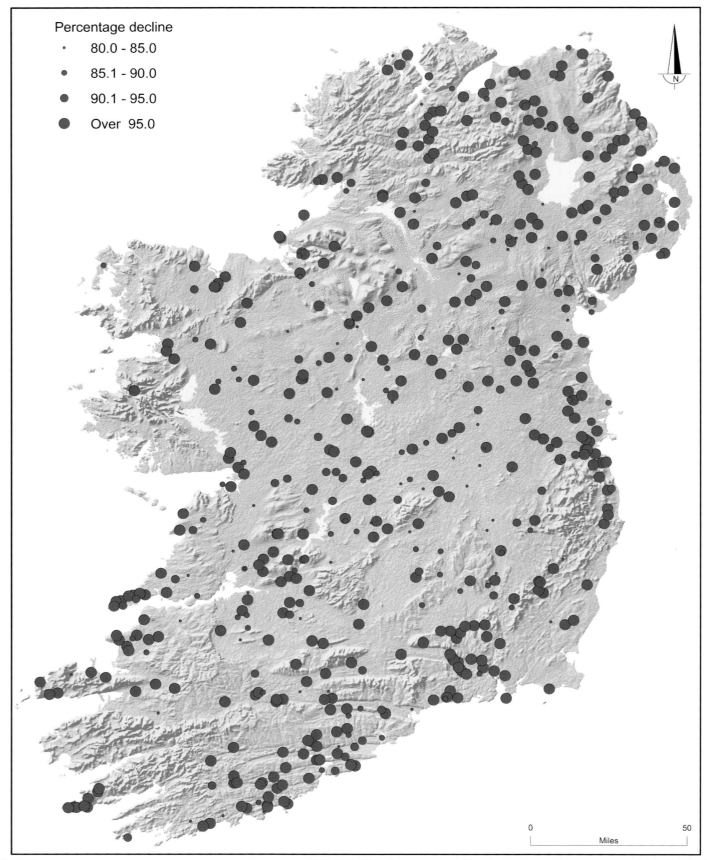

Fig. 9 THE DISAPPEARANCE OF FOURTH-CLASS HOUSES FROM IRISH TOWNS, 1841–51. In 1841, the proportion of fourth-class houses in towns was much less than in the countryside, ranging from 29% in 'Census towns' under 500 to less than 1% of the housing stock in Dublin city and averaging *c*.17% across all categories. By 1851, like its poorest inhabitants, the fourth-class house had almost vanished from the urban scene, now constituting less than 5% of the urban housing stock ranging from 0.2% in Dublin to 8.4% in the smallest 'towns'. Figure 9 shows the dramatic island-wide reduction of this one-room mud cabin from the towns, not only in the small 'Census towns' (many of which had disappeared completely) but also in towns of all sizes. For example, the proportion of fourth-class houses in the sturdy towns with populations of 5,000-9,999, decreased from 16.5% to 2.7% and in towns with 1,500 to 1,999 populations from 23.9% to 4.5%.

238

category except the smallest villages. Even for the latter though, the situation had improved considerably, from 32% in 1841 to over 46% in 1851. Both the numbers and proportion of the third- and fourth-class houses were considerably lower in 1851 than before the Famine.

The occupational data in the table illustrate other changes that occurred over the decade. Agriculture accounted for less than a quarter of employment in all towns except the smallest; even in those villages agriculture provided less than one-third of jobs, compared with over 45% in 1841. Manufacturing and trade also changed, employing over 40% of workers in all towns except the smallest, where the figure was 37%, compared with 40% ten years earlier. Manufacturing's share of employment was lower in many size groups than in 1841. Some of this may be due to towns switching from one category to another because of population loss, although, of course, the collapse in demand because of the national catastrophe must also have adversely affected manufacturing and trade.

This is also evident in the data on people's means. In 1841, over 50% of all town families (and 66% in Dublin) depended on vested means, professions and the direction of labour (as usual, the smallest villages were the exception, at 45%). The corresponding levels in 1851 were considerably lower. Dublin was highest, at 30%, and the other groups ranged between that and 20%. The 1841 figures suggest an emerging urban bourgeoisie, which was badly affected by the economic collapse, resulting in the lower figures after the Famine. Conversely, their own manual labour was the only support for about 60% of all city and towns people in 1851, compared with far lower levels ten years earlier.

Adult literacy levels improved slightly over the decade. In 1841, most towns were around the 50% level (with the cities higher), and in 1851, all towns had improved a few percentage points.

## CONCLUSIONS

The Famine had a huge impact on the cities and towns of Ireland. In 1841, they were growing in size and expanding in number. Although the country had a small number of cities and large towns, there were a substantial number of medium-sized towns with urban-type characteristics, which would probably have become catalysts for economic and social change. In addition, there were almost 1,000 villages with less than 1,000 people, and these were improving in terms of housing, employment and literacy levels. Without the disaster of the Famine, all of the 1841 towns would almost certainly have continued to grow and develop.

The Famine brought enormous change. The cities' populations expanded, but every other category of town lost population. Of every five towns with populations exceeding 2,000, over four declined during the decade. Many of the smaller settlements disappeared for census purposes, and in real life also, many never recovered from the loss.

If there was any positive outcome for the towns from the Famine, it was the reduction in the numbers of the mud cabins, the so-called fourth-class homes, and the slight improvement in adult literacy, but this was negated by the employment and occupational changes which must have adversely affected the towns' capacity for future development.

# The roles of cities and towns during the Great Famine

## *William J. Smyth*

Apart from the dynamism of the major port cities – of the national capital Dublin and the regional capitals of Cork, Belfast, Limerick and Waterford – quite a number of other coastal towns still commanded a considerable maritime trade in the early 1840s. Likewise, some inland towns were important trade and communication centres as they acquired increasing commercial traffic through road and, in some cases, canal links. But, as T.W. Freeman points out 'in aggregate the towns shared the problem of widespread unemployment and underemployment with the countryside'.[1] This was particularly true of urban communities such as Bandon, Drogheda, Kilkenny, Limerick and indeed the Dublin Liberties where 'the living standards of the semi-skilled and unskilled declined most palpably' after the Napoleonic Wars and 'where the power of the money-lender and petty speculator in meal compounded the misery of a swelling proletariat'.[2] Life became even more problematic as one moved down to the smaller urban centres. Both a hierarchical and regional analysis is necessary to identify the strengths and weaknesses in the urban economy in the years before and during the Famine.

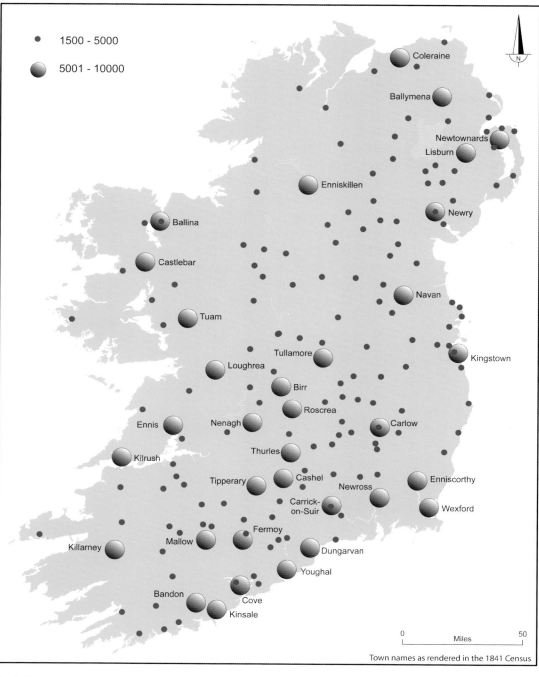

Fig. 1 DISTRIBUTION OF TOWNS WITH POPULATIONS OF 1,500–5,000 AND 500 TO 10,000 IN 1841. This map shows the distribution of relatively small towns (1500–5000) and more significant market towns (5001–10,000). Of the latter, it is striking that twice as many of these substantial market towns lay south of the line from Galway to Dublin city than to the north. This emphasises the strength of a mixed farming economy in the southern region of substantial farms which were intimately linked to agriculture-related industries in these strong market towns. In contrast, apart from a narrow urban corridor from Ballina to Tuam in central Connacht and the mainly coastal towns of the industrial northeast, there are only two inland towns in this category – Enniskillen and Navan –located in the rest of the northern half of the island. Neither the small farm world of much of the north and west, nor the extensive pastoral worlds of the midlands were generators of strong towns. Towns from 1500-5000 are more evenly distributed across the island although gaps in the far west and southwest, in east Connacht and the northwest, point to even less sophisticated local economies.

240

Only five of the towns with a population exceeding 10,000 were inland towns. Armagh – handsomely patronised by its wealthy primates – was an important market centre. Kilkenny had a large market hinterland, good road connections and still some industry. Carlow with its canal and road connections was a market and milling town, its industrial centre linked to the Castlecomer coalfields. Clonmel, on the River Suir, had still a significant export traffic in grain via Waterford. Many of its mills were on Suir Island and it was also the centre of the expanding Bianconi coach network. In contrast, the former woollen manufacturing town of Carrick-on-Suir was in decline and – like many of the textile centres outside the Belfast region – was characterised by serious underemployment. The port towns of Galway, Drogheda, Derry, Sligo, Newry, Tralee, Wexford and Dundalk – with populations ranging from Galway's 17,275 to Dundalk's 10,782 – all served important regional functions, their extensive quays and warehouses pointing to the historic importance of external trade.[3] However, Tralee and Dundalk were less vibrant and were already characterised by impoverished urban quarters.

As Figure 1 confirms, half of the strong towns with 5,000 to 10,000 populations in 1841 were in Munster. Some (like Fermoy, Mallow and Bandon) were significant military garrisons as well as local market centres. Other important inland market towns were Tipperary, Thurles and Ennis. Kinsale was still a lively port and fishing town and the shipping activities of both Youghal and Dungarvan had not yet declined. Queenstown (Cobh) had

become an important naval base while the market town of Killarney – set amongst the lakes and mountains – had begun to blossom as one of Ireland's first tourist towns.[4] Leinster had seven such towns: Athlone was a major military stronghold, Navan was an industrial and market centre in a rich agricultural zone, Kingstown (later Dun Laoghaire) was an outport of Dublin, New Ross and Enniscorthy were still active as port and market centres, Tullamore was already a thriving centre, but the landlord town of Birr had seen better days. Ulster had six such towns: Lisburn and Newtownards – the latter a lively town yet characterised by already impoverished lane populations – lay in Belfast's shadow,[5] while Coleraine, Ballymena, Enniskillen and Strabane all served as strong local market towns. Connacht – the least urbanised province – had only four towns in the 5,000 to 10,000 range: Tuam, Loughrea and Castlebar were all important market centres for extensive hinterlands while Ballina had also minor port functions.

Hardly less significant in the Irish urban scene of the 1840s were towns of 1,500 to 5,000 inhabitants as indeed were the many small towns in the 500 to 1,500 category – the latter most notably over an extensive region in east Connacht. Trade was central to the life of these towns, all characterised by lively, colourful fairs and markets and very little significant industry and where a considerable number of their inhabitants were farmers or farm labourers. The 1,500+ category included such small but thriving estate and milling towns as Clogheen in southwest Tipperary; it included landlord towns like Gort, Mitchelstown and West-

MAY 10, 1851.]　　　THE ILLUSTRATED LONDON NEWS.　　　387

THE EMIGRATION AGENTS' OFFICE.—THE PASSAGE MONEY PAID.

Fig. 2 Emigration Agent's Office, Cork, *The Illustrated London News*, 10 May 1851.

port. But it also included the formerly buoyant but now declining river towns of the southeast – Callan, Thomastown and Graignamanagh. It also included urban centres like Arklow, Dingle, Bantry, Skibbereen, Rosscarbery and Clonakilty – all small port and fishing towns already in decline. And included here also are impoverished inland towns like Baltinglass[6] and Kilmallock. In many such towns, little work was available 'and a significant proportion of the population already lived in miserable circumstances'.[7]

### CENTRAL PLACES

Cities and towns, given their existing employment, market, health and administrative functions, and their roles as workhouse and union centres, occupied a central place in the years of the Great Famine. The combination of private charities – quite a number originating in eighteenth century Protestant philanthropic endeavours – and government and urban/municipal initiatives had already by the 1820s and 1830s established maternity, fever and mental hospitals as well as houses of industry and gaols in the cities and bigger towns.[8] Port cities, especially those of the south and west, were central to the importation of American corn and other foodstuffs. It was the 130 towns, originally selected as the union and workhouse centres, which came to bear the brunt of the famine catastrophe. Many smaller towns saw the all too often temporary establishment of food depots – and all towns, great and small, were central in the marketing and selling of foodstuffs. In this context, the activities of small town meal-dealers and money lenders and their furtive pursuit of money and profiteering needs to be recognised. Merchants and shopkeepers were crucial in the supply of provisions to the workhouses and related institutions. As the Famine crisis deepened all cities and most towns were to be inundated with the starving poor, begging in the streets and/or passing through to the emigrant ships. Their many streets were to witness scenes of protest by the hungry poor just as their military garrisons, police barracks, bridewells and gaols were to be used to deflect and control such desperate populations. Heart-rending scenes involving destitution, disease and death were to be enacted and witnessed on these streets.

Apart from London – the seat of Parliament and Government and key institutions (such as the Treasury) responsible for determining a range of policy decisions

Fig. 3a *Market scene, Ennis County Clare, 1820* by William Turner De Lond. The population of Ennis declined by 16% between 1841 (9,318) and 1851 (7,841) [Source: Private Collection]

Fig. 3b  The County Courthouse in Ennis, designed by local architect Henry Whitestone, was built between 1846 and 1850 and supplied work to starving labourers for much of the Famine. [Photo: Frank Coyne]

shaping life and death in Ireland during the Great Famine – Dublin, Ireland's metropolis, was the pivotal place for implementing and enforcing these decisions. It was from here that all Poor Law Commissioners operated, regulating every aspect of the administration of the Poor Law throughout the island. It was here – as in Dublin Castle – that the Commissary General, Sir Randolph Routh, endeavoured to direct the distribution of food supplies to the most needy, pressed for more food imports and defended the relief committees. Dublin was the headquarters of the Board of Works where an understaffed and overwhelmed division struggled to establish and supervise the public works relief schemes under Sir John Burgoyne. It was to confer with Burgoyne that, in the first week of 1847, Charles Trevelyan made his one visit to Dublin where he wrote to *The Times* about the Government's new Poor Law plans, stressing that he wrote as one 'being constantly in the habit of receiving information, both written and oral, from all parts of Ireland'[9] as to the condition of the people. He only spent a few days in Ireland and never ventured westwards or southwards to engage with these famine conditions at first hand. We will never know if the direction of relief policies and funding would have changed if he had made that journey of dis-

covery. He returned after a few days to London – his imperial gaze remaining austere, dedicated, distant and unbending. In the following year (1848), in recognition of his work on the Irish Famine, Charles Trevelyan was knighted.

## SCARCITY

Back in March 1846, it is already reported 'that the tradesmen and others in the town of Ennis are severely suffering from want of food' and that the people are expressing 'a determination not to starve whilst food can be procured'.[10] In the town of Killaloe an alarming scarcity prevails with its working class amounting to 500 to 600 persons unable to procure one meal per diem. Likewise, in Clonakilty, a great distress 'is beginning to be felt amongst the poorer classes'. Given their 'spirit shown in consequence of the scarcity of provisions and employment' as their stocks of potatoes are nearly exhausted, the Earl of Bandon applies for a military detachment to be stationed at Clonakilty. In Dingle distress and fever are very much on the increase in a town and district with only one dispensary and no fever hospital existing nearer than Tralee. In the town of Galway, the people were suffering 'under the most trying privations; not a stone of potatoes could be purchased at market for the use of 20,000 inhabitants', and in its western suburb, in the Claddagh, the fishermen 'have been living on half rotten potatoes'. In Limavady, very great distress is reported amongst labourers and cottiers. The Mayor of Cork City, A.F. Roche, reports 'great distress prevails' while in Mallow 'one half of the inhabitants of the town are in actual distress and . . . are nearly as badly off as in country parts'. In Roscrea town the 'supply of potatoes at market [is] scanty and dear'; in the neighbouring village of Moneygall a memoir of working-class petitioners report 'a state of utmost destitution, being without food or the price of it' and that 'many of its poor would gladly walk to Roscrea (five miles) for Indian corn at famine price'. Close on 400 labourers are unemployed in New Ross 'who together with the families dependent on them, amount to 1170 individuals'. Already in Tubbercurry, 'the want of a permanent fever hospital is severely felt'.

In the city of Limerick, the population is suffering 'and require immediate relief' while in the country town of Askeaton families 'were in hopeless distress and on hearing that public works would probably be commenced by the latter end of April cried out that "they were hungry and relief would be too late"'. Of the labouring population of Nenagh, 600 out of at least 700 families 'are constantly idle and are now suffering all the horror of starvation, considering themselves fortunate if able to procure one scanty meal each day'. Even in Kingstown, County Dublin, '695 persons are now suffering privation from the high price of provisions; 317 are in extreme distress, their means of buying food being more inadequate than that of others'. Out of a population of 8,000 in the Graignamanagh District, 3,000 are reported 'in destitution; and that £200 are already collected for their relief'. In the Kilkenny village of Freshford 'distress is daily spreading', amounting to all but starva-

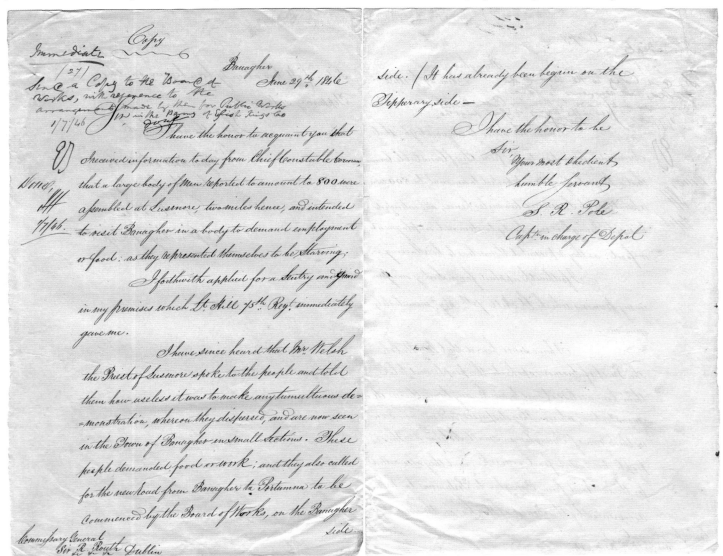

Fig. 4  A letter from Captain R.S. Pole, Banagher, County Offaly to the Commissary General Sir Randolph Routh, 29 June 1846. Pole was in charge of the food depot in Banagher. He referred to 'a large body of men reported to amount to 800 were assembled at Lusmagh, two miles hence, and intended to visit Banagher in a body to demand employment or food: as they represented themselves to be starving'. A local priest, Fr Walsh, intervened and 'told them how useless it was to make any tumultuous demonstration, whereon they dispersed'. Smaller groups made their way to Banagher where they 'called for the new road from Banagher to Portumna to be commenced by the Board of Works, on the Banagher side'. It had already commenced on the Tipperary side. [Source: Relief Commission Papers 3/1/3857, National Archives Ireland]

tion. 'Its Church of Ireland rector is daily beset by starving people' and finds it 'impossible to provide even a scanty supply for his numbers perishing'. Across the county border it is recorded for Killenaule (County Tipperary) that many were perishing of fever in the nearby collieries. In Mountmellick a number of decent women applicants to the local Board of Guardians 'form but a small proportion of these actually subsisting on food made from "the wash" of a starch-yard but indifferently suited for pigs'. The town of Athlone reports similar deplorable conditions. The destitution of the poor of Clifden and its locality is reported on several times – including the death of 'a father of five children'. In Mohill, County Leitrim, 'the cottiers are almost destitute' and 'armed parties have visited the homes of dealers in oatmeal for the purpose of forcing them to lower their charges'. Already food prices were escalating.

FOOD DEPOTS

That spring of 1846 saw the establishment of provision or food depots, involving a hierarchy of urban places administered from Dublin and governed from London. Port cities were central to supplying these food depots to second-order urban places in their hinterlands. Cork was the most important port and centre for both importing and distributing tons of oatmeal biscuit, Indian corn but particularly Indian cornmeal. This central reserve depot was established on 18 January 1846 and opened on 27 February. Cork port acted as the distribution centre for seven urban depots: Cork City and district, Cobh, Kinsale, Skibbereen, Bantry and Castletown-Berehaven and their surrounding districts.[11] (Bandon was denied a depot.) In turn these seven depots were responsible for supplying their dependent centres – Cobh endeavoured to supply seven such local centres, Kinsale another seven. Skibbereen served six 'dependencies', Bantry two and Castletown two. These second-level depots and their dependent stores were opened between mid April and late June (Castletownsend, Bantry, County Cork, and Ballinskelligs and Kells, County Kerry) but all were again closed by August 1846 when the public works were ushered in. Such government depots and subdepots were guarded by police and/or troops. Commanding the Shannon estuary and the southwest, the Limerick central depot was established on 6 January 1846 and opened in April. It was responsible for twelve second-order depots – in the city of Limerick, Knightstown (Valentia), Dingle, Ballybunion, Kilrush, Clarecastle, Banagher, Doonbeg, Killaloe, Cahirciveen, Castletown-Berehaven (December–January 1847) and Skibbereen. There were nine dependent centres in the Limerick sphere of distribution. In contrast and reflecting the weakness of the urban hierarchy in southwest Connacht, Galway (not established until April 1846) had no second-order depots but was directly responsible for ten dependent centres from Ballyvaughan in County Clare to Clifden

in the west.

Westport and Sligo were the two key depots for serving the famine-stricken west and northwest. Apart from serving its own district, Westport (established 7 March 1846) also supplied Clifden, Keel (Achill Island), Newport, Belmullet, Ballinrobe, Hollymount and Castlebar. (The people of Louisburgh were bitterly disappointed that their town was not so designated.) Sligo (established February 1846) supplied fifteen second-order centres in the northwest from Bunbeg in Donegal across to Ballina and inland to Swinford, Ballaghdereen and Tubbercurry. These in turn served a total of eleven dependent centres. In the Midlands, Longford (opened March 1846) served six urban districts including Strokestown, Castlerea, Roscommon, Drumsna and Carrick-on-Shannon. On the east and southeast coasts, Dundalk (opened late March 1846) served its own district as well as Armagh and Monaghan. Dublin (established March 1846) served six urban centres reaching inland as far as Mountmellick, Castlecomer, Castledermot, Athy and Tullamore. Provision depots at Clonmel, Dungarvan, Carrick-on-Suir, Fethard, Arthurstown and Bunmahon were supplied from the port city of Waterford (established March 1846). As famine conditions worsened in the winter of 1846, Banagher, Clifden and Belmullet were constituted as *separate* depot centres – and remained open until early 1847. Practically all of the other provision depots named above were formally abolished between August and November 1846. Amongst others, the peoples of Swinford, Ballyhaunis and Ballina protested that the closing of their depots would provoke the most extreme misery and that they should be kept open.[12] But government policy had changed.

CRY FOR FOOD

The provision of food supplies in the under-urbanised west and northwest remained a central issue. Trevelyan's failure to permit the ordering of adequate supplies from America, while its markets still remained open in the autumn of 1846, exacerbated famine conditions generally. Numerous shiploads of American corn only arrived in Cork harbour in early February 1847. In the meantime, even bread was scarce not only in the baker's shops in towns like Longford and Dungarvan but also in cities such as Cork and Limerick. People in the starving town of Longford resented the troop of dragoons galloping through their town on their way to repel a hungry protest in County Roscommon. In the desperate conditions that prevailed in Westport, a peaceful march by townspeople was made to Westport House to seek the aid of the landlord. Ballinrobe – like many other towns – reported starvation conditions as the Government sent additional troops into distressed districts. In September 1846, in the market town of Skibbereen, not a single loaf of bread was to be found in the shops. Similar conditions were reported in Skull, Bantry, Bandon, Balti-

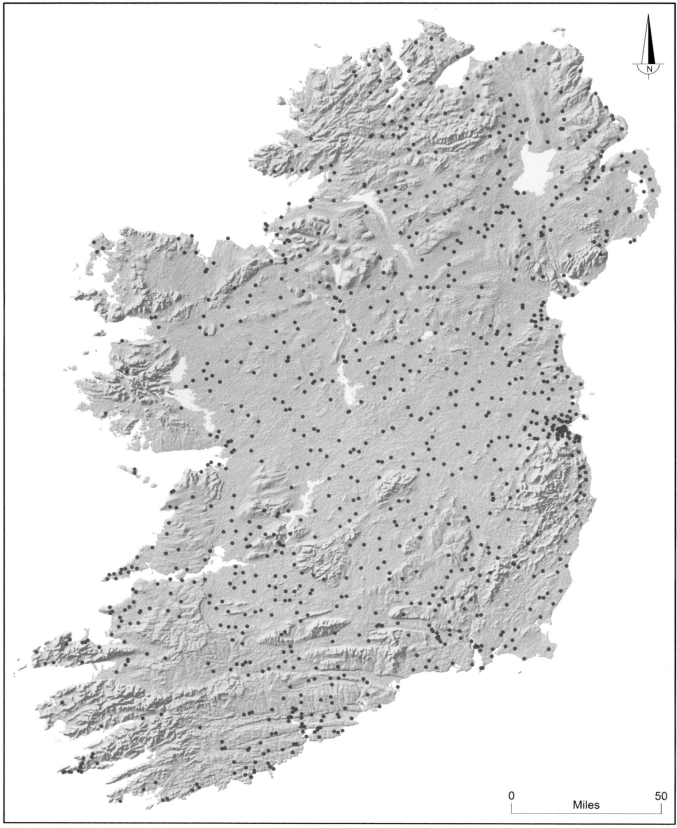

Fig. 5 DISTRIBUTION OF TOWNS WITH LESS THAN 1,500 POPULATION IN 1841. There were 89 towns with populations of 1,000 to 1,499, making up 5.3% of the total island-wide urban population. As many as 233 towns contained populations of 500–999 (6.6% of urban total) and a further 745 in a group of census 'towns' (cum villages) with populations of less than 500. These smallest settlements still constituted 11.2% of the total urban population as defined by the 1841 census. All these smaller towns played significant roles in their local economies, particularly as centres for fairs and markets. At least 40% of families (in the smaller 500 population group) and close on 50% (in the 1,000+settlements) were chiefly engaged in trade and manufacturing. In the less than 500 population group (some of which were essentially farm clusters), 45% of families were chiefly employed in agriculture and in the somewhat bigger towns (500–1,500) about a third of families were so employed. The Famine was to wreak devastation in many of these settlements. Across all three categories at least three-quarters of these towns lost populations between 1841 and 1851.

246

OLD CHAPEL-ROAD, DUNGARVAN, A SCENE OF THE LATE FOOD RIOTS.

Fig. 6  Old Chapel Road, Dungarvan, scene of the recent food riots, *The Illustrated London News*, 7 November 1846.

more, Crookhaven and Castletownbere. In all these towns, as in Abbeyside, Dungarvan and Rosbercon, across the bridge from New Ross, populations of destitute beggars, evicted families, penniless widows and starving children cried out for bread and often starved and died in crowded back lanes.[13]

The Soup Kitchen Act was introduced in early 1847. Numerous ships were, therefore, engaged to supply cargoes of meal to key ports serving distressed regions in the southwest, west and northwest of Ireland. In February 1847, five ships were anchored at Cork City (the *Geyser*, the *Dee*, the *Zephyr*, the *Mercury*, and the *Rhadamanthus*) to carry Indian meal to relief committees at 'West Cobh' (in Kenmare Water) and Dingle and elsewhere in southwest Munster. Baltimore, Cahirciveen, Castletownsend, Kenmare, Kildysart, Tarbert, Limerick, Galway, Westport, Sligo and Killybegs likewise all acted as vital links between at least seventeen supply ships and their own hinterlands. One of the most striking features of the supply strategy was the roles of ships anchored at Tarbert, Long Island Sound, Galway, Westport, Sligo and Killybegs as *floating depots* in supplying Indian meal to their surrounding distressed hinterlands.[14] This linking of food imports via these depots and port towns with the work of inland relief committees in charge of soup kitchens represented the single most effective intervention by central government during all of the Great Famine years.

BATTLE FOR SURVIVAL

Almost from the beginning of the Famine, the towns became key *sites in the battles for survival*. Some hungry families simply closed their doors, turned their backs on this world, and died of starvation and fever. Others did not. Early in 1846, a crowd of about 100 men, women and children blocked carts going to the Commissariat store in Mitchelstown and took almost two tons of meal. All across

Munster, there are numerous reports of horses being shot or their traces cut so as to allow cartloads of flour or meal to be stolen by hungry crowds. Likewise, throughout the rich grain-growing counties of southern and southeastern Ireland, cornstores and mills were attacked in the towns. Troops were drafted in to escort convoys – like the barges leaving Clonmel with grain and flour for export via Carrick-on-Suir and Waterford. Likewise, grain barges on the Fergus River were attacked, requiring a naval escort to protect such boats plying their trade from Ennis to Limerick port.[15] Troops and police were put in place to defend the mills. Port towns also witnessed attempts to block exports. In September 1846 at Youghal, a port then active in the exporting of grain, a large crowd of country people attempted to hold up a boat ready to export grain. The police called in the troops and the crowd was stopped. However, two protestors were shot (one died subsequently) in a similar if more explosive incident at Dungarvan, where a crowd of starving unemployed workers entered the town. They threatened merchants and shopkeepers, ordering them not to export grain and plundered some bakeries. A riot ensued, the Royal Dragoons were called in, stones were thrown and shots fired. Fishermen at Dungarvan were also involved in blocking ships leaving with grain and when out fishing the fishermen's wives – bodies of them, relieving each other at intervals – remained at the quays, intimidating the ship's merchants and workers, insisting that they would not allow the ship to leave until a supply of Indian meal arrived at Dungarvan. The artist, who sketched the riot scenes for *The London Illustrated News* reported:

The distress, both in Youghal and Dungarvan, is truly appalling in the streets; for, without entering homes, the miserable spectre of the haggard looks, crouching attitudes, sunken eyes and colourless

## Pawnshops

■ Shop location

□ Shops closed
   in 1847

Miles
0                    50

Town names as rendered in the 1841 Census

Fig. 7 DISTRIBUTION OF PAWNSHOPS BY 1847. The pawnshop was an essential feature in the life of the poor in the cities and most towns. As this map shows, by 1844 a total of 160 towns listed at least one pawnshop and the cities had many more. Between 1844 and 1845 the number of pawnshops increased from 462 to 504. New pawnshops had emerged in Arklow, Balbriggan, Cavan, Cahir, Kells, Maghera, Moate, Tarbert, Tuam and Wicklow. In 1846, as the famine crisis deepened, pawnshops had started business in Ardee, Castlewellan, Killenaule, Moy, Newmarket (County Cork) and Tullow (County Carlow). But by the bitter year of 1847, pawnshop business had peaked and pawn offices closed in Askeaton, Callan, Carrickmacross, Carrick-on-Shannon, Clones, Cloyne, Cootehill, Sligo, Tullow (County Clare) and Westport. By 1848, for the ragged poor, lack of access to adequate clothing was added to the dearth of food. It is clear from this map that east Ulster, northeast Leinster and much of Munster and south Leinster contained a reasonable concentration of pawnshops. But in the pastoral midland towns and especially in Connacht, the pawnshop was not a feature of urban life.

248

Fig. 8 *Cottage Interior, Claddagh, Galway, 1845* by Francis William Topham (1808–77). Topham was invited to the fishing village of Claddagh by his artist friend Frederick Goodall where he took a keen interest in the working lives of the local women. His depiction of the interior of this cabin is sparse. A young woman holds a child in the foreground while an older woman is mending a net behind her, the latter a familiar subject in Topham's paintings of the Claddagh. Such fishing communities also endured great hardship during the Famine. Many fishermen had pawned their tackle in order to survive the initial onslaught of famine. Unable to redeem their nets they were left without the means of sustaining themselves and their families. [Source: Ulster Museum, Belfast]

lips and cheeks, unmistakably bespeaks the suffering of the people.[16]

'Towns and villages are invaded and plundered by armies of idle labourers' the *Cork Examiner* of 30 September 1846 reported, 'who famish for want of bread and will not be put off'.[17]

## WORK RIOTS

Work riots were also characteristic. In March 1846, a crowd marched through the town of Carrick-on-Suir demanding work. Troops were called out. In this case, the promise of temporary employment quietened the rioters. Likewise, starving and unemployed labourers marched on towns like Clogher, Dungarvan and Macroom, demanding employment on the public works. In Cork, a crowd of 400 labourers marched into the city carrying their spades and demanding work. Limerick city also witnessed such angry demonstrations. But in a number of cases – as in the town of Clogheen, County Tipperary – the townspeople did not support hungry protests by people of the surrounding district.[18] Other desperate and hungry groups invaded Petty Sessions meetings in the courthouses of a number of towns, threatening violence and insisting on relief works for their parishes. Kilfinane and Hospital in County Limerick were witnesses to such demonstrations as was Lismore. The protesters there are described as 'hunger maddened' with deep marks of starvation and famine written on their faces.[19] Relief committees – as in Carlingford, Castlebar, Nenagh and Thurles, as well as Skibbereen – were also intimidated to augment the list of those qualified for relief work. Shopkeepers elsewhere – as in Castleisland, County Kerry – were also threatened with plunder when men and women could no longer bear the cries of their hungry children for food. In Thurles, a half-starving population poured in from the surrounding countryside, and begged in the streets before being driven away.[20] Beggars and displaced people roamed the streets and tramped the roads everywhere.

By the summer's end of 1846, as the new potato crop lay rotting in fields and gardens and as the price of foodstuffs rocketed, the plight of the urban poor reached new depths. Panic set in. The inhabitants of Athy are reported as having 'pawned everything and cannot bear it much longer'.[21]

For many of the poor, every piece of clothing had already been pawned to buy food. By August 1846 in Cork

city, the starving poor wondered how they might find food. Having already pawned their clothes, they had nothing to exchange and nothing to buy food with. They slept in their rags and pawned their bedding. And as in Newtownards and other towns, some women felt unable to go abroad for work or beg or queue for food, as they had already pledged their clothes. The pawnshop was already a central feature in the life of the poor in the cities and towns. By 1844 there were 462 such pawn offices located in 160 towns and cities across the county, giving an average of three pawnshops per town.[22] However, Dublin had forty-two, Belfast and Cork as many as forty-one and thirty-nine respectively, Limerick nineteen and Waterford thir-

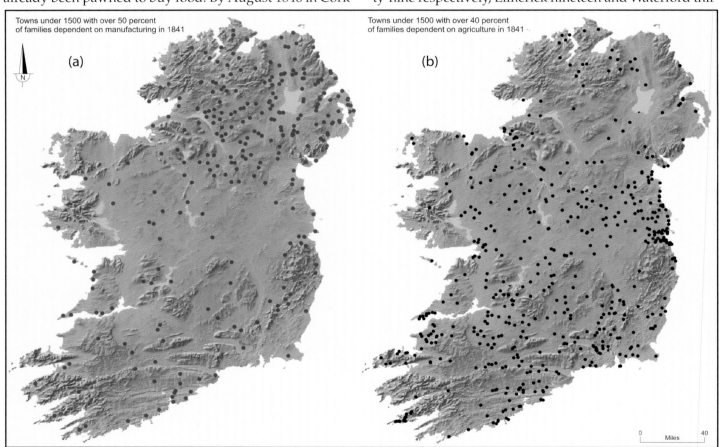

Towns under 1500 with over 50 percent of families dependent on manufacturing in 1841

(a)

Towns under 1500 with over 40 percent of families dependent on agriculture in 1841

(b)

Fig. (9a) and (9b) TOWNS UNDER 1,500 POPULATION: ECONOMIC AND POPULATION STRUCTURES, 1841–51. The distribution of small towns (under 1,500 population) with over 50% of families chiefly dependent on manufacturing, trade and commerce is in one respect very predictable. (9a) The striking density of such 'industrial' towns in Ulster and its borderlands is to be expected. However, there were quite a number of such towns with a strong manufacturing and commercial base scattered throughout the rest of the island, most notably around the coasts and in Munster and southeast Leinster. (9b) In contrast, 'agrarian' small towns with over 40% of their families involved in agriculture are 'few and far between' both over much of Ulster and in upland areas generally. In contrast, across Munster, south Leinster, much of Connacht and the Leinster/Connacht borderlands a reasonable number of such towns could be found in 1841. Unlike their 'industrial' equivalents, many such 'agrarian' small towns – like their rural hinterlands – were to lose significant populations between 1845 and 1851. County Galway's Headford (population in 1841 of 1403) lost one-quarter (-353) of its population in the Famine years, as did Lusk (-162) in County Dublin. County Mayo's Killala population (1446) was reduced by one-third (-476) as was that of Balrothery (-129) in County Dublin and Kilmacthomas (-210) in County Waterford. Binghamstown in Ennis, County Mayo (-183) lost over 40% of its population. The ancient town of Castledermot in County Kildare lost more than half of its population (-750) in those devastating five years as did Freshford in County Kilkenny (-999). Even in the rich lands of County Meath, an old centre such as Dunshaughlin lost one-quarter (-102) of its population. Newtownforbes in County Longford saw a reduction of 40% (-147), typical of small agrarian towns in that region of high emigration and high mortality along the Leinster/Connacht/Ulster borderlands. In addition, there were at least fifty towns with over 1500 population where over 40% of their families were dependent on agriculture. The two most striking zones with a high number of such large 'agrarian' towns were (i) the north Connacht/Leinster/Ulster borderlands and (ii) the province of Munster and its borderlands. In the latter region, population decline by 1851 amongst such 'agrarian' towns averages as high as 27%. But the Munster group included a number of Cork/Waterford towns – Charleville (-37.9%), Bunmahon (-35.5%), Newmarket (-34%), Tallow (-33.1%), Rosscarbery (-32%) and Millstreet (-31%) – where losses exceeded 30%. On the northern borderlands of this Munster zone, Maryborough (-42.8%), Urlingford (-33%), Mountrath (-30.7%) and Killenaule (-30%) also saw massive losses in population. In the northern zone, the average loss of population amongst these large 'agrarian' towns was c.20% but the County Meath towns of Athboy (-34%) and Oldcastle (-30%), Leitrim's Carrick-on-Shannon (-35%) and Claremorris (-30.9%) in Mayo were most severely affected by the Famine catastrophe.

teen. By 1845, the number of pawnshops had increased by 9% to 504 and remained at this level for 1846. By 1848, the Medical Inspector, Mr Phelan, was reporting that many were seeking admission to the workhouse, partly for want of clothes along with the want of food. In consequence, the Poor Law Commissioners asked Poor Law inspectors to report on 'Distress indicated in the clothing of the Peasants' and sought returns from the pawnbrokers in their districts.[23]

The compulsory reduction in the number of people employed in the public works during March and April of 1847 sparked a series of disturbances and 'outrages' in some parts of Ireland. Youghal – which had already seen violent protests early in 1846, given the lack of employment there – saw further violent protests as bodies of men were dismissed from the public works before new forms of relief (i.e. the soup kitchens) had been put in place. In Ballinasloe, as elsewhere, given the deadly delays in the opening of their soup kitchens, hundreds protested against this delay by marching through the town and attacking the local food stores. Likewise, there were violent disturbances in Gort following on from the closure of the public works. Some of the soup kitchens were attacked as in Castlemartyr, County Cork, because the people preferred either work or money to 'that greasy stuff'. In Corofin, County Clare, and Kells, County Meath, local people objected to the indignity of receiving cooked food – the latter a Poor Law strategy to prevent the selling of foodstuffs. The striking feature of most of these protests is that they were not the work of agrarian organisations but initiated by desperate people worn out by famine conditions.[24]

## WORKHOUSE TOWNS

It was the workhouse towns which witnessed the greatest distress and disturbance. With men on the public works starving on a seven penny rate of pay, hungry labourers forced their way into Mallow workhouse, demanding to be admitted as paupers rather than be abandoned to die slowly of hunger on the public works. Cahirciveen, Dungarvan, Galway, Kilrush, Nenagh, Scariff and Sligo all witnessed the gathering of crowds at meetings of the Board of Guardians. Some of these protests were sparked by new regulations about outdoor relief and particularly in relation to demands that such relief should be extended to larger groups of people. In November 1847 a crowd of about 300 people threatened to attack the New Ross workhouse unless either food or employment were provided. A similar protest took place in Newcastlewest, while at Kilrush workhouse a great gathering of c.3,000 people congregated outside the workhouse, seeking and demanding outdoor relief. Police and troops were regularly called out to maintain order and disperse the crowds. In early November 1847, a crowd of starving labourers broke down the gates of Tralee workhouse and marched into the yard. They

declared they would enter the workhouse by force. Queues outside workhouses were also lengthening. In Carrick-on-Shannon, 100 persons gathered for admission but only thirty vacancies existed. The rest were refused amidst painful and heart-wrenching scenes. As the workhouses filled up, police were regularly stationed at the doors to keep the numerous applicants out.[25]

In the country gaols across the country, the Famine led to a dramatic increase in the number of prisoners – possibly a fourfold increase. As documented elsewhere, the number of hunger-related robberies – of cattle, sheep, grain, flour and Indian meal – rose exponentially during the Famine. Likewise, 'shops and stores were plundered in classic "moral economy" fashion and petty larceny was widespread'.[26] Prison convictions often followed. Quite a number of these prisoners died in these badly overcrowded city and county gaols. A total of 5,443 are officially returned as dying in prisons and prison hospitals between 1841 and 1851 – 4,567 males and 876 females. Nine out of ten of these prisoners died between 1846 and 1851. Only 9.9% died in Ulster jails and 19.0% in Leinster prisons. As many as 2,428 (44.6%) died in Munster's prisons and prison hospitals and a disproportionate number, 1,443 (26.5%) in Connacht's jails. These prison mortality figures are consistent with other mortality figures for the Famine.

It is striking that of Leinster's twenty-two prisons, only two, Richmond and Grangegorman – both *convict* depots as well as bridewells – record more than 100 deaths. Ulster's prisons record no such high figures; Enniskillen reports the highest with eighty-five deaths. In contrast, in Munster, Ennis gaol (231), Cork County gaol (984), Tralee (229), Limerick County gaol (293), Nenagh (238) and Clonmel (144) all massively exceed 100 prison deaths. Waterford's divergence from Munster famine conditions is again emphasised by only thirty-three deaths at its county gaol. What is also striking is 154 deaths in the Spike Island convict depot, the halting site for so many prisoners destined for transportation to Australia, Tasmania and elsewhere.[27] John Mitchel was incarcerated there. The unmarked graves of the convict dead are scattered across the western end of the island.[28] Across a narrow but deep channel to the east was the great emigration port of Cobh/Queenstown.

By 1849, a profound quietude had fallen over much of the Irish countryside. However, it was not a peaceful quiet but a bitter silence, born of defeat, disease, death and often decimated populations. In most country towns, 'as the population of the rural hinterland emptied, so the population of their agricultural service towns fell too'.[29] Apart from the larger cities and a few strong market towns, the populations and businesses of the remaining towns had contracted. In Athlone, for example, it appears that the best shops had closed and their owners had emigrated. He describes Kildare as reduced to wretched village status – 'full of ragged beggars'[30] – nevertheless its small town character and func-

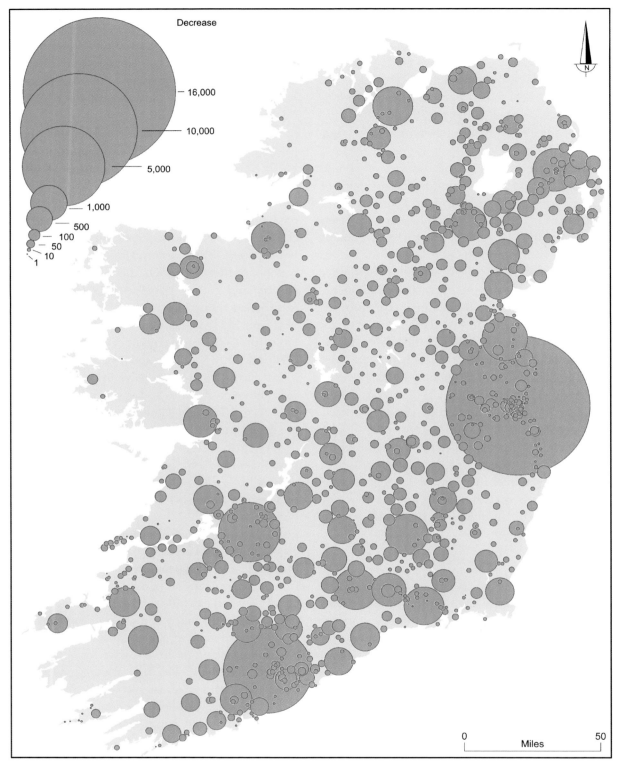

Decrease

— 16,000

— 10,000

— 5,000

— 1,000

— 500
— 100
— 50
— 10
— 1

0                    50
Miles

Fig. 10 DECREASE IN NUMBER OF FAMILIES DEPENDENT ON 'VESTED MEANS' AND THE 'DIRECTION OF LABOUR' BETWEEN 1841 AND 1851. The impact of the Great Famine on Irish rural communities has been well documented. Much less attention has been focused on the dramatic transformation of Irish urban communities. Some towns lost close on half their populations: Charleville (-2,165) was one such town, losing 45% of its 1841 total. Towns such as Cashel (-2,386), Loughrea (-1830), Rathkeale (-1,213) and Roscrea (-1,886) all lost between 30 to 36% of their populations. Many Munster towns were devastated, reflecting the depth of the Famine crisis in that province. A host of towns – including Armagh (-2,291), Callan (-760), Carlow (-1574), Castlebar (-1,121), Carrick-on-Suir (-2,150), Dungarvan (-1,760), Kilmallock (-334), Kinsale (-1550), Mallow (-1412), Nenagh (-1584), Newcastlewest (-655) and Youghal (-2299) lost between 20 and 25% of their 1841 populations. But as this dramatic map shows, there were even more devastating losses amongst the emerging bourgeoisie of these towns (i.e. those involved in the direction of labour and those with vested means). Here the proportionate losses are even greater than population losses: Armagh, Ballina, Callan, Clonmel, Drogheda, Loughrea, Mallow and Rathkeale all lost at least three-quarters in this class. A further array of towns such as Castlebar, Dundalk, Roscrea and Sligo all lost close on two-thirds in this category. And practically all the big cities – Dublin, Cork, Limerick and Galway – lost around half of this class, and this in spite of the fact that Galway's population increased by 16%, Dublin by 6% and Cork by 2.4% (Limerick city barely increased its population [+0.8%], again reflecting the depth of the Famine impact in north and mid-Munster). Dynamic Belfast, with a 30% population increase, was the only exception to this massive decline amongst the bourgeoisie – it only shows a 19% decline in this class. Waterford city lost 38%, the best performance of the southern cities.

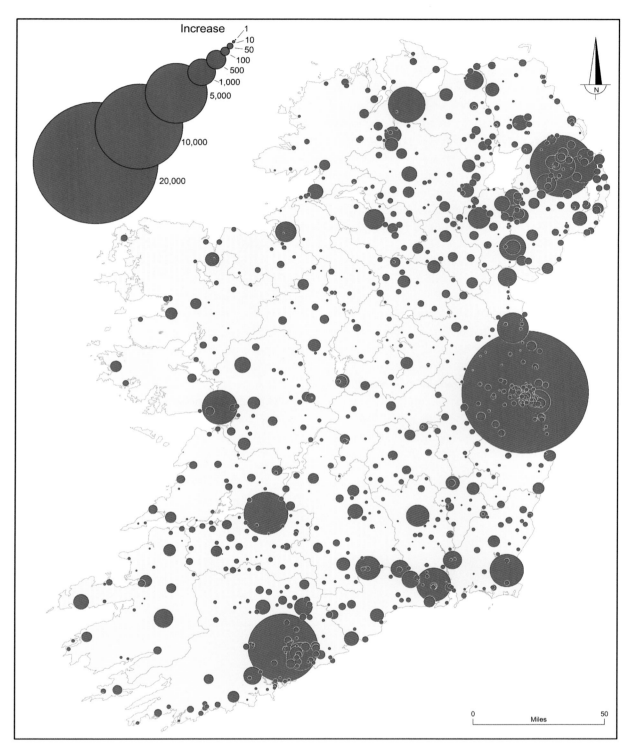

Fig. 11 INCREASE IN NUMBER OF FAMILIES DEPENDENT ON MANUAL LABOUR BETWEEN 1841 AND 1851. If the decline in the number of people with vested means and involved in the direction of labour was dramatic between 1841 and 1851, the increase in those dependent on manual labour – as this map shows – was even more striking. While acknowledging that the emergence of bigger industrial and retailing establishments would correlate with these two major trends, nevertheless the extraordinary increase in those dependent on their own manual labour also points to the pauperisation and further proletarianisation of most Irish towns and cities. Dublin saw an almost 21,000 increase in this class, an increase of two-and-a-half times the 1841 figures. Cork's manual labouring class more than doubled in this period as did Galway's, while Belfast and Waterford – increased by 84 and 91% respectively. Limerick experienced the least dramatic change, yet still saw a 66% increase on its 1841 manual labouring component. Regional centres like Carlow (+40%), Drogheda (+103%), Dundalk (+48%), Sligo (+74%), Newry (+150%) and Tralee (+23%) saw varied patterns of increases in this class. Clonmel's manual labouring component doubled, Armagh almost did so while Derry city increased by 70%. Most of Ulster's middle order towns with populations of 2,500 to 5,000 retained or slightly increased their overall population numbers during the Famine years yet their manual labouring class increased on average by 80 to 100%. Elsewhere, equivalent towns of this size – Ballina, Ballinasloe, Birr, Callan, Castlebar, Edenderry and Loughrea – saw much smaller percentage increases (25.50%) in this class. Two dominant emigration ports reveal exceptional profiles. Kingstown (Dún Laoghaire) was to increase its population from ,7729 to 10,458, not only increasing its middle-class component but almost doubling its manual labouring component during the famine decade. Queenstown (Cobh) saw an even more dramatic increase in population – from 4,929 to 10,985 – a significant reduction in its middle class but an astonishing increase from 278 to 1,242 (+347%) in its labouring (cum impoverished) class, many of whom were waiting to board the next emigrant ship.

tions continued. Carlyle depicts Dublin as patched and dilapadated.[31] It certainly had become 'a gigantic refugee camp' during the Famine.[32] About half of its population lived in fourth-class accommodation, that is where one or more families lived in a fourth-class house (one room with window), two or more in a third-class house; four or more in a second-class house and more than six in a first-class house. Dublin's tenements had expanded since 1841. Most strikingly, close on 40% of its residents were not Dublin-born. Many of them were starving famine migrants in search of short-term relief before gathering sufficient resources to emigrate.[33] Dublin's growth later in the nineteenth century would depend much more on its commercial rather than its industrial functions.

Between 1841 and 1851, Cork city had also seen a significant decline in its industrial base. While the commercial and service sectors were to expand in this city ruled by a merchant class, its overall population did not grow over the next century. In the late 1840s, Waterford's commerce was described as ruined with most of its industries, especially its bacon-curing, reduced or closed, and its butter and cattle trade at a standstill. Although it would recover, Waterford city's limited growth over the second half of the nineteenth century was still below the Irish mean. Belfast – even though its poorer working-class neighbourhoods suffered during the early years of the Great Famine – was the

great exception. New industrial plants continued to be developed during the Famine years, not only in linen but also in a host of ancillary and other industries, most notably in its eastern suburbs of Ballymacarret on the Down side of the Lagan.[34]

In much of the rest of Ireland in the late 1840s, the biggest trade was in cartloads of Indian meal winding their way to still overcrowded workhouses. But one other trade had grown dramatically in the coastal towns and most especially in the port towns and cities – that of emigration. The interior towns had witnessed the extraordinary exodus of over one million people, deserting every parish in the island and tramping across the land, sometimes with inadequate food resources, begging as they passed through the country towns before reaching the emigrant ships. One of the most telling features of southern Ireland's urban geography in the second half of the nineteenth century is that of the few towns that grew substantially, two were ferry ports – Kingstown (Dun Laoghaire) and Queenstown (Cobh) – both involved in the business of exporting Irish people to Liverpool and other cities in Britain and North America.[35]

Many towns not only lost populations but also a more diverse social and economic base. They would remain museum pieces to the nineteenth century[36] and would not recover for a hundred years.

# The impact of the Great Famine on subsistent women

## Dympna McLoughlin

The Famine had a far-reaching impact on women's lives, especially the lives of labouring women. These were the very poorest women in Irish society, many of whom lived subsistent lives. By subsistence, I mean, an economy of makeshifts, women basically living a hand-to-mouth existence, with no secure employment. This included petty traders, tramps, peddlers, petty criminals, dealers, beggars and a high proportion of labourers. The subsistence economy involved a constantly changing stratum of Irish society right up to the Famine. The aim of this chapter is to present the reasons why subsistent women came under such stress in the Famine period. Labouring women and their children were particularly hard hit by the Famine and those that survived it faced extreme prejudice that militated against them finding work. Therefore, they had no option but to enlist on various assisted emigration schemes.

The factors that severely impacted on subsistent women included the reluctance of employers to allow female labourers to have their children with them while they worked, famine mortality rates and the overcrowded and disease-ridden nature of the workhouse, the quarter-acre clause, the ideology of respectability and, finally, workhouse-assisted emigration and transportation.

By 1820, before the Poor Law Act of 1838, there was a growing concern about deserted children. Once the workhouses were established the numbers of these children increased dramatically. Many mothers paid the Master of the workhouse for the upkeep of their child, while they travelled the country seeking work. These children were very carefully watched and regularly visited by their parents and relatives to make sure that no harm came to them. In most cases the mother reclaimed the child at Christmas time and over other short periods. The reasons why mothers had to relinquish their child to the workhouse, was that employers would not take them on with children. Many farmers were unwilling to take on the extra burden of feeding labourers' children or even allowing them onto their farms.[1]

Although some mothers paid for the upkeep of their child in the workhouse, there were many others who could not. One strategy some of them used was entering a workhouse with their children and subsequently absconding over the workhouse wall, leaving the children behind. In response to this, several Poor Law guardians decided to send these children out to work so that they could pay for their maintenance in the house.

## MIGRATORY HABITS

The migratory habits of the poor were one of the key ways to offset starvation and distress in the pre-Famine period. The workhouse facilitated their subsistence lifestyle by allowing them to enter en masse in winter and then releasing them any time they wanted, but most often in spring. These people used the workhouse on their own terms, entering and leaving when they liked, but usually in large numbers in spring. Popular occasions for women to leave the workhouse included fairs, market days, horse racing, keeping Christmas, as well as family events such as funerals, court cases and visiting the local hospital. It was the flexibility of the workhouse practices that ultimately facilitated this lifestyle.

Fig. 1 Workhouse walls in Birr. Women who entered the workhouse with their children often absconded over workhouse walls leaving their children behind them. [Photo: William J. Smyth]

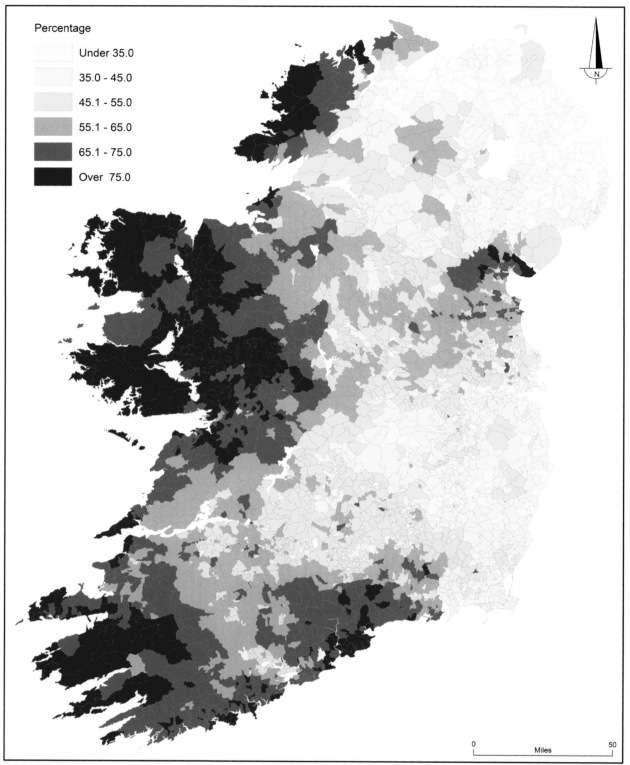

Percentage

Under 35.0

35.0 - 45.0

45.1 - 55.0

55.1 - 65.0

65.1 - 75.0

Over 75.0

0     Miles     50

Fig. 2 PERCENTAGE OF FEMALE POPULATION (OVER 5 YEARS OF AGE) WHO COULD NOT READ OR WRITE IN 1841. The ability to read and write or read only were impor-tant life-saving skills during the Famine. People who could not read public health and Poor Law Union notices (all in the English language) could be at a disadvantage in availing of these necessary supports. Levels of literacy in early- and mid-nineteenth-century Ireland were above the European norm for this period. A commitment to education was a striking feature of many in the society and literacy levels rose rapidly from the late eighteenth century onwards. However, there still remained sharp gender differences in the proportion of men and women who were literate and equally striking regional differences – as this map demonstrates – in women's ability to read and write. Amongst the older population (aged 66–75) in 1841, there was a 20% dif-ferential between the number of male illiterates (45.8) vis-à-vis women (65.8%). However, this gender gap was closing amongst the younger age group (aged 16–25) with only a 10.8% difference between a reduced illiteracy amongst both men (34.6%) and women (45.4%). However, amongst this younger age group, there were still striking provincial differences as between Leinster and Ulster where the gender gap was only 6.5% and 8.6% respectively, vis-à-vis Munster and Connacht, where the gap was 14.9% and 16.0% respectively. This map, therefore, reveals long-standing differences in the expansion of English speech across Ireland and the degree to which fee-paying schools were supplemented by the evangelical Sunday School movement – the latter a particular feature of east Ulster. Literacy levels were, therefore, profoundly influenced by a family's income, way of living, location, religious affiliation and language. And it is clear that the areas with very high levels of female illiteracy – especially from 65% upwards – were profoundly influenced by the dominance of the Irish language, by relative remoteness from the centres of English speech and by very, very poor living conditions.

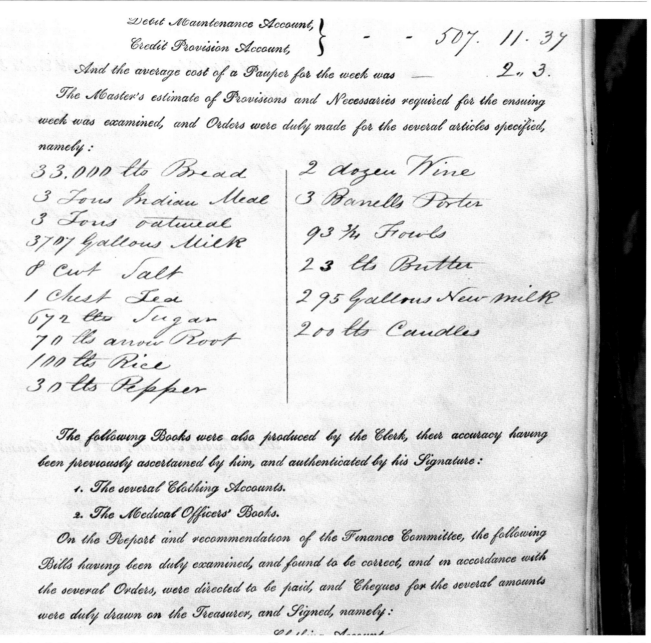

Debit Maintenance Account,
Credit Provision Account, } - - - 507. 11. 3¼

And the average cost of a Pauper for the week was — 2 „ 3.

The Master's estimate of Provisions and Necessaries required for the ensuing week was examined, and Orders were duly made for the several articles specified, namely:

33.000 lbs Bread                2 dozen Wine
3 Tons Indian Meal              3 Barrels Porter
3 Tons oatmeal                  93 ½ Fowls
3707 Gallons Milk               23 lbs Butter
8 Cwt Salt                      295 Gallons New milk
1 Chest Tea                     200 lbs Candles
672 lbs Sugar
70 lbs arrow Root
100 lbs Rice
30 lbs Pepper

The following Books were also produced by the Clerk, their accuracy having been previously ascertained by him, and authenticated by his Signature:

1. The several Clothing Accounts.
2. The Medical Officers' Books.

On the Report and recommendation of the Finance Committee, the following Bills having been duly examined, and found to be correct, and in accordance with the several Orders, were directed to be paid, and Cheques for the several amounts were duly drawn on the Treasurer, and Signed, namely:

Fig. 3 Sample provision list from a minute book of the Cork Union workhouse. The deterioration in workhouse diets during the Famine often sparked riots amongst inmates, as was the case with the women in the Dublin and Limerick unions. [Source: Cork Archives Institute]

In the winter months when there was no work available, female labourers went to the workhouse in droves. In the workhouse they were assured of food, drink, shelter, medical attention, and especially the company of other women of the same class. During the Famine the workhouses were massively overcrowded with other groups competing for survival with the subsistent. The Poor Law guardians reluctantly broke with the key principle of the Poor Law and allowed outdoor relief. These new groups who would never willingly enter the workhouse included farmers and their families, male labourers and tradesmen, the sick of all classes, large numbers of orphans as well as whole communities in Munster and Connacht, the provinces most badly affected by the Famine. The extent of the overcrowding cannot be underestimated. The number of people in the workhouse in 1847 was 417,139, rising to 932,284 in 1849 and thereafter slowly declining. The emergency measure of outdoor relief provided for 207,683 persons in 1848, falling to 135,019 in 1849 and thereafter dropping dramatically.

During the Famine workhouses also provided accommodation for the sick. Sheds, verandas and all sorts of basic accommodation were set up to separate the sick from the healthy. This was because many of the fever hospitals, such as the Cork Street Hospital in Dublin, refused to take in these patients, fearing they would be completely swamped by them. Labouring women used to having the workhouse to themselves and their friends now had to put up with thousands of other people. Many of these new inmates, unused to the workhouse, were shocked and traumatised by it. For these formerly independent people, many of them of middle-class origins, the workhouse rep-

Fig. 4 From 6 June 1841 to 30 March 1851, 2,193 inmates are recorded as dying in Dungarvan workhouse of which 1,107 were males and 1,086 females. The separate Dungarvan fever hospital contains no records of deaths previous to May 1847. By 30 March 1851, 430 had died there, close on two-thirds from 'fever', all the remainder from other causes. More males (230) perished there than females (200). William Fraher writes that 'towards the end of October 1847, the police had to guard the entrance to the workhouse to allow the guardians to pass through the crowds of people seeking relief' (William Fraher in Des Cowman and Donald Brady, eds, *The Famine in Waterford 1845–1850*, Dublin, 1995, p. 146). Given its overcrowded conditions, the guardians rented Kiely's store in Quay Lane to accommodate a further 350 people. Another store was later acquired to cope with the growing number of applicants. Conditions in the workhouse were poor and riots and disturbances were a repeated feature. The poem 'Amhrán na Prátaí Dubha' remembers these inhumane conditions and the many that are buried at Reilig an tSléibhe (The Mountain Graveyard) that overlooks the town a few miles to the west. [Photo: William J. Smyth]

resented a complete loss of status. Their very negative view of the workhouse is the perspective that has lasted to the present day.

A very difficult issue for all workhouse inmates was the reduction in the workhouse diet during the Famine. The response of the women took the form of food riots, as was the case in the Dublin and Limerick unions. Other injustices in their treatment resulted in them setting fire to their bedding and destroying workhouse property. Labouring women were used to standing up for themselves and their children, and they certainly had the ability to challenge the workhouse regime. However, it became impossible to employ these survival strategies during the Famine. Probably more than 50% of this class of women died during this period. Because of their geographical mobility they had a higher chance of contract-

ing fever and cholera and dying. The lifestyle of subsistence inevitably took its toll on the most vulnerable in this group.

Another area that impacted disproportionately upon subsistent women was the quarter-acre clause, which was brought into law in June 1847. A Galway landlord, William Gregory, who along with several other landowners who did not want subsistent people holding land in any capacity, very carefully introduced this clause. They effectively succeeded in having the workhouse removed as a lifeline to those holding more than a quarter acre.[2] In terms of the cottiers, or 'scoresmen' as they were known in Cork, the annual renting of a small patch of land on a yearly basis was achieved by the cottier migrating to neighbouring counties or indeed further afield to Scotland to secure paid work, while the women and children remained in the local

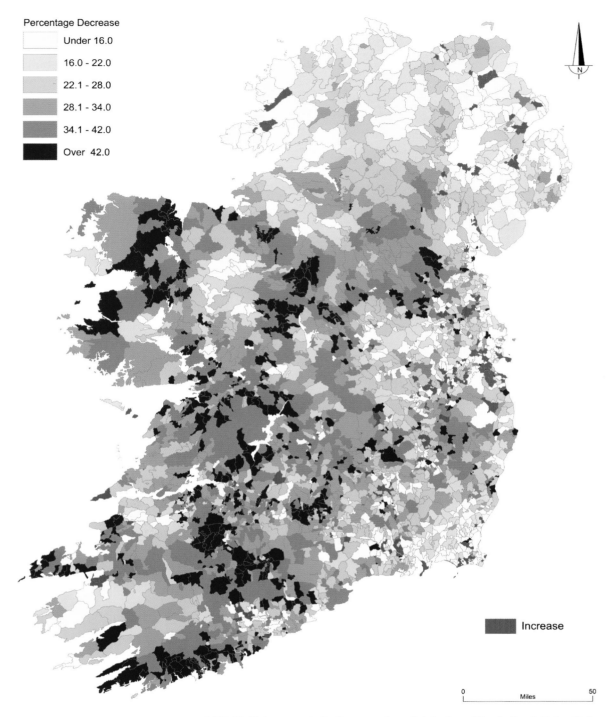

Percentage Decrease

Under 16.0

16.0 - 22.0

22.1 - 28.0

28.1 - 34.0

34.1 - 42.0

Over 42.0

Increase

0   Miles   50

Fig. 5 PERCENTAGE DECLINE PER PARISH OF FEMALE POPULATION, 1841–51. Not unexpectedly, the percentage distribution of the decline in Ireland's female population between 1841 and 1851 is almost identical to that of the population as a whole. One encounters similar patterns of low, medium and high levels of decline across the country. The few pockets of increased populations overall are also almost identical, although a few parishes register an increase in the number of women but not in the parish population as a whole. A striking and notable universal feature of famine mortality everywhere is that males are more likely to succumb to famine conditions than females. The census figures record that of the total recorded dead over the Famine decade, 53% were male and 47% female. The mortality gap was less in urban districts – 52.5% male versus 47.5% female deaths – and greater in the country districts – 54.3% male vis-à-vis 45.7% female deaths. Gender-based death rates were similar in the hospitals but varied between union workhouses. Research has shown (The National Famine Commemoration Project) that the fate of inmates admitted to the Parsonstown (Birr) workhouse in 1849 differed greatly by gender and age. Mortality was greatest amongst children under five (64.7% of this age group), followed by a high mortality rate amongst the 5–14 year olds (25.2%) with the proportion of inmates over sixty (23.4%) signalling the third most vulnerable group. But there was a striking difference between the fate of males and females: 21% of the former died in this workhouse in 1849 as against 14.8% of the females. The gap was even greater amongst the adults: 11.5% of adult males died in this workhouse as against 4.1% of the females in that year. In the County Wicklow workhouse of Rathdrum, the gender difference is less severe with close on 7% of all male inmates dying between 1849–52 as compared with 4.3% of female inmates. So destinies varied between different workhouses and in the north Dublin Union it appears that the risk of dying was shared equally between females and males. Research has indicated that the greater capacity of females to survive is a consequence of 'physiological rather than cultural causes' (see Ó'Gráda this volume). But unlike other emigrant groups from European countries, Irish women's propensity to emigrate was as great as Irish men's and the literature confirms that many such women were prepared to travel alone to a foreign destination. These latter behaviours, therefore, help to explain why the overall patterns of population decline compared with that of females is strikingly similar.

area begging.[3] These families were often reunited just before Christmas time. Having earned the money for the rent of conacre, their survival was guaranteed for over six months of the year before they would have to take to the road again.

Temporary residence in the workhouse was the vital component for this partnership to work. For many subsistent people, the workhouse was a safety net where the woman and children could go in the winter when it was too wet and cold to beg. If a child was sick when the mother was on the road, they could easily be brought into the workhouse to avail of medical attention and particularly the services of the apothecary in compounding and dispensing drugs. If the mother chose to, she and her children could remain on in the workhouse indefinitely. Once enough money had been earned to rent the quarter acre or so for a term, the man returned to Ireland and joined up with his partner and children. Together they rented the quarter acre and its small cabin.

The quarter-acre clause had a twofold impact on this class. Women and children could no longer avail of workhouse relief while they begged. This was a devastating blow to them and impacted on their survival. Furthermore, with the passing of the Poor Law Extension Act in June 1847,

those holding more than a quarter acre could not avail of any workhouse relief without giving up their cabin and land. Despite their protestations to their landlords many had no choice but to relinquish their holdings. Quarter-acre holdings were essentially another type of subsistence that ended with the Famine.

## SURVIVING THE FAMINE

The small numbers of female labourers and subsistent women who survived the Famine, probably less than 40% of the original number, were now faced with an ideology that was extremely hostile to them. Respectability was exclusively concerned with the behaviour of women and was based on the two concepts of reference and reputation. Both these requirements attested to a woman's virtue and good name in the local area. For aspiring and politically ambitious farmers in the immediate post-Famine period, respectability was an essential code for their daughters to live their lives. Pregnancy outside marriage for these women meant a large economic cost to their father. Money had to be spent in fixing up the errant daughter in some kind of marriage. The actions of an 'immoral' daughter resulted in a massive loss of status to a family no matter how wealthy they were. While this ideology of respectabil-

IRISH SKETCHES : MARKET WOMEN OF THE OLD BOOTHS, GALWAY.—SEE PAGE 48.

Fig. 6 'Market women of the Old Booths, Galway', *The Illustrated London News*, 22 November 1879. As in many other cultures, some poorer women earned their living as peddlers and dealers travelling from market to market. The shop name 'Burke' is a strong indication of the Galway location.

Fig. 7 Labouring women in the fields as depicted in the engraving entitled 'Harrowing under difficulties in a mountain farm in County Mayo', *The Illustrated London News*, 17 January 1880. The farm was located close to Pontoon Lough on the road from Castlebar to Ballina.

ity kept middle-class women in line, it had severe consequences for female labourers and reduced their numbers dramatically.

Geographical mobility was an essential part of life for labouring and subsistent women. They had to travel from place to place in order to survive. Therefore, they had nobody to vouch for their character in a reference. Neither did labouring women have a reputation, as they were not known in the areas they quickly moved through. The absence of these basic requirements made labouring women suspect. Usually they secured work during the harvest times when they worked in the fields alongside men. They were never let into the yard or even near the house of the farm they were working on. Most importantly they were never let near the respectable daughters, safely contained within the house. The separation of the moral and respectable women from geographically mobile and subsistent women was essential practice at this time, as it was believed by middle-class men, that female immorality was contagious to other women.

A couple of weeks' work at harvest time were about the most that these female labourers could secure. The remainder of the time they were employed in opportunistic endeavours such as selling briars, seaweed and sticks. Sometimes they were employed as rough servants in male-only households. These households did not care for references or reputation and as a result treated these women wretchedly. There was an assumption that these women were sexually available. Without a reference or reputation, male employers believed that these women were no better than common prostitutes. In the absence of a reference to attest to their character they were unemployable in respectable households, and had no option but to take up any kind of work available, whatever the consequences. Some of these rough servants ended up back in the workhouse awaiting the birth of their child. Few of their employers took any responsibility for their offspring. Some of these women then had no option but to set themselves up as peddlers of small goods and travelled up and down the island selling their wares. They often hired young girls of eight years out of the workhouse to mind their babies for them as they worked. Other women in desperation had no option but to resort to theft and larceny.

THE STATE OF IRELAND: WOMEN CARRYING HOME MEAL-SACKS FROM THE RELIEF COMMITTEE.

A SKETCH NEAR HEADFORD, GALWAY, BY OUR SPECIAL ARTIST.

Fig. 8 'Women carrying home meal-sacks from the Relief Committee, Headford, County Galway', *The Illustrated London News*, 20 November 1880. The long shadow of Famine conditions persisted well into the late nineteenth century and outdoor relief remained a feature of life especially in the congested western unions.

## EMIGRATION

The seasonal pattern of subsistence had come to an end for many female labourers by 1848. Many of them had no option but to crowd into the workhouse. The terms 'redundant' and 'superfluous' were applied to them. By 1850 many realised that subsistence as a way of life was over and that there was simply no way of overcoming the prejudice against them as women without references or reputation. The only option available to them was emigration. Since they had no means of their own that meant, in effect, assisted emigration.

The first method for 3,000 women was transportation.[4] There was nothing easy about this process as it required serving some time in prison, usually in terrible conditions, and then enduring a very long and difficult journey to Australia. Once they arrived the prisoners had to work out their sentences before they were free women. A more popular type of emigration to Australia was the Bounty scheme that started in 1848. This allowed selected women out of the workhouse during the height of the Famine. This was free emigration for Irish women to Australia on the basis that

they would marry lonely male colonists and therefore make Australia into a stable settlement. Hardly any subsistence women married in Ireland as the financial cost of getting married was outside their ability to pay. Some of this class of women preferred common-law partnerships and had several such relationships. These women were not going to Australia to get married but to have a chance of an independent life. To prevent this situation the Poor Law guardians decided instead to send young girls under eighteen years of age. At this age they hoped that immoral habits had not yet set in. The youthful appearance of these Bounty scheme recipients, along with the very feminine ways in which they were dressed made them very attractive as wives.

In Killarney, County Kerry, in 1848, twenty-four orphans were selected under the Bounty scheme. They were listed as follows

Ann Lovitt, aged 14 years, Mary Murphy 16, Mary Shea 18, Mary Connor 18, Joyce Foley 17, Catherine Sullivan 18, Margaret Sullivan 18, Mary McCarthy

Fig. 9 *The Potato Gatherers in the West* (1902) by Charles McIver Grierson, pastel on paper [Source: Crawford Art Gallery]

Fig. 10 Monument erected at workhouse burial site in Boyle, County Roscommon. [Photo: William J. Smyth]

17, Margaret Foley 17, Mary Regan 16, Mary Shea 16, Norrie Sullivan 18, Margaret Murphy 17, Mary Sullivan 17, Julia Shea 17, Catherine Manning 18, Margaret Cronin 18, Ann Hubbard 17, Jane Shea 18, Eileen McCarthy 18 years, Catherine Dowling 18, Mary McCarthy 18, Mary Dineen 18, Mary Corkery 18, and Fanny Riordan, 17 years.[5]

They were well dressed and supplied with necessary items for their journey and new life. In a cost-saving measure most of the items were either sewn or knitted by the female inmates of the workhouse. The remainder were purchased from local suppliers at competitive prices and made up by female workhouse inmates.

Items included: 150 yards black stuff for 50 pairs of worsted stockings, 100 pairs of cotton stockings, 200 yards cotton for dresses, 150 yards wool plaid for dresses, 50 aprons, 12.5 yards linen for collars, 25 pairs of stays, 25 woollen plaid shawls, 150 yards black lining, 25 yards of muslin for caps, 25 black bonnets, 75 yards ribbon for bon-

nets, 60 yards ribbon for caps, 50 pairs of shoes for girls between 12 and 18 years, 50 toothbrushes, 25 pairs of mittens and 25 boxes (two feet long and fourteen inches deep, with locks and hinges). The emigrants' names were printed on the front of each box. Soap and religious books were also included.

The need for women in Australia was far more important than any other criteria.[6] As a result, scandal followed in the wake of some of the women selected for these schemes. Probably the most notorious were the girls who were sent out from the Belfast workhouse in 1848. Some of these 'girls' were over fifty years old and most of the women in this scheme had sexual relations with the sailors while on the journey, fought with each other and spoke in the crudest terms imaginable. Even the protection afforded by the presence of a matron did not save these women from obloquy.

Institutionalised young Irish girls, on getting their freedom from the workhouse, were never going to behave like ladies. One could go as far as saying that this fighting spirit and the ability to stand up for themselves, to survive against the odds, was in fact exactly the type of frontier spirit that was needed in Australia.

The estimated total number of orphans that took up this scheme according to Magdwick was 4,175.[7] While the Bounty scheme was popular in Ireland, the scheme that followed it was not. This was the 'Remittance scheme' where a person in Australia would pay a portion of the passage of a person they wanted to assist to emigrate. The Bounty schemes were the only realistic way for pauper women to leave Ireland and try life in Australia as a free settler.

One of the most successful schemes was that of assisted emigration from the workhouse to North America. This involved a very careful selection of paupers based on their health, time in the workhouse, and moral character. All the remaining subsistent women were on this scheme, perhaps up to 50,000 of them, and were assisted to emigrate to various destinations in North America. The women were to be employed as domestic workers. This scheme ultimately failed because many women left their destinations and sought out paid factory work in the major cities where they could live their lives on their own terms.

The contracting opportunities for subsistent women before the Famine and the intolerance towards them after it made assisted emigration a necessity. Many of these women, who lived on the margins of Irish society, did very well for themselves in both North America and Australia. They were in fact the ultimate survivors. Other groups and classes of women fared differently. For many subsistent women who did not make it through the Famine, the workhouse became their final resting place.

# The landed classes during the Great Famine

## *David J. Butler*

Undoubtedly it is the landlord's right to do as he pleases, and if he abstained he conferred a favour and was doing an act of kindness. If, on the other hand, he choose to stand on his right, the tenants must be taught by the strong arm of the law that they had no power to oppose or resist . . . property would be valueless and capital would no longer be invested in cultivation of the land if it were not acknowledged that it was the landlord's undoubted and most sacred right to deal with his property as he wished.

> Lord Broughman's speech on 23 March 1846 in
> the House of Lords

In folk memory, Irish landlords have generally been condemned for their callous attitude towards their poor tenants. However, research has shown their response was very varied. While some used the distress to evict their tenants, others gave relief in different ways. When the blight came a second time some landlords lowered their rents or provided employment. These actions tended to be short-term, especially because landlords themselves had financial problems when taxes rose steeply and income from rents fell. This chapter will endeavour to look at the behaviour of the Irish landlord class during the Famine period, its benevolent and malevolent aspects, and the overall context of its time.

### LANDLORD MALEVOLENCE AND FAMINE CLEARANCES

Mass evictions or 'clearances' will forever be associated with the Irish Famine. It has been estimated that, excluding peaceable surrenders, over a quarter of a million people were evicted between 1849 and 1854. The total number of people who had to leave their holdings in the period is like-

THE EJECTMENT.

Fig. 1 'The Ejectment', *The Illustrated London News*, 16 December 1848.

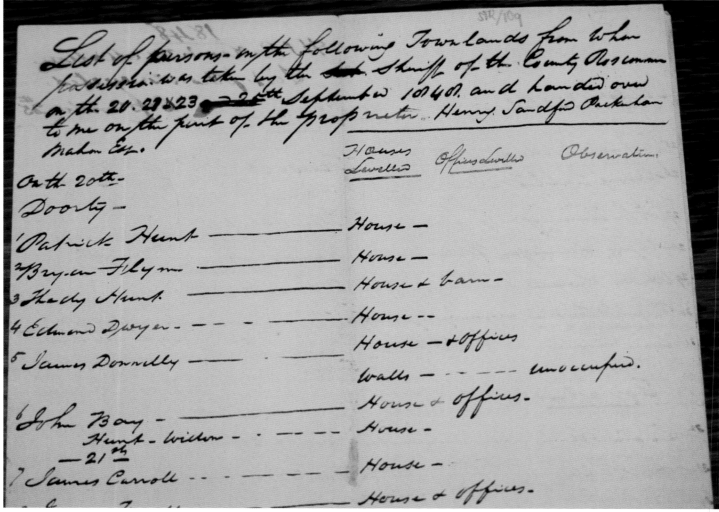

Fig. 2 List of persons from whom possession of holdings was taken by the sheriff of County Roscommon and handed over to a representative of Henry Sandford Pakenham Mahon, Esquire, between 20 and 23 September 1848. The list is organised by townland. [Source: Strokestown Estate Archive, OPW-NUI Maynooth Archive and Research Centre at Castletown]

ly to be around half a million and 200,000 smallholdings were obliterated.[1] To become eligible for relief under the Gregory clause, the tenant had to surrender his holding to his landlord. Some tenants sent their children to the workhouse as orphans so they could keep their land and still have their children fed. Other tenants surrendered their land, but tried to remain living in the house; however, landlords would not tolerate it and, as Donnelly has contended, 'in many thousands of cases estate-clearing landlords and agents used physical force or heavy-handed pressure to bring about the destruction of cabins which they sought'.[2]

With regard to the Famine clearances between 1847 and 1851, their origin as an exercise in Poor Law taxation avoidance on the part of the landlords has for some time been the subject of attention. As early as 23 January 1846, Mr Todhunter, a member of the Central Relief Committee of the Society of Friends, had noted evidence of 'some landlords, forgetful of the claims of humanity and regardless of the Public Welfare . . . availing themselves of the present calamity to effect a wholesale clearance of their

estates'.[3] As Ó Murchadha has argued, a small number of landlords and agents indeed seized the opportunity presented by the prostrate state of tenants, to push ahead with estate consolidation policies. Furthermore, he has convincingly presented the case for a revenge motivation in the Famine evictions,

in that the social protest and secret society activity of the early years of the Famine had driven landlords into such a state of physical and psychological insecurity that collectively they were in extremely vindictive humour with regard to their tenants by the end of 1847.[4]

Among the mass evictors, great landowning magnates featured prominently, few more so than Colonel Crofton Moore Vandeleur of Kilrush, County Clare, who ejected some 1,000 of his own tenants, and intimidated their neighbours from sheltering them by the threat of sharing their fate.

Irish Poor Law reform made landlords responsible for

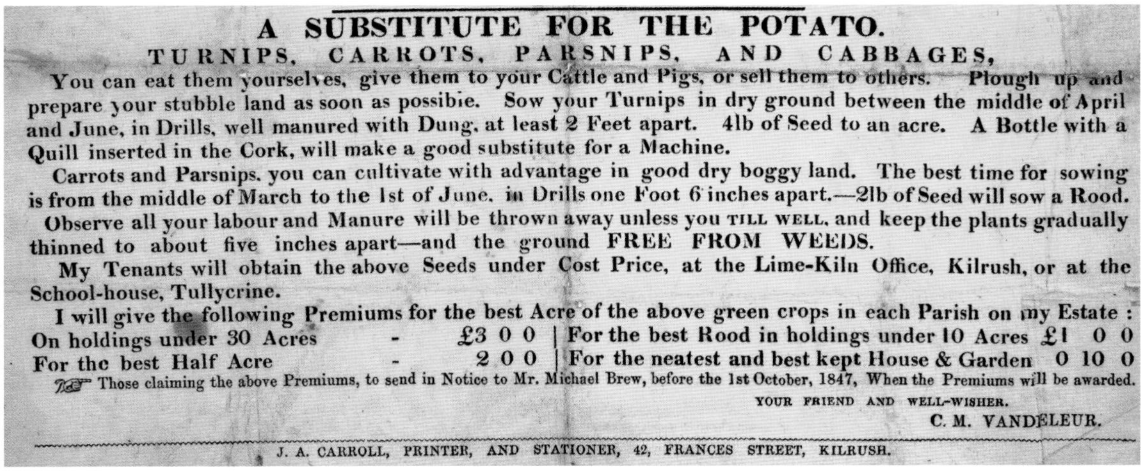

relief of the poor on the smallest properties – those valued at £4 or less, per annum – giving them a strong incentive to rid themselves of tenants who were in that category and unable to pay rent. Many landlords did at least initially attempt to provide relief and some suffered great financial hardship in so doing. Others refused to help, contending they were already paying enough in the rates that funded the new workhouses

**A SUBSTITUTE FOR THE POTATO.**
**TURNIPS, CARROTS, PARSNIPS, AND CABBAGES,**
You can eat them yourselves, give them to your Cattle and Pigs, or sell them to others. Plough up and prepare your stubble land as soon as possibie. Sow your Turnips in dry ground between the middle of April and June, in Drills, well manured with Dung, at least 2 Feet apart. 4lb of Seed to an acre. A Bottle with a Quill inserted in the Cork, will make a good substitute for a Machine.
Carrots and Parsnips, you can cultivate with advantage in good dry boggy land. The best time for sowing is from the middle of March to the 1st of June, in Drills one Foot 6 inches apart.—2lb of Seed will sow a Rood.
Observe all your labour and Manure will be thrown away unless you TILL WELL, and keep the plants gradually thinned to about five inches apart—and the ground FREE FROM WEEDS.
My Tenants will obtain the above Seeds under Cost Price, at the Lime-Kiln Office, Kilrush, or at the School-house, Tullycrine.
I will give the following Premiums for the best Acre of the above green crops in each Parish on my Estate :
On holdings under 30 Acres    -    £3  0  0  | For the best Rood in holdings under 10 Acres  £1   0   0
For the best Half Acre        -         2  0  0  | For the neatest and best kept House & Garden   0  10   0
☞ Those claiming the above Premiums, to send in Notice to Mr. Michael Brew, before the 1st October, 1847, When the Premiums will be awarded.
YOUR FRIEND AND WELL-WISHER.
C. M. VANDELEUR.
J. A. CARROLL, PRINTER, AND STATIONER, 42, FRANCES STREET, KILRUSH.

Fig. 3 Landlord Crofton Moore Vandeleur's instruction to his tenants on his Kilrush estate in County Clare with regard to planting substitutes for the potato crop bears all the hallmarks of the improving landlord. Vandeleur regarded improvement as essential for the future of his estate and diversifying one's produce was deemed a worthy objective. His Kilrush estate was 17,000 acres in extent with the town at the heart of his improving zeal. However, improvement came at a price. Vandeleur, although financially secure, evicted over one thousand of his tenants during the Famine with little regard for their welfare. [Source: National Library of Ireland]

created by the Irish Poor Law Act (1838). Even the infamous Lord Lucan initially involved himself in relief measures but, by 1848, he was enforcing wholesale evictions of tenants unable to pay rents on his lands around Castlebar and Ballinrobe, evicting 187 families (913 persons) in eighteen months. A follow-up report by a Galway newspaper found that of the total number evicted, 478 were receiving public relief, 170 had emigrated, and 265 were dead or left to shift from place to place.

Equally infamous was Sir Roger Palmer, who owned 90,000 acres in Mayo. In July 1848, the *Telegraph* reported how:

> at Islandeady his 'crowbar invincibles', pulled down several houses, and drove forth the unfortunate inmates to sleep in the adjoining fields. On Thursday we witnessed the wretched creatures endeavouring to root out the timber of the houses, with the intention of constructing some sort of sheds to screen their children from the heavy rain falling at the time. The pitiless pelting storm has continued ever since, and if they have survived its severity, they must be more than human beings.[5]

There can be little doubt that the actions of these, and other prominent landlords, were crucial in dispelling the lingering moral scruples of lesser landowners in regard to eviction.[6] And yet, in many instances, cheek by jowl with these, were others who, in sharp contrast, refrained from evicting their tenants. Once more citing the example of County Clare, William Nugent MacNamara and Cornelius O'Brien, the managers of the bankrupt Stratford estate near Ennistymon and a number of smaller landowners, behaved with humanity towards their tenants, when they might easily have joined in the eviction fray.

## LANDLORD BENEVOLENCE AND TENANT ASSISTANCE

Tenant assistance was, in itself, a strongly contested phenomenon. Public reaction to landlord assistance was usually influenced by the political perspective of the observer or commentator. Assistance by way of forgiveness of debts or supply of relief in any form by landlords was typically lauded, while any question of assisted emigration led to divisions. In this way, the example of Colonel Wyndham's scheme of transporting tenants to Canada was held up by the *Clare Journal*, an establishment paper, as an example of his being a 'truly generous and benevolent landlord. Let the landlords of Ireland take a lesson from his example'.[7] Predictably, the nationalist *Limerick and Clare Examiner* utilised colourful and emotive language in expressing incredulity as to how that landlord

> deserved to be eulogised [when he] decimates his land and exports the culled stock of his human farmyard. How can any man be ranked as a good landlord who clears his estate from human rubbish . . . and transport[s] a cargo of human beings to the swamps and interminable forests of Canada.[8]

A number of Irish landlords engaged in schemes of assisted emigration to North America in the years before, during and following the Famine. Research has shown almost 30,000 persons to have been sent by the combined resources of Colonel Wyndham in Clare, Lord Monteagle in Limerick, Earl Fitzwilliam in Wicklow, Lord Palmerston and Sir Robert Gore-Booth in Sligo, Lord Lansdowne in Kerry, Lord Bath in Monaghan, the Wandesfordes in Kilkenny, Francis Spaight in Limerick, Clare and north Tipperary and Major Denis Mahon in Roscommon. Assisted emigration schemes usually formed part of a landlord's scheme of general estate improvements and the concept of the model farm through

267

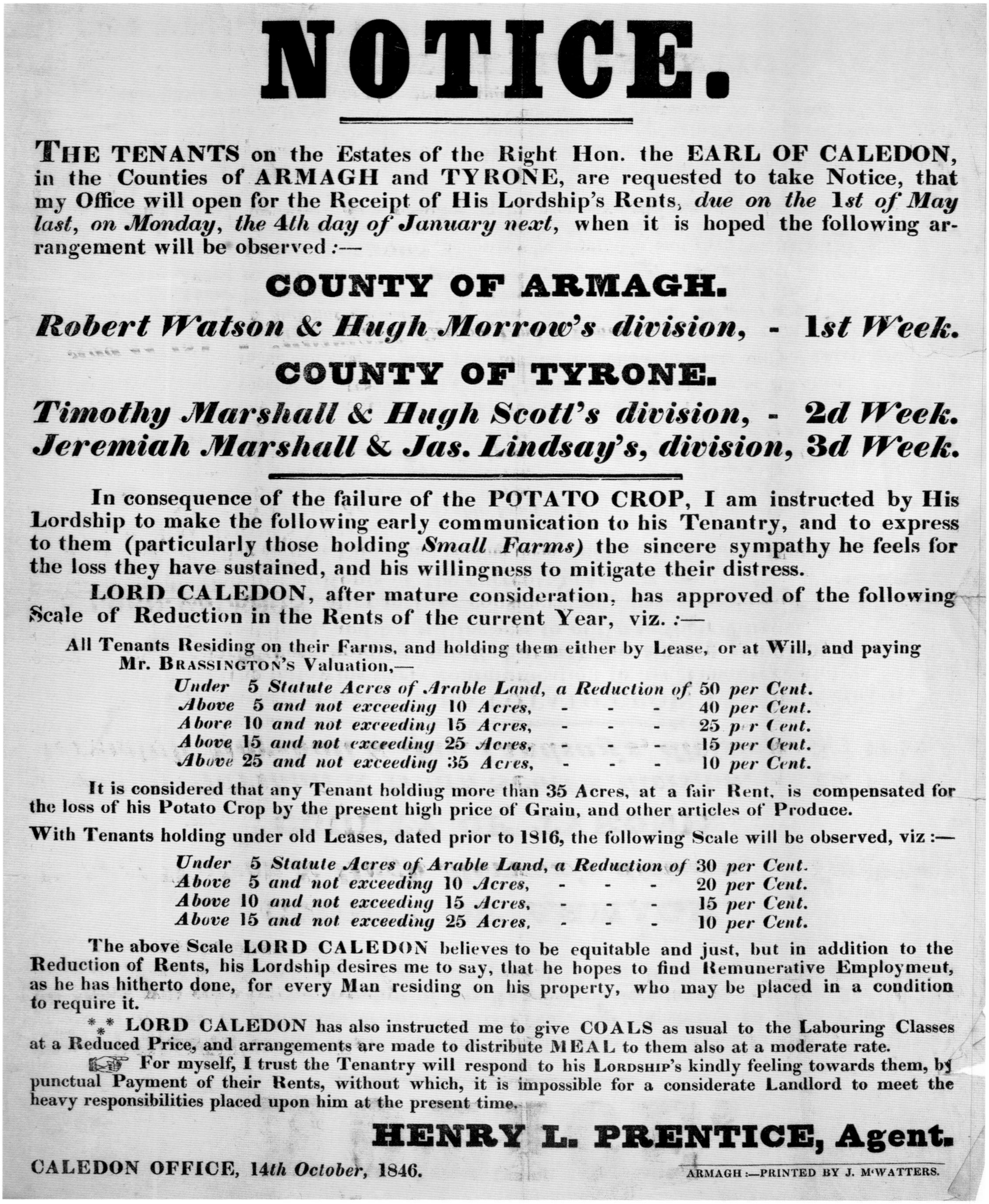

# NOTICE.

THE TENANTS on the Estates of the Right Hon. the EARL OF CALEDON, in the Counties of ARMAGH and TYRONE, are requested to take Notice, that my Office will open for the Receipt of His Lordship's Rents, *due on the 1st of May last, on Monday, the 4th day of January next,* when it is hoped the following arrangement will be observed :—

## COUNTY OF ARMAGH.

*Robert Watson & Hugh Morrow's division,* - *1st Week.*

## COUNTY OF TYRONE.

*Timothy Marshall & Hugh Scott's division,* - *2d Week.*
*Jeremiah Marshall & Jas. Lindsay's, division, 3d Week.*

In consequence of the failure of the POTATO CROP, I am instructed by His Lordship to make the following early communication to his Tenantry, and to express to them (particularly those holding *Small Farms)* the sincere sympathy he feels for the loss they have sustained, and his willingness to mitigate their distress.

LORD CALEDON, after mature consideration, has approved of the following Scale of Reduction in the Rents of the current Year, viz. :—

All Tenants Residing on their Farms, and holding them either by Lease, or at Will, and paying Mr. BRASSINGTON'S Valuation,—

*Under* 5 *Statute Acres of Arable Land, a Reduction of* 50 *per Cent.*
*Above* 5 *and not exceeding* 10 *Acres,* - - - 40 *per Cent.*
*Above* 10 *and not exceeding* 15 *Acres,* - - - 25 *per Cent.*
*Above* 15 *and not exceeding* 25 *Acres,* - - - 15 *per Cent.*
*Above* 25 *and not exceeding* 35 *Acres,* - - - 10 *per Cent.*

It is considered that any Tenant holding more than 35 Acres, at a fair Rent, is compensated for the loss of his Potato Crop by the present high price of Grain, and other articles of Produce.

With Tenants holding under old Leases, dated prior to 1816, the following Scale will be observed, viz :—

*Under* 5 *Statute Acres of Arable Land, a Reduction of* 30 *per Cent.*
*Above* 5 *and not exceeding* 10 *Acres,* - - - 20 *per Cent.*
*Above* 10 *and not exceeding* 15 *Acres,* - - - 15 *per Cent.*
*Above* 15 *and not exceeding* 25 *Acres,* - - - 10 *per Cent.*

The above Scale LORD CALEDON believes to be equitable and just, but in addition to the Reduction of Rents, his Lordship desires me to say, that he hopes to find Remunerative Employment, as he has hitherto done, for every Man residing on his property, who may be placed in a condition to require it.

\*\*\* LORD CALEDON has also instructed me to give COALS as usual to the Labouring Classes at a Reduced Price, and arrangements are made to distribute MEAL to them also at a moderate rate.

☞ For myself, I trust the Tenantry will respond to his LORDSHIP's kindly feeling towards them, by punctual Payment of their Rents, without which, it is impossible for a considerate Landlord to meet the heavy responsibilities placed upon him at the present time.

## HENRY L. PRENTICE, Agent.

CALEDON OFFICE, 14*th October,* 1846.

ARMAGH :—PRINTED BY J. M'WATTERS.

Fig. 4 Landlords responded in different ways to the Famine. In a notice issued by Lord Caledon to tenants on his Armagh and Tyrone estates, he firstly sympathises with their plight while also declaring a reduction in their rents. Such a benevolent attitude was not always in evidence amongst the landholding gentry. [Source: National Library of Ireland Proclamations Collection] the introduction of new breeds of stock, land fertilisation and reclamation, erection of new farm buildings, and the general education of the tenantry.

The fourth Earl of Donoughmore, from his Knocklofty estate on the South Tipperary-Waterford border, near Clonmel, on succeeding to the estate in 1851, encouraged emigration to the United States, being an enthusiast about opportunities there. In a letter to the *Clonmel Chronicle*, he described how he had 'paid a little' towards the passage of his tenants and had given each a Christian bible. This was sufficient to incur the wrath of a local parish priest, Canon Michael Burke of Clonmel, who claimed the assisting of some five hundred persons to America amounted to their 'extermination', listing their names to support his claim. At a time when there was a vigorous campaign of proselytism in other regions of Ireland, and faced with his own declining congregation, Burke was especially exercised about the religious aspect of Donoughmore's activities, citing the good example of one tenant, Mary Cleary who, in the spring of 1853, en route to America, threw her bible into the River Suir near Clonmel, noting the local parson to be 'a good angler; let him go and fish for that'.[9]

### FEEDING THEIR TENANTRY

Other charitable landowners chose to feed their tenantry *in situ*, such as the Marquis of Sligo, a liberal landlord, who was chairman of a committee that set up a private soup kitchen in Westport in January 1847. He made an opening donation of £100 and promised a subscription of £5 a week. Yet he was forced to inform Lord Monteagle in October 1848 that he had received no rent from his tenants for upwards of three years. Certainly he must have received only a small fraction of his nominal rental of about £7,200 per year for, in Westport Union, up to 85% of the occupiers had holdings valued at £4 or less annually. By March 1848, Lord Sligo was almost £1,650 in debt to the Westport Board of Guardians, a body that he served as chairman. This debt he only discharged by borrowing £1,500 – thus adding to his already heavy encumbrances, amounting to some £6,000 annually – a situation which, in his own words to Lord Monteagle, placed him 'under the necessity of ejecting or being ejected'.[10]

Invariably, those landlords who tolerated their tenantry by refusing to evict for non-payment of rent were despised by those landlords who, in grasping the nettle, as they saw it, had already commenced the eviction or assisted emigration processes on their estates. Such landlords were not above expressing some measure of satisfaction when so-called indulgent landlords were eventually forced to evict on a large scale, having previously forecast that delayed action would lead only to greater consequences. Indeed, landlord indebtedness, a pre-Famine phenomenon, was greatly exacerbated by the Famine and agriculturally depressed years of 1849–52. Lost rents, heavy Poor Law rates and, in some cases, significant expenditure for employment and relief schemes, wiped out what was already a narrowing margin between estate income and expenditure, even before the outbreak of famine.

The existing cumbersome machinery of the court of chancery was superseded by the passing of the Encumbered Estates Act in July 1849, which established a new tribunal with drastic powers for land sale and eradication of landlord indebtedness. The early operations of the court served only to confirm the worst fears of heavily indebted landowners, with the estate of Earl Mount Cashell – comprising some 62,000 acres in Cork and Antrim, a combined annual rental of £18,500 – being bought for £240,000 or thirteen years' purchase. The pre-Famine rate of purchase had been twenty-five years' purchase, and the frustration of Lord Mountcashell was such that, during the proceedings, he was heard to exclaim that it was bad enough having the estate confiscated, 'but to be sold up by a dwarf in a garret was more than he could endure!' – a reference to Encumbered Estates Commissioner Charles Hargreave, a man of small stature whose office was located on the uppermost floor of a house on Henrietta Street, in Dublin.[11]

The percentile of townlands in each of the thirty-two counties of Ireland sold through the Encumbered Estates Courts between 1849 and 1855 is displayed in Figure 5. A primary core of landlord indebtedness in Counties Mayo, Galway and Tipperary – where in excess of 15% of townlands were sold – swiftly becomes apparent, with a largely adjacent secondary core of Counties Cork, Kilkenny, Offaly, Westmeath and Louth, where in excess of 13% was auctioned off.

Despite considerable levels of indebtedness, landlord benevolence, in varying degrees and for varying periods, was in evidence as often as malevolence, with particular bursts of generosity towards the tenantry displayed at times of celebration. In November and December 1846, Viscount Lismore of Shanbally Castle, Clogheen, County Tipperary, received news of the birth of his first two grandchildren. On both occasions, two hundred of his tenants and employees were entertained at Shanbally Castle to 'sumptuous dinners of roast beef and plum pudding', the music for the after-dinner revelry supplied by the Clogheen Amateur Band. Bonfires illuminated the neighbourhood from the Knockmealdowns across the valley to the Galtees and dancing was kept up to a late hour.[12] Crucially, in a letter to the *Tipperary Free Press*, 'Benevolus' was at pains to emphasise that this was no isolated occurrence. Lord Lismore was quite unlike some other landlords,

> who revel in foreign countries out of reach of interruption from the wailing of their fellow creatures . . . when an appalling famine and its awful consequences threaten the land . . . Lord Lismore does not feast the people today and let them starve

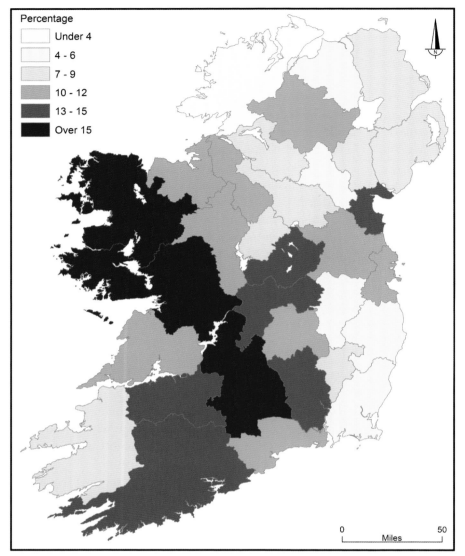

Fig. 5 PERCENTAGE OF TOWNLANDS IN EACH OF THE THIRTY-TWO COUNTIES, AUCTIONED THROUGH THE ENCUMBERED ESTATES COURT, 1849–55.

the people. When he saw the awful plight of his tenants, he caused a mill to be built half a mile below our village . . . When the mill was ready the landlord bought Indian meal in Cork City and got his tenants to go with their horses and bring the meal free of charge to the mill where, when it was ground, everyone who needed it got a measure or scoop of meal for each one of their family.[14]

The landlord class were not always to be blamed when evictions took place. Middlemen and well-to-do farmers often played a part and, occasionally, land 'grabbing' was encountered, where unscrupulous farmers with spare cash reserves approached a landlord or his agent with an offer to pay rent arrears on an adjacent property, on the condition that they would be given possession.

## PRIVATE RELIEF

One of the remarkable aspects of the Great Famine was the amount of private relief collected on behalf of the Irish poor, especially following the second crop failure in 1846. Although this money is difficult to quantify, it likely surpassed £2m. There was extensive fund raising from all sections of Irish society, with resident landlords generally involved, although many absentees were criticised for their indifference. Within Ireland, these diverse groups included: The Irish Art Union, which organised an exhibition of Old Masters, the proceeds being dispersed between various relief organisations; the Irish Benchers, who gave £1,000 to the General Relief Fund; the Irish Coast Guards, who raised £429; and the brewer, Arthur Guinness, who made two separate donations of £60 and £100. Even in rural parishes, efforts were made through the creation of fundraising committees, as in South Tipperary, where a surviving manuscript headed 'Mullinahone Relief Committee – A list of landlords, clergymen, etc., who gratuitously subscribed and paid towards the poor infirm in Mullinahone locality . . . [Signed] James Kickham, Treasurer. June 8th 1846' lists ninety-five subscribers, and a significant sum collected, £154 2s.[15]

All over Ireland, local landlords, gentry and clergy contributed in small ways, particularly in the early Famine years of 1846 and 1847. In Belfast, a privately funded relief committee in Ballymacarrett gave soup to over 12,000 people daily, about 60% of the local population. On some estates, practical assistance was given: on his Kerry estate,

tomorrow. No, his Lordship's bounty flows as a constant stream . . . during this season of famine over 50 people of the most destitute are daily fed at the castle and 48 families of 250 persons supplied with meal for their families at home.[13]

While the identity of the writer, 'Benevolus' remains unknown, references concerning other caring landlords – both resident and non-resident – remain on the historical record. One post-Famine writer from west Cork, in emphasising that not all landlords were malign, cited his grandfather, who had lived through the Famine, who on going to 'pay part of his rent to his landlord, a Bantry man [was told], "Feed your family first, then give me what you can afford when times get better."' In another district, it was contended that the reason the residents of the locality were comparatively unaffected by famine was owed to the landlord of the time, Mr Cronin Coltsman. He earned the everlasting gratitude of

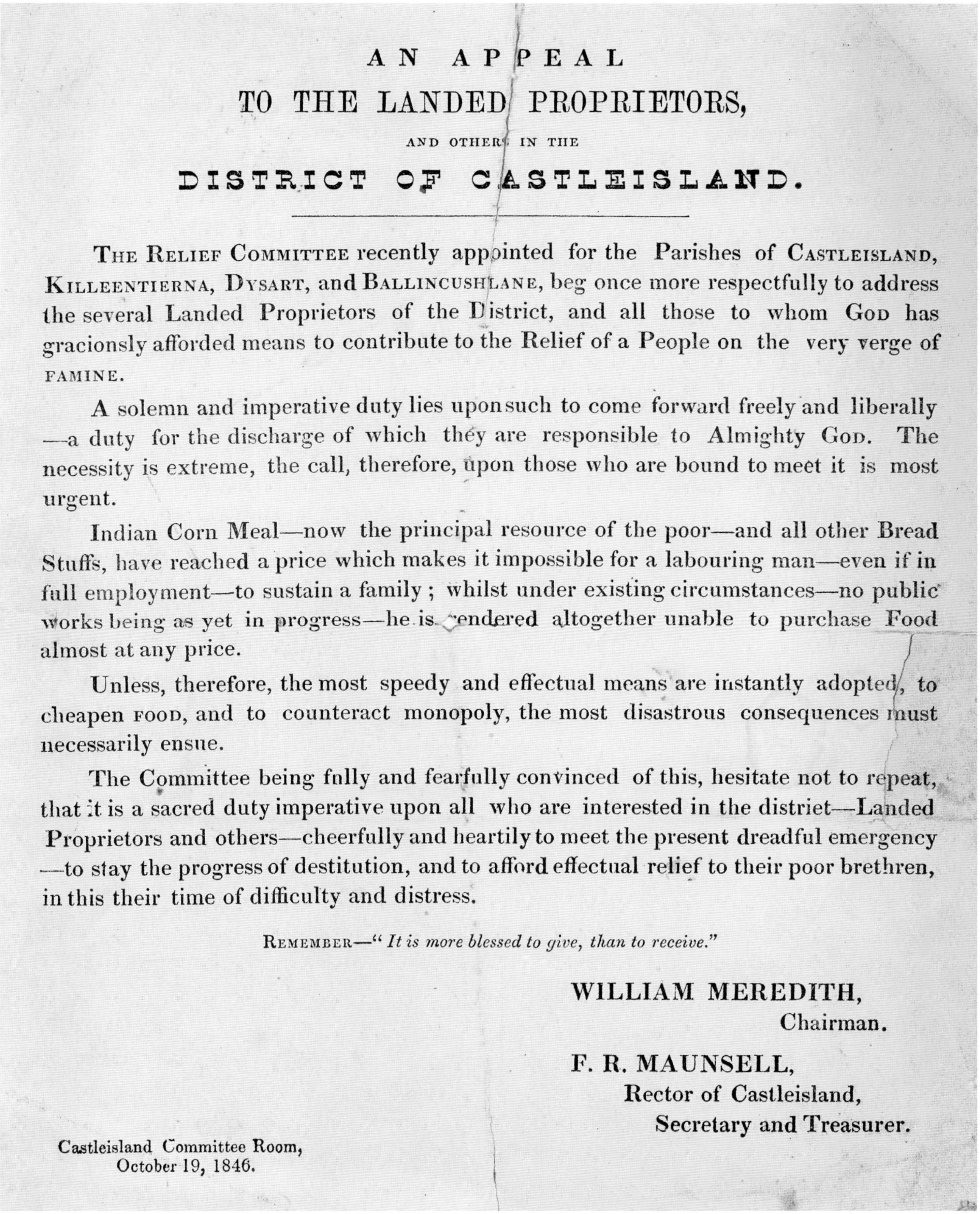

# AN APPEAL
## TO THE LANDED PROPRIETORS,
### AND OTHERS IN THE
# DISTRICT OF CASTLEISLAND.

THE RELIEF COMMITTEE recently appointed for the Parishes of CASTLEISLAND, KILLEENTIERNA, DYSART, and BALLINCUSHLANE, beg once more respectfully to address the several Landed Proprietors of the District, and all those to whom GOD has graciously afforded means to contribute to the Relief of a People on the very verge of FAMINE.

A solemn and imperative duty lies upon such to come forward freely and liberally —a duty for the discharge of which they are responsible to Almighty GOD. The necessity is extreme, the call, therefore, upon those who are bound to meet it is most urgent.

Indian Corn Meal—now the principal resource of the poor—and all other Bread Stuffs, have reached a price which makes it impossible for a labouring man—even if in full employment—to sustain a family ; whilst under existing circumstances—no public works being as yet in progress—he is rendered altogether unable to purchase Food almost at any price.

Unless, therefore, the most speedy and effectual means are instantly adopted, to cheapen FOOD, and to counteract monopoly, the most disastrous consequences must necessarily ensue.

The Committee being fully and fearfully convinced of this, hesitate not to repeat, that it is a sacred duty imperative upon all who are interested in the district—Landed Proprietors and others—cheerfully and heartily to meet the present dreadful emergency —to stay the progress of destitution, and to afford effectual relief to their poor brethren, in this their time of difficulty and distress.

REMEMBER—" *It is more blessed to give, than to receive.*"

**WILLIAM MEREDITH,**
Chairman.

**F. R. MAUNSELL,**
Rector of Castleisland,
Secretary and Treasurer.

Castleisland Committee Room,
October 19, 1846.

Fig. 6 An appeal to the landed gentry in the district of Castleisland, County Kerry, 19 October 1846, to contribute to the relief of the distressed in their locality. The exorbitant price of Indian corn had put it beyond the reach of the labouring poor, while public works had yet to commence, hence the earnest plea for greater assistance. [Source: National Library of Ireland]

271

Daniel O'Connell gave a 50% reduction in rent, while on their Portlaw, County Waterford, estate, Lord and Lady Waterford financed a soup kitchen.

Some absentee landlords sent financial assistance to their Irish tenants or organised schemes of employment through their land agents. In general, however, they were not particularly noted for their generosity. Consequently, their land agents bore the brunt of both the criticism of their employers concerning the lack of rental income and the pressure from local relief committees to further alleviate distress. At Fermoy, in north Cork, Matthias Hendley, agent for Sir Robert Abercromby's estate and himself a small landowner, finding himself on the Fermoy Relief Committee, was 'obliged to attend many meetings connected with the procuring of food and work for our unfortunate paupers'. At one meeting, 'absentee landlords were spoken of with so very little respect that I thought it right (agreeably to your permission) to put down your name at once for £50, which I have paid'. He himself, as agent, had donated £20, but revealed further pressure to donate to the Kilworth Relief Committee, as he held some land in that adjoining parish. It was becoming increasingly the case that a chronic lack of money was preventing tenant assistance.[16]

Occasionally, absentee landlords were lauded, as in the June 1849 epistle of the Very Revd James Browne, parish priest of Ballintubber and Burriscarra, who had 'never heard of a single tenant being evicted from the estate of George Henry Moore Esq., either by the landlord or his agent', he having 'sent over from London at an early stage of the famine, a sum of £1,000 for the poor on his estates, as a free gift, besides orders to his steward to give a milch cow to every widow on his property'.[17]

### BUSINESS AS USUAL

The drastic reduction of Ireland's population through death and emigration over a ten-year period has been seared into the Irish psyche and is not easily laid to one side when researching those years. However, quite aside from the positive and negative aspects of landlord–tenant relations during this period, contemporary newspaper reports and advertisements contain copious examples of the prevalence of a 'business as usual' approach to social and commercial life. In highlighting this, it is not intended to in any way minimise the devastation and horror of those years or detract from the memory of the suffering that existed but, rather, to provide a greater context through which the social and cultural aspects of the middle and upper classes in the Famine period can be better understood.

A perusal of contemporary provincial newspapers shows a 'business as usual' attitude was adopted by the mercantile and landowning classes during the Famine period, as in north Tipperary in January 1846, when the correspondents felt compelled to observe that 'seldom, indeed we may say never, have we witnessed a more splendid Ball in Nenagh . . .', in connection with the soirée given by the officers of the 1st Royals:

> As early as nine o'clock the rank and beauty of the country poured in and arrivals were continuous up to twelve . . . Several rooms handsomely decorated were thrown open, and refreshments abundantly provided. The ballroom was magnificently decorated.

Supper that evening consisted of 'every delicacy that the season could afford or the most fastidious appetite desire' with the 'old Baronial Boar's Head' decorating the table, the tables being laid for two hundred people. Those attending included the aristocracy and 'many families of the *respectable portion* [emphasis added] of the residents of Nenagh'.[18]

As the year progressed, the provincial entertainments calendar became ever more lavish. In August, the Royal Agricultural Improvement Society of Ireland held their show in Limerick where cattle were exhibited and agricultural implements displayed. The report from the 'General Banquet' at the theatre noted 'About 400 people sat down to an excellent dinner, provided, as on the former day, by Mr John Goggin . . . The wines were . . . as on the previous night, of the very best quality.' Toasts were drunk to the royal family, with loud cheers, applause, and the 'usual honours'. The only apparent discordant note was when a Captain Kennedy stood and suggested that things were not all well in the country but such were the 'expressions of dissatisfaction', loudly and frequently repeated, that Captain Kennedy was forced to sit down.[19]

The reader of the *Cork Examiner* of 1 January 1847 would be forgiven for immediately assuming a front-page column headline, announcing 'Ireland's Greatest Difficulty', to be famine-related, certainly not contending: 'The Public will readily admit that the greatest difficulty in Ireland is that of getting good tea. To remove "the difficulty", buy at Harman Dilis's, Prince's Street, Cork.'[20] Perhaps, having purchased one of the many teas on offer in Dilis's, the discerning purchaser could host, as at Cahir, County Tipperary, that July, 'a picnic on a very elegant scale . . . at Caher Cottage. There were over fifty persons present, chiefly from the neighbourhoods of Clonmel and Caher. An amateur band attended, and after the dinner, which presented all the delicacies of the season, dancing was commenced and kept up much spirits until a late hour.'[21]

Further evidence of the pursuits of some of the upper classes comes through an exotic advertisement of February 1848 concerning an 'Extraordinary Exhibition of Aborigines' at the Theatre Royal, Cook Street, Cork, namely

> Two women, two men, and a baby of . . . The Bush Tribe, from the interior of South Africa, belonging to a race that, from their wild habits, could never before be induced to visit a place of civilisation.

Admission: 2s. to boxes, Gallery 6d. Children under ten – half price. Private interviews . . . 2s. 6d.[22]

It is surely safe to speculate that these were the same 'Bush people' who were on exhibition in Dublin earlier in the month.[23] The advertisement was deeply ironic, given that malnourished locals, some scarcely in recognisable human form abounded, particularly in the west of the county. The social and cultural life of the port city of Cork clearly continued as before for those who could afford it, with advertisements for Christmas 1848 by Woodford Bourne and other firms of an array of Christmas supplies, including coffee, port, whiskey, rum, cigars, 'Prime Wicklow Hams', sugar, spices and candles.[24]

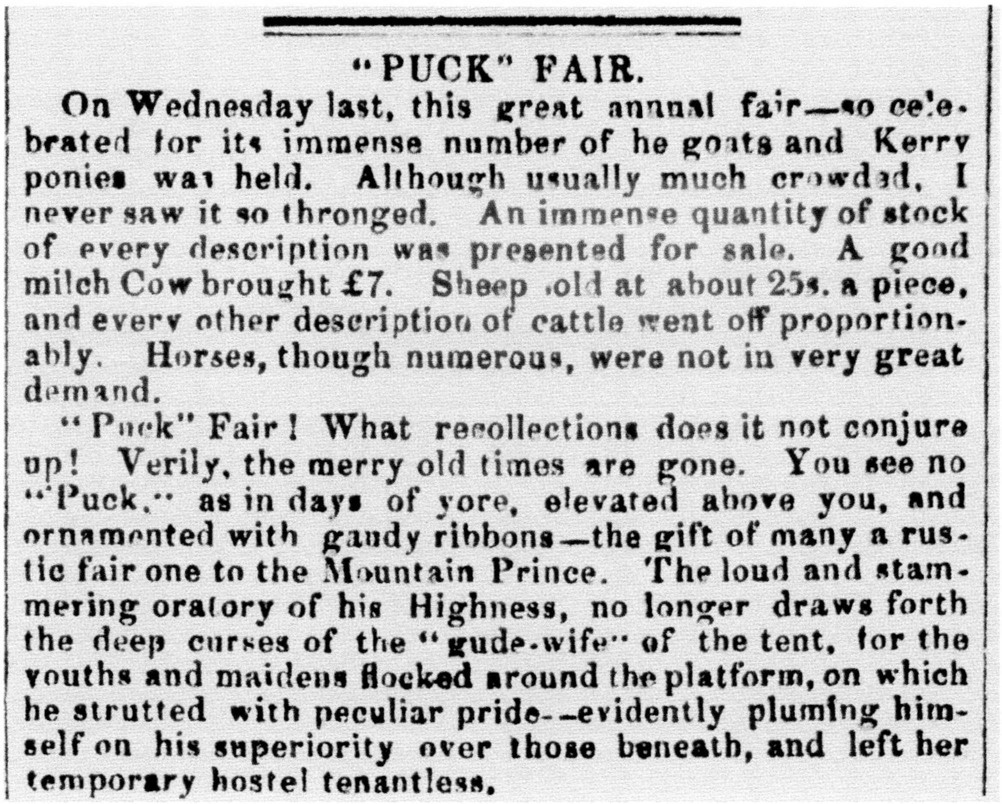

The sporting pursuits of the upper and middle classes – namely, horse racing and fox hunting – also continued apace in late 1840s and early 1850s Ireland, judging by the number of meetings and reports in the media. Colonel Wyndham-Quin, writing in 1919, in referring to the Ormond and King's County pack of fox hounds, provides some glimpses of hunting in 'those days' of the late 1840s, noting the November 1847 and February 1848 meetings of the Kilkenny hunt as being of two weeks duration, with dinners held at night notable for 'Sneyd's claret largely fortified with Hermitage and Old Port'.[25] The January 1848 meetings for hounds in Tipperary noticed seven separate meets in the second half of that month alone,[26] while in east Cork, the Castlemartyr Hounds gave notice of six meetings for the first half of February 1847.[27] In December 1847, in the Rosscarbery district of west Cork, the Castle Freke Hounds caused excitement when they put up fifty or sixty partridges, considered to be an unusual sight at that time of year, as they are a migratory bird.[28]

On the racing front, the Irish Turf Appointments for 1846 were twenty-six in number and were scheduled from April to November.[29] John Welcome has written that Irish racegoers returned 'again and again' to Liverpool during the 1840s, a point in favour being the easy access from Irish ports.[30] Indeed, the 1847 Aintree Grand National was won by an Irish horse, 'Mathew', ridden by Denny Wynne, whose victory 'was celebrated on both sides of the Irish Sea in a manner that may well have disconcerted the worthy Apostle of Temperance in whose honour he had been

## "PUCK" FAIR.

On Wednesday last, this great annual fair—so celebrated for its immense number of he goats and Kerry ponies was held. Although usually much crowded, I never saw it so thronged. An immense quantity of stock of every description was presented for sale. A good milch Cow brought £7. Sheep sold at about 25s. a piece, and every other description of cattle went off proportionably. Horses, though numerous, were not in very great demand.

"Puck" Fair! What recollections does it not conjure up! Verily, the merry old times are gone. You see no "Puck," as in days of yore, elevated above you, and ornamented with gaudy ribbons—the gift of many a rustic fair one to the Mountain Prince. The loud and stammering oratory of his Highness, no longer draws forth the deep curses of the "gude-wife" of the tent, for the youths and maidens flocked around the platform, on which he strutted with peculiar pride--evidently pluming himself on his superiority over those beneath, and left her temporary hostel tenantless.

Fig. 7 A report in the *Tralee Chronicle*, 14 August 1847. Even at the height of the Famine, life went on as this report on Puck Fair appears to confirm. A correspondent observed that he had never seen it 'so thronged' and that 'an immense quantity of stock of every description was presented for sale'. [Source: Local Studies and Archives Department, Kerry County Library]

named'.[31] Even at provincial level, race going reached new heights, assisted by the progress of the new Irish railways, as with a report carried in the *Tipperary Free Press* of 12 May 1847, when the largest train 'that had ever been started' on the Great Southern and Western Railway since its inception conveyed twenty-three carriages containing 1,500 racegoers from Carlow to the steeplechase at Lucan.

### CLEARANCES AND LEGACY

During the Great Famine and in its immediate aftermath, Irish landlords engaged in a campaign of mass evictions that was unprecedented in its extent and severity. Substantial landlord debt was exacerbated, rather than caused by, the Famine. The Government-inspired solution, the Encumbered Estates Court, was part of the widespread negative opinion in Britain with regard to Irish landlords generally; it functioned from 1849 until 1858 when, in recognition of its success, it was replaced by the Landed Estates Court.

Although few parts of rural Ireland escaped clearances altogether, as a rule they occurred most frequently in the more remote, poorer regions of the country, where subdivision of holdings had been carried on to its most extreme degree. Regions of the west and south of Ireland were therefore most affected by the clearances, with residents of counties such as Clare, Tipperary, and Mayo suffering more than others. The level of evictions in Tipperary was some twenty times that of Fermanagh, the county with the lowest inci-

Fig. 8 Emo Court, County Laois. Built during one of the most expansive epochs in Irish history in the 1780s and 1790s, the construction and embellishment of Emo Court almost broke its owners – the Dawson-Damer family, earls of Portarlington. Located at the centre of a magnificently planted and very large demesne, one might imagine that the events of the Great Famine might seem remote to such a landlord, ensconced in such a sylvan setting. However, the earls of Portarlington earned a reputation as good landlords and subscribed generously to, amongst other relief schemes, the soup kitchen at Portarlington. Likewise, the earl's agent Henry Scroope in Roscrea town – then part of this vast estate – was a generous and dedicated member of the Board of Guardians of Roscrea union. Yet Roscrea town was to lose one-third of its population between 1845 and 1851, and the union lost even more. In areas badly affected, even the better landlords could not and did not arrest the accumulating horrors of the Great Famine catastrophe.

dence of clearance, and in Clare it has been calculated that one in every ten persons was permanently expelled from house and holding in the years between 1849 and 1854.

The sudden onset and exceptional severity of the Famine clearances were the consequence of new government relief policies that added greatly to the economic troubles of landlords. A massive loss of rental income from successive years of crop failure and extreme deprivation, including actual starvation, together with encumbrances inherited from pre-Famine times, had already brought many landlords to the brink of insolvency. To these difficulties was added a hugely increased tax liability under the Poor Law Amendment Act of June 1847, which transferred the major responsibility for poor relief to Irish property owners. Most landlords, therefore, acted in the belief that the only way to avoid potentially ruinous liability was to eliminate their tax-bearing smallholdings altogether by the wholesale expulsion of the occupiers and the destruction of their dwellings. For the owners of large estates who were not in difficulties, the new pressures fur-nished a reason to finally resolve the problems of overcrowded properties and unprofitable holdings; for them the dislocation of the period presented a convenient opportunity to complete the estate consolidation begun before 1845.

Although many landlords carried out evictions directly, increasingly, the services of land agents with specialised knowledge of cost-cutting legal procedures and the innumerable practical difficulties were utilised at eviction sites, thus enabling the landlord to distance himself from distressing aspects of the eviction process. It could be argued that behind the landlord rush to clear unviable smallholdings lay the fear that the eviction option might soon be closed off forever in the event of the introduction of a tenant-right measure by government. Because of the frenzied manner of so many clearances, estates were voided of occupiers to an extent that went beyond what the landlords had originally intended, or what was economically wise for the owners.

It is thought-provoking to realise that in January 1847, around the same time the *Cork Examiner* carried an adver-

Fig. 9 Bellegrove House(below) near Ballybrittas in County Laois. The Great Famine marked the beginning of the end of landlordism in Ireland. Everywhere in Ireland the Big House and its demesne – like the landlord system it epitomised – rested uneasily on a deep and resilient social and cultural infrastructure. It appears that Bellegrove House was destroyed by accidental fire in 1887. This Big House was built *c*.1835 by Mr George Adair and further embellished by his wealhy American wife, Cornelia. George Adair was an evicting landlord and his son, John George, even more so. The latter became infamous for his making homeless by forcible eviction (with the aid of 203 constables) forty-seven families comprising 244 people from his Donegal estate at Glenveagh Castle – an estate and castle later enhanced by American Mr Henry McIlhenny and now in the state's care. The magnificent mansion of Bellegrove House – once a monument to the great wealth of its eighteenth-century owners – now stands as a magnificent ruin – *fotrach follamh gan áird*. The Irish landscape is littered with the ruins of institutions – such as the Big House – which failed to negotiate a landed history scarred by displacement and discontinuity. [Photo: Tarquin Blake, *Abandoned Mansions of Ireland*, The Collins Press, Cork 2010, courtesy of the photographer-historian]

tisement claiming 'the greatest difficulty in Ireland is that of getting good tea', it carried an article about a man and woman being arrested in Youghal, County Cork, for attempting to sell the body of a seven-year-old boy, so that they could buy food.[32]

Antiquarians collecting gold and silver were well served by the Famine as families sold off the pieces that had become family heirlooms in order to feed themselves, their tenants, or a combination of both. As J.F. Maguire has asserted, 'the potato-rot stripped the side-board of its gorgeous ornaments . . . the late crowning disaster glutted the shops of Dublin, Cork, Limerick, and other large towns, with the first sad offering to the evil genius of the hour'.[33] And yet, contemporary newspapers poured forth evidence of a fashion-conscious, race-going, banquet-attending, rail-travelling, sherry-drinking section of Irish society at the height of the Famine, which poses the question – was it due to this that, in 1847, Britain handed the problem of Irish poverty over to Irish proprietors? Was it callous indifference or congenital inability to be concerned for the poorer classes that made the four hundred diners at the Limerick banquet in the autumn of 1846 shout down the warning voice of Captain Kennedy? Perhaps, after all, some truth lay in John Mitchel's claim that the Famine Irish who died, did so 'in the midst of abundance, which their own hands created'.[34]

Not surprisingly, the Famine clearances left behind many bitter memories in Irish rural communities. The cruelty of particular evicting landlords and agents was remembered sharply for generations – far more than the considerable amount of landlord and gentry kindnesses – and general culpability was assigned to the British Government for the Poor Law Amendment Act and its notorious Gregory clause. More than any other aspect of the Great Famine tragedy, the evictions provided ammunition for the nationalist belief that a genocidal intent lay behind British Government famine policies. Transmitted memories of the clearances supplied much of the enraged energy behind the nationalist movements of the later nineteenth century, from physical-force separatism to constitutional demands for self-rule for Ire-

land and agitation for agrarian reform. There is little doubt, too, that in the long term, by engaging in clearances during the Great Famine, Irish landlords helped seal their own fate. At the end of the nineteenth century, a series of land-purchase acts, inspired by determined campaigning on the part of agrarian and constitutional nationalists, initiated the legal processes by which Irish landlordism would disappear within a generation.

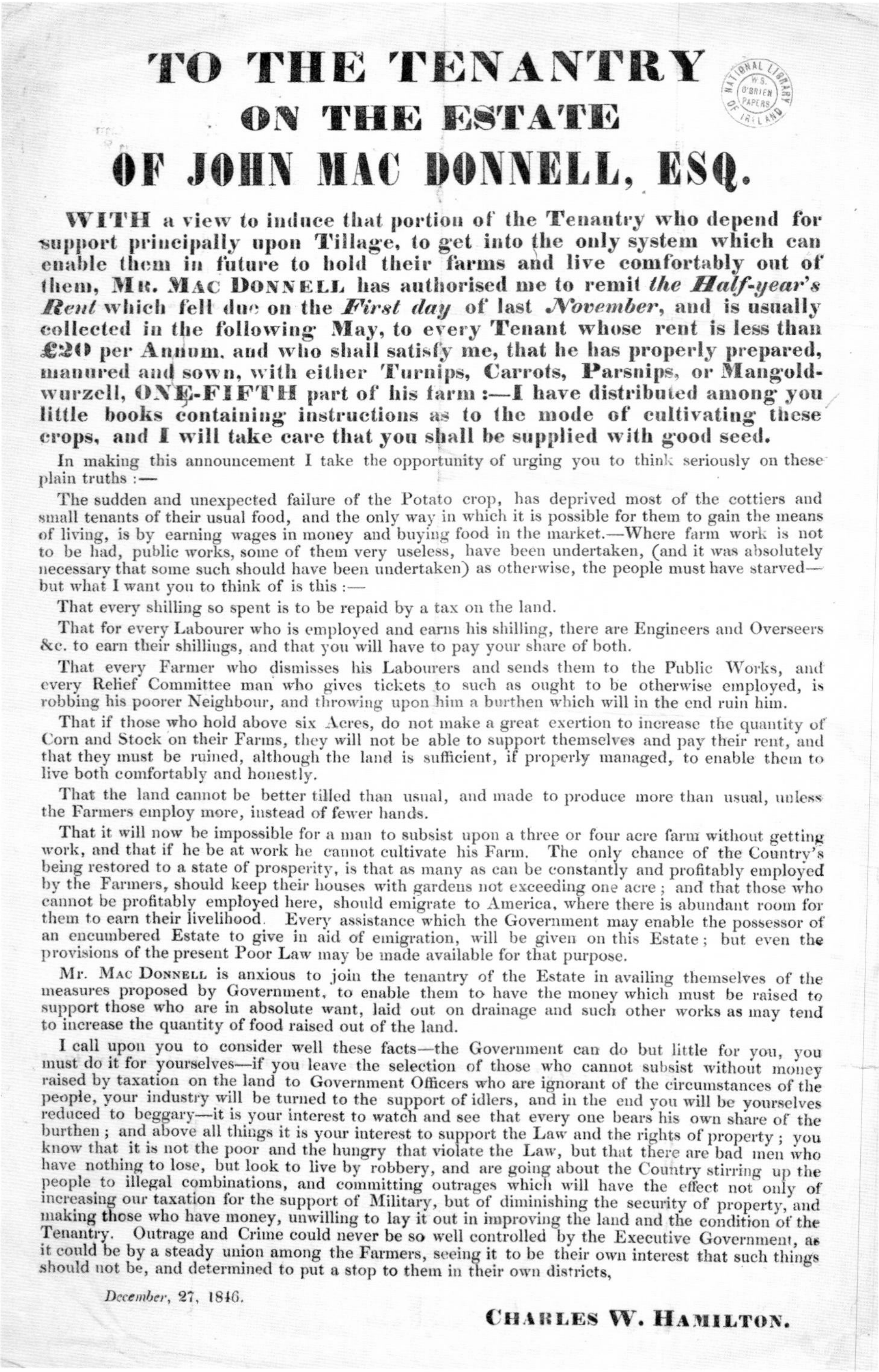

## TO THE TENANTRY ON THE ESTATE OF JOHN MAC DONNELL, ESQ.

WITH a view to induce that portion of the Tenantry who depend for support principally upon Tillage, to get into the only system which can enable them in future to hold their farms and live comfortably out of them, MR. MAC DONNELL has authorised me to remit *the Half-year's Rent* which fell due on the *First day* of last *November*, and is usually collected in the following May, to every Tenant whose rent is less than £20 per Annum, and who shall satisfy me, that he has properly prepared, manured and sown, with either Turnips, Carrots, Parsnips, or Mangold-wurzell, ONE-FIFTH part of his farm :—I have distributed among you little books containing instructions as to the mode of cultivating these crops, and I will take care that you shall be supplied with good seed.

In making this announcement I take the opportunity of urging you to think seriously on these plain truths :—

The sudden and unexpected failure of the Potato crop, has deprived most of the cottiers and small tenants of their usual food, and the only way in which it is possible for them to gain the means of living, is by earning wages in money and buying food in the market.—Where farm work is not to be had, public works, some of them very useless, have been undertaken, (and it was absolutely necessary that some such should have been undertaken) as otherwise, the people must have starved—but what I want you to think of is this :—

That every shilling so spent is to be repaid by a tax on the land.

That for every Labourer who is employed and earns his shilling, there are Engineers and Overseers &c. to earn their shillings, and that you will have to pay your share of both.

That every Farmer who dismisses his Labourers and sends them to the Public Works, and every Relief Committee man who gives tickets to such as ought to be otherwise employed, is robbing his poorer Neighbour, and throwing upon him a burthen which will in the end ruin him.

That if those who hold above six Acres, do not make a great exertion to increase the quantity of Corn and Stock on their Farms, they will not be able to support themselves and pay their rent, and that they must be ruined, although the land is sufficient, if properly managed, to enable them to live both comfortably and honestly.

That the land cannot be better tilled than usual, and made to produce more than usual, unless the Farmers employ more, instead of fewer hands.

That it will now be impossible for a man to subsist upon a three or four acre farm without getting work, and that if he be at work he cannot cultivate his Farm. The only chance of the Country's being restored to a state of prosperity, is that as many as can be constantly and profitably employed by the Farmers, should keep their houses with gardens not exceeding one acre ; and that those who cannot be profitably employed here, should emigrate to America, where there is abundant room for them to earn their livelihood. Every assistance which the Government may enable the possessor of an encumbered Estate to give in aid of emigration, will be given on this Estate ; but even the provisions of the present Poor Law may be made available for that purpose.

Mr. MAC DONNELL is anxious to join the tenantry of the Estate in availing themselves of the measures proposed by Government, to enable them to have the money which must be raised to support those who are in absolute want, laid out on drainage and such other works as may tend to increase the quantity of food raised out of the land.

I call upon you to consider well these facts—the Government can do but little for you, you must do it for yourselves—if you leave the selection of those who cannot subsist without money raised by taxation on the land to Government Officers who are ignorant of the circumstances of the people, your industry will be turned to the support of idlers, and in the end you will be yourselves reduced to beggary—it is your interest to watch and see that every one bears his own share of the burthen ; and above all things it is your interest to support the Law and the rights of property ; you know that it is not the poor and the hungry that violate the Law, but that there are bad men who have nothing to lose, but look to live by robbery, and are going about the Country stirring up the people to illegal combinations, and committing outrages which will have the effect not only of increasing our taxation for the support of Military, but of diminishing the security of property, and making those who have money, unwilling to lay it out in improving the land and the condition of the Tenantry. Outrage and Crime could never be so well controlled by the Executive Government, as it could be by a steady union among the Farmers, seeing it to be their own interest that such things should not be, and determined to put a stop to them in their own districts,

*December*, 27, 1846.

CHARLES W. HAMILTON.

Fig. 10 A broadside issued on 27 December 1846 by Charles W. Hamilton on behalf of his landlord, John Mac Donnell, to his tenants. While stipulating the changes that need to take place in order for the tenant to benefit from a reduction in rent, it also points to emigration to America as a satisfactory solution to those cottiers and labourers who cannot be 'profitably employed'. [Source: National Library of Ireland]

# 'Turned out . . . thrown down': evictions in Bunkilla and Monavanshare, Donoughmore, County Cork

## John O'Connell

The parish of Donoughmore, in mid-Cork, was severely affected by evictions, mortality and emigration during the period of the Great Famine, with the parish records noting for 1847: 'This was the Famine year. There died of famine and fever, from Nov. 1846 to Sep. 1847 over fourteen hundred of the people . . .'[1] Information in two sets of documents, the house books (1849) and the perambulation books (1850) – notebooks of the survey conducted by the Valuation Office which formed the basis of Griffith's Valuation – provide indications on the level of eviction that took place in the adjoining Donoughmore townlands of Bunkilla and Monavanshare.[2] Located at the southern end of the parish, and only 20 km from Cork city, these townlands were well connected to local markets through good roads, including the Cork –Kerry butter road which ran through Monavanshare (Fig. 1). The potato crop, however, remained pivotal to the local economy. When John O'Donovan visited these townlands, as part of his work for the Ordnance Survey in 1841, he noted the poor quality of the soil, some of which was 'spent bog in a state of tillage', and that oats and potatoes 'of a very poor quality' were grown there.[3] The poor quality of the land, combined with the reliance on the potato crop for food and rent, would prove to have disastrous consequences.

Landlords responded in different ways to the crisis resulting from the Great Famine, with some behaving responsibly towards their tenants. The majority, however, moved to evict if rents were unpaid. Mounting landlord indebtedness, along with their liability to pay the poor rate on smallholdings, increased the likelihood of eviction and it is estimated that over 70,000 families were evicted throughout Ireland in the period 1846–53.[4] At the micro-level, the sur-

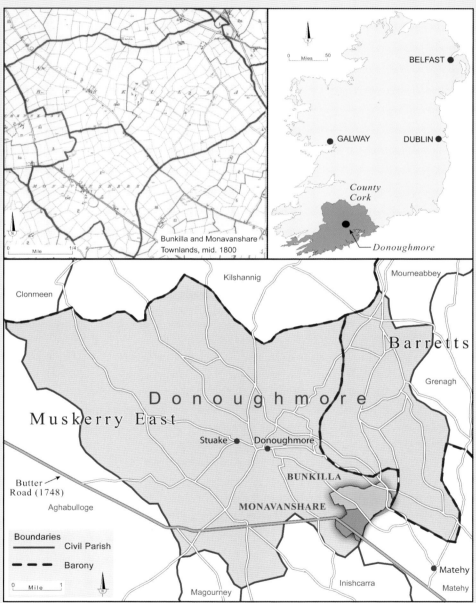

Fig. 1. Townlands in the parish of Donoughmore, with Bunkilla (Bun Coille/Bottom or Foot of the Wood) and Monavanshare (Moin an Mhainseir/Bog of the Manger) highlighted.

veyor's notes and alterations to the house books and perambulation books for Bunkilla and Monavanshare provide a glimpse into what can only have been devastating outcomes for these Cork tenants, documenting that their landlords – John O'Callaghan, and later Henry Wise – oversaw the eviction of family after family from their holdings. The lines

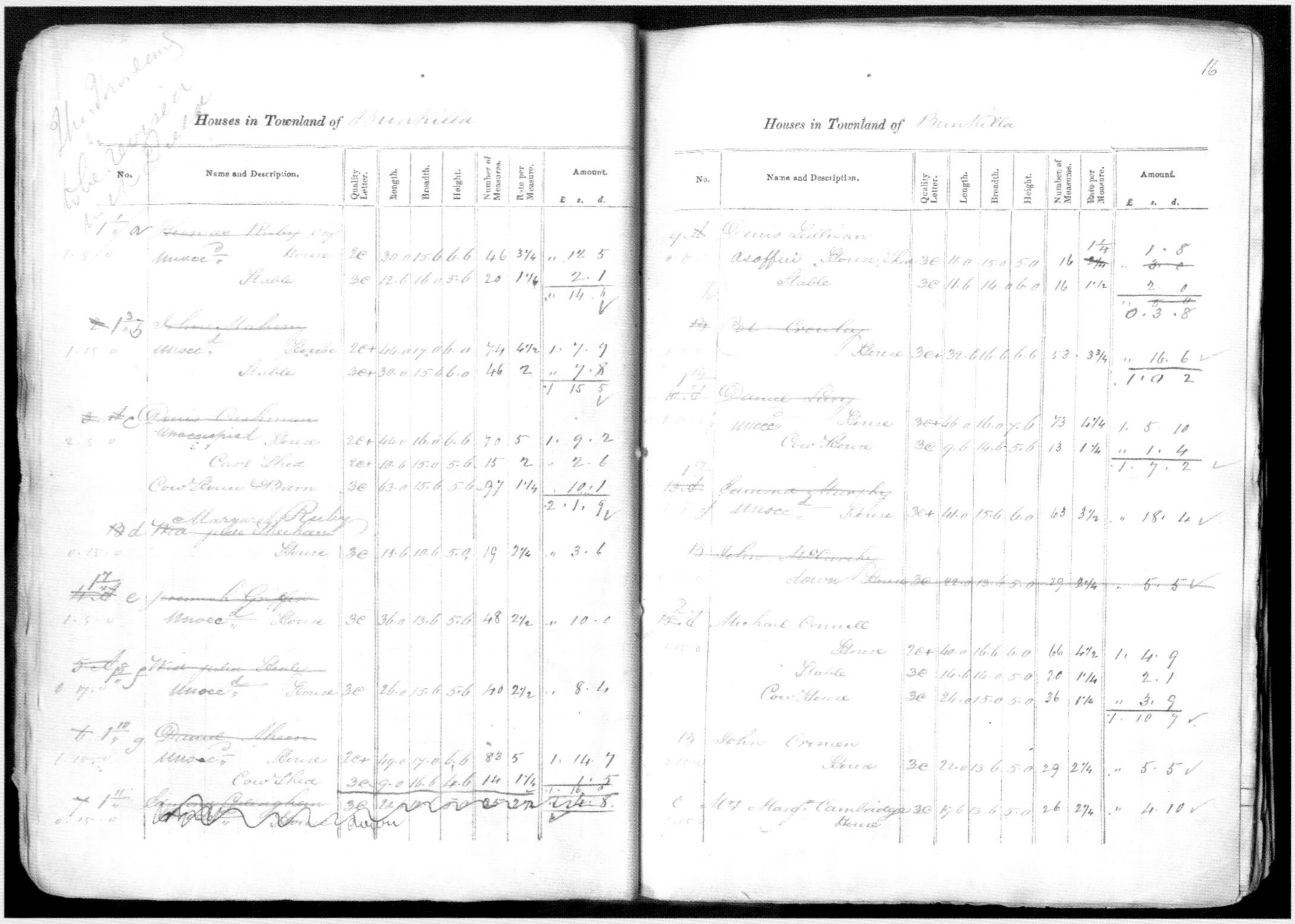

Fig. 2. The house books, which formed part of the basis of Griffith's Valuation, provide a valuation of dwellings in each Irish townland. The Donoughmore townlands of Bunkilla and Monavanshare were surveyed in 1849 and the lines drawn through the names of their occupiers reveal the extent to which eviction took place here during the period of the Great Famine. [Source: National Archives of Ireland]

drawn through the names of each tenant reveal in precise detail the stark reality of evictions that were occurring on a large scale throughout the country (Fig. 2). The 1850 perambulation book for Bunkilla also notes these evictions, stating 'Since this townland was perambulated the immediate lessors have been evicted and all the tenants turned out by the head landlord . . . who has . . . thrown down some of the tenants' houses' (Fig. 3).

The records testify to the fact that the entire population of Bunkilla and Monavanshare, twenty families in total, had been evicted by 1851. Although little is known about the subsequent fate of the majority of these people, it is recorded that some of the Bunkilla families emigrated.

Various members of the Linehan family, for instance, emigrated to the United States, entering through the ports of New Brunswick, Connecticut, New Orleans and Boston, and up to thirty members settled in what came to be known as Linnahan Valley, Monroe County, Wisconsin, where they farmed extensively. In the early 1860s some of the family moved to Minnesota, where they purchased Winnebago Indian Reservation land from which the Native Americans had been removed.

The Cashmans settled in the Boston area, where they succeeded in developing a successful construction and timber business. They purchased one of the finest quarries in Quincy, the product of which was a handsome granite from which many large bridges and public works were made, and were involved with the building of the Provincetown Monument, a tower commemorating the first landfall of the Pilgrims on Cape Cod.

The Mahonys settled in New York and worked in construction. Four of the brothers were bricklayers, and three of these later became successful contractors. Eugene, the fourth brother, having worked as a bricklayer, was ordained to the priesthood in 1879 and built the Lady of Good Counsel Church, Putnam Avenue, Brooklyn, which was financed by the Mahonys.

The Connells, the last remaining Bunkilla tenants listed in Griffith's Valuation in 1851 (Fig. 4), were subsequently evicted. They later emigrated to South Carolina, where two of their uncles were serving as missionary priests. Denis Connell, the youngest casualty of the Bunkilla evictions, became Bishop of Richmond, Virginia, in 1912.

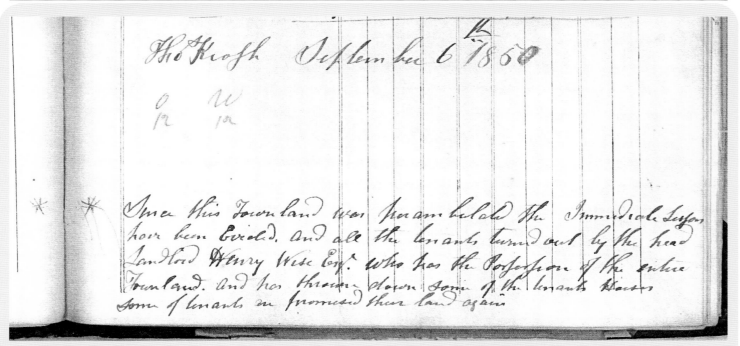

Fig. 3 Before making a rate assessment, valuators in the field were supplied with the surveyor's perambulation book and a map of the townlands in their assigned area. This operation was conducted in Bunkilla in 1850, and the valuator's handwritten note refers to the evictions: 'Since this townland was perambulated the immediate lessors have been evicted and all the tenants turned out by the head landlord Henry Wise Esq. who has the forfeiture of the entire townland. And has thrown down some of the tenants' houses. Some of [the] tenants are promised their land again.' [Source: National Archives of Ireland] One of the families, the Connells, was reinstated, appearing as tenants in Griffith's Valuation in 1851 (Fig. 4), but they were subsequently evicted and eventually settled in the Carolinas.

### Parish of Donaghmore

| Reference to Map | Names | | Description of Tenements | Area | Net Annual Value | | |
|---|---|---|---|---|---|---|---|
| | Townlands & Occupiers | Immediate Lessors | | | Land | Buildings | T. |
| | | | | A. R. P. | L. s. d. | L. s. d. | L. |
| | Barrahaurin — con. | | | | | | |
| 31 | Ellen Murphy | Repts. Henry Longfield | House office & land | 27. 1. 16 | 10. 5. 0 | 0. 10. 0 | 10 |
| | | | Total | 2527. 1. 8 | 327. 7. 0 | 23. 6. 0 | 380 |
| | Bunkilla (Ord. S. 61) | | | | | | |
| 1 | Henry Wise | In fee Henry Wise | Land | 370. 1. 6 | 162. 10. 0 | — | 162 |
| a | Unoccupied | same | House and office | | — | 0. 6. 0 | 0 |
| b | Unoccupied | same | House and office | | — | 0. 18. 0 | 1 |
| c | Unoccupied | same | House and office | | — | 0. 2. 0 | 0 |
| d | Margaret Luby | same | House | | — | 0. 5. 0 | 0 |
| e | Unoccupied | same | House | | — | 0. 4. 0 | 0 |
| f | Unoccupied | same | House | | — | 0. 18. 0 | 0 |
| g | Unoccupied | same | House & office | | — | 0. 10. 0 | 0 |
| h | Unoccupied | same | House & office | | — | 0. 14. 0 | 0 |
| i | Unoccupied | same | House & office | | — | 0. 10. 0 | 0 |
| j | Unoccupied | same | House | | — | 0. 8. 0 | 0 |
| k | Unoccupied | same | House & office | | — | 1. 0. 0 | 1 |
| l | Unoccupied | same | House & office | | — | 0. 16. 0 | 0 |
| m | Unoccupied | same | House & offices | | — | 0. 4. 0 | 0 |
| n | Unoccupied | same | House offices & land | 23. 1. 15 | 11. 0. 0 | 0. 55. 0 | 11 |
| 2 a | Michael Connell | same | House & sm garden | | — | 0. 2. 0 | 0 |
| b | John Crown | Michael Connell | House | | — | 0. 2. 0 | 0 |
| c | Margaret Cambridge | same | House | | | | |
| | | | Total | 393. 2. 21 | 173. 10. 0 | 8. 8. 0 | 181 |
| | Commeenaplaw (Ord. S. ) | | | | | | |

Fig. 4 Details of Bunkilla townland, Griffith's Primary Valuation of Tenements, January 1851.

# CONNACHT

**Ón Ghaillimh go Meiriceá**

Lá áirithe thíos bhí sé a' báisteach
De mhéid an ghála agus on stoirm mhór,
Chrocamar na seolta suas in airde
Nó gur bhualamar Árainn agus Iorras Mór.
A Oileáin Phádraig, mo chúig chéad slán leat,
Mar is ann a d'fhás mé agus mo mhuintir romham,
Agus gurb é lobhadh na bprátaí a chuir muid go na Státaí,
Agus a Rí na nGrásta cuir díriú orainn anonn.

**A Galway Emigrant Poem**

One day out and it was raining
blowing a gale and a mighty storm,
We hoisted sail aloft and upwards
And struck past Aran and Errismore.
To Patrick's island, five hundred farewells,
Where I was raised and my people too,
The potato blight sent us to the States,
O King of Grace direct us there!

**Black Ball Line packet ship *Fidelia* by Samuel Waters (1811–82), oil on canvas [Source: Hart Nautical Collections, MIT Museum]**

# The province of Connacht and the Great Famine

## *William J. Smyth*

The people of Connacht suffered most grievously during the Great Famine. According to the 1841 and 1851 Censuses, Connacht's population declined by 408,828 persons (from 1.4m to 1.0m) in that decade. That constitutes a reduction of 28.8%, well above Munster's devastating loss of 22.5% and about double that of both Leinster (-15.3%) and Ulster (-15.7%).[1] However, Connacht's population by the middle of the 1840s was likely to have reached *c*.1.55m[2], so total population loss is probably over half a million and close to one-third of its peak population. In these five years (1846–51), as many as three out of every ten persons in the province had disappeared from their homes and neighbourhoods and parishes. Some had emigrated and many had died. Connacht's society and landscape had been cruelly and utterly transformed.

Connacht was clearly least best prepared for the shock of the recurring potato failures, the awful hunger and the consequent spread of many deadly famine-related diseases. Although the province constituted over one-fifth of Ireland's territories, only one-sixth of the land was classified as arable. A third of the province was rough, uncultivated land, by far the greatest proportion of all the provinces. Another third of the province was covered by the water of rivers and many lakes, including Loughs Corrib and Mask.[3] Average land values per acre stood at £0.4, less than half that of Leinster's £0.95.[4] In 1841, with almost four-fifths of its families 'chiefly employed in agriculture' and that on very small farms (60.6% under ten acres), Connacht was the

least industrialised and least commercialised province. Only 15% of families were 'chiefly employed in manufacturing and trade'. Its independent and professional classes (and farmers of over fifty acres) only constituted 7% of its families, compared with, say, Leinster's 15%. Labourers, smallholders and other persons 'without capital in land, money or acquired knowledge' constituted 79% of its population. Only 5.6% of its people lived in towns with 2,000+ populations – and County Leitrim had no such town. The absence of local retailing/provision centres – particularly in some inland parts of the province – was to prove a fatal flaw in its human infrastructure when the crisis of the Famine struck. Compared with 26% in Leinster, 19% in Ulster and 18% in Munster, only 9% of Connacht females (over five

Fig. 1 *Lazy Beds*, Jay Murphy, oil on canvas, 36 x 56 cm. {Courtesy of the artist]

years of age) could read and write. Its male literacy figure at 24% was likewise significantly below other provincial levels.[5] The province of Connacht was, therefore, the least well-endowed and least well-equipped to deal with the horrors of famine conditions.

Characterised by the poorest material endowment and quality of life, yet Connacht had an average population density of nearly 400 per sq. mile of arable land – only industrialising and urbanising Ulster exhibited higher densities. But the average disguises the level of congestion in some upland and bogland communities and in particular all around the coastal fringes of the province. In these latter communities, population densities sometimes exceeded 1,000 people per sq. mile of arable land – similar to densely populated countries like Belgium and the Netherlands, well above that of France and about three times the densi-

ty of Denmark's population at the time.[6]

Connacht was exceptional in terms of sustained levels of population growth (2.0% per annum 1791–1821 and 1.2% p.a. 1821–41) and settlement expansion in the pre-Famine decades. This population explosion was fuelled by a partible inheritance system, the subdivision of land, a looser and labyrinthine estate structure, and above all the spread of potato cultivation into the most marginal lands. Here potatoes were sown (and harvested) by the very labour-intensive, spade-based, and highly efficient and high yielding lazy bed (ridge) cultivation system. Underpinning this social structure was a clachan ('village') settlement pattern and a rundale system of land organisation. The classic western clustered settlement pattern involved a group of families where landholding was organised in a cooperative fashion, generally on a townland basis and usually involving kin-related households. Beyond the individual gardens of each household, was the permanently cultivated 'infield' – a large, enclosed, open field, with its numerous arable strips, separated by sods and stones and balks. Each family had its own scattered shares where potatoes and/or oats and/or rye were cultivated. Beyond the core area was the 'outfield', poorer upland or boggy land or coastal marshes (*machair*), which was used for common pasture and for turf harvesting. Communities along coastal strips were characterised by intricate arrangements in the sharing of boats, seaweed, sand and *cnuasach trá* (shore food).[7] Knitting and spinning by women and seasonal migration by *spailpíní* (smallholders-cum-labourers), were also part of this intensive, mainly subsistence economy.

It is still not clear why Connacht, in particular, should exhibit such a specific landholding and settlement regime. Was its enduring features reinforced by an essentially Irish pattern of landholding following on from the Cromwellian transplantations? Did the consequent survival of so many Irish landowners in this province make for greater tolerance of more cooperative landholding systems? Whatever its origins – and ecological conditions may also have been significant – Connacht was by

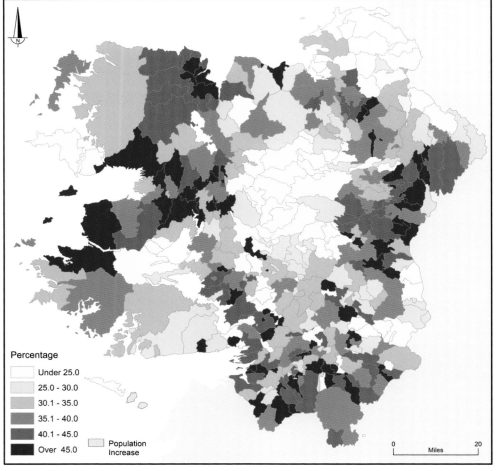

Percentage

- Under 25.0
- 25.0 - 30.0
- 30.1 - 35.0
- 35.1 - 40.0
- 40.1 - 45.0
- Over 45.0
- Population Increase

0     Miles     20

Fig. 2 PERCENTAGE DISTRIBUTION OF DECLINE IN POPULATION BETWEEN 1841 AND 1851. In 1841, the density of rural population reached as high as 386 – and in County Mayo 485 – per square mile of cultivated land. The province was a land of tiny farms along the western coasts and patches of cultivated land high up the mountain sides or between bogland and lakeland landscapes over much of the inland regions. A core of relatively low declines in population (under 25 or 30%) occurs in the east-central part, stretching from Killasser, Bohola, Kilconduff, Killeden and Kilcolman in the west to Annagh through Bekan, Aghamore, Kilmovee and Kilbeagh to the east along to the Mayo/Roscommon borderlands. As well as some northern and eastern parishes in County Leitrim (Rossinver, Kilasnet, Calry, Drumlease, Cloonclare to the north and Drumreilly and Carrigallen to the southeast), this core laps up against significant regions of massive population declines all across north, west, south and east Connacht. On the west side of Killala Bay the parishes of Killala and Ballysakeery actually lost over 50% of their populations. So did Ballintober and Kilmaclasser (inland from Clew Bay), Kilcoona (east of Lough Corrib), Kilbecanty further south on the Clare border and Annaghduff and Kilglass due north of Lough Ree to the east. This pattern of major declines (at least over 35%) is only broken in a number of parishes west of Athlone, in Ross west of Lough Mask and most interestingly, given its specific evangelical history, on Achill (see Fig.3).

far the most dynamic rural settlement frontier as the Famine approached. As Kevin Whelan notes 'new areas of settlement were concentrated along the ragged Atlantic fringe, and on bog and hill edges. Rundale villages, powered by the potato acted as a mobile pioneering fringe – the spade and the spud conquered the contours'.[8] By the 1840s, impoverished families and communities were colonising the very poorest land in upland regions, reaching even above 800 to 1,000 feet.

Characterised by both high marital fertility if still significant levels of infant mortality, the generations multiplied. As they subdivided holdings and eventually settled permanently on the former grazing lands, families became increasingly impoverished, living in the poorest of mud-walled cabins, almost entirely dependent on the potato as the oats crop graduated to become a cash crop. Others were pushed out onto bog edges, roadsides and cabin suburbs, as landlord consolidations turned many smallholders into poverty-stricken landless labourers. In

Fig. 3 The nineteenth-century Protestant mission at Dugort on Achill Island was part of a wider effort by Irish and English evangelicals to convert Catholics from the 'superstition of Rome'. Much of the missionary activity took place in the west of Ireland with significant colonies in Achill and Dingle. Rev Edward Nangle's Protestant mission on Achill Island had been successful in winning converts; however, the fact that conversions took place during a period of great scarcity raised the spectre of proselytism. Those Catholics who 'turned' were called 'jumpers' while those who dispensed the food were known as 'soupers'. Nangle's abhorrence of Roman Catholicism was deep-seated and consequently he was in little doubt about the causes of the Famine and the necessity for conversion. Saint Thomas' church in Dugort (shown above) was an integral part of Nangle's missionary colony and stands as a reminder of a controversial period in the island's history. [Source: Mayo County Library]

the northern half of the province, impoverishment was further exacerbated by the erosion of a host of artisan-based industries including the retreat of domestic weaving and spinning of flax and wool from the villages and countryside

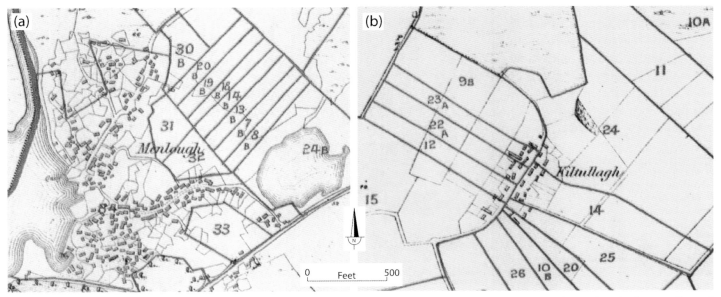

Fig. 4 THE AGRICULTURAL VILLAGES ('CLACHANS') OF (A) MENLOUGH AND (B) KILTULLAGH. Menlough was one of the largest of agricultural villages in Connacht in 1841. With a population of 1,100 and 220 houses it was classified as a single 'census town' in that year. Of the 223 families living in this large, irregular cluster, as many as 201 were mainly dependent on agriculture and the great majority were smallholders and labourers (203), dependent on their own manual labour. Essentially an Irish-speaking settlement, 83% of Menlough's population five years and over were illiterate in the English language. By 1851 the population of Menlough was reduced by almost one-third to 764 persons but it is clear that some consolidation of holdings has occurred as there are now fifty-seven families involved in the 'direction of labour' whereas only fourteen were so engaged in 1841. The number of families dependent on manual labour had been more than halved. In contrast, Kiltullagh agricultural village was a much smaller settlement with nine dwelling houses and a population of sixty-two in 1841. Unlike Menlough it is clearly a deliberately designed *sráid* or street village, a product of the rule of the adjacent castle-mansion. However, the famine was more devastating here and it was to lose two-thirds of its houses in population between 1845 and 1851.

Fig. 5 Dooagh village, Achill *c.*1900, an example of a clachan settlement. [Source: The National Library of Ireland]

as the products of Britain's industrial revolution spread into the West.[9] A depressed and distressed proletariat was created in a situation of rising populations and shrinking job opportunities outside of farming. Volatility, mobility and marginality became the fate of more and more individuals and families. Already vulnerable, the failure of the potato crop – not once but often twice or three times in the Famine years – was utterly devas-

Fig. 6 POPULATION CHANGE AND THE DISTRIBUTION OF CLUSTERED FARM SETTLEMENTS. It is argued in the Introduction (above) that congestion and overcrowding in the clustered farm settlements in Connacht may have facilitated the spread of famine diseases and so increased mortalities. Figure 6 seeks to explore this thesis in more detail. While it is likely that clustered settlements exacerbated mortality levels in the Killala to Castlebar axis of parishes, more especially in the Castlebar–Westport zone, in northeast Roscommon and some parishes in the very south of Galway, it is clear that in east-central Mayo, west Connacht and southeast Roscommon that clustered settlement is equally dominant in parishes registering the lowest population declines. Indeed some clustered settlements may have emerged or expanded in these zones during the Famine. As noted elsewhere, monocausal explanations of Famine population decline are clearly insufficient. Vulnerability to famine conditions was always complex and many-sided.

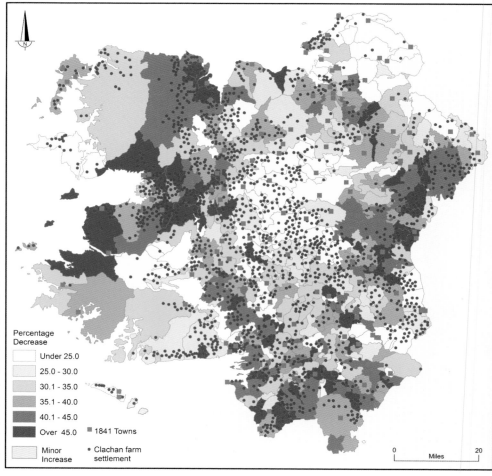

Percentage Decrease

- Under 25.0
- 25.0 - 30.0
- 30.1 - 35.0
- 35.1 - 40.0
- 40.1 - 45.0
- Over 45.0
- Minor Increase

■ 1841 Towns

• Clachan farm settlement

0    Miles    20

tating (see Mary Kelly below). Amongst the coastal villages, fishermen's nets and tackle were pawned to buy a little food. The many deserted village ruins and the fossilised remnants of many lazy beds today bear silent witness to the many families which vanished in these desperate and despairing years. The tight-knit villages or clustered settlements had become deadly vehicles for the dissemination of infectious famine diseases.[10]

Mokyr's lower-bound estimate of Connacht's share of excess deaths island-wide averages out at 39.3% while

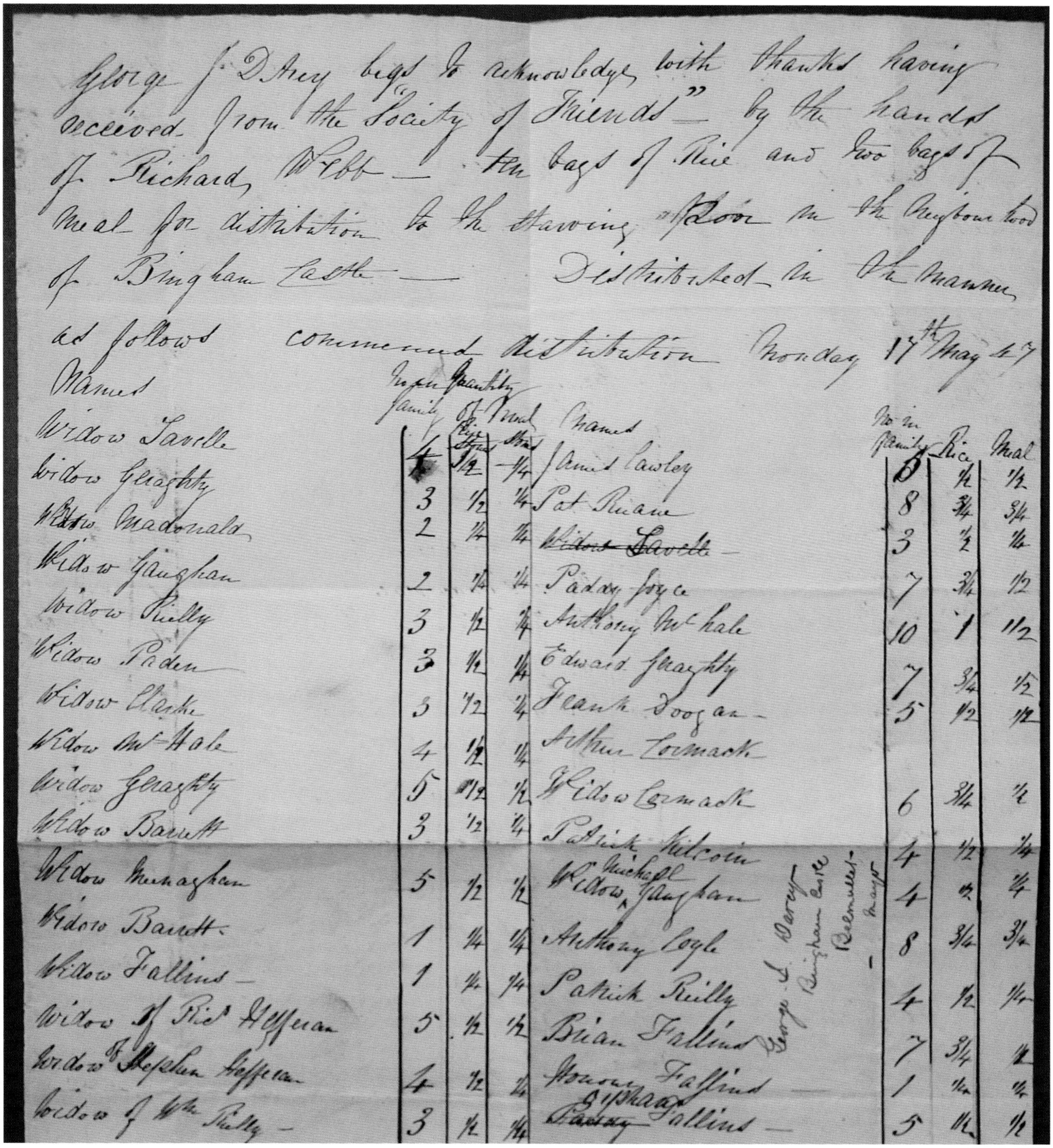

George J. D'Arcy begs to acknowledge with thanks having received from the "Society of Friends" by the hands of Richard Webb — ten bags of Rice and two bags of meal for distribution to the starving poor in the neighbourhood of Bingham Castle — Distributed in the manner as follows commenced distribution Monday 17th May 47

| Names | No in family | Quantity of Rice | Meal | Names | No in family | Rice | Meal |
|---|---|---|---|---|---|---|---|
| Widow Tavelle | 4 | 1/2 | 1/4 | James Cawley | 5 | 1/2 | 1/2 |
| Widow Geraghty | 3 | 1/2 | 1/4 | Pat Ruane | 8 | 3/4 | 3/4 |
| Widow Madonald | 2 | 1/4 | 1/4 | ~~Widow Tavelle~~ | 3 | 1/2 | 1/4 |
| Widow Gaughan | 2 | 1/4 | 1/4 | Paddy Joyce | 7 | 3/4 | 1/2 |
| Widow Reilly | 3 | 1/2 | 1/4 | Anthony McHale | 10 | 1 | 1/2 |
| Widow Peden | 3 | 1/2 | 1/4 | Edward Geraghty | 7 | 3/4 | 1/2 |
| Widow Clarke | 3 | 1/2 | 1/4 | Frank Doogan | 5 | 1/2 | 1/2 |
| Widow McHale | 4 | 1/2 | 1/4 | Arthur Cormack | | | |
| Widow Geraghty | 5 | 1/2 | 1/2 | Widow Cormack | 6 | 3/4 | 1/2 |
| Widow Barrett | 3 | 1/2 | 1/4 | Patrick Malcolm | 4 | 1/2 | 1/4 |
| Widow Monaghan | 5 | 1/2 | 1/2 | Widow Michael Gaughan | 4 | 1/2 | 1/4 |
| Widow Barrett | 1 | 1/4 | 1/4 | Anthony Coyle | 8 | 3/4 | 3/4 |
| Widow Fallins | 1 | 1/4 | 1/4 | Patrick Reilly | 4 | 1/2 | 1/4 |
| Widow of Richd Heffernan | 5 | 1/2 | 1/2 | Brian Fallins | 7 | 3/4 | 1/2 |
| Widow of Stephen Heffernan | 4 | 1/2 | 1/4 | Honor Fallins | 1 | 1/4 | 1/2 |
| Widow of Wm Reilly | 3 | 1/2 | 1/4 | Bartly Fallins | 5 | 1/2 | 1/2 |

George J. Darcy
Bingham Castle
Belmullet
— Mayo

Fig. 7 An acknowledgement by George Darcy of ten bags of rice and two bags of meal sent by the Society of Friends at the request of Richard Webb to the starving poor in Binghamstown, County Mayo. The distribution commenced on 17 May 1847 with the names of the recipients and the amount allocated recorded. Webb, a member of the Central Relief Committee, had toured County Mayo and observed the starvation and misery for himself. [Source: National Archives Ireland]

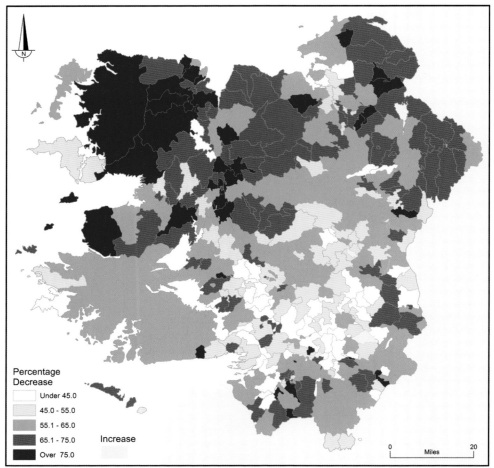

Percentage Decrease

| | Under 45.0 |
| | 45.0 - 55.0 |
| | 55.1 - 65.0 |
| | 65.1 - 75.0 |
| | Over 75.0 |

Increase

0    Miles    20

Fig. 8 THE CHANGING DISTRIBUTION OF FAMILIES DEPENDENT ON THEIR OWN MANUAL LABOUR BETWEEN 1841 AND 1851. At least three-quarters of the population of the province were dependent on manual labour for survival. Underemployed labourers cum seasonal migrants, servants, fishermen and domestic textile workers and smallholders survived in poor, sometimes wretched living conditions. Outside County Leitrim, three-fifths of all farms were under five acres. In 1841, over 114,000 people across Connacht were employed in home spinning (mostly women) and weaving of flax and wool (mostly men). Although textile activities provided an additional source of income, already domestic production was being challenged by factory-imported goods, threatening livelihoods. Over 250,000 of the actively employed were 'servants and labourers'. Many holdings were long subject to subdivision, fragmentation and a rundale system of management. Yet even in Connacht, these patterns were uneven in their distribution and intensity. Once again the parishes of Kilmovee and Aghamore in east Mayo stand out as returning over 90% dependent on manual labour, while many of the west Mayo and west Galway parishes return at least 87%. Usually regionalised between west and east, on this measure the crucial divide is between north and south Connacht. By 1851, over two-thirds and often over three-quarters of those dependent on manual labour had disappeared across Mayo, west Sligo, and practically all of Leitrim (Figure 5). North Connacht (as well as northwest Leinster and south Ulster) was to experience both devastating levels of famine-related deaths and very high levels of emigration. South Connacht was more resilient.

with a combined population of 336,662, had disappeared off the map.[12] Assuming Connacht's population was of the order of 1.55m at mid-century, this suggests that Connacht lost between a fifth and a quarter of its population to famine-related mortalities. Many of the lost generation were monoglot Irish speakers – bearers of a rich oral and aural heritage which involved folk customs and stories, poetry, ballads, music and dance. Neither maps nor words can attempt to render the scale or particulars of this catastrophe.[13] Only music comes close to remembering the cry of want, the mournful wail of hordes of people as they faced starvation and death.

However, all of the above estimates need to be treated with some caution. Mr Dobree, a very experienced Commissariat official, involved in trying to feed the hungry out of his poorly supplied Sligo food depot, reported to Trevelyan: 'there are no records, even round figures [of the number of the dead]. Thousands have disappeared'.[14] It was then estimated that the population of Leitrim had been reduced by a quarter. There, as elsewhere in the province, many who had died of fever were buried in ditches, fields and hillsides – 'many deaths were unrecorded because of the Irish horror of "fever" [which] even conquered the bond of family affection, which is the strongest bond in Ireland'.[15] The official census record for Connacht reported that 6.6%

Cousens' estimate comes to 24.2%.[11] Mokyr's figures appear too high and Cousens' are clearly too low. We will never know how many died of famine conditions in Connacht but the likely figure is close to a third of the national total of excess deaths. That would mean that one-third of a million (c.330,000) of Connacht's men, women and children died of famine-related causes between late 1845 and mid-1851. (This figure excludes averted births – that of the children who remained unborn because of the traumas of the Famine years.) To try and put the deaths of so many starving and disease-ridden people into some kind of perspective, the above figure means that almost as many men, women and children died of famine-related causes in *rural* Connacht as might have died if the cities of Cork, Dublin and Waterford

of the deaths between 1841 and 1851 occurred in civic districts, 68.7% in rural districts and 24.7% in public institutions, especially in the workhouses.[16] These ratios may be indicative – if more reliable for the institutions – but the actual numbers returned are likely to be deficient by the order of 50%.

That close on two-thirds (fourteen) of the twenty-two government-designated 'distressed' unions were in Connacht is a further measure of its desperate state – as was the need to create so many new unions: Belmullet, Claremorris, Newport, Dromore west, Tobercurry, Strokestown, Glenamaddy, Mountbellew, Oughterard and Portumna – in that province. The poverty of so many unions – which crippled and literally bankrupted the proper functioning of so many workhouses – was also

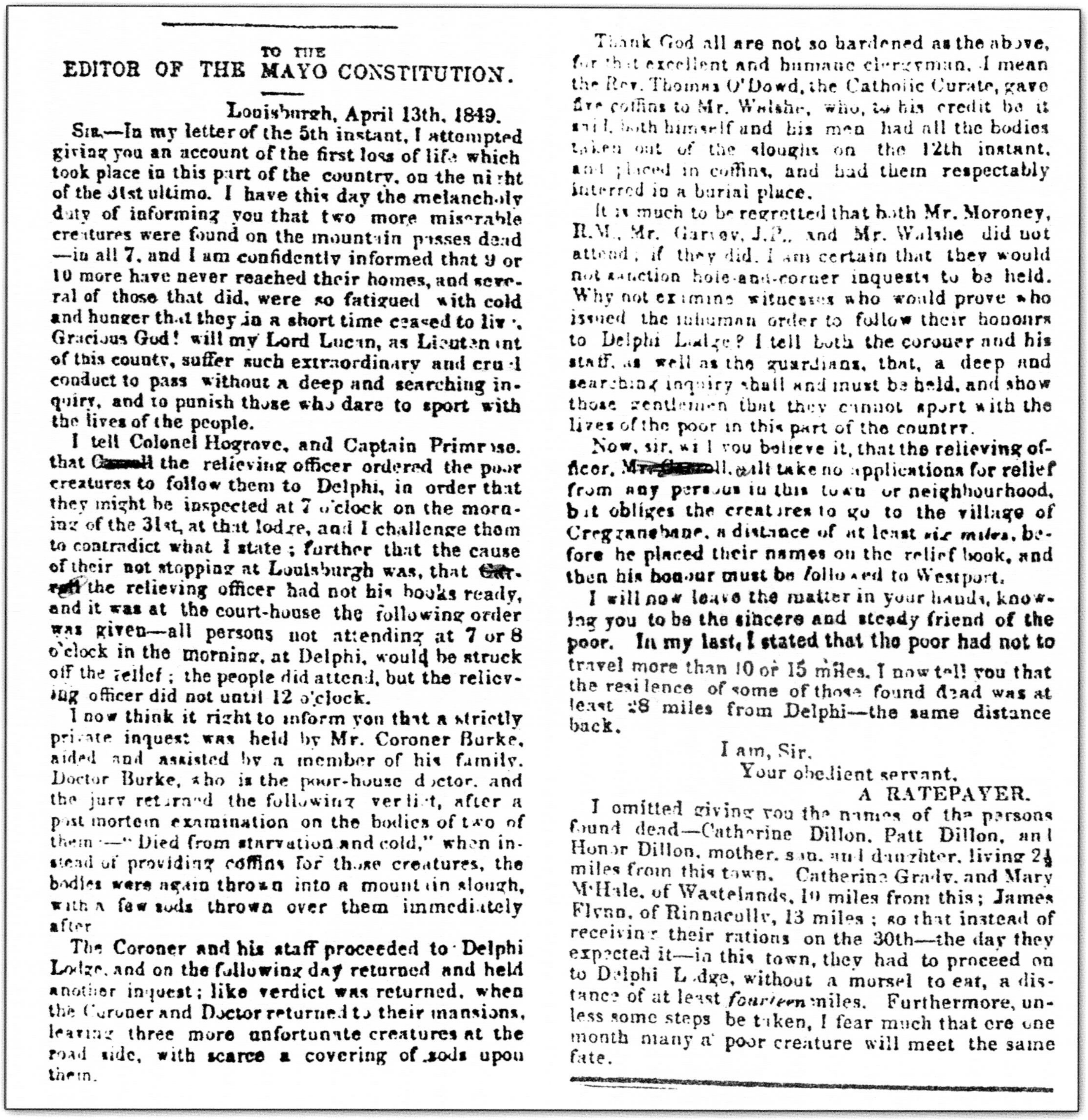

## TO THE
## EDITOR OF THE MAYO CONSTITUTION.

Louisburgh, April 13th, 1849.

Sir,—In my letter of the 5th instant, I attempted giving you an account of the first loss of life which took place in this part of the country, on the night of the 31st ultimo. I have this day the melancholy duty of informing you that two more miserable creatures were found on the mountain passes dead —in all 7, and I am confidently informed that 9 or 10 more have never reached their homes, and several of those that did, were so fatigued with cold and hunger that they in a short time ceased to live. Gracious God! will my Lord Lucan, as Lieutenant of this county, suffer such extraordinary and cruel conduct to pass without a deep and searching inquiry, and to punish those who dare to sport with the lives of the people.

I tell Colonel Hogrove, and Captain Primrose, that Carroll the relieving officer ordered the poor creatures to follow them to Delphi, in order that they might be inspected at 7 o'clock on the morning of the 31st, at that lodge, and I challenge them to contradict what I state; further that the cause of their not stopping at Louisburgh was, that Carroll the relieving officer had not his books ready, and it was at the court-house the following order was given—all persons not attending at 7 or 8 o'clock in the morning, at Delphi, would be struck off the relief; the people did attend, but the relieving officer did not until 12 o'clock.

I now think it right to inform you that a strictly private inquest was held by Mr. Coroner Burke, aided and assisted by a member of his family, Doctor Burke, who is the poor-house doctor, and the jury returned the following verdict, after a post mortem examination on the bodies of two of them—"Died from starvation and cold," when instead of providing coffins for those creatures, the bodies were again thrown into a mountain slough, with a few sods thrown over them immediately after.

The Coroner and his staff proceeded to Delphi Lodge, and on the following day returned and held another inquest; like verdict was returned, when the Coroner and Doctor returned to their mansions, leaving three more unfortunate creatures at the road side, with scarce a covering of sods upon them.

Thank God all are not so hardened as the above, for that excellent and humane clergyman, I mean the Rev. Thomas O'Dowd, the Catholic Curate, gave five coffins to Mr. Walshe, who, to his credit be it said, both himself and his men had all the bodies taken out of the sloughs on the 12th instant, and placed in coffins, and had them respectably interred in a burial place.

It is much to be regretted that both Mr. Moroney, R.M., Mr. Garvey, J.P., and Mr. Walshe did not attend; if they did, I am certain that they would not sanction hole-and-corner inquests to be held. Why not examine witnesses who would prove who issued the inhuman order to follow their honours to Delphi Lodge? I tell both the coroner and his staff, as well as the guardians, that, a deep and searching inquiry shall and must be held, and show those gentlemen that they cannot sport with the lives of the poor in this part of the country.

Now, sir, will you believe it, that the relieving officer, Mr. Carroll, will take no applications for relief from any person in this town or neighbourhood, but obliges the creatures to go to the village of Cregganebane, a distance of at least six miles, before he placed their names on the relief book, and then his honour must be followed to Westport.

I will now leave the matter in your hands, knowing you to be the sincere and steady friend of the poor. In my last, I stated that the poor had not to travel more than 10 or 15 miles. I now tell you that the residence of some of those found dead was at least 28 miles from Delphi—the same distance back.

I am, Sir,
Your obedient servant,
A RATEPAYER.

I omitted giving you the names of the persons found dead—Catherine Dillon, Patt Dillon, and Honor Dillon, mother, son, and daughter, living 2½ miles from this town. Catherine Grady and Mary M'Hale, of Wastelands, 10 miles from this; James Flynn, of Rinnacully, 13 miles; so that instead of receiving their rations on the 30th—the day they expected it—in this town, they had to proceed on to Delphi Lodge, without a morsel to eat, a distance of at least fourteen miles. Furthermore, unless some steps be taken, I fear much that ere one month many a poor creature will meet the same fate.

Fig. 9a An account of the events (*Mayo Constitution*, 17 April 1849) which led to the deaths of seven people and more in the Doolough valley, County Mayo. The letter writer highlights in particular the poor creatures' harsh treatment at the hands of the relieving officer at Louisburgh, who insisted that they make the journey to Delphi Lodge in order to be inspected the next morning. [Source: Mayo County Library]

indicative. Ballina, Clifden, and Westport Union workhouses became bywords for the terrible conditions which prevailed in so many western unions.[17] Already in the spring of 1847, workhouses in the western province were 'overcrowded and frequently disease-ridden, particularly with fever and dysentry'.[18] Given the levels of destitution, Relief Committees struggled everywhere to meet local needs because of poor food supplies, lack of funds and frequent bureaucratic delays and restrictions (see Gerard Mac Atasney below). Adding further obstacles to the provision of relief were both the enormous size and populations of so many of Connacht unions (in sharp contrast, for example, to the closely packed, if densely populated unions of Ulster). On average, each of the seventeen provincial unions had to serve a population of the order of over 90,000 by 1845–46. And some of the unions were of

Fig. 9b shows part of the road which runs through the Doolough valley. [Photo: Michael Diggin]

immense size – Ballina Union encompassed half a million acres and was expected to serve over 120,000 people; the Westport Union covered one-third of a million acres. Sligo Union also covered a very extensive catchment area of one-quarter of a million acres. In County Galway the unions of Ballinasloe, Loughrea, Galway and Tuam all exceeded 200,000 acres in size – the Galway City Union (centred on that city) came close to 300,000 acres in area. And the shape of the unions also mattered. The Westport Union stretched over a coastal region for over seventy miles. How could the destitute poor from either its southern end in the Killeries or from its northwestern extension into Achill be expected to survive, to travel, reach and seek admission and relief in its workhouse? Both physical and human geographic realities combined to make Poor Law relief even more remote (see Kathleen Villiers-Tuthill below), not to speak of the effects of 'inappropriate social and economic policies, which refused to recognise the facts that when land had ceased to be productive, it no longer had the means to support its own poor'.[19]

Adding to the trauma of many during the Famine was the level of evictions carried out by so many landlords – the latter seeking to consolidate farms and increase pastoral production (see Mary Kelly below). At the beginning of the Famine, many Connacht landlords reacted with compassion by reducing or deferring rent payments. Funds and employment were provided to alleviate the starvation and some landlords continued these practices throughout the hungry years. In County Mayo, landlords such as the Marquis of Sligo, Sir Robert Blosse Lynch, Sir Compton Donville and others were applauded by both local newspapers and tenants for their generosity.[20] Most conspicuous in this group was George Henry Moore whose horse Coranna won the Chester Cup in 1846, netting for its owner £10,000. In a letter to his mother at Moorehall he stated: 'No tenant of mine shall want for plenty of everything this year'.[21] By 1850 and 1851, the same Marquis of Sligo was responsible for evicting and levelling the houses of at least 150 families; Sir Roger Palmer and George Bingham, 3rd Earl of Lucan, were also involved in major 'clearances' in County Mayo as was the bankrupt estate of the Martins in Connemara while Christopher Taaffe was involved in many evictions in Counties Mayo and Roscommon. As Tim O'Neill has argued, evictions played a major if not central role in the catastrophe that was the Great Famine.[22] In Connacht alone, the official court and constabulary records suggest that c.30,000 families or c.150,000 people were put out on the road in the Famine years. We have little knowledge of either the thousands who were evicted without any legal decree or those who simply abandoned their holdings and emigrated.

Although the province of Munster was most deeply affected by the level of evictions between 1849 and 1852 alone with over 95,000 persons put out on the road, Connacht with at least 58,000 individuals forced out of their homes was equally traumatised by these brutal and brutalising actions.[23] These figures constitute about 5% of the province's population in 1849. Earlier, between 1846–48, court records confirm that 7% of all evictions island-wide are recorded for each of counties Galway and Roscommon with Mayo registering 5.4% of this total.[24] It seems that Sligo and Leitrim were less affected by evictions in these earlier years. For the Gort Union, the local Poor Law inspector reported that many people had been evicted: 'their cottages pulled down, whilst the large proprietors were doing nothing to support the destitute'.[25] Stories like that of December 1847 when eleven boatloads of destitute people came into Galway Harbour from Connemara 'most from the estate of Christian Saint George. . . who, I am told, is ejecting them without even a rag to cover them'[26] recur and reverberate across the whole province. However, the landlords did not always have life their own way; resistance to landlords, and not only in counties Roscommon, Sligo and Leitrim, meant that for some of the property-owners their daily experience most resembled living 'in an enemy country'[27] (see Charles E. Orser below). Yet rents were still demanded, rate collections were enforced with the help of both the police and the military and evictions still continued.

So began the great exodus from the west. It is almost certain that the well-worn pathways created by the seasonal migrants, led by the many Mayo *spailpíní* and their companions from Counties Roscommon, Sligo and Leitrim, helped shape the first phase of Famine emigration. But after the second almost universal failure of the potato in 1846, the floodgates opened. Thousands of destitute

men, women and children embarked onto the high roads, leaving their cabins and memories behind, moving from west to east, to spread out over the eastern counties, begging all the way until they managed to get a boat to Liverpool or Glasgow. Others emigrated via the ports of Galway and Sligo while some scrambled to escape from small harbours at Ballina, Westport and Killala. The greatest numbers were from Mayo and Roscommon; County Galway contributed the smallest share.[28] It is likely that at least one-tenth of Connacht's 1845 population emigrated between 1846 and 1851. During those years, somewhere between 200,000 and 230,000 people deserted their own western homes and communities, seeking food and hope in a new land.

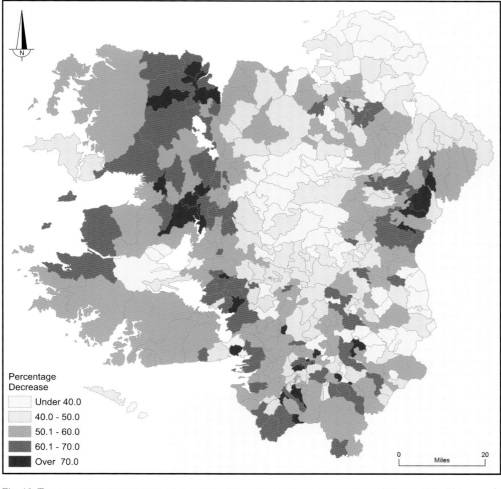

Percentage Decrease

☐ Under 40.0
☐ 40.0 - 50.0
▨ 50.1 - 60.0
▨ 60.1 - 70.0
■ Over 70.0

0    Miles    20

Fig. 10 THE CHANGING DISTRIBUTION OF CHILDREN UNDER FIVE YEARS OF AGE BETWEEN 1841 AND 1851. This map for Connacht reveals very different kinds of communities – some aged, some still vibrant and many devastated – by 1851. Along the western shores of Killala Bay, in parishes such as Lackan, Templemurry, Rathreagh and Ballysakeery (as well as inland Moygawnagh), close on three-quarters of the equivalent age group in 1841 were no longer present by 1851. Likewise, pockets of massive decline, high child mortality and – one must assume – many averted births are evidenced from Castlebar south through Aghagower, Ballyhean, Ballintober and Burriscarra, in the Roosky-Slieve Bawn area in east Connacht, around Roscommon town as well as parishes such as Taghmaconell and a scatter of smaller parishes in south Galway. In contrast, north Leitrim and a very interesting and highly adaptive block of communities including Kilkelly, Castlemore, Kilmovee and around Ballaghderreen and Ballyhaunis – as well as vibrant pockets in southeast Roscommon and Joyce Country in west Galway return a much smaller decline. Declines in County Roscommon, south-central Galway and central and west Mayo indicate high child mortality and high levels of family outmigration. Evictions from the central lowlands of Mayo – from Ballina through Westport and Lord Lucan's Castlebar – as well as from the pastoral lands of central Roscommon, led to colonisation of the poorest land by displaced families along the borderlands of east Mayo and west Roscommon. These factors may help explain the exceptional demographic character of the parishes in and around Kilmovee.

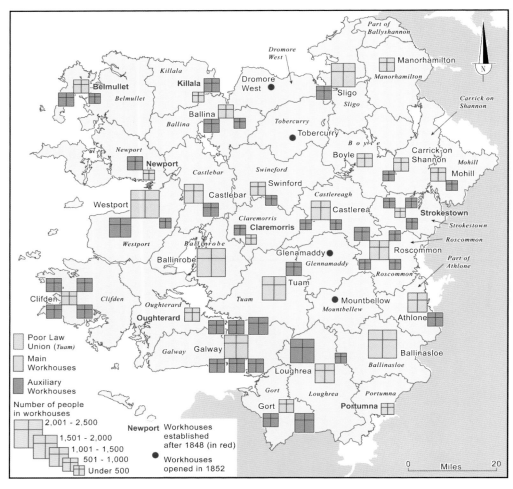

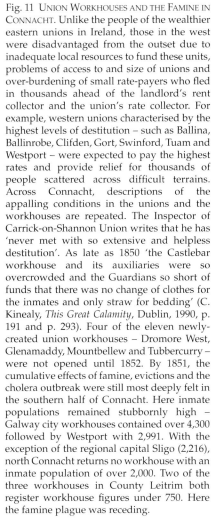

Fig. 11 UNION WORKHOUSES AND THE FAMINE IN CONNACHT. Unlike the people of the wealthier eastern unions in Ireland, those in the west were disadvantaged from the outset due to inadequate local resources to fund these units, problems of access to and size of unions and over-burdening of small rate-payers who fled in thousands ahead of the landlord's rent collector and the union's rate collector. For example, western unions characterised by the highest levels of destitution – such as Ballina, Ballinrobe, Clifden, Gort, Swinford, Tuam and Westport – were expected to pay the highest rates and provide relief for thousands of people scattered across difficult terrains. Across Connacht, descriptions of the appalling conditions in the unions and the workhouses are repeated. The Inspector of Carrick-on-Shannon Union writes that he has 'never met with so extensive and helpless destitution'. As late as 1850 'the Castlebar workhouse and its auxiliaries were so overcrowded and the Guardians so short of funds that there was no change of clothes for the inmates and only straw for bedding' (C. Kinealy, *This Great Calamity*, Dublin, 1990, p. 191 and p. 293). Four of the eleven newly-created union workhouses – Dromore West, Glenamaddy, Mountbellew and Tubbercurry – were not opened until 1852. By 1851, the cumulative effects of famine, evictions and the cholera outbreak were still most deeply felt in the southern half of Connacht. Here inmate populations remained stubbornly high – Galway city workhouses contained over 4,300 followed by Westport with 2,991. With the exception of the regional capital Sligo (2,216), north Connacht returns no workhouse with an inmate population of over 2,000. Two of the three workhouses in County Leitrim both register workhouse figures under 750. Here the famine plague was receding.

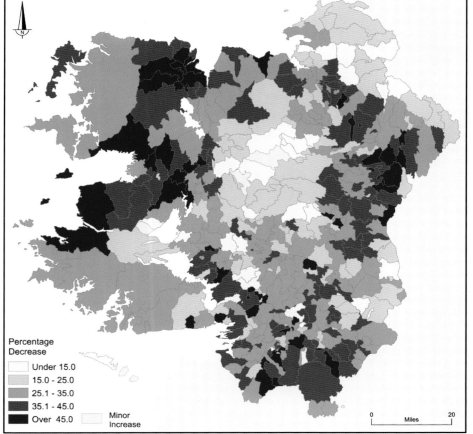

Fig. 12 THE CHANGING DISTRIBUTION OF FAMILIES LIVING IN FOURTH-CLASS HOUSES BETWEEN 1841 AND 1851. Mud-cabins with only one room dominate the crowded landscapes of pre-Famine Connacht. Pockets of better-class housing are found in only a few regions. Elsewhere, the overcrowded and desperate living conditions associated with a fourth-class house characterise more than half the housing stock. In a belt of parishes from Clifden and Leenane north by the Partry Mountains and on through central Mayo, Achill, the Mullet and large swathes along the Sligo/Mayo/Roscommon borderland parishes, the single-roomed mud cabin has overwhelming dominance. South of Ballina close to the Ox mountains, in the parishes of Ballintober, Mayo and Tagheen, in the far west of Connemara around Omey and Ballynakill and on the Galway–Roscommon borderlands around Ballymoe and Glenamaddy, over 85% of all houses were single-roomed, mud-walled cabins. By 1851 (Fig. 8), the Mullet peninsula was the only region where fourth-class houses still constituted over half the housing stock. Across the rest of Connacht, the mud cabin and the class of people who had lived in it had been swept from the land. It is a landscape of silence, utterly and radically transformed and the areas of great transformation are not necessarily the poorer areas (such as northwest Mayo and west Galway) but rather the better farming lands of central Mayo and north Sligo and particularly central Roscommon and east Galway where landlord clearances and farm consolidation had been most actively pursued, especially after 1847.

# Clifden Union, Connemara, County Galway

## Kathleen Villiers-Tuthill

The Clifden Union came into operation on 24 August 1840. It covered 191,426 statute acres and had a population of 33,465. Geographically the union covered the barony of Ballynahinch and was comprised of four parishes: Ballynakill, Ballindoon, Moyrus and Omey. The town of Clifden was the centre for administration and the proposed site for the workhouse. Joseph Burke, the Assistant Poor Law Commissioner responsible for setting up the Clifden Union, used the four parish boundaries to divide the union into four electoral divisions: Clifden, Renvyle, Roundstone and Ballindoon.

Burke, in his report to the Poor Law Commission, described a region with many advantages: fishing, possible mineral wealth and land suitable for reclamation. And although the potato crop had failed repeatedly in recent decades, the region had the ability to meet such emergencies and was well capable of supporting its poor.[1]

Many of the landed proprietors of the union had been in possession of their lands for two hundred years or more and almost all were resident in the area. The 1841 Census recorded 5,909 families in the barony, of whom 4,881 were listed as deriving their income from their own manual labour, with 4,665 employed in agriculture. The average holding was five acres, with some acres of mountain and bogland. Those living on the coast supplemented their food supply with fish, but there were few who derived their income solely from the fishery. The majority of the people were self-sufficient, although living at subsistence level: 'Tending their small holdings, cutting turf for fuel, harvesting the oats and potato crop and fishing for herring, were the chief occupations of the men, while the women knitted stockings, made flannel-yarn and nets, and drew seaweed from the shore to be used as manure on the potato plot.'[2] There was little or no employment to be had and cash was almost never used; the barter system continued to be the preferred mode of doing business.

### ESTABLISHING THE UNION

The election that followed the setting up of the union was bitterly contested and claims of bribery and vote rigging were made to the Poor Law Commissioners and published in the newspapers. A valuation of the area for the poor rate was commenced and it took two years to complete. The Board of Guardians, however, refused to accept the report and the valuation team was compelled to begin again. Burke estimated that workhouse accommodation for 300 would be sufficient for the union. A site was purchased and the tall four-storey building erected east of Clifden. The workhouse was declared fit to receive paupers on 22 December 1845, but it was fifteen months before it admitted its first inmate. The Board of Guardians delayed the opening, although the effect of a partial failure of the potato crop of that year was already impacting on the very poor. Frustrated by their actions, the Poor Law Commission dissolved the board and ordered a second election.

The new board was made up of sixteen guardians: Hyacinth D'Arcy was elected chairman, Henry Blake, vice-chairman, Major-General Thomson, deputy vice-chairman, John Griffin, clerk, with the Bank of Ireland, Galway, acting as treasurer.[3] The Commissioners warned the new board that, should it attempt to follow the actions of its predecessors, it too would be dissolved and replaced by paid guardians. The board, however, was experiencing difficulty

Fig. 1 Remains of lazy beds taken from across Lough Muck near Killary Harbour to Benchoona. [Photo: Clare Cashman]

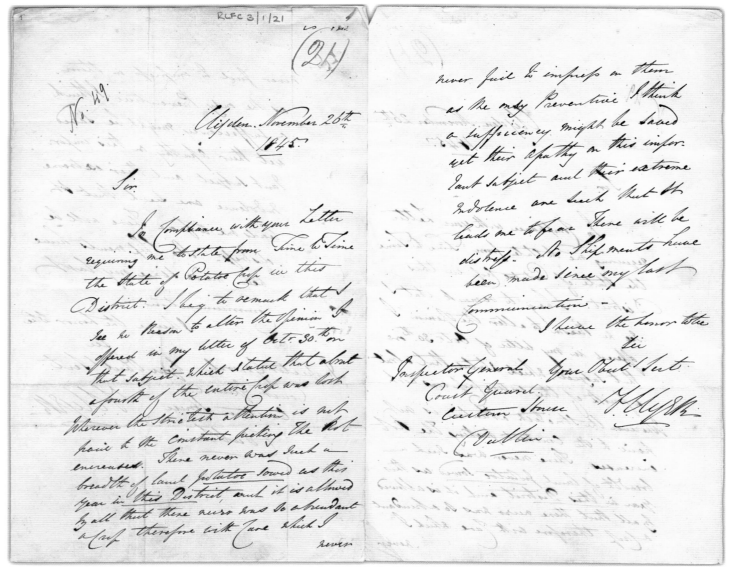

Fig. 2  The early work of the Relief Commission in Dublin concerned itself primarily with assessing the impact of the blight. Letters were received from interested parties throughout the country, including members of the Board of Works as well as coastguard officers. This letter from the coastguard officer in Clifden, County Galway, 26 November 1845, states that about a fourth of the entire crop has been lost. While optimistic in part in relation to the abundance of the crop, he is very dismissive of those dependent on the potato and their indolent ways: 'there was never such a breadth of land potatoe (sic) sowed as this year in this district and it is allowed by all that there never was so abundant a crop,  therefore with care what I never fail to impress on them as the only preventative, I think a sufficiency might be saved yet their apathy on this important subject and their extreme indolence are such that it leads me to fear there will be distress'. [Source: Relief Commission Papers, 3/1/21, National Archives Ireland]

in collecting the poor rate and this further delayed the opening of the workhouse. By law the board was forbidden to administer relief other than inside the workhouse; this left it free of responsibility to the starving poor for the early years of the Famine. Individual members were, however, to the forefront of the local relief committees.

Relief committees were set up in Clifden, Ballynakill and Roundstone in 1846. Their members were well meaning and worked tirelessly for the poor in their district. But in a region as remote and underdeveloped as Connemara, there were too many obstacles to overcome and, as events will show, they never quite came to grips with the task.

The committees were instructed by the Relief Commission to investigate into the conditions of every family in their parish, to raise subscriptions locally and to oversee the public works in their district; it was an immense task, when

one considers the extent of Connemara and the high percentage of its population affected by the failure of the potato crop. Its remote, isolated communities scattered along the coast and among the foothills made it impossible to ascertain the true condition of all of the people. Raising subscriptions would prove difficult in a region where those with means were few when compared with those in need. The Roundstone Committee in particular repeatedly complained of the absence of what it termed, 'respectable persons' residing in its district. Providing a cheap food supply for the poor of the union would prove a challenge for the committees throughout the Famine. Lack of funds would restrict their purchasing power and seriously hamper their efforts to curtail prices on the open market.

Local merchants too found it impossible to keep up a regular food supply. Bringing large quantities of food into

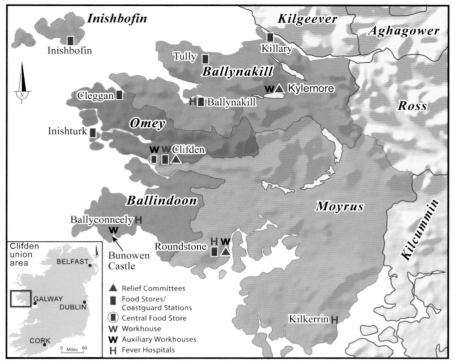

Fig. 3 THE DISTRIBUTION OF FAMINE INSTITUTIONS IN CONNEMARA. This map represents the provision of relief of all kinds in Connemara during the Famine. It not only indicates the location of workhouses and fever hospitals, but also illustrates where relief committees were established. Most particularly, it illuminates where vital food stores were established to try and deal with the early years of the famine crisis.

an area that was previously self-sufficient required ingenuity and a business aptitude that had not been in evidence heretofore. There were no major importers in the area, just small shopkeepers importing groceries and manufactured goods. Insufficient piers and poor quality roads created logistical difficulties, making the distribution of food to remote communities difficult and costly.

## FOOD DEPOTS

In April 1846, government food depots were set up at Galway and Westport. The depot at Galway was responsible for supplying food to Galway city, Oughterard and Clifden, as well as the Aran Islands and the south Connemara coast. The depot at Westport supplied the north coast of Connemara and the coast of Mayo to Belmullet.

At first, small stores were set up at each of the coastguard stations: Killary, Ballynakill, Tully, Cleggan, Clifden, Roundstone, Inishbofin and Inishturk. However, in August 1846, the Relief Commission closed down the coastguard stores and replaced

Fig. 4 Clifden Union Workhouse. Opened very late on 8 March 1847 with accommodation for 300 inmates, the workhouse cost over £4,800 to construct and equip with furniture, fixtures and fittings. As many as 1,626 died there (756 females and 870 males) and the union as a whole lost 27.3% of its inmates between 1841–51. [Source: *The Illustrated London News*, 5 January 1850]

them with one central store at Clifden. The Commission consequently left the cost and difficulty of supplying food to the remote regions to the local relief committees. In the years that followed, the Government supply of food to the area would prove to be erratic, frequently leaving the relief committees, and later the Clifden Board of Guardians, frantic with frustration as they desperately tried to feed a starving population.

## PUBLIC WORKS

Public works, the only means the poor had of acquiring cash for the purchase of food, commenced in the union on 17 June 1846 and by 1 August there were reported to be 7,237 men, women and boys employed. Hyacinth D'Arcy protested to Dublin Castle that those who succeeded in getting employment on the public works were still handicapped by the high price of provisions and the low wages provided. Wages of 6d per day were insufficient for a man to feed a family of six or eight persons. But any wage was

Fig. 5 Thomas Martin, MP, Ballynahinch Castle, proprietor of almost 200,000 acres in Connemara and principal rate-payer in the Clifden Union. The death of Thomas Martin on 23 April 1847, from fever caught while visiting tenants in the workhouse, caused alarm throughout Ireland. [Source: © Martin Family]

better than none and whenever works were opened, large numbers would turn up seeking employment. Numbers were restricted, however, and works were sporadic, leaving many people unemployed. One public works official described as 'subordinate in the extreme' those fortunate enough to obtain employment.[4]

With the irregular supply of food and the coming together of large numbers at the feeding stations and the public works, sickness in the form of dysentery and fever spread through the people. The workhouse, with accommodation for 300 inmates, eventually opened on 8 March 1847. A separate fever hospital, with beds for forty-six, was opened nine days later. In time this would prove inadequate and it was later estimated that workhouse accommodation for 2,700 would be needed.

However, in a region almost devoid of substantial buildings, finding suitable accommodation for workhouses and hospitals was difficult and converting these into functional buildings took time and delays cost lives. Accommodation was eventually provided for 1,700, in 1848, with the setting up of auxiliary workhouses at Kylemore, Roundstone, Bunowen Castle and Clifden, and fever hospitals at Kilkerrin, Ballyconneely, Roundstone and Ballynakill. The sheer vastness of the union, however, meant that it was only ever possible to bring medical attention to a small percentage of those in need of it. This left the vast majority of the fever sufferers to die in their own homes or along the roadside as they attempted to reach the nearest hospital.

## TOTAL DEPENDENCE

The appalling conditions to be found in Connemara in 1847 were well documented by members of the Society of Friends visiting the region in January and April of that year. Sickness, starvation and poverty had brought the majority of the population to total dependence on the relief committees and the Poor Law guardians. Food was coming on to the market and prices were falling, but the depressed circumstances of the people meant that many were in no position to purchase food at any price. The public works, it was argued, were keeping the people from the land and the fishermen from the sea.

It was hoped that the food supply in the west would be improved by the operation of a government curing station set up at Roundstone and Board of Works employees were sent to teach the people how to cure fish. However, the fishing was poor throughout the Famine and fish supplies to the curing house were unreliable. Many of the fishermen had already pawned their tackle or were unable to replace worn tackle. Bad weather and the weakened state of the fishermen left others reluctant to leave the public works and the certainty of pay, to take on the boisterous Atlantic. To force the fishermen on to the sea, an inventory of boats was carried out and employment on the public works withheld from the owners of seaworthy boats. After this, the supply

Fig. 6  Clifden, 1850. 1. Twelve Pins. 2. Road to Galway. 3. Poorhouse. 4. Jail. 5. Mr. Griffith, Poor Law Inspector. 6.-7. Waterfall & Bridge. 8. Church. 9. Parochial school. 10. Carr's Inn, all public conveyances stop here. 11. Hart's Hotel, just opened. 12. Road to Clifden Castle. 13. Road to school and church. 14. Mitchell's shop. 15. National school, temporary fever hospital. 16. Road to quay. 17. Children's auxiliary poorhouse. 18. The sea. 19. Infant's school. [Source: National Library of Ireland]

of fish to the station improved for a time, but it remained erratic and caused problems for its continuous operation.[5]

Under the Temporary Relief Act (1847), the public works were wound down and soup kitchens, financed by the poor rates, were set up for the free distribution of soup. From May to July the number of people fed at the soup kitchens in the Clifden Union rose steadily to peak on 3 July at 24,403, almost two-thirds of the population. The potato crop of 1847 was free of blight, but the small quantity sown in the union was only expected to feed the people for three months. The relief committees had encouraged the people to cultivate the land, but seeds were expensive and difficult to obtain, with the result that, out of an acreage of 191,426, only 5,500 acres were under seed.[6]

Under new measures introduced in the summer, all future relief measures would be financed entirely by the poor rate. The food depots and soup kitchens were to close and the board of guardians, aided by the Poor Law

Commission, would take responsibility for distress in their own area.

Shifting the responsibility for the poor on to the ratepayers eventually caused the collapse of the Clifden Union. There were simply insufficient funds to maintain the large numbers of destitute poor in the union. By autumn 1847, the union was in deep financial difficulty and was being maintained almost exclusively by government loans. All classes were buckling under the strain. Rents were falling due, but the tenants were unable to pay. Rates were proving difficult to collect, as the ratepayers were protesting that they too were out of funds. Many of the ratepayers were already in severe financial difficulty and the two largest in the district, the D'Arcy and Martin estates, were bankrupt.

The Government listed Clifden among the 'distressed' unions designated to receive financial assistance from the British Relief Association. Financial aid, however, would

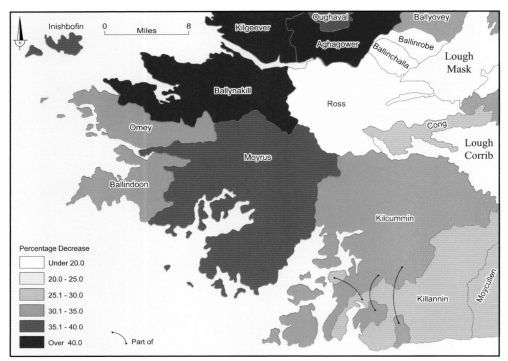

Fig. 7 THE DISTRIBUTION OF POPULATION DECLINE PER PARISH IN CONNEMARA, 1841-51. Even within the single territory of Connemara, this map demonstrates that famine conditions and outcomes varied tremendously. Population decreases were less than 20% in Ross and adjacent parishes whereas in nearby Aghagower, Kilgeever and Ballynakill, population losses were more than double that percentage. To the south, Moyrus lost over 35% of its population – that is, well over 4,000 inhabitants. In contrast, Omey and Ballindoon parish communities lost under 1,500 inhabitants each. It should be noted that there is no consistency in losses as between adjacent coastal or inland parishes. Detailed work by local geographers and historians is necessary to explain such varied contrasts in human destinies.

only be extended when every effort to collect rates had been made. In October 1847, a temporary inspector, John Deane, was appointed to assist the union in the distribution of the funds. Deane found the Board to be in debt to over forty creditors, among them many local tradesmen and dealers, who, he felt, had charged exorbitant rates for the goods they supplied. Under Deane, the management of the workhouse was improved, maintenance work on the building carried out and the interior altered to accommodate more inmates. He also oversaw the distribution of 527,723 rations to 4,698 children, between November 1847 and May 1848, saving many children in the union from certain death.[7]

COLLECTION OF RATES

The Relief Commission put pressure on the Clifden Board to increase all efforts to collect outstanding rates. What ensued was a prolonged, and sometimes violent, conflict between the rate collectors, backed by the forces of the law, and the ratepayers. The four rate collectors of the union, Joseph McDonnell (Renvyle), John Flynn (Ballindoon), John Lydon (Roundstone) and Francis Mullin (Clifden), met opposition in almost every attempt to seize livestock and crops in lieu of rates. They were frequently attacked with stones and bludgeons and driven away empty handed, as the small farmers tried to hold on to the few livestock and small amount of crops that remained.

The Resident Magistrate, John Dopping, was reluctant

to provide a police escort for the collectors as he felt they overcharged for their services. He was also called upon to protect landlord agents and bailiffs, who were meeting similar opposition in the collection of rents. Dopping protested that the constabulary were already stretched, protecting food depots, arresting thieves and escorting prisoners to the county prison in Galway. He was, however, overruled by Dublin Castle and instructed to personally accompany the constabulary when aiding the collection of the poor rates.

Crime, born out of desperation, was on the increase. Among the many harrowing cases investigated by Dopping at this time were an accusation of cannibalism made by a man against his late wife and a complaint of a brother having buried his sister alive, because he could not lose another day's rations to come again to bury her. The number of burglary and larceny incidents was rising and in January 1848 alone seventy-nine people were committed to Galway jail for sheep stealing. Clifden jail, built to hold eighteen, regularly held four times that number. Fever was rampant among the prisoners and, still, Dopping told Dublin Castle, 'the poor people are most anxious to be committed, and look upon the gaol as an asylum'. Dominick Kerrigan, keeper of the jail, was breaking down under the strain. Writing to Dublin Castle, he described the inmates as 'half starved, half naked beings in human form' and ended his letter with a plea, 'May the Lord look to us in the midst of fever and dysentery, overcrowded with felons and beggars. Amen.'[8]

The order, issued in January 1848, to extend outdoor relief to the able-bodied, eventually brought about the dissolution of the Board of Guardians. Deane told the Commissioners that the order 'required too much vigilance' and the Clifden guardians 'for the most part, men of the more humble (indeed I may say of the lower class of life) . . . from their want of business-habits and experience', were simply not up to the job. The exception was the chairman, Hyacinth D'Arcy, and to his 'indefatigable exertions and ready co-operation at all times' Deane wished to bear testimony.[9]

The Commissioners sent Richard Burke, Poor Law Inspector, to investigate and report on the capability or otherwise of the Clifden Board. Burke found that the entire operation of the Board was left to D'Arcy. The rest of the

Board seemed unwilling to properly supervise the work-house, the relieving officers and the rate collectors. They were relying almost totally on John Deane to administer the union. The finances of the union were in such a state that respectable merchants and tradesmen were refusing to deal with it. The Board, Burke contended, would be unable to cater for the large numbers expected to apply for relief in the coming months. He recommended that the Board be dissolved and replaced by paid guardians. The Commission concurred and in February 1848, Denis O'Leary and Joseph Jackson took up their appointments as vice-guardians of the Clifden Union, with Hamilton Smith acting as secretary; James Copland would later replace Jackson. For the next twenty months these men, along with John Deane, were responsible for the well-being of almost the entire population of Connemara.

The vice-guardians proved to be efficient and diligent in their efforts to manage the union and humane in their attempt to relieve the suffering of the people. However, the complete failure of the potato crop in 1848 meant that they would prove as ineffectual as the previous Board in the collection of rates. Government grants would still be needed to assist with the financial burden of running the union. Disease was widespread among all classes in the union throughout 1848 and 1849. During February and March 1848, fever was reported to be in every house of every village. Measles and dysentery were also prevalent and the people were reported to be little more than skeletons, living in dirt and squalor, too ill to do anything other than wait for

death. Dr Bodkin, the workhouse doctor, died of fever in February, just two months after a similar fate had befallen his brother, who had acted as his assistant.

January 1849 brought reports of fever, diarrhoea and dysentery again attacking the inmates of the workhouse and there was whooping cough among the children. A second doctor in the union, Dr Gannon of Roundstone, died of fever. A year earlier, Dr Gannon had been severely criticised for his neglect of the sick. Many of the officials of the union and staff of the workhouse and auxiliary workhouses became ill and some resigned in fear for their health.

In April a cholera epidemic struck and the number of deaths recorded in the workhouse and auxiliary workhouses between 14 April and the 16 June, the period of the epidemic, came to 208. However, it is impossible to estimate the number that died outside of the workhouses, in their own homes, in ditches, in hillside caves and by the roadside.[10]

A healthy crop in 1849 saw the official end to the Great Famine. The vice-guardians were removed and the administration of the union returned to an elected Board of Guardians. The Board took over a union in debt, with still a large number of the population dependent on them for relief and many of the ratepayers offering their estates for sale in the newly established Encumbered Estates Court; 181 townlands, out of a total of 278 in the barony of Bally-nahinch, went up for sale. The census figures for 1851 show a population drop of 12,116 on the 1841 figure; one-third of the population was lost to starvation, fever and emigration. The level of suffering, however, is impossible to quantify.

# In the shadow of Sliabh an Iarainn

*Gerard Mac Atasney*

Even though the first potato blight of 1845 only partially affected the crop it had a devastating impact on County Leitrim where almost half of the population (46.8%) lived in the worst type of housing – usually a one-roomed cottage – and were almost entirely dependent on the potato for their livelihood. The population loss in the mountain districts varied. In Ballinamore around one-third of the crop was lost while in Drumshanbo it was slightly less, at one-quarter. The area worst affected was that of Kiltubrid, where the loss

was estimated at some two-thirds. However, if the initial blight varied in its impact, the second in 1846 was devastating as indicated by an estimate of 80% loss in and around Ballinamore. A member of the local police constabulary commented how 'the state of the crop is deplorable. There is scarcely a sound potato to be had in the district and the decay is rapidly progressing.' In addition, the estimates of unemployed labourers ranged from 80% in Ballinamore to total unemployment in Drumshanbo. The consequence was

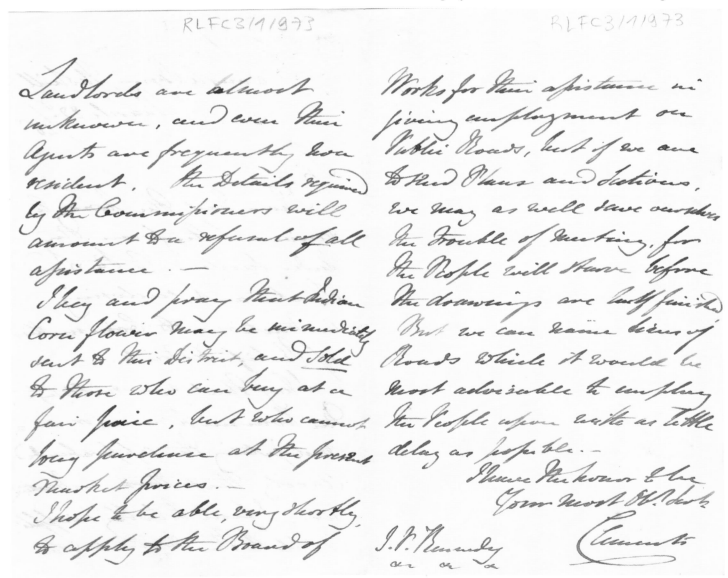

Fig. 1 The organisation of local relief committees could prove cumbersome. This letter from a resident of Mohill, County Leitrim, underlines the difficulties in complying with the directions of the Central Relief Commission in Dublin as regards the organisation and membership of local committees: 'Landlords are almost unknown and even their agents are frequently not resident. The details required by the Commissioners will amount to a refusal for all assistance'.' The letter writer begs and prays that Indian corn be immediately sent to the district and sold at a fair price to those who 'cannot today purchase at the present market price'. Public works are urgently needed in the district. Unless they are introduced immediately 'the people will starve while the drawings are half-finished'. [Source: Relief Commission Papers, 3/1/873, National Archives of Ireland]

that in Garradice approximately 2,000 were in need of relief while in Ballinamore, the figure was 10,000 out of a total population of 14,000.

## RELIEF

In the harsh conditions of the winter of 1846, the poor of Leitrim, as in every other county, rushed to local workhouses in an attempt to obtain relief. The mountain area was served by two workhouses – one in Mohill and the other in Carrick-on-Shannon. The distance to each varied with the Mohill house situated ten miles from Ballinamore while the Carrick institution was four miles from Drumshanbo and ten from Keshcarrigan and Annadale. The poor, sick, starving and disease-ridden had to travel these distances if they wished to avail of the scanty relief available. While the workhouses were bleak the alternative was even more so. In late 1846 John Hack-Tuke, a member of the Society of Friends, reported on a scene he witnessed in Ballinamore:

We entered many cottages by the roadside, the inmates of which were generally huddled together for warmth around a few turf embers. Their emaciated forms and sunken features testified but too truly to their statement, 'that they were nearly starved', and many told us 'that they had tasted

nothing that day', and knew not where to get anything, and that they had lived on one meal of cabbage or a few ounces of oatmeal gruel for many days together.

By January 1847 the workhouses at Carrick and Mohill were both filled to capacity and had become synonymous with diseases such as fever and dysentery. With people entering and leaving the workhouses the spread of disease was inevitable. In early February, William Percy commented that fever was not prevalent in the Ballinamore area 'to an extraordinary degree' except in the union workhouse in Mohill. However, he added that 'bowel complaints' were 'daily carrying off numbers'.[1]

Similarly, in early March the rector of Kiltubrid, George Mansfield, remarked that although cases of fever and dysentery had occurred, they had not proven either very numerous or fatal. However, less than a month later, William Noble, writing from Prospect near Drumshanbo, noted that both fever and dysentery 'prevail to an alarming extent'. At the end of April, George W. Peyton of Driney House, Keshcarrigan, lamented how 'hundreds are dying by fever, dysentery and starvation' with the people 'burying even without coffins'. In the beginning of May, disease was extending its pestilence throughout the area and by the end

Fig. 2 Part of the Famine road which runs from Gubnaveagh (Aughnasheelin) to Slievenakilla (Ballinaglera). The closure of public works (including many road schemes) and the delay in opening soup kitchens under the new Temporary Relief Act (Soup Kitchen Act) resulted in a hiatus in the provision of relief and consequently further suffering for those reliant on such schemes. [Photo: Leitrim County Library]

Fig. 3 POOR LAW UNIONS, DISTRICT ELECTORAL DIVISIONS AND KEY SETTLEMENTS IN COUNTY LEITRIM. This map shows the distribution of all district electoral divisions within the three Poor Law unions in County Leitrim – those of Carrick-on-Shannon, Manorhamilton and Mohill – as well as that part of the union of Ballyshannon in the extreme north of the county. The map also identifies the key settlements in the county, many of which were also the location for soup-kitchens – marked 'S' on the map – in 1847.

equally graphic description of the scenes he witnessed on a daily basis:

It is not money we want but food – I have no wish to deny that I am also desirous to be in some degree exonerated from the pressure of distress which officially falls upon myself. I am, at the moment I am writing this, afraid to appear at my own gate or to open my back door, knowing what starving crowds I have to encounter. They latterly linger in my yard or in part of my house and say they may as well die there as anywhere else.

### PUBLIC WORKS

For those unable to gain entry to the workhouses, the British Government established a programme of public works. This initiative was the chosen vehicle of relief by an administration determined to make Irish men and women, and occasionally children, work for their relief. In the majority of cases throughout the country they were put to work on road building and earned a maximum of one shilling per day in one of the coldest and harshest winters on record. George Mansfield reported that at its peak between 600 and 700 men were employed in the Kiltubrid area but noted:

Families often consist of ten and more individuals and in such cases it would require the wages of three men to maintain them at the present prices of food. Females can bring seldom anything to the aid of their family. Indeed, at present they feel their destitution so great that they seek to be put on the Relief Works.

However, despite its many shortcomings the scheme was beginning to show some benefits and provide money and food for the populace. Nevertheless, the authorities, in anticipation of a healthy potato crop in August, decided to halt such works in April/May 1847 and establish instead a

of that month Annadelia Slack of Annadale, Drumshanbo noted that both fever and dysentery were 'raging throughout the district'. Similarly, Mary Johnston of Aghacashill stated that these diseases were now prevalent to 'a very frightful extent'. Matilda Shanly, of Riverdale, Drumshanbo, stated that she did not know any place 'more afflicted than this is with fever'. She claimed that without a local fever hospital the people were 'obliged to lye (sic) along the road sides and not even a shed was made for them'.

The vicar of Oughteragh, Richard Clifford, in writing from Drumdartan, Ballinamore, revealed how death was 'a matter of everyday occurrence around me' and gave an network of soup kitchens to enable the direct provision of food to the people by means of the Temporary Relief Act (also known as the Soup Kitchen Act). Thus, George Peyton of Driney House reported on 26 April that there were now very few employed 'in consequence of the roads having been done away with'. He added that no alternative employment was now available. Mary Johnston of Agha-cashill, noting that she lived in 'a very mountainous district where the entire potato crop failed' claimed that since the cessation of the public works, the people were 'in the great-est possible distress particularly the poor females who are anxious to get employment of any kind'. For her part Matil-da Shanly of Riverdale, Ballinamore, noted that as all the public works had been stopped some local men had been forced to travel to Scotland to find work.

David Mansfield, writing to the Relief Commissioners on behalf of the Kiltubrid and Keshcarrigan Relief Commit-tee, stated that 'men who can dig but are ashamed to beg, are literally in the grasp of famine and cannot extricate themselves'. Expressing his indignation at the treatment of local people he continued:

> Roads begun without discretion or forethought have been abandoned without reflection and men who were known to be supporting themselves and their families by their earnings are now cast off to perish. Give work to men who are more willing to receive your wages than your alms.

## ABSENTEE LANDLORDS

One of the main contributory factors to distress was the absence of the majority of local landed proprietors. George Mansfield, the rector of Kiltubrid, remarked that 'the prin-cipal proprietors are absentees' while William Percy of Gar-radice, the sole resident proprietor in his locality, attributed the lack of both manufacturing and indoor employment to such absenteeism.

Thus, with the reduction of the public works and the lack of indigenous industry, local applicants to the Society of Friends endeavoured as best they could to provide an outlet for some of the local population. At Prospect, Drumshanbo, William Noble afforded employment to ninety-two women at spinning and sixteen men at weaving, while George Pey-ton of Driney House, Keshcarrigan, noted how his female relatives were 'exerting themselves to get all the women and girls employed knitting, etc but are greatly at a loss for funds to carry out this much desired object'. Similarly, Mary Noble of Prospect, Drumshanbo, revealed that her brother had employed twenty-eight men as weavers and 170 'poor women' in spinning. However, such attempts, although highly laudable, hardly made a dent in the misery then enveloping the district.

The new Soup Kitchen Act contained punitive restric-tions and for those who were either able-bodied or landhold-

## CLOONE SOUP-SHOP.

**Days of Distribution:**

WEDNESDAYS AND SATURDAYS,

WEEKLY.

RULE 1.—That Mrs. Hogg be requested to act as Treasurer, and superintend the management of the Cloone Soup Shop.

2.—That Soup be sold to the destitute at 1d. per Quart.

3.—That, in order to provide some Subsistence for the totally destitute, who are *wholly* without means, a copy of these Rules be sent to the Clergy, Gentry, and Farmers of the Parish of Cloone, to afford them an opportunity of supporting this be-nevolent object, and providing substantial relief for the Poor in their localities.

4.—That each Subscriber shall have power to recommend persons for gratuitous *weekly* supplies of Soup, according to the following order:

Subscribers of £1, to dispose of 16 Quarts of Soup, weekly, for 16 weeks, on Recom-mendation Tickets, to be supplied by the Treasurer.

Subscribers of 10s., to dispose of 8 Quarts, weekly, for 16 weeks, &c.

Subscribers of 5s., to dispose of 4 Quarts, weekly, for 16 weeks, &c.

Subscribers of 1s., to dispose of 2 Quarts, weekly, for 6 weeks.

The Glebe, Cloone,
December, 1846.

P.S.—Bailiffs to have power to recommend on the Subscriptions of absentee Landlords, as above.

[BRENNAN, Printer, Ck.-on-Shannon.

Fig. 4 Advertisement for Cloone Soup Shop, December 1846. With reports of death from starvation increasing during the winter months of 1846–47, local relief committees came under pressure to respond to the growing crisis. Meal was largely replaced by soup as the main form of relief. In Cloone, Mrs Hogg, wife of the local rector, oversaw the work of the 'Cloone Soup Shop' which in January was distributing 1,500 quarts of soup gratuitously to 400 people on a weekly basis. Andrew Hogg anticipated that at least 4,000 gallons would have to be distributed 'to prevent thousands perishing from starvation'. [Source: Gerard Mac Atasney, *Leitrim and the Great Hunger* (Carrick- on- Shan-non, 1997)]

ers it proved less than useless. George Peyton, writing on 26 April, remarked that the relief lists had not been submitted by that date and estimated that no relief would be disbursed for at least another three weeks. He added that the numbers eligible for such relief would represent only a small propor-tion of the actual numbers in want. Annadelia Slack com-mented that there were so many in need, 'the committee will not relieve any person holding above two acres of ground'. For her part, Mary Johnston estimated that at least 200 people would be unable to avail of food from the Government-spon-sored relief committee 'in consequence of having land'. Richard Clifford of Drumdartan, Ballinamore, made the stark observation that 'we do not expect any relief from Govern-ment for some weeks to come. The requirements of the Com-missioners are unreasonable and it is the belief of the people that the Government wish to starve them'.

## SOCIETY OF FRIENDS

In light of the obvious deficiencies of the new Act, the role of the Society of Friends as an alternative source of relief was critical to those who lived in the mountainous areas of Ballinamore, Drumshanbo and Kiltubrid. Unlike the British

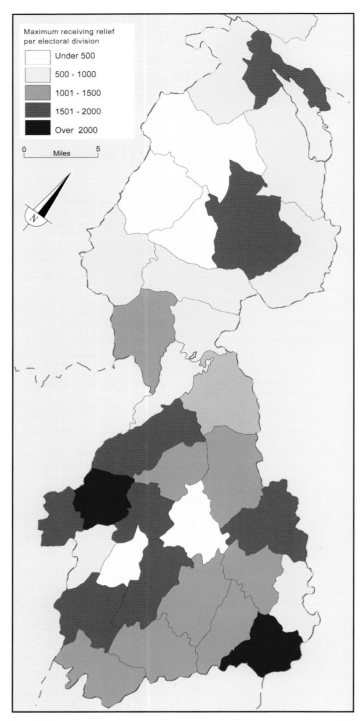

Fig. 5 MAXIMUM POPULATION RECEIVING RELIEF DURING THE SUMMER OF 1847. This maps the maximum distribution of the population receiving relief under the Soup Kitchen Act in the summer of 1847. There is a clear distinction between north and south Leitrim. In north Leitrim, only two district electoral divisions (DEDs) – Kinlough and Manorhamilton – saw over 1,500 of their populations receiving relief. In contrast, eight such DEDs saw populations of over 1,500 receiving relief and in Leitrim and Carrigallen over 2,000 of the population of these DEDs were in receipt of food relief in local soup kitchens.

comfortable circumstances, has undergone a painful change from actual want and misery.' Thus, the applicants, with the aid of the Quakers, established their own relief operations.

By February, the Ballinamore Relief Committee had been forced to suspend its activities due to lack of funds. Prior to this it had distributed 'one quart of good soup and one pint of oatmeal for one penny'. On the occasion of each distribution, 100 gallons of soup were distributed. However it was enabled to continue its exertions by means of a £40 grant to support a soup shop for the town. George Mansfield secured a grant of £50 towards the maintenance of two soup kitchens already established in Drumshanbo.

At Prospect, William Noble had been distributing meal and rice for three months but by late April he reported that 'rapidly decreasing funds will oblige me to give up in a very few days'. The Quakers made him a grant of a boiler and £20 and sent one ton of rice to be distributed, in accordance with the stipulations of the Friends, in a cooked state. Noble's gratitude for such was obvious: 'I have no hesitation in saying that but for this seasonable assistance numbers would perish during the coming weeks', adding how 'it has become absolutely appalling to witness the rapid strides destitution and disease have made during the last few days'.

George Peyton sought assistance for about 120 individuals 'in great distress [but] industrially inclined' in the townlands of Driney, Rossey, Gubnaveigh and Corglass and informed the Quakers that in the event of a grant being made he intended to work in conjunction with the Slack family of Annadale. He received a grant of one ton of Indian meal, which was to be distributed 'in small portions to the most necessitous of the poor, carefully selected, with strict impartiality'.

Annadelia Slack sought aid for 200 people ineligible for government aid in seven townlands. She had been selling meal at reduced prices but 'in consequence of the poverty of the country rents have not been paid and landlords are unable to do anything further for their tenantry'. She stated that she proposed to work alone in her endeavours as 'the surrounding districts have been already supplied'. She received a supply of half a ton of Indian meal.

Mary Johnston of Aghacashill, who had already been distributing soup and 'Indian meal porridge' received half a ton of Indian meal and half a ton of rice to feed those landholders 'who cannot get any assistance from the relief committee'. She was aided in her endeavours by her brother, Joseph, and sister, Kate. Mary Anne Noble of Prospect had been daily serving food to children 'independent of the Relief Act' and acknowledged that for this she was 'chiefly indebted to the beneficent assistance of the Society of Friends'. However, she admitted there was 'still urgent necessity for private charity, there being numbers in a state of destitution'. Hence, she received a further grant in June 1847 of half a ton of oatmeal and a similar quantity of rice.

Government, the Quakers realised that there were many in a starving condition who were neither destitute nor landless. This class had been able to withstand the early part of the Famine, but by the middle of 1847 they too had succumbed, a point noted by William Noble of Prospect, who commented: 'The appearance of many, a few months ago in

302

## CLOTHING DISTRIBUTED BY MATILDA SHANLY AT RIVERDALE FROM 27 FEBRUARY TO 24 MARCH 1848 (BY TOWNLAND)

Aughoo: Joseph Matthews (1); James Mc Carter (1); Biddy Mc Teague (4); 8 orphans; 4 old men; 4 women; 7 poor old people. Riverdale: Michael Roarke (2); John Bannin (1); Peggy Carter (1); Peter Magohan (8); Thomas Magohan (6); Biddy Murphy (1); T. Roarke (5); John Magohan (7); James Brien (6); Hugh Conolly (6); Anne O'Donnale (2); Fanny Johnston (4); Bessey Mc Guire (2); Tally Reilly (6); Thomas Magorn (1); Biddy Galin (3); Hugh Conolly (3); Biddy Scollan (1); Biddy King (4); Kitty Mc Brien (2); M. Parks (4); Ally Brien (3); James Conolly (1); Bartly Murphy (3).

## CLOTHING DISTRIBUTED BY WILLIAM NOBLE AT DRUMSHANBO FROM 29 FEBRUARY TO 2 MARCH 1848

Carricknabrack: Anne Jones (7); Biddy Holand (8); Honor Giblin (6); Anne Cowan (1); Mary Mc Keon (1); Sally Reilly (5); Bryan Mc Shaney (2); Keith Magorty (2); James Curran (1). Drumkeelan: Catherine Anderson (7). Drumhael: Anne Mc Donogh (6); Anne Rosmond (8); Mary Brown (1). Lisbrockan: Mary Adams (7); Patt Donelly (3). Drumderg: Catherine Fanning (6); Catherine Mc Nallan (8). Cornamuddagh: Fanny Higgeson (8); Jane Higgeson (6); Elizabeth Higgeson (8); Elizabeth Scales (3). Curlough: Mary Foley (9). Blackrock: Mick D'Olsay (1); Tom Allen (3). Currahill: Sally Maguire (6); Tom Cowan (6); Margaret Cowan (3); Molly Mc Cavina (2); Betty Mac Kay (8). Drumhalwy: John Cowan (4). Derryhallagh: John Sadleir (4). Drumshanbo: Mary Noon (5); Paddy Breen (1); Francis Morron (1); John Burk (1); Widow Hill (1); Nancy Brennan (2); Tom Mc Manus (4); Biddy Shanley (1); Mark Killerlia (4); Stephen Kilhooley (1); Pater Mc Namee (3); Winnifred Tigh (4); Willy Guckeen (7); Mary Magorty (5). Drumcoora: Mary Monaghan (5); George Reilly (5). Creenagh: John Curren (3). Dernaseer: Tim Shanley (12); Margaret Shanley (5). Aughnagallop: Jane Knott (7). Ardcolum: Peggy Flynne (5). Shancurry: William Taylor (6); Ellen O'Brien (5). Lisbrackill: James Berne (6). Drumhauver: Mary Mc Donogh (9). Drumherriff: Bridget Barry (7). Drumduff: Margaret Abraham (4); Robert Cowan (8). Mahanagh: Biddy Sanders (7). Lisbruckill: Widow Cowan (4). Aughriman: Ally Gallon (3). Diffier: Judy Horan (5).

## CLOTHING DISTRIBUTED BY ELIZABETH PEYTON AT DERIGVON AND GUBNAVEIGH FROM 20 APRIL TO 27 APRIL 1848

Derigvon: James Wynne (5); John Wynne (2); Andrew Guckian (7); James O'Hara (7); Mary Cull (widow) (4); Michael Guckian (1); Pat Mc Glynn (6); Thomas Corrigan (4); Bernard Felan (2); J. O'Hara (4); Pat Templeman (deserted) (1); Mary Flynn (2); Tom Plunkett (2). Gubnaveigh: Laurence Mc Glynn (4); John Mc Glynn (2); Owen Cull snr (4); Owen Cull jnr (3); Widow Lache (1); Mary Magourty (1); Bridget Cafferty (widow) (6); Widow Cull (1); Michael Maguire (3); Pat Faulen (6); James Gannon (3); Rose Gannon (3); Hugh Mc Kiernan (5); Bryan Gallogly (7); John Murphy (5); Michael Brady (3); John Mc Cabe (5); F. Magourty (4); Dan Shanan (3); Peter O'Hara (2); Gilheeny (6); Pat Gannon (3); John Guckian (4); Darby Quinn (4); Mark Boyle (4); Peter Shanly (5); Mc Manus (4); Mulvanerty (4); Michael Mulvy (7); James Horan (9); Mc Laughlin (4); Pat Magourty (1); Michael Monaghan (5); Widow Mulvanerty (4); Hugh Maguire (8).

Fig. 6 Grants of clothing became an integral part of the relief operations of the Society of Friends from mid-1847 onwards. The lists of names included here bring the reader face to face with the destitute of Riverdale, Drumshanbo, Gubnaveigh and Derigvon. (The number in each family is included in brackets after each name.) [Source: Gerard Mac Atasney, *Leitrim and the Great Hunger* (Carrick-on-Shannon, 1997)]

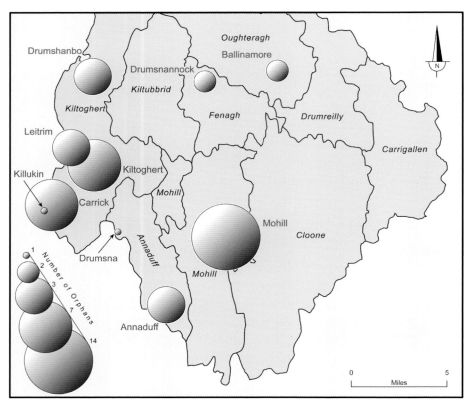

To assist her endeavours Shanly received six hundredweight of rice for distribution to the 'sick and convalescent'.

As the Famine stretched into 1848 the policy of the Society of Friends was altered to reflect a long-term approach to aid. This was demonstrated in attempts to start model farms in some areas and fisheries in others. However, in the vast majority of districts throughout Ireland the policy found expression in the distribution of clothes to those in need. The fact that previously independent and proud people, who had survived the worst excesses of the Famine, were now required to beg for clothing represents in itself the terrible extent of the ravages of these years. The standard clothing bundle distributed consisted of the following: Shoes, blueprint, fustian, bed rugs, blankets, calico, guernseys, flannel, corduroy and sheets.

The first Leitrim grant was made to Mary Johnston of Aghacashill in July 1847 and between 17 July and 9 September she distributed seventy-four grants of clothing to aid 117 people. By early 1848, the distribution of such clothing was the main source of relief in County Leitrim and between 27 February and 15 March Matilda Shanly was enabled to help 115 individuals. While clothing parcels were usually requested and subsequently distributed by women, William Noble helped in the clothing of 296 individuals in the town of Drumshanbo in the same period. For her part, Elizabeth Peyton was able to help clothe 186 people through forty-seven grants made to those in the townlands of Gubnaveigh and Derigvon in the month of April 1848. The lists included in Figure 6, contain the names and addresses of the men, women and children who received clothing and in this way bring us face to face with those who lived in the shadow of the mountain in the time of the Great Hunger.

FIG. 7 SOURCE-AREAS FOR ORPHAN GIRLS WHO LEFT ON THE *LADY PEEL* AND THE *TIPPOO SAIB* FOR SYDNEY. During the period 1848–50 over 4,000 young women between the ages of fourteen and twenty were sent from workhouses in Ireland to the Australian colonies. Orphan girls from the Carrick-on-Shannon workhouse left for Australia on 27 February 1849 on board the *Lady Peel*. They were first brought to the workhouse in Mullingar and later to Dublin, where they boarded a ship for Plymouth. From Plymouth they began their long journey to Australia. After a journey lasting four months the ship arrived in Sydney on 3 July. A second shipload of female orphans arrived in Australia the following year. The map shows the source areas for orphans from the Carrick-on-Shannon and Mohill Unions. [Source: Gerard Mac Atasney, *Leitrim and the Great Hunger* (Carrick-on-Shannon, 1997), pp. 77–79]

Matilda Shanly sought aid for the distressed of the townlands of Riverdale and Aughoo. She informed the Quakers that 'I know of twelve or fourteen families in the townlands mentioned to be in the most wretched state of poverty, some of which consist of six and eight children.' She also revealed how she had been struggling to help as best she could:

> Any relief I could give has been out of my own small income besides a few trifling subscriptions I got for work in knitting for old women and sewing, etc., for the children of an adjoining school and which, as far as I can, I will pursue. I [only] have a boiler that used to be made use of for potatoes for cattle.

# Mohill Union workhouse

## Gerard Mac Atasney

In March 1846 the Mohill Board of Guardians informed the Poor Law Commissioners that very high prices were being paid for potatoes in the local market. They also remarked that cottiers were almost destitute while farmers of six and seven acres were in great want with provisions only until May. On 2 April the use of potatoes in the workhouse diet was supplanted by oatmeal but the extent of distress in the union was attested to by the fact that, in spite of poor diet being available, numbers still sought refuge in the workhouse. In one week in October 132 paupers were admitted and by December the workhouse was filled to capacity (700). Indeed, the latter month saw the transfer of all fever patients to the town fever hospital in an increasingly desperate attempt to procure more workhouse space.

With increased numbers came the risk of widespread disease and in January 1847 fever and dysentery were rife in the building, claiming the lives both of the medical officer and the master of the workhouse. Throughout this period the maintenance costs of the workhouse had risen exponentially and this caused serious difficulties for the administrators. The Mohill Union had always experienced problems with rate collection (the Cloone area described as the most lawless in the union) and with weekly costs reaching £50, the equivalent rate collected totalled only £30. Throughout

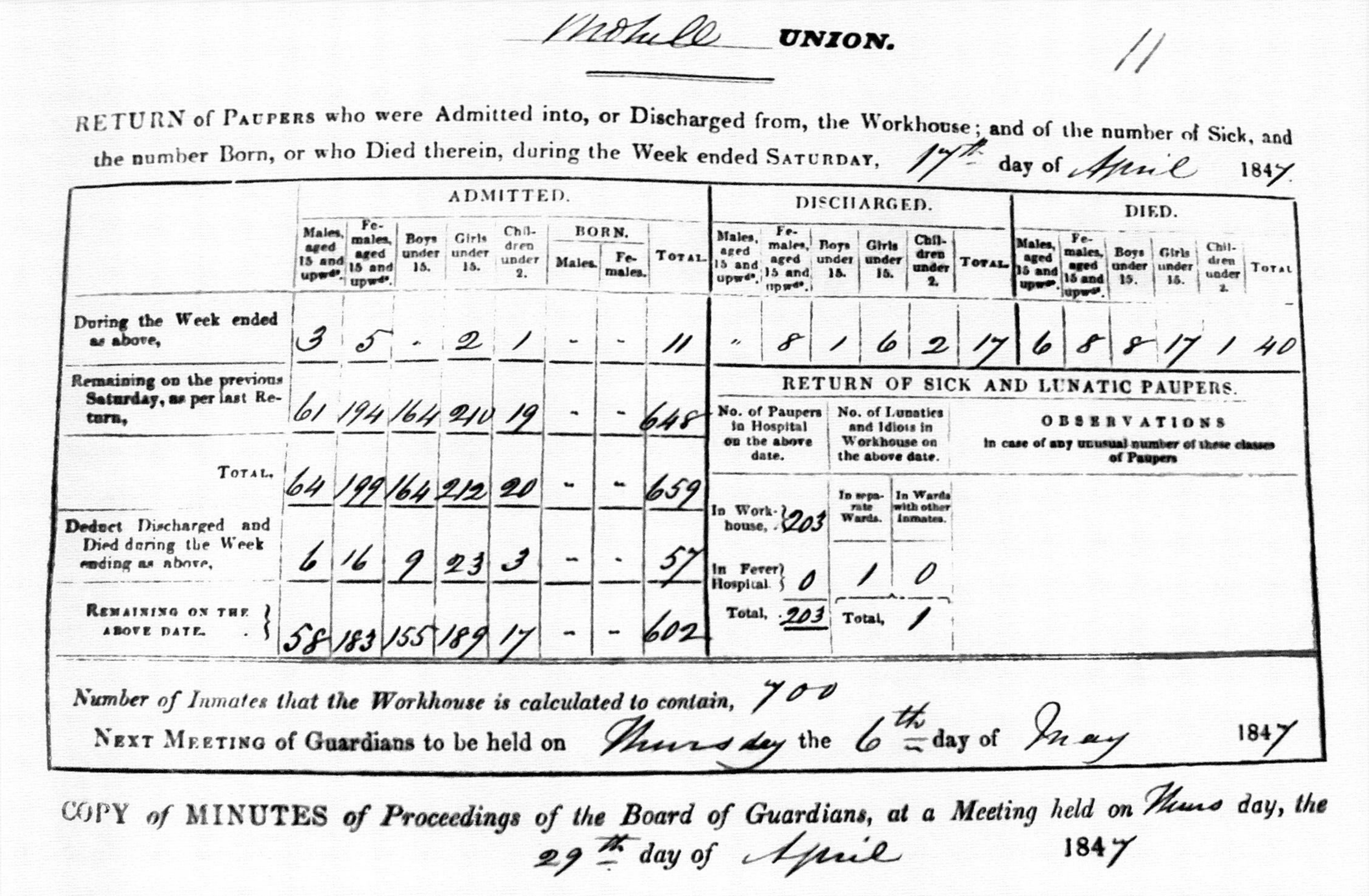

**Mohill UNION.** — 11

RETURN of PAUPERS who were Admitted into, or Discharged from, the Workhouse; and of the number of Sick, and the number Born, or who Died therein, during the Week ended SATURDAY, 17th day of April 1847

| | ADMITTED | | | | | BORN | | | DISCHARGED | | | | | | DIED | | | | | |
|---|---|---|---|---|---|---|---|---|---|---|---|---|---|---|---|---|---|---|---|---|
| | Males aged 15 and upwds. | Females aged 15 and upwds. | Boys under 15. | Girls under 15. | Children under 2. | Males. | Females. | TOTAL. | Males aged 15 and upwds. | Females aged 15 and upwds. | Boys under 15. | Girls under 15. | Children under 2. | TOTAL. | Males aged 15 and upwds. | Females aged 15 and upwds. | Boys under 15. | Girls under 15. | Children under 2. | TOTAL. |
| During the Week ended as above, | 3 | 5 | - | 2 | 1 | - | - | 11 | " | 8 | 1 | 6 | 2 | 17 | 6 | 8 | 8 | 17 | 1 | 40 |
| Remaining on the previous Saturday, as per last Return, | 61 | 194 | 164 | 210 | 19 | - | - | 648 | | | | | | | | | | | | |
| TOTAL. | 64 | 199 | 164 | 212 | 20 | - | - | 659 | | | | | | | | | | | | |
| Deduct Discharged and Died during the Week ending as above, | 6 | 16 | 9 | 23 | 3 | - | - | 57 | | | | | | | | | | | | |
| REMAINING ON THE ABOVE DATE. | 58 | 183 | 155 | 189 | 17 | - | - | 602 | | | | | | | | | | | | |

RETURN OF SICK AND LUNATIC PAUPERS.

| | No. of Paupers in Hospital on the above date. | No. of Lunatics and Idiots in Workhouse on the above date. | | OBSERVATIONS In case of any unusual number of these classes of Paupers |
|---|---|---|---|---|
| | | In separate Wards. | In Wards with other Inmates. | |
| In Workhouse, | 203 | | | |
| In Fever Hospital. | 0 | 1 | 0 | |
| Total, | 203 | Total, 1 | | |

Number of Inmates that the Workhouse is calculated to contain, 700

NEXT MEETING of Guardians to be held on Thursday the 6th day of May 1847

COPY of MINUTES of Proceedings of the Board of Guardians, at a Meeting held on Thursday, the 29th day of April 1847

Fig. 1 An extract from the minute book of the Mohill Poor Law Union showing the number of paupers in the workhouse on 17 April 1847 and the number of those who had died in the previous week. Girls under fifteen accounted for 38% of those who had perished.

1847 debts were allowed to increase and many contractors, owed substantial amounts of money, refused to supply desperately needed goods unless they were paid on delivery. For example, in September George Church of Carrick-on-Shannon began legal proceedings against the Board and in the same month the master was forced to purchase supplies of meal on a weekly basis. An indication of the dire straits in which the Board found itself was a resolution in April 'that the dead should for the present be interred without coffins'. When this was objected to by the Poor Law Commisioners the guardians replied that 'due to the awful state of the union it is more advisable to feed the living than to provide coffins for the dead'. Consequently, a bier for carrying the dead to the place of burial was purchased and throughout 1847 this item saw regular usage.

### Mortality

For the first week in January to the last week in July there were 712 deaths in the workhouse – the worst month being April with 162 fatalities. With fever rampant the workhouse was closed to all admissions at the end of the month and in August a number of guardians resigned. In November the Commissioners appointed Major Halliday as a temporary inspector and within a week he provided an in-depth report on the institution which made grim reading. It was £2,500 in debt, contractors were owed more than £1,000 and the workhouse itself was described as being 'little better than a large shed – a bare protection from starvation to 700 ill-sheltered paupers'. Halliday's appointment was simply the prelude to a more permanent move by the Commissioners and on 8 December 1847 the Board of Guardians was dissolved and replaced by two paid vice-guardians.

The new administration, with no ties to the local area, was quick to identify the problems in the workhouse, commenting:

> Every department of the workhouse is in a lamentably neglected and disorganised state. The building itself is most dilapidated and fast advancing to ruin. Everything is out of repair – the cess pools are full of filth and every ward is filthy to a most noisome degree. The paupers are defectively clothed with many still in their rags and impurity. Dietary is not adhered to, the food is given in a half-cooked state and breakfast is not completely dispensed until late in the evening. The school children are in a diseased and emaciated state and there are no means for the proper treatment of the sick.

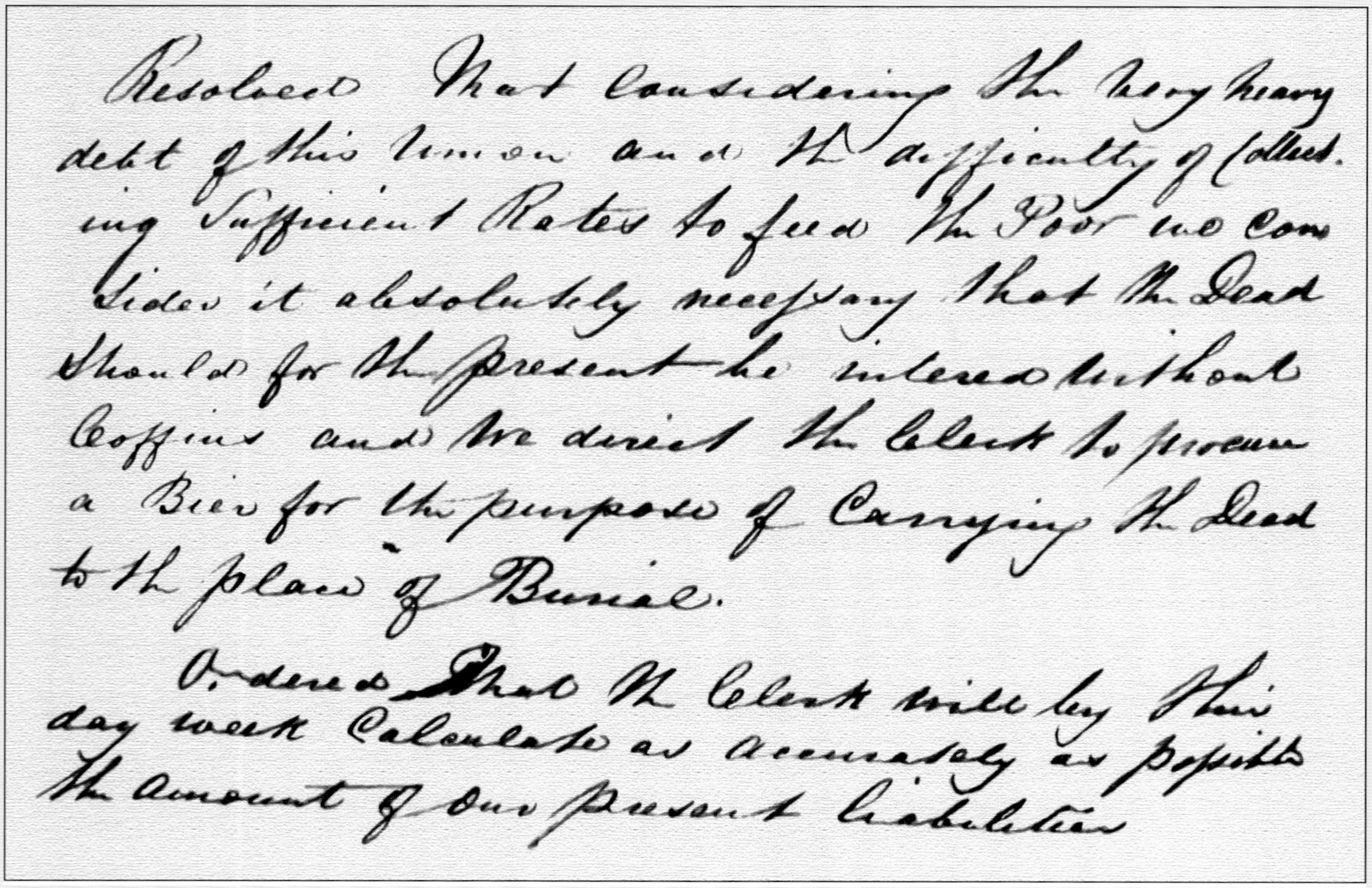
Resolved That considering the very heavy debt of this Union and the difficulty of collecting sufficient Rates to feed the Poor we consider it absolutely necessary that the Dead should for the present be interred without Coffins and we direct the Clerk to procure a Bier for the purpose of Carrying the Dead to the place of Burial.

Ordered That the Clerk will by this day week Calculate as accurately as possible the amount of our present liabilities

Fig. 2 The Mohill Board of Guardians resolved in April 1847 to bury the workhouse dead without coffins, given the union's mounting debts and increased mortality. They direct 'the clerk to procure a bier for the purposes of carrying the dead to the place of burial'.

It was quite evident that either as a result of being inundated with large numbers seeking relief, or through inefficiency, or a combination of both, the Board of Guardians had proved unequal to the task of managing Mohill Union. Hence, the vice-guardians set about rectifying the situation as quickly as possible. In order to increase workhouse accommodation a number of buildings were hired on a temporary basis. Two houses in Mohill were obtained – one for infant children and their mothers; the other to act as an infirmary for those suffering from infectious diseases. At the same time, a temporary fever hospital was established in Carrigallen.

## OUTDOOR RELIEF

The original workhouse building was restricted to able-bodied men thereby allowing for the support of women and children by means of outdoor relief. The latter enterprise was aided to a great extent by grants from the British Relief Assocation who supported thousands of children in local schools. Their assistance was vital given the huge numbers then applying for outdoor relief. In January 1848 this number totalled almost 1,000 but less than two months later, at the end of February, it had reached more than 7,000. Of course, with increased numbers came greater expense and in the above period the cost rose from £30 to £218 per week. Thus the vice-guardians embarked upon a concerted effort to ensure collection of the poor rate, actually gaining the assistance of the local constabulary to accompany collectors on their rounds. This policy achieved significant results and as the year progressed amounts averaging over £200 were lodged into the union accounts on a weekly basis. Reputations were of no consequence to the new regime and the solicitor to the board, O'Brien, was dismissed for non-payment of rates on estates for which he was agent and receiver.

As 1848 progressed matters improved in the union and by the end of that year temporary sheds had been constructed in the workhouse yards bringing total capacity to 1,300. In the first week of January 1849 there were 1,189 people receiving indoor relief and 4,496 on the outdoor lists. While the latter figure peaked at over 11,000 in June it had been reduced to 1,575 by the end of September.

In October 1849 the vice-guardians vacated their posts and the local elected board resumed control. Whilst the latter felt embittered about many aspects of the role played by the government appointees, not least a union debt of almost £6,000, there can be little doubt that the vice-guardians succeeded in reversing a culture of neglect and inefficiency in the Mohill Union. When Dr O'Higgins, Catholic Bishop of Ardagh and Clonmacnoise, attended the workhouse to confirm 400 Catholic children, he found a much-improved institution:

I have minutely examined the several departments of the establishment and I feel bound in justice to state that I was most agreeably surprised to find that the letter and the spirit of the law was carried out to perfection in the workhouse. The harmony and high-minded feeling which evidently exists among all those connected with the administration of the house guarantees the continuance of discipline, good order and efficiency.

# The Famine in County Roscommon

## Mary Kelly

Over the Famine decade, County Roscommon lost 31% of its population, the highest population loss of any county in the country. The impacts of the Famine were neither shared equally among the populace nor distributed evenly across the county. The worst affected barony was Ballintober North in the east, which lost 48% of its population, followed by neighbouring Ballintober South, Roscommon and Ballymoe all losing over 40% of their populations. The west of the county in general suffered less severe losses. However, baronial averages mask more localised impacts. Of the sixty-nine parishes in the county, twenty-five parishes lost over 40% of their populations, a number of which were located in western baronies. Examination of population losses at townland level reveals a more complex geography of decline. A number of townlands in the west of the county lost over 50% of their pop-

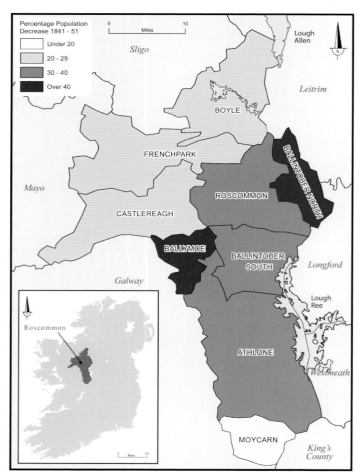

ulations. However, in general the more severe (over 86%) and concentrated losses were located towards the eastern part of the county. Why did Roscommon suffer so severely during the Famine and why did certain parts of the county suffer more severely than others? To answer these question this chapter looks at pre-Famine population pressure on marginal land, the loss of the potato crop, hunger and starvation and famine relief.

The particularly acute nature of population pressure on marginal land in County Roscommon was recognised by John Longfield in 1814. In his report to the Bogs Commission he stated that:

> the population of the county of Roscommon (although generally considered as a grazing county) is exceedingly great, so much so, that every little island or peninsula in the bogs contains more than an ordinary proportion of inhabitants; as an instance of which, I shall mention one island near Lough Glynn of 107 acres, called Cloonborny, that contains no less than 21 families, being little more than five acres to each house.[1]

This situation however was to worsen significantly over the next three decades. The population of the county increased by 20% between 1821 and 1841, reaching just over 250,000 on the eve of the Famine. Some parts of the county experienced significantly higher rates of population growth than others, meaning that pressure on land was greater in some areas than in others.[2] This pressure was exacerbated by an agricultural policy that involved the expansion of grazing and the clearance of excess tenants from estates to make way for more viable holding sizes. Evidence given to the Devon Commission in 1844 from all over the county indicates that Roscommon landowners were actively pursuing such policies.[3]

### REORGANISATION OF FARMS

Morgan Crofton, agent to the Lorton estate in Boyle, outlined the procedure through which he reorganised farms when leases fell in. Properties that had been occupied by multiple families were divided into ten-acre holdings which were then redistributed to those who held the most land, had lived longest on the estate, were the most solvent and had 'the best characters'. This process usually resulted in the dispossession of about 50% of the original occupiers, who continued to live on the estate as landless cottiers under the new holders. Denis H. Kelly, owner of 10,000 acres on the Roscommon-Galway border, outlined how he created a three-tier system on his estate, cutting out a proportion to give to a farmer who 'could keep it in good state of cultivation', dividing the rest among the remainder but setting a few acres aside for paupers.

In other areas those cleared were given a small compensation and turned out. Consequently, in pre-Famine Roscommon, as holding sizes on well managed estates increased and the conditions of those lucky enough to hold 8–10 acres or more improved, population pressure on marginal lands into which those who had made way for improvement also increased. Here living conditions worsened. One respondent reported that the wretchedness of Roscommon labourers was 'beyond anything you could calculate' while in Frenchpark it was reported that the tenantry were 'all paupers in this district'.[4] In these marginal areas into which the dispossessed had been expelled practices such as subdivision and rundale, which had been curtailed on the newly leased small farms, continued leading to ever increasing numbers existing on ever decreasing holdings. Moreover, while agricultural improvements and crop diversification had been introduced on the new farms, here people continued to exist on the potato.

A measure of the poverty in which Roscommon people lived in can be seen from the house classifications recorded in the 1841 Census, which shows that 89.6% of all housing in the county was in either the third- or fourth-class category. However, thirty-four parishes in the county returned higher than average percentages. Greatest concentrations of poor house accommodation were located in those parts of the county that saw the highest population increases in the decades preceding the Famine and which suffered the most severe population losses when the Famine struck.

### SPREAD OF THE POTATO BLIGHT

Bourke's analysis of the potato survey of 1844 notes that just before the Famine there were 60,000 acres of potatoes in the county.[5] As a result of the first attack of the blight in 1845, the 1846 planted crop fell by 20%. The blight, striking earlier and more severely in 1846, led to the further devastation of what had already been a reduced cultivation. By 1847, there was limited seed for planting. This is reflected in the agricultural census of that year, which shows that the potato acreage for the county was a mere 6.5% of what it had been three years previously.[6] Feeding a population of approximately 227,000 dependants (those living in third- and fourth-class housing), meant that there were approximately fifty-eight people per acre of potatoes, in 1847, the highest dependence in Connacht.

Dependency was not even across the county. In Kilglass, in the east, for example, there were only 11 acres of

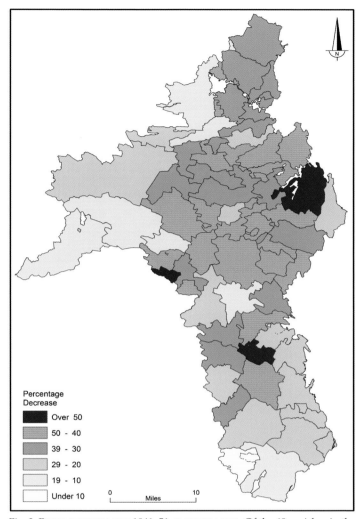

Fig. 2 POPULATION CHANGE 1841–51 AT PARISH LEVEL. Of the 69 parishes in the county, 25 parishes lost over 40% of their populations.

potatoes planted for a dependent population of 3,000 while on the other side of the county in Cloonygormican there were only 7 acres for a similar number. Not surprisingly, these were parishes which suffered high population losses. Thus, while the blight did not strike in 1847, there was scarcely a crop to harvest. An attempt at recovery was made in 1848 when 20,000 acres of potatoes were planted. However, by August that year it was recognised that the crop was again affected by blight, although many reported that while the leaves were blackened, the roots could be eaten. Potato cultivation declined again in 1849. Reports from several of the unions in January of that year indicate that people were living on Indian meal supplemented with turnips. From 1850 onwards potato cultivation began to gradually recover, but never to reach its 1844 extent.

### STARVATION AND HUNGER

People in County Roscommon were living on the verge of starvation on the eve of the Famine. William Murray, from Tisrara in the barony of Athlone, reported to the Devon Commission that a great many in his parish were starving and

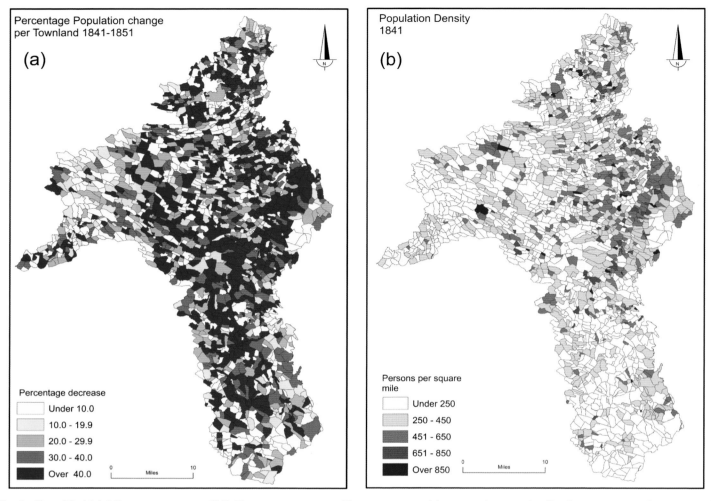

Figs 3a, 3b and 3c (right) POPULATION CHANGE 1841–51 AT TOWNLAND LEVEL. The eastern part of the county in general suffered more severe and concentrated losses than the west. This was the part of the county in which density per square mile was highest and land valuations low (3b and 3c). However, also evident here are pockets of high population loss in the north of the county where valuations were higher and the social geography more mixed as well as a consistent belt of high population loss running from the more valuable lands around Frenchpark and the plains of Boyle southwards towards less valuable and less densely populated lands in the south of the county.

similar reports came from other parts of the county.[7] William Wilde recorded a number of cases of death by starvation in the early years of the 1840s. These, however, increased sharply in 1845 (twenty deaths), 1846 (123) and 1847 (480).[8] This corresponds with newspaper reports of starvation deaths, which became most voluminous during 1847.

In March *The Nation* carried the story of how two orphan girls had been found dead on the streets of the county town and stated that 'in Roscommon deaths by famine are so prevalent that whole families who retire at night are corpses in the morning'. On the same day it also published details of an inquest into the death of a man who had died from starvation outside Lanesborough, which found that neither he nor his family had any food in the house or eaten any for the previous four days. Starvation was particularly common in this locality; seventy others had already died under similar circumstances. The destitution found in this district was explained by the lack of local agents or organisations who could administer relief, there being not 'a priest, a parson, church, a chapel, a resident landlord, a magistrate, a policeman, a soldier or

a relief committee' in the district and while the people of the town had reportedly raised £20 for relief, there was nobody to distribute it.[9]

Despite the establishment of soup kitchens in 1847, starvation continued. In December 1847, reports of a number of people who had died of starvation, despite having applied to the authorities for relief, came to the attention of the Relief Commissariat, while in February 1848 two brothers aged eleven and fourteen from the parish of Cam, perished after being turned out of the Athlone workhouse.[10] Deaths by starvation gradually declined after 1847, but hunger persisted. In the Roscommon Union in 1848 it was reported that 'there are numbers . . . in every part of the union in a state bordering on actual starvation' while in Carrick-on-Shannon, it was feared that destitution had reached 'the entire population'. By January 1849, the Castlerea Union reported that due to 'the great distress existing at present in this union . . . even a greater number of persons will require relief before next harvest than during the previous year', while in Athlone a visible change 'in the emaciation of the applicants for relief' was noted.[11]

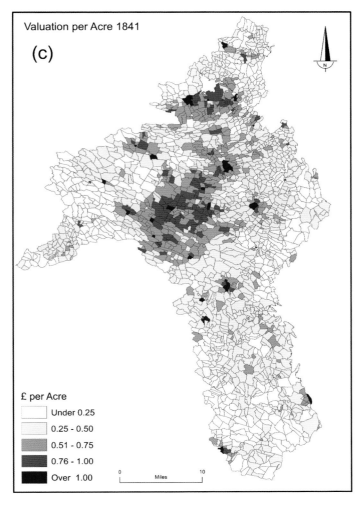

Valuation per Acre 1841

(c)

£ per Acre

| | |
|---|---|
| | Under 0.25 |
| | 0.25 - 0.50 |
| | 0.51 - 0.75 |
| | 0.76 - 1.00 |
| | Over 1.00 |

0    Miles    10

## RELIEF MEASURES

By July 1846, thirteen relief committees were operating in Roscommon and by November this had increased to thirty, the third highest of any county in the country.[12] These committees were actively lobbying for depots, supplies of meal and seed, financial aid as well as for the establishment of public work schemes. Initially County Roscommon was to be supplied with corn from depots at Athlone, Banagher, Longford and Sligo. However, as the situation worsened, the inadequacy of supplying Roscommon from external depots was recognised and by August depots had been established at Roscommon, Castlerea and Strokestown. By October, however, these depots were empty and throughout the autumn months relief committees made repeated calls for the establishment of additional depots around the county. However, despite the high level of applications for donations, meal, seed and depots, most were rejected, due to the delayed arrival of corn into the country, to committees not having raised the appropriate subscriptions locally, having exhausted their funds on gratuitous relief, or not supplying their accounts in order.

The ability of Roscommon committees to raise subscriptions locally was particularly limited. Of the £98,000 raised in subscriptions in the country as a whole between March and July 1846, just over 1% came from Roscommon commit-

tees.[13] Thus, while there was certainly an early willingness within the county to respond to the disaster, relief efforts were frustrated by a lack of compliance or co-operation with Commissariat regulations. This is not to suggest that local agents did not make their own contributions. One land owner, Sir Charles Coote, for example, 'declined aiding the Relief Fund, or any *public* fund . . . [but did] . . . much good privately'.[14]

Applications for public works schemes were more successful. By August 1846 over £33,000 had been issued to the county. The greatest proportions were granted to Ballintober north and south, Roscommon, Athlone and Moycarn while baronies in the west of the county received less. Monies peaked in March while the numbers employed on schemes peaked in June with 40,000 people employed, although numbers remained high throughout the year. In December, 30,000 people were still employed on public works in Roscommon, the highest number for Connacht, and following only Clare and Kerry nationally.[15]

By December 1846 the inadequacy of both corn depots and public works was clear. Rioting had been reported in

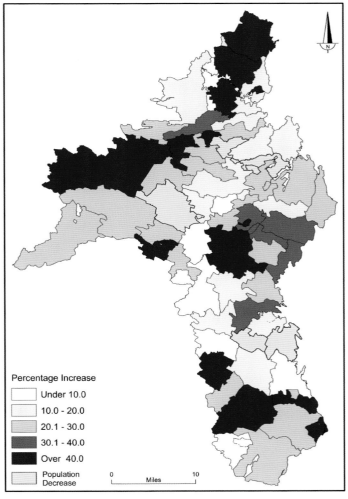

Percentage Increase

| | |
|---|---|
| | Under 10.0 |
| | 10.0 - 20.0 |
| | 20.1 - 30.0 |
| | 30.1 - 40.0 |
| | Over 40.0 |
| | Population Decrease |

0    Miles    10

Fig. 4 POPULATION CHANGE 1821–41 AT PARISH LEVEL. Some parts of the county experienced significantly higher rates of population growth than others, meaning that pressure on land was greater in some areas than in others.

311

Roscommon town in August when paupers 'broke open all the provision shops'. In September, officers were trapped inside the Strokestown depot by a blockade of people seeking relief.[16] Pressure on supplies was also increasing. In early September Trevelyan was informed that he could 'have no idea of the demand in Galway, Mayo Roscommon, Sligo, Longford and Donegal', while later in the month it was reported that conditions in Roscommon, like Cavan and Monaghan were 'likely to be most deplorable'.[17] Provisions in the Roscommon depots were stagnant over the autumn and winter of 1846/7 and while they were re-stocked in January they were not open.[18] In early 1847, as criticisms that the provision of public work schemes created a culture of dependency as well as labour shortages locally and as reports of fraud, corruption and death on the road works increased, government relief policy moved towards the establishment of soup kitchens.

Uptake of the Soup Kitchen Act was fastest in Boyle where by May fourteen out of sixteen DEDs were participating in the distribution of over 9,000 rations per day. Uptake was slower in Roscommon, where only six out of eighteen electoral divisions were participating, while in Castlerea only four out of eighteen were distributing. However by June, all electoral divisions were operating under the Act, supplying over 96,000 rations per day, while in early July ration distribution peaked at 125,000 per day. When the Temporary Relief Act ended in August, all of the Roscommon relief committees were dissolved under the third wave of closures, an indication of the high level of need in this county. Quantities of gratuitous relief being distributed also declined, although both the Roscommon and Carrick-on-Shannon unions were still distributing over 20,000 rations per day at the end of August.[19]

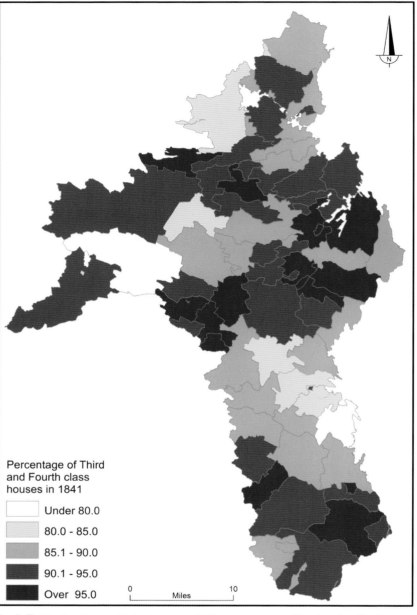

Percentage of Third
and Fourth class
houses in 1841

◻ Under 80.0
◻ 80.0 - 85.0
◻ 85.1 - 90.0
◼ 90.1 - 95.0
◼ Over 95.0

Fig. 5 THIRD- AND FOURTH-CLASS HOUSING IN 1841 AT PARISH LEVEL. Housing classification provides a measure of poverty in Roscommon as recorded in the 1841 Census. Thirty-two parishes contained higher-than-average percentages of third- and fourth-class housing (above 90%), while in thirteen parishes over 95% of all accommodation was of this category. Such parishes saw the highest population increases in the decades prior to the Famine and suffered severe population losses when the crisis struck.

## WORKHOUSES

When the Soup Kitchen Act terminated in August 1847, responsibility for the poor came to rest with the unions. Roscommon had been divided into four unions on the eve of the Famine and had three workhouses, Boyle (opened in 1841), Carrick-on-Shannon (1842) and Roscommon (1843). Castlerea workhouse opened in 1846 and an additional union and workhouse was established in Strokestown in 1850 to cater for the particularly acute needs of the people in that district. The workhouse system was wholly inadequate to deal with the situation, due to both the continued levels of destitution in the county and the imbalance that existed between rate-payers (who funded the workhouse) and non rate-payers (who came to depend on it). In some parts of the county, 90% of the population did not pay rates. Consequently, responsibility for the destitute was transferred to the unions at that time when they were least able to cope with it.

In October 1847 the Carrick-on-Shannon Union was collecting only 5% of its rates and despite the 'multitudes of destitute . . . crowding the roads in every direction', the workhouse could not afford to admit them.[20] While the subsequent appointment of rate collectors led to the re-opening of the workhouse and an improvement in conditions therein, the numbers being admitted were still only about one-fifth of the number in need and those that were admitted were in such a state of destitution that workhouse deaths

---

ENCLOSURE.

*County of Roscommon, District of Strokestown.*

DOCUMENT found pasted on the townland of Moyglass, in the parish of Kilglass and Barony of Ballentobber, on Monday, the 6th day of July, 1846.

To the Honorable and Committee of Public Works.

We the indigent and needy and distressed class of Workmen of this part of the Vicinity having no means to procure a subsistance, can no longer bear the merciless pangs of hunger, humbly deprecates the Committee will take into consideration and commisserate the awful and melancholy state of these humble and peaceful People, and give them Employment, according to every other part of the Country, before they are exposed to the impending danger of present famine which has neither shame or honesty, and before We violate the ties of honesty which we were bred to. We desire Work and nothing but Work, and hope the Committee and Gentlemen of the Vicinity will find that for us, and hopes the honorable Gentlemen will not be offended at this Notice, because We are no Mollys, We distain it.

Let no Person take this down.

Fig. 6 While criticisms that the provision of public work schemes created a culture of dependency as well as labour shortages locally, the above notice posted by the people of Kilglass, County Roscommon, in July 1846, imploring the local relief committee and the gentlemen of the district to provide them with employment, indicates that the scarcity of employment was a genuine issue at this time. [Source: Correspondence explanatory of the measures adopted by Her Majesty's government for the relief of distress arising from the failure of the potato crop in Ireland', HC 1846 (735), p. 203]

continued to rise. In 1848, destitution had increased 'to a fearful extent' and had a more 'formidable character' while many townlands in the area exhibited 'strong marks of the march of the enemy' evident from:

> the multitudes of ruined cottages or cabins, the absence of every description of cattle, and the neglected state of the land; yet these contain less destitution, and stand less in need of relief, than the most favoured townlands in the majority of the electoral divisions in this . . . union.[21]

The situation was not much better in the Roscommon Union. In December 1847 it was reported that the workhouse was in a deplorable state both in terms of overcrowding and a lack of hygiene regulations. The union owed over £6,000 pounds to creditors, £3,000 of which was to the local baker alone.[22] Rates had not been collected since the previous March, rate collectors and their books were missing, guardians were paying exorbitant amounts for supplies and paupers were still being admitted. Immediate steps were taken to remedy the situation. The board was dissolved and a paid board appointed. Tents were erected in which fever patients could be isolated and additional accommodation for children was acquired. A loan of £300 was granted from the British Relief Association which was to be put forward for the establishment of outdoor relief, clothing was dispatched from the Dublin Commissariat and procedures for the collection of rates were put in place. However, despite numerous reports of improvements in early 1848, by March the board's

finances were again all but exhausted, the workhouse was overcrowded, conditions unsanitary and provisions lacking. Despite this, the Roscommon Union continued to provide workhouse relief to increasing numbers of people. The average numbers maintained in the workhouse in April, May and June were 1,234, 1,599 and 1,767 respectively. At the same time, the Roscommon Union was providing outdoor relief to between 17,000 and 21,000 people a week.

Rate collection problems also obstructed the Castlerea Union. In February, there were over 8,000 people in the union in need of relief, but the board did not have the funds to relieve them. Many rate collectors were tenants on large local farms and were consequently reluctant to enforce rate collection in their own areas. Rate-payers hid their goods so as to avoid confiscation in lieu of payment and rate-payers delayed payment as long as possible. While many were processed for their dues, magistrates were 'afraid to act', concerned for their own safely. Members of the Castlerea Board of Guardians also feared for their personal safety. Some stated that they would not continue to attend meetings because 'the poor blame them for not giving outdoor relief' and, given the state this country was in, they were 'in a very dangerous position'.[23] Board members were also criticised for not paying rates themselves. However, most were members of the lesser landowning class and not members of the gentry who reportedly neither participated on the board nor provided employment locally. Eventually the constabulary was deployed to assist in the sale of goods in lieu of rates, £300 was secured from the British Relief Association and clothes were issued from the Commissariat

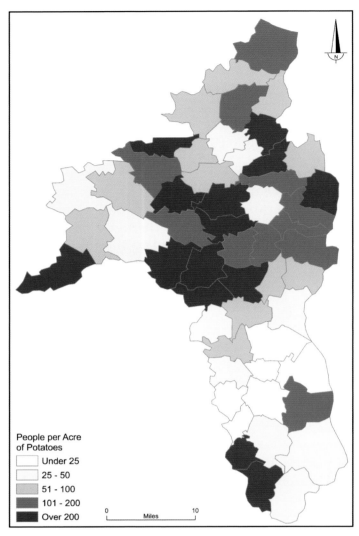

People per Acre
of Potatoes

☐ Under 25
☐ 25 - 50
▨ 51 - 100
▨ 101 - 200
■ Over 200

Fig. 7 PEOPLE PER ACRE OF POTATOES, 1847. Potato dependency was not even across the county. In Kilglass, in the east, for example, there were only eleven acres of potatoes planted for a dependent population of 3,000 while on the other side of the county in Cloonygormican there were only seven acres for a similar number.

stores. Outdoor relief began in March 1848 and by July over 19,000 people were being supplied every week.

Administrative difficulties also beset the Boyle Union, which began to provide outdoor relief in February 1848. However, in March the Commissariat had received communication from a parish priest in the Sligo part of the union regarding persons having died of starvation despite having applied for relief. In response, the Boyle Board of Guardians outlined the difficulties that pertained to the 'herculean labour of commencing the out-door relief' when many of the relieving officers were inexperienced, new to their districts and faced with the challenge of selecting 'out of a whole population seeking for relief, such classes as were entitled to receive it'.[24] Another problem that beset the union was the persistent absenteeism of guardians from particular districts, thus depriving 'the board of the necessary information concerning their districts, which would have enabled the board to lessen the calamities' therein. In April the board was dissolved and a paid board appointed.

Outdoor relief increased gradually in the subsequent months peaking at about 16,000 a week in late June/early July before tapering off thereafter.

### ACUTE LEVELS OF POPULATION LOSS

While Roscommon had a higher proportion of arable land than its Connacht neighbours, as well as a lower population density, a declining rate of population increase, and average percentages of first- and second-class houses, it suffered the most acute levels of population loss during the Famine decade. A culture of estate improvement and the move towards a less labour intensive but more land intensive grazier economy in the decades before the Famine resulted in the creation of communities of landless labourers who in the absence of employment opportunities were totally dependent on the potato. The worst affected part of the county, an area stretching from the parish of Kilglass just north of Strokestown, moving southwards along the Slieve Bawn Mountains, was a part of the county that experienced continued population increase in the two decades before the Famine, and was characterised by poor land valuations and high population densities. Over 95% of the housing in a number of the parishes in this district belonged to either the third- or fourth-class category and there was a high imbalance between the rate-paying and non rate-paying populations, particularly towards the south of the region where over 90% of the population were non rate-paying.

This part of the county had been recognised as a 'bad tract' by the Relief Commissioners in the early years of the Famine, and was also the part of the county made infamous by the Ballykilcline rebellion, evictions, assisted migration of paupers and the eventual murder of Major Denis Mahon. These incidents had an impact on the region. In December 1847 it was reported that 'almost all the resident gentry have left this neighbourhood' while the few who remained were 'afraid to leave their homes, or take part in public business'. The murder of Mahon also resulted in the withdrawal of any assistance then being provided by the British Relief Association.

High, but more dispersed, population losses also occurred in the north of the county in an area stretching westwards from the parishes of Boyle and Kilbryan, through Ardcarn and into Tuma. Most of Boyle was owned by Viscount Lorton, whose demesne overlooked Lough Key. Lorton was recognised as an improving landlord, having established two schools and a dispensary for tenants on his estate. He had also been active on the local relief committee and had made repeated applications for the establishment of corn depots in this area.[25] However, a number of respondents to the Devon Commission were people who had been evicted from the Lorton estate and, as outlined above, a policy of tenant clearance was actively pursued there.

Weld's 1830s' description of this part of the county

*Soup to be provided for Sale.*

It is recommended to Relief Committees to establish soup-kitchens; and also to provide ingredients for soup to be sold to persons who can prepare it according to printed directions.

The soup No. 1, in Count Rumford's Essay on Food, appears to be best adapted for general use, as not containing any green or unseasoned vegetables, and may consist only of barley, peas, salt, water, with cuttings of wheaten bread, or biscuit.

A land proprietor in the county of Waterford, whose labourers use this soup for dinner, has supplied the following practical information in recommending its general adoption.

"The soup No. 1, in Count Rumford's Essay, has been used in the Lismore Union Workhouse, for many months, and has been adopted in the Fermoy Union, and I believe in Macroom also.

"For the last year I have given this soup, one quart each to my labourers for dinner. Each quart is about *two pounds four ounces* in weight, and costs *three farthings.**

"It is composed of barley, ground whole, with all the bran, *whole* peas, pepper salt and water. (See proportions below.)

"In each quart are placed small cuttings of wheaten bread on which the boiling soup is poured, so as to fill each quart.

"The whole meal of barley answers as well as pearl barley, and is much cheaper.

"Of course, meat would improve the soup, but then the price would be greatly increased; and the object is to produce a nutritious food at the lowest price.

"A quantity of peas and barley, *used in soup*, will support a much greater number of persons than if cooked separately."

"The soup used in Lismore Workhouse is composed of pearl-barley, peas, pepper and salt, *in the proportion* of one pound of peas, and one pound of barley, to one gallon of water.

"For dinner, each adult gets thirty ounces of this soup, with six ounces of bread, as only two meals are given in the day; and the bread is given separately."

"Count Rumford's Essay is sold by J. McGLASHAN, D'Olier-street; ROBERTSONS, Sackville-street, Dublin; and by HAMILTON, Youghal."

In preparing this soup, the peas should be soaked in cold water for some hours, not less than two, before being put into the boiler; and the soup must be made with soft water, as peas will not mix with *hard* water, unless a small lump of soda is put into it. The water should be boiling when the peas are put in; and they must be let boil separately until tender. Do not add the salt until they are boiled, or they will not become soft. They should be stirred occasionally to keep them from the bottom of the boiler. When they are quite soft, stir in the barley, and let the soup simmer gently for a couple of hours. In the mean time put some pepper into a vessel with a little of the soup, mix them well, and pour them into the boiler;— then stir the soup thoroughly and season it with salt.

If biscuit is to be used with the soup instead of bread, put it separately into the vessels like the cuttings of bread, otherwise it cannot be equally distributed.

*Commissariat Relief Office, Dublin Castle, December* 31, 1846

---

Fig. 8 One of a selection of recipes collected by Routh, which he proposed be posted in provision shops around the country so as to instruct the people on the making of cheap but nutritious soups and broths. [Source: Correspondence from July, 1846, to January, 1847, relating to the measures adopted for the relief of the distress in Ireland', Commissariat series, HC 1847 (761), pp.482-90]

noted that a similar policy of clearance and improvement had been carried out on the neighbouring Coote Hall estate.[26] While it is not possible to trace the movements of evictees, a number of townlands on the opposite side of the lake to Lorton had population densities in excess of 650 people per square mile and may have been places where evictees found refuge. A large number of townlands on the Lorton estate, and on neighbouring estates, lost over 50% of their populations between 1841 and 1851, while some parishes to the northwest of the lake saw an 86–94% decline in fourth-class houses. What differentiates the pattern of decline around the Boyle area from that around Slieve

| DISEASES—continued. | YEARS. | | | | | | | | | | |
|---|---|---|---|---|---|---|---|---|---|---|---|
| | 1841. 203 days. | 1842. | 1843. | 1844. | 1845. | 1846. | 1847. | 1848. | 1849. | 1850. | 1851. 89 days. |
| **VIOLENT OR SUDDEN DEATHS.** | | | | | | | | | | | |
| Burns and Scalds, | 1 | 9 | 12 | 13 | 9 | 11 | 22 | 33 | 19 | 21 | 3 |
| Drowned, | 5 | 19 | 13 | 12 | 19 | 16 | 13 | 20 | 19 | 19 | 8 |
| Injuries of the Head, | . | 1 | . | . | 2 | . | . | 1 | . | . | . |
| Intemperance, | . | 3 | 1 | . | 2 | 2 | 3 | 1 | 3 | 4 | 2 |
| Homicide, | 4 | 8 | 5 | 7 | 3 | 7 | 8 | 7 | 10 | 4 | 2 |
| Starvation, | 5 | 9 | 9 | 8 | 20 | 123 | 480 | 306 | 188 | 65 | 14 |
| Executed, | . | . | . | 2 | . | . | . | 4 | 3 | . | . |
| Poison, accidental, | . | . | . | 1 | 1 | 2 | . | . | 1 | . | . |
| Suicide, | 3 | 2 | 2 | 1 | 1 | 1 | . | 3 | 1 | 1 | . |
| Lightning, | . | . | . | . | . | . | . | . | . | . | . |
| Accidental, unspecified, | 4 | 19 | 17 | 19 | 17 | 25 | 30 | 49 | 39 | 20 | 10 |
| Total, | 22 | 70 | 59 | 63 | 74 | 187 | 556 | 424 | 283 | 134 | 39 |
| Causes not specified, | 34 | 194 | 192 | 186 | 202 | 341 | 1,170 | 324 | 708 | 356 | 69 |
| Total Males, | 200 | 1,042 | 1,030 | 1,023 | 1,129 | 1,784 | 4,267 | 3,149 | 3,196 | 1,864 | 458 |
| Total Females, | 132 | 823 | 871 | 906 | 1,053 | 1,568 | 3,479 | 2,684 | 2,704 | 1,864 | 391 |
| Total Males and Females, | 332 | 1,865 | 1,901 | 1,929 | 2,182 | 3,352 | 7,746 | 5,833 | 5,900 | 3,728 | 849 |

Fig. 9 William Wilde's table of deaths for County Roscommon recorded a number of cases of death by starvation in the early years of the 1840s. These, however, increased sharply in 1845 (20 deaths), 1846 (123 deaths) and 1847 (480 deaths) and correspond to the overall increasing death rate for this period. Wilde's recorded starvation deaths, however, only account for 5% of deaths that occurred between 1845 and 1849. Dysentery, fever and miasmas were the primary causes of reported deaths in County Roscommon. The weakened state of the hungry, however, may have led many who were suffering from starvation to fall victim to death by other means. In Carrick-on-Shannon in 1848, it was reported that people were 'a mass of indefinable diseases' when they arrived at the workhouse, having left it so late to look for help, and the high death rates within were explained by the emaciated state that people were in when admitted. [Source: Papers relating to proceedings for relief of distress, and state of unions and workhouses in Ireland', sixth series, HC 1847–48 (955), p. 749]

Bawn, is that while the latter was characterised by high densities of impoverished communities living on marginal uplands in the absence of the gentry, Boyle was characterised by better land values and a more mixed social geography. While poverty and overcrowding existed in the Boyle/Lough Key area, this part of the county also contained the highest number of first- and second-class houses in the county and a number of affluent demesnes. This may have provided a level of protection, however limited, that did not exist around Strokestown.

Finally, a consistent tract of higher-than-average population losses was also evident in an area of low population densities stretching southwards from more valuable lands between Frenchpark and the plains of Boyle into the less valuable lands in the south of the county. This part of the county had its fair share of first- and second-class housing as well as affluent demesnes. Thus, while areas with high population densities on marginal lands with limited gentry presence may have been areas in which the Famine hit hardest, areas with higher values, lower densities and a gentry presence were not immune from 'the march of the enemy'.[27]

As outlined in this chapter, interrelated processes operating in County Roscommon created a context for famine. Ejectments for improvement or for the expansion of grazing led to the growth of a landless population, who, in a county that did not have employment opportunities for those who did not hold land, became dependent on the easily grown and high calorific potato. The failure of the potato upon which so many were dependent consequently led to destitution. As outlined by the inspector to the Castlerea Union in 1848:

In this union, in former years, a great portion of the good land was appropriated for grazing purposes, and in the hands of a few larger occupiers; the poor being generally squatters on the brink of bogs, or collected in large numbers, in villages, on the poor and unprofitable lands; the con-acre potato system, their chief means of support . . . To the disastrous failure of the potato crop, and the almost total want of employment, must consequently be attributed to the great destitution now existing.[28]

This situation, however, was exacerbated by a Poor Law in which responsibility for destitution was to be borne by the landholding rate-payers, who consequently sought to rid their lands of the financial burden of a pauper tenantry, and by the Gregory clause, under which the destitute who managed to hold on to their land were forced to become landless in order to receive relief. This meant that while the underclass was wiped out in the early part of the Famine, this class was replenished by those who became the landless in the second part under a Poor Law which while designed to deal with poverty had the effect of exacerbating it. As outlined in the Athlone Union:

The quarter acre clause and ejectments have filled the workhouse; and where, by mutual agreement, the cottier has surrendered his holding for a sum of money, and thrown his cabin down, it is more than probable the parent or parents have emigrated to America . . . This is most frequent on the Roscommon side.[29]

Finally, while in the early part of the Famine there was a concerted effort locally to deal with the disaster – Roscommon being the third most active in 1846 in terms of the numbers of relief committees in operation – as the Famine drew on, and responsibility was to be managed locally, a certain

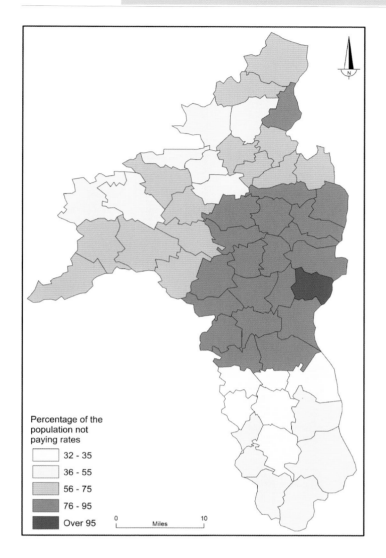

Percentage of the
population not
paying rates

| | |
|---|---|
| | 32 - 35 |
| | 36 - 55 |
| | 56 - 75 |
| | 76 - 95 |
| | Over 95 |

0        Miles        10

Fig. 10 (left) PERCENTAGE DISTRIBUTION OF POPULATION NOT PAYING RATES IN 1846. The particularly acute impact of the Famine in County Roscommon might be explained by the growing imbalance that existed between the moderately wealthy landed and the impoverished landless; between rate-payers and non rate-payers. As early as 1846, in some parts of the county 90% of the population did not pay rates. As the prolonged destitution of one class grew, so too did the inability of the other to deal with it. Those parts of the county where destitution and population losses were heaviest were also those parts of the county where this imbalance was greatest.

amount of relief fatigue set in. In December 1847 it was reported that the most active guardian in the Roscommon Union had left the country while in early 1848 it was reported that not one member of the Castlerea gentry attended union meetings.[30] By the middle of the year the boards of guardians for all of the Roscommon unions were dissolved in favour of paid guardians. Members of the resident gentry were frustrated by their inability to deal with the disaster and were fearful both for their personal safety and their financial security, due to the encumbered nature of many estates that were not receiving rents but burdened by poor rate. However, apathy and a declining concern for others was also apparent. The opportunity to distribute seed potatoes to 'the small and needy farmers' of the Carrick-on-Shannon Union in 1848 was passed over by the inability of the temporary relieving officer to mobilise committees to do so: 'nobody [he argued] appears inclined to stir in the matter'. Here farmers showed 'no tendency' towards providing employment locally. Many looked on 'with seeming indifference' as their fields went untilled. Others who had not held a farming implement for twenty years were now working their own lands such was 'the scarcity of money, and the anxiety of those who have it, to hold it'.[31]

317

# Ballykilcline, County Roscommon

## Charles E. Osner Jr.

Compared to other townlands, Ballykilcline is both mundane and special. Like thousands of other places throughout the countryside, the townland was inhabited by small farmers who paid annual rents in two instalments to landlords. And, like thousands of their fellows, they struggled to survive during the Great Hunger as best they could. On the other hand, Ballykilcline has the unique character of having been a Crown Estate, one that witnessed a long-lasting rent strike that terminated in the almost complete eviction of its people.[1]

Ballykilcline is located in the barony of Ballintober North in Kilglass Parish, north County Roscommon about 8 km (5 miles) northeast of Strokestown. The earliest history of the roughly 246 ha (609 acres) townland is largely unknown, but documents confirm that it was confiscated by royal troops around 1688 and designated a Crown Estate. Rather than allow the land to lie fallow, the British monarch ordered it leased to tenant farmers for rents that would increase the public treasury. Around thirty families lived at Ballykilcline in 1749.

### THE MAHON FAMILY
The ascendancy family most closely associated with Ballykilcline was the Mahons. In the seventeenth century, Nicholas

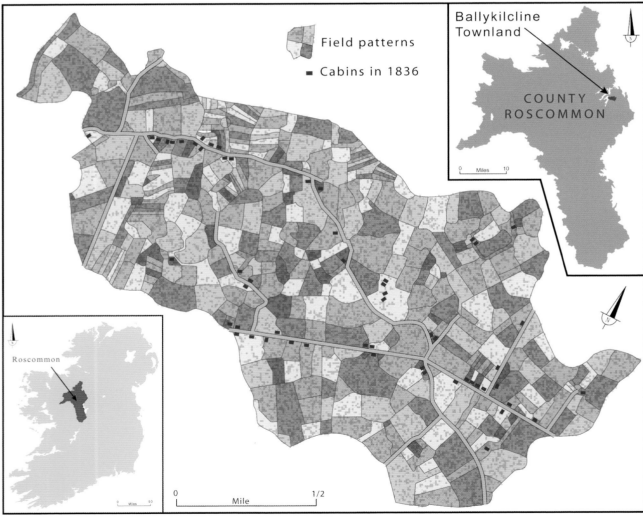

Fig.1 THE BRASSINGTON AND GALE MAP PROVIDES A UNIQUE SPATIAL UNDERSTANDING OF BALLYKILCLINE IN 1836. The survey revealed that the townland was divided into seventy-four individual tenancies (accounting for seventy-nine holders) with individual plots ranging in size from 0.15 to 9.8 ha (0.37–24.3 ac). Forty-nine of the tenants (62.0%) farmed between 0.81 and 4.0 ha (2–10 acres). Only nineteen (24.1%) farmed between 4.0 and 12.1 ha (10–30 acres) and eleven11 (13.9%) farmed less than 0.81 ha (<2 acres). The map also makes it possible to locate the sites of the cabins of the individual families. Their houses were located along the main roads, with the exception of three possible clachans. The individual fields were small and irregular.

Mahon, a Roscommon sheriff, had received just over 2,000 ac (809 ha) around Strokestown as payment for his governmental service. In 1659, he began constructing a grand house called 'The Bawn' (later Strokestown Park House). The name of the house, though located near Slieve Bawn mountain, also recalled ironically that the location was originally the site of the bawn, house and ancestral lands of the displaced Gaelic leader, the O'Conor Roe (Ruadh). During the same period, Mahon also began purchasing huge tracts of land with borrowed money.

In 1793, Charles, Viscount Dillon of Costelloe, acquired the Ballykilcline lease from the Crown for a term of forty-one years. That year, he turned it over to Maurice Mahon, the first Baron Hartland (who had obtained the title by consenting to the Act of Union). The Mahons thus held the lease and administered it from their Strokestown mansion until 1 May 1834, when they surrendered it due to Maurice's illness and family debt. Maurice Mahon was the last Mahon to hold the Crown's lease to Ballykilcline. Denis Mahon inherited the Mahon lands in 1845, but he never held the lease to Ballykilcline because by this time it was already under the direction of the Commissioners of Her Majesty's Woods, Forests, Land Revenues, Works and Buildings. Mahon, who was always known as 'Major Mahon', had attained the rank of major in 1830, but had retired as a captain in the 98th Foot in 1834. He had acquired the lease after having his cousin Maurice (the Third Baron Hartland) declared mentally unfit and after winning a legal judgment against another cousin.

## SURVEY

Upon taking direct control of Ballykilcline, the Commissioners ordered a complete and thorough survey, one that would plot the individual parcels and identify each occupying family. James Weale of the Dublin firm of Brassington and Gale performed the survey and drafted a map that provides a unique spatial understanding of the townland in 1836. The survey revealed that Ballykilcline was divided into seventy-four individual tenancies (accounting for seventy-nine holders) with individual plots ranging in size from 0.15 to 9.8 ha (0.37-24.3 ac). Forty-nine of the tenants (62.0%) farmed between 0.81 and 4.0 ha (210 ac). Only nineteen (24.1%) farmed between 4.0 and 12.1 ha (1030 ac) and eleven (13.9%) farmed less than 0.81 ha (<2 ac).

In addition to learning the spatial layout of the estate, the Crown's agents also discovered that the tenants had begun a rent strike as soon as the Mahon lease had expired in 1834. Agrarian unrest was common in County Roscommon in the early nineteenth century, with most of it arising because of the unequal distribution of land, the anti-tithe war, and the landlord-led shift from farming to grazing.[2] By the third decade of the nineteenth century, Kilglass parish had developed a reputation for unruliness. John O'Donovan asserted in 1837 that Kilglass was 'proverbial in this part of the county for its wickedness',

Fig. 2 Landlord Denis Mahon of Strokestown House, fearing the influence of the Ballykilcline rent strike on his own tenants, carried out extensive evictions in neighbouring townlands. Mahon was murdered in an act of retribution. [Source: Stephen J. Campbell, *The Great Irish Famine* (The Famine Museum, Strokestown, 1994), p. 48].

and George Knox, the Crown's agent for Ballykilcline, observed that the townland's tenants were 'the most lawless and violent set of people in the county of Roscommon'.[3] It remains debatable whether such comments were in fact true, but the salient point is that the tenants of Ballykilcline were known to be men and women who were likely to protest what they understood to be unfair treatment.

## SURRENDERING HOLDINGS

Two years after the rent strike had begun, and with no amiable resolution seeming likely, the Commissioners issued notices requiring the tenants to surrender possession of their holdings. Of the seventy-nine tenants, fifty-two agreed to the arrangement and were reinstated as 'care-takers' with a monthly allowance of 6d. The remaining third refused to accept the terms of the agreement and began to sway the resolve of those who had initially consented to the Crown's offer. When the Crown's rent collectors appeared in the townland, they were met with threats of violence. With the refusal of the local police to protect their representatives, the Crown instituted legal proceedings against eight men they perceived to be the strike's 'ring leaders' in 1842.[4]

In 1844, with the legal battle dragging on, the Commis-

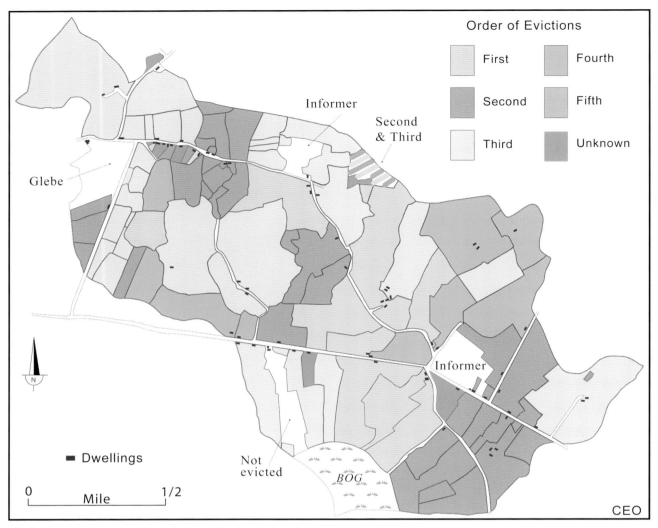

Fig. 3 MAP SHOWING THE SEQUENCE OF EVICTIONS AT BALLYKILCLINE WHICH TOOK PLACE BETWEEN MAY 1847 AND MARCH 1848.

sioners attempted to resolve the strike by simply locking the doors of the houses belonging to the most recalcitrant tenants. They secured the doors with iron staples, hasps and locks, but learned upon their retreat that the tenants simply broke the locks open and reoccupied their homes. This sequence of action and reaction led agent Knox to advocate for the eviction of the tenants and the levelling of their houses. The Commissioners finally agreed with Knox and began the removal of the tenants.

At the same time, Denis Mahon, who still held leases to neighbouring townlands, was growing concerned that his tenants would be empowered by the Ballykilcline strike action and, like other local landlords, he wanted to redivide, reassign and re-lease his holdings to Protestant tenants who would not follow the communal farming practices (rundale) of the Irish. Accordingly, in 1847, Mahon began evicting 605 families from his twenty-seven townlands.[5] Local lore maintains that the local parish priest declared from the pulpit that 'Major Mahon is worse than Cromwell' (but he later denied saying it).[6] Regardless, the view that Mahon was an evil, rack-renting landlord circulated throughout the region. And, in apparent retribution for the evictions, Mahon was murdered on the road

Fig. 4 Luke Nary, one of those evicted who later settled in Illinois. [Source: Robyn Frendling, 'Irish rebels settled in LaSalle County 150 years ago, ancestors search for truth.', *The Daily Times* (Ottawa, Illinois, 1999), 11 January 1999, p. 7]

320

Fig. 5 The remaining wall stones of the Nary house in Ballykilcline after eviction and upon excavation. According to the Brassington and Gale map, Mark Nary and his sons Edward, Luke and James held 44.04 acres on the extreme western edge of the townland. The Nary family was evicted in 1847–48 after which the holding was consolidated and used for pasture. [Photo: Charles Orser]

from Roscommon town on 2 November 1847, an event that caused great consternation in the landlords' homes and in the halls of government.[7] Many of the families he evicted were friends and relatives of the Ballykilcline tenants and a resident of Ballykilcline was an early suspect in his murder in November 1847.

For their part, the tenants of Ballykilcline petitioned the Commissioners either to be allowed to remain in their homes or to be provided with the means to emigrate. The Commissioners approved the assisted-emigration scheme. Agents Henry and William Scott, of Eden Quay, Dublin, handled the arrangements, charging £2 15s for a child under the age of fourteen and £4 for an adult. The Commissioners also provided provisioning funds for the emigrants and a modest amount of landing money (paid in American currency).

The Ballykilcline tenants left the townland in five groups, beginning in May 1847 and ending in March 1848. As of 1847, the families at Ballykilcline had been in arrears from between 9.5 and 12 years. Families in arrears

twelve years constituted the group who initiated or at least originally agreed with the strike action. The Crown termed this cohort the 'Defendants', and judged them to be violent and dangerous. They were the first to be ejected. Upon removal, the tenants travelled to Dublin then to Liverpool; from there they embarked for New York in seven ships. In all, 366 individuals can be identified as being aboard these vessels (189 males, 177 females). Upon reaching the United States, the Ballykilcline immigrants tended to settle in clusters in several states, with Vermont, Illinois and Maryland being principal among them. Many of them followed earlier immigrants who had journeyed to North America before the Great Hunger. The immigrants generally prospered in their new homes as they became involved in agriculture and quarrying.

## A GEOGRAPHY OF EVICTION

Weale's map of Ballykilcline, drafted in 1836, permits a rare look at the geography of eviction. The first eviction emptied large plots of land in the east-central portion of

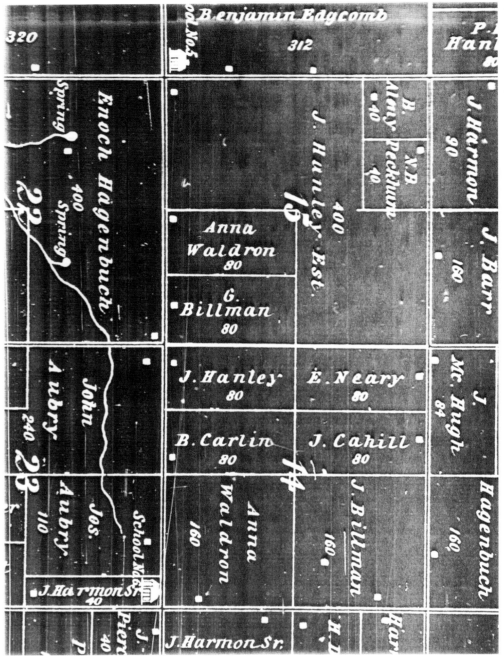

Fig. 6  Plat map of part of Waltham Township, Illinois, showing where the Narys (Neary above) from Bal-lykilcline settled. [Source: *Atlas of LaSalle County and the State of Illinois* (Warner & Beers, Chicago, 1876)]

the evicted cohort on the *Roscius*, the first ship to take Ballykilcline tenants to the United States in September 1847, indicates that the largest category were men and women between the ages of 16 and 25 (17, or 30.9%); the second largest group were men and women in the 26–35 age category (11, or 20.0%). These figures suggest that the authorities desired to remove the age groups that were most able to protest. This conclusion is supported by the realisation that the tenants who sailed on the *Metoka* (the following week in September 1847) tended to be slightly younger. Here, the 16–35 groups accounted for 39.3% of the cohort. On the *Metoka*, the 0-15 age group accounted for 41.7% of the cohort, whereas on the *Roscuis*, this age group constituted only 29.1%.

Once the townland was essentially vacant, the Commissioners required that the doors and windows of the empty houses be removed and the stone walls demolished and dispersed. Archaeological research verifies that these actions were indeed taken. The Commissioners further required that two or three houses be repaired and renovated as police barracks. Only five dwellings – three houses (those of strike informers), a 'Herd's house, and a Police-barrack' – remained in the townland in 1850.[8]

the townland, as well as a medium-sized plot in the centre and a small plot on the west side. Both the eastern fields and the small plot on the west side were situated at or near important crossroads that allowed access to the townland's interior. The Commissioners were especially concerned to maintain outside access to the townland and they perceived these roads as vitally important. The second eviction cleared the eastern part of the townland, on both sides of the road into the interior and in the northern section at a cluster of houses. The third eviction appears to have been designed to empty the settled portions that remained along the main roads. The fourth and fifth evictions were merely designed to clear the rest of the tenants. An analysis of

## EFFECTS OF THE GREAT HUNGER

The effects of the Great Hunger on the people of Bal-lykilcline are difficult to assess with confidence. Entire families did perish in their homes,[9] but the available documentation does not address the full extent of distress throughout the townland. Historical records imply that the evictions were precipitated by the rent strike rather than the want and desperation of the Hunger, but this conclusion may represent merely an attempt at memory creation or historical revisionism. Little doubt exists, however, that if Denis Mahon had held the lease in 1847 he would have evicted the tenants even in the absence of the rent strike. Mahon had considerable debts and depended upon the tenants' rents for his livelihood. The presence of the blight in his townlands significantly reduced and imperilled his income.

Mahon's agent during the Great Hunger conducted a survey of only eight of his twenty-seven townlands and discovered that 479 families, totalling 2,444 individuals, had paid no rent in two years. Their arrears totalled over £600. Applications to Mahon by his tenants indicate that many families experienced severe want. For example, the petition of James Smyth in 1846 states that he 'Respectfully begs your honour will cause him to get work at Cutting down Curraghroe hills. The Applicant is a poor Starving Man and has six in family.'

At the same time, distress because of the Famine was widespread throughout the parish of Kilglass. In June 1847, Joseph Kincaid, of the Stewart and Kincaid land agency, observed that in the parish 'the People were extremely distressed; Numbers were dying.' In 1841, the Irish Census recorded 11,391 people in Kilglass; ten years later, the population was 5,118. Henry Brennan, Kilglass parish priest, reported in the *Freeman's Journal* that 'Fever has made its way into almost every house. The poor creatures are wasting away and dying of want. In very many instances the dead bodies are thrown in waste cabins and dykes and are devoured by dogs.'[10] Clearly, the women, children and men living at Ballykilcline faced the same conditions as other tenant farmers in the parish and suffered accordingly.

# LEINSTER

**The Famine Year (The Stricken Land)**

Weary men, what reap ye? – Golden corn for the stranger.
What sow ye? – Human corpses that wait for the avenger.
Fainting forms, hunger-stricken, what see you in the offing?
Stately ships to bear our food away, amid the stranger's scoffing.
There's a proud array of soldiers – what do they round your door?
They guard our masters' granaries from the thin hands of the poor.
Pale mothers, wherefore weeping – Would to God that we were dead;
Our children swoon before us, and we cannot give them bread.

- 'Speranza'
Lady Jane Wilde

View of Dublin Castle
[Photo: Therese Kenna]

# The province of Leinster and the Great Famine

## *William J. Smyth*

The people of the provinces of Connacht and Munster suffered most severely during the Great Famine – Leinster and Ulster were also deeply affected, but not to the same catastrophic levels. Leinster benefited from containing the best land, a good communications and urban network and a diverse, relatively robust, if deeply stratified social structure. Comprising close on a fourth of the island's territory, it contained over 27% of the island's arable land, a little less than Munster and very similar to that of Ulster. But whereas Munster returned 29.6% and Ulster 23.9% of boggy and mountain land, Leinster was blessed with only 13.3% in the category of 'uncultivated land'. Water bodies were also practically non-existent at 8.3% versus Munster's 24.0%, Connacht's 33.7% and Ulster's 34.6%. In 1841, Leinster had the highest amount of land under cereals and other crops (36.6%) followed by Ulster at 24.9%. Such intensive corn cultivation was underpinned by the hard-working spadesmen of the labouring and cottier classes. But Leinster also matched Munster (45.3%) in the extent of its rich grasslands (44.7%). The wealth of the province's resident landlords, middlemen and big farmer classes is reflected not only in the highest land values but also by the fact that over one-third of the island's plantations, demesnes and treescapes were in Leinster. Bolstered by the capital, Dublin's metropolitan status and size, two-fifths of Ireland's urban land measured by the size of civic districts (2,000+ population) was returned in 1841 for the Leinster province. Over one-quarter of its families were then engaged in 'manufacturing and trades'. In a province deeply committed to schooling and literacy, 52% of its population over five years of age could read and write. Only 16.7% of its houses were classified as fourth-class whereas over one-third of Munster's houses were in this class.[1] Its labouring families earned almost twice that of their Connacht counterparts.[2] Overall, more prosperous Leinster appeared better prepared to handle the disaster of the Great Famine.

However, by 1841 these overall configurations and generalisations may obscure very significant regional variations and deep class divisions in this extensive territory of twelve counties. In a province characterised by greater propertied and social controls and smaller family size, it is not surprising that its density of population per square mile of arable land (226) is well below that of the other three provinces. But within Leinster densities vary from 187 per square mile of arable land in County Kildare to

close on double that density not only in County Dublin but also in its two western counties of Longford and King's (Offaly). And whereas the provincial average was a little over one-third, arable-cum-grain cultivation in Louth at 57.8% and Wexford at 44.7% is very different to its more pastoral counties. Meath's 38.9% arable should also be noted.

One interesting indicator of provincial variations in the immediate after effects of the Great Famine is the numbers returned for the poor and the ill still resident in public institutions by 1851. Only 1.4% of Ulster's and 3.8% of Leinster's population were so domiciled; in contrast 4.3% of Connacht's and a staggering 7.8% of Munster's population were still resident in poorhouses and other

SUPPLEMENT TO THE IRISH FIRESIDE, SEPTEMBER 2ND, 1885.

"SPERANZA."
LADY WILDE.

Fig. 1 Lady Jane Wilde (1821–96). Poet, nationalist and wife of William Wilde, 'Speranza' (the pseudonym under which she wrote) contributed a number of poems to the weekly newspaper *The Nation*, which was a vehicle of the Young Ireland movement. She was a trenchant critic of British policy during the Famine years and her poetry captures her anger and despair at the loss of life in Ireland (see introductory page). [Source: National Library of Ireland]

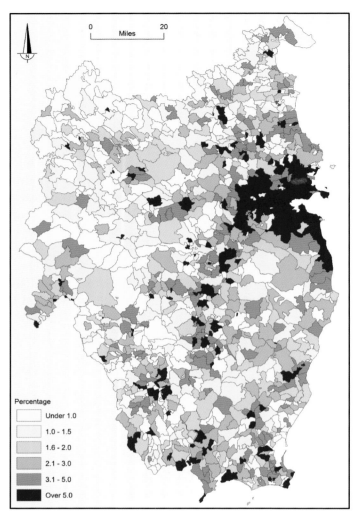

Fig. 2 PERCENTAGE OF FAMILIES LIVING IN FIRST- CLASS HOUSES IN 1841. The first-class house was mainly made up of landlord and gentry big houses, very substantial farmhouses, mill-owner residences and substantial townhouses along main streets or in estate villages. In this map, which identifies the percentage of first- class houses at above 3%, one can track from north to south the villas in Carlingford Bay, the big houses and demesnes around Drogheda and the Boyne Valley as far as Trim. The Dublin hinterland dominates, with very substantial residences of landlords and well-to-do commercial and professional classes and at the core of industrial villages along the Liffey Valley at Lucan, Celbridge and Leixlip. Further west, Edenderry and the Grand Canal had their own attractions. Along the east coast, there are demesnes and estate villages around Powerscourt, Enniskerry and Kilruddery. Further to the southeast, coastal vistas still attract their share of big houses while south Wexford contains both its old, often thatched and very substantial farmhouses as well as demesne landscapes around villages like Arthurstown. A second major area of first-class houses – of gentry, strong farmers and millers – extends down the Barrow and Nore valleys by Kilcullen, Athy, Carlow and Kilkenny. The northwest counties of Leinster have the lowest percentage of big houses, apart from the lakeland country northwest of Mullingar. It is the boggy, hummocky worlds of northwest Leinster and its Ulster borderlands which contain less than 1% of houses in the first classes.

public institutions.[3] As is widely known, there were very significant regional and social variations in the annual intensity of famine conditions and mortalities. Excess mortality was lower in Leinster than in any of the provinces – but again this varied from the lowest levels along the eastern seaboard counties from Louth through to Wicklow – as against excess mortality levels in Longford and King's County, which were above the national average. Queen's County, Carlow, Meath and indeed Wex-

ford also show very substantial famine-related deaths. Even in this relatively wealthy province, vulnerabilities to potato failures and famine-related diseases varied substantially. It was a deeply stratified society: 23.7% of Leinster's families lived in fourth-class houses in 1841 and 39.0% in the two-roomed mud cabins classified as third class.[4] Leinster was a land of great extremes – poverty and wealth juxtaposed, 'mud cabins and fat cattle',[5] landlords with elegant lifestyles and the desperate poor scavenging and begging for food (see Peter Connell, pp. 334–340). And its many urban slums and cabin suburbs were full of undernourished and poorly housed communities.

Unlike Connacht and Ulster – both dominated by smaller farms – Leinster and Munster display a bi-modal distribution of farm sizes. Close on one-fourth of Leinster's holdings were between one and five acres. Kildare heads the list with 30.2% in this category, closely followed by Louth, Dublin and King's County. On the other hand two-fifths (43.8%) of farms were over fifteen acres in size. County Wicklow had 63.3% in this category, Wexford 55.9%, Westmeath 54.3%, Kilkenny 52.7% and Carlow 52.5%.[6] Apart altogether from a wealthy landlord class, Leinster had a cohort of well-to-do comfortable farmers – over a quarter held farms of over twenty acres. Conscious of their status, not subdividing their farms and marrying later than in any other province, these families were either oriented to a mixed cattle and tillage economy in the south or emphatically geared to fat cattle production in the lush grasslands of the central lowlands. But both of these rural societies were propped up by smallholding farmer-labourers and a vast landless labouring class – a classic interweaving of two economies. One economy was either geared to commercial cattle production in Dublin's shadow or geared to grain and other crop production in the deeply urbanised south with its ancillary trades and industries. The other economy was geared to a localised subsistence and labouring lifestyle, increasingly dependent on the potato (and a little milk). Even in the rich county of Kilkenny 'where beans, barley and oaten bread had been common, labourers and their families had switched over to potatoes'[7] as early as 1800. The failures of the potato and the spread of epidemic diseases exposed the vulnerability of small farmers, cottiers and labourers – as well as the poor of both moorland, bogland, roadside and canal edges and the slums, backlanes and cabin suburbs in the province's cities and towns.

The tragedy of the Great Famine in Leinster provides a kind of microcosm of what happened on the island as a whole. The most desperate conditions were in its western areas and the least among its east coast communities. The most devastating consequences of the Famine were exhibited in an arc stretching from its northwestern borders with Ulster and Connacht – involving all of County Long-

Fig. 3  Stradbally Hall.  A two-storey house built in 1772, Stradbally Hall was remodelled in the 1860s in the Italianate style. It was described in the early 1840s as a handsome mansion adjoining a well-embellished demesne that included the ancient castle of the O'Mores of Laois. It has been the chief seat of the Cosby family in Queen's County since the mid-sixteenth century, a family that stubbornly and determinedly defended their landed interests up to and including the years of the Land League. Stradbally was a landlord town and its relief committee reported on 27 June 1846 that the poorer classes of the town and its vicinity 'are supplied with plenty of Indian meal. Oatmeal was sold at the rate of four shillings per hundred weight and given out at half price, and gratis according to the needs of the recipients.' [Photo: Frank Coyne]

ford and parts of north County Meath and Louth and curving southwards along its western border through King's and (part of) Queen's Counties and also including parts of County Kilkenny. A second order of devastation extends in a broad belt from the rest of County Meath and Westmeath in the north Midlands southwards via the eastern half of Queen's County, Kildare, Kilkenny and Carlow to Wexford. The most prosperous counties less devastated in the Famine stretched along the east coast from Louth to Wicklow. Finally, the Dublin city region presents a very complex face to the realities of the Famine. Regions of the city and its suburbs remained unaffected by its reach and life went on as comfortably as usual. In contrast, its western inner city communities suffered even more. But Dublin was also the scene of much immigration by desperate migrants from the stricken west, seeking succour in its two union workhouses (especially the North Dublin Union)[8] or scrambling to get a boat and escape the stricken land. It also was to witness 'thousands of destitute persons sleeping out on the streets; partly as a consequence of English Poor Law unions sending back Irish emigrants'.[9]

In 1841, farms progressively diminished in size as one moved from east to west Leinster. In the broken hummocky lands of north Meath, much of Longford, King's and the western half of Queen's, Poor Law valuations per head were generally lower – an indicator of fewer rural comforts. The intermixture of good land and bogland created a mosaic of mixed-cum-arable farming on smaller holdings and the intensification of squatting on bogland edges and commons by a growing and impoverished stratum in the population.[10] Consequently, population pressures were greater here than further east. Unlike Westmeath and Kildare, full of resident proprietors, absenteeism was a feature of the landlord culture further west – most conspicuously in County Longford – and eviction rates were also higher (see Ciarán Reilly below). A proto-industrial culture was also a feature of north and western Louth and Longford and especially in the two Meaths. But such cottage industries were on the retreat as was cloth manufacturing in a city like Kilkenny – adding to levels of unemployment and underdevelopment there (see Jonny Geber below). The peripheral nature of these fringe areas of Leinster is also suggested by the movement of harvest labourers – not only from Connacht, but also from these western counties – to work in

327

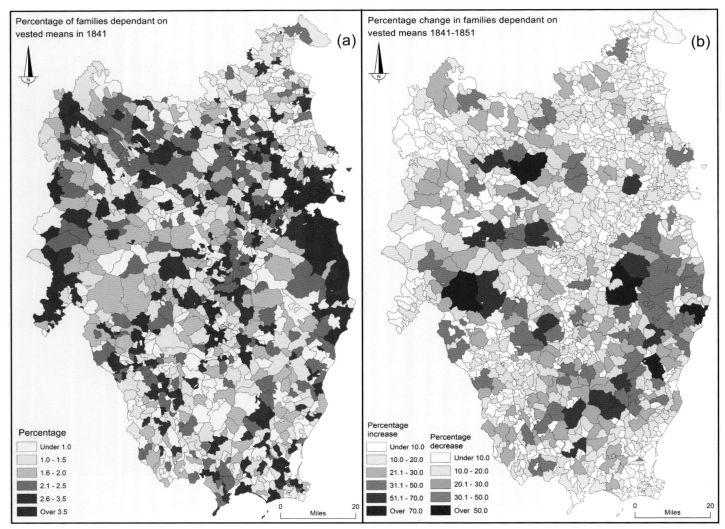

Figs. 4(a) and 4(b) PERCENTAGE OF FAMILIES DEPENDENT ON VESTED MEANS IN 1841 AND PERCENTAGE CHANGE IN THIS CLASS BY 1851. 'Vested means' includes people of independent means, members of professions and, what is sometimes forgotten, farmers holding 50 acres or more. Located here are big farmers in the north midlands, especially in south County Meath, Westmeath and parts of Longford (+2.6% of all families). Likewise, it identifies the large sheep farms on each side of Slieve Bloom and across the Wicklows and the Leinster chain. It is important to note that the 1841 and 1851 methodologies for identifying bigger farms differ. In 1841, the census-makers measured the areas of 'arable' (i.e. farmed) vis-à-vis 'uncultivated' land from the maps of the Ordnance Survey, whereas these were taken from the Agricultural Statistics in 1851. Poor land adjacent to farms previously classified as 'uncultivated land' were now correctly included as integral components of farms. Consequently, Figure 4b exaggerates somewhat the increase of the 'vested interest/big farmer' class in the Leinster chain stretching from the Dublin Mountains south to Mount Brandon and the Blackstairs. However, Figure 4b clearly emphasises how this class of strong farmers (with 30–40 acres) had expanded considerably their farm sizes by 1851 at the expense of the now absent smallholding tillage farmers. It is clear that the Famine had shaken the confidence (and incomes) of people of independent means all around Dublin and Carlingford Bay as well as on the outskirts of towns such as Birr, Longford and Wexford. Hence, the reductions in their distribution.

'saving' the corn and potatoes in the richer counties to the east.[11] Given these conditions, it was not surprising that higher excess famine deaths characterised this zone. Emigration levels were even greater. For example, smallholders with farms valued between £4 and £6 deserted their homes and sought new lands.[12] Longford was the leading county in this respect, and the core of the region of the highest levels of emigration, which included the adjacent counties of Connacht and Ulster.

The rest of inland Leinster comprised two very contrasting regions of commercialised farming. The north Midlands centred on Meath, Kildare and much of Westmeath was a region of demesnes, big grazier farms and large enclosed fields, fattening cattle for the Dublin or English markets. Here was the best land in Ireland in a region of low urbanisation. In contrast, in what was economically, perhaps, the strongest region in Ireland, came the arable, mixed-farming lands of south Leinster stretching from Queen's County to Wexford and including most of Kilkenny, south Kildare and Carlow. This was a zone of deeply rooted and stratified rural communities, living in well-furnished lands with substantial farmhouses and good barns, bespeaking a long settled land. These were communities characterised by impartible inheritance and the outmigration of non-inheriting sons and non-dowried daughters either overseas or to the strong local towns – with their milling, brewing and distillery industries. Large smallholding, artisan and labouring classes characterised both these farming regions. Labour-intensive spade cultivation of grain crops was not only a feature of the southern

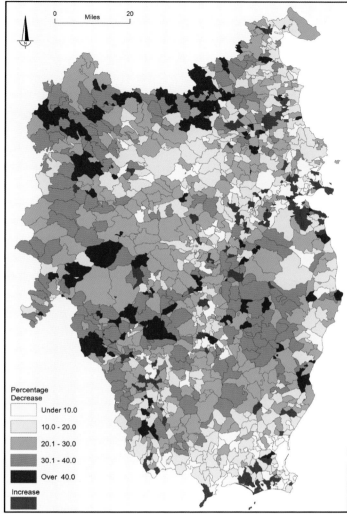

Fig. 5 PERCENTAGE DECLINE IN POPULATION 1841–51. Although the intensive arable communities of Louth suffered losses of population, these were much lower than in the Kells–Oldcastle region of County Meath and much of County Longford, especially from Granard south to Kilglass, both of which suffered high mortalities and high out-migration. Heavy declines also characterise the western half of Westmeath, west Offaly and especially on each side of the Slieve Bloom–Rosenallis region as well as the Rathdowney–Fartagh area on the Laois/Kilkenny borders. Upland Kilkenny especially and Castlecomer and upland County Wicklow also saw at least one-third of a disappearance. Further along the flanks of the Wicklows and all bogland margins saw at least one-quarter of a loss. In contrast, the sturdy arable counties of south Wexford weathered the plague more successfully as did strong farming communities along the Barrow Valley. Mortalities in these zones were class-based amongst the squatter settlements and cabin suburbs. The contrasting fortunes of Leinster counties is most emphasised in parishes which record a population increase. Here urban and port-city influences are striking – around Kilkenny city, Dundalk and Drogheda – but squatter settlement on common lands around Dundalk is a feature. The Dublin hinterland has pronounced increases – in a ring from Howth around to Rathfarnham through to Stillorgan. 'Refugee' settlements also bolstered the population of small parishes along the roads to Dublin. Elsewhere, some villages like Borris-in-Ossory also increased their population in the midst of population decline.

counties but also helped feed the mills along the north Leinster rivers, especially along the Boyne.[13] However, when the potato failed and failed again, the intertwining and mutual dependence of these various strata in these communities collapsed. Levels of evictions during the Famine years were higher in the southern zone than the northern Midlands. Yet it is striking to note that excess mortality levels at around 8% in County Meath were high-

er than in County Donegal (see Peter Connell below). More dramatic than the roadside clustering in County Meath was the way poor 'refugees from the countryside had overwhelmed the outskirts of towns and villages especially those with defunct burgher or church lands. Inland towns such as Ardee, Navan, Trim and Kildare – the historic guardians of the Pale – were particularly affected.'[14] Such towns were dominated by agricultural labourers living in single-room cabins. In this prosperous pastoral zone, many of its poor withered in the face of famine conditions. Likewise, excess mortality levels have probably been underestimated in the south Leinster zone. For example, it is striking that right throughout the Famine years from 1847 to 1850, Wexford witnessed consistently high mortality levels and also formed part of a more extensive southeastern region long attuned to emigration overseas.[15]

The lowest Famine death-rates occurred along the eastern coastal counties of Leinster (and also included Counties Down and Londonderry in the north). Centred on the Dublin metropolitan region and county as well as the counties of Louth and Wicklow, this was a zone where dependence on agriculture was less, where commercial and industrial activities were pronounced and where incomes from 'other pursuits', e.g. gentry rentals, independent means and other professional practices, were higher than in the rest of the province. As Tom Jones Hughes notes, 'the Louth plain through north County Dublin to north Wicklow, an area which had been closely settled by a farming community from early times . . . [was] distinguished by the fact that the proportion of improved land that was devoted to permanent pasture was among the lowest in the country'.[16] This reflected the intensity of arable – mainly barley – and garden cultivation by mainly farmers of six to thirty acres using the hand implements of spade and sickle or scythe in conjunction with a large cottier labourer element benefiting from conacre facilities. Inshore fishing was also a feature of these counties – and also involved some inland refugees. It was these parishes in easy reach of the coast and a countryside of varied cultivation and close settlement which recorded population losses well below the national and indeed provincial averages. However, in the upland Wicklows, especially on its southwestern flanks, population losses were greater. This was a zone where many poor labourers had long competed for wages and potato plots, colonising high up the mountain sides. In summer, such families went begging or survived on cabbage and nettles.[17] The number of these travelling poor grew as famine conditions worsened. Some towns were also very vulnerable to the famine crisis – pre-Famine Arklow had 1,200 destitute families out of a total population of 3,000 and Baltinglass had its share of impoverished slum-dwellers.[18] When the famine struck, Wicklow's workhouses came to be dominated by the unemployed former servants, labourers, charwomen, knit-

Fig. 6 Cherry Orchard is the name of the pauper graveyard in Enniscorthy town. As many as 1,440 died in the Enniscorthy workhouse during the Famine decade (721 male and 719 female), somewhat less than the 1,896 inmates who died in the larger New Ross workhouse. A quarter of all County Wexford's deaths occurred in Enniscorthy but a far greater proportion (42% of all Wexford hospital deaths from fever) died in its fever hospital (968 comprising 459 males and 509 females). One in every seven patients in Enniscorthy fever hospital died in these Famine years. Overall, the population of Enniscorthy Union declined by 17.2% — from 65,031 to 53,862 – during the Famine decade. [Photo: William J. Smyth]

ters and, most noticeably, redundant artisans.[19] Yet the contrasts with even the neighbouring counties of Wexford and Carlow were quite sharp. At the height of the Famine in 1848–49, none of Wicklow's unions provided outdoor relief for more than 4% of their populations. In Enniscorthy, the figure was 12%.[20] And Wicklow's mortality levels from infectious diseases paled in comparison with their deadly effects in the unions of the west of Ireland.

Early Victorian Dublin – like much of Leinster – was a society of great extremes. The middle and upper classes lived in fine townhouses while the poor congregated in the west of the city. The elegance of its magnificent squares contrasted with the squalor of the Liberties, the old congested quarter outside the city wall. With its noxious industries, small traders and huxters, this was the receiving area for so many poor refugees fleeing the countryside.[21] Even before the Famine conditions were appalling in these neglected, filthy tenement streets, alleyways and courtyards where contagious diseases flourished. In contrast, the

**Table 1.** Mortality rates from contagious diseases 1851 census of population

| Census ranking of streets | Deaths per thousand people | | |
|---|---|---|---|
| | Cholera | Fever | Consumption |
| 1st Class private: south | 0.9 | 3.4 | 12.3 |
| 1st Class private: north | 1.3 | 2 | 11.8 |
| 2nd Class private: south | 4.5 | 7 | 21.1 |
| 2nd Class private: north | 4.1 | 7.6 | 18.8 |
| 1st Class shop: south | 3.3 | 4.8 | 12.8 |
| 1st Class shop: north | 3.3 | 2.8 | 17.8 |
| 2nd Class shop: south | 9.5 | 9.5 | 28.5 |
| 2nd Class shop: north | 6.3 | 7.7 | 28.5 |
| 3rd Class shop: south | 8.8 | 11.8 | 31.5 |
| 3rd Class shop: north | 8.1 | 12.2 | 33.3 |
| Mixed Streets: south | 6.1 | 8.6 | 23.8 |
| Mixed Streets: north | 6.4 | 7.4 | 23.7 |

Source: J.H. Martin in W.J. Smyth and Kevin Whelan (eds), *Common Ground: Essays on the Historical Geography of Ireland* (Cork, 1988).

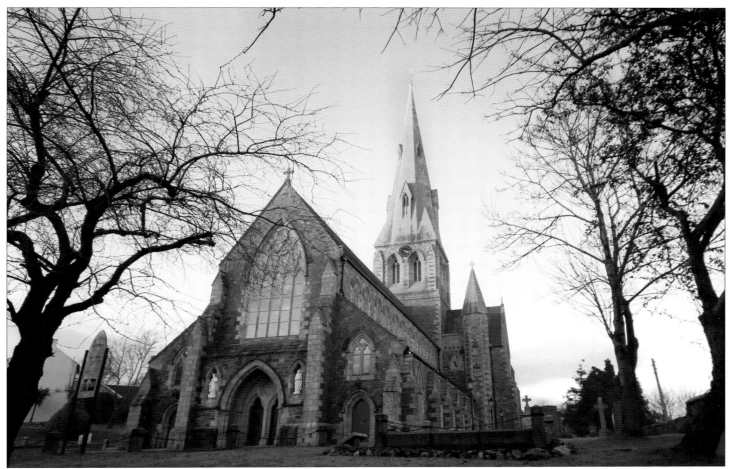

Fig. 7a Pugin's Catholic cathedral in Enniscorthy, County Wexford, which was opened in 1846. Fig. 7b (below) Its colourful interior. Building work continued on the cathedral during 1847, one of the worst years of the Famine. The construction of the cathedral during the Famine raises many questions about the nature of Irish society. As Colm Tóibín explains: 'The story of the cathedral and those who subscribed to it makes clear to us that Catholic society in Ireland in the 1840s was graded and complex, that to suggest that it was merely England or Irish landlords who stood by while Ireland starved is to miss the point. An entire class of Catholics survived the Famine; many, indeed, improved their prospects as a result of it, and this legacy may be more difficult for us to deal with in Ireland now than the legacy of those who died or emigrated'. (See Colm Tóibín, *The Irish Famine* [London, 1999], pp. 12–15.) [Photos: Frank Coyne]

splendid suburbs of the southeast were occupied by nobility, gentry and members of the professions while its wealthy northeastern section was dominated by merchants and officials. In 1846, the pawnbrokers saw a rush by the poor to pawn goods for either food or the price of a boat ticket. By 1847 and 1848 even this trade had declined as famine conditions worsened.[22] Famine conditions were also to intensify and deepen class contrasts and destinies across the city. By 1850–51 people living in insanitary and crowded third-class streets in the city were eight times as likely to die of cholera, four times of fever and three times of 'consumption' as those resident in first-class private dwellings on the south side of the city (see Table 1).[23] For the decade 1841 to 1851, 69.0% of all recorded deaths in the city occurred between 1846 and 1851 while in Dublin's public institutions the proportion is 71.6%.[24] If the recorded mortality levels in 1845 are assumed to carry through for

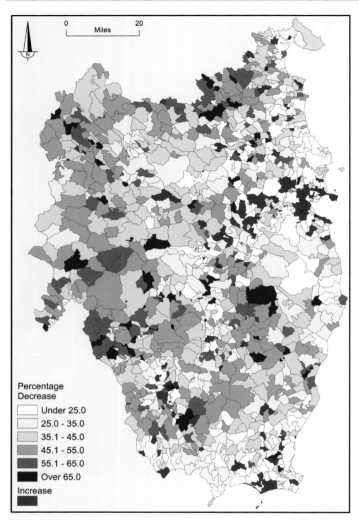

Percentage
Decrease

☐ Under 25.0
☐ 25.0 - 35.0
☐ 35.1 - 45.0
☐ 45.1 - 55.0
☐ 55.1 - 65.0
■ Over 65.0
Increase

Fig. 8 (left) THE PERCENTAGE CHANGE IN THE DISTRIBUTION OF CHILDREN UNDER FIVE YEARS OF AGE BETWEEN 1841 AND 1851. This map strikingly mirrors the overall pattern of population decline and is indeed a very strong measure of the distribution of Famine-related mortalities. The upland parishes of Wicklow and north Wexford, from Donaghmore to Carnew, the Walsh Hills parishes from Callan across to Inistioge and Graiguenamanagh in Kilkenny and parishes such as St Mullins and Killann on the Carlow/Wexford border lost at least half of this young cohort. Similar losses – pointing to deeply traumatised and divided communities – were experienced in the Castlecomer region and in south Laois from Rathdowney towards Abbeyleix as well as the northern and western flanks of the province stretching from upland parishes on each side of Slieve Bloom through the mixed-farming bogland parishes of Westmeath and Longford as well as the Kells–Nobber region in north County Meath. The remaining pattern is highly uneven with adjacent parishes characterised by very different destinies and stories. However, the demographic vitality of strong farming communities of central Kilkenny, south Wexford, the Barrow and scenic valleys and parts of east Meath is clear, as is the fact that County Dublin suffered less. The most striking contrast occurs where there are increases. In many respects, these latter communities mirror the parishes characterised by an increase, as in south Wexford, around the leading towns with the Dublin hinterland and roads leading into the city augmented by in-migration from surrounding counties.

ever, the ratio of famine deaths to emigrant numbers is very different to, for example, Connacht. It is probable that somewhat less than one-third of a million people left the twelve counties of the province during the Famine years; excess famine deaths may have exceeded 140,000. Leinster was to experience one person dying from famine-related causes to *c*.2.4 persons emigrating. In sharp contrast, for every three persons dying from famine conditions in Connacht, only two managed to emigrate. Profound differences characterised the fate of communities with sharply diverging capacities to withstand the horrors of potato failures, starvation and disease.

each year from 1846 to 1850, the resultant proportion of 'excess' deaths for civic districts in the city comes to 24.4% and reaches 34.4% in public institutions. Overall, given a city population of 232,726 in 1841, this suggests excess famine deaths of less than 5% – at the bottom end of the national pattern of fatalities.[25]

Overall, it is likely that Leinster lost just over 20% of its 1845 population during the Famine years. How-

Fig. 9 (right) VALUATION OF DUBLIN CITY C. 1830. This composite valuation map of pre-Famine Dublin city (*c*.1830) – compiled by John Martin – shows two V-shaped high value (+£50) sectors extending north/northeast and south/southeast from the then Carlisle (later O'Connell) Bridge. Adjacent to the wealthiest sectors were comfortable middle-class streets in the £30-£50 bracket. In contrast, to the west of the city and in the eastern docklands, the poorest areas with the lowest valuations (below £10 and £20) predominated. The contrast between the wealthiest and poorest residential districts had sharpened further by 1850. During the Famine years, deaths from cholera, fever and consumption were three to four times more likely to occur amongst the inhabitants of the poorer wards and streets.

River Liffey

Mountjoy Square

Trinity College

St.Stephen's Green

House valuation in £

■ 50 and Over
☐ 30 - 49.9
☐ 20 - 29.9
☐ 10 - 19.9
☐ Under 10

J.H. Martin *Common Ground* CUP 1988

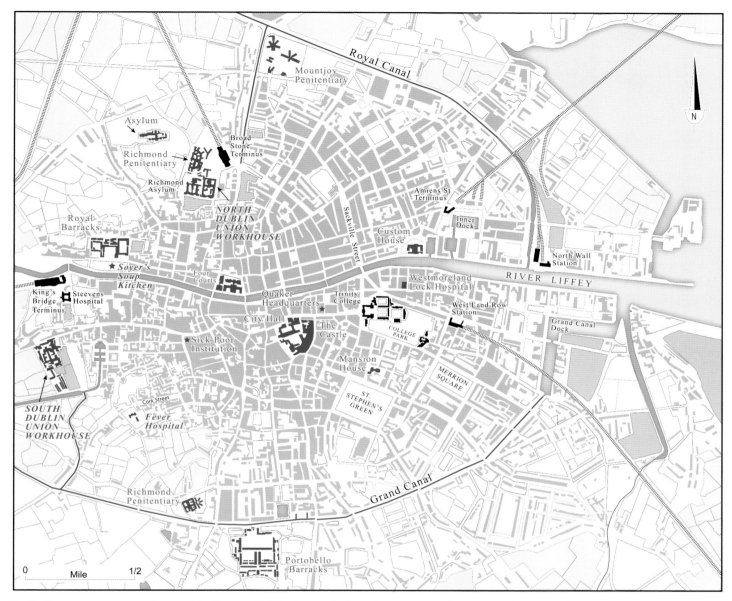

Fig. 10 DUBLIN CITY DURING THE FAMINE. After London, Dublin city was the key administrative and decision-making centre for all aspects of the Famine island-wide. Here were the residences of the Lord Lieutenant and the officers of the Crown in Ireland, the offices of the Poor Law Commission, the Relief Commission, the Board of Works and the Central Board of Health. Dublin Castle was at the heart of this centralising authority, ensuring the detailed supervision, inspection and auditing of every aspect of relief, whether exercised by the Office of Public Works, relief committees or the Poor Law unions. Within the city, two unions were established with the River Liffey as the boundary between the North Dublin and South Dublin Unions, located on the poorer northwestern and southwestern edges of the built-up area. The 1841 city population of the North Dublin Union numbered 97,032 persons, but the union territory also extended into eight DEDs encircling the city from Blanchardstown to Howth, making for a total union population of 123,095. The 1841 city population of the South Dublin Union was 135,694, but again this union included a ring of settlements and boroughs from Clondalkin to Whitechurch and comprised a total population of 178,408. The South Dublin workhouse made use of the Old Foundling Hospital and the original City of Dublin workhouse dating from 1703. The cost of rebuilding and adaptations came to over £10,000 to house an inmate population of 2,000. It opened on 24 April 1840. The North Dublin Union took over the House of Industry on North Brunswick Street, which had been established as a private charity but it had long depended on government funding. Refurbishment costs to house 2,000 inmates came to £8,000 and it was opened on 4 May 1840. As famine conditions intensified in 1847, the south city Fever Hospital in Cork Street became crowded and another house was hired nearby while temporary fever sheds were erected at Kilmainham. The North Dublin Union obtained premises in Glasnevin for a fever hospital. Elsewhere, in 1847 a French chef, Alexis Soyer, opened his famous model soup kitchen in front of the Royal (later Collins) Barracks. Eventually, this kitchen was given to the South Union and installed in a house in Dolphin's Barn. By late 1847, the capacity of both workhouses had been increased to house up to 4,000 inmates, reflecting not only levels of distress in the poorer western areas of the city but also both the influx of destitute people from the south and west of Ireland as well as the reflux movement of emigrants forcefully returned to the North Wall quays from Liverpool and other British cities. As many as 60,000 of the often migrant poor were in receipt of outdoor relief at the height of the city's famine crisis in 1848–49. Nevertheless, it should be emphasised that Dublin city and its unions never had to face the scale of the famine horrors, disasters experienced in Connacht and Munster. The death rate in the North Dublin Union was the equivalent of 4.9% of its 1841 population, while that in the South Dublin Union was 2.9%. As Cormac Ó Gráda and Timothy Guinnane have confirmed ('Mortality in the North Dublin Union during the Great Famine', *Economic History Review*, 55.(3), 2002, pp. 487–506), death rates in the North Dublin Union were concentrated amongst the young children, especially those who entered the workhouse alone and those who had originated from the south and west and had managed to make their way to Dublin.

# County Meath during the Famine

## Peter Connell

You see rich meadows and luxuriant fields of potatoes, wheat and oats in every direction and still the
people are starving – 'starving' they say 'in the
midst of plenty'. There is something wrong in the
organization of Society, but to set it right is the difficulty.[1]

In the summer of 1836 John O'Donovan spent six weeks in
Meath travelling around the county investigating the
orthography of names to be used in the six-inch-to-the-mile
Ordnance Survey maps. O'Donovan's letters contain little
social commentary. The quotation above from a letter written in Kells on 14 July is a striking exception and encapsu-
lates the observations of a number of visitors to the county
in the pre-Famine years on the stark contrasts between the
evident wealth of the countryside and the shocking deprivation of much of its population. The marginalised poor
lived hidden in clusters on the edges of big fields of grass

and corn, behind high hedges, in huddled cabins along the
roadsides and in the squalid suburbs and lanes of the county's towns. Their poverty had nothing to do with distance
from markets or the poor quality of land or 'overpopulation'. Outside of County Dublin, Meath had the highest
Poor Law valuation per head of population in the country.
The county's agriculture was closely integrated with both
national and international markets for its produce. Over
5,000 tons of corn was sent from Navan to Drogheda each
year, much of it for export to England and Scotland. A further 1,000 tons of corn were sent to Dublin together with
10,000 pigs and 27,000 sheep and lambs. Meath's cattle, destined for Dublin butchers or the growing live export trade,
numbered 100,000 on the eve of the Famine and were valued at £700,000. 80% of the county's wealth in the form of
livestock was owned by 2,500 grazier families who occupied most of the best land and represented just 7% of the
population in 1841.

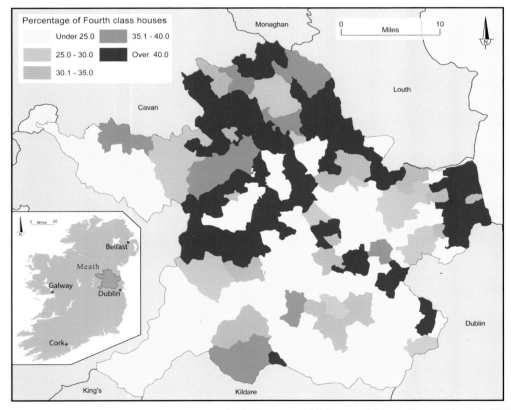

### IMPOVERISHED FAMILIES

At the bottom of the social pyra-
mid, 11,700 families lived in
fourth-class housing, one-roomed
mud cabins as defined in the 1841
Census. Along with County Louth,
this represented the highest proportion of cabin dwellers in the
population in Leinster. Even before
the partial failure of the potato
crop in the autumn of 1845, the
position of these impoverished
families had been progressively
marginalised by rising conacre
rents for land on which to grow
their potatoes, by falling demand
for their labour as some commercial farmers switched from labour
intensive tillage to capital intensive livestock and by the drastic
decline in the domestic linen
industry from the 1820s onwards.
Figure 1 shows that cabin dwellers
made up over 40% of the population across much of the north of
the county, also in a band of
parishes west of Navan and

Fig. 1 DISTRIBUTION OF FOURTH-CLASS HOUSES IN 1841. The nature of living conditions in County Meath in 1841
– as measured by its housing patterns – presents a highly variegated picture. In some of the wealthier parishes
of the southeast – from Navan south to Dunboyne – and in its two western 'peninsular' areas, the percentage
of one-roomed mud-walled cabins falls below 25%. Yet both along the narrow seafront from Colp to Stamullen
and in much of the northern half of the country (including the parishes of Moybolgue, Kilskeer, Girley and
Burry) and extending south to Rathmoylyan and Rathcore, over 40% of houses were in this category – the
dwellings of the very poorest in the county.

334

towards the town of Kells, and in a strip of coastal parishes from Drogheda south to the Dublin border. It is in the first two of these regions, together with the Oldcastle area in the west of the county, where the Famine had its most devastating impact. This is the context in which the Famine evolved in the county from the autumn of 1845.

The vulnerability of Meath's labouring poor and the paucity of their resources, particularly in the areas of the county described above, is evident by how quickly their circumstances deteriorated once the potato crop partially failed in the autumn of 1845. As early as the first week of February 1846 the scale of the crisis in north Meath was evident. Along the Cavan border in the parish of Moybolgue, one-third of the population were described as being 'in great distress'. In the parish of Kilskeer, west of Kells, half the population was described as being 'in a state bordering on actual destitution'.[2] In the parishes of Girley and Burry, near Kells, another 900 out of a population of 2,300 were destitute. The relief committee reported that 'families had for some time been living on potatoes thrown out into the ditches as too bad for any use, even for pigs'.[3]

From the spring of 1846 right through to 1849 the town of Kells was at the eye of the Famine in Meath. In 1847 three-quarters of the land within the hinterland of the town was given over to grazing. So, while the suburbs of the town of Kells were described as consisting of cabins of single rooms, some home to a couple of families, a huge swathe of land to the east of the town – Headfort demesne, Grange glebe, Rossmeen and Fyanstown – consisting of 2,700 acres of prime agricultural land, had a population of just 118. As early as February 1846 the Deputy Lieutenant for the county identified 3,000 people as destitute in the Kells area, with 1,000 unemployed and seeking work. In March Rev. Nicholas McEvoy, the Roman Catholic parish priest of Kells, wrote to the Relief Commissioners, pleading for relief and stating that 'many many of my people are already fainting for want of food'. McEvoy identified the lack of employment as critical, commenting that 'even agriculture affords a very limited source of employment in consequence of the vast tracts of grass ground by which we are in all directions surrounded'.[4]

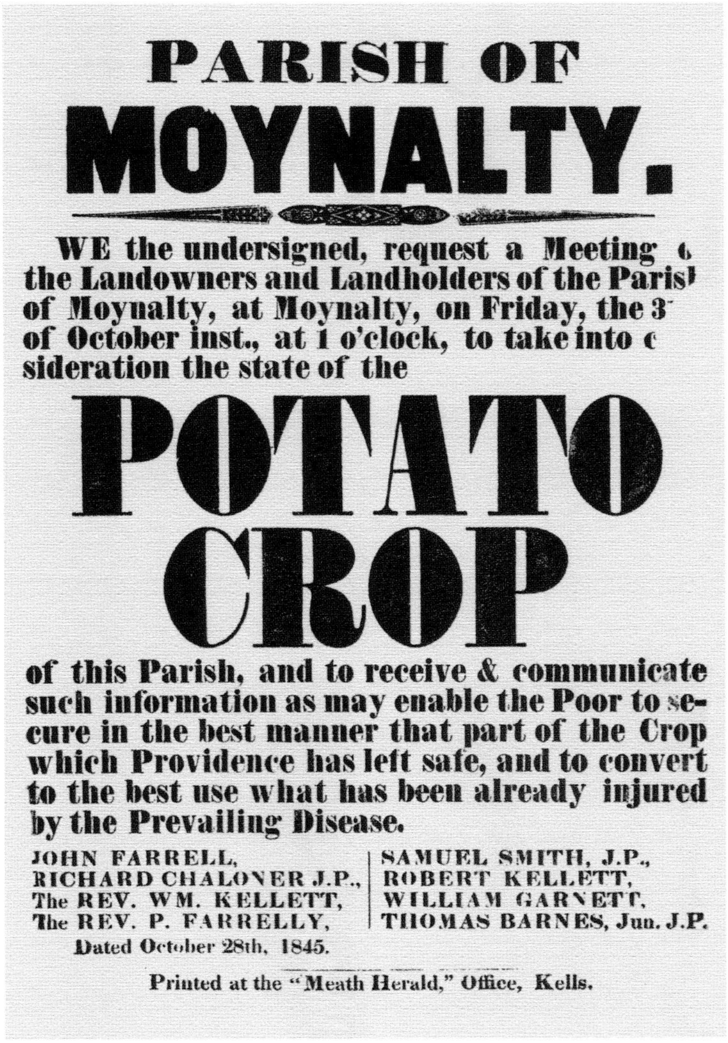

PARISH OF

MOYNALTY.

WE the undersigned, request a Meeting o the Landowners and Landholders of the Paris of Moynalty, at Moynalty, on Friday, the 3 of October inst., at 1 o'clock, to take into c sideration the state of the

POTATO

CROP

of this Parish, and to receive & communicate such information as may enable the Poor to secure in the best manner that part of the Crop which Providence has left safe, and to convert to the best use what has been already injured by the Prevailing Disease.

JOHN FARRELL,
RICHARD CHALONER J.P.,
The REV. WM. KELLETT,
The REV. P. FARRELLY,

SAMUEL SMITH, J.P.,
ROBERT KELLETT,
WILLIAM GARNETT,
THOMAS BARNES, Jun. J.P.

Dated October 28th, 1845.

Printed at the "Meath Herald," Office, Kells.

Fig. 2 Notice of a meeting at Moynalty to discuss the failure of the potato crop, 28 October 1845.

## INCREASING DISTRESS

As conditions deteriorated later in the year the editor of the *Meath Herald*, published in Kells, remarked:

> Our town is becoming one entire Bazaar of Beggars. Daily and hourly are they increasing. Scores of famished women and children prowling about from morning until night, from door to door shivering with cold – attacking every individual that may chance to come into the town on any business whatever, with wailings for relief to save them from perishing.[5]

Conditions in Navan, where over 60% of the housing stock consisted of one-roomed mud cabins, deteriorated rapidly through 1846. With the workhouse in the town in an overcrowded condition the local relief committee was feeding 2,000 people. While more successful in collecting subscriptions than the Kells committee, the secretary reported that 'this is one of the poorest and most destitute districts in this part of Ireland'.[6]

Reflecting the fact that, apart from the town of Navan, distress was largely confined to the north and west of the county in early 1846, most local famine relief committees up to the summer of that year were located in this region. In total about £2,200 was raised in subscriptions between March and August with a further £1,500 contributed by the Central Relief Committee. By the end of 1846, with the complete failure of that season's potato crop confirmed, a whole raft of new committees were established so that by the end of the year fifty-one were in regular correspondence with the Central Relief Committee.

Based on this correspondence it is apparent that some

committees were more effective than others. Indeed the Inspecting Officer for the county claimed that 'many relief committees have become worse than useless, one individual (or two) obtaining such ascendancy that the others from indolence or intimidation absent themselves'.[7] Despite the fact that some committees had small memberships and may have been dominated by local dignitaries, they nevertheless raised about £7,000 in subscriptions between October 1846 and March 1847 and received over £6,000 in funding from the Central Relief Committee. All the evidence suggests that during these months, often driven by Catholic and Protestant clergy working together, these committees sustained thousands of families and saved them from starvation.

With distress spreading beyond the north and west of the county, relief committees were set up for the first time in the sparsely settled parishes of southeast Meath where landless labourers constituted a significant proportion of the population. In the midst of a countryside dominated by large grazing farms, the Kilmessan committee described the area as 'a wretchedly poor one . . . we have three wretched villages to look after'.[8] From Drumconrath on the Louth border where over 2,500 were being fed in March 1847 and with great distress prevailing in the neighbourhood, to Athboy in the southwest where 'there is an immense and very poor population in most instances on the estates of proprietors contributing nothing to the relief funds and leaving . . . the poor on their properties to starve', relief committees struggled to meet the demands for food.[9] The response of landlords to appeals for subscriptions was mixed. Resident landlords such as J.L.W. Naper of Loughcrew, John Preston of Bellinter near Navan and Lambert Disney of Clifton Lodge near Athboy are amongst many listed in the subscription lists returned to the Central Relief Committee. On the other hand, absentees such as Charles P. Leslie, MP for Monaghan, who owned land on the outskirts of Trim, was castigated by the local committee for failing to contribute to its fund. It urged his agent to 'come and be witnesses to an amount of wretchedness unparalleled'.[10]

## GOVERNMENT RESPONSE

Through the autumn of 1846 and into the spring of 1847 public works, together with the assistance to local relief committees for the purchase of food, represented the main government response to the deepening crisis. From 4,500 in early November 1846, numbers employed on schemes in the county climbed to over 17,000 in mid-March 1847 before numbers fell away as all schemes were closed down by June. Grand Juries in County Meath appear to have been particularly effective in applying for funding for schemes. At its peak in March 1847 almost a quarter of Meath's workforce, as enumerated in the 1841 Census, were employed on public works schemes, ranking the county second to Long-

ford in Leinster in this regard and well ahead of neighbouring counties such as Louth (14%), Westmeath (16%) and Monaghan (10.5%). 60% of the employment was concentrated in the four northern baronies of Kells Lower, Kells Upper, Morgallion and Slane Lower. In the barony of Kells Upper, west of the town of Kells, in February £730 per week was being paid in wages to 4,000 people employed on twenty-one different schemes. This partly reflected levels of distress in this region but, probably more significantly, the effective lobbying of local landed proprietors and prominent individuals involved in local relief committees.

Notwithstanding the relatively high levels of employment available through these schemes, given escalating food prices, the inadequate level of wages was a recurring issue in much of the relief committee correspondence. Three prominent landlords on the Moynalty Relief Committee wrote that the labourer earning the 10d per day wage available in their area 'even supposing he can work six days in each week and be blessed with uninterrupted good health, he cannot possibly support himself and his family. We find that many in such circumstances are perishing.'[11] Robert Skelly, secretary of the Navan committee, argued that at 10d per day a family of five was obliged to live on 21oz of the cheapest meal per day, an allowance well below that available in the workhouse.[12]

The switch in government policy from providing relief via public works to the direct supply of food via soup kitchens in the spring of 1847 ultimately succeeded in feeding tens of thousands of people in the county during the summer of 1847. As elsewhere in the country, though, the public works were run down much more quickly than the new network of soup kitchens could be established. Almost 10,000 were discharged from schemes in March and early April, yet across most of the Kells and Oldcastle Poor Law unions the funding of soup kitchens did not commence until late April. The closing of the public works schemes exacerbated the crisis in employment for agricultural labourers. The vice-lieutenant, Robert Fowler, writing from Rathmolyon in the southwest of the county in March, reported that farmers were employing fewer labourers than in previous years as few potatoes were being planted and corn was being scattered on the ground and ploughed in, rather than being dug in using spades.

## DEPENDENCE ON SOUP KITCHENS

Between April and August 1847 over one-third of the population were fed at soup kitchens across large parts of the county. In the Culmullin and Skreen electoral divisions over 60% of the population were fed in an area where large farms dominated, but where the population largely consisted of landless labourers, some of whom were migrants. The medical officer of the nearby Dunshaughlin workhouse reported that the high mortality rate in the house during the summer of 1847 'the full half of which resulted from the previous privations to which poor harvest men and their families were subjected to before leaving home, several having been cases of absolute famine and proved fatal in a few days after their admission'.[13]

At its peak over half of the population of the electoral divisions of Navan and Ardbraccan were being fed at soup kitchens, totaling over 8,000 people. Seven years earlier the Poor Law Commissioners, when devising the boundaries for electoral divisions in the area,

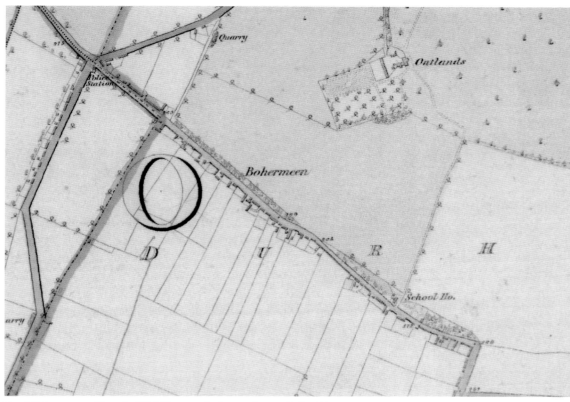

Fig. 3 Bohermeen village in 1836. [Source: Ordnance Survey Ireland]

had commented on the huge pauper population both in the town of Navan and in the nearby parish of Ardbraccan. The geography of the area around Ardbraccan, west of Navan, provides one of the more extreme examples in the county of the juxtaposition of wealth and poverty, of deprivation in the shadow of demesne landscapes. Bohermeen, as shown in Figure 3, was little more than lines of roadside cabins but was designated as a town with a population of 831 in the 1841 Census. The whole settlement was based on complex patterns of subletting and subdivision which allowed a desperately poor population to congregate southeast of the demesne of Oatlands House. Immediately to the northwest lay the 650 acre demesne of Allenstown House owned by the Waller family while just to the south of the demesne was a 250 acre grazing farm owned by the same family. A mile to the southwest lay an extensive tract of bogland, the edges of which were densely settled by a large pauper population. In February 1847, Rev Stopford, secretary of the Ardbraccan Relief Committee, reported that 'we have 196 families who will require gratuitous relief in soup at the average of two quarts per diem . . . There is great distress in our district but it arises entirely from the properties of non-residents.'[14] At its peak in June 1847, 2,700 out of a population of about 5,000 in the Ardbraccan electoral division were being sustained by these soup kitchens.

The closing of the soup kitchens in August 1847 and the passing of the Poor Law Amendment Act meant that the destitute were faced with entering the workhouse or applying for outdoor relief under the strict provisions of the new Act. The potato crop in Meath was largely blight-free in

1847 but there was a much reduced acreage. As the conacre system had virtually collapsed, most labourers were still obliged to buy their food. While food prices fell – a hundredweight of oatmeal cost 15s 6d in August in Kells market compared to £1 6s earlier in the year – the end of harvest work meant that many became dependent on outdoor relief. But outdoor relief was not approved in Kells until January 1848 while in October a report from the fever hospital presented to the Kells Board of Guardians stated that

> a great number of houses are now infected and the sick are generally not fit to be moved. They are all lying by hundreds without food, clothes, medicine or attendance [and] in many cases whole families being ill have no one to apply for relief and the measures hitherto taken have been quite ineffectual in practically relieving all these people.[15]

Outdoor relief for able-bodied men was discontinued in March 1848 based on the rationale that seasonal work was now available and an additional 300 workhouse places were provided by acquiring extra accommodation in the town. But a meeting of rate-payers in Kilskeer, west of the town, was told that 'when the house is filled, a few of its inmates are induced to leave it that an apology may be furnished for the denial of food to thousands of starving creatures'.[16] Even the editor of the *Meath Herald*, who repeatedly railed against the level of Poor Law rates, argued that 'the withdrawal of this little relief, at the present season, is a very ill-judged step'.[17] The Trim Board of Guardians granted relief to able-bodied men on Christmas Day 1847 without the permission of the Poor Law Commissioners based on a report that 'great distress among the labouring population of the Athboy Electoral Division, as, notwithstanding the exertions made by the gentlemen of the district to provide employment, many are without work and in a condition tending to starvation'.[18] The board was subsequently dismissed and replaced by vice-guardians who implemented the Poor Law Commissioners' policies to the letter.

In 1848 the potato acreage in Meath increased fourfold to 17,000 acres, but production was little better than in 1847 as blight returned in many areas. Again smallholders and labourers would be obliged to buy food and, although the price of Indian meal and oatmeal was low compared to the first half of 1847, this meant they might have to default on the payment of their rent for another year, bringing the prospect of eviction ever closer. The corollary of low food prices was low prices for agricultural produce and a Poor Law Inspector in January 1849 attributed the continuing destitution of smallholders to 'the low state of markets. The

smaller class of occupiers are, I fear, entirely exhausted.'[19] Conditions in the Kells area continued to be particularly bleak as reported by Thomas Finnigan, a pawnbroker from Newmarket Street:

> The peasantry, as well as the great majority of tradesmen and women in the town, are in such a miserable state of nudity, that immense numbers of them are precluded from attending their respective places of worship; and when they do attend, it is remarkable that their dress in general consists of some ragged outside cloak or coat to cover their scanty rags and emaciated bodies.[20]

The final crisis of the Famine years in Meath occurred during the summer of 1849 when cholera struck, spreading inland from the port of Drogheda. Kells was by far the most seriously affected town with 330 cases and 156 deaths between June and August. In one week in July alone sixty-six died in the fever hospital and the guardians adopted a

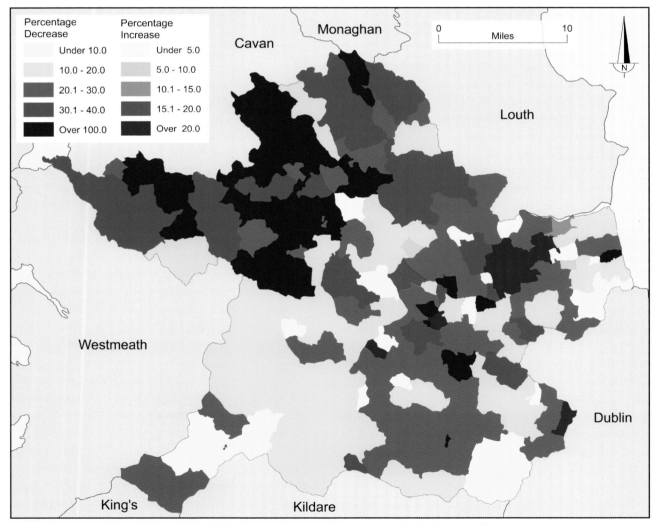

Fig 4  POPULATION DECLINE IN COUNTY MEATH, 1841–51. In what was in many other ways one of Ireland's most affluent counties, County Meath's poorer families represented a very significant proportion of its total population. The Famine was to wreak havoc amongst this class. Parishes in the northwest of the county – including Kilbeg, Moynalty, Moybolgue and Loughan – lost well over 40% of their population as did the densely settled parishes west of Navan. In contrast, the poorer families in the parishes along the sea coast saw losses of less than 20% and weathered the Famine trauma more successfully.

Fig. 5 Mass burial site in Kells, which was opened for the poor people of the district in the latter years of the Famine. [Photo: Frank Coyne]

resolution 'that in consequence of the mortality at present prevailing in the workhouse that a horse and cart be employed for the purpose of conveying the remains of the paupers to their respective graveyards'.[21]

The year 1849, by which time the very poorest sections of the population had endured three years of deprivation, marked the peak year for deaths in Meath in the 1840s. Our best estimate is that between 13,000 and 18,000 famine-related deaths occurred in the county between 1845 and 1851, while a further 30,000 emigrated. Overall, the county's population fell from 183,828 in 1841 to 140,748 in 1851. This decline of 23.4% places the county on a par with the losses experienced by Cork (24.0%), Clare (25.4%) and Leitrim (27.9%). About 4,000 Meath people died in workhouses during the Famine years and a further 821 died in the county's fever hospitals. Of course, not all of these deaths were famine-related, but a huge proportion was. For example, thirteen inmates died in Navan workhouse in the first eight weeks of 1846 before famine conditions had taken hold in the area, while fifty inmates died in the same period in 1848. Based on evidence from the Poor Enquiry and other sources ,emigration from Meath does not appear to have been extensive before 1846. By the end of that year, however, the *Meath Herald* was reporting that 'in the memory of the old-

est inhabitant in this part of the country the spirit of emigration was never known to have arrived at the height it is at present. Numbers who can muster sufficient funds are wending their way towards the shipping ports for America.'[22] Around this time the local newspapers carried prominent advertisements for the City of Dublin and Drogheda Steam Packet companies offering cheap carriage to Liverpool.

The geography of population loss shown in Figure 4 accurately reflects the distribution of pre-Famine poverty and of distress during 1845–50. The adjoining parishes of Kilbeg, Moynalty, Moybolghue and Loughan in the northwest corner of the county lost well over 40% of their population, amounting to over 5,000 people. Despite extensive public works, the efforts of local relief committees and some local landlords, the cabin dwellers of the region were decimated. The number of one-roomed mud cabins in the area fell from 879 in 1841 to just 106 ten years later. In the densely settled parishes west of Navan similar patterns were experienced. The parish of Ardbraccan, which included the village of Bohermeen, lost 35% of its population. The village of 160 houses in 1841 was no longer considered an urban settlement in the 1851 Census and only about ninety houses, mostly cabins, remained by 1854. Townlands such as

Ongenstown (-45%) and Jamestown (-48%), bordering bog-land to the southwest, also suffered huge population loss. Just north of this area, and south of Kells, the three parishes of Rathmore, Girley and Balrathboyne also lost over 40% of their population, with the number of mud cabins falling from 247 to just 69. In the west of the county the parishes of Oldcastle (-41%) and Diamor (-44%) suffered the heaviest losses. The townland of Boolies, just east of the town of Old-castle, which was in the hands of absentees, saw its population fall from 909 to 233. The townland of Oldtully, owned by J.L.W. Naper of Loughcrew, was cleared of its population of 262. In the sparsely settled southeast of the county, population decline was largely concentrated on poverty stricken villages. Several were little more than roadside settlements, smaller versions of Bohermeen. The 'cluster of mud cabins on the Dublin Road' near Tara melted back into the landscape and the 'small scattered village' at Kilmoon Cross on the road from Dublin to Derry had a similar fate.

From the autumn of 1846 through to the spring of 1847 thousands of weakened men (and hundreds of women) toiled on public works schemes in the county, breaking stones for new roads, building walls and cleaning drains. For most, their wages were inadequate to buy sufficient food for their families, given the inflated price of oatmeal and Indian meal. During these same months, August 1846 to April 1847, 37,828 cattle and 64,092 sheep were exported from the port of Drogheda along with 44,975 hundred-weights of oatmeal, 11,026 quarters of wheat, 4,946 quarters of barley and 4,877 quarters of oats.[23] Based on patterns of trade identified in the Railway Commission Report in the 1830s, much of this produce would have originated in County Meath. This level of exports of grain at 8,850 tons was only about half what it had been in 1845 and in these eight months the equivalent of 16,857 tons of grain, including over 42,000 quarters of Indian corn, were imported through the port of Drogheda. However, taking into account the huge number of livestock exported through the port, it is not easy to dispute the claim made by a contemporary commentator that the region was a net exporter of food during these months when thousands were on the edge of starvation.

It is clear, in this region at least, that the affordability of food was at least as important as its availability. The famished labourers and their families who crowded into the towns of Kells and Navan in 1847 could not afford the oatmeal and meat destined for Drogheda and Dublin, just as they could not afford it before famine conditions developed in 1846. Their plight was defined by their inability to earn adequate wages to buy food. At the same time a recurring appeal, articulated by members of relief committees, the clergy, by Poor Law inspectors and by the editor of the *Meath Herald*, was for the county's graziers to plough their fields of grass and grow crops as a means of providing employment for the thousands of idle smallholders and labourers whose potatoes had failed. One small farmer was quoted as predicting 'if the graziers do not break up some of their farms to allow employment, the labourers will eat the farmers and the farmers will eat the landlords'.[24] In most cases these appeals found no response. As we have seen, the geography of the Famine in Meath reflected these sharp divisions. And so, while the mud cabins of Bohermeen, Moynalty and Oldtully were flattened or melted back into the ditches, Meath's graziers in adjoining townlands and across the county stocked their farms with an additional 12,000 fat cattle between 1847 and 1851. The future would be theirs.

# Burying the Famine dead: Kilkenny Union workhouse

## Jonny Geber

When Kilkenny Union workhouse opened in April 1842, it was with a built capacity for 1,300 inmates, the fifth largest of such institutions in Ireland. The construction of the house had begun in 1840 in Pennefatherslot townland within the parish of St John's, at the northeastern fringe of the city. The union included the city and twenty-one electoral divisions from the north part of the county, and the seemingly huge size of the house reflected the local need. Kilkenny was plagued by persistent unemployment, mainly due to the decline of the local textile industry, and it was reported to be the poorest county in all of Leinster. On the first day of admission, thirty applications were accepted.

Many pre-Famine accounts and descriptions remarked on the noticeably high incidence of poverty in Kilkenny. The poor in the outskirts of the town of Callan were said to inhabit cabins which were mere holes, 'without a ray of comfort or a trace of civilization about them', and the people themselves were described as being in 'either a state of actual starvation or barely keeping body and soul together'.[1] In the parish of Fiddown, the poor were reported to sleep 'on a wad of straw, or perhaps heath laid on a damp clay floor . . . [T]hrough the scanty thatch, the rain would sometimes descend upon their beds, and bringing down the sooty substance lodged there by the smoke of the cabin, wets and stains the bed itself and those who are stretched upon it'.[2]

The industry of the workhouse reflected the traditional local economy; the inmates produced blankets, clothes and

Fig. 1 Aerial photograph of Kilkenny Union workhouse, taken some time during the early 1960s. Construction of the house began in 1840, and it opened for the first time in April 1842. The management of the workhouse was taken over by the Sisters of Mercy in 1875, and during 1921–42 the buildings functioned as the Kilkenny Central Hospital. Thereafter, the buildings were used as a depot by Kilkenny County Council. Since 2007, the remaining structures of the workhouse constitute a part of the MacDonagh Junction Shopping Centre. [Source: Kilkenny County Library, Local Studies, published through kind permission from Karyn Deegan]

341

pins while the boys were taught the skills of shoemaking. Inmates also broke stones and worked on the agricultural plots attached to the workhouse. A strict regime was adhered to, even during the height of the Famine. For instance, four able-bodied male inmates were sentenced to three to four weeks of hard labour in the gaol in June 1848 after having refused to work when told to do so. Two years previously, the newspapers reported on an incident when some of the boys had been severely beaten by their schoolmaster. Eighteen boys were undressed before the Board of Guardians, who were then able to identify several bruises on their bodies. The board then moved for the immediate suspension and dismissal of the schoolmaster from his position.

## THE FAMINE CRISIS

The extent of the blight across the county was first reported in the *Kilkenny Journal* in October 1845, and in a document from the Irish Constabulary to the Government in the same month it was noted that the 'crop [from Johnstown was] more or less diseased throughout the district: on some farms nearly half quite rotten'.[3] Kilkenny City began to see a considerable influx of people from distant counties such as Clare and Limerick. The newspapers described these non-locals as being people of bad moral character, and they were reported to stay in camps at Grange's Road and Brougemaker's Hill in the northern districts of the city, as well as around John's Green close to the workhouse. Large crowds gathered daily at the gates of the workhouse, and in December 1847 it had become necessary to station the police and a group of able-bodied inmates outside the institution to keep order. Deaths by destitution and starvation became more and more prevalent. Destitute people were found lying dead on the streets, and in March 1848 the corpse of an eight-day-old infant, half eaten by dogs and 'frightfully mutilated', was found in an old house opposite the workhouse.[4] In the workhouse itself, the death rate was about eighty people a month, with the highest numbers noted in 1847 when more than 200 people died each month at the beginning of that year.

The deepening of the crisis meant further logistical and economic strains on the workhouse, from desperate people seeking refuge from hunger and destitution. Despite it being periodically illegal, outdoor relief was provided.[5] Wooden sheds had to be erected on the grounds to provide further accommodation within the house, and at least seven auxiliary buildings were rented at various locations within the city. Many of these buildings were clearly derelict; the auxiliary workhouse at St Francis was infested by rats, and the rented premises on Patrick Street, where 'children of tender age' were accommodated, had no windows. In March 1845, there had been about 870 people receiving indoor relief. This had increased to 2,340 by July 1847. The highest number was recorded in June 1851, when a total of 4,357 were dependent on indoor relief from the workhouse.

## BLACK '47

The notorious 'Black '47' saw a vigorous spread of epidemic typhus and consequential mass deaths in the city and its environs. From 1845 and until December 1846, the average number of patients in the fever hospital had been between five and forty individuals. These figures then changed dramatically: in December 1846 more than 100 patients were treated; in January 1847 there were almost 300; and between February and May there were between 400 and 500 patients. In April, both the workhouse chaplain and the schoolmistress had succumbed to fever while the Assistant Master died of fever in the same month. The number of ill peaked in late June 1847, when there were more than 600 patients. Thereafter the numbers fell quickly, and by August there were again less than 100 patients treated for fever.[6]

Like most of the new union workhouses elsewhere in Ireland, there was no designated burial plot assigned to the institution when it was established. From the very beginning, the need for a pauper cemetery associated with the workhouse had been recognised. In January 1844, parishioners complained about the interment of deceased paupers in St Patrick's cemetery in an article published in the *Kilkenny Journal*. The cemetery was evidently crowded at this stage, and there were demands for the establishment of a new burial ground at a convenient distance from the city. In March 1846, the board received a highly critical letter from Dean Vignoles, who protested against the burials of paupers who had no parish claim to the churchyard, referring to the ever increasing and critical overcrowding of the cemetery.

After this complaint, the cemetery of St Maul's, located close to the fever hospital, was put to use. The mortality rate in the house at this time was at its peak, and by early March 1847 St Maul's was full. The mayor received complaints from local residents, as well as from the Dean and the Colonel, who had noted that about ten corpses were carelessly interred in the burial ground every day. The guardians therefore reserved £10 to be used to buy a plot of land adjoining this cemetery. It had been ordered that at least three feet of earth should cover the interred coffins, and that an additional three feet was to be added over the original ground level, but this was not adhered to, and some graves were reportedly even left unfinished. The interments took place in large mass burial pits, where several coffins were put in and finally covered with a few shovels of earth flung over them.

## INTRA-MURAL BURIALS, 1847–51

In April 1847, it was noted in the minute books that 'the new plot of burial ground had been taken by the Sheriff, and the workhouse-men turned off the ground, and threatened with law proceedings'.[7] It appears as if corpses had been illegally buried on a plot adjacent to St Maul's. At the same time, it was reported that the mortuary was overcrowded. The

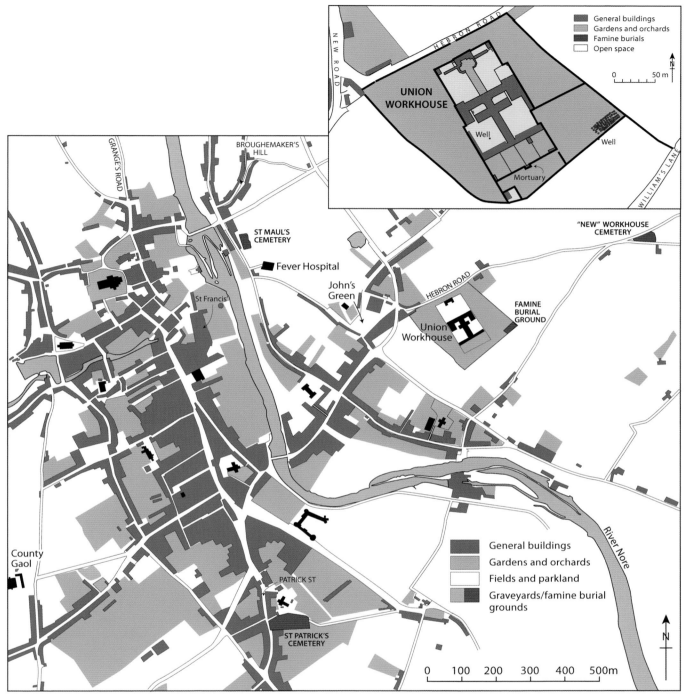

Fig. 2 MID-NINETEENTH-CENTURY KILKENNY CITY, WITH THE LOCATIONS OF THE BURIAL GROUNDS USED BY THE UNION WORKHOUSE DURING THE FAMINE AND OTHER PLACES MENTIONED IN THE TEXT. [Map by Maura Pringle, Queen's University Belfast]

board was in negotiation with a Mr Loughnan, the landowner, about purchasing the land, but the legalities had not been sorted with the previous land tenant. Once again, the union workhouse resorted to using St Patrick's cemetery for burial, and in August Dean Vignoles yet again complained about the number of paupers buried there. From this point there was no other choice than intra-mural burial within the grounds of the workhouse itself. The minutes from the meeting of the Board of Guardians in the last week of October read that 'the Commissioners notified their desire that the Guardians should consider the propriety of obtaining a burial ground at a proper distance from the

Workhouse; as they considered it most desirable that burials in the Workhouse grounds should be discontinued'.[8]

The intra-mural burial ground was discovered in 2005 and made the subject of an archaeological excavation in 2006. The area had after the Famine been used as the workhouse garden, and throughout the decades any local knowledge or awareness of the history of the burials taking place there had been forgotten. The archaeological excavation revealed the existence of a minimum of sixty-three pits, measuring 1.5–2m in length and 1.5m in width, located in the northeast corner of the workhouse grounds. The skeletal remains of at least 970 individuals were identified in

Fig. 3 The skeleton of an older adult male, who was buried in a coffin along the edge of a mass burial pit which contained a further seventeen other interments. The bones of the skeleton in the coffin underneath are visible along the left side of the skeleton. [Photo: Margaret Gowen & Co., Ltd.]

these mass burials. The location of the burial ground suggests that it was intentionally placed the furthest possible distance away from the workhouse buildings or any other houses. The pits were dug close to each other and were roughly arranged in rows of a southwest to northeast alignment. The often very close proximity between two adjacent pits suggest that they were never opened at the same time, at least not if placed next to each other.

One of the pits was empty, which is interesting, as it indicates that after a burial pit had been backfilled, a new one was dug in anticipation of further deaths. There was a variation in the number of individuals buried in each feature, from only six individuals in four pits to twenty-seven individuals in one pit, with the majority of the mass burials containing between fourteen and twenty-two interments. The mortality rate, as recorded in the minutes, suggest that each pit probably catered for the total number of deaths per week. Adults and children of both sexes were buried in each pit, and it is clear that the segregation of the living within the workhouse, where men and women and boys and girls were kept apart, was not upheld in death.

The archaeological evidence from the burial ground indicates that the use of the notorious 'sliding coffin' did not take

Fig. 4 The skeleton of a five-year-old child. A minimum of 970 individuals were interred in the intra-mural burial ground at the Kilkenny Union workhouse. The majority of these were non-adults, with the largest proportion being small children aged two to five years. The skeleton displayed lesions consistent with scurvy, which is a direct reflection of the Famine as the potato was virtually the only source of Vitamin C in the diet of the poor. [Photo: Margaret Gowen & Co., Ltd.]

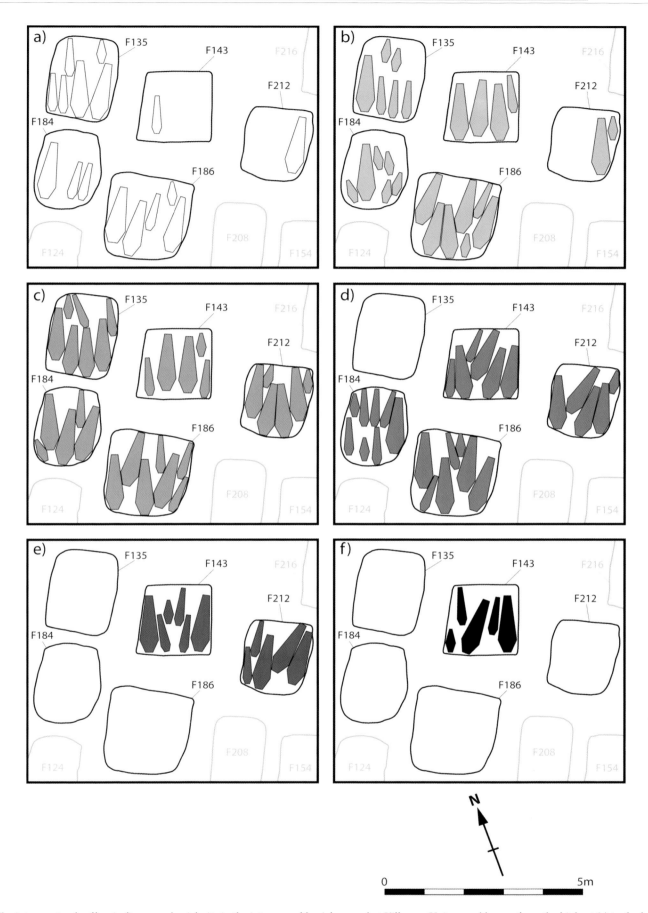

Fig. 5 The interments of coffins in five mass burial pits in the intra-mural burial ground at Kilkenny Union workhouse, from the highest (a) to the lowest (f) level. Both adult males and females and children were buried in each pit. Segregation by age and gender, which was the case in the workhouse, was evidently not upheld in death. [Illustration: Jonny Geber]

345

place, but rather that all individuals were interred in coffins. The evidence for these was mainly represented by soil stains and coffin nails in a clear hexagonal shape outlining the skeletons. In some cases, preserved fragments of pinewood were also found. The coffins were evidently simple constructions, with no ornaments or furniture. They were bought by the union by tender, and eventually became a significant expense. Between March and June 1846, the board received a bill of £108 for delivered coffins, based on a price of nine pence a foot. A year later, a bill of £80.1.5 was paid. Some of the purchased coffins were used by the fever hospital, to the disapproval of the board, who eventually in the spring of 1848 ordered that 'no coffins be given out from [the] Workhouse'.[9]

The coffins had been stacked on top of each other in the pits, in varying numbers of levels. In some pits it was evident that as many coffins as possible had been interred, and there were cases where a coffin had been slotted into the pit on the side between a previously placed coffin and the inner side of the pit. After the addition of the coffins was complete, the pits had been immediately backfilled with the material from their excavation. The local papers did not include any articles or notes regarding burials from the weekly meetings of the Board of Guardians until early January 1850. Mr Lanigan, one of the guardians, had told the board during the first weekly meeting of that year that 'it was most desirable that ground should be obtained at once for a cemetery'. The same week, an advertisement was placed in the *Kilkenny Journal* seeking a portion of land of not less than one acre. The advertisement sparked a response from two readers who wrote in the following edition of the paper:

> INTRAMURAL BURIAL – KILKENNY. The following letter, which we received yesterday, refers to two or three matters of very great local interest. It is most desirable that the Vice-Guardians should, if at all practicable, select ground for cemeterial purposes which lie out of town. The mischievous influence of intramural internment has been long an acknowledged evil.
>
> In London, Liverpool, Dublin and Belfast – in fact in any town where attention is paid to sanatory [sic] regulations – the practice has altogether disappeared. It is impossible that any place can be free from a vitiated atmosphere where the dead are housed almost among the living; and in times of epidemic the evil is lamentably increased by the neglect invariably paid to burial in such cases, because seldom anything beyond mere surface burial is obtained, from a want of proper officers to see that all graves are sunk to a proper depth.
>
> It is a very great abuse that the poor people who die in the hospital are not buried in consecrated ground. To whom is this to be attributed? Once the

ground was procured, where was the difficulty in having it consecrated? This is, indeed, a matter that requires explanation.

> Our correspondent's suggestion that there should be a town meeting to deal with the general question is an excellent one. It is for the people themselves, who are the parties most interested, to make a move in the matter. It concerns the health of themselves and their families; and a very little exertion will suffice to obviate a great and growing evil.[10]

Immediately underneath the article, was a second letter published:

> TO THE EDITOR OF KILKENNY JOURNAL. Kilkenny, August 23, 1849. Sir – I have seen in yesterday's number of your paper, an advertisement from the Vice-Guardians, for an acre of ground, for a cemetery. I trust it is their intention that in future no interments shall be allowed at the rear of the Fever Hospital, or on the Workhouse grounds. It is for many other reasons also, most desirable, that they may succeed in procuring a suitable place of interment, and one in particular which will relieve the inhabitants of Blackmill, Vicar, and Green-Street, from a repetition of the scenes of outraged decency they were frequently obliged to witness during the last year.
>
> It is also a cause of complaint that the poor people who die in the Hospitals or Workhouse, unless claimed by their friends, are not buried in consecrated ground; and such has been the case with regard to one place for the last three years.
>
> In connexion with this matter I think it would be well if the citizens of influence and position, both clergy and laity, would come together and consult about the grave yards within the town, with a view to ascertaining if the opinions of some are correct as to the great necessity that exists for a new cemetery, and whether it would be advisable to enlarge the present ones or establish a new one. [11]

The published letters indicate that the local awareness of the practice of intra-mural burial at the workhouse was very much present, and that there were sincere objections to it from both a sanitary and ethical point of view. In February 1850, the board started negotiations with a Mr Greene, for the purpose of either buying or renting a plot of land to be used as a cemetery. The board offered Mr Greene £75 for one acre of land, but the offer was rejected.

## THE 'NEW CEMETERY'

In June 1850, the guardians were made aware of a suitable

## KILKENNY UNION.

## LAND WANTED.

**T**HE VICE-GUARDIANS of this Union, will, at any time up to THURSDAY, the 13th SEP-TEMBER, prox., receive Tenders from persons willing to SELL or HIRE to the Poor Law Com-missioners, a quantity of LAND, not less than ONE STATUTE ACRE, to be used as a CEMETERY, for the Burial of deceased inmates of the Work-house.

A Site not more than One Mile distant from the Workhouse would be considered preferable.

Sealed Tenders, con·aining full particulars, as to terms, tenure, &c., may be forwarded, addressed to the Vice Guardians, Kilkenny.

By Order,
MICHAEL MOLONY,
Acting Clerk of the Union.

Board-Room, Workhouse,
21st August, 1819.

Fig. 6 Advertisement placed in the *Kilkenny Journal* by the Vice-Guardians of the Kilkenny Union in August 1849, asking for tenders for a plot of land that could be used as a workhouse cemetery. The advertisement led to the publication of two critical letters, regarding the practice of intra-mural burials at the workhouse, which were published in the following edition of the paper. [Source: *Kilkenny Journal,* 21 August 1849]

On 3 March 1851, the *Kilkenny Moderator* published, in its report-ing of the weekly meeting of the Board of Guardians, a discussion concerning the contractors having sought permission to continue building the cemetery wall as the task had been postponed due to bad weather during the winter. The discussion that followed highlighted the need of discontin-uing the practice of intra-mural burial, not only at the workhouse but also at the fever hospital. It was decided that the new ceme-tery was to be taken in use imme-diately, in a seemingly light-hearted atmosphere:

Mr. Burke thought they might use a portion of the new cemetery at once.

Sir Wheeler Cuffe – Yes, let them stop the burials . . . immediately and begin to bury in the new cemetery to-morrow.

The Mayor – Tomorrow! Wouldn't you wait if they have no corpse to bury Sir Wheeler? (laughter.)[12]

A final indirect reference to the intra-mural burials at the workhouse dates to 13 March 1851, where it was recorded in the minutes that the enclosing wall of the burial ground was to be com-pleted and that all future inter-ments were to be made 'in the new cemetery'. Burials within the grounds of the workhouse had ceased to take place at that time.

The intra-mural burial ground was never consecrated; a fact which would have been of great grievance and prob-ably also a sense of shame, which perhaps explains why the existence of the cemetery had been forgotten. In May 2010, however, the skeletal remains of the people buried there were, after detailed osteological and palaeopathological analysis, finally reinterred at a new Famine memorial gar-den in Kilkenny. The re-burial included a multi-denomina-tional religious ceremony to the memory of all those who

plot of land, just northeast of the workhouse, by Hebron Road. The owner, Major Helsham, was willing to sell the piece of land for only £30. This generous offer was acknowl-edged by the board, who wrote in their minutes that a sim-ilar piece of land they had previously queried about was offered at a price of £200. The purchase of the land was resolved in the first week of July, and it was bought for that price. The new workhouse cemetery was more than suffi-cient in size so that the board allowed the burial of ordinary Kilkenny citizens within it. An iron gate was erected in December 1850, and work began in the same month on the enclosing wall, which was a prerequisite for having the bur-ial ground consecrated.

Fig. 7. The re-burial ceremony at the Famine memorial garden in Kilkenny on 19 May 2010, which included a multi-denominational religious ceremony involving St John's Catholic Church, the Church of Ireland, the Kilkenny Presbyterian Church and the Kilkenny Methodist Church. [Photograph: Jonny Geber]

died during the Great Famine, and the people, whose remains now rest in the memorial garden, were given their final respectful treatment in death, which they were denied when they died about 160 years previously.

# King's County during the Great Famine: 'poverty and plenty'

*Ciarán Reilly*

On 17 October 1846 the *King's County Chronicle* reported that 'at the Wakely estate at Ballyburley in the barony of Warrenstown such is the scale of the widespread hunger that even the crows have been reduced to skeletons'.[1] Such was the universal panic amongst the county's inhabitants, that those perceived to be profiting in the midst of crisis were threatened about their actions: 'Landlords use no tyranny, keep your trumpeters at home, tenants gather all your corn into your farmyards; also threaten agents, landjobbers, moneylenders and millers'. Such threatening letters accompanied the almost daily plundering of flour, corn and sheep which characterised the early stages of the Great Famine in King's County (now known as County Offaly). Many landlords chose to provide abatements of rent and let arrears accumulate but by the end of 1847 (and with the introduction of the Gregory or 'quarter acre' clause in 1848) heretofore lenient landlords undertook extensive clearances of their properties and helped in the assisted emigration of others. The number of murders and attacks on estate personnel indicated the desperate situation that the majority of the county's inhabitants were placed in. The aim of this chapter is to show the impact of the Famine in King's County; it will also show that in the midst of such a calamity there were numerous festivities, dinners and social events enjoyed by the gentry and others, who were, it seems, oblivious to the plight of those around them.

## COMING OF THE BLIGHT

Writing in 1895, William O'Connor Morris of Mount Pleasant House, near Tullamore vividy recalled the impact that the sight of many starving people had on him: 'The lean and wolfish faces of many of those are stamped on my mind even as I write now.' He had first noticed the potato blight in September 1845 while partridge shooting when the 'sickly smell of corruption' assailed his nostrils.[2] A month later Lord Ponsonby's agent at Philipstown (now Daingean), Joseph Grogan, reported to the Dublin land agency firm of Stewart and Kincaid:

> The crop is still in the fields in stacks and can't be got into the haggards as it is raining same every day and night and the corn has received some damage in the stacks. With regard to the potatoes at the first time I wrote to you there was not the least appearance of damage on them but at this moment there appears to be great damage to the potato crop in this county or any other part that I am in the habit of travelling along the canal line but it is damaged more or less and the people appears [*sic*] to be greatly alarmed on that account.[3]

Other reports were more alarming. Daniel Manifold, Colonel Bernard's agent at Kinnitty, feared the worst and predicted that the blight would result in famine. Sir Andrew Armstrong of Gallen warned that 'there will be more than the usual destitution this year'. In October James F. Rolleston reported a riot in Dunkerrin over the shortage

Fig. 1 William O'Connor Morris of Mount Pleasant House at Pallas. [Source: Offaly Historical Society]

of potatoes and requested troops to be sent to that part of the county. Later that month *The Times* reported that the 'rot is more or less extensive' in King's County. William Parsons, 3rd Earl of Rosse and lord lieutenant of the county, appears to have mishandled the initial investigations into the effect of the potato blight in King's County, which included an account by Lord Charleville's agent Francis Berry, who reported that a third of the potato crop was lost and he feared 'excitements if not disturbances' would result in further crop failures. Almost immediately, and predictably, there was considerable resentment towards the exportation of corn and other foodstuff. As a result, Arthur Rolleston claimed that his tenants near Moneygall refused to pay rents, while George Crampton, agent of the Carter estate at Eglish, received several threats about the export of corn.

### THE PROVISION OF RELIEF

There appears to have been a period of procrastination on the part of the gentry in providing relief, but as O'Connor Morris contended, 'the memory of the distress of 1818–22 led many of the county's proprietors to believe that the failure of the potato crop would be short lived'. Thus he

Fig. 2 Birr Castle, the residence of the 3rd Earl of Rosse. [Photo: Frank Coyne]

believed that it was 'not heartlessness but the dangerous ignorance of a class kept apart from the classes beneath it'. Individual efforts to provide relief temporarily relieved the failure of coordinated efforts. Henry L'Estrange's daughter provided work for 100 women spinning and knitting at Moystown, while Thomas Manifold offered to mill flour free of charge at Kinnitty. William Johnson and his agent Dawson French were praised for their generous efforts in providing tenants at Tullamore with seed oats and peas. However, such schemes had a limited effect such was the scale of the crisis. Rev. J.P. Holmes at Ferbane wrote in February 1846 that 'all the horrors of starvation will be experienced by half at least of the population'. However, local rivalries and squabbling delayed the formation of relief committees and many were unhappy with Lord Rosse's division of relief boundaries. A reluctance to establish a single relief committee for each of the baronies of Ballycowan, Geashill and Kilcoursey delayed the provision of poor relief for a large part of the county's population. There was also considerable resentment towards those in charge of the relief works.

In 1846 a petition from tenants at Ballyboy complained that 'the gentry of our parish are negligent in our regard and the farmers who could not go to the helm of relief and shout for work and hire, they will not because they are wallowing in the riches of this world'. In June Fr Walsh of Lusmagh dispersed a crowd of 800 men in search of food and employment. When the relief works at Bell Hill, Clareen, were cancelled in the same month, the labourers protested that 'they would not die like cowards, all we want is work so as not to be allowed to starve. If we don't get that we will be obliged to procure food with the bayonet.' In the same month over 150 tenants visited Lord Rosse's demesne looking to have over forty men put to work and if not they threatened to go to Parsonstown and take what they could. A threatening notice posted at Philipstown in October 1846 warned that if the poor were not soon supplied with relief they would 'resort to harsh measures'. That same month Edenderry workhouse, built to provide shelter for 600 people, was accommodating nearly 1,800 'wretched souls'. Amongst the areas most affected were those in the west of the county, particularly Banagher, Lusmagh, Gallen and Rynagh, where by 1847 an average of eight robberies a day were reported.

Despite the high levels of destitution, Henry Sheane, agent on the Bell estate, noted the complete aversion of the poor to the workhouse who would 'die in the ditch rather than go there'. But where did responsibility lie? John A. Burdett, a landlord at Coolfin, near Ferbane, stated that he would not allow any of his tenants to take relief because as their landlord he was responsible for them.[4] Some landlords had their own stereotypical impressions of what they perceived to be a lazy tenantry unwilling to help themselves and who were 'unsuited to work'; they contended that relief works were not the best method of solving the crisis. Lord

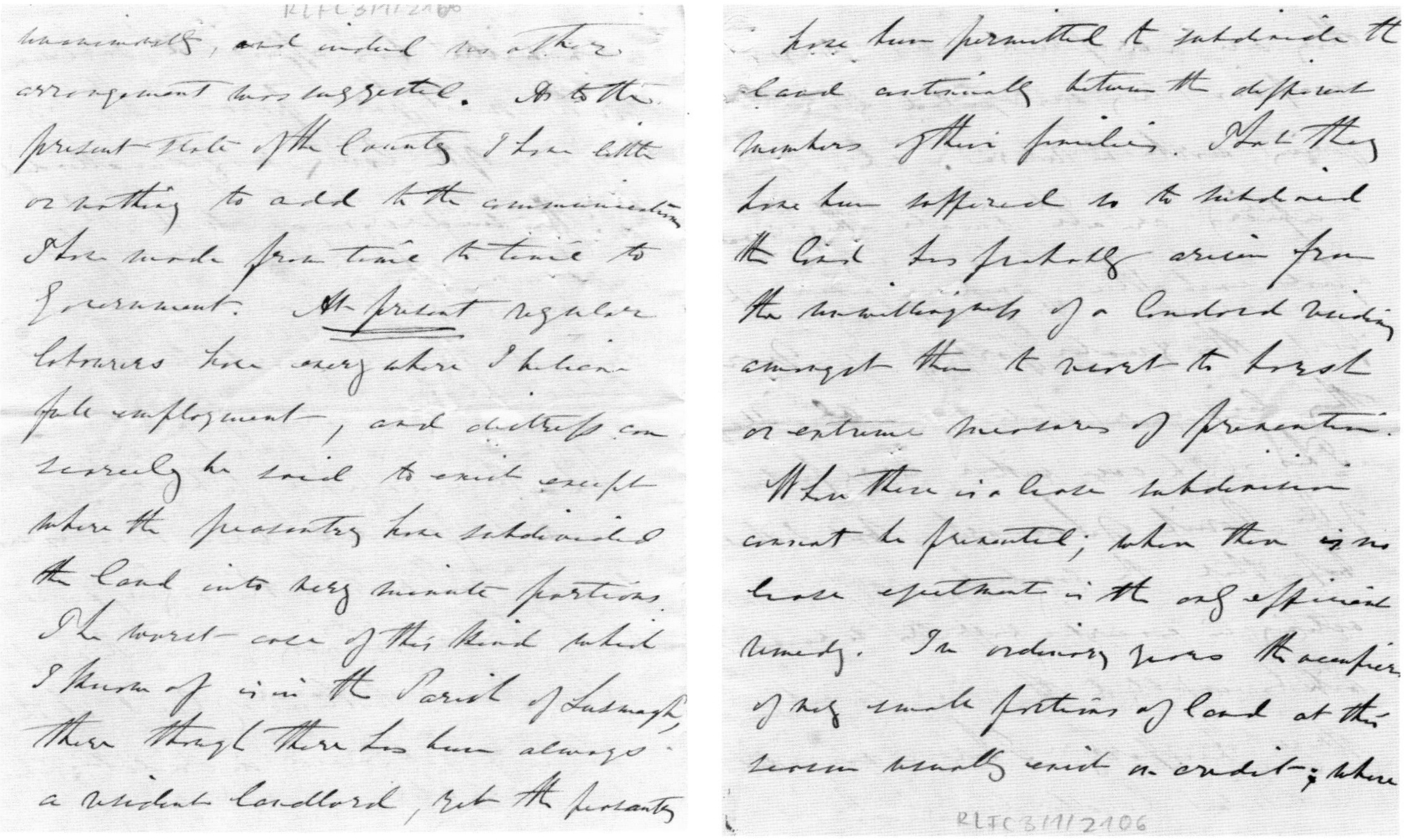

RLFC 3/1/2106

unanimously, and indeed no other arrangement was suggested. As to the present state of the County I have little or nothing to add to the communications I have made from time to time to Government. At present regular labourers have every where I believe full employment, and distress can scarcely be said to exist except where the peasantry have subdivided the land into very minute portions. The worst case of this kind which I know of is in the Parish of Lusmagh there though there has been always a resident landlord, yet the peasantry

have been permitted to subdivide the land continually between the different members of their families. That they have been suffered to subdivide the land has probably arisen from the unwillingness of a landlord residing amongst them to resort to harsh or extreme measures of prevention. Where there is a large subdivision cannot be prevented; when there is no large ejectment is the only efficient remedy. In ordinary years the occupiers of very small portions of land at this season usually exist on credit; when

RLFC 3/1/2106

Fig. 3 In an early letter to the Central Relief Commission in Dublin, the Earl of Rosse explained that 'distress can scarcely be said to exist except where the peasantry have subdivided the land into very minute portions. The worst area of this kind which I know of is in the parish of Lusmagh . . . . [T]hough there has always been a resident landlord, the peasantry have been permitted to subdivide the land continually between the different members of their families.' He clearly underestimated the level of destitution across the Parsonstown (Birr) Union. Apart from the many deaths in the open countryside, as many as 3,159 people died in its workhouse between 1841 and 1851. [Source: National Library of Ireland]

Rosse believed that smallholders were 'little accustomed to work' and he was reluctant to join the public work scheme. Despite this, the numbers employed on work schemes rose from 718 at the beginning of July 1846 to over 3,750 by the end of that month.[5] Other efforts to provide relief included a large-scale drainage scheme on the River Brosna, which was initiated in 1846 and gave employment to thousands of labourers in the baronies through which it passed. Despite the existence of Quaker communities at Edenderry and Clara, there was no great effort on their part to provide relief in contrast to Friends elsewhere. Travelling through the county, Alexander Somerville noted that the people of Parsonstown had broken the bridge leading from the town to prevent meal intended for export from reaching Shannon Harbour. Without any pity, Somerville noted that 'the peasantry here are very ignorant', failing to mention the fact that they were also starving.[6]

### CLEARING THE LAND

The year 1848 marked the turning point in the clearances, although large numbers had been evicted prior to this. Indeed, King's County had the highest number of evictions in Leinster as the decade came to a close. The drafting and publication of the Rosse estate 'rules' in 1847 highlighted that there would be a change in the management of the estate. Such 'rules' were necessary for landlords to avoid public censure similar to what had occurred to Mrs Gerrard in County Galway in 1846 following the eviction of over 300 tenants. In two years over 500 people were cleared from the Rosse estate at Newtown and Fadden. The evictors also included Repeal supporters such as Sir Andrew Armstrong and Robert Cassidy (a Catholic brewer) who undertook large-scale clearances of their properties. Others followed suit.

In August 1849 George Greeson evicted a number of families at Grogan and Lebeg, part of Holmes estate, while in December the same agent oversaw the removal of thirty-one families in Lemanaghan while levelling five houses in the process. Of those evicted, twenty-six families were subsequently allowed to re-occupy their properties as caretakers. Many of these tenants had not paid rent for three to five years. On this occasion no mercy was shown from Greeson, who took one man lying in bed with fever and put him on the ground. Other evictions included twenty-seven families (comprising 126 people) evicted from Forelacka for arrears of rent in March 1849. In May at George Walpole's estate at Glosterbeg twenty families were evicted. Six families, a total of thirty-nine people, were evicted and their homes levelled at the Harden estate near Parsonstown while three families numbering twenty persons were evicted from Rev. William Minchin's estate at Barnagrotty.

However, those evicted did not leave quietly and in a

number of cases they sought to gain retribution for what had occurred. This resulted in the murder of several landlords and agents. These included William Lloyd, a landlord near Birr, in December 1846; William Lucas, a landlord near Brosna, in December 1848; Charles Trench Cage, agent of the Gore estate, in October 1849; Robert Pyke, agent of the Cassidy estate, in August 1850; Roger North, a landlord near Croghan, in September 1850; and William Ross Manifold, agent of the O'Connor Morris estate, in October 1852, while scores of other agents and estate personnel were assaulted and shot at.

### PLENTY IN THE MIDST OF WANT

While the Famine undoubtedly interupted the 'Big House' building boom in Ireland, it did not deter some landlords from embellishing their houses and demesnes and maintaining their lavish lifestyles. It could be argued that by doing so they provided much needed employment and therefore relief. From 1840 to 1845 large-scale improvements were carried out at Birr Castle which included a 'bell ceiling', a mock gothic structure housing the great telescope and iron gates set into the gate keep of the castle. Then, from 1846 to 1848, came the construction of the Vaubanesque fortifications at Birr Castle, while plans were also put in place in 1850 for two gardens to be set out in front of the castle. During the Famine it was noted that visitors to the castle enjoyed 'pretty good fishing' as there were large quantities of fish in the lakes. Many years later, Laurence Parsons, 6th Earl of Rosse (1906–1979), noted that his great-grandparents spent most of their time engaged in relief work and that astronomical pursuits only began in earnest after 1848.

The rather contradictory contemporary evidence suggests that Birr Castle was a recognised international scientific centre during the Famine and many visitors travelled there to see the great telescope, including Lord Stanley and the Prince Imperial, son of Napoleon III.[7] To celebrate what was perceived to be the end of the Famine in 1851, Lord Rosse provided an extravagant display of fireworks for his tenants in February, which included the wheel piece, roman candles, rockets and tourbillons. According to the *King's County Chronicle*, 'no pains or expense was spared in their procurement'. The final bill was estimated to be £400 and the Earl's son, although only ten years old, published a programme of the night's events. The Earl and Countess of Rosse continued to entertain the gentry of the county and surrounding areas hosting elaborate balls where they received their guests with 'the usual urbanity and politeness'. In January 1852 a ball was held at Birr Castle and attended by over 300 guests.

In his personal diaries for the years 1843–48, John Plunkett Joly (1826–58) of Hollywood, Bracknagh appeared unperturbed by the Famine or the suffering which must have occurred in the barony of Coolestown in which the family's estate was located. Joly's description of everyday life in King's County during these years contrasts greatly with the scenes of destitution and the daily pleas of the relief committees. His carefree lifestyle included listening to the 'blackbirds singing in the morning and evening'; the growing of flowers and vegetables and daily observations on the weather. Throughout this period Joly seemed ignorant of the plight of the masses and indeed the murder of a local land agent, John Gatchell, in May 1843 only merited a fleeting mention amongst his description and sketches of the local landscape.

William O'Connor Morris' memoirs recall that he had been left the owner of an 'embarrassed legacy' during the Famine and that his family had done much to relieve the plight of their tenants despite not having the resources to do so. Yet in January 1846 the *King's County Chronicle* reported on the lavish dinner which was hosted at the family home of Mount Pleasant to celebrate the coming of age of William himself. It was reported that upwards of 160 people enjoyed the meal that was served and 'a merry and well prolonged dance, in which our national character for fun was well kept up'. A 'Ball and Supper' were celebrated at Tisaran, the home of Edmund L'Estrange, in August 1846, while Mr Armstrong of Balliver gave a picnic on a 'magnificent scale' at Strawberry Hill House. Similarly in February 1847 a lavish dinner was celebrated and attended

Fig. 4 The Great Telescope (52 feet focus; 6 feet clear opening of speculum) erected at Birr Castle in the early 1840s, by William Parsons, 3rd Earl of Rosse and president of the Royal Society. The drawing shows Lord Rosse directing the conveyance of the Great Speculum to its position at the base of the tube, north side. *On Stone* by W. Bevan, from a drawing by Miss Henrietta M. Crompton. [Source: National Library of Ireland]

Fig. 5 James Plunkett Joly, of Hollywood House, Bracknagh, near Clonbullogue and later Church of Ireland rector at Clonsast, compiled a series of diaries (1843–49) which provide an alternative view of the Famine years. Included above is a sketch from his diaries showing music and dancing in the Clonbullogue Constabulary Barrack at which Lewis and Campion played. [Source: Offaly Historical Society]

by upwards of 150 people at Thomastown House for the coming of age of Francis Bennett. Again, two years later, while there were reports of whole districts being cleared of smallholders and landless labourers, Bennett threw a feast for all the tenants at his estate, at which it was once again reported that nothing was spared.

Likewise, great festivities were celebrated on New Year's Day 1849 for Col Westenra's tenants at Sharavogue, at which the celebrated Peter Cunningham the piper played. Other examples of entertainment in the midst of Famine are to be found in the aforementioned Joly diaries. In September 1847 Joly notes that thirty-six loads of hay were drawn from Clonbullogue, which was followed by lively entertainment at which Ned Charmychael played the fiddle while John Connell and Patsy Kelly danced. Another dance in May 1846 was hosted by George Redding at which Joly played the drum and Corcoran the fife. Remarkably, these diaries show an altogether different perspective of the Famine at local level. The leisure pursuits of the ascendancy were also undisturbed by the Famine. In particular, the Ormond and King's County hunt continued to meet regularly during this period. Other race and hunt meets included those at Banagher, at Parsonstown in 1846 and 1850, the Geashill Associated Hunt at Ballymooney in 1846, and Tullamore when it was hosted at Ballykilmurray. In January 1849 the hunt met four times in ten days covering the track at Woodfield, Ballyapple, Rathrobin and Glasshouse. At a meeting of the King's County and Ormond Hunt, led by Colonel Westenra, at Golden Grove in March 1849, it was noted that 'not since the praties ceased to grow' had such a crowd assembled.

For the majority of the population, the Famine brought about considerable change as the population of King's County declined by 34,000 people or 23% in the period 1841 to 1851, while emigration continued unabated throughout the 1850s. About 6,000 people died in the county's workhouses at Birr, Edenderry and Tullamore, where there were several outbreaks of cholera. Could more have been done to relieve the plight of the people? It appears that if landlords

and agents had been prepared to cooperate at barony level rather than resort to the provision of relief for their own tenants, progress might have been made in terms of the relief of hardship. While some landlords did alleviate distress at a local level, questions remain to be answered about the perceived benevolence of others. As many as sixty landlords were forced to sell their estates in the Encumbered Estates Court in the 1850s, indicating that they were themselves in a precarious state. What were the motives that lay behind schemes of assisted emigration? Did the largest of these in King's County, involving over 350 people on the Ponsonby estate at Cloghan in 1847, result from the benevolence of the landlord or his intention to make the estate attractive for a sale to Earl Fitzwilliam in the same year?[8] For many landlords the Famine brought the chance for the reorganisation of their estates. Although some, like John Julian, a solicitor, noted the tranquility of the county by 1850, a new wave of clearances began in the years which followed. In fact, the clearances of the early 1850s in King's County were more numerous than at any period during the Famine.

Fig. 6 Tullamore workhouse was known locally as the 'Gorm' (blue), because of the colour of its admission ticket. One might also suggest that the term captures the dark brooding character of the institution. A total of 1,681 people died in the workhouse between 1841 and 1851 (775 females and 906 males). [Source: Offaly Historical Society]

# The Smith estate of Baltyboys, County Wicklow

## Matthew Stout

The Smith estate of Baltyboys corresponded to the townland of Baltyboys Lower, which lies within two miles of Blessington, in west County Wicklow.[1] The large townland of 462 hectares is a roughly triangular shaped ridge with the King's river and Liffey river forming its northeast and northwest sides, respectively. The 'base' of the townland (and the limit of the estate) is demarcated by a straight townland boundary. The ridge bounded by the rivers rises sharply from below the 180m contour (the level of the modern Blessington Lake) to 303m.

Due to the steep gradient, most of the individual holdings displayed an egalitarianism, typical of holdings in environmentally marginal areas such as this. Holdings include both rough upland pasture and waterlogged lowlands. This compact townland estate makes an ideal study area for four key reasons. First, Baltyboys House stands near the apex of the triangular townland; nonetheless, it stood no more than 3km from all the Smith's tenants and this is a rare example where the landlord (and the landlord's wife) knew and interacted with all the tenants on the estate.

Secondly, its location in Wicklow provides a less common, eastern-Ireland perspective on the landscape implications of the Famine. Thirdly, the Smiths were very conscientious landlords who carefully and reliably prepared statistical data dealing with their estate; a late (1836) entry in the tithe applotment books took advantage of new Ordnance Survey mapping, and the first reliable Census of June 1841:

> Busy filling up the Census papers which are very complete as to information, the use of which I don't exactly know, the poor people here are all terrified that they were to have been kidnapped or pressed or murdered on the night of the 6th. Half of them were not to go to bed and had barricaded their doors.

Lastly, this estate is the subject of a remarkable diary kept by Elizabeth [née Grant] Smith (1797–1885), the landlord's wife.[2] Elizabeth Smith wrote professionally for British journals,[3] but she is best known for the posthumously published memoirs of her early life in Scotland and her experience in Ireland during the Great Famine (she also wrote about her first-hand knowledge of India and France).

Elizabeth Smith's diaries begin in Ireland on New Year's day in 1840 and continue until her death in 1885. Published 'selections' of her work extend only to 1850, and the full diaries deserve to be in print along with her published writings. The memoir offers a complete picture of life on this small Wicklow estate; from the conditions of its poorest tenants and sub-tenants to the lives of their wealthy neighbour, the Earls of Milltown of 'Russboro' house. Literature, politics, economics, and pure gossip are all featured. An entry from 24 June 1843 typifies her range of concerns:

> In the evening, when we were wandering about among the flowers, Lady Milltown and her two daughters arrived. They staid three hours or more. She was most amusing – the lord and she are rather at variance about Mr Fitzleeson [Lord Milltown's illegitimate son with an Italian mistress] – he is still in England making his tour of the race-courses, while she is left alone without a penny in that Cathedral of a house [Russborough].
>
> O'Connell has so unsettled people that many dreading evil to come . . . occupying themselves with preparations for running off to America or anywhere whenever the outbreak threatens. . . . Sir Robert Peel will be a wonderful man if he weather[s] all the storms.

As her Irish diaries were not intended for publication, Smith is frank about her family, friends and tenants. Com-

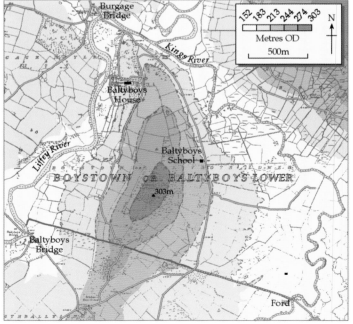

Fig. 1 THE SMITH ESTATE, BALTYBOYS LOWER TOWNLAND, NORTHWEST COUNTY WICKLOW.

bining this unique qualitative source with ubiquitous quantitative data restores the humanity to the individuals behind anonymous statistics.

## PRE-FAMINE

Tithe applotment books, the later Griffith's valuation, Census results, Valuations Office records and the remarkable detail provided in Smith's diaries all permit a precise mapping and classification of pre-Famine population and land holdings. Prior to the Famine, Baltyboys was held by twenty-eight individuals in thirty separate holdings totalling (in the tithe books) 456ha. Although the average holding size was 15ha, just four men held half of the estate: Protestants Thomas Darker, the estate manager, and his brother John held 107ha, including the then vacant house and demesne lands of 38ha; Thomas and Hugh Kelly held 87ha between them.

The 1841 Census recorded 260 people on the Baltyboys estate. Approximately one-fifth of the population (21%, fifty-five people) gained a livelihood from the Smith estate. This includes the Smiths themselves, their household servants, live-in outdoor farm labourers and the aforementioned Darkers. Five dwellings outside the demesne gates housed a retired nurse-maid, the gardener, herd, stableman and a general labourer. Three craftsmen and their families comprised another twenty-five persons (10%) on the estate.

Large tenants, their families and labourers made up the largest percentage of the population. The ten largest holdings (all over 15ha) accounted for eighty-seven persons, one-third (33%) of the townland's population. In her diaries, Elizabeth Smith provides detailed pen-pictures of her larger tenants. Tom Kelly, for example, was the estate's largest Catholic tenant farmer. He had a wife and seven children and seven servants/labourers. His house was thatched, but tellingly, his outbuildings were always slated. Smith begrudges the prosperity of this tenant because of his 'backward' farming methods. In January 1847 she wrote:

Tom Kelly, an old man now, with old untidy ways, married at fifty, a girl with a hundred pounds who has made him an excellent wife. They have a large yard, new good offices, a garden, house of three large rooms, and seven children, four boys and three girls; the four elder ones at school; plenty here but in an uncomfortable manner and the worst farming though the rent is never behind; no draining, no turnips, not sufficient stock.

The remainder of the population (ninety-three persons, 36%) was made up of the smaller tenant farmers, former tenants who still held houses from which the land had been dispossessed, and sub-tenants, those who had a house through one of the Smith's larger tenants. For the most part, these were the very poor who survived on their plot of pota-

toes and acted as casual agricultural labourers. As Famine struck, the worsening poverty of this class was vividly described by Elizabeth Smith:

I went up the hill again first calling on the Widow Quinn, who being left some years ago on her husband's death insolvent with a large and very young family and she an ailing woman, the Colonel [Smith] relieved her of her land, forgave her seven years' rent, gave her the stock and crop to dispose of and left her the house and garden for her life. I put mother and daughter on the souplist, times being so hard. Two of the daughters are very well married, the third made a wretched one; she took a sickly labouring lad who is often laid up, but to whom she has brought seven children. They live in the mother's cowhouse where she had no right to put them

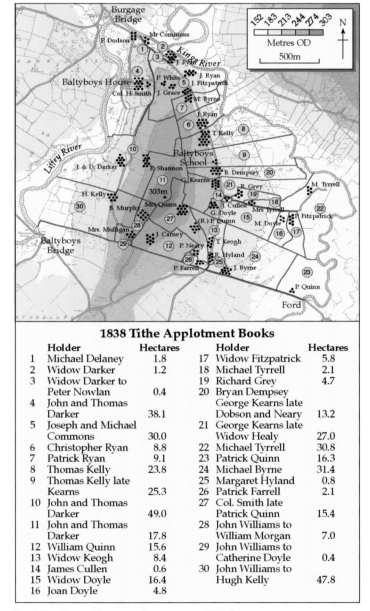

### 1838 Tithe Applotment Books

| | Holder | Hectares | | | Holder | Hectares |
|---|---|---|---|---|---|---|
| 1 | Michael Delaney | 1.8 | | 17 | Widow Fitzpatrick | 5.8 |
| 2 | Widow Darker | 1.2 | | 18 | Michael Tyrrell | 2.1 |
| 3 | Widow Darker to | | | 19 | Richard Grey | 4.7 |
| | Peter Nowlan | 0.4 | | 20 | Bryan Dempsey | |
| 4 | John and Thomas | | | | George Kearns late | |
| | Darker | 38.1 | | | Dobson and Neary | 13.2 |
| 5 | Joseph and Michael | | | 21 | George Kearns late | |
| | Commons | 30.0 | | | Widow Healy | 27.0 |
| 6 | Christopher Ryan | 8.8 | | 22 | Michael Tyrrell | 30.8 |
| 7 | Patrick Ryan | 9.1 | | 23 | Patrick Quinn | 16.3 |
| 8 | Thomas Kelly | 23.8 | | 24 | Michael Byrne | 31.4 |
| 9 | Thomas Kelly late | | | 25 | Margaret Hyland | 0.8 |
| | Kearns | 25.3 | | 26 | Patrick Farrell | 2.1 |
| 10 | John and Thomas | | | 27 | Col. Smith late | |
| | Darker | 49.0 | | | Patrick Quinn | 15.4 |
| 11 | John and Thomas | | | 28 | John Williams to | |
| | Darker | 17.8 | | | William Morgan | 7.0 |
| 12 | William Quinn | 15.6 | | 29 | John Williams to | |
| 13 | Widow Keogh | 8.4 | | | Catherine Doyle | 0.4 |
| 14 | James Cullen | 0.6 | | 30 | John Williams to | |
| 15 | Widow Doyle | 16.4 | | | Hugh Kelly | 47.8 |
| 16 | Joan Doyle | 4.8 | | | | |

Fig. 2 PRE-FAMINE BALTYBOYS (BASED ON THE 1841 CENSUS, THE TITHE APPLOTMENT BOOKS AND THE SMITH DIARIES)

and thus settle a whole family of beggars upon us, but we did not look after things then as we have learned to do now. It is the most wretched abode imaginable, without window or fire-place, mud for the floor, neither water or weather-tight, nor scare a door, all black with smoke, no furniture scarcely.

Smith first mentions the potato failure on 26 October 1845, a mere fifty-one days after blight was first reported in Ireland. This passage records the early, and mistaken belief, that the food value of blighted potatoes could be salvaged:

The Colonel has been very much occupied with plans for the prevention of such extreme distress as the failure of the potato crop threatens the poor with . . . The potato once attacked is quite unfit for food, it rots away, infecting all its companions, but the farina the nourishing part of the root is uninjured even in the worst cases so that by scraping down the potato at once and making it into what

they call starch nothing fit for food is lost.

A year later, on 26 September 1846, the implications of the potato's failure is more fully understood:

Here comes the famine too, the rain has spoiled the few miserable potatoes left, the markets are higher than they were ever known to be since the war, harvest work is over, the Irish landlords generally are bankrupt, three fourths of the land mortgaged to full value, with, therefore, nominal large rent rolls they have not a penny to spend in labour. From some hitch between the government and the Board of Works, no public works are going forward, the ministry don't choose to interfere with the provision trade; so here we are, the peasantry starving.

During the course of the Great Famine, these diaries tell of the estate's attempts at caring for the starving, while at the same time expressing enthusiasm for the notorious Gregory clause. Accounts of the ravages of the famine diseases; dysentery, inflammatory attacks, influenza and fever,[4] are juxtaposed with meals in the Gresham Hotel in Dublin. The cumulative effects of death and emigration were so extensive that it led to the closure of her boys' school. On 7 April 1850 Elizabeth Smith recorded:

There are very few boys left on our side of the country; there will be few men soon for they are pouring on in shoals to America. Crowds upon crowds swarm along the roads, the bye roads, following carts with their trunks and other property. We have forty children as yet in the girls' school; but really I don't think there will be half that number by autumn.

Potato failures are recorded as late as 6 August 1850, at which point Smith's entries are mainly concerned with the marriage of her daughter. It is a reminder, nonetheless, that famine did not end neatly with that disastrous decade.

## IMPACT

The immediate impact of the Famine can be assessed using Griffith's Valuation and the 1851 Census. After the Famine, Baltyboys was held by eighteen individuals in twenty-one separate holdings totalling (in Griffith's Valuation) 447ha. The number of landholders fell by ten during the Famine years (-36%) and consolidation resulted in a 30% reduction in the number of holdings. The average holding size increased from 15ha to 21ha but the Darker and Kelly holdings were virtually unchanged.

The 1851 census recorded 207 people on the Baltyboys Estate. The drop of 20% compares favourably with the information extracted from the Smith diaries and Griffith's Valuation. A population decline of one-fifth is also compara-

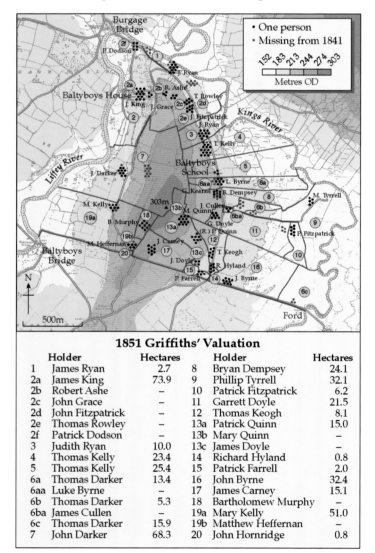

### 1851 Griffiths' Valuation

| | Holder | Hectares | | Holder | Hectares |
|---|---|---|---|---|---|
| 1 | James Ryan | 2.7 | 8 | Bryan Dempsey | 24.1 |
| 2a | James King | 73.9 | 9 | Phillip Tyrrell | 32.1 |
| 2b | Robert Ashe | – | 10 | Patrick Fitzpatrick | 6.2 |
| 2c | John Grace | – | 11 | Garrett Doyle | 21.5 |
| 2d | John Fitzpatrick | – | 12 | Thomas Keogh | 8.1 |
| 2e | Thomas Rowley | – | 13a | Patrick Quinn | 15.0 |
| 2f | Patrick Dodson | – | 13b | Mary Quinn | – |
| 3 | Judith Ryan | 10.0 | 13c | James Doyle | – |
| 4 | Thomas Kelly | 23.4 | 14 | Richard Hyland | 0.8 |
| 5 | Thomas Kelly | 25.4 | 15 | Patrick Farrell | 2.0 |
| 6a | Thomas Darker | 13.4 | 16 | John Byrne | 32.4 |
| 6aa | Luke Byrne | – | 17 | James Carney | 15.1 |
| 6b | Thomas Darker | 5.3 | 18 | Bartholomew Murphy | – |
| 6ba | James Cullen | – | 19a | Mary Kelly | 51.0 |
| 6c | Thomas Darker | 15.9 | 19b | Matthew Heffernan | – |
| 7 | John Darker | 68.3 | 20 | John Hornridge | 0.8 |

Fig. 3 BALTYBOYS IMMEDIATELY AFTER THE FAMINE (BASED ON THE 1851 CENSUS, GRIFFITH'S VALUATION AND THE SMITH DIARIES)

ble to the decline in population experienced in Lower Tal-botstown barony and in Wicklow county as a whole.

The Famine only began the haemorrhaging of people from the Irish landscape. In Baltyboys, the long-term empty-ing out of the estate can be better assessed by examining the population of Baltyboys in 1883. On this date, two years prior to the death of Elizabeth Smith, the valuation records reveal that she was once more in possession of Baltyboys House.

Thirty years after the end of the Famine, Baltyboys was held by eleven individuals in twenty separate holdings totalling (according to Valuation Office records) 442ha. Stability in land-holding patterns is shown by the fact that both landholders and holdings were just one fewer than in 1851. The same large ten-ants, or their heirs, are still in situ. Eleven of the fifteen major tenants – those with holdings over 14ha – survived the period 1836–83. For nearly half a century, years that included the cata-clysm of the Famine, the landholding pattern remained virtual-ly unchanged. In Baltyboys, just as was seen in the Catholic parish of Clogheen/Burncourt in County Tipperary,[5] and as was the case in early medieval Ireland, the 14ha holding ensured viability in pre-industrial pastoral farming.

Stability in landholding stands in marked contrast to population change. The 1881 Census records only 136 people living in the townland, down 48% from the 260 recorded four decades earlier. The valuation records indi-cate that most of the decline in population came from on or near Baltyboys demesne. Most of the houses recorded here in 1851 were empty or gone by 1881. The withdrawal of patronage on the part of the resident landlord accounted for as much as 41% of the overall decline in population during those thirty years.

The Smith estate demonstrates the major dichotomy in post-Famine Ireland. On one hand, there was profound population decline, and an emptying out of the landscape.[6]

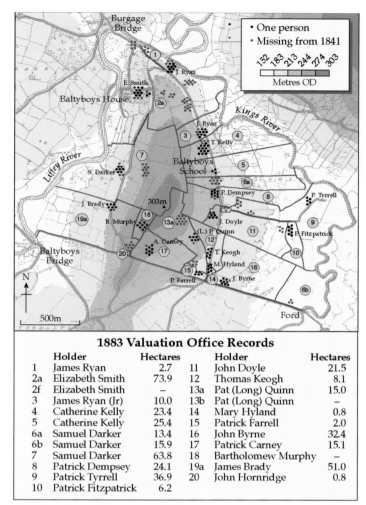

**1883 Valuation Office Records**

| | Holder | Hectares | | Holder | Hectares |
|---|---|---|---|---|---|
| 1 | James Ryan | 2.7 | 11 | John Doyle | 21.5 |
| 2a | Elizabeth Smith | 73.9 | 12 | Thomas Keogh | 8.1 |
| 2f | Elizabeth Smith | – | 13a | Pat (Long) Quinn | 15.0 |
| 3 | James Ryan (Jr) | 10.0 | 13b | Pat (Long) Quinn | – |
| 4 | Catherine Kelly | 23.4 | 14 | Mary Hyland | 0.8 |
| 5 | Catherine Kelly | 25.4 | 15 | Patrick Farrell | 2.0 |
| 6a | Samuel Darker | 13.4 | 16 | John Byrne | 32.4 |
| 6b | Samuel Darker | 15.9 | 17 | Patrick Carney | 15.1 |
| 7 | Samuel Darker | 63.8 | 18 | Bartholomew Murphy | – |
| 8 | Patrick Dempsey | 24.1 | 19a | James Brady | 51.0 |
| 9 | Patrick Tyrrell | 36.9 | 20 | John Hornridge | 0.8 |
| 10 | Patrick Fitzpatrick | 6.2 | | | |

Fig. 4 POST-FAMINE BALTYBOYS IN 1883 (BASED ON THE 1881 CENSUS AND VALUA-TIONS OFFICE RECORDS)

On the other hand, there was a marked continuity in land tenure on viable holdings. The basic layout of farms was unchanged.

# MUNSTER

**The Hungry Grass**

Crossing the shallow holdings high above sea
Where few birds nest, the luckless foot may pass
From the bright safety of experience
Into the terror of the hungry grass.

Here in a year when poison from the air
First withered in despair the growth of spring
Some skulled-faced wretch whom nettle could not save
Crept on four bones to his last scattering,

Crept, and the shrivelled heart which drove his thought
Towards platters brought in hospitality
Burst as the wizened eyes measured the miles
Like dizzy walls forbidding him the city.

Little the earth reclaimed from that poor body,
And yet remembering him the place has grown
Bewitched and the thin grass he nourishes
Racks with his famine, sucks marrow from the bone.

                                        - Donagh MacDonagh

Cill Rialaigh, County Kerry.
[Photo: John Crowley]

# The province of Munster and the Great Famine

## *William J. Smyth*

The Munster province is a land of contrasts – and the level of human devastation wreaked by the Great Famine is in some respects surprising for this rich but complex territory. Munster contains 29.2% of the total area of Ireland and in 1841 its share of arable land was practically the same (29.1%). As an indication of the relative wealth of its land-lords, middlemen, big farmers and merchants, 34% of the island's demesnes, plantations and tree-lined landscapes were in Munster – an even higher proportion than in Leinster. Like Leinster, Munster was a land of both small and big farms. Over 17% of its holdings were in the 1–5 acre category but, more significantly, some 52% were over 15 acres.

Figs 1(a) PERCENTAGE DISTRIBUTION OF FAMILIES LIVING IN FOURTH-CLASS HOUSES IN 1841 and 1(b). THE CHANGING DISTRIBUTION OF FAMILIES LIVING IN FOURTH-CLASS HOUSES, 1841–51. The fourth-class house – a 'mud cabin having only one room' –- is seen as a great symbol of poverty in pre-Famine Ireland. One can make a broad distinction between (i) the eastern Munster counties of Tipperary and Waterford (as well as the lower Lee and Blackwater valleys), where families living in these houses were least prevalent in 1841, and (ii) western peninsular and upland Munster where over 60% and often, as in parts of the Dingle, Beara, Sheep's Head, and Mizen peninsulas, over 85% of all houses were in this class. However, there were also exceptionally high levels in many small parishes around Kinsale, and in a cluster of similar parishes around Fedamore and Knockainy in lowland east Limerick. This map (Fig. 1a) thus reveals very sharp variations in living standards as between west and east Munster. In middle Munster from Clare through much of Limerick, south and mid-Kerry and much of Cork, fourth-class dwelling houses made up 45–60% of the housing stock. During and after the Famine these cabins were swept from the landscape (see Fig. 1b). Over much of north and south Munster, less than 20% of this house type survived by 1851. Three major regions of greater stability are revealed for the north Kerry/west Limerick borderlands, east Limerick/west Tipperary and southeast Tipperary. These areas, with smaller pockets around Waterford and Cork cities and in peninsular Kerry, also reveal the lowest decline.

Indeed more than a third were over the critical threshold for famine survival at 20 acres or more. Cork was par excellence the county of big farmers followed by Waterford and Kerry. Small farmers were more characteristic of the north Munster counties, particularly County Clare. Close on one-third of the island's civic districts (2,000+ population) were located in Munster – led by the three port cities of Cork, Limerick and Waterford. Some one-quarter of the 1841 population lived in towns and villages, but much of the populations of some of these – for example, Bantry, Carrick-on-Suir, Fethard, Kilmallock – were already in a semi-destitute condition. Population densities were high, especially in the far west whose communities were to suffer so severely during the Famine.

Yet Munster's overall density figure of 305 per square mile of arable land was below the national average at 335 and well below that of Ulster (406) and Connacht (386). Keen on schooling, like Leinster, one-fourth of its children aged from five to sixteen were attending school in 1841, yet 52% of its males and 68% of its females could then neither read nor write.[1] While famous for its lush grasslands and the out-wintering of its cattle and cows in its very temperate climate, yet as late as 1851 one-quarter of Munster's cultivated land was devoted to cereals and other crops. It was a land rich not only in cattle, cows, pigs and dairy products but also a land of many mills and strong towns like Clonmel, Tipperary, Tralee and indeed Skibbereen.[2] Munster's population at the end of 1845 was likely to have been a little over 2.5 million – the most peopled province on the island.

But that is only half the story. Nearly 30% of the island's rough uncultivated land was in Munster. Apart from the boggy upland plateaus of parts of Limerick and Clare, much of these difficult lands were part of the east–west trending Armorican foldings, which carved the province into an oscillating series of uplands and lowlands: the Galtee, Knockmealdown and Slieve Felim Mountains – and the Golden Vale in the east – and the deeper valleys to the west amid the mountainous peninsulas of Kerry and west Cork. Thus, Munster was also split into an oscillating series of upland parishes which supplied servants and migrant labourers (*spailpíní*) to the richer lowland parishes below and those further to the east. The ancient province of Munster was known to be the land of both music and serf-cum-servant.[3] Even in the mid-nineteenth-century, Munster had the island's greatest number of rural servants, working mainly on the big farms of the province. Almost one-quarter of the island's

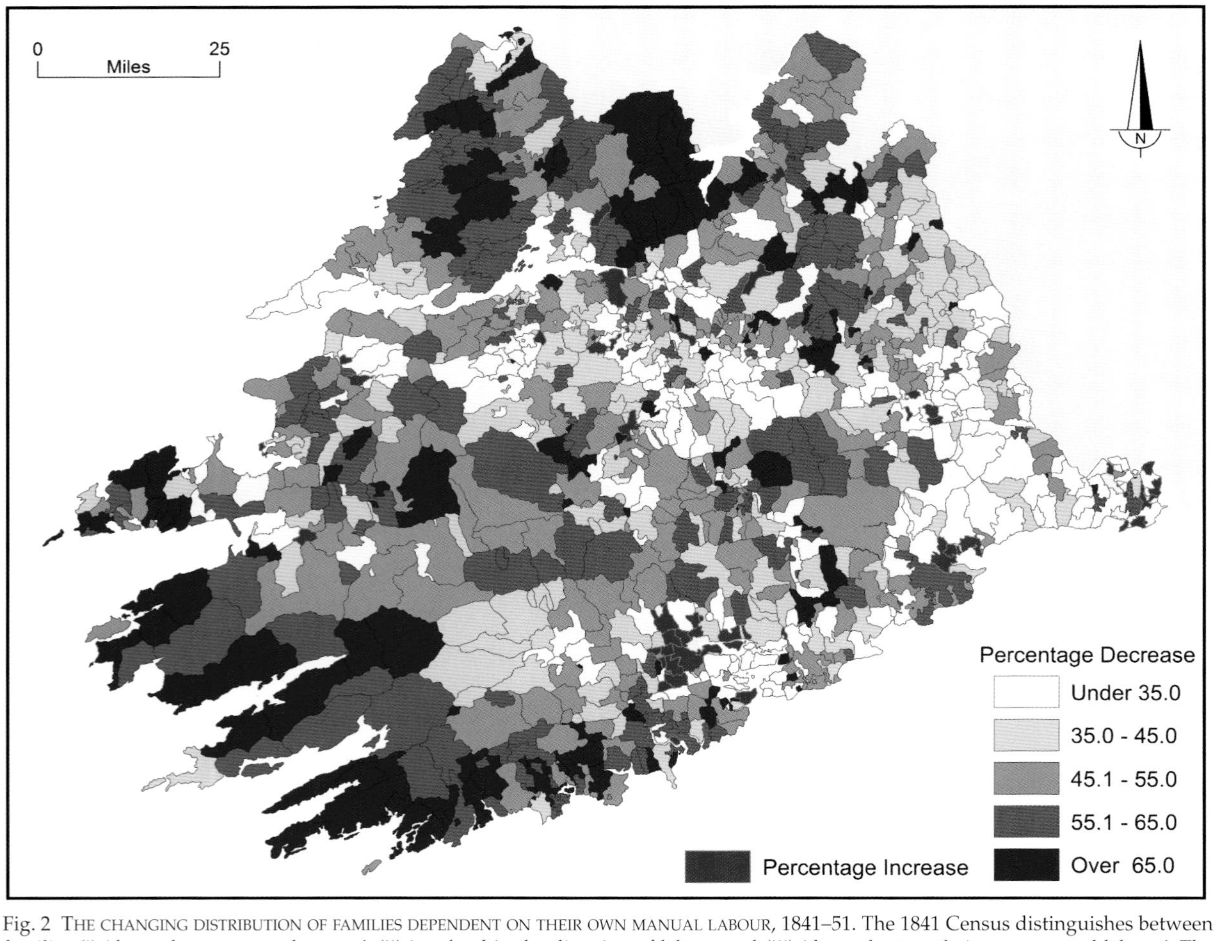

Fig. 2 THE CHANGING DISTRIBUTION OF FAMILIES DEPENDENT ON THEIR OWN MANUAL LABOUR, 1841–51. The 1841 Census distinguishes between families (i) 'dependent on vested means'; (ii) involved in the direction of labour and (iii) 'dependent on their own manual labour'. The third category is, therefore, most indicative of the distribution of smallholders, artisans, cottiers and landless labourers, i.e. those most likely to be badly affected by the Famine. There are four major regions in Munster where up to three-quarters of all families were in this third class in 1841: almost all of County Clare; upland mid-Tipperary; the Waterford/Tipperary/Cork borderlands; and the southwestern peninsulas. In contrast, the Feale and Laune valleys in Kerry, those of the Maigue and the Deel in Limerick, and the Golden Vale, stretching from east Limerick into all of south Tipperary, mid-Waterford and the Cork/Charleville axis, were regions where people 'with independent means' and/or who 'directed labour' constituted close on one-half of the rural families. By 1851, the labouring and smallholder classes of Clare and upland and peninsular Munster had been devastated. With some exceptions, families dependent on their own manual labour were more resilient in strong farming areas where there was still a demand for farm labourers and areas in proximity to towns and cities. In these latter areas, in particular, a greater diversity of employment opportunities, especially for artisans, and internal patterns of migration may have helped to ensure a more than two-third 'survival rate' amongst this class by 1851.

water bodies were also in Munster – adding further to this complex and often beautiful mosaic of good land, poor land, wet land, moorland, extensive coastlands, remote rural regions and sophisticated port cities.

A deeply class-stratified province, it is not surprising that in 1841 Munster had the greatest proportion of one-roomed mud cabins – containing one-third of the island's share as compared with one-quarter each for Connacht and Ulster and a mere 16.3% for Leinster. Not surprisingly, almost one-third of families were dependent on their own manual labour, the same as in Connacht.[4] On a number of other social indices, it ranks below Leinster and

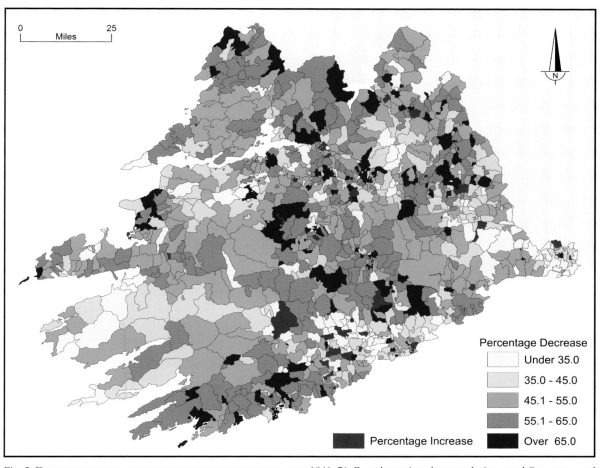

Fig. 3 DECLINE IN NUMBER OF CHILDREN UNDER FIVE YEARS OF AGE, 1841–51. By subtracting the population aged five years and upwards from the total population in both 1841 and 1851, this map seeks to address the fate of young children during the Famine. On average, Munster in 1851 only retained half the equivalent population of under five years in 1841. The major reductions (over 55%) are in the strong farming regions of north Cork, east Limerick and mid-Tipperary and in the poorer regions of southwest Cork and north and east Clare. Here the combination of high mortality amongst the labouring and smallholder classes, as well as significant reductions in the number of marriages and births amongst the wealthier classes, changed dramatically the age profile of the young by 1851. Parishes which reveal a devastating two-thirds decline include Kilfintinan, Killeely and Tomgraney in County Clare, Ballysheehan, Youghalarra, Templeneiry and Thurles in County Tipperary, Kilmeedy and Tullylease in County Limerick, Mallow, Monanimy and Rahan in north Cork and Kilmocomoge and Desertserges in west Cork. In contrast, youthful populations prevail in southeast Munster, in the Cork city hinterland as well as amongst smallholding populations of Iveragh, the Kerry/Limerick borderlands and the Tipperary hills. This transformation appears to have had the most impact on overall population decline in west Munster, in mid-Waterford and the Tipperary/Limerick borderlands, as well as in urban areas, where the percentage of children under five years of age was highest (+14%) in 1841.

Ulster and comes closest to conditions in Connacht. Its infant mortality rates for 1,000 live births at 239 was greater than Ulster (200) and Leinster (231) but less than Connacht (253).[5] The census of 1841 defines three major class-groups – the third comprising 'labourers, smallholders and other persons without capital in either land, money or acquired knowledge'.[6] Almost two-thirds of the population of Ulster and Leinster were in this category – Munster is four points higher at 68.3% but Connacht is emphatically the poorest with 79% in this class-group. Munster, therefore, presents many faces: proletarian and middle-class, 'strong', comfortable and poor farmers and shopkeepers, many artisans, servants, labourers, huxters, beggarmen and women, the well-fed and the already impoverished. When the Famine ended, in absolute terms it had lost the greatest number of people of any province through death and emigration and in relative terms ranked closer to Connacht than the other

two provinces. And one of the key reasons for this status was that famine conditions were sustained throughout much of this province for five years or more. This sad state is confirmed by the fact that 7.8% of Munster's population were still confined in public institutions in 1851 – seven times that of Ulster, twice that of Leinster and almost twice that of Connacht's population.[7] This status is also confirmed by the phenomenal levels of emigration out of the province in both 1850–51 and 1851–55.

When looked at in detail, as in the parish-based computerised maps, Munster is an even more varied place. Its western flanks and peninsulas were more like the west of Connacht and famine conditions were very similar. In contrast in the east, parts of Tipperary and much of County Waterford shared features common to the midland and south Leinster counties. Middle Munster reveals even more complicated social terrains. Land hunger was endemic in this province as was the level of agrarian violence, not only against agents and landlords but also within and between different labouring and farming classes. Conflict over conacre was a central aspect. Freeman notes the Drummond Commission's reporting many of Munster's poorer pre-Famine populations 'having a diet at best of potatoes and milk and no meal . . . yet robust, active and athletic, capable of great exertion but often exposed to great privations'.[8] As elsewhere, poorer people were still colonising high up the sides of uplands and moorlands, and on wetland edges – particularly in the west and southwest but also in mid-Munster as in the Ryan–Dwyer hill county of Tipperary. In addition, poor labouring families congregated in roadside agglomerations (alongside mills and quarries, in cabin suburbs in many towns such as Carrick-on-Suir and Listowel, along arterial roads leading out of towns such as Thurles and Ennis) or colonised the fair greens in many towns.[9]

The hiring of conacre for potato growing was most pronounced amongst Munster's poor. In Ulster, labourers were seven times more likely to be paid in wages than in conacre, in Leinster three times as likely and nearly twice as likely in Connacht. In sharp contrast, in Munster conacre was almost

as important a mode of payment as wages.[10] When the potatoes failed, this poor labouring population were thus most exposed. In a province where upland and lowland parishes interdigitated, a dual economy had been very much a feature yet these two economies and societies were clearly not geographically separate. They coexisted in mutual interdependence in the good times even if the material world, status and quality of life of employers were so much superior. The Great Famine was to rupture these complex interrelationships, compounding class antagonisms and exposing many of the labouring poor, cottiers and even smallholding farmers to the terror of the famine.

Judging by the evidence of recorded deaths, all the Munster counties and boroughs headed by Limerick city (described as a 'town of grace and squalor'), Clare and West Cork and with the possible exception of Tipperary, were affected by early famine conditions and the onset of diseases such as typhus and dysentery by late 1845. Only Mayo and Longford report equivalent levels of early distress.[11] And when the Famine had run its deadly course, every county's population in Munster (except south Tipperary) had registered *above average* excess famine deaths. County

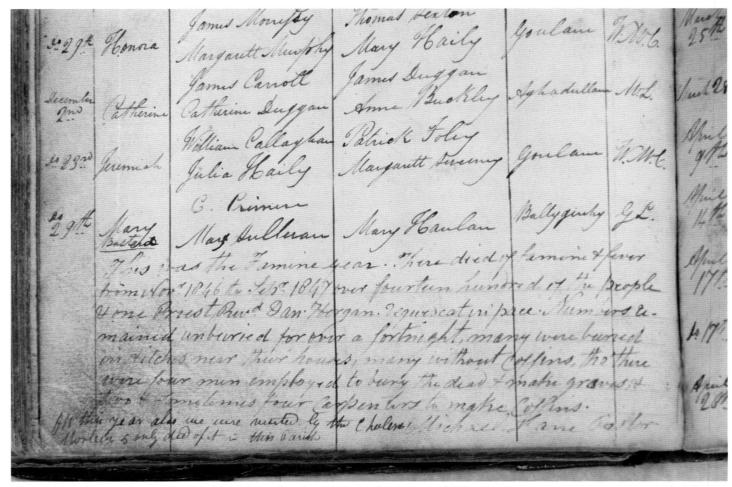

Fig. 4 Fr Michael Lane, who was transferred from the combined parishes of Baile Mhúirne and Cill na Martra to Donoughmore in 1845, made the following entry in the Baptismal Register for the parish of Donoughmore in March 1847: 'This was the Famine year. There died of famine and fever from Nov. 1846 to Feb. 1847 over fourteen hundred of the people and one priest, Rev. Dan Horgan. *Requiescat in pace*. Numbers remained unburied for over a fortnight; many were buried in ditches near their houses, many without coffins, tho [*sic*] there were four men employed to bury the dead and make graves and two sometimes four carpenters to make coffins.' [Source: Donoughmore Baptismal Register]

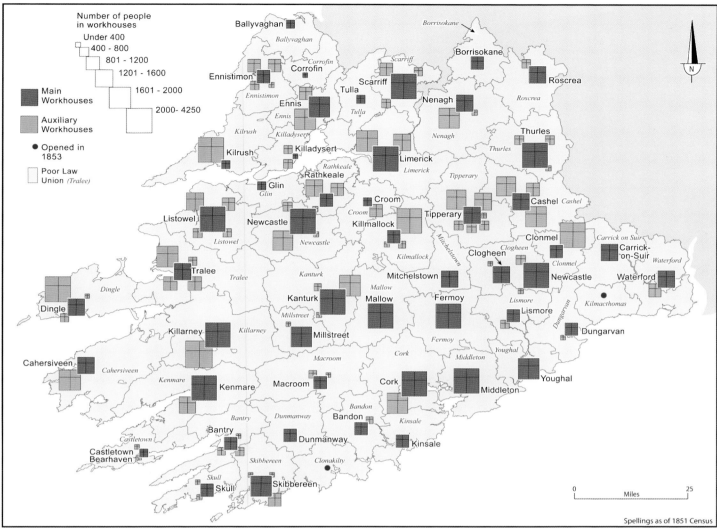

Fig. 5 THE MUNSTER WORKHOUSE POPULATION IN 1851. The workhouse or 'poorhouse' carries with it powerful memories of degradation and shame. In 1845, the workhouse population in Ireland was 38,497; in 1847 it rose to 83,283 and peaked in 1851 with 217,000 people. This map reveals the widespread distribution of workhouse inmates in Munster at its peak. As many as 145,139 people, almost 8% of Munster's population, were inmates in public institutions, 92% of which (134,064) were in workhouses. By 1851, workhouse numbers indicate that both north and west Munster (and not the south and east of the province) were most severely affected. North of a line from Cashel to Kenmare, the great majority of workhouses had inmate populations of over 3,300. Tralee (5,199) and Listowel (5,087) workhouses contained 9% and 12%, respectively, of their union populations. The workhouses of Kilrush (4,706), Ennis (4,481), Killarney (4,425), Kanturk (4,326), Newcastlewest (4,268), Tipperary (4,260), Cashel (4,206) and Dingle (4,128) were still dealing with overcrowding. A further measure of the depth of Famine conditions is the number of auxiliary buildings (see map) – often unsuited for the purpose – acquired to deal with distress. Tipperary Union workhouse had five such buildings and Ennistymon, Newcastlewest and Listowel all required four. Cashel, Dingle, Kanturk, Kilmallock and Scarriff needed three additional workhouses to deal with the desperate conditions. However desperate life was within the workhouse walls, they often came to represent the last refuge and only hope of survival for the starving people who clamoured at their gates. Conditions were particularly distressful in unions such as Kanturk, Newcastlewest and Kilrush. The workhouse population of Kilrush was greater than that of the town (4,471), a pattern repeated for eight other workhouses in County Clare. In 1851 the population of Schull workhouse was 1,311 – that of the village, 535; the Kenmare workhouse population (3,553) was also more than double that of the town (1,501).

Clare's population was the most severely affected of a deeply affected province. In many respects the people of County Clare can be seen to have shared in the worst horrors visited on the adjacent communities in Connacht. But all of Munster suffered in terrible ways. By September 1846, the people of Clashmore in County Waterford were living on blackberries and those of Rathcormack in County Cork on cabbage leaves.[12] By the winter of 1846/47, people were perishing in vast numbers across the province. In the period 1847 to 1850, excess death rates of over 3% per annum were experienced in all four years by the people of County Clare, in at least three of these years in Cork and Kerry and

for at least two years in communities in Waterford and Tipperary.[13] In the official returns for deaths by starvation, while Connacht is the most deeply traumatised with 47.2% of the island's total, Munster registers over one-quarter of the total at 27.2%. Ulster's population starvation deaths are returned at 5.2% and Leinster's 4.2%.[14] But these are the official and obviously faulty returns. If one examines Patrick Hickey's statistics for the six parishes in the Skibbereen Union (see pp. 371–379), there is a clear underestimation in these returns and this is most likely for Munster and Connacht generally.

Other parish records reveal the depth of the impact of

363

*Gentlemen*

There is a little boy named Michael Rice of Lahinch aged about 4 years he is an orphan, his father having died last year and his mother has expired on last Wednesday night, who is now about being buried without a coffin!! unless ye make some provision for such. The child in question is now at the workhouse gate expecting to be admitted if not he will starve.

Robs S. Constable

Fig. 6 *An Gorta Mór* memorial is situated on the Lahinch–Ennistymon Road , County Clare. Located near the site of the now-demolished workhouse, it commemorates the victims of the Great Famine. The memorial was sculpted by Alan Ryan Hall and was dedicated on 20 August 1995. It depicts an orphan child at the gates of the workhouse. The inscription is taken from the Ennistymon workhouse records. As many as 3,843 inmates (1,955 males/1,888 females) died in the workhouse between 1841–51. One-quarter of all the workhouse deaths in Clare, in a county devastated by the Famine, took place in this workhouse. [Photo: Frank Coyne]

the Famine. In Donoughmore parish in County Cork, the average number of marriages per annum in the years 1840 to 1846 was close to fifty-four. Between 1847 and 1852 the average declined to sixteen per annum. Only one-quarter of the pre-Famine numbers of marriages occurred in the Famine years. Between 1840 and 1846 there were 1,728 births (including thirty-nine abandoned babies). Between 1847 and 1852, only 599 babies were born and only one was abandoned. The average birth rate per annum had declined by 60%. The figures suggest a suddenness to the 1847 decline – 1846 appears to be representative of pre-Famine years. But the deadly cliff line was actually in late 1846. The then parish priest, Fr Michael Lane, reported that between November 1846 and February 1847, (i.e. in those short four winter months), over 1,400 people died of famine and fever, including the parish curate, Rev. Dan Horgan. Many of the dead remained unburied for over a fortnight and 'many were buried in ditches near their houses'.[15] Further north on the borders of Cork and Limerick, in the parish of

Charleville (*Ráth*), there were only three baptisms in October 1846 compared to an average of seventeen per month previously – confirmation of the depth of the human crisis in the winter of 1846/47. These figures suggest a reduction in the order of 60–80% in births from November 1846 to November 1847. This pattern is confirmed by Cousens' map of the decline of baptisms for the year 1847 (versus 1842 to 1845) for much of west Munster, i.e. in a line westwards from the Kerry/Limerick border to south Kerry and south-west Cork, especially its coastal-cum-peninsular regions.[16] The parishes west of Dingle were in this category. By late spring 1847, these parishes – full of clustered farm villages – are described as a virtual 'charnel house of death' (see Kieran Foley below). The decline in baptisms in east Munster parishes for 1847 were not as steep but still average only half of pre-Famine levels. East Leinster counties such as County Kildare reveal much less dramatic falls in parish baptisms.[17] The overall picture for Munster's poor is of a deeply traumatised and frightened population.

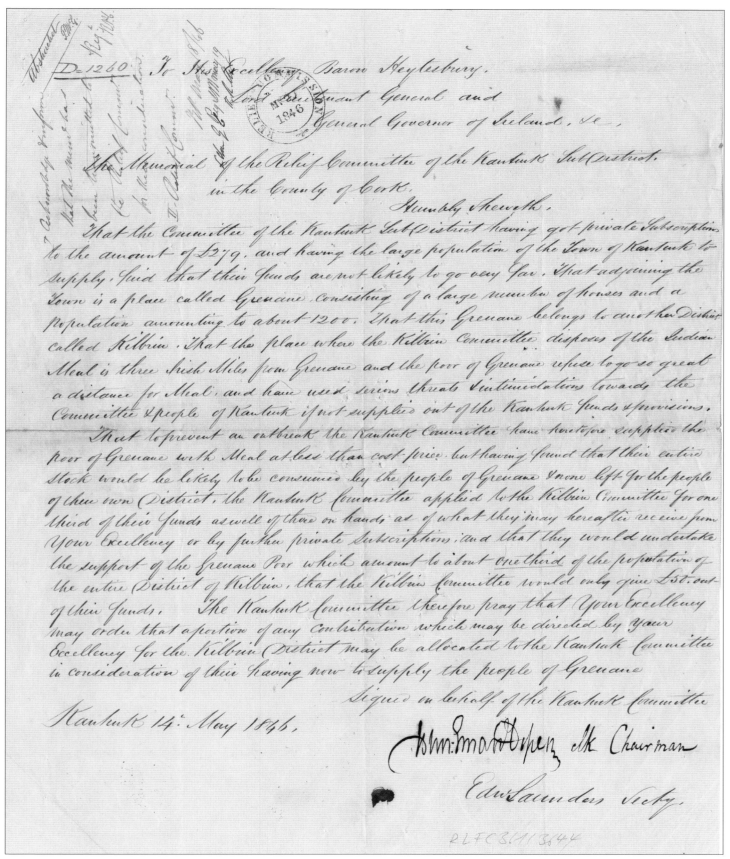

Fig. 7 A letter from Mr Edward Tierney, chairman of the Kanturk Relief Committee, County Cork, to the Lord Lieutenant, 14 May 1846, outlining the committee's concerns with regard to the provision of relief to the distressed people of Grenane ('population amounting to about 1,200'). The committee contends that it is not their responsibility to provide for the poor of Grenane but that of the neighbouring Kilbrin committee: 'That the place where the Kilbrin committee disposes of the Indian meal is three Irish miles from Grenane and the poor of Grenane refuse to go so great a distance for meal and have used serious threats and intimidation towards the committee and people of Kanturk if not supplied out of the Kanturk funds and provisions.' They request that part of the funds directed to the Kilbrin committee be now allocated to Kanturk in order to provide for the people of Grenane. [Source: Relief Commission Papers, 3/1/3644, National Archives of Ireland]

365

To the Right Honorable and Honorable, the Knights, Burgesses, &c., in Parliament assembled.

# THE PETITION

OF THE

# BOARD OF GUARDIANS, THURLES UNION,

SHEWETH,

THAT Petitioners approach your Honorable House with feelings of deep regret at the awful state of destitution into which the people of this country are plunged. Amidst the general calamity of famine, pestilence, and direful disease with which Ireland is visited, the County Tipperary is destined to be pre-eminently unfortunate. She is again stained with human blood; and her peaceful inhabitants horrified with another barbarous murder. On the 21st of May last, THOMAS DILLON went to the lands of Kilmakill, near Thurles, to serve some notices relative to the eviction of tenants, where he was brutally murdered. Sometime ago, a man named MAGRATH, in the same occupation, met a similar fate at the same place.

Your Honorable House has been often surprised at the extraordinary misery, and shocked at the unexampled crimes, with which this country has been afflicted. Her most Gracious Majesty has issued Commission after Commission, in order to discover the sources of these enormous evils. The Land Commission has at length laid before the world clear and conclusive evidence sufficient to show that most, if not all, of these evils arise from the inefficiency of the laws between landlord and tenant, and the oppressive manner in which they are administered. It may be argued that the failure of the Potato crop is the cause of our present distress. Supposing it to be the immediate cause, your Petitioners respectfully submit that if the rights of the tenants had been protected during the last century as well as the rights of the landlords, the failure of the Potato crop, or any other particular crop, could never have entailed such misery on an industrious and well-disposed people. Had such been the case, the farmers of Ireland would be long since elevated in their moral as well as social condition, and periodical famine, and misery, and crime would be banished from our land. The want of security to the tenant, that his labour, skill, and capital expended shall be fairly compensated for, has damped his exertions, paralyzed his energies, and often drove him to despair, which led him ultimately to the commission of the most barbarous crimes. All the stimulants of farming societies, all their verbose theoretical doctrines of improved systems, will never cause any advance in agricultural improvement, until there is a certainty of tenure and a just remuneration for profitable expenditure.

In administering the Relief Act, your Petitioners cannot but deplore the sad spectacle daily presented to them of farmers, holding between five and fifty acres of land, coming before them as paupers seeking relief. Had there been anything like fair protection, or encouragement from their landlords, no such class would become a burden on the state. Had the misfortunes of a hard-worked and brokenhearted tenantry terminated in their extreme poverty and privations, which they bear with unexampled patience, your Petitioners perhaps would have remained silent; but when they see this numerous class, inured to sorrow and misery, afraid to come forward in open day and lay their grievances before the Parliament; plotting and seeking wild revenge, and imbuing their fertile soil with the blood of their fellowmen; they feel called on to endeavour to draw the attention of your Honorable House to the absolute necessity of affording to the tenants of Ireland that legislative protection to which the landlords themselves acknowledge they are entitled.

Your Petitioners by no means want to infringe on the rights of the landlords; they are free to confess that many landlords, when evicting their tenants, make allowance for permanent improvements. But, while they possess three legal modes of recovering their rents—namely, distress, civil action and ejectment, all at the same time—the tenants claim only one legal mode of recovering compensation for their productive expenditure. The landlords have the most stringent and extraordinary powers to enforce their part of the contract; yet they do not wish the legislature would interfere on the part of the tenants, who they think ought to be left to their honor, their caprice, or their tender mercy. Petitioners beg to state that this country has been involved in the most disastrous calamities by the continuance of this system. From the burning of the SHEES, some twenty years ago, down to the recent massacre of DILLON, including the murders of the Messrs. COOPER, CHADWICK, BOURKES, O'KEEFFE, BYRNE, SCULLY, &c., and hundreds of murderous attacks on other individuals; all arose out of the eviction of tenants without compensation, and uncertainty of the tenure of land.

During the last ten years a landlord and tenant bill has been promised by the late, as well as the present, Government; but, alas! little or no progress is yet made, now that Parliament is about to be dissolved. Your Petitioners respectfully state that this is not a time to trifle with the feelings of an impoverished, a starving and infuriated people, who only desire a pretext for outbreak—and when that mighty Man, whose magic influence could quell an insurrection, is now no more.—Your Petitioners regret to see a well-organised Police, and a well-disciplined Military force engaged in the ignoble exploits of protecting our Merchants' provisions from plunder—in escorting our Sheriff while ejecting our fellowmen from their homes, and the homes of their ancestors—and harassed night and day in pursuing the murderers of those persons whose only crime is, that they enforce the landlord laws with the accustomed severity.

The Kilmakill murder occurred under peculiar circumstances. The poor tenants paid eight years' rent within the last eight years; but there appeared to be old arrears and law costs. In all other dealings between man and man, the statute of limitation would have protected the creditor. The landlord, however, should have unlimited power; he sums up to the very farthing all arrears accruing for twenty years, and thus brings the unfortunate tenants in debt: then ejects them; and, under a newly discovered, refined mode of eviction, is about to turn them out to starve. He got the Sheriff to take possession; but, in his clemency, he let them in as caretakers. In a short time he orders them to quit: they refuse. He then sends DILLON to summons them for forcible possession: while obeying his orders, DILLON is murdered,—Your Petitioners most earnestly request that your Honorable House be pleased to order an inquiry into the facts of this case, in order to add another to the many convincing proofs already adduced of the want of legislative interference on this subject.

Your Petitioners yield to none in loyalty and attachment to our gracious and beloved Sovereign, in respect for your Honorable House, or in zeal and anxiety for the public peace. But they feel called on to express their firm conviction, that if that justice which has been so long promised to the tenants of Ireland be much longer delayed, the consequences may be most disastrous to the peace and security of this part of the Empire. They, therefore, most earnestly entreat, implore, and beseech your Honorable House to bring forward, before the closing of this Session of Parliament, a comprehensive measure of protection for the tenants of Ireland.

And your Petitioners will ever pray.

Signed on behalf of the Board,

**P. B. RYAN,**

Chairman.

Board-room, 29th June, 1847.

M. QUINLAN, PRINTER, THURLES.

Fig. 8 The Board of Guardians of the Thurles Union petition parliament for the reform of the landholding structure, 28 June 1847. The murder of Thomas Dillon, who had gone to serve eviction notices to tenants on the lands of Kilmakill, is but a symptom of a much deeper crisis. The Famine has further underlined the injustices of a system where there is 'no certainty of tenure' and where 'evictions occur without compensation'. The petitioners argue that agricultural improvement cannot take place within the present system where the landlords' rights are protected while no such legislative protection exists for the tenants: 'In administering the Relief Act, your petitioners cannot but deplore the sad spectacle daily presented of farmers holding between five and fifty acres of land coming before them as paupers seeking relief. Had there been anything like fair protection or encouragement from their landlord, no such class would become a burden on the State.' [Source: National Library of Ireland]

366

Munster's plight is epitomised by the creation of fifteen new unions and workhouses by 1850 – almost half of the island-wide total. Of all the provinces, it is Munster's population which reveals the most sustained excess famine mortality from 1847 onwards. In the case of Counties Clare and Tipperary, famine mortalities even continued into the year 1852. Workhouse records for 1850 and 1851 in County Clare confirm severe mortality levels in the county at the end of the Famine period. Records exist for deaths in Kilrush and Ennistymon workhouses for the year ending 25 March 1851. Kilrush and its auxiliary workhouse recorded 1,590 deaths and Ennistymon 1,412 in that year. These figures alone represent mortalities of 31 per 1,000 of the Kilrush Union's total population and 45 per 1,000 of Ennistymon's total union population. If these were the mortality figures *within* the workhouses alone, it is abundantly clear that excess mortality among the general population was much greater. Excess mortalities for the Ballyvaughan Union are equally extraordinary.[18] Back in late 1847, famine is reported as making 'fearful havoc' among the people of

Ennistymon Union – in Kilfenora parish 'the poor were perishing in ditches'.[19] And by the end of the Famine, destitution would reach such a level that the population of the workhouse amounted to over half that of the county capital Ennis itself. Ciarán Ó Murchadha is scathing about government and Poor Law policies 'that were grotesquely misconceived and indefensible'.[20] And when government policy shifted radically in mid-1847, he notes that the influx of poor people into the county town of Ennis became a torrent: 'evicted, famished and pauperised individuals from the parishes [around] flocked towards the union workhouse and when refused entry then huddled in crowds outside the gates or haunted the streets and alleyways in search of shelter'.[21] Clare, like all the Munster communities, was seeing, first the gradual, and then the rapid acceleration of the collapse of its society.

However, it is important to note that social disintegration was preceded by waves of protest and intimidation by both agrarian organisations and the desperate poor clamouring for either food or work. The Munster province had

Fig. 9 Robert George Kelly, *An Ejectment in Ireland (A Tear and a Prayer for Erin), 1847–48*, oil on canvas. [Source: Collection of Anthony J. Mourek on loan to the John J. Burns Library, Boston College]

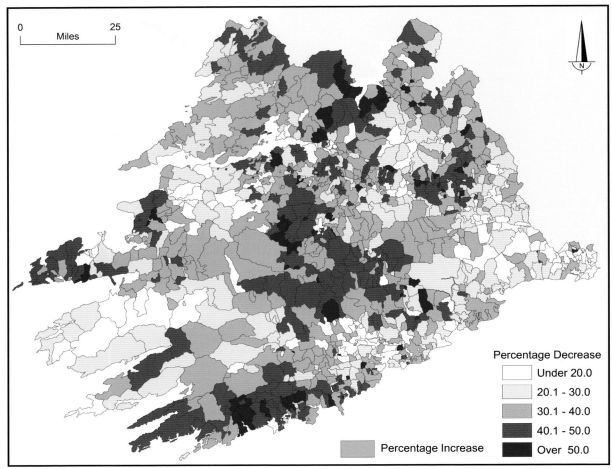

extends north into the west Midlands to middle Roscommon (8.2%), Longford (5.5%), (east) Galway (4.9%) and Leitrim (4.3%). It is also clear that Munster's role in these actions was intensifying between 1845 and 1846 while that of Connacht was diminishing somewhat.[23]

The nature of agrarian offences had also dramatically changed. Whereas the records of 'offences against the person' and 'offences against the public peace' had remained relatively stable, there was more than three times the increase in 'offences against property' between 1845 and 1846. Many of

Fig. 10 PERCENTAGE DISTRIBUTION OF POPULATION CHANGE FROM 1841 TO 1851. The Great Famine in Munster devastated most communities. One can distinguish three major types of communities suffering different levels of devastation. What is often not recognised is that the zone of the wealthiest parishes and best lands in Munster suffered massive losses. Regions which lost at least 40% and often well over 50% of their populations include the champion lands of north Cork, east Limerick and mid-Tipperary. Here, commercial farming and urban life was underpinned by a large number of labourers, mill workers and cottiers. Many landless and small-holding families suffered major hardships and mortalities in these zones and evictions and emigration were also significant features. Munster towns also witnessed dramatic population losses. Poorer parishes to register such major losses were concentrated in southwest Cork, the Dingle peninsula and north and east Clare. In contrast, while obviously deeply affected by famine conditions, other parishes which lost less than 30% and often under 20% of their populations were mainly located in southeast Tipperary and much of County Waterford, the Cork city hinterland, the hill country of Tipperary and upland regions in west and north Kerry. Finally, parishes suffering 30–40% losses constituted the greatest number in the province and were characteristic of most of Clare, Tipperary and the Limerick/Cork borderlands as well as the upland regions of inland Cork and Kerry where youthful populations were still colonising marginal land into the early 1840s.

been the primary domain for agrarian protest movements since the eras of the Whiteboys and Rightboys in the mid to late eighteenth century and Tithe Agitation in the early 1830s. It is, therefore, not a surprise that Munster was the core area of so called 'agrarian outrages' as reported by the constabulary island-wide in 1846. Of the protests – many famine related – 40% were in Munster, 25% in Leinster, 22% in Connacht and 13% in Ulster.[22] County Tipperary, as heretofore, was at the heart of Munster's agrarian-cum-famine protests with 13.1% of the island's total, followed by Cork (9.4%), Limerick (6.9%) and Clare (5.8%). County Kerry at 2.5% reflects a much lower level of protest all along the western seaboard counties while Waterford – at 2.2% – like many other indices – behaves more like a Leinster county. Indeed, a very significant faultline divides County Tipperary from all the adjacent Leinster counties, which return very low levels (on average 2.7% per county) for agrarian offences. Rather, the Munster heartland of agrarian protest

these latter offences related to food issues. Cattle (and sheep) stealing came to dominate in over half of the total in this category of 'offences against property' in 1846. Its incidence had increased six times over that of 1845. 'Burglary and housebreaking' almost trebled and 'highway robbery' increased by two and a half times. And 1846 reveals two *new* categories: 'plundering provisions', which occurred 416 times, and 'obstructing the transport of provisions', thirty-five times.[24] The foci of agrarian protests and actions had changed dramatically. Intimidation and angry demonstrations on relief works and by the desperate, starving poor crowding town streets, crying out for food and work, all became familiar occurrences.

Thus, in the early months and years of the Famine, both formal and informal protest groups endeavoured to ensure that food supplies would remain local. Quays were regularly blockaded – from Clare Abbey in the north to Youghal and Dungarvan in the south – to prevent the movement or export of grain. Grain, Indian meal and flour carts were disabled by the regular shooting of their horses and then robbed. The stealing of sheep and cattle – gathering pace from 1845 to 1846, peaking in 1847 but still remaining at a very high level until 1852 – became so frequent an occurrence as to go unnoticed in the local newspapers. Conflicts within and between classes of labourers, cottiers and smallholders and with bigger farmers and lesser gentry were clearly important. But equally important was the intimidation of, and threats made against, both certain landlords and their agents. These latter actions belong most especially to the years 1845 and 1846 (but they were still significant until 1852) and were motivated by landlords' failure to support famine relief efforts and to provide employment, in relation to continued rental demands and, ultimately, in response to accelerating rates of evictions. Frightened, insecure and cash-strapped landlords sought the introduction of the New Coercion Act, which was legislated for early in 1846.

It is clear that in the early stages of the Famine, agrarian organisations remained strong and vital. But what is also clear is that social protest peaks with the deadly closure of the public works schemes in the summer of 1847.[25] With the introduction of the soup kitchens and the later institutionalisation of outdoor relief work via stone-breaking and more road works, the situation changed dramatically. The now weakened and reduced populations – their status officially transformed from free labourer and smallholders to 'paupers' in need of relief – were less capable of still mounting organised resistance.[26] In County Limerick, the incidence of agrarian protests returned for 1851 is six times less than that recorded in 1846. Even in turbulent Tipperary, the reduction in 1851 was two and a half times less than the level of resistance in 1846.[27] In contrast, landlords and public officials further empowered by the Gregory clause, by the deaths or transportation of local agrarian leaders, and by police and troop saturation of 'disturbed' localities, regained control of what was previously an often anarchic situation. Any protests that now occur are the desperate expressions of a people literally maddened by hunger, disease and the fear of death. What follows is likely to be the greatest wave of tenant farmer evictions ever seen in Munster. According to the court and constabulary records, possibly as many as 45,000 families and one-quarter of a million family members lost their homes and land in Munster and were put out on the road in the hungry years between 1846 and 1852.[28]

In the four years between 1849 and 1852, it is recorded by the constabulary that 24,431 families comprising 131,706

Fig. 11  The post-Famine landscape is often one of desolation and silence. The photo shows the ruins of a deserted house near Kenmare, County Kerry. [Photo: Frank Coyne]

persons were evicted in Munster; 6,304 families were read-mitted to their holdings. Thus, a total of at least 17,927 fam-ilies and 95,535 people were put out on the road. Overall, Munster's share of the total number of evictions for these four years was over two-fifths (43.1%); Connacht experi-enced just over one-quarter (26.1%); Leinster one-fifth (20.5%) and Ulster – then the least disturbed – only one-tenth (10.3%). In these years Munster's share peaked in 1850 at 46% of the island-wide total. And as with the generation of agrarian conflicts and protests, Tipperary's families were the major recipients of eviction notices and expulsions (17.5% of its 1848 holdings), followed by Clare (14.9%) and Limerick (13.0%), both counties also key epicentres of agrar-ian troubles. Kerry, followed at 10.3% and Waterford at 6.4%. Cork's 4.5% suggests that the county's experiences were affected by the remaining farmers' greater capacity – after earlier clearances – to still pay their rents.[29]

The evidence of evictions for the previous three years – 1846 to 1848 – comes from court records.[30] Over these three years, evictions registered by the courts in 1846 constituted 13.9% of the total. 'Black' 1847 saw a very significant accel-eration in evictions to 36.4% of the total. With the Gregory clause now coming into deadly effect, evictions in 1848 increased to almost half of the total for these three years. This indicates that a staggering number of c.30,000 families were expelled from their farms in 1848 alone. Between 1846 and 1848, Munster's share in these court-recorded evictions comes to 35%, Connacht 23% and both Ulster and Leinster 21% each. Far greater stability comes to Ulster as both famine conditions decline thereafter 1847/8 and some land-lords come to play a more supportive role in relation to their tenants. Hence, its level of evictions is halved by 1849 while Munster and Connacht tenants faced the continuation of forceful evictions, initiated by so many landlords. Apart from the structural reasons for the reformation and enlarge-ment of farms – particularly the landlord's drive to establish viable commercial pastoral farms at the expense of small-scale tillage holdings – it could also be argued that some landlords may have been taking revenge on communities which had been to the forefront of agrarian intimidation and threats to their persons at a time of poor rental incomes and heightened insecurity. Be that as it may, the human conse-quences of evictions were immense. The already weakened families – brutally dispossessed of their homes, their dwellings deliberately smashed or burnt – were now not only to experience hunger and the greater threat of disease but also were now literally exposed to the elements. Images proliferate of displaced families – still wandering around their parishes – scratching to construct makeshift shelters in bogholes, roadside ditches or adding further to the teeming, starving masses wandering or lying in the streets of nearby towns and villages.[31] Some may have managed to emigrate; some few may have managed to find another smaller hold-

ing; others ended up dying either in the field or workhouse. As an example, the Kilrush Union in County Clare was notorious for 'the horrendous mortality and suffering that obtained there . . . fuelled by a colossal level of evictions that had no equivalent anywhere in Ireland'.[32] Combined with the spread of cholera in the first half of 1849, it is little won-der that County Clare had the greatest excess mortalities and indeed the largest number of evictions of any county in 1851. The heartland county of Tipperary was not far behind – losing a staggering 20% of its population from either famine deaths or emigration over the Famine period. Even County Waterford, with one of the lowest eviction rates in the province, registered over 31% of its total famine deaths in 1849.[33] But emigration from this county was to make an even more dramatic impact on its population losses.

Munster may come closest of all the province's popula-tions in reflecting the national average of a relatively even ratio in the number of excess famine deaths to the number that managed to emigrate between 1846 and 1852. South Munster – especially its ports and hinterlands – had long witnessed migration to the New World. And as Jack Burtchaell points out 'a long tradition of emigration to Atlantic Canada, easy access to the ports of Waterford, Dun-garvan and Youghal, and cheap fares across St George's Channel to the colliery ports of south Wales and the Cum-brian coast ports',[34] all were to augment the emigration opportunities for Waterford people. Famine conditions also saw the first great exodus of Irish speakers to America. Kerby Miller estimates that Munster and Connacht 'where in 1841 over half of the inhabitants spoke Irish constituted at least 50% of Famine emigrants'.[35] Artisans, labourers and smallholders may have been in the vanguard of the emi-grant exodus in the early years of the Famine. However, by the spring of 1847 even substantial tenant farmers in Tipper-ary and elsewhere packed their bags and belongings on a cart to head for Waterford or Cork ports (see Marita Foster below) and sailed for America. By early 1851, people from Munster counties constituted 40% of the total number of emigrants in that year, almost double that of both Leinster and Ulster and three times that of the Connacht exodus. Only one of four Munster men and women born around 1831 died at home in their own province of old age.

Out of a total population of c.2.5 million in 1845, Mun-ster was to lose c.650,000 of its population in the Famine years. This constitutes over one-quarter (c.26.0%) of its total population and also constitutes the greatest absolute popu-lation loss of all the provinces. How many died of famine-related causes and how many actually emigrated will never be fully known. But the likely figure of famine dead is in the region of 340,000 – and the likely number of famine emi-grants was only a little less. By 1901, the population of Mun-ster (1.08m) had been reduced to less than half its 1841 total.

# Mortality and emigration in six parishes in the Union of Skibbereen, West Cork, 1846–47

## Patrick Hickey

The devastation of the potato crop by a strange disease caused deaths by August 1846, or probably earlier. The road works carried out under the Labour Rate Act were generally a failure since some labourers actually died while on them from cold and hunger. The soup kitchens bravely set up by people such as Dr Robert Traill, rector of Schull,[1] James Barry, the parish priest, the Society of Friends and others were simply inadequate to deal with the sudden calamity. It was a 'visitation of Providence' or an ecological disaster striking a poor country much like the tsunami which hit southeast Asia in 2005 or the earthquake that shattered Haiti in January 2010.

The Temporary Relief Act (Soup Kitchen Act) was introduced into Parliament in January 1847 but it would be a long way from parliament to parish. A Captain Coffin of the H.M.S. *Scourge* landed a large cargo of meal in Schull from the Society of Friends. Dr Traill took him on a visit around the area. The captain wrote that 'famine exists in a frightful degree with all its horrors' and concluded that it was not possible for human power 'to stay the evil but it might be possible to alleviate it'. Coffin continued to deliver food along the west coast and wrote from Belmullet, County Mayo, that famine scenes 'are all alike, getting worse as you go south, and at Schull and its neighbourhood the very climax of misery finds its resting place'.

### TREVELYAN'S RESPONSE

Coffin's letter was forwarded to Charles Trevelyan, Assistant Secretary to the Treasury, and was also published in the press in Ireland and England, including *The Times*. This letter shocked him out of his complacency; he described it as 'awful' and sent a copy to Sir John Burgoyne, Chairman of the Relief Commission in Dublin. Trevelyan promised some medical aid for Schull but added in a rather defeatist manner that

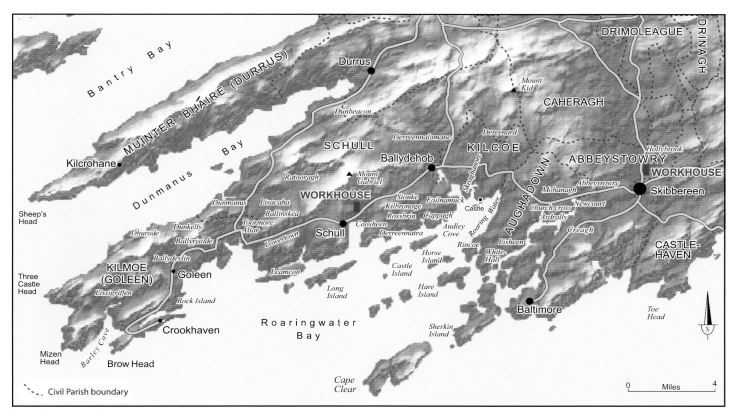

Fig. 1 THE MIZEN PENINSULA SHOWING PARISHES, SETTLEMENTS AND THE LOCATION OF WORKHOUSES

This sailor was seeing the results of hunger oedema. His letter appeared also in the press in both countries. By February 1847 Schull and Skibbereen were fast becoming bywords for famine.[2] This was reinforced by the sketches of James Mahony in *The Illustrated London News*. He also vividly described the terrible famine scenes he had witnessed during his visit to west Cork.[3]

In March effective aid came at last to the western parishes. A Church of Ireland clergyman, Rev. F.F. Trench, curate of Cloughjordan, County Tipperary, visited Ballydehob, Schull and Kilmoe (Goleen). He found James Barry 'utterly paralysed by the desolation around him' and was in danger of starving himself.[4] Trench was soon joined by his cousin travelling from England, R.C. Trench, Professor of Divinity at King's College, London, and later Archbishop of Dublin.[5]

Trench considered that 'Skibbereen had the appearance of a flourishing place' compared to Ballydehob and Schull. The Trench cousins together with the relief workers already in the field organised many 'eating-houses'. F.F. Trench claimed that by the middle of April 'the mortality, though it had not ceased . . . yet it had been arrested'. Mortality certainly had not ceased as fever soon swept away, Dr Traill himself[6] who had worked so tirelessly amongst the distressed in Schull and its environs.

## SOUP KITCHEN ACT

By April, the Soup Kitchen Act was being brought into operation all over the country. The inspector who was appointed to the union of Skibbereen was a J.J. Marshall,

**BOY AND GIRL AT CAHERA.**

Fig. 2  Boy and girl at Caheragh, *The Illustrated London News*, 20 February 1847. The artist James Mahony visited west Cork in the early months of 1847. He hoped that his drawings would make the affliction known to the charitable public. The sketches which appeared in the pages of the *The Illustrated London News* highlighted the suffering in many districts throughout the peninsula. Of the above sketch of a forlorn boy and girl searching for potatoes on the road to Drimoleague, Mahony reports: '[N]ot far from the spot where I made this sketch and less than fifty perches from the high road, is another of the many sepulchres above ground, where six dead bodies had lain for twelve days, without the least chance of interment, owing to their being so far from the town.'

it would 'do good as far as it goes, and the calamities of the Irish are so great and pressing that it is only by bringing every available means to bear on them that we can hope to make an impression. Let us save *as many as we can* [his emphasis]'.

The next report on famine conditions was even worse than Coffin's. A sailor from the H.M.S. *Tartarus* delivering a cargo of food to Ballydehob gave a close up description of what he had witnessed:

> The deaths here average 40 or 50 daily; 20 were buried this morning and they were fortunate in getting buried at all. The people build themselves up into their cabins so that they may die together with their children and not be seen by passers-by. Fever, dysentery and starvation stare at you in the face everywhere – children of 10 and 9 years old I have mistaken for decrepit old women, their faces wrinkled, their bodies bent and distorted with pain, the eyes looking like those of a corpse. A dead woman was found lying on the road with a dead infant on her breast.

Fig. 3 Professor R. C. Trench, later Archbishop of Dublin (1864–84), who followed in the footsteps of fellow clergymen in establishing 'eating houses' in West Cork for the relief of the starving. Having established three eating houses in Ballydehob, he still despaired at the levels of distress around him –'the mass of wild hunger there is unimaginable'.

Fig. 4 Dr Robert Traill, Rector of Schull (1830–47), worked selflessly in administering relief to the sick and starving in his own parish before eventually succumbing to fever.

recommended by Charles Trevelyan. Evidently Marshall paid special attention to the following six parishes, beginning from the western end of the Mizen Peninsula: Kilmoe (Goleen), Schull/Ballydehob, Kilcoe, Caheragh, Drimoleague and Drinagh. The Soup Kitchen Act finally came into operation in these areas on 10 May, except for Kilmoe (Goleen), which had to wait until 24 May.

Although this measure was criticised by some (e.g. Fr Laurence O'Sullivan of Kilmoe) for being 'tardy', it was really appreciated by many others (e.g. Fr James Barry). A meeting of the Ballydehob Relief Committee was held at the end of June. A resolution of gratitude was sent to F.F. Trench. Barry's covering letter summed up the latest state of affairs:

> The face of the country is changed for the better – the people look healthier, sickness is less prevalent and deaths so few that the burial staff and the slide-bottomed coffins are no longer in requisition. The daily ration is evidently the cause. Many noble-minded and charitable Christians had contributed largely to the alleviation of our suffering, and much had been dispensed; yet, there was a want of combined and systematic action – the administration of relief did not embrace all the afflicted community .

. . Next, the Government measure, so ably conducted as it is under the guidance of a wise and indefatigable inspector, J.J. Marshall, affords a hope, if not of plenty, at least of few or no deaths from dire want. There is also hospital treatment with the aid of a second medical officer for fever patients.

This general improvement was also taking place all over the country, as the Poor Law Commissioners were pleased to announce: 'The absolute starvation that was spread over the land has been greatly arrested, as also the progress of the particular diseases engendered by the great destitution prevailing extensively.' They gave the example of the union of Skibbereen, 'the sufferings of which district were so notorious'. The last rations under the Soup Kitchen Act were distributed on 12 September. In their final report, the Commissioners concluded that there could not be 'the slightest doubt' but that this act 'had succeeded in its object'. They even admitted that on the score of economy many relief committees regretted that the act had not been originally introduced instead of the Labour Rate Act.

The reason was simple; the Soup Kitchen Act 'reached the helpless destitute, whether capable or incapable of labour, [yet] it cost only one-third of the expenditure' of the Labour Rate Act. Yes, on the score of humanity alone it was the fundamental fault of this Labour Rate Act that hungry men were expected to work whereas in 1822–23, when Richard Griffith made the road through the Mizen Peninsula, food was distributed as wages or part wages and not placed in depots. However, such direct dealing in meal in 1845–47 would have been seen as unduly interfering in the free trade of the corn merchants and anathema to *laissez-faire* thinking. By September 1847 the tide of famine and fever had at last been turned. Trevelyan boasted that 'the famine was stayed . . . upwards of three millions of persons were fed every day'. This was indeed true. Nevertheless, the Famine had not been stayed – at least not to the extent that he would have liked the world to believe – because the calamity had already taken a heavy toll. For whom and for how many did the Famine bell toll?

This is a very difficult question. William Wilde (father of Oscar Wilde) gave the reason why in his analysis of the 1851 Census:

> No pen has ever recorded the numbers of the forlorn and starving who perished by the wayside or in the ditches, or of the mournful groups, sometimes whole families who lay down and died, one after another, upon the floor of their miserable cabins and so remained uncoffined and unburied till chance unveiled the appalling scene.[7]

Fig. 5 A sketch of the village of Meenies, north of Drimoleague, which was wiped out during the Famine. [*The Illustrated London News*, 20 February 1847]

## MARSHALL'S RETURN

The parishes of our study area provide a rare exception to this lack of recording. At the end of September the relief committees of Schull and Ballydehob held a joint and final meeting at which both chairmen attended. They were Fr James Barry and John Limerick, a Schull landlord, who had succeeded Dr Traill as chairman. The priest had called the landlord 'a good magistrate . . . devoted to deeds of benevolence'. The meeting thanked J.J. Marshall for 'the zeal and untiring perseverance' with which he had laboured to overcome the difficulties of introducing the Soup Kitchen Act. The meeting declared that the act had done 'great good' in its own district and as 'a criterion by which the public may judge the good results of that act generally', they presented 'A return of deaths and emigrations . . .' from the six parishes which comprise our study area.[8] The meeting described the return as follows:

> A copy of the statistical return made out with scrupulous exactness under the direction of J.J. Marshall, showing at one view the very great mortality which preceded, and the equally great decrease of such mortality which followed, the introduction of that measure.

Marshall's return provides the numbers of those who died in each parish whether men, women or children, from September 1846 to September 1847 on a month-to-month basis (although the figures for the period from September 1846 to January 1847 are combined). The causes of death are added. Figures for emigrants as well as their destinations are also given. The return was published by the dispensary doctor, Daniel Donovan of Skibbereen, in the *Dublin Medical Press*, which was edited by William Wilde, an eminent physician and brilliant analyst of famine data. Donovan stated that the document 'exhibits the sudden falling off in mortality, even from fever, that took place on the introduc-

tion of the Temporary Relief Act [Soup Kitchen Act] . . . and establishes the fact that food is the best cure for Irish fever and . . . that employment would be the best preventative'.[9]

According to the 1841 Census, the six parishes had a total population of 43,266. As baptismal records indicate, this had undoubtedly increased by 1845 but the increase may not have been very significant because emigration was by now a steady stream. Fr James Barry had told the Devon Commission in 1844 that 'many people' were leaving. A ship or two had been freighted every year for the previous four or five years from Ballydehob ('a small inlet'), and he wondered how many were leaving from ports such as Castletownbere, Bantry, Crookhaven or Schull.[10] Out of this population of 43,266, Marshall states that the number of people who died of hunger and disease was as high as 7,332, or 17.0%. Did these relief workers exaggerate the mortality in order to claim credit for implementing the Soup Kitchen Act? We can check their figures against estimates made by other people on the ground. On 2 January Dr Traill wrote that deaths in the parish numbered twenty-five daily. The Commissariat officer, William Bishop, reported the same figure. This would yield about 775 deaths for the month but Marshall gives 'only' 349 for that parish for the whole period from September 1846 to January 1847. In February Traill and the dispensary doctor, Stephen Sweetnam of Schull, reported that mortality in the parish was running at thirty-five deaths daily. This would yield about 980 casualties for the month where Marshall gives 'only' 449 for the whole period from September 1846 to this month of February 1847.

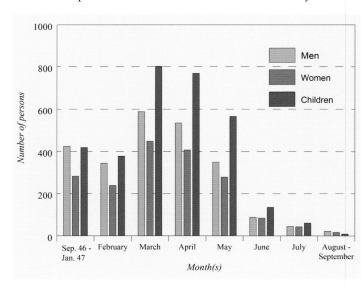

Fig. 6 MORTALITY IN SIX PARISHES SEPTEMBER 1846 TO SEPTEMBER 1847. Marshall's Return was 'a return of deaths and emigrations' for the six civil parishes of Kilmoe, Schull/Ballydehob, Kilcoe, Caheragh, Drimoleague and Drinagh. This statistical return was compiled under the direction of Poor Law Inspector J.J. Marshall with the primary intention of assessing the impact of the Soup Kitchen Act.

Dr Jones Lamprey was sent to Schull by the Central Board of Health in Dublin at the end of March 1847. William Wilde sent a circular to doctors all over the country inquiring about famine fevers. In his reply, Lamprey stated that 2,000 people had died of famine and fever in the parish in l846–47.[11] This is the only figure which is lower than that of Marshall (i.e. 3,094), and is clearly far too low. In the middle of March 1847 Traill announced that it had been 'computed' that 2,000 of his parishioners had already fallen victim.

In the parish of Kilmoe (Goleen), the dispensary doctor, James McCormick, wrote that the deaths in January numbered seven per day. Bishop similarly reported eight per day. This would amount to about 248 deaths for the month whereas Marshal gives 'only' 236 deaths for the whole period from September 1846 to January l847. On 5 February the parish priest, Laurence O'Sullivan, lamented that 1,000 of his flock had now fallen but, as already stated, Marshall gives 'only' 236 deaths for the entire period from September l846 to January l847.

Marshall reports the number of soup rations given out

Figs 7 Chapel Lane graveyard in Skibbereen. Inset shows the hut or watch-house in the graveyard as sketched by James Mahony in the *The Illustrated London News*, 13 February 1847. On 20 February 1847, American philanthropist Elihu Burrit visited the town to see for himself the devastation wrought by starvation and disease. On visiting the same graveyard, he wrote: 'We entered the graveyard, in the midst of which was a small watch-house. This miserable shed had served as a grave where the dying could bury themselves . . . . And into this horrible den of death, this noisome sepulchre, living men, women and children went down to die – to pillow upon the rotten straw – the grave clothes vacated by previous victims surrounding them.' [Photo: John Crowley]

on 19 June as 22,616, or 52.3% of the total population. At first glance this may appear rather high, but it was not nearly as high as in parts of Connacht, where it ranged from 70% to 100%. It is sometimes concluded that since the uptake of soup rations was much lower in the Skibbereen district than in parts of Connacht, that the Famine was therefore less severe there. But this thinking is invalid.

By the time the Soup Kitchen Act had come into operation in these parishes (as in much of the country) in May, as many as 6,135 (or 14.17%) of the people were already dead. So the reason why the number of people on soup rations in this district was not so terribly high is not that the people

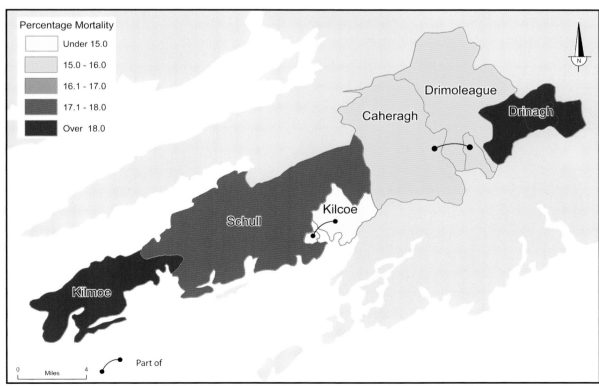

**Percentage Mortality**

- Under 15.0
- 15.0 - 16.0
- 16.1 - 17.0
- 17.1 - 18.0
- Over 18.0

Drimoleague
Caheragh
Drinagh
Kilcoe
Schull
Kilmoe

Part of

0 Miles 4

Fig. 8 LEVELS OF MORTALITY IN THE SIX PARISHES AS DOCUMENTED IN MARSHALL'S RETURN, SEPTEMBER 1846 TO SEPTEMBER 1847.

were not hungry but simply that they were dead. The very high uptake in other areas means that at least the people there were still alive. The acid test of the impact of the Famine must surely be mortality itself.

Let us now examine Marshall's return in relation to the timing of all these deaths. The first period is the five months, from September 1846 to January 1847, in which there were 1,125 deaths, or 15.3% of the total mortality for the whole period. This is, of course, high but it is not much higher than the figure for the short but hard month of February when 962 died (13.1% of the total mortality). In March, the number of deaths rose still higher, to 1,838 (or 25.1%), mercifully coming to a peak. But this can well be said to be little more than a plateau because in April mortality fell only slightly (to 1,710, or 23.0%). The district had to wait until May when a significant but not dramatic decline took place: 'only' 1,194 or 16.3% perished. This decline was, of course, due to the Soup Kitchen Act, which came generally into operation on the tenth of the month.

A dramatic decline in mortality did not occur until June when it fell from 1,194 to 307. It then declined further to 148 in July and finally to 48 in August-September, when the Relief Act finally expired. One observes this mortal spring of 1847 claiming nearly two-thirds (61.5%) of the total mortality for the whole period of one year, September l846 to September l847.

There were significant differences in mortality as between men, women and children, as is shown in the following diagram: More men than women died in these parishes. The Census Commissioners also noticed this for the whole country. Deaths among road workers must have accounted for some of the deaths. Women were the best sur-

## Table 1. Mortality and property/poverty

| Parish | Mortality (%) | Poor Law Valuation (PVI) |
|---|---|---|
| Kilmoe (Goleen) | 18.8 | 0.75 |
| Schull | 17.7 | 0.80 |
| Ballydehob | 18.0 | 0.93 |
| Kilcoe | 9.7 | 1.31 |
| Caheragh | 15.7 | 1.22 |
| Drimoleague | 15.7 | 1.17 |
| Drinagh | 18.4 | 1.52 |

vivors. The very high mortality among children comes as no surprise as it appalled those who had witnessed it. Dr Traill found that 'the children . . . were disappearing with awful rapidity . . . and are almost all swollen and ripening for the grave'. To sum up; mortality among men, women, and children was roughly in the ratio of 3:2:4. In simple figures: out of every nine persons who perished, three were men, two were women and four were children.

Marshall knew only too well of the relation or nexus between mortality and property or lack of property, i.e. poverty, because he presented the Poor Law valuation in his return. These parishes were placed among the poorest categories in the country.

Examining Table 1 we see that the highest rate of mortality, 18.8%, and the least valuable property, 75 c, were to be found in the most westerly parish, Kilmoe. As has been noted, this was the last place in which the Soup Kitchen Act had been put into operation. Schull and Ballydehob similarly show a very high mortality rate, 17.7% and 18.0% respectively, and a very low valuation, 80c. Kilcoe shows the lowest mortality rate, 9.7%, and this is combined with a high valuation rate, 1.31c. Caheragh and Drimoleague show a moderately high mortality rate, 15.7% each, together with a moderately low valuation, 1.26c. Drinagh, however, is an apparent exception: it has a very high mortality rate, 18.4%, combined with a very high valuation – in fact, the highest of all, 1.52c. With the exception of Drinagh, therefore, mortality varied inversely with valuation, the lower the valuation the higher the mortality.

George Robinson of the Drimoleague Relief Committee explained why Drinagh was an anomaly, its valuation and mortality both being high. It had no resident rector or gentry. Its labourers were always 'miserably poor' and there was even a higher proportion of them there than in the parishes where Skibbereen was situated. Most of the larger farmers dismissed their labourers when the Famine crunch came. The thatched outhouses of one such farmer were set on fire; four cows were burned to death although a horse and some sheep escaped. Even the small farmers had been reduced to 'abject misery'. Accordingly, the case of Drinagh serves only to reinforce the general rule: mortality varied inversely with property, the less the property, the greater the mortality. As the Skibbereen Soup Commit-

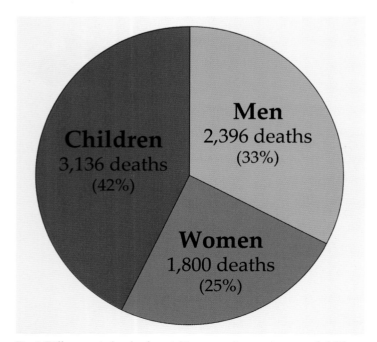

Fig. 9 Differences in levels of mortality amongst men, women and children.

376

## CAUSES OF DEATH

Marshall next presents the causes of death. William Wilde in the 1851 Census pointed out that fever had ever been 'lurking in hovels and corners . . . but ever ready like an evil spirit to break out at the slightest provocation'. Marshall categorised the causes of death under the headings of 'fever', 'dysentery' and 'destitution and other causes'. As regards what 'destitution and other causes' might mean, Wilde bluntly pointed out that it was a matter of 'want, destitution, cold and exposure, neglect; in Irish, it is *gorta*, starvation'. Dr Donovan gave the causes of mortality as simply 'fever, dysentery and starvation'.

Summing up for the six parishes, 43.6% died of fever, 22.1% of dysentery and 34.3% of starvation. If fever and dysentery taken together designate famine fever, then 65.7% died of famine fever and 34.3% of starvation.

A death census was compiled by Fr Thomas Synnott, who was involved in the distribution of funds which came from Archbishop Murray of Dublin. Returns for the numbers of 'deaths from starvation' and 'deaths from disease produced from starvation' were made from certain districts around the country up to September 1847. These deaths numbered 22,241, of which 30% were from starvation and 70% from disease. These percentages are remarkably close to those of Marshall. Dr Donovan finally declared that a physician was forced to admit that his art by itself could do little about diseases which owe their origin to 'squalor, misery and starvation'. Marshall also provided figures for those who emigrated giving their destinations as either England or America.

Fig. 10 Part of the ruins of Schull workhouse. While the census commissioners made no claims to have been able to count the numbers of those who died in the cabins and ditches, they did give figures for those who died in institutions. The Skibbereen workhouse was opened in 1842. Between 1842 and 1851, 4,346 people died in the workhouse. Schull workhouse opened in 1850 and in little over a year 189 people had perished. [Photo: John Crowley]

tee put it, the calamity was generally causing 'a mortality proportioned to destitution'. Thus there was a definite mortality/poverty nexus.

The location of a parish was also important. However, it was not a simple case of the further west the worse the famine. Drinagh, which is located in the direction of Dunmanway, had almost twice the mortality of Kilcoe, which is west of Skibbereen, 18.4% as against 9.7%. The two highest mortality rates occurred in the two extremes of the union, namely Drinagh, 18.4% and Kilmoe (Goleen) on the Mizen, 18.8%. Drinagh was, of course, inland and therefore remote from the ports where food was landed.

Out of a total population of 43,266 in these six parishes, only 997 persons emigrated of whom 535 (53.7%) headed to America and 262 (46.3%) went to England. As regards destination, there is a certain difference between the peninsular parishes (Kilmoe, Schull and Kilcoe) and the inland ones (Caheragh, Drimoleague and Drinagh). In the peninsular parishes, more people went to America (430 compared with 313). In the inland districts, however, more went to England than to America (149 compared with 105). The main reason why more people from the peninsula went to America was undoubtedly that they were nearer the harbours facing the

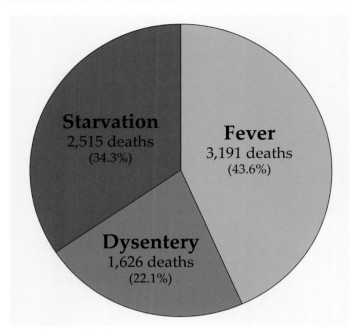

Fig. 11 Causes of death.

**Table 2.** Number and destinations of emigrants

| Parish | England | N. America | Total |
|---|---|---|---|
| Kilmoe | 45 | 22 | 67 |
| Schull | 155 | 225 | 380 |
| Ballydehob | 96 | 105 | 201 |
| Kilcoe | 17 | 78 | 95 |
| Caheragh | 85 | 38 | 123 |
| Drimoleague | 12 | 54 | 66 |
| Drinagh | 52 | 13 | 65 |
| TOTAL (%) | 462(46.3) | 535(53.7) | 997(100) |

New World while those from the inland districts around Drimoleague would have found it less difficult to make their way to Cork and go by steam to England.

The relationship between emigration and mortality is very interesting. It is usually inverse – the higher the mortality the lower the emigration, and the lower the mortality the higher the emigration. In January 1847 Francis Webb, rector of Caheragh, ruefully remarked that he had heard much about the emigration that was going to take place all over the country to the New World but that in his own district, at least, it was more a matter of 'an awful mode of emi-

Fig. 12 Emigration advertisement, *Cork Constitution*, 9 February 1847. Early in the spring of 1847 people were preparing to emigrate, if only they had the money 'to pay for the steam'. As John Triphook told James Mahony of *The Illustrated London News*, anybody in Ballydehob 'who could command £5 was emigrating for dread of fever'. Fares to Canada were cheaper than those bound for the United States. Hence the former tended to be overcrowded, fever-filled and even untrustworthy – coffin ships – but for some it was a stark choice between the coffin ship and the hinged coffin.

gration to the Next World, without even the expense of a coffin!'

It is revealing in many respects to compare and contrast the percentage rates of mortality and emigration in each of the six parishes. These are shown in Figure 13.

Kilmoe, the most westerly parish, has the highest mortality (18.8%) and the lowest emigration rate (0.9%). Kilcoe, further east (between Ballydehob and Skibbereen), possesses the lowest mortality rate (9.7%) and the second highest emigration rate (4.1%). These two parishes are the two most extreme examples. The others show correspondingly high or moderately high mortality rates combined with low or moderately low emigration rates. The only exception is Schull, where mortality is very high (17.7%) and emigration is the highest of all (4.4%). Nevertheless, the general correlation between emigration and mortality is striking. In simple figures, out of every forty-three persons living in all these parishes in 1841, as many as seven died while only one emigrated. In sum, the highest mortality rate, the lowest emigration rate, the lowest valuation rate, and the remotest location were all to be found together in one and the same parish: Kilmoe (Goleen) on the Mizen Head. It was not as if these people lacked a harbour; Crookhaven was in the parish and Bantry was not very far away, either. Famine, however, prevented many of them from taking the coffin ship to the New World and forced them to take instead the

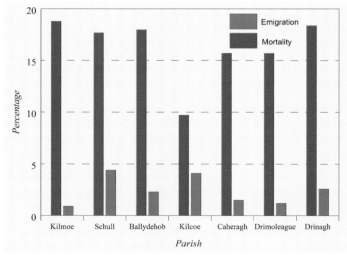

Fig. 13 Percentage of mortality and emigration in six parishes, Marshall's Return, September 1846 to September 1847.

Fig. 14 *Emigrants Awaiting Embarkation, West Cork, 1852*, by Robert Richard Scanlon. Emigration remained central to life in west Cork throughout the second half of the nineteenth century and for much of the twentieth century. [Source: Crawford Art Gallery]

hinged coffin to the next World.

Marshall's return is an authoritative document in that it was signed by three men who struggled together courageously to face famine and fever: John Limerick, the landlord, James Barry, the parish priest, and Daniel Donovan, the dispensary physician. It is an apolitical and matter-of-fact report. We have seen how its figures have been cross-checked from data presented by other relief workers and found to be conservative, as might be expected from its rather official provenance. Those who died or emigrated may have been slightly undercounted. On the other hand, it is possible that some relief workers may have been inclined slightly to exaggerate mortality and emigration in order to attract sympathy and funds. In conclusion, therefore, when the Poor Law inspector, the landlord, the doctor, and the priest all agree on numbers, these figures cannot be too far from the truth concerning the Great Famine in these six parishes of west Cork. Every figure tells a story – a sad one. Such was the mortality which earned Schull and Skibbereen the unenviable title of the 'Two Famine-slain Sisters of the South'. Already in July 1847 *The Nation* newspaper was campaigning against the Whigs and politicising the calamity. Its slogans were 'By the memory of Schull and Skibbereen, oppose them!' and 'By the souls of the two million dead, oppose them!' The song 'Dear Old Skibbereen' was soon to be sung; loud and high it would raise the cry 'Revenge for Skibbereen!'

Epilogue: J.J. Marshall was fated to join the victims; cholera swept him off less than eighteen months later, on 2 February 1849.[12]

# From 'Famine roads' to 'manor walls': the Famine in Glenville, County Cork

## Mike Murphy

'What is to become of the farmers and labourers of this impoverished district under the pressure of the triple oppression of the rules of the Board of Works, of the rule of Whig political economy, and of scathing heartless land-lordism'. So ends a letter written by Fr E. McCarthy P.P. to the *Cork Examiner* on 1 March 1847.[1]

Glenville in north Cork lies at the centre of a triangle comprising Cork City, Fermoy and Mallow (see inset map Figure 1). The village itself owes its existence to the local manor house and demesne and was established in the 1700s

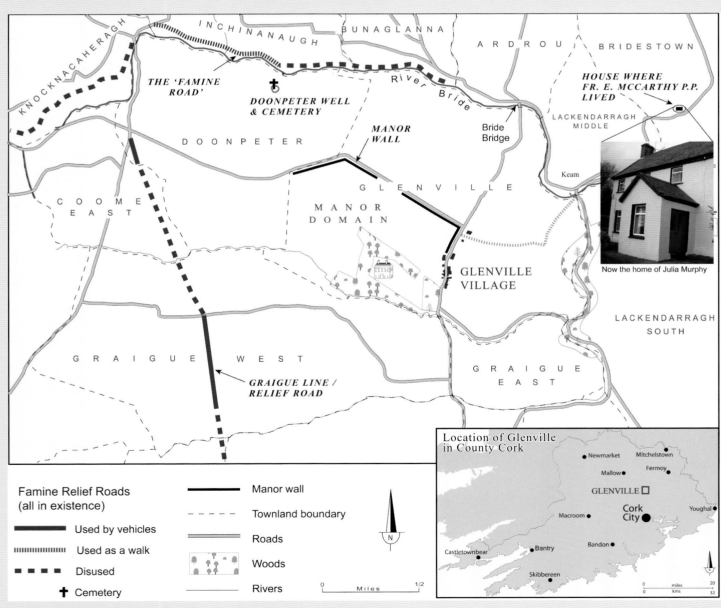

Now the home of Julia Murphy

Fig. 1  A MAP OF THE GLENVILLE AREA SHOWING THE LOCATION OF ROADS, RELIEF ROADS, TOWNLANDS AND OTHER PHYSICAL FEATURES. The inset photograph is of Fr. McCarthy's house as it is today. Inset map shows the location of Glenville in County Cork.

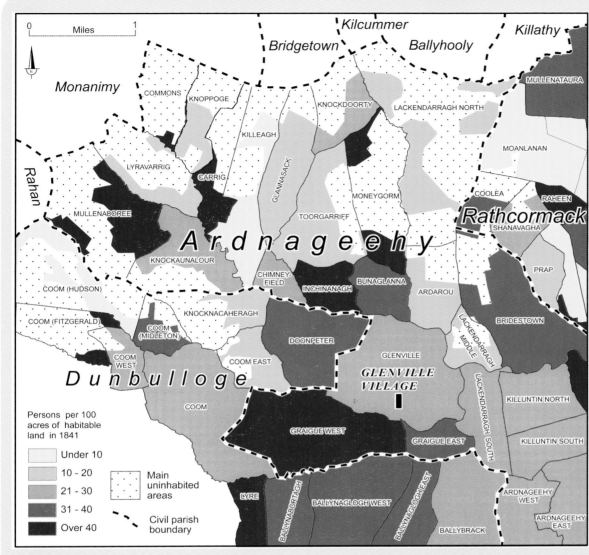

Persons per 100
acres of habitable
land in 1841

Under 10
10 - 20
21 - 30
31 - 40
Over 40

Main uninhabited areas

Civil parish boundary

Fig. 2 TOWNLANDS IN THE GLENVILLE AREA, SHOWING THE POPULATION DENSITY PER ONE HUNDRED ACRES OF HABITABLE LAND. The main uninhabited areas of each townland (dot shading pattern) have been excluded from the calculation of population density.

by Dr Edward Hudson to house and provide local services for the estate and its workforce. As can be seen in Figure 2, the greater area of Glenville includes not only townlands in the northern portion of Ardnageehy Parish, but also townlands in the parishes of Rathcormack and Dunbulloge with the village at its centre. For practical purposes the walking distance to the local village and not the administrative boundaries (such as townlands) was the important factor in defining a person's local area. However, administrative boundaries including townlands, parishes and Poor Law unions became crucial when it came to the provision of support and relief, often making

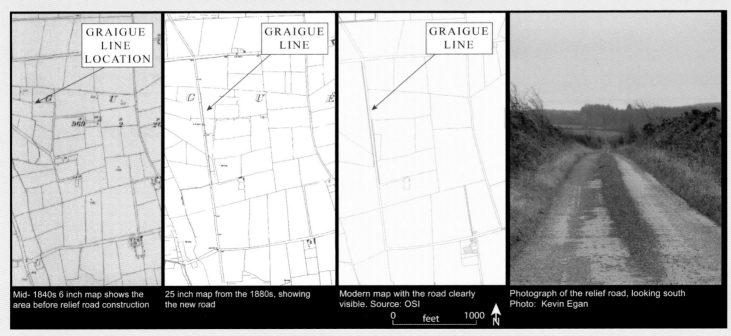

GRAIGUE LINE LOCATION

GRAIGUE LINE

GRAIGUE LINE

Mid- 1840s 6 inch map shows the area before relief road construction

25 inch map from the 1880s, showing the new road

Modern map with the road clearly visible. Source: OSI

Photograph of the relief road, looking south
Photo: Kevin Egan

Fig. 3 Timeline images of the construction of the relief road known as the 'Graigue line'. [Source: Ordnance Survey Ireland]

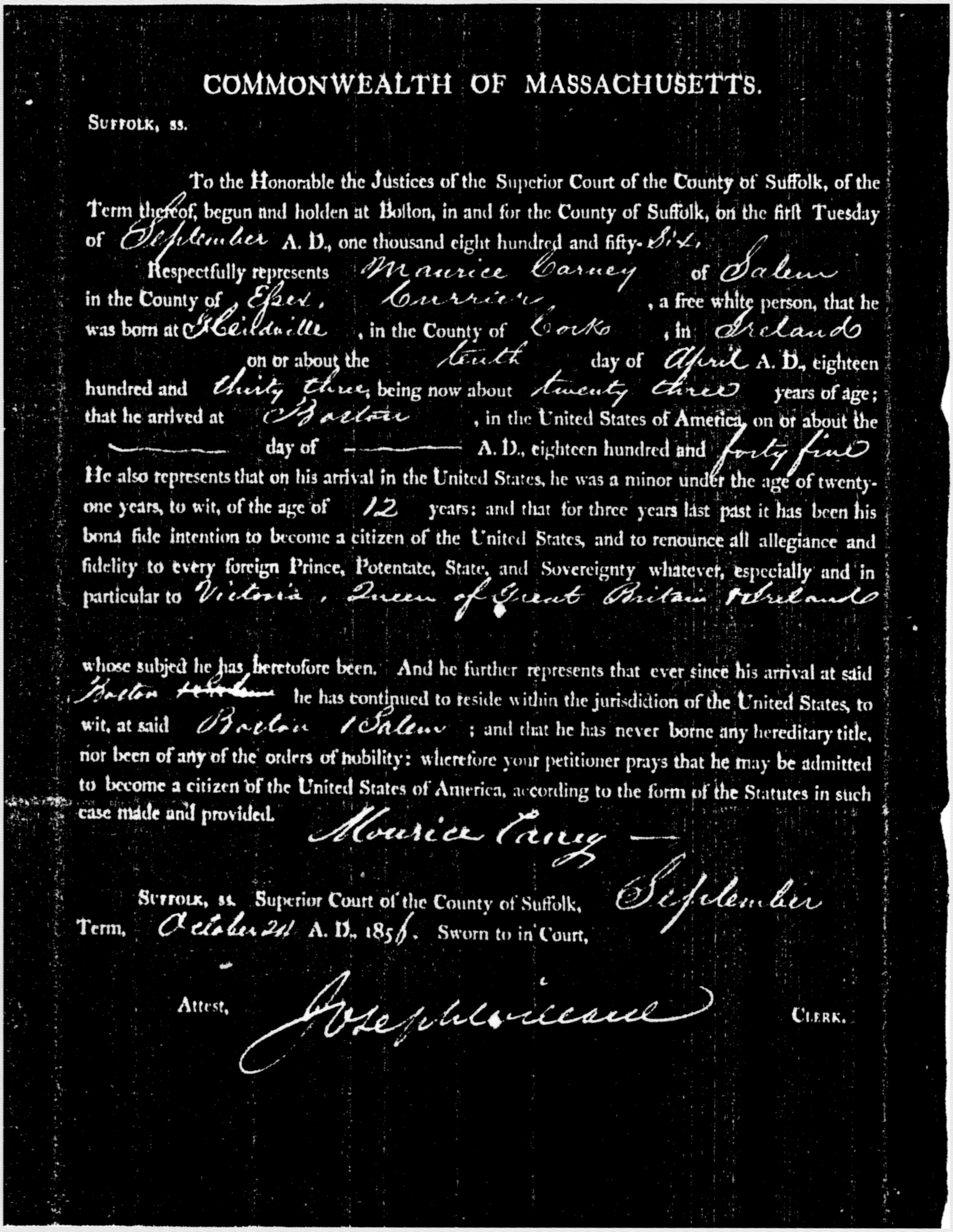

# COMMONWEALTH OF MASSACHUSETTS.

Suffolk, ss.

To the Honorable the Justices of the Superior Court of the County of Suffolk, of the Term thereof, begun and holden at Boston, in and for the County of Suffolk, on the first Tuesday of *September* A. D., one thousand eight hundred and fifty-*Six*.

Respectfully represents *Maurice Carney* of *Salem* in the County of *Essex, Currier,* , a free white person, that he was born at *Kildville* , in the County of *Corks* , in *Ireland* on or about the *tenth* day of *April* A. D., eighteen hundred and *thirty three*; being now about *twenty three* years of age; that he arrived at *Boston* , in the United States of America, on or about the ———— day of ———— A. D., eighteen hundred and *forty five* He also represents that on his arrival in the United States, he was a minor under the age of twenty-one years, to wit, of the age of *12* years: and that for three years last past it has been his bona fide intention to become a citizen of the United States, and to renounce all allegiance and fidelity to every foreign Prince, Potentate, State, and Sovereignty whatever, especially and in particular to *Victoria, Queen of Great Britain & Ireland* whose subject he has heretofore been. And he further represents that ever since his arrival at said *Boston* he has continued to reside within the jurisdiction of the United States, to wit, at said *Boston & Salem* ; and that he has never borne any hereditary title, nor been of any of the orders of nobility: wherefore your petitioner prays that he may be admitted to become a citizen of the United States of America, according to the form of the Statutes in such case made and provided.

*Maurice Carney*

Suffolk, ss. Superior Court of the County of Suffolk, *September* Term, *October 21* A. D., 1856. Sworn to in Court,

Attest, *Joseph Willard* CLERK.

Fig. 4 Maurice Carney's application for American citizenship in 1856.

the difference between life and death.

Pre-Famine population pressure can be seen in Figure 2 which shows population density per townland in 1841. Of particular interest are the townlands of Graigue (West and East) and Doonpeter, which are centrally located on the map. The outer townlands with high densities, such as Commons in the northwest, show up because the map has been corrected to highlight the population density of habitable land only (as per Griffith's Valuation). The townland of Commons comprised 389 acres, however 385 acres of this was mountain. By looking at the first edition Ordnance Survey map, it is clear that no physical evidence of human activity in the mountainous area existed, so the area of human occupation in Commons amounted to only four acres, with a total population in 1841 of twenty persons. By contrast, Graigue West had a total of 969 acres of which only twenty-one acres were planted woodland, leaving 948 habitable acres. In 1841 it had a population of 422 persons and sixty-nine houses. Doonpeter comprised 556 acres, all of which was habitable. In 1841 it had a population of 220 persons and thirty-five houses. In pre-Famine Glenville, both Doonpeter and Graigue witnessed substantial population pressure. These townlands experienced contrasting fortunes, one of relief works, starvation and death, the other, clearances and transportation.

Thomas Dennehy was the landlord of Graigue West at the time. Graigue West's pre-Famine population consisted of tenant farmers and labourers with a population density of over forty-four per hundred acres. The people were predominantly dependent on potatoes for their subsistence. In 1846, when the potato crop failed, their world fell apart with unimaginable consequences. A relief programme of road construction was put in place with one new 'line' passing through Graigue West. Figure 3 shows the area of Graigue West prior to the road's construction (first edition, Ordnance Survey six-inch map). In the later twenty-five inch map (c.1880s) the road is clearly visible. The photograph shows the road as it is today where it forms the entrance to Aidan Ford's farm.

Two sources from the time provide us with an insight into the levels of destitution experienced. The first is a further extract from Fr McCarthy's letter. In reference to Graigue (West) he writes: 'On the 4th Patrick Manning died at Graig [ue] of Dysentery. On the 5th Corns. Sullivan of Graig[ue] was found dead in a field at some distance from his own house having fallen the preceding evening on his way home from Graig[ue] line – an inquest was held on Saturday. This morning Michael Foley of Graig[ue], one of five I prepared, last week in this doomed townland, died of sheer starvation. I fear more that half the miserable creatures of this locality will die before substantial relief reaches them.'

The second source, again from the *Cork Examiner*, forms part of a report to the constabulary in Watergrasshill, the

Fig. 5 Famine relief road crossing through the townland of Inchinanaugh. [Photo: Kevin Egan]

383

neighbouring village, also in Ardnageehy parish: 'In this locality, [referring to Ardnageehy townland] we are assured, absolute famine stalks abroad with fearful pace, as also in the localities of Gragg [Graigue] and Glenville; and if some steps be not immediately taken to meet the dreadful wants of the famishing population, the districts must ere long be tenanted alone by the dead.'[2]

Between 1841 and 1851 Graigue West experienced a population decline of over 47%. While it is impossible to quantify the exact percentage of mortality within these figures, an estimate of 50% would be conservative. This rate would point to between 20 and 25% of the population perishing, or in real terms, upwards of one hundred persons. In reality the figure may have been greater, if those who died on the Graigue line relief works who originated outside the townland were added. These people were not included in the townland census data and so are not taken into account here. The number of houses dropped from sixty-nine to fifty, a reduction of over 27%.

The people of Doonpeter suffered a different fate. They were predominantly tenant farmers. The failure of the potato crop coincided with early developments in mechanised farming. The townland was owned by Edward Hudson of the manor house in Glenville. With the population of the townland in a state of destitution, Hudson decided to purchase the tenant agreements from the majority of the Doonpeter farmers, paying between one and five pounds per holding depending on size. Transport to America was also arranged. While this was a process of population clearance rather than eviction, it was very much resented by the local population. It did, nevertheless, offer some hope of a future to the poor desperate people of the townland. In 1841 Doonpeter had thirty-five houses and by 1851 it had been reduced to just fourteen, a reduction of twenty-one or 60%. The stone from these houses and field boundaries was used to build the manor perimeter wall. It stands up to twelve feet high and is one and a half miles long.

The following is an example of one family's experience after being cleared from Doonpeter. An advertisement appeared in the *Boston Pilot*, enquiring as to the whereabouts 'Of Mrs Joanna Kearney (Carney) and her children, Mary, Ellen, Thomas, Maurice, Patrick, William, Richard and Peter, native of Doone, parish of Ardnageehy County Cork on

the 1st of May 1847, and landed in Quebec; afterwards proceeded to the State of Vermont.[3] Any information respecting them will be thankfully received by Michael Riordan, care of John Foley 21 Hamilton Street, Boston Ms'. Subsequently three of her sons (Maurice, Patrick and William Kearney) applied for American citizenship. Maurice's submission to the Superior Court, Suffolk County, Massachusetts, in October 1856 is shown in Figure 4. He stated the following in his application: 'that he was born at Glenville on the tenth day of April A.D. eighteen hundred and thirty three being now about twenty three years of age. He arrived at Boston in eighteen hundred and forty five aged twelve years.' His descendant, William Fawcett, returned to Glenville in the early 1990s and with the help of local historian, Norma Buckley, tracked down his roots in Doonpeter.

Another relief road ran from Bride Bridge along the northern bank of the River Bride and is known locally as the 'Famine Road' (Figure 5). It cost *c.*£1,300. The Board of Works rules governing relief works provide some idea of the working conditions. Labourers had to work from six in the morning until six in the evening. Anyone turning up late got docked a quarter of a day's pay while those who arrived for work after nine in the morning were not employed that day. A temporary fever hospital was set up at the western end of the works which was opened in June 1847 and closed in November 1848. A total of forty-one people perished in the hospital, nineteen women and twenty-two men. Many of those who died on the works and in the hospital were buried in Doonpeter Cemetery, which locals say contains at least one mass grave.

Fr E. McCarthy's letter also states: 'On Tuesday, a man brought to my door a corpse of a Girl, about ten years old on his back, craving for food'. The priest was living in the townland of Bridestown. The door and house referred to can be seen in the photo inset in Figure 1. This is now the home of Julia Murphy and is the home in which I grew up. The memory of the Famine lives on in Glenville to this day. From 'Famine roads' to 'manor walls', many physical reminders to the past are still in evidence as can be seen in the maps and illustrations. It also lives on in the hearts of the people whose ancestors survived the tragedy. It has become part of the culture and heritage of the area, ensuring the Famine will never be forgotten.

# The Famine in the County Tipperary parish of Shanrahan

## William J. Smyth

The present-day population of the civil/medieval parish of Shanrahan is about 1,400, a little less than its mid-seventeenth-century population but substantially less than its peak of close on 8,000 people in 1845. There are about 150 farms in the parish today, about the same as in the 1660s but very different to its *c.*530 holdings (over 1 acre in size) in the early 1840s. By 1851, after the devastation of the Famine, as many as 200 of those family farm holdings had disappeared from the landscape. In addition, close on over half of the cabins and gardens of the poorest labourers and some artisans had vanished in these deadly years.[1] The censuses record a population decline of 2,539 (or 34.1%) between its 7,437 figure in 1841 and 4,898 in 1851[2] – but parish losses were likely to have been greater than this. Close on two-fifths of the rural population had disappeared – over one-fourth of the village population of Burncourt and close to one-fourth of the town of Clogheen. Indeed Clogheen town was one of the nine Munster towns that were no longer classified as 'civic'/urban districts in 1851 since its population had dropped by over 500 from an estimated 1845 figure of 2,190. In the parish as a whole, families whose main source of livelihood was in agriculture had declined by over a half (54.8%) by 1851, those in manufacturing, trade and related activities by one-third while those in the curious classification of 'other pursuits' had more than doubled (from 89 to 186 people) or 109%.[3] It is also clear that many more of Clogheen's townspeople were dependent on the land. Clogheen town had also been a union/workhouse centre since the opening of its workhouse to 'inmates' in June 1842.[4] In 1851 there were as many as 1,322 paupers still resident there (and 545 more in its auxiliary children's workhouse at Tincurry).[5] This workhouse had been built to house a capacity of 500 inmates.

Practically coterminous with the modern Catholic parish of Clogheen–Burncourt, the civil parish of Shanrahan is situated in southwest Tipperary. County Tipperary occupies a transitional economic and cultural location between the east and west of Ireland. The parish of Shanrahan is likewise characterised by similar transitional features, including a wide range of land values from the poorest land on the mountain edges to the north and south and a more gently and improving slope in land quality as one moves from the northwest to the highly valued lands at its centre and along its eastern flanks. Located as it is between the Galtee and Knockmealdown mountains to the north and south respectively, Shanrahan parish can be simply described as comprising twenty-two 'lowland' or 'valley' townlands with richer limestone soils and eighteen poorer 'mountainous' townlands fringing the old red sandstone blocks to the north and south. Climate and ecological factors have favoured a pastoral grassland regime in this wider region with dairying the predominant mode. However, in the early 1840s, the parish was more strongly associated with a grain-growing economy.[6] This was symbolised in the seven mills that distinguished the then lively estate/market town of Clogheen with a census population of 2,049 in 1841.[7] There were then four other flour mills in the rural part of the parish – and even as late as 1853 over 60% of its cultivated area was devoted to wheat, oats and barley. The parish also contained the small village of Burncourt with a population of 194 in 1841.

Figure 1 represents a composite picture of the pre-Famine landscape and society using the 1835 Tithe Applotment books, the 1839–41 Ordnance Survey first edition six-inch sheets and the very earliest of the Griffith's Valuation Survey from 1847. It needs to be stressed that the composite map portrays the culmination of a phenomenal population expansion during the previous half-century and more. The population of the parish more than trebled between 1766 and 1841.[8]

### TRANSFORMATION AND EXPANSION

The period from 1770 to 1815 was one of those powerful yet exceptional epochs in Irish history when intensive mixed farming – both dairying and grain production – gained the upper hand. This was a phase of massive elaboration in both the society of the parish and its landscape expressions. A new dramatic landlord's demesne of over 1,000 acres complete with a magnificent John Nash-designed Big House, Shanbally Castle, was created at the centre of the parish. The functions, streetscape and population of the estate town of Clogheen were also transformed. There was an impressive expansion in the communications network, both along the edges of the long-settled, well-endowed central area of the parish and connecting the parish with the towns of Cahir, Cappoquin, Lismore and Mitchelstown. All of this further accelerated small-farm colonisation along the stubborn moorland edges. At the same time, there was a significant intensification of enclosure on existing bigger farms and a related expansion in the number of new farms created. Probably as many as 200 to 250 new farm holdings were carved out by subletting, subdivision or moorland colonisation between 1766 and 1821. In addition, landless families – renting small patches of potato ground – proliferated in this dynamic phase. Approximately one-third (*c.*260) of the total number of rural households were landless cottiers in 1821.[9] A further 63% of all farm holdings on the O'Callaghan/Lord Lismore estate – comprising *over four-fifths* of the parish area – were then under 15 Irish acres (24

statute acres).[10] This great boom period in the economy thus saw a disproportionate increase in those sectors of the population who benefited temporarily from the huge demand for labour in town and countryside.

As many as half (910) of the workers on the O'Callaghan estate in the parish are described in the 1821 Census as 'labourers'. A further one-fifth (345) are categorised as 'farmers'. One-fifth (175) of the workforce were

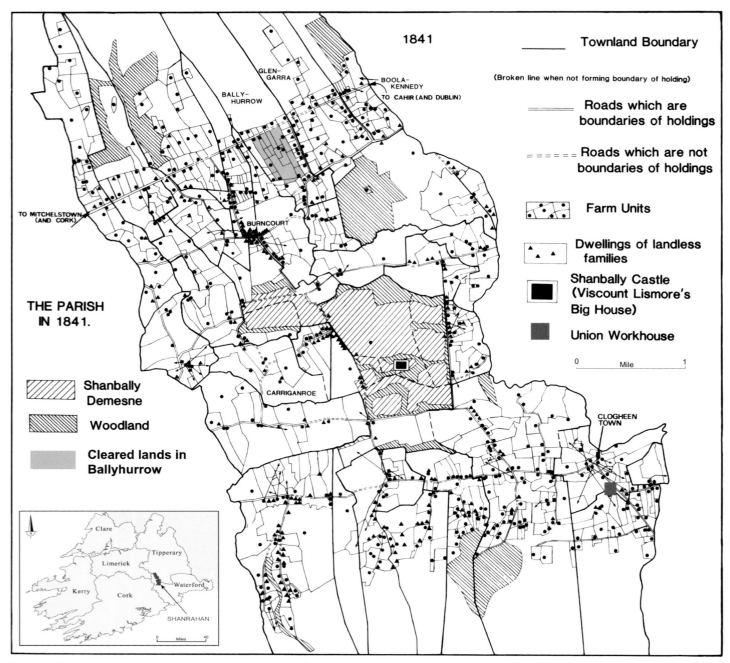

Fig. 1 PRE-FAMINE SETTLEMENTS AND LANDSCAPES OF THE PARISH OF SHANRAHAN. Located between the Galtee and Knockmealdown mountains in southwest Tipperary, Shanrahan parish (modern parish of Clogheen–Burncourt) comprises twenty-two 'lowland' or 'valley' townlands with richer limestone soils and eighteen poorer 'mountainous' townlands fringing the old red sandstone blocks to the north and south. By the early 1840s there were 530 holdings over 1 acre in the parish with 'big' (100+ acres) and 'comfortable' (30–50 acres) farms dominant along the better lowland corridor while smaller holdings (under 30 acres) were concentrated in the mountain townlands. As many as 250 of these smallholdings, so dependent on potato cultivation, were carved out by subletting, subdivision and moorland colonisation between 1766 and 1821. Over 260 landless families congregated along the roadsides, in small estate villages attached to the 1,000-acre demesne of landlord Viscount Lismore or in the back lanes of the estate town of Clogheen. It was a world of great social diversity and great social extremes – dominated by labourers, farmers, craftsmen, women servants and estate employees as well as a minority of shopkeepers, millers and professionals in and around the town of Clogheen. Clogheen town saw the foundation of a fever hospital and a Poor Fund as early as 1811 and was selected as a union centre, its workhouse built between 1840 and 1842. The population of the parish trebled between 1766 and 1841.

Fig. 2 The early nineteenth-century neo-classical Shanbally Castle, the residence of the O'Callaghan landlord family, was designed by John Nash and was located at the centre of a late eighteenth century, 1,000-acre demesne and an estate which comprised over 30,000 acres. The housebooks of Griffith's Valuation take three and a half pages to describe Lord Lismore's mansion and associated buildings, valued at £348/10/11, fifty times the value of the average dwelling plus outbuildings of strong farmers in the parish. The proprietor of a well- managed estate, Viscount Lismore in his generosity maintained the good reputation of the O'Callaghan family throughout the Famine years, while cautiously and unobtrusively utilising the specific Poor Law regulations to rationalise farm sizes on the estate. [Source: Irish Architectural Archive]

craftsmen and women. These included forty-six shoe- or broguemakers, twenty-seven tailors, and twenty-two each in the trades of carpenter, mason and smith. There were also twelve weavers as well as seven coopers, six nailers, five wheelwrights, three harness makers, three mill-wrights and two wool spinners. Another one-tenth (174) of the workforce in 1821 were women servants, mainly described as 'maids' but also including other specialist functions within the household. This group of female servants were mainly employed on the big farms and also in and around the town of Clogheen in the big houses of its mill-owning, merchant and professional families. Only 2% (30) are described as 'menservants' or 'servant-boys' but it is clear that the catch-all description of 'labourer' includes others in this specific occupational category as well as some family members assisting on farms and in craft-houses. Shopkeepers of all ranks (including huxters) comprise only 3.4% (60) of the estate's occupations. Another 40 (2.2%) were estate employees – gatekeepers, stewards,

mountain keepers, gardeners and nurserymen, woodrangers, 'sportsmen', horsebreakers, stablemen, henwomen and milkwomen. 'Pauper' families – originating from other counties with no roots in the local community – number 16 (0.9%). All other occupational categories – teachers, doctors, attorneys, millers, brewers, clerks and mail-coach agents – each number ten or less. Bringing up the rear in this teeming world of diverse occupations are three pedlars, one musician, one dancing master, one 'cyderman', one 'turnpike man' and one excise officer.[11] It was a world of great social diversity and great social extremes.

Up to 1815–20, the estate records reveal little of the growing problems of destitution and poverty in town and countryside. The foundation of Clogheen fever hospital and the Clogheen poor fund in 1811 are simply straws in the wind of the approaching storms. However, from 1815 to the beginning of the Famine years, one notes a transitional phase, one of reorientation of policy and farm amalgamation on the part of the landlord and one of increasingly bitter competition for land between the bigger grazier farmers – able to swing back reasonably quickly from mixed farming to a more specialised pastoral economy – and the still proliferating tillage farmers and the even more desperate labouring population. Cottiers, labourers and possibly some artisans now found that the original economic impetus for their labour services was often declining at precisely the time when the population of these sectors of society was increasing rapidly. Rural conflicts once again erupt. Clogheen town requires a new police barracks and a new bridewell in 1826 and a new courthouse in 1832 when the estate agent's house windows are protected for the first time with iron bars.[12]

INCREASING COMPETITION
In the period 1815–45, a battle was waged and a delicate kind of balance struck between competing sections of the society. The needs of the poor saw further fragmentation and subdivision of holdings on the one hand while deliberate landlord policies, reinforced by the interests of the bigger farmers, fostered the maintenance and enlargement of more stable farm holdings. In this period, the O'Callaghan landlords were seeking to introduce innovative, substantial Catholic farmers, to rationalise farm-holding size and enforce impartible inheritance sys-

Figs 3a and 3b (right) The housebooks of Griffith's Valuation tell the very different stories of (a) the mountain townland of Ballyhurrow and (b) the lowland townland of Carriganroe during the Great Famine. John Brennan's valuation survey of 26 April 1847 itemises in brown ink the pre-Famine houses and outhouses in Ballyhurrow. Later house and farm valuations are outlined in blue ink by surveyor Thomas Hogan for October–November 1849. This latter survey records the total obliteration of all the holdings in the townland, following the intervention of the landlord the Earl of Glengall (Cahir). The adjacent townlands of Boolakennedy and Glengarra were to suffer a similar fate. In contrast, the housebook records comfortable farmhouses and families of 60–70 acres in the townland of Carriganroe, which survived the Famine crisis without too much change – typical of the destinies of the better-off farms in the lowlands. [Source: National Archives of Ireland]

tems, particularly on the better, lowland farms. There was a deliberate attempt to deflect population pressures both onto the adjacent peripheral mountain townlands and into the burgeoning lanes of the town of Clogheen and to a lesser

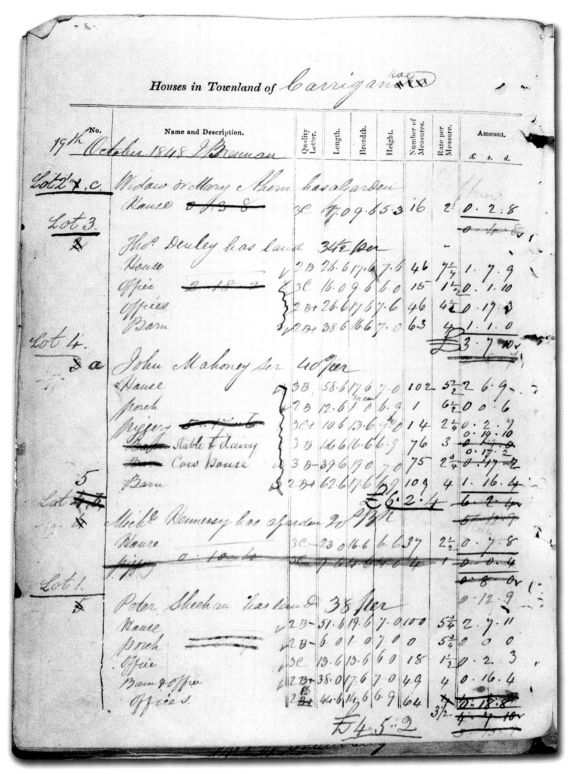

decline in the living conditions for a number of people in town and countryside is also indicated by sharp increases of 32%, 42% and 52% in the number of families crowding into Chapel, Pound and Cockpit Lane, respectively, in the town of Clogheen between 1821 and 1846. However, much of these population increases more likely reflected a still vital milling industry in and around the town as well as a boom in the building of public institutions – bridewell, police barracks, national school, Catholic and Church of Ireland churches, courthouse and the new workhouse, the latter built between 1840 and 1842.

In contrast to the strategic management of the O'Callaghan estate, including the deliberate development of Clogheen town, it is important to note that the administration of the Cahir Butler estate in the northeast of the parish was still in the hands of now parasitic middlemen. Hence the concentration of dwarf holdings in this zone. To summarise, between 1821 and 1845, it is probable that the parish of Shanrahan increased its population by more than the total population of the parish today, i.e. by more than 1,600 people or a 30% increase on the parish's population of 6,040 in 1821.[13]

### SHATTERING IMPACT OF THE FAMINE

The delicate equilibrium between lowland consolidation and moorland deflection (as well as urban congestion) was shattered by the Famine, thus opening up the fragile small farm communities to colonisation by the adjacent bigger

extent into surrounding villages like Burncourt. Between 1821 and 1841, there was only a small increase (14%) in the total number of farms in the 'lowland' townlands. In sharp contrast, there was an increase of at least 30% in the number of holdings on the 'mountain' townlands while the population of Clogheen town increased by close on 40% over the same period.

This 'mountain' colonisation represented the strenuous efforts of impoverished families to extract a livelihood from among the rocks and acidic soils of the mountain edges. A farmers and the disappearance of so many of the cabins of the landless in town and countryside. As we have seen, the Famine broke the symbiosis between farmers' needs for both labour and suitable grain rotations and the labourers' needs for life-sustaining work and potato ground. Elsewhere, the apparatus of the Poor Law was now well established in the Clogheen Union: workhouse officers in place, rates being collected and parish wardens appointed. In Shanrahan parish, Clogheen mill owner William Wade and strong farmer Alex Mahony of Old Shanbally (near Burncourt) were selected as the parish wardens – William Connor and Timothy Casey in the nearby western parish of Templetenny (modern Ballyporeen), and James Fennessy and Edmund Heffernan, Edward Ryan and James Williams, and James Connolly and William Walpole acted as wardens in the nearby eastern parishes of Tullaghhorton, Tubbrid and Whitechurch, respectively.[14]

As famine conditions deepened by mid-April 1846, a relief committee was established for the Clogheen area under the chairmanship of the landlord, Viscount Lismore. Its membership included the estate agent, the parish priest and two Catholic curates, two leading millers, and two medical doctors. The Church of Ireland rector was made secretary of the committee, which included a number of strong farmers and shopkeepers. The first major subscriptions to the relief committee's funds were led by Lord Lismore, who contributed £100 (his sister the Hon. Mary O'Callaghan contributed a further £10); £40 each came from two leading Grubb millers; £20 from the parish priest, Rev. James Kelly, as well as from the Cahir estate landlord, the Earl of Glengall, and £15 from the Shanbally estate agent, Edwin Taylor. The total came to £436.[15] As Edmund O'Riordan has noted, the town and the surrounding area was divided into ten 'walks' and those walks were visited by the Relief Committee members; they selected 387 families containing 2,017 persons 'as fit objects of relief'.[16] In the week of 18 April 1846, oatmeal and coarse flour was distributed to over 1,000 people in the Clogheen area. By the summer of 1846, relief works were also in operation, building new roads and repairing roads, bridges, walls and even public buildings. In building the new road from Clogheen to Cahir – still called 'the New Line' – folk memory suggests that some people died at work on this famine road and were buried in the ditches along the way.

By early June 1846, the relief committee of the adjacent parish of Templetenny reported high levels of distress in the community with '3000 people in immediate need of relief and assistance'.[17] Commencing the sale of Indian meal at the reduced price of one penny per pound, the Templetenny Relief Committee was selling three tons per week in relieving over 1,660 people. All along the mountain edges of the Knockmealdowns and Galtees, townland communities were in desperate straits and crying out for

relief. As that crisis deepened, more and more families joined the ranks of the starving poor and many were to die of want and starvation. Already in the spring of 1846, military escorts were needed for conveying cartloads of flour on to Clonmel for export. Lord Lismore then reported that the carriages of Alfred Grubb, 'a great miller', which were conveying flour from Clogheen to Lismore (and on to Youghal) were 'plundered by a tumultuous body of people'.[18] He succeeded in having the Third Dragoons dispatched immediately to Clogheen Military Barracks. (He was again to seek the provision of extra dragoons in October 1847 to protect the corn buyers attending the mills in the district.) Mills were being attacked around Clogheen, Cahir and the county town of Clonmel – then linked by boat to the port of Waterford. In the village of Kilsheelan below Clonmel, boats conveying goods between Clonmel and Waterford were attacked and flour taken off by starving men, women and children. Police were drafted in to defend the mills.

## PANIC

Then in the autumn of 1846, panic set in as the poor people realised that the new potato crop was almost totally destroyed. The women of Quaker milling families in Clogheen played an early and significant role in seeking to alleviate these people's sufferings. Hence, the supreme irony that the military and police defend the convoys of flour carts making their way from the Grubb family mills to be exported via Clonmel while the wives of the owners seek to defend the poor. Early in January 1847, Mrs Grubb of Clashleigh House, Clogheen (one of the big houses associated with the Grubb milling families), wrote to the Undersecretary at Dublin Castle seeking further aid from the Government to enlarge the scope of their soup depot so as to provide support to the people of the adjacent mountain district who 'are already dying of famine'.[19] Mrs Grubb reports that the 'Ladies Association' of Clogheen town had from December 1846 established a soup depot, had already relieved over 7,800 persons with quarts of soup and a ½lb of bread, that they continued to support 260 persons daily and that the numbers seeking relief continued to increase. Mrs Grubb later confirmed in a letter to Sir Randolph Routh, Commissary General – then in charge of the distribution of Indian corn – that the Ladies soup depot had brought great relief in the town 'as the improved looks and health of many of the people evince'.[20] She persists in seeking further help for the still 'unprovided for people' of the surrounding countryside, especially those living at the foot of the Knockmealdown Mountains ('starving wretches imploring them for relief which they cannot give'). Mrs Grubb continues: 'disease in the rural districts is making rapid strides, where grass, and bran, and donkeys, they are here resorted to for food; the two former they know are not uncommon. Can the rest of Ireland,' she pleads, 'which has excited well merited support exceed the misery we are fast approaching to?'[21]

Mrs Grubb may well have been in touch with the Central Relief Committee of the Society of Friends and with Robert Davis, who shortly afterwards travelled to this region. On 27 February 1847, Davis visited the districts of Ballyboy (just east of Clogheen town), Burncourt and Tubbrid. He reports that

> active measures in progress for the daily distribution of prepared food to the distressed people around [Ballyboy], and here I may literally say that active famine first met my view. There was no mistaking the shrunken looks and sharpened features of the poor creatures, who were slowly and with tottering steps assaulting to partake of the accustomed bounty. Sheer destitution marked their attenuated countenances too legibly to admit of a doubt that it was all a sad reality . . . From Ballyboy I next went to Clogheen and visited the soup, or rather porridge establishment there, it was at full work and appears to be well attended to. From Clogheen we proceeded to the village of Burncourt situated at the foot of the Galtee mountains, a locality where destitution abounds to a fearful degree. This place, though five miles distant, belongs to the parish and relief district of Clogheen: but from its remote situation, it has been so far neglected, . . . as it was I could learn that deaths from actual starvation were becoming of daily occurrence; whilst the corpses were buried in some instances at night and without coffins! However, it was truly gratifying to me to find, that, by means of the kind contributions of a few individuals (some in England) and a small grant from our auxiliary relief committee, . . . there is now a well regulated and well supplied porridge shop, or kitchen, opened and at full work in the little village of Burncourt and daily dispensing its benefits to the multitudes of famishing objects.[22]

Davis then proceeded from Burncourt along the base of the Galtee mountains 'through a desolate and wretched district, to Tencurry where another porridge kitchen is just set up and at work'.[23] Davis was alarmed at this apparent abandonment of the land in that district between Burncourt and Tincurry where 'desolation abounds to a fearful degree' and the land 'lying desolate and uncultivated'.[24] The people he

Fig. 4 Looking south towards the wealthier lowland townlands and beyond to the Knockmealdown mountains and including the castle mansion of the Everard landlord family at Burncourt (the previous landlords before the O'Callaghan Lord Lismore family), the most critical feature is the single great field of over 50 acres in the townland of Ballyhurrow (in the foreground – see highlighted area in Fig. 1), which housed and provided a subsistence to eight smallholders in pre-Famine times. This landscape was cleared by the Earl of Glengall during the Famine and now incorporates the motorway between Cork and Dublin. [Photo: William J. Smyth]

observed on the way projected a total absence of anything bordering on 'pleasantry or cheerfulness . . . all seemed to be downstricken and rejected yet had refrained from outrage in a remarkable manner.'[25]

What Davis may not have known is that he was passing through a series of townlands – Ballyhurrow, Boolakennedy and Glengarra in Shanrahan parish – which had experienced the proliferation of a vast number of tiny holdings on the Cahir Butler estate of the Earl of Glengall. These townlands had long been left in the hands of 'rentier' middlemen shopkeepers from Cahir town. Up to 1845, these townland communities of pauperised sub-tenants had subsisted on these overall plots of often recently colonised inferior land. They had increased their meagre subsistence and paid their rents by selling turf and turf mould off the mountain to lowland farms, villages and small towns and by providing labour to the big farmers in the wider region.[26] With the second failure of the potato, these families were in desperate straits. Some people had already died from starvation and famine fever.

### EVICTIONS

The *Tipperary Free Press* printed a letter in the first week of January 1847 entitled 'Extermination Systems' when reporting on sixty-two ejectments at Clogheen court that winter week. The letter writer reflected that such events are 'calculated to fill every thinking mind with the horrifying suspicion that the present terrific scourge of famine may be precursory to a still more appalling catastrophe, the extermination, by legal process, of the smaller tenantry on the estate of this landlord'.[27] As Edmund O'Riordan notes, 'many of the ejectments granted were against tenants who were able to produce receipts of the previous March rent'.[28] The landlord responsible is not named in the newspaper, but is made clear that it was not Viscount Lismore, who is praised for reducing the rents due in the previous year, for his judicious estate management and for the improving quality of his tenant farmers. Through his activities on the Clogheen Board of Guardians, in promoting public relief works, in providing a soup depot at the castle gates and directly assisting forty-eight other families in their homes, Viscount Lismore maintained the good reputation of the O'Callaghan landlord family throughout the Famine years.[29]

The very earliest valuation maps confirm that the Clogheen ejectment proceedings were against – amongst others – the tenants of Ballyhurrow, Boolakennedy and Glengarra. It is clear from other valuation records that the Earl of Glengall sought to avoid liability for paying the full amount of the poor rates for the many holdings valued at £4 or less in this area. An early valuation map states: 'the Earl of Glengall has received possession of the whole of the present occupiers of the townland of Glengarra' and gave instruction, as per the valuation map

entry, that 'their houses were to be thrown down'.[30] The associated cabins of the landless were also demolished. Perhaps as many as 380 men, women and children had been put out on the road in these bitter spring months of 1847. Hence the desolate and impoverished families of dwarf holdings that Robert Davis encountered. Hence the battering of the social structures of these northern townlands by these Famine evictions. Following these clearances, a small number of favoured tenants were placed on these townlands by the landlord. On the central Shanbally estate, Lord Lismore – if in a far more cautious and unobtrusive manner – also capitalised on this traumatic period by using the specific Poor Law regulations to further rationalise farm structures in some of the intermediate townlands between the mountains and the better and favoured lowland farms.[31] The latter had survived intact, despite the devastation that Famine conditions and Poor Law regulations were wreaking all around them.

Important and underutilised source materials in reconstructing the impact of the Famine locally are the Housebooks of Griffith's Valuation. The Valuation Housebook for Shanrahan parish covers the period from April 1847 to February 1851. John Brennan's valuation survey of 26 April 1847 clearly precedes the worst effects of the Famine and landlord consolidations in this parish. Later house and farm valuations now outlined in different ink – carried out by Thomas Hogan in October and November 1849 – records the fate of each house and family in the intervening traumatic two years.[32] The valuation maps and the Housebook pages reveal the devastation wrought throughout the townlands of Ballyhurrow, Boolakennedy and Glengarra in 1847. The brown-ink writing itemises the pre-Famine homes and outhouses. The later survey which strikes out so many homes in blue ink records the almost total obliteration of these townland communities by 1849.

In sharp contrast, the Housebook takes three and a half pages to describe and value Lord Lismore's mansion from the house proper, valued at £90/17/7, on to the basements, towers, greenhouse, coach-house, numerous stables through to the cowsheds, piggeries and seven fowl houses. All these made for a total valuation of £348/10/11.[33] Flourmills in the parish were valued at between £50 and £150 and the estate agent's big house was valued at £41.

The average valuation of the dwelling house and outbuildings of the 'strong' farmers (with over 100 acres) in the middle of the parish ranged from £5 to £10 while the average valuation of 'comfortable' farmers' houses (30–100 acres) was *c*.£3. For these farmers, the Famine period marked a reduction in living standards and a more demanding work routine but not destitution. The pages of the Housebook for well-to-do townlands with average farm sizes of 60–70 acres – as in Carriganroe – shows that little changed between 1847 and 1851. The valuation of the fourth-class cabins of the landless families rarely exceeded five shillings. The names of many of these families have long since disappeared from parish lists.

It is recorded in the folklore of the wider region that some strong farmers defended their turnip crops, sheep and cattle with the assistance of armed watchmen housed in field-huts. The nearby county town of Clonmel was then widely known for its brisk auctions for guns of all sizes. The Irish Folklore Commission records the following observations about the Famine and its effects on social life in these parts of southwest Tipperary:

> The Famine brought untold misery and hardship. Thousands and thousands were forced to roam the county and beg for anything that might keep them alive. Robberies and breaking into houses became an everyday occurrence. Often these poor robbers, who were robbers only through necessity, met their death in the raids. Some were shot in the act of a very small robbery while those who were caught were sentenced to severe terms of imprisonment. As a result of such robbery, one member of a family would have to remain at home when the others went to Mass.[34]

This passage suggests both the terror and frenzy of the Famine at its height and also the revolution in social mores that accompanied it.

Fig. 5  Paupers' burial place at the Reigh above Clogheen town. [Photo: John Crowley]

## CLOGHEEN UNION WORKHOUSE

Built on former mill grounds at Mountanglesby, it was the Clogheen Union workhouse which bore the brunt of these Famine devastations. Built to accommodate 500, its first pauper admissions occurred on 29 June 1842. Like most other workhouses in Ireland, it was only half full with c.230 inmates until the winter of 1845/46.[35] By 5 December 1846, there were 452 inmates there; by 30 January 1847 the numbers had climbed to 524.[36] In the meantime store sheds had been adopted to accommodate fever patients and a nearby cornstore leased to house 100 paupers. In the spring of 1847, because of overcrowding in the work-

house, many applicants were now being refused admission. In the summer of 1847, over half of the inhabitants of Clogheen Union as a whole were receiving food from soup kitchens under the Soup Kitchen Act. When the provision of soup was terminated in that August, 15.9% of the population of Clogheen district electoral division (DED) were on rations, 30.4% in Ballyporeen DED and only 7.3% in Tullahorton DED, east of Clogheen town. What is most striking is that in Tubbrid DED 40.4% of the population was still in receipt of soup rations in August 1847 – from a peak of 56.5% that summer. In 1851 Tubbrid DED reports the lowest population loss (9%) in the whole

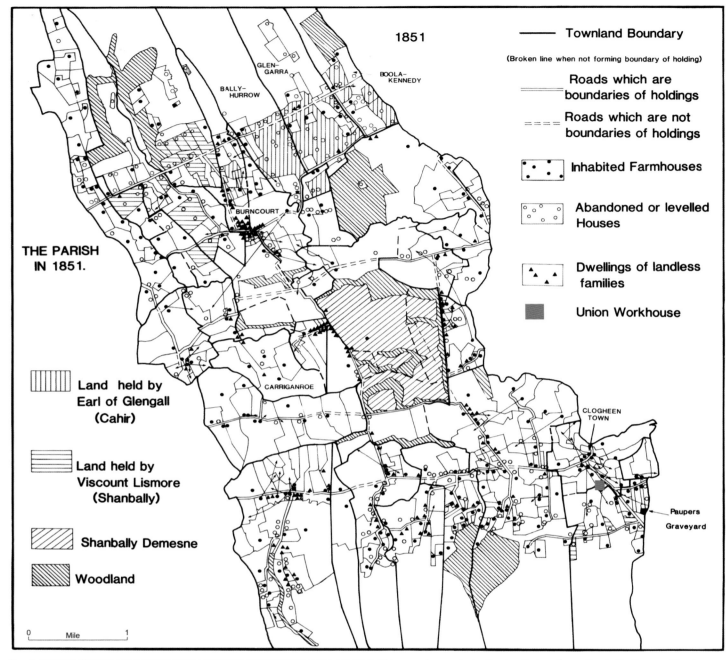

Fig. 6 THE POST-FAMINE SETTLEMENTS AND LANDSCAPES OF THE PARISH OF SHANRAHAN. This map demonstrates the drastic transformation in the lives and landscapes of the people of Shanrahan parish by 1851. As many as 200 family farms (out of 530) had disappeared during the Famine and close on half of the cabins and gardens of the poorest labourers and artisans had vanished in these deadly years. The greatest devastations occurred in the northern Galtee townlands where Famine conditions were ruthlessly exploited by the Cahir Glengall estate to demolish many smallholdings, formerly developed under exploitative shopkeeper/middleman administration. The more long-settled smallholdings at the southern end of the parish survived better but were to disappear over the next half century while bigger farms in the central townlands were augmented by often aggressive processes of amalgamation. Close on two-fifths of the rural population of the parish had disappeared while the village of Burncourt and the town of Clogheen were both reduced by one-fourth. In the Clogheen workhouse, 1,322 paupers were still resident in a building designed to house 500 inmates and a further 545 were resident in the auxiliary children's workhouse at Tincurry. A teeming pre-Famine landscape of great social diversity had been simplified, denuded and reduced to silence.

union.[37] The soup kitchens were clearly saving lives, but they were not left in place long enough.

By the end of 1847, when there were 584 paupers in Clogheen workhouse, it was decided to relocate the children elsewhere so as to make way for the inevitable influx of able-bodied paupers who could not receive any outdoor relief under the new legislation. So over 400 children were sent to a disused textile factory on 12 acres at Tincurry (near Cahir). Leased from William Walpole for £80 per year, some

of this land was used for agricultural instruction and part became a cemetery for the many children who died there.[38] By 4 March 1848, 1,159 paupers were now resident in the main workhouse and its auxiliary at Tincurry. In addition, in June of that year, a further 8,000 people were receiving outdoor relief across the union – a very significant proportion, only surpassed by unions in the west of Ireland. By the winter of 1848–49, the Old Courthouse at Clogheen was also being used to house some paupers. By 6 March 1849, the

Clogheen Union housed 1,510 paupers, 981 in Clogheen workhouse itself and 529 at Tincurry in a week when twenty children under fifteen and six babies under two years of age died.[39] Numbers continued to increase into 1851 when there was a total of over 1,800 resident paupers of all ages. Clogheen workhouse and union was part of the extensive Munster region that still suffered severely from famine and disease into the early 1850s.

Conditions in Clogheen workhouse were typical of a large number of workhouses. There were problems with overcrowding and ventilation, with smoky dormitories, poorly trained staff coming and going, cost-cutting measures in diets in attempts to reduce expenditure, poor food suppliers, problems with rate collectors and rate-collecting, misappropriation of union property, the abandonment of wives and children in the workhouse by errant husbands/fathers and tensions between Catholic and Protestant chaplains. There is clear evidence of problems in the distribution of food with children neglected and pauper nurses selling some of their food to purchase whiskey. There was probably much more coming and goings of 'inveterate' 'travelling' paupers than the literature has reported. Certainly there was a policy attempt at Clogheen to discharge the able-bodied paupers at harvest time so as to reduce costs.[40] The union had problems with debts but these were not too severe – the workhouse seems to have been reasonably well managed. It certainly did not receive any significant reprimands from the Poor Law Commissioners.

## MORTALITY

A total of 1,890 inmates died in the workhouse between June 1841 and March 1851 – 1,009 males and 881 females. Many died of famine-induced diseases which thrived in such congested surroundings. Yet, inmate mortality rates per week in April 1847 were less than 3% as opposed to over 5% per week in the unions of the west of Ireland and the west Midlands.[41] By October 1848, as the number of the workhouse dead accumulated, 12 acres of land high up on the mountainside in Mountanglesby (on the border with the townland of Kilballyboy) were rented from Lord Lismore, part to be used as a workhouse burial ground, the rest for cultivation. Now known as 'the Paupers Cemetery', it is located on the mountain flat or 'rea' (from the Irish réidh – flat, even). It appears that earlier victims of the workhouse were buried in a corner of Shanrahan graveyard known as 'the heap'.[42]

Across Clogheen Union as a whole it is likely that many more died of famine-related causes than managed to escape via the emigrant ship. By 1851, the pre-Famine population of Shanrahan parish had declined by over one-third. It therefore suffered both higher mortality and emigration levels than the union as a whole, which lost a quarter of its pre-Famine population, a loss of 10,202 people. However,

pointing up the complexity of the core factors that favoured survival or otherwise, two adjacent DEDs in the parish, those of Kilcoran and Clogheen, experienced two very different population histories during the Famine. Kilcoran's population declined by over a half (-56.3%) while that of Clogheen by only -4.5%. Kilcoran's decline – while staggering – is explained by the Earl of Glengall's sweeping clearances in these townlands during 1847. Clogheen's marginal decline strongly reflected the contrasting fortunes of landless families either employed on the Lismore demesne and estate or in the many mills along the Rivers Duag and Tar near Clogheen town.

Estate employees remained a privileged class and received special food supports from the landlord right through the Famine. Mill workers also appear to have survived the Famine conditions in a better state than landless families dependent on seasonal labour and the renting of potato ground from farmers. The more difficult lands of much of Burncourt saw a 30% decline in population. Likewise, to the west of Shanrahan in the more poorly endowed, small-farming world of Ballyporeen and Coolgarranroe DEDs – neither with any resident gentry – were each characterised by population losses of one-third. As already noted, Tubbrid on the better lands to the east may have been a particular beneficiary of extended soup-kitchen support – as well as a gentry-led active relief committee which employed 280 to 375 people working in the many local limestone quarries.[43]

Overall, in Shanrahan parish male heads of families and male children declined by over one-third between 1841 and 1851, whereas female heads and children declined by only six percentage points. However, the cumulative traumatic effects of the Famine saw the number of children under five in 1851 reduced to half the 1841 figure. Both male and female 'visitors' – mainly extended kin residing with their families – declined by about a half. On the other hand, the number and proportion of male servants increased by 6% whereas female servants declined by one-fifth. These gender shifts may reflect the fact that gainfully employed males declined by over one-third between 1841 and 1851 whereas the number of gainfully employed women hardly declined at all. Indeed among persons classified as 'ministering to food', male decline was more than two-fifths of the 1841 figure whereas women registered an increase. This pattern reinforces the view of the greater survival of widows and female farmers and shopkeepers as well as the phenomenal decline of labouring and small-farming males.[44] So, despite the reinforcing of patriarchy in the post-Famine world, a greater proportion of women were empowered in the economic sphere in this parish.

In this predominantly Irish-speaking parish, literacy levels by 1851 had not been dramatically transformed. People with an ability to read and write had increased by only 13.4% – there was some decline in the number of those

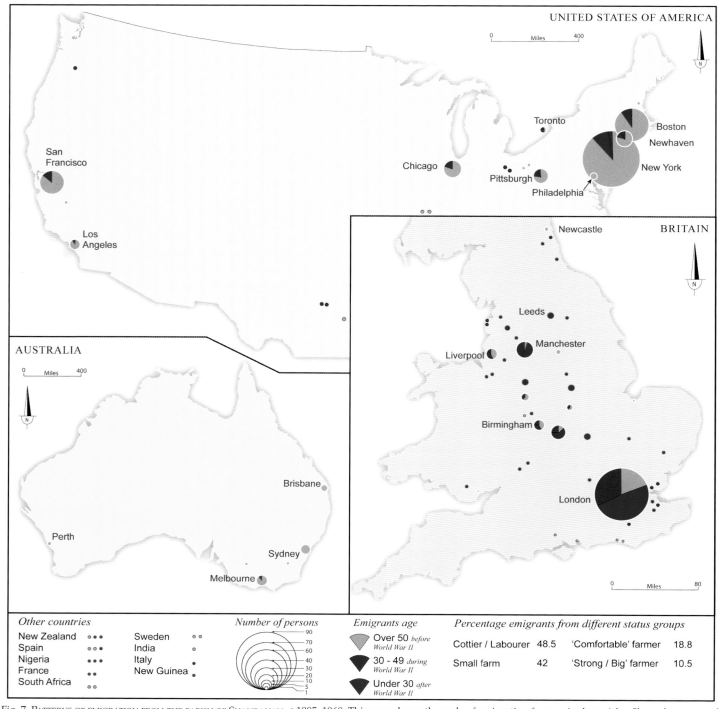

**Other countries**

| | | | |
|---|---|---|---|
| New Zealand | ● ● ● | Sweden | ● ● |
| Spain | ● ● ● | India | ● |
| Nigeria | ● ● ● | Italy | ● |
| France | ● ● | New Guinea | ● |
| South Africa | ● ● | | |

*Number of persons*

90
70
60
40
30
20
10
5
1

*Emigrants age*

Over 50 *before World War II*

30 - 49 *during World War II*

Under 30 *after World War II*

*Percentage emigrants from different status groups*

| | | | |
|---|---|---|---|
| Cottier / Labourer | 48.5 | 'Comfortable' farmer | 18.8 |
| Small farm | 42 | 'Strong / Big' farmer | 10.5 |

Fig. 7 PATTERNS OF EMIGRATION FROM THE PARISH OF SHANRAHAN, C.1885–1968. This map shows the scale of emigration from a single parish – Shanrahan – out of Ireland. (Multiply this pattern by *c*.2,500 other parishes and one arrives at overall emigration from the island.). The destination sought by these emigrants break down into three phases. The United States dominated nineteenth-century and early twentieth-century emigration patterns. There was a transitional phase in the inter-war years with Britain becoming the dominant focus of emigration after the Second World War. Throughout this whole period, however, certain cities remained the favourite places for emigrants – New York, Boston and Chicago in North America and Liverpool, Manchester, Birmingham and London in Britain. Yet what is most striking about all these patterns is the dominance of migrants from the landless and small farming classes – close on half of whose family members emigrated in every generation. In contrast, family members from comfortable and big farms saw only one-fifth or one-tenth of their family members leaving home.

who could 'read only' whereas illiteracy levels declined by about 40% for both men and women.[45] Housing transformations were more dramatic with four-fifths of the fourth-class houses cleared from the landscape – almost mirroring the level of decline in the families dependent on their own manual labour. Continuing relative poverty is suggested by only a decline of one-fifth in third-class houses. Thirty-three new

solid second-class houses (+15.6%) had emerged by 1851 and the number of large first-class houses had increased by only four – from 33 to 37. Overall, these housing figures reflect the strengthening of the strong and comfortable farming classes especially – a feature confirmed by the doubling of the census class 'those dependent on vested means'.[46] They also suggest the disappearance of the many poor.

On the other hand, the reduction by one-fourth in the number involved in 'the direction of labour' is far more a reflection of the decline in Clogheen's urban economy than that of the countryside. By 1901, the number of shopkeepers in the town was much the same as in 1821, albeit with a much stronger merchant class. The number of farmers had been reduced by 60% but the labouring class had been eroded by a massive 77%. Even more poignant, artisan tradesmen and women of all types had been more than decimated. Only twelve craftspeople were left in a parish that had close on 200 in 1821.[47] Factory goods from Britain's Industrial Revolution had penetrated deep into the society and economy of Shanrahan.

## EMIGRATION

Travelling in the opposite direction were the many emigrants from Shanrahan who during and after the Famine had escaped to new worlds either in Britain or North America. We know that some tradespeople were among the persons queuing for soup in Clogheen when hunger was at its greatest. Some tradespeople managed to escape as emigrants, but the greater impetus to emigration came from the labouring and small farming classes. The convoys of flour carts regularly making their way to Clonmel were soon followed by cartloads of emigrants on their way to the ships with their few belongings. Some died on the way – John Bourke's wife from Tubbrid died onboard ship at Liverpool while David Ryan wrote from St Louis to his cousin, Father James Hickey of Shanrahan parish, to confirm that his sister had died of cholera on arrival in quarantine in the harbour of Halifax, Nova Scotia.[48]

Their emigrant companions – the Burkes, Ryans, Hickeys, Keatings, Breedys and Sharkeys – left behind a silent world, emptied of people and the bustling, chattering vitality

iof a pre-Famine world of great social extremes.[49] They also left behind the 'survivors' who would remain silent as to why and how they had survived. Figure 6 demonstrates the denudation and simplification of both the landscapes and social structures of the parish. For example, the contrasts in the patterns of farm occupation between the period of the Tithe Survey (1835) and Griffith's Valuation (1851) – a time span of only sixteen years – are as great and as sharp as the differences between the 1851 picture and what prevails today 160 years later. Having lost out to Cahir in acquiring a railway link, the mills gradually closed, fairs and markets declined and the population shrank as the town of Clogheen became more isolated from the main currents of life and commerce.

On the landlord's demesne, the encircling demesne walls are built higher, the mansion is redecorated and a 'Bullock House' is built in the farmyard. The wheel has come almost full circle as the economy gradually reverts to an extensive pastoralist regime, somewhat similar to the kind of economy prevailing over much of the eighteenth century. The processes of farm and shop amalgamation, consolidation, displacement and depopulation accelerated during the crisis of the Famine. It is striking that the more substantial tenant farmers of the lowlands remained for the most part unaffected by the often catastrophic changes occurring in quite a number of mountain townlands. Thus, they emerged unscathed from the crisis of the late 1840s, to wax stronger during the agricultural boom of the 1850s and 1860s – frequently enveloping smaller farms as they moved into the growing power vacuum. These farmers helped to pave the way for the final phase of the estate system which had ironically fostered this section for its own interests.[50]

# The Famine in the Dingle Peninsula

## Kieran Foley

All the evidence points to poverty being very much a feature of the Dingle Peninsula in the years before the Famine. The more densely populated coastal districts were worst off, but even the town of Dingle itself showed few signs of prosperity. This was acknowledged by *Slater's Directory* (1846), which described the town as being 'little more than a fishing village'. The peninsula's hilly uplands were mainly devoted to pastoral farming and, while farm size was often above average, joint tenancy was very prevalent. Tillage predominated in the low-lying areas but many of the holdings were small. Fishing in the region was primarily a part-time activity that gave meagre financial returns. The setting up of a fisheries board and the introduction of a system of bounties on boats and catches provided a much-needed stimulus, but the board was abolished and the bounties withdrawn in 1829. The bounty on catches had been particularly important for the poorer fishermen and, according to Dingle's parish priest, they now began 'sinking into poverty'.[1] For almost seventy years a successful domestic linen industry had enabled both the farming and fishing families to supplement their incomes, but this was in rapid decline by the 1820s and had soon become extinct. This deepening poverty may help explain why the population of the barony of Corkaguiny, which took in most of the Dingle Peninsula, increased by a mere 0.3% between 1831 and 1841 when the corresponding figures for Kerry and for the country as a whole were 11.7% and 5.3%, respectively.[2]

### THE POTATO BLIGHT STRIKES

The initial appearance of the potato blight in the autumn of 1845 caused little anxiety in Kerry. By early 1846, however, the state of the potato crop in various parts of the county, including the Dingle Peninsula, was giving rise to real concern. In mid-February Corkaguiny was said to have lost two-thirds of its crop.[3] The Government encouraged the setting up 'relief committees' to sell food at cost to those in need. In all, fourteen such committees looked after the people of Kerry during the summer of 1846. A Dingle-based committee assumed responsibility for Corkaguiny but the parishes of Ballinacourty and Ballinvoher later formed their own committee. The coastguard was also involved in the relief effort. Thomas deMoleyns, a member of the Ventry family who were the Dingle Peninsula's main landlords, informed the government's relief commission in May 1846 that the crop failure was 'much more general and severe' in the parishes to the west of Dingle but that setting up a separate relief committee for that region was out of the question. The reasons he gave were that the district contained 'several wretched villages' but no town that could act as a focal point; that not a single magistrate or 'gentleman of property' resided within it; and that cooperation between the Catholic and Protestant clergy was highly unlikely since 'conversions from amongst the lower orders' had brought about a state of 'religious warfare'.[4] The relief committees were funded by Government grants and local donations. By August 1846 Kerry's committees had raised an average of £460. Contributions to the Dingle committee, however, came to £695-5-6, with Lord Ventry and the Earl of Cork each contributing £100.[5]

The arrival of a Board of Works engineer in Dingle in early April 1846 to carry out preliminary road surveying was warmly welcomed as public works were part of the Government's relief operation. Some works got under way later that month and Corkaguiny benefited from nine of the forty-nine

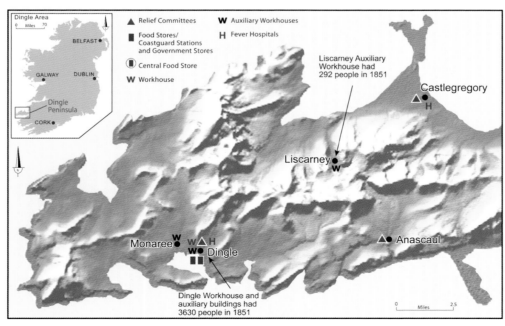

Fig. 1 MEDICAL AND RELIEF FACILITIES IN THE DINGLE PENINSULA DURING THE FAMINE

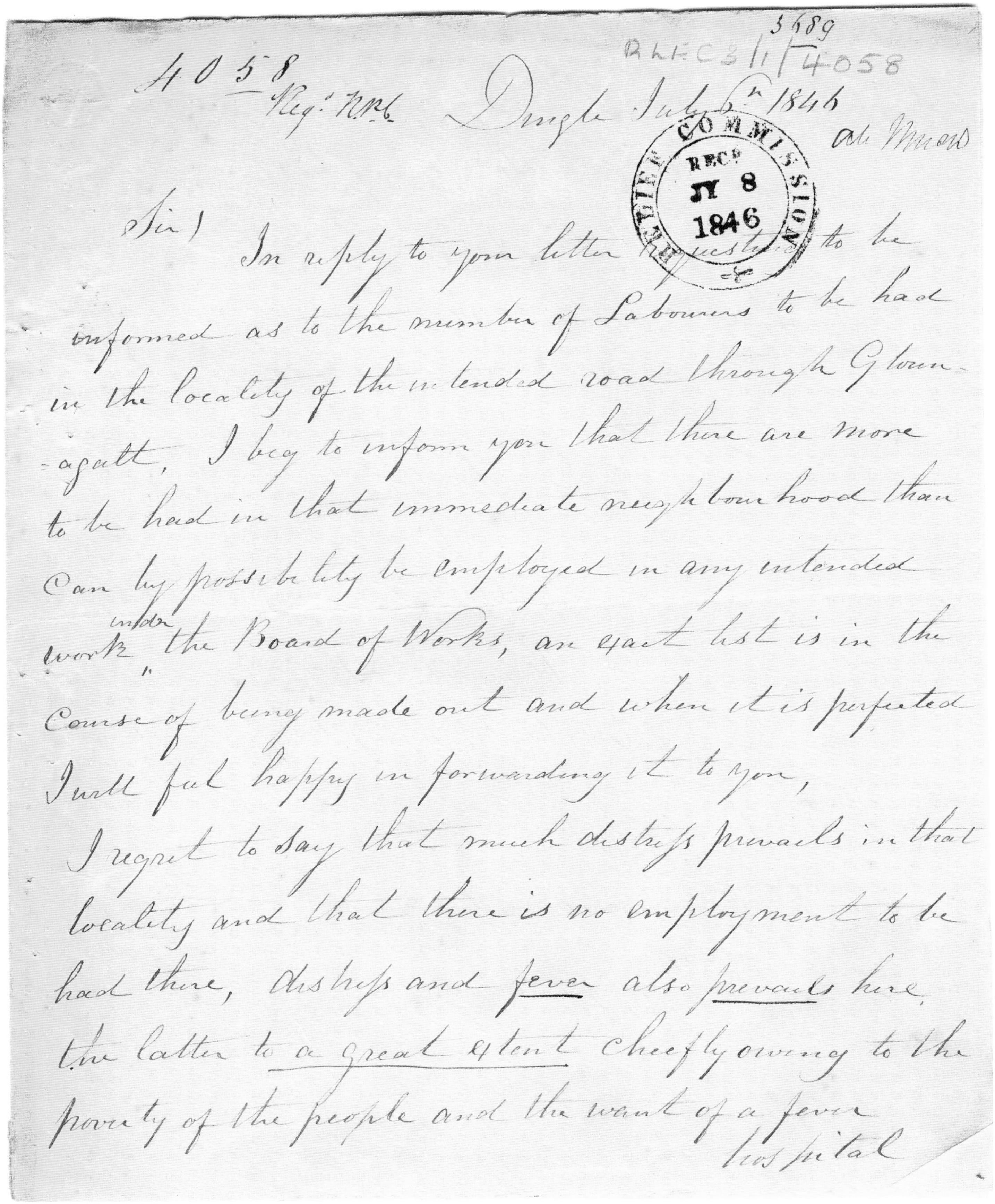

4058

3689

RLF C3/1/4058

Dingle July 6th 1846

RELIEF COMMISSION

RECD

JY 8

1846

Sir,

In reply to your letter requesting to be informed as to the number of Labourers to be had in the locality of the intended road through Glown-agatt, I beg to inform you that there are more to be had in that immediate neighbourhood than can by possibility be employed in any intended work under the Board of Works, an exact list is in the course of being made out and when it is perfected I will feel happy in forwarding it to you,

I regret to say that much distress prevails in that locality and that there is no employment to be had there, distress and fever also prevails here, the latter to a great extent chiefly owing to the poverty of the people and the want of a fever hospital

Fig. 2 A letter from Thomas Trant, secretary of the Dingle Relief Committee, to the Secretary of the Relief Commission, 6 July 1846. Trant explains that there are more labourers 'in the locality of the intended road through Glownagatt [*sic*] than can by possibility be employed in any intended work under the Board of Works'. He also refers to the distress and fever in this specific neighbourhood and 'the want of a fever hospital'. [Source: Relief Commission Papers, 3/1/4058, National Archives of Ireland] projects sanctioned for Kerry up to July.[6]

The response to the partial potato failure of 1845 proved to be adequate and people now looked forward to the new season's crop. But hopes that the worst was over were soon dashed. As early as 19 August 1846 the *Kerry Evening Post* accurately predicted that 'the scarcity of the year 1846 will be mere child's play to the famine of 1847'. Meanwhile, a new Government had come to power in the summer of 1846 and employment on public works formed the centrepiece of its relief policy. The relief committees continued to operate but only in a subsidiary role. The number of committees in the Dingle Peninsula increased to three when a new committee was established in Castlegregory. In addition, one of the four Government food depots in Kerry was located in Dingle.

The sum now sanctioned for road works in Kerry was over seven times greater than that for the previous season;

---

VENTRY.

TO THE EDITOR OF THE KERRY EVENING POST.

Ventry Cottage, March 18, 1847.

DEAR SIR—Unwilling as I am to trespass on your columns, the feelings of your readers, or my own time, I cannot resist adding one more to the tales of woe I have already told you of this ill-fated parish.

I could give you facts connected with the moonlight and coffinless burials equal to any which have happened in the most destitute parts of Ireland, but will confine myself to one.

Out of the litte village of Ballintlea, which is in the centre of this parish, twenty deaths have taken place from actual starvation up to Monday the 7th of this month.

On Thursday last a poor man living in it was alarmed by seeing a fire break out in an adjoining cabin, and immediately hastened towards it with the intention of waking and assisting the inmates—supposing they were asleep—when, to his horror, he found the only occupants two lifeless bodies—the straw on which they lay lighting around them. They were two sisters of eighteen and twenty years of age, the sole survivors of a family of six, all of whom have died within the month from the same cause, starvation. Having succeeded in putting out the fire he went to inform some friends of the deceased, all of whom refused, through dread of infection, to enter the cabin. The next day a dog was seen dragging about one of their hands, on which there was made some exertion to procure a parish coffin for the mutilated bodies.

But on Saturday, when they went to collect the remains of both into it, a head was also missing, having doubtless followed the fate of the hand!

On their way to the church-yard with the coffin in a mule's cart, they were met by a poor woman striving to take a coffin to the grave, but unequal to the task, it was thrown also into the cart. While in the church yard another woman was brought in a decomposed state in a basket and thrown into a hole there.

Such, Mr. Editor, is the state to which we are reduced by starvation with its train of diseases, and I will only express my hope in conclusion that some who may cast an eye on this painful narrative will think with pity on those poor sufferers—with compassion on this once favoured spot—and send us a mite to help in keeping alive those yet remaining.

Yours very faithfully,

MATTHEW T. MORIARTY.

---

Fig. 3 A graphic account of Famine distress penned by Matthew Moriarty in a letter to the *Kerry Evening Post*, 20 March 1847. [Source: Local Studies and Archives Department, Tralee, County Kerry]

and statistics for the week ending 30 January 1847 show 5,410 people being employed in Corkaguiny, which was far more than in any of the other Kerry baronies. Included in that total were 115 women, 428 boys and two people who were classed as 'infirm'.[7] These workers, many of whom were weak from illness and/or hunger, were engaged in road making in the middle of a cold and bitter winter and the wages they earned did not keep pace with rising food prices. Moreover, the works could be interrupted or suspended as happened when heavy snow in mid-December 1846 brought all works in the Dingle area to a halt. The flawed nature of this form of famine relief was clearly recognised by a concerned local resident who, in a letter to a newspaper, despairingly asked, 'With the price of provisions so high, the rate of wages so low, and the weather so bad . . . what are we to do?'[8]

### HUNGER, DISEASE AND DEATHS

On 16 November John Boland, a labourer, collapsed while working on a new road to the west of Dingle. He was carried to his home, where he died. The inquest verdict of 'death from hunger and cold' was the first of many.[9] A local clergyman wrote at the end of December that the people seemed to be 'dying by inches', in that they had some food but not enough to 'support life'.[10] Eight people from John Street in Dingle died in a single day in January 1847 from dysentery and starvation. The town already contained a large number of poor residents who were struggling to survive but their number was augmented by an influx of impoverished people from the surrounding areas. Eyewitnesses spoke of famine, fever and dysentery wreaking havoc among the poor and a local charity provided 'a shell to convey the remains of the unfortunate victims to the churchyard' where they were buried 'without a shroud or a coffin'.[11] The relief committee, the Presentation Sisters, the St Vincent de Paul Society, Rev. Charles Gayer and others were doing their utmost to relieve the distress, but their best efforts fell far short of what was needed. And their task was not made any easier by the local food retailers, who were described as 'famine mongers' by one local newspaper and 'a heartless set' by another; the town's bakers also came in for criticism because of an alleged 'deficiency of weight' in their bread.[12]

Harrowing scenes were now being enacted all over the peninsula but, particularly, in the parishes to the west of Dingle which in early April were deemed to be 'a very charnel house of death'.[13] A correspondent bemoaned the fact that the press and local gentry had made the plight of the people of Skibbereen and other distressed areas widely known 'while the poor famishing creatures' living at the western end of the Dingle Peninsula were being left 'to the tender mercies of famine, with all its attendant horrors'.[14] This was not quite correct as Matthew Moriarty, a

Fig. 4 Eask Tower was built as a Famine relief project intended to signal to sailors that they were approaching the 'blind' entrance to Dingle Harbour. It did not form any part of the Government's own relief measures and was erected at the instigation of Rev. Charles Gayer. [Photo: Frank Coyne]

member of a prominent local family, sent numerous letters to the press highlighting the awful scenes that he witnessed on a daily basis in Ventry. He graphically described coffinless burials, corpses part-eaten by rats and dismembered by dogs, whole families wiped out by starvation and disease, and a people broken by the suffering and death that surrounded them.[15] John Busteed, a surgeon attached to the Castlegregory dispensary, drew attention to Killiney and the neighbouring parishes, claiming that they too were suffering greatly, but doing so in silence. He named a number of people who had died of hunger or disease and described in detail the fate of one particular family:

> About a fortnight ago a boy named John Shea of Tullaree died of starvation – such was the verdict of a jury. On yesterday week his sister died, entirely from the same cause: she lay naked and uninterred on what had been the hearth, for four days, during which time she had been gnawed by rats. On Friday evening last a brother of hers died from dysentery, brought on by hunger, and on Saturday the father also fell a victim to this desolating scourge. They had no food for many days . . . The door was hasped on the outside, and the famishing family abandoned by every relative. Only one child of all this family is now alive; his days too are numbered, the dysentery of starvation has marked him as its own.[16]

## SOUP KITCHENS

The enactment of the 'Soup Kitchen Act' in February 1847 was an acknowledgement that the employment-based relief policy had failed. An extensive network of soup kitchens was now to be put in place. Soup kitchens were not unknown in the Dingle Peninsula as they were already being operated at various locations by the relief committees and by private individuals. This policy change was well received and distribution centres were set up throughout the peninsula but, faced with having to feed such large numbers of people, the different committees decided that it would be more practical to provide uncooked food. This new relief system was fully operational by June and its scale is shown by the fact that the Castlegregory committee alone had issued a total of 498,222 rations by 12 September.[17] As most of this food was distributed gratuitously, instances of fraud were inevitable. An examination of the relief lists for the parish of Kilquane, for example, led to the removal of farmers with land and animals, tradesmen, labourers in constant employment and 'huxters with some money'.[18]

The problem of starvation was now being addressed but large numbers continued to fall victim to famine-related diseases. The Irish Fever Act of April 1847 empowered the relief committees to implement various anti-fever measures, including the whitewashing of cabins, the providing of coffins to bury the destitute dead and the opening of temporary fever hospitals. Two of the fourteen such hospitals established in Kerry served the

Fig. 5 'Hussey's Folly' was also built as a Famine relief project and paid for by landlord Edward Hussey. [Photo: Frank Coyne]

Dingle Peninsula. One was located in Dingle and the other in Castlegregory. These initiatives had the desired effect and there was soon a marked reduction in the number of fever deaths.

### RELIEF UNDER THE POOR LAW

The soup kitchen system began to be wound down in August and September 1847 and the Poor Law assumed responsibility for all famine relief. The Dingle Peninsula formed part of the Tralee Union and its workhouse was located in Tralee town. The number of inmates in this workhouse frequently exceeded the 1,000 persons it was meant to accommodate. Yet it was not unusual for large crowds to assemble at the workhouse gates, only to be turned away. This was highlighted by one of the Tralee guardians during a board meeting in December 1847:

> Many of you were present on the last and preceding day of meeting and saw hundreds of paupers from these windows, many with children on their backs and others by their sides, from the most remote districts, mostly without clothing and in a state of half starvation, dripping with wet and shivering with cold seeking admission here, a place

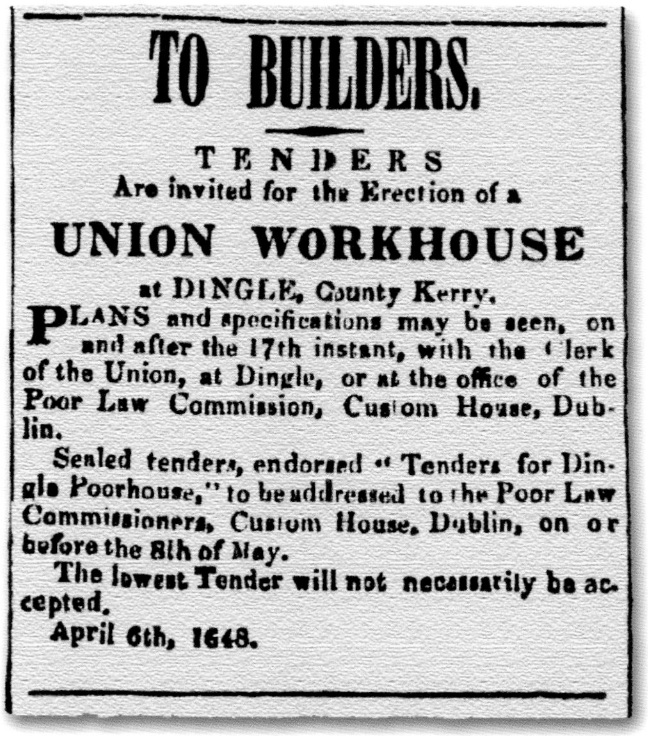

**TO BUILDERS.**

TENDERS
Are invited for the Erection of a
**UNION WORKHOUSE**
at DINGLE, County Kerry.

PLANS and specifications may be seen, on and after the 17th instant, with the Clerk of the Union, at Dingle, or at the office of the Poor Law Commission, Custom House, Dublin.

Sealed tenders, endorsed "Tenders for Dingle Poorhouse," to be addressed to the Poor Law Commissioners, Custom House, Dublin, on or before the 8th of May.

The lowest Tender will not necessarily be accepted.

April 6th, 1648.

Fig. 6  An advertisement for tenders for the building of Dingle workhouse, *Kerry Examiner*, 11 April 1848.

which the people of the country dislike, and to which nothing but starvation drives them. Those poor people, whose condition no language of mine can describe, we were unable to admit because there was no room.[19]

The problems that the sheer size of the Tralee Union posed for both the guardians and the destitute prompted the authorities to order the creation of a separate Dingle Union in February 1848. The new union covered most of the peninsula, stretching from Dunquin in the west to Killiney and Ballinvoher in the east and its valuation of 16s 4d per head of population was only marginally higher than that of Caherciveen and Kenmare, Kerry's poorest unions. The peninsula had earlier been identified as a region that was likely to require external financial assistance in providing for its destitute and this proved to be the case. The union received funding from the British Relief Association at first, and later from the 'rate-in-aid', a levy placed on all unions to help those whose resources were insufficient to meet their commitments. Dingle contributed a mere £916 of the £11,207 levied in Kerry and received £14,784 of the £42,998 distributed.[20] But this was not enough and the Government had to advance further

sums as creditors regularly threatened to stop supplying the workhouse and the wages of the union's employees went unpaid. In April 1851 the board pleaded for its own dissolution, saying that the poverty of the rate-payers themselves meant that the funds necessary to run the union just could not be collected. This request was turned down and so the board had to struggle on. The sheriff seized beds, bedding and furniture from the workhouse, as well as crops belonging to the union, in August 1851, but he then agreed to postpone their sale to give the board time to raise the money owed.[21]

The escalating numbers seeking relief forced boards of guardians to increase their workhouse accommodation. The Dingle board erected temporary sheds in the workhouse grounds and was soon renting virtually every vacant building in the town and neighbourhood for this purpose; auxiliary workhouses were also opened at Liscarney and Monaree. None of these buildings was purpose-built and only minimal sums were spent on fitting them out. During the week ending 21 June 1851, the number of workhouse inmates in the Dingle Union peaked at 4,841, which was 17.7% of the union's population.[22] An amendment to the Poor Law allowed outdoor relief for specified groups of people who could not be accommo-

Fig. 7 Dingle Union workhouse was built in 1848, the first new union and workhouse created to deal with rising levels of distress. From 1849 onwards a further thirty-two were established to deal with the continuing Famine crisis. [Photo: Michael Diggin]

dated in the workhouses. The numbers in receipt of this form of relief were at their highest in the Kerry unions in 1848–49 and they dropped rapidly thereafter. Dingle was the only Kerry union in which it was still available in 1851, but this was only for a nine-week period from May to July.[23] Able-bodied recipients of outdoor relief were required to perform some type of work as proof that their need was genuine. The Poor Law Commissioners were so keen that stone-breaking should be used for this purpose that they told their Dingle inspector that 'it should be adopted even if the stones, when broken, cannot be advantageously disposed of'.[24]

### EVICTIONS

The available records relating to evictions are incomplete, but anecdotal evidence and newspaper reports suggest that a sizable number of families in the Dingle Peninsula may have lost their holdings during the Famine years. Kerry's relieving officers were notified of evictions involving a total of 560 persons during the twelve months to July 1849; 89% of these resided in the Dingle Union and were tenants on the Ventry estates.[25] Landlords frequently claimed that tenants 'voluntarily' vacated their holdings. However, it is difficult to imagine hard-pressed tenants being in a position to resist too strenuously if their landlords wanted to get rid of them. Moreover, resistance could well prove futile as thirty families in Kilquane found in February 1848 when they were all evicted after they had refused inducements to hand over possession.[26] It is also likely that some who returned home after a stay in the workhouse found that

their cabins had been levelled in their absence.

### PROSELYTISM

Dingle and some of the neighbouring parishes witnessed major religious controversy during the Famine years. However, this had started long before the potato blight appeared and it would be very wrong to allow it obscure the major contribution made by clergymen, Catholic and Protestant, to the relief of famine distress. Rev. Charles Gayer, an Englishman, arrived in Dingle in 1833 as private chaplain to Lord Ventry. A low-key proselytising campaign had begun in the area two years previously and this now gathered momentum, with Rev. Gayer as its driving force. An appeal to the Irish Society in 1836 led to twenty Irish-speaking teachers being sent to assist the proselytising effort; and a further boost was received when Rev. Thomas Moriarty, a native of Dingle and a convert from Catholicism, began ministering in the area. Protestant colonies were established in Dingle and Ventry, with a lesser presence in other locations. A major row broke out towards the end of 1844 when the *Kerry Examiner* launched a scathing attack on Rev. Gayer and his supporters in a series of articles laden with such terms as 'souper', 'soup-bloated tribe', 'soup-gang', 'soup-fattened followers' and 'souper-perverts'. Rev. Gayer sued Patrick Byrne, the newspaper's proprietor and editor, for libel and the jury awarded him £40 in damages.

The widely-reported court proceedings attracted support for the Protestant colonies from evangelical Protestants at home and in England, but the controversy served to increase local animosity towards both the pros-

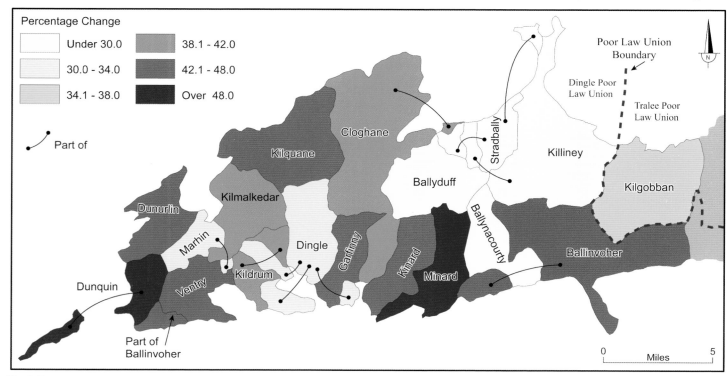

Fig. 8 POPULATION CHANGE IN THE DINGLE PENINSULA, 1841–51

elytisers and the converts. This hostility intensified when the Famine struck. Rev. Gayer was constantly being accused of bribing desperate Catholics to abandon their faith. He staunchly defended his proselytising efforts but rejected out of hand any suggestion of 'souperism'. Bearing in mind the awful circumstances of the time, however, it is hard to believe that none of the converts were enticed by the prospect of food, employment and even housing. The Vincentian fathers conducted a seven-week mission in Dingle in 1846 and this marked the beginning of a vigorous counter-offensive against the proselytisers. Two years later the proselytising movement was dealt a particularly severe blow when Rev. Gayer died from typhus. By now, the Protestant colonies were in decline with increasing numbers of converts returning to their former faith and others emigrating. And this was accelerated by the appointment of Fr Owen O'Sullivan as parish priest of Dingle, following the death from cholera of Fr Michael Devine in 1849. Fr O'Sullivan's opposition to the proselytisers bordered on the obsessive and he used every means at this disposal to undermine them and their work.

## POPULATION LOSS

The population of the Dingle Union fell by 23.7% between 1841 and 1851 compared with 18.9% for the county as a whole, and this pattern continued in the post-Famine decades. Between 1851 and 1891, for example, Kerry's population dropped by 24.8% while that of the Dingle Union decreased by 30.4%.[27] Catholic parish registers show that contracting marriage and birth rates contributed to this population decline; emigration, however, was the most significant factor. Very few labourers, farm servants or smallholders emigrated in the early years of the Famine as they

generally lacked the necessary financial resources. But this later changed and the poorer classes began to dominate the emigration statistics. In the period from 1 April 1851 to 31 March 1852, for example, 1,443 Kerry people were helped to emigrate by the Poor Law; and 357 of these were from the Dingle Union.[28] But remittances from friends and family members who had already left, rather than the poor law, would provide the main source of funding in the years ahead.

The Famine brought starvation, disease and death to the Dingle Peninsula, with the western parishes being particularly badly affected. While most of the deaths occurred in the first half of 1847, people continued to succumb to hunger and disease over the following months, and even years. For example, verdicts of 'death from starvation' were returned at inquests during the winter of 1847–48 and again in 1848–49. In the Dingle Peninsula, as elsewhere, however, it was principally the poor who starved to death. Disease was less discriminating, but the vast majority of disease victims also came from the poorer classes. The members of the Dingle relief committee believed that the tragic consequences of the potato failure in their area were predictable:

> In our case, we can only say that the sea-shore character of our district, presenting, by its facilities of manure, great inducement to the cultivation of the potato, and, from its dense population, equally great inducements to the minute sub-division of the ground, and to entire dependence on the production of the potato as the great means of life – these causes combined to make the total failure of the potato crop a sentence of starvation to the great mass of the people.[29]

# Famine relief in Cove and the Great Island, April 1846–March 1847

*Marita Foster*

By early 1846 Cove was a prosperous town, which during the previous thirty years, had greatly increased in size, population and importance. *Slater's National Commercial Directory of Ireland 1846* described a town which had:

> handsome ranges of houses, well stored shops, elegant hotels, convenient lodging-houses, an intelligent population, and, above all, an active trade. Provisions of nearly all kinds are cheap, and articles of a more luxurious kind are obtained with facility from Cork – with which a communication is constantly maintained by steam vessels.[1]

The directory continued:

> The trade of the town, exclusive of a good retail business, consists of exports and imports – the latter comprising timber, coal, guano, and various goods; among the former a large quantity of stores for the army and navy. It is the great port for the embarkation of troops to Canada and the Colonies, and also the great southern station for government emigration, for which latter purpose there is an efficient agent stationed here.[2]

There was a daily market for fish, vegetables and various commodities, with the market, especially on Saturdays, abundantly supplied. The population of the town as recorded in the 1841 census was 5,142, while the total population of the Great Island (parishes of Clonmel and Templerobin) was 9,955.

## ESTABLISHMENT OF A COVE RELIEF COMMITTEE

Despite the prosperity of Cove a relief committee of the clergy, gentry and other inhabitants of the town was established in April 1846 in response to 'the prevailing distress among the poor of Cove and the Great Island'. At a meeting on 9 April discussions focused on the establishment of a subscription list 'for the purpose of contributing, in whatever way was most desirable, to lower the price of food and occasion relief to the poor'.[3] The requirement that non-resident and resident landowners alike contribute to the sub-

scription list was addressed by many of the speakers at the meeting. It was agreed that the sum obtained 'by the subscription list now opened be immediately applied to the relief of the present distress by selling food at cost price'.[4]

The extent of destitution in Cove was addressed at the meeting by the Reverend P.D. O'Regan, a Catholic curate. He stated that in the town itself there were over 500 families whom:

Fig. 1 Reverend P.D. O'Regan, a Catholic curate in the parish of Cove from 1844 to 1849, was a member of the Cove Famine Relief Committee. In April 1847 Fr O'Regan reported to Captain Forbes of the relief ship the *Jamestown* of the daily suffering he was witnessing in his parish. 'As a Catholic clergyman, on whom devolves the sad and laborious office of administering the rites of the Church to some ten victims of disease every day, of visiting them in their wretched hovels at the peril of my own life, I have opportunities of witnessing scenes of misery which cannot be known or relieved by public committees, however zealous. In fact, within the last month, I have been obliged out of my own small means to furnish coffins to fifteen of our poor people.' He went on to serve as parish priest in the parishes of Kanturk, Mallow and Mitchelstown and as vicar general of the diocese of Cloyne. He died, dean of Cloyne, in June 1898, aged ninety-one, having served as a priest for sixty-six years. [Source: Cork Public Museum]

From his inspection and from their own statements (which he believed to be true) he knew to be in a state of destitution (hear, hear); for he considered it destitution when a man could not afford himself any more than one meal of potatoes, or even of worse food, in the twenty-four hours.[5]

Fr O'Regan referred to the difficulties that tradesmen engaged in labour were having in feeding their families and that if they were having such difficulties:

> How much worse then must be the condition of the labouring class of Cove, and worse still of those who have no means of subsistence except the precarious relief of the benevolent, or the still more precarious assistance which they may glean from persons in a state of distress little less severe than their own (hear, hear)? He would not be making a very incorrect statement if he multiplied that 500 by five, and that would give them 2,500 destitute poor in the town of Cove.[6]

He also recommended that the gentlemen of the town of Cove and the landed proprietors, who were engaged in giving employment to the people, and thereby diminishing the extent of poverty in the town, should:

> give that employment in every place where they could to the inhabitants of the town, and not to bring strangers from other parts of the country (hear, hear); for the influx of those persons only brought additional distress. He would also urge on the people of Cove, and he hoped he would not be taxed with want of charity when he recommend them that they should not encourage the system of

begging on the part of strangers, and to administer their charity as judicious as possible; because whilst they gave to strangers they were doing a certain share of injustice to those who had claims on them.[7]

## ALLEVIATING THE DISTRESS

From the outset the members of the Cove Relief Committee applied themselves diligently to the task of alleviating the distress of the inhabitants of Cove and the Great Island. Meetings were held regularly – usually twice weekly. One of the first tasks undertaken was the division of the general committee into sub-committees, 'each to be assigned a particular district for the purpose of ascertaining by minute personal enquiry the exact amount and character of the distress which now prevails or may be apprehended'.[8] The 'district visitors', as they were known, were to report back to the general committee. Various other sub-committees were established whose tasks included the solicitation of subscriptions, the distribution of Indian meal, oatmeal and other food stuffs, and the commencement of public works.

W.M. Drew, a Justice of the Peace and the secretary of

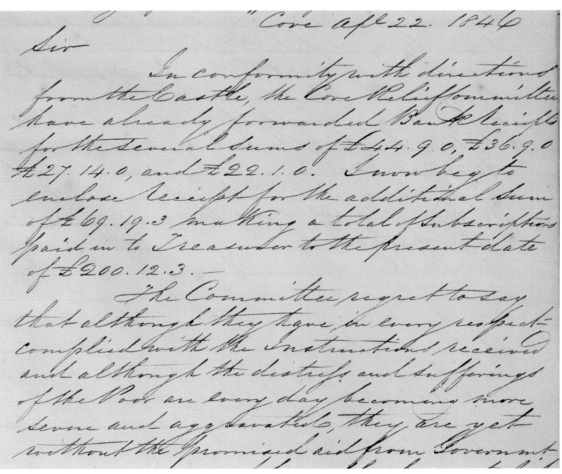

Fig. 2  Extract from a letter sent by the Cove Famine Relief Committee to the secretary of the Poor Law Commissioners, 22 April 1846, expressing regret that the promised financial help from the Government had not yet been received. Such tardiness in responding to the crisis caused even greater suffering: 'In conformity with directions from the Castle, the Cove Relief Committee have forwarded bank receipts . . . to the total sum of £200.12.3. The committee regret to say that although they have in every respect complied with the instructions received and although the distress and suffering of the poor are every day becoming more severe and aggravated they are yet without the promised aid from government.' [Source: Minute book of the meetings of the Cove Famine Relief Committee, p. 26, Cork Public Museum]

the Relief Committee, was in regular correspondence with the Central Relief Commission in Dublin, advising the secretary of that body of the efforts being undertaken to provide relief. Local relief committees were to receive state donations equal to the amount collected from subscriptions. In the months following the establishment of the Cove Relief Committee, correspondence from the committee to the Relief Commission requested the payment of such donations. On 22 April, in a letter to the Commission, Drew pointed out, that in conformity with the directions of the Castle, the Cove Relief Committee had already submitted bank receipts for several sums of money and was now enclosing a receipt for an additional sum of £69.19.3, making a total subscription paid to the treasurer of £200.12.3. He continued:

> The Committee regret to say that although they have, in every respect, complied with the instructions received and although the distress and sufferings of the Poor are every day becoming more severe and aggravated, they are yet without the promised aid from Government.[9]

In May Drew advised the Commission that a further sum of £263.6.0 had been lodged in the Bank of Ireland in Cork, bringing the total subscriptions collected to a sum of £463.18.3. Drew stated:

> Having on two or three occasions described the severe and extensive distress prevailing in the locality, I would now merely add that in few districts, perhaps, was the Government System of Relief more required, or carried into effect with more advantage to the Poor, than in the Town and Island of Cove.[10]

In June the committee was advised that the Lord Lieutenant had granted a donation of £225 in aid of the subscription fund which the Commissary-General in Cork was authorised to pay once the necessary paper work was completed by the committee.[11]

The subscriptions raised by the committee were used to purchase Indian corn, oatmeal, flour and other food stuffs which were sold at cost price to the poor. However, due to the enquiries of the District Visitors into the extent of destitution in Cove and on the Great Island, it was evident to committee members that many of the inhabitants were not in a position to purchase provisions at cost price. The poor were classified under three headings: (i) those who were able to purchase provisions at cost price, taking into account their earnings and the number in their families; (ii) those who from want of employment or from incapacity of giving a fair day's work were unable to provide a sufficiency of food for their families at cost price; (iii) the destitute. While

enquiries were made to the Chairman of the Board of Guardians to ascertain whether there would be room for the Cove paupers in the union workhouse in Cork city, the Cove Relief Committee, on its establishment, had recognised the importance of providing employment through public and other relief works for those who could work in order to support themselves and their families, but who were unable to find employment.

## PUBLIC WORKS

At a public meeting on 9 April it was resolved that:

> The Board of Public Works be requested to send their Engineer to decide on the most suitable part of the Harbour for the construction of a Pier, and that subscriptions be now entered into for the purpose of defraying the expenses of the Survey in accordance with the requirements of the Board.[12]

This proposal followed an earlier memorial from the gentry, clergy and other inhabitants of Cove which had been submitted to the Board of Works outlining the advantages to be derived from the construction of a pier in the town. From April onwards the Relief Committee endeavoured to persuade the Board of Works, the Admiralty, the Cork Harbour Commissioners, Lord Midleton[13] and James Hugh Smith Barry (the two most important landowners on the island) that the construction of a pier 'would give such extensive employment to the Poor and would be of such vast utility to the Public'.[14]

While the initial decision of the board was not 'to entertain the application for a grant to build a pier at Cove', the committee continued to argue in its favour, pointing out that:

> The Committee presume that the Board must have come to this unfavourable conclusion before they had received the report of their Engineer Captain James, who after due consideration and a minute Survey of the locality highly approved of the measure.
>
> Should the Board, on receiving the circumstances of the case be willing to contribute half the cost of the work, the Cork Harbour Commissioners would probably give one third, and the remainder would, doubtless, be supplied by private Subscriptions.[15]

In addition to the pier, the committee also forwarded a number of other proposals for public works, including the construction of a road from the east end of Harbour Row to the East Ferry, the provision of main sewers in the town and the lowering of the hill entering Cove from the west side.

By the end of October 1846, the frustration of the committee in relation to the issue of the commencement of pub-

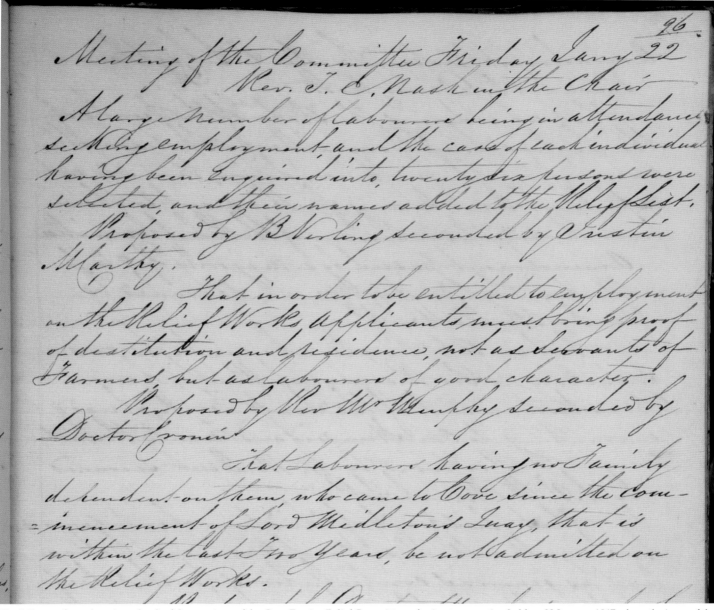

Fig. 3 Extract from the minute book of the meetings of the Cove Famine Relief Committee referring to a meeting held on 22 January 1847 where the issue of the provision of employment for labourers was discussed. The committee resolved 'that in order to be entitled to employment on the relief works applicants must bring proof of destitution and residence, not as servants of farmers but as labourers of good character . . . [and] that labourers having no family dependent on them, who came to Cove since the commencement of Lord Midleton's reign, that is within the last two years, be not admitted on the relief works.' [Source: Minute book of the meetings of the Cove Famine Relief Committee, p. 96, Cork Public Museum]

lic works was evident in a letter from Drew to the Secretary of the Board of Works:

> The Cove Relief Committee have been during the last three or four weeks, in daily expectation of seeing Public Works commenced in this District, but find with bitter regret that as yet, no step has been taken to give employment to our destitute labouring classes.
>
> A list of 331 persons, now out of work, has been forwarded to Captain Broughton, and an additional number are anxiously waiting to give in their names. We have, however, heard nothing since from the gallant Officer.
>
> The Poor of this locality are, at present, suffering the greatest privations. Food has risen to Famine price. The Union Workhouse is crowded to suffocation, and unless the Board of Works take promptly the necessary measures to enable our unemployed and famishing labourers to procure food for themselves and their families, the most deplorable results may be expected.
>
> The Committee earnestly entreat that the required works may forthwith be commenced, and beg you will have the goodness to bring their application, with as little delay as possible under the consideration of the Board of Works.[16]

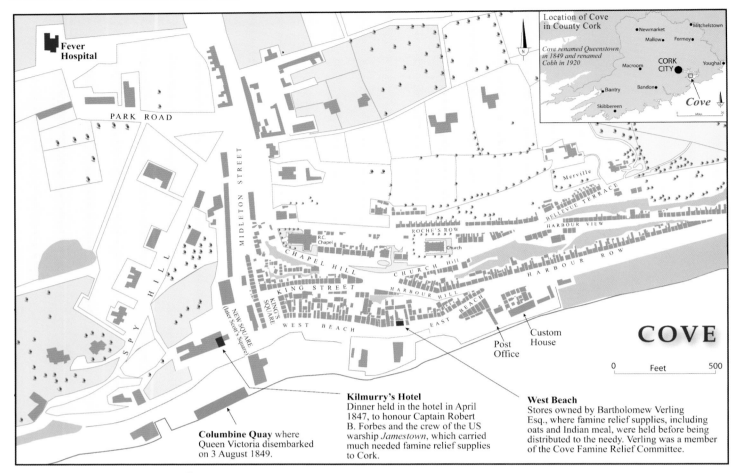

Location of Cove in County Cork

Cove renamed Queenstown in 1849 and renamed Cobh in 1920

Newmarket  Mitchelstown
Mallow  Fermoy
Macroom  CORK CITY  Youghal
Bantry  Bandon
Skibbereen  Cove

Fever Hospital

PARK ROAD

MIDLETON STREET

SPY HILL

CHAPEL HILL

KING STREET

KING'S SQUARE

NEW SQUARE (later Scott's Square)

WEST BEACH

EAST BEACH

R.C. Chapel

ROCHE'S ROW

Church

Church Hill

HARBOUR HILL

MERVILLE

BELLEVUE TERRACE

HARBOUR VIEW

HARBOUR ROW

Post Office

Custom House

COVE

0  Feet  500

**Kilmurry's Hotel**
Dinner held in the hotel in April 1847, to honour Captain Robert B. Forbes and the crew of the US warship *Jamestown*, which carried much needed famine relief supplies to Cork.

**West Beach**
Stores owned by Bartholomew Verling Esq., where famine relief supplies, including oats and Indian meal, were held before being distributed to the needy. Verling was a member of the Cove Famine Relief Committee.

**Columbine Quay** where Queen Victoria disembarked on 3 August 1849.

Fig. 4 LOCATION OF RELIEF FACILITIES IN COVE.

However, in November, the committee received word that the Government had approved the application for 'the construction of a public pier and landing place with a harbour of refuge for small craft at Cove'. The Cork Harbour Board agreed to build the jetty at the outlay of £750, and to keep it permanently in repair. One of the conditions attached to the approval of the project was that Lord Midleton and James Hugh Smith Barry would give permission to tank the water running regularly from the hill behind the town in order to supply the inhabitants with water and to provide the necessary facilities for watering naval ships in the harbour.

In seeking such approval from James Hugh Smith Barry, Drew wrote to him informing him that Lord Midleton had consented to give the right to water as required. Similar consent was now required from Smith Barry:

It would be superfluous to point that the great benefit which must be conferred on the Town and Island of Cove should the intentions of the Government be carried into effect. The Committee would however, submit to your consideration the peculiarly advantageous nature of the proposed Works under the present afflicting circumstances of the country. With the exception of the comparatively small outlay to be made by the Harbour Board, the entire expense is to be defrayed by the Admiralty.

The employment, so indispensible during this period of distress and suffering would thus be extensively afforded, while the Rate Payers would escape the direct taxation consequent on the adoption of other Works for the relief of our labouring Poor.[17]

Smith Barry acceded to the request. Approval for other public works in the town was confirmed by Captain Broughton of the Royal Engineers, at the end of November.[18] While there was relief that the public works had been approved there was tension between the committee and Captain Broughton regarding the works which actually commenced. At a meeting on 14 December the committee resolved:

That a statement be made to Captain Broughton that the road at which the people are now employed from Cove to Glenmore is such as would not be of advantage to this town and Island, but would be of the most serious injury to the welfare of this place, and that he be requested to send the people now at work there to the other roads presented.[19]

Committee members also expressed their concern over the rates of pay on the works. At a meeting on 8 January it was stated that the wages paid to labourers were insufficient to support their families and that Captain Broughton should consider the introduction of task work for the labourers who were able for it or if that was not feasible wages should be increased to one shilling per day.

## PROPOSED WORKS FOR HAULBOWLINE AND SPIKE ISLAND

In addition to the public works proposed for Cove and the Great Island, a series of relief works were also proposed for Haulbowline and Spike Island. On 7 September 1846 a public meeting, chaired by the Earl of Mountcashel, was held in Cove to discuss the necessity of introducing a series of relief works. A memorial was submitted to the British Prime Minister, Lord Russell, requesting that work be undertaken on the construction of building slips and docks at the naval establishment on Haulbowline which would combine 'useful labour with public utility'.[20]

Following a report by Captain James of the Royal Engineers on the proposed works at Haulbowline, Mr Ward of the Admiralty, in a letter, dated 26 October 1846, to Charles Trevelyan at the Treasury, stated:

It is the wish of my Lords, with the sanction of the Treasury, to begin upon the wharfs, the embankment, the road, the landing, and the watering place at Cove. The cost of these works would be about £15,000. The more expensive works of the dock, and the buildings connected with it, my Lords propose not to commence during the present financial year.[21]

The Admiralty also suggested that ordnance works at Spike Island, which were in an unfinished state, could provide employment for 'any given number of common labourers, . . . . nothing but the spade and the pick-axe being required'. In November 1846 Assistant Commissary-General Bishop, the Inspecting Officer for the county of Cork, was sent to Cove, to investigate:

Whether there is any such urgent necessity for providing employment for destitute persons in the neighbourhood of Haulbowline, as would render it desirable to commence the Ordnance works on Spike Island in addition to the Naval works already in progress.[22]

Bishop's report gives an insight into the official mindset and provides details regarding conditions in Cove at the end of November 1846:

I do myself the honour of stating that I proceeded to Cove, and having instituted a careful inquiry on the spot, I am led to report that at that moment there is no such urgent distress in the district of Cove, or in

the immediate locality of Haulbowline, as to call for commencement of the Ordnance works suggested at Spike Island, as a measure of necessary 'relief' to the destitute poor in that vicinity.

The number of labourers at present provided for, who seek employment through the Relief Committees of the Cove district do not exceed 150. Presentments for Relief Works to the extent of about £4000 have been passed in the Cove district, and the Committee is advised that the Board of Works will commence their operations immediately, which will give employment to the greater part of the unemployed labourers of the district.

The Naval works now carrying on at Haulbowline give employment to an average of 140 labourers daily; this number will be greatly increased as the works which have been sanctioned come into more extensive operation.

Spike Island ought, however, to be regarded as a resource, offering employment for a large number of labourers, should an extraordinary pressure of distress in this or any immediate locality render their employment desirable, and it would be, to a certain extent, reproductive labour, as tending to the completion of a military work which would otherwise, in all probability, be hereafter estimated for.[23]

Following the receipt of the report, the Treasury advised the secretary to the Ordnance, that 'my Lords do not consider it necessary that the works on Spike Island should be undertaken'.[24]

## THE ESTABLISHMENT OF SOUP KITCHENS

Despite the efforts of the of the Cove Relief Committee to relieve distress in the town and surrounding districts by the end of 1846, members believed that the measures undertaken were inadequate to meet the needs of the poor. At a meeting on 4 December it was considered:

Most desirable to establish a Soup Depot in this Town for the more effectual relief of the destitute Poor, and that the expense of providing a Boiler and the necessary utensils, and putting the Establishment in working order be defrayed by the Committee.[25]

It was also agreed that:

The proposed measure would be better carried into effect if the Ladies of the Town consented to undertake the management and that the Secretary be requested to address Circulars to the Ladies of the Town and Island respectfully inviting them to assemble on Tuesday the 8th at Kilmurray's large

Fig. 5  Subscription list for the Cove Ladies Soup Relief Depot. [Source: National Archives of Ireland]

At the meeting of 11 February the committee was informed that Routh had recommended to the Lord Lieutenant the payment of a donation of £150 in aid of subscriptions raised locally for the running of the soup kitchens. At the same meeting, a decision was also taken that gratuitous relief should be provided. It was resolved:

That to all reported by the District Visitors as incapable of labour from age or infirmity, and also as having no one naturally bound and able to maintain them – to desolate Widows and Orphans, and to children, when the supporting member of members of the Family are from sickness or any other cause unable to maintain them, gratuitous relief be given at the rate of not more than One Pound of Bread, and one quart of Soup daily, for every individual of or over Twelve Years of age, and not more than half a Pound of Bread and one quart of Soup daily for every person under that age.[29]

room to consider the necessary arrangements for that purpose.[26]

At the end of January 1847, W.M. Drew wrote to the Commissary-General, Sir Randolph Routh, advising that as the committee had found:

The measures which they have hitherto taken insufficient to meet the fearful, and still increasing distress of the Poor, they have decided it their duty to establish a 'Soup Kitchen' for the Cove District. The benevolent Ladies of the Town and Neighbourhood have kindly undertaken to assist them in soliciting Subscriptions, and administering relief under the direction of the Committee. Contributions amounting to £151.2.1 as per list enclosed, have been already received by the Treasurer for this object, but, as the charity has been now nearly four weeks in operation, and at least twelve hundred destitute persons are relieved at each distribution, the Fund is rapidly diminishing.
At this inclement season, when the Poor find it so difficult to supply themselves with *Fuel*, and can scarcely procure sufficient *Food* to sustain life, the aid afforded by the 'Soup Kitchens' has contributed greatly to alleviate their sufferings, and to check the spread of disease in this locality.[27]

The letter concluded with a request for a donation to enable the committee 'to continue and extend a mode of relief so well adapted to the present emergency'.[28]

Despite the valiant efforts of the Cove Relief Committee distress and destitution prevailed. An article entitled 'Destitution in Cove' appeared in the *Cork Examiner* of 19 March 1847 outlining the pressure that the relief efforts faced due to the influx of paupers from the countryside into the town:

The acute distress which exists in this town, is aggravated, in a degree unprecedented, by the want of habitations, for the multitude of poor, attracted there from the country, by the chances for obtaining a subsistence at a watering place much frequented, as well as by the generous conduct of the townspeople, who are able, in relieving destitution. Rooms and other small tenements are so dreadfully crowded, that life in them is merely fuel for disease, which consequently rages unchecked amongst the lower inhabitants. But the extent of the privation, which the poor endure from the want of shelter, may be judged best from the following fact.
On one of the quays, where a soup kitchen is established, are to be seen some water casks, or large hogsheads, lying on the side with the head out; and each of these throughout the day contains its quota of human beings. Some of the creatures

Fig. 6 SS *Jamestown Leaving Cove* by E.D. Walker. The US warship the *Jamestown*, captained by Robert B. Forbes, arrived in Cork Harbour on 12 April 1847 carrying much needed relief. Its cargo included cornmeal, rice, flour, bread, beans, peas, oats, rye, pork, ham and sixteen barrels of clothing. The cargo was dispatched into government stores on Haulbowline and was subsequently distributed to relief districts throughout County Cork. Forbes was determined to see the plight of the people for himself and was escorted on his journey around Cork by Fr Theobald Mathew. According to Forbes, he had been witness 'to the valley of death and pestilence itself'. On 22 April the *Jamestown* left Cork Harbour for its return journey to the United States. A second US warship, the *Macedonian*, captained by George DeKay, and carrying a cargo of relief supplies, departed New York on 19 June and arrived in Cork Harbour on 14 July. The supplies were dispersed through the Society of Friends, with the exception of fifty barrels of foodstuffs, which were delivered to the novelist Maria Edgeworth, at her estate at Edgeworthstown, for distribution to her distressed tenants. [Courtesy of the artist]

take up a temporary residence in this novel kind of tenement, only waiting to drink the soup which they receive, and then leaving it. Others, however, it appears, find the cask their sole refuge, not quitting it even during the night except, perhaps to straighten their limbs. In several hogsheads, four or five children, with their mother, are thus lodged, wedged and packed together, the young tenants half suffocated and struggling and fighting in their prison.[30]

The only extant minute book of the Cove Famine Relief Committee records the work undertaken by the committee over the period covered in this piece (April 1846 to March 1847). It is clearly evident from this invaluable record and from other available sources that the Cove Famine Relief Committee made tremendous efforts to alleviate the distress and destitution which prevailed in the town of Cove and on the Great Island. Through various relief measures – the collection of subscriptions, the provision of affordable food, the introduction of public works and the establishment of soup kitchens – the committee endeavoured to respond to the unprecedented disaster which developed from early 1846 onwards. While clearly frustrated at times by what they perceived as the tardy response by government to their requests for support in addressing the unfolding crisis, the committee 'resolved not to neglect their duty'[31] in ensuring that prompt and effective aid be afforded to their fellow citizens. By their actions they ensured that the suffering of the residents of Cove and the Great Island and those who flocked to the town seeking relief was somewhat alleviated.

# Visit of Queen Victoria to Cove, August 1849

## Marita Foster

The decision to have Queen Victoria undertake a 'private' visit to Ireland in August 1849 was taken in the hope that her presence in Ireland would mark the symbolic end of the Famine. On 3 August 1849 when she stepped ashore in Cove, Victoria became the first Queen of England to visit Ireland. The royal yacht, *Victoria and Albert*, entered Cork Harbour at 10 p.m. on 2 August. Bonfires lit up the harbour to welcome the Queen. She wrote in her diary, later published under the title, *Leaves from the Highlands*, 'The harbour is immense though the land is not very high, and entering by twilight it had a very fine effect.'[1] At 2 p.m. on 3 August the Queen boarded the *Fairy*, the smaller of the royal yachts, and following a tour of the harbour she landed on Columbine Quay in Cove. The *Cork Constitution* of 4 August stated that the Queen's arrival was received with a 'tremendous cheer from the gentlemen on the Columbine Quay and the waving of many handkerchiefs from the hands of a vast number of ladies who filled the Quay'.[2]

In her diary the Queen recorded the reception as follows:

We then went into Cove, and lay alongside the landing place, which was very prettily decorated, and covered with people; and yachts, ships, and boats crowding all round. The two members, Messrs. Roche and Power, as well as other gentlemen, including the Roman Catholic and Protestant clergymen, and the members of the yacht club, presented addresses. After which, to give the satisfaction of calling the place Queenstown, in honour of

Fig. 1 *The Arrival of Queen Victoria at Queenstown, August 1849* by George Mounsey Wheatley Atkinson, oil on canvas. [Source: Port of Cork]

its being the first spot on which I set foot upon Irish ground, I stepped on shore amidst the roar of cannon (for the artillery were placed so close as quite to shade the temporary room which we entered), and the enthusiastic shouts of the people.[3]

A temporary pavilion had been erected on the quay and following the speeches of welcome by the various gentlemen, the Queen announced: 'I have much pleasure in giving my sanction to the change of name which has been sought by the inhabitants and directing that this town shall in future be called Queenstown.'[4] A flag bearing the name Queenstown was then raised over the pavilion.[5]

The changing of the name from Cove to Queenstown was a matter of some debate in the newspapers in the lead up to the Queen's visit, with accusations of 'servility' and 'sycophantic behaviour' being levelled against the townspeople of Cove who were in favour of the change of name.[6] In response to these charges, W.M. Drew, justice of the peace, who had been the secretary of the Cove Famine Relief Committee, and a member of the committee established to welcome the Queen to the town, stoutly defended the decision. In a letter to the *Cork Examiner*, he wrote:

The question we have really to consider is, would it be likely to benefit Cove if the name were changed to Queen's Town? If you could think that it would have that effect I am sure you would be rather inclined to assist us than to throw difficulties in our way. Our views are these. We think, in the first instance, that the Queen would feel complimented by the request, and if she accedes to it, that it is likely she will have a pleasing recollection of the town to which she has given a name; that she will take some interest in it, and have a desire to revisit the locality. The occasional visits of royalty would be of the greatest importance to the place. It would become more frequented and fashionable. The many beautiful sites on the shores of our Harbour would be rapidly built on and improved, employment would be given to our artisans, our labourers and our watermen. Every kind of agricultural produce would find a better market, the value of the surrounding property would increase and a new impulse would be given to the general prosperity of this part of the country. We would also have opportunities of reminding the ministers of their duty, and bringing under the immediate notice of the Queen the neglect and injustice which have been evinced towards our noble harbour. Some may think these reasons of little weight, but with those who are interested in the prosperity of the place they have some influence.[7]

Drew also argued that:

'Cove' is not properly the name of a town. In Johnson we find the meaning of 'Cove' to be 'a small creek or bay', and the term is calculated to give strangers an insignificant idea of the place, and that there is, in reality, no town here worthy of notice or of a name. This has been found to be the case, practically in many instances, and has operated greatly to the injury of the town.[8]

In his concluding paragraph he asked: 'How it can be inconsistent with "independent feeling" or "patriotism" to change the name of the town, if it be considered advantageous to do so, is what I cannot so clearly perceive.'[9] Despite Drew's hopes, Victoria did not return to Queenstown on her subsequent visits to Ireland. However, throughout the remainder of the nineteenth century the town did prosper, due primarily to its development as the major port of departure for emigrants seeking a new life in the United States of America.

# ULSTER

Stained glass window commemorating the Famine in Belfast City Hall (right)
[Photo: Kelvin Boyes]

## The Scar
*For Padraic Fiacc*

There's not a chance now that I might recover
one syllable of what that sick man said,
tapping upon my great-grandmother's shutter,
and begging, I was told, a piece of bread;
for on his tainted breath there hung infection
rank from the cabins of the stricken west,
the spores from black potato-stalks, the spittle
mottled with poison in his rattling chest;
but she who, by her nature, quickly answered,
accepted in return the famine-fever;
and that chance meeting, that brief confrontation,
conscribed me of the Irishry forever.

Though much I cherish lies outside their vision,
and much they prize I have no claim to share,
yet in that woman's death I found my nation;
the old wound aches and shews its fellow scar.

– John Hewitt

John Hewitt, *The Collected Poems of John Hewitt*, ed. Frank Ormsby (Blackstaff Press, 1991) reproduced by permission of Blackstaff Press on behalf of the Estate of John Hewitt.

# The province of Ulster and the Great Famine

## William J. Smyth

The 1841 Census confirmed that Ulster's nine counties comprised 26.3% of the entire surface of the island, second only to Munster's 29.2% and that Ulster shared with Leinster approximately the same proportion (27%) of the island's arable land, behind Munster at (29%) but well above Connacht's 17%. On the other hand, almost one-fifth (24%) of the island's rough, uncultivated land was located in Ulster, almost double that of Leinster's proportion (13.3%) but behind Munster's 29.6% and well behind Connacht's one-third (33.3%) share. With some of the island's largest lakes – including Lough Neagh and Lough Erne – Ulster also contained over one-third of the island's water bodies. Yet despite the extent of its difficult lands and water surfaces,

Ulster was the most intensely settled province with its density of 406 people per square mile of arable land well ahead of the other provinces and most particularly that of Leinster.[1] Ulster almost matched Belgium's density of population.[2] Paddy Duffy's reconstruction of pre-Famine Monaghan (see pp. 440–449) succinctly evokes the densely packed, congested nature of life in south Ulster with quite a number of people apparently 'living on their wits'.[3] That intensity of occupation is still reflected in 1851 in the extent of land under cereals and other crops (34%), six points above the national average (28.2%). Over half of the land of counties Armagh and Down was devoted to such intensive cultivation and Monaghan (at 48.2%) came close to such intensity. Indeed, only Counties Donegal (19.1%) and Fermanagh (23.6%) fell below the national average under this criterion.[4] Ulster was indeed a land of smallholdings with 55% of its farms under 10 acres and only 14.4% over 20 acres.[5] Armagh was the core of the small farm world followed by Monaghan and Down. North Ulster from Donegal to Antrim contained the bigger farms. And just over two-thirds of the province's pop-

ulation was classified by the Census of 1841 as 'labourers, smallholders and other persons with no capital'.

That almost two-fifths of Donegal and 28% of Derry's and Tyrone's land was classified as 'bog and waste' points to the diversity of physical conditions across Ulster. That profound diversity is further emphasised in that after Armagh (511), County Donegal yet reveals the second highest density of rural population per square mile of arable land in the province (472), one and a half times that of both Counties Antrim and Fermanagh. In contrast, land values generally are much higher in the northeastern counties vis-à-vis its western and southwestern counties. Whereas 43% of Donegal's mainly Irish-speaking families lived in the

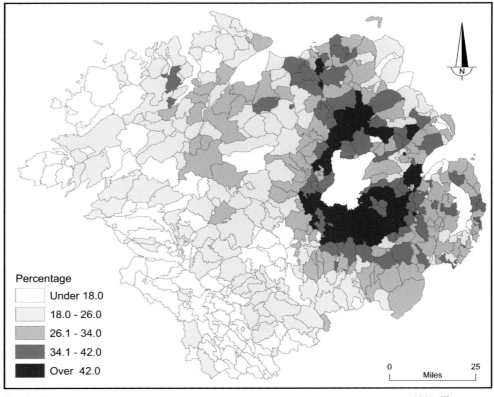

Percentage

| | |
|---|---|
| | Under 18.0 |
| | 18.0 - 26.0 |
| | 26.1 - 34.0 |
| | 34.1 - 42.0 |
| | Over 42.0 |

0 — 25 Miles

Fig. 1 PERCENTAGE OF FAMILIES EMPLOYED IN MANUFACTURING TRADE AND COMMERCE IN 1841. There were significant variations across the province in patterns of employment in manufacturing, trade and commerce. East of a line from Magilligan through Lissan and Pomeroy and south to Newry, at least a quarter and usually at least a third of families were so engaged. Indeed, a ring around Lough Neagh – from Artrea and Clonoe in the west, Kilmore and Tartaraghan, Tullylish and Seagoe in the south and around through Magheralin, Dromore, Moira and Ballinderry back up to Connor and Ahoghill – registered over 40% of their families involved in these activities. In contrast, much of western Donegal, south Fermanagh and west Cavan registered under 18% so engaged. Mid-Ulster, its western borders stretching from Kilmacrenan and Conwal south by Clogher and Clones to Donaghmoyne, constituted a traditional zone with at least 18% and in parts of the Derry region – such as Ardstraw, Donaghhedy, Burt, and Tullyfern – over 26%. After the Famine, this middle zone had all but merged with the western region. To the west of a line of parishes along the Bann south to Newry, half had suffered over a 50% decline and, with some exceptions, the remainder had suffered losses of at least 30%. The Great Famine had a powerful role in splitting the province into an industrialising, urbanising zone to the east and a deindustrialising zone to the west and south.

very poorest fourth-class houses, only 0.2% did so in 'Belfast Town'. Counties Cavan (34.4%), Fermanagh (34.9%), Tyrone (32.7%) and Londonderry (31.9%) also record proportions of fourth-class houses above the provincial average of 29.7%. This latter figure, however, highlights Ulster's similarity with wealthy Leinster's housing patterns and diverges strongly from Munster and Connacht where over two-fifths and nearly one-half of all houses respectively were in the fourth-class category.

Ulster's distinctiveness emerges even more clearly in its relatively high literacy levels (58%); Leinster records 52% but Munster's 36% and Connacht's 27% are much lower.[6] As has been emphasised, the ability to read health-related, Poor Law or other notices (e.g. ship sailings) was a crucial skill in dealing with the challenge of famine conditions. Ulster's communities were clearly advantaged and Connacht's and Munster's disadvantaged in this respect. A second and even more important series of skills and aptitudes related to the level of industrialisation and monetisation that characterised different communities. Here again Ulster scores highest with 32% of its families engaged in manufacturing, trades and related activities, over twice that level in Connacht (15%) and also far ahead of Munster's 19%. The industrialisation of Ulster's textile trade – especially its linen manufacturing in Belfast and other key towns – as well as the survival of at least some of its cottage industries gave much of Ulster a distinctive stamp. The average annual labourer's income in Ulster was £14.6, second only to that of Leinster. Likewise, the practice of taking conacre in lieu of wages was by far the lowest of all the provinces. Only 5% of Ulster's potato ground was in conacre in 1845, just one-fifth of that in Munster.[7] Ulster's population, therefore, was a more waged society, more familiar with the use of money in purchasing food stuffs in a province which – while not outstanding in terms of its territorial share of the island's urban/civic districts – benefited from access to a dense distribution of smaller market towns.

Yet despite these advantages, economic vulnerability and extreme destitution became widely apparent in the province. Many smallholding, artisan and labouring communities in Ulster were to suffer grievously during the Great Famine.[8] The consequences of famine conditions – distress, disease, excess mortality, evictions and emigration – were all to affect severely such communities. Across much of the province, population losses by 1851 average from 15 to 30% of its 1841 totals. However, it appears that the very specific ethno-religious, political and economic structures of this province saw the construction of rather different myths and ideologies about the impact of the Famine. Two of the major myths to emerge stated (1) that Ulster was not greatly affected by the Famine and (2) if it was, it was only its poorer Catholic population that was so affected. While both these interpretations were to be reinforced later in the nineteenth century, contemporaneous judgements already emphasised Ulster's very dif-

ferent famine experience. In opposing the rate-in-aid tax in 1849, the Lisnaskea Board of Guardians objected to this tax being imposed on 'peaceable and industrious inhabitants of the north of Ireland for the support of the lazy, vicious and indolent population of the south and west'[9] of Ireland. Likewise, at a meeting in Lurgan in 1849 (at a time when famine conditions were receding in the northeast), a Robert Dolling – noting that the potato failure had occurred across all of Ireland – argued that it was the capabilities of the North's 'painstaking, industrious, laborious' people which sustained them and prevented famine in the province. He went on: 'if the people of the south had been equally industrious with those of the north, they would not have so much misery among them.'[10] The ironic feature of this latter statement is that it was made only two years after the famine conditions and suffering of the poor in these parts of north Armagh had equalled the worst scenes reported from the southwest of the country. Despite the earlier famine experiences, a new memory and myth was in a process of construction.

Trevor McCavery, in his review of the impact of the Famine in County Down, notes that 'in Ulster as a whole there was a reluctance to accept that there was any destitution at all because it would be a 'disgrace to the province' and would 'sully the credit of Ulster'.[11] For example, the powerful Lord Londonderry, who had extensive estates across Ulster, was very opposed to any relief committees or relief works being established in his north Down bailiwick. Rather he, with many other landlords and their agents, were to stress the prevailing ideologies of the time – the virtues of self-reliance and adherence to a *laissez-faire* philosophy. Yet Londonderry's own town of Newtownards was to suffer grievously during the early years of the Famine. Conditions were even more severe in south Down, especially around Rathfriland and the Mournes. Captain Brereton, the Board of Works officer observing the landlords' reluctance to strike a rate and establish relief works there, noted 'the great desire of the landed proprietors to hide the poverty of the people'.[12] Kerby A. Miller, Brian Gurrin and Liam Kennedy (see pp. 426–433) highlight the later solidification of a perspective amongst Irish Unionists and its perpetuation even in some scholarly works – emphasising that '"Ulster" – that is its Protestant inhabitants – eluded the Famine because of the province's superior "character" for industry, virtue and loyalty'. In contrast, what their study illuminates in particular is the vulnerability of deindustrialising Protestant communities – particularly its Presbyterian component – to devastating famine conditions. The Presbyterian communities in mid-Antrim and in and around Maghera, County Londonderry, lost *c.* one-third of their populations between 1841 and 1851. Likewise Gerard Mac Atasney and Christine Kinealy (see pp. 434–439) challenge the long-established view that Belfast and northeastern Ireland 'escaped lightly' from the famine onslaught. This was clearly not the case.

Reading recent literature on the Great Famine in Ulster is to be reminded of the similarities with the conditions and concerns of the other three provincial communities. There are numerous references to pre-Famine destitution and impoverishment. The decline of domestic spinning and weaving in particular saw many small tenants and cottiers in this highly industrialised province – including those of Armagh, Cavan and Monaghan – fall into destitution. A striking feature of this impoverishment is that of the many hand-loom linen weavers, and the mainly women spinners, living in their cottages with small plots of land attached. As their functions and incomes slumped, this once vibrant class were increasingly forced back more on potato consumption – a process of dietary simplification characteristic of the poorer families across much of Ulster.[13] Others – less skilled – were even more impoverished and marginalised. And behind many main streets, were small, crowded, unhealthy backstreets.

Then comes the fear associated with the blight in 1845 and more particularly the panic that seized so many poor with the widespread and

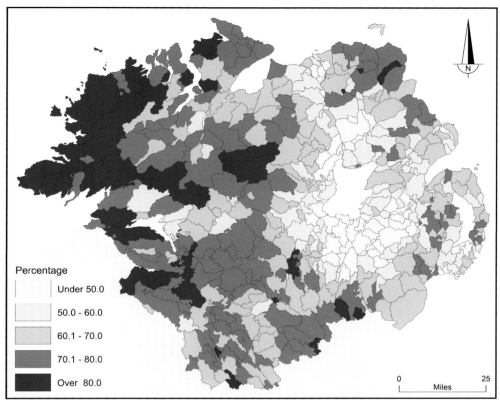

Percentage

| | |
|---|---|
| | Under 50.0 |
| | 50.0 - 60.0 |
| | 60.1 - 70.0 |
| | 70.1 - 80.0 |
| | Over 80.0 |

Fig. 2 PERCENTAGE OF FAMILIES DEPENDENT ON THEIR OWN MANUAL LABOUR IN 1841. This map depicts three types of communities in pre-Famine Ulster. In the parishes shaded brown or dark brown and where at least 70% of families were dependent on their own manual labour, impoverishment was generally highest. In much of west Donegal, mid-Tyrone, south Fermanagh, Cavan, south Monaghan and the Glens of Antrim families were predominantly labourers, artisans or small-holders. Around Shercock in County Cavan the average farm size was then 7 acres. Others tried to survive as domestic textile workers in an era when factory goods were spreading into the Ulster countryside. Along the coast some 'made a living' by fishing and harvesting *cnuasach trá* (shore food). The folk-memory of, for example, Teebane in County Tyrone and around Castleblayney in County Monaghan tells of the poor stealing and eating *praiseach* (wild cabbage) from the turnip fields and dying along roadsides. A more robust social and economic structure with 50–70% of families dependent on manual labour is revealed, most dominantly in east Ulster and pockets around Derry city, mid-Cavan and mid-Monaghan. However, the most sturdy and compact social structures encircle Lough Neagh, including Ballymena, Antrim, Magherafelt, Cookstown, Dungannon, Armagh, Lurgan, Lisburn and Dromore. This was clearly the most economically diverse and dynamic region in Ulster – having sturdy market-cum-industrial towns with the highest proportions dependent on either 'the direction of labour' or 'vested means'.

devastating failure of the potato in 1846. Judging by a reduction of at least one-quarter in the acreage of potatoes planted in 1846 versus 1845, it was the east coast counties of Down and Antrim and the inland counties of Cavan and Monaghan that were most affected by early potato failures. In Counties Armagh, Fermanagh and Londonderry, while the amount of potatoes planted was reduced by *c*.15%, these counties are still above the national planting average (-20%) in 1846. On the other hand, communities in Counties Tyrone and Donegal seem least affected by such early failures, although they did occur in these counties, especially in Inishowen. In 1846, Counties Tyrone and Donegal managed to plant close to the same amount of potatoes as in 1845. However, it should also be noted that County Donegal had only 11.1% of its acreage of crops and pasture set in potatoes. Oat crops and oat-based foods still remained important in the northwest as they did throughout the province of Ulster. In contrast, County Down, probably the nucleus of early potato-growing, had 27% of its total acreage of crops and pasture planted with potatoes in

1845.[14] This is a county, which like Antrim and Londonderry in particular, had a more varied diet. Apart from Antrim, where only 14.7% of the cultivated land was potato ground, the overall picture of potato cultivation in Ulster suggests expansion from its eastern core in County Down (and Louth to the south) and weakening as it spread westwards. Apart from Donegal, the lowest percentage of potato acreages were in Fermanagh (13.4%) and Tyrone (14.1%). Dependence on the potato varied, therefore, and it may be no coincidence that many communities in Tyrone and Donegal were less affected by famine conditions in Ulster. It may also not be irrelevant that whereas only 5% of Ulster's potato land was held in conacre in 1845, Cavan, Monaghan and Armagh (with, respectively, 12.8%, 12.1% and 11.2% of potato ground in conacre) were well over twice that average.[15] It is most likely that it was the poor conacre families who were first exposed to the horrors of the famine conditions when the potato – their only source of food – failed. However, as elsewhere in Ireland, vulnerabilities were always many-sided. As

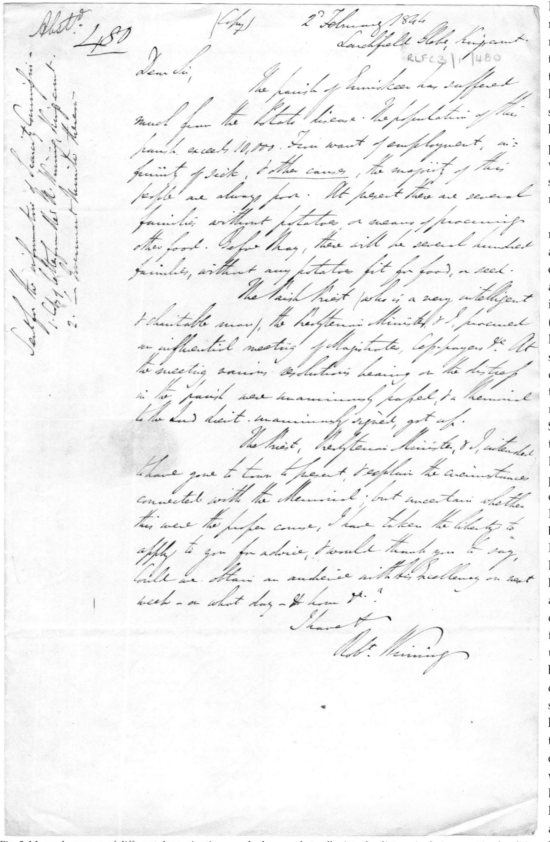

Paddy Duffy points out, the most vulnerable rural communities in Monaghan were those where there was a multiplicity of often absentee landlords, much unregulated subdivision of already small holdings with overcrowded populations where no relief was provided and no leadership available to seek such relief.[16]

This Ulster literature reveals similar concerns about the onset of famine as elsewhere. As early as February 1846, a Presbyterian minister in Carndonagh Union (Inishowen) reported that 'a large proportion of 3,400 souls in the parish is in great distress in Upper Fahan and the workhouse can offer no relief as it is already full'.[17] Similarly, in May of that year, the clergy of the parish of Donagh confirm that of c.440 people suffering and in need of relief, 40% were Anglican Protestants, 27% were Presbyterians and 33% were Roman Catholic.[18] The same literature reveals the fear of hunger and the terror of fever and reflects on the provision of relief and the relative performance of the Poor Law unions, many of which behaved poorly. Across much of the province, there was the same need to extend workhouse accommodation as these became engulfed by the end of 1846. Ballyshannon workhouse, serving south Donegal and parts of west Fermanagh, first stopped admitting paupers as early as November 1846. Subsequently, that winter an increased influx of the Protestant poor is evidenced by additional orders for Protestant prayer books and bibles. Such orders

Fig. 3 Many clergymen of different denominations worked earnestly to alleviate the distress in their respective localities. They also provided the Relief Commission in Dublin with first-hand accounts of the conditions they were daily encountering in their parishes. In a letter dated 2 February 1846, Rev. Robert Winning of Larchfield Glebe, Kingscourt, described the extent of the poverty in the parish of Inniskeen, County Cavan: '[T]he majority of the people are always poor. At present there are several families without potatoes, or means of procuring other food. Before long there will be several hundred families, without any potatoes fit for food, or seed.' Along with the local Roman Catholic priest and Presbyterian minister, Winning organised a public meeting to address the rising levels of destitution in the parish. [Source: Relief Commission Papers, 3/1/480, National Archives of Ireland] continued throughout 1847. Although boardroom conflicts among the guardians may have sometimes reflected ethno-religious tensions and cleavages, the evidence from Enniskillen Union is suggestive of an impartial administration. The proportions dying in its workhouses from its opening on 1 December 1845 to early April 1847 (when the board was dissolved) was almost the same for both Catholics (29%) and Protestants (28.6%).[19]

Overcrowding accelerated the spread of diseases, especially the deadly fevers, in workhouses where poor diet, lack of clothes, often both poor administration and uncaring guardians all added to further mortalities. As elsewhere, children – often in a majority in the workhouse – were major victims. County Armagh's Lurgan Union – whose mortality levels were the highest in Ulster – required, with Cork and Bantry unions, a special investigation by the Central Board of Health into its management and appalling conditions.[20] Lowtherstown (Irvinestown), poorly administered by its guardians, also came under central control. Other unions (like the hard-pressed Armagh workhouse and Ballycastle in County Antrim) earned much better reputations. However varying famine pressures obviously affected union and workhouse performance – Donegal's northern unions at Dunfanaghy, Milford and Stranorlar performed better but were under less pressure. In contrast, those at Glenties and Ballyshannon were faced with larger numbers, more crowded conditions, higher mortalities and poorer finances. County Tyrone reveals similar contrasts between hard-pressed unions such as Omagh and Clogher vis-à-vis unions like Castlederg and Strabane which reported less pressure.[21]

As elsewhere, public relief works were deemed to be ineffective. There were inordinate delays in getting public works established and much disagreement amongst landlords at presentment sessions about what works – if any – should be initiated. By the time these were put in place many people were already dying from dysentery, fever and diarrhoea. The provision of soup kitchens in the first half of 1847, nevertheless, does highlight variations in both the intensity of famine conditions and administrative responses to these conditions across Ulster and the island as a whole. There is no doubt that west and south of a line from Sligo to Waterford, the proportion of the population on the Temporary Relief soup-kitchen scheme was at least 50% and in the western half of Connacht over 80%. Only in west Donegal and south Cavan does any of Ulster's unions reveal such distress levels for over 30% of the population – the Ulster average was 17.5%.[22] In contrast, in the northern and eastern coastal unions in Ulster, the proportion is often under 10%. However, this latter figure may be a little misleading for in some of these unions there was a reluctance to institute outdoor relief of this or any other kind. Privately-subsidised soup kitchens were substituted in some instances. Certainly this was the case in Newtownards Union in County Down where there were boardroom battles about the provision of

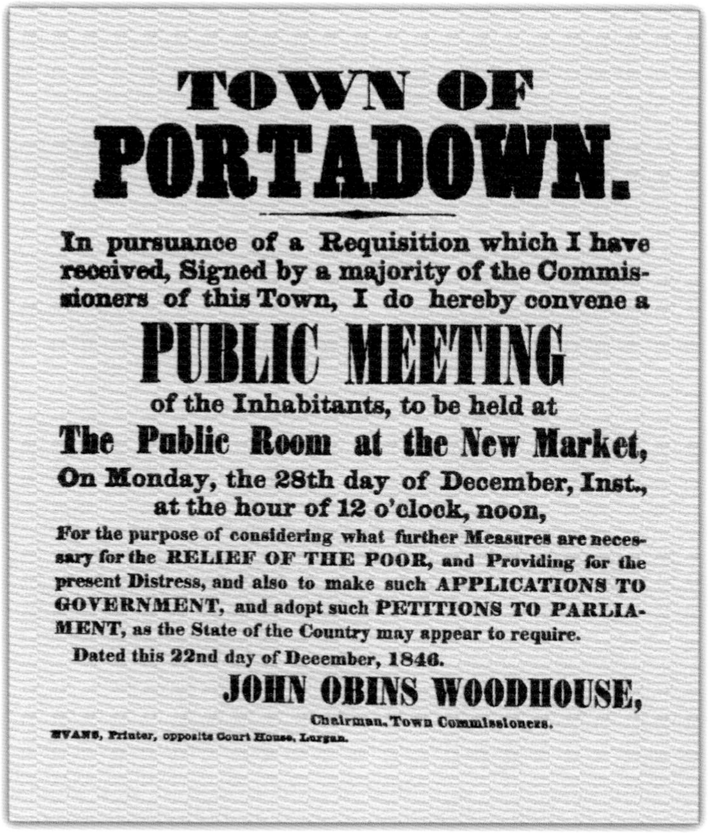
TOWN OF
PORTADOWN.
In pursuance of a Requisition which I have received, Signed by a majority of the Commissioners of this Town, I do hereby convene a
PUBLIC MEETING
of the Inhabitants, to be held at
The Public Room at the New Market,
On Monday, the 28th day of December, Inst.,
at the hour of 12 o'clock, noon,
For the purpose of considering what further Measures are necessary for the RELIEF OF THE POOR, and Providing for the present Distress, and also to make such APPLICATIONS TO GOVERNMENT, and adopt such PETITIONS TO PARLIAMENT, as the State of the Country may appear to require.
Dated this 22nd day of December, 1846.
JOHN OBINS WOODHOUSE,
Chairman, Town Commissioners.
EVANS, Printer, opposite Court House, Lurgan.

Fig. 4 By September 1846, the condition of the poor was described as desperate in the Portadown district, then characterised by a great concentration of population. It was noted that not only agricultural workers but also weavers were in great distress with 'starvation pictured on their countenances'. A relief committee was established in Portadown in this month of September. The nearby workhouse of Lurgan was described as resembling a morgue on either side of Christmas 1846. In late May and, early June of 1847, a temporary fever hospital was established in Portadown and later on a small famine hospital. [Source: G. Mac Atasney, *'This Dreadful Visitation': The Famine in Lurgan/Portadown* (Belfast, 1997), p. 41]

outdoor relief. The majority conservative view – paralleling that of the London Treasury's policy to minimise the cost of public relief schemes (and their own rate payments) – prevailed. Yet in nearby Bangor, where the soup kitchen was placed in the town hotel, one-fifth (600) of a population of 3,000 were receiving free soup.[23] Overall, there remains a strong probability that quite a number of unions' boards of guardians, especially in northeast Ulster, were less than generous in their support for public relief schemes.

The contemporary descriptions of the Famine in Ulster are equally devastating and harrowing. Newtownards people queuing at the soup-kitchen are described as 'emaciated and half-famished souls', many of whom are without sufficient clothes to cover them. It appears that the men were obliged to go collect the soup there 'when the females could not find a garment to cover their squalid wretchedness'.[24] From County Antrim comes the report that 'pallor and anxiety appeared on every face and hunger knowing no law forced many an individual of previous good character into crime'.[25] In Drumcree, County Armagh, the condition of the poor was one 'of extreme deprivation and

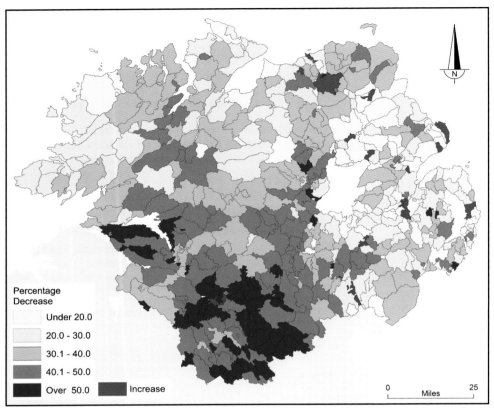

Fig. 5 PERCENTAGE CHANGE IN THE POPULATION UNDER FIVE YEARS OF AGE BETWEEN 1841 AND 1851. Unlike many of the 1841 Census measures, this one does not divide Ulster into an eastern and western half. Rather, significant clusters with a very high young child component are all over the province. By 1851 the situation was dramatically different. Apart from the rare increases as around Ballymoney, on Islandmagee, at Lambeg and in the Newry environs, the extent of parishes which return losses of more than 40% and in many cases over 50% in this young cohort by 1851 is striking. These parishes dominate much of Cavan, Monaghan and Fermanagh with outliers in mid-Armagh, south Tyrone and the Donegal/Londonderry borderlands. These massive declines reflect three critical Famine processes: high child mortality, averted births and the out-migration of whole families. These were, therefore, the communities that suffered the greatest trauma in Ulster. But the distribution of loss and pain also extends over the rest of the province, most noticeably where at least 20% and often 30 to 40% of these young had disappeared as in east Donegal, east Tyrone and Londonderry, north Armagh and north Antrim and south Down. With some exceptions in the northwest in parishes such as Tulloghbegley and Clonca in Donegal, Faughanvale and Magilligan in County Londonderry, the major region of least change comprises urbanised and industrialised south Antrim, north Down and northeast Armagh. Yet even here, communities had lost up to 20% of this age cohort.

distress' suffering from awful want and destitution; the Drumcree Relief Fund was giving 'weekly aid to 450 destitute families among the 2,300 people'.[26] People perished not just in the workhouses but also in the ditches, on the roads and in their tiny mud-walled huts. A letter in the *Belfast Newsletter* from a person employed in administering the charity of Christian Friends of England describes the scene in a poor cabin on the old road leading to Portadown where first the man of the house, then his wife, then their daughter died. Later that week when he visited he found 'a young man about fourteen or fifteen, on the cold dark floor, off the rubbish, dead, without a single vestige of clothing, the eyes sunk, the mouth wide open, the flesh shrivelled up, the bones all visible, so small around the waist that I could span him with my hand'.[27] To carry out the required dismissal of 20% of those employed on the public works in March 1847, lots were drawn in Kilnaleck, County Cavan. The report goes on: 'the wretched creatures on whom the lots fell raised a cry that still rings in my ears, it was like a death

sentence to them.'[28] In Ballyshannon workhouse, a Society of Friends observer reported that two corpses were 'carried to a graveyard in an open cart, without ceremony or procession of any kind'.[29] The *Enniskillen Chronicle & Erne Packet* noted that '[f]ever and famine are making havoc on human life in the heretofore healthy district of Ederney. On Sunday last a woman, named Walker, was to be seen in the street seeking charity, with two children, one dead on her back and the other dying in her arms.'[30] As the Famine crisis deepened, multiple burials became characteristic around workhouses. 'There are frequently twenty bodies in one grave' is reported for Lurgan while at Ballyshannon and probably elsewhere the burying of uncoffined dead in mass graves is indicated.[31]

Many of the contemporary descriptions come from the pens of clergymen or voluntary relief workers. It is clear that the clergy of all persuasions played leading roles on relief committees, in pressing for better relief and in highlighting the failures of the Poor Law system. Catholic priests were particularly active in defending their starving parishioners as were Presbyterian clergymen. The picture for landlords is much more uneven. It is clear that some landlords were indifferent to the suffering of their tenants and many took advantage of escalating crises and Poor Law legislation to 'thin out' and 'improve' their estates and create a more viable tenantry. There also appears to be a prevailing ideology among many landowners such as Lord Londonderry and the Marquess of Downshire which resisted the establishment of anything beyond the provision of minimum relief. Other landlords became 'notorious' like Alexander Hamilton in the Ballyshannon district for the level of evictions while John Joseph Whyte in the Banbridge area became 'the talk of the whole county' for the large number of tenants he evicted.[32] In contrast, there were many landlords who stood by their tenants. William Sharman Crawford was one such radical landlord. It would also appear that the Londonderry companies provided rent rebates for many of their tenants. Likewise, the landlords of north Donegal, led by Lord George Hill 'defied regulations and sold Indian meal below cost price and sooner than directed, thus preventing the fatal delays which

Fig. 6 The entrance block and only surviving structure of the Coleraine workhouse. It was formerly part of Coleraine Hospital. [Photo: Brian Graham]

occurred in other areas'.[33] However, as elsewhere in Ireland, absentee landlords were the object of much criticism, particularly by the clergy who mourned the lack of gentry leadership in either providing employment or assisting the relief committees.

The landscapes and societies of Ulster were radically transformed during the Famine. Over four-fifths of its fourth-class houses were cleared from the landscape with 87%, 89% and 92% disappearing from the counties of Londonderry, Antrim and the borough of Carrickfergus respectively and 85% each for Counties Down and Tyrone. In contrast, significant increases in the number of first-class houses reflected the consolidation of wealth amongst the ruling elites, traders and industrialists (see Jim McLoughlin, pp. 450–457).[34] Some of these societal and landscape changes reflected excess mortality levels amongst the poorest populations – especially in Counties Fermanagh, Monaghan and Cavan and to a lesser extent in Counties Antrim, Armagh, Donegal and Tyrone. Mortality rates in Counties Down and Londonderry paralleled the lowest levels along Leinster's east coast. But the greater changes in the society resulted from mass emigration. Ulster had long been a major zone of outmigration and the Famine years continued this trend. Here, there are strong suggestions of the role of chain migration. Ulster workhouses had by far the largest

population of women inmates. It appears that in some instances the husband emigrated and, once established, then managed to bring out his workhouse wife and children.[35] However, of far greater importance was assisted emigration ('eviction by another name') by landlords anxious to rid their estates of the poorer tenants and more especially the effects of many forceful evictions. Almost 20% of Ireland's legally enforced evictions between 1846 and 1852 happened in Ulster – and close on 84% of these took place between 1846 and 1848, during the deadliest years of the Famine. In the earlier Famine years, eviction levels were highest in both Antrim and Armagh (17.8% each of the provincial total) and Cavan (15.2%) followed by Donegal (11.2%), Tyrone (9.9%) and Monaghan (8.1%). Counties Down (8.0%), Fermanagh (6.4%) and Londonderry (6.5%) record the lowest proportions.[36] For the later years (1849–52), it is noticeable that it is the 'outer' counties of Cavan (18.9% of the provincial total), Donegal (15.6%) and Monaghan (5.2%) which head the eviction list.[37] The parish curate of Drung, County Cavan, describes the consequences of a winter eviction in 1848: 'in this parish at present there are fifty farms vacant, 200 human beings sent adrift in an inclement season to beg or die. Many of them have since died. As I met them on the highways livid corpses raised . . . I can give but a faint idea of their wretched appearance . .

# NOTICE

## TO

# THE EARL OF CHARLEMONT'S TENANTRY.

IN consideration of the extensive failure in the POTATO CROP this Season, willing to bear his share in the general calamity, and anxious to relieve, as far as in him lies, his Poorer Tenants from an undue share of suffering under the Divine Will, LORD CHARLEMONT has directed that the following Scale of Reduction, in Payment of Rent, shall be adopted for this Year, upon his Estates in the COUNTIES of ARMAGH and TYRONE, viz. :—

| | |
|---|---|
| 25 per Cent. on Rents under £5 | 10 per Cent. on Rents under £20. |
| 20 per Cent. on Rents under £10 | 5 per Cent. on Rents under £30. |
| 15 per Cent. on Rents under £15 | No Discount on Rents exceeding £30. |

Abatements, according to the above Scale, shall be made only to Tenants holding under Lease paying the present Annual value; and Tenants-at-will, not being occupiers of Town Parks, upon their paying the Year's Rent now in course of Collection, on or before the days appointed underneath :—

| | | | |
|---|---|---|---|
| ALTATURK, AUGHNACLOY, ANAGHA, & ANAGHMACMANUS, | On TUESDAY, 3d Nov., 1846. | GRANGEBLUNDELS, GRANEMORE, GRANGEMORE, | On WEDNESDAY, 25th November, 1846. |
| AUGHMAGORGAN, BALLYLEAN, | On WEDNESDAY, 4th November, 1846. | | |
| BALLYMACNABB, BALLYBRANNAN, BALLYMACAULLY, | On TUESDAY, 10th November, 1846. | KILLMAKEW, KILLMAKEW, DRUMMONBEG, LURGABOY, | On TUESDAY, 1st December, 1846. |
| CARRICKATOAL, CARNAVANAGHAN, CAVANAGROUGH, | On WEDNESDAY, 11th November, 1846. | LARAGHASHANKILL, MAGHERY, RATHDRUMGRANA, TASSAGH, | On WEDNESDAY, 2d December, 1846. |
| CASHILL, CLADYMORE, | On SATURDAY, 14th November, 1846. | | |
| CLADYBEG, CLOGHFIN, CREEVEROE, | On TUESDAY, 17th November, 1846. | TERNASCOBE, TYREARLY, TULLYSARRIN, | On TUESDAY, 8th December, 1846. |
| CORR and DONAVALLEY, CORCLEA, | On WEDNESDAY, 18th November, 1846. | DRUMCART, DRUMGRANNON, LISROAN, | On WEDNESDAY, 9th December, 1846. |
| DAMULLY, DRUMATEE, DRUMACHEE, | On SATURDAY, 21st November, 1846. | | |
| DERRYLARD, FOLEY, ENAGH, | On TUESDAY, 24th November, 1846. | LISTAMNET, MOY, TYRLEENAN, | On SATURDAY, 12th December, 1846. |

\*\*\* Where a Tenant is subject to the payment of more than One Rent, the abatement shall be made according to the Gross Annual Amount to which he is liable.

☞ Where Two or more Occupiers hold under one Lease, the Total Rent reserved by the Lease shall be taken as the sum to regulate the per Centage to be allowed.

# W. W. ALGEO.

*ARMAGH, 13th October, 1846.*

ARMAGH:—PRINTED BY J. M'WATTERS.

Fig. 7 This 2nd Earl of Charlemont, Francis William Caulfield, was the heir to a rich liberal tradition, epitomised by his father, James Caulfield, 1st Earl of Charlemont and commander in chief of the Volunteers in 1780. It is not surprising that this landlord's family was supportive of its tenantry as evidenced in this notice. Lord Charlemont, in recognising the levels of distress amongst poorer tenants on his Armagh and Tyrone estates, sanctions a scaled reduction in the payment of rents. [Source: National Library of Ireland]

. wishing for the happy release of death.'[38] In County Donegal, the thatched roof was burnt 'to prevent the tenant entering the house again after the bailiff and his assistants had left the scene'.[39] The officially recorded number of evictions for Ulster over the full Famine period (1846–52) suggests that perhaps 120,000 family members were put out on the road.

We may never know the number of people evicted without any warrant or decree; likewise the numerous families who simply abandoned their holdings to escape rent and rate payments and emigrated is unknown. However, we do have a reasonably reliable picture of the levels of emigration from the different Ulster counties. Not surprisingly, a classic contrast emerges between the northeastern and southwestern counties. Cavan is the leading emigration county, with 17.8% of the province's emigrant total, followed by Tyrone (16.7%), Monaghan (14.2%) and Fermanagh (10%). In contrast, Counties Donegal, Down and Antrim record well below 10% as does County Londonderry – but even here the county proportions mask significant localities of heavy emigration, as from the Magherafelt district of south Derry.[40] It is probable that well over one-third of a million people left Ulster during the Famine. As many as 150,000 to 170,000 people likely died of famine-related causes. Out of a probable 1845 total of over *c.*1.9 million, Ulster lost *c.*480,000 to 500,000 people – or *c.*19% of its population.

Overall, there were significant regional and class variations in the impact of the Great Famine in Ulster. The major divergence is between the northern and eastern counties, communities which suffered over a less lengthy period, and the southwestern communities which suffered more and for longer. Famine conditions prevailed longest in the south and west – in County Cavan mortality levels were greater in 1849 than 1847.[41] On the other hand, many communities to the north and east suffered considerable, even extreme distress between 1846 and 1848 and especially in the winter of 1846–47. Conditions improved by 1849 and – as in Counties Armagh and Tyrone – mortality rates were returning to normal levels by 1850.[42] During the Famine, Ulster's level of industriali-

sation and commercialisation was probably its most outstanding saving grace – hence its lower overall numbers receiving relief in 1847 and 1849 and its related lower rates burden. However, that is not to say that the horrors of the Famine did not strike most communities – not only amongst the poorer Catholic populations but including the working-class communities in Belfast and other towns and the many Presbyterian small-farming and weaver communities across the province. But the weavers that survived the Famine

were not the same men they were before it. Saturday night squabbling had ceased; the public house might as well have been closed for all the business done; prayer meetings were established in different localities, in out-of-the-way places where cock-fighting, dog-fighting and rat-hunting-on-Sunday characters lived: and a tone of seriousness pervaded the people.[43]

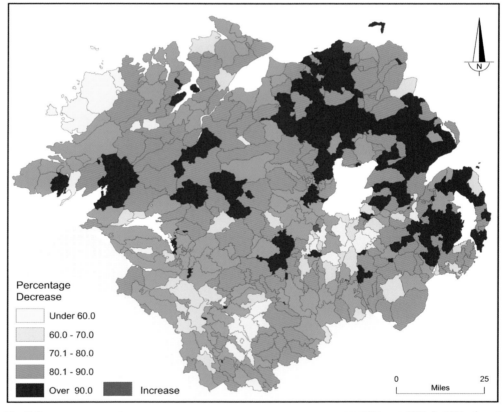

Fig. 8 PERCENTAGE CHANGE IN FAMILIES LIVING IN FOURTH-CLASS HOUSES BETWEEN 1841 AND 1851. In 1841, almost 30% of Ulster families were living in fourth-class (i.e. one-room, mud-walled) houses. However, this varied dramatically across Ulster. With the exception of a cluster of parishes, Ulster west of a line from Magilligan south to Clones had well above 30% of families in such houses. Indeed, in much of Donegal, Tyrone, Londonderry and mid- and south Fermanagh, at least 40 to 55% of families lived under these desperate conditions. Aside from the upland parishes in County Antrim, less than 30% suffered such conditions in east Ulster. However, the Great Famine was to dramatically transform this. By 1851, only 6.5% of Ulster families lived in a single-room, mud-walled cabin whereas 38% now lived in second-class and 52% in third-class houses. As shown, the social landscape was radically transformed as variations in housing conditions were reduced. In only a few pockets across Ulster – Templecrone and Tulloghbegley parishes in west Donegal, a cluster of Armagh parishes stretching from Tullylish and Donaghcloney to Grange south of Lough Neagh and from Ematris south to Lavey on the Monaghan/Cavan borderlands – did the decrease in the families living in fourth-class houses fall beneath 60%. Across parishes in the rest of Ulster there was at least a 70% decrease, with the majority in excess of 80%. In the most prosperous districts of the east Ulster region, the census returns show that nine out of every ten fourth-class cabins had disappeared.

425

# The Great Famine and religious demography in mid-nineteenth-century Ulster

*Kerby A. Miller, Brian Gurrin and Liam Kennedy*

Until recently scholars generally neglected the Great Famine's impact on the northern province of Ulster and especially its impact on Ulster's Protestant inhabitants.[1] This neglect stemmed in part from historians' reading of published census and other data that indicate that the North's *general* experience of excess mortality and emigration in 1845–52 was indeed less catastrophic than that of southern and western Ireland. Thus, whereas between 1841 and 1851 the populations of Munster and Connacht declined by 22.5 and 28.8%, respectively, that of Ulster fell 'only' 15.7%.[2] To be sure, Joel Mokyr and other scholars have noted that several counties in south or 'outer' Ulster – particularly Cavan and Monaghan – witnessed high rates of Famine mortality, but this is commonly understood by reference to the fact that their populations were composed predominantly of poor Catholic smallholders and cottier-labourers.[3] By contrast, conventional wisdom holds that northeast Ulster or, even more broadly, the six counties that later became Northern Ireland – and particularly their Protestant inhabitants – escaped the Famine with comparatively minimal damage, whether measured in excess mortality or in abnormally heavy out-migration. To explain this perceived phenomenon, historians often have cited socio-economic and cultural factors relatively unique to northeast Ulster, such as industrialization and urbanization, the prevalence of tenant-right and comparatively congenial landlord-tenant relations, and, among the rural populace, a greater variety of income sources and less dietary dependence on potatoes than prevailed in Munster and Connacht.[4]

Inadvertently, however, some scholars may unconsciously have repeated contemporary and subsequent claims by Irish Unionists, who argued that 'Ulster' – that is, its Protestant inhabitants – eluded the Famine because of the province's superior 'character' for industry, virtue, and loyalty. But in reality, many Protestant as well as Catholic Ulstermen and -women suffered grievously. Between 1841 and 1851 Ulster's population fell by nearly one-sixth – slightly more than the 15.3% decline that occurred in heavily Catholic Leinster. During the same period the number of inhabitants of the future Northern Ireland (not including Belfast) fell 14.7% (or 13.0% if Belfast's burgeoning population is included), and in the four northeastern counties that

in 1861 had Protestant majorities (Antrim, Armagh, Down and Londonderry), the comparable decline was 12.1% (or, including Belfast, nearly 10%).[5] Of course, it is likely that northeastern Catholics suffered more severely than did Protestants, and it is probable that population losses in the region, particularly among Protestants, were primarily due to out-migration rather than to the effects of starvation and disease.[6] However, as David Miller has argued, in the pre-Famine decades the contraction of rural weaving and spinning had created in Ulster an impoverished Protestant underclass whose members' vulnerability to the crisis of 1845–52 can be compared with that of Catholic cottiers and labourers in the south and west. Furthermore, Miller points out, some poor Protestants in northeast Ulster *did* perish of malnutrition or 'famine fever', even in areas adjacent to busy industrial centres. Mokyr's estimated excess mortality rates for heavily-Protestant County Antrim, as well as for the roughly half-Protestant counties of Armagh, Fermanagh and Tyrone (all four in the future Northern Ireland), exceed those in most parts of Leinster.[7]

## RELIGIOUS AFFILIATIONS

Unfortunately, the Irish census did not begin to record religious affiliations until 1861, and so it is impossible to gauge precisely or compare population losses among Ulster's Protestants and Catholics between 1841 and 1851. And although the Irish Commissioners of Public Instruction compiled parish-based religious censuses in 1831 and 1834, scholars rarely have tried to correlate these data with those of 1861.[8] Thus, the authors of the most recent comprehensive study of the Famine in Ulster made few attempts to distinguish between Protestant and Catholic experiences, and the subject awaits detailed research in church, estate and other records.[9] Yet much evidence indicates that Protestants suffered heavy losses, primarily through emigration but also, to a lesser degree, from disease and malnutrition, in many areas of northeast Ulster.[10] For example, David Miller concludes that between 1845 and 1861 the Presbyterian population of Maghera, County Derry, fell by about 30%.[11] Likewise, between 1841 and 1851 the number of inhabitants in ten heavily Protestant, contiguous parishes in east and mid Antrim declined overall by more than 14%, and losses in some parishes were comparable to those in parts of Munster and Connacht.[12] In 1841–51, for instance, the population of Glenwhirry parish (92% Protestant in 1831) fell nearly 23%, in Raloo (84% Protestant) by more than 23%, and in Killyglen Grange (81% Protestant) by nearly 21%.[13]

## KILWAUGHTER PARISH, COUNTY ANTRIM

Adjacent to Glenwhirry and Killyglen Grange is Kilwaughter parish, which experienced even greater famine attrition and is worthy therefore of close examination.[14] Kilwaughter seems to conform to David Miller's suggestion that Ulster's deindustrialized but still heavily populated rural parishes were especially susceptible to famine conditions, regardless of their inhabitants' religious affiliations. In 1831 over three-fourths of Kilwaughter's inhabitants were Protestants, and of these some 96% were Presbyterians.[15] Formerly a centre of domestic cotton spinning, linked in trade to the nearby town of Larne, by 1841 Kilwaughter's economy was overwhelmingly agricultural, its landscape crowded with petty farms, mostly under 20 acres in size, which at best generated precarious livelihoods for most of their occupiers. By 'market' criteria, Kilwaughter was best suited for grazing livestock (only one-third of the parish consisted of arable soils), but in 1841 over 87% of its small-holdings were devoted to subsistence crops – oats and potatoes. Over four-fifths of Kilwaughter's families lived in one- or two-roomed thatched cottages, and only half the males – and less than one-third of the females – were literate.

The fate of Kilwaughter's inhabitants was linked inexorably to the fortunes and management of the Agnew estate, which covered the entire parish. The proprietor of the estate in the mid-1840s, Margaret Jones, was resident and reputedly paternalistic, but when she died in 1848 her heirs not only rescinded her charity to the estate's tenants but apparently also carried out wholesale clearances of Kilwaughter's smallholders, cottier-weavers and labourers.[16] Whether tenants were forced to leave or did so, ostensibly, 'voluntarily' is unknown, but between 1841 and 1851 Kilwaughter's population declined by a remarkable 36.4%, compared with a 9.0% overall decline in County Antrim (not including Belfast). (To put Kilwaughter's experience in wider perspective, its 1841–51 rate of population decline

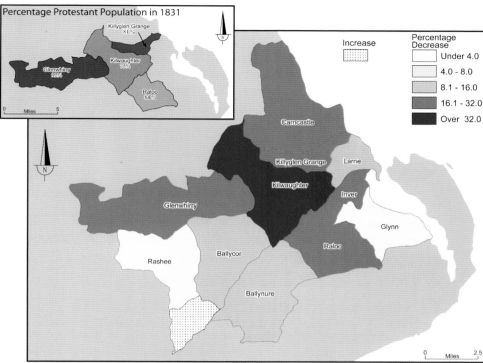

Fig. 1 POPULATION DECLINE IN EAST AND MID-ANTRIM, 1841–51. Between 1841 and 1851 the number of inhabitants in ten heavily Protestant, contiguous parishes in east and mid-Antrim declined overall by more than 14%, and losses in some parishes were comparable to those in parts of Munster and Connacht. In 1841–51, for instance, the population of Glenwhirry parish (92% Protestant in 1831) fell nearly 23%, Raloo (84% Protestant in 1831) by more than 23%, Killyglen Grange (81% Protestant in 1831) by nearly 21% and Kilwaughter (75% Protestant in 1831) by 36.4%. The Protestant population of Kilwaughter was overwhelmingly Presbyterian, as were the Protestant inhabitants of those adjacent east- and mid-Antrim parishes, which in 1841–51 also suffered abnormally high demographic attrition.

was greater than County Roscommon's -31.6%, which was the highest of all Irish counties.) By 1851 nearly a third of Kilwaughter's families, enumerated in 1841, had disappeared, including nearly half of those that had occupied the poorest dwellings. As a result, by 1851 a consolidation of holdings had radically altered the local landscape: nearly half of Kilwaughter's farms were now over 30 acres in size, and more than three-fourths of the parish's arable land had been converted to pasture.[17]

As noted earlier, 1841–51 parish (and other) population losses cannot be distinguished by religious affiliations. However, between 1831 and 1861, the three decades spanning the Famine, the size of Kilwaughter's Presbyterian-majority community fell by 36.0%, roughly the same as the 1831–61 decline of -35.6% in the parish's entire population.[18] Relatively few of Kilwaughter's inhabitants may have perished from malnutrition or disease, but out-migration – hitherto reportedly rare – clearly was extensive. Many no doubt moved to Belfast, the population of which rose by nearly one-fourth, to 97,784 inhabitants, between 1841 and 1851; many of the city's newcomers were Famine refugees; in 1847 alone, 14,000 persons were admitted to Belfast's workhouse, while hundreds perished in the streets. Other poor migrants probably died soon after settling, since mid-nineteenth-century Belfast – its working-class districts perennially afflicted by typhus, typhoid, and tuberculosis –

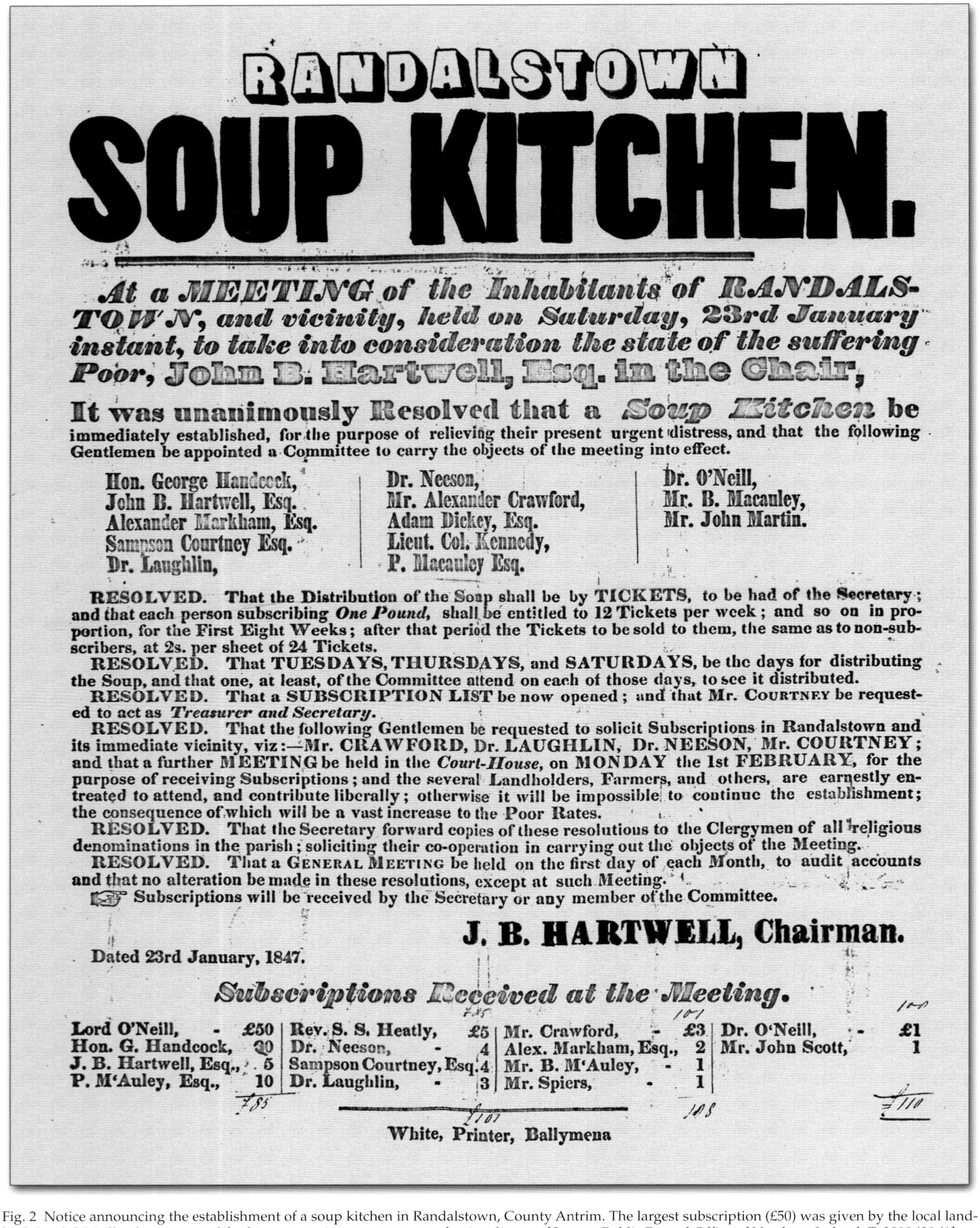

# RANDALSTOWN SOUP KITCHEN.

At a *MEETING* of the *Inhabitants* of *RANDALS-TOWN*, and vicinity, held on Saturday, 23rd January instant, to take into consideration the state of the suffering Poor, John B. Hartwell, Esq. in the Chair,

It was unanimously Resolved that a *Soup Kitchen* be immediately established, for the purpose of relieving their present urgent distress, and that the following Gentlemen be appointed a Committee to carry the objects of the meeting into effect.

| | | |
|---|---|---|
| Hon. George Handcock, | Dr. Neeson, | Dr. O'Neill, |
| John B. Hartwell, Esq. | Mr. Alexander Crawford, | Mr. B. Macauley, |
| Alexander Markham, Esq. | Adam Dickey, Esq. | Mr. John Martin. |
| Sampson Courtney Esq. | Lieut. Col. Kennedy, | |
| Dr. Laughlin, | P. Macauley Esq. | |

RESOLVED. That the Distribution of the Soup shall be by TICKETS, to be had of the Secretary; and that each person subscribing *One Pound*, shall be entitled to 12 Tickets per week; and so on in proportion, for the First Eight Weeks; after that period the Tickets to be sold to them, the same as to non-subscribers, at 2s. per sheet of 24 Tickets.

RESOLVED. That TUESDAYS, THURSDAYS, and SATURDAYS, be the days for distributing the Soup, and that one, at least, of the Committee attend on each of those days, to see it distributed.

RESOLVED. That a SUBSCRIPTION LIST be now opened; and that Mr. COURTNEY be requested to act as *Treasurer and Secretary*.

RESOLVED. That the following Gentlemen be requested to solicit Subscriptions in Randalstown and its immediate vicinity, viz:—Mr. CRAWFORD, Dr. LAUGHLIN, Dr. NEESON, Mr. COURTNEY; and that a further MEETING be held in the *Court-House*, on MONDAY the 1st FEBRUARY, for the purpose of receiving Subscriptions; and the several Landholders, Farmers, and others, are earnestly entreated to attend, and contribute liberally; otherwise it will be impossible to continue the establishment; the consequence of which will be a vast increase to the Poor Rates.

RESOLVED. That the Secretary forward copies of these resolutions to the Clergymen of all religious denominations in the parish; soliciting their co-operation in carrying out the objects of the Meeting.

RESOLVED. That a GENERAL MEETING be held on the first day of each Month, to audit accounts and that no alteration be made in these resolutions, except at such Meeting.

☞ Subscriptions will be received by the Secretary or any member of the Committee.

## J. B. HARTWELL, Chairman.

Dated 23rd January, 1847.

### Subscriptions Received at the Meeting.

| | | | | | | | |
|---|---|---|---|---|---|---|---|
| Lord O'Neill, | £50 | Rev. S. S. Heatly, | £5 | Mr. Crawford, | £3 | Dr. O'Neill, | £1 |
| Hon. G. Handcock, | 20 | Dr. Neeson, | 4 | Alex. Markham, Esq., | 2 | Mr. John Scott, | 1 |
| J. B. Hartwell, Esq., | 5 | Sampson Courtney, Esq. | 4 | Mr. B. M'Auley, | 1 | | |
| P. M'Auley, Esq., | 10 | Dr. Laughlin, | 3 | Mr. Spiers, | 1 | | |

White, Printer, Ballymena

Fig. 2  Notice announcing the establishment of a soup kitchen in Randalstown, County Antrim. The largest subscription (£50) was given by the local landlord, Lord O'Neill, who was noted for his compassionate response to famine distress. [Source: Public Record Office of Northern Ireland, T. 2890/38/1] had the highest death rate of any city in Ireland and possibly in the entire United Kingdom. Others, probably more fortunate, soon re-migrated to Britain, North America or Australia.[19]

The Protestant population of Kilwaughter was overwhelmingly Presbyterian, as were the Protestant inhabitants of those adjacent east and mid-Antrim parishes, which in 1841–51 also suffered abnormally high demographic attrition. For example, in 1831 Presbyterians comprised nearly 100% of the Protestants in Glenwhirry, 92% in Raloo and 97% in Killyglen Grange. Apparently, this was no coincidence. Indeed, much broader evidence suggests that the Famine's effects were *not* evenly distributed among Ulster's Protestants, and that Presbyterians experienced substantially greater losses than did members of the Established Church. For example, during the period 1831–61, spanning the Famine crisis, Ulster's Presbyterian population fell by nearly 18% (only slightly less than the 19% decline among Ulster Catholics), compared with a less than 13% decline among Ulster Anglicans.[20] In 1831–61 Presbyterians suffered greater proportional losses than did Anglicans in eight of Ulster's nine counties; only in Fermanagh, with its miniscule Presbyterian population, did the percentage decline among communicants of the Church of Ireland exceed that experienced by Presbyterians (or by Catholics). Moreover, only in Antrim (excluding Belfast) and in Down were Presbyterian attrition rates less (and only slightly less) than those of Catholics. In Antrim (excluding Belfast), for instance, between 1831 and 1861 the Presbyterian and the Catholic populations declined by 7 and 10%, respectively, but the number of Anglicans increased by more than 12%. Likewise, Armagh's Anglican population fell merely 7.8%, compared with a startling 31% decline among Presbyterians (and a 16% decrease among Catholics); and in County Londonderry the number of Anglicans rose nearly 1%, while that of Presbyterians fell by a remarkable 28.5% (and of Catholics by 13.3%). Even in the predominantly Catholic 'outer' Ulster counties of Cavan, Donegal and Monaghan, proportional losses among Presbyterians in 1831–61 exceeded those among Anglicans and Catholics alike.

## ULSTER'S PRESBYTERIAN AND ANGLICAN POPULATIONS

To be sure, between 1831 and 1861 the Catholic proportion of Ulster's total inhabitants declined from 53 to 51%. However, whereas the Famine and the emigrations immediately preceding and following that crisis made Ulster more heavily Protestant, they also made the North and its Protestant populace less Presbyterian and more Anglican. Thus, between 1831 and 1861 the Presbyterian proportions of Ulster's overall and Protestant populations declined from 27 to 26% and from 57 to 53%, respectively. In nearly all the counties that comprised the future Northern Ireland, the changes in the balance between Presbyterians and Anglicans were particularly striking. For instance, in Antrim (excluding Belfast), the Presbyterian percentage of the Protestant population declined from 76 to 70.5, while the Anglican proportion rose from less than 22 to more than 24%; in Armagh the comparable Presbyterian decrease was from 40.5 to 32%, and the Anglican rise from 58 to 60%; in Down the Presbyterian decline was from 71 to 66%, and the Anglican increase from 27 to 30%; and in Londonderry the Presbyterian decrease was from 73 to 64%, while the Anglican share of the county's Protestants rose from 25 to 31%. [21] These trends would continue for at least the next half-century: between 1861 and 1926 the Protestant share of the total population in the area that in 1920 became Northern Ireland rose from 59 to 66.5%, whereas the Presbyterian proportion of the future statelet's Protestant inhabitants declined from 55 to 47%, while the percentage of Protestants who were members of the Church of Ireland rose from 39 to 40. By 1961 Presbyterians comprised only 44.5% of Northern Ireland's Protestants.[22]

Scholars have scarcely examined these demographic trends, although the shifting balance between Ulster's Presbyterians and Anglicans may have begun back in the early eighteenth century, with the onset of heavy Presbyterian emigration to North America. Nor have historians considered their possible political ramifications – for the consolidation of Ulster Protestant loyalism and conservatism, both traditionally Anglican projects, for instance – although the remarkable attrition of Presbyterians in many mid-Ulster parishes between 1766 and 1831, accompanied by equally startling proportional increases among the area's Anglicans, suggests that local Dissenters, no less than Catholics, may have suffered from the rise of Orangeism and the triumph of loyalism in the 1790s and early 1800s.[23] More pertinent to this essay, however, is that quantitative as well as qualitative evidence indicates that many of Ulster's Protestants, especially its Presbyterians and even in its most economically 'developed' counties, did not escape the horrors of Black '47 and other Famine years.

## RESPONDING TO THE FAMINE

But how did ordinary northern Protestants, particularly Presbyterians, respond to the travails they endured and witnessed between 1845 and 1852. In the Famine's aftermath contemporaries observed, and historians subsequently have confirmed, that the Famine – and Irish and Irish–American nationalists' Anglophobic interpretations of that crisis – engendered lasting bitterness among Irish Catholics both at home and in the United States, fuelling desires for vengeance against the British government and Ireland's Protestant landlords that found expression, from the 1860s through the early 1920s, in Catholic Irish and Irish–American support for the Fenian, Land League, Home Rule, and Independence movements. In addition, several scholars, including Kerby Miller, one of this essay's authors, have argued that such expressions also served hegemonic

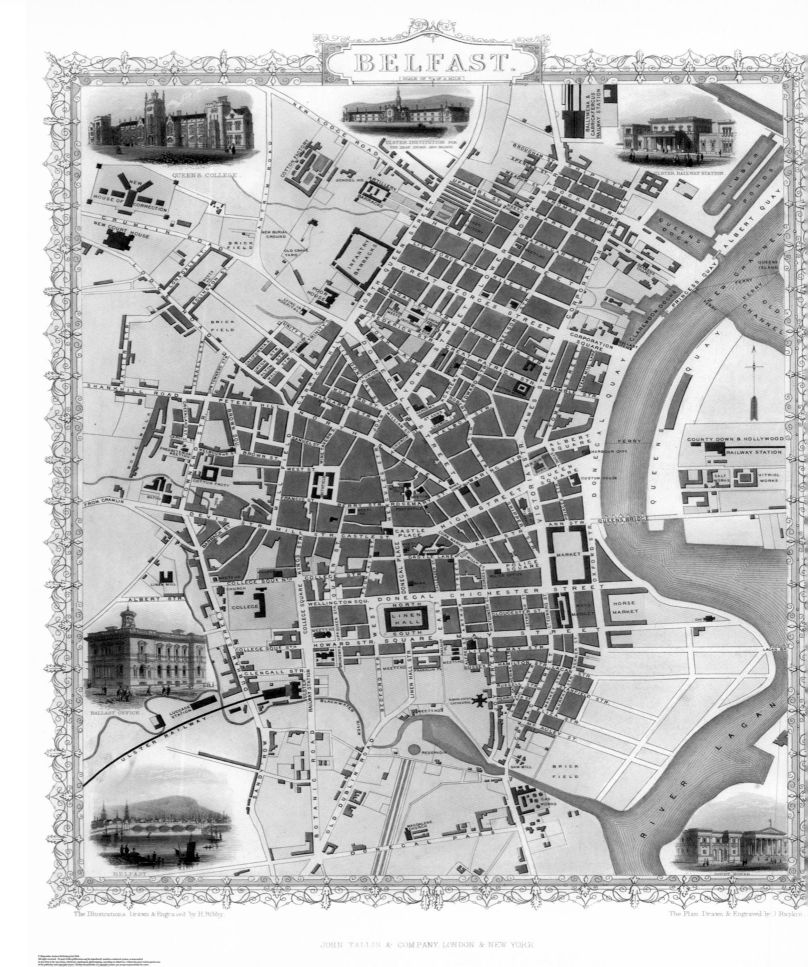

Fig. 3 Tallis map of Belfast, 1851. Belfast, a growing industrial hub, experienced a large population increase between 1841–51, rising by a quarter to 97,784 inhabitants. Many of the newcomers were Famine refugees. The overcrowded conditions in its working-class districts were responsible in the main for the spread of disease and the extremely high mortality rate in the city during this period. [Source: Mapseeker Archive Publishing]

and psychological functions, enabling Catholics in Ireland and overseas to project onto alien 'others' feelings of anger and shame: anger that might have been directed against wealthier co-religionists – merchants, shopkeepers, and, perhaps especially, 'land-grabbers' – who benefited from the plight of starving peasants and evicted neighbours; and shame – for their poverty, humiliation, and self-saving violations of communal ties and constraints – which, if not externalised, might have had destructive personal consequences.[24]

To be sure, during the Famine years some Ulster Presbyterian emigrants did write letters that revealed anti-British and anti-landlord sentiments comparable to those expressed by Irish and Irish-American Catholic nationalists. Thus, from the safety of New Orleans in 1849, young David Kerr cried 'Down with landlordism' and told his uncle in County Antrim that he prayed for a revolution that would overthrow 'the vile British Government', establish an Irish 'Republick', and banish 'all the pampered aristocracy from the country'.[25]

However, although the Famine could rekindle the United Irishmen's spirit among at least a few Ulster Presbyterians, in general northern Protestants' political culture, as it had developed on both sides of the Atlantic since the Act of Union, allowed for neither a nationalist nor a class-based interpretation of the Famine experience. In Ulster itself, although Anglican–Dissenter and landlord–tenant conflicts remained common, between the early 1800s and the 1840s a combination of socio-economic, religious and political factors (not least of which was mass emigration by disaffected Presbyterians) had virtually eradicated among northern Protestants the ecumenical radicalism of the 1790s – creating instead a pervasive, hegemonic loyalty to the union with Britain and to its Irish upper- and middle-class Protestant champions, as well as a corresponding hostility to Irish nationalist movements that were now almost exclusively Catholic in composition and identity. Likewise, by the mid-1800s Irish–American Protestant political culture was dominated by what later critics would call a 'Scotch–Irish myth' that encompassed nearly all non-Catholic Irish immigrants and their descendants in a shared sense of social and cultural superiority.[26]

## UNIONIST IDEOLOGY

Indeed, it is arguable that the Famine in Ulster played a crucial role in the consolidation of unionist ideology (just as Famine immigration, heavily Catholic and generally impoverished, undoubtedly spurred Irish-American Protestants' efforts to distin-

guish themselves as 'Scotch–Irish').[27] Ironically, this was because Ulster Protestant distress during the Famine belied and challenged unionists' most basic assumptions in at least three crucial respects. First, it contradicted their fundamental conviction that Protestantism and its associated social virtues would inevitably produce material rewards, win God's favour, and thus shield its adherents from poverty, famine, and eviction – that is, from the 'natural' consequences of the social and moral degradation that Irish Protestants conventionally attributed to Irish Catholics, especially to the 'feckless' peasantry, and from the divine punishment that Catholics allegedly deserved for their wickedness and disloyalty to the Crown. Second, Ulster Protestant suffering in 1845–52, and especially the deficiencies of official relief, had the potential to call into question the practical value of the union with Britain even among the Queen's most proverbially dutiful subjects. Not only revolutionaries like John Mitchel (from Newry, County Down) saw that possibility; in 1849 the Ulster MP, William Sharman Crawford, warned the British government that its rate-in-aid bill, which levied extra taxes on solvent Poor Law unions in east Ulster for relief of bankrupt unions in western Ireland, might dissolve the ties of loyalty that bound the North's Protestants to the 'British connexion'.[28] And third, Famine conditions and the inadequacy of local relief had the

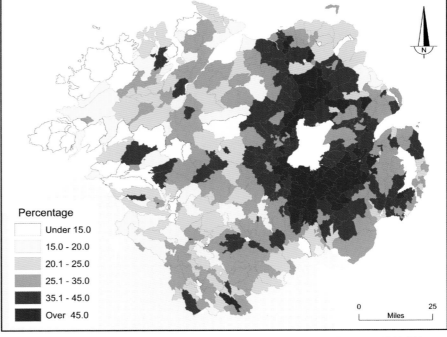

Fig. 4 PERCENTAGE OF FAMILIES DEPENDENT ON THE DIRECTION OF LABOUR IN ULSTER IN 1841. This map highlights significant contrasts in class structures and the distribution of wealth in pre-Famine Ulster. In the powerful core area of east and northeast Ulster, centred on the burgeoning town of Belfast and encircling all of Lough Neagh and extending northwards along the Bann, at least 35% and often over 45% of families were involved in the direction of labour. This was the Protestant heartland of big farmers, shopkeepers, mill owners, industrialists and members of the professional classes. This was also the core area which saw the consolidation of Unionist ideology during the Famine, where some if not many Protestant proprietors and middle-class rate-payers justified the implementation of less than generous relief measures. Apart from a small number of exceptions, the western half of Ulster contains a much lower proportion of families – under 25% and often under 15% – then engaged in the direction of labour. For the most part, the Famine crisis was to reinforce these regional, class and ethno-religious divisions.

Percentage

Under 15.0
15.0 - 20.0
20.1 - 25.0
25.1 - 35.0
35.1 - 45.0
Over 45.0

Fig. 5 *William Sharman Crawford, MP (1781–1861)* by John Prescott Knight, *c.* 1843. A prominent landowner, politician and reformer, Crawford remained a firm advocate of tenant rights during his lifetime. As chairman of the Newtownwards Board of Guardians and despite local opposition by other vested interests he recognised the distress caused by the Famine and appealed to parliament in March 1847 to allow Poor Law guardians to provide outdoor food relief to the able-bodied poor. [Source: © National Museum's Northern Ireland Collection, Ulster Museum]

potential to expose and even exacerbate the overlapping class and denominational resentments and conflicts that had long existed within Ulster Protestant society.

Thus, ideological and political imperatives converged with economic and social concerns to ensure that Anglican landlords, clergymen and other Ulster Protestant spokesmen would interpret or 'explain' the Famine by escalating unionist and sectarian rhetoric so as to counteract the crisis's divisive (and politically educational) possibilities. For example, as rents fell and relief costs and poor rates rose, Protestant proprietors and middle-class rate-payers became less likely to be charitable and more prone to contend that, thanks to the thrifty, Protestant character of 'Ulster', there was no Famine in 'their province' at all. Moreover, loyalist pronouncements not only denied the Famine's very existence in loyal, industrious, and Protestant 'Ulster', but ascribed hunger and misery only to the 'lazy, vicious and indolent' Catholics of southern and western Ireland, and attributed the latter's plight to 'the almighty's wrath' against 'idle', 'sabbath-breaking repealers'.[29]

Such arguments – repeated in Protestant newspapers,

speeches, sermons, and public resolutions – helped justify the exceptionally parsimonious relief measures implemented (or denied) by many northern Poor Law boards, especially in eastern Ulster. Those measures won high praise for 'efficiency' and 'frugality' from Whig officials in London, but must have exacerbated distress among lower-class Protestants as well as Catholics. Hence, public works, soup kitchens, and outdoor Famine relief, generally, were employed less often in Ulster (especially in its northeastern counties, such as Antrim) than in any other province, while local landlords and Poor Law guardians publicly rejected accusations of misery and starvation among their dependents as malicious slanders on 'the peaceable and industrious inhabitants of the north of Ireland'.[30]

### THE FAMINE'S HARSH REALITIES

This rhetoric, of course, obscured the harsh realities of contemporary experience for poor northern Protestants, but it also served to cloak the actions of many Anglican landlords – and of affluent Protestant head tenants and employers – who, in east Ulster as elsewhere, often evicted insolvent farmers, cottiers, and labourers or, at the least, viewed with equanimity the Famine's 'thinning' of their properties.[31] Furthermore, as David Miller has argued, unionist rhetoric during the Famine also reflected Ulster Presbyterianism's contemporary transformation from 'an inclusive communal faith' to a bourgeois, 'class-based denomination' – and, in consequence, its clerical and lay leaders' increasing tendencies to ignore poor, un-churched Presbyterians and to interpret 'class' problems, such as posed by the crisis of 1845–52, in crudely sectarian terms.[32] Finally, therefore, it may be very significant that the greatest outpouring of unionist and sectarian rhetoric occurred in the Famine's *latter* years and coincided not only with the controversy over the rate-in-aid, which threatened upper- and middle-class Ulstermen with higher taxation, but also with the beginnings of Sharman Crawford's tenant-right movement, designed to mobilise ordinary Presbyterian farmers against the authority of landlords and their middle-class allies. Likewise, it may not be coincidental that the single bloodiest event in nineteenth-century Ireland, the Orangemen's massacre of at least thirty Catholics, including women and children, at Dolly's Brae (1849), in southwest County Down, also occurred at this time; at the least, this incident helped ensure that 'normal' sectarian polarisation and strife, not renewed social conflict among Ulster's Protestants (as in the 1760s–1810s), would be the Famine's principal legacy in the northern province.[33]

Thus, as a result of both long-term trends and short-term elite strategies, Ulster Protestant victims of famine, evictions, and parsimonious relief measures could not express their pain, their grievances and resentments, within the context of a hegemonic religious and political culture that denied their very existence. Consequently, whereas the

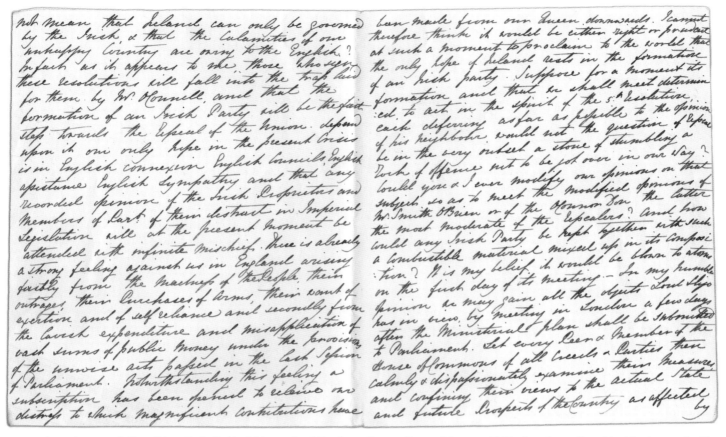

Fig. 6 A letter from Lord Clare, Wrest Park, Bedfordshire, to Lord Farnham, County Cavan, 9 January 1847, where he outlines his objections to the idea of creating an Irish party at Westminster in opposition to the Government. It was his considered view that Irish interests would not be best served by such a move. Ireland's difficulty could only be resolved within an imperial context: ' . . . Depend upon it, our only hope in the present crisis is in English connection, English councils, English assistance, English sympathy, and that any recorded opinion of the Irish proprietors and members of parliament of their distrust in imperial legislation will at the present moment be attended with infinite mischief. There is already a strong feeling against us in England arising from the madness of the people, their outrages, their purchases of arms, their want of exertion and self reliance, and secondly, from the lavish expenditure and misapplication of vast sums of public money under the provisions of the unwise acts passed in the last session of Parliament. Notwithstanding this feeling, a subscription has been opened to relieve our distress to which magnificent contributions have been made from our Queen downwards. I cannot therefore think it would be either right or prudent at such a moment to proclaim to the world that the only hope of Ireland rests in the formation of an Irish party . . . ' [Source: Public Record Office of Northern Ireland, D3078/3/34/4]

letters of some Famine immigrants suggest that the crisis of 1845–52 scarred them psychologically and adversely affected their adjustment to American life, it is possible that this may have been particularly true of those who were poor Protestants. In contrast to Irish Catholic immigrants, Protestant migrants from Ulster generally lacked large, cohesive, and supportive working-class ethnic communities and subcultures in a mid- and late-nineteenth-century America where the prevalent 'Scotch–Irish myth' also denied that Irish Protestant immigrants might be permanently destitute, culturally alienated, politically disaffected, or psychologically disoriented by their harsh experiences. More

crucially, as loyalists to both the British Crown and the ideology of Protestant superiority, Ulster Protestant immigrants could only internalise feelings of anger and shame that Irish Catholics could project outwards on their traditional oppressors.[34] In short, Irish Catholic diasporic nationalism, in the United States and elsewhere, may have been a socially and psychologically healthy phenomenon – a rational individual and communal response to otherwise nearly intolerable conditions and memories – but one that culture and politics denied to Ulster and other Irish Protestant victims of the Great Famine and its attendant miseries and injustices.

# The Great Hunger in Belfast

## Gerard Mac Atasney and Christine Kenealy

The belief that the Great Hunger did not affect the northeast corner of Ireland is long established.[1] By the mid nineteenth century this part of Ireland was at the forefront of industrial advancement based largely on the textile industry and, increasingly, ship building. The town of Belfast was at the heart of these changes. As a result, some historians have suggested that the eastern part of Ulster was protected from the ravages of the Famine and, in the words of the historian, Roy Foster, 'escaped lightly'.[2] Other historians of the Famine have simply ignored the northeast part of the country in their research and writings.[3] This myth of Ulster 'exceptionalism' has its roots in the Famine period itself when, as early as 1849, the *Newry Telegraph* proclaimed:

> It is true that the potato has failed in Connaught and Munster; but it has failed just as much in Ulster; therefore, if the potato has produced all the distress in the South and West, why has it not caused the same misery here? It is because we are a painstaking, industrious, laborious people, who desire to work and pay our just debts, and the blessing of the Almighty is upon our labour. If the people of the South had been equally industrious with those of the North, they would not have had so much misery among them.[4]

The experience of Belfast after 1845 demonstrated that no part of Ireland escaped from the devastation triggered by the failure of the potato crop. It also shows that being part of the United Kingdom provided no protection to the poor of Ireland as the country was increasingly forced to depend on its own resources.

In the decades prior to 1845, Belfast was undergoing a number of changes. The growth of textile production had resulted in a rapid growth of population from approximately 20,000 in 1801 to 75,000 by 1841. This was largely due to immigration, mostly from the local surrounding countryside. The relationship between the town and the countryside remained significant in a number of other ways. There was a high dependence by the local textile workers on potatoes grown in the surrounding areas, which provided them with cheap and nourishing food.[5] This interdependence meant that a poor harvest or an industrial downswing would inevitably have an impact on both town and countryside. In 1846 and 1847, Belfast suffered from a collapse in both agricultural and industrial production.

The pre-Famine prosperity of Belfast was summed up by the Halls, who visited in 1840, and pronounced that 'the clean and bustling appearance of Belfast is decidedly unnational'.[6] Yet, Belfast also shared the urban squalor of many Victorian towns and cities in the 1840s. The rapid economic and industrial expansion disguised an underbelly of poverty, disease, dislocation and vulnerability, which were shared by all areas that had undergone rapid industrial expansion. This vulnerability was exacerbated by insufficient housing and inadequate medical and social welfare provisions. In a number of ways, therefore, the town of Belfast had more in common with the industrial towns of Britain rather than the major cities of Ireland. The population of Belfast also differed from that of other towns in Ireland in that its inhabitants were predominantly Presbyterian.

Prior to the introduction of the Poor Law, private philanthropy and local benevolent organisations provided a safety net for the sick and the destitute. The latter included the Belfast Charitable Society, which provided local facilities such as the poorhouse, graveyards and water supply. The provisions of the 1838 Poor Law had divided Ireland into 130 Poor Law unions, each with its own locally financed workhouse. Belfast's workhouse had opened in 1841, at the centre of a union that extended beyond the town's boundaries and included the highly industrialised area of Ballymacarret. The underpinning ethos of the Poor Law, and of most philanthropy, was that the individual was solely responsible for his/her own poverty and relief should only be available to those who were destitute and deserving. The experience of Belfast after 1845 exposed the vulnerability of the local population to the horrors that were being experienced by the poor and vulnerable in other parts of Ireland. They also demonstrated that religion and allegiance to the union with Britain provided no protection as the impact of the food shortages extended to all parts of Ireland.

### FAILURE OF THE POTATO
The onset of famine was triggered by the failure of the potato crop in 1845, which reappeared in varying degrees for a further six years. Part of the tragic timing of the Irish Famine was that it coincided with a Europe-wide credit crisis and industrial downswing that had affected British markets in particular. A consequence was to throw many industrial workers out of work or put them on short time hours. For people in Belfast, this presented the double prob-

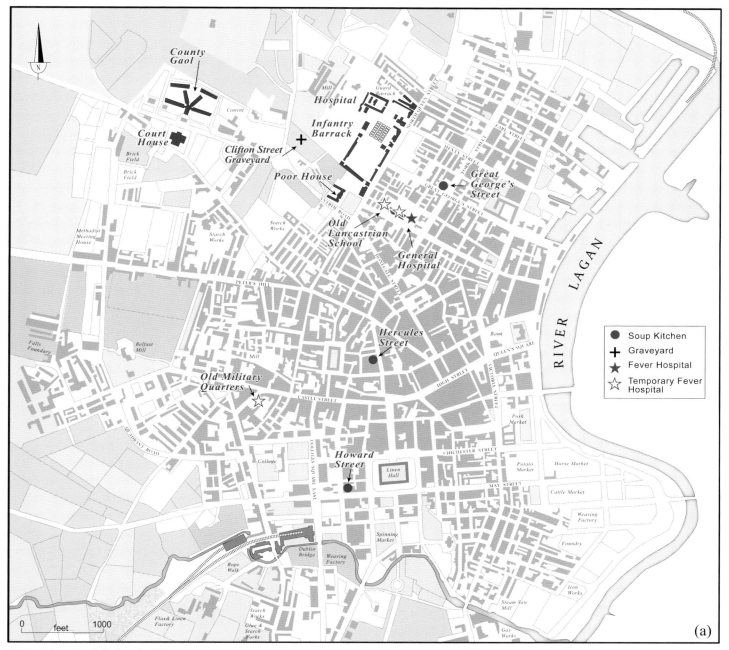

Figs 1a (above) and 1b (overleaf) LOCATION OF MEDICAL AND RELIEF FACILITIES AND BURIAL GROUNDS IN BELFAST AND ITS ENVIRONS DURING THE FAMINE.

lem of having either no or a low income at a time when food prices were rising.

By the end of 1846, the workhouse was full, which was not helped by an influx of poor from the surrounding areas – a situation that was experienced by all towns in Ireland. The fact the Irish Poor Law (unlike in the English and Scottish systems) did not include a Law of Settlement, meaning that the poor could not be refused relief in any workhouse in Ireland where they sought relief. Inevitably though, it put a particular burden on workhouses situated in towns and ports.

As was the case elsewhere, people flocked from the rural areas into the towns – seeking work, relief, or a route to escape from Ireland. Belfast was also the recipient of a number of paupers deported from Britain where they were

not eligible to receive relief. Inevitably, this put pressure on the already stretched resources of the local Poor Law and the tax-payers.

### INTRODUCTION OF SOUP KITCHENS

The first indication of distress in Belfast emerged with the opening of a soup kitchen by a group of butchers based in Hercules Street. At the end of October 1846 they contributed meat and vegetables together with financial assistance to this project. Within days hundreds of people were obtaining a daily meal by this means.[7] Subsequently, a meeting at the town hall in late November heard evidence of the 'very great distress' prevalent in the town and it was decided to support two further soup kitchens; one in the old House of Correction in Howard Street and the other in an unoccupied

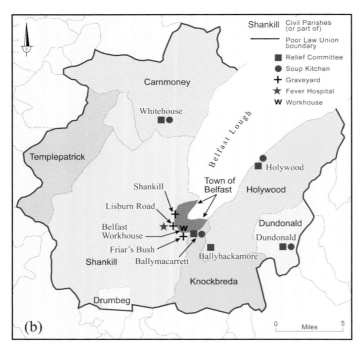

(b)

house in Great George's Street.[8]

The extent of distress was further highlighted by a march for food in mid December by some 200 men who had been made unemployed from their work on the railway. They decided to march to a number of bakeries in the northern area of town and after threatening to resort to violence unless fed, they eventually dispersed when bread to the value of twenty shillings was distributed amongst them.[9] Such actions stimulated the town fathers into action and after a long debate they decided to appoint a deputation to meet the Chief Secretary and request the closure of all distilleries in an attempt to save grain for those in need. However, despite this being a traditional response to shortages, their request went unheeded.[10]

In the meantime the two kitchens under the auspices of the council were providing increasing numbers with food; by mid December they were distributing a weekly average of 1,500 quarts of soup together with 22 cwt of bread to 1,200 families – 80% of whom received this gratuitously.[11] Throughout the Belfast Union, guardians in other electoral divisions were also attempting to feed their poor and relief committees, with associated soup kitchens, were formed in Ballymacarret, Whitehouse, Dundonald and Holywood.[12]

In February 1847 a meeting of subscribers to the Belfast General Dispensary was told that 'at no period within our memory has such an amount of destitution prevailed in the town'.[13] By the end of that month the two town soup kitchens were now distributing 20,000 quarts of soup and 42 cwt of bread per week.[14] In Ballymacarret the local committee was supplying 800 quarts of free soup per day together with five tons of coal on a weekly basis to 300 families.[15] Such was the demand that by the beginning of March the Belfast Ladies Clothing Society had provided blankets and clothing to almost 1,000 families in Ballymacarret, Bal-

lyhackamore and Ballynafeigh.[16]

An indication of the extent of the relief operation is shown in the figures for the Belfast town soup kitchens. From 20 December 1846 to 20 March 1847 they distributed 278,671 quarts of soup and 775 cwt of bread to 3,008 families (approximately 15,000 people).[17] The existence of such relief facilities saw the ingress of thousands of people into Belfast from the surrounding countryside. After complaints in the press about large-scale vagrancy on the town's street it was decided to open a day asylum. To achieve this goal, a local textile merchant Andrew Mulholland donated an unused factory at May's Dock near Queen's Bridge. In this building the poor could receive, until 7 p.m., food and industrial training. The latter demonstrated that even during a period of intense distress, relief was to be combined with 'improving' the condition of the poor. It opened on 12 April 1847, admitting just over 100 men, women and children. Within three days more than 650 people were daily making their way to this establishment – this number peaking at 902 on 27 April.[18]

## WORKHOUSE

The demand for relief in such temporary establishments was also reflected in the main instrument of poor relief in the town – the Belfast Workhouse. This building had been constructed to accommodate a maximum of 1,000 paupers but by November 1846 it had exceeded its capacity with a figure of 1,103.[19] As in workhouses throughout the country, the Belfast guardians were forced to utilise every possible space on the workhouse grounds in order to meet demand. Hence, the piggery, stable and straw houses were converted into wards capable of accommodating a further 600 paupers. By the end of January there were more than 1,500 inmates in the workhouse and inevitably diseases such as diarrhoea, dysentery and typhus fever were widespread. Indeed the medical attendant to the institution, Dr Coffey, succumbed to the latter in this period. So stretched were resources that eighteen beds in the fever hospital contained two patients each.[20]

In an attempt to alleviate the situation, the guardians managed, after much debate, to convince the management of the Belfast General Hospital to accept patients suffering from smallpox and dysentery. The hospital was a surgical establishment and thus loathe to accede to such a request, but the acquiescence of its management allowed the workhouse infirmary to concentrate solely on cases of fever.[21] However, such were the number of fever cases (253 on 23 March 1847) that the guardians had to again ask the General Hospital for further assistance. Indeed, it was only after the guardians revealed that all future fever admissions would have to be refused that the General Hospital agreed to limit the admission of surgical patients to 'extraordinary cases only', thereby allowing for more cases of smallpox and dysentery.[22]

## Fund for the Temporal Relief of the Suffering Poor of Ireland.

### THROUGH THE INSTRUMENTALITY OF THE CLERGY OF THE ESTABLISHED CHURCH.

At a MEETING of MEMBERS of the ESTABLISHED CHURCH, held in Belfast, on Monday, January 4th, 1847 (after several preliminary conferences on the present alarming state of distress in Ireland),

**J. B. SHANNON, Esq., in the Chair,**

After prayer for the Divine guidance, and lengthened consideration, it was unanimously resolved:—

"That the present awful state of destitution in which so many millions of our countrymen are involved, through the providential dispensation of God, and the consequent incessant demands upon the Clergy of the Established Church, especially in the South and West of Ireland, urgently call upon us to take prompt and vigorous measures for their relief; and that a fund be forthwith commenced for that purpose, to be called, 'Fund for the Temporal Relief of the Suffering Poor of Ireland, through the Instrumentality of the Clergy of the Established Church.'"

Resolved—"That all money entrusted to the care of this Committee shall be expended in the purchase of food."

Resolved—"That the following gentlemen be appointed a Committee, to carry out the objects of the preceding resolutions, with power to add to their number:—

| | |
|---|---|
| The Rev. T. Drew, D.D., | The Rev. E. J. Hartrick, |
| .. R. W. Bland, | J. B. Shannon, Esq., |
| .. R. Oulton, | S. G. Fenton, Esq., |
| .. A. Oulton, | James Crawford, Esq., |
| .. C. Allen, | Dr. C. Purdon. |

Treasurer—Dr. Purdon.

Hon. Secretaries—Rev. W. M'Ilwaine; Rev. T. Campbell."

Resolved—"That an address, embodying the substance of the foregoing resolutions, be drawn up, and extensively circulated."

Signed,         J. B. SHANNON, Chairman.

Several Contributions to the Fund have been already received, which will be duly acknowledged. Further Donations will be thankfully received by any member of the Committee; or, by

71)     WM. M'ILWAINE,
THEOPH. CAMPBELL, } Secretaries.

Fig. 2 *Belfast Newsletter*, 8 January 1847. Report of a fund created for the relief of distress in Ireland by members of the Established Church. The tendency of philanthropists to look beyond Belfast and ignore suffering in an industrial suburb like Ballymacarrett did not go unnoticed. The Presbyterian newspaper, the *Banner of Ulster*, claimed 'that the people of Belfast have been benevolent at a distance and heedless of distress on their own doors'.

### SPREAD OF DISEASE

The spread of disease was exacerbated by the arrival in port of a vessel, the *Swatara*, containing 296 passengers, many of whom were afflicted with fever. The local medical establishments attempted to aid them as best they could but nevertheless by mid-April typhus was reported to be making rapid progress throughout the town.[23] On 25 March 1847 the workhouse hospital contained 254 patients; one month later this figure reached 503. In many cases up to four people shared a bed – the healthy lying with the diseased.[24] An indication of the conditions endured by the poor at this

time is given by the following account of the Rev. William Johnston, a member of the town soup kitchen committee:

> In one house there were lying ill of contagious diseases, four persons in one small room. The poor afflicted people had no straw to lie down upon, only a piece of dirty sackcloth. On this miserable bed nine persons, including the fever patients, were obliged to sleep every night . . . In another part of the same room resided another family consisting of seven people who also slept in the apartment – not near nine foot wide – four of whom were afflicted with a dangerous fever.[25]

Under such circumstances death became commonplace. Fatalities in the union workhouse exceeded 600 in the first four months of 1847.[26] In some cases, as reported in the local press, people simply lay down and died on the streets – a woman in Chichester Street, another in York Street; a beggarman on the Shankill Road; a two-year-old child at May's Bridge.[27]

On 2 July it was reported that the Catholic graveyard at Friar's Bush was 'so much choked with the dead' that the sextons were obliged to dig deep square pits capable of holding forty coffins. At the main Protestant burial ground on the Shankill Road the local Anglican minister, Rev.

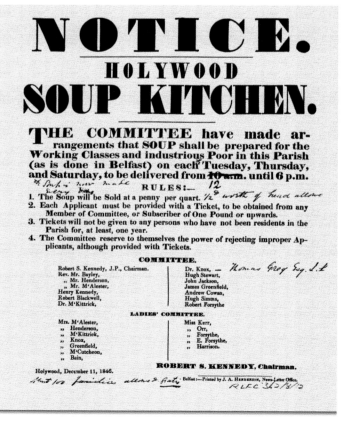

Fig. 3 Soup kitchen poster, December 1846. In the spring of 1847 soup kitchens began to replace public works as the main form of government relief. By the end of March over 3,000 families were receiving rations at Belfast's soup kitchens, which roughly translates to over 15,000 people.

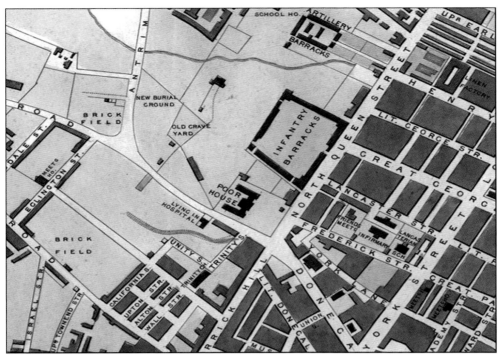

Fig. 4 Belfast Town grew rapidly in the first half of the nineteenth century, reaching a population of 75,308 and increasing rapidly again during the Famine decade to 100,301. Prior to this, the foundation of the Belfast Charitable Society in 1752 led to the establishment of a poorhouse and infirmary by 1771 on land donated by the Earl of Donegall in the open countryside at the north of Belfast near Antrim Road. The Belfast Poor Law Union – catering for a union population of 100,595 in 1841 – saw the first admission of paupers to the new workhouse on 1 January 1841. Built to accommodate 1,000 inmates at a cost of nearly £10,000 pounds, the workhouse was located to the southwest of the city between the new Lisburn Turnpike Road to the east and Blackstaff Loaning (now Donegal Road) to the north. In the early phases of the Famine in the city, soup kitchens were established in Hercules Street, in the old House of Correction on Howard Street and in an unoccupied house on Great George's Street. During the crisis of the Famine, sheds and sleeping galleries were added to the workhouse to provide accommodation for a further 747 inmates. As many as 5,060 inmates died in the workhouse during the Famine decade, constituting 5% of the union population. A large fever hospital to accommodate c.160 patients was also opened in January 1847. Over 5,200 were treated and 700 died there in 1847 – the darkest year of the Famine in Belfast. [Source: Detail from Tallis map of Belfast, Mapseeker Archive Publishing]

Richard Oultan, reported how 'Coffins are heaped upon coffins until the last one is not more than two inches under ground and in finding room for others, bodies that have not been long buried are often exhumed.'[28] His colleague, Dr Drew, related gruesome details of a recent interment in the same cemetery:

> A few days since I turned away in disgust when I observed the manner in which bones and skulls were thrown up and about and in which the spade was stuck into coffins and dead bodies which had seemingly been but a very short time deposited.[29]

Eventually, as with Friar's Bush, the sextons in the Shankill graveyard had to dig huge pits in order to accommodate forty coffins at a time.[30]

## POOR LAW EXTENSION ACT

In August 1847 the British Government introduced new relief measures based on an extension of the existing Poor Law. As a result of the Poor Law Extension Act, responsibility for all relief fell to boards of guardians. This measure sig-

nalled the closure of soup kitchens throughout the Belfast Union, even though in Belfast the soup kitchens were private and not government-sponsored. The Howard Street kitchen ceased operations in July while the Great Georges Street establishment, despite still feeding 1,300 families, was closed on 27 August.[31]

The day asylum continued to operate, the only alteration in its status being that both it and the Old House of Correction were placed under the control of the Belfast guardians, thereby increasing the workhouse capacity by more than 400.[32] To counter the problem of ingress of non-residents, the Belfast Charitable Society established a committee in July 1847 to oversee the return of paupers from Belfast to their native districts. Within the next eighteen months they had returned more than 11,000 paupers from Belfast to various parts of Ireland.[33]

Given the much-publicised problem with burial space, the Belfast guardians successfully negotiated the purchase of a three-acre site as an additional burial ground. The first burial took place on 14 June 1847. In that same year an extension to the

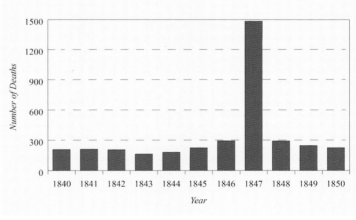

Fig. 5 Mortality in the Belfast workhouse, 1840–50. During the summer months of 1847 there was a fourfold increase in mortality in the workhouse which, in turn, increased the pressure on burial space. The Poor Law Commissioners were adamant that only those who died within workhouse walls could be interred in the workhouse graveyard. The overcrowded conditions which prevailed simply mirrored that which existed in Belfast's public graveyards. Friar's Bush cemetery, for example, was described as 'so much choked with the dead' that the sextons were obliged to dig deep, square pits capable of holding forty coffins. Unlike the pattern of mortality in western or southern unions, mortality in Belfast was massively concentrated in a single year.

Shankhill graveyard allowed for an increase in capacity by one-half.[34]

Although the worst year of the Famine had passed, in terms of fatalities, demand for relief in the Belfast workhouse remained constant. In July 1849 the numbers receiving relief inside the various workhouse buildings was 2,643.[35] Even into the 1850s demand for relief tended to be higher than in the pre-Famine era. In December 1852 the workhouse contained 1,749 able-bodied inmates and 443 paupers. By 1854 the average daily number of paupers in the workhouse was 2,008, with only the Cork, Dublin and Limerick unions providing more relief.[36] Of course, some of this demand may well have been due to Belfast's sustained population growth together with returned paupers and the continuing influx from the countryside.

## AFTERMATH

The population of Belfast was 97,784 in 1851. A somewhat similar growth was experienced by other big towns in Ireland, reflecting the tendency of people to flee from agricultural areas during a period of famine.[37] Unusually though, while the population of other parts of Ireland continued to decline after 1851, Belfast's population grew rapidly. From the 1850s, Belfast's industrial base expanded rapidly. The success of the Harland and Wolff shipyard after 1861 gave a stimulus to other associated and auxiliary industries. By 1886, Belfast was the third largest port in the United Kingdom in terms of the customs revenue collected.[38]

After 1851, as the rest of the Ireland declined in terms of population and industry, the success of Belfast was particularly remarkable. The union with Britain was regarded by many Protestants as being responsible for the town's economic and industrial success. The years of famine in Belfast, however, suggest that the Act of Union with Britain was no protection against poverty, suffering and death, even for those who supported the union and who professed the Protestant religion. As had been the case in other parts of Ireland, the poor of Belfast had been left increasingly to their own resources. Moreover, their suffering had been aggravated as a consequence of inadequate and inappropriate government interventions and the parsimonious way in which relief was provided. Even as the tragedy was unfolding, however, there were attempts made by some supporters of the union to minimise the Famine's impact on Ulster, in an effort to make the point that northern Protestants were superior to people in the rest of the island.[39]

The suffering of the poor was forgotten as Belfast presented itself as being different from, and superior to, other towns in Ireland. As a consequence, the experiences of those who suffered during the Famine years were forgotten or marginalised in the quest to create a version of Ulster's past in which famine and death – and abandonment by the British Government – played no part.

# Mapping the Famine in Monaghan

## Patrick J. Duffy

Monaghan county in the mid-nineteenth-century did not contain the poverty-stricken wilderness landscapes of the west which have come to symbolise the social and environmental tragedy of the Great Famine. However, in terms of population loss, reports of destitution and deaths from starvation, expenditure on relief measures, soaring Poor Law taxation, and emigration, Monaghan shared more experiences with the west and north west of Ireland than with the rest of Ulster, which had a lower regional population loss. The distinctiveness of Monaghan's demographic crisis was prefigured in earlier decades by soaring rural population densities, pressure on land resources, and escalating social poverty, a landholding crisis reflected in rent arrears and growing interest in emigration.

### OVERPOPULATED DISTRICTS

By 1841, the county contained some of the most extensively overpopulated districts in the country, part of a belt of countryside running from south Cavan through Monaghan into Armagh and the parishes of north County Louth, which contained up to and over 400 persons per square mile, densities that were shared with the narrow coastal belts along the west coast of Ireland. Excluding populations in towns, there were 185,000 people living in the Monaghan countryside, representing an average rural density of 58 persons per 100 acres (or 370 per square mile). One-quarter of the 1,853 townlands in the county had extremely high population densities of more than 76 persons per 100 acres; many of these townlands in the south and west of the county had densities which when converted amounted to from 600 to 1,300 persons per square mile. As in much of rural Ireland, at townland level there were local contrasts in popula-

tion pressure, with hugely overcrowded townlands being juxtaposed with virtually empty districts, coinciding with demesnes and large farms, though large-farm areas were comparatively limited in Monaghan.

This population largely depended on a landholding structure which had become increasingly fragmented over the previous several decades. Apart from the miniscule holdings, there were large numbers of cottiers and labourers with limited or no access to land, and by the 1830s fewer of these had access to other work. The linen industry's spin-

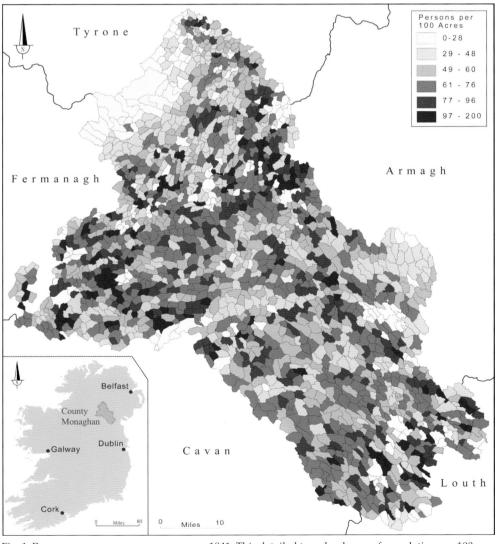

Fig. 1 POPULATION DENSITY PER TOWNLAND IN 1841. This detailed townland map of population per 100 acres in 1841 highlights the diversity of conditions within this crowded county with a population density per square mile of arable land well over 400. Many townlands contain over sixty and often over one hundred persons per 100 acres, reflecting extremely congested and difficult conditions. But there were also a significant minority of less-well-populated townland communities with less than fifty and often less than twenty-eight persons per 100 acres, existing side-by-side with highly congested townlands. This map, therefore, highlights contrasting tenurial and living conditions in the county before the Famine.

440

ning and weaving crafts were in rapid decline in the 1840s, leaving a huge population of underemployed rural dwellers in a crisis situation throughout the decade.

These population and landholding trends took place within a template of landownership in which a management 'policy' operated to a greater or lesser extent depending on the involvement or interest of the owner. In practice, estates representing segments of land containing tenant occupiers with variable legal relationships to the owner, provide an important territorial context for understanding the repercussions of the Famine. The more extensive properties contained very large populations. The neighbouring Shirley and Bath estates in the south of the county, for instance, contained c.50,000 acres, inhabited by more than 40,000 people. Both proprietors lived mostly on their English estates and usually employed agents, bailiffs, and clerks whose principal duties were to get in the rent. On the large Shirley estate, a variety of measures were imposed to 'squeeze' the tenants, with watchers and keepers for surveillance, and extra charges imposed for use of peat bogs and lime. There were subsidiary objectives, sporadically implemented, of making orderly and efficient use of the land by preventing subdivision and subletting of farms. Shirley's large estate employed a surveyor and an agriculturist who supervised a model farm.

Smaller properties, frequently parts of a more extensive but fragmented estate with the owner living elsewhere, had no discernible presence or management policy beyond the twice yearly rent collection. As was often the case, these properties may have had complex layers of 'ownership' and title. Eighty-eight out of 154 properties of 100–500 acres were owned by persons not resident on their estates in County Monaghan in 1858, but in neighbouring counties or in other counties ranging from Dublin to Derry. Of the twenty-eight largest estates in the county, seven were non-resident, like Shirley of Carrickmacross, living much of the year in England.

## MISMANAGEMENT

Decades of poor management on many estates had frequently resulted in the build-up of large numbers of tenants and cottiers with no tenurial connection to the estate: many were sub-tenants or cottiers of the estate's tenants. As far back as 1795, agent Norman Steel warned the Bath and Shirley estates about 'the little interest felt by the occupier from the shortness of the present tenures and the attendant discouragement that must be the consequence of past changes in the managers of so extensive an absentee property, and also the many instances in which the occupier might have been the *second*, perhaps the *third* tenant'.[1] At the height of the Famine in 1847, there were 591 cottier families on the Shirley estate, many of them tenants or under-tenants of tenants of Shirley. The neighbouring Rothwell estate of 2,300 acres had been indifferently managed for many years and in 1835 the new owner evicted fifty-two cottier families who were 'not known even by name to Mr Rothwell or his agent'. The Presbyterian minister of Smithboro in the west of the county reported in February 1847 that the local estate had been 'in the courts for the greater part of the last century' and as a result of 'having been so long deprived of any immediate acknowledged proprietor, vast numbers of cabins were built from time to time in spots of waste ground in the village and on patches of spent bog in the neighbourhood . . . [and the inhabitants are] at present reduced to a state of destitution bordering on starvation.'[2]

Where the occupiers of the land were left alone in such circumstances, the crowded and impoverished landscapes of the mid-nineteenth century were the unsustainable consequences. As Peter Mohan, a witness before the Devon Commission in 1845, observed: 'The [eleven households] in my townland have ten acres among them all. You see my condition. I am the best man that can pay rent in the townland and this is the best suit of clothes I wear.'[3] William Steuart Trench, land agent on the Shirley estate in the early 1840s, reported that there were 'many tenants houses where there are neither windows, bedsteads, tables nor chairs, and hundreds destitute of one or more of these comforts'.[4] In the west of the county in 1835, Lt Taylor of the Ordnance Survey reported that the houses were divided into three apartments, containing 'an earthen floor with no ceiling and universally thatched with straw'. One room was a bedroom for the family, the opposite end was for the cattle and in the centre was a living room for the whole household. 'Nothing can surpass the filth and dirtiness of these cabins and the enclosures around them.'[5]

The fourth-class house was the most inferior category of house occupied by the poorest classes in the country in 1841, mainly landless labourers. It was usually one-roomed, frequently windowless, though the classification was often left to the discretion of the local constabulary. Monaghan did not have the ubiquitous housing deprivation of the west, where many districts had from 60 to 80% of their housing in this category. Monaghan was part of an extensive region extending from south Leinster to northeast Ulster with 20-40% fourth-class houses. The economic role played by the linen industry and the opportunities for non-farm earnings contributed to the paradox of population pressure and lower proportions of poorer housing. Unlike Leinster, where landless populations had a labour relationship with the farm population, the Monaghan cottier was in a very vulnerable situation by mid-century. Some were linked to the larger farms in the northern and the southern extremities of the county. The Devon Commission noted that the largest farmers in Magheross parish had 40 acres; there were, however, only about ten of these in the entire parish, each having from four to six cottiers.

Correspondence on the Shirley estate indicates that a great many of the small tenant farmers had become accus-

**Clones, 11th February 1847**

In consequence of the very awful distress which prevails in this town and parish, I can no longer refrain from bringing under immediate attention of the government of this unfortunate country the fearful situation of the labouring population; I shall therefore feel obliged by your drawing the benevolent consideration of his Excellency the lord lieutenant to the following facts. The labourers of this locality have been totally deprived of employment under the Board of Works for many weeks past and, inasmuch as we are at present visited with a hard frost and deep snow, the small amount of private work has also ceased. The consequence is that hundreds of poor labourers, heads of large and starving families, are literally reduced to the situation of strolling beggars and destitute of any possible means of saving the lives of themselves, their wives and their starving children. No later than last evening upwards of 120 labourers came to my house and told me the melancholy tale of their sufferings and their woe – that they were without fuel, without clothing, without food even to supply a morsel to their famishing families. I immediately purchased, out of a small fund received from England for the purpose of relieving distressed householders, a quantity of bread to save the lives of the unhappy creatures. Yet alas! Today presents the same sad and gloomy picture, labourers begging alms from door to door and unless we get some immediate relief I have not the slightest doubt but that many deaths must take place in this locality and the fearful and heart-rending scenes of Skibberreen [sic] must disgrace this once flourishing and plentiful parish. We have exhausted local resources in the establishment of a soup kitchen under the auspices of my venerable and respected rector Dean Roper, and with the view of receiving aid from the commissariat department, we addressed a letter some weeks ago and have never been noticed by even a reply and I have no hesitation in stating and repeating that unless some instant help be sent the people must die in hundreds. Parliament may debate and do hereafter something for our land, but the power of parliament can never restore the loss of health and energy daily inflicted upon our people - the power of parliament can never affect much in removing the hourly increasing prostration and degrading demorilization [sic] of our unhappy population. For the sake of God, let something be done for us. Presentment sessions are called for Tuesday next but in the interim how many deaths may take place here none but God can tell. Our poor house is thronged – 300 over its number. I trust you will pardon the energy of this letter but our circumstances loudly call for instant aid.

*Charles Welsh, curate of Clones*

Fig. 2  Local curate Rev. Charles Welsh in a letter to the Relief Commissioners highlights the plight of the labouring poor in Clones. [Source: *Clogher Record*, Vol. 17.2, No. 2 (2001), p. 537]

holdings. The Lucas estate's tenants increased from 170 in the mid-eighteenth century to 570 in 1845 – a characteristic example of land division and demographic expansion facilitated in the early years by the development of the linen industry. This industry had been seen as an economic panacea by landowners; the Bath and Shirley estate agent noted in 1795 that 'lands in more linen manufacturing parts let for at least 25% higher than they would be worth to a farmer, and that it is also remarkable that all those who manufacture linens in the Barony of Farney, are more industrious and pay their rents more punctually than those who do not'.[7] By 1845, however, a great many of the cottiers were unemployed for two-thirds of the year. In 1841, the linen industry

tomed to subletting portions to one or two labourers. The agent on the Lucas estate further north in the county reported that often a labourer built his own house on a corner of a four- or five-acre farm, married the farmer's daughter and became his labourer. Belated attempts to restrict or remove such cottier houses by Shirley agents Trench and Morant in the years immediately before the Famine were resisted by farmers. Owen Fitzpatrick pleaded in 1844 to be allowed to keep his labourer permitted by the previous agent; that he had built a house for him, 'roofed with timber before your honour prohibited'.[6]

Many of the cottier populations were legacies of an earlier, more vibrant rural textile economy: in the Lucas estate in Castleshane there were eight mills, for example. The mid-county and western districts had a great many scutch and beetling mills, as well as bleach greens. Flax growing, spinning and weaving in the later eighteenth century, by providing increased off-farm income opportunities for tenants and cottiers, ensured more stable rental income for landowners and was an incentive for occupiers to fragment their land-

was in serious decline in the county: the 1841 Census, for instance, recorded 24,687 women engaged in the industry, mostly in spinning, and 3,400 men, all mainly concentrated in the parishes of central and west Monaghan. By the 1851 Census, their numbers had fallen to 2,331 and 1,283 respectively, many of course victims of the Famine.

Small tillage holdings were the most characteristic feature of the rural landscape and demographic context of mid-nineteenth-century Monaghan. More than a quarter of all farm holdings in much of south Monaghan and around Monaghan and Clones towns were less than 5 acres. Well over 75% of the holdings throughout most of south and mid-county districts were less than 15 acres.

## CRISIS

All this data provides a context for the onset of famine. More direct evidence from contemporary observers such as Ordnance Survey officers in the 1830s, Devon Commissioners, estate agents, as well as the pleas of clergy and some landowners during the crisis itself in the Distress Papers and Relief Commission correspondence, highlight the poverty and destitution of sections of the population before and during the Famine. The introduction of the Poor Law in the early 1840s quite quickly brought into focus the imbalances in the territorial ratios of land to people, as well as the reckless mismanagement of many estates in the previous half century.

The extent of potato failure can be conjectured by mapping the agricultural census data which commenced in 1847. Although the data are not very reliable due to what was noted as 'the disturbed conditions', they hint at the extent of potato failure by comparing the acreage of potatoes in 1847 to that of 1851, when a semblance of normality may have returned. The extent of all cultivated crops in 1847 and 1851 was not very different due largely to increased grain growing by farmers in 1847. It was the potato acreage, therefore, which changed substantially. Potatoes were most widely cultivated in those areas where the smallholders and cottiers where most numerous. At the first hint of failure, the larger farmers resorted to other crops, while the poorer classes had little alternative but to try potatoes again on their small plots. Where the 1847 acreage was low and where there were substantial numbers of smallholders, there was probably a high degree of failure in 1846 with no seed left to plant. These areas must have been particularly distressed. Great distress which ultimately caused huge population losses also occurred in the western and the northeastern districts of the county where there were large numbers of landless labourers and where the potato apparently failed greatly. In winter 1846 there was evidence of growing rebelliousness by labourers in the west and north of the county. In September, the *Northern Standard* was appalled at the destitution outside the towns with the poor peasantry subsisting on green cabbage and wild herbs: in 'some of the country villages a stranger immediately perceives a most offensive odour, which proceeds from the boiling of those coarse and unwholesome vegetables'.[8]

**SEVERE POPULATION LOSS**

County Monaghan had some of the most severe population losses in the country, part of a region extending westwards through Counties Cavan, Leitrim, Longford, Roscommon, Fermanagh, Sligo and Mayo, which lost more than one-quarter of their populations in the Famine years. Monaghan's population fell from more than 200,000 in 1841 to 141,000 in 1851. When one excludes the towns, Monaghan experienced the third heaviest rural decline in Ireland, almost 30%. Within the county, twenty-five out of its sixty-five electoral divisions had losses of more than 35%, eleven of these losing more than 40% of their populations in the decade. The decline in house numbers is perhaps the most dramatic reflection of the sweeping nature of the changes across the countryside. Aghnamullen parish in the south of the county lost more than 1,000 houses in the decade (and 5,636 people). Some townlands on the outskirts of towns and villages had extraordinary declines, like Mullanary outside Carrickmacross, whose house numbers fell from 133 in 1841 to four

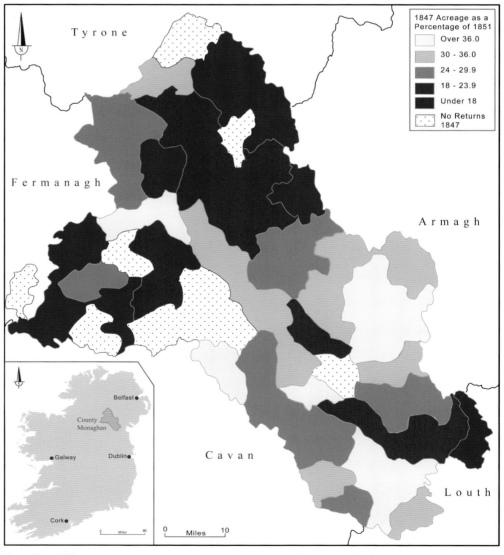

Fig. 3 THE 1847 ACREAGE OF POTATOES AS A PERCENTAGE OF 1851. This map highlights the devastation wreaked on the potato crop by 1847. In some parishes in the northeast, west and southeast of the county, less than one-quarter and sometimes less than 18% of the crop of potatoes cultivated in 1851 were sown in the more populated world of 1847. In only a few parishes did the 1847 crop even reach one-third of that sown in 1851. This map also reveals the uneven impact of the potato failures in adjacent parishes.

Fig. 4a (above)  A large number of paupers in the Carrickmacross workhouse had been evicted from the Shirley estate. Between 1841 and 1851, 1,054 paupers (540 males/514 females) died in this workhouse. The total number of deaths in workhouses in County Monaghan was 5,352. Fig. 4b (below) The fever hospital in Carrickmacross was opened in 1842 but there are no returns of deaths prior to July 1847 when it became connected to the Central Board of Health. In the period 1841–51, 367 deaths are recorded. [Photos: Patrick Duffy]

in 1851, clearly a catastrophic collapse in cottier cabins. The landscape impact of such housing decline in the post-Famine period (from Griffith's Valuation in the 1850s) is illustrated for selected townlands. While there was some alteration in holdings structure, there was not a straightforward relationship between population and house/farm decline, as a large proportion of the population decline, especially in farm households, consisted of individual members of household. In the case of cottier houses, however, there was more likelihood of the whole family abandoning house and home together. The time lag between population and house decline (with family members leaving in a trickle until the household was extinguished) was more significant in the decades after the Famine crisis: during the Famine years the immediate pressures of rents, rates and hunger among the poorest farmers led to family emigration.

As the crisis deepened in the late 1840s pressure on the rates (Poor Law taxation) for the maintenance of poor relief increased. In 1847 and 1848 the workhouses of the county were grossly overcrowded. Clones workhouse was supporting 2,600 inmates in 1848 alone, with a further 4,000 obtaining outdoor relief in auxiliary houses and sheds. Carrickmacross supported 4,000 in thirteen auxiliary houses in 1848, while Castleblayney with 3,600 inmates also supported 5,300 in outdoor facilities. Destitution, which was mirrored in the level of rates in each Poor Law Union, mainly affected the landless, cottier or smallholder population with farms of less than £4 valuation. Of the population which held land, over one-tenth in Monaghan Union was under £4 in contrast to between one-quarter and one-third in Clones and Carrickmacross unions. Holdings between £4 and £5 valuation in the county generally were broadly in the 5–15 acre category. In Castleblayney Union there were large numbers of tenants with farms valued between £4 and £5 who were under great pressure in 1847 when Poor Law rates exceeded 3s in the £ (compared with 8d prior to the Famine). As late as summer 1850 Carrickmacross Union struck a rate of 5s in the £ in two electoral divisions on the Shirley estate – a move by the 'rascally Guardians' which, in Shirley's view, would ruin them.[9]

Official state response to the crisis was exacerbated by the geographical complexities of local conditions. Active relief committees which succeeded in raising local funds were often deemed ineligible for public funds in the late 1840s. There were continuing tensions around the disjunction between relief committees' areas of responsibility, estates with resident and active owners and those which were non-resident, and estates such as Shirley's which generated disproportionate numbers of destitute families for union support.

As the crisis deepened, many landowners and farmers in the county were increasingly anxious to have rates charged on individual electoral divisions, in that 'it would

be well for some of them if they had only to support their own paupers. One portion of the union was robbed by another.'[10] A great proportion of the paupers in Carrickmacross workhouse were from the Shirley estate where an active programme of emigration and cottier reduction was taking place. The principal landowners in the county petitioned the Lord Lieutenant in November 1846 to adopt townlands in preference to electoral divisions in administering rates for relief works so that proprietors who engaged in public works would not be have to carry the burden of higher rates because of 'negligent neighbours' who refused to get involved.[11]

## DESPERATION

The desperation of smallholders being pressed by the potato failure on the one hand and rent and rate demands on the other is reflected in the appeal of Thomas and Mary Marron to Shirley's agent in February 1848:

> [We] exhort your honour . . . [O]ur forefathers for centuryes past were tenants to Mr Shirley and always paid his rent punctually . . . The emergency of the present crysis and the expense of the Burial of our parents which we had to encounter left us inadequate to pay . . . [B]ear with us until harvest as we have a good promise of a wheat crop . . . together with oats which we are about to sow, our friends will help us in putting our crops in.

The military was brought in to assist with the collection of rates in Castleblayney Union and in many cases, tenants sold up where they could and emigrated to avoid paying rates and rents. Day Books on Shirley's estate recorded the expenses incurred in 'pulling down' houses in numerous townlands: for example, fifteen houses between 1 and 6 October 1849, thirteen houses between 1 April and 25 May 1850, eleven houses between 1 May and 20 June and five houses between 28 June and 8 August.[12] Shirley was alleged to have thrown down at least 100 houses in Enagh electoral division in 1849, leaving c.500 occupants in ditches. In fact this and neighbouring divisions had the worst population losses in the county – over 47% (or 1,364 people and 231 houses) in Enagh. The numbers of landlord-assisted emigrants, however, was relatively small by comparison with those who emigrated under their own resources. However, the subsidised emigration of more than 5,000 people on the Shirley and Bath estates (and smaller numbers on other Monaghan properties) was important in priming a subsequent voluntary outflow of rural migrants.[13]

The decline in holdings of less than fifteen acres during the Famine illuminates the nature of the population decline. The most notable trend is the comparative stability in holdings in the light of the massive social and demographic

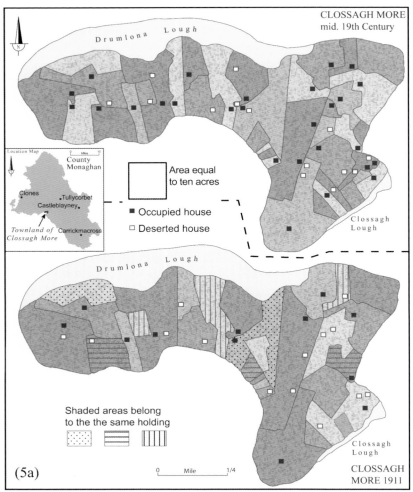

CLOSSAGH MORE
mid. 19th Century

Drumlona Lough

Area equal
to ten acres

■ Occupied house
□ Deserted house

Clossagh
Lough

Location Map

County
Monaghan

Clones
Tullycorbet
Castleblayney
Carrickmacross

Townland of
Clossagh More

Drumlona Lough

Clossagh
Lough

Shaded areas belong
to the the same holding

(5a)

0   Mile   1/4

CLOSSAGH
MORE 1911

upheaval that was taking place. The poorly-clad Peter Mohan who stood before the Devon Commission was present in Griffith's Valuation in 1860 on a 16 acre holding. This trend hints at a persistent underlying characteristic of the Famine experience for landowners and farmers – an appearance of normality in the midst of crisis. During the 1840s the Improvement Books of the large Shirley estate recorded grants and assistance given to tenants for planting hedge quicks, and for house improvements (mainly windows and roof timbers). Although the pace of such grants noticeably slowed in the late 1840s, they did not cease – in 1848 there were scores of applications for quicks (by the thousand) and pairs of windows. (The years 1847 and 1848, were also distinguished by the scores of applications for lime 'to clean house after fever'.[14]) By 1850 large

Figs 5a, 5b and 5c. THE CHANGING DISTRIBUTION OF HOUSES AND FARMS IN FOUR TOWNLANDS FROM THE MID-NINETEENTH CENTURY UNTIL 1911. These maps of the townlands of (a) Clossagh More, (b) Tattyreagh, (c) Billeady and Corlealackagh reveal the high population densities and often tiny holdings of so many families in mid-nineteenth-century County Monaghan. It also demonstrates the drastic reduction in the number and distribution of families, their houses and holdings both during and after the mid-nineteenth century as hope and life ebbed out of these once densely occupied drumlin townlands, since immortalised in the writings of Patrick Kavanagh. County Monaghan as a whole lost close on 30% of its population – from 200,442 to 141,823 – between 1841 and 1851. By 1911, its population was reduced to 71,455, just over one-third of its pre-Famine population.

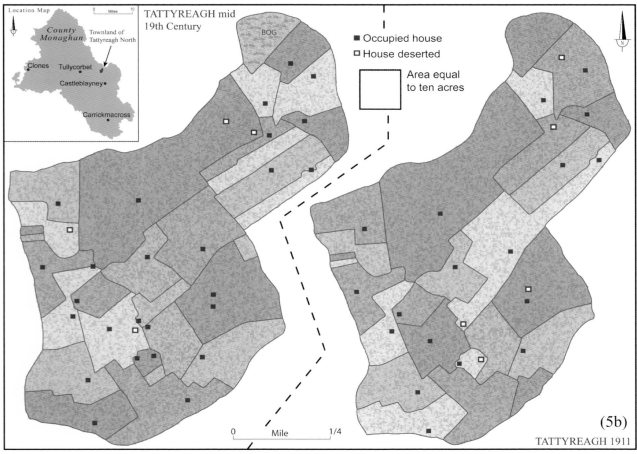

Location Map

County
Monaghan   Townland of
Tattyreagh North

Clones   Tullycorbet
Castleblayney

Carrickmacross

TATTYREAGH mid
19th Century

BOG

■ Occupied house
□ House deserted

Area equal
to ten acres

0   Mile   1/4

(5b)

TATTYREAGH 1911

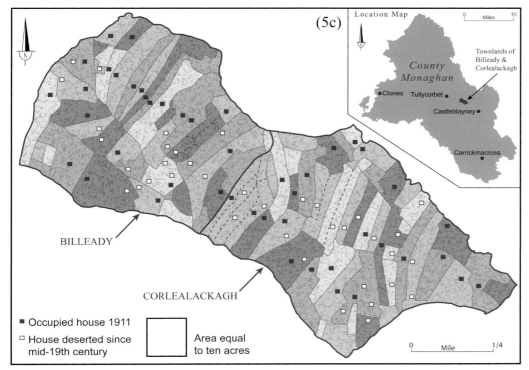

(5c)

Location Map

County Monaghan

Townlands of Billeady & Corlealackagh

Clones  Tullycorbet

Castleblayney

Carrickmacross

0 Miles 10

BILLEADY

CORLEALACKAGH

■ Occupied house 1911
□ House deserted since mid-19th century

Area equal to ten acres

0  Mile  1/4

comparatively easy, which probably helped to offset some of the local famine mortality. Traditionally, there had been a strong pre-Famine harvest migration, especially from south Monaghan into Louth and England.

## CHANGES IN HOUSE NUMBERS IN EMATRIS PARISH

Table 1 shows the changes in the house numbers in the most densely populated townlands in Ematris parish in 1841. It shows the catastrophic reduction in houses which occurred in this region after the Famine and, by implication, the character of changes in much of rural Monaghan.

Figures are given for house numbers as they appeared in the first edition of the six-inch Ordnance Survey (1835). These are not wholly reliable estimates as it is impossible to distinguish between dwellings and outhouses on the map. Where there are small groups of buildings, a range from the lowest to the highest number of

quantities of lime were being sought to accompany drainage works on farms on the estate – much of this the result of 'reproductive' relief works in the form of land drainage from 1846 onwards, which was particularly sought by relief committees in the south of the county. Elsewhere in Monaghan, 'unproductive' public relief in the form of road works ('lowering hills and filling hollows') was more common.

## DECLINE IN FOURTH-CLASS HOUSES

As many as 3,770 holdings under 15 acres (c.25% of the total) were lost at a time when the rural areas of the county lost more than 50,000 people. Clearly the massive reductions in population as a result of the Famine bore heaviest on those with no land. The dramatic decline in fourth-class houses, inhabited by the poorest sections of the population, is indicative of this social consequence. The fourth-class house was virtually eliminated in County Monaghan by 1851. Eighteen out of twenty-three parishes suffered losses of more than 75% in fourth-class houses, ten of them with losses of around 90%. The landless cottiers, in particular, were in absolute destitution following the second potato failure in 1846–47. Most of the coroner reports on sudden death at this time relate to landless families who spent the winter begging. This class, therefore, was truly transient; they seldom speak in the pages of the Devon Commission report; fleeting glimpses of them appear in the descriptions of others. In the post-Famine period, a great many of them had disappeared, like ghosts, from the local scene. Of the fifty-two cottiers evicted from the Rothwell estate in the late 1830s, 'some went to America, and some are begging and some are cottiers'.[15] Monaghan's walking distance to the ports of Dundalk and Newry made the trip to Liverpool

Table 1. Changes in house numbers in Ematris parish

| Townland | OS (1835) | 1841 (Census) | 1851 (Census) | Griffith's Valuation (1858) |
|---|---|---|---|---|
| Drumgole | 22 | 23 | 14 | 11 (2)* |
| Drumcall | 21 | 27 | 18 | 12 |
| Cornawall | 20 | 21 | 9 | 8 |
| Cordressigo | 11-12 | 16 | 8 | 5 |
| Dundrannan | 14-16 | 16 | 8 | 5 |
| Crosslea | 9-10 | 12 | 8 | 4 (1) |
| Dernamoyle | 30-34 | 49 | 21 | 12 (3) |
| Annaghybane | 17-18 | 18 | 9 | 8 |
| Derrylossett | 22-24 | 16 | 8 | 4 (2) |
| Kinduff | 25-29 | 29 | 19 | 12 |
| Derrykinard | 17 | 17 | 8 | 5 |
| Drumintin | 27 | 22 | 7 | 4 |
| Corranewy | 21-25 | 25 | 14 | 13 |
| Corragarry | 18-22 | 20 | 11 | 10 |
| Drumlona | 12 | 11 | 4 | 4 |
| Aghadrum-keen | 15-17 | 22 | 9 | 5 |
| Claraghy | 14-17 | 19 | 6 | 6 |
| Drumulla | 30-32 | 34 | 7 | 5 (1) |
| Lislynchahan | 16 | 14 | 6 | 4 |
| TOTAL | 361-391 | 411 | 194 | 145 (10) |

*houses in brackets were landless in 1858*

447

projected houses is given. By using the information on houses and holdings in Griffith's Valuation (and its accompanying map), farmhouses and landless houses in 1858 can be fairly certainly identified for 1835. Thus in Dernamoyle townland, at least ten farmhouses can be identified on the six-inch map. There were also three landless houses in the townland in Griffith's Valuation, which were there in 1835. The vast majority of the remaining houses in 1835 (from fifteen to eighteen) were therefore landless houses. There was a 5%-14% increase in houses in the six years between 1835 and 1841 – between the lowest and the highest house count for 1835. There were 411 houses in the nineteen townlands in 1841 and 194 in 1851 – a decline of 53%. There was a further reduction of one quarter between 1851 and 1858, so that in less than twenty years this small area in west Monaghan had undergone a radical transformation in population and settlement. Since the continuity of farms and farmhouses between 1835 and 1858 can be identified on the six-inch valuation maps, it is clear that the overwhelming majority of the reduction in houses in these townlands was caused by cottier houses.

## OFFICIAL RESPONSE

As elsewhere in Ireland, the official response to the crisis was marked by ponderously bureaucratic relief measures at local level. Relief committees which were not established according to regulations were ineligible for funding. Committees had to be set up by the county lieutenant. In Monaghan's case, Lord Rossmore was generally absent from the county in Britain or Europe, and gentry leadership often failed to appreciate the seriousness of the situation that was emerging locally, so that local relief measures were slow in starting and were ineffective. Committees were established a couple of months late in 1846 and many of the nominated members, especially in cases where there were no resident landowners, were inactive.

The Monaghan grand jury decided in April 1846 that there was no need to summon a meeting under the legislation to hold presentments for public works. In early May 1846 a meeting of magistrates in Dartrey barony in west Monaghan met to consider setting up local relief committees, had a desultory discussion on the potato crop, postponed setting up committees until later in the month and adjourned to landlord Kerr's mansion in Newbliss 'where a splendid *dejeuner* was in readiness for the occasion'.[16] The disjunction between the lives of the landowning (and larger farming classes) and the realities of starvation was demonstrated the following year in August 1847 when all the local relief committees in the west of the county were wound up in the expectation of a good potato crop and the passing of the new Outdoor Relief Act and a sumptious banquet was held in Clones to celebrate the erection of a local steam mill. In November 1848, at the height of the

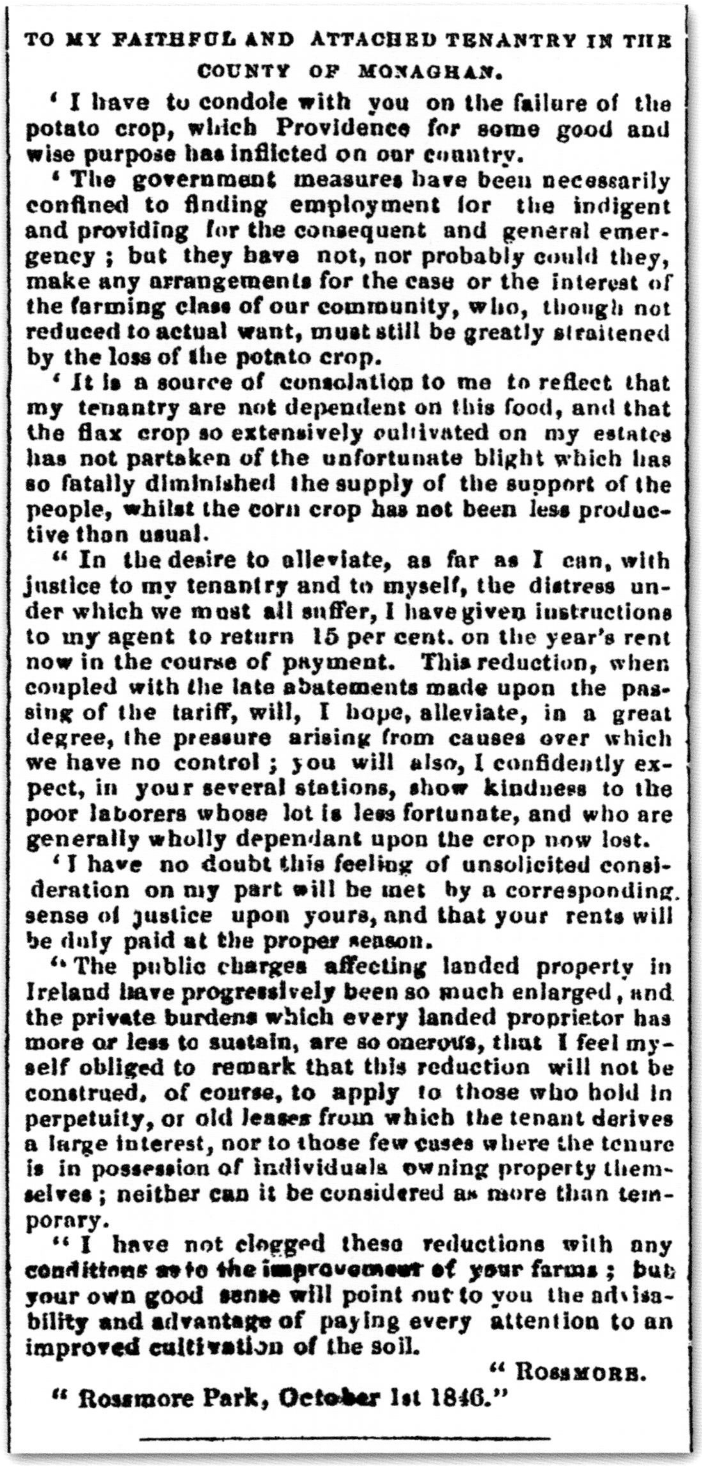

TO MY FAITHFUL AND ATTACHED TENANTRY IN THE COUNTY OF MONAGHAN.

' I have to condole with you on the failure of the potato crop, which Providence for some good and wise purpose has inflicted on our country.

' The government measures have been necessarily confined to finding employment for the indigent and providing for the consequent and general emergency ; but they have not, nor probably could they, make any arrangements for the case or the interest of the farming class of our community, who, though not reduced to actual want, must still be greatly straitened by the loss of the potato crop.

' It is a source of consolation to me to reflect that my tenantry are not dependent on this food, and that the flax crop so extensively cultivated on my estates has not partaken of the unfortunate blight which has so fatally diminished the supply of the support of the people, whilst the corn crop has not been less productive than usual.

" In the desire to alleviate, as far as I can, with justice to my tenantry and to myself, the distress under which we must all suffer, I have given instructions to my agent to return 15 per cent. on the year's rent now in the course of payment. This reduction, when coupled with the late abatements made upon the passing of the tariff, will, I hope, alleviate, in a great degree, the pressure arising from causes over which we have no control ; you will also, I confidently expect, in your several stations, show kindness to the poor laborers whose lot is less fortunate, and who are generally wholly dependant upon the crop now lost.

' I have no doubt this feeling of unsolicited consideration on my part will be met by a corresponding sense of justice upon yours, and that your rents will be duly paid at the proper season.

" The public charges affecting landed property in Ireland have progressively been so much enlarged, and the private burdens which every landed proprietor has more or less to sustain, are so onerous, that I feel myself obliged to remark that this reduction will not be construed, of course, to apply to those who hold in perpetuity, or old leases from which the tenant derives a large interest, nor to those few cases where the tenure is in possession of individuals owning property themselves ; neither can it be considered as more than temporary.

" I have not clogged these reductions with any conditions as to the improvement of your farms ; but your own good sense will point out to you the advisability and advantage of paying every attention to an improved cultivation of the soil.

" ROSSMORE.

" Rossmore Park, October 1st 1846."

Fig. 6 Landlord Lord Rossmore addresses his tenantry in the *Northern Standard*, 10 October 1846. He is adamant that the Famine which presently afflicts the people is the work of an all-wise Providence. To ameliorate the condition of his own tenants he orders a reduction in their rents and requests them to extend a similar kindness 'to the poor labourers whose lot is less fortunate, and who are generally wholly dependent on the crop now lost'. [Source: Monaghan County Library]

Famine, Shirley hosted a lavish ball with up to 200 guests to celebrate the completion of various works to his mansion, marked by '500 coloured lamps' in the Conservatory and dancing until six in the morning.

A common complaint throughout the county was the

448

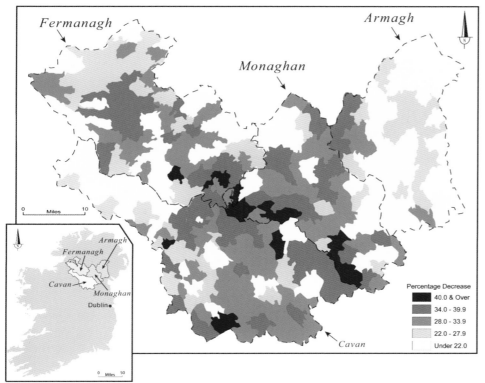

Fig. 7 POPULATION DECLINE IN COUNTIES ARMAGH, CAVAN, FERMANGAH AND MONAGHAN BETWEEN 1841 AND 1851. In a region which suffered severe population losses due to mortalities and, more particularly, high levels of out-migration, this map highlights how uneven these processes were across the four counties. Three patterns stand out. It is noticeable that most of County Armagh and the upland country of northwest Cavan return the least population losses. In sharp contrast, and apart from core areas in Counties Monaghan and Fermanagh, it is striking that the greatest population losses are in parishes which are aligned along county boundaries, possibly reflecting greater remoteness from urban areas and their support systems. Finally, the map also reveals how locally varied were the fortunes of different communities and how difficult it is to generalise about famine conditions and their effects, either within counties or across the island.

that with the Famine crisis and the elections of boards of guardians a shift in the balance of power was taking place locally, that

in any civilized country we not only *ought* to have, but would have a fair and just and preponderating influence but I believe not only that all was done at the Election of the Boards in 1846 to maintain the landlord's influence, . . . but the Priests put their whole power into the scale and the landlords were beaten.[19]

Indeed while on his journey from England in August 1848, E.J. Shirley saw first signs of blight in south Monaghan, but he was more preoccupied with a possible upsurge of violence and the arrest of William Smith O'Brien in Thurles.

Some landowners were sceptical about the value of unproductive road works, and were keen on getting works in drainage which would improve the land (and presumably the landowners' estate). There was a dawning awareness among landowners of the geographical repercussions of local relief measures as the link between local taxation (rates) and past estate management (destitute tenantry) was realised. Many landowners in 1846 favoured charging rates for public works by townland rather than electoral divisions, so that proprietors 'shall not be subject to any additional charge in consequence of other proprietors declining to take advantage of such works'.[20]

The bureaucracy of the Poor Law Commission and the Board of Works was a frequent source of frustration locally – the *Northern Standard* noting in December 1846 that the proceedings of [the Board of Works] are 'enveloped in a mystery dark and impenetrable'. The strongly unionist newspaper excoriated the government in 1847 for its policy of non-interference in the market. Clones and the western districts of the county were suffering while

we see droves of bullocks . . . winding their weary way to some port to be shipped to Liverpool. This week the dead-cart of the workhouse most impertinently intercepted a drove of those bloated natives in a narrow street of our town and the dead-cart stopped, that the living luxuries walking into the maw of England might pass on.[21]

failure of absentee proprietors to respond to requests for subscriptions from relief committees. In general, districts which lacked the support and leadership of a resident landowner, who could most effectively represent their poverty to the authorities and relief committees, suffered most. In September 1846 several hundred tenants in the parish of Aughnamullen west petitioned the Lord Lieutenant stating that their large parish contained over 9,000 people with twenty-eight landed proprietors, none of whom 'save two, have been known to look to the distresses of their tenantry during the last hard summer'.[17] Clergy tried to fill the gap and the parish priest of Currin parish, for example, submitted a list of fifteen absentee landlords to the Lord Lieutenant.[18] Smithboro failed to get support from any neighbouring relief committees because of the absence of a landed proprietor to procure a local subscription as matching funds for public relief. Local relief committees in the west of the county were meeting weekly in 1846 to receive subscriptions and employ destitute persons, each of whom had to be assessed for employment by a Poor Law inspector. The *Northern Standard* complained about the officiousness of regulations which prohibited persons with even the smallest quantity of flax from being eligible for employment on the public works.

Some landlords like Shirley in south Monaghan sensed

449

# The Management of Famine in Donegal in the Hungry Forties

## Jim MacLaughlin

If nationalists and historians generally produce poor partnerships, this may be because nationalists generally regard history as little more than a source of political legitimacy. For the historian, on the other hand, historical research brings its own rewards that often challenge the cherished dogmas of political establishments. In the case of nineteenth-century Ireland, local studies are a particularly effective means of demythologising nationalist explanations that have simplistically ethnicised the causes of the Great Famine and nationalised its solutions.[1] Thus three basic assumptions underlie most nationalist interpretations of the Famine experienced in mid-nineteenth-century rural Ireland. Firstly, it is usually implied that poverty and social disadvantage were almost exclusively confined to a rural Catholic population that had fought continuously to regain land taken from it by colonial confiscators in the sixteenth and seventeenth centuries. Secondly, it is widely assumed that the Catholic population was socially homogenous, and therefore largely devoid of the social class and status differentials that were such a feature of other European societies at that time. Thirdly, it is often suggested that the rural ascendancy in late colonial Ireland consisted, with few exceptions, chiefly of Church of Ireland Protestants or Scots–Irish Presbyterians. It is now widely recognised that none of these assumptions stand the test of historical scrutiny.[2]

### LANDHOLDING

In the case of pre-Famine Donegal, there was a small and widely dispersed Protestant ascendancy that derived its wealth from land and shared its cultural values with their social peers in lowland Scotland and the north of England.[3] This group was much thicker on the ground in the east and southwest than in the marginal lands of the rural interior and coastal fringe of the county. However, few areas were entirely devoid of a scattering of substantial landholders, estate managers and well-off tenant farmers. Of the 6,000 dwellings in the comparatively prosperous Poor Law Union of Inishowen in the early 1840s, a mere forty-five were valued at or above £50 per annum, while another fifty were in the £40–50 category. In the ethnically mixed and rich agricultural land around Raphoe, thirty-eight of the union's 1,800 dwellings were in the £50+ category, while a further

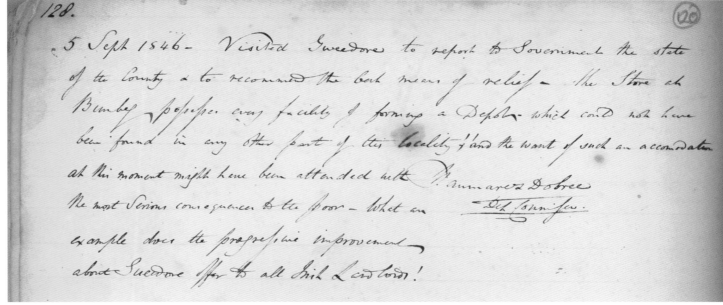

Fig. 1 An entry in the visitor's book of the Gweedore Hotel, 5 September 1846. The hotel was owned by the local reforming landlord, Lord George Hill, who was recognised for the improvements carried out on his landholdings which were c.24,000 acres in extent. It is noted in the entry that the store at Bunbeg provides every facility for the operation of a food depot, unlike other localities, while the efforts of Hill are also praised: 'What an example does the progressive improvement about Gweedore offer to all Irish landlords.' [Source: Archive Services, Donegal County Council, Lifford]

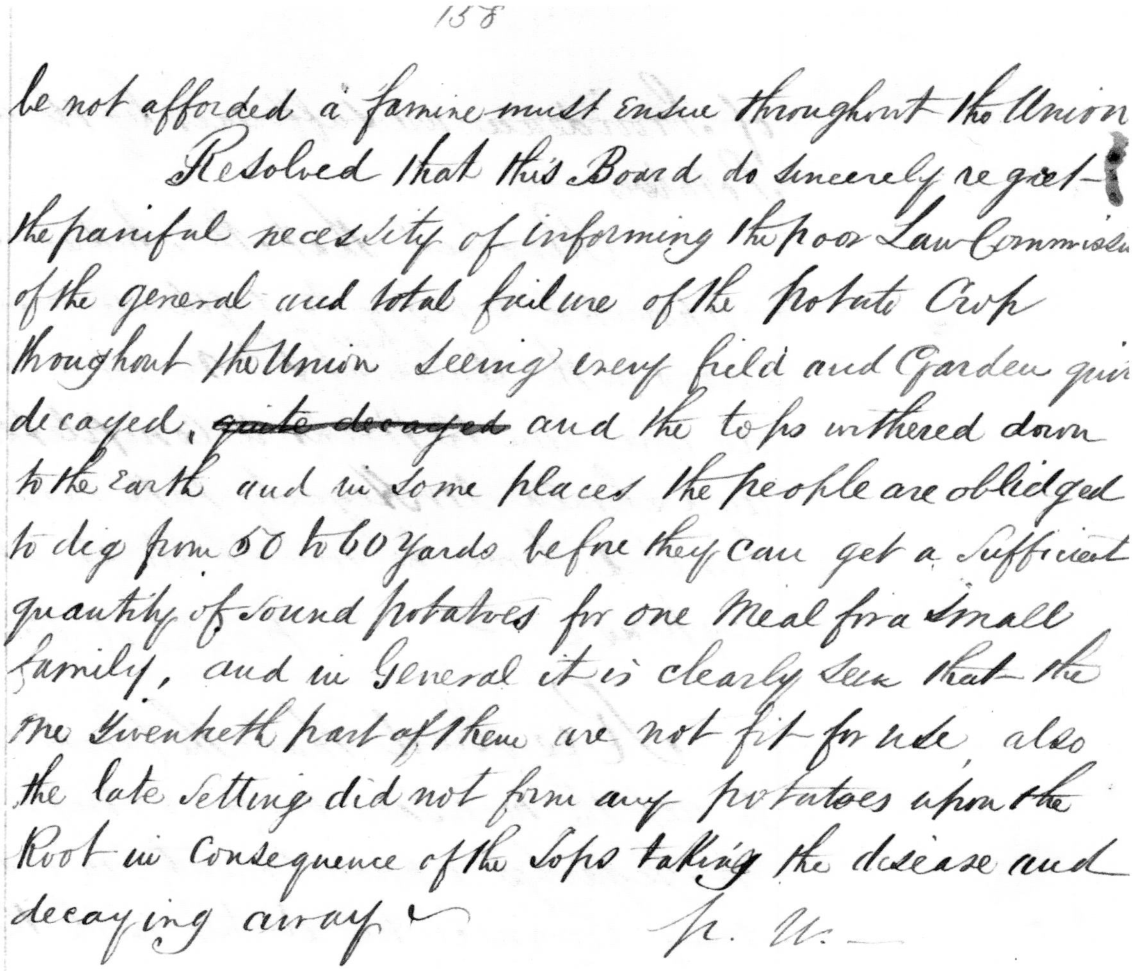
158

be not afforded a famine must ensue throughout the Union
Resolved that this Board do sincerely regret
the painful necessity of informing the Poor Law Commissi
of the general and total failure of the Potato Crop
throughout the Union seeing every field and Garden qui
decayed, ~~quite decayed~~ and the tops withered down
to the earth and in some places the people are oblidged
to dig from 50 to 60 yards before they can get a sufficient
quantity of sound potatoes for one Meal for a small
family, and in General it is clearly seen that the
one twentieth part of them are not fit for use, also
the late setting did not form any potatoes upon the
Root in Consequence of the Tops taking the disease and
decaying away —
P. U. —

Fig. 2 The failure of the potato crop in the Glenties Union as documented in the minute books of the Poor Law Guardians, 7 August 1846: 'Resolved that this Board do sincerely regret the painful necessity of informing the Poor Law Commissioners of the general and total failure of the potato crop throughout the Union seeing every field and garden quite decayed, and the tops withered down to the earth and in some places the people are oblidged (*sic*) to dig from 50 to 60 yards before they can get a sufficient quantity of sound potatoes for one meal for a small family.' The union was comprised 'principally of mountainous districts' and the Board later warned the Commissioners of the baneful consequences of famine unless 'the people be immediately relieved by the speedy intervention of government'. [Source: Board of Guardians Minute Books, Glenties Poor Law Union, Archive Services, Donegal County Council, Lifford]

thirty-five were between £40-50. Only twelve dwellings in the densely populated and much more marginal districts around Glenties in south Donegal had valuations of £30 or more, while another six were between £20 and £30 pounds. Almost two-thirds of the houses around the coastal enclaves of Killybegs and Dungloe had valuations of £5 or less in 1841. Finally, less than 8% of the dwellings in the barony of Boylagh, and 11% of those in Kilmacrennan were substantial, five-bedroomed houses or dwellings superior to that.

These were the homes of the small but influential petty bourgeoisie from whose ranks were drawn members of the Poor Law boards of guardians, and recruits to the clergy and the Royal Irish Constabulary. Accounting for around 15% of families in parts of the east and south of the county, they wielded social and political influence out of all proportion to their actual numbers. This 'rising' group of improving farmers and substantial tenants also accounted for the bulk of Donegal's agricultural exports throughout the 'Hungry Forties'. Even at the height of the Famine they sent surpluses of eggs, butter, oats, pork, wheat and flax to local markets and to the larger border towns such as Derry, Strabane and Letterkenny. In January 1847, the *Londonderry Standard* recorded a 'fair supply' of oats and wheat at the Derry market, adding that 'the supply of butter continues to be large'. At Strabane 'the quantity of oats and wheat was increased, while butter was plenty and much cheaper'.[4] Ominously also this newspaper noted that famine relief commodities such as Indian meal, bran and turnips were 'in very great demand' at this time.

For the more substantial sectors of Donegal society the Famine was a mixed blessing. It cleared whole swathes of the indigent poor from the land, and from isolated coastal areas where small fishing communities survived on the produce of inshore waters and the shoreline. However, famine also threatened widespread social disruption and caused the local rates to increase between 300 and 500% from 1844 to 1847. The management of famine relief fostered a peculiarly Irish Victorian work ethic among more substantial townsfolk and country folk, encouraging some sectors to accumulate capital and expand production on a scale that was by no means insignificant in a marginal county such as Donegal. In so doing, it contributed to the development of an indigenous business-class elite, and an organic intelligentsia and professional elite whose descendants went on to dominate the political and cultural landscape of the county in the aftermath of the Famine. Towards the end of August, 1846, when the first calamitous signs of famine were looming in the northwest, the Glenties Board of Guardians recorded the following:

Deeply deplored the melancholy disaster to which 13,752 human beings in the union are subjected to in consequence of the total destruction of the potato crop. Of the entire population, seven-eighths of householders are small farmers and occupiers whose existence at all times depended upon this article of food. This union is composed principally of mountainous districts in many parts of which grain neither fills or ripens in many places, and in many places where it does, its progress is so slow in coming to that state of perfection that the people have no relief from it.[5]

So close to the edge of subsistence were the majority of the inhabitants of this densely-populated union, that the Board of Guardians felt that 'famine, with all its baneful consequences' was unavoidable 'unless the people be immediately relieved by the speedy and benevolent intervention of Government in affording them some general system of employment'.[6] In the event, the Poor Law Commissioners advanced £35 per week to relieve starvation here in the autumn and early winter of 1846–47, raising this to £50 per week in the second half of 1848. Ironically, even

before the onset of famine, leaders of public opinion in Donegal's poorest districts often pleaded for exemption from central Government provisions for the provision and administration of welfare facilities in their localities. Thus in 1842, when many of Ireland's workhouses were already operating, a motion before the Glenties Union stated that 'a workhouse capable of accommodating five hundred inmates, rather than the standard six hundred, would be more suitable'. William Walker, who represented the local gentry who would have to meet the expense of famine relief, insisted that a house capable of accommodating 300 inmates would suit everyone's needs. Such a workhouse, he claimed was:

> In the best interests of the union – from its extreme poverty and the circumstances of the population of this wild and mountainous district who have almost all small holdings of land and are not likely to afford as many applicants for workhouse relief as the populations of other districts in the country.[7]

## POOR LAW RELIEF

Although an act for the effectual relief of the poor in Ireland

Fig. 3  Those who perished in the Glenties Union workhouse during the Famine years were buried in a paupers' plot just north of the workhouse site. During May 1847, the Poor Law Commissioners insisted that the Board of Guardians be more vigilant in the burial of those who died within the workhouse walls. [Photo: William J. Smyth]

was passed in 1838, it was not until the early 1840s that workhouses began to appear in Donegal. The prime considerations in the organisation and administration of relief were economy and restraint. In September 1846 the *Londonderry Standard* spoke for a significant minority of landowners when it advocated caution in the allocation of Poor Law relief, adding that relief of the poor was best left to those capable of developing the local economy. As a strong advocate of tenant rights, the *Standard* insisted that:

> Were landlords to set to work generally and with vigour under the Drainage Act, and were they to grant their tenantry pecuniary assistance to employ their own cottier population in the work of draining farms in their occupancy, the value of the land would be enhanced, its fertility multiplied so as to avert the dangers of periodical scarcity, and a profitable return would be ensured for every farthing of money expended.[8]

Supporting private investment for rural regeneration over the widespread allocation of poor relief, it was felt that:

> The case is very different in regard to public works, which are, in reality, only public causes for sinking a vast amount of capital, without any chance or even expectation of pecuniary returns. When a million or two of public money is to be expended for the benefit of the Irish population, it is necessary that, if possible, it should be applied in the way of a beneficially productive investment, so as to add to the permanent capital of the nation, instead of being swallowed up in the 'bottomless pit' of transient and elementary relief.[9]

In April 1847, after a 'good deal of discussion' among local officials and church leaders, it was agreed to spend £10,000 still remaining out of the sum allocated for the relief of poverty in Inishowen to improve roads linking Derry to its Donegal hinterland.

The Board of Guardians in the Glenties Union sought to ensure that the alleviation of poverty in this part of the county would not constitute a debilitating or constant burden on local landholders and improving tenant farmers. Rarely was an opportunity missed for reducing the costs of building, equipping and maintaining workhouses throughout the county. The usual procedure for furnishing workhouses was for the Poor Law Commissioners to place a standard order for furniture and make the local rate-payers meet the costs. In 1843 the Inishowen guardians petitioned the Commissioners 'not to furnish the workhouse with furniture of any kind, as it is the opinion of the Board of Guardians that they will be able to furnish the house on better terms than the Commissioners'.[10] Only at the height of

the Famine did local rate-payers even consider extending relief to those with valuations lower than £5 per annum, and even then this came with the stipulation that relief would only go to those who abandoned all claim to their tiny holdings – as per the Gregory clause. This meant that many tenancies in remote upland areas reverted to scrubland, while those in low-lying areas near the coast were available to improving farmers and well-off tenants. This was particularly the case in coastal districts where the potato famine drove many smallholders off the land and sounded the death knell of mixed farming and fishing communities which for centuries depended on the rich, but commercially under-exploited, resources of Donegal's shoreline and inshore waters.

## RURAL BOURGEOISIE

Although somewhat below the status of the substantial landlord class in the rural heartlands of the country, Donegal's scattered rural bourgeoisie was growing in wealth and influence in the period prior to the Famine. With the introduction of Poor Law legislation its interests were represented alongside those of substantial Church of Ireland and Presbyterian landholders on Poor Law boards of guardians throughout the county. Social class allegiances were as important as religious affiliations for membership of this social collectivity, whose members were social Darwinists before Darwinism was used as a political doctrine to advance laissez-faire rural capitalism in the county.[11] Steeped in the philosophy of the free market, they resisted central government attempts to effectively make the socially advantaged the guardians of the poor in their districts. Thus local boards of guardians implemented strict rules governing the administration of relief throughout the county in the 1840s and pragmatically tailored these to suit local conditions.

Despite the sanctity of family life in rural Catholic Ireland, the Inishowen guardians in the autumn of 1847 resolved that 'no part of a family should be admitted to the workhouse without the head of the family'. In June of that year, a number of cases were tried before the Carndonagh Petty Sessions to establish whether or not nine female inmates of the workhouse were eligible for relief. In their patriarchal wisdom the authorities resolved that the women and their children, a number of whom were from the Presbyterian and Church of Ireland community, should be discharged until such time as the husband of each should come into the workhouse with his wife and children. In so doing the guardians clearly signalled that Donegal's workhouses were not to become women's refuges, places where unmarried mothers could feel protected and where their children could be nurtured.[12]

Another ruling stipulated that if any inmate left the workhouse, for whatever reason, they would not be readmitted until they remained outside it for more than three weeks. In December 1847, the Glenties Board of Guardians urged the Poor Law Commissioners to establish only one outdoor relief station to cater for the needs of the rural poor in Carrick and Glencolumcille, rather than one depot for each of these densely populated districts as recommended by an officer appointed by the Commission. The guardians of the union, half of whom were Roman Catholics, insisted that this would improve the supervision of outdoor relief, while simultaneously reducing administrative costs. They sought:

> To assure the Commissioners that the allocation of relief stores was an act of mature deliberation [which sought] to carry out the provisions of the Extension Act with the greatest possible economy, and that it is most essential to have a relief store in the centre of each district in order that the weak and infirm who are the real objects of relief may be forced to attend in person for their allowance and not through proxies.[13]

Incidences and responses to the Famine varied significantly throughout Donegal in the Hungry Forties. Conditions in the west and northwest more closely resembled those along the west coast of Ireland than the rural interior and east of the county. That is not to say that extreme rural poverty was unknown in the richer agricultural lands around Raphoe, Inishowen and Dunfanaghy. However, because these areas already possessed the rudiments of a health-care system at the start of the 1840s, they were somewhat better placed to tackle the problem of poor relief during and immediately after the Famine. In 1841, for example, the Poor Law Union of Inishowen had dispensaries for treating contagious diseases at Buncrana, Moville, Clonmany, Carndonagh and Culdaff. A qualified medical officer attended each of these on a monthly basis. In the late 1830s these centres received almost £300 from private subscriptions, and an equal amount from public funds. Ministering to approximately 10,000 inhabitants, they spent around £350 on medical salaries, and a mere £150 went on medicines. In contrast

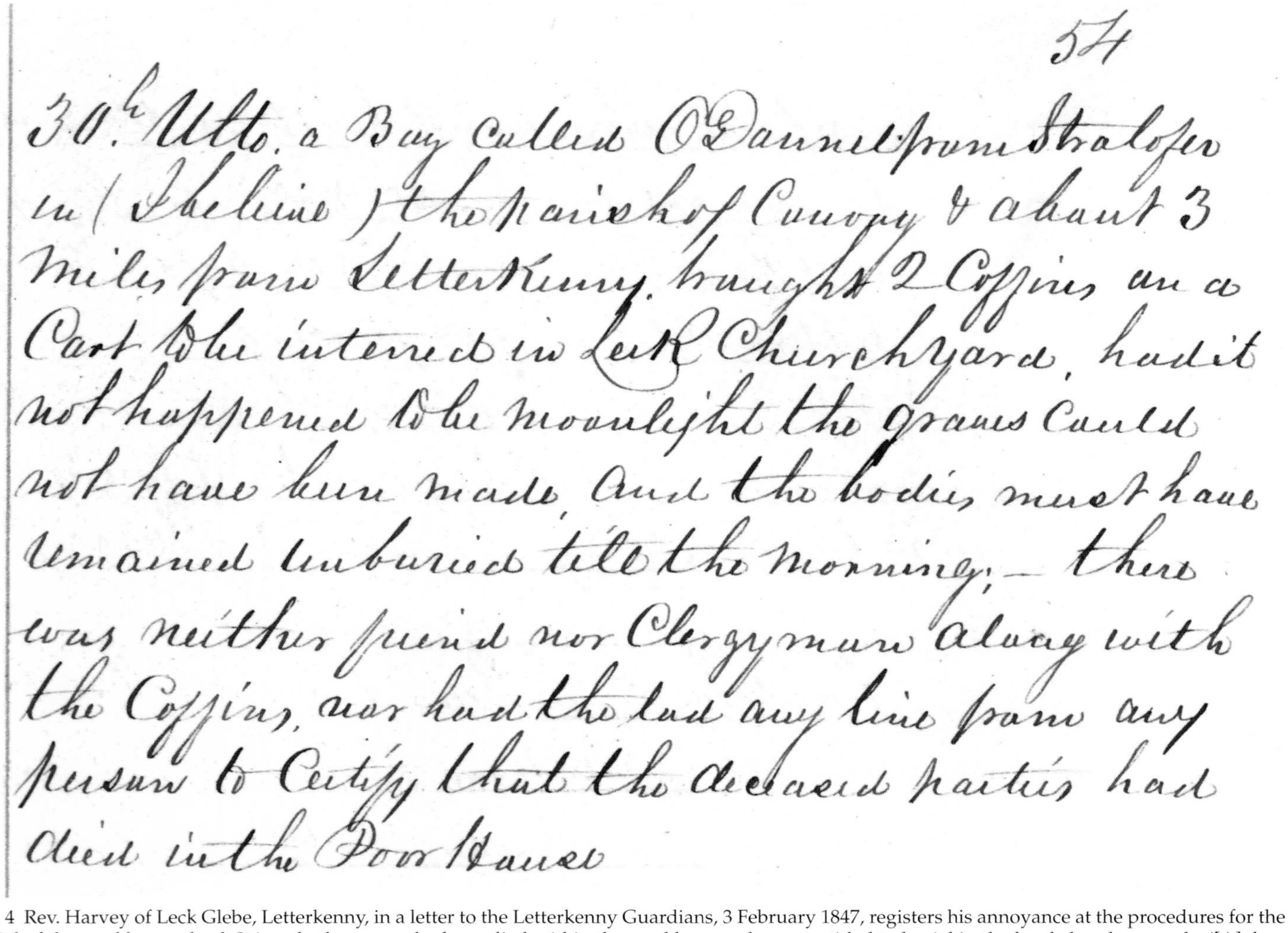
54

30th Ulto. a Boy called O'Donnell from Stranorlar in (I believe) the parish of Convoy & about 3 miles from Letterkenny, brought 2 Coffins on a Cart to be interred in Leck Churchyard, had it not happened to be moonlight the graves could not have been made, and the bodies must have remained unburied till the morning; – there was neither friend nor Clergyman along with the Coffins, nor had the lad any line from any person to certify that the deceased parties had died in the Poor House

Fig. 4 Rev. Harvey of Leck Glebe, Letterkenny, in a letter to the Letterkenny Guardians, 3 February 1847, registers his annoyance at the procedures for the burial of the workhouse dead. It is only the poor who have died within the workhouse who are entitled to burial in the local church grounds: '[A] boy named O'Donnell from Stranorlar in the parish of Convoy, about three miles from Letterkenny, bought two coffins on a cart to be interred in Leck churchyard. [H]ad it not happened to be moonlight the graves could not have been made and the bodies must have remained unburied till the morning – there was neither friend nor clergymen along with the coffins, nor had the lad any line from any person to certify that the deceased parties had died in the Poor House (sic) . . . ' Such situations were widespread during the Famine, given the extent of the mortality and the extreme pressure on burial plots. [Source: Archive Services, Donegal County Council, Lifford] to this, the extensive Poor Law Union of Glenties had only three dispensaries, and was so hard pressed for medical personnel that the local apothecaries were enlisted as medical officers to deal with the tremendous upsurge in rural illness and disease throughout the Famine years and well into the 1850s.[14]

## MAINTAINING PAUPERS

Nowhere was greater economy taken than in measures to reduce the costs of maintaining paupers in workhouses. While Poor Law Commissioners were largely responsible for setting dietary regulations in the workhouse system, local guardians had considerable autonomy over the workhouse diets and placed orders for food and other workhouse materials with local businesses. Indeed, the costs of maintaining paupers in Donegal workhouses were constantly under review. On the eve of the Famine, it was estimated that paupers in the Carndonagh workhouse could be fed for two shillings per person per week. By August, 1847, when the numbers of relief applicants was on the increase, that figure was trimmed back to one shilling and six pence. In the early 1850s, when several workhouses were still filled to capacity, the cost of maintaining inmates was reduced as low as ten pence per week per pauper. Strict economy also surrounded the disposal of the workhouse dead.[15]

'Famine fever' made its first appearance in Donegal in the winter of 1847 and rapidly became endemic in impoverished and densely populated districts in the southwest of the county. In inaccessible mountainous and remote coastal districts, medical officers often had great difficulty in accessing the sick poor. Many of those affected by fever in the Glenties Union could only be reached by sea. The incidence of fever was so great in some workhouses that guardians insisted that they should be 'immediately emptied' to prevent contagious disease 'breaking out throughout town and country'. In May 1847, the Poor Law Commissioners felt it necessary to urge the board of guardians at Glenties 'not to bury paupers nearer the walls of the workhouse than can be possibly avoided, and that the graves made near the walls be covered with at least six feet of clay'.[16]

In Carndonagh, where the workhouse was located at an elevated site on the outskirts of the town, famine fever struck in the winter of 1847. Here, as in the areas around Glenties, great care was taken to ensure that the disposal of the workhouse dead would not contaminate local water supplies. Thus paupers who died of fever were generally buried within the confines of the workhouse grounds. Care was also taken to ensure that burial costs would be kept to a minimum. In a number of unions, coffins with sliding false bottoms were used to dispose of the dead, and black shrouds were occasionally also used to cover the dead. In 1847, the Poor Law guardians in the comparatively prosper-

Fig. 5 Ballyshannon workhouse. Between 1841–51, 1,152 people died in Ballyshannon workhouse (589 male/563 female), by far the greater number than in any other workhouse in County Donegal and constituting more than a quarter of workhouse deaths in the county. [Photo: William J. Smyth]

ous region in the south of the county accepted a contract which priced 'large size' coffins at 3s 11p, and 'half size' coffins at 2s. In June 1847, the guardians of Glenties Union accepted the terms of a local carpenter who contracted to supply coffins at the following rates:

Persons not above three years one shilling and nine pence
Persons three to nine years two shillings and five pence
Persons nine to fifteen years two shillings and ten pence
Persons fifteen years and upwards three shillings and five pence.[17]

Burial costs were only paid for those who died within the workhouse, and did not apply to the hundreds of rural destitute who passed away in their own cabins. Thus in 1847, the Inishowen guardians passed a ruling that 'persons who die while their names are on the Outdoor Lists cannot be legally provided with coffins out of the Poor Rates'. In the spring of the following year it was resolved that 'husbands whose wives and families are in the House are not entitled to Relief'.[18]

## BUSINESS GENERATED BY POOR RELIEF

The parsimonious approach to payments of relief and bur-

ial costs did not extend to the imbursement of the salaries of petty officials, or other running costs of the county's workhouses. In remote rural areas with large workhouse populations, the incomes of poor relief officials, and the amount of business generated by poor relief, were not inconsiderable. This was especially the case in areas where opportunities for professional employment were scarce, and where cash incomes were so small as to be practically non-existent. Thus Thomas Doherty, a former land agent and 'improving landed proprietor' from the relatively prosperous area around Redcastle in the Inishowen Union, told the Devon Commission that:

The poor-law tax is . . . a heavy burden both on the landlords and their tenantry and is effecting but very little good for the poor. The greater part of the costs of supporting the workhouses is occasioned by the defrayment of the expenses of the staff which it is considered expedient to put into requisition, and not in anything having relation to the sustenance of the poor themselves.[19]

The construction and management of workhouses, together with the disciplining of the poor, clearly benefited some sectors of Donegal society more than it did others. The

Fig. 6 Milford workhouse cemetery, County Donegal. 283 (160 males/123 females) people died in Milford workhouse, constituting the second lowest death rate in County Donegal – representing only 6.9% of the total number of workhouse deaths in the county. Stranorlar recorded only 227 deaths. Both of these unions in the north of the county were under least pressure during the Great Famine benefiting from the complex of conditions including landlord benevolence, less dependence on the potato and access to coastal resources. [Photo: William Gallagher]

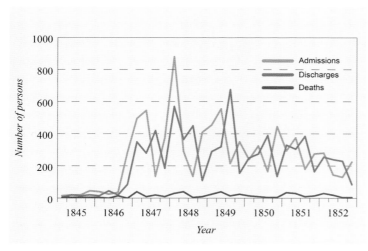

Fig. 7 Estimated quarterly figures for Inishowen workhouse, 1845–52. At Inishowen workhouse, numbers admitted averaged twenty-eight per quarter year until October–December 1846, when admissions surged to 285 and reached 545 in April–June 1847. Numbers declined somewhat over the remainder of the year, but they reached 880 in January–March 1848. There were wintertime peaks subsequently, but overall admission numbers gradually declined to c.200 by 1852. High levels of discharges in the workhouse seem to follow on from peak admissions. As compared with southern and western union workhouses, death rates remained relatively low, peaking at forty in January–March 1847, April–June 1848 and April–June 1849. Only five died in the October–December quarter of 1852. [Source: National Famine Research Project, Dublin]

regular and assured purchases of food, clothing and other goods required in the day-to-day running of large workhouses often went a long way towards guaranteeing the solvency of businessmen and medical officers in remote areas. In March 1848, when the workhouse at Carndonagh was filled to capacity, the workhouse clerk had his salary increased from £30 to £50.[20] The minutes of January 1843 recorded that William Wilson, Valuator of the union, received £162 for services rendered to the guardians. In addition to clerical staff, each workhouse employed a master, a matron, a porter, a teacher and his/her assistants.[21] In the Inishowen workhouse the master received an annual salary of £30, while the matron was paid £20. The corresponding figures for the much poorer Glenties Union were £22 and £15, respectively. Workhouses also employed up to four medical officers at dispensing centres scattered throughout the county, each of whom was paid between £25 and £30 per annum.

Payment for workhouse duties also supplemented the meagre cash incomes of Roman Catholic and Protestant clergymen in the county. The Roman Catholic priest who ministered to the poor in the workhouse at Carndonagh was paid £30, while other chaplains received £20 per annum

A considerable number of jobs were also created through the administration of outdoor relief. In 1847, the guardians of Glenties Union appointed fifty wardens to supervise the administration of outdoor relief in each electoral division of the union. The total salary of this group was approximately £600. When famine stress increased in the autumn of 1847, the Inishowen Union was also divided into four relief districts and a relieving officer, who was paid a salary of £35 per annum, was appointed to each of these. This was in addition to twenty other officers already employed in that union on similar salaries.

Two of the most important government agencies operating in Donegal from the 1840s to the dawn of the twentieth century were the Poor Law boards of guardians and the Congested Districts Board. The middling tenantry and improving landholders dominated the boards of guardians from the start. As a result, they became platforms where substantial farmers and petty merchants voiced their concerns about everything from the rates question to the relief of the poor, from tenant rights to rural destitution, and from the need for assisted emigration, to the state of local government. This group literally managed the Famine in their interests, ensuring that poor relief would not constitute an excessive drain on their comparatively meagre resources.

Throughout the Famine and its immediate aftermath local landholders controlled the market for agricultural goods, fostered the development of rural tourism, provided credit facilities for successful farmers, and practised 'rate-capping' on a large scale. From their socially strategic positions in small towns and rural communities, they imposed their own Hiberno-Victorian worldview, with its puritanical ethos and parsimonious attitudes, on the more profligate and pauperised sectors of Donegal society. Boards of guardians also fostered the formation of a cohesive rural middle class, complete with its own 'priestocracy' and 'shopocracy'.[22] These sectors of Donegal society cut their political teeth in the meeting rooms of the boards of guardians. The latter in turn became platforms for the protection and advancement of their class interests in a plebeian environment not all that suited to the process of capital accumulation and the growth of a salaried middle class. In so doing, they helped these 'men of the highest respectability' to take their first faltering steps towards political maturity, causing them to literally carve a new county out of what they considered the human debris and social flotsam of the Famine.

An Irish Eviction (oil on panel) by Frederick Goodall (1822–1904). [Source: New Walk Museum & Art Gallery, Leicester, UK/ Photo © Leicester Arts & Museums/ The Bridgeman Art Library]

# The Great Famine in Gaelic manuscripts

## Neil Buttimer

Irish was no longer the language of a ruling class or of public administration after 1700. Nevertheless, it remained widely spoken in the eighteenth and early nineteenth centuries. The circulation of handwritten Gaelic documents which prevailed in the Middle Ages also continued during the latter period. This situation resembles that of other societies marginalised on geographic, cultural or alternative grounds.[1] Among those, access to print as a publishing outlet was limited. Copyists entered into manuscripts their experience of contemporary happenings. These were retold in both prose and verse. Poetry was the age-old medium for commentary on the affairs of the day, being easily memorised and resonant. In line with this tradition, Gaelic authors active in the mid-1800s and afterwards gave us their witness of the Great Famine as well as its impact. None of the statements is as extensive as ones issued in official or governmental compilations. This could reflect the reality that Irish-language composers were occasional rather than full-time chroniclers, being engaged in other occupations for their livelihood.

In addition, modern accounts, because often short, may mirror the medieval practice of conciseness in recording events, however important. Such brevity might have resulted from concerns like a desire to save space when using costly or valuable writing materials. The laconic nature of certain contributions could have a deeper foundation also. Here, the challenge for us is to identify what people in the past believed constituted an action or an occurrence or even a fact, and how or to what degree they relayed those phenomena. Further clarification of such epistemological topics must be left first to research into earlier phases of human existence. The debate, of necessity, will have parameters both philosophical and linguistic,[2] each of these categories being essentially inseparable from one another. Suffice it to say that, previously, incidents of critical significance were often encapsulated in nothing more extensive than one solitary phrase. Condensing matters thus could arise from a variety of reactions, some emotional: shock, bewilderment or incomprehension. Simultaneously, a single statement, a concentrated act of narration, capturing time momentarily, might have represented an intellectual challenge: a call to consider in a focused way what was or was not held to be important and with reference to which scheme of things. These expressions, even if scarcely as evocative as aphorisms, would have held complex latent messages. It is likely that the earlier approach of conveying much in a small amount left a legacy to the writings under review here. One would wish to deliberate further on the compositional process in question for enlightenment on perception, cognition, meaning and identity in Ireland. However, that enquiry would take us beyond our immediate aims. The chapter turns instead to the primary task of outlining what the compilers of the documentary sources under discussion knew of the Famine, and particularly their thoughts on it.

### BACKGROUND

Reports of the Great Hunger in Irish-language compendia are part of an established convention of noting instances of societal or natural upheaval from pre-Norman times onwards. Information from the seventeenth century shows this type of recording endured into the early modern period. The 1640s were particularly troubled. Ulster's Irish population revolted against the province's recent settlers.[3] They took advantage of the difficulties posed to English authority in Ireland by civil war then in train throughout Britain. Attacks on planter landholdings and residences were followed by their proprietors' reprisals, aided by Scottish reinforcements. This resulted in sustained warfare during that decade. The activities and their consequences were described in a quasi-military diary, most likely by the Franciscan friar, Toirdhealbhach Ó Mealláin.[4] Already towards early to mid-1643, substantial sections of the community throughout counties like Antrim and Down were reduced to lawlessness and starvation (Fig. 1a and 1b). Theft of cattle, horses, sheep and goats appears to have been endemic. So was the stealing of available milk supplies from 'churns' (cunneog). Any 'poor person' (duine lom) was to be punished severely for such misdemeanours by measures like 'hanging' (crochadh), while a transgressor who was otherwise 'well-to-do' (fer suime) would be fined (togbhail suas ar a mhaoin). This suggests pilfering was widespread among the lower orders. Those in demanding circumstances were 'snatching cats' (fuadach cat) and 'dogs' (madradh), or engaged in cannibalism (ag ithe daoine). They also attempted to derive sustenance from unlikely products like leather trappings (leathar carbaidhi. agus leathar fo na aol.). The immediate link between these incidents and conflict cannot be doubted. They were recorded by a participant in the fray, a supporter of the insurgent interest. The fact that those who took measures to counteract cases of social unrest were his own allies must lend the churchman's chronicle of extreme behaviour particular validity. In the present context, it may be worth remarking that Ó Mealláin's work, cast self-consciously in annalistic style, was much sought after well into the nineteenth century for its reportage of the occurrences at issue (for transcripts or translations, see Royal Irish Academy (RIA), Mss 23 H 7 and 12 K I).

Later Gaelic commentators distinguished between bouts of hardship originating in civil strife and those whose main causes were environmental. This may be seen in descriptions of unusually harsh weather from late 1739 and afterwards. Its devastating effects on staples like the potato lead to widespread mortality throughout the years to follow.[5] A Dublin resident, Tadhg Ó Neachtain, son of a County Roscommon historian father who moved to the metropolis in the late 1600s seeking employment following dispossession during the Cromwellian period, noted these matters. Tadhg made entries into his Irish-language codices of happenings in his own private life and that of his neighbourhood, drawing frequently on contemporary newspapers.[6] He speaks of the arrival of 'severe frost' (*sioc anmhor*) in December 1739, recounting its impact on shipping in the harbours of Ireland and Britain, with vessels and their crews becoming 'ice-bound' (*siocioghe a leacaibh oidhre*). He shows awareness of a steep increase in commodity prices by summer 1740, as food shortages began to affect both the availability and cost of bread, meat and milk products, as well as potatoes. An item of his from 1741 talks about mass deaths and burials in Munster, and, in Con-

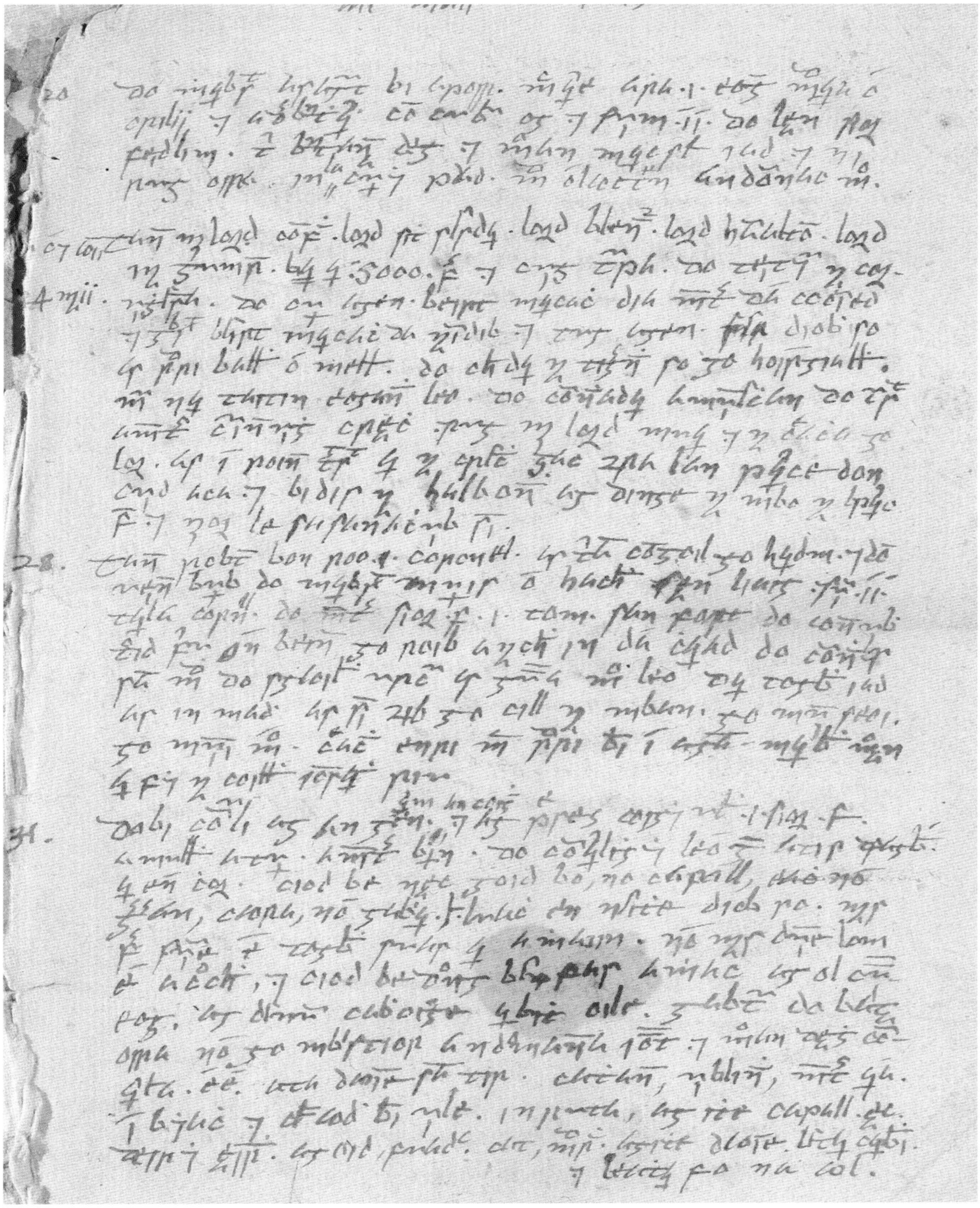

Fig. 1a  Conflict and distress throughout Ulster, from Antrim (*Trian Conghail*) to Monaghan (*Muineachan*), during May 1643, as reported in Friar Ó Mealláin's Diary (from original document in University College, Cork, Murphy MS 3, p. 15, courtesy of Crónán Ó Doibhlin). Actions listed include troop movements of Irish insurgents, countermeasures by settler and Scottish forces, plundering for supplies (*cruinnuigh creach*), together with their distribution (*roinn*) or hoarding (particularly with reference to cattle, *ag dingne na mbo 'na bpairc féin*) by various parties, in addition to widespread fatalities (*Marbhadh moran*). [Photo of UCC manuscript by Tomas Tyner]

nacht, stories of sickness (*tinneas fiabhrasach*) and 'tragedy' (*oidheadh*) resulting from eating unsuitable greens like nettles and weeds. Ó Neachtain is loud in his praise of Lord Mountjoy's and his wife's 'charity' (*carrthanach*) and 'humanity' (*daonnacht*) during their unceasing endeavours to elicit aid from Ascendancy and other Irish public figures so as to finance relief schemes for Dublin's 'indigent' (*boicht*).

461

Do bhī Comhuirli ag Gen.[4] Airm an Chōigidh[5] agus ag Preses Cōigidh Uladh .i. Sior F[eidhlim] i Mullaigh a' Tuir i Muinteir Bhirn. Do comhairligheadh leó gan a' tīr d'fhāgbháil ar énchor. Ciodh b'é neach ghoid bō nó capall, each nó gearrān, caora nó gabhar no luach ēn-neithe dhīobh so, mās fer suime é tōgbhail suas ar a mhaoin, nó mās duine lom é a chrochadh ; agus ciodh b'ē drong bhenfas amach[6] ag ōl cuinneog, [nó] ag dēnumh cabhoige ar bith oile, gabtur do bhata orra nō go mbristior a ndromanna ionnt[a] ; agus mōrān deagh-chomharleadha eile. Atā daoine san tīr, Cathānaigh, [D]uibhlinigh, muinter Ára, Íbh Eathach,[7] agus Clann Aodh Buidhe uile, in Rūta, ag ithe capall, each ; deireadh Earraigh ; a' goid ; fuadach cat ; madraidh ; ag ithe daoine ; lethar carbaidhi ; agus leathar fo na aol.[8]

Fig. 1b  Famine-induced deprivation and hardship noted for 31 May 1643 in Friar Ó Mealláin's Diary, as edited by Tadhg Ó Donnchadha, 'Cín Lae Ó Mealláin', *Analecta Hibernica*, No. 3 (September, 1931), p. 20. [Photo: Tomas Tyner]

In one passage, he says 4,000 persons were helped daily by such measures. This confirms the crisis frequently elicited a non-sectarian response which also transcended class divides. Tadhg's views counter the assumption that Gaelic sources are entirely anti-authoritarian in their outlook.

A unified approach to mitigating the same adversity also comes across in the poetry of the east-Cork author, Séamus Mac Coitir.[7] One of his works, *Ní cogadh ná caragail fhada idir ardríthibh* ('It is not warfare or prolonged dispute between high kings'), states unequivocally that the 1739 disaster was climate-induced. Although it bore all the harmful hallmarks of conflict, this time the unwelcome outcome was generated by a 'frost war' (*cogadh . . . an tseaca*) rather than a struggle between rulers. The evocation of combat in this latter citation as well as the verse's first line might have been intended to contrast current affairs with what had happened previously in the 1600s. The poem claims the loss of the potato crop (*na potátaí*) was widely lamented by the people (*is fairsinge ghnáthchaoinid*). Its absence brought 'misery and want' (*ainnise is airc*), 'sighing, crying and sorrow to housewives' (*osna is atuirse is mairg ar mhnáibh tí*) and others. Penetrating physical disability (*orchra im scartaibhse*) was visited on the poet himself, apparently. In a subsequent composition, *Créad an fhuaimse ar fuaid na dtíortha* ('What is this rumour throughout the land?'), Mac Coitir lauded a member of the local aristocratic Barry family for assisting the needy. A third piece, *M'atuirse ghéar, mo phéin, mo bhrón, mo bhroid* ('My harsh sorrow, my distress, my grief, my trouble'),

Fig. 2  Kerry winter landscape, 2011. References to calamitous events like the great frost and famine of 1740–41 can be found in the writings of Dublin resident, Tadhg Ó Neachtain, who recorded not only the arrival of a severe frost (*sioc anmhor*) in December 1739 but also its dire consequences in terms of starvation and mortality. The impact of the 1740–41 famine is also captured in the poetry of Séamus Mac Coitir from east Cork. [Photo: Frank Coyne]

recalled how efforts on behalf of the disadvantaged on the part of the Barrys or other notables in east Munster's Power Country were complemented by those of ecclesiastics in Cloyne (*déirc is daonnacht i nEaspag Chluanach*).

Assertions within the same poetic tracts of rent being demanded while the potatoes rotted (*glaoch ar airgead fearainn is fataí a' lobhadh*) do not seriously diminish that feeling of communal solidarity otherwise present in the poem. This is despite the writer's depiction, as late as 1739, of denominationally based disputes locally in the Bride River valley concerning the management of tithes. Such tensions are manifest throughout his verse text, *Is mé an chrínbhean chnaoite gan aird* ('I am an old withered woman without esteem', in RIA Ms 23 M 11: 206–10). In it, Séamus Mac Coitir speaks plaintively as Ireland personified (a mode of expression which we shall encounter later below) as he decries machinations to deprive a Catholic clergyman, based in the barony of Kinnatalloon, of his entitlements. It is worth reflecting briefly on the implications of such a composition. The

Blue text = 1640s
Red text = 1739 - 40s
Purple = pre-Famine
Black text = Famine era

ESRI Topographic map, (not to scale)

Fig. 3 INSTANCES OF HUNGER, DISEASE AND MORTALITY ARISING FROM FAMINE CONDITIONS THROUGHOUT IRELAND (MID-1600S TO MID-1800S) MENTIONED IN CONTEMPORARY GAELIC MANUSCRIPT SOURCES (WITH REFERENCE TO PLACE OR DISTRICT).

downturn of 1739 and afterwards might not have been sufficiently lasting when compared with its successor in the mid-1800s to bring about that psychological reaction to disaster now known as 'donor fatigue'. However, had the distress of the early 1740s gone on for longer, one wonders to what extent the prevailing benevolence could have been affected by negative sentiment rippling below the surface. Redaction of various of these Mac Coitir works at different points in the next century (such as a recension of *Ní cogadh ná caragail fhada* found in RIA Ms 23 0 39: 198, possibly to be dated to 1818) may reveal the extent to which circumstances described in them continued to seem relevant to future copyists. Thus the Dublin-based bookseller and Irish-language enthusiast, Seán Ó Dálaigh,[8] wrote *Créad an fhuaimse* and *M'atuirse ghéar* out again in the course of the 1850s (in RIA Ms 24 M 5: 93–96, for example). That Waterford-born writer has to have sensed those works' resonance during the recent debacle of his own era.

Annotating contemporary difficulties, actual or potential, via the medium of Irish persisted in the early 1800s. The County Kilkenny-based diarist, Amhlaoibh Ó Súilleabháin, mentions in that language the subsistence crises of 1827, before the same year's potato harvest became fully available in autumn, or those of 1830, when exigencies in Kerry, his

native county, led to reminiscing about privations in 1740.[9] Information concerning conditions of the previous century may have been conveyed to him as a family memory. There were extensive cholera outbreaks in the mid-1830s which Ó Súilleabháin describes as well and whose effects are also the subject of commentary in Gaelic homilies of the time.[10] In light of the diverse ways the tradition notes such occurrences (Fig. 3), works more overtly literary than factual may nevertheless accurately portray events about to unfold as the nineteenth century progressed. Take, for instance, a piece beginning *Céad míle fáilte romhat a bhanríon na scéimhe!* ('One hundred thousand welcomes to you, o beautiful queen!', from RIA Ms 23 E 12: 258–59). Its Drogheda author, Brian Ó Tumaltaigh, could have composed the tract when a visit by Queen Victoria was thought likely in 1845. While praising her, the poem suggests her Irish subjects require whatever support the monarch can make available:

*Uch! a bhanríon mhín! 's gan aon nduine leár n-éagaoin!*
*'gus inn creachta, 'gus gointe, 'gus scaipthe chum gach réigiúin,*
*gan éadach, gan oideas, 'nár seachránaithe ' sclábhaithe,*
*is dream an uabhair 'ár ndiaidh sa mbaile go cumhachtach! . . .*

*'S na mílte ' fáil bháis tré anródh 's na críochaibh!*
*A Dhé uilechumhachtaigh! cá bhfuil creideamh an*
*Bhíobla?*

Alas! gentle queen!, there is no one to lament us! We
are destroyed and injured and scattered to every
region, unclad, unlettered, like wandering slaves,
and a haughty crew pursue us powerfully at home!
. . .

There are thousands dying of distress in the land!
Omnipotent God! where is the faith of the Bible?

If the Famine was not indeed under way when those
lines were penned, the work may anticipate already the
backdrop against which the tragedy would soon develop.
Optimism that Victoria's intervention could prove positive
might not have been shared universally. Writing in 1849,
William Hackett, member of a successful distilling family
from Midleton, County Cork, reported to his correspondent,
the County Louth Gaelic scholar, Nioclás Ó Cearnaigh, then
living in Dublin, that 'The country people here have a tradition that the reign of a queen is portentous of evil to Ireland',
referring to the 'fire sword famine' of Elizabeth I's time (RIA
Ms 24 E 20: 286). Martin Luther's excommunication,
imposed during the Council of Trent, was also set to expire
in 1845, according to another Irish-language text (National
Library Ireland (NLI), Ms G 306: 129). However unlikely the
connection between this latter consideration and subsequent
happenings, it at least shows that a range of sentiment and
perspective permeates the pre-Famine Gaelic record. Different types of reportage and attitude would also characterise
accounts of the catastrophe set shortly to unfold.

### AN DROCHSHAOL ('THE BAD LIFE')

This is how speakers of Irish designated the Famine after it
had occurred. The term, *gorta*, was also used to depict it
when in progress and subsequently. That word is a deriva-
tive abstract noun from the adjective, *goirt* ('bitter'). Here, a
link with a root denoting 'heating' lead to the development
of meanings like 'scalding', if the exterior surface of the
body was burned, or 'searing, piercing pain', namely, from
sharp pangs of hunger felt internally in the stomach,
whence the concept of 'famine'. *Gorta*, in a primary and a
range of other senses, is well represented in the culture.[11]
The origin, progress, duration and impact of its major mid-
nineteenth-century attestation have received much attention. The following outline of the event's more important
moments is intended as a guide to the various kinds of
Irish-language evidence considered subsequently.[12]

An unfamiliar disease (*Phytophthora infestans*) struck the
potato crop – the primary food source of large sections of
the population – in autumn 1845. Matters deteriorated

when the 1846 harvest failed, leading to the cataclysm of
1847. Illnesses coinciding with mass starvation proved as
harmful as the food shortages themselves. Privately supported or publicly sponsored relief measures were developed or enhanced, including construction schemes or the
operation of the workhouse system. Substitute staples like
meal were imported in response to ongoing need. The fact
that hundreds of thousands of people perished before the
situation eased reveals the scale of the disaster.

Gaelic manuscript materials illuminate each of these
stages, as the following survey suggests. Contemporaries
were aware of the problems confronting primary food supplies. In a piece entitled 'Laoi coscartha na bpotátaí' ('A
poem on the potatoes' destruction', from NLI Ms G 199:
330–34), the Midland's composer and scribe, Peadar Ó
Gealacáin (Peter Gallegan), speaks of 'our noble, auspicious
crop' (*ár saorbharr breá séanmhar*) being 'in death's hands' (*i
lámha an éaga*). In its absence, he claims other kinds of nourishment were of little value:

*Níl rófhlaith gan eolchaire is éagnach*
*'s ní sómasach a dhéantar a bhféasta,*
*fíon Spáinneach, beoir ársa nó tea glan*
*ní áirím gur sású sin d'aoinneach.*

There is no great leader without sorrow or lamentation, and their feasting is not relaxed. Spanish
wine, mature beer or clear tea, I do not believe these
satisfy anyone.

Ó Gealacáin suggests the following steps taken to protect the harvest are to no avail:

*Ní díon dóibh balla daingean dá thréine*
*scioból nó lafta nó cagework,*
*nó beannacht na sagart nó éigse*
*i n-uaimh thalmhan dá gcasadh 'na sréathaibh.*

A firm wall, however strong, does not shelter them,
neither does a barn, a loft or cagework, or the
priests' or poets' blessing when they are in a pit in
the ground being turned in series.

Practical measures to protect the crop were the subject
of other forms of commentary, for instance via a printed
sheet ascribed to a west-of-Ireland rector (now in RIA Ms 3
C 7: 364, and also accessible elsewhere[13]). Issued in Irish and
English, it comprises illustrative diagrams as well as this
guidance on potato conservation:

*Togh iond tirim spearumhail don bpoll. Ann sin dean*
*poll-gaoithe leathan go leor air barra na talmhan, a*
*bhfoirm thrinse osguilte no abhfoirm linteire, le gearradh*

*trinse naoi norluighe no troig ar leathad ⁊ ar doim-*
*neachd, ⁊ le cuir mion cloch air a dtreasna air. Tarraig an*
*trinse no an linteirse ar fhad an phoill ⁊ fag osguilte 'na*
*da cheann e, ionus go ngeabhach an ghaoth thrid go*
*thaosga. Chum na gaoithe a ghabhail nios fearr (an nidh*
*is nios [sic] riochdanaiche), dean poill-gaoithe a dtaob-*
*haibh an phoill a-mballaibh go reasanta a bh-fad o cheile.*
*Air urlar an t-rinse se deantar an poll, ag tabhairt aire*
*air poill-gaoithe d'fagailt ag an bharra, chum an gal a*
*leigint amach. Is uraisd e so a dheanamh le fóid a chasadh*
*tiomchuil feac ráine.*

Let a dry and airy site be chosen for the pit; then let
an air-pipe or funnel be made, of tolerable width,
either on the surface of the ground, in form of a
French drain, or in that of a lintern, by cutting a
trench nine inches or a foot in depth and breadth,
and laying stones loosely across it; and let this funnel be carried the whole intended length of the pit,
and left open at both ends, freely to admit the air. To
render the ventilation – and ventilation is the great
desideratum – still more complete, let air-holes be
made in the sides of the pit, at moderate distances.

With the foregoing in mind, the composition gave further instructions for keeping the pit cool to prevent fermen-
tation in stored tubers. If associated with a Protestant
clergyman, the item is fur-
ther confirmation of those
many efforts by members of
the Established Church to
counter the worst effects of
the infestation. In this case
also, dialect features in the
text's Gaelic version probably mirror actual discussion
about how to cope with the
blight.

Such measures were to
little avail in the absence of a
proper understanding of the
disease. The latter's consequences were momentous.
They may be seen in this
description (in St Patrick's
College, Maynooth, Ms R 70:
490) from northwest County
Clare by a scribe, Mícheál Ó
Raghallaigh (Fig. 4), well
used to chronicling contemporary happenings in his
manuscript annotations:

AD 1847 Bliaidhain na gortan .⁊ an riachtanais. Oir
do sgrios an ghaothruadh blath .⁊ gasa na bpotá-
tuídhe. ionnus gur loibh siad uile. Ni raibh potátá le
buaint as talamh ag aon duine san bfomhar mur
badh gnáth. bliadhanta eile. Ni raibh an corcaidh go
maith mur badh gnáth. na an mhin ann. Dá bhrigh
sin bhí gorta .⁊ riachtannais air gach aon duine san
ríoghacht acht tanaig iliomad minne .⁊ earbhuir go
hEirinn as *America* .⁊ as rioghachtuibh eile. D'eug
mórán do na daoine an gach áit san rioghacht.
Fiabhrus .⁊ tinnios cuirp do thanaig orra do bhár an
oicrais .⁊ is leis a déug na daoine san tir seo. Do
thuit breis .⁊ míle duine san bporóiste so. Ar feadh
tri mhídh .i. Cill Mhainnithinn a cCorcamruadh.

AD 1847 The year of famine and need, because the
strong wind destroyed the potatoes' flowers and
stems, so that they all rotted. Nobody had a potato
to pick from the earth in autumn as was usual in
other years. Oats were not as good as usual, nor
was there meal. Therefore everyone in the kingdom
was famished and in want, but much meal and corn
came to Ireland from America and other realms.
Many people died everywhere in the kingdom.
Fever and sickness overcame them as a result of
hunger, and that is how people in this country died.
More than a thousand fell in this parish in three

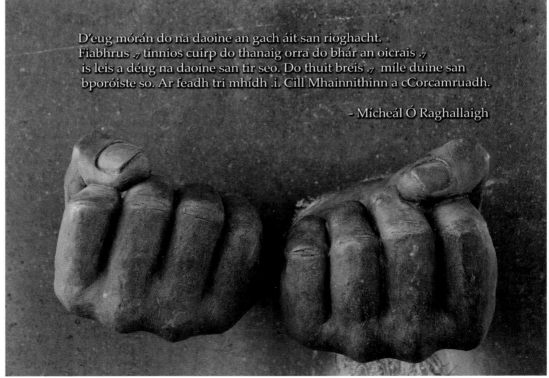

D'eug mórán do na daoine an gach áit san rioghacht.
Fiabhrus .⁊ tinnios cuirp do thanaig orra do bhár an oicrais .⁊
is leis a déug na daoine san tir seo. Do thuit breis .⁊ míle duine san
bporóiste so. Ar feadh tri mhídh .i. Cill Mhainnithinn a cCorcamruadh.

- Mícheál Ó Raghallaigh

Fig. 4 Mícheál Ó Raghallaigh, a scribe from northwest County Clare, details the extent of the devastation wrought by the
Famine across the 'kingdom' while also recording the number of dead in his own parish of Kilmanaheen in Corcomroe:
'Many people died everywhere in the kingdom. Fever and sickness overcame them as a result of hunger, and that is how
people in this country died. More than a thousand fell in this parish in three months.' Ó Raghallaigh's description is
superimposed here on a detail from the 'An Gorta Mór' memorial, sculpted by Alan Ryan Hall, which is situated on the
Lahinch–Ennistymon Road, County Clare. [Photo: Frank Coyne]

465

months, i.e. Kilmanaheen in Corcomroe.

Another Gaelic copyist, Séamus Ó Caoindealbháin (James Quinlivan), from near Askeaton in County Limerick, wrote out 'An oration in time of plague and other diffficulties' ('Oráid a naimsir plágha et doghruingeádha eile', in NLI Ms G 326: 391) during late January 1847. This is a probable parallel to the difficulties experienced in the preceding north-Clare citation. An English-language formula after Quinlivan's prayer may indicate what 'plague' he had in mind: 'One drop of Hydrocyanic acid, and one drop of creasote, with an ounce of cinnamon water immediately arrests the spasmodic action of cholera.' It is hard to envisage that most of the citizenry would have had access to those ingredients, although many of them, including Irish speakers, had extensive experience of cholera arising from the disease's many attacks throughout Ireland in the 1830s referred to above. Fertility and reproduction were affected by famine conditions and also elicited supplications for divine aid. The writer, Riocard Paor (Richard Power), an employee of the Waterford Lunatic Asylum in 1850, when transcribing one composition (NLI Ms G 326: 410), claimed in this introduction to it (marked by Gaelic orthographic conventions):

The follóing prayer hath ma[n]y truly remarkable properties, so as to obtain agood death to any person who says it debhoutly once aday, with a good intention to the glorí of God, and debhótion of the Blessed Bhirgin. And saying it debhoutly for any woman in labour, it forwards with God's blessing, a speed and safe delibherí, with many other benefits.

Documents of the kind under review show awareness of other more down-to-earth types of relief. These include accounts of payments to road workers during November 1846 to January 1847 found in a manuscript (NLI Ms G 400: 253–74) of Gearóid Mac Gearailt (Garret FitzGerald) from near Fieries in north County Kerry (Fig. 5a–b). Other forms of assistance appear to have dried up, however. When writing in October of the latter year from Croom, County Limerick, to the aforementioned Dublin-based Seán Ó Dálaigh, one Edmund Bennett claimed his income had declined 'as school teaching has in a great degree failed in my neighbourhood' (NLI Ms G 389: 179–81). Circumstances like these reduced Gaelic scribes to drafting begging letters such as the following (from NLI Ms G 691: 22) by an east-Cork copyist to an unidentified patron:

Gaibh leathsgeal na locht do cidhfir annso am dhíaig da bhrigh gur tré bhuaireamh aígne, 7 riachtanas an tsaoghuilsi mé féin 7 mo mhuirrear air easba bídh 7 eadaig, do sgríobhas an beagán so, 7 aithcim air tonóir feachuinn le suil na truadhmheile

orruinn 7 comhair éigin do thabhairt orruinn. do bhrigh nach fuil dfalltas agam acht corroin annsa tseachtmhuin a faire lae 7 oidhche. Guídhim fad saoghail fa meanamna 7 fa luthghair an sláinte mhaith, 7 a crich mhaith do bheith air dhéire do beatha. Is mise do seirbhiseach dileas go bás; Seádhan Ó Moihill Gleantán.

Please excuse the errors you see in what follows, because it is on account of mental distress and the necessities of life – I and my family being in want of food and clothing – that I have written this little amount. I beseech your honour to look mercifully upon us and to assist us in some way, because my only income is a crown a week for guarding day and night. I wish you a long, high-spirited, happy and healthy life, and a good end at the conclusion of your days. I remain your faithful servant until death, Seán Ó Moithill, Glounthaune.

Help might not have been readily forthcoming. Suspicion caused a person's appearance or complexion to be examined closely for signs of contagion (see NLI Ms G 662: 84–85), leading to avoidance of contact with the infirm or infected. This hesitancy may have encouraged Catholic priests, such as Rev John Meany of Kilrossanty, County Waterford, to preach 'On Charity or Love of Neighbour' ('Air Charthanacht nó Grádh na cComharsan'), as a work bearing this title (RIA Ms 23 O 71: 206) he copied in the 1850s indicates.

The survival of Irish itself as a vernacular came into question while its speakers suffered. The language activist, Seán Ó Dálaigh, addressed the challenges confronting it at a Dublin Confederate Club meeting in November 1847, where, in his lecture (NLI Ms G 416), he stated, 'Alas poor Ireland! and that you are poor and hungry and starved every thing about you plainly indicates.' Its parlous condition may have motivated the Cork antiquarian and court offical, John Windele, to request the Registrar General to include a question about its usage in the 1851 Census (RIA Ms 12 C 2: 583). This was the first in a continuous and valuable set of enquiries to feature in all such censal investigations down to the present day. Census data from throughout the nineteenth century in particular show the steady decline of Irish and the major impetus the Famine and its aftermath gave to its retreat. These events also affected the vitality of Irish oral tradition. William Wilde, Dublin-based physician and folklore enthusiast, strove to record elements of popular culture before these were swept away, noting a greatly diminished vitality in this domain due to rural depopulation in mid-century.

Emigration soon followed these other losses and augmented them significantly. The flight out of Ireland features in Gaelic handwritten records also. Some of those departing

## The Famine Road

'Idle as trout in light Colonel Jones,
these Irish, give them no coins at all; their bones
need toil, their character no less', Trevelyan's
seal blooded the deal table. The Relief
Committee deliberated: 'Might it be safe,
Colonel, to give them roads, roads to force
from nowhere, going nowhere of course?'

> *one out of every ten and then*
> *another third of those again*
> *women – in a case like yours.*

Sick, directionless they worked, fork, stick
were iron years away; after all could
they not blood their knuckles on rock, suck
April hailstones for water and for food?
Why for that, cunning as housewives, each eyed –
As if at a corner butcher – the other's buttock.

> *anything may have caused it, spores*
> *a childhood accident; one sees*
> *day after day these mysteries.*

Dusk: they will work tomorrow without him.
They know it and walk clear. He has become
a typhoid pariah, his blood tainted, although
he shares it with some there. No more than snow
attends its own flakes where they settle
and melt, will they pray by his death rattle.

> *You never will, never you know*
> *but take it well woman, grow*
> *your garden, keep house, good-bye.*

'It has gone better than we expected. Lord
Trevelyan, sedition, idleness, cured
in one; from parish to parish, field to field;
the wretches work till they are quite worn,
then fester by their work; we march the corn
to the ships in peace. This Tuesday I saw bones
out of my carriage window. Your servant Jones.'

> *Barren, never to know the load*
> *of his child in you, what is your body*
> *Now if not a famine road?*

– Eavan Boland

**Fig. 5a** Road at Dreenagh on the Kerry Head peninsula. A road in this area is represented in Figure 5b 'from the top of Drinagh bog to the village of Tiershanahan'. This seldom-used roadway comes to an end at boggy ground. (Photo: Tomás Kelly)

**Fig. 5b** Roads constructed in North Kerry during the course of the Famine. Over 114 miles of road built by those on outdoor relief in the baronies of Clanmaurice (Clann Mhuiris) and Iraghticonnor (Oireacht Uí Choncubhair) are represented here. Straight lines on the map show roads that were built between two given locations, while the numbers indicate the distance of the roads built (in miles). In cases where the mileage was not available, the *financial* cost of the project is given in its place. £93,806 was presented for relief works, £63,607 (67.8%) of which was for the construction of roads. The remaining £30,199 (32.2%) was presented for the repair of roads and miscellaneous projects such as building walls, repairing fences and 'filling the hollow below the church of Tarbert'. £68,906 had been expended by August 1847, with £19,882 estimated to complete the projects. A cluster of roads is evident around Listowel, the seat of Lord Listowel and the location of the Union workhouse. In addition to Lord Listowel, Sir John Walsh and 'Mr. Bateman' – both large landholders in the area – had roads referred to as being theirs, at Tullamore and Clievragh respectively. Three roads – represented on the map at Ballyheige, Kilmore and Letter – finished at a strand. A further three roads finished at the strands of Ballyardcane, Fenit and Killeen in the nearby barony of Trughanacmy. [Source: *The Tralee Chronicle*, 14 August 1847, Kerry County Library, Tralee; map and research by Tomás Kelly]

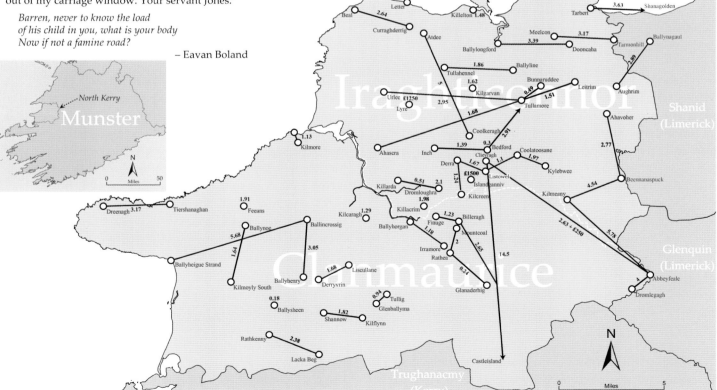

embarked in port towns like Galway and experienced the dread of an ocean crossing before beginning an uncertain stay in locations like the eastern American city of Baltimore (NLI Ms G 250.186 [3]). A number of Irish scribes brought their manuscripts with them, perhaps as reminders of their cultural inheritance. Those heirlooms could easily become commodities to be traded. This latter type of exchange may explain how the privately funded, independent research library, the Boston Athenaeum, founded in 1807, came to acquire items previously owned by one Patrick O Keeffe. He is likely to have reached New England among the substantial arrivals there from Ireland in the late 1840s and might have conveyed his collection to more prosperous patrons as a source of income.[14] The County Kerry copyist, Dáth Mac Gearailt (David FitzGerald), from Ardnagragh east of Castleisland, quit the country in 1845, his leaving possibly spurred on by the incipient problems of that year. He would live out the remainder of his days in Ohio. Later generations of his family retained as treasures this FitzGerald's Gaelic manuscript writings, where testimony of his travels across the northeastern United States was also included. Others contemplating getting out may have taken guidance from texts like the poem *Ar farraige má thaistilir le cúrsa an tsaoil* ('If you travel overseas on life's journey') found in a compilation by made Mícheál Ó hÉalaithe (Michael Healy) of Kilcorney, County Cork, in 1846–52 (NLI Ms G 422: 343). Persons who left or even those remaining might have found consolation in nostalgic compositions about separation, as can be sensed from works such as 'The Emigrant's Farewell by Patrick Higgins'. This poem, beginning *I'm leaving you at last, Mary*, now survives in a largely Gaelic document completed in the years 1850-60 (NLI Ms G 634 (a): 54).

## INTERPRETATION

While noticing the Famine or experiencing its circumstances, Gaelic writers sought equally to account for is causes and consequences. The aforementioned Peadar Ó Gealacáin felt it happened for the following reason:

*'Sé shílim, 's ní scríobhaimse bréaga,*
*'s bíodh a fhianaise ag saoithibh atá aosta,*
*gurb é dhíbir ar saorbharr breá séanmar*
*ceart Chríosta ar dhaoithibh gan chéadfa.*

It is my view, and I write no lie – may venerable learned people be my witness – that what banished our noble, auspicious crop was Christ's vengeance on senseless fools.

Untoward absorption with mundane matters, dancing, dressing and disputation, incurred the Lord's wrath. He was equally angry at 'evil' (*olc*), 'perverse ambition' (*mírún*), 'theft' (*goid*), 'ravishing' (*fuadach*), 'treachery' (*feall*), 'ill-judgement' (*daorbhreith*) or other manifestations of

sinfulness. Warnings of improper behaviour were ignored, with this outcome:

*As siocair gach olc dár tharla in Éirinn*
*d'éag na potátaí, mo chrá 's mo ghéarghoin,*
*ach a Rí na nGrása, a bhásaíos na céadta,*
*go sábhála tú feasta iad trí do dhaonnacht.*

As a result of all of Ireland's evils the potatoes died, my grief and torment! But, O graceful King, who dispatches hundreds, save them henceforth through your humanity.

The copying by the scribe, Aindrias Ó Súilleabháin, from Cahirciveen, County Kerry, of an Irish-language tract, 'Craobhsgaoile No Miniughadh Leabhar An Taisbeanach' ('An Exploration or an Explanation of the Book of Revelations', in NLI Ms G 368: 329–47) during 1854, with its reflections on the pain to be visited on humanity in general and on sinners in particular at the world's end, may also suggest that the Irish merited punishment because of their innate deficiencies. Moralising poetry read and written out at the time, such as 'The Conversation between Death and the Patient' ('Comhrá an Bháis agus an Duine Thinn'), argues that Man should seek assistance in prayerfulness and in the devout life rather than from earthly goods. Recourse to religious literature may thus have furnished psychological means for coping with disaster analogous to practical strategies for confronting shortage often transmitted by other means in unwritten lore.[15]

Different commentators appear to claim that the Famine was visited wrongly on the people of Ireland, who did not deserve such an imposition. This may be sensed from a statement (Maynooth MS R 69: 427) by the Clare writer, Mícheál Ó Raghallaigh, also mentioned earlier, who, when finishing his copy of a devotional text, noted he ceased on 'the 22 August AD 1848 i.e. the year of slaughter and hunger during which thousands died for want of food' ('a dtarradh lá fithchiod do Lúmhnas AD 1848 .i. bliadhain an áir 7 an ocrais ionnar éag na millte duine le huireasbadh bígh'). What precisely the term *ár* ('slaughter') could have meant to Ó Raghallaigh may perhaps be sensed from a remark by fellow countyman, Brian Ó Luanaigh. On transcribing the emigration work, *I'm leaving you at last, Mary*, spoken of above, he said it was 'Written after the odious extermination of 47' (NLI MS G 634 (a): 54). Explorations of the event lengthier than these brief entries are also extant. They include a Gaelic poem (NLI G MS G 545) of one hundred and twenty-five quatrains by the northerner, Nioclás Ó Cearnaigh, mentioned previously as well, Ulster poets taking a particular interest in the event.[16] Entitled 'Cruadhghorta na hÉireann noch chrádh a clannain go díocrach feadh 1846.7.8' ('Ireland's harsh famine, which grievously tormented its children during 1846.7.8'), it is cast in a metre and form reminiscent of Irish-language verse lamenting the country's condition during the mid-1600s and later, a type of writing also recopied abundantly throughout and after the 1840s. Ó Cearnaigh explores the calamity in the context of this island's historic relations with Britain. Such contact never favoured Ireland, when one considers suffering inflicted in Oliver Cromwell's day or following enactment of the Penal Laws. Ó Cearnaigh holds the English Government responsible for this latest example of wilful disregard, naming in this connection persons like Prime Minister, Lord John Russell, and Lord Lieutenant, George William Frederick Villiers, 4th Earl of Clarendon:

> Seán beag Ruiséal, pocán gan éifeacht,
> bhí an tan ina cheannphort ós na réigiúin;
> Fear Ionaid an Rí in Áth Cliath níorbh fhearr é
> Clarendon ciapach, cíorlach, scléipeach.

Little John Russell, a bloated, ineffectual fellow, was at that time commander of the regions; the King's Deputy in Dublin was no better, the tormenting, upsetting braggart, Clarendon.

Irish grandees such as William Gregory merit censure equally for heartless conduct towards their tenantry, particularly introducing steps (like the 'Gregory clause') leading to eviction for non-payment of rent in greatly straitened circumstances:

> Bhí stócach bríobach i gcríochaibh Chonnacht,
> Greagoire íocas, fíor a ainm,
> do rinn' sé dlighe do dhíchuir céadta
> i ngach crích de chríochaibh Éireann.

There was a bribing youth in the province of Connacht, paying Gregory – his name is accurate – who made a law which banished hundreds in each of the territories of Ireland.

The Famine era elicited proposals for political reform or action on the ground, with each of these strands represented in the Gaelic record as well. Irish speaker and scholar, Eugene O'Curry, from County Clare but living in the capital by mid-century, reflected on them in a short verse text (Maynooth MS C 71 (c): 8) of which the following are the opening stanzas, normalised here and also with my translation:[17]

> Go mbeannaí Dia fá thrí dhuit, a Sheanbhean Bhocht,
> is fada riamh ó scaoileadh ort lom agus nocht,
> do gheal do chiabh le críne, is do chas do ghiall ó chaoineadh,
> is do shreath ort rian na síne, mo Sheanbhean Bhocht.

> Monuar! is fíor do ghlórtha, ars' an tSeanbhean Bhocht,

> is buartha bhíos gan fóirithin, in amhgar go docht,
> ó scar liom Brian na mórghal gur éirigh suas mo Dhomhnall
> ní bhfuaras suan ná sóchas, ars' an tSeanbhean Bhocht.

'May God bless you thrice, Shanvan Vocht, you have long been left thin-sparing and bare, your hair has whitened with age with your cheek deformed from crying, while the trace of inclement weather has marked you, my Shanvan Vocht.'

'Alas! your sayings are true,' said the Shanvan Vocht, 'I have been distressed, without aid, firmly in difficulty, since valorous Brian left me until my Domhnall rose up, never did I gain rest or riches,' said the Shanvan Vocht.

The Clareman speaks to Ireland, personified above as a woman. This normally stock sovereignty motif (at issue previously here in the eighteenth-century output of Séamus Mac Coitir) seems replete with echoes of the era itself. The lady's appearance in the poem as one traumatised, impoverished and emaciated looks like a pen-picture of sights to be seen in everyday encounters at the time of writing. She reposed hope in Daniel O'Connell (the *Domhnall* of the foregoing citation), successor to the fabled tenth-/eleventh-century leader, Brian Boru (*Brian na mórghal*). In subsequent lines, the female figure expresses regret that the likes of O'Connell was not at the Battle of the Boyne in the 1690s to aid the patriot, Patrick Sarsfield, such that she would probably not now be left 'sick' (*tinn*) or 'wounded' (*leointe*). The text highlights an event in 1782 (*san ochtó 's a dó*) which 'shocked' King George III (*bhain bíog as Seoirse*), specifically, the granting of increased powers to Ireland's local assembly in light of colonial, particularly North American, restiveness. The inference is that a return to domestic parliamentary autonomy must be sought once more. Therefore, O'Curry appears as a supporter of the O'Connellite Repeal platform. That agenda sought to overturn the Act of Union of 1800, which had deprived the country of control over its internal affairs and the capacity immediately to intervene in response to current requirements.

O'Curry characterised the work as 'A *Ráiméis* of my own 1847 –' in what is possibly a later marginal note, entered transversely. This confirms it was completed at the height of the Famine and most likely before Daniel O'Connell's death in that year. Self-description (perhaps retrospective) of the item as 'doggerel' (*Ráiméis*) should not be taken to signify its author was dismissive either of the composition or its contents on the occasion of writing. While the poem is unfinished, the Clare-born author made various attempts to correct or improve the draft. One emendation to the second stanza above, in speaking of Ireland's enemies being determined (*do namhad go docht*), hints at the resolve required to recast current arrangements. Eugene O'Curry was employed by a number of public bodies, whether the Ordnance Survey or various Commissions. This suggests he was anti-establishment neither in outlook nor in temperament, but sought amelioration within existing structures. Others, however, took a more radical tack. The recently formed Young Ireland movement's dissatisfaction with Britain grew as a result of the Famine. The organisation endorsed insurrection in 1848 against a state apparatus which could allow a tragedy of such proportions to take place, in its view. The survival among Gaelic sources of verse texts (in NLI MS G 634 (a): 32–33; cf. RIA MS 12 O 17 (3)) supporting various rebel leaders like William Smith O'Brien may strengthen the impression that certain speakers of Irish viewed the crisis as an injustice deserving a more assertive response.

Supplementary reactions are forthcoming in Irish-language material completed overseas as well as from within Gaelic Ireland. The compositions of Pádraig Phiarais Cúndún provide a prominent external point of view on current affairs. This native of the east-Cork Ballymacoda district emigrated to upstate New York during late 1820s in search of a better life. By 1834, seven years' hard work had enabled him to buy out a farmstead at Deerfield, near Utica in Oneida County, close to where relatives of his father's settled before him. His verse and prose correspondence in Irish with friends and neighbours from his home area circulated in manuscripts throughout the Cork region, our author having become one of Irish–America's first literary representatives as much as a European writer. Significant portions of it happily survive the apparent loss of the originals and are given in a modern edition.[18] The impact of the Famine is unmistakable in them. It cannot be discounted that coverage of Irish affairs in the local New York press could have heightened Cúndún's awareness of conditions in his native shore. A publication like the Geneva *Gazette* from the state's more westerly reaches might have given a pithy summary of recent incidents, for instance those of late 1847 mentioned in an entry dated 9 November: 'The reports from Ireland come with alarming amounts of distress and outrages.' Normally, however, such broadsheets are replete with accounts of malnourishment and disease throughout various Irish districts while they also followed the public debate the crisis engendered in Britain, Ireland and elsewhere. A major gap in Famine scholarship will be filled when the extensive body of American journalism on the event is collated and appraised. In this connection, it should be noted that United States newspapers, particularly on the east coast, reported repeatedly down to 1900 on the status of the Irish potato harvest, particularly during years when the crop appeared at risk. That suggests ongoing sensitivity on the part of survivors or their descendants to the recurrence of famine as an existential threat, a lasting aftershock from the pivotal event under discussion in this chapter.

Cúndún appears principally to have heard directly from

Cork about this debacle. Although no items from those who wrote to him seem to be extant, there could be independent confirmation that he was indeed receiving such communication. Our writer may be identified with one 'Patrick Condon' named among a list of persons for whom letters were 'Remaining in the Post-Office at Utica, May 1' 1850, as stated in the *Oneida Morning Herald* of that year. The inventory has a large complement of Irish family names. Some, like that of 'John Mc Craith', are rendered in a spelling which suggests the three pieces awaiting this addressee also came from a sender conversant with Gaelic. Early in 1849, Pádraig Phiarais undertook to answer his acquaintance, Tomás Ó Briain (Fig. 6a–b). As happens when people correspond, the reply most likely retraces what the latter had told Cúndún in the first instance. Pádraig states the news Ó Briain dispatched to him from home was 'sad and melancholy' (*doilbh dolásach*). There is thus in this composer's statement a virtual reverberation of tidings heard in Geoffrey Keating's lamentation, *Óm sceol ar ardmhagh Fáil*, when news of distress in his country of origin saddened that clerical student, then based in France, two and a half centuries earlier. On learning of it, Pádraig Cúndún encouraged those enslaved and disadvantaged in Ireland (*sclábhaidhthe bochta Éireann*) to come to America to secure their well-being (*luach bhur sláinte*). He detailed the availability for cultivation of land both fertile, abundant as well as freehold (*saor go brách*), particularly further west, with its inviting climate of short, two-month-long winters (*Níl de gheimhreadh ann acht dhá mhí*). These and other inducements would continue as a steady refrain in Cúndún's messages to the Imokilly area well into the 1850s as he contrasted the Old World with the New. He never tired of emphasising how he and his wider family circle prospered after they moved abroad. The case of one J. Francis Condon may illustrate the claim was well-founded. This lawyer, based in Utica, was quite likely connected to Pádraig Phiarais. A resident of Deerfield, he sought the office of United States consul at Cork (as reported in the journal, *Rome Semi-Weekly Citizen*, on 29 March 1893) from no less a personage than Grover Cleveland, soon after the latter's second term as America's twenty-fourth President commenced. Previously of Oneida County as well, Cleveland's Democratic affiliation probably also matched the applicant's own allegiance. The example makes it equally clear that the Condons' contact with their old homeland remained as long-lasting as it was cherished.

Pádraig Cúndún's responses were not confined to practical advice about escaping the Great Hunger's impositions. The writer's verse texts from the late 1840s onwards reflect on the reasons for Ireland's predicament. He saw events in the period as a further instance of the enduring torment of the island and its people visited on them by those then in power. In works like *Is truagh san treabha chlanna Mílidh thréan* ('Alas for the descendants of Míl the Brave'), from 1847, lamenting the country's plight, adherents of Reformed

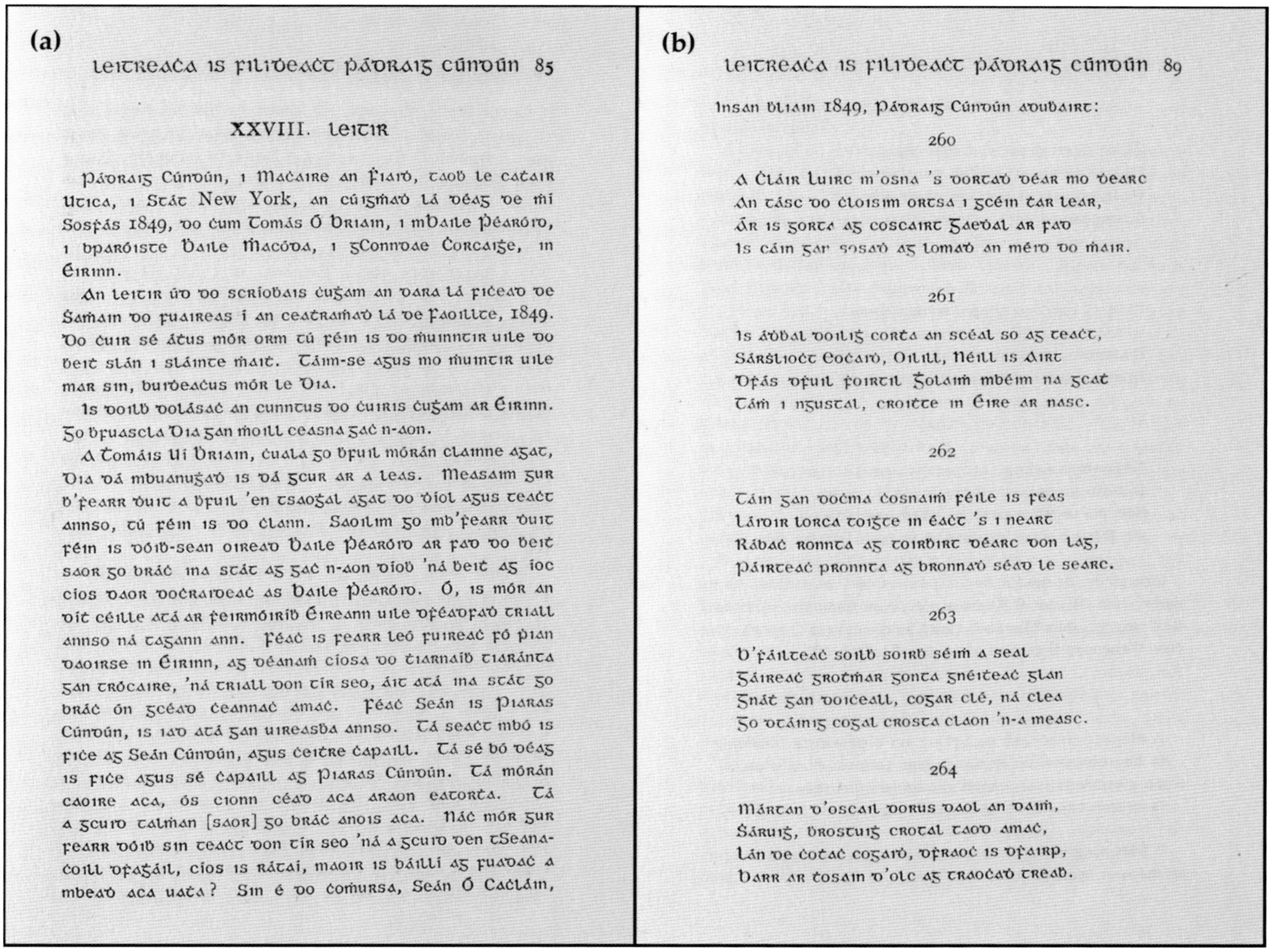

**(a)**

Leitreaca is filideact Pádraig Cúndún 85

### XXVIII. Leitir

Pádraig Cúndún, i Macaire an Fiaid, taob le catair Utica, i Stát New York, an cúigmad lá déag de mí Sospás 1849, do cum Tomás Ó Briain, i mbaile Péaróid, i bparóiste Baile Macóda, i gConndae Corcaige, in Éirinn.

An leitir úd do scríobais cugam an dara lá ficead de Samain do fuaireas i an ceatramad lá de Faoillte, 1849. Do cuir sé átus mór orm tú féin is do muinntir uile do beit slán i sláinte mait. Táim-se agus mo muinntir uile mar sin, buideacus mór le Dia.

Is doilb dolásac an cunntus do cuiris cugam ar Éirinn. Go bfuascla Dia gan moill ceasna gac n-aon.

A Tomáis Uí Briain, cuala go bfuil morán clainne agat, Dia dá mbuanugad is dá gcur ar a leas. Measaim gur b'fearr duit a bfuil 'en tsaogal agat do díol agus teact annso, tú féin is do clann. Saoilim go mb'fearr duit féin is dóib-sean oiread Baile Péaróid ar fad do beit saor go brác ina stát ag gac n-aon díob 'ná beit ag íoc cíos daor docraideac as Baile Péaróid. Ó, is mór an dít céille atá ar feirmóirib Éireann uile dféadfad triall annso ná tagann ann. Féac is fearr leó fuireac fó pian daoirse in Éirinn, ag déanam cíosa do tiarnaib tiaránta gan trócaire, 'ná triall don tír seo, áit atá ina stát go brác ón gcéad ceannac amac. Féac Seán is Piaras Cúndún, is iad atá gan uireasba annso. Tá seact mbó is fice ag Seán Cúndún, agus ceitre capaill. Tá sé bó déag is fice agus sé capaill ag Piaras Cúndún. Tá morán caoire aca, ós cionn céad aca araon eatorta. Tá a gcuid talman [saor] go brác anois aca. Nác mór gur fearr dóib sin teact don tír seo 'ná a gcuid den tSeanacoill dfágáil, cíos is rátaí, maoir is báillí ag fuadac a mbead aca uata? Sin é do comursa, Seán Ó Caclám,

**(b)**

Leitreaca is filideact Pádraig Cúndún 89

Insan bliain 1849, Pádraig Cúndún adubairt:

260

A Cláir Luirc m'osna 's dortad déar mo dearc
An tásc do cloisim ortsa i gcéin tar lear,
Ár is gorta ag coscairt Gaedal ar fad
Is cáin gar sosad ag lomad an méid do mair.

261

Is adbal doilig corta an sceál so ag teact,
Sárslioct Eocaid, Oilill, Néill is Airt
Dfás dfuil foirtil Solaim mbéim na gcat
Tám i ngustal, croitte in Éire ar nasc.

262

Tám gan docma cosnaim féile is feas
Láidir lorca toigte in éact 's i neart
Rábac ronnta ag toirbirt déarc don lag,
Páirteac pronnta ag bronnad séad le searc.

263

D'fáilteac soilb soirb séim a seal
Gáireac grotmar gonta gnéiteac glan
Gnát gan doiceall, cogar clé, ná clea
Go dtáinig cogal crosta claon 'n-a measc.

264

Mártan d'oscail dorus daol an daim,
Sáruig, brostuig crotal taob amac,
Lán de cotac cogaid, dfraoc is dfairp,
Darr ar tosain d'olc ag traocad tread.

Fig. 6a Text of letter sent in 1849 by Pádraig Phiarais Cúndún from Deerfield, near Utica, in upstate New York, to Tomás Ó Briain of Ballypherode townland in the east Cork barony of Imokilly, expressing upset at recent bad news from Ireland, encouraging him to emigrate, and speaking about his own extended family's prosperity since their arrival in America in the 1820s. Cúndún repeats similar views about Ireland's woes in his verse composition (Fig. 6b), *A Chláir Luirc m'osna 's dortadh déar mo dhearc*, also from 1849. The opening sections of both letter and poem are reproduced here from Risteard Ó Foghludha (eag.), *Pádraig Phiarais Cúndún* (Baile Átha Cliath, 1932), pp. 85 and 89, respectively. [Photo: Tomas Tyner]

religious sects (*Cuallacht Chailbhin bhradaigh*) were mentioned in adverse terms. Persons of questionable probity who implemented perverse legislation (*Cuaine is measa bearta dlighe agus méinn*) are indicted. They include arrogant and acquisitive land agents (*maor / Ag suathadh ag smalcadh ag sracadh ó shaoithe a séad*) responsible for physically assaulting tenants (*Dfhuagadar alta ar bhaitheas cinn gach aon*). The harshness of their measures caused distress to hundreds of thousands (*Cruadhas a reachta chealg mílte céad*), while those stewards themselves tasted greedily of the good times (*suaimhneas seascair, fleadhtha, fíonta is feast . . . le craos*). By 1849, in his poem *A Chláir Luirc m'osna 's dortadh dear mo dhearc* ('O Ireland, my sigh and tears shed from my eyes'), Pádraig Piarais also juxtaposed the term *gorta* ('famine') with *ár* ('slaughter') when accounting for what had happened. He highlighted how unending taxation continued to burden those who had outlived the Famine (*Is cáin gan sosadh ag lomadh an méid do mhair*). The author's sentiments in this regard may have been shaped by recalling factors which probably occasioned his own earlier removal from Ireland. Forced evictions in the Ballymacoda area are rehearsed at length in the writer's earliest known letter, from 1823.[19] This was compiled during a phase of marked economic downturn and associated violence, particularly in the south of Ireland.[20] Occurrences of such a kind had undoubtedly provided Cúndún and his likes with substantial motivation to leave.

### EVALUATION

The evidence reviewed here merits attention for various reasons. It is expressed in the ancestral voice of sizeable sections of Ireland's population (especially those most seriously affected by the Famine), Irish being the country's other principal vernacular besides English. So far as I am aware, there appears to be no further Gaelic material in existence which is directly contemporary with the subject-matter at issue.

Given the diminished status of the Irish language, the data are neither hugely abundant nor systematic. However, the facts derive from tradition- bearers' close involvement with the incidents as portrayed, or from their credible reportage of them to others. The information's provenance is widespread in geographic terms, while consistency between sources is apparent, regardless of point of origin. The range of genres, whether prosaic or imaginative, through which the testimony is mediated does not yield profiles of the incident that are essentially incompatible with one another. The documentation's potential may be felt from the diversity of alternative source types one needs to consult to clarify its context and import. Therefore, the pieces we are considering, although seeming fragmentary, should scarcely be underestimated. They tend to be overlooked even in major research on the Great Hunger, where the cultural aspects to this crisis frequently attract less notice than topics such as its influence on Ireland's economy.[21]

We have seen that our Gaelic manuscript materials show a spectrum of response to what had taken place. They comprise recognition that the calamity may be credited to the community's own immorality as well as examples of Irish speakers' possible inhumanity towards each other, especially to the infirm, when the downturn was in train. This latter element, almost imperceptible but hinted at nonetheless, calls for further investigation in light of considerable supporting testimony for same. Thus, from the mid-1840s onwards, publications like the *Freeman's Journal* appear to show a marked increase in advertisements for firearms. Notices of this kind suggest a highly developed sense of self-preservation on some people's part rather than their altruistic concern either for the promotion of the weapons trade or for those less fortunate in society. The ethos of the newspaper in question tends to argue for the prevalence of a strong feeling of cautiousness towards their fellow human beings among the majority element of the population as much as within its ruling Ascendancy component, particularly persons who could afford to take measures to defend life, property or limb. Therefore, scholars who claim reactions to the circumstances of the time had multiple layers[22] are doing nothing less than describing the complexities of the situation as it surely unfolded.

Such commentators, when identifying extenuating circumstances, however exiguous, do not propose that the Famine never happened, unlike those who reject the notion that other compelling incidents in world history were real.[23] The Irish-language texts reviewed in the present chapter confirm that the event did occur. There is, furthermore, a preponderance of opinion in them as to causation and the way matters were handled. Responsibility is apportioned directly to the existing system and governing authorities. One sees as much both in Pádraig Phiarais Cúndún's pieces

and alternative compositions. In his case, this Corkman's works provide insights into evolving attitudes to the catastrophe among Irish emigrants (with the Great Hunger set to become a touchstone of their self-consciousness, as similar happenings would determine other exiled people's sense of identity), in addition to thoughts about it of informants at home. What lends all such items credence is their capacity to measure action against a specific set of criteria deriving from a written record extending backwards into the history of recent centuries as known to later copyists from their manuscript contents. It was a yardstick capable of differentiating between disasters exhibiting different circumstances and motivating factors. In this context, the Famine stood out for its singularity even if not its uniqueness, its extremity being rendered in wording already noted above. How to understand such expressions must give pause for reflection. The Gaelic sources explored here could not yet incorporate the concept of holocaust in the sense that such phrasing would be understood after the mid-twentieth century. Neither did they include the notion of genocide such as that idea was defined technically from the early 1900s.[24] Therefore, to attribute to Cúndún and his likes the impression that the incident is to be characterised using either of those descriptors is basically anachronistic. However, if they had an awareness of the terminology under review, one may conclude many of them would probably invite others to demonstrate that the Famine was not genocidal in its tendencies.

The writers we have discussed report the ruination of their people and the reduction of their civilisation. While not having experienced for oneself anything that they saw, it is difficult to gainsay what they relate. They appear as men of no little erudition, integrity or sophistication. Although it is not now possible to restore their loss, some further lessons might be learned from the story they relay to us. Comparative studies of food shortages suggest an admixture of facets in their circumstances, that politics, for instance, can play a role either in their alleviation or their aggravation.[25] In this connection, the Great Hunger may enable a further hypothesis to be proposed. This is that a community which has known repeated instances of politically induced want in the past stands a far greater chance of a recurrence of the same traumatic conditions in the future. That Ireland was in such a situation, notably from the 1500s onwards,[26] appears to be acknowledged increasingly. Continuing instability in Irish life from the mid-nineteenth century down to the present seems proof positive of the realisation that, even if other explanations must also be adduced, contemporary society is still grappling with volatility consequent on and reflective of those underlying trends.[27] In deliberating on the origins and the out-turn of such a disaster, therefore, the Gaelic evidence asks one to consider famine's teleology as much as its actuality.

# The artist as witness: James Mahony

## Julian Campbell

Best-known for his illustrations of the Great Famine in Ireland for *The Illustrated London News*, James Mahony was a versatile artist, also painting genre subjects, seascapes, watercolours of France, Italy and Spain, and interiors of Continental cathedrals. He was admired for his large panoramic watercolours of the Great Industrial Exhibition held in Dublin in 1853. His work spans contrasting historical themes: witnessing scenes of poverty and distress in West Cork during the Famine, to celebrating the visit of Queen Victoria to Dublin in 1853. Mahony was a co-founder of the Cork Art Union, and he was a keen traveller. Uncertainty surrounds the dates of the artist's birth and death, and he has been confused with a near-contemporary of similar name.

James Mahony was born in Cork in *c.*1810.[1] He was the son of a carpenter and the brother of Patrick Mahony, who later became an architect. James Mahony first exhibited at the Cork Society for Promoting the Fine Arts in 1833. He spent some years travelling on the Continent, visiting Milan, Venice and Florence, and studying in Rome, gaining skills as a watercolour painter. He returned to Cork in *c.*1841, staying at his father's house at 34 Nile Street. With Samuel Skillen (*c.*1819–1847), Mahony established the Cork Art Union in 1841. The first exhibition was held at Marsh's Rooms, South Mall, in September, and Mahony showed four Italian watercolours there. He also worked in oil, painting beach scenes and seascapes, including *After the Storm* (1842), relating to the storms that occurred along the County Cork coastline in 1839 and 1842. From 1842 to 1846 Mahony exhibited Cork and Continental scenes, and subjects taken from Shakespeare, at the Royal Hibernian Academy, Dublin, and at the Cork Art Union. He won the Royal Irish Art Union prize in 1843.

### REPORTING THE FAMINE

During the years from 1846 to 1852 Mahony was employed as an artist and reporter by *The Illustrated London News* (*ILN*), founded in 1842. Sketches made by him on location were sent to London, engraved by resident artists, and pub-

**WOMAN BEGGING AT CLONAKILTY.**

Fig. 1 'I started from Cork, by the mail (says our informant), for Skibbereen and saw little until we came to Clonakilty, where the coach stopped for breakfast; and here, for the first time, the horrors of the poverty became visible, in the vast number of famished poor, who flocked around the coach to beg alms: amongst them was a woman carrying in her arms the corpse of a fine child, and making the most distressing appeal to the passengers for aid to enable her to purchase a coffin and bury her dear little baby. This horrible spectacle induced me to make some inquiry about her, when I learned from the people of the hotel that each day brings dozens of such applicants into the town.' [Source: *The Illustrated London News*, 13 February 1847] lished by the magazine. Mahony's first sketch was of the grounding of a ship in Dundrum Bay, County Down. In 1847 he made illustrations for the funeral of Daniel O'Connell. With the advent of the Famine, Mahony's work became focused on this catastrophic event and its aftermath. He made drawings of scenes which he witnessed on the south and west coasts of Ireland. Some were signed and others were unsigned, but have been attributed to Mahony.[2] He also wrote a series of articles about the Famine for the *ILN* as well as other Irish newspapers. He was not the only illustrator of the Famine for the *ILN* during this period – others included Ebenezer Landells, F.G. Smyth, Edmund Fitzpatrick and H. Smith[3] – but he is the best-remembered.

In 1846–47 Mahony made illustrations, and wrote two articles, relating to the Famine. In 1849–50 he wrote seven articles, and in 1851–52 his illustrations relate to the aftermath of the Famine and emigration. Mahony's studies show a progression of events: from the sale of Indian corn in Cork (*ILN*, 4 April 1846), to the aftermath of food riots in Dungarvan and Youghal (7 November 1846), to distressing scenes in West Cork and County Clare in 1847. *The Illustrated London News* wrote: 'We have commissioned our artist, Mr. James Mahony of Cork to visit the seat of extreme suffering . . . Skibbereen and its vicinity; and we now submit to our readers the graphic results of his journey.'[4] In February 1847 Mahony published two articles entitled 'Sketches in the West of Ireland', the first with seven illustrations of Clonakilty and Skibbereen (13 February 1847), the second with five studies (20 February 1847).

Upon arriving at Clonakilty crowds of famished people gathered around Mahony's coach and begged for food. One woman carried the body of her small child. Beyond Clonakilty he encountered many funeral parties, for example, at Shepperton Lakes. At Skibbereen, in the company of Dr D. Donovan (who had been recording famine events in his diary) and his assistant, Mr Crowley, Mahony visited badly-hit areas. They saw houses of the destitute without doors and windows, and at Bridgetown they encountered terrible sights, such as a group of figures in rags, living, dying and dead, lying close together.

In the company of a Mr Everett, Mahony travelled towards Ballydehob. They observed 'many sepulchres above ground, where six dead bodies have lain for twelve days'.[5] At Aghadoe, Mahony and Everett witnessed four bodies lying in a hut, and at Schull there were 300 women queuing for Indian meal.

## HARROWING SCENES

In 1849–50 Mahony wrote seven articles entitled 'Condition of Ireland: Illustration of the new Poor Law', four of which were illustrated. Some of his sketches were made on a visit to County Clare. Among Mahony's most harrowing Famine illustrations are his most simple and spare, for example: *A Boy and Girl at Cahera Searching for Potatoes* (20 February 1847), *Woman in Clonakilty Begging for Money to Bury Her Dead Child* (13 February 1847), *Bridget O'Donnell and Her Children Searching for Potatoes* (22 December 1849), and *Bridget O'Donnell and Her Children* (22 December 1849), set in County Clare, the latter showing the ragged emaciated figures standing together. Such pictures shocked readers of the *ILN* in Ireland and England, and helped to draw the attention of the English-speaking world to the nature and sever-

Fig. 2 *The Stone Bridge at Blarney, 1850* by James Mahony, watercolour on paper. [Source: Crawford Art Gallery]

ity of the Famine.

On 10 May 1851 Mahony wrote that eleven vessels had left Cork in only eight days. His illustrations show calmer scenes than those of the Famine, depicting groups of emigrants assembled on the quaysides of Cork, waiting to embark on ships. On the occasion of the opening of the National Industrial Exhibition in Cork, the *ILN* published a supplement with illustrations by Mahony (19 June 1852). During this period he also painted a number of watercolours of local and genre scenes, including *A Country Dance*, *The Wren Bush* (National Gallery of Ireland [NGI]), *Stone Bridge at Blarney*, 1850 (Crawford Art Gallery, Cork) and *Queen's College, Cork*. Ten watercolours of local and Italian subjects were shown at the Exhibition of Arts and Manufactures, Cork in 1852.

The occasion of the Great Exhibition in Dublin in 1853, held to show a spirit of revival in Ireland after the Famine, provided Mahony with the opportunity to paint several large-scale watercolours of architectural subjects and crowds, including scenes depicting the visit of Queen Victoria and Prince Albert to the exhibition. Mahony's watercolour *The Nave of the Chapel Royal* (the Church of the Holy Trinity), Dublin Castle, 1854 (NGI), shows his skill in conveying architectural perspective. His best-known watercolour *Dublin from the Spire of St George's Church, Hardwicke Place*, 1854 (NGI), gives an atmospheric, panoramic view from the spire of the church towards the Dublin and Wicklow Mountains. Mahony also made a journey to Spain, painting watercolours of Cadiz, Cordoba and Granada.

At home many of his watercolours were acquired by Captain G.A. Taylor. On Taylor's death in 1855 a collection of watercolours was bequeathed to the National Gallery of Ireland. In 1856 Mahony exhibited seventeen watercolours of Irish and Continental scenes and historical subjects at the Royal Hibernian Academy (RHA). That year he was elected an Associate of the RHA. In 1858 eleven watercolours from the Taylor Bequest were exhibited at the Irish Institution, Dublin, and the following year two scenes of Cordoba at the RHA. Mahony also painted two watercolours of Cork Harbour.

In 1859 Mahony resigned from the RHA. There is some confusion about what happened next to Mahony. It had long been generally believed that Mahony then moved to London, where he pursued a busy career as an illustrator and watercolourist. It is possible, however, that Mahony has been confused with a London-based artist of similar name 'James Mahoney'.[6] The possible mix-up first came to light in the early twentieth century, following the publication of W.G. Strickland's *Dictionary of Irish Artists* (1913), in which Mahony is mentioned. In 1914, Mr Campbell Dodgson, Keeper of Prints at the British Museum, wrote to inform Strickland that there were two artists of similar name. The second James Mahoney (1847–79), his name spelled with an 'e', was an artist based in London, who executed illustrations for graphic magazines and children's books, and for

the Household edition of Dickens's novels, and who painted watercolours of working-class men and boys in a skilled, realist and sometimes humorous manner. Strickland noted this error in an annotated copy of his dictionary, which is kept in the National Library of Ireland.[7]

Confusion over the activities of Mahony after 1859 continues to this day, but I believe that after resigning from the RHA in that year Mahony left Dublin and returned to Cork, where, as a result of an illness, he died in November 1859. In the early 1880s, his illustrations were admired by the Dutch artist Vincent Van Gogh (1853–1890).

## BEARING WITNESS

For a period of several years in the middle of his career Mahony was a first-hand witness of the Great Famine in Ireland. Although his name is little-known outside of academic circles in Ireland, and some of his Famine drawings may lack sophistication, Mahony belongs to an important tradition in the history of art – that of Callot, Goya, Daumier, Käthe Kollwitz, Otto Dix and George Grosz – the tradition of artist as witness, or social critic, of historical events, of wars, of suffering or impoverished peoples.

In the seventeenth century Jacques Callot (c.1592–1635) saw French troops enter the city of Nancy, and he created two series of etchings entitled *The Miseries of War*, 1633. According to Edwin de Bechtel: 'Callot ... presents the facts so overwhelmingly that over the centuries he has helped to awaken the public conscience against War.'[8] Francisco Goya (1746–1828) witnessed the invasion of Madrid and subsequent horrors committed by French troops, and also the Famine in Madrid (1811–12) in which 20,000 people died. In response, he created a series of etchings called *The Disasters of War* (1809–15), described by Ralph Shikes as 'the most powerful and unforgettable indictment of War in the History of Art'.[9]

Lorenz Eitner asserts: 'The treatment of war as misery rather than glory, and its presentation from the victim's point of view, is rare in art before Goya.'[10] Yet Goya's etchings were little-known during his lifetime, and were not published until 1863, several years after Mahony's Famine illustrations. The lithograph *Rue Transnonian, April 15, 1834*, by Honoré Daumier (1808–1887) poignantly shows the effects of police suppression of a popular uprising in Paris on one working-class family. During her life Käthe Kollwitz (1867–1945) witnessed the poverty and suffering of working-class people, women and children in Germany, and executed a series of etchings related to an uprising by weavers, woodcuts relating to the First World War, and lithographs showing post-war poverty and hunger.

Mahony's Famine illustrations have a raw, first-hand quality that find echoes in Kollwitz's images of desperate peasants, women with hungry children in Vincent Van Gogh's drawing *Sorrow* (1882), and, as late as 1951, in Peter Peri's engraving *Korea*,[11] made in response to the Korean War.

# Asenath Nicholson's Irish journeys

## Lorraine Chadwick

The reader of these pages should be told that, if strange things are recorded, it was because strange things were seen; and if strange things were seen which no other writer has written, it was because no other writer has visited the same places, under the same circumstances . . . they *are* realities, and many of them fearful ones – *realities* which none but eye-witnesses can understand, and none but those who passed through them can *feel*.[1]

Penned by Asenath Nicholson in the mid nineteenth century, *Ireland's Welcome to the Stranger* and *Lights and Shades of Ireland* are two narratives which provide unique insights into Ireland and its people. Nicholson travelled to Ireland on two separate occasions; her first visit was on the eve of the Great Famine and her detailed accounts of social conditions in the country are rich and varied. Her second journey through the towns and villages of Ireland, undertaken during the Famine itself, is a searing account of the anguish and agony endured by the starving. In writing about her own personal and harrowing experiences amongst the poor and hungry, Nicholson not only gives a voice to the famished, she also bequeaths to her readers a realistic and disturbing portrayal of life at the time of the Famine.

### NICHOLSON'S BACKGROUND

Asenath Nicholson was born Asenath Hatch in the village of Chelsea, eastern Vermont, in the United States on 24 February 1792. She was the youngest child and only daughter of Michael Hatch and his wife, Martha. Asenath was something of a prophetic name for her; the Asenath referred to in the book of Genesis (Chapter 41) was the daughter of an Egyptian priest, given as a wife to Joseph, who was responsible for the management of the famine food supply in Egypt. Asenath Nicholson would in time mirror the efforts of her biblical predecessor, managing her own scarce resources in order to help feed and clothe the poor of Ireland: 'the greatest suffering was, during the few hours devoted to sleep, when I was occasionally awaked by hearing some moan of distress under my window . . . [E]very day the quantity of meal lessened, and my purse grew lighter.'[2]

Nicholson acknowledges in her narratives that the upbringing she received from her parents was instrumental in the way she approached others. She stated that her home

education was of 'a most uncompromising kind' and that her parents were descended from puritanical stock who taught her that goodness alone was greatness. Nicholson's family were members of the Protestant Congregational Church, whose teachings emphasised not only the autonomy of local churches but also the absolute importance of the Bible. Her narratives are infused with biblical quotations and references. The precepts of her church also underlined the importance of the freedom of the individual and it is perhaps this principle which is most apparent in Nicholson's writing; she was never afraid to speak her mind when she saw an injustice or a neglect of duty.

Nicholson initially worked as a teacher in her home village of Chelsea. However, in the early 1830s she moved to New York and opened a small school. While teaching in New York, she met and married Norman Nicholson, a merchant whose interests also included abolition, temperance, reform and philanthropy. Both became interested in the work of Sylvester Graham and his popular health movement of the period. In essence, Grahamites believed that it was possible to develop bad habits, not alone in terms of food and drink, but also in terms of one's own physical

Fig. 1 *Asenath Hatch Nicholson* (1792–1855) by Anna Maria Howitt. [Source: *Annals of the Famine in Ireland*, Edited by Maureen Murphy (Dublin, 1998), p. 2]

well-being. Practices such as not bathing regularly, not taking exercise and not breathing in fresh air, were all violations of what Graham determined were nature's physiological laws.

Norman and Asenath Nicholson opened their first temperance boarding house in 1832 in a borough of New York City to accommodate and provide for the faithful through Grahamite principles. Nicholson's fiercely held belief regarding temperance surfaces repeatedly in her writings; her narratives, for instance, speak highly of Father Theobald Mathew, an advocate of temperance, who worked tirelessly to promote sobriety, conscientiousness and industry amongst the Irish people.

### ENCOUNTERING THE IRISH IN NEW YORK

While operating the boarding houses in New York, Nicholson visited the nearby impoverished slums known as the Five Points. It was here she made her initial contact with the Irish poor:

> It was in the garrets and cellars of New York that I first became acquainted with the Irish peasantry, and it was there I *saw* they were a suffering people. Their patience, their cheerfulness, their flow of blundering, hap-hazard, happy wit, made them to me a distinct people from all I had seen . . . God will one day allow me to breathe the mountain air of the sea-girt coast of Ireland – to sit down in their cabins, and there learn what soil has nurtured, what hardships have disciplined so hardy a race – so patient and so impetuous, so revengeful and so forgiving, so proud and so humble, so obstinate and so docile, so witty and so simple a people.[3]

Protestant missionaries worked together in the Five Points district during the 1830s and the 1840s; however, Nicholson chose to work amongst the poor unaided, a practice which would be observed again when she visited Ireland. Her husband Norman died in 1841. It was at this juncture that she decided to travel to Ireland, to read and distribute the Bible and to learn more about the people she had come to respect while working in the slums of New York City.[4] Nicholson would bring much more to the people of Ireland than the Bible; her narratives provide a vivid picture of the social, economic and political conditions which prevailed in Ireland on the cusp of and during the Famine years.

It was Nicholson's intention not 'to tax the Irish public with another volume, added to the huge pile already written on Ireland. It was my design to go silently through among the poor, and tell the story to my own countrymen; that they might be induced to labour more untiringly and effectually for the destitute portion of this nation, who are daily landing upon their shores.'[5] She had little time for those whom she perceived to be casual observers of Ireland:

Fig. 2 *Fr Theobald Mathew* (1790–1856) by Edward Daniel Leahy (1846, oil on canvas). Nicholson lavished praise on the Temperance Movement and Theobald Mathew's own personal crusade. She had a great deal of sympathy and admiration for the Capuchin priest who laboured so selflessly amongst the poor during the Famine years. [Source: National Portrait Gallery]

'we have had many "Pencillings by the Way", and "Conciliation Halls" and "Killarney Lakes" from the tops of coaches and from smoking dinner tables. But one day's walk on mountain or bog, one night's lodging where the pig, and the ass, and horned oxen feed, "Like Aaron's serpent, swallows all the rest".'[6]

Nicholson chose to be an intimate observer whose sole intention was to write factually and first-hand about the Irish poor; it is the intimacy of her observations which allows Nicholson to construct narratives which bear witness in a unique and compelling way: 'I resolved to avail myself of every invitation to ride on any vehicle, however humble; for two reasons – to rest me, and to learn more of the people than I could by walking alone. To be a peasant myself, was the only way of getting at facts which I was seeking.'[7]

### NICHOLSON'S PRE-FAMINE VISIT

Nicholson's first journey to Ireland began in May 1844 when she set out from New York on a fifteen-month visit. She travelled on foot throughout much of the island, reading the Bible to the local people and sharing their hospitality. Nicholson was wholehearted in her praise of the welcome extended to the stranger, particularly in rural Ireland. She initially visited people and places where she had introductions from her New York connections.

Given her own strongly-held beliefs, Nicholson clearly had to steer a path between the religions she encountered. Bible-reading strangers were very often viewed with mistrust by Catholics, while Nicholson's independent spirit and determination were viewed with equal suspicion by Protestant missionaries with whom she came in contact.[8] Literacy and education were the two main areas which Nicholson viewed differently to other Protestant

missionaries. She firmly believed that the Irish could only be delivered from 'the superstition of Rome' through education and a thorough understanding of the Bible. The latter conviction was not always shared by her contemporaries in the field, in particular evangelical New Reformers who actively engaged in proselytism by promising food to those Catholics who converted. It was a charge levelled at missionary colonies established in Dingle and Achill.

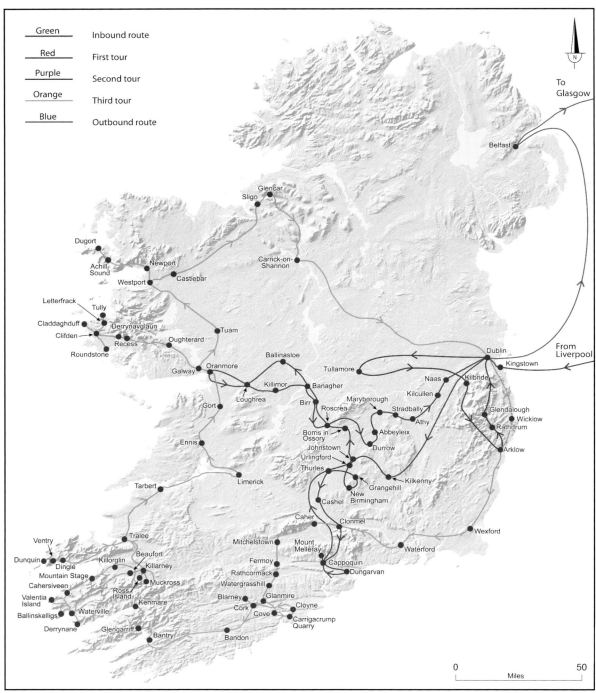

Fig. 3 PLACES VISITED BY ASENATH NICHOLSON DURING HER FIRST JOURNEY TO IRELAND, 1844–45. It was in May 1844 that Nicholson first set out on her journey to Ireland. Her sense of duty and thirst for knowledge would take her to the remotest parts of the country. Initially she stayed in Dublin, familiarising herself with the lanes and streets of the capital. While she had cut her cloth so to speak in the cellars and garrets of New York, little had prepared her for the squalor and dirt she encountered in the lanes and back streets of Dublin. Leaving Dublin she ventured out into the heart of the Irish countryside, confining much of her travels to the south and west of the country.

478

## MISSIONARY COLONIES

The fact that Nicholson was an educator herself shaped her views of Protestant educational societies and the educational establishments which they organised. She was keenly interested in visiting the schools of two missionary colonies that had received specific attention in the 1840s: those situated in Dingle and Achill. Rev. Edward Nangle established the Achill mission in 1831, being drawn to the island by its rugged beauty and the 'primitive but noble savagery of its people'.[9] While Nicholson initially approved of the work of both missions she also cautioned that such places should be carefully monitored. She visited both colonies during her first visit to Ireland but it was Nangle's mission in Achill which was of most interest to her.

Nicholson's first impressions were positive and she wrote that the mission appeared to be prosperous and the inhabitants well nourished. However she became disturbed when Nangle informed her that converts at the mission were not taught to read as it 'would be too difficult'. Nangle was opposed to Nicholson's ideals about literacy and education and relations between the two deteriorated when Nicholson read an article written by Nangle in the *Achill Herald* published in July 1845, detailing her visit to the mission. He

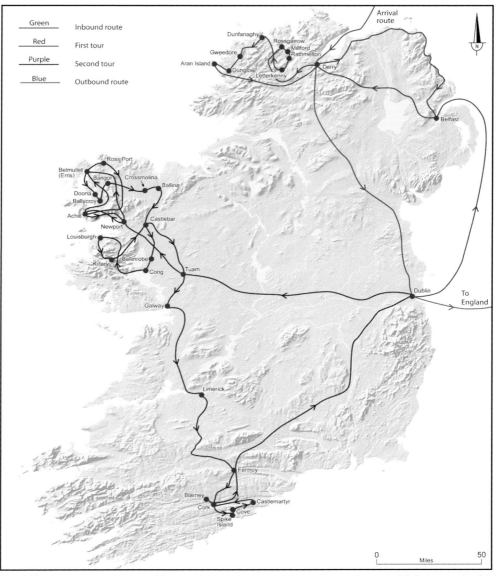

Fig. 4 PLACES VISITED BY ASENATH NICHOLSON DURING HER SECOND JOURNEY TO IRELAND. Nicholson arrived in Ireland in May 1846 determined to play her part in famine relief efforts. Administering relief initially in Dublin she desired to view for herself the worst affected regions. Her travels would take her to a number of villages and towns in the west and northwestern parts of the country. Such was the extent of the distress that Nicholson witnessed on her first visit to County Mayo that she could not bear the thought of confronting such 'realities' again.

noted that 'the principal object of this woman's mission is to create a spirit of discontent among the lower orders, and to dispose them to regard their superiors as so many unfeeling oppressors. There is nothing in her conduct or conversation to justify the supposition on insanity, and we strongly suspect she is the emissary of some democratic and revolutionary society.'[10]

*Ireland's Welcome to the Stranger* is a valuable record of social conditions in Ireland. Nicholson provides detailed descriptions of the one-roomed cabins, which often reeked of poverty, and the routines of cabin life. She found it difficult to reconcile the wealth that was visible in the Irish countryside with the extremes of destitution she witnessed. She believed that those who had been endowed with the riches of the earth had a responsibility to those less fortunate; hence the landlords had a duty towards their impoverished

tenants. There was little doubt that the suffering of the people she encountered was keenly felt. Yet the poor had extended the hand of friendship and given of themselves and their few possessions to an extent that shamed the 'coldly proffered bread' of the gentry.

In settlements in the west of Ireland, Nicholson was particularly struck by the burdens of work placed on women. Her independent spirit did not mean that she was untouched by contemporary beliefs about the proper role of women in society.[11] She refused to accept the inevitability of the poverty which she surveyed. In the final pages of *Ireland's Welcome*, however, Nicholson prophetically warned her readers that Ireland and its people was teetering on the edge of a great calamity. Two year later she would return to Ireland to bear witness to the ravages wrought by famine and disease.

## FAMINE IRELAND

*Lights and Shades of Ireland* is Nicholson's account of her travels in Ireland during the Famine years. Compassionate and heartfelt, it is a narrative shaped by Nicholson's own particular 'way of seeing' Ireland and the suffering of its people. Having taken up what she believed to be a divinely appointed undertaking, she never complained about her own personal travails but only grumbled that she did not have the resources to do more for those who were suffering in her midst. During her second visit to Ireland, Nicholson spent time in Dublin, Cork and in the west (Fig. 4). In January 1847, at the height of the Famine, she began her one-woman relief operation in Dublin: organising a soup kitchen, visiting the homes of the poor and distributing bread in the street. Her depictions of the starving are graphic:

A cabin was seen closed one day a little out of the town, when a man had the curiosity to open it, and in a dark corner he found a family of the father, mother and two children, lying in close compact. The father was considerably decomposed; the mother, it appeared, had died last and probably fastened the door, which was always the custom when all hope was extinguished, to get into the darkest corner and die where passers-by could not see them. Such *family* scenes were quite common, and the cabin was generally pulled down upon them for a grave. The man called, begging me to look in. *I did not,* and *could not* endure, as the famine progressed, such sights, as well as the first, they were too *real,* and these realities became a dread.[12]

Nicholson made it clear from the outset that she believed the Famine's devastation was not providential in design, 'but rather the failure of *man* to use God's gifts responsibly'; she saw Irish dependence on the potato as the principal reason for the people's ultimate demise.[13] However, Nicholson also readily acknowledged their perseverance in the face of absolute adversity and in their unwavering faith in God, using the example of how some would persist in saving, sometimes by stealth, some part of a sound potato, and keep it from the hungry mouths of their children so that they might put it in the ground, while praying fervently to God that the potato would grow without disease once more.

Nicholson was highly critical of the absentee land-owning class. However, she did recognise the burden which some of the landlords shouldered during the Famine. Neither was she afraid to blame the government of the day, as illustrated in the following excerpt from *Lights and Shades*:

The government of England might possibly have dozed a little too long, regardless of what these her thriving landlords in that green isle were doing; they might not have precisely understood how they

were *feeding, housing* and *paying* their serfs that were squatting 'lazily' upon their soil; they might not have applied the laws of mind precisely to *this* point, that these laws possess the unvarying principle of fixing deeply and firmly in the heart of the oppressor a hatred towards the being that he has unjustly coerced, and the very degradation to which he has reduced him becomes the very cause of his aversion towards him.[14]

Criticism also rained down on those religious who were found wanting, for example, 'those full-fed, government-paid clergymen, who had learned the law of love through her own bread and wine exclusively, and whose jaundiced eyes saw dark and foul spots on all her surplices but her own'.[15]

Lack of employment opportunities for the poorer classes was the principal economic reason which Nicholson put forward to explain why the failure of the potato had such a calamitous impact on Ireland. In *Lights and Shades* she stressed the fact that the economy of rural Ireland, especially those areas most affected by the Famine, was completely different to that of England and that it was this *ignorance* of prevailing conditions in Ireland by the British Government which also helped to contribute to the disaster. She observed that the poorer classes in rural Ireland rarely handled money and even more rarely used it for the purchase of food. Rent was paid to the landlord through labour on the land and families lived on the potato which they grew themselves. When the potato failed those on the bottom rung of the social ladder were left helpless. Nicholson correctly saw that there was little use in paying the poorer classes a money wage for their labour on any type of relief works without also creating some type of market distribution system to enable them to convert their wages into food.

Other writers of the period did not see the lack of work as a problem for the rural poor but preferred to label them as 'idle'. Nicholson addressed this issue in a subtle way, *inverting* the characterisation and re-labelling the upper classes: 'that idleness and improvidence (which are generally companions) are two great evils of Ireland, must be acknowledged. The rich are idle from a silly pride and long habits of indulgence; and the poor, because no man "hires them".'[16] Nicholson's narratives are distinctive in this respect because in a sense, she deconstructs the then popular views of the Irish as an indolent race, denouncing them as uninformed and unjust.

In both of her narratives, Nicholson frequently compared the lot of the Irish poor with that of the slave. She observed that the Irish poor were enslaved in their situation, enslaved to their employers, enslaved to the system and, worse still, enslaved to the potato. Class distinctions and how these were played out and characterised within Irish society were also observed in her writings. For example, she contrasted the burial of a *respectable* young woman in a churchyard with

Fig. 5 Potato ridges in Newport, County Mayo. Nicholson journeyed from Tuam to Newport in an open car remarking that the 'wretchedness of the country made it altogether a dismal ride'. On reaching her destination she was met by the naked, cold and dying: 'I found here, at Newport, misery without a mask'. [Photo: Frank Coyne]

that of two peasant children being buried by their brother in the same burial ground on the same day. The bell tolled for the upstanding woman; no bell tolled for those who had starved. The respectable young woman was afforded the dignity of a coffin, entombed the correct distance under the ground while the children were buried in sacks in a shallow, hand-excavated grave quarried by their brother.

> I never witnessed a more stirring striking contrast between civilized and savage life – Christianity and heathenism – wealth and poverty, than in this instance; it said so much for the *mockery* of death, with all its trappings and ceremonies – the *mockery* of pompous funerals, and their black retinue. This poor boy unheeded had staid in the dark cabin with those dead brothers, not even getting admittance into the gate, till some *respectable* one should want a burial; then he might follow this procession at a suitable distance, with two dead brothers upon his back, and put them in with his own hands, with none to compassionate him![17]

Nicholson's narratives are powerful and poignant accounts of conditions in Ireland both on the eve of and during the Great Famine. Her's is a unique account; it is personal, intimate and focuses chiefly on the human suffering endured by the people. Nicholson knew that despite the graphic nature of her accounts, she would never truly capture the misery, grief and horror of those she wrote about: 'should any of these facts appear exaggerated, let it be said that no language is adequate to give the true, the real picture. One look of the eye into the daily scenes there witnessed would overpower what any pen, however graphic, or tongue, however eloquent, could portray.'[18] She was also cognizant of the fact that the written word could have a profound effect into the future: 'some hap-hazard expression, made to give the sentence a lively turn or happy ending, may fix a label on a people, which will be read and believed by many generations.'[19]

Nicholson departed Ireland in early 1849, eventually returning to America in 1852, the year when famine conditions finally began to abate. She died in Jersey City, New Jersey, on 15 May 1855. On leaving Ireland Nicholson vowed that she would not forget 'this Jerusalem'.[20] She did not. Her writings are a powerful testimony to the sufferings of the people she encountered.

# Thomas Carlyle and Famine Ireland

## *John Crowley*

Many distinguished writers arrived in Ireland during the Famine years. Some were commissioned by newspapers such as *The Times* or *The Illustrated London News* to report on the condition of Ireland and the scenes they had witnessed. Others, like the Scots-born imperialist Thomas Carlyle (1795–1881), journeyed across the country to see for themselves the extent of Irish distress. A historian, essayist and social critic, Carlyle pronounced widely on many of the important issues of the day. The influx of Famine refugees to the ports of Glasgow and Liverpool had alerted him to the grave dangers of ignoring the Irish problem. Fears were aroused that such cities could not cope with the rising tide of destitute Irish in their midst and the threat they could pose to the established social order. Having witnessed the extremes of poverty amongst the Irish in Glasgow, Carlyle asked, rhetorically, where the true capital of Ireland was now located? 'Has Ireland any capital and where is its future to be? Perhaps Glasgow and Liverpool is the real capital now.'[1] Carlyle was stridently opposed to the tide of reform which was sweeping Europe. 'Fundamentally he had wanted to assault the priggishness and smugness of the liberal and philanthropic consensus that believed the lower orders could be reformed and improved and entrusted with greater responsibility.'[2] His writings on Ireland must be seen in this light. Perhaps in the end they tell us as much about the politics and personality of Carlyle as the country he was visiting.

### YOUNG IRELAND

Carlyle's reputation was such that he had attracted the attention and admiration of Young Irelanders such as John Mitchel and Charles Gavan Duffy. His friendship with Gavan Duffy was one of the reasons for undertaking his journey to Ireland in July and August 1849. It was an unlikely friendship to say the least, for Carlyle was deeply antagonistic to the aims of the Young Irelanders. He had been highly critical of Daniel O'Connell's campaign for repeal and was equally dismissive of the aspirations of the Young Irelanders:

> I cannot find that the Irish were in 1641, are now and until they conquer all the English ever again be a nation, anything but an integral constituent part of a nation – anymore than the Scotch highlanders can, than the parish of Kensington can.[3]

Despite these obvious political differences, it was Duffy who accompanied Carlyle for much of his travels in Ireland. Carlyle's record of his journey was published posthumously in 1882 under the title *Reminiscences of My Irish Journey* and constitutes a minor work when seen in the context of his overall *oeuvre*. By 1849 Carlyle had published widely on topics such as *The French Revolution* (1837), *Chartism* (1840) and *Oliver Cromwell's Letters and Speeches with Elucidations* (1845). Duffy maintained that Carlyle would never have allowed *Reminiscences* go to print had he lived, 'claiming that the account was no more than "hasty notes" written with a "license of language" fit only for a private communication'.[4] *Reminiscences* bears all the hallmarks of a journey endured. The writing style is harsh, uncompromising and at times despairing.[5] Clearly Carlyle was troubled by much of what he had seen. His language coarsened as his views

Fig. 1 *Portrait of Thomas Carlyle (1795–1881)* by John Everett Millais. [Source: © National Portrait Gallery]

on Ireland hardened. Not only was his anger directed at the landlords but also at Russell's Liberal Government, which he sensed had all but relinquished its moral authority in Ireland by its refusal to provide work for the starving and destitute. Carlyle displayed at most a paternalistic concern for the Irish 'peasantry': 'the toiling inferior can find a superior that should lovingly and wisely govern. Happiness will consist in being given work and being compliantly grateful for it.'[6] He was convinced that Ireland needed the strong arm of government if it were to awaken from the paralysis which threatened to destroy her.

## THE EXAMINER

Carlyle's views on Ireland must be seen in the context of a series of articles he wrote in 1848 for *The Examiner* newspaper in which he roundly condemned the repeal movement. He was also scathing in his criticism of the governing classes, especially a landholding elite who in his eyes had been buttressed by the union but had failed miserably in their primary duty. They were a class 'quite unconcerned with governing, concerned only to get the rents and wages of governing and the governable ungoverned millions sunk meanwhile in dark cabins, in ignorance, sloth, confusion, superstition and putrid ignominy, dying the hunger death or what is worth living the hunger life'.[7] Yet Britain was destined to rule Ireland by virtue of its civilising mission. Carlyle the imperialist shuddered to think what would become of the country if the union should ever be repealed. He zealously dismissed the repeal movement as well as the militancy of the Young Irelanders, describing the relationship between Ireland and Britain in jingoistic terms:

> Deduct what we may call Teutonic Ireland, Ulster and the other analogous regions, leave only the Ireland that clamours for Repeal at present, and in spite of its size on the map and in the population returns we must say that its value hitherto approaches amazingly to zero, so far as Britain is concerned . . . Not out of the Tipperary regions did the artillery that has subdued the world and its anarchies and devils and wild dog kennels proceed hitherto. No it was out of other regions than Tipperary, by other equipment than are commonest in Tipperary, that England built up her social constitution, wrote her literature, planted her Americas, subdued her Indias, spun her cotton webs and got along with her enormous job of work so far. This is true, and Tipperary ought to be made to know this, and even will be made to know it – by terrible schooling if mild will not serve.[8]

Carlyle's time in Ireland in 1849 only served to reinforce his views about the country which, in many respects, were already well defined before his visit. Given the tenor of his

Fig. 2  Charles Gavan Duffy (1816–1903). Journalist and Young Irelander, Duffy accompanied Carlyle for much of his Irish journey in 1849. Duffy wrote his own account of the 'terrible realities' he witnessed for the *Nation* newspaper, a paper that he had recently revived. His was a much more sympathetic record of the hardships endured by the starving and dispossessed. Duffy highlighted in particular the callousness of the landlords and their 'pitiless extermination' of their tenants. A reluctant revolutionary, who had supported the failed rebellion of 1848, he was later elected MP for New Ross in 1852. Land reform and the disestablishment of the Church of Ireland became central to his political beliefs. He subsequently grew tired of Irish politics and emigrated to Victoria in Australia where he later became governor. [Source: National Library of Ireland]

reports on Irish affairs in 1848, it is not that difficult to understand the bleak picture which he painted of the country and its people. On 8 July 1849, for example, he visited Kildare, 'a wretched and wild village' where he was greeted by a 'swarm of clamorous mendicants; men, women and children . . . [H]ere for the first time was Irish beggary itself.'[9] The stark poverty and vagrancy which he witnessed in Kildare fitted neatly his characterisation of the island and its people as an unwieldy mass of beggars.

## ENCOUNTERS WITH FAMINE IRELAND

Carlyle's itinerary would take him from Dublin, through Kildare, Carlow and Kilkenny to Waterford. From there he would travel to Cork and Limerick and a number of towns and villages in the west of Ireland. The abiding image was

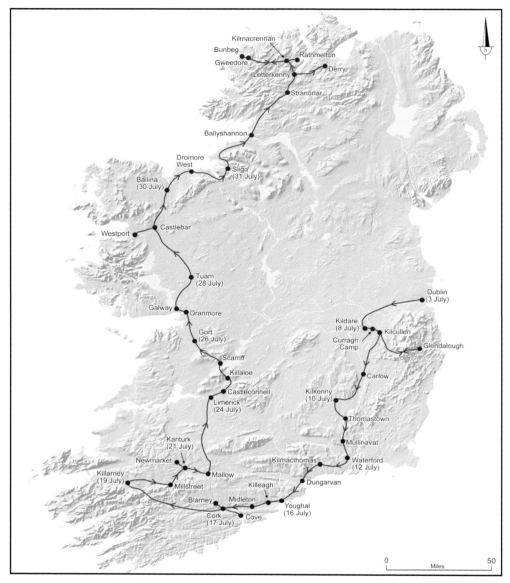

Fig. 3 THOMAS CARLYLE'S IRISH JOURNEY. Carlyle arrived in Ireland on 3 July 1849. He would spend just over a month in the country travelling in a clockwise direction from Dublin to Cork and then taking in most of the western counties. His carping spirit never deserted him throughout his journey. [Adapted from David Nally, *Human Emcumbrances: Political Violence and the Great Irish Famine* (Notre Dame, 2011)]

had all but succeeded in turning society into a breeding ground of pauperism. His remedy was the provision of schemes which would give real work to the people.

The larger circumstance of the Famine, at times, sat uneasily in the background. On the journey from Lismore to Youghal, Carlyle pointed to 'the ragged barrenness of the landscape, with many roofless huts being the main characteristic'.[12] He found laudable the efforts of the Duke of Devonshire to employ the poor on the embankment of a Government money had been borrowed by the duke to carry out such works. In Carlyle's view the Duke of Devonshire was a rare exception. In general he reproached the landlords for the neglect of their tenants. Millstreet was described 'as one mass of mendicancy, ruined by the Famine. Its main street was filled with beggars – people in another coach throw halfpence; the population run at them like rabid dogs, dogs of both sexes and whelps.'[13] In Killarney he referred to beggars waiting at solitary corners –'who start with us, run sometimes miles – get nothing'. His retort 'get nothing' hints at his own discomfiture at such an encounter. The extent of the begging which he witnessed in the town appalled him: 'poor wretches after all but human pity dies away into stony misery and disgust in the excess of such scenes'.[14]

Carlyle regarded the successive failures of the potato crop as a blessing in disguise – 'all of us thank God for the merciful destruction of the potato' – as it would end both Irish dependence upon it and more importantly the culture it spawned.[15] He distanced himself at every turn from the wretched creatures he encountered on his journey. Little of his writing conveys genuine sympathy for the plight of those afflicted by the Famine. In addition, as Geary observes: 'there is a distinct lack of curiosity about the event itself, the catalyst for the social conditions he had encountered. There is a sense of detachment almost, typified by his silence on evictions, the callousness and crudity and scale of which in the south and west of Ireland in the late 1840s so shocked visitors and other commentators.'[16]

one of cities and towns populated with ever increasing numbers of destitute. For many of the latter the workhouse was a final resort. On 11 July Carlyle visited the workhouse in Kilkenny: '1000 or 2000 great hulks of men lying piled up within brick walls is such a country, in such a day. Did a greater violence to the law of nature ever before present itself to sight if one had an eye to see it.'[10] He was brutal in his depiction of these 'human-infested' institutions. In Ballina, County Mayo, he visited an auxiliary workhouse which catered for children, who in Carlyle's eyes were being weaned on a diet of pauperism – 'a thatched subsidiary workhouse this; all for the children: really good, had the children been bred towards anything but pauperism – pauperism in geometrical progression'.[11] He was bitterly opposed to the Poor Law in principle and had little but disdain for the architects of this failed policy. He considered the workhouse a vile imposition on the Irish people which

## THE NATION.     September 1

too long, a whole narrative poem; and too like Day and Martin's poetic puffs (which B. O'N. will please to recollect some one accused Lord Byron of writing). We will take an extract, however, in consideration of its being so Irish :—

"Oh! glory, glory, be to God, my own, my heart's delight, And sure 'tis Him we ought to thank both morning noon and night.

Dear Mary, call the neighbours in, I'm sure 'tis glad they'll be,

Their darling, and their favourite, you were *asthore machree.*

The dances were neglected, love, the hurlers would not play—

The patrons were deserted, too, since that unhappy day; But now as you're at home, my love, they'll sing and dance once more,

And hurlers brave will meet again as in the days of yore.

Run, brothers run, to Slievenamon, and light a noble fire, Till every hill all round about will cheer my heart's desire. Let grief and sorrow fly away, my faithful love is here, And bid the harpers play for me the wedding day is near. Oh! a hundred thousand welcomes, *asthore, asthore, machree.*

Oh! sure I never thought before you were so dear to me! Oh! welcome, welcome, &c. &c."

"A Spectator;" "P. K.;" the subject and object are unworthy of your care. "He who washes an ass's head," says the Italian proverb, "loses his soap." How are you off for soap that you expend it so wastefully? "A Future Pauper;" "Letter to Mr. Webb on American slavery;" "J. P. N.;" of your sixteen pages we have diligently read six to discover your object, but utterly to no purpose. *Nota bene*—gentlemen who mean nothing are respectfully requested to say ditto.

## THE NATION.

"To create and foster public opinion in Ireland, and to make it racy of the soil."—CHIEF BARON WOULFE.

SATURDAY, SEPTEMBER 1, 1849.

### The New "Nation."

An Irish "Rebel" for whom the transport ship floated in Dublin harbour but four months ago; who has since seen his dearest friends and comrades carried away into penal exile; who sees the wrongs they rose up to redress at peril of their heads, daily widening and aggravated since their fall; and who knows that the country they hoped to save is sinking deeper and deeper into an ignominious lethargy, is called upon to-day to show cause, if there be any, for still believing in the deliverance of Ireland.

Such a position is one that forbids all romantic hopes and exaggerated promises, and I am rejoiced that it does. It calls upon whomsoever speaks of deliverance now, to be sure as life or death that he is walking on the solid earth, and towards a goal that may actually be attained, and I am rejoiced that it does. To me it has always been a first and imperative necessity in political movements to know where I am going, and how. I cannot walk in the dark. I cannot follow, and I cannot play, a Will of the wisp. Breaking

solid sense and integrity lapsing into inaction, while vigorous effort and moral courage were never so essentially necessary as at this moment—neither is that a creditable attitude for a people.

Speaking for one man, who has not come to the conclusion without anxious thought and investigation, and who has not published it with raw or indecent haste, I declare that the struggle for Ireland *can* be renewed with just hopes of success, and that it must be renewed forthwith. This is my assured conviction. At that midway of life when illusions disappear and reality is the only basis on which we can stand erect, I rest upon this belief. Not unacquainted with men, nor unfamiliar with the resources or with the faults of Ireland, and not unwarned of the penalty at which her cause is sometimes advocated, I deliberately take it up anew. And so sure does the ultimate end appear, and so clear the present duty, that though our country lies in ruins—morally a beggar, physically a spectre—I for one man, declare before God, I would not exchange the task of helping to bind her wounds and lead her anew to strength and honor for the right of ruling among the proudest people on the earth.

I am not blind to the actual condition of the country, nor to the vices of the country. As far as a conscientious investigation of facts with my own eyes could enable me to judge, I have laboured to understand them to the bottom. I have visited the famine districts and the "rebel" districts; and conversed with many of the wisest and best men in Munster and Connaught. Of the physical and moral state of the people, and of our actual political condition I believe there is little which I am capable of understanding, that I have not learned.

No words printed in a newspaper or elsewhere, will give any man who has not seen it a conception of the fallen condition of the West and the South. The famine and the landlords have actually created a *new race* in Ireland. I have seen on the streets of Galway crowds of creatures more debased than the Yahoos of Swift—creatures having only a distant and hideous resemblance to human beings. Grey-headed old men, whose idiot faces had hardened into a settled leer of mendicancy, simeous and semi-human; and women filthier and more frightful than the harpies, who at the jingle of a coin on the pavement swarmed in myriads from unseen places, struggling, screaming, *shrieking* for their prey, like some monstrous and unclean animals. In Westport the sight of the priest on the street gathered an entire pauper population, thick as a village market, swarming round him for relief. Beggar children, beggar adults, beggars in white hairs, girls with faces grey and shrivelled, the grave stamped upon them in a decree which could not be recalled; women with the more touching and tragical aspect of lingering shame, and self-respect not yet effaced; and among these terrible realities, imposture shaking in pretended fits to add the last touch of horrible grotesqueness to the picture! I have seen these accursed sights, and they are burned into my memory for ever.

Away from the towns other scenes of unimaginable horror disclose themselves. The traveller meets groups, and even

In Ballina, which sprung up like a miracle of prosperity on the distant shore of the West, with desolate Erris on one hand, and the wide Atlantic on the other—where fostering help is specially invited by so providential a success—an entire street of the working classes has been pulled down. Even in Erris itself, where men are thinly scattered, and wide tracts of fertile land call for labour, there has been active and pitiless extermination. Between Killala Bay and Sligo, for half a day's drive, every second house is pulled down; and not cabins alone or mainly, but substantial stone houses not unfit for a thriving yeomanry.

In my native county, where tennnt-right lately prevailed, in a barony which has won a reputation for independence and gallantry proverbial throughout Ulster, I have seen the same system in its very worst aspect. The poor "Farney Freeholders" have been scattered like the Electors of Clare, and for the same offence. I stood upon hill in Maheracloon within the present week, from which the levelled houses could be counted by the dozen, wherever the eye turned. Within two years and principally within the last six months, upwards of eighteen hundred human creatures have been ejected from one-half of the barony in which an Englishman named SHIRLEY is the landlord; while in the second half, situated in all other respects alike, extermination is almost, or absolutely, unknown And to my unspeakable astonishment I was shown in several instances the crop, sowed and tended by the exterminated tenant now ripening in possession of the Exterminator, and to be sold by him for rent, weeks after he had flung the owner out on the high road. And this is in the region of tenant-right—at the very "gap of the North."

In this physical and social condition I found large tracts of the country. A condition before which exaggerated hopes stand rebuked, and silent. But a condition too that carries in itself assurance, to whoever believes in GOD's justice, that it will sooner or later be resisted and overcome. These things cannot continue. Queen, monarchy, law, rights of property, which of these words sound so awful as the name of GOD whose people we see massacred Which of them weigh against the lives and souls of our race and kindred, rotting away in unspeakable misery and degradation. If any just man on the face of the earth wonders that Irishmen meditated insurrection in 1848, he need but look on these scenes for a solution.

For myself, no Herculaneum or Pompei covers buried memories so venerable to me as the memories that sleep under the ashes of these ruined Irish hamlets. It may be that the miserable serfs yielded their rights in a base submission that makes manhood ashamed to name them dying in some ditch, or living a protracted and viler death, but they are not the less our own race and people. Poor, mutilated and debased scions of a tender, brave, and pious stock, they were not less martyrs in the battle of centuries for the right to live on our own soil.

And close to the levelled cottage, close to the thronged poorhouse lie thousands of acres out of cultivation. Multitudes are dying on one hand, on the other the fruitful earth bears only weeds; any other crop being practically forbidden! Before all things this system must end. It has arrived

Fig. 4 An extract from Duffy's account of his journey which appeared in *The Nation* newspaper on 1and 8 September 1849 [Source: National Library of Ireland]

## IMPROVEMENT AND INDUSTRY

There was no disguising Carlyle's contempt for Irish society's 'indolent' ways. Improvement could only be achieved by adopting the industrious methods of his fellow countrymen. It would be wrong to categorise such depictions of idleness and waste as unthinking as they clearly reflected more widespread attitudes towards the Irish during the period of the Famine. As Peter Gray explains:

In Britain the Great Irish Famine occurred in an existing ideological context that had already pathologized the backwardness of Ireland and prescribed a reconstructive regime. Ireland differed from other famine-stricken European regions in being interpreted through the lens of colonialism . . . What made the Irish experience unique in terms of state response was the British perception of the potato failure as an opportunity rather than an obstacle, an opportunity to deny the benefits of common nationality until Irish society had been remodelled according to British norms.[17]

A rural landscape shaped by a 'class of improvers' was central to Carlyle's vision for the country. The human cost of achieving such an objective was not something which weighed too heavily on his mind. On his return to London

485

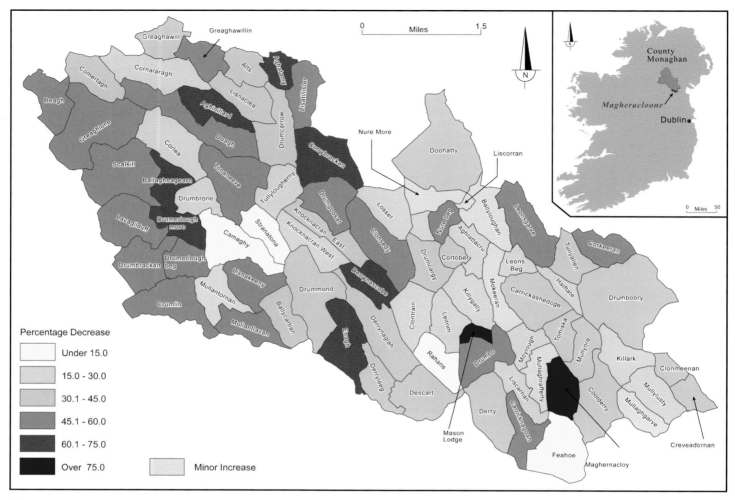

Fig. 5 THE PARISH OF MAGHERACLOONE IN COUNTY MONAGHAN, referred to in Duffy's account (previous page), suffered a population decline of 43% between 1841–51 (from 9,012 to 5,141). Much of the parish was located within the Shirley estate at Lough Fea, Carrickmacross. The decline was due in the main to the policy of eviction which was rigorously enforced on the estate. [Source: *Clogher Record*, Vol. 17, No. 2 (2001), pp. 528–529]

he 'thanked heaven for the sight of real human industry', while on the train journey home he enthusiastically made reference to 'the fenced fields, the weeded crops and the human creatures with whole clothes on their backs'.[18]

In general Carlyle offered a very depressing view of Ireland and its people. He had seen the unploughed fields, the clusters of cabins unfit for human habitation and the cities and towns rife with beggars and paupers. He described the countryside on his journey from Gort to Galway as 'fifteen miles of the stoniest, barest barrenness I have ever seen yet'. On reaching Westport 'he concluded that society is at an end here with the land uncultivated and every second soul a pauper – society here would have to eat itself and end by cannibalism in a week, if it were not held up by the test of our Empire still standing afoot'.[19] His anger and despair at the depths of Irish poverty and the inadequacy of the official response to it was expressed in language which was ofttimes 'savage, harsh and inhumane' but no different, as Morrow contends 'to his reactions to the breakdown of effective authority in other parts of Britain'.[20] His most trenchant criticism in the end was reserved for those social

and political elites who failed miserably to live up to his sense of moral duty and mission. Such a failure in Ireland had devastating and profound consequences.

The key point for Carlyle was that Ireland and its people were not beyond redemption. He had been a bitter opponent of the English Poor Law and his visits to workhouses in Ireland only served to confirm his abhorrence of such institutions: 'Brutallist stupidity can hardly be more brutal than those human swineries had now grown to seem to me.'[21] The Poor Law was not an effective means of dealing with Irish distress. Work was what the Irish required most of all and in Carlyle's view it was the duty of those who governed to provide it. In that regard he was at different times vexed and angered by what he saw as the Liberal government's mismanagement of Irish affairs. He was acutely aware of the impact of this 'bad and thoughtless governance'. The hordes of starving and destitute Irish descending on English cities only confirmed Carlyle's worst fears, a stark reminder if any was needed that Ireland's problem was indeed England's problem.

486

# 'Le pays classique de la faim': *France and the Great Irish Famine*

*Grace Neville*

Despite triggering seismic shifts across Irish society, the Great Famine has often been shrouded in silence and secrecy in Ireland itself. One might wonder what, if anything was known of it elsewhere, for instance, in Ireland's nearest Continental European neighbour and age-old ally, France? A lot, it would appear. It featured prominently in public discourse there: Lacordaire mentioned it twice in his funeral oration on Daniel O'Connell delivered in the Cathédrale de Notre-Dame on 10 February 1848[1] and sermons appealing for help for impoverished Irish Catholics were preached in churches in prosperous Paris neighbourhoods.[2] In fact, the Bibliothèque Nationale in Paris contains several thousand nineteenth-century texts published mainly in Paris but also in provincial cities like Grenoble and Clermont, and even further afield, for instance in Montréal,[3] which focus briefly or at length on the Great Irish Famine. The French commentators were a motley crew of journalists, priests, poets, playwrights, novelists, satirists, statisticians, scientists, lawyers, horticulturalists, botanists, epidemiologists, postgraduates, aristocrats and proletarians, conservatives and revolutionaries. Their reactions ranged from empathy and searing passion to clinical detachment: in an award-winning 1862 study, the editor-in-chief of *L'Economiste français*, Jules Duval, commended the Famine for reducing the Irish population and heralding happier times.[4]

## A LAND OF FAMINES

Far from seeing the Great Irish Famine as something unique or exceptional, French observers repeatedly considered it as part of something larger. From at least the seventeenth century until the late nineteenth century, they depicted Ireland not as a land of famine but of famines: *'le pays classique de la faim'*.[5] The Great Famine was thus just one of many famines, albeit the worst. Furthermore, hunger in Ireland, though catastrophic, was not essentially any different from the myriad hardships visited on other countries – political oppression in Poland, for example. The Famine was also contextualised within the European-wide revolutions of 1848, with the starving Irish merging into the oppressed European proletariat. Most frequently, however, the Great Famine emerged as a sideshow in the story of the massive pan-European potato failure that saw famine spread from Belgium, through France and Germany, into Portugal, Spain and Lombardy in the 1840s.

Sources of information on famine(s) in Ireland include London and regional Irish newspapers, Quaker activists and illustrious earlier French visitors like Gustave de Beaumont. As for actual French eye-witnesses, a visitor to Ireland in the summer of 1844, journalist Amédée Pichot, graphically tracked the unstoppable emergence of famine: hoards of beggars in Dungarvan, people besieging workhouses before being thrown into ditches like animals, even 'strong' farmers sliding into misery.[6] In June 1846, Edouard Déchy noticed a skeletal woman in a dark tumbledown cabin near Waterford: her bones were sticking out through her body (*'les os perçaient la peau de ses pieds nus'*); she was so weak that he had difficulty establishing whether she was dead or alive.[7]

## EXPLAINING THE FAMINE

What did the Famine mean for these French commentators? At an immediate level, of course, they concentrated on the calamitous loss of life accompanied by a general collapse in morale throughout the country. At the same time, however, their focus was often elsewhere for they were keen to draw lessons for France from disaster in Ireland: famine in Ireland highlighted the risks posed by rapid population growth; unless France's population grew more slowly it would, like starving Ireland, become one huge cemetery: *'Grace à la famine, la France menace de devenir, comme l'Irlande – un grand cimetière.'*[8] They warned, too, of the dangers of a people made desperate by famine: a novel set in the west of Ireland depicted visitors hounded by hoards of frantic Medusa figures – women beggars who no longer looked human.[9] After food riots in Rouen and Lyon in the fateful year of 1848, Charles Marchal suggested that social unrest throughout an entire famine-stricken continent could be sparked by people with nothing to lose, like the starving Irish; he recalled the ominous warning of poet/politician, Lamartine: *'le pauvre a faim et la France a peur'*.[10]

The scientific origins of the Famine were baffling (*'la maladie de la pomme de terre est restée un mystère, comme le choléra'*[11]); that potato blight could strike in apparently optimum weather conditions was bewildering.[12] Nonetheless,

IRELAND. - Every day brings us news of more menacing unrest in Ireland. On 25 September, Youghal was once more the location of scenes that were even more fearful and particularly more heart breaking than those that we have already reported. Subscriptions that were opened spontaneously produced £2,500 sterling which will be used for the purchase of maize destined for the poor.

In Crookhaven, misery has reached its ultimate limit. On 25 September also, a huge crowd of individuals suffering from the most horrible distress rushed like an avalanche into the village of Goleen, declaring that their misery was unbearable, that it went beyond anything that can be expected of human patience. 'We can hardly make a single meal in twenty four hours', cried the unfortunates. 'We are near death from hunger. We would prefer to die of need rather than to touch anything that belongs to someone else if this concerned ourselves alone; but we cannot stand the cries of our children who are asking us for bread that we do not have to give them. For too long we have been nourished by hope alone, the work that we are promised will arrive too late. We will no longer have the energy to work!'

When people remonstrated with these misfortunates over the unrest that their demonstration could cause, violent murmurs broke out and their faces became animated in extreme exasperation. Once a priest had finished telling these unfortunates that they should resign themselves and be patient for a few days more, they left in gloomy despair and went back to their miserable homes.

In Cork, a house that was meant to provide the poor with help in the form of meals has been besieged from the Tuesday of the week before last by an ever- growing crowd of 217 people at the start, then 301, then 579, then 742, then 1,000 and finally 1,419. In the space of three weeks, the price of a barrel of maize has risen from £10 sterling to £15 sterling. One can see unfortunate people selling their most vital possessions, their beds and even their clothes in order to obtain goods that are 50% above their true value. Everywhere, pitiful representations of near naked peasants are crowding into the towns, crowds of men, women and children, gaunt, with no flesh on them, ghost-like, walking the streets asking for bread. In Dungarvan, on the 29th, a baker, Mr James Morgan, encouraged the crown passing in front of his shop to take some bread; the unfortunates rushed to take up his offer. 'In any case' added the correspondent from the Standard, 'they made do with just a small amount of bread and left after giving profuse thanks to generous Mr Morgan'. But other bakers did not display the same charitable prudence and a riot broke out in the midst of which the troops opened fire seriously wounding three men'. The correspondent added that it is a painful sight to see misfortunate starving people laid low by gunfire, even though this appalling, extreme measure may be needed for the maintenance of peace and the protection of property'.

Troops have boarded ship in all the ports of England for transportation to Ireland. But the Cork Examiner says on this occasion: 'If the government does not hurry and come to the aid of our starving population, and does not take strong measures in order to give it work and food, the gift of prophecy will not be needed to predict appalling calamities which will strike this crushed, impoverished population maddened by hunger and despair. If famine causes an uprising, I doubt whether England has enough troops at her disposal to suppress it because it will be widespread. I am convinced that 60,000 men would not be enough to accomplish this task'. {Translation by author}

Fig. 1 A report on Famine conditions in villages and towns in Counties Cork and Waterford, as highlighted in *L'Illustration: Journal Universel*, 10 October 1846, p. 82 [Source: National Library of Ireland]

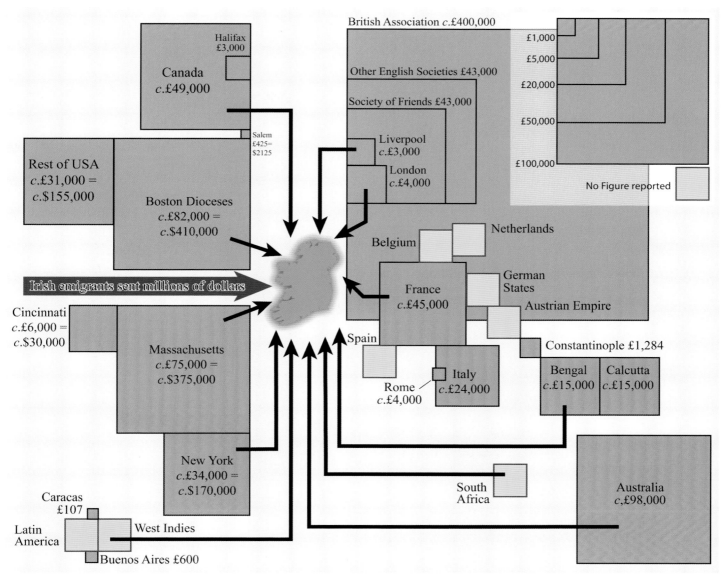

Fig. 2 GENERALISED SKETCH-MAP OF EXTERNALLY GENERATED NON-GOVERNMENT CONTRIBUTIONS TO IRISH RELIEF EFFORTS DURING THE GREAT FAMINE. The extent to which Irish relief committees and key institutional figures – such as the Catholic Archbishop of Dublin, Dr Murray – were in receipt of non-government funds generated outside of Ireland may not be well known. Funding initiatives were inspired by key organising individuals and societies, church sermons, newspaper reports and a papal encyclical from Pius IX. One cannot be very precise about the actual levels of funding. We do know that the 'British Association for the Relief of Extreme Distress in Ireland and Scotland' contributed as great a sum as c.£400,000 to famine relief in Ireland, much of it focused on the most distressed western unions. The Society of Friends in Britain raised £42,506 and other societies in England £70,916, bringing the total of privately-generated funding in Britain for famine relief in Ireland to over £0.5m. Including the Choctaw Indians of Oklahoma, the people of the United States were also most generous, subscribing well over $1,000,000 (c. £230,000) to famine relief. Millions of dollars also flowed back to Ireland via emigrant remittances, saving some lives and funding the emigration of other family members. Australia, Canada, South Africa and the Irish diaspora everywhere across the British empire also played their roles as did a variety of other groups and influential leaders – the Sultan in Constantinople, Abd-el-Medjid, as well as bishops, ex-slaves, mayors, priests and soldiers – in seeking to assist Ireland. Catholic bishops and their diocesan communities on the continent of Europe – particularly those in France and Italy – contributed generously to the support of their distressed co-religionists across the sea on the island of Ireland. (Source: Based mainly on Donal A. Kerr's, *The Catholic Church and the Famine* [Blackrock, 1996] pp. 28-41)

famine in Ireland, and the cholera and typhus that so often accompanied it, generated extensive if inconclusive analyses among the French scientific community.[13]

If science could not explain the Great Famine, perhaps politics would. For many French writers, the Famine was not an accident or a natural calamity but a deliberate stratagem devised by English colonisers whose true colours it unmasked: callous and indifferent in the face of never-ending famine in Ireland.[14] Others apportioned blame more widely, suggesting that all of Europe knew about it but chose inaction. Famine followed colonialism in Ireland and

throughout Europe according to several French commentators who pointed to contemporary famines elsewhere in colonies like India[15] and Algeria. Whether the Famine had indeed finally broken age-old Irish resistance to domination was widely debated.

Religion, rather than science or politics, was sometimes called upon to 'explain' the Famine. Here, famine sometimes became a 'test' of faith visited on Catholic Ireland. C.R. Girard concluded that famine was a punishment for sinners; in any case, science could not cure famine in Ireland or France because 'notre science est athée autant qu'immorale'.[16]

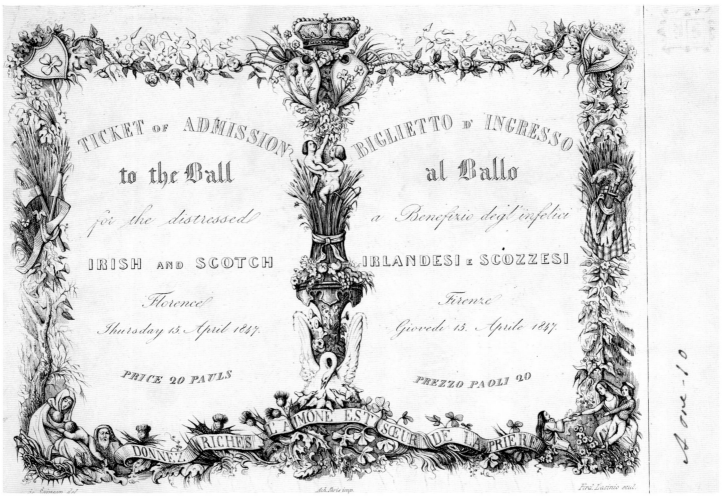

Fig. 3 Admission ticket to charity ball in Florence, 14 April 1847. Continental European countries and communities responded generously to appeals for help to famine-stricken Ireland. This was true for all of Catholic Europe and particularly of France. As early as February 1847, the French Catholic community requested Pope Pius IX to make a general appeal for assistance towards the stricken Irish. In May, a powerful committee – led by many of the French aristocratic elite – was established to co-ordinate aid for Ireland. All across France, diocesan contributions from bishops, priests and lay people poured in – headed by Strasburg which contributed 23,365 francs. Various social events were initiated to gather in subscriptions. Italian dioceses and communities were equally generous. Again many events – as, for example, this Florentine ball of 15 April 1847 – were organised to collect funds for the relief of distress in both Ireland and Scotland.

English Famine relief efforts, like the building of pointless roads, were derided by French writers. At the same time, French help for the starving Irish, which predated 'Black '47', was a constant theme: in 1831, Montalembert, learning that famine had again struck Ireland, organised a collection among French Catholics through the newspaper, *L'Avenir*. In just three months, 80,000 francs were donated. In 1847, the St Vincent de Paul Society in Ireland, through its council-general in Paris, received 154,199 francs for famine relief.[17]

## MEMORY
Famine memories surfaced in Ireland in 1870 to play a perhaps unexpected though major role in Franco–Irish relations. As the Irish newspapers of the day, especially the *Cork Examiner*, made clear, massive fundraising among rich and poor produced regular dispatches of hundreds of tons of food, clothing and other necessities for the victims of the Franco-Prussian War: starving peasants, besieged Parisians

and post-war refugees. So spectacular was this Irish largesse that the citizens of Caen flocked to view some of it which had been put on public display there in October 1870. What exactly prompted this massive outpouring of war relief is debatable. What is clear is that earlier French famine relief for Ireland was frequently mentioned at the highest levels, by both religious and state authorities. A public meeting at the City Hall, Cork, in February 1871, called for monies to be collected 'towards relieving the pressing necessities of a nation so intimately bound to us by ties of amity, and which so nobly came to our aid in the fearful crisis of the Irish famine'.[18] State was joined by church as a Carrigaline priest pleaded in a letter to the *Cork Examiner*, 3 February 1871 for aid for France:

[T]he records of our own country reveal the misery that followed the failure of the potato crop in '46 and '47. Far gloomier is the French peasant, without any crops . . . Relief in aid of the peasantry, while it would complete the measure of our charity, would at the same time be a grateful tribute to the memory of that generosity with which France, in '46 and '47, relieved the sufferings of our poor people.[19]

What is striking and, indeed, moving here is to witness the extreme generosity of the poor, particularly the poor of Cork city and county, and especially West Cork, often seen as the epicentre of the Great Famine. Money poured from 'poor and remote' parishes in west Cork and Kerry 'for the relief of distressed and suffering France'.[20] The food sent often carried Famine associations: 'two sacks of potatoes from Mr J.T. Rearden, Ballincurrig . . . for the suffering French peasantry'.[21] It is surely not fanciful to surmise that still-raw Famine memories prompted such generosity.

What is equally arresting is to see the St Vincent de Paul Society's role in this war relief effort. With exquisite symmetry, this organisation with its international headquarters in Paris, which had organised massive French relief for the starving Irish during the Great Famine, now organised and distributed Irish largesse to the war-stricken French. For instance, the Cork branch of the St Vincent de Paul Society organised a collection, stating:

> We have received a circular from the Council of Ireland, suggesting that all the Conferences in this country should contribute towards alleviating the deep distress now prevailing in France in consequence of the war. In the famine years, 1847-48, a sum of more than £6,000 was sent over here by our Council General in Paris, being the contributions of the French and other foreign conferences towards the relief of the sufferers in Ireland. At the same time, the bishops of France sent a sum of above £15,000 for the same purpose. Again a few years ago, on another appeal being made by our President-General, £3,000 more were remitted in Ireland, in aid of the poor visited by our Conferences. It is now hoped that the Society in Ireland will worthily reciprocate the charity of France.[22]

Ireland and France would, it was believed, continue to support each other into the future:

> Ireland has done her duty. The gratitude and astonishment of the French people at such generosity is unbounded, and a day may come, *as it once before did*, when France will repay the debt she contracts now to the only country that remains faithful to her in her hour of need [my emphasis].[23]

Thus, France and Ireland, two countries already closely allied in countless different ways over many centuries, witnessed new links of solidarity being forged between them thanks to the disaster that was the Great Irish Famine.

# SECTION VI
## THE SCATTERING

*An Emigrant Ship, Dublin Bay, Sunset*
by Edwin Hayes (1820–1904), oil on
canvas, 58 x 86 cm.
[Source: National Gallery of Ireland]

# Exodus from Ireland – patterns of emigration

## William J. Smyth

Ireland's dramatic population decline between 1841 and 1852 was profoundly influenced by emigrant/refugees abandoning Ireland in their thousands and seeking by whatever means to reach safe havens in the New World. Close on a million Irish people emigrated overseas between 1846 and March 1851 with a further 464,000 leaving Ireland by the end of 1852. In addition, at least a quarter and probably as many as one-third of a million of famine-stricken people ended up in the slums of Liverpool, Glasgow, London and other British cities. For passage money of a few shillings, they could cross by steamer to land in ports in England and Scotland or cross (as did some 'emaciated, ragged men and children') as ballast in the coal ships plying between south Wales and the south of Ireland.[1]

A striking feature of emigration rates from Ireland to overseas countries (excluding emigration to Britain) is the almost exact correspondence between the proportion of documented mortalities and the proportion of emigrants for the years 1846 to 1849. For the decade 1841 to 1851, the national proportion of deaths recorded in 1846 is 9.1% and emigration overseas is 9.0%; in 1847 the two figures were 18.5% and 18.4%. In 1848, the estimated mortality proportion is 15.4%, and overseas emigrants constitute 15.2% of the year's total of emigrants and in 1849 the proportions were 17.9% and 18.3%, respectively. This suggests a profound interrelationship between the intensities of the Famine catastrophe and the levels of emigration overseas in these years. However, in 1850, 1851 and 1852, mortality and emigration proportions diverge dramatically. In 1850 the estimated national mortality proportion for that census decade is 12.2% but emigration soars to 17.8%; in 1851, the equivalent mortality figure is 10.2% but the emigration equivalent is about double that to 21.3%. In these two years the exodus from Ireland is both massive and now self-sustaining. Almost half a million emigrated overseas in these two years alone and in 1852 another 220,428 people abandoned Ireland for a hoped-for better life abroad. The catalyst of the Great Famine was seeing the beginning of a social revolution which would reverberate even into the twenty-first century.

However, the above is not to suggest that the emigrant source regions were identical to the regions of the dead and the despairing. Fitzpatrick's map (see Fig. 2)depicts the depletion of the cohort initially aged between five and twenty-four years between 1841 and 1851.[2] The core area of depletion is constituted by the counties of Cavan, Longford, Leitrim and Roscommon with second-order depletions encircling the core from Monaghan, Fermanagh and Sligo around from Mayo to Clare and curving back to include Tipperary, the midland counties and Meath. The regions of lowest age depletions include southwest Munster and northwest Ulster but most particularly the counties of southeast Leinster and northeast Ulster.

### EMIGRANT SOURCE AREAS

Cohort depletion, however, does not necessarily confirm regional gradations in the distribution of emigrant source-areas since these figures also include depletion due to excess mortality in these age groups. While recognising the limitations in the estimates of famine mortality, it seems valuable to calculate the number of emigrants as the total decline in population from 1841 to 1851 minus famine mortalities. Cousens' map details this picture at the county level. County Roscommon is seen as the epicentre of emigration in this decade with emigration levels between 1846 and 1851 exceeding 20% of the total population in 1841.[3] Roscommon is followed by the counties of Sligo, Longford, Cavan and Monaghan in addition to the midland county of Queen's (Laois) with a 17.8% to 19.9% decline. A third zone of heavy emigration with a 15–17.4% decline is constituted by a further circle of counties including Mayo, Leitrim, Fermanagh and Meath with an outlier in County Wicklow. Counties Tyrone, Westmeath, Offaly and Kilkenny record 12.5% to 14.9% declines while counties Louth, Kildare, Carlow, Tipperary and Cork record considerable declines of between 10 and 12.4%. A less than 10% decline is experienced by the counties of northeast Ulster and County Donegal, the western coastal counties of Galway, Clare, Limerick and Kerry and the southeastern coastal counties of Waterford and Wexford plus County Dublin. The complex living conditions of very different Irelands are again revealed in these emigrant patterns.

My concern is to try to map estimated emigration levels at the Poor Law Union scale. Following Cousens, I calculate emigration levels as a 'residual' after subtracting estimated mortalities from the total population in 1841. Not surprisingly, this figure confirms in more detail the county patterns identified by Cousens. The Poor Law unions of Roscommon, Carrick-on-Shannon, Mohill, Longford and Granard (+20%) constitute a major core area of emigration. An axis from Kells through Cootehill and Monaghan constitutes a second core (17.5%+). These two cores connect up and expand into a significant zone

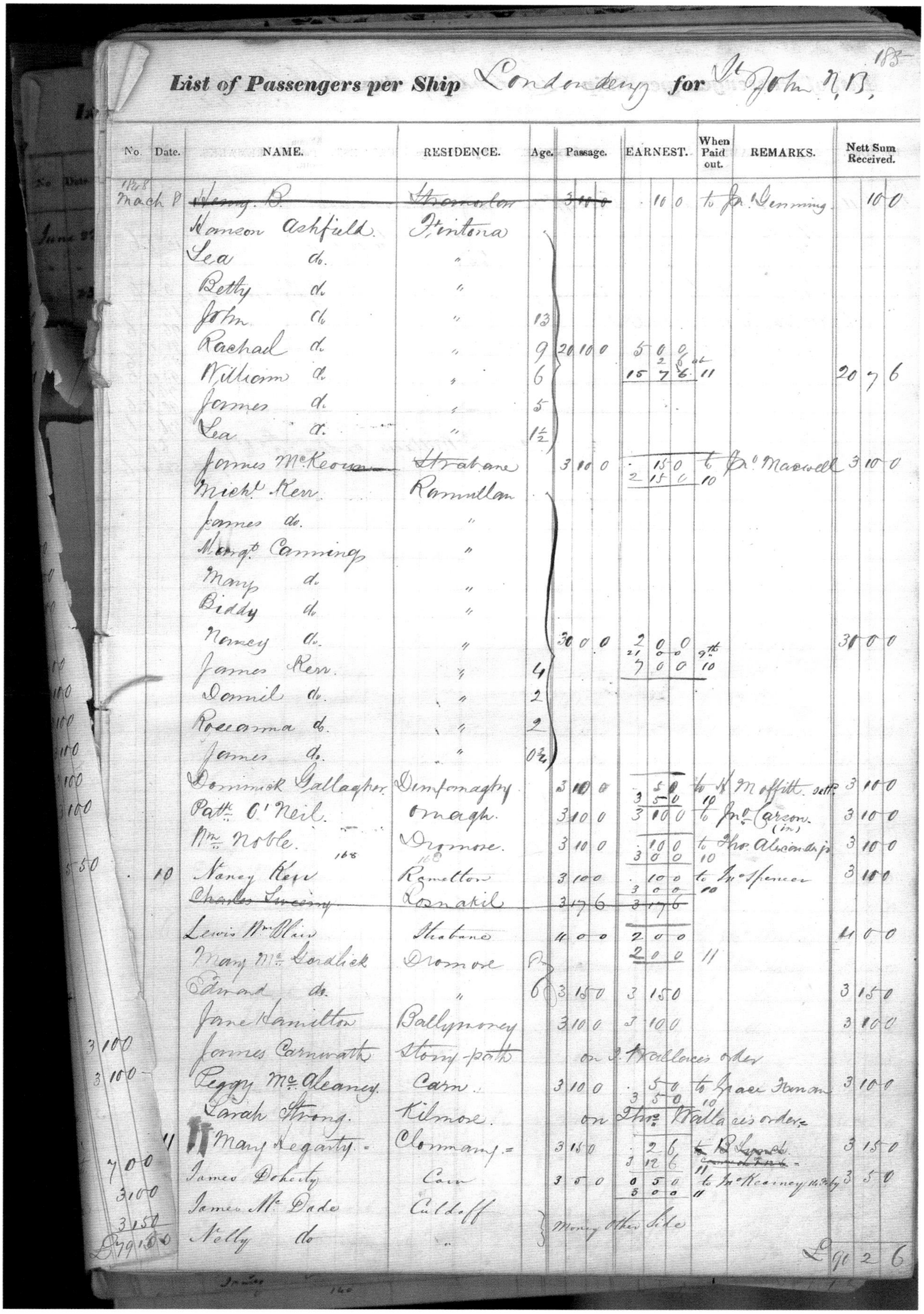

List of Passengers per Ship *Londonderry* for St John N.B.

| No. | Date. | NAME. | RESIDENCE. | Age. | Passage. | EARNEST. | When Paid out. | REMARKS. | Nett Sum Received. |
|---|---|---|---|---|---|---|---|---|---|
| | March 8 | ~~Henry D.~~ | Stranorlar | | 3 10 0 | 10 0 | | to Jas Denning | 10 0 |
| | | Hanson Ashfield | Fintona | | | | | | |
| | | Lea do. | " | | | | | | |
| | | Betty do. | " | | | | | | |
| | | John do. | " | 13 | | | | | |
| | | Rachael do. | " | 9 | 20 10 0 | 5 0 0 | | | 20 7 6 |
| | | William do. | " | 6 | | 15 7 6 2 8 11 | | | |
| | | James do. | " | 5 | | | | | |
| | | Lea d. | " | 1½ | | | | | |
| | | James McKeown | Strabane | | 3 10 0 | 1 5 0 2 15 0 10 | | to Jas McDowell | 3 10 0 |
| | | Michl. Kerr | Ramullan | | | | | | |
| | | James do. | " | | | | | | |
| | | Margt. Canning | " | | | | | | |
| | | Mary do. | " | | | | | | |
| | | Biddy do. | " | | | | | | |
| | | Nancy do. | " | | 30 0 0 | 2 0 0 21 0 0 9th 7 0 0 10 | | | 30 0 0 |
| | | James Kerr. | " | 4 | | | | | |
| | | Daniel do. | " | 2 | | | | | |
| | | Roseanna do. | " | 2 | | | | | |
| | | James do. | " | 0½ | | | | | |
| | | Dominick Gallagher | Dunfanaghy | | 3 10 0 | 5 0 3 5 0 10 | | to H Moffitt sett | 3 10 0 |
| | | Patk. O'Neil. | Omagh. | | 3 10 0 | 3 10 0 | | to Mr Carson (in) | 3 10 0 |
| | | Wm. Noble. | Dromore. | | 3 10 0 | 1 0 0 3 0 0 10 | | to Thos Alexander Jr | 3 10 0 |
| 5 50 | 10 | Nancy Keys | Ramelton | | 3 10 0 | 1 0 0 3 0 0 10 | | to Jas Spencer | 3 10 0 |
| | | ~~Charles Sweeny~~ | Lonakil | | 3 17 6 | 3 17 6 | | | |
| | | Lewis McBain | Strabane | | 11 0 0 | 2 0 0 2 0 0 11 | | | 11 0 0 |
| | | Mary Mc Gorlick | Dromore | | | | | | |
| | | Edward do. | " | 6 | 3 15 0 | 3 15 0 | | | 3 15 0 |
| | | Jane Hamilton | Ballymoney | | 3 10 0 | 3 10 0 | | | 3 10 0 |
| 3 100 | | James Carnwath | Stony path | | on J. Wallaces order | | | | |
| 3 100 | | Peggy Mc Aleaney | Carn | | 3 10 0 | 5 0 3 5 0 10 | | to Grace Hanon | 3 10 0 |
| | | Sarah Strong. | Kilmore. | | on Thos Wallaces order | | | | |
| | 11 | Mary Legarty | Clonmany | | 3 15 0 | 2 6 3 12 6 11 | | ~~to B Lynch~~ | 3 15 0 |
| 7 0 0 | | James Doherty | Carn | | 3 5 0 | 0 5 0 3 0 0 11 | | to McKearney Novy | 3 5 0 |
| 3 100 | | James Mc Dade | Culdaff | | | Money other side | | | |
| 3 150 | | Nelly do. | | | | | | | |
| £79 15 0 | | | | | | | | | £90 2 6 |

Fig. 1 Page from the passenger list of the ship *Londonderry* bound for Saint John, New Brunswick, March 1848. The ship was part of the J. & J. Cooke line operating from the port of Derry. [Source: Public Record Office of Northern Ireland, D2892/1/1]

495

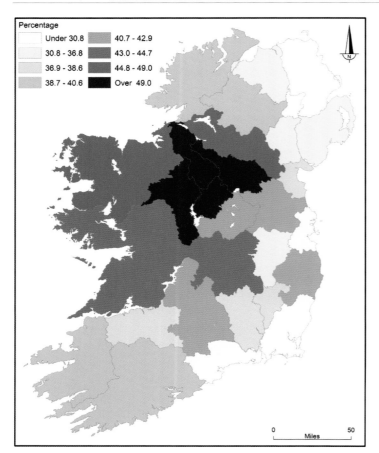

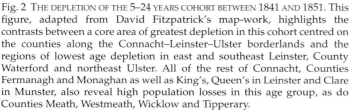

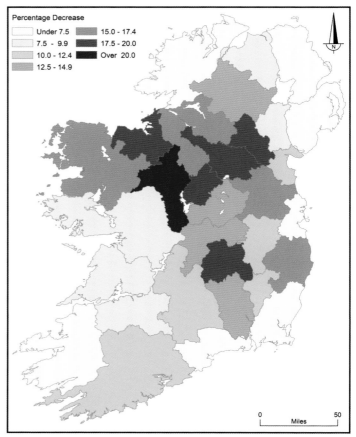

Fig. 2 THE DEPLETION OF THE 5–24 YEARS COHORT BETWEEN 1841 AND 1851. This figure, adapted from David Fitzpatrick's map-work, highlights the contrasts between a core area of greatest depletion in this cohort centred on the counties along the Connacht–Leinster–Ulster borderlands and the regions of lowest age depletion in east and southeast Leinster, County Waterford and northeast Ulster. All of the rest of Connacht, Counties Fermanagh and Monaghan as well as King's, Queen's in Leinster and Clare in Munster, also reveal high population losses in this age group, as do Counties Meath, Westmeath, Wicklow and Tipperary.

Fig. 3 PATTERNS OF POPULATION DECLINE PER COUNTY DUE TO EMIGRATION BETWEEN 1841 AND 1851 (AFTER COUSENS). Cousens' 1960 map highlights very significant variations in levels of emigration, pointing up very sharp differences between neighbouring counties as, for example, Armagh vis-à-vis Monaghan, or Roscommon vis-à-vis Galway. Having established levels of excess mortality per county, Cousens was in a position to estimate emigration levels as a percentage of the population in 1841. County Roscommon emerges as the epicentre of this great exodus, losing over 20% of its population with the adjacent counties of the Connacht/Leinster/Ulster borderlands acting as the fulcrum for the remaining very high emigration at between 17.5% and 19.9%. In contrast, it is the very poorest countries of the west and the most stratified and economically more vigorous counties in the northeast and east which show the lowest emigration proportions. It should be noted that percentage figures may obscure the actual numbers emigrating. For example, County Tipperary, with a 12% decline, loses as many people (at least 54,000) as does the core county of Roscommon and Cork city and county lost double that amount (+ 100,000). Likewise, County Meath, with a 16% decline, equals the losses (c.30,000) of Queen's (19%) while Limerick city and county loses a similar number with a percentage loss of 9%. And in the latter part of 1851 (1 May to 31 December) the province of Munster contributed 61,285 (40.3%) to a phenomenal emigration stream (152,060), with Leinster contributing 38,719 (25.4%), Ulster 28,884 (19%) and Connacht only 20,094 (13.2%). Between 1851 and 1855 a further three-quarters of a million people had emigrated, joining the c.1.3 million who had escaped the Famine catastrophe in the previous five and a half years.

of high emigration (+15%), focused on mid and south Ulster and north Leinster. This emigrant region stretches from Magherafelt south through Armagh to Navan, Edenderry and Parsonstown (Birr) and continues westwards from Enniskillen through Sligo to take in most of the County Mayo unions.[4] Abbeyleix, Shillelagh, Listowel and Skibbereen constitute outliers for this level of emigration (17.5 to 19.9%) although the status of the latter two unions may be complicated by overstating emigration and understating mortality levels. Nevertheless, a weaker third focus of emigration is suggested for at least some of these communities. This emigrant zone extends from Listowel and Newcastlewest south to Macroom, Dunmanway and on to Skibbereen. The unions of mid-west Ulster, east Connacht, much of Queen's (Laois), north and west Tipperary and on into Kilmallock in Limerick display moderate (10 to 12%) levels of emigration.

## LOW LEVELS OF EMIGRATION

Equally striking are the regions and communities with little or no emigration (and in a few cases where emigration levels are balanced by in-migration flows). Donegal

stands out in the northwest as do a number of unions in south Galway, much of County Clare and mid-Kerry. Significant too, are the low levels of emigration from the southeastern, eastern and northeastern unions from Ballymena and Larne in the North, south through the coastal communities of east Leinster and extending westwards from Enniscorthy to Midleton and Kinsale. Finally, the three major city unions – those of Belfast, Cork and Dublin – all return population increases, reflecting both greater economic capacity, especially in the case of Belfast, and also reflecting very significant internal 'refugee' movements from their surrounding hinterlands. The cities – but *not* the unions – of Limerick, Waterford and Derry also reveal both substantial in-migration and institutional populations from their surrounding countrysides. Incidentally, the 1851 county figures suggest an average *increase* over the 1841 figures of *c*.5% in rates of *internal* migration from adjacent counties to the counties of east Ulster and mid Leinster. In contrast, internal migration from other counties into the most distressed counties of the West was practically non-existent in this decade. In these regions the exodus was overseas or more likely to the workhouse and/or to the grave.

There are, therefore, two outstanding regions where emigration levels are low. One is this western region south of County Mayo, where populations were so poor that a significant proportion relied on statutory reliefs between 1846 and 1851. More than 50% of the populations of the following essentially Irish-speaking unions were in receipt of some form of relief for at least two years between 1847 and 1851 : Castlebar, Clifden, Westport, Ballinrobe, Swinford, Gort, Ennistymon, Scariff, Ennis, Kilrush, Listowel, Newcastlewest, Dingle (from 1848), Killarney, Cahersiveen, Kenmare

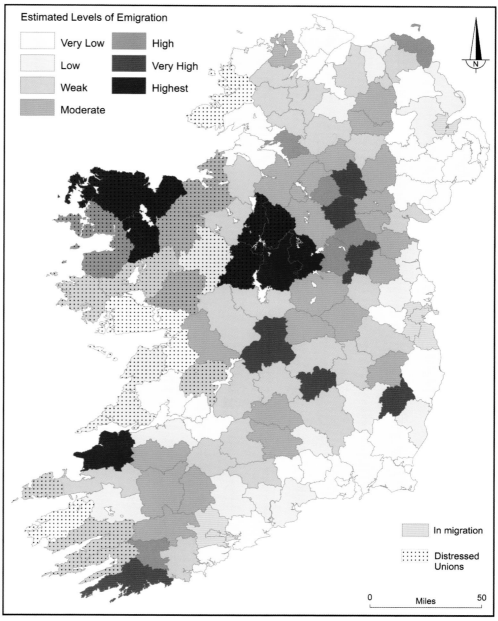

Fig. 4 ESTIMATED LEVELS OF EMIGRATION 1841–51 AT POOR LAW UNION SCALE. This map seeks to refine Cousens' county map by estimating levels of emigration from each Poor Law Union. Contrasting emigration patterns within Counties Antrim, Donegal, Derry, Galway, Clare, Limerick, Kerry, Cork, Wicklow and Meath are highlighted. Likewise, zones of both in-migration and/or the lowest levels of emigration are emphasised for the Belfast, Dublin, Waterford, Cork and Limerick city hinterlands.

and Bantry. With one or two exceptions – notably Castlebar and Listowel – none of these unions were conspicuous emigrant source-areas. Whereas the national average for rateable tenements valued at under £5 was 53.4%, 90.0% of Westport's holdings were in this category and in the west Connacht unions as a whole the proportion averaged between 75 and 85%. All the west Kerry unions registered well over 60% of their rateable tenements valued at less than £5. These household populations with their highly fragmented and subsistence holdings were generally too poor and too destitute to be able to muster either the seventy shilling fare to the USA or the fifty to sixty shilling fare to Canada. However, some of the most destitute 'bringing pestilence on their backs' may have man-

aged to get to Britain. Hence, the major concentration of destitute Irish emigrants in Liverpool, Glasgow, Manchester, London and other industrial towns in lowland Scotland, Lancashire and the Midlands. Whatever the judgement on British Government policy during the Famine, it needs to be recognised that most of these Irish emigrants – although threatening to engulf the support systems in British cities and towns – nevertheless managed to establish homes and gain livelihoods across industrial Britain.

## COUNTY DONEGAL

County Donegal reveals an exceptional low emigration level but for different reasons. Firstly, over each of the four

497

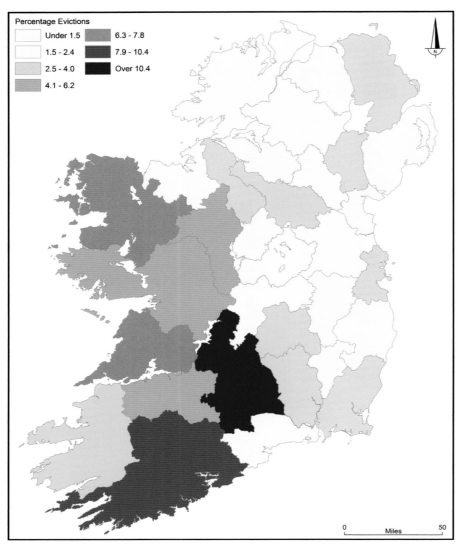

Percentage Evictions

| | |
|---|---|
| Under 1.5 | 6.3 - 7.8 |
| 1.5 - 2.4 | 7.9 - 10.4 |
| 2.5 - 4.0 | Over 10.4 |
| 4.1 - 6.2 | |

0    Miles    50

Glenties region suffered badly, especially in 1847.[5] The particular economy of the county where oats was more important in the diet, where the potato crop recovered more rapidly after 1847, and where seasonal migration was a very significant support may all have been stabilising factors. However, it appears that the very distinctive role of its landlords may have been crucial here. Lord George Hill and other landlords in north Donegal strove valiantly *not* to lose their tenants either through death or emigration.[6]

It is striking therefore, that Donegal (with County Down) has by far the lowest rate of court-based landlord evictions (2.5% of the island-wide total) in the whole country between 1846 and 1848. The national average was 4.9%. County Tipperary recorded the most court-based evictions with 9.4% of its holdings suffering this fate. These evictions involved as many as 13,200 people in Tipperary – as compared with 3,500 from Donegal.[7] However, these court-based figures are rather incomplete. An official police tally of people formally and permanently evicted from their holdings between 1849 and 1852 exceeds 220,000. If one were to guesstimate the equivalent figures for 1846–48 and take into account the 'thousands pressurised with involuntary surrenders', the resulting figure for 1846 to 1852 would likely be greater than two-thirds of a million (660,000+) – with counties Tipperary, Clare, Mayo, Limerick, Galway and Kerry (see Figs 5 and 10) suffering most.

The second zone of low emigration includes in the first case the highly literate, English-speaking and well-to-do unions of the industrialising and urbanising northeast, where in the countryside weaving and farming were combined with high density populations in unions like Ballymena, Lisburn and Lurgan. All of these factors constituted a deterrent to emigration. Secondly, the urbanised, better-educated and commercialised farming regions of the east and southeast did not foster high emigration levels. Here, all the way from Ardee to Athy, from Balrothery to Bandon, from Car-

Fig. 5 PERCENTAGE DISTRIBUTION OF EVICTIONS PER COUNTY 1846–52. For the years 1846 to 1848 and the first law term (Hilary) of 1849, court records have survived of ejectment proceedings for both the three superior courts and the much less costly assistant barristers' courts. Very different interpretations have been placed on these court records. However, all the available evidence for the 1840s as a whole suggest the following conclusions: (i) that on average only *c.*two-thirds of ejectment proceedings ended up with evictions (many ejectment proceedings were used as threats to ensure the payment of rents); (ii) the average number of defendants/tenants incorporated in any one ejectment procedure was *c.*2.7–3.0; (iii) the assistant barristers' courts were by far the dominant vehicles to ensure that evictions were realised. Using these guidelines, Fig. 5 summarises the combined data for the courts and police records to illustrate the percentage share of evictions per county between 1846 and 1852. It is not dramatically different from the 1849–52 picture. There remains a strong western and southern emphasis with Tipperary (10.4%) again leading in the eviction stakes, followed by Cork (9.0%), Mayo (7.8%) and Clare (7.2%). But apart from Cork, it is also clear that the three Ulster counties of Antrim, Armagh and Cavan – as well as Counties Roscommon and Leitrim – saw much greater 'thinning out' of estate tenantry in the earlier period (1846–48) while north Leinster counties saw an acceleration of evictions from 1849. The court evidence for the Hilary term 1849 also strongly suggests that the police returns for 1849 are deficient, possibly by the order of *c.*20–25%. Overall, these official records of evictions from the two sources suggest that at least 100,000 families – or *c.*half a million people – were put out on the road during the Famine years. But apart from these legal processes, many landlords cleared and rationalised their estate holdings by compelling surrenders, by 'assisting' tenant mobility or emigration for trifling sums and by even more devious and/or aggressive means. In addition, in the counties of Connacht and south Ulster, the threat of pending ejectment proceedings saw many smallholders desert their farms after harvesting the crops and before rents were due. All these 'clearances' resulted in an economic and social revolution of enormous proportions. The more realistic human figure for all these 'clearances' is that between two-thirds and three-quarters of a million people lost their homes and way of living. Many were forced onto relief, some managed to emigrate, many others died.

worst years of the Famine from 1847 to 1850, Donegal never registered excess death rates above 3% although the

low to Cork, Kells to Kilkenny and from Mullingar to Mallow on to Rathdown and Rathdrum, each union boasted

# THE NATION.

Fig. 6 Advertisements for a line of packet ships bound for New York, Boston, Philadelphia and New Orleans, *The Nation*, 8 September 1849. [Source: National Library of Ireland]

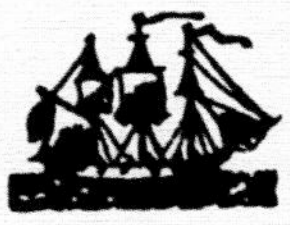

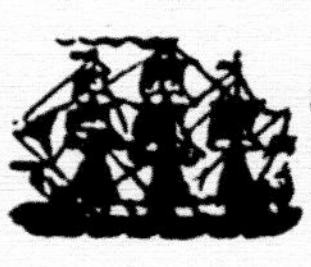

well over 400 rateable tenements valued at over £50 – all benefiting from a well-developed market and central-place system, pivoting around the cities of Dublin, Waterford and Cork (and to a lesser extent, Limerick city). This was not emigration territory – even more so since its very significant landless labouring population could not afford the passage monies. The unions of the southeast constituted very different social terrains to those in Ballyshannon, Cahersiveen, Castleblayney, Swinford and Westport, where in each case less than fifty holdings were valued at more than £50.

The core area for emigration was an inverted triangular region with its base stretching from Ballina to Monaghan and its pivot focused on the south Midlands. It would appear that this belt with the highest rates of emigration was located between the regions of greatest destitution in the west and those of least destitution in the east of the island. This, for the most part, was a relatively poor zone but not so poor as to prevent a significant number of households finding the precious passage money – firstly, possibly to Liverpool and then across the Atlantic to either British North America or the United States. There they settled in the cities of Boston, New York, Philadelphia, Scranton, Pittsburgh and many other smaller industrial cities in New England and the Middle Atlantic states. It is clear that the panic following the first failure of the potato crop in 1845 and more especially after its almost total failure in 1846 saw numerous small farmers harvest and sell their crop of oats and whatever stock was left, avoid paying the next round of rents and rates and emigrate before being evicted. This was particularly true of areas like the barony of Tyrawley in County Mayo (Ballina Union) where as early as January 1847 13,000 processes for eviction were lodged at Ballina court. Here the dominant small-farming families fled, selling what they could before it was distrained for rent. County Mayo had been a leading county for emigration from 1821 and this pattern still prevailed during the Famine.[8]

### BLACK '47 – HEADLONG FLIGHT

By January 1847 the exodus from Ireland becomes a mass, almost indiscriminate riot as thousands embarked for North America 'running away from fever and disease and hunger with money scarcely sufficient to pay passage for and find food for the voyage'.[9] The 1847 exodus 'bore all the hallmarks of panic and hysteria; it was less an emigration than a headlong flight of refugees'.[10] And for small-

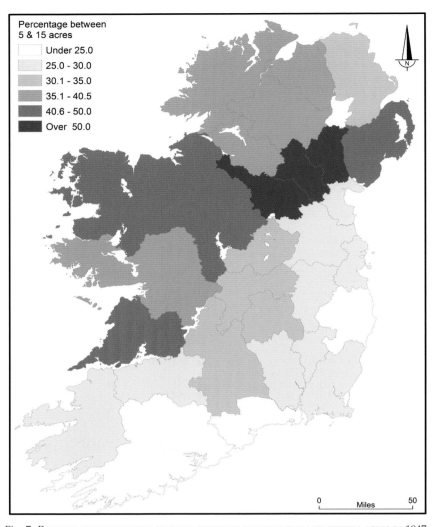

Fig. 7 PERCENTAGE DISTRIBUTION OF FARM HOLDINGS BETWEEN FIVE AND FIFTEEN ACRES IN 1847. This map seeks to identify the distribution of smallholders (5–15 acres) in 1847. Already between 1845 and 1847, 13.4% of this group of farmers had disappeared from their holdings. With the exception of Counties Antrim and Down, the region with the greatest concentration of these smallholders corresponds with the major zones of both high emigration and high mortality in the early, bitter years of the Famine. By 1851, only 191,854 out of a total of 311,133 of these 5–15 acre holdings had survived – an almost 40% reduction in this class. Between 1845 and 1851, close on one-third of a million holdings (327,382) – including those of less than one acre – had disappeared. This constitutes a staggering reduction of 35% over the traumatic Famine years.

Map legend:

Percentage between 5 & 15 acres
- Under 25.0
- 25.0 - 30.0
- 30.1 - 35.0
- 35.1 - 40.5
- 40.6 - 50.0
- Over 50.0

holding farmers with a rated valuation of say £4 to £6 and so liable and pressed for rates, escape seemed the only option. This was particularly true of south Ulster counties, centred on Counties Cavan and Monaghan. In a majority of unions in these counties, less than a third of all rateable tenements were under £5 in value.[11] On the other hand, in the western half of the core zone of highest emigration centred on County Roscommon, over two-thirds of the rateable tenements were valued at less than £5. More relevant perhaps was the distribution of 5–15 acre farms right across this emigrant region. In Cavan and Monaghan over 50% of the farms were in this category with over 48% in Roscommon, Sligo and Leitrim and 46% in Mayo. Across Ireland as a whole, these smallholders with 5–15 acres declined by almost 40% between 1845 and 1851. The Famine also saw the rapid disappearance of over 93,000 1–5 acre small holdings.[12] If holdings under one acre are included the overall number comes to *c.*330,000. Half of the very smallest holdings had disappeared between 1845 and 1847; one-quarter of the cottier holdings (1–5 acres) were gone by 1847 and over one-half (51.6%) by 1851 whereas the rate of decline of the 5–15 acre farmers doubled *after* 1847. Even the 15+ acre farms, after increasing by 16% from 1845 to 1847, declined by nearly 10% by 1851. The pre-Famine landscape and society was being utterly transformed.

It is also important to note the shifting axis of emigration over the decade 1841–52 as a whole. The 1821–41 emigration field had a bimodal distribution – much of it came from the literate, English-speaking Presbyterian communities of Ulster, especially its western half, who were suffering from the contraction of the domestic textile industry. The second core was the north-central Midlands of east Connacht and west Leinster. The *overall* pattern of emigration over the decade 1841–51 remained strongly anchored over these north Midland counties, suggesting amongst other things, the sustained importance of emigrant networks and remittances in helping other kinsfolk to emigrate.

However, it is also clear that this pattern did *not* prevail in the last years of the Great Famine. When one examines emigration out of Ireland from 1 May to 31 December 1851, a very different picture emerges. This pattern is likely to have been gaining momentum from 1848/49 – especially in the regions where cholera was later to be particularly devastating. The zone of greatest emigration is now centred on Counties Tipperary and Clare with a second intense zone of high emigration extending from Kerry around to Kilkenny, Laois, Offaly and northwards to Meath and Westmeath. Beyond these zones there are still significant emigration levels from Galway through to Cavan, Monaghan and Louth and in the south from Wexford to Waterford and Cork. Practically all

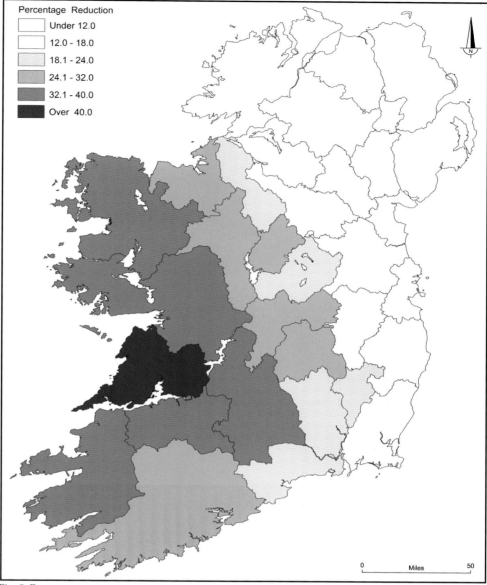

Percentage Reduction

| | |
|---|---|
| | Under 12.0 |
| | 12.0 - 18.0 |
| | 18.1 - 24.0 |
| | 24.1 - 32.0 |
| | 32.1 - 40.0 |
| | Over 40.0 |

0     Miles     50

Fig. 8 PERCENTAGE REDUCTION IN THE NUMBER OF HOLDINGS (OVER ONE ACRE IN SIZE) BETWEEN 1847 AND 1853. Whatever about ambiguities and uncertainties in relation to the scale of evictions, whether legal or 'illegal/enforced', we are on much safer ground in assessing the overall decline in the number of farm holdings between 1845 and 1851 – and also between 1847 and 1853. Between 1845, 1847 and 1851, almost one-quarter of a million holdings over one acre in size disappeared during these Famine years or almost 30% of a total of 800,000 holdings. The introduction of a specific agricultural census from 1847 onwards allows for further insights. Figure 8 demonstrates the percentage distribution of the reduction in the number of holdings between 1847 and 1853. Once again, Ireland is divided between a northern and eastern world where the number of holdings were least disturbed and a western and southern world which suffered enormous losses. County Clare lost a staggering four farms out of every ten (42.4%) between 1847 and 1853 and this kind of devastation had already begun there in 1845 and 1846. The western counties of Galway (38.3%), Mayo (36.9%), Limerick (32.5%) and Kerry (32.9%), as well as Tipperary (37.5%), also saw massive losses while a crescent of counties from Sligo and Leitrim and curving southwards to Cork saw at least one-quarter of farm holdings disappear during these years. In sharp contrast, County Down lost only 8.5%, Antrim, Armagh, Donegal and Londonderry less than 12% and Tyrone only 13.2% of their holdings. Not surprising, the level of correlation (0.83) between evictions and loss of holdings is very high – particularly in Munster and south Leinster – whereas it is clear that in most western counties the overall losses greatly exceed official eviction figures. It should also be noted that the greatest loss in number of holdings peaked in 1848 (*c.*one quarter) and then in 1849 (*c.*one fifth). Overall, there was a steep rise in holdings lost from 1846 to 1848/49 and a continuing if less steep decline to 1853. It is likely that four out of every ten of these holding losses were due to official evictions.

of Ulster, north Connacht and the Dublin–Kildare–Wicklow region have by far the lowest number of emigrants. This new regional pattern of emigration intensifies over the period 1851–55 when a further

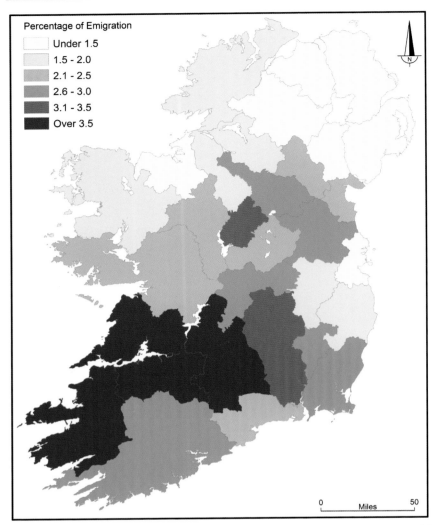

**Percentage of Emigration**

| | |
|---|---|
| | Under 1.5 |
| | 1.5 - 2.0 |
| | 2.1 - 2.5 |
| | 2.6 - 3.0 |
| | 3.1 - 3.5 |
| | Over 3.5 |

0    Miles    50

Fig. 9 PERCENTAGE DISTRIBUTION OF EMIGRATION PATTERNS BY COUNTY FROM 1 MAY TO 31 DECEMBER 1851. This map shows the significant shift in emigration patterns between the early years of the Famine and the later years. Beginning c.1849 and coinciding with massive levels of evictions (and the spread of cholera), it is the Munster/south-Leinster counties which now experience the full force of emigration and the scattering of families and communities. Parallel to this, the old north-Midland migrant core shifts eastwards to County Meath. By 1848–49 much of Ulster was beginning to recover from Famine conditions and, with a sharper economic recovery, records the lowest levels of emigration by 1851.

800,000 left the island in search of a better life.[13]

It is particularly noticeable that this second pattern of emigration is linked to those counties in the Munster province suffering continuing high mortalities in the latter years of the Famine. These levels of emigration, therefore, reflected this cumulative deterioration in living conditions for many communities – even the better-off communities – in the latter years of the 1840s. And these desperate conditions were further exacerbated by landlord eviction policies. The police records for 1849–52 show that this Munster core centred on Tipperary (15.2% of total number of holdings evicted), Clare (9.2%), Limerick (7.0%) and Kerry (5.5%) were the counties most exposed to the demolition squads and their police enforcers (see *Atlas* cover).[14] Counties Mayo (9.0%) and Galway (8.3%) constitute a second core and there are above average levels of evictions (i.e. 3% or more of holdings evicted) in all of the remaining Mun-

ster and southern and western Leinster counties (except Waterford [1.0%] and Westmeath [1.8%]). None of the northern counties suffered even an over 2% rate of evictions – Cavan (1.9%), Donegal (1.7%), Monaghan (1.5%) and Armagh (1.0%) reveal lower levels of evictions while counties Fermanagh, Londonderry and Tyrone record less than 1% of the island-wide total of evictions. It is clear, therefore, given these levels of evictions, that there was a very significant shift in the axis of emigration proper in the last years of the Great Famine, from the north Midlands to Munster and adjacent counties with a striking extension into the better lands of west Leinster.

**MORTALITY AND EMIGRATION**

To conclude this section, it is important to recognise that Ireland's massive population loss between 1845 and 1852 has two main components. When we look at the distribution of the dead, there are clear east/northeast versus west/southwest gradients. The communities most dramatically affected by famine deaths were located in the western counties and unions from Mayo to Cork. And there is a second high level of mortalities stretching from Leitrim through the central Midland counties to Tipperary. While all counties witnessed excess mortalities, all of Ulster and much of east Leinster and County Waterford were much less deeply affected by famine deaths. In contrast, the core emigrant region is centred on north Connacht and south Ulster (plus Leinster's County Longford). A second significant zone of emigration extends through the middle of the county from Tyrone south through Meath and the counties of west Leinster (plus Wicklow) and also includes Tipperary and Cork in Munster. And the counties with the lowest levels of emigration stretch along the west coast from Galway to Kerry and along the east coast from Londonderry south to Dublin, Wexford and Waterford (and also including that most exceptional county, Donegal).

Some regions, therefore, suffered both very high mortalities and very high levels of emigration. This is particularly true of communities in Mayo, Roscommon, Leitrim, Longford and Sligo. On the other hand, a whole range of communities from Donegal across to Antrim and south by Down, Louth, Dublin, Kildare, Wexford to Waterford witnessed moderate to low levels of emigration and not as many famine deaths. Other counties such as Cavan and Monaghan and Wicklow experienced very high levels of emigration and much less dramatic famine mortalities. Fermanagh, Meath and a broad swathe of communities in west Leinster (in Westmeath, Offaly, Laois, Kilkenny and

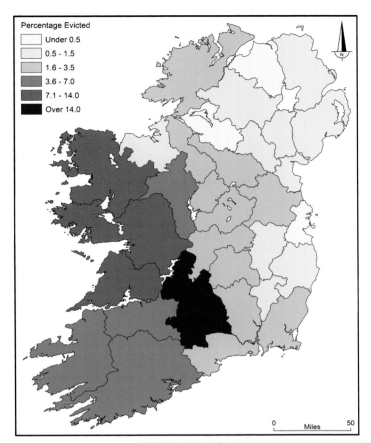

Percentage Evicted
- Under 0.5
- 0.5 - 1.5
- 1.6 - 3.5
- 3.6 - 7.0
- 7.1 - 14.0
- Over 14.0

0    Miles    50

Fig. 10 PERCENTAGE DISTRIBUTION OF EVICTED FAMILIES PER COUNTY 1849–52. The long-running catastrophe that is the Great Famine could also be referred to as 'The Age of the Great Clearances'. Even before the onset of the Famine in the mid-1840s, the rate of landlord evictions had accelerated over the previous decade, facilitated by new legislation which made it both less costly and less cumbersome for the landlord to evict certain categories of tenants. The 1843 amendment to the Poor Law which made landlords responsible for all the rates on holdings valued at £4 or less and more particularly the infamous Gregory clause of mid-1847 which prohibited relief for any family holding more than one-quarter acre further facilitated landlords in the rationalisation of tenants and farm sizes on their estates. Taking advantage of the Famine crisis, evictions and the levelling of dwelling houses intensified – processes which also enhanced greatly the British Government's policy of 'agrarian anglicisation' in Ireland. However, the determining of the number and rate of evictions is still very much a contested domain. Figure 10 of police records of evictions for the Famine years 1849–52 shows the percentage distribution of families evicted per county. A Munster core centred on Tipperary (15.2% of national total of evictions), Clare (9.2), Limerick (7.0%) and Kerry (5.5%) were the counties most affected while Mayo (9%) and Galway (8.3%) constituted a second eviction core. Northern counties suffered very low rates of evictions in these years.

Carlow) as well as counties Tipperary and Cork witnessed relatively high numbers of both the famine dead and the emigrant leaving. No parish in Ireland escaped unscathed. But it is also clear that the pain and suffering were combined in extraordinary different ways across a social and economically diverse island – an island that was deeply fragmented along cultural and political lines. The distribution of evicted families is strongly correlated with both the distribution of the dead and the distribution of emigrants from 1846 onwards.

Fig. 11 Scanlan's *The Famine*. The work of Robert Richard Scanlan (1826–76) shows a fascination with ordinary people or the poorer members of society. He observed scenes of suffering and distress during the Famine period and made two distinguished wash drawings, *The Famine* (1852) – depicted here – and *Emigrants Waiting in Embarkation*, West Cork (1852) [see Patrick Hickey above]. The theme of the little known *The Famine* centres on the drastic consequences of evictions. In the upper half of the drawing, at least two – if not three – houses are shown with the roofs thrown/burnt down. A long winding country road, a number of ejected and disconsolate families trudge along, fathers and mothers carrying their infant children as the younger children cling to their garments. One family remains in a dejected state at the gable end of their roofless house, their few 'belongings' scattered beside them. In the foreground, more pitiful scenes are enacted – probably two evicted families are shown here. On the left, the father carries on his back either a very ill or dying companion and is accompanied by young children. Perhaps a better off family (to the right) – complete with horse and cart – carry a few belongings as they traipse along the Famine road, possibly trying to get to an emigrant embarkation point as depicted in Scanlan's *Emigrants* drawing. Special thanks to Dr Julian Campbell for drawing our attention to *The Famine* and for providing a copy of the wash drawing from the Sotheby catalogue of 16 May 1996. Thanks also to Sothebys for permission to use this image

# Liverpool and the Great Irish Famine

## Carmen Tunney and Pat Nugent

In 1831 the population of the town of Liverpool was 165,175. Twenty years later it had more than doubled to 375,955.[1] The most significant factor in this increase was the influx of Irish migrants during the Irish Famine. However, the Irish had been making their way to the port for some years. Irish communities were already well established not only in Liverpool but in nearby Manchester and Chester as well as further afield in Lancashire, Yorkshire and Cumbria. The common link that attracted predominantly Irishmen to these areas was the availability of unskilled jobs. The industrial revolution taking place in Britain and America was an opportunity for many to leave Ireland in search of work. And so it is unsurprising to find that on the eve of the Famine there were already 49,639 Irish inhabitants in Liverpool, some 17% of the total population.

The employment market in Liverpool had little to offer Irishmen and women who chose to stay there. It appears to have been the Irish who were offered the most unpleasant and poorly paid work whilst their employers congratulated themselves on having a workforce who would accept such low wages and harsh conditions.[2]

### BLACK '47

By 1847 (or Black '47 as it was to become known), Liverpool was experiencing a massive wave of Irish immigration. The docks were continuously thronged by passengers arriving from Ireland. Many took onward passage to America, Canada and Australia, but others remained, seeking a new life in Liverpool and in the northwest of England. The need for a new landing stage to take the increased number of ships was evident and on 12 June 1847 *The Illustrated London News* reported that 'this stupendous work has just been completed at Liverpool, for the convenience of the public'.[3]

The vast numbers of people who arrived in Liverpool in 1847 seeking either temporary or permanent accommo-

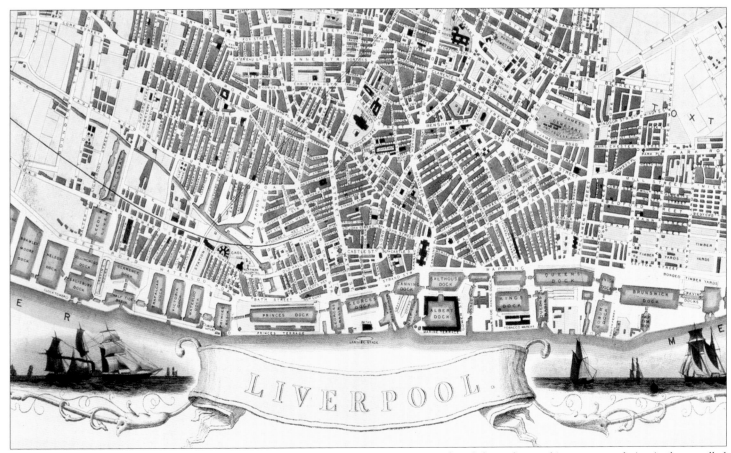

Fig. 1 Tallis map of Liverpool *c*.1851. Many of the already impoverished Famine migrants found themselves seeking accommodation in the so-called 'courts' – back-to-back housing in areas such as Vauxhall, Scotland Road and Exchange located in close proximity to the docks. [Source: Mapseeker Archive Publishing]

dation were soon faced with the harsh realities of life when they walked through the gates of Clarence Dock into what Dr William Duncan, the first medical officer of health, had already dubbed 'the most unhealthy town in England'.[4] New arrivals who were already impoverished found themselves seeking accommodation in the 'courts' – back-to-back housing located in areas such as Vauxhall, Scotland Road and Exchange in close proximity to the docks. Many of these premises were already in an extremely poor state of repair prior to 1847. Cellars were often utilised to house the poorest families. Prone to frequent flooding with contaminated water, these cellars with their overcrowded and unsanitary conditions allowed disease to spread unchecked; inevitably, typhus or 'Irish fever' soon became a distressing part of life in Liverpool. Dr Duncan called for emergency measures to be put in place and soon a number of lazarettos (quarantine stations for maritime travellers) were moored on the River Mersey while fever sheds were erected in the area around the workhouse. Duncan's then groundbreaking research confirmed a link between areas of high-density Irish settlement and fever outbreaks. The death toll was immense both from typhus and diarrhoea: 8,434 souls perished in 1847.

Blame was placed squarely at the door of the incoming Irish; in reality, the arrival of the newcomers had merely exacerbated an already dire situation. A significant tide of resentment began to build in response to the arrival of so many Irish in the city. The year 1847 was pivotal: the point at which sympathy in Liverpool for these people had effectively run out.[5] Primarily this resentment was in response to the heavy rates, which were being levied on the rate-payers of the town who were called upon to support the poor via the select vestry of the parish of Liverpool, the governing body of the parish that acted more or less as borough council. This resentment is clearly evident in the many petitions that were raised and directed at the Government via the Houses of Parliament. The rate-payers were predominantly

Protestant while the beneficiaries of the rates collected by the select vestry were predominantly Catholic. The evidence surrounding the collection and distribution of rates is not always clear. For example, whilst a figure of 55,385 instances of relief paid out is given for six days in June 1847, how many individuals this accounts for is not known. Given the lack of information it is impossible to extrapolate exact numbers of those claiming relief. Using a rule of thumb and taking an average per day produces a figure of 9,231 although this method of arriving at an estimate of the number of those claiming relief is less than satisfactory.[6]

## REMOVING IRISH IMMIGRANTS

The costs of maintaining the health and welfare of the Irish in Liverpool were growing. Not only that, the cost of removing immigrants back to their homeland had increased. Again, the findings for actual costs are often unclear, but the best evidence comes from the records of the Select Committee on Poor Removal for the years 1844 to 1854. During 1847 some 15,000 Irishmen and women were taken back to Ireland, however their stay was often short-lived and they made the journey back to Liverpool when they could.[7]

Figures which have been calculated to take into account the many variances surrounding the costs of supporting the incoming Irish poor show a dramatic increase for the financial year of 1845/6 from £2,916 to £25,926. This financial burden proved an extremely difficult pill for many of Liverpool's more affluent inhabitants to swallow. Many of these same individuals were well-known philanthropists who were asked to dig even deeper to help ease the desperate situation. Distinctions were now made between the 'deserving' and the 'undeserving' poor.

Those who looked for help in Liverpool had a choice of whether to seek 'outdoor' or 'indoor' relief. 'Outdoor' relief for the Irish, contrary to the belief of some at the time,

Fig. 2 Detail from Tallis map *c.*1851 revealing an extremely busy waterfront. By the mid-nineteenth century many of Liverpool's docks had already been built to accommodate the increased shipping traffic and trade at the port. While the docks dominated, other industries such as shipbuilding, glass manufacture and soap making also flourished. [Source: Mapseeker Archive Publishing]]

Fig. 3 CONTAGION AND DENSITIES OF IRISH IMMIGRANTS. Many deaths resulted from fever and diarrhoea. [Adapted from Frank Neal, *Black '47: Famine in Britain* (Basingstoke, 1998), pp. 130-131]

fied individuals and families to the authorities. The workhouse in Liverpool, situated on Brownlow Hill, was the largest institution of this type outside of Ireland and yet it was still unable to cope with the sheer demand; outdoor relief remained the only viable option for many.

Those who could work were thought to have had a better chance in life. It is true that Liverpool's position as an increasingly busy port provided employment for large numbers of Irishmen. The influx of unskilled Irish labour, however, called into question the extremely poor rates of pay being offered by employers. Whether the reality was that the availability of Irish labour was serving to keep wages low or whether that was merely the belief at the time, the issue raised important questions – and also anti-Irish sentiment. A report in the *Liverpool Albion* in 1849, for example, suggested that Irish workers were being taken on at the expense of experienced dockers simply because they were willing to work for less. Further reports in the *London Times* questioned 'whether every English working man is always to carry an Irish family on his shoulders'.[8]

Begging was rife and presented a huge problem for the town officials. Liverpool was already the focus of those who thought 'the Irish are more addicted to begging than the English and there are more impostors among the Irish than the people of any other country'.[9] To highlight their plight, beggars often 'borrowed' children, although this was not a uniquely Irish habit. There is some evidence of professional begging becoming increasingly prevalent amongst the Irish and it became a feature of Liverpool life during this period. In 1849 a large group of professional beggars were taken to court and, when sentenced, were given the option to either go to jail or be taken back to Ireland. Unsurprisingly, most chose jail, creating another burden to the borough by joining the growing number of inmates detained at 'Her Majesty's pleasure' who could be identified as Irish.[10]

Visits to the local jail were to be a regular feature of the Irish experience in nineteenth-century Liverpool. As early as 1836 it was reported by Liverpool's superintendent that a third of all the people he had in custody were Irish. He estimated at the time that Irish people made up around a quarter of the population. By 1849 Edward Rushton, a magistrate, demonstrated to the Home Secretary, George Grey, that of all those who appeared in the Liverpool magistrates courts, the Irish made up 40% of the total. He went on to say that they were better fed and cared for in prison, which made the proposition of a jail sentence hardly a deterrent. The prison, which had been built originally to house 500 inmates now found itself housing 1,100.[11]

### GROWING RESENTMENT

Resentment towards the Irish poor quickly became a feature of life in Liverpool. Such feelings were easily absorbed by

did not provide for much more than the most basic of existences and was comparably less than that given to English paupers by as much as 2d. Again, the total per year is difficult to determine. A rise in the cost of 'outdoor' relief was particularly noticeable and may be attributed to the fact that the Irish, on the whole, would fight to avoid admission to the workhouse, which is where 'indoor' relief was provided. 'Indoor' relief carried with it a considerable amount of shame and stigma and would also have identi-

DEPARTURE OF THE "NIMROD" AND "ATHLONE" STEAMERS, WITH EMIGRANTS ON BOARD, FOR LIVERPOOL.

Fig. 4 Emigrants boarding the steam ships *Nimrod* and *Athlone* in Cork bound for Liverpool. [Source: *The Illustrated London News*, 10 May 1851]

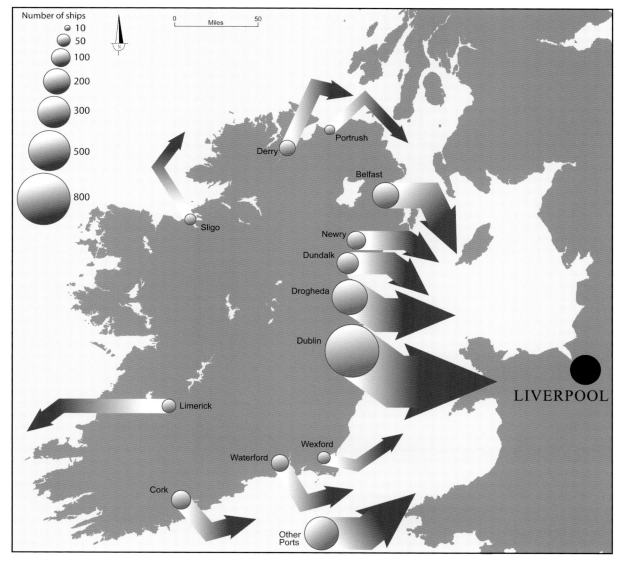

Fig. 5 THE NUMBER OF VESSELS ARRIVING AT LIVERPOOL FROM IRISH PORTS DURING 1847. While Dublin was the principal port of departure for those seeking a passage to Liverpool, the majority of refugees were from the famine-stricken western counties. [Adapted from Frank Neal, *Black '47: Famine in Britain* (Basingstoke, 1998), p. 55]

507

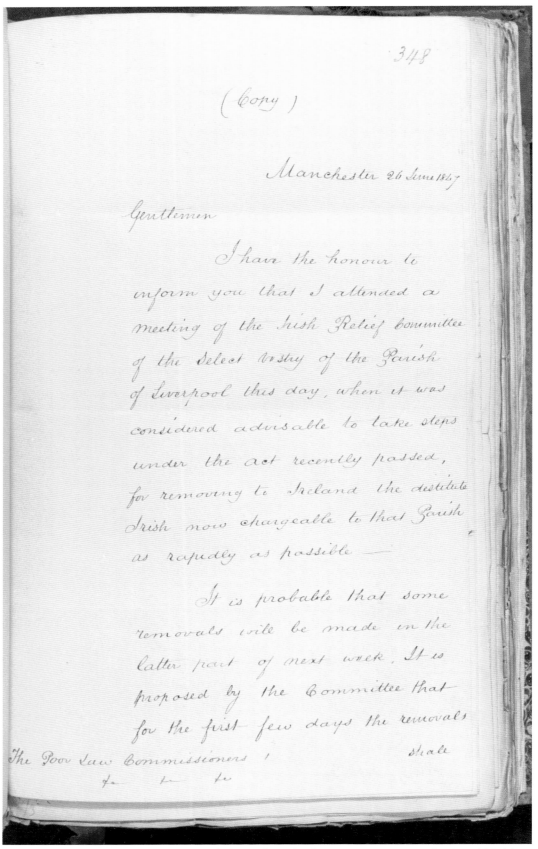

those who carried anti-Catholic sentiments. A note in the *Liverpool Mail*, 6 November 1847, attested:

That the scum of Ireland come to Liverpool and die in thousands is true. But whose fault is that? Misgovernment in Ireland – idleness on the part of the peasantry and ignorance and extravagance on the part of the gentry . . . The people that come here are not labourers . . . they are beggars and paupers. They were never labourers. They never did an honest day's work in their lives. They lived by begging, as the Roman Catholic *prelate* regrets to say they cannot do now, for the potato crop has failed and when they arrive here, begging is their profession, the workhouse their retreat, the penny loaf per day a certainty and medical aid, port wine, soup, a coffin and a Christian burial.[12]

Thus the feelings of sectarianism that were later to become so evident in Liverpool began to manifest themselves.

The Irish habit of 'enjoying' a drink also became the topic of much scrutiny and its link to crime was inevitable. In reality, much of the drink imbibed by the Irish poor was taken at the weekends. As a section of the population who were living on the brink of destitution even when employed, drink became something that was only accessible when payday arrived. The superintendent

Fig. 6 Liverpool authorities could not cope with the numbers of Irish immigrants arriving in the city in 1847. Measures were quickly taken to remove the destitute Irish. During 1847 some 15,000 Irishmen and women were sent back to Ireland. This letter included in the Minute Books of the Cork Board of Guardians refers to a meeting of the Irish Relief Committee of the Select Vestry of the Parish of Liverpool 'where it was considered advisable to take steps under the Act recently passed, for removing to Ireland the destitute Irish now chargeable to that parish as rapidly as possible'. [Source: Cork Archives Institute]

Table 1. Number and percentage of sailings carrying Irish passengers to New York

| Port(s) | 1846 | 1847 | 1848 | 1849 | 1850 | 1851 | Total |
|---|---|---|---|---|---|---|---|
| Liverpool | 214 (79.6%) | 241 (59.1%) | 337 (57.8%) | 349 (53.0%) | 322 (60.5%) | 382 (62.2%) | 1845 (60.2%) |
| London | 24 | 23 | 37 | 45 | 27 | 23 | 179 (5.8%) |
| Glasgow | 13 | 26 | 41 | 50 | 50 | 45 | 225 (7.3%) |
| Other UK ports | 3 | 3 | 14 | 25 | 9 | 2 | 56 (1.8%) |
| Irish ports | 14 (5.2%) | 106 (26.0%) | 145 (24.9%) | 186 (28.2%) | 123 (23.1%) | 162 (26.4) | 736 (24.0%) |
| European ports | 1 | 9 | 9 | 4 | 1 | - | 24 (0.8%) |
| TOTAL | 269 | 408 | 583 | 659 | 532 | 614 | 3065 |

Source: Tepper, Michael, (Assoc. ed.) *The Famine Immigrants: Lists of Irish Immigrants Arriving at the Port of New York 1846-1851, Forward, Volume 2.* Genealogical Publishing Co., Inc. Baltimore, US, (1983), p. viii.

of Liverpool himself observed of the Irish that it was their habit *en masse* to spend whatever earnings they received on Saturday nights in local hostelries. There were two main reasons for this. Firstly, it was the custom for Irish labourers to be paid in public houses at the end of the week. Secondly, the 'pub' was to many a place of refuge from the bleak conditions which awaited them in their accommodation in the courts and cellars. By comparison, the public houses were warm, friendly and a source of social interaction with people from their own country who understood the terrible hardships which had been endured.

John Denvir, an Irish nationalist who lived and worked in Liverpool and Birkenhead, revealed what he saw were the subtle but important differences in the English and Irish drinking habits. He claimed that the Irish were merely more demonstrative as a nation and let this be evidenced whilst they were drinking. By comparison, he observed that the English, when drunk, would simply go quietly away to sleep it off. However, the prevalence of so-called 'wabble shops' where illegally imported Irish liquor was sold, together with illegal stills set up in boarding houses, only served to fuel the stereotype of the Irish drunkard who brawled in public with his equally intoxicated 'friends'. Unsurprisingly, there were those who dismissed Denvir's view and such behaviour became another focus for those who wished to fuel anti-Irish sentiment for many years to come.[13]

## LIVERPOOL'S ROLE AS A TRANSIT PORT (1846–51)

On average 250,000 Irish arrived in Liverpool every year from 1846 to 1851.[14] Between one-half and two-thirds continued their generally prepaid journeys on more seaworthy ships to the United States and Canada annually.[15] Those who remained stayed in Liverpool or migrated to other towns and cities in the northwest of England.[16] Most of these migrants had traveled on deck on the generally

inferior ships that crossed the Irish Sea. This was the cheapest possible fare and consequently these passengers were classified as paupers.[17]

The Liverpool–New York route became the primary channel of transatlantic emigration traffic because it offered the safest passage at competitive prices and on superior quality vessels that could travel throughout the year, unlike the ships that traveled from Irish ports. Liverpool's competitive advantage was also aided by the practice of charging deck passengers on ships from Ireland a very low (or even no) fare if they were prepared to act as human ballast. (This arrangement was financially viable for Liverpool shipowners due to the lucrative business of transporting of American timber to England on the return voyage from New York City.)[18] Of the 301 ships carrying Irish passengers that docked in New York City in 1846, 214 came from Liverpool. Throughout the Famine years, Liverpool was the origin of just over 60% of crossings carrying Irish migrants to New York City (see Table 1).

However, focusing on voyages alone gives a distorted picture. Ships from Liverpool carried the greatest number of Irish passengers per ship. In the early years of the Famine, Irish passenger numbers averaged about 200 per ship. However, in late 1849, some ships were regularly carrying between 600 to 1,000 Irish passengers. Throughout the Famine years, the 738 ships that sailed departed from one of the following Irish ports: Belfast, Cork, Dublin, Drogheda, Donegal, Galway, Killibegs, Kilrush, Derry, Limerick, Moville, Newry, New Ross, Queenstown, Sligo, Tralee, Waterford, Wexford and Youghal. They rarely carried more than 300 Irish passengers. Ships travelling from Glasgow had similar passenger numbers while those from London and other English ports rarely carried more than fifty.[19]

Ships that originated in continental European ports such as Bremen and Le Havre carried even fewer Irish. These passengers probably alighted at the English ports to which these ships called before continuing on their transatlantic voyage. Consequently, while Liverpool was the port of origin for 60% of the 3,065 transatlantic voyages between January 1846 and December 1851, these ships carried close to 90% of all Irish passengers to New York. Given the detail of the shipping records, it is possible to analyse the following: changes over time relating to the numbers of passengers, the frequency of voyages, the demographic profile of the emigrants, the ratio of individual to group emigration,

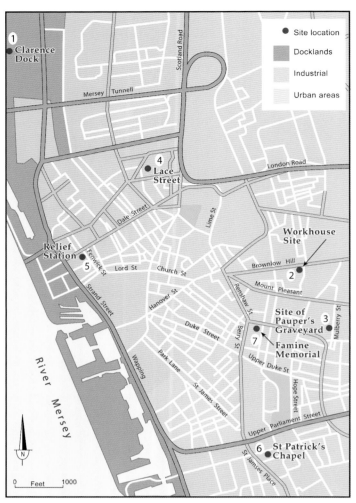

Fig. 7 (left) SITES ASSOCIATED WITH THE FAMINE IN LIVERPOOL including Clarence Dock, Regent Road (1) which was the arrival point for *c.*1.3–1.5 million refugees fleeing Ireland during the period 1845–52. Many of the destitute Irish ended up in the workhouse at Brownlaw Hill (2) while those who perished there were buried in the nearby Pauper's Graveyard at Mulberry Street (3), now the site of a college car park. Given their impoverished circumstances the Irish tended to gravitate to areas like Lace Street (4) which was predominantly Irish speaking in 1850. During a three-month period in 1847 the rapid spread of disease in this street resulted in the deaths of 181 people. Meagre rations were distributed to the destitute by parish authorities at relief stations such as that established on Fenwick Street (5) while a memorial in St Patrick's Chapel, Park Place (6) commemorates ten priests who died while administering relief to a disease-stricken population. Liverpool's principal Famine memorial is located at St Luke's Gardens, Leece Street (7) and was unveiled in 1998. The centrepiece of the memorial is a traditional standing stone behind an empty bronze bowl and was designed by sculptor Eamonn O'Doherty. [Adapted from *Liverpool and the Irish Great Hunger: A Heritage Trail* produced by the Great Hunger Commemoration Committee, Liverpool]

the socio-economic status as reflected in listed occupations and death rates per voyage. An exploratory analysis reveals between ten and twenty ships operated throughout the six-year time period, including the *Fidelia*, which was one of the ships in regular use during the Famine years.

## TRANSFORMATION

The Famine would leave an indelible mark on Liverpool. The arrival of the Irish in such tragic circumstances and in such vast numbers rapidly changed the socio-economic

and cultural complexion of the city. A generation after the-Famine, people of Irish origin accounted for *c.*24% of the population of Liverpool. Lawton's research, based on a 10% sample of household heads in the census enumerators' books of 1871, revealed that the Irish remained at the lower end of the employment market and social hierarchy (for example, 42% of the households were headed by dock and warehouse workers).[20] These families were still concentrated in the low-cost, poor-quality 'court' housing areas such as Vauxhall, Scotland and Exchange.

Beckingham's recent research on the 'drunken' Irish reveals that problems identified during the Famine period continued at least into the next generation until there were attempts by the Irish community to address these problems and their impact on the negative perception of the Catholic-Liverpool Irish. These attempts did little to dispel this stereotypical view and some Irish Liverpudlians continued to experience 'marginalisation and discrimination for much of the following century'.[21]

Throughout the latter half of the nineteenth century, Liverpool would maintain its position as the primary transit port for Irish emigration to the United States and Canada, completely eclipsing the role of any other port in Ireland or Britain.

# The Fidelia

## Carmen Tunney and Patrick Nugent

The *Fidelia* was one of the ships in regular use during the Famine years. It disembarked in New York on the following dates having left Liverpool four to six weeks previously; 23/02/46, 01/06/46, 05/10/46, 23/02/47, 27/05/47, 06/10/47, 03/02/48, 01/06/48, 30/09/48, 21/02/49, 31/05/49, 17/01/50, 11/05/50, 07/09/50, 08/01/51, 15/04/51, and 05/08/51. Irish passenger figures ranged from eighty-nine on the first voyage, peaking at 377 on 31 May 1849 and returning to 274 during the last voyage on 5 August 1851. In total, 2,268 males (49.8%), 2,234 females (49.1%) and fifty-two 'unknowns' (1.1%) travelled on the *Fidelia*. Unknowns usually referred to passengers whose names were phonetic renditions of Irish language personal or pet names. Their occupational classifications reveal them as being of the lowest socio-economic strata, and consequently insignificant to those compiling the manifests.

The level of detail in the ship's manifests facilitated the identification of the following five categories of immigrants; A. Unaccompanied individuals, B. Same surname groups, C. Young couples with children (nuclear families), D. Single parents with children and E. Extended kin groups. These categories represent a modification of Glasier's seven basic family types in his seminal work on the socio-demographic characteristics of Irish immigrants from 1846–51.[1]

Unaccompanied individuals were the largest contingent on all ships, averaging at 49.9% but ranging from 30.9% to 62.9%. The six lowest percentages coincided with the winter crossings in each year. Same surname groups accounted for 18.0% over the time period. Again there was some seasonal fluctuation but it was not as pronounced as in the previous category. Same surname groups invariably consisted of two to three males or females with the same surnames and of the same generation. Males and females with the same surname also fell within this category. Some of these may have been young childless couples.

The third category consisted of young couples with children. These nuclear families accounted for 11.3%. However, there was a dramatic range within this category, where they accounted for 38.3% of the passengers on the February 1848 crossing but only 1.1% of the September 1850 crossing. While they were proportionally more significant on winter crossings until 1850, these vessels had below average num-

Table 1: Categories of immigrants

| Year | Month | A | B | C | D | E | Total |
|------|-------|---|---|---|---|---|-------|
| 1846 | February | 29 | 18 | 26 | 8 | 8 | 89 |
| | June | 178 | 78 | 28 | 36 | 24 | 344 |
| | October | 135 | 47 | 42 | 27 | 7 | 258 |
| 1847 | February | 79 | 21 | 47 | 43 | 16 | 206 |
| | May | 165 | 66 | 29 | 24 | 23 | 307 |
| | October | 99 | 18 | 26 | 24 | 18 | 185 |
| 1848 | February | 46 | 18 | 57 | 20 | 8 | 149 |
| | June | 116 | 56 | 26 | 11 | 21 | 230 |
| | September | 152 | 50 | 18 | 62 | 20 | 302 |
| 1849 | February | 98 | 40 | 54 | 23 | 38 | 253 |
| | May | 188 | 72 | 40 | 36 | 41 | 377 |
| 1850 | January | 106 | 37 | 38 | 33 | 47 | 261 |
| | May | 231 | 62 | 20 | 21 | 33 | 367 |
| | September | 177 | 34 | 3 | 35 | 20 | 269 |
| 1851 | January | 172 | 85 | 16 | 53 | 35 | 361 |
| | April | 163 | 64 | 10 | 16 | 69 | 322 |
| | August | 138 | 51 | 33 | 25 | 27 | 274 |
| TOTAL (%) | | 2,272 (49.9) | 817 (18.0) | 513 (11.3) | 497 (10.9) | 455 (9.9) | 4,554 (100) |

bers of Irish. There was also a noticeable decline in this category from mid 1848. Single parents with children accounted for 10.9% of all passengers. On midsummer sailings they fell significantly below this average. Close to 90% were headed by a female adult. The final category consisted of extended kin groups. These were usually two or three generational groups bearing the same surname. These groups could exceed ten individuals. The overall average of 9.9% concealed a considerable range from 2.7% on the October 1846 crossing to 21.4% on the April 1851 crossing.

The seventeen passenger lists of the *Fidelia* were compiled from the original ship manifest schedules on deposit in the National Immigration Archives in the Balch Institute in Philadelphia.[2] It is clear from the preceding analysis that there was a lack of standardisation in the original manifests. There appears to be a negative correlation between the standard of record keeping and ships with above average numbers of Irish passengers and winter crossings. Nevertheless, there is sufficient detail in all lists to arrive at the following conclusions. Over the six-year period, female passengers had a younger age profile than their male counterparts. The ratio of male to female passengers increased slightly. Analysis of the socio-economic profile over time suggests that there was greater diversity until 1849. Some passengers' lists suggest the arbitrary allocation of 'labourer', 'servant', 'unknown' as

one progresses through the manifests in relation to occupational status particularly on ships with over 300 Irish passengers. Nevertheless, the vast majority of passengers were potential blue-collar workers or domestic servants and this profile appears to become more pronounced with time.

While there was an annual seasonal variation in the proportion of unaccompanied individuals on each crossing, they were always the most numerous. There was also a steady stream of sibling groups of the same generation and a growth in multi-generational kinship groups. Fragmented families lead by a young female with two to three children remained significant but there was a marked decline in the number of nuclear families. Such a profile supports the explanation that men emigrated initially and then sent remittances so that their wives and families could emigrate later.[3] The increase in multi-generational kinship groups represented a growing tendency for cutting all ties with the home country possibly because of eviction.

By any standards the number of deaths at sea was low. The February 1849 crossing was the only sailing that conformed to some degree to the 'coffin ship' stereotype with eight deaths. Ships plying the Liverpool–New York trade route were invariably of superior quality to the infamous 'coffin ships' which sailed directly from Irish ports or ships that were bound for Canadian ports. The *Fidelia* was clearly one of the former.

**Fig. 1** Black Ball Line packet ship *Fidelia*, oil painting by Samuel Walters (1811–1882). The *Fidelia* was a typical packet ship which served the Liverpool–New York trade route during the Famine years. Built by William H. Webb of the celebrated New York shipbuilding family, it carried thousands of Irish emigrants to the New World in search of better lives. Unlike the infamous 'coffin ships' few deaths occurred on the *Fidelia*. [Source: Hart Nautical Collections, MIT Museum]

# Irish Famine refugees and the emergence of Glasgow Celtic Football Club

## John Reid

Out of adversity and struggle is born defiance, resilience, self-reliance and innovation. All of these accompanied the birth of Glasgow Celtic Football Club. Celtic's character and culture was fashioned in the struggle to overcome poverty, deprivation, discrimination and exclusion. In a sense, of course, these were features of quite a few of the ultimate destinations of the Irish diaspora that flowed from the Famine, but it was in nineteenth-century Glasgow that the response took the concrete form of a sporting institution. Central to its birth was the experience and consequences of the Great Hunger.

Eighteenth-century Glasgow was a relatively modest settlement; it had a small population of 20,000 with grazing animals kept on the banks of the Clyde, a river which most people could wade across and where salmon were caught regularly. At that time Glasgow was only at the beginning of that great journey that culminated in it becoming a principal commercial city of the British Empire. Much of the city's subsequent wealth was derived from international trade, especially the exploitation of resources in the Americas and West Indian colonies including tobacco, sugar, cotton and people. These were all essential facets of the slave trade and it is to the plantation economy of the West Indies that Glasgow owed much of its early wealth.

### 'Workshop of the world'

Its mercantile and commercial stimulus resulted in Glasgow becoming a magnet, attracting people from all over Scotland to provide the manpower required for a period of rapid industrialisation. This transformation also led to significant urbanisation. Even before the influx of Famine refugees the city had expanded to take in Anderston, Calton and Gorbals, all areas to be significantly settled by the Irish. From the 1830s Scotland, particularly the west-central belt, had shown itself to have an abundance of coal and iron, important in their own right and massively so in making Glasgow a world centre of shipbuilding; so much so that by the 1850s and 1860s the city produced 70% of the iron tonnage launched in Britain every year.[1]

Glasgow's place as the 'Workshop of the World' and 'Second City of the Empire' was consolidated during the latter half of the nineteenth century. Its industrial and commercial rise was reflected in its population. The city experienced a rapid increase from 77,000 at the beginning of the century to 202,000 in 1831 and by 1861 it had become Scotland's largest city with 448,000 inhabitants. In 1891 the population stood at 858,000, having increased ten-fold in the course of the nineteenth century.[2]

Economic growth marched inexorably on. Despite experiencing uncontrolled booms and slumps, the British economy was during this period the most highly developed in the world. Progress and prosperity were not for everyone, for wealth distribution was massively unequal. Alongside the rich and lavish lifestyles bestowed by commercial or industrial ownership sat the dire poverty of the vast majority of the population. It was a period that also coincided with the Great Irish Hunger of the mid-nineteenth century.

Initially, Glasgow's new dwellers had come from all over Scotland, especially from the Highlands. Most of these native Scots were Protestant; a small number, however, were Catholic, leading to the opening of the first Catholic Chapel in 1792 near Argyll Street for the few hundred Catholic Highlanders in the city – a significant event in what was then recognised as a fiercely anti-Catholic city. Indeed, there had been a series of anti-Catholic riots in Glasgow just a few years previous to the opening of this new chapel.

Whereas estimates placed the Catholic population for the whole of Scotland in the mid-eighteenth century at no more than 16,490 – or just over 1% of the population[3] – this gradually but significantly changed when from the early nineteenth century the Catholic Irish began to make their way to Scotland, in the main as seasonal workers and cheap labour.[4] For several decades before the onset of the Great Hunger immigrants from Ireland were thus indigent labourers meeting the demand created by the expansion of industrial and agricultural Scotland in the late eighteenth and early nineteenth centuries. From 1845 the Irish immigrant to Scotland came mainly from the starving Catholic 'peasantry' and 'underclass' escaping from the wrath of the Great Hunger.

This influx of Catholics from Ireland over several decades, in particular from the period of the Great Famine, would dramatically change the social, cultural, ethnic and religious face of Glasgow and the west-central belt of Scotland. During the Famine years approximately 100,000 Irish arrived in the Glasgow area, spreading out to surrounding areas like Lanarkshire. These were destitute refugees from the most appalling mass social catastrophe in nineteenth-century Europe.

Proximity and access to means of transport rendered

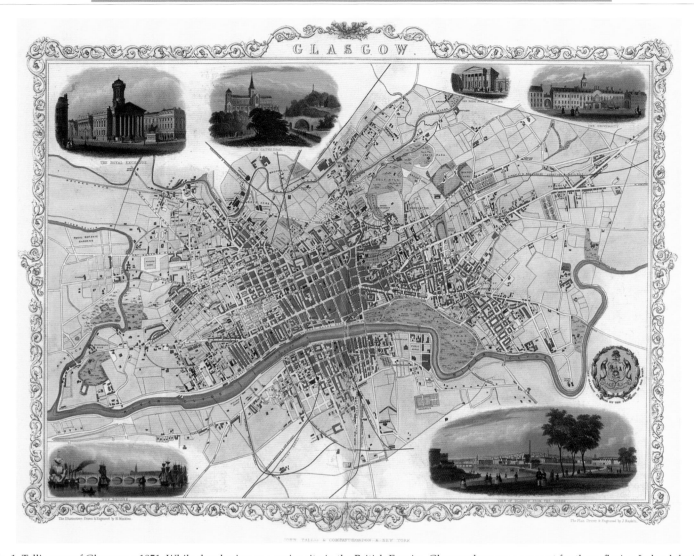

Fig. 1 Tallis map of Glasgow, *c.*1851. While developing as a major city in the British Empire, Glasgow became a magnet for those fleeing Ireland during the Famine and its aftermath.

Scotland a viable choice for these refugees. By 1845, for instance, there were some twenty steamers operating from Glasgow, Ardrossan and Stranraer to Belfast, Newry, Dundalk, Dublin, Cork, Derry and Sligo. Nevertheless, this journey was an arduous undertaking with passengers more often than not required to share space with other cargo, including livestock. In addition, hunger and disease made certain that the narrative of immigration to Scotland was one dominated by trauma.

## BLACK '47

Records from 1847 provide examples of the upsurge in Irish Famine migration to Glasgow. For instance, in the two weeks between 6 August and 18 August 1847 alone, several ships – the *Shamrock*, *Aurora*, *Londonderry* and *Tartar* – all left either Belfast or Derry for Glasgow, carrying in total over 11,000 passengers.[5]

Their impoverished condition is equally evident from contemporary records. During the first twenty-five days of 1847 alone, no fewer than 783 men, women and children, classed as 'vagrants', were rounded up and taken

before the police court. The vast majority of these were from Ireland. By March 1847 'about fifty cases of vagrancy, chiefly Irish', were being brought before the same court every day, and a number of them deported back to Ireland.[6]

In the same year, Glasgow city's parochial board complained about the condition of the immigrants. The board members submitted that between 15 June and 12 September, 33,267 passengers from Ireland landed at Glasgow, 2,370 of whom were reported to belong to the class able to support themselves, 708 were old and infirm, unable to do anything whatever for their own maintenance, and the remaining 30,189 consisted of men, women and children in the last stage of wretchedness, thousands of whom at once made their way from the quays to the office of the parochial board for temporary relief.[7] Many of the people who fled Ireland were completely destitute 'disoriented, passive and fatalistic'.[8]

Throughout the Famine years the number of refugees fleeing to Scotland gathered pace. But, while for some Scotland held out at least the prospect of a new life, for others it proved all too soon to be no more than a final resting place. As the Irish arrived in Glasgow in greater numbers there was a dramatic increase in the number of deaths recorded in the city. At the onset of Famine in 1845 there were 8,259 deaths in Glasgow's population of 322,100: a rate of one in thirty-nine. By 'Black '47' the death rate had more than doubled to one in eighteen, or 18,886 in a population of 344,200. Most of this increase can be attributed to the massive rise in cholera deaths in Glasgow as a result of the Famine influx.[9]

Most of the authorities in British recipient cities fulfilled their basic responsibilities with regards Famine refugees, though, given the poor physical condition of many of those landing at British ports, 'it is not surprising that the poor law system immediately came under severe strain', a factor accentuated by the downturn in the British economy of the time.[10] The authorities were not generous but neither were they generous to their own poor. By the winter of 1847 there was much charity forthcoming from various sections of the community to set against the many examples of rejection: a soup kitchen set up in St Enoch Square, Glasgow, for example, several hundred yards from the docks where thousands of migrants disembarked, was feeding 4,000 to 5,000 starving Irish a week.[11]

### DREAD OF INFECTION

But not all were as charitably disposed: 'It was the dread of infection of famine fever that kept the public authorities continuously on the alert. They resented the coming of the Irish as certain to add to the evils of native unemployment and ultimately to the burden of the poor rates, but their immediate concerns were to prevent a recurrence of the epidemics that were familiar visitors to the industrial towns of Scotland in the early nineteenth century.'[12] The *Glasgow Herald* (11 June 1847) reported on the 'Irish Invasion', stating that:

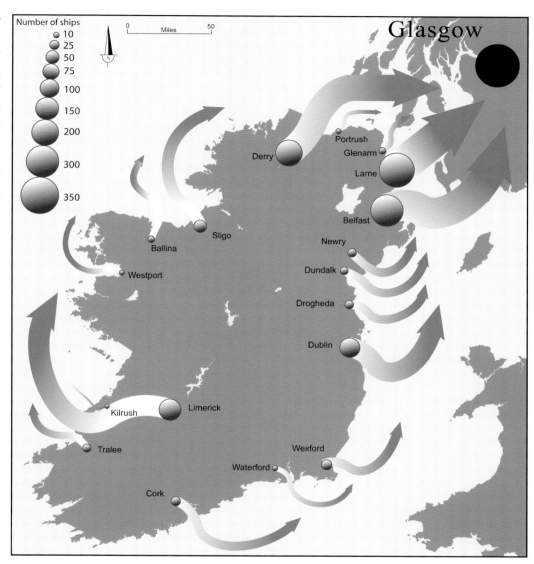

Fig. 2 THE NUMBER OF VESSELS ARRIVING AT GLASGOW FROM IRISH PORTS DURING 1847. Many of the Famine refugees arriving in Glasgow in 1847 came via ports located in the north of Ireland. Belfast, Larne and Derry accounted for 62% of the tonnage of vessels entering Glasgow in that year. Many of the steam ships were not suitable for passenger services, having been built mainly for the transport of agricultural products and livestock, hence the terrible conditions experienced by the refugees in transit. [Source: Frank Neal, *Black'47: Britain and the Famine Irish* (Basingstoke, 1997), pp. 56-57]

The streets are literally swarming with vagrants from the sister country and the misery which many of these poor creatures endure can scarcely be less than what they have fled or been driven from at home. Many of them are absolutely without the means of procuring lodging of even the meanest description and are obliged consequently to make their bed frequently with a stone for a pillow.

Like the *Glasgow Herald*, the *Glasgow Chronicle* of January 1847 expressed concern at the numbers of Irish arriving in the city and blamed them for the ongoing typhus epidemic.[13] This malignant influence was perceived as spreading well beyond public health, into social ills. Articles decrying the Irish appeared regularly in the Scottish press after 1846, usually blaming them not only for 'importing typhus fever',

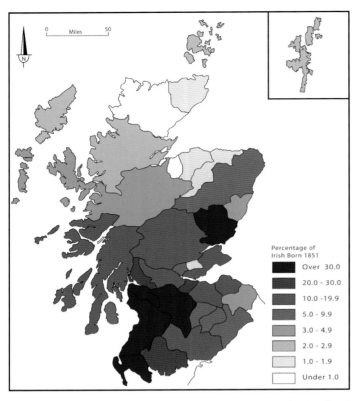

Percentage of
Irish Born 1851

| | |
|---|---|
| ■ | Over 30.0 |
| ■ | 20.0 - 30.0 |
| ■ | 10.0 - 19.9 |
| ■ | 5.0 - 9.9 |
| ■ | 3.0 - 4.9 |
| ■ | 2.0 - 2.9 |
| ■ | 1.0 - 1.9 |
| ☐ | Under 1.0 |

Fig. 3 DISTRIBUTION OF IRISH-BORN IN SCOTLAND IN 1851. Given Scotland's relatively small population size in 1841, the scale of Irish emigration there meant that the ratio of Irish to Scottish was greater than any other emigrant country over the latter half of the nineteenth century. This factor is striking when one considers that the vast majority of Irish and their offspring eventually settled in a thirty mile radius around the greater Glasgow and Lanarkshire areas of the west-central belt.

al areas of Irish Catholic settlement – places such as Gallowgate, Trongate, Calton, Briggate, Saltmarket, Tradeston, Hutchesontown, spreading out to more modern Parkhead and Shettleston – still retain some of the worst levels of social and economic deprivation in contemporary Europe.

By 1851 almost 20% of Glasgow's population had been born in Ireland with the peak of Irish-born in Scotland occurring in the 1880s.

## CATHOLICISM IN SCOTLAND

Famine migration irrevocably changed the nature of the Catholic Church in Scotland. The number of Catholics in Scotland rose from around 50,000 at the onset of the Famine to 150,000 by 1850 and 332,000 in 1878 (and around 750,000 by the new millennium).[16] From being a tiny organisation geographically and numerically limited to a few parts of the Highlands, the Catholic Church in Scotland was transformed with the influx of Irish Catholics. This change began early in the nineteenth century but took off spectacularly from the 1840s and 1850s. From this period on, Catholic churches were built by the immigrants in Glasgow, Lanarkshire and to the west in Greenock and Dumbarton, in particular.[17] The number of clergy in the same period more than doubled and in 1878 the Catholic hierarchy in Scotland was restored. The minority of Irish immigrants to Glasgow that prospered and made their way in business significantly assisted the financing and construction of these churches, as well as Catholic schools, in Glasgow and beyond, as did many of the impoverished Irish themselves.[18]

As a result primarily of the arrival of the Famine, Irish Catholicism re-emerged in Scotland and as Catholic churches began to be founded so also did Catholic charities. The St Vincent de Paul Society was founded in Scotland during the Famine in 1846 amongst the Irish Catholic poor of Edinburgh before rapidly spreading throughout the Catholic population of the urban west-central belt. Its aim was to succour the poor in spiritual and material ways. The Catholic Men's Society was introduced to Scotland from Ireland in the 1850s while the League of the Cross was established in the 1870s. Other Catholic organisations followed as the nineteenth century progressed.

but also for 'corrupting the lower orders of Scotland by setting the most pernicious example of dependency on parochial aid' and accused them of spreading criminality alongside disease.[14]

As ever, ignorance and unfamiliarity bred fear and suspicion. The overtly Catholic nature of the Famine immigration added to the overall picture of fear and confusion created in the Protestant host country. Prejudice towards Irish Catholics came not only from traditional religious or political foes but was endemic throughout society. In 1847, when the anti-Catholic journal, *The Witness*, associated Roman Catholicism with dependence and indigence, and Protestantism with vitality and progress, 'it was merely repeating a widely-held Victorian nostrum'.[15]

Narratives of family breakup, humiliation, death, suffering, poverty, hardship, begging, charity, disease, squalor and desperation followed the Famine Irish wherever they landed and settled. Indeed, as far as Glasgow is concerned, it can be argued that aspects of Irish disadvantage and deprivation remain as a legacy several generations on. In Glasgow, although many of Irish descent have moved from traditionally impoverished areas and greatly improved and even matched the rest of the population in terms of their material and personal well-being, it is noticeable even in the new millennium that the tradition-

## SOCIAL DIVISION

As Catholics struggled to establish their civil rights in Scotland, and, with an absence or lack of state relief at this time, abject poverty could mean deportation back to Ireland – even if a person had been in Scotland for ten or more years. Even by 1849 when a number of conditions had marginally improved in and around Glasgow the parochial authorities were still repatriating 1,000 a month back to Ireland.

For those remaining, geographical and social division

increasingly imposed itself. Just a few years after the worst excesses of the Famine, and with many people still suffering its effects, the vertically segregated residential pattern of pre-modern urban Scotland in which different social classes occupied the various storeys of the same tenement was replaced by a horizontally segregated residential pattern. Inner-city Glasgow was completely abandoned to the poor, and disproportionately, the Irish poor. Even after the Famine, the infamous Drygate district of Glasgow, where many Irish had settled, produced an incredible density of people that could only shorten the lives of its inhabitants. One thousand persons to an acre characterised an area where contagious diseases, poverty, unemployment, malnourishment and premature death flourished in confined conditions.

## CELTIC FOOTBALL CLUB

The processes of urbanisation, industrialisation and the concomitant rise in population, yielded great extremes of wealth and poverty in Glasgow. In such an environment it is not difficult to see how the growth of organised sport, particularly football for the working classes, represented a bright light in the dark lives of many people. But in the case of Celtic there were driving forces other than leisure and recreation.

Despite some advances in the provision of support for the poor on the part of the Board of Supervision and Poor Relief, during the period of Celtic's founding the vast majority of Glasgow's poor had no safety net. This was at a time when medical science had no answers to the tuberculosis, whooping cough and measles that contributed to the persistence of appalling mortality rates amongst infants. Around six out of 1,000 pregnancies ended with the death of the mother.

Ill-health accompanied poverty and social deprivation, even among the unemployed. In the 1880s almost 27% of the adult male workforce in Glasgow earned no more than the basic minimum of £1 per week. Many people were frequently unemployed while some of the worst housing in Europe existed in the Glasgow area. Despite Glasgow being well on its way to becoming the shipbuilding capital of the world during the 1880s, with the Clyde producing almost a fifth of the world's shipping output by the time of the First World War, the life expectancy for men in Scotland was forty-two and for women forty-five.

In the decades after the Great Hunger had subsided, football had become a highly popular game throughout Britain, especially amongst the working classes. In Glasgow, Sligo-born Brother Walfrid, a member of the Catholic Marist order, and some of his Irish–Catholic immigrant compatriots, saw in the development of the game an opportunity to raise money and feed poor immigrant Irish Catholics in the east end of the city. Walfrid, whose real name was

Fig. 4 Sligo-born Brother Walfrid (1840–1915) who as a child witnessed firsthand the suffering caused by the Famine is generally credited as being the driving force behind the founding of Glasgow Celtic Football Club in 1887/1888. [Photo: Glasgow Celtic Football Club]

Andrew Kerrins, had been a child in Ballymote, County Sligo, during the Famine and had witnessed much suffering firsthand. In promoting his idea of founding Celtic, Walfrid, a teaching missionary to the Irish-Catholic community in Glasgow, intended also to keep Catholics within the faith (and out of the reaches of proselytism via Protestant soup kitchens), while also raising the confidence and morale of that community. Although several men were crucial to the foundation and success of Celtic Football Club it is Brother Walfrid who is generally credited as providing the main driving force in its foundation.[19]

At the time of Celtic's founding in 1887–88, the words Catholic and Irish were interchangeable in the west of Scotland. And charitable, social and political activities were equally intertwined. Celtic's donations to charity frequently included causes such as the Evicted Tenant's Fund, then an important feature of Irish nationalist politics; and like many other members of their community they were also preoccupied with the perennial question of Irish politics, Home Rule. For example, John Glass (of Donegal parentage), president and director of the club in its formative years, was an outstanding figure in nationalist circles, prominent in the Catholic Union, a founder of the O'Connell branch of the Irish National Foresters and treasurer of the Home Government branch of the United Irish League. Another member, William McKillop, became MP for North Sligo whilst celebrated Irish patriot Michael Davitt (revolutionary/Fenian and founder of the Irish Land League), was one of the club's original patrons. And the efforts and energies of all associated with Celtic often extended well beyond just Home Rule-related issues. For instance, they were directed into supporting the contentious Catholic endeavour to have their schools brought within the state-funded system in Scotland.

## AN INCLUSIVE CULTURE

So, while the origins of Celtic can certainly be placed within the context of the spread of football and football clubs as a recreational phenomenon accompanying the growth of the industrial and working class it is equally certain that, with Celtic, there were unique additional characteristics. The founding of Celtic Football Club from within the Irish Catholic immigrant community became a symbol of pride while reflecting a capacity to celebrate heritage and cul-

Fig. 5 *Michael Davitt* by William Orpen (*c*.1905), oil on canvas [Source: Dublin City Gallery The Hugh Lane. In 1892 Irish revolutionary leader and one of the original patrons of Celtic Football Club, Michael Davitt (1846–1906) laid the centre sod, 'fresh from Donegal that morning with a clump of shamrocks growing in it', at the newly-built Celtic Park in Glasgow's east end. Davitt's family was evicted from their home in Straide, County Mayo, an event which he never forgot. The family would eventually settle in Haslingden, east Lancashire: 'Straide was my birthplace and almost my first remembered experience of my own life and of the existence of landlordism was our eviction in 1852, when I was about five years old. The eviction and the privations of the preceding famine years, the story of the starving peasantry of Mayo, of the deaths from hunger – and the coffinless graves on the roadside – everywhere a hole could be dug for the slaves who died for "God's Providence" – all this was the political food seasoned with a mother's tears over unmerited sorrows and sufferings which had fed my mind in another land, a teaching which lost none of its force or directness by being imparted in the Gaelic tongue, which was almost always spoken in our Lancashire home'. [Source: Michael Davitt, *The Fall from Feudalism* (1904)]

ture, despite often-abject misery and poverty and religious and social marginalisation.

But much more than this, this new Scottish football club, though steeped in its Irish heritage, chose through its very name – Celtic – to build a linking bridge between the Irish and the Scottish, between past and present, and signalled from the beginning in its aspiration and approach a rejection of the very discriminatory conditions which surrounded it. Crucially then, though Celtic was founded by and primarily for Irish Catholics, it was never exclusively so. The club's subsequent history of employing as players and staff, and being supported by people, of all religions and none, has reflected this ethos.

And so, although of Irish heritage, Celtic's involvement in football allowed its supporting Catholic immigrant community to integrate with and share in a popular cultural activity of many people in Scotland. Football and Celtic provided avenues for interaction and co-operation with the host community, despite ethnic cleavage in the wider society. Celtic's hybrid nature as a central aspect of the Irish diaspora in Scotland positioned it as a Scottish institution of Irish heritage. It was in that way that it became known locally, internationally and then globally. By the 1960s and 1970s Celtic had become one of the greatest teams in world football, winning the European Champions Cup in 1967.

It was members of the Irish community in Glasgow who had lived through the Famine and its consequences in both Ireland and Scotland who founded Celtic Football Club. The club was initially supported by members of the same community while many of its first players were the direct offspring of people who had survived the Great Hunger. In this new millennium, and as the jewel in the sporting crown of the Irish diaspora, most of the club's support is made up from descendants of Famine and subsequent generations of Irish immigrants to Scotland. Unlike any other such sporting institution, Irishness is celebrated and can be witnessed at Celtic matches and social gatherings through the songs, colours and flags of its army of supporters. Since the early 1990s one of the club's most significant anthems has been the Irish ballad, 'The Fields of Athenry', which tells about one small though important Famine story of love, rebellion and emigration.

So it was fitting that in 2009 Celtic Football Club joined in with others in Ireland and amongst the Irish diaspora worldwide to remember Ireland's Great Hunger by wearing a match jersey embroidered with a commemorative Celtic Cross and the words 'National Famine Memorial Day' included.[20]

'Man's inhumanity to man', wrote Burns, 'makes countless thousands mourn.' The Great Irish Hunger of the mid-nineteenth century destroyed and rendered desolate the lives of millions. The legacy of the Famine lives on in

Fig. 6 Celtic's 1967 European Cup winning team. From its humble beginnings Celtic would eventually make its mark in European and World football with a team managed by Jock Stein and then very much locally based. [Photo: Glasgow Celtic Football Club]

the economic, social, cultural and political lives of subsequent generations of people who remain on the island of Ireland as well as amongst the multi-generational diaspora abroad. Amongst the many relevant narratives of the Irish Famine experience in Ireland and particularly the diaspora, those pertaining to Scotland have often been marginalised or omitted in relevant commentary. This short history of some aspects of that experience reveals that accounts of how the Great Irish Famine subsequently affected life in Scotland reflect comparable as well as rich and distinctive features amongst the narratives that comprise the broader Famine story.

In the coming year, as in previous years, all associated with Celtic Football Club will commemorate the Irish Famine and those whose lives were lost or blighted as a result. Without the Great Hunger, it is unlikely that there would ever have been a Celtic Football Club. Perhaps those of us at Celtic could claim, though in a much more modest way, that without Celtic Football Club there would be one less living, breathing, celebrated reminder of the awful consequences of that terrible and historic tragedy, the Irish Famine.

Fig. 7 The crest embroidered on the jerseys of Celtic players when they played Hibernian in the Scottish Premier League (SPL) on 17 May 2009 to mark National Famine Memorial day. The Cross embodies the connection between Scottish and Irish cultures and is a symbol of the club's charitable arm, established to continue the work initiated by Celtic's founder Brother Walfrid. [Source: Glasgow Celtic Football Club]

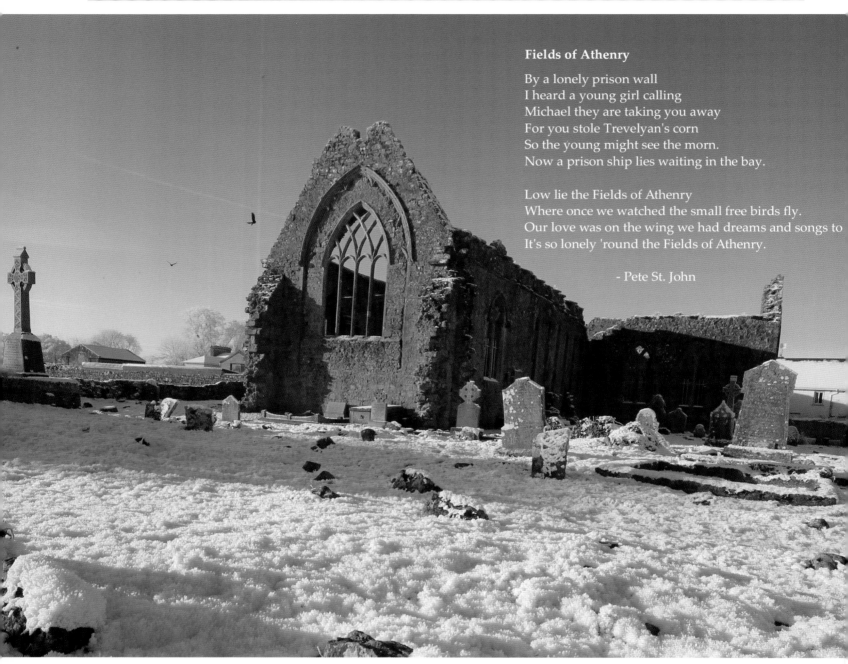

**Fields of Athenry**

By a lonely prison wall
I heard a young girl calling
Michael they are taking you away
For you stole Trevelyan's corn
So the young might see the morn.
Now a prison ship lies waiting in the bay.

Low lie the Fields of Athenry
Where once we watched the small free birds fly.
Our love was on the wing we had dreams and songs to
It's so lonely 'round the Fields of Athenry.

- Pete St. John

Fig. 8 The *Fields of Athenry* was composed by Pete St John in the mid-1970s. The most popular and successful version of the song was recorded by Paddy Reilly in 1983. It is a song of love, rebellion and exile framed by the tragic events of the Famine years. It has been adopted as a sporting anthem both in Ireland and its wider diaspora. It was initially sung by Irish supporters at the World Cup finals in 1990 in Italy. It was then adopted by Glasgow Celtic's supporters and has become intimately connected with the club. The song is also strongly identified with the more recent success of the Munster rugby team. [Photo of Athenry Priory by Frank Coyne with verse from the *Fields of Athenry*]

520

# Archaeological evidence of Irish migration? Rickets in the Irish community of London's East End, 1843–54

*Don Walker, Michael Henderson and Natasha Powers*

Excavations by Museum of London Archaeology (MOLA) between September 2005 and January 2006 recovered 705 individuals (268 adults (>17 years of age) and 437 children) from the cemetery of the Catholic mission of St Mary and St Michael, Lukin Street, Tower Hamlets, London E1 (NGR 535260 181145). The parish church burial ground was purchased in 1842, consecrated on 24 July 1843 and closed, with no space remaining, after only eleven years of use, on 1 May 1854. Burials in wooden coffins were found placed on top of each other in shared plots, with infant burials placed at the top of the stacks, older children below them and adults towards the base.

The mission was located in an area of Irish Catholic occupation, conveniently situated between the city and the

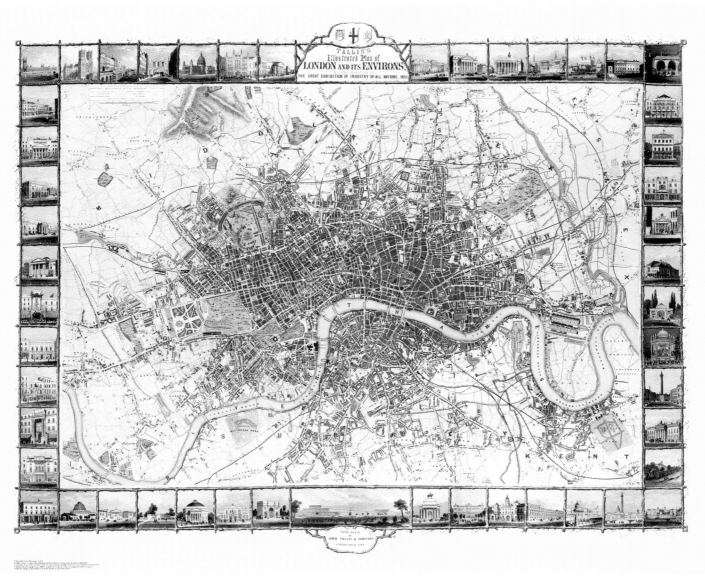

Fig. 1 Tallis map of London *c.*1850s.

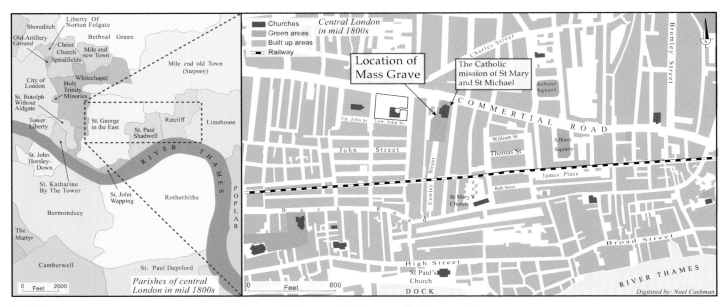

Fig. 2 SITE LOCATION PLAN OF THE CEMETERY OF THE CATHOLIC MISSION OF ST MARY AND ST MICHAEL, WHITECHAPEL.

docks. Epigraphic data from coffin plates suggested that many of the excavated individuals were of Irish extraction and analysis has afforded a unique opportunity to investigate whether the health of the buried population reflects that reported in contemporary written sources carrying signatures of the Famine. Analysis had demonstrated clear differences between those buried at St Mary and St Michael and their contemporaries buried elsewhere in London. These differences are seen in the demographic composition of the group, in cultural behaviour (specifically pipe-smoking) and in their health.[1]

Urban living conditions had deteriorated to a great degree even before the main influx of migrants from Ireland during the Great Famine of 1847–48. Although the Irish community was already well established in London at this time, it expanded further and by the 1851 Census, 4.6% of the population of London was recorded as Irish-born.[2] Contemporary writers, including Henry Mayhew, John Garwood and Edwin Chadwick, described the living conditions of the immigrant populations of London in the mid-nineteenth century. However, while these sources provide remarkably detailed accounts of the lives of London's poor, they must be interpreted in the light of contemporary prejudices and preconceptions: to many of these writers, the Irish were not just immigrants, but potentially dangerous 'Papists'. *The Times* newspaper also provides a valuable insight into the attitudes of the period, with numerous references to the disease and squalor of the poorer areas of London. One article in 1847 claimed that areas such as Whitechapel and Spitalfields 'contain the greatest amount of poverty, and therefore the greatest amount of disease, in London'. During the cholera epidemic of 1848–49, when 62,000 deaths were recorded in London, the medical officer of the Whitechapel Union wrote to *The Times* describing the overcrowding, unhygienic conditions and lack of sanitary

facilities in some of the Irish areas. Does the osteological evidence support the contemporary accounts and were those buried at St Mary and St Michael, the impoverished and malnourished victims of the Famine?

## OSTEOLOGICAL EVIDENCE OF DECLINING HEALTH

While the adult mortality profile was similar to other low-status sites in the capital, with a relatively high proportions dying aged 26–35 years, 62% of the burials from St Mary and St Michael were those of subadults, a large proportion of whom died between birth and three years of age. As there is no reason to believe that the Irish community in Whitechapel enjoyed higher than average levels of fertility, it appears that infant mortality was in excess of that in neighbouring communities, suggesting a population under increased stress.

Dental enamel hypoplasia is associated with nutritional deficiency, fever, infectious disease or low birth weight. Perhaps surprisingly, a relatively low proportion of adult teeth were affected (16.5%) when compared to high-status burials from St Marylebone, Westminster (20.1%).[3] This may indicate that the adult population had lived a relatively stress-free childhood. In marked contrast, osteological indicators of stress in the subadult population were seen almost twice as frequently than in the population from St Marylebone. Further comparison of subadult bone measurements, dental development and epigraphic evidence of age showed a 'lag' in growth of up to four years and also suggests that those who died young suffered chronic stress.

Vitamin D deficiency in infancy and childhood can lead to inadequate levels of bone mineralisation; the weight-bearing and loaded bones may bend and areas of the skeleton become porous. Once rickets develops, it can lead to muscle weakness, spasms and apnoea (a temporary inability to breathe). In historic populations, the under-exposure

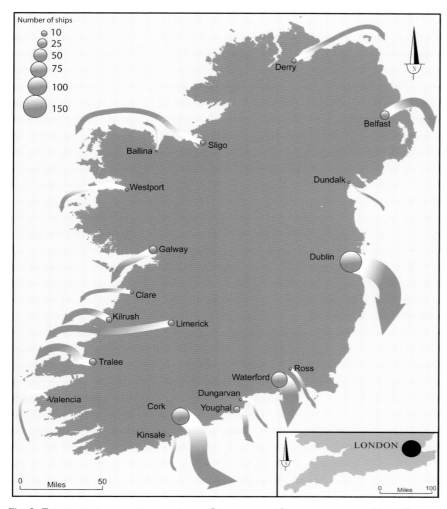

Fig. 3 THE NUMBER OF VESSELS ARRIVING AT LONDON FROM IRISH PORTS DURING 1847. The map reveals the greater diversity of ports involved in emigrant traffic to London, albeit of lesser volume than that to Liverpool and Glasgow. [Adapted from Frank Neal, *Black '47: Famine in Britain* (Basingstoke, 1998), p. 57]

revealed a strong correlation between infantile rickets and maternal malnutrition during pregnancy and lactation. A weaning diet low in vitamin D rich foods would have exacerbated the problem, leading to diarrhoeal disorders that reduced the body's ability to absorb nutrients even further, resulting in spiralling ill health.[5] Children with symptoms may have been kept indoors for longer periods of time and fitted with extra clothing and blankets, thus reducing their potential vitamin D intake even further. Although rickets is only active in childhood, residual effects in the form of bowed limbs may be observed in adults; but despite the high levels of the disease in chil-

of the skin to ultraviolet rays from the sun was the chief cause of rickets,[4] as sunlight is vitally important for the synthesis of vitamin D and vulnerable infants need at least two hours of exposure to per week. Diets containing inadequate levels of vitamin D rich foods, such as eggs and oily fish, also contribute to deficiency. The crowded tenements of Whitechapel, domestic and industrial air pollution and unhygienic streets which may have encouraged residents to remain indoors, would all have reduced the opportunity for exposure to sunlight. Documented examples from nineteenth-century autopsies carried out in other European cities show infant rates of rickets running at 90% or higher and demonstrate the severity of the problem.

Seventy-eight children from St Mary and St Michael had been suffering from rickets: 11.1% of the population or 17.8% of the children. The high levels of rickets may result from a combination of poor nutrition, crowded living conditions and ill health. Maternal vitamin D deficiency can contribute to the development of rickets in infants, and even when stores are passed on to the foetus they can be used up within a month of birth, after which exposure to sunlight or diet supplementation is essential. Modern studies have

5cm

Fig. 4 The left tibia of an infant buried at St Mary and St Michael who was suffering from rickets when he/she died. Substantial bowing of the bone shaft can be clearly seen.

523

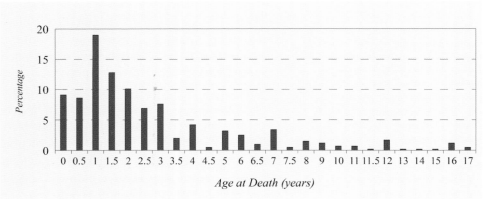

Fig. 5   Age at death in years for children from St Mary and St Michael. In those children for whom specific ages were assigned; 19% (77/406) died around one year of age, representing a peak in child mortality.

they tended to settle in overcrowded and poorly sanitised 'slums' in places such as Whitechapel. The archaeological evidence does not suggest a uniformly poor or malnourished group. For example, dental treatment was extremely expensive, yet one woman had been buried with a gold dental prosthesis. Not only could she afford to purchase such an expensive item, but those burying her were not in such desperate straits as to reclaim the precious metal, though perhaps cultural

dren, there was no evidence of resolved rickets in the adults of St Mary and St Michael.

Rickets provides some clue as to the reasons behind the shortened life span of many subadults, and its frequency is high when compared to overall rates for post-medieval Britain (3.7%).[6] However, a greater proportion of children (21/78: 26.9%) from St Marylebone had rickets – a finding which appears at odds with their relative status. One possible explanation may be found in the writings of Mrs Beeton, who encouraged her readers to let their children play in the open air, like those of poorer families to improve their health.

### EVIDENCE OF DIET

The skeletal sample also provides direct indications of dietary status: the rate of dental caries was high (20.2%), which suggests that the Irish population of Whitechapel had access to, and resources to buy, sugar and sweet goods. A low prevalence of diffuse idiopathic skeletal hyperostosis (DISH), a condition affecting predominantly the spine, suggests that the day-to-day diet was not rich and evidence of vitamin C deficiency in the subadult population was plentiful (9.4%, compared to St Marylebone's 5.1%), though as little as two months of deficiency can cause scurvy to develop.

The staple diet of Irish country people, that of potatoes, buttermilk, occasional meat and vegetables, was actually reasonably healthy when compared to that of poor Londoners. However, during the period of the Famine, migrants from Ireland may not have been adequately nourished and though they may have previously lived in open, rural areas,

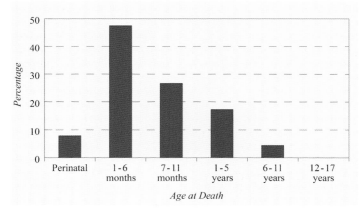

Fig. 6   Percentage distribution of age of children with skeletal evidence of rickets from St Mary and St Michael, showing a clear peak amongst infants who died between one and six months of age.

mores precluded them from doing so. However, overall the osteological data suggests a population under stress.

Although local environment and cultural behaviour form part of a complex aetiology for rickets during the industrial growth of the nineteenth century, the nutritional status of the mother was undoubtedly an important factor in levels of rickets in infants from poor communities. The prevalence of rickets certainly suggests that only those born in London were likely to suffer severe vitamin D deficiency, while older individuals, many of whom would have been raised in pre-Famine Ireland, were not affected. This and other contrasts between the adult and subadult populations may reflect the health divide between those who were fully grown before the Famine struck and those born during it.

# Black '47 and Toronto, Canada

## *Mark G. McGowan*

In the spring of 1847, amidst the calamity caused by two consecutive years of the failure of Ireland's potato crop, the *Limerick Reporter* observed that there were few options left for the starving masses of that country. In reflecting upon the future of the Irish, the editor mused, 'In the present day there is a refinement on the edict of the Protector [Cromwell's "to hell or Connaught"], and the word is "Death or Canada".'[1] He continued to observe that 'The grand inducement held out is that death awaits the people in their own country, and they ought, therefore, to leave as quickly as possible, without knowing whether as speedy a death does not await them in the wilds of Canada.' What was clear to the Irish during the years of the Famine, yet it appears less clear to survivors and future generations, was the important role Canada would play in what would become one of the largest diasporic moments in Irish history.

In the memorialisation and commemorations of our own time, the inherited and collective historical memory of the Famine readily conjures up images of the coffin ships leaving Ireland and Britain for Australia, and 'America', but rarely is Canada acknowledged as a principal recipient of Irish refugees. In fact, during the sailings of Black '47, the British North American ports of Quebec, Saint John (New Brunswick), Halifax and St John's (Newfoundland) scrambled to receive a reported 110,000 Irish fleeing from Irish and British ports.[2] Fewer observers of the Famine might recognise that the deadly *Phytophthora infestans* fungus that attacked Irish potato crops may have originated in the St Lawrence Valley and eastern North America, where local populations witnessed their own potato crop failures from 1842 to 1845 and at least one reported 'famine' in Cape Breton, Nova Scotia, in 1845.[3] During the early years of the Famine, the Canada–Ireland connections were strong, and, as predicted by the *Limerick Reporter*, passage from Ireland and Britain to the Canadian ports of Quebec, Montreal, Kingston and Toronto, did not guarantee Irish migrants security of life or limb.

### TAKING REFUGE

In 1846, in the wake of the first crop failure in twenty-three

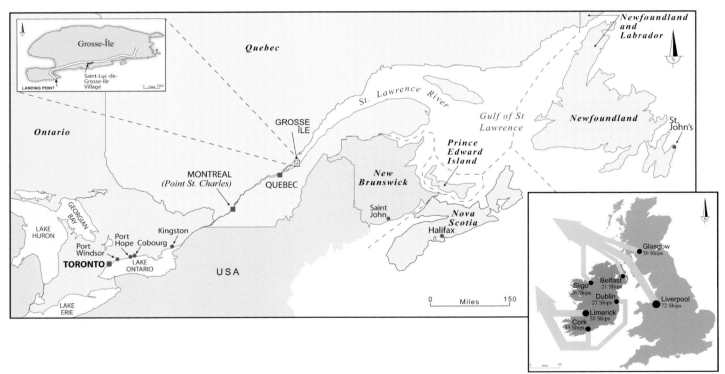

Fig. 1 FAMINE EMIGRANT DISEMBARKATION SITES IN CANADA. During Black '47, 441 ships landed at Quebec carrying over 80,000 passengers. The principal ports from which the ships sailed were Liverpool (72), Glasgow (30), Limerick (50), Cork (33), Dublin (27), Sligo (26) and Belfast (21). Important ports where the Irish disembarked included Saint John (New Brunswick), Halifax and St John's (Newfoundland). Those migrants who passed the quarantine station at Grosse Île (48 km north of Quebec) were taken to Quebec. Those who were passed fit at Quebec but who later succumbed to illness were quarantined at fever sheds at Point St Charles along the shores of the St Lawrence River – many of whom subsequently perished. A similar story was repeated in Kingston. Montreal was in many respects a dispersal point with migrants heading south to New York, north to Bytown (now Ottawa) or further west to Upper Canada and the major commercial centre of Toronto. Rather than land at Toronto a small number of Irish emigrants disembarked at small lake ports such as Cobourg, Port Hope and Whitby (Port Windsor).

of Ireland's counties, emigration to Canada constituted nearly 32,750 persons.[4] After a brief stay at the quarantine station at Grosse Île (see pp. 532–35), some 48 km northeast of Quebec City, Irish passengers were transported to Quebec, and then hundreds of kilometres west to Montreal and Toronto, which frequently became points of departure for the agricultural hinterlands of Canada or the United States. Many Irish migrants had relatives or friends already settled in Canada who often wrote open letters, to be published in Irish newspapers, boasting of the availability of cheap freehold farmland, good wages in the Canadian labour market, and the abundance of 'plums, apples, and pears in endless variety and almost unlimited quantity'.[5]

Looking forward to 1847, Canadian officials took note and planned upgrades of the facilities at Grosse Île and the emigration sheds in the inland ports, in knowledge of the fact that the potato crop had failed again in the autumn of 1846 and more migrants were expected with the spring sailing season. They had reason to be anxious. By the end of the sailing season, in Black '47, 441 ships landed at Quebec carrying over 80,000 passengers;[6] the largest number of these ships had come from Liverpool (72) and Glasgow (30), where Irish refugees had sojourned and waited for transatlantic passage. Limerick and Cork dominated the direct Irish routes to Quebec, sending fifty and thirty-three ships respectively. Over twenty ships came from each of Dublin (27), Sligo (26), and Belfast (21).[7] Such a variety of ports of departure meant that the Irish who ventured to Canada came from nearly every county and both English and Irish speakers could be counted among their numbers. Contrary to popular belief, however, only 6,000, of these passengers, or roughly 7.5%, had been subsidized by their landlords;[8] the vast majority had paid for passage from what meagre funds they possessed, from the charity of friends or from remittances from those already settled in Canada.[9]

## HUMAN BALLAST

Horrendous conditions were found aboard the ships, whose holds had been refitted from their usual cargo of timber, grain and other chattels. The Irish were simply human ballast for ships returning to Canada or intending to pick up cargo at Quebec. In addition, most passengers were subject to poor food and abysmal sanitary conditions in steerage, crowding below decks, and six to eight weeks rough passage atop the powerful swells of the north Atlantic. While waiting in port and in their cubicles below decks, passengers were bitten by lice carrying the bacteria *Rickettsia prowazekii*, which caused outbreaks of typhus, a disease that tormented the carrier with headaches, rashes, intense thirst, an enlarged liver and skin eruptions. Without knowledge of antibiotics and no effective cure, one-half to three-quarters of those afflicted by 'ship's fever' died at sea, or later, in quarantine or in hospital.[10] The *Syria* arrived at Grosse Île, on 20 May 1847, having made a gruelling forty-six day passage across the Atlantic with its 241 passengers. Nine died before they reached Quebec; forty died at Grosse Île; and the haggard remnant of the human cargo was pushed on to Quebec and Montreal.[11] They became the harbingers of a grotesque story of sickness, death and negligence on the high seas. Scenes described to the Select Committee of the British Parliament by Stephen De Vere, a Limerick landlord who travelled to Canada with his tenants, neatly summed up what one author called 'the ocean plague':

> Hundreds of poor people. Men, women, and children of all ages, from the driveling idiot to the babe just born, huddled together without light, without air, wallowing in filth and breathing in a fetid atmosphere, sick in body, dispirited in heart, the fevered patients lying between the sound, in sleeping places so narrow as almost to deny them the power of indulging by a change of position, the natural restlessness of the disease.[12]

By the end of the sailing season of 1847, nearly one in every five migrants who set out from Irish and British ports to Canada had died either at sea or in the new land that had held out the promise of a better life.

Those who passed the quarantine or survived at Grosse Île were taken upriver to Quebec, and then to Montreal, which became the principal dispersal point for migrants headed south to New York, north to Bytown (now Ottawa) or farther west to Upper Canada (also called Canada West) and its major commercial centre, Toronto. Over 3,000 Irish migrants,[13] however, never made the journey beyond Montreal. Many carried typhus undetected, because the infection has a ten-day incubation period before the display of symptoms. Thus, some who were passed at Grosse Île and Quebec as fit, became ill and quarantined in fever sheds at Point St Charles, along the shore of the St Lawrence River in Montreal. Typhus claimed both migrants and people in Montreal who offered charity and medical aid: physicians, nurses, priests, Sisters of Charity (Grey Nuns), and other citizens. The same story was repeated at Kingston, Canada West, where the St Lawrence River is fed by Lake Ontario, a giant inland sea. At this former Canadian capital, some thirty hours by lake boat and steamer from Montreal, perhaps as many as 1,200 more Irish migrants died.[14] From this eastern terminus of Lake Ontario, the healthy, the infected but undetected, the weary and the hopeful continued their trek west, subsidised by the Canadian government on uncovered boats exposed to the merciless sun, biting and bloodsucking insects and rain. If they were fortunate, and conditions optimal, they could count on making the 850 km journey from Quebec to Toronto in twelve days.[15]

## ARRIVAL IN TORONTO

Although some elected to disembark at small lake ports such

Fig. 2 Toronto Courthouse and Gaol c.1829. By the 1840s Toronto had established itself as an important commercial and transportation hub. [Courtesy: Library and Archives Canada]

as Cobourg, Port Hope and Whitby (Port Windsor), some 38,500 elected to land at Toronto, the former provincial capital, and the largest town in the province. Despite its growing prominence as a commercial and transportation hub, Toronto had a population of 20,000 people who lived in wood frame, stone, and brick buildings along mainly dirt (often muddy) thoroughfares; in 1847, only two streets Yonge (running north–south) and King (running east–west) were macadamized with a gravel surface. The town rested on the northern shore of a beautiful natural harbour, which was protected by a crescent-shaped peninsula that joined the mainland in the east and allowed for an opening in the west. The harbour opening was protected by Fort York on the mainland and by a battery and lighthouse on the western tip of the peninsula, known locally as Gibraltar because it had reminded town founders of the British landmark in the Mediterranean.

In Black '47, Toronto's citizens would have little control over the direction of policy regarding the processing, treatment and transportation of migrants. These decisions were made in Montreal, the temporary capital of Canada, and specifically by the Provincial Secretary, the Honourable Dominick Daly, who was in charge of the immigration portfolio. Reporting directly to Daly were Alexander C. Buchanan, the Chief Emigration Agent, who was headquartered in Quebec City, and his lieutenant, Anthony B. Hawke, who was responsible for the western section of Canada, formerly known as Upper Canada. Hawke was stationed at Kingston and therefore selected agents to represent him in each major entrepot outside of Kingston. In Toronto, on the advice of Bishop Michael Power, Hawke had selected a local Catholic, Edward McElderry, who was tasked with repairing the emigrant sheds and preparing for a 'large emigration' that year.[16]

Although Buchanan had warned leaders in the west of Canada that the year's influx of immigrants from Ireland would be larger than the previous years, preparations in Toronto were competent but slow. Toronto's mayor, William Henry Boulton, was a well-connected conservative, whose Council was almost equally divided between his own sup-

porters and a 'reform' faction. Each improvement of existing facilities and recommendation for additional assistance to the immigrants would have to be navigated carefully though municipal governance. In February 1847, Boulton's Council established a Board of Health, headed by Boulton's political ally and former mayor, George Gurnett. Council appointed Constable Jonathan B. Townsend board clerk, and together with Gurnett, he would be responsible for creating much of the infrastructure to assist the newcomers to Toronto, including healthcare, the rationing of food, public safety, and transportation.

RECEIVING EMIGRANTS

Toronto's citizens envisioned the following orderly plan for receiving emigrants: ships would be landed at only one quay, Dr. Rees' wharf, where they would be met by McElderry and triaged. The sick would be sent to the wharf's shed and to the hospital facilities and the healthy would be hurriedly sent out of Toronto by boat and wagon. It was Hawke's intention that the indigent be scattered 'far and wide',[17] in the hopes of avoiding a massing of potentially sick and impoverished Irish immigrants in Toronto, a town noted for its Protestant ascendancy, with little relish for an increase in the Roman Catholic population. Hawke had given the Royal Mail Steamship Company a monopoly in transporting the immigrants from Kingston and Toronto, and his department would also subsidise further movement of the migrants out of Toronto to the rural hinterlands and perhaps, eventually, the American frontier. In the early spring, the procedures all seemed to be working according to plan. Several hundred Irish entered Toronto, via Rochester, New York, on the other side of the lake, and were ushered into the rear townships and counties of Canada.[18]

By the end of May, however, amidst reports from Quebec of rampant sickness and disease among the thousands of Irish arriving in the St Lawrence daily, Toronto's Board of Health scrambled to accelerate their preparations. Hawke instructed McElderry to improve the sheds at Rees' Wharf, while the Board of Health planned to build a hospital on the peninsula, out of fear of 'the probability of contagious [sic] fever and other diseases injurious to the general health of the

Fig. 3 View of Toronto c.1850. [Courtesy: Library and Archives Canada]

City'.[19] Negotiations between the city and the doctors at the Toronto General Hospital had not rendered the result Gurnett had wanted; emigrants would not be welcome there. By 7 June, the Government ordered all municipalities to provide sheds and a hospital, to appoint an attending physician, to draw up sanitary regulations and to make contracts for the provision of bread and meat for migrants, according to specific daily allotments to be managed by the local emigrant agent. The Government's new regulations, and the promise of state funds to Toronto, came none too soon. Local authorities reckoned that 2,592 migrants had already landed in the city and thousands more were nearby.[20]

The scene at Rees' Wharf became increasingly chaotic as some days witnessed the arrival of hundreds of migrants. In the seventeen days following 7 June, an additional 4,608 Irish refugees arrived at Toronto, an average of 300 migrants per day. By August, McElderry and his officers at Rees' Wharf processed over 450 persons per day.[21] An eyewitness from the steamer *Princess Royal* described the swarm of migrants at dockside: 'We got rid of most of our living cargo, whom they treated just like cattle driving them out, and tried to do the same to us, but we rebelled. They were all turned out and kept back with sticks til their luggage would be tumbled out after them.'[22] In addition to the sheer volume of immigrants, McElderry and others were overwhelmed by the poverty and sickness they witnessed among those who disembarked. Their condition was not at all helped by the conditions found on board the steamers and lake boats that had brought them from Kingston. One observer reported: 'The poor creatures . . . were crowded together like herrings in a barrel, and many had difficulty gasping for a breath of fresh air. Our informant . . . remarked that the condition of the unfortunate cargo reminded him of accounts of Negroes on slave ships.'[23] The passage was made worse if passengers had been exposed to the elements for the entire five days required to travel on the lake from Kingston to Toronto. In the summer, Hawke made arrangements with the Royal Mail Line that more steamships be deployed, thereby eliminating many of the barges and lessening the trip by three days.[24]

EMERGENCY ACTION

The volume of migrants and their condition necessitated emergency action by Toronto authorities. On 14 June, Gurnett chaired his first full meeting of the Board of Health and made immediate attempts to secure a hospital site. The great fear was the spread of typhus, and the certain knowledge that at least 40,000 more refugees had already set sail from the United Kingdom and were headed for Canada and a potentially disastrous situation at Grosse Île and at every landing place from Quebec to Lake Ontario. According to the local Tory newspaper, the *British Colonist*, the people of Toronto were now in the grips of panic: 'We are not alarmists in this matter, but these figures show a fearful

Fig. 4 Irish Catholics who were victims of the Famine were buried in unmarked graves in the churchyard adjoining St Paul's Parish, which was the cathedral parish for the Diocese of Toronto. [Source: Courtesy Library and Archives Canada]

state of things . . . This is a most important matter for pestilence once let loose spares neither rich nor poor'.[25] Within days, Gurnett and his Board secured the use of the General Hospital at King and John Streets, several blocks north of Rees' Wharf, for the emigrants, in exchange for giving the local doctors use of the Temple Chambers, farther to the east on King Street, for the use of general medical cases.[26] Originally built in 1819, the General Hospital building had initially been the home of the Upper Canadian legislature and had only reverted to its hospital status in 1829.[27] Conveniently located on a large grounds to the west of the city, the isolation of the sick emigrants at King and John Streets gave some comfort that the principal residential areas of Toronto might be spared any contagion. Due to the hundreds of sick and typhus-bearing migrants sent by McElderry up to the hospital each day, the board ordered the building of sheds on the grounds of the hospital. By the end of August 1847, thousands of migrants, the ill and their families, were occupying at least sixteen sheds, some open sided, some closed and windowed, ranging in size from 50 feet by 10 feet, to 75 feet by 20 feet.[28] The Board of Health also tried to relieve pressure on the hospital by establishing a temporary convalescent hospital, at Front and Bathurst Streets, for those patients who appeared to be recovering from typhus and other ailments. Shortly after opening in August, this second hospital was caring for 300 patients each day. Nearby, at Bathurst and King Streets, the city also created a 'House of Refuge for Widows and Orphans'.

By the end of the year Constable Townshend reported that 38,560 migrants had passed through the port of Toronto and that over 75% of these were Irish. He indicated that McElderry and his team moved 35,630 emigrants through the port very quickly, although 4,355 migrants had to be triaged through one of the three local health facilities. By his own accounts, Townshend reported that 1,124 people had died, of whom 863 died at the General (also known as the Emigrant) Hospital itself.[29] The Roman Catholic dead, perhaps as many as 75% of the dead, were buried in unmarked graves in the churchyard adjoining St Paul's parish, which was the cathedral for the Diocese of Toronto. The remaining dead, mostly Protestants and those without any declared religious affiliation, were buried at St James Anglican cemetery, northeast of the city, or in a potter's field directly north of Toronto. The financial cost was also staggering. In 1848, the Imperial Government reimbursed the Canadian Government £150,000 for the care of the emigrants during the previous shipping season, but it was stipulated that there would be no more such grants. The costs in Canada West, which included Toronto, were estimated at £35,635, a very large sum when one considered that, in 1846, Hawke's agency had spent only £2,000.[30]

## BISHOP MICHAEL POWER (1804–47)

The events of 'Black '47' in Toronto brought out the best and the worst of the local community. One of the city's leading figures, Catholic Bishop Michael Power, was born of Irish parents in Halifax, Nova Scotia, in 1804. He had studied for the priesthood in Quebec and Montreal and had served as a missionary priest on the Canadian frontier until his appointment as the first Bishop of Toronto, in 1841. In May 1847, Power had witnessed the Famine in Ireland firsthand, while on a trip recruiting the Loretto Sisters of Rathfarnham to teach in his diocese.[31] He issued pastoral letters begging alms for the relief of Ireland and its victims and making impassioned pleas in Toronto for charitable relief of the Irish without prejudice. In September, he rose in a public meeting, chaired by Mayor Boulton, and delivered a reasoned plea for a mature response to the crisis. 'The disease seemed to be of an insidious character,' he commented, 'as to baffle all the skill that might be employed in treating its cure and it did not seem to be affected by the change of season.'[32] He urged those present to resist from blaming the Irish for typhus and assist them with all compassion. Power lived by his words. With all of his priests bedridden with the disease, he alone made a daily trek to and from his rectory to the sheds, the hospital and the cemetery at St Paul's. In late Sep-

tember, he began to show symptoms of the disease and became bedridden himself. On 1 October, less than ten days shy of his forty-third birthday, Michael Power died. Thereafter, he was known by contemporaries in Toronto as a martyr of 'charity'.[33]

Other tales of sacrifice and courage were witnessed that summer. In July, George Grasett, a young physician and brother to the Anglican archdeacon of Toronto, assumed the post of chief physician at the Emigrant Hospital. Within a month he was stricken with typhus and died. A similar fate awaited his head nurse, Susan Bailey, who died while serving the Irish in the sheds. Edward

Fig. 5 Michael Power (1804–47), Bishop of Toronto. Born in Halifax, Nova Scotia in 1804 the first of eight children, he would play a pivotal role in the relief of suffering amongst the Irish who arrived in Toronto in 1847. Educated for the priesthood in Quebec and Montreal, and fluent in several languages, he was destined for higher office in the Catholic Church. In 1841 he was appointed Bishop of Toronto. Returning to Canada from Rome in 1847 he visited Ireland with the objective of inviting Loretto Sisters to come to his diocese to open schools. During his stay he witnessed firsthand the condition of the starving. He quickly informed his own flock in Toronto of the desperate plight of the Irish. Between June and November 1847 almost 39,000 migrants fled to the city, many of them infected with typhus. Power worked tirelessly to help the sick, provide comfort to their families and to bury the dead. Over 1,000 people perished, with Power also succumbing to fever on 1 October 1847. He was buried in the crypt of the then unfinished St Michael's Cathedral. [Source: St Michael's Cathedral, Toronto]

McElderry, the father of seven children, worked tirelessly throughout the summer and autumn at Rees' Wharf. On 29 October, exhausted and weakened by his work, McElderry died of fever. Despite pleas from local officials (and even from Stephen De Vere, who admired McElderry's work greatly), the Governor General Elgin denied McElderry's widow, who was pregnant with their eighth child, any pension for his service.[34] Such sacrifice stands in sharp contrast to the initiatives of Councillor John Ritchey, political ally of Boulton and Gurnett, who managed to secure the contracts for all of the fever sheds for £250 each.[35] One might also question how Constable Townshend's figures of the number of patients in the hospital and the sheds, in August, appeared to be overstated by 300 persons, causing some in Toronto to wonder if hospital workers might be pocketing the funds allotted for these 'invisible invalids'.[36] Finally, there was the case of Catholic undertaker Thomas Ryan, who was paid to transport the Catholic dead to St. Paul's, bury each in a single coffin at the depth of three feet of earth between the coffin lid and level ground. On 14 August 1847, one of his hearses hit a rut on King Street, broke a wheel, and witnesses watched four coffins tumble off the cart and smash open on the street. Onlookers were horrified to see 'nearly, if not quite naked corpses' tumble out of their caskets in front of them and worse when it was discovered that there were two bodies in one casket. Local pundits suggested that

someone somewhere was profiting from this human misery. Ryan was never charged, but the rumours of malfeasance in the operations of the hospital did not die.[37]

### THE WILLIS FAMILY

Of the emigrants themselves little is known, although fragments of stories have emerged that have restored names and identity to some of the Famine migrants while painting portraits of sorrow. A farmer named Willis, his wife and five children were likely Protestants from either Tipperary or Offaly. They boarded the *Jessie* at Limerick, 18 April 1847, and prepared to set sail for Quebec as part of a human cargo of 482 people. Tragedy struck immediately as the youngest Willis took ill in port and had to be left on the Limerick pier. During their fifty-six-day voyage across the Atlantic, twenty-six passengers died and were committed to the deep, including the Willis' eighteen-year-old son and a daughter, ten-year-old Martha. When they arrived at Grosse Île, seventeen-year-old Mary Ann Willis was removed from the ship and died at the quarantine station. Mother, father, and remaining son made it as far as Toronto. By July, only Mrs Willis survived, and was in the care of Brantford's Anglican minister, James Campbell Usher.[38] The Willis tragedy could be seen as a microcosm of the pain and suffering experienced by thousands of their countrymen, Catholic and Protestant, as they sought a new life in Canada. After 1847, increased government regula-

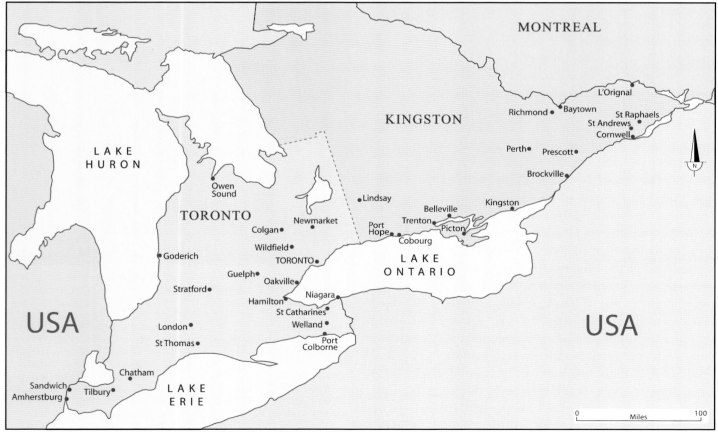

Fig. 6 LOCATION AND EXTENT OF TORONTO DIOCESE. In 1841 Michael Power was appointed the first Catholic Bishop of Toronto, a diocese that was four times the size of Ireland.

Fig. 7 Famine memorial in Toronto harbour which was unveiled on 21 June 2007. The names of 660 of the 1,124 victims have been carved into the crevasses of a massive Kilkenny limestone wall that separates the park from the rest of the harbour front. [Photo: Gail Edwin-Fielding]

tion of migration in Canada, and the greater attractiveness of the United States in the minds of immigrants themselves, limited the number of Irish Famine migrants who sought refuge in Canadian ports and cities. In 1848, only 31,065 passengers landed in British North America, less than one-third of the numbers in Black '47. In 1849, the number increased to 41,367, but this marked the beginning of a decline of Irish migrants to Canada and Britain's neighbouring Atlantic colonies.[39]

The migration of Black '47 had in fact been the height of the last mass migration of the Irish to Canada, but because of the tragic circumstances experienced by the Irish and their hosts across the colonies, the Famine migration remained a lens through which much of the Irish experience in Canada came to be viewed.[40] During the memorialisation and commemorations marking the 150th anniversary of the beginning of the Famine tragedy, Canadians too began to reflect and build monuments to remember the Famine migration. In 1995, President Mary Robinson visited Grosse Île, where the Ancient Order of

Hibernians had erected a giant Celtic cross to tower over the graves of more than 5,400 Irish buried at the quarantine station in 1847. In Montreal, the local Irish make visitations to the 'Black Stone', which was erected by construction workers at Point St Charles in 1859, when they discovered the remains of some of the 3,000 Famine victims who died in the sheds there in 1847. Celtic crosses mark the Famine in other Canadian centres. Most recently in Toronto, a local committee has built Ireland Park (on the shores of Lake Ontario on Éireann Quay at the foot of Bathurst Street), to commemorate the Famine migration. The names of over 660 of the 1,124 victims have been carved into the crevasses of a massive Kilkenny limestone wall that separates the park from the rest of the harbour front. In recent years Canadians of Irish descent have rediscovered the Famine moment, its history, and its current relevance as the world faces new challenges of equitable food distribution, economic development in the 'two-thirds world', and social justice.

531

# Grosse Île, Quebec

## Mark McGowan

Lying in the St Lawrence River approximately 48 km northeast of Quebec City one will find Grosse Île, Canada's best-known immigrant quarantine station and Irish Famine memorial. Sitting as the largest island within an archipelago, hence its name 'The Big Island,' Grosse Île is approximately 2.5 km long and just slightly less than 1 km across at its widest point. Yet, for well over a century this rather diminutive island was the first stop for immigrants travelling by ship to the interior of Canada, and for the most unfortunate of these migrants, it was their final stop as well.

In 1832, the Imperial Government established a quarantine station on the island, replacing one at Point Levis close to Quebec City, which had been in operation since the French occupation of Canada in the eighteenth century. The station at Grosse Île provided for an ice free landing area from early May until mid-November.[1] In the year of its founding its medical personnel were forced to deal with victims of cholera, many of whom were migrants from Ireland. Susannah Moodie, the famed chronicler of pioneer life in Canada, and herself an English immigrant who passed through the quarantine station in 1832, commented that the natural beauty of the island and its surroundings was ruined by the sight of wretched and sickly Irish beggars seen clamouring over its rocky landings.

> Here, the shores of the island and mainland, receding from each other, formed a small cove, overhung with lofty trees, clothed from the base to the summit with wild vines, that hung in graceful festoons from the topmost branches to the water's edge . . . The sun-

beams, dancing through the thick, quivering foliage, fell in stars of gold, or long lines of dazzling brightness, upon the deep black waters, producing the most novel and beautiful effects. It was a scene over which the spirit of peace might brood in silent adoration; but how spoiled by the discordant yells of the filthy beings who were sullying the purity of the air and water with contaminating sights and sounds![2]

### REQUIRED TO ANCHOR

From its inception as a quarantine station to the year 1860, all ships sailing up the St Lawrence, and particularly passenger vessels were required to anchor at the island and prepare for inspection. Passengers who evidenced symptoms of any communicable disease were evacuated from their ships to the island, which was equipped with a hospital, lazarettos, two chapels (Roman Catholic and Anglican) and residential housing for the attending physicians and medical staff and the soldiers stationed at the island for its security. In fact, for its first seven years, the military controlled the island and the medical staff consisted of army surgeons.[3]

With the failure of the potato crop in Ireland in 1845, there was anticipation among civil servants and politicians in the United Province of Canada (an organic union of the former provinces of Upper and Lower Canada, 1841–67) that there might be an increase in the number of Irish migrants to the region in the sailing season of 1846. The civilian physician in charge of the island, Dr George Mellis Douglas (1809–1864), treated about 892 migrants, out of the 32,753, who departed from Irish and British ports, destined for Quebec, in the May to November sailing season. Only sixty-six deaths were recorded at Grosse Île.[4] Since the potato crop failed for a second time in the autumn of 1846, that year's migrants from Ireland and Britain who passed through Grosse Île were not technically 'famine' migrants. None had remained in Ireland to live through the horror of the winter of 1846–47, when some of the worst cases of poverty, starvation, and death were recorded, particularly in the counties within Munster and Connacht. When reflecting on the sailing season of 1846, Douglas commented that the Irish that he saw were primarily Catholics and Irish speakers from the southwest of Ireland. In rather disparag-

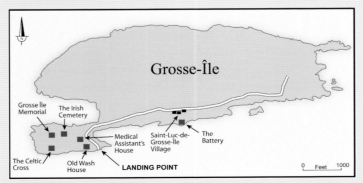

Fig. 1 FAMINE SITES AT GROSSE ÎLE.

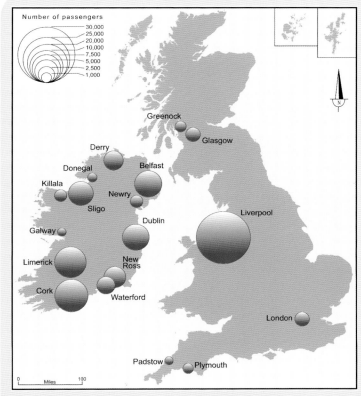

Fig. 2 THE NUMBER OF PASSENGERS ARRIVING IN QUEBEC AND GROSSE ÎLE AND THE PRINCIPAL PORTS OF DEPARTURE BASED ON LIST OF SHIPS INSPECTED AT GROSSE ÎLE AND A LIST OF ARRIVALS IN THE PORT OF QUEBEC IN 1847. [Adapted from Geneviève Duguay, 'Echoes of a tragedy: Grosse Île, summer of 1847' in Audrey Horning and Nick Brannon (eds) *Ireland and Britain in the Atlantic World* (Dublin, 2009) p. 256]

ing terms he commented: 'They came out ignorant of everything beyond the use of the spade, and in point of intelligence and civilization are little superior to our Indians . . . the children of these people are found to be active, shrewd and intelligent and become useful and valuable settlers both here and in the United States.' It was clear that Douglas preferred the less impoverished, more self-sufficient and better educated migrants from the north of Ireland, the Scottish lowlands, southern England, and the German states.[5]

## DISEASE AMONGST PASSENGERS

Reports of the worsening situation in Ireland in early 1847 prompted further warnings to Douglas who had added fifty new beds to the 150 that had been used the previous year.[6] Douglas had underestimated how many of the reported first wave of 10,000 migrants[7] would be carrying 'ship fever' (typhus), an incurable bacterial contagion that would spread among passengers in the tightly packed holds of ships and would necessitate far more evacuations to the quarantine station than its chief physician had imagined and for which his preparations would scarcely accommodate. In the first three weeks of May, however, Douglas may have thought that his calm approach to improvements in his facilities on the island had been the proper course of action. Of the twelve ships inspected, only one spent a single day in quarantine, and only two deaths were recorded

at the quarantine hospital.[8] On 20 May, with the arrival of the *Syria* and its 241 steerage passengers from Liverpool, Douglas' world was about to be turned upside down. During its forty-six days at sea, nine passengers had died. The ship spent a further six days in quarantine and forty more passengers died at Grosse Île. The *Syria* had lost a staggering one-fifth of its passengers. The worst was yet to come. By the end of the shipping season, 441 ships had landed at Quebec, accounting for approximately 90,000 passengers who had boarded these vessels in Ireland and Britain. Of these over 15,000 died before the dawn of 1848, and at least 5,424 were buried in a massive cemetery at the southwestern end of the island.[9]

Some of the most tragic stories of the passage and quarantine came from the 982 tenants whose passage was paid for by Major Denis Mahon, the landlord of estates in Strokestown, County Roscommon. Mahon had sent his tenants across Ireland by land to Dublin, where they boarded ships for Liverpool. There most of the tenants boarded the *Virginius* (476), *Erin's Queen* (100), and the *Naomi* (350), with the remaining fifty-five joining the *John Munn*. When the *Virginius* arrived at Grosse Île at the end of July, after a sixty-three-day passage, 158 passengers had already died at sea. Nineteen more of their colleagues perished while on board ship during the thirteen-day quarantine and another ninety died at Grosse Île. On this single ship 56% of the passengers perished. In total, perhaps as many as 500 of Mahon's tenants, or nearly one-half, may have perished before reaching Quebec City.[10] It is not surprising that the ledgers of orphans from Grosse Île are filled with the names of children from Roscommon.[11] Nor is it surprising that, given his tactics of relieving the effects of the Famine on his tenants at Strokestown, assassins struck Mahon down on 2 November 1847.[12]

Fig. 3 The authorities responded to the rapid spread of typhus in the summer of 1847 by setting up hundreds of tents at the eastern end of the island which were later replaced by twelve wooden structures. The only remaining building of the twelve is the lazaretto (hospital for treatment of contagious diseases) which has been restored. A number of artefacts dating to the Famine years including personal items were found during excavations at the site. [Photo: Mark MacGowan]

Fig. 4 The Famine plot at Grosse Île. [Photo: Piaras Mac Éinrí]

## HORRIFIC CONDITIONS

Conditions on Grosse Île were terrible as physicians, nurses, orderlies and chaplains were overwhelmed by thousands of sick and dying migrants. The building of new sheds barely kept up with the demand which came from hundreds of new diseased migrants who arrived every week throughout the summer.[13] Many in the station were huddled into tents because there was no room in the wooden structures. On his second visit to the island, in August 1847, Anglican Bishop G.J. Mountain described one of the harrowing scenes outside the lazarettos: 'Inmates of one tent, three widows and one widower, with remnants of their families, all bereft of their partners on the passage. Filth of person, accumulated in cases of diarrhea. Three orphans in one little bed in corner of tent full of baggage and boxes, one of the three dead, lying by his sick sister.'[14] Similarly, a young priest and future bishop, Father E.A. Taschereau (1820–1898), reported to Roman Catholic Bishop Joseph Signay of Quebec, on the fetid conditions aboard ships he found anchored by the dozens off the island, waiting to land their sick:

> Most of them have for a bed the boards or a few
> filthy wisps of straw that do more harm than good:
> still how many more, after a month and a half of the
> crossing, are wearing the same clothes and the

same shoes that they had when they came on board ship, and which they have not taken off . . . I have seen people whose feet were so stuck in their socks that I could not anoint them![15]

By year's end it was clear that Douglas and his company were completely overwhelmed and underprepared. Several members of his own staff joined the lists of the dead.

Grosse Île continued to exist as a quarantine station beyond the tragedy of Black '47, but its staff never had to process the numbers witnessed that year, nor had to experience such an enormous loss of life. Famine Irish migration dramatically trailed off in 1848 to a little more than 31,000 and perhaps as many as 41,367 the following year.[16] By 1857, the military control of the island passed formally to civilian authorities. Douglas held the post of chief medical officer on the island until 1864. British migrants still dominated the passengers who were inspected at the island, but the island's historian, the late Marianna O'Gallagher, has indicated that Germans, Norwegians and other Europeans became more common in the immigrant groups passing through the island in the late nineteenth century.[17] It was her grandfather, Jeremiah Gallagher, and the Quebec Council of the Ancient Order of Hibernians (AOH), however, who endeavoured to put an indelible Irish stamp on the island's identity.

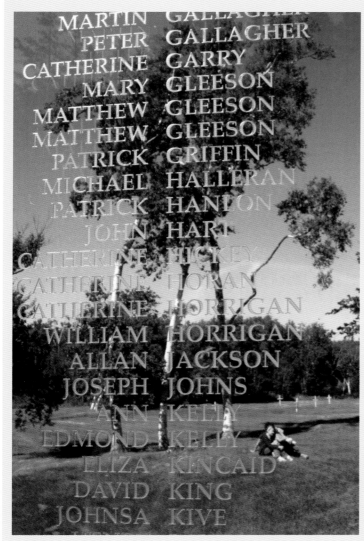

Fig. 5 A memorial was erected in 1997 in close proximity to the 1847 grave-yard. The glass panels contain the names of all who died in Grosse Île in the period 1832–1937. The names of those who perished in Black '47 occupy the most panels. [Photo: Piaras Mac Éinrí]

## MEMORIAL SITE

In 1909, with donations from AOH branches from across North America, Gallagher's group erected a massive Celtic cross on Telegraph Hill, the highest point on Grosse Île (about 140 feet above the river). The forty-six-foot-high cross faces the St Lawrence River on one side and casts its gaze over the Famine cemetery to the south. Four bronze panels adorn each side of its base; one bears an inscription memorialising the clergy who served on the island during the Famine and those who died tending to famine victims across Canada and the other three – one in English, one in French, and one in Irish – offer a tribute to those who died on the island. The French panel places the memorialisation within the context of the Catholic Faith, while the Irish inscription departs from the politically neutral expressions of the English and French panels by stating that these 'children of the Gael' died fleeing from 'foreign tyrants and an artificial/ treacherous famine in the year 1847–48'.[18] As is

the case in many commemorations, the memorial speaks as much about the commemorators as it does about those being commemorated.

The island continued to be an immigrant-processing station through the late nineteenth and early twentieth centuries. In 1901, during a new wave of immigration to Canada, over 400 vessels stopped at Grosse Île.[19] The island was officially closed in 1937, although its use by the Canadian Government did not cease. It is somewhat ironic that this immigrant 'cemetery' became host to Government experiments in chemical warfare, including the use of anthrax. By the 1990s, and with the approach of the sesquicentennial of the Famine, Parks Canada and the Ministry of Heritage converted the long-abandoned island into a National Park commemorating the quarantine of all immigrant groups and in particular memorialising the Irish tragedy on the island in the 1840s. In the summer and autumn, Parks Canada provides historical interpretation to visitors who can only access the island by boat from Montmagny, Quebec.

Fig. 6 The 46 foot high Celtic Cross commemorating the Famine which was erected in 1909 with donations from the Ancient Order of Hibernians (AOH) branches from across North America. [Photo: Piaras Mac Éinrí]

# The Famine and New York City

*Anelise H. Shrout*

Between 1845 and 1855, over 900,000 Irish emigrants entered the port of New York, and by the end of the nineteenth century New York was the largest urban Irish settlement in the world.[1] Irish immigration resulted in both the development of a New York Irish community and in changes to New York's hospitals, reception of immigrants and political organisations. These changes were deeply conditioned by the historical development of New York City, by the structures of nineteenth-century immigration, and by the physical condition that Irish immigrants found themselves in upon arrival. Before the mid nineteenth century, New York City had certainly been troubled by inadequate public health systems, insufficient care for the poor, anti-Catholic and anti-immigrant biases, and the dangers that immigrants posed to politics and labour. However, the 'Irish influx' of the 1840s and 1850s pushed these issues to the forefront of public debate, and fundamentally changed the social, political and institutional character of the city.

## NEW YORK CITY BEFORE THE FAMINE

Irish enclaves of both elite Irish Americans and working-class Irish immigrants developed in New York in the years before the Famine. These neighbourhoods were the seeds of post-Famine Irish settlement in New York, and piqued anti-immigrant, and particularly anti-Irish sentiment. Preconceptions about the Irish vis-à-vis health, political involvement and education both coloured popular responses to Famine immigrants, and shaped institutional responses to the Irish in the city.

The early nineteenth century was a turning point for Irish immigration to New York. In the sixteenth, seventeenth and eighteenth centuries, most Irish immigrants to New York were Protestant, but after the early nineteenth century, the majority of Irish émigrés were Catholic and working-class.[2] In New York of the early nineteenth century 'native' Anglo–Americans held most of the political and social power. However, demographically New York was becoming a city of recent immigrants.[3] This early Catholic, lower-class Irish immigration provoked New Yorkers' anxieties about the relationship between Irish immigrants and the spread of disease, the danger that immigrants posed to American jobs, and (after the 1821 elimination of property qualifications for voting) the role that lower-class Irish labourers would play in politics. This pre-Famine anti-Catholicism and anti-Irish sentiment

profoundly affected the reception and impact of Irish immigrants after the 1840s.[4]

This new mode of Irish immigration also prompted anxiety amongst established Irish-–American families. Prior to the Famine middle- or upper-class Irish–American families had worked to develop an established elite Irish–American community in the city, through organisations like the Friendly Sons of St Patrick, the Hibernian Society and the Shamrock Friendly Association of New York.[5] The immigration of lower-class, and mostly Catholic Irish labourers threatened these families' place in the city's social hierarchy. The fears about the influx of lower-class Irish immigrants were somewhat justified. By the end of the nineteenth century, Irish New York would be more associated with slum life and Tammany Hall than it would be with Irish–American societies and fetes.

In the early years of the nineteenth century, New York City reached from the Battery, at the southern end of Manhattan, to 42nd Street, and was expanding northwards. Downtown neighbourhoods which had previously been home to professionals were beginning their transition into slums, as the well-to-do moved north and labourers moved in, cramming either into re-purposed houses, or into 'tenements' built to maximise occupancy in a minimum of space. Pre-Famine Irish immigrants settled in these slum neighbourhoods in Manhattan, and in scattered working-class enclaves in the Bronx and Brooklyn, which were separate cities until the late nineteenth century. Irish settlement before the Famine fundamentally informed settlement patterns after 1845 with these working-class communities continuing to draw newly arrived immigrants.[6]

## 'NUMEROUS HORDES OF PASSENGERS'[7]

In 1845, there were 97,000 Irish men, women and children in New York City. By 1855, that number was almost doubled, and Irish-born New Yorkers comprised almost one-third of the city's total population.[8] New York State began to record immigration in May of 1847, and by December of that year 52,946 Irish had entered the port of New York. Irish immigration peaked in 1851 at 163,306, and declined very gradually there-

**Table 1.** Incoming Irish immigrants by year

| Year | Number of Immigrants |
|------|---------------------|
| 1847 | 52,946 |
| 1848 | 91,061 |
| 1849 | 112,591 |
| 1850 | 117,088 |
| 1851 | 163,306 |
| 1852 | 118,131 |
| 1853 | 118,164 |
| 1854 | 82,802 |
| 1855 | 43,048 |

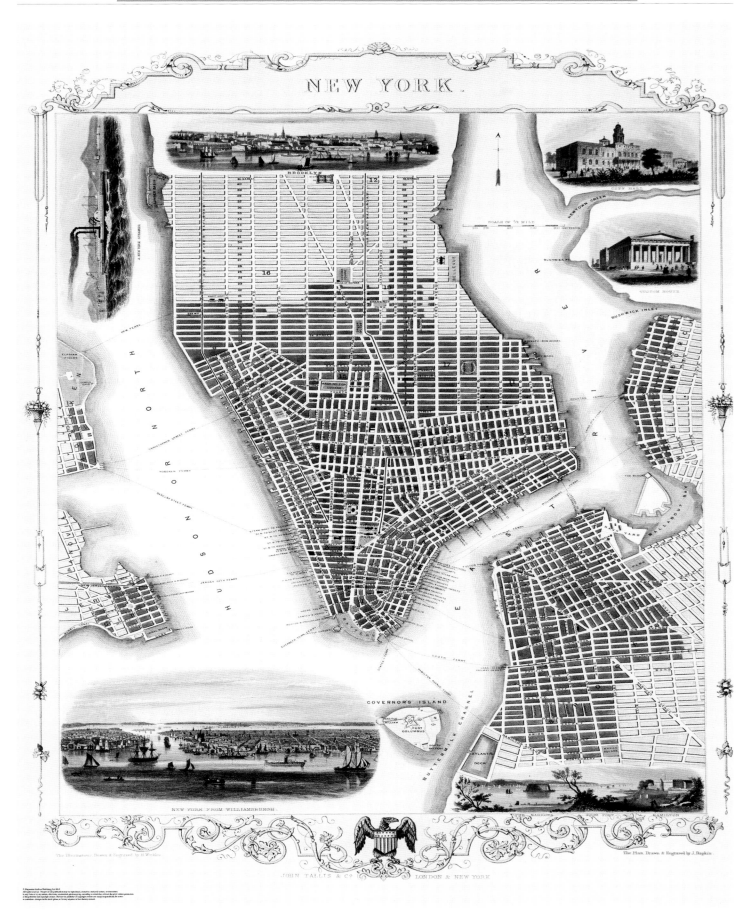

Fig. 1  Tallis map of New York City in 1851. Although the area between 23rd Street and 42nd Street was beginning to be developed, most of the population of the city was concentrated below the lower twenties. [Source: Mapseeker Archive Publishing]

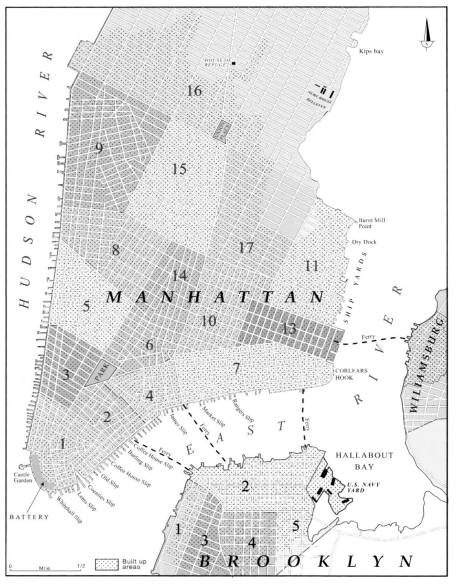

Fig. 2 THE WARDS OF NEW YORK CITY IN THE MID-NINETEENTH CENTURY. [Adapted from the outlines of the wards in the Tallis map with ward numbers included]

often targeted as easy victims of fraud. In 1855, New York State built the Castle Garden immigrant reception centre to better manage, and care for, the influx of bodies into New York City. Castle Garden remained the point of arrival for immigrants until Ellis Island was opened in 1892. Some of these immigrants simply passed through New York on their way to other destinations, but many stayed in the city temporarily or permanently. Often, the decision to stay in New York was determined by an immigrant's health upon arrival, the availability of work, and financial obligations to the shipping agents who had provided passage. Both those who immigrated in the immediate wake of the potato failures of 1845–52, and those that followed in subsequent years would make an indelible mark on New York City.

## THE IMPACT OF THE FAMINE

From their initial landing to their permanent settlement, each stage of Irish immigrants' entry and eventual residence changed the character of the city. Systems for quarantining, counting, caring for and housing immigrants were institutionalised, and the political machine of New York underwent fundamental changes. None of these was due solely to Irish immigration – indeed, the German immigration of the mid-nineteenth century added to New Yorkers' concerns about the 'immigrant menace'.[11] However, because the first Famine immigrants tended to be, or at least appeared, less healthy and less prosperous than their German counterparts, they were often cited in contemporary discussions of changing laws and social structures. Whether justified or not, these Irish Famine immigrants became symbols of all immigrants, and representatives of the changes that those immigrants wrought on New York City.

## PUBLIC HEALTH

New Yorkers faced two sets of public-health concerns with regard to Irish immigration. The first was for the health of the city. The second was for the health of the immigrants. In the first decades of the nineteenth century, Irish immigrants had been associated with the spread of cholera, and New Yorkers feared that the renewed waves of Famine immigrants would bring new diseases to the city.[12] Eighteenth-century legislation mandated that immigrants be assessed before entering the port of New York at the

after, settling around 40,000 per year after 1855.[9] Between 1847 and 1855, Irish immigrants comprised between 23% and 56% of all those entering the port of New York each year.

These 'numerous hordes' often finished the transatlantic journey in a state of starvation, and were almost always destitute. Irish immigrants travelled on ships rife with typhus, smallpox and cholera, and often in steerage, deprived of air and space. Many immigrants had been ill when they left Ireland, or were simply too young or too old to safely make the six-week transatlantic journey. In consequence, as many as one in ten of the immigrants who arrived in New York were sent directly to one of the city's hospitals.[10]

Before 1855, immigrants would have stopped first at the quarantine station on Staten Island, before proceeding to one of the many docks along the Battery, located at the southern tip of Manhattan Island, where they were

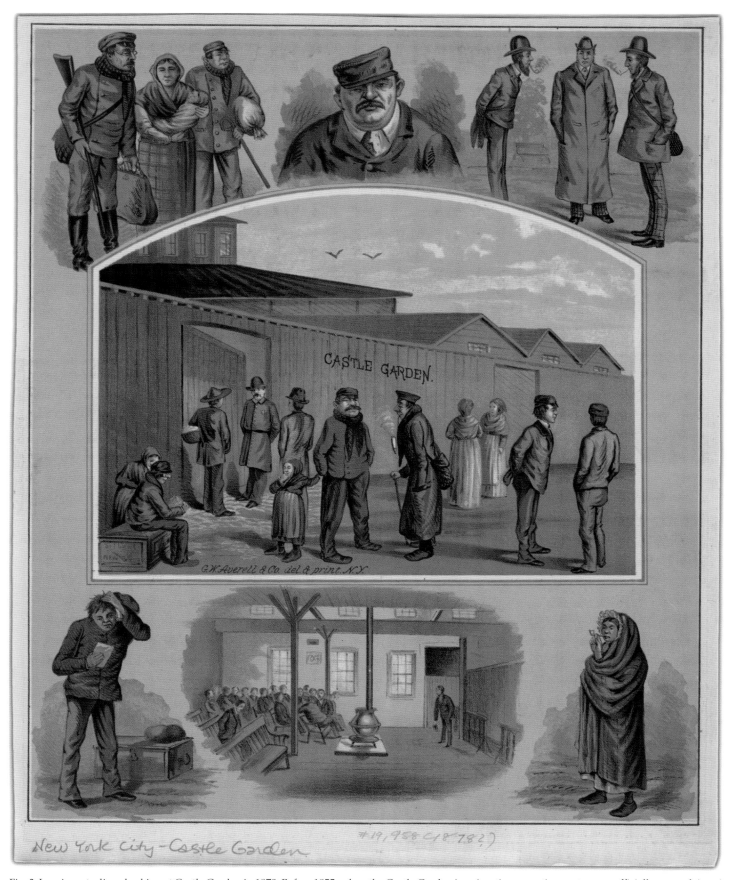

Fig. 3 Immigrants disembarking at Castle Garden in 1878. Before 1855, when the Castle Garden immigration reception centre was officially opened, immigrants would have simply disembarked along the Battery. Between 1855 and 1890, seven million immigrants – most of Irish and German extraction – would enter New York City through Castle Garden. [Source: *Pictures of New York life & character* (New York, 1878), Held at New York Public Library]

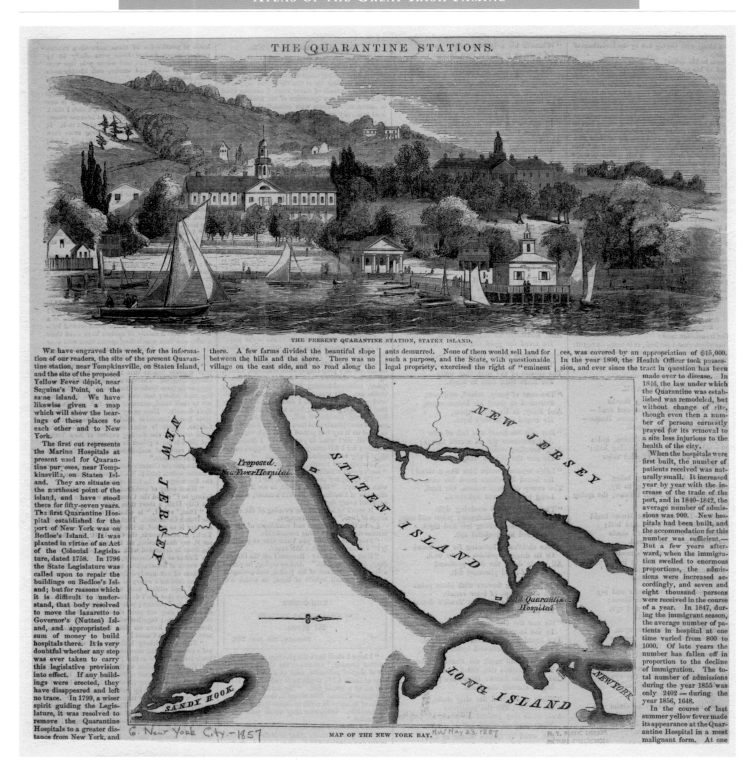

Fig. 4 Marine Hospital Quarantine Station. Legislation drafted in the wake of fever epidemics in the late eighteenth century mandated that visibly sick immigrants be deposited at the marine hospital, originally intended for sick sailors, and later used as a quarantine station. During the nineteenth century, it was used alternatively to house sick immigrants and as a hospital for contagious diseases. [The present quarantine station, Staten Island; Map of the New York Bay, 1857, New York Public Library]

Marine hospital on Staten Island so that doctors could determine whether they posed a risk to New Yorkers. However, during the immigration boom of the 1840s, there were not enough regulators to ensure that all ships stopped at the Marine hospital, and many sick immigrants bypassed medical inspection altogether. As a result, the city's hospitals were inundated with sick immigrants, most of whom could not pay for medical care, and who

became wards of the city.

While the implementation of mechanisms for quarantine and the screening of immigrants had been considered prior to the mid-nineteenth century, the sheer numbers of Irish, and the state of health in which they arrived required immediate action. In 1847, the Commissioners of Emigration of the State of New York were formed, both to protect immigrants from nefarious New Yorkers, and to protect the city from 'the number of such diseased emigrants'. The Commissioners' first report noted that 'the overcrowding of the vessels' resulted in 'great suffering and much mortality', and that increased immigration 'even threatened danger to the public health'.[13]

One of the first acts of the Commissioners was to build an immigrant reception centre. The centre was eventually built in 1855 at Castle Garden, on the southern tip of Manhattan. The first proposed site for an immigrant depot was rejected after the residents of the area complained that it would 'bring into a quiet part of the city a noisy population, without cleanliness, or sobriety, would endanger the health and good morals of the ward, and seriously affect the value of real-estate'.[14] Despite general interest in regulating immigration, most New Yorkers were not keen to have that regulation take place in proximity to their homes.

The Commissioners enforced the previous requirement that all ships carrying immigrants stop at the Marine Hospital, so that inspectors could record the number of passengers, the number of shipboard deaths, and assess the severity of illness among passengers. Immigrants were either admitted to the city or diverted to one of the city's hospitals: the marine hospital, the 'city of asylums' on Blackwell's Island, or to the newly-built hospital complex on Ward's Island.[15]

In the later 1840s and early 1850s the Commissioners worked to find space for the numerous sick and sometimes contagious immigrants entering New York. In 1848, the first buildings on Ward's Island, in the East River, were completed and partially occupied, and in 1863 Ward's Island fell

under the purview of the newly created Board of Quarantine Commission for contagious cases. After 1849, the Marine Hospital was restricted to contagious diseases, while smallpox patients were sent to the smallpox hospital on Blackwell's Island. By 1850, 60% of the patients on Blackwell's Island were Irish.[16]

The Commissioners of Emigration also worked to ensure that immigrants were treated fairly upon arrival, but did not become a burden on the city. Before 1847, the captains of ships were obligated to cover the costs of any passenger who fell ill or otherwise became wards of the city within two years of arrival. Captains frequently sold their liability onto bondsmen, who nominally agreed to pay for any immigrant who was sent to a city hospital, asylum or almshouse. While this system was effective when there were relatively few immigrants and sufficient inspectors to prevent non-payment of fees, the immigration of the 1840s gave bondsmen an opportunity to perpetrate fraud and avoid paying the city.

One of the most common frauds was to send ill or destitute passengers to private hospitals or private poor houses in lieu of better run, but more expensive, city hospitals. Passengers who were sent to these private hospitals often died for want of care.[17] Recent immigrants also fell prey to the fraudulent dealings of ticket agents. Shipping agents in Dublin, Liverpool and London often distributed transatlantic tickets in advance of payment; promising immigrants that they would find ample work in America. When work was not forthcoming, or when immigrants could not pay back the price of their tickets,

WARD'S ISLAND BUILDINGS, N.Y. 1860.

Fig. 5 The Emigrant Refuge and Hospital began on Ward's Island in 1848 as a few temporary buildings, but expanded throughout the 1850s to become the largest hospital complex in the world. By the time this image was drawn, Ward's Island was populated with solid buildings intended to withstand the immigrant influx. [Source: Ward's Island Buildings, N.Y. 1860, drawn by G. Hayward, 171 Pearl St. New York. for *D.T. Valentine's Manual for 1860*, Eno collection of New York City views] they were 'allowed' to enter the agents' private hospital and poorhouse, where they were required to work off their passage with hard labour, and with little or inedible food.

The Commissioners of Emigration attempted to protect immigrants by providing emergency medical services at the marine hospital and on Blackwell's and Ward's Islands. In addition, the Commissioners established labour boards to help immigrants find work, employed clerks to help them avoid fraud, and mandated prices of tickets away from New York to prevent price gouging. These new mechanisms for immigrant welfare, though triggered by Irish immigration, ultimately affected all immigrants entering the port of New York in the nineteenth century.

NEIGHBOURHOODS

For contemporary New Yorkers, the most obvious change wrought by the Famine was the presence of many more Irish people in the city. In 1850, 26.2% of Manhattan resi-

dents were born in Ireland, and many more would have been the children of first generation immigrants. By 1855, the number of Irish-born had risen to 27.9%.[18] Despite the presence of elite Irish-American families in the city from the mid eighteenth century, Irish settlement in New York after the Famine came to be associated with poverty, tenement life, and with particular neighbourhoods and wards. Slums, like the notorious Five Points neighbourhood in Manhattan, and others in Brooklyn and in the Bronx became home to many of the Irish who settled in the city. These neighbourhoods often developed according to networks transported from Ireland. For instance, the tenants of Lord Lansdowne who emigrated together also settled together in Five Points.[19]

Irish neighbourhoods developed in the sixth, first and fourth wards, and to a lesser extent in the fourteenth, second and seventh wards, along the East River. While many Irish men positioned themselves at the heart of the city, near projects that required labour, the most destitute drifted to the edges of the expanding metropolis where

Fig. 6  New York City acquired Blackwell's Island in 1828, intending it to be a 'city of asylums'. The Smallpox Hospital was built on the Island in 1848, and replaced by a larger hospital in 1856. However, before these hospitals were built the extant buildings on Blackwell's Island, which included a lunatic asylum, served the Irish immigrants of the 1840s. [Source: Smallpox Hospital, N.D., held by the New York City Municipal Archives]

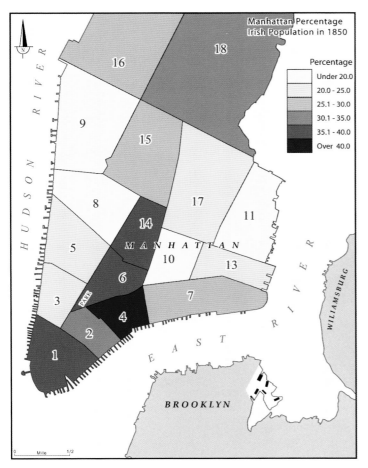

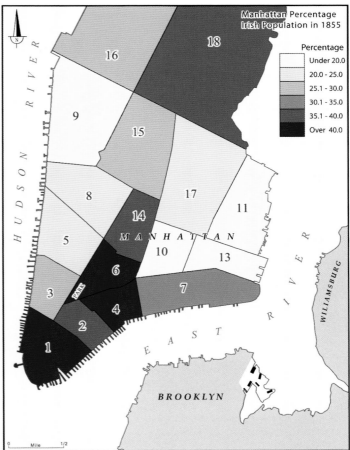

Fig. 7 DISTRIBUTION OF PEOPLE OF IRISH DESCENT BY WARD IN 1850. While the Irish were present in every ward of the city, they settled into enclaves in the first, sixth and fourth wards. The first ward was comprised of the Battery, where the Famine Irish would have found themselves after disembarking. The sixth ward contained the infamous Five Points neighbourhood, and the fourth ward ran along the East river near the Brooklyn Bridge.

Fig. 8 DISTRIBUTION OF PEOPLE OF IRISH DESCENT BY WARD IN 1855. By 1855, the Irish presence had increased across the city, and especially in lower Manhattan, where buildings were less well maintained and rents were cheaper. These lower wards also had a greater need for unskilled labour. Similarly, many settled in the upper wards of Manhattan, in an effort to take advantage of building work that expanded the city northwards. These numbers only reflect the number of Irish-born in New York City. The Irish population, consisting of both immigrants and their children, would have been larger.

they lived in shantytowns, farmed meagrely, or scavenged for food.

Women provided a peculiar anomaly in patterns of Irish settlement. Irish women and girls made up a considerable part of New York City's domestic workforce, and lived in the upper-class houses in which they worked. Many Irish also settled outside of Manhattan, in Brooklyn and the Bronx. In Brooklyn, between 1850 and 1865, the Irish outnumbered all other non-native residents. In the Bronx, Irish neighbourhoods were considerably smaller, but workers' enclaves formed around large public projects like the Harlem Railroad, the Hudson River Railroad and the Croton Aqueduct.[20]

A less tangible effect of the Famine was the impact that news of Irish distress had on New Yorkers. Between 1845 and 1852 tens of thousands of articles describing distress in Ireland, and requests for aid designed to appeal to New Yorkers appeared in the popular press. In response, New Yorkers donated generously to famine relief, giving over $170,000 to Irish aid projects. These charitable efforts, organized by the Society of Friends, synagogues, the Catholic Church and local committees for the relief of distress in Ireland provided a counter-

narrative to anti-Irishism and nativism prevalent in New York of the day.[21]

## POLITICS

Irish immigrants quickly became involved in New York City politics. The 1821 repeal of property qualifications for voting meant that the Irish who were naturalised were eligible to vote, and after 1845 the party that carried the Irish vote controlled a significant amount of political power. This political agency enabled the Irish, particularly Irish men, to use politics as a buffer to ease the difficulties of immigration. However, not all politicians celebrated Irish visibility in the political sphere. The Whig Party saw Irish immigrants as a danger to white, Protestant American privilege, and particularly a danger to the availability of jobs and political control.

The Democratic Party's Tammany Hall political machine, which controlled New York City politics in the nineteenth and early twentieth centuries, expertly courted the Irish vote. Tammany Hall was famous for dispensing

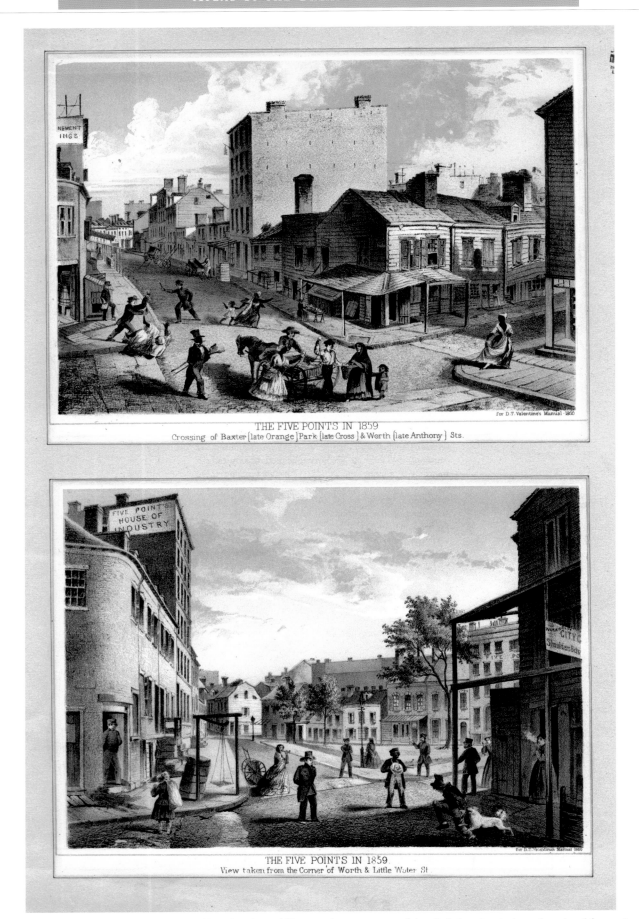

Fig. 9 The Five Points in 1859. The Five Points neighbourhood would become known as one of the city's 'most notorious slums' and for a mix of lower-class Irish, African–American, and immigrant residents. [Source: The Five Points in 1859: crossing of Baxter (late Orange) Park (late Cross) and Worth (late Anthony) Sts.; The Five Points in 1859: view taken from the corner of Worth and Little Water St., New York Public Library]

patronage to the Irish, in particular in the form of city contracts and political positions. Tammany Hall also helped recent immigrants to naturalise, making them eligible to vote. This patronage evolved over the years to full-blown participation in New York politics, typified by the election of John Kelly, the son of Irish immigrants, as alderman in 1854.[22]

This kind of patronage both drew the Irish into New York City politics, and angered native New Yorkers, who thought that the Democratic Party was helping the immigrants to put them out of business. In response, anti-immigrant nativists formed the 'Know-Nothing' Party in 1853, with the objective of protecting white 'native' American interests. Additionally, many new labour organisations were formed to protect the rights of white – that is to say non-immigrant – American workers. In the years after the Civil War, Irish labourers would re-purpose the rhetoric used against them to define themselves in opposition to African Americans, in order to argue for an Irish place in white American society.[23]

Irish immigration immediately after the Famine introduced a new voting bloc into New York City politics, and invited the extant political parties to determine the best ways to woo the new votes. In consequence, from a very early stage the Irish became involved in New York politics, and in doing so perpetuated systems of patronage that favoured the Irish over other immigrant groups.

## A PLACE IN NEW YORK

Despite the difficulties of life in New York, Irish communities solidified their place in New York life in the latter half of the century. These communities were supported by extant social networks begun in Ireland, by political patronage, but perhaps most importantly by the Catholic Church. The Catholic Church not only embraced new Irish congregants, but also worked to expand available Catholic education and to protect newly arrived immigrants from anti-Irish sentiment and anti-Catholicism.

After 1842, and under the bishopric and then archbishopric of John Hughes, the Catholic Church began a proactive battle to protect its congregations' rights from perceived attacks by the city. One of the most visible battles for the Irish community in New York was that for Catholic education. From the 1820s, the Irish in New York, in conjunction with the Catholic Church, had been working to open Catholic schools and to remove anti-Catholic rhetoric from the Protestant-run New York City public school system. 'Dagger John' Hughes, an immigrant from County Tyrone, enthusiastically joined this debate. Throughout the 1840s, Hughes fought for state funding for Catholic schools, a demand that was intensified after 1847 when many more Irish Catholic children in New York needed education. When he was unable to secure state funding for Catholic schools, Hughes oversaw the con-

HARPER'S WEEKLY.

Fig. 10 John Kelly would come to be known as 'honest' John in the 1870s, when after Boss Tweed fell from power, he orchestrated Irish control over City Hall that would last until after the Second World War. Kelly was famous for differentiating between 'honest' and 'dishonest' graft, claiming that money paid for services rendered, even if payment was rendered in ways not strictly legal, was far superior to outright theft from the public – payment for no services at all. In this way, he was able to rationalise bribery, patronage and nepotism to the people of New York. [Source: New York Public Library]

struction of parochial schools to serve New York's Catholics.[24]

Under Hughes the Catholic Church in New York expanded dramatically, in large part to cater for newly arrived immigrants. The church provided a familiar social structure for Irish immigrants in New York City, and those immigrants provided an impetus for the continued expansion of the Church. Similarly, the Emigrant Industrial Savings Bank (EISB) helped the Irish to build communities in New York, and to maintain connections with friends and relatives at home. Founded in 1850 for the use of immigrants, the EISB provided another social structure around which immigrants could coalesce, and by 1860 the Emigrant Savings Bank alone had ten thousand depositors, most of whom were Irish.[25] Both the Catholic Church and the EISB helped the Irish community in New York to develop and solidify in the wake of the Famine.

After its peak in 1851, Irish immigration to New York slowed, though it by no means abated. Between 1851 and 1860, rates of immigration fell, and in 1858 only 25,075

Irish-born passengers entered the port of New York. The Irish population in New York decreased along with immigration. In 1860, there were 203,740 people of Irish descent living in Manhattan, and by 1900, that number had dropped to 166,066. However, it was not until 1930 that the Irish-born population of the city dropped below pre-Famine levels.[26]

## LEGACY

After the immediate subsistence crisis was over, the Famine would continue to have an effect on New York City. Between May of 1847 and 1853, more than three-quarters of a million Irish men, women and children had come to New York, setting up social networks that would continue to draw Irish immigrants well into the late nineteenth century.[27] The systems of public health that had been created in response to large-scale Irish migration would continue to function until 1892, when Castle Garden was supplanted by Ellis Island, although Ward's Island still housed patients into the 1920s and Blackwell's Island continues to serve as a site for New York's hospitals to the present day.

Although anti-Irish prejudice was a feature of New York politics as late as the 1880s, the Irish in New York continued to build communities, and to rise socially. Steady immigration continued between the late 1850s and 1914, with spikes during the economic depression of the late 1870s and famines of the early 1880s. These immigrants were demographically similar to those who had emigrated forty years earlier, but they would have come to a New York that was very different from that of their predecessors. After the mid-nineteenth century, New York was a city deeply affected by, and still adjusting to the Irish Famine.

Fig. 11 John Hughes served as the Archbishop of New York between 1842 and 1864. Hughes was born in County Tyrone in 1797, and became known for his successful efforts to expand the Catholic Church in New York. In contrast to John Kelly, and because of his dogged commitment to supporting Catholics in New York, Hughes became known as 'Dagger John'. [Source: Library of Congress Prints and Photographic collection]

# New York Famine Memorial

## Joe Lee

*The Irish Hunger Memorial* in New York City, sponsored by the Battery Park City Authority, designed by Brian Tolle, and landscaped by Gail Wittwer-Laird in collaboration with 1100 Architect, was dedicated on 16 July 2002. Occupying a half-acre site at the corner of Vesey Street and North End Avenue, it lies close to where nearly a million Irish immigrants disembarked during or immediately after the Great Famine – close, too, to the site of the Twin Towers and the horrors of 9/11.

Among Famine memorials it is unusual in that it is not focused on human figures representing victims of hunger, eviction or emigration. Instead, it blends four interpretive themes that, though restrained in exposition, dominate the conceptualisation of the site.

The first theme quietly conveys the sense of identity of the survivors, reflected in a belief in the antiquity and continuity of Irish history, variously symbolized by limestone more than 300 million years old containing fossils from the Irish seabed, the formal ceremonial entrance passageway reminiscent of Neolithic graves, thirty-two scattered stones, one for every Irish county, and more than sixty varieties of Irish flora. In this composition, the Famine occurred not on some ephemeral sandbank or to transitory vagrants, but to a people with a distinctive historical sense who conceived of themselves as belonging to a culture whose roots extended far into a distant past and spread throughout the whole island. It was this instinctive sense that contributed to their feeling of banishment, banishment by a catastrophe that originated in, but was not caused by, a natural disaster, a sentiment expounded by Bishop John Hughes of New York in his powerful philippic of March 1847 denouncing the human agency behind famine deaths.

This second theme, the human genesis of the Famine, is reflected, firstly, in the ruined, unroofed stone cottage that was brought to New York from the townland of Carradoogan in the parish of Attymass, County Mayo, and reconstructed, stone by stone, on the site, and, secondly, in the size of the adjacent cultivated area within the site, a quarter acre. This was no arbitrary choice. It resonated with memories of the quarter-acre clause of the Poor Law Act of 1847, which in its eagerness to clear people off the land, denied relief from poor rates to any occupier of

Fig. 1 *The Irish Hunger Memorial* created by Brian Tolle near Battery Park, Manhattan. [Photo by Nicoleta Coman@ Brian Tolle Studio]

Fig. 2  To encounter the Irish Hunger Memorial is to have an experience rather than to see an object or group of statues. Human absence rather than presence stimulates the imagination. Almost invisible amongst the skyscrapers, the roof of the memorial is a sloping green field below which the ruins of an authentic Famine era cottage (donated by the Slacks of Attymass, County Mayo) has been reconstructed. Evoking a passage grave, the memorial is also a funeral monument built from limestone, remembering the many dead of the Irish and other famines. The quarter-acre site allows the visitor to explore the thickly planted native Irish flora including the blackthorn, the foxglove, the purple heather and the rushes. While the primary experience is of being in an Irish Famine homestead, the emotional impact is intensified by the horizontal stripes of text wrapped around the exterior and along the passageway leading to the cottage. The range of people who donated to the relief of famine in Ireland – Quakers, American Indians, children and others – is juxtaposed with narratives about many other world famines. [Photos: William J. Smyth]

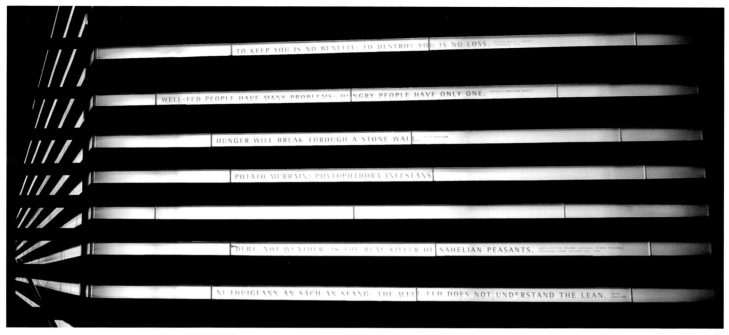

Fig. 3 The illuminated bands of quotations which wrap around the base of the memorial. [Photo: Gail Edwin-Fielding]

more than a quarter acre (and initially even to their depen-dants). This refusal sowed the seeds that would ripen into a bitter harvest. It contributed substantially to not only the scale of death and emigration, but to the hatred of the per-petrators caused by the memory of dispossession that would fuel the rage for revenge, the dominant sentiment in perhaps the most familiar of all Famine ballads, 'Revenge for Skibbereen'.

The third theme is the emphasis on the generosity of the American reception of immigrants, in stark contrast to the cruelty of the circumstances that drove them from their homeland. At the summit of the memorial, 25 feet higher than the point of entry far below on the pavement, a can-tilevered overlook brings suddenly into sight the Statue of Liberty and Ellis Island. Though belonging to a later gener-ation, they stand as symbols of America's welcome to the tide of nineteenth-century transatlantic immigrants, howev-er harrowing the adjustment might be for some. But it is natural that their symbolism should rouse particularly pow-erful responses in the descendants of those who fled from the horrors of the Great Hunger. The history and the inher-ited memories conjure up striking images blending in a seething cauldron of instincts and feelings that can still evoke so powerful a surge of emotion in many of the heirs of the immigrants who have climbed up the winding path from the entrance.

More concretely, and more contemporaneously with the Famine, the list of donors to relief recorded on the entrance wall serves to remind the visitor who has time to stand and

read, of the scale of sympathy for the famine suffering among many New Yorkers, and not only Irish New Yorkers, even if a degree of famine fatigue did set in. However great the Great Hunger was, many more would have died but for the escape route of emigration offered mainly by America, a route closed to the victims of so many other famines, before and since.

The fourth theme is a logical corollary of New York's sympathy for the sufferings of the time, the expression of solidarity with victims of more recent famines. Nearly two miles of text merging accounts of older and later famines have been installed in illuminated bands that wrap around the base of the memorial. The 110 quotations, ranging from autobiographies, letters, oral traditions, poems, recipes and songs through official parliamentary reports and statistics, signify the similarity of the horrors suffered by victims of famine across cultures and centuries.

For a memorial to so searing a tragedy, Tolle's design strives to rouse intellectual as well as emotional responses in the visitor. In some ways this possibly most cerebrally conceived of all Famine memorial monuments may lack something of the immediate emotional impact of emaciated figures clinging to the hope of life, familiar from more visu-ally evocative monuments. But for those who know some-thing of the history, the claim to enduring distinction of the New York Memorial lies in its remarkable ability to blend powerful cumulative emotional and intellectual responses that move heart and mind to simultaneously capture and transcend the Irish experience.

# The Great Famine and Australia

## Thomas Keneally

Australia was at a prodigious distance from Northern Europe and its griefs, the Irish Famine amongst them. Those who would come to Australia, voluntarily, 'semi-voluntarily' (for there were a form of evictees involved), or involuntarily, as in the case of convicts, became acquainted along the way with four oceans, the Atlantic, the Indian, the Southern and the Pacific. The traveller faced a journey which would last more than 120 days.[1]

Exclusive of the thousands of Irish convicts of the Famine period, Australia received in the ten years from 1845 to 1855 only 70,000 Irish immigrants.* This number becomes more impressive when one understands that in 1850 the European population of the entire continent was 405,000, and takes into account the fact that in the five years between 1855 and 1860, a further Irish immigration of about 175,000 occurred. This more numerous immigration was influenced by two realities, post-Famine want in Ireland, and the discovery of gold at the beginning of the decade in New South Wales and Victoria.[2]

### PRE-FAMINE IRISH

The 77,000 Irish of 1845–55 joined a pre-existent Irish community of considerable relative size (20% of the population), and of at least some influence. John Hubert Plunkett, for example, associate of O'Connell, was a former pioneering attorney-general of New South Wales, the first holding that office to prosecute white men for the murder of Aboriginals. In the early 1850s he was engaged in the committee framing a New South Wales constitution which would ultimately lead to what was for the times a remarkable degree of representative democracy, including universal male suffrage. Another notable Irishman was Roger Therry, justice of the Supreme Court of New South Wales. Ned Ryan of Galong was a former convict transported in 1816 for burning a tithe-proctor's house in Tipperary but was now, Magwitch-like, a great New South Wales landowner and pastoral grandee. And Dan Deniehy, a diminutive son of two Cork convicts who had made a success as the head of a merchant family, dazzled his way across public life in vast New South Wales, calling on 'the sons of the South' to seize their freedom and independence through a new constitution, and lashing the proposed concept of a colonial peerage as a 'bunyip [bush monster] aristocracy'. But most Irish were small tradespeople, shepherds, agricultural labourers, servants, and serving and former convicts.[3]

The motives of some of the immigrants at the time of the Famine are, as everywhere else, rendered ambiguous by the fact that famine and land issues in Ireland coincided so neatly with the discovery of Antipodean gold and the sudden booming of the Australian colonies. The Lalor brothers, Peter and Richard, brothers of James Fintan Lalor and children of a County Laois anti-tithe activist, had their own resources to meet the expense of their journey to Melbourne in 1852. But colonial maladministration would so come to mimic that of Ireland that in late 1854, Peter would lead the rebel miners of the Eureka Stockade on the goldfields of Ballarat against a corrupt colonial police and units of the British army. (Shortly after, having lost an arm in the fracas, he would be elected to the Legislative Assembly on the introduction of universal male suffrage, which his actions had helped accelerate.) The part the Famine as such played in his emigration from Ireland, and in his Australian career afterwards, is hard to define exactly, but that it was present as a motivation seems indisputable.[4]

### 'BOUNTY IMMIGRATION'

In the Famine and immediately post-Famine years, the majority of Irish emigrants came to Australia under a scheme called 'bounty immigration'. Since the United States and Canada attracted so much emigration, including even the hapless and fever-haunted evictees of Mahon, Lucan and Palmerston, the Australian colonies each appointed Agents General for Emigration in London, and gave them the task of employing sub-agents throughout Britain and Ireland to attract emigrants to Australia.

The scheme was run collaboratively by British and colonial authorities, the latter being the authorities in New South Wales, which at the time of the Famine's outbreak included present Queensland and Port Phillip or present Victoria, and south Australia. In Britain emigration committees and the agents sought and selected suitable emigrants, individuals and families. In some cases, emigrants were accepted for free passage to New South Wales, Port Phillip or South Australia, and in others the payment of a generally achievable deposit was required. It was not a perfect system, since it attracted speculative sub-agents who tried to exact further payments from the emigrants, and discipline aboard ship was not always of the first order. The vessels

---

*The terms 'emigrant' and 'emigration' are used where the context involves departure from Ireland, and 'immigrant' and 'immigration' when the perspective of the passage is to do with schemes for populating the colonies.

involved were, however, the antithesis of coffin ships. They were sound and hygienically run, and shipowners were paid a bounty by the colonial government for each immigrant landed in good health. If it had not been so, passengers and crew would have perished on the great voyage. The cost of this new version of transportation was met out of revenue from sales of Crown Land in Australia.[5]

## LORD MONTEAGLE

The scheme had been abandoned in 1840, in part because of a colonial depression, but was revived in 1847 at the Famine's height. In Ireland, Lord Monteagle, Thomas Spring Rice, MP, former Speaker of the Commons and now Comptroller of the Exchequer, was one who had early and enthusiastically used the scheme to relocate many of his tenantry from his estates either side of the Shannon estuary in the region of Shanagolden. Thereby, he, and others who availed themselves of the bounty system, had a not inconsiderable impact on Irish emigration to Australia.

Previous to the Famine, indeed as early as 1838, Monteagle had urged tenants to avail themselves of the Australian bounty immigration schemes. It seems from their later letters to him to have been by robust persuasion rather than by coercion. His was an example of a responsible if paternalistic landlord, and paternalism and compassion was combined in him with a mixed view of his tenants. On the one hand, in September 1846, he had written an excoriating letter to Trevelyan acquainting him with the intensity of want in the west. But in the Commons in March 1847, he would speak of the 'idleness of the people, of their reliance on others, their mendicant propensities'. He would oppose the Poor Law Extension Act in June 1847, which increased the number of Poor Law unions but which also contained the infamous Gregory clause. Yet earlier, in 1846, when the Shanagolden Office of Public Works was in arrears, Monteagle spent £4,500 of his own money to keep relief work going. This was in accordance with his belief in giving 'all benevolent assistance', and his conviction that, 'he [the landlord] may not only assist their distresses, but may enable them to assist themselves'. He hoped that his tenantry would 'look up to the landlord as to a protector and friend'.

So he was one of those landlords, who – like the future convict Smith O'Brien's family in Dromoland Castle in Clare – believed in the appropriateness of large-scale emigration, but emigration according to humane standards.[6]

It is undeniable that Monteagle pressed this form of immigration on his tenants. They were to sell up their assets to pay for part of the rents owing and in return he would help them emigrate. Indeed, sometimes those needing to pay a margin of the cost had the money advanced by Monteagle on the basis that they would repay him out of their Australian wages. The alternative to emigration would be eviction, though even the resistant came to comply rather

Fig. 1 *Portrait of Thomas Spring Rice, Lord Monteagle* (1790–1866) by Martin Shee. Spring Rice was a paternalistic landlord and politician who firmly believed in Ireland's union with Britain. His response to the Famine was complex, exhibiting on the one hand compassion for those suffering while on the other being highly critical of the people's 'indolent' ways. He supported large-scale immigration from Ireland as a humane solution to the crisis of the Famine years. His son Stephen Spring Rice while also defending landlords' interests, sought to alleviate the sufferings of the poor and was very involved in the establishment of the 'British Association' which funded much relief in the most distressed parts of Ireland. [Source: Limerick Chamber of Commerce]

than face that reality. In encouraging some of the sceptical emigrants of 1848–50, he was helped by a letter from Melbourne composed by a former tenant, Pat Danaher. 'I, as in duty bound, feel called upon to inform your Lordship How the Emigrants who obtained a passage through your Lordships intercessions are situated.' All the girls were working in Melbourne at £25 or £26 per annum, he reported. 'The general hire of labourers of every description, my lord, is from £28 to £32 per annum, with board lodgings . . . Ellen Shanahan is married to one Rockford in this town and

## LETTER FROM AN IRISH EMIGRANT TO LORD MONTEAGLE

Melbourne, Port Philip,
20th of March, 1848.

My Lord,

I, as in duty bound, feel called upon to inform your Lordship how the Emigrants who obtained a passage through your lordship's intercession are situated. All the Girls are employed in the Town of Melbourne, at the rate of Twenty-five to Twenty-six pounds per annum; they are all in respectable places. Thos. Sheahan is employed in the Town adjoining, attending Bricklayers at Four Shillings and Six pence per day - John Enraght on Public work, at the same rate. The general hire for Labourers of every description, my lord, is from Twenty-eight to Thirty-two pounds per annum, with board and lodgings. There is nothing in such demand in this Colony as Male and Female Servants: I was employed myself, my lord, on board the Lady Peel, by the Colonial Doctor, filling up forms of agreement between Masters and Servants, so that I had an opportunity of knowing all the particulars concerning wages, term of employment, occupation &e.&c.

I would mention all, but I consider your lordship will feel satisfied when you know they are all in good situations, and with respectable masters and mistresses. I have seen a good deal of the Emigrants whom I knew at home, that obtained a passage through your lordship's intercession, about eleven years ago, some of them live in the Town of Melbourne, and are living comfortably. Ellen Shanahan (Loughill), is married to one Rockford, in this Town, and keeps a Hotel. Maurice Conners, of Foynes, is living in this Town, and has as much money spared as exempts him from personal labour. I have heard from some more of them who live in the Country, and as far as I can learn, my lord, they are living independently. Ellen Sheahan is just going up to her brother accompanied by her first cousin, Daniel Mulcare, of Clonalikard, himself and his brother has lived some time in this Town, and kept a Grocer's Shop. They have acted the part of a brother to me, my lord, they gave me the best of entertainment, and procured a situation for me with one Mr. Ham, a Surveyor. I am going up the Country to the Avoca River to survey a Station; my wages are Twenty-one pounds for six months. Mr. Hurley has sent for his nephew and his aunt, they are on their way up by this time. I expect, my lord, to be able to remit some money to your lordship in recompense for the expenses incurred on my and my sisters' account by your lordship, as well as some relief to my poor mother, brothers and sister. I hope, my lord, this humble but imperfect epistle will find your Lordship, Lady Monteagle, Mr. Spring Rice, and all his family in good health. Any information I can give your lordship respecting the interior of this Country, will not be lost sight of on my part. Mr. Thos. Ham, of Great Collins Street, Melbourne, would forward any commands to me, my lord, if your lordship should want any more information concerning any of the late or former Emigrants. Every thing in this Colony, my lord, is from three to four times as dear here as it is in England or Ireland, except Bread, Beef, Mutton, &c., the best of which is obtained at Three half-pence to Two-pence per lb.

I am, My Lord, with profound veneration,

Your Lordship's most devoted Servant,

P. DANAHER,

P.S. My sisters also, my lord, beg leave to return their most sincere thanks to your Lordship and Lady Monteagle.

John Flanagan and Wife are both employed by a man of the name of Murphy, a Brewer, about twelve miles out in the Country, wages Fifty pounds per annum.

Fig. 2 A letter from one of Monteagle's former tenants, P. Danaher which was used to convince the more sceptical of his tenants of the better economic conditions to be found in the Australian colony. [Source: National library of Ireland]

keeps a hotel.'[7]

Lord Monteagle 'emigrated' in the near term somewhere near 1,000 people, many of whose progeny are generally aware of their origins and still honour Monteagle's name.[8] By the end of the Famine, further emigration from Lord Monteagle's various properties was based upon money sent home to those who had failed somehow the tests for bounty immigration, or had not been offered it; men and women, perhaps, who, at the height of the Famine, had questionable health but who were now ready to travel. Having missed Monteagle's initial culling, therefore, they intended to follow on and join relatives.

Monteagle emigrants' money sent back to Ireland was generally remitted home by way of Monteagle himself, either in repayment of advances he had made to cover any deposit on their passage, or else to support the household economy or emigration of family members. Many letters from Monteagle immigrants in Geelong or Sydney, Goulburn or Yass, acknowledged the debt burden to Monteagle and enclosed whole or partial repayment – a repayment to which only honour and the consciousness that their relatives were still dependent on Monteagle's benevolence compelled them. Some of his former tenants now in Australia also asked him to assist personally in bounty or fully paid emigration of family members left behind. There seemed to be considerable affection for Monteagle amongst emigrants and those who stayed on his estates. In a private letter from Thomas Kennelly in Shanagolden to his daughter Ellen in Tumut, New South Wales, Kennelly told her that they offered 'a prayer of the longevity and eternal bliss of our good and noble patrons, my lord Monteagle and his most amiable and generous daughter'. Whether or not this was a form of flattery which the correspondents might have hoped would reach the ears of the Monteagles, many of the emigrants to Australia expressed similar sentiments in both private letters as well as letters to Monteagle himself.

As everywhere the Irish settled, emigration begot emigration. By 1850–51, when gold was discovered in New South Wales and Victoria, and goldfields, much-reported on in Irish news, proliferated across both colonies, tenants needed less persuasion than ever to leave Ireland.[9]

## FEMALE ORPHANS

There was one other version of famine emigration to Australia. Between October 1848 and August 1850, more than 4,000 Irish girls, aged mainly between fourteen and nineteen years, sailed on eleven Australia-bound ships, each vessel under the direction of a surgeon superintendent. This scheme, devised by Earl Grey, Secretary of State for the Colonies, involved the shipping of female 'orphans' from the workhouses of Ireland. Their immigration was to be paid from the same purse which enabled that of the Monteagle and other emigrants, but none of the young women were required to contribute any amount to their passage. Earl Grey's reasons for instituting this emigration were the Irish pressure on the workhouses, the Australian imbalance between the sexes, and the need of female servants in the Australian rural regions. To relieve the girls of their workhouse rags, and to impose respectability on them, the Poor Law unions fitted them out with a uniform which consisted of two gowns, six shifts, six pairs of stockings, two pairs of shoes, and other items.

Apart from Earl Grey, one of the instigators of the emigration of the orphan girls was Caroline Chisholm, a Roman Catholic Englishwoman domiciled in Australia who had begun her remarkable career by meeting every emigrant ship which arrived in Sydney, and giving advice to immigrants. From 1842 onwards, she conducted parties of newly-arrived single women along the roads of the interior to resting shelters and employment agencies in bush towns. From these centres, women were recruited to employment in town itself, and on farms and sheep and cattle stations. Chisholm envisaged that Irish orphan girls could be similarly distributed. During the Famine, she visited Britain and Ireland and wrote a pamphlet to Earl Grey entitled *Emigration and Transportation Relatively Considered*. In New South Wales, her lobbying of the Secretary of State in Whitehall and of the Lord Lieutenant of Ireland caused outrage amongst the colonial anti-Irish. Earl Grey and the Lord Lieutenant, said one commentator, were 'dupes of an artful female Jesuit', and Chisholm's success in the matter was considered part of a supposed plot to Romanise the Australian colonies.[10]

The first group of such girls came from the north, from Armagh, Banbridge, Downpatrick, Dungannon and other workhouses in Ulster, including Belfast. They were sent to Plymouth from which they began their 122 days' voyage to New South Wales on the *Earl Grey*. Not all of them were, in the strictest sense, orphans, and this was particularly so of this first shipload. Famine scholars frequently mention the

Fig. 3  Henry George Grey, 3rd Earl Grey by Camille Silvy, albumen carte-de-visite, 1866. Grey was one of the principal architects of the orphan girl immigration scheme and an influential voice at Cabinet level in determining famine policy. [Source: © National Portrait Gallery, London]

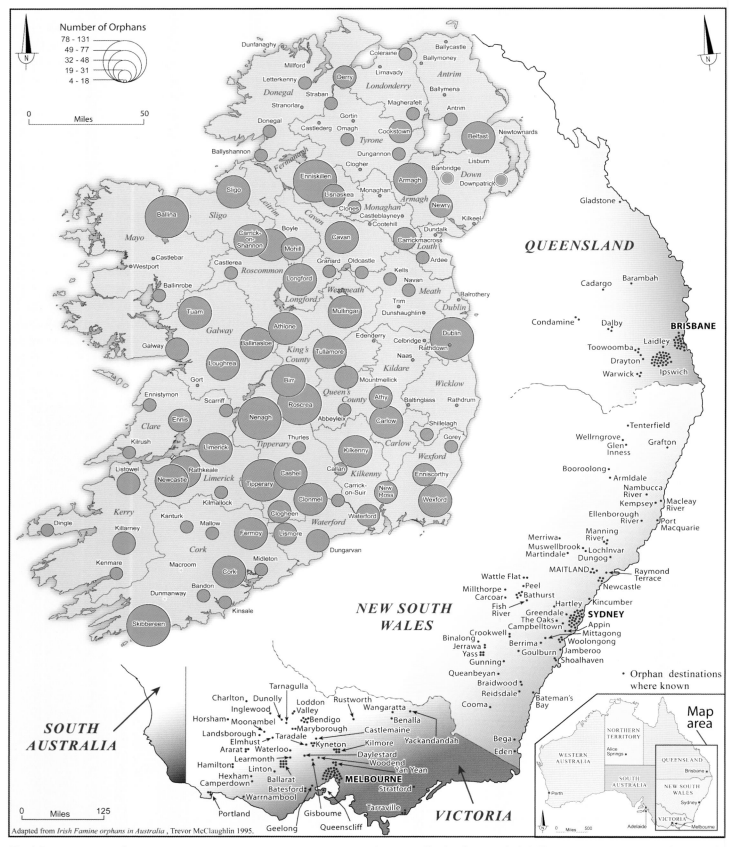

Fig. 4 SOURCE AREAS FOR IRISH FEMALE ORPHANS AND THEIR FINAL DESTINATIONS IN AUSTRALIA. During the period 1848–50 over 4,000 young women between the ages of fourteen and twenty were sent from workhouses in Ireland to the Australian colonies. Earl Grey, Secretary of State for the Colonies had devised the scheme in order to reduce the pressure on Irish workhouses while also meeting the demand for female servants and marriageable young women in the colonies. Map shows the destinations of many of the female orphans in eastern Australia in 1861. [Source: Trevor McClaughlin, *Barefoot and Pregnant? Irish Famine Orphans in Australia*, Volume 2 (Melbourne, 2001), pp. 79-80]

loosening of family ties under the impact of starvation. Many of the girls had parents who had emigrated to England or the United States. Indeed, three of the woman who would immigrate then and in the succeeding months had parents already in Australia. From the *Earl Grey*, which sailed into Sydney in October 1848, to the final ship, the *Maria*, which arrived in August 1850, surgeon superintendents of good character and evangelical stripe were appointed to look after the women. In terms of the material welfare of the orphans they seem to have done an excellent job, despite one of weak character permitting relationships between older girls and sailors – something that probably happened to an extent on other ships as well. Some Belfast girls who had passed themselves off as workhouse orphans had worked in factories in Belfast, and were notorious for singing bawdy songs they had picked up there. The surgeon superintendents in general tended to mistake Irish rowdiness for lowness of soul. But as the surgeon on the *Thomas Arbuthnot* came to realise, his charges were 'a decent set a girls'.

The arrival of the orphan girls in Sydney, Melbourne and Adelaide, where care of them passed to orphan committees, was treated with civic abhorrence by some. Many colonials were angry with Earl Grey for trying to renew transportation under another name, for the importation of these girls was considered the equivalent of the introduction of criminality into their communities. In Sydney the orphan girls were described as 'professed public women and little country beggars'. The Belfast girls in particular were 'violent and disorderly, obscene and profane in their language, many of them prostitutes and many of them not orphans at all'. The repute of the girls of the *Earl Grey* was influenced by the opinions of the strait-laced surgeon superintendent Dr Douglass, who was later criticised for tarring the girls with the one brush.[11]

In fact, it was only a minority of these young women who chose to live outside the limits of 'acceptable' society. Even of the first ship, Governor Sir Charles FitzRoy, wrote, 'more than two-thirds conducted themselves, both during the passage and since their arrival in Sydney, in an extremely satisfactory manner'. Like some of the more unruly convicts of Sydney, the minority of girls who were considered most unruly and profane were sent north to Moreton Bay (Brisbane), then a remote settlement and now capital of

Fig. 5 Memorial to the orphan girls at Hyde Park Barracks, Sydney designed by artists Hossein and Angela Vlimanesh. Sandblasted on the two glass panels are the names of many of the young women who were part of the Earl Grey scheme. [Photo: Kevin Kenna]

Queensland. But later orphan ships contained more 'satis-factory' girls from the west of Ireland, even though some of them were still afflicted by famine-induced *amenorrhoea* (lack of periods).

In fact, the great majority of the girls, scattered over tremendous distances in the bush or in country towns, mar-ried within three years; and on the basis, as Caroline Chisholm had promised them, of 'Meat Three Times a Day!', they flourished in health. Given the enlarged calorie intake of the orphan girls and the reality that land-holdings in Australia consisted of hundreds if not thousands of acres, and were demanding of intense and determined labour, the women of the orphan ships were able to bear a large num-ber of offspring to help in the working of their properties, and the average number of children they gave birth to was nine.

Jane Duff, a Presbyterian from Newtownards, County Down, was characteristic in that she had already given birth to five children when at thirty-five years, in 1868, she died prematurely of a fever in the hinterland of Queensland. In 1861, Cathy O'Donnell of Limerick was living some 260 miles north of Sydney with her husband and five children on rich farming land on the Manning River. One of the orphan girls, Mary Green, who laboured as a farm wife on a selection (320 acres), is a forebear of an Australian Prime Minister, Kevin Rudd.

Given their input into Australia's progeny, a monument stands to their honour in Sydney's Convict Barracks where they had been temporally accommodated after their arrival. But under colonial pressure, the scheme was abandoned after the arrival of the *Maria*, the last of eleven ships in 1850.[12]

## IRISH CONVICTS

Despite the spirited 1842 decision of the populace of New South Wales not to accept any further convict transports, Irish convicts of the Famine years were still arriving in other regions of the continent. During 1847 alone, three ships from Dublin, the *Arabian*, the *Tory* and the *Waverley*, arrived in Van Diemen's Land carrying between them some 470 female convicts, and since 1846 was a peak year for crimes of stock-stealing and larceny (to be surpassed only by 1847), one can be justified in the surmise that some of these women had committed famine-induced crime. The same could be said of the 1,300 men who arrived in Van Diemen's Land in 1848 for crimes committed in greater part in the previous year. In 1846, 60% of all agricultural outrages in Ireland occurred in the adjoining counties of Limerick, Clare, Tipperary, Roscommon, Longford and Leitrim. The historian George Rudé argues that this figure is specifically related to the Famine, since those counties were an epicen-tre of famine. Most crimes committed in County Clare dur-ing the Great Hunger were larceny and stock-stealing. There were also a number of Ribbon-type crimes – less

notable than that of the assassination of Mahon at Stroke-stown. Such crimes of agrarian protest or aggression, how-ever, would diminish as the Famine went on, and the surmise is that this was due to the growing debilitation of the peasant Irish and their preoccupation with personal and family survival.[13]

As for Irish – and particularly County Clare – crime, outrages and otherwise, the incidence remained high. At the Kilbride mine in 1847, John Hannon was accused of assault-ing the manager and a clerk, and was transported. Thomas Britt was sentenced to ten years' transportation for stealing a gun, an act often associated with Ribbon activism, though he might simply have stolen it for sale. Michael Frawley was convicted of filching money from the drainage section of the Board of Public Works. He pleaded 'his young and helpless family of brothers and sisters in consequence of no room being at present in the workhouse'. He was nonethe-less transported. Some of the men and women sentenced to transportation, such as the Sheridan sisters, claimed they were about to emigrate to America at the time of their crimes. Perhaps they were trying to convince the magistrate or judge that they were willing to transport themselves rather than put the Government to the expense of doing it. The following year, when John Benn pleaded guilty to sheep stealing, he claimed that 'himself and his family were two days without eating one morsel of life-sustaining food'. Despite this, his sentence of ten years' transportation was not commuted to anything less severe. In view of the dimin-ishing number of penal colonies, not all of those condemned to transportation were actually transported. But thousands were. Many of them considered themselves not as criminals but as something along the lines of what Rudé would call 'social bandits', that is, people who were convinced that their officially illegal acts wore the coloration of protests against inequity and assertions of natural justice. We can thus justifiably imagine them at their ultimate Australian hearths passing on to their Australian children a set of sim-ilar beliefs as they had harboured themselves.

It is indeed an eloquent statistic of the pressure of want in Ireland that Irish convicts in Van Diemen's Land (the future Tasmania) made up 6,000 of the 10,000 prisoners transported from the United Kingdom between 1845 and 1849. They were notable amongst other convicts for being speakers of the Irish tongue as their first language, and for their pre-industrial attitudes and unworldliness. The gentry of Van Diemen's Land found that the men were 'ignorant and insubordinate' and the women 'unfitted to engage in domestic service'. Many of the women were detained, as earlier convict women had been, in the notorious 'female factories', workhouses-cum-prisons-cum-refuges, in Hobart and elsewhere.[14]

Meanwhile, a great deal of Famine relief was collected in Australia, most but not all of it through parish churches, where former Irish convicts joined settlers in giving. The peasant convicts were not immune from news and concern for families, any more than the Irish in the free community were. For example, Hugh Larkin, serving a life sentence for Ribbonism, received his conditional pardon in 1848, and thereafter, with his time-served Irish convict wife, Mary Shields, heard news of the Famine from the pulpit of Sts Peter and Paul bush cathedral in the town of Goulburn, and listened to the Famine Encyclical of Pope Pius IX. From a previous, Irish marriage, he had two sons in Ireland (and perhaps a still-living wife) when the Famine struck.

General committees for relief were established in the various colonies, including one chaired by the governor of New South Wales, Sir Charles FitzRoy, son-in-law of the Marquis of Londonderry. The town of Brisbane, with its high Irish proportion in a general population of 20,000, donated £10,000, and altogether the Australians collected £98,000, a higher proportion than that of any other national group. One of the mediators of the relief was the Catholic Archbishop of Sydney, the Benedictine Bede Polding.[15]

During the Famine period, Van Diemen's Land became the receiving penal colony for a species of convict far removed from the norm but equally victims of the Famine. These were the more economically privileged members of the movement known as Young Ireland, the most distinguished of whom was the County Clare landlord and Member of Parliament, William Smith O'Brien. O'Brien's property in Clare was named Cahirmoyle, but the family seat was the imposing Dromoland Castle.

Typically of the movement's members, a Young Irelander named Thomas Francis Meagher – nicknamed 'Meagher of the Sword', ally of Smith O'Brien and son of a mayor of Waterford – addressed himself to the question of Irish produce exported each year of the Famine, and saw in it the ultimate indifference of Westminster towards the starving. John Mitchel, the son of a Unitarian Presbyterian minister from Newry, was a passionate young advocate of physical force (and even of the destruction of railway lines) who wrote for the Young Ireland newspaper *The Nation*, founded in 1842 by Charles Gavan Duffy. As the famine began, the tone of *The Nation*'s correspondence and poetry departed more and more from the moral force ethic of O'Connell. The total divorce between Young Ireland and Old Ireland occurred in May 1845. But it was the onset of the Famine which accentuated the gulf between the two groups. The schism between the two wings of the Repeal movement deepened in 1846.

In the spring of 1848 Meagher had visited France, where a bloodless revolution had occurred, and now he and other Young Irelanders, on the basis of their widespread Confederate Clubs, believed that they should lead a rising should the harvest of 1848 be shipped to Britain. John Mitchel preached revolution in his new organ, the *United Irishman*, and was arrested for sedition and transported for

fourteen years. He would first be transported to Bermuda, but ultimately would be sent to Van Diemen's Land.[16]

The other Young Irelanders were not allowed to wait for a harvest-time rebellion. In mid-summer, warrants were issued for their arrest, and wandering through the countryside they attempted unsuccessfully to rouse a famished people to rebellion. While some of them campaigned in the west, hoping for a spontaneous rebellion, Smith O'Brien and his associates, including Terence Bellew McManus and Patrick O'Donohoe, travelled westwards from Dublin to Tipperary. Ultimately, after attempting to ambush an armed column of police, who then took refuge in the house of a widow named McCormack, O'Brien's small force was scattered. The leaders of Young Ireland in the south and southwest were picked up and the leaders tried in Clonmel.

*John Mitchel*

Fig. 6 John Mitchel (1815–75). The dominant view in British circles during the Famine was that Ireland's tardiness in conforming to British models of progress had left her susceptible to such a calamitous event. It was a view which absolved the British Government of all blame for the Famine. Progress was very much linked in the British mind with moral improvement. Such morality in Mitchel's eyes was largely defined by British self interest. 'Britain being in possession of the floor' and being the dominant power determined to a large extent how the Famine was interpreted. In telling Ireland's story Mitchel would redress this imbalance. In his eyes Britain had relinquished its moral authority to govern Ireland by its refusal to deal effectively with the Famine. An impassioned writer and advocate of physical force, he preached revolution in the pages of *The United Irishmen*. He was subsequently arrested for sedition and transported to Australia, eventually ending up in Van Diemen's Land and subsequently in the United States. [Source: National Library of Ireland]

O'Brien, Meagher, McManus and O'Donohoe were found guilty of treason and condemned to the same barbarous death which Robert Emmett had suffered. This sentence meant the Young Irelanders were 'divested of their farcicality', and they became to many liberals, in France and America, in particular, but in Britain as well, the unjustly suppressed spokesmen for a famine-beset, misgoverned Ireland. Less spectacularly, John Martin and the young physician Kevin Izod O'Doherty received ten years' transportation.

By a special act of Parliament, the treason sentences were transmuted to transportation for life. The four 'state prisoners', as they were called, travelled to Van Diemen's Land in reasonable comfort as the only convicts aboard a ship named *Swift*, which arrived in Hobart in late October 1848. Here they encountered the determination of Governor William Denison, who considered penal reform to be 'maudlin sentimentality' but who was under instructions to provide the

Fig. 7 William Smith O'Brien (1803–64), a Protestant nationalist who was elected MP for Ennis in 1828. An early advocate of repeal he later joined the militant Young Ireland movement. He was convicted of high treason for his part in the failed rebellion of 1848 and transported to Tasmania. This statue of O'Brien by sculptor Thomas Farrell on O'Connell Street, Dublin was unveiled in 1870. [Photo: John Crowley]

state prisoners with tickets-of-leave as long as they gave their parole (word) as gentlemen that they would not try to escape. In return, they would be able to live and work in a specified region of the island. Other recipients of tickets-of-leave were able to work and wander wherever they chose in Van Diemen's Land, and there was immediate outrage that the Young Irelanders were so restricted. William Smith O'Brien would not give his word to the governor and so was subjected to a period of great loneliness at Maria Island and, after an escape attempt from there, at Port Arthur. There even his guards were not permitted to speak to him.

News of Smith O'Brien's confinement was spread around the world by Van Diemen's Land sympathisers, and he became a famed political prisoner, provoking moral outrage against Britain, particularly in the United States, and re-concentrating attention on the Famine as an administrative crime rather than an act of God. He who had adopted a physical force position was now, by his very prison situation, a figure of moral force, and though 14,000 miles away from Ireland, was synonymous with its woes.[17]

When John Mitchel arrived in Van Diemen's Land, he would take up residence in the town of Bothwell with his fellow transportee, John Martin, under the same conditions which applied to the others, and he too was not averse to letting the world know what he was enduring for his convictions. Against the advice of the others, Patrick O'Donohoe improbably ran a newspaper, the *Irish Exile and Freedom's Advocate*. His editorial policy could not be as strident as that of *The Nation* at the height of its popularity, but he made up for that by attacking the local administration as a continuation of the same follies as afflicted Ireland. Hobart was a place, he said, where the authorities 'think nothing of hanging five or six people every morning; some of them, if old offenders, on very trifling charges'. Ultimately, for being considered seditious, he would have his ticket-of-leave suspended and be sentenced to what was known as 'secondary punishment' at one of the bitter hard-labour camps on the Tasman Peninsula.

The Young Irelanders, in their various districts and in their public struggle against the unpopular colonial governor, also became a focus of colonial dissent and of popular sentiment in favour of self-government for the colony. Smith O'Brien, whose health was failing from a form of solitary confinement in Port Arthur (again a cause of international outrage), was under pressure from friends to give in to Denison and accept the limited freedom of a ticket-of-leave. His point had been proved, they argued. He acceded and began to live under the same terms as the others.[18]

When Meagher, McManus and Mitchel devised means to retract their word of honour and escape the colony to take up careers in the United States, they did so with the sympathy and help of a range of settlers, English, Scottish and Irish. Meagher and Mitchel, in particular, went on to evoke extraordinary New York demonstrations of joy at

Fig. 8  The McCormack house in Ballingarry, County Tipperary was the site of William Smith O'Brien's ill-fated rebellion of 1848. His small force was scattered after a brief altercation with the local constabulary. [Photo Frank Coyne]

their escapes, as well as to achieve civic eminence, at least until the Civil War, which saw Mitchel on what history would prove the wrong side of the conflict, and Meagher by contrast a Union general.[19]

Smith O'Brien, still Ireland's Mandela, was serving his sentence in Van Diemen's Land when that colony's constitution was framed. He himself had written and published anonymously a draft constitution for a polity which was about to drop the shame-ridden name of Van Diemen's Land and to become Tasmania. Interestingly, his version of a constitution was not totally Chartist and required considerable property qualifications for the franchise, and retained the connection with the Crown as well. His last entry in his Van Diemen's Land journal is political and concerns a meeting of the colony's Legislative Council with the governor in which an end to transportation was the leading issue. Of the councillors he said, 'The combined moderation and firmness which they have evinced appear to me to deserve the approval of every reasonable man', and declared that, 'despite the narrowness of the colony, the lowborn nature of its gentry, if Ireland had such a constitution as that settled upon for Tasmania, there would be peace within that kingdom.'[20] Despite his belief in the Crown's claim on Australian loyalties, he would never express regret for the uprising he had led during the Famine.

After his conditional pardon, which would permit him to be at large anywhere except in the British Isles, political pressure, particularly that exerted by the Democrats in the United States, the voices of fifty members of the Commons, and those of the Canadian Legislature, led in 1856 to a full pardon and his return to the famine-ravaged and depopulated Ireland.[21]

It is easy to argue that another Young Irelander, the Irish MP and editor of The Nation, Charles Gavan Duffy, was also a Famine emigrant to Australia. In an editorial published in The Nation on 15 August 1855, he lamented the decline in numbers of the Irish Party and the squandering of 'the special opportunity sent by Heaven for our deliverance . . . Till all this be changed, there seems to be no more hope for the Irish Cause than for a corpse on the dissecting table.'[22]

During the high days of Young Ireland, he had faced five trials under the Treason Felony Act, before being elected as the member for New Ross to the Commons. He was acquainted with what we call the leading figures of his time but now, after two frustrating years in Parliament and under the assurance of a friend that there were good bookshops in Melbourne and that it was a coming place, he decided to depart with his family for that 'golden' city. He took with him the same principles as had characterised The

*Nation*, but now that Melbourne hinterland had become the colony of Victoria and was framing its own bourgeois democratic constitution, he could see the possibility of progressive legislation, something thwarted in Ireland. He was also aware that the land issue could be addressed there in a way that was not possible in post-Famine Ireland. Within a few months of his arrival, he received by subscription £500 on condition he stand for the new Victorian Legislative Assembly. Appointed Lands Minister, he engaged in his passionately felt and chief cause, legislation to enable former miners, immigrants and others to select land in a countryside previously dominated by the large landowners known as squatters. His inspiration was the land-reforming League of North and South, of which he was one of the founders in 1850. Due to the chicanery of squatters in using proxies ('dummies') to select good land and thus retain it for themselves, his legislation was only partly successful, but it was followed by a number of further attempts at more watertight lawmaking. The squatters, however, would only ever be partially defeated.

Land was an Irish issue translated from pre-Famine and Famine Ireland. But very early in his Australian residence, he had taken up a cause above all particular to geographically immense land-masses – federation of the colonies,

which were soon to be called states. 'You are not Australians,' he declared, 'till there is some federal connection between the separate members of Australia.' But the states were not ready yet for such a patently rational arrangement and were on their way to being divided along the lines of free trade and protection. 'The flowers gathered from so much seed,' he lamented on the matter of federation, 'make only a scanty bouquet.'[23]

Despite Gavan Duffy serving as Premier of Victoria between 1871 and 1872 and being knighted in 1877, it was widely believed that his Catholicism and his seditious past inhibited the advance of his political career. His regular correspondence with Gladstone, Carlyle and other notable figures can be read in his collected letters. His *Four Years of Irish History* (1883), like his other works, show his conviction that the Famine demanded, at the very least, a restoration of an Irish legislature. Dying in Paris in 1903, he was buried in Glasnevin Cemetery, the burial place of many nationalist heroes whose histories were shaped by experience of the Famine.[24]

His career, amongst humbler Irish–Australian ones, is a demonstration of the reality that there was no reach of the earth, however remote, which was not potently influenced either politically or demographically by *An Gorta Mór*.

# 'Week after week, the eviction and the exodus': Ireland and Moreton Bay, 1848–52[1]

## Jennifer Harrison

On 21 October 1848 the coastal schooner *Ann Mary* discharged thirty-seven Irish female teenagers at Moreton Bay in the sub-tropical northern regions of New South Wales.[2] These were the first of nearly 200 orphan girls dispatched from workhouses in twenty-seven Irish counties at the height of the Great Hunger destined to spend the rest of their lives in this remote outpost.[3] After arriving in Sydney on the *Earl Grey* on 6 October 1848, two weeks afterwards the young women were welcomed nearly 600 miles to the north by the local police magistrate, Captain John Wickham, and the majority of Brisbane merchants and tradesmen who would employ the newcomers. Among those from Ulster was Anne Hartley of Dungannon, County Tyrone, who in May 1849 married John Connors, had three children after working for Mr Richardson in North Brisbane for six months.[4] How did this seventeen year old end up over 12,000 miles distant, far from family and friends? She was just one of thousands of Irish female orphans and prisoners who were dispatched to Australia as a result of decisions made by imperial policy-makers in the years between 1848 and 1852.

### IMPERIAL POLICY

Three British Cabinet ministers, in particular, were responsible for devising strategies that brought these people to Australia and eventually to Moreton Bay. They were Earl Grey, Sir George Grey and Sir Charles Trevelyan. While always endeavouring to impose guidelines applicable to all colonial situations throughout the British world, these officers in Lord John Russell's 1846 Whig Government sought solutions to the multiple problems that faced famine-stricken Ireland and the labour-desperate Australian colonies.

Earl Henry Grey at the Colonial Office, as Viscount Howick, had been involved with Australian decisions including the Ripon land regulations and as a member of the Molesworth Enquiry, despite learning of the evils of transportation, encouraged it as the answer to two problems: Britain could rid itself of criminals, and colonies could use their labour. He already had earned seething criticism. 'His acidulous, assertive individualism made him difficult to patronize and earned him the perilous reputation of a young man in a hurry, preoccupied with his own ideas and impatient of opposition.'[5] As a firm advocate of free trade, Grey ignored advice from the House of Commons' Irish members and concurred with Treasury decisions concerning Ireland's export arrangements and the limitation of financial compensation by transferring all impositions to exhausted Irish resources. The resulting neglect, carelessness and laissez-faire policies left a grim legacy.

Sir George Grey of the Home Office, a cousin of the Earl, had extensive, but not always successful, experience with colonial matters during his years as Under Secretary for War and the Colonies during the 1830s.[6] He worked closely with former Irish chief secretary, Charles Grant, later Lord Glenelg, for the emancipation of slaves. From 1846 George Grey was involved with Irish affairs, including relief efforts and the Young Irelander rebellion in 1848. Both issues were reflected in decisions which echoed at Moreton Bay.

Charles Trevelyan was a member of the evangelical Clapham Sect, and a firm believer, 'renowned for his iron integrity, strong principles and unswerving commitment to duty'.[7] From 1840, as Assistant Secretary to the Treasury, his influence was much more extensive than appeared from his title. He was determined to refuse lending or giving money in the certainty that the misery and distress would eventually finish despite the improvident behaviour of the Irish. In this role, he became one of the most reviled names in Ireland. Even among his colleagues, Trevelyan's ultimatums evoked disparaging comments.

> C. Wood [Sir Charles Wood, later Lord Halifax], backed by Grey, and relying upon arguments (or rather Trevelyanisms) that are no more applicable to Ireland than to Loo Choo, affirmed that the right thing to do was to do nothing – they have prevailed and you see what a fix we are in.[8]

In 1846, when Lord John Russell's Government took control in Britain, the Moreton Bay and Darling Downs districts of New South Wales, with a population numbering 2,257, were all that existed of the area later designated the colony of Queensland. The main centre, Brisbane, neglected by Sydney decision-makers, was a convict relic relying heavily on rural produce. The most urgent need was for settlers, particularly labourers, 'muscle and bone', to ensure growth into the ever-widening acres that were being discovered by explorers and defined by surveyors.

### DESPERATE FOR SERVANTS

Emigration to New South Wales and eastern Australia was cancelled from June 1842 and then after a short revival in

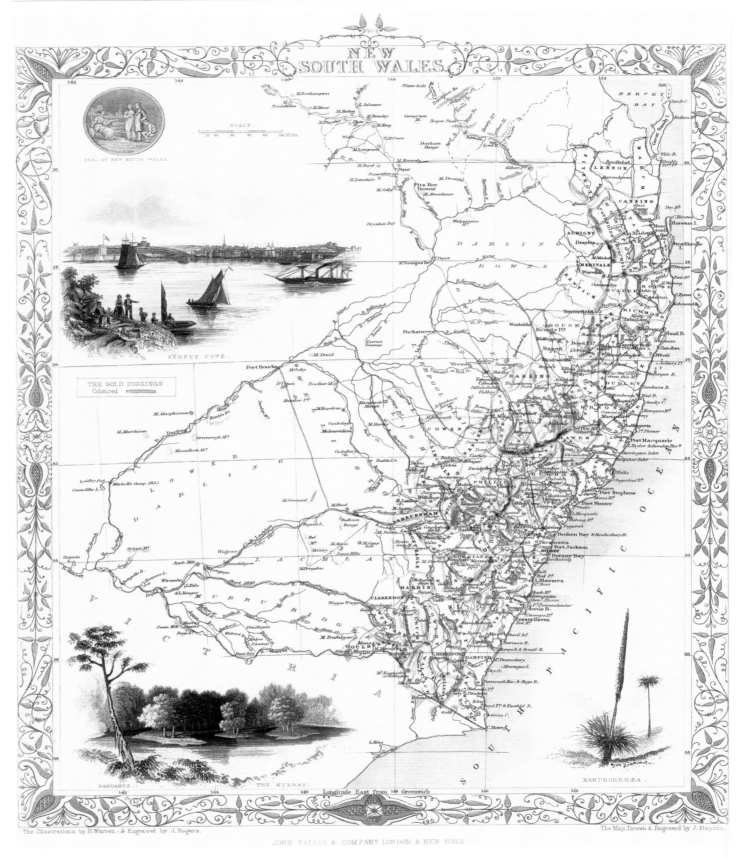

Fig. 1 Tallis map of New South Wales 1855. The colony of Queensland did not separate from New South Wales until 1859 but was the first British colony to be granted responsible government from the outset. By the end of 1852, four years after receiving its first immigrants, 1,051 Irish had arrived as settlers which represented 57% of the growing population. More than of half of these came from Counties Tipperary and Clare. [Source: Mapseeker Archive Publishing]

1844 and just two shiploads in 1845, it was again curtailed until the beginning of 1848. Earl Grey championed Mrs Caroline Chisholm's recommendation urging the resumption of single girls' migration, which had brought thousands during the 1830s.[9] Despite complex problems associated with transferring young women across the world, Grey persisted, knowing that New Zealand and the Cape Colony also were desperate for servants, and he firmly believed that gender imbalance caused many colonial social evils. His insistence on this point produced a modified female emigration between 1848 and 1851, with most unfortunate results to the women themselves and to the state of colonial society.[10]

With the resumption of travel in 1848, the Land and Emigration Commissioners in London handled the determination of immigrant fitness. While the regulations clearly stated that habitual paupers were ineligible to receive fare assistance from colonial funds, home government officials sought their sponsorship to relieve local conditions. Trevelyan, who was well aware of this restriction (his correspondence with Ireland's Chief Secretary specifically mentioned Australian resources) and also conscious of the condemnation of the overwhelming Catholicity of the orphan girls, artfully suggested that Protestants should be chosen initially and that this preselection be concealed from Ireland's Catholic Bishop Murray.[11] New South Wales

Fig. 2 Location map of both Sydney and Moreton Bay.

authorities, who deplored the suspension of migration, were prepared to accept people under almost any conditions leaving the northern areas of the colony completely at the mercy of decisions by southern officers as much as of English ones.

Constant petitioning by Moreton Bay and squatter interests to both Sydney and London authorities finally was rewarded by the arrival of the first immigrant ship despatched directly from London to Moreton Bay. This was the *Artemisia*, which, on 13 December 1848, disembarked 240 welcome settlers, including several children from Lord Shaftesbury's ragged schools. The haste with which these travellers were selected was a desperate attempt by Earl Grey to deflect widespread disapprobation. On 9 August 1850 the *Emigrant* was ushered into quarantine at Stradbroke Island in the bay with its exhausted and debilitated, mainly Irish, passengers, who had survived a serious typhoid outbreak. The arrival at the end of January 1851 of

the third vessel, the *Duchess of Northumberland*, with 172 Irish among 228 passengers, many past the prime of life, only emphasised the lacklustre nature of the attempts by the English triumvirate to populate this emerging territory between 1848 and 1852, when Earl Grey surrendered his office.[12]

### ARRIVAL OF IRISH ORPHANS

Among local problems Brisbane was experiencing a dire lack of housing, which prompted more land sales. Despite appointing an immigration officer, George Watson, on 2 September 1848, a dedicated reception house was not established for another twenty years. Watson's first responsibility was to care for the *Earl Grey* orphans. What were the thoughts of County Down natives, Margaret McDougall and Biddy McGuire, when they arrived at Brisbane Town with its dusty, unmade streets, grassy paddocks and clear, dry October weather? Watson's sympathy for the young girls extended to his later employing a *Thomas Arbuthnot* passenger, Margaret Raymond, from Listowel, Kerry.

Over the next two years almost 200 orphans arrived at Moreton Bay, many of whom had known misery, which exceeded that experienced by the Ulster contingent. Twenty-one of the fifty-eight on the *Thomas Arbuthnot* had originated in County Clare. As early as November 1845, the parish priest of Kilfearagh and Killard, Father Michael Comyn, described local conditions to the Relief Commission in terms that caused great alarm. Locally, the state of emergency persisted for six years.[13] The Poor Law Union of Kilrush included a number of impoverished parishes. One newspaper reported in 1849:

> Kilrush will be celebrated in the history of pauperism. With Clifden, Westport and Skibbereen and other places, it forms one of the battlefields of Ireland . . .[14]

In 1847 when the Poor Law Extension Act was passed, local Kilrush landlord, Colonel Crofton Moore Vandeleur, sought to avoid responsibility for his tenants by combining his holdings. He distributed over 6,000 eviction notices, which culminated in hundreds of demolished cabins with their former occupants condemned to vagrancy. Poor Law Inspector Captain Arthur Kennedy, posted to Kilrush late in 1847, reported: 'Their lamentable state of filth, ignorance, destitution and disease must be seen to be comprehended', especially with all stages of fever quite obvious among those seeking workhouse admission.[15] This sole remaining source of public benefit was now quite inadequate. At a dismally low time in November 1849, the *Limerick Chronicle* reported that Dr Patrick Kennedy (no relation), the Roman Catholic Bishop of Killaloe, had sent Kennedy's eldest daughter, seven-year old Elizabeth, a gift of £10 'to dispose in clothing to the naked'.[16] With her family's help she distributed garments, the event recorded by an *Illustrated London News* journalist who described her as 'filling the place of a saint, and performing the duties of a patriot'.[17]

During the famished forties, the distant station of Moreton Bay, New South Wales, may not have been known to the County Clare residents, the orphan girls, the Kennedy family or the Vandeleurs. Nevertheless, all three were to become quite familiar with the place. Of the *Thomas Arbuth-*

Fig. 3 Kangaroo Point was one of three districts which formed the emerging town of Brisbane during the late 1840s and early 1850s. The orphan girls who arrived on the *Thomas Arbuthnot* including sixteen-year-old Mary Byrnes from Ballynakill, County Galway, Mary Fitzgibbon (fifteen) from Ennis, County Clare and Belfast-born Jane Kirkwood (eighteen), lived, worked and married in these pioneering surrounds. [Source: Henry Scott-Montagu sketchbook, John Oxley Library, State Library of Queensland]

*not* girls, Mary Marrinan had travelled from Milltown Malbay, in the Ennistymon Poor Law Union adjacent to Father Comyn's parish. Others from there, close to Liscannor Bay, were Mary Clune, Mary Foran, Ellen Lydon and Margaret Stack. Another contingent, including Mary Carigge, Mary Connolly, Mary Fitzgibbon, Alice Gavin and Catherine Smith, had been sent from the workhouse in the county town of Ennis. As Sir Arthur Kennedy, the fourth governor of Queensland, the former solicitous Poor Law Inspector arrived in Brisbane in April 1877 where he served until May 1883, often contributing to local Irish relief appeals.[18] His 'saintly patriotic' daughter joined him briefly in August 1881 when her husband, Admiral Clanwilliam, was in charge of the squadron conveying their Royal Highnesses, Princes Edward and George, on their world tour. Coincidentally, also in the colony during the royal visit were Walter and Michael Vandeleur, who had migrated as free settlers. They later were joined by a further four young men from within the extended family.[19] Moreover, one contemporary writer on the redistribution of land in Ireland following the Famine, James Godkin, also had relatives in Queensland.[20]

### CONVICT EXILES

The late 1840s would see the arrival of 3,734 men who were sent to the Australian colonies as convict exiles. Between 1844 and the end of April 1850, fifteen ships brought this category of prisoner to Port Phillip, Geelong, Hobart, Sydney and Moreton Bay. Following strenuous objections about the unpopular revival of convict transportation, the policy was modified so that after serving half their detention time, the detainees were awarded a ticket-of-leave so they arrived as free men. Earl Grey convinced New South Wales officials that as the British Government was responsible for the cost of shipping these men, they should be distributed throughout the colony to relieve labour shortages and, as an extra incentive, gave assurances that a similar number of free emigrants would be sent at Britain's expense. The 'exiles' arrived but not the much-wanted and promised free settlers.

This Earl Grey scheme was yet another which, between 1849 and 1850, had ramifications at Moreton Bay, the destination of two 'exile' ships. Because the earlier penal settlement had been populated by second offenders from Sydney, these were the only two convict ships to ever arrive at Moreton Bay directly from overseas. They were the *Mountstuart Elphinstone* which berthed on 1 November 1849 and the *Bangalore* in April 1850. This decision ensured that 517 ticket-of-leave men were let loose on the small towns of Brisbane and Ipswich, where they celebrated being free and on dry land again by happily patronising local hostelries and generally running amok. Court cases, suspension of freedom, and then employment in the outback pastoral districts followed.

Only one 'exile' ship, the *Havering*, carried Irish prison-

Fig. 4 Margaret Stack, then fourteen years of age, came from Ennistymon in County Clare. Her parents Peter and Bridget were both deceased. She was employed by Mr Charles Windmill of north Brisbane at a wage of £6 to £9 per year but these indentures were later cancelled after she appeared before the Bench for neglecting her work. On 4 September 1852 Margaret married James Smith, a carrier and bullock driver and had twelve children. She died on 21 November 1919. Her sister, Mary, also arrived in Moreton Bay by the *Irene* in 1858. [Photo: Trevor McClaughlin, *Barefoot and Pregnant? Irish Famine Orphans in Australia*, Vol. 2 (Melbourne, Victoria, 2002) p. 120]

ers to Australia. After sailing from Dublin to Sydney where it anchored on 8 November 1849 with 334 men, thirty-six of them were sent to Moreton Bay and the Darling Downs where, within a short time, several like Thomas Grealish, Cornelius Mahony and Patrick Monaghan acquired small plots of land and married into the local population or moved back into western New South Wales. The 'exile' system permitted the clearance of over-populated English and Irish gaols but increasingly modified policies were required to provide punishment in their home countries.

### YOUNG IRELANDER REBELLION

Prime Minister Russell, with decreasing influence in Cabinet, dispiritedly reported in February 1849:

> We have granted, lent, subscribed, worked, visited, clothed the Irish, – millions of money, years of debates, etc etc – the only return is calumny and rebellion. Let us not grant, lend, clothe etc etc any-

more, and see what that will do.[21]

The rebellion to which Russell alluded was that organised by William Smith O'Brien and the Young Irelanders, with which Home Secretary, Sir George Grey, became closely involved. The result of this unsuccessful armed attempt protesting at the British Parliament's ineffectual Irish policies was the transportation of seven revolutionaries to Tasmania.[22] Among them was Kevin Izod O'Doherty (1823–1905), having been found guilty of 'compassing to levy war against Her Majesty the Queen, for the purpose of compelling her by force and constraint to change her measures and counsels'.[23] O'Doherty and fellow rebel, John Martin, joined O'Brien, John Mitchel, Thomas Meagher, Terence McManus and Patrick O'Donohue in Tasmania.

Five years later, O'Doherty returned to London to marry Mary Ann Kelly of Killeen House, near Portumna, County Galway, yet another site of Famine misery. Kelly although only eighteen years of age (the same as many of the twenty-two Galway orphan girls in Moreton Bay), already was renowned as 'Eva of the *Nation*'. In 1860 the family migrated to Brisbane, Queensland. During the next twenty years as a member of the Legislative Assembly, O'Doherty introduced the first Health Act passed in

Queensland, was closely associated with the opening of St Stephen's Cathedral and was appointed a member of the Queensland Legislative Council. He also chaired the first Irish National Convention in Melbourne before travelling back to Ireland for a year where he became an elected member for Meath in the House of Commons. When O'Doherty died in 1905, he had spent more than half his life in Queensland.[24]

In the decade following the Famine the colonies became more economically viable and by underwriting a variety of programmes exerted greater control over the selection of migrants. At Moreton Bay the Irish continued to stream in, taking the total to 5,500 among 30,059 by the time of the 1861 Census. After attaining full responsible government as the colony of Queensland on 10 December 1859 and taking command of its own migration policies, an unprecedented flow increased Irish numbers to 20,384 in a population of 120,104 by 1871 and 37,636 at the turn of the century at the time of federation.[25]

By now traditions were established and the incomers were those who wanted to relocate rather than following precedents set by Famine orphan girls, prisoners and paupers. These had been reluctant and unwilling tools foisted on the emerging settlement by British officials more deter-

404      THE ILLUSTRATED LONDON NEWS.      [Dec. 22, 1849.

MISS KENNEDY DISTRIBUTING CLOTHING AT KILRUSH.

Fig. 5 Miss Kennedy distributing clothing at Kilrush. [Source: *The Illustrated London News*, 22 December 1849]

Fig. 6 *The Mountstuart Elphinstone* was one of two vessels that brought 'exiles', convict workers, to Moreton Bay in November 1849 and carried rebel, Kevin Izod O'Doherty to Sydney before his imprisonment in Tasmania where he joined other Young Irelanders including John Mitchel and William Smith O'Brien. [Source: National Maritime Museum, Greenwich]

mined to solve their own problems. They had used dubious schemes, enforced by assuming all financial obligations to ship the unwanted out of Britain and Ireland. When the costs became too high, they simply reneged on promises. Nevertheless, while some Irish did not achieve the status of which they dreamed in their new land, most did make significant contributions to small outback towns and large coastal ports as well as pastoral and mining districts, on their way to becoming Queenslanders and parenting families. Each of these categories of pioneer, the orphan girls, the Poor Law inspector, the landlord's family, the 'exiles' and the Young Irelander, having survived the drastic physical, economic and social effects of the Famine, tolerated change, loneliness and distance because 'there the road ended'.[26]

SECTION VII
LEGACY

News of the Land League, 1891 by
Howard Helmick, oil on canvas.
[Source: National Gallery of Ireland]

# Land reform in post-Famine Ireland

## Willie Nolan

In what a contemporary reviewer described as 'a truly astounding sentence', the Commissioners of the 1851 Census informed the Lord Lieutenant in their general report:

> In conclusion we feel it will be gratifying to Your Excellency, to find that although the population has been diminished in so remarkable a manner, by famine, disease, and emigration, and has been since decreasing the results of the Irish Census are on the whole satisfactory.[1]

The benefits of the Famine were enumerated by the Commissioners. The surplus mass of the population had been reduced; the system of minute division of land had 'been happily got rid of', and the class of pauper holdings was 'rapidly giving place to the large sized grazing farms, which from time immemorial have produced the cattle exports, the great source of wealth to this country'. Furthermore, the Encumbered Estates Act had 'placed land within the power of a comparatively solvent proprietary class'. They enrolled Sir Charles Trevelyan as an auxiliary, quoting from his *Irish Crisis*:

> Unless we are much deceived, posterity will trace up to that famine the commencement of a salutary revolution in the habits of a Nation long singularly unfortunate; and will acknowledge in this, as in many other occasions, supreme wisdom has produced permanent good out of transient evil.

John O'Donovan who had 'visited and examined ten thousand Irish cabins', many of them we can presume classified as fourth-class houses in the censuses, was not as sanguine as the Census Commissioners or Sir Charles. Writing to his friend Daniel MacCarthy at Bath he confided:

> The theory of Parson Malthus is to my mind most completely demonstrated by the condition of the Irish. The cottier and con-acre population must dwindle into a small number and the most of them must die of want. The gentry will all be broken.[2]

O'Donovan, who from his labours with the Ordnance Survey knew the country better than any living man, was struck by the silence which pervaded Ireland. Advising his expatriate friend not to return, he described the desolation:

> Do not think of coming here to view our wretched cabins, and our ghastly visages, and famine-stricken bodies. You will see nothing to cheer or please you; not a song is heard from the ploughman or a whistle from the ass driver; but solemn and awful stillness reigns which seems to forebode some dreadful reaction and frightful commotion.[3]

The voices of the two great nationalist political groups, the Loyal National Repeal Association and the Young Ireland/Irish Confederation, its seceding wing, were also stilled. It was claimed that on 15 August 1843, a short few years before the deadly blight was borne on the wind to Ireland, one million people had attended the monster meeting at Tara Hill to listen to the Liberator tell them he would bring them to the promised land by breaking the accursed Act of Union. But by 1851 the Liberator and his party were silenced forever. Conciliation Hall, Ireland's surrogate parliament, was closed and empty; its great library sold by auction. The military Rising of the Young Irelanders on 29 July 1848 was ridiculed alike by friend and foe. Some of its leaders, who had inaugurated and directed the most extraordinary crusade of national reconstruction through *The Nation* newspaper, were transported for high treason to Van Diemen's Land; others escaped across the Atlantic.[4]

The political exiles had plenty of company in the 1850s. 'In round numbers,' wrote the reviewer in the *Irish Quarterly Review*, 'out of a total ascertained emigration from Ireland during the period 1851 to 1855 of 2,000,000, fully 1,100,000 went to a foreign country and only the remainder to our own colonies.'[5] The reviewer was certain that the 'stern compulsion of exile in a famine driven emigration' had and would result in 'a deadly aversion and hostility to England and all belonging to her'. It was a prescient comment. Both the nature and scale of the contribution of Famine emigrants and their descendants to their new homes have been amply documented. But they never forgot the people at home. It is estimated that emigrant's remittances increased from £460,000 in 1848 to £7,404,000 in 1852, and they contributed to household income in areas of heavy outmigration well into the twentieth century.[6]

### THE LAND QUESTION

One voice, though silenced by premature death in 1849, was to resonate through the half century after the Famine. James Fintan Lalor, the delicate, hunchbacked, son of a middleman farmer from County Laois, and descendant of the chieftains of the Lalor sept, who had been dispossessed in earlier confiscations, believed that the Famine had terminated the social contract between landlord and tenant. In his celebrated letter to the editor of the *Irish Felon* in July 1848 he stated it clearly:

> The principle I state, and mean to stand upon, is this, that the entire ownership of Ireland, moral and material, up to the sun, and down to the centre, is vested of right in the people of Ireland; that they and none but they, are the land-owners and law-makers of this island; that all laws are null and void not made by them; and all titles to land invalid not conferred and confirmed by them; and that this full right of ownership may and ought to be asserted and enforced by any and all means which God has put in the power of man.[7]

But the government's guiding principle, through the Famine years and the long decades which followed, was to resist any changes to the land settlement on which both its claim to Ireland and the country's parliamentary representation resided. As late as November 1880 this credo was expressed in the words – 'no amount of agitation will ever induce England to give way to pretensions which are inconsistent with the welfare of the realm'.[8] Even when the landed gentry were found guilty by many of failing the realm during the crisis of subsistence, the government's first reaction was to strengthen the establishment by luring new money from mainland Britain into old bankrupt estates. A number of Encumbered Estates Acts were introduced during the parliamentary sessions of 1848 and 1849, which enabled creditors to petition for the sale of estates. From 1849 to 1855 about 2,500,000 acres of land were purchased under the provisions of the Act.[9] The Encumbered Estates Act made no new arrangements for tenant farmers and many of the purchasers, who were mainly local speculators, were determined to make a return on their investments by focusing on sheep and dry cattle.

The politicisation of the land question had its origins in the autumn of 1849 when a tenant's protection society, with the objective of forcing down rents by combination against the landlord, was formed in Callan, County Kilkenny, under the leadership of Fathers O'Shea and O'Keeffe. James Fintan Lalor and the Repeal Association had separately attempted but failed in efforts to establish similar organisations in late 1847. When the Callan initiative was repeated it seemed to political activists, such as Charles Gavan Duffy and Frederick Lucas, that the basis for a new political grouping presented itself and the Tenant League was founded in August 1850.[10] Its objectives were to obtain fixity of tenure, lower rents and legal protection for the Ulster custom through an independent opposition at Westminster.

But the new party became enmeshed in political controversies, which had little to do with the land question, and folded in 1859. Evictions persisted as landlords extended demesnes and large graziers removed the communities of the clachans to either estate boundaries or cabin suburbs in towns. William Sharman Crawford, a County Down landlord but an indefatigable proponent of land reform, was utterly opposed to such a policy:

> In place of adequate security for tenants, I fear that the exterminating and consolidating system is largely operating. It is the fashionable doctrine to call this improvement; but the extermination of human beings and the substitution of brute animals for the human race on the soil of Ireland, is not an improvement grateful to my mind.[11]

Advocates of land reform publicised clearances as evidence of the capriciousness and greed of individual landlords, un-restrained by any legal code. When Thomas Plunket, the Church of Ireland archbishop of Tuam, evicted tenants on his estate in the remote Partry Mountains, County Mayo, in 1860, it offered a splendid opportunity for Fr Patrick Lavelle, an able advocate of land reform, to come to the defence of beleaguered tenant victims of a rapacious landlord, who happened to be a Protestant bishop.[12] In the following year John George Adair, originally from Queen's County, cleared his estate at Derryveagh, County Donegal, to create a sheep farm, highlighting the absolute power of owners.[13] One of the more celebrated cases was the attempt by William Scully, son of Denys Scully, Daniel O'Connell's great ally in the quest for Catholic Emancipation, to evict tenants in August 1868 from lands he had purchased at Ballycohey near Tipperary Town.[14] In the affray which followed a police constable and Scully's land steward were shot dead and Scully, though reputedly wearing body armour, was wounded. Such violence was anathema to a resurgent Catholic establishment, who feared that the release of dormant passions on the land issue could derail its post-Famine reconstruction project, scrupulously confined to constitutional politics under the leadership of Archbishop Paul Cullen.[15] The Catholic Church gave its support to the National Association, very much a carbon copy of O'Connell's Repeal Association, founded in 1864. Its policies were focused, not on land reform but on the disestablishment of the Church of Ireland and the vexed question of denominational education.

The political philosophy of the Irish Republican Brotherhood, founded in 1858, borrowed more from militant Young Irelanders, such as John Mitchel and James Fintan Lalor rather than papal encyclicals, but it did not have a specific land policy. It believed that it was only after political independence from Britain was secured that the land question could be tackled. But the pages of the *Irish People*, the Fenian paper, had an enormous influence on public opinion as its master propagandists, such as Charles Kickham, projected an image of a rural arcadia being dismembered by ruthless capitalist graziers.[16] The IRB, with help from Irish America, attempted an uprising in March 1867, but it was quickly suppressed. Yet the shadow of the gunman was a powerful if unacknowledged driver of land reform in Ireland.

### BEGINNINGS OF TENANT PURCHASE SCHEMES

The Disestablishment Act of 1869 was not a land purchase act, but it contained limited provision for tenant purchase of church or 'bishops' land and, significantly, it was the first time that state funds were advanced to enable occupying tenants to become owners in fee.[17] Each holding was sold for cash, but tenants could secure farms on payment of one-fourth of the purchase price and the balance could then be secured on a mortgage of the holding to be paid off in thirty-two years by sixty-four half-yearly instalments. Some 6,957 occupiers became owners of 34,924 statute acres under the Act. William Gladstone's first Land Act which followed in 1870 provided compensation for both disturbance and improvements and it legalised but did not define what was

Fig. 1 *Portrait of Charles Stewart Parnell in 1892* by Sydney Prior Hall. The establishment of the Irish National Land League (1879) with Parnell as president and Michael Davitt as one of its secretaries, marked the beginning of an extraordinary campaign to shape Ireland from below. [Source: National Gallery of Ireland]

known as the 'Ulster Custom'. The land purchase provisions of this Act were so restrictive that only 800 tenants availed of them. Because the Act, in recognising that tenants had an interest in the land, hinted at the concept of dual ownership, it is seen as an important stage in the transition to eventual 'peasant proprietorship'.

James Fintan Lalor had presumed that there were 8,000 estates in Ireland but until 1876 there was no inventory of landed property. The *London Times* was so impressed by the returns that it published a map showing, by county, the number of landowners and the identity of the major landowners.[18] The published returns were subsequently analysed by Tom Jones Hughes, who in a stimulating paper identified 'the powerful territorial preferences of "English landlordism"' in Ireland.[19] Jones Hughes, using valuation rather than acreage as his measure, identified 4,000 estates with total valuations of £500 and over in 1876. Ireland, he concluded, was a country dominated by relatively small estates and only thirty-three of the estates valued at £5,000 and over could be described 'as truly great estates, each valued at over £20,000'.

The conjunction of a series of bad harvests and competition from America on the British market reduced both the volume and return from agricultural produce in Ireland during the 1870s. The crisis was especially bad in the western small farm fringe, which produced young cattle for the midland graziers.[20] Michael Davitt, son of an evicted Mayo emigrant, released on a ticket-of-leave from over seven years imprisonment at Millbank and Dartmoor for Fenian activities, was the new champion of the hillside men. More surprising was the fact that his future ally would be Charles Stewart Parnell, heir to the Avondale estate in county Wicklow. Davitt was present at the inaugural meeting of the Land League of Mayo held at Irishtown near Claremorris on 20 April 1879 where he advocated 'the land for the people'. He went far beyond the demands for the three F's – free sale, fixity of tenure and fair rents – to reiterate James Fintan Lalor's call for the establishment of a 'peasant proprietary'. At Westport on 19 September 1879, Parnell commanded them 'to hold a firm grip of your homesteads' in defiance of rack-renting landlords.[21] The establishment of the Irish National Land League on 21 October 1879, with Parnell as president and Davitt as one of its three secretaries, heralded the beginning of an extraordinary campaign to shape Ireland from below. Davitt later claimed that by 1881 the Land League had 1,000 branches and 200,000 members. It brought together remnants of the Fenian militants and the constitutional Home Rulers in what has become known as the 'New Departure'.

Parnell's advocacy of social ostracism for tenants who occupied lands from which previous occupiers were evicted was the most dramatic weapon of the new organisation. His celebrated boycott speech was delivered at Ennis, County Clare, on 19 September 1880 to a cheering crowd

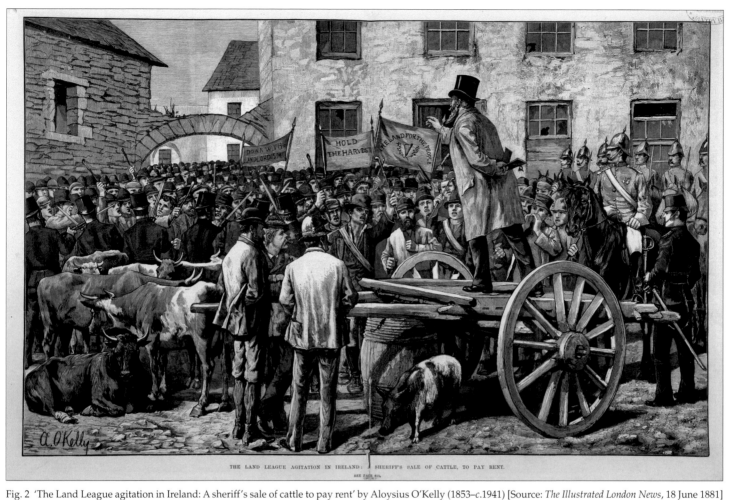

Fig. 2 'The Land League agitation in Ireland: A sheriff's sale of cattle to pay rent' by Aloysius O'Kelly (1853–c.1941) [Source: *The Illustrated London News*, 18 June 1881]

who illuminated the event with burning turf sods held aloft on pitchforks:

> When a man takes a farm from which another has been evicted you must shun him on the roadside when you meet him, you must shun him in the streets of the town, you must shun him at the shop-counter, you must shun him at the fair and at the market place and even in the house of worship by leaving him severely alone, by putting him into a sort of moral Coventry, by isolating him from the rest of his kind, as if he were a leper of old.[22]

The Land League had a splendid propaganda victory in what appears to have been a carefully targeted test case for the new policy. Captain Charles Cunningham Boycott was agent to the County Mayo fragment of the 3rd Earl of Erne's estate.[23] The greater part of the Erne estate was located adjacent to the splendid family seat at Crom Castle near Newtownbutler, County Fermanagh. The Mayo fragment consisted of 2,184 acres of the total property of 40,365 statute acres. Boycott resided at Lough Mask House and farmed its 300 acres of relatively good land near the village of The Neale in south Mayo. Because of the conjunction of wet weather and poor prices in late 1880, Erne's Mayo ten-

ants asked for a 25% reduction in their rents but the earl would only allow 10%. Boycott issued ejectment processes, but the constabulary were unable to ensure the safety of the process server, and when Boycott's domestic household staff and his agricultural workforce withdrew, the captain and his family were isolated. The *Daily Express* and *Daily Telegraph* organised a fund to finance an expedition to save Boycott's crops and a group of fifty sympathisers, drawn from the counties of Monaghan and Cavan and led by Captain Somerset Maxwell (Farnham), came to Boycott's assistance, taking up residence in tented villages on the demesne. Over 1,000 troops and police had to be deployed to protect the Boycott Relief Expedition and the Government, in Parnell's words, paid 'one shilling for every turnip dug from Boycott's land'. On 13 December 1880 the *Daily Mail* headlined its account of what had transpired in Mayo with the single word 'Boycott'.

Persistent agitation led to the setting up of a Royal Commission under the chairmanship of the Earl of Bessborough, whose recommendations became the basis for the Land Act of 1881.[24] This Act by establishing the principle of dual ownership revolutionised the relations of landlords and tenants in Ireland. The fair rent provision, by which rents were fixed by the newly constituted Irish Land Commission, was of great importance and the rents thus fixed

Fig. 3 Organised resistance to eviction increased during the Plan of Campaign. This illustration from *United Ireland*, 30 October 1886, depicts the defence of Hurley's Mill at Castleview near Clonakilty, County Cork where the tenant Tim Hurley lived with his wife and five children. The arrival of the sheriff and bailiffs resulted in a violent altercation eventually forcing the evicting party to withdraw. Hurley, along with six other men, was arrested several days later. [Source: National Library of Ireland]

became the basis for purchase annuities under the provision of later acts. The land purchase arrangements were improved with tenants enabled to borrow three-quarters of the purchase price as compared to two-thirds in 1870. But there was little enthusiasm to take up this offer – only 731 tenants purchased holdings – reflecting both the depressed state of agriculture and the attractiveness for the time being of the rent reductions. The Land Commission, though its remit changed through the years, became one of the great shaping institutions of twentieth-century Ireland.

The Land Act of 1881 although offering significant concessions did not mollify the Land League. Agitation persisted to qualify tenants in arrears for the provisions of the Act. Its leaders were imprisoned under a variety of coercion acts and the No-Rent Manifesto urging a rent strike was issued by Parnell from Kilmainham Jail on 18 October. Almost immediately the Land League was suppressed. As Joseph Lee has argued, the No Rent Manifesto failed because the tenants in good standing with their landlords enthusiastically accepted rent reductions, whereas those in arrears – calculated by Lee as one-third of tenants throughout the country and nearly two-thirds in Mayo – could not, thereby

dividing the tenant body into two groups.[25] Agrarian outrages increased, compelling Gladstone to enlist Parnell's help in calming rural Ireland. The subsequent Kilmainham Treaty gave assurances that coercion would be dropped and the arrears of rent wiped out, so that the ineligible tenants could take advantage of the 1881 legislation under the Arrears Act of 1882. Class divisions based on farm size meant that Davitt's utopian nationalisation of land and its redistribution in equal measures would never be countenanced. Even rundale agriculture, the most 'Irish' of landholding systems, was a mixture of individual plots in the arable section with joint, not communal, use of the commonages.

The Ashbourne Act in 1885 advanced the full purchase price for tenants and the repayment period was extended to forty-nine years with the annuity calculated at 4% per annum. A subscribing tenant would therefore not have to pay more by way of terminable annuity than what he was already liable for as a perpetual rent. The Act was oversubscribed, but it did not solve the problem. The uncertain political climate in England with the Tories and Liberals, sometimes with the support of Parnell's party, alternating in power and with the land question enmeshed in the constitutional issue of Home Rule meant that there was no clarity of purpose. In 1886 the extraordinary Plan of Campaign, prompted by another periodic agricultural crisis brought about by falling prices and bad harvests, was initiated.[26] In an unparalleled communal effort some one hundred landed estates were targeted; landlords were offered 'fair' rents by local management committees and when they refused, these rents were retained by the committee. The rents were then used to support evicted tenants and construct what became known as Land League huts to house them. An unusual consequence of the Plan of Campaign was the building of the 'new' town of Tipperary in 1890 to house tenants evicted by A.H. Smith-Barry of Fota House, County Cork, from the old town.[27]

The Land League mounted a major propaganda campaign by focusing on the estates of politically active landlords, such as Lansdowne (Queen's County) and Smith-Barry (Tipperary town). The Perpetual Crimes Act (or Irish Coercion Act) introduced by Balfour in 1887 to break the power of the League was widely used, but state violence, such as at Mitchelstown, where the police fired into a crowd, killing three people, gained martyrs and sympathy for the Land League. Photography enabled images of eviction scenes (such as at Clongorey, County Kildare, and Kilrush, County Clare) to be publicised at home and abroad and the United Ireland newspaper founded by Parnell and edited by William O'Brien, the politician and journalist, became more popular than *The Nation*.[28] With such a well-oiled propaganda machine it was no surprise that the battering ram became an enduring symbol of landlordism.

Under the terms of the Purchase of Land (Ireland) Act, 1891, landlords were to be paid in guaranteed Land Stock, equal in nominal amount to the purchase money. The repayment terms were the same as in the 1885 Act. All Land Acts up to now had focused on relationships between landlord and tenant, but the 1891 Land Act gave special prominence to the problems of the western counties by instituting the

Fig. 4 Thomas Bermingham's house, Moyasta, County Clare with battering ram and soldiers outside. One of the estates where the Plan of Campaign was put into effect was on the Vandeleur estate in Moyasta, County Clare. The reduction in farm prices caused by an agricultural depression in the 1880s had forced the tenants to seek a reduction in rents. The landlord, Captain Hector S. Vandeleur, refused and subsequently served eviction orders on those tenants withholding rents. Thomas Birmingham was evicted on 31 July 1888. Such forced evictions received widespread coverage in the Irish and British press, with the battering ram becoming the symbol of landlord oppression. [Source: National Library of Ireland]

Fig. 5 'Houses not burnt on account of the corn, Clongorey, County Kildare'. The Plan of Campaign was also adopted by tenants in Clongorey, three miles north of Newbridge in County Kildare. Despite the poor quality of the land, principally cutaway bog, the tenants were generally able to produce sufficient potatoes and cut enough turf to pay their rents when they were due. However, events could intervene. In this case the attempt to negotiate a fair rent failed. There were a series of evictions in Clongorey between 1883 and 1892 with many of the tenants' houses burned in the process. The houses shown in the above photograph avoided such a fate. [Source: National Library of Ireland]

Congested Districts Board (CDB) under Part Two of the legislation. Instead of promoting emigration to the colonies as the panacea for Ireland, the CDB attempted to ameliorate the persistent disequilibrium between population and resources by rearranging the local distribution of land and people. The tenant rather than the landlord was its central concern. Now regarded as an early model for sustainable development, the area under the CDB remit was extended in 1910 to over 7,658,292 statute acres or over a third of Ireland.[29] The Board engaged in major infrastructural improvements along the western seaboard and encouraged the establishment of industries based on local raw materials and introduced new breeding stock across the whole range of livestock and fowl. Convinced, as all improvers were, that rundale agriculture was an impediment to improvement, the Board was determined to eradicate it.

New individual houses in splendid isolation replaced the old nucleated settlements with their emphasis on communal space and joint farming. The open landscapes of the west coast were transformed through striping into single farms, which ran in spectacular fashion from sea level to mountain. Between 1891 and 1919 the CDB built a total of 13,216 houses, usually tall, two-storey structures with distinctive lozenge shaped tiles. During its lifetime the CDB reorganised the internal structure of individual townlands through the consolidation of fragmented holdings and carved out new farms in grazing lands, which in some instances had been created through clearances during the Famine. In all, the CDB redistributed some two million acres encompassing over 1,000 estates. Its programmes were badly disrupted by the First World War and then by the War of Independence and Civil War. The CDB was dissolved under the terms of the 1923 Land Act, the first such act passed by a native government.

It may have seemed with Parnell's premature death on 6 October 1891 that land reform had lost one of its most formidable champions. Yet it was inexorably moving to the ultimate conclusion of James Fintan Lalor's peasant proprietorship. In 1898 William O'Brien founded the United Irish League (UIL) at Westport, County Mayo. Just like its precursor organisation, the Land League (founded in 1879), the UIL was a response to the recurring crises in the congested districts. The League, presided over by Michael Davitt, spread rapidly beyond Connacht and by 1900 was claiming 462 branches. Its philosophy was pure Land League fundamentalism encapsulated in the slogan 'The land for the people'. Dismayed at the slow progress of the CDB it called for a massive programme of land redistribution. But once again an organisation focused on land reform was subsumed into a political party and the UIL became the constituency organisation of the Irish Party.

Legislation enacted since 1870 in respect of land had been confined to changes in the conditions of tenure with limited reference to ownership. Sales of land were carried out by holdings. However, Wyndham's Land Act of 1903 introduced the revolutionary system of sales by estate. Landlords could sell directly to tenants or the Land Commission could purchase estates, provided that at least three-fourths of the tenants in number and rateable valuation were committed to purchase their holdings from the Commission. Landlords could also sell their demesnes and untenanted lands to the Commission and then re-purchase them back as tenant purchasers. In effect, the landlord had now the status of a tenant farmer, subject, like their former tenants, to paying annuities to the state. It is noteworthy that the 1903 Act was recommended for acceptance to the Irish Landowner's convention by The O'Conor Don, who claimed descent from the last high king in the twelfth century:

They [the landlords] will submit to it with diminished incomes, with the loss of that ownership, the desire to possess which seems to be imbued in every human breast, but with the hope that the change may lead to the pacification of their country and the cessation of that social strife and war of classes which has done so much mischief in the past, and which would be perpetuated and intensified by the loss of this Bill, and by the continuance of the present exasperating system of land tenure, a parallel for which cannot be found in any civilised country in Europe.[30]

A new body, the Estates Commissioners, was instituted to carry out the provisions of the 1903 Act. Apart from its focus on estates, the Commissioners could acquire untenanted land – usually consisting of the grazing farms despised by agrarian activists – and allocate it as auxiliary land to existing smallholdings or to former evicted tenants or their representatives. A separate Evicted Tenant's Act was passed in 1907 to deal specifically with this category of claimants. In order to encourage landlords to sell, a 12% bonus on all sales was to be paid. Tenant's annuities were more favourable than in previous Acts at 3.25% per annum payable over 68½ years

With such a great slice of occupied land now settled, the state turned to the untenanted land that existed as demesne parklands associated with the great houses or was used as non-residential grazing farms. A parliamentary enquiry in 1906 calculated that some 2.6 million acres could be defined as untenanted. Although the 1909 Land Act introduced compulsory acquisition for the relief of congestion in the CDB districts, it was not until the Irish Free State was established in 1922 that the untenanted lands, neatly identified in the 1906 report, were targeted for division. The 1923 Land Act provided for the compulsory acquisition of surviving landlord estates and transferred almost four million acres to 127,000 tenants in the Free State. By 1925, in Northern Ireland 805,000 acres were transferred to 38,500 tenants under similar legislation. With the wars over and Ireland partitioned, the 1923 Land Act effectively terminated landlordism in the Free State. It abolished the concept of

Fig. 6 *The United Ireland* newspaper was founded by Parnell and edited by William O'Brien. It became an integral part of the propaganda campaign waged against landlordism in Ireland. [Source: Cork Archives Institute]

**Table 1.** Tenant Purchasers under Parliamentary Acts 1869–1923

| Legislation | Number of Tenant Purchasers | Observations |
|---|---|---|
| Irish Church Act 1869 | 6,057 | |
| Landlord and Tenant (Ireland) Act 1870 | 877 | |
| Land Act (Ireland) 1881 | 731 | Irish Land Commission established |
| Purchase of Land (Ireland) Act 1885 | 25,368 | Commonly known as Ashbourne Act |
| Land Act (Ireland) 1891 | 36,994 | Congested Districts Board established |
| Land Act (Ireland) 1903 | 252,000 | Commonly known as the Wyndham Act - 8,220,000 acres transferred |
| Land Act (Ireland) 1909 | 66,500 | 2,413,000 acres transferred |
| Land Act 1923 (Saorstát Eireann) | 127,000 | 4,000,000 acres transferred |
| Land Act 1925 (Northern Ireland) | 38,500 | 805,000 acres transferred |

dual ownership and introduced compulsory purchase powers for both tenanted and untenanted lands. These compulsory purchase powers were later extended to land already vested under earlier acts.

The landlord system was not without its champions. In his poem 'Upon a House Shaken by the Land Agitation',[31] William Butler Yeats lamented that the possible dismemberment of the demesne and Big House of Coole Park, County Galway, and its replacement by smallholdings, would signal the destruction of a high civilisation that had nurtured the arts and all that was civil and civic in society:

> How should the world be luckier if this house,
> Where passion and precision have been one
> Time out of mind, became too ruinous
> To breed the lidless eye that loves the sun?
> And the sweet laughing eagle thoughts that grow

Where wings have memory of wings, and all
That comes of the best knit to the best? Although
Mean roof-trees were the sturdier for its fall,
How should their luck run high enough to reach?
The gifts that govern men, and after these
To gradual Time's last gift, a written speech
Wrought of high laughter, loveliness and ease?

It was ironic that many would have held Sir William Gregory, the late proprietor of the Coole Park estate and husband of Lady Gregory, responsible for much greater dismemberment by introducing a clause in the Labouring Poor (Ireland) Bill 1847 of the provision that persons in possession of more than a quarter acre of land should not be entitled to Poor Law relief.

But if the Big House symbolised excellence for Yeats, it was for others a symbol of dispossession, conspicuous waste and political servitude. Fr Timothy Corcoran, the reputed author of the Tipperary ballad 'Carden's Wild Domain', captured the alternative:

> It grieves me sore to see this land oppressed by tyrant's laws,
> To strike a blow for this fair land would be in righteous cause,
> To see our sons and daughters fair compelled to cross the main
> And leaving such a land behind as Carden's Wild Domain.
> So raise you men around Barnane and hasten to the fray,
> And join the noble general McSweeney from Killea,
> Led on by this great mountaineer, these lands we will regain,
> We'll plant our homesteads once again on Carden's Wild Domain.[32]

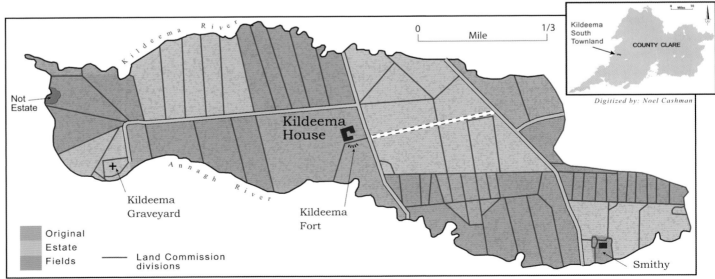

Fig. 7 NEW FIELDS CREATED IN FORMER GRAZING FARM OF LORD LECONFIELD IN TOWNLAND OF KILDEEMA SOUTH, KILFARBOY PARISH, COUNTY CLARE UNDER THE PROVISIONS OF THE WYNDHAM LAND ACT OF 1903. [Source: Land Commission Records relating to Lord Leconfield's Estate now in National Archives, Dublin]

## CONCLUSION

In many respects the insensitive commentary of the Commissioners of the 1851 Census and James Fintan Lalor's vision had both been realised by the early twentieth century. Demographic change had continued apace since the haemorrhage of people associated with the Famine years. By 1901 some two million people born in Ireland were resident overseas. Marriage rates had declined and the replacement of multiple by single inheritance produced its own dynamic or, in many cases, stasis. Cattle and sheep, as the Census Commissioner's had predicted in 1851, were numerically dominant and the decline of arable farming was amply demonstrated in the comparable acreages under wheat and oats for 1851 and 1901. There was also a new dynamic in local government inaugurated by the Local Government Act of 1898, which, along with the extension of the franchise under the Reform Act 1894, further eroded landlord influence. As landlordism waned a revived and robust Catholic Church established an unparalleled network of influence and control. In the hundred years after Emancipation, twenty-four cathedrals or pro-cathedrals and over 3,000 substantial churches were erected giving form and function to towns and villages.[33]

The landlord estate, however inadequate, had been a kind of collective economic and social unit. Ownership had been transferred by the state, an outcome that could not have been foreseen by James Fintan Lalor. Land reform had been primarily redistributive, aimed more at equity and social justice than with increasing productivity. Extensive agriculture persisted in the new farms and fields, and, apart from the co-operative societies in the dairy districts, there was little change in a structural sense. One class which did not benefit was the agricultural labourer, described in the Bessborough Commission as 'a farmer without land'. By default therefore the Land Acts had widened the divide between farmer and labourer. The focus in the half century after the Famine on land reform also ensured that the decline and decay in the tenement sectors of Irish cities continued unabated. But possession of the country had been regained and even the Great Famine could be consigned to history.

Fig. 8 Borris House is the residence of the Mcmorrough Kavanagh's, one of the few old Gaelic aristocratic families in Ireland who still live on their ancestral lands. Originally – as shown on the Down Survey map – an important castle guarding the River Barrow, Borris House was rebuilt in 1731 by Bryan Kavanagh and further modified and enlarged on the marriage of his son to Lady Suzanne Butler. In the 1820s, the distinguished father and son architectural team of Richard and William Morrison 'clothed Borris House in a thin gothic dress and concealed the roof behind a tall, crenallated parapet' [*Carlow: History and Society*, ed, Thomas McGrath (Dublin, 2008), p. 744]. Set in over 650 acres of a walled demesne, Borris House retains its place as the centre of the carefully nurtured estate town of Borris. Through the centuries, the Mcmorrough Kavanaghs sustained their reputations as 'benevolent and kind' landlords. However, in the later Land Acts most of the former 16,000-acre estate was divided amongst a tenantry still bearing mainly Gaelic names. During the Famine, Borris town lost 24% of its population – declining from a population of 950 to 720 – and the losses were particularly noticeable amongst its middle-classes. The number of its second-class houses declined by 27% °– from 112 to 88 – while the families engaged in 'the direction of labour' declined from 101 to 39. The surrounding parish of Clonagoose lost 17.5% of its population in the Famine decade, declining from 1,706 to 1,408 but here the big losses -- from 109 to 39 (-64%) - were amongst the families with fourth-class houses. [Photo: William J. Smyth]

# Legacy and loss: the Great Silence and its aftermath

## *Máiréad Nic Craith*

The Famine is often euphemistically called 'The Great Silence', thereby re-affirming the common perception that this event was primarily responsible for the decline of Irish in Ireland. While it is true that the catastrophe had a severe, irreversible impact on the speaking of Irish, it must also be recognised that the language was already in decline by the time the potato blight occurred in 1845. As Seán de Fréine notes: '[c]innte, bhí tionchar ag an Ghorta ar an Ghaeilge. Ach ní féidir a mhaíomh ar an ábhar sin gurbh é bunchúis caillte na teanga é. Bíonn difríocht idir uirlis agus cúis. Maidir le cúlú na Gaeilge de, ní raibh sa Ghorta ach ceann de na huirlisí.'[1]

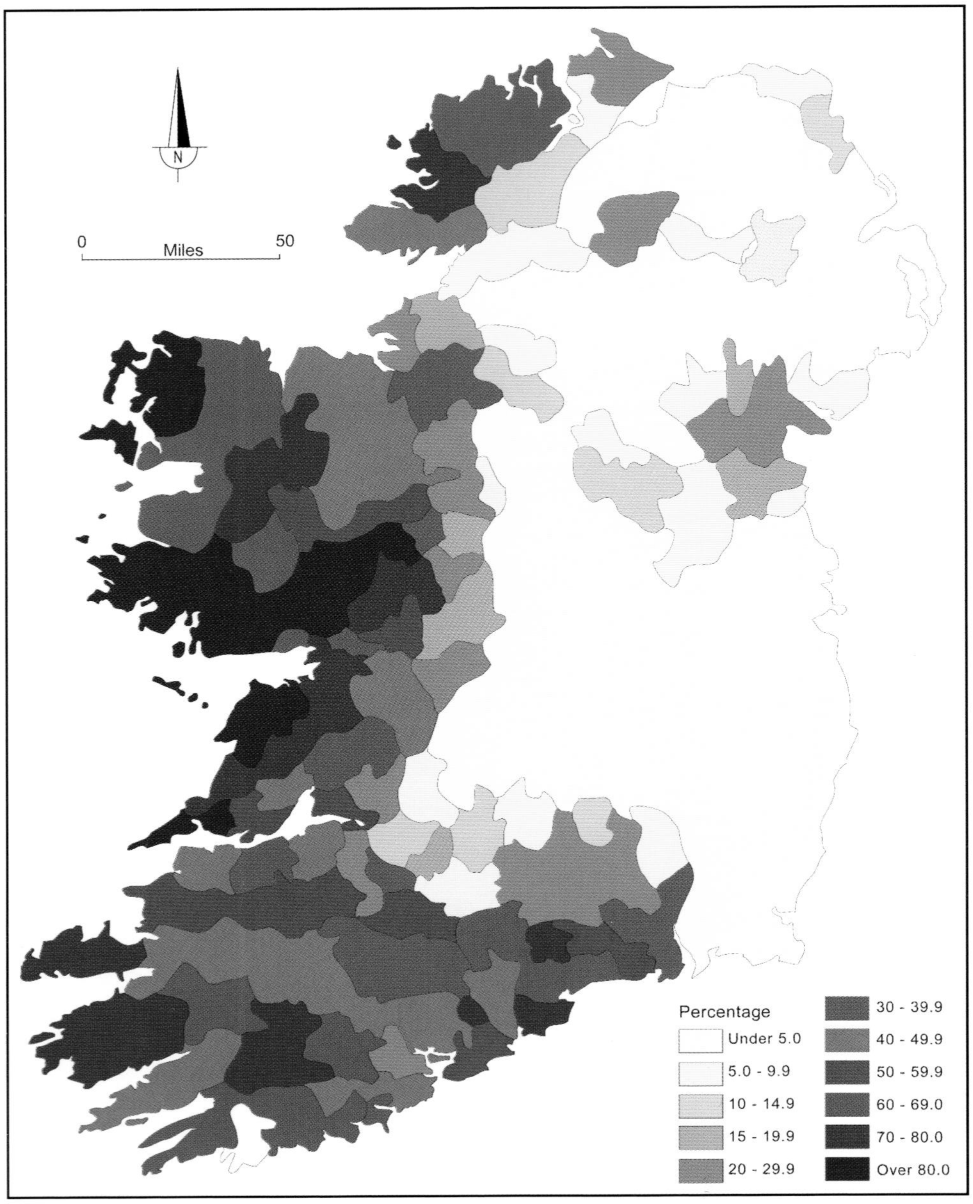

A number of factors had already influenced the process of Anglicisation in Ireland. This chapter will briefly highlight some key factors responsible for the shift from Irish to English at the beginning of the nineteenth century. Using statistics, it will also examine minimum levels of Irish-speaking at the time of the Famine as outlined in the Census of 1851, but the substance of the chapter will focus on the implications of the loss of a native tongue for a national psyche.

## PROCESS OF ANGLICISATION

One of the more significant tools in the spread of English was the 'national' system of education, established in Ireland in 1831. This British model of education offered skills in literacy and numeracy entirely through the medium of English even where children were largely speakers of Irish. Many national school inspectors' reports throughout the country lamented the problems encountered by the use of English as a medium of instruction in Irish-speaking areas.[2] Parents colluded with the teachers in persuading their children to acquire English at the expense of Irish. Continuing to speak the native language was regarded as

Fig. 1 THE DECLINE OF THE IRISH LANGUAGE AT BARONY SCALE BY 1851. The erosion in the distribution of Irish-speakers had begun much earlier than the Famine decade. Already in the early seventeenth century, an unequal relationship had begun between an imperial, urbanising, print-based and aggressively expansive English culture and language, and an Irish language and culture that was more rural-based, more oral/aural in style and far more manuscript dependent. By the mid-eighteenth century, English speechways and levels of literacy had expanded strongly over much of Ulster and mid- and south Leinster. Salients of English speech were also advancing across the Shannon and more particularly into north Munster and along an axis extending from north Kilkenny into Waterford city. Even by then Connacht and Munster (and County Donegal) remained the great bulwarks of Irish speech and traditional ways of living. As populations increased disproportionately in these two provinces from the late eighteenth century onwards this pattern of Irish speech is sustained even up to 1851 as shown on the barony map. Significant pockets of Irish speech also survived in the Glens of Antrim, mid-Tyrone and the Leinster/Ulster borderlands.

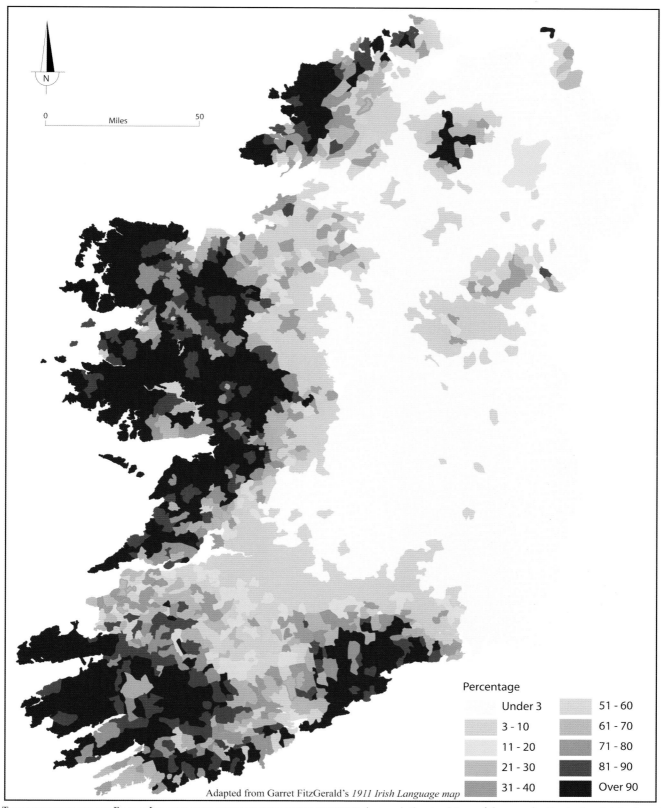

Percentage

| | |
|---|---|
| Under 3 | 51 - 60 |
| 3 - 10 | 61 - 70 |
| 11 - 20 | 71 - 80 |
| 21 - 30 | 81 - 90 |
| 31 - 40 | Over 90 |

Adapted from Garret FitzGerald's *1911 Irish Language map*

Fig. 2 THE DISTRIBUTION OF PRE-FAMINE IRISH-SPEAKERS BY DISTRICT ELECTORAL DIVISIONS. A more intimate picture of the complexities in the distribution of English and Irish is illustrated here. This map, based on Garret FitzGerald's in-depth analysis of the returns of the 1911 census, demonstrates the intricate pathways along which English expanded and Irish retreated at the DED level of resolution. Critical vectors in the expansion of English included the developing road and canal network, the expansion of pedlar-networks selling inexpensive English books (chapbooks), the expansion of a more commercial economy especially in those parishes in the hinterlands of major cities including Derry, Limerick and Waterford. This map also highlights the retreat of Irish and the advance of English between Limerick and Waterford cities and particularly between the cities of Limerick and Cork. The grey areas on the map demonstrate decisively the dominance of English throughout two-thirds of the island by 1841. But the Famine itself was to deal a devastating blow to the Irish language. Many poor monoglot Irish speakers died in the west and the south, and many others scrambled to escape to the New World. Kirby Miller has estimated that close on half of the Munster and Connacht emigrants to America were Irish speakers. [See also Garret FitzGerald's 'Estimates for baronies of minimum level of Irish speaking amongst successive decennial cohorts, 1771–81 to 1861–71', *Proceedings of the Royal Irish Academy*, 84C (1984), pp. 3-155] detrimental to the honing of skills in English. Along with the decline of the native tongue, the colonial process had also engendered a sense of shame in traditional Gaelic culture and the Irish themselves conspired in the efforts to destroy the indigenous culture.

The status of English among the Catholic clergy in the nineteenth century was also a significant influence on the Anglicisation process.[3] While there may have been individual enthusiasts of Irish among the clergy in the mid nineteenth century, the clerical infrastructure operated in English. With the establishment of Maynooth College in 1795, Irish priests trained in an English-speaking environment. Those from the poorer, Irish-speaking environs were the least likely to be able to afford training for the priesthood.

Indeed by the time of the Famine the English language had acquired significant (what Bourdieu terms) economic and 'cultural capital'.[4] The English language was associated with cities, education, emigration, economics and the rule of law. Irish was the language of the hearth – 'cosy' but useless. English was associated with capitalism and print technology and paved the path for new 'imagined communities'. Irish, on the other hand, was the language of manuscripts and the past – a hindrance rather than a help. English was for the middle classes. Irish was the language of the peasantry – or at least that was the perception.

### THE 1851 CENSUS

It is virtually impossible to gauge the real level of Irish-speaking in the country when the Great Famine wrought its destruction. Sometimes interested parties point to the 1851 Census as a numerical indicator of the strength of the language at that time, because a question about language was added as a footnote to the census form. The 1851 Census required that Irish should be added to the name of every individual who spoke Irish only. In the case of bilinguals, it was requested that the words 'Irish and English' should be added against the names of the individuals concerned. There was no indication of how a person who spoke English only would respond. Indeed it was assumed that a blank response implied an English monoglot.[5]

The results of the 1851 Census at the time suggested that 23.3% of the population could speak Irish. Of these, 4.88% were Irish-speaking monoglots while 18.38% could speak both Irish and English. There were considerable variations across the baronies of Ireland.

As one might expect, the largest proportion of Irish-speakers (50.77%) was located in the province of Connacht. Of these, the census indicated that 13.59% could speak Irish only, and a further 37.18% spoke both Irish and English. Munster contained the greatest actual number of Irish-speakers. Here, 815,785 individuals (or 43.91%

of the population) indicated knowledge of Irish. A general pattern of language decline was easily discernible at this time, with the highest proportion of Irish-speakers in the western half of the country. In Ulster and Leinster, the results suggested that there were only 6.78% and 3.54% respectively with Irish. A more detailed breakdown is given in Table 1.

**Table 1.** Knowledge of Irish by Province

| Province | Population | Irish only | | Irish + English | | % with Irish |
|---|---|---|---|---|---|---|
| | | Total | % | Total | % | |
| Leinster | 1,672,738 | 200 | 0.01 | 58,976 | 3.53 | 3.54 |
| Munster | 1,857,736 | 146,336 | 7.88 | 669,449 | 36.03 | 43.91 |
| Ulster | 2,011,880 | 35,783 | 1.78 | 100,693 | 5.00 | 6.78 |
| Connaught | 1,010,031 | 137,283 | 13.59 | 375,566 | 37.18 | 50.77 |
| TOTAL | 6,552,385 | 319,602 | 4.88 | 1,204,684 | 18.38 | 23.26 |

Source: 1851 Census, Part IV

Apart from the general westerly direction of the decline, a rural-urban divide was clearly discernible in the pattern of decline. For eight counties, the General Report of 1851 returned separate summary rural and urban figures (see Table 2 below). (Further details on Irish-speaking

**Table 2.** Knowledge of Irish in Counties with Distinct Urban Areas

| County | Population | Irish only | | Irish + English | | % with Irish |
|---|---|---|---|---|---|---|
| | | Total | % | Total | % | |
| Antrim | 251,383 | 11 | - | 3,022 | 1.2 | 1.2 |
| Belfast Town | 100,301 | - | - | 295 | 0.29 | 0.29 |
| Carrick-fergus | 8,520 | - | - | 17 | 0.20 | 0.20 |
| Cork | 563,576 | 46,486 | 8.25 | 249,548 | 44.28 | 52.53 |
| Cork City | 85,732 | 123 | 0.14 | 10,258 | 11.97 | 12.11 |
| Dublin | 146,778 | 5 | - | 1,276 | 0.87 | 0.87 |
| Dublin City | 258,369 | 27 | 0.01 | 3,399 | 1.32 | 1.33 |
| Louth | 90,815 | 50 | 0.06 | 18,712 | 20.60 | 20.66 |
| Drogheda Town | 16,847 | 1 | 0.01 | 598 | 3.56 | 3.57 |
| Galway | 297,897 | 72,075 | 24.19 | 135,574 | 45.51 | 69.70 |
| Galway Town | 28,787 | 3,511 | 12.19 | 11,084 | 38.50 | 50.69 |
| Kilkenny | 138,773 | 99 | 0.07 | 20,731 | 14.94 | 15.01 |
| Kilkenny City | 19,975 | 5 | 0.03 | 585 | 2.93 | 2.96 |
| Limerick | 208,684 | 6,800 | 3.26 | 71,182 | 34.11 | 37.37 |
| Limerick City | 53,448 | 313 | 0.58 | 3,891 | 7.28 | 7.86 |
| Waterford | 138,738 | 21,845 | 15.75 | 64,978 | 46.84 | 62.59 |
| Waterford City | 25,297 | 140 | 0.55 | 3,963 | 15.67 | 16.22 |

Source: 1851 Census, Part IV

Table 3. Knowledge of Irish for the remaining 24 Counties

| County | Population | Irish only | | Irish + English | | % with Irish |
|---|---|---|---|---|---|---|
| | | Total | % | Total | % | |
| Armagh | 196,084 | 148 | 0.08 | 13,588 | 6.93 | 7.01 |
| Carlow | 68,078 | - | - | 243 | 0.36 | 0.36 |
| Cavan | 174,064 | 54 | 0.03 | 12,973 | 7.45 | 7.48 |
| Clare | 212,440 | 25,446 | 11.98 | 101,550 | 47.80 | 59.78 |
| Donegal | 255,158 | 34,882 | 13.67 | 38,376 | 15.04 | 28.71 |
| Down | 320,817 | 2 | - | 1,151 | 0.36 | 0.36 |
| Ferman-agh | 116,047 | 10 | 0.01 | 2,694 | 2.32 | 2.33 |
| Kerry | 238,254 | 44,455 | 18.66 | 102,043 | 42.83 | 61.49 |
| Kildare | 95,723 | 1 | - | 513 | 0.54 | 0.54 |
| King's (Of-faly) | 112,076 | - | - | 403 | 0.36 | 0.36 |
| Leitrim | 111,897 | 144 | 0.13 | 14,859 | 13.28 | 13.41 |
| London-derry | 192,022 | 28 | 0.01 | 5,378 | 2.80 | 2.81 |
| Longford | 82,348 | 3 | - | 1,462 | 1.78 | 1.78 |
| Mayo | 274,499 | 49,643 | 18.08 | 130,435 | 47.52 | 65.60 |
| Meath | 140,748 | 7 | 0.01 | 8,956 | 6.36 | 6.37 |
| Monaghan | 141,823 | 243 | 0.17 | 10,712 | 7.55 | 7.72 |
| Queen's (Laois) | 111,664 | - | - | 244 | 0.22 | 0.22 |
| Roscom-mon | 173,436 | 1,326 | 0.76 | 44,970 | 25.93 | 26.69 |
| Sligo | 128,515 | 10,584 | 8.23 | 38,644 | 30.07 | 38.30 |
| Tipperary | 331,567 | 728 | 0.22 | 62,036 | 18.71 | 18.93 |
| Tyrone | 255,661 | 405 | 0.16 | 12,487 | 4.88 | 5.04 |
| Westmeath | 111,407 | 1 | - | 920 | 0.83 | 0.83 |
| Wexford | 180,158 | 1 | - | 799 | 0.44 | 0.44 |
| Wicklow | 98,979 | - | - | 135 | 0.14 | 0.14 |

Source: 1851 Census

in baronies and other towns were provided in the 1851 Report on Ages and Education). In most instances, the numbers with knowledge of Irish in the countryside far outweighed their urban counterparts. There were a mere two exceptions to the rule – both of which are hardly surprising. In Galway, there was very little difference in the numbers speaking Irish in urban versus rural districts. In Dublin City, the number with knowledge of Irish in the city exceeded that in the rural environs. This might be a consequence of inward migration from Irish-speaking areas. However the numbers are so small that they could hardly be regarded as significant.

Results in the remaining counties also display a level of predictability (see Table 3). Populations in western counties, such as Donegal, Mayo, Clare and Kerry, had a substantive knowledge of Irish whereas counties in the east, such as Wexford, Wicklow and Kildare, had significantly less knowledge of Irish. Many counties in the north of the country registered surprisingly low levels of Irish

– note, for example, the figure of 2.8% for Londonderry.

RELIABILITY OF THE RESULTS

Although these figures suggest that the Irish language was in considerable decline at the time of the Great Famine, it is highly likely that they *seriously* underestimate the levels of Irish-speaking in the country at that time. In the first instance, the language question (and the census form itself) was entirely in English. A monoglot Irish-speaker would not have understood the question and would have been utterly reliant on the enumerator (who did not necessarily have Irish) to draw his attention to this element in the form. As it is probable that most enumerators focused on the body of the form, it cannot be assumed that a blank space genuinely indicated competence in English and ignorance of Irish.

Even if the Irish had understood the question, it is possible that many of them choose to ignore it and conceal their fluency in the language.[6] Apart from the fact that Irish was associated with ignorance and poverty, it was commonly suspected that the British government may have had an ulterior motive in seeking information regarding linguistic skills. As a consequence, many may have opted to infer that they were monolingual English speakers. In consequence, those census results can only serve as absolute minimal indicators of the extent of Irish-speaking in the country.

In 1881, the census form changed and the Irish language question was incorporated fully into the main body of the form. The results returned an 'almost universal pattern of very much higher percentages for Irish-speaking for each cohort in each barony recorded in 1881'.[7] This would strongly indicate that previous censuses were inaccurate in relation to the language question and should not be needlessly repeated as accurate or as proof that the language had disappeared before the Famine.

Although the process of Anglicisation had begun much earlier than the Famine, it is highly likely that Irish-speakers still predominated in large tracts of the country in the mid-nineteenth century. As they lived in the poorer, more rural regions, it is also probable that they suffered the effects of the Famine more acutely than their English-speaking counterparts and large numbers of Irish-speakers died at this time. The deaths of a large proportion of Irish-speakers undoubtedly added great impetus to the Anglicisation process and hastened the loss of the language.

LOSS OF CULTURAL WORLDVIEW

There is a theory that your language is not just your home but that it represents your cultural worldview – that your understanding of the world is mediated or filtered through your language. The idea of an essential link between language and worldview was originally promoted by Johann Herder (1744–1801) and Wilhelm von Humboldt (1762–1835) who argued that people who speak

Fig. 3  The hearth has always been the central place in Irish rural life. When the home fire was finally extinguished it marked the end of one family history and with it went the family's practical and symbolic relationship to a specific place. [Photo: Frank Coyne]

distinct languages think differently. This happens because their specific languages filter the way they understand the world.

This theory of linguistic relativity was later developed by other scholars, such as Franz Boas (1858–1942), Edward Sapir (1884–1939) and Benjamin Lee Whorf (1897–1941). These scholars were not suggesting that it was entirely impossible to translate from one language to another. Instead, they proposed that there is what Claire Kramsch calls 'an incommensurable residue of untranslatable culture' associated with different languages.[8] In other words, when a language is lost, that 'incommensurable residue' can never be brought into another form. It is lost forever.

In its more extreme form, this theory of linguistic relativity is generally not accepted today, but it is also acknowledged that language is more than a simple means of communication. It is more than words and grammar. Instead it is the medium in which we live and interpret the contemporary world. All languages are local dictionaries of the world. They have vocabularies which have emerged and evolved from the everyday lives of people living in a particular environment. Languages express the

insights and folk wisdom that have accumulated over centuries through a history that is specific to a community and a place. There are old sayings and superstitions that offer guidance on life stages from one generation to the next. The creativity of past generations is frequently accessed through a traditional language. Languages have a specific rhythm that can be heard in the music of their people.

Hans-Georg Gadamer suggested that it is only through language that we can understand the world. Moreover, our traditions are primarily verbal in character. Very significantly, he says that 'linguistic tradition is tradition in the proper sense of the word – that is, something handed down. It is not just something left over, to be investigated or interpreted as a remnant of the past'.[9] It is the mirror in which we look – and see not just ourselves, but our ancestors and their understandings of the world.

Different worldviews filter through different languages and part of the cultural capital of any nation-state with its own language is the unique worldview that is preserved in that language. A multiplicity of languages implies a range of perspectives and worldviews which are not necessarily at odds with – but can complement one another. For George Steiner, the story of Babel was not a curse but a blessing. It was a gift of tongues that was reinforced at Pentecost. Each language is a unique gift. 'The memories stored, the empirical surroundings inventoried, the social relations which the language organises and mirrors (kinship, for example), the colours distinguished in its vocabulary of perceptions, differ often radically, from tongue to tongue.'[10]

In Irish, one of the more common examples of the distinctive nature of the language is the adjective *glas* often used to describe green grass and grey horses but not green eyes. The name *An Ghlas Ghaibhleann* refers to a famous grey and white-forked cow in Irish mythology. Dineen's dictionary also gives the example of *glas-aighne* to refer to a 'green' advocate – that is, one knowing only one language.[11]

Much more fascinating is the idea that there are two verbs 'to be' in Irish – one to express a temporary position and the other to represent a permanent state of being. While 'I am a girl' and 'I am going to the shop' will use just one verb 'to be' in English, this does not happen in Irish. Instead *'is cailín mé'* denotes my femininity as a permanent aspect of my nature, whereas *'tá mé ag dul go dtí an siopa'* refers to a temporary action that will be completed.

### HERITAGE LOSS

When there is a break in linguistic transmission, there is inevitably a significant loss of insight from earlier generations that is often unrecoverable, and the current generation in Ireland has hardly begun to understand or appreciate the significant impact of the loss of Irish on the native psyche. This is not to lament the acquisition of English, particularly since the time of the Famine – but it is to seriously regret that the gain of a new language was accompanied (unnecessarily) by the decline of an ancient and precious national resource.

In her *Fifty Minute Mermaid*, Nuala Ní Dhomhnaill conducts a powerful exploration of the impact of loss of linguistic heritage on a community. The original idea for this volume of poetry was based on the Hans Christian Andersen's fable of a beautiful little mermaid who falls in love with a human prince and longs to live with

him. In order to get permanent access to the human world, she trades her exquisite singing voice and ends up living as a dumb companion to her beloved prince. Her silence was the price she paid for gaining access to the love of her life.[12]

In Ní Dhomhnaill's volume, the 'merfolk' (Paul Muldoon's translation) get access to dry land and leave the water behind them. However, their gain is accompanied by many problems of assimilation. Adjusting to life on dry land brings stiffness and a debilitating skin condition. Moreover, while they have not entirely forgotten their language, they do not feel any inclination to speak it. Instead they are busy trying to accommodate to a new rhythm of life in a foreign country. As each mermaid adjusts to local customs, popular culture and Catholicism, she becomes 'a kind of embittered, silenced, confounded caricature of the culture she lands up in'.[13] She dries up literally, linguistically and creatively. Her endeavours to assimilate and mimic

Fig. 4 *Vespers* by Linda Graham, oil on board, 25 x 20 cm [Courtesy of the artist].

## An Logainmneoir

*do Bhreandán Ó Cíobháin*

Stopann sé scathaimhín ag Carraig Coiscéim,
Ag meá rithim an uisce a scéitheann isteach
Agus amach de réir rúibricí na haimsire.

N'fheadar sé an guth na n-áitreabhóirí
Nó foghar na toinne, nó seanchas ar foluain
Fós ar an ngaoth a rug go dtí an ball seo é.

Ach tuigeann sé chomh tromchúiseach
Is atá an choiscéim seo, cé gur beag
Idir an charraig seo agus an charraig thall.

Tuigeann sé gur beag idir ainm is anam,
Gur mór idir friotal agus balbhacht,
Gur beag idir taobh tíre agus iontaobhas.

Tógann sé an choiscéim, coiscéim a fhágann
Lorg ar an aer. Cromann sé láithreach
Ar nótaí a bhreacadh dá leabhar athgabhála.

— Pádraig de Buis

## Toponomist

*For Breandán Ó Cíobháin*

He lingers for a space at Carraig Coiscéim,
Weighing the rhythm tide that surges in
And out following the weather's rubric.

He doesn't know if it is the inhabitants' voice,
The utterances of the tide, or folklore floating
Still in the air that brought him here.

But he knows well just how crucial
This footstep is, although there's little between
This rock over here and that rock over there.

He knows there is little between naming and animating,
That there is much between articulation and silence,
That there is much between landscape and inscape.

He takes the footstep, a footstep that leaves
An imprint on the air. He begins on the spot
To jot down notes for his book of repossession.

— Paddy Bushe

Fig. 5 Seeking to articulate the silent layers of language and memory buried in the landscape is central to the work of the toponymist as captured in Paddy Bushe's poem dedicated to Breandán Ó Cíobháin. [Photo: Valerie O'Sullivan] local culture are not quite successful and she will always be different.

This is a classic example of the art of mimicry as described by Homi Bhabha in his *Location of Culture*. Although colonised subjects endeavour to imitate or mimic the behaviour of the coloniser, the mimicry is always imperfect – 'almost the same, but not quite'.[14] This clearly happened in post-Famine Ireland. Despite our endeavours to acquire pure English – at the expense of our native language – we have failed to speak 'proper English' – or at least 'the Queen's English'.

James Joyce, one of Ireland's most notable writers in English, remarked that even when an Englishman and an Irishman utter the same words, their experience of English is different.[15] In his *Portrait of the Artist as a Young Man*, the principal character, Stephen Dedalus, feels the shadow of imperialism while conversing with an English priest. Dedalus feels that the language in which they are communicating originally belonged to the priest before it became his. He remarks on the difference between 'the words *home, Christ, ale, master*' on the priest's lips and on his own. Dedalus 'cannot speak or write these words without unrest of spirit'. The priest's language, 'so familiar and so foreign', will always remain 'an acquired speech' for Dedalus because he has not made or accepted its words. His voice holds them at bay. His 'soul frets in the shadow' of the priest's English (original emphasis in Joyce, 1977).[16] And the impact of loss is not confined to the speaking of particular languages.

## LOSS OF PLACELORE

The polymath George Steiner suggests that different languages map our different worlds.[17] Language is inherently linked with the landscape and here, too, the loss of the language has severely impacted on the way the Irish landscape is viewed. In his *The Sailor in the Wardrobe*, Hugo Hamilton quotes his father on the effect of language loss after the Famine. 'He says they lost their language and now they're all walking around like ghosts, following maps with invisible streets and invisible place names. He says the Irish are still in hiding in a foreign language.'[18]

British rule and the acquisition of English ensured the translation of many indigenous placenames from Irish to English. While the original placenames in Irish often referred to local stories and folklore, the translation was usually meaningless and much Irish placelore was lost. Many Northern Irish writers have lamented this loss, most notably Brian Friel, whose celebrated play *Translations*, first produced in Derry in 1980, deals with the ordnance survey of Ireland, carried out by the British Army Engineer Corps in the 1830s. In this play, Owen, the son of the hedge-school master, who helps the British army with the mapping and renaming of places in Donegal, is portrayed as betraying his ancestral Gaelic home for a modern English world.

*Translations* devotes considerable attention to the historical significance of placenames and to the legends associated with them.[19]

Of course, the translation of placenames was more than a simple process of Anglicisation – more than a loss of placelore. It also changed the way in which people looked at the landscape. In reviewing a parallel example of a British soldier surveying the land in India in the nineteenth century, Gayatri Chakravorty Spivak suggests that the process of 'map-making' defines the alien as master.[20] The coloniser is appropriating the territory and distancing the 'native' from his homeland. He is claiming ownership of their territory, which now becomes a foreign territory. The coloniser becomes the local, the native become the alien. He is 'worlding *their own* world'.

## GAIN OF HIBERNO–ENGLISH

But there was some gain. The Irish acquired the English language and some of us have begun to regard our use of English as an important aspect of a distinctly Irish heritage – although generally speaking the Irish have failed to claim ownership of Hibernicised English. 'Green English' is the term given by Loreto Todd to this 'grafted tongue', which she describes as being 'an English foliage on an Irish stem, still nourished by an Irish root'.[21]

Differences in vocabulary between the English spoken in Ireland and that spoken in England are not necessarily significant but some variations in vocabulary can create occasional difficulties for Irish migrants. When I first went to live in Liverpool, not only had I great difficulty understanding 'Scouse', it was also impossible to purchase food items, such as a 'sliced pan' (sliced loaf of white bread), rashers (sliced bacon), or 'taytos' (potato crisps). My vocabulary differences also extended to hardware items such as 'jar' (hot water bottle) or 'press' (cupboard) or to articles of clothing, such as the word 'slip', which I commonly use for a petticoat. Apart from differences in vocabulary, the Irish language has also had a significant influence on the syntax of Hiberno–English. There is no doubt that the acquisition of the English language has been a great asset – and some of the best writing in English today *is written* by writers in Ireland. Ireland can boast a number of Nobel prizewinners for literature in the English language – including William Butler Yeats (1923), George Bernard Shaw (1925), Samuel Beckett (1969) and Seamus Heaney (1995). The Irish are effortlessly speaking and writing a language that enables them to communicate with millions worldwide. And yet there is the niggling suspicion that more has been lost than has been gained. If English had been acquired and the Irish language maintained, what could have been achieved? Why was it assumed that only one language could be spoken properly when the rest of Europe seems perfectly capable of speaking several without difficulty?

Fig. 6 Brian Friel's *Translations,* directed by Art O Briain, was first performed in Derry in 1980 to launch the Field Day Company. Set in Donegal in the 1830s the events depicted concern the work of the Ordnance Survey. It is a play very much about cultural imperialism as the Irish language is replaced by the coloniser's language. The English officer Yolland admits that the work of the Ordnance Survey represents 'an eviction of sorts'. The deep layers of cultural meaning embedded in Irish placenames are lost in the work of translation contributing to what Declan Kiberd refers to as a 'geography of disin-heritance'. Situated in the historical context of the Survey and related processes of Anglicisation via the new national schools, central concerns of the play are how a people have to learn to speak a language 'that is not their own', and the cultural consequences arising from such a dramatic transformation in modes of communication. While the Famine would deal a serious blow to the Irish language, nevertheless the play also raises questions as to the extent to which the Irish people themselves were complicit in its demise throughout the nineteenth century. [Source: John Baldwin graphics]

# Famine and the Irish diaspora

## Piaras Mac Éinri

### Introduction

The volume and quality of scholarship on the Famine and its legacy produced in recent decades contrasts sharply with the previous one hundred and thirty years.[1] The centenary of the Famine in the 1940s received relatively little academic attention in Ireland or elsewhere, with the notable exception of the Irish Folklore Commission's commendable decision to collect material from the oral tradition in English and Irish concerning the Famine.[2] The first major study of the Great Famine, edited by R. Dudley Edwards and T.D. Williams, appeared in 1956.[3] The two following decades had been dominated, in popular terms at any event, by just one book, Cecil Woodham-Smith's *The Great Hunger*,[4] a work whose influence continued to be felt far beyond Ireland in the years which followed.[5] But, in general, historical research into what Graham Davis calls the 'central event of nineteenth-century Irish history'[6] was remarkably limited. Yet from the mid-1980s onwards, new research and new publications in the field began to proliferate.

The Famine was not a simple narrative of exploitative English landlord and victimised Irish poor. There were many other actors as well, including officialdom, land agents and other middlemen, clergy of various confessions, Poor Law guardians, the Irish middle classes and the neighbours of those who had perished or fled. One literary critic suggests in discussing Liam O'Flaherty's *Famine* (1936) that it may have been easier to capture these complexities in fictional rather than historical terms.[7] O'Flaherty's novel fully recognises the perfidious role played by the British authorities, but its characters also include the bigoted and sectarian Fr Roche, liberal Protestant minister Mr Coburn, a corrupt relief works engineer, greedy farmers and an avaricious shopkeeper:

> The shopkeeper, Johnny Hynes, strives only to protect his own profits, which are safe as long as food is not sold at cost price from government depots . . . The shopkeeper's greed for profit, combined with rising prices, eventually makes it impossible for the poor to buy food, especially if they have been refused relief work. The farmers are implicated in taking bribes and favouring their own class when granting tickets for the works.[8]

The intolerable intimacy of what was done, and what was known, must have been one reason why the folklore of the Famine often recounted that the greatest mortality occurred in the next parish, not one's own, or that only 'vagrants and strangers' actually died.[9] Many had indeed died or been forced out, but others had profited. For some who survived, the material conditions of life actually improved in the decades that followed.

The Great Famine and the Great Exodus were thus followed, at least initially, by the Great Silence. Ó Cíosáin captures the ambivalence of remembrance and denial, when he says, referring to the folklore sources in Ireland, that 'they give a vivid picture of a society both remembering and refusing to remember a harrowing catastrophe in its recent past'.[10] In the case of those Irish who fled abroad, a myth of exile and longing for home[11] had to be balanced against the more pragmatic reality that traumatised survivors had escaped to a better place, but also one in which they needed to forge a new way of being in the world.

The link between Famine and Diaspora is thus different from the inheritance of the Irish who remained. Those who fled saw themselves as victims. Some of their descendants regarded themselves, with some justice, as entitled to a more 'authentic' claim to the legacy of the Famine than people in Ireland itself. Yet literary scholar Jason King points out that early narratives of Famine migration voyages did not support the later theme of English oppressor and Irish victim as part of a generalised discourse of 'famine as genocide'.[12] Research drawing upon folklore sources in Ireland tends to corroborate this. Ó Gráda and Ó Cíosáin note that such accounts do not generally reflect the view that the 'State had deliberately exploited the Famine in order to solve an economic and social crisis that was seen in Malthusian terms as being due to overpopulation.'[13] Such deterministic interpretations emerged over time and crystallised into a specific diasporic narrative somewhat later, notably in the 1860s, influenced above all by John Mitchel's *The Last Conquest of Ireland (Perhaps)*.[14] This powerful polemic inspired a more politicised, radicalised and confessionalised Irish–American identity, which in turn was to shape the Irish contribution to American public life and identity in new and different ways. Such narratives had as much to do with a way of being in America as they had to do with understanding the Irish Famine. As Akenson puts it:

> In a brilliant analysis of the changing place of the Famine in Irish-Catholic history, Patrick O'Farrell has shown that this national folk memory was replaced by a 'contrivance', a synthetic substitute

**25 September 1847**
Of Bridget Fahey, a native of
Co. Galway, parish of Killyma,
Co. Galway. She landed in Quebec,
where a sister of her's died. She is
supposed to be in Montreal. Any
information (whether dead or alive)
will be thankfully received by her
sister, Mary, care of the Editor of
the Pilot, Boston, Ms.

**23 October 1847**
Of John Connors and Bridget, his
wife, natives of Karney Kelly,
parish of Kiltullagh, Co. Galway,
who sailed from Galway in the brig
Napolean, on the 18th of May last,
and has not been heard of since.
Any information respecting them
will be thankfully received by Mary
Carroll (sister to the said Bridget),
at No. 4 Prince street, Boston, Ms.

**1 January 1848**
Of Rose Dillon, aged about 20 years,
a native of Ballinturly, parish of
Oran, Co. Roscommon, who arrived
in this country in May last, and when
last heard from (August last) she was
in Boston and about going to Andover,
Ms. being hired by a Lady. Any
information respecting her will be
thankfully received by brother-in-law
John Early, in care of the Rev.
Thomas Lynch, Roxbury, Ms.

**15 January 1848**
Of Mary McCabe, aged about 13 years,
daughter of Owen McCabe, formerly of
Drumdufla, Co. Leitrim. Said Owen died
at Quebec in October in 1847. Mary left
there to come to Providence, R. I., where
some of her friends reside, but has not
reached there yet. Any information
respecting her will be thankfully received
by her uncle, Mr John Prior, Reynalds
Street, Providence, R. I.

**25 March 1848**
Of Miss Winifred Clara aged 19, who
arrived at quarantine in New York in
April, 1847, in ship Lady Hunkley,
from the parish Dinary, Co. Galway.
Any information will be thankfully
received by John Lynch, Meredith
Bridge, N. H.

**15 April 1848**
Of James Kenny, of Ballaghaderrine,
Co. Mayo, parish of Kilcoleman near
Loughlinn, who sailed from Sligo,
March 2d, 1847, in the brig Imperial,
Capt George Salter, and landed in New
York, April 19th, 1847. Any information
respecting him will be thankfully received
by his wife and two children, Ann, Mary
and Bridget Kenny by addressing Francis
Newell, 55 Norfolk Street, New York.

(Ruth-Ann Harris and Donald M. Jacobs
(eds.), <u>The Search for Missing Friends</u>,
Boston, 1989, Vol. 1, pp. 223-274)

Fig. 1 The search for missing friends and relatives in the United States assumed greater significance given the scale of emigration from Ireland during and after the Famine. The notices carried in the 'Missing Friends' column in *The Boston Pilot*, especially during the Famine years, provide an important insight into the often shattered lives of those who left Ireland.

cumstances directly encountered, given and transmitted from the past. The tradition of all the dead generations weighs like a nightmare on the brain of the living.[16]

In the case of the post-Famine diasporic Irish, Marx's phrase captures an apparent paradox. People *do* have agency, but as he noted within parameters over which they may have little control. The assertion of that agency, especially by an oppressed people, requires the construction of narratives which they can 'own' and which enable them to make sense to themselves of their own pasts. Such narratives are the very condition upon which they can inhabit the present, escape from victimhood and achieve a degree of

that was, in its domestic form, anti-Protestant and in its external visage, anti-British. The greatest touchstone in this transformation was John Mitchel's *The Last Conquest of Ireland (Perhaps).*[15]

In twenty-first-century debates in Ireland concerning the abuse of children by Church and State authorities, the term 'victim' has been replaced by 'survivor'. The distinction is an important one, as relevant to the post-Famine diasporic legacy as to the later case cited. Victims do not have agency, whereas survivors do. Karl Marx famously noted that,

Men make their own history, but they do not make it just as they please; they do not make it under circumstances chosen by themselves, but under cir-

agency. In the case of those who have involuntarily left an ethno-national homeland, the need to construct a continuing link with that nation is all the more pressing. Yet these narratives may involve what David Lowenthal calls the fabrication of heritage[17] and, at the very least, the simplification or outright distortion or falsification of historical record.

All of the above prompts a number of questions. Can the Famine be described as a 'foundational moment' in nineteenth-century Irish emigration history? Did the Famine bring about a fundamental shift in the way in which individuals in the Irish Diaspora imagined themselves and their identities? How were differing and sometimes competing versions of these identities negotiated and memorialised in recent decades, notably on the occasion of the 150th commemoration of the Famine? Is the legacy of the Famine still unfinished business, or is it relevant at all, for the modern Irish Diaspora?

## IRISH EMIGRATION BEFORE THE FAMINE

Irish emigration, on a substantial scale, began well before the Famine. In that sense, as Akenson has argued, 'the Famine was not the cause of the Irish Diaspora'.[18] Eighteenth- and early-nineteenth-century statistics are not especially reliable, but there seems little reason to question a statistic of at least one million Irish emigrants in the period up to the Famine. Miller suggests that between 800,000 and 1,000,000 persons left in the period 1815–44 alone, 'about twice the total for the preceding two hundred years'.[19] Initially the majority were Protestant, although the number of Catholics was already increasing in the pre-Famine period. Some poorer migrants travelled to America as indentured servants, especially in the colonial period. But by and large the very poorest of the poor, notably landless labourers and their families, had not the means, the knowledge or the motivation required to depart.

By the 1820s emigration from Ireland was running at dramatic levels by general European standards. For the five-year period, 1825–30, for instance, emigration (excluding emigration to Britain, which was simply viewed as internal migration) was more than 50,000 to the USA and almost 80,000 to Canada. In the following years, 1831–40 emigration to North America as a whole jumped dramatically to almost 438,000 persons, a decadel increase of 59%. By contrast, Australia, New Zealand and South Africa attracted very modest numbers in that period.

The story of Irish emigration in that period was therefore focused in part on Britain (including migration to other places connected with British military service, where Irish men and the Irish wives of British Army soldiers were disproportionately over-represented[21]), but more especially on North America.

## FAMINE AND AFTERWARDS: A LASTING LEGACY

The Famine turned the river of emigration out of Ireland into a torrent. The precise figures for deaths and departures have been the subject of much controversy. Kevin Kenny suggests that 2.1 million emigrated in the period 1845–55, of

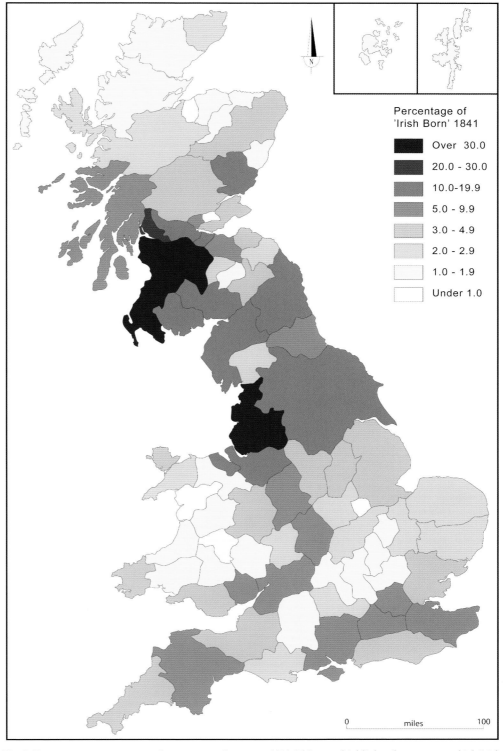

Percentage of 'Irish Born' 1841

| | |
|---|---|
| ■ | Over 30.0 |
| ■ | 20.0 - 30.0 |
| ■ | 10.0-19.9 |
| ■ | 5.0 - 9.9 |
| ■ | 3.0 - 4.9 |
| ■ | 2.0 - 2.9 |
| ■ | 1.0 - 1.9 |
| □ | Under 1.0 |

0        miles        100

Fig. 2 DISTRIBUTION PER COUNTY OF IRISH-BORN IN BRITAIN IN 1841. This map highlights the extent to which Irish migration to Britain was already a long established feature in the decades prior to 1841. In some counties, as in the Glasgow–Clydeside and industrial Lancashire regions, over 30% of the population were Irish-born. Mid- and south Scotland and northern England also received significant numbers of Irish migrants and there is a band of Irish settlement extending southwards from Liverpool and Cheshire to Birmingham and Coventry, and onwards to Bristol and the south Wales coalfield. Southeastern England and the West Country were also receiving areas for the Irish emigrants.

whom 1.5 million went to the USA, 340,000 to British North America (at least as their initial destination), 200,000 to 300,000 to Britain and 'tens of thousands more (generally the better-off)' to the Antipodes.[22] In the single year of 1847, 90,150 passengers, of 98,649 who had left, disembarked at Grosse Île, Québec, six out of seven being Irish, not including, obviously, those who died at sea. The total who died on board ship, at the quarantine station, or subsequently in local hospitals or other places, was estimated at 17,477, a mortality rate of over 17%.[23] Grosse Île, the subject of a separate chapter in this book, is the largest Irish Famine mass grave outside Ireland. While 1847 is remembered as the blackest Famine year, emigration actually rose in subsequent years. In the five years 1851–55 almost three-quarters of a million people (740,216 persons), left for the United States.[24]

The Famine also led to an upsurge in emigration to Britain. In 1841 the number of Irish-born residents of England and Wales was 291,000; for Scotland it was 126,000. By 1861, these figures stood at 602,000 and 204,000 respectively – increases of over 200% for the first and 62% for the second. For Scotland, the Irish-born percentage of the population as a whole increased from 4.8% to 6.6%. Such statistics mask the far higher local concentrations of Irish in cities like Glasgow as well as specific English and Welsh cities or counties such as Bradford, Liverpool and Glamorgan. The outstanding example is Liverpool, where by 1851 fully 22.3% of the population was Irish-born, making Liverpool Britain's most Irish city.[25]

## DIFFERENT DIASPORAS

The main locations of the diasporic communities which emerged from this exodus were therefore Britain, Canada and the USA. However, the experiences, profiles and subsequent fates of each of these communities were very different.

In Britain, the arrival of large numbers of destitute Irish migrants, many suffering from typhus or 'Irish fever',[26] occurred against a backdrop of a society which was itself experiencing all the upheavals of rapid industrialisation. Moreover, the response of the national authorities was similar to their attitude in Ireland itself and cities and rate-payers were largely left to foot the bill through the Poor Law system. Inevitably, the newly arrived migrants crowded into the most marginal and rapidly ghettoised parts of the city, where disease and poverty were their lot. To say the least, they were not popular. The Famine Irish were frequently victimised, while a policy of removal back to Ireland was largely a failure. Nevertheless, as Neal notes:

The Irish death rates, in many areas, were massively higher than the corresponding rate among the British working classes. However, many English, Scottish and Welsh sacrificed their lives helping the Irish Famine immigrants: policemen, doctors, nurses, relieving officers

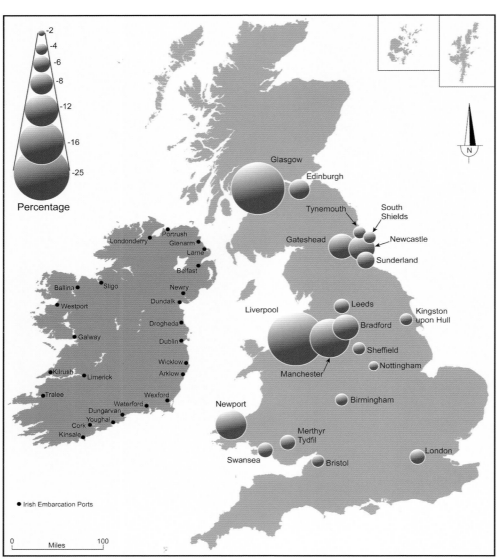

Fig. 3 PERCENTAGE IRISH-BORN RESIDENTS IN THE CITIES AND TOWNS OF BRITAIN 1851. This map emphasises that it was the cities of Britain, especially those in northern England and central Scotland, which were the great receiving areas for often desperate Irish populations. With over 22% of the city's population, Liverpool (93,874) and Glasgow with 18% (59,801) dominate the pattern of Irish immigration followed by Manchester with 13% (53,662). As many as 108,000 Irish had settled in London but this represented less than 5% of the capital city's population. Yet the size of London's Irish population meant that only Dublin city in Ireland housed a greater number of Irish people. Significant concentrations are also found in the industrial cities of northeastern England and south Wales.

and most of all Catholic priests. Mistakes were made in the Poor Law Unions but there were few villains and many heroes.[27]

Notwithstanding the existence of already substantial Irish populations throughout Britain, the Famine period saw the further ethnicisation, confessionalisation and ghettoisation of the Irish in Britain. Although they ultimately became a significant and largely successful community within British life, the legacy of the Famine years, racism and discrimination, ongoing political tensions between the two countries and the continuing influx of Irish labour into Britain since that time has made relations between host community and migrants a fraught one on occasions, notably in those areas, such as Liverpool and parts of Scotland, where sectarian tensions further complicated the picture.

The case of Canada was also a particular one. For one thing, many of those who fled there were actually bound for the USA. The Canadian route was cheaper but they did not plan to stay. Secondly, the main, although not the only, port of arrival, was Grosse Île. It is clear from the records of the quarantine station that it was overwhelmed by the sheer numbers of Famine migrants arriving at its quays, creating particularly dreadful conditions of arrival and settlement.

That said, Irish Famine migrants to Canada need also to be seen in their wider historical context. There was already a significant Irish presence in Canada before the Famine, but one which took many different forms. Bruce Elliott notes the relatively more positive, or at least more mutually non-confrontational, relations between Catholic and Protestant Irish–Canadians, a situation which could certainly not have been said to be the case in parts of the USA.[18] Many Irish–Canadians became loyal members of Canadian society. The form of devolved administration in British North America was relatively benign from an Irish standpoint, in a country which was conveniently distant from Britain. Nothing illustrates this better than the career of Thomas D'Arcy McGee, who moved from being a nationalist Young Irelander in the 1840s to becoming one of the architects of the Canadian Confederation, and a man who is still honoured in Canada today. Yet McGee was assassinated by a dissident Fenian in 1867, one year after the abortive Irish American Fenian 'invasion' of Canada. It has been argued that, until then at least, Fenianism was a significant force in Canadian–Irish politics.

Ultimately the balance of confessional and political power was different in Canada than in the USA. The absorption of Québec in 1763, notably, had involved the *de facto* acceptance of what would nowadays be called a multicultural framework, even if tensions have persisted between English- and French-speaking Canada down to the present day. By 1867, the Irish in Canada were the second largest European ethnic minority (after the French) and they became a force to be reckoned with in Canadian life.

Finally, in the Famine context, there is a real poignancy in the hidden diaspora represented by those Irish orphan children in John Francis Maguire's[29] and Marianna O'Gallagher's[30] accounts, who were absorbed into French-speaking life in Québec and whose identities might seem to have been erased in the process, although many kept their Irish names. In recent years, with the increasing interest in ethnicity in multicultural Canada, much has been done to explore these hidden histories. A fascinating recent exhibition on the Irish in Québec at the Montréal McCord Museum was jointly organised with the non-sectarian St Patrick's Society and the Irish Protestant Benevolent Society.[31] If Irish migrants, especially children, *were* 'absorbed', it was not least because of the quite extraordinary generosity extended to them by Québecois society, French- and English-speaking, Catholic and Protestant.

## THE IRISH IN THE USA

However convoluted the relations between different varieties of Irish nationalism . . . the memory of the Famine became the focal point around which crystallised Irish America's search for historical understanding of why they found themselves where they were.[32]

The Catholic post-Famine Irish were the single most important community of 'ethnic others' to arrive in the USA in the mid-nineteenth century. If one place and one city, more than any other, stands out as a place profoundly influenced by the Irish Famine, it has to be New York, dubbed 'America's Most Irish City'.[33]

Of the 1.8 million immigrants who disembarked at New York City between 1847 and 1851, 848,000, or 47%, were Irish; most of the rest were German. Of course, not all stayed there, but nevertheless New York evolved into what Hasia Diner calls a 'heavily Irish city'. The 1850 US Census recorded that fully 26% of the total population of New York City was born in Ireland. When second-generation ethnic Irish are included, the size and impact of the Irish may be imagined.[34]

These immigrants not only developed their own narratives and ways of being in the new society; they also changed that society profoundly in many ways.

The Famine was therefore central to the type of country America became, for the Irish who poured in left their distinctive mark on politics, on religion, and on the labor movement, to mention only the three most obvious examples.[35]

As David Noel Doyle points out, these new immigrants changed the face of the city and the nation, challenging a largely Protestant country to find new ways of accommodating a numerically significant minority and pre-figuring

Fig. 4 President John Fitzgerald Kennedy's motorcade makes its way along St Patrick's Street, Cork city during his visit to Ireland in June 1963. Kennedy was the first representative of Catholic Irish America to become president of the United States. Members of the Fitzgerald family from Bruff in County Limerick left Ireland during the period 1846–55, while Patrick Kennedy, a cooper, also left his home in Dunganstown, County Wexford in 1848 to make a new life for himself in Boston. In a speech given at New Ross President Kennedy paid due respect to his Irish inheritance: 'When my great-grandfather left here to become a cooper in east Boston, he carried nothing with him except two things: a strong religious faith and a strong desire for liberty. I am glad to say that all of his great-grandchildren have valued that inheritance.' [Photo: Robert Knudsen, White House, in the John F. Kennedy Presidential Library and Museum, Boston]

by a half-century the ever more diverse migrant communities which were to settle there. This was not an easy process, nor were the results wholly beneficial. To quote J.J. Lee on the Catholic identity of the post-Famine Irish: 'It was forged in opposition to a common enemy, identified as Anglo Saxon and Protestant at home, WASP in America. A common enemy can be a great unifier'.[36] In fairness, the post-Famine Catholic Irish found themselves struggling as an underclass in a heavily Protestant society. They had to fight their own corner and find their own champions in such redoubtable figures as Archbishop John Hughes of New York.[37] Without in any way minimising the specific and more oppressive experiences of African–Americans, Native Americans and Asian–Americans, the Catholic Irish presence ultimately provided a disruptive but creative game-changer for mainstream American society, even if more than a century was to pass before one of their own would be elected President and even if they themselves contributed their share of a negative ethnic legacy, notably in their frequently fractious relations with the African–American community.[38] In the process, they helped to re-invent urban America:

The urban and laboring Irish population, newly populous, more wholly Catholic, salved its trauma and poverty and maintained its self-esteem by constructing a peculiar subculture around the familiarities of the neighbourhood, the saloon and the parish . . . The formal sides of these concerns saw the creation of trade unions and fraternal clubs, the support of the urban organizations ('machines') of the national Democratic Party and the multiplication of Catholic churches, schools and hospitals.[39]

It is only after the Famine that it becomes possible to conflate, albeit inaccurately, 'Irish emigrant' and 'Catholic'. It also explains why 'Irish–American' as a term, whether defined in political, literary or cultural ways, henceforth reflects a specific, largely confessional and partially ghettoised notion of identity.

Although the Famine fell hardest on Irish Catholics, who were strongly overrepresented in the very poorest levels of society, it affected Protestants, too. They experienced privation and economic distress and many were obliged to emigrate. Protestants died during the Famine, even if the numbers were not on the same scale as their Catholic counterparts. However, they developed no collective mythology about the Famine, save for an attenuated tradition concerning how selfless some of their clergy had been in serving Protestant and Catholic poor alike, and how generous many Protestant landlords had been in supporting relief efforts.[40]

Overall, it seems clear that in the case of those Irish who were forced to depart, in more or less catastrophic circumstances and to countries and to cultures where they were often unwelcome, the Famine and its aftermath represented a far-reaching, confessionalised and exclusionary reorientation concerning the meaning of Irishness in the Diaspora at least in the main destination, the USA.

A question which must be posed, in relation to post-Famine Irish emigration as a whole, is the extent to which it changed the composition of the main Irish diasporic communities. In spite of the Canadian, British and other discussions mentioned above, one can but cite Doyle's nuanced view:

> For the major scholars of Irish migrations to Britain, Australia and Canada have by now demonstrated that, while their Irish populations increased after 1845, that event neither reshaped nor originated Irish subcultures and communities therein to anything like the degree that was the case of the United States.[41]

Nevertheless, the contributions of Protestant Irish America, before and after the Famine, should in no way be minimised. As Akenson points out, a majority of Irish Americans today are Protestant, not Catholic.[42] Of the twenty US Presidents claiming Irish descent, including the present incumbent Barack Obama, all but one have been Protestant.

### THE LONG-TERM EFFECTS OF THE FAMINE ON PATTERNS OF EMIGRATION

Famines, however traumatic, are usually followed by the recovery of the population within about two generations. In the Irish case this did not happen, primarily because of a shift towards delayed marriage patterns and changes in family farm inheritance patterns,[43] but most of all because of the way in which an expectation of emigration, or at least the normalisation of departure, became embedded in the life choices of young people. The *Commission on Emigration and Other Population Problems* put it starkly. If one tabulates Irish emigration in terms of the number of Irish-born persons living outside Ireland as a percentage of the total number of persons born in Ireland (excluding 'non-Irish born in Ireland', which in those days generally meant 'British'), the figures are dramatic. In 1841 it was 6.2%, but by 1851 it had jumped to 22.8%. By 1891 it had reached an unprecedented 38.8%.

Such data tell us two things. First, to repeat the obvious, the Famine led directly to a dramatic increase in emigration from Ireland. Second, it set in train a long-term pattern of high emigration: children were raised for export and the rate of emigration consistently outstripped the natural growth in the population. As the Reverend A.A. Luce put it so vividly in one of his contributions to the *Commission on Emigration and Other Population Problems*:

> The hard core of the problem is the sad stark fact that one Irish child (more than one, statistically) in every three is born to emigrate, and grows up in the knowledge that he or she must emigrate. The moral and psychological effect of that fact is immense. It paralyses certain areas. It is a dead weight upon the spirit of the whole country, a dead hand upon her economy.[44]

### MYTH-MAKING AND MEMORIALISATION: DIASPORIC PARALLELS

The Irish in the US diaspora were not the only group to

Fig. 5 President Barack Obama addresses an Irish audience at College Green, Dublin, 23 May 2011. [Photo: Maxwell Photography]

experience some of the unnerving effects of the transition to a more complex world of modernity as well as a layered world of identity politics, but also one in which, following the African–American experience, discourses of victimhood and redemption were central. The case of American Jews, with whom comparisons were frequently made, offers interesting parallels to the Irish experience.

Critical writing on the 'Holocaust industry' has stressed the ways in which Holocaust commemoration became a highly contested site of memory, identity and ownership. Historian Tim Cole in *Images of the Holocaust* explores how Shoah commemoration reflects the differing perceptions and ideological views of Israelis, European and American Jews. Many of these debates crystallised around the reception of two key visual works: Frenchman Claude Lanzmann's 1985 *Shoah* and Steven Spielberg's 1993 *Schindler's List*. Revisionist historians in Israel like Tom Segev, as well as Lanzmann himself, were critical of what they saw as an attempt to Americanise the Holocaust, erasing the reality that it was not the story of the majority of American Jews and that others arguably had a more authentic claim to its legacy.[45] Cole also points to the narrative of *Schindler's List* as being a classic Hollywood one of intervention by a flawed but good hero (Schindler) and a very American tale of redemption, something which hardly accorded with the experiences of the vast majority of European Jews during the Second World War.

How is this relevant to the Irish and issues of Famine commemoration in 1990s America? Pierre Nora argues that recent decades have been marked by an almost obsessive trend in memorialisation,[46] with the proliferation of museums, monuments and events as ethnic communities staked their differing claims to an identity in which victimhood was central. These themes were also typical of Famine commemoration, including the erection of memorials, the inclusion of Famine Studies in the curricula of a number of US states and, more generally, issues of 'ownership' of the agenda, with competing discourses on the part of the Irish Government and a variety of civil society groups within the USA itself. On a broader level, Cole argues that commemorations always tell us more about the era in which they take place than about the event being commemorated. In an era of shifting identity politics, they may serve either as a present-day insistence on an exceptionalist past in which all such events and their discourses are grist to a narrow, victimised and exclusionary mill, or as templates for a broader exploration of the human condition, including experiences of structural human oppression.

Omer Bartov, writing on the Holocaust, discusses two broad strands:

> Holocaust museums seem to offer two narrative options: one that presents Zionism as the ultimate answer to Jewish persecution by host gentile

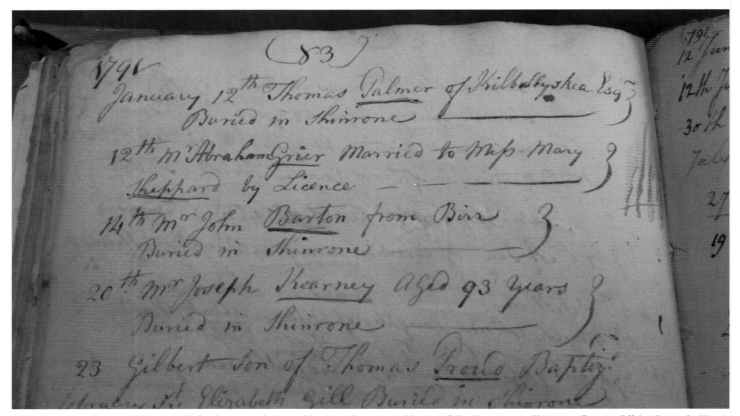

Fig. 6 President Barack Obama's Irish forebears can be traced back to the ancestral home of the Kearneys in Shinrone, County Offaly (formerly King's County). The President's seventh-great-grandparent, Joseph (who was born in 1698) died at the age of ninety-three as this Shinrone Church of Ireland burial record shows. Joseph's wife Cicely's death is recorded for 1769. Many other members of the Kearney family are also buried in Shinrone graveyard. [Photo: William J. Smyth, with thanks to Rev. Michael Johnston, Church of St Mary, Shinrone]

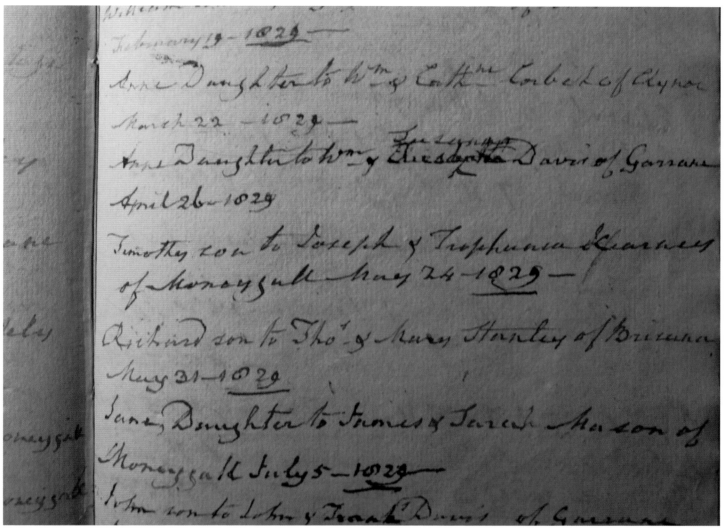

Fig. 7 One of Joseph and Cicely Kearney's four sons, also called Joseph, married a woman from nearby Moneygall and eventually went to live in that village. His eldest son William was the grandfather and Joseph, the father of (Timothy) Falmouth Kearney born on 24 May 1829 (see above), who emigrated to America during the Great Famine. Falmouth Kearney, listed as a 'labourer', was one of 289 passengers who boarded the ship *Marmion* in Liverpool, which reached New York on 20 March 1850. He first settled in Ohio but later lived and worked as a farmer in Indiana. One of his daughters, Mary Anne Kearney, married Jacob William Dunham and their grandson Stanley Dunham was the father of Ann Dunham, President Obama's mother. [Photo: Courtesy of Canon Stephen Neill]

nations; another that argues in favour of toleration and understanding for cultural and ethnic minorities. The first is a nationalist narrative, the second a humanist one. These are not mutually contradictory messages, but they do reflect the social and intellectual environment in which they tend to be disseminated.[47]

These elements are also present in the Irish debates of the 1990s. The website IrishHolocaust.org does not mince its words:

Irishmen and Irishwomen!
Read this site and weep. Weep for the agonies and deaths of your people at the hands of genocidists. The authorities who imposed the curriculum, the teachers and professors who funneled it into you, have carefully kept you uninformed as to which

British regiment, or that any regiment, murdered your people. Until now, that information was kept from you. You had no access to it. You do now – you read it on your computer screen! Commit the regiment's name to memory.
Never, ever, forget it!
. . . As no Jewish person would ever refer to the 'Jewish Oxygen Famine of 1939–1945', so no Irish person ought ever refer to the Irish Holocaust as a famine.[48]

Their targets, it will be noted, are not simply the British, but also the 'authorities who imposed the curriculum' and the 'teachers and professors who funnelled it into you'. Particular bile is reserved for then President of Ireland, Mary Robinson, the Irish authorities and those Irish–Americans who are held to agree with them. The authors of the site, on the other hand, legitimate their claims by their ancestry:

597

Fig. 8 *News from America, 1875* by John Brenan RHA, oil on canvas. The Famine was indeed a watershed that turned a river of emigration out of Ireland into a torrent. In Brenan's painting, members of a West Cork family listen attentively to the contents of a letter sent from America and read aloud by a young girl. As Irish emigrants forged new lives and identities for themselves such letters frequently became their only link with their homeland. [Source: Crawford Art Gallery]

'we, the descendants of the survivors of that starvation, will no longer be silenced'.

The real agenda of such people, however, has as much to do with the present as with the past. The 1990s saw a major breakthrough in Anglo–Irish political relations, a process in which the Irish Diaspora in the US played a key role. The peace process was not universally supported there (to quote Irish Holocaust.org again):

Thus the Irish government advertises its quisling status by ending the commemoration prior to the anniversaries of the murders of more than half of the 5.2 millions. What else can one expect from the government whose Consuls spoke in Illinois' State Legislature in opposition to the McBride Principles for Fair Employment in Northern Ireland? They pose as anti-terrorists while collaborating with the British terrorists who, since 1969, have murdered over six times 16 as many noncombatants as have the IRA.

In reality, as scholars such as Professor Liam Kennedy of QUB have shown, comparisons between the Famine and the Holocaust are never considered in a detailed and rigorous way. He examines such comparisons under four headings – the pre-crisis phase, workhouses and ghettoes, mortality and intentionality – and shows that such comparisons are ultimately both facile and futile.[49]

The Irish Famine memorial in Boston shows another dimension of the commemorative projects within the Diaspora which, again, reflects aspects of the Holocaust debates and indeed echoes a theme already touched upon in

*Schindler's List*: the redemption narrative. Two groups are depicted, one starving and emaciated, the other striding confidently into the future. It is America as a place of escape and safety, but without the overly ethno-nationalist content of the narrative above.

The 1990s was also a propitious time for the Famine to be re-visited, not least because the aforementioned President Mary Robinson, elected in 1990, had made the building of closer links with the Irish Diaspora a key part of her own presidential mission. Irish Presidents had traditionally paid some degree of lip-service to this constituency but Robinson was the first to highlight the Diaspora and to give substance to her mission by visiting Irish communities worldwide. Many of her speeches, including one entitled 'Cherishing the Irish Diaspora', made to a joint session of the Houses of the Oireachtas on 2 February 1995, explicitly referred to the impact and legacy of the Famine, but in terms which reflected Bartov's alternative, more humanist vision of commemoration:[50]

> We cannot have it both ways. We cannot want a complex present and still yearn for a simple past. I was very aware of that when I visited the refugee camps in Somalia and more recently in Tanzania and Zaire. The thousands of men and women and children who came to those camps were, as the Irish of the 1840s were, defenceless in the face of catastrophe. Knowing our own history, I saw the tragedy of their hunger as a human disaster. We, of all people, know it is vital that it be carefully analysed so that their children and their children's children be spared that ordeal. We realise that while a great part of our concern for their situation, as Irish men and women who have a past which includes famine, must be at practical levels of help, another part of it must consist of a humanitarian perspective which springs directly from our self-knowledge as a people. Famine is not only humanly destructive, it is culturally disfiguring. The Irish who died at Grosse Île were men and women with plans and dreams of future achievements. It takes from their humanity and individuality to consider them merely as victims.

President Robinson also opened the Irish Famine Museum in Strokestown, County Roscommon, in 1994 and also visited Grosse Île, with which it was subsequently twinned, in one of her many global journeys. As noted above, she sought frequently to stress the relevance of the Irish legacy in addressing other famines in other parts of the world in the present day, in fostering closer connections between poorer and richer countries and in promoting a particular sense of Ireland's role in such developments.

## CONCLUSIONS

What is the legacy of the Famine in the Diaspora today? Undoubtedly, the commemorative events of the 1990s saw a great flowering of interest, with the erection of Famine memorials, the incorporation of the teaching of the Famine into American and British school curricula and the many other controversies and debates about the Famine across the diaspora from the Americas to the Antipodes. Many questions remain, including the challenge of keeping the issue in the public mind. Will the visitor numbers to all those monuments and museums remain strong? History might suggest otherwise.

And yet. The sheer strength and resilience of Famine narratives are sometimes most evident in the unlikeliest of places. Any Irish sporting team playing in an international game – whether soccer, rugby or the GAA/Australian Rules compromise code – will be serenaded by supporters, homeland and diasporic, singing Pete St John's popular and enduring, albeit recently written 'Fields of Athenry', a song about the Famine:

> For you stole Trevelyan's corn
> So the young might see the morn.
> Now a prison ship lies waiting in the bay.

Questions remain. How will the Irish at home and abroad re-invent their identities when myths of Famine, victimhood, poverty and oppression no longer serve? And will such identities reflect the many strands of Irish experience – confessional, cultural, political, ethnic – in more pluralistic and inclusive ways? There is some way to travel.

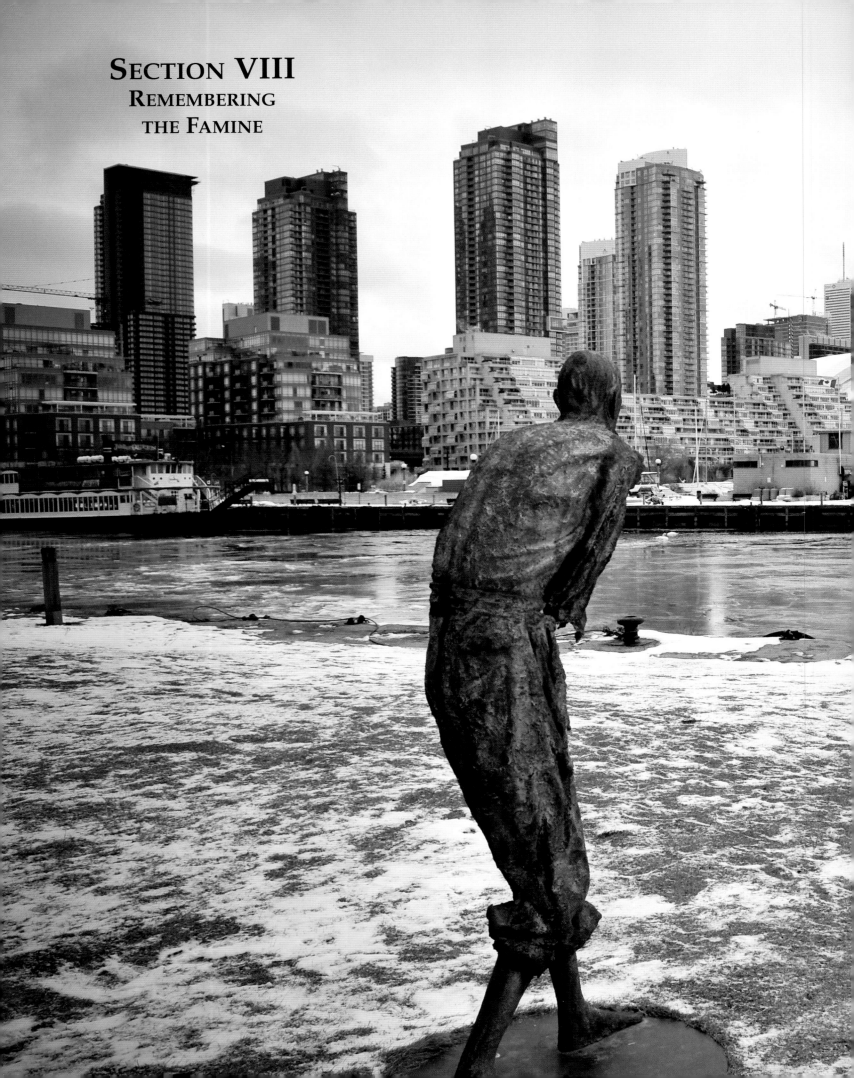

SECTION VIII
REMEMBERING
THE FAMINE

Figures from sculptor
Rowan Gillespie's Famine memorial
located on Toronto's waterfront.
[Photo: Gail Edwin-Fielding]

# The folklore of the Famine: *Seanchas an Drochshaoil*

## *Cathal Póirtéir*

'*Tá dhá insint ar gach scéal agus dhá leagan déag ar gach amhrán.*' This traditional Irish saying highlights the variety of traditional oral narrative and song. It is those variations on a theme that make the oral tradition in Ireland a fascinating source for researchers. While the proverb promises more versions of a song than a story, the recorded folklore of the Great Famine is rarely reflected in the traditional songs that have come down to us. It has however provided extensive narrative accounts of the Famine, many of these collected by the Irish Folklore Commission. Nevertheless, some fine songs dealing with the events of the Famine have survived in the living tradition into the twenty-first century. There are easily available commercial recordings of 'Na Prátaí Dubha'[1] and 'Johnny Seoige',[2] probably now the best known songs concerning the Great Hunger.

My own research into the folklore of the Famine was originally carried out as research for a number of radio programmes broadcast by RTÉ Radio 1 as part of the 150th anniversary of the Famine period beginning in 1995 and was confined to material in the main manuscript collection in the National Folklore Collection, UCD. As well as themed programmes, in both English and Irish, I published two compendia of famine folklore based on that research: *Glórtha ón Ghorta*[3] and *Famine Echoes*,[4] reflecting the language in which the material had been collected. Much of it had been gathered as the result of a concerted effort to collect the folklore of the Famine to mark the 100th anniversary in 1945. This work included responses to Irish Folklore Commission (IFC) questionnaires.

### COLLECTING FOLKLORE

The IFC questionnaire system was designed to provide information to the Commission from many parts of the country that would not otherwise have been represented in the collection due to the small number of full-time collectors available to the Irish Folklore Commission. Many of those who replied to IFC questionnaires were teachers who had previously been involved in the IFC's Schools' Collection in

Fig. 1 Tadhg Ó Murchú interviewing the informant/storyteller Pádraig Ó Súilleabháin at An Spuncán, Waterville, County Kerry, in 1948. [Photo: Caoimhín Ó Danachair of the Irish Folklore Commission/Courtesy of the Delargy Centre for Irish Folklore and the National Folklore Collection, University College Dublin]

Fig. 2 *The Discovery of the Potato Blight in Ireland* by Daniel MacDonald (1821–53), gifted to the Irish Folklore Commission by Cecil Woodham Smith in 1966. [Courtesy of the Department of Irish Folklore, University College Dublin]

1937–38 and who subsequently volunteered to collect folklore through the questionnaire system in their own areas.

Thousands of manuscript pages also resulted from the work of the commission's small team of full-time collectors who were experienced in all areas of collecting and transcribing folklore material and who worked particularly in the Gaeltacht areas. There was a concentration of collectors in these areas because it was felt that, while the oral tradition was strongest in the Irish-speaking communities, the language itself and the lore it carried were being lost. As the use of English became more widespread as a community language, the transmission of Irish language lore to the next generation was endangered. The quality of the Famine folklore collected in Irish is notably richer than the material collected in English-speaking areas, both in quantity and quality.

It should be remembered that many of the informants who contributed to the questionnaire system were not recognised tradition bearers and that responses to a ques-

tionnaire would have differed from those elicited by the questions of skilled and sympathetic collectors whose own knowledge might have influenced the questions asked of an informant particularly well-versed in the *seanchas* or traditional historical lore of the area.

The oral traditions of the Famine that we encounter in the National Folklore Collection in UCD flow from recollections of contemporary events by eyewitnesses which were later transmitted to members of their own communities, perhaps a generation or two removed from the events described. It is a commonplace among folklorists to note that oral transmission of songs and stories can often be passed directly from a grandparent to a grandchild, bypassing a generation which might be too busy with daily survival to have the time to listen and learn. This type of transmission is well-attested in the study of structurally complex and detailed folk narratives. The retentiveness of a young person's memory can appear prodigious to many in middle and old age, as can the memory of practiced and conscious tradition bearers who can provide identically worded folktales recorded decades apart.

The absolute accuracy of these memories is, of course, debatable because of possible distortion over time. Nevertheless, the material collected by the IFC is undoubtedly what was remembered in the communities where Famine lore was collected. It provides a historical perspective otherwise unavailable by allowing access to the experiences of those inside the communities who experienced the Famine. Indeed, it is the variety of family and local lore, linking individual and community experience, which brings a unique dimension and quality to the pictures of the Famine.

## HUMAN DIMENSION

Often, valuable administrative, statistical, ideological and economic studies may hide or obscure the human dimension which is one of the strengths of the oral material. Folklore can provide vivid and evocative accounts of what was experienced in a particular locality. Indeed its advantages may lie in its more personal telling of that people's own history and how it was remembered by those communities immediately after the Famine. That is not to say that folklore contradicts the information in contemporary written data but rather that it humanises statistics with vivid heart-felt descriptions. Undoubtedly, attention to a number of accounts of a single event can give a more rounded or nuanced overall picture. To ignore folklore as a source is to limit the number and variety of sources for local or national studies.

During the period of the 150th anniversary of the Famine in the late 1990s I was invited to give lectures on the folklore of the Famine at thirty or forty local conferences, along with many academic researchers in the history and economics of the period. It was remarkable to hear how well papers from various disciplines complemented, rather than contradicted, each other in providing a coherent overall picture of events.

The larger economic, historical or ideological contexts of the Famine are rarely found in the folk material. Explanations of what happened at national or governmental level do not feature prominently. What is recalled is how the Famine impacted on an individual's family or community. The folklore of the Famine allows us to hear local voices recall local events and gives us glimpses of how the cataclysm made a lasting impact on a community's past and its understanding of it.

So while informative and important parliamentary debates and official records are absent from the folklore record, it is rich with references to how policy impacted on a wide spectrum of communities and individuals. This ranges from those whose relatives were on the receiving end of the public works, soup kitchens and workhouses, to those others whose predecessors had been employed in administering these schemes locally. Where a community's account might lack scientific understanding of potato blight

Fig. 3 Inscribed in the landscape were physical memorials of the devastation wrought by the Famine including burial plots, deserted houses and abandoned plots and fields. The empty shells of houses spoke of dispossession and loss and were daily reminders to those who survived of what had happened. [Photo: John Crowley]

or how famine-related diseases were spread, they did remember and describe, in harrowing human terms, how hunger, starvation and infectious diseases affected individuals and families within their own locality.

It is within the folklore material that we discover that stories of individual cruelty and kindness outlasted the Famine itself by generations and that it was the actions or inactions of people at a local level which were vividly recalled, rather than government policy or its national administrators who were far removed from their communities.

## LOCAL EVENTS AND MEMORY

Particular individual items of folklore do not in themselves give the general or complete picture of what was happening on a national level, but cumulatively we can build up images of what happened and what was remembered in a locality. It is worth acknowledging the degree of conformity and consistency within the oral tradition as well as comparing them with other primary sources. In these accounts we can access the memories and descriptions of what happened on the ground within the communities who were hit by hunger, disease, homelessness and eviction and who needed the soup kitchens, public works, workhouses and assisted emigration. These were the people who continued to populate a landscape which contained daily reminders of what had happened. These connections to the events were often physical memorials to the Famine in the form of deserted and dilapidated homes, abandoned plots and fields, official and unofficial burial places, results of relief works and the imposing presence of the workhouses.

On another level there were letters and remittances from those who emigrated, fields, farms and estates which had changed hands. Much of their sense of place and cultural landscape was marked by reminders of the Famine and often provided a frame of reference for the accounts given. The people had an intimate knowledge of the landscape in which they lived. Placenames reflecting Famine events anchored social memory, offering regular opportunities to explain, recall and interpret the events which gave rise to a name. There are numerous examples of Famine-related names, with Famine Roads, New Lines, 'Male' (Indian Meal) Roads and so on, some still serving the present with a reminder of the past. Sometimes places were pointed out and identified as locations for certain events, unmarked burial places or emergency food distribution, even though the physical evidence may have disappeared.

Referring to folklore material about the 1798 rebellion in Ireland, Guy Beiner notes that the folk history of the events is 'propagated through various genres, including stories, songs and ballads, poems, rhymes, toasts, prophecies, proverbs and sayings, placenames and a variety of commemorative ritual practices. Each of these models of expression needs to be examined on its own terms and placed within a wider historical context.'[5] The folklore of the Famine shares many of those genres, from simple proverbs like 'a wilful waste makes a woeful want' to easily recognisable genres of oral narrative.

### LEGENDS AND ADAPTATIONS

One specific genre worth noting is a small number of migratory legends about generosity being rewarded by a miraculous abundance of food. These Irish Famine versions are adaptations of international legends predating the Irish Famine by many centuries. The narrative detail in each version differ as legends involve specific places and people in a locality, but the moral message of the legends are more or less the same: generosity or prayer is rewarded by divine intervention and the miraculous replacement of lost crops or food.

The first time I heard a version of one of these legends was in Rinn Ó gCuanach, County Waterford, in the 1990s and it concerned the generosity of Máire Ní Dhroma, also identified by local tradition as the composer of the song 'Na Prátaí Dubha'. Versions of the same legend were recorded in several places around the country and the example I give below was collected from Pádraig Ó h-Arrachtáin, born 1886, a farmer, na h-Insí, Eyeries, Castletownbere, County Cork, and is typical of this migratory legend:[6]

> To the west of Castletownbere there is a place called Drom. In this townland there is a field known to many of the older people as 'The Field of the Crop', and this is how it got its name.
>
> At the time when the famine was in Ireland, a man of the Hurleys lived here. He had a small farm and was married to a small charitable woman. This farmer was a hard worker and he always tried to be up to time with his crops and to have everything down *blasta* (tastefully). He could not bear to hear

anyone say that he was a lazy or untidy man. That was an *asachán* (accusation) he could not stand.

Well, the Great Famine came in 1848. Times got very bad entirely. The potatoes all blackened and other crops, too, especially oats were very bad the same year. This poor man was struck hard for he had only two bags of oats, as he thought.

When he had everything gathered in the first thing he did was to fill a firkin of potatoes and put them aside as seed for the coming year. Then he sieved the oats and found that it was all chaff and only a grain here and there. He gathered chaff and grain all into one bag and put that aside also.

That was all right till the winter came, and the hunger and the cold. The place was full of poor people going around looking for something to eat. Again and again they came to the farmer's house. His good wife never let them go empty. She couldn't bear to refuse a thing to anyone who asked for it for God's sake. Soon she found that her store was getting very small, yet in spite of all, the number of the poor people who came to the house increased daily. In the end she was up against it as she hadn't anything left but the firkin of seed potatoes and the few bags of chaff. Often and often the husband told her not to meddle with the seed, whatever else she would do.

Now the poor people who came to the house had to go away empty-handed. Still they continued to come day after day. The poor woman was very troubled when she had to put them off day after day like this. She thought it very wrong to be refusing it when they asked it for 'God's sake', and when she had a little still left. In the end it came so hard on her that she commenced on giving out the potatoes now and again.

When the spring came her husband went to examine the seed one day and when he found that the firkin of seed potatoes was half-empty he became very angry. He abused his wife left and right. He said that they would be shamed for ever by the neighbours when they would have no crop in the fall or in the harvest, a thing, he said, never happened in their family before. The only answer the wife made him was to leave it to God, that he was strong and that he had a good mother.

About Patrick's Day when the farmer had the field ready for the *sciolláns* (seed potatoes) he went again to the firkin to get as much seed as he could out of what remained. He was amazed this time when he saw the firkin was full of fine potatoes. When he told his wife she was more surprised. They cut them into *sciolláns* and planted them.

The farmer thought the oats he had was no

good and was not going to sew it at all. His wife made him plough the field and shake it anyhow.

When the harvest came round again, the talk and wonder of that neighbourhood was the crops that were grown by that farmer. Their like was never before seen or, perhaps, since.

Obviously, migratory legends such as this reflect social attitudes, wishful thinking and communal *mentalité* rather than events as they occurred. The folklore material not only gives us descriptions of what happened locally but also provides access to some of the feelings and interpretations which accompanied the events and their aftermath. It is here we find invaluable popular expressions of the community's reaction to events and some forms of popular remembrance.

### COMMUNAL MEMORY

The material in the National Folklore Archive was collected from the descendants of those who survived the Famine. That is not to say that these families escaped deprivations. In many families, the weakest perished, often old people and infants, while others survived to see better times. In badly hit areas of the West, even those who survived were likely to have lost relatives and neighbours and to have witnessed the ravages of malnutrition, abject poverty and deadly disease. While we are dealing with accounts that originate with those who survived, what they describe is part of their community's recent history and all of them carried the scars of the Famine to a greater or lesser extent. Given the passage of time, it is possible that memories in a particular community may have interacted with each other after repeated recollection and narration, and in some cases may have merged over time into a sort of composite community memory.

In 2110 Famine historian Mary Daly outlined the reservations academic historians held about folklore sources but also hinted at a more recent nuanced appreciation of this material:

> Given the centrality of myths, legends and folktales in the material collected by the Irish Folklore Commission it may not be altogether surprising that the relationship between Irish history and Irish folklore has been problematic in the past. However, in

Fig. 4 *Deserted Dwellings* by Seán McSweeney, oil on board 46 x 61 cm. [Courtesy of the artist]

Fig. 5 *Emigrants at Cork, c. 1840,* artist unknown, oil on canvas. [Courtesy of the Department of Irish Folklore, University College Dublin]

defence of historians, I would also argue that the use of folklore sources for historical inquiry requires a methodological training and a sophisticated understanding of the material that evolved many decades after the founding of Irish Historical Studies, and it is only in recent decades that historians have begun to actively engage with historical memory as a research topic . . . The explosion of interest in local history and in history written 'from below'– the search for the voices of ordinary people and their lives – all promise a growing interest in folklore material as a source for topics such as diet, health and medicine, material culture and popular politics.[7]

The need to close the gaps in inter-disciplinary understanding and methodologies has now been recognised and a number of publications have resulted[8] but it remains to be seen if this will lead to a stronger emphasis on the use of folklore as a source for Irish social history. *Is maith an scéalaí an aimsir.*

Fig. 1 (overleaf) *Na Prátaí Dubha* is a traditional song/poem from Ring, County Waterford, attributed to Máire Ní Dhroma of Baile na nGall, Ring, and dated *c.* 1850 by the editors of *Londubh an Chairn.* Michael Coady's translation is based upon the text published in *Duanaire Déiseach* (Nioclás Tóibín; Sáirséal agus Dill, 1978) supplemented by the recitation of Peig Bean Uí Riagáin of Ring. 'The mountain graveyard' is Reilig an tSlé, west of Dungarvan, on the road to Youghal which was opened to bury the workhouse dead when all the other graveyards were full. [Our thanks to Michael Coady, both for these notes and this translation. Photo: William J. Smyth]

## Na Prátaí Dubha

Na Prátaí Dubha a dhein ár gcomharsana a scaipeadh orainn,
A chuir sa phoorhouse iad is anonn thar farraige,
I Reilig an tSléibhe tá na céadta acu treascartha
Is uaisle na bhFlaitheas go ngabha a bpáirt. …

Más mar gheall ar an bpeaca claon a tháinig an chéim seo eadrainn,
Oscail ár gcroí agus díbir an ghangaid as;
Lig braon de do fhíorspiorad arís chun a chneasaithe,
Is uaisle na bhFlaitheas go ré ár gcás. …

Tá na bochta seo Éireann ag plé leis an ainnise,
Buairt is anacair is pianta báis,
Leanaí bochta ag béiceadh is ag screadadh gach maidin,
Ocras fada orthu is gan dada le fáil.

Ní hé Dia a cheap riamh an obair seo;
Daoine bochta a chur le fuacht is le fán,
Iad a cur sa phoorhouse go dubhach is glas orthu,
Lánúineadha pósta is iad a scartha go bás.

Mo thrua móruaisle a bhfuil mórán coda acu,
Gan tabhairt sásaimh san obair seo do Rí na nGrás,
Ag feall ar bhocta Dé nach bhfuair riamh aon saibhreas
Ach ag síorobair dóibh ó aois go bás.

Bíonn said ar siúl ar maidin, ar an dóigh sin dóibh,
Is as sin go tráthnóna ag cur cuiríní allais díobh.
Níl aon mhaith ina ndícheall mura mbíd go cuíosach seasmhach,
Ach téigí abhaile is beidh bhur dtithe ar lár. …

Beidh Rí na Glóire fós ag freagairt dóibh,
Is an Mhaighdean chumhachtach go humhal á nglacadh isteach;
Beidh an dá aspal déag ag déanamh dóibh caradais'
Sin stór nach mbeidh caite acu go Lá an Bhráth'. …

- Máire Ní Dhroma

## The Blackened Potatoes

The black potatoes scattered our neighbours,
Sent them to the poorhouse and across the sea,
They are stretched in hundreds in the mountain graveyard,
May the heavenly host take up their plea. …

It was sin brought this penance down on us,
Open our hearts and banish gall,
Anoint our wounds with your spirit's healing
And heavenly host take up our cause. …

The poor of Ireland truck with misery
With the pain of death and the weight of grief.
Little children scream each morning
From hunger pains, with no bite to eat.

It can't be God that brought this down on us,
The starving scattered under freezing skies,
Or the poorhouse door bolted cold and dark on them
With wives and husbands set apart to die.

Alas there are those endowed with wealth enough
Who do not serve the King of life,
They abuse the poor who never had anything
But constant labour for all their time.

From early morning they toil unceasingly
Each sweated day until dark comes on,
Little gain their best can earn for them
But cold dismissal and tumbled homes. …

The King of Glory will surely answer to them
And the Virgin Mary unbolt the door,
The twelve apostles will make good friends of them
To share in plenty for evermore. …

- Trans. Michael Coady

# Tadhg Ó Murchú (1842–1928)

## Cathal Póirteir

*Scríobh an bailitheoir béaloideasa Tadhg Ó Murchú tuairisc óna chuimhne ar sheanchas a athar, Tadhg Ó Murchú (1842-1928) a bhí ar an Sceachánaigh i bParóiste Chathair Dónaill. Is é an tuairisc aonair is faide agus is iomláine ar an drochshaol atá ar fáil i gCnuasach Béaloideas Éireann, imleabhar 1070:418-584. Ta súil agam go dtugann na sliochtanna thíos blaiseadh den 166 leathanach seanchais sin.*

Bhí sé thíos ag Crois na Trá Báine, Seán Ó Dubhghall agus do tháinig gátar an tsaoil chomh docht san ar an nduine mbocht agus go mb'éigin dó imeacht agus cúpla caora a ghoid ó dhuine des na comharsain agus iad a mharú agus d'ithe dhó féin chun an t-anam a choiméad ann.

Cuardaíodh an tig agus do fuarthas na heireaball agus craiceann na gcaorach sa tig aige. Tógadh leis na caoraigh é agus do déineadh *transporting* go dtí *Spike Island* air. Mhair sé agus chuir sé an drochshaol de agus d'fhill sé ar a dhúchas arís tar éis a théarma príosúin a thabhairt. Ach níor chaladh chun suain an baile dhó tar éis filleadh dhó, mar do bhí cailín bocht nach raibh ró-mhaith sa cheann. Bhí sí ina cónaí ar an dtaobh theas den Chrois, agus ní fhéadfadh Seán bocht a cheann a chur thar doras ná go mbíodh sí seo ina chochall agus an bhradaíocht a chaitheamh sa tsiúl aici air, gach aon 'Spaidhcín Beag Burdach na Leadhbhach' agus 'Spaidhc na n-Eireaball Cnuímhtheach' aici á bháisteadh air.

Bhí eachtra eile aige i dtaobh buachaill muinteratha dó a ghaibh isteach chucu maidin fhuar seaca, é féin agus a mháthair. *Cousin* dó ba é, a dúirt sé, darbh ainm dó Peter Crowley. Tháinig sé féin agus a mháthair isteach chucu an mhaidin so go háirithe agus sé a raibh d'éadach ar Pheter, a dúirt sé, sean-mhála stracaithe agus a ghéaga sáite amach ann agus chífá an craiceann glégeal, a dúirt sé, ag nochtadh tar éis na pollaibh a bhí sa tsean-mhála, agus an fear bocht ar sionna-chrith leis an bhfuacht agus leis an ocras.

Do leath sé féin ar an dtine, ag siúl rompu a bhíodar, féachaint cá mbuailfeadh greim bia leo, agus do tugadh greim éigin bia dó féin agus don mháthair agus do bhailíodar leo sa chuardach arís.

Mhair Peter, ar éigin, go dtí gur bhris Cogadh an Chruimé amach. Thóg sé an scilling agus an seacéad dearg, agus ní le grá don tSasnach é ach gur chuir an t-ocras chuige é, agus do bhí sé páirteach in gach aon chath agus in gach aon bhualadh ar tharlaigh sa chogadh san ó scaoileadh an chéad urchar go dtí gur fógraíodh síochán. Tháinig sé abhaile ar a dhúchas tar éis an chogaidh agus do stad sé i dtig mo shean-athar, Pádraig Bán Ó Murchú, ar feadh tamaill, é féin agus an mháthair. Bhíodh sé ag eachtraí dhóibh ar an gcogadh agus deireadh m'athair leis 'Muise a Pheter, is dócha gur mó scanradh a chonaicís an fhaid a bhís sa chogadh?'

'Dhearú, éist do bhéal a dhuine,' a deireadh Peter. 'Chonac-sa scanradh ba sheacht mhó agus ba sheacht mheasa ná aon chogadh. Ba mheasa an t-ocras ná é, a Thaidhg, nuair a bhíos ag dul ó thig go tig ag brath ar ghreim bia a fháil ó dhaoine nach raibh sé acu féin. Nár bhreá an rud duine a leagadh i gcogadh nuair a bheadh a bholg lán, seachas bheith ag fáil bháis leis an ocras.'

Is gnáthach go leanann plaigh agus breoiteacht an t-ocras agus b'shin é a tharla aimsir an drochshaoil leis. Do chloisinn m'athair á rá go raibh feaimlí de Mhuintir Raithille ina gcónaí ann aimsir an drochshaoil, seisear nó mór-sheisear pearsa acu. Buaileadh síos leis an droch-thaom iad agus ní thiocfadh éinne ina gcoire. Cailleadh gach aon mheidhil bheo acu a raibh sa tig, slán beo sinn, agus do leagadh an tig anuas orthu agus d'fhágadh ansan iad.

Chloisinn é á rá go bhfeicfeadh aintín a bhí aige an gadhar ag imeacht agus ceann cailín óig aige á stracadh chun siúil leis an folt brea fada buí a bhí ar an gceann ag scuabadh an bháin.

Asachán mór a ba é ó aimsir an drochshaoil anuas go dtí gur cuireadh deireadh lena leithéid sa tír seo, an *poor-house* a chasadh le duine, agus bhíodh scathalach i gcroí an duine bhoicht roimis, ab é bacach an bhóthair é, b'fhearr leis síneadh siar chun báis ar thaobh an bhóthair ná aghaidh a thabhairt ar an b*poorhouse*.

Fiú amháin an libhré a ghabh leis, asachán a ba é 'Tá *brand* an *Union* ort' a deirfí le duine, mar ba dheabhrach le culaith an phríosúin an éide seo a bhíodh ar na *pauper*.

Aimsir an drochshaoil, sa mbliain 1848, is dóigh liom, is ea do cuireadh na *poorhousaí* suas. Do bhí ceann acu i Neidín, i gCill Eoin agus ceann eile acu ar na Beathachaibh, tuairim is dhá mhíle ar an dtaobh thoir de Chathair Saidhbhín.

609

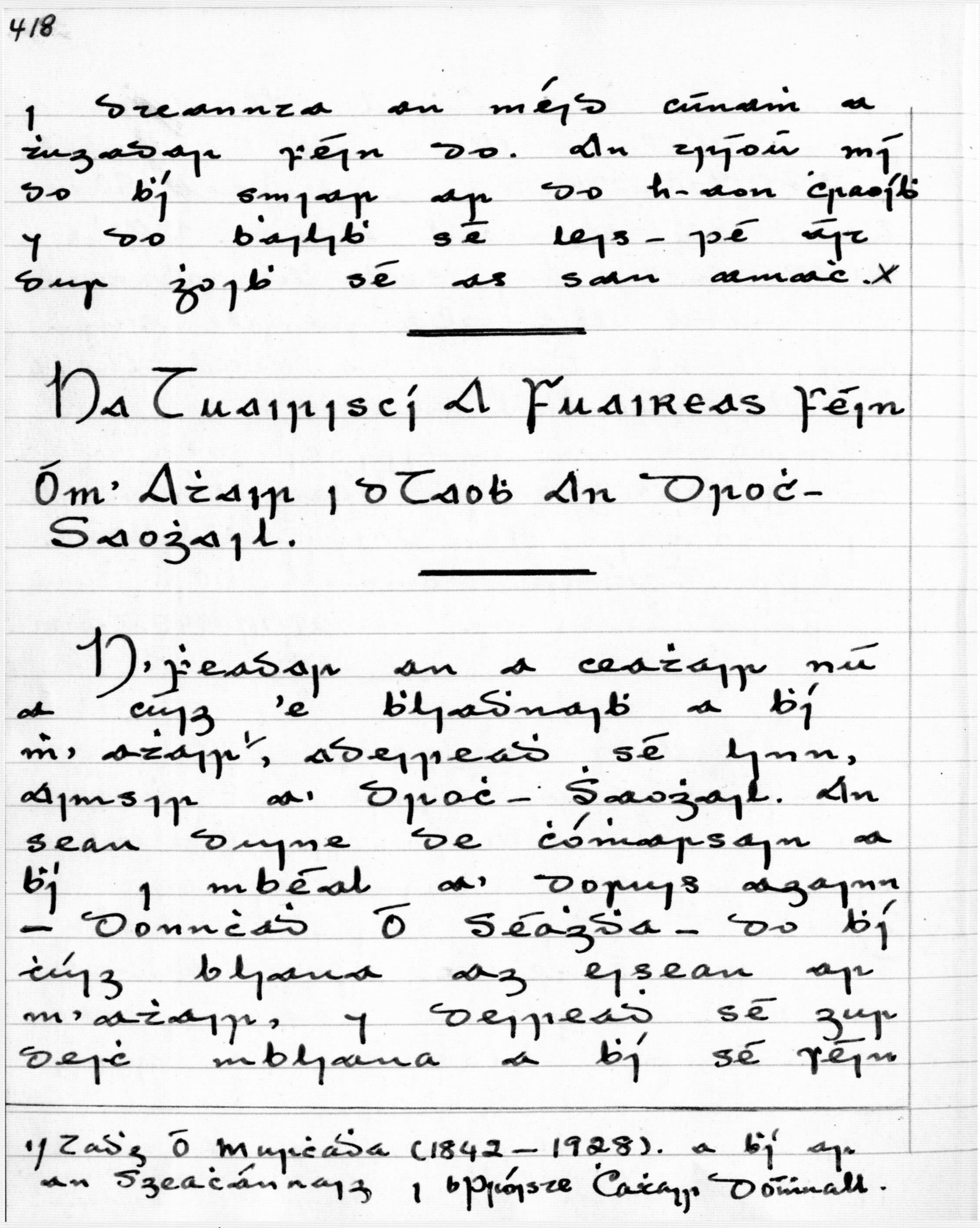

418

i dteannta an méid cúnaimh a
thugadar féin do. An tríú mí
do bhí smear ar do h-aon chraobh
y do bhainfí sé leis – pé áit
ar ghoirb sé as san amach. X

———

Na Tuairiscí a Fuaireas Féin

Óm' Athair i dTaobh An Droch-
Shaoghail.

———

D'fheadar an a ceathair nú
a cúig 'e bhlianaibh a bhí
m'athair, adeireadh sé linn,
aimsir a' Droch-Shaoghail. An
sean duine de chómharsain a
bhí i mbéal a' dorais againn
– Donncadh Ó Séaghdha – do bhí
cúig bliana ag eisean ar
m'athair, y deireadh sé gur
deich mbliana a bhí sé féin

y Tadhg Ó Murchadha (1842–1928). a bhí ar
an Sceachánach i bparóiste Cathair Dónall.

Fig. 1 The first page from Tadhg Ó Murchú's manuscript detailing his father's memories of the Famine in the Waterville/Cahersiveen area of south Kerry.
[Source: Delargy Centre for Irish Folklore and the National Folklore Collection, University College Dublin]

Bailíodh na daoine bochta isteach iontu so fé mar a bhaileofaí scata ainmhithe isteach go póna. Seift mhaith a ba é chun a gcúram a chur des na daoine a bhí freagrach don ghátar – rialtas Shasana agus na tiarnaí talún. B'fhearr, dar leo san, iad a bhailiú i dteannta a chéile in aon láthair amháin agus ligint dóibh bás a fháil ná iad a bheith ag titim ar thaobh na mbóithre. B'fhusa iad a chur nuair a scarfadh anam le colainn acu. Mórán Éireann acu a cuirtí ina mbeathaidh. Thit sé sin amach in *Workhouse* na mBeathach. Botaí a bhíodh á dtarrac sa reilig, i reilig Shruth Gréine a cuirtí bochtáin na mBeathach.

Déintí uaigh mhór sa reilig, poll doimhin leathan, go bhfaigheadh céad éigin corp, b'fhéidir, slí ann. Bhíodh tóin fhallsa sa bhota so. Cuirtí carnán corp air agus nuair a thaigidís ar bhruach an phoill leis, ní raibh moill orthu ach pé ceangal a bhíodh ar thóin an bhota, é sin a scaoileadh agus na coirp a scaoileadh síos insa pholl, idir mharbh agus leath-mharbh. *Buggy* a tugtaí ar an mbota so a bhíodh ag tarrac na gcorp agus do lean an ainm sin den *ambulance* a bhíodh ag Oispidéal an Fhiabhrais go dtí mo chuimhne féin.

Éagóir agus cos ar bolg agus ocras a ba saol na mbochtán sa *Phoorhouse*. Bhíodh na ceanna ag slad chucu féinig agus chun a lucht leannúna, agus ní raibh le fáil ag na *paupers* bhochta ach an caolchuid – 'an ceann ba chaoile den bheatha agus ceann ba ramhaire den bhata.' Déintí na leannaí a dheighilt ós na máithreacha nuair a cuirtí sa *phoorhouse* iad. Cuirtí i seomra leo féin iad agus glas orthu, agus do chloisinn m'athair á rá go mbíodh garsún linbh ann agus go sáthadh sé a mhéirín amach tré scoilteán a bhíodh sa doras agus go ndeireadh sé leis an mháthair: 'Mhuise féach an aithneofá mo mhéar a mham.' Ghoileadh m'athair go faíoch nuair a bhíodh sé ag insint an scéil seo dúinn. D'imigh mórán leanbh as aithne na máithreacha agus na n-athracha ar an slí seo, aon chuid acu a mhair agus ba bheag é.

Chloisinn m'athair ag eachtraí ar bhuachaill óg a bhí ag obair ar fhalla an Chomhaid agus lá dá raibh sé san obair, do ráinig le corp a theach sa reilig, á chur. Pé stíobhaird a bhí ar na fearaibh, is dóigh liom go mb'é gurbh é Sullivan Dubh é, d'fhiafraigh sé de dhuine des na fearaibh cérbh é an corp nó céarbh as é. Is dócha ná déintí puinn suim de chorp ag teacht go dtí an reilig sa tsaol san, Dia linn, nó dhá chorp. Dúirt an fear leis gurbh é a leithéid seo é 'athair sin

Fig. 2 Many of those who died in Bahaghs workhouse near Cahersiveen, the nameless victims of famine and disease, were buried in the nearby graveyard at Srugreana. [Photo: John Crowley]

ansin', ar seisean, ag pointeáil an bhuachalla so amach dó. Briseadh an buachaill as an obair ar an láthair sin. Dúirt an stíobhard leis nach raibh coinsias aige a bheith ag obair agus a athair á chur. Ag tagairt a bhí m'athair gur mhúch an gorta agus an gátar mórán den sean-nadúr a bhí i gcroíthe na ndaoine. Bhí an buachaill ag iarraidh a phá lae a thuilleamh féachaint an bhféadfadh sé an t-anam a choiméad ann féin.

Níor chuala aon bhreis moladh riamh ag m'athair ar Mhuintir Chonaill, Doire Fhinneáin. Níor chuala sé, a dúirt sé, gur dhéin an Couinsiléar (Dónal) aon fhóirthint puinn ar éinne, ach amháin go dtugadh sé scilling d'aon gharsún a dhúiseódh giorria dó lá fiaigh; nó an mhuintir a tháinig ina dhiaidh (cailleadh Dónal i dtosach an drochshaoil), níor chuala gur dheineadar aon fhoirithint ar éinne, ach amháin a gcuid cíosa a bhailiú ar nós na coda eile, agus dian go maith a bhíodar san éileamh leis, a dúrthas.

Na daoine a mhair agus do chonaic an drochshaol, do bhí scathalach ina gcroíthe ar eagla go mbearfadh aon sciúirse eile mar í orthu. Níor mhaith leo aon scubháiste a dhéanamh ar an mbia, nó aon tarcaisne a thabhairt dó. Dá b'é an craiceann prata é a bhuailfeadh leo ar an mbóthar, do thabharfaí abhaile chun an tí é i gcóir na circe nó i gcóir na muice, agus dá bhfeicfí éinne ag déanamh aon bhasta ar bhia nó ag tarrac ró-bhog air, bhagrófaí go dóite air tarrac socair ar an mbia agus gan é a bhastáil, agus dearfaí leis 'Mar sin, ní fhacís-se an drochshaol fé mar do chonac-sa.'

B'fhada siar a lean cuimhne an drochshaoil sin, agus do mhúch sé mórán den sean-daonnacht agus den tsean-fhéile a bhí bainte riamh i gcine Gael (1,579 focal)

*A translation from Tadhg Ó Murchú's account of the Famine memories told to him by his father, Tadhg Ó Murchú (1842-1928) from the Parish of Skeahanagh near Waterville, County Kerry. His full account is in the National Folklore Collection, UCD, volume 1070:418-584. It is the longest individual account of the Famine in the collection.*

He was down at White Strand Cross, Seán Ó Dubhghall, and the poor man was so sorely hit by hardship that he had to go and steal a couple of sheep from one of the neighbours and kill and eat them to keep himself alive. The house was searched and the sheep tails and hides were found there. He was taken off and transported to Spike Island. He lived and survived the Famine and returned home after serving his time in prison. But returning home wasn't a return to a peaceful harbour because of a poor girl who wasn't too good in the head. She was living south of the Cross and poor Seán couldn't put his head out the door without her getting it up for him, throwing the thieving up to his face, calling him every 'Little Thieving Spike of the Tatters' and 'Spike of the Maggoty Tails'.

There was another incident involving a boy who was related to him who came in one cold snowy morning, himself and his mother. He was a cousin, he said, called Peter Crowley. He and his mother came in this morning anyway and all Peter was wearing, he said, was a ripped old sack and his limbs shoved through it and you could see his bright naked skin, he said, through the holes in the old sack, and the poor man shivering with the cold and the hunger.

He spread himself by the fire. They were wandering about hoping to come across something to eat and he and his mother were given a bite of something and they set off on their search again.

Peter survived, somehow, until the Crimean War broke out. He took the shilling and the red jacket, and it wasn't for love of the English that inspired him but hunger, and he took part in every battle and confrontation that happen in that war from the first shot until peace was announced. He returned home to his own after the war and he stayed in my grandfather's house, Pádraig Bán Ó Murchú, for a while, himself and his mother. He would tell them about the war and my father would say 'Peter, I suppose you saw many frightful things while you were in the war?' 'Be quiet man,' Peter would say. 'I've seen worse and more horrors than I saw in any war. The hunger was worse, Tadhg, when I was going from door to door, looking for a bite to eat from people who didn't have it. Wouldn't it be a fine thing to fall in war with your stomach full, rather than dying from hunger.'

It is normal for plague and sickness to follow hunger and that's what happened in Famine times, too. I used to hear my father say that there was a Reilly family living during the Famine, six or seven of them. They were hit by a bad attack of illness and no one would come near them. Every single one of them in the house died, save us all, and the house was levelled on top of them and they were left there.

It was a great insult dating back to the time of the Famine until an end was put to the likes in this country, to reproach someone with the poorhouse and a poor person was deeply frightened by it, even a homeless beggar would prefer to lie down and die by the side of the road than face the poorhouse. Even the livery that was used, it was an insult to say to someone, 'You have the brand of the Union on you', because this suit the pauper wore looked like a prison uniform.

The time of the Famine, in 1848 I think, was when the workhouses were built. There was one in Kenmare, in Killowen and another one in Bahaghs about two miles east of Cahersiveen.

The poor people were herded into them the way animals would be herded into a pound. It was a clever device by those responsible for the hardship to fulfil their duties – the English government and the landlords. It was preferable, according to them, to gather them together in one place and let them die than to have them falling by the side of the road. It would be easier to bury them when the soul left the body. Many were buried alive. That happened in the

Bahaghs Workhouse. 'Botaí' would draw them to the grave-yard, Shrugreana graveyard was where the poor of Bahaghs were buried. A mass grave would be dug in the graveyard, a deep wide hole where there was space for, maybe, a hundred bodies. This 'botaí' would have a false bottom. A pile of bodies would be put on it and when they would come to the edge of the hole, they would not delay in releasing whatever tied the bottom of it to let the bodies fall into the hole, dead or half-dead. This 'botaí' which carried the bodies was called a buggy and that name stuck to the fever hospital ambulance until my own time.

Injustice and subjugation and hunger were the life of the poor in the poorhouse. Those in charge were plundering for their own benefit and for their followers but the poor paupers only got the least bit – 'the thinnest bit of the food and the thickest bit of the stick'.

The children were separated from their mothers when they were put in the poorhouse. They would be put in a locked room and I used to hear my father say that there was a young boy who would stick his little finger through a gap in the door and say to his mother: 'See if you can recognise my finger, mam.' He would cry bitterly when he was telling us that story. Lots of children became unrecognisable to their mothers and fathers this way, any who lived and they were few.

I used to hear my father talking about a young boy who was working on the Coad wall and one day when he was at work, a corpse came along going to the graveyard for burial. Whichever steward was in charge of the men – I think he was Sullivan Dubh – he asked one of the men whose corpse it was or where it was from. Probably not much heed was paid to a corpse coming to the graveyard in those times, God save us, or even two corpses. The man said it was such a person, 'the father of your man there', he said, pointing the boy out to him. The boy was sacked on the spot. The steward said he had no conscience working while his father was being buried. My father was referring to the way the Famine and the hardship extinguished the old nature in the people's hearts. The boy was trying to earn pay to keep body and soul together himself.

I did not hear my father express any great praise for the O'Connell family of Derrynane. He did not hear, he said, that the Counsellor (Donal) came to anyone's aid, apart from giving a shilling to a boy who raised a hare for him on a day's hunting; or the people who came after him. (Donal died early in the Famine times.) I did not hear that they came to anyone's aid, apart from collecting their rents like the rest of them, and they were fairly tough in their efforts.

The people who lived through and saw the Famine, they lived in fear that they would suffer a similar scourge again. They didn't like to waste any food or to misuse it. Even a potato skin, if they came on it by the roadside, they would take it home for the hen or the pig, and if they saw anyone wasting food or eating reluctantly, they would scold them severely to eat up well and not to waste it, and he would be told 'So, you didn't witness the Famine as I did.'

The memory of the Famine lasted a long time, and it killed off a lot of the old human nature and generosity that had always been associated with the Irish.

# Sites of memory

## John Crowley

Over the last number of years I have taken students on field-work in the Iveragh Peninsula in County Kerry. One of the geographical skills I try to impart is the ability to read different cultural landscapes. On one of the field days we visit the ruins of a workhouse at Bahaghs which is situated 4km from the town of Cahersiveen. What remains of the building is unremarkable in many respects. It did not follow one of George Wilkinson's uniform designs having previously served as a private residence. (p. 87) Yet there is something haunting about the site. The road which we travel on is now known as the Paupers' Road. The poorest of the poor who travelled this road at the height of the Famine must have been filled with fear and trepidation. Their instinct for survival would have taken them here in the hope that their admission would bring an end to their torment. There is little to remind the visitor to Bahaghs today of the hardships endured by those who felt compelled to enter such an institution. Instead of ensuring their survival such workhouses very often hastened their demise. The overcrowded conditions resulted in the rapid spread of disease. Colonel Clarke, who was appointed Temporary Inspector at the workhouse in the early months of 1848, having witnessed conditions in Bahaghs, quickly revised his initial objectives which were expressed in a cold and bureaucratic language:

I considered my appointment – Temporary Inspector in the Cahersiveen workhouse – to embrace a two-fold duty: in the first place to see that the laws for the relief of the poor were carried out to their fullest integrity and in the second to produce a moral revolution in the minds of the people by convincing them that their well-being depended on their own industry and exertions and not in becoming craving recipients of food wrung from the means of those scarcely better-off than themselves.[1]

Clarke's central mission to chastise the poor out of their idle ways quickly altered given the circumstances which he encountered in the house. Those who perished in Bahaghs were buried in the nearby Srugreana cemetery, one of the loneliest sites I have visited while researching the Famine.

Union workhouses like Bahaghs are central to the history of this tragic period. The ruins of this workhouse and the burial place at Srugreana are sites of memory which in their own understated way capture the essence of the Famine story. There are no signposts leading to Bahaghs or the unmarked graves at Srugreana – they are largely out of sight and out of mind which mirrors indeed the attitude of contemporaries who wished to remove the poor from their 'gaze'. The preservation of such sites

Fig. 1 The ruins of Cahersiveen workhouse at Bahaghs about 4 km from the town. [Photo: John Crowley]

Fig. 2 Maurice McGonigal's painting *An Ghorta 1847* (The Famine 1847) was exhibited in 1946 in the National College of Art and Design as part of an exhibition commemorating Thomas Davis and the Young Ireland movement. It was one of the few representations of the Famine produced to mark the one-hundredth anniversary. [Source: National Museum of Ireland]

should be uppermost in the minds of those who value the island's Famine heritage. Such relic features in the landscape bear witness to the horrors of the Famine in ways that are difficult to emulate or replicate in the work of contemporary artists and sculptors who have created new sites of memory which are the principal focus of this chapter.

## OFFICIAL NEGLECT

The spate of commemorative events relating to the Famine, especially since the mid-1990s, disguises the fact that the traumatic events of the mid-nineteenth century had long been overlooked by officialdom. In Ireland's capital city, Dublin, a memorial to the Famine was not constructed until 1967 when Edward Delaney's memorial was unveiled. It was one of a series of works sculpted by Delaney which also included monuments to Theobald Wolfe Tone and Thomas Davis. The memorial was positioned in a quiet corner of St Stephen's Green, separated by a granite wall from the Wolfe Tone monument on the other side that looked out on the busy Merrion

Row. Delaney's monument afforded the memory of the Famine a physical presence in the capital city, albeit one which was initially eclipsed by the imposing figures of Davis and Tone. Given that 1966 marked the fiftieth anniversary of the 1916 rising, it was perhaps not altogether surprising that the Famine should have taken a back seat in the commemoration stakes. This had also been the case in 1945, the year that marked the one hundredth anniversary of the Famine as well as the centenary of Thomas Davis' death. While the Davis commemoration took centre stage the Famine was relegated to the margins. The bleak socio-economic conditions that prevailed in the new Irish state help explain the rather muted official response. As Daly explains:

The strong and unqualified belief in Irish nationalism during the 1940s is immediately obvious from the uncritical attitudes paid to figures such as Davis and Parnell. Although the Famine is often seen as giving a boost to the cause of Irish independence, the fact that the centenary was ignored suggests that the event conveyed some less comforting messages, such as the failure of the independent state to reverse a century of emigration and population decline, or its difficulty in feeding and heating its citizens adequately during 1947.[2]

In this case the official response merely reflected a wider public apathy. Indeed the neglect of the Famine in this period lends weight to Declan Kiberd's contention 'that far from being worshippers of the past, what Irish people really worship is their own power over it, including the power to bury it at a time of their own choosing'.[3] It goes without saying that along with the power to bury the past comes the power to resurrect it. In this respect the State's and indeed the wider public's willingness to embrace the sesquicentenary commemoration of the Famine in 1995 stands in marked contrast to 1945. Gray and Oliver explained the surge in interest

Fig. 3 Edward Delaney's Famine Memorial, St Stephen's Green, Dublin. This memorial was unveiled in 1967 and exhibits many of the qualities which Delaney was searching for in his art. The style is modern expressionism rather than conventional realism. It is a piece of sculpture which transcends time; it speaks clearly and powerfully of the suffering and indignity of famine: 'One figure stands with arms up stretched towards the sky, while another weakly holds a cup of running water to the mouth of a seated figure. But the water is running over, out of the bronze cup – a sculpture cannot drink obviously. This adds to the poignancy of it all: the water trickles outwards and down over the base of the monument, suggesting wastage, or aid coming too late, or a stream of tears'. Eamon Delaney, *Breaking the Mould: A story of art and Ireland* (Dublin, 2009), p. 194. [Photo: John Crowley]

in terms of the pursuit of cultural stability in a rapidly changing society.

> While the symbols of a largely Catholic, inward-looking and autarkic nationalism may appear increasingly problematic in Ireland's secularising and internationalising society, there remains a demand for some historical continuity, a collective identity, rooted in a distinctive past; and the Famine appears to many to offer a focus that is at once catastrophic, local, diasporic and relevant to the modern world.[4]

Artistic works commissioned since the mid-1990s on the theme of the Famine must be seen within this wider context.

### BEHAN'S FAMINE SHIP

> The Great Irish Famine of 1845–52 is embedded in the folk memory of all Irish people as an unresolved phenomenon – memories of history lessons at school are of unspeakable sadness and suffering to me personally. Like the generations before me, my peers and I have not faced up to the facts of the Famine. Perhaps the complexities of the Famine have not been properly laid out for us to understand in total. We have tended to highlight incidents such as Queen Victoria's meagre contribution, something we can deal with rather than view in a detached way the reasons why the Famine occurred.[5]

> – John Behan

To mark the one-hundred-and-fiftieth anniversary of the Famine, the Irish government embarked on a series of commemorative events and memorial projects. One such memorial commission was awarded to the sculptor John Behan who works in the medium of bronze. Behan carried out a great deal of research into the history and folklore of the period before ultimately deciding on the form of the monument. The proposed site of the memorial in Murrisk at the foot of Croagh Patrick in County Mayo had a profound influence on the artist. The mountain has been a focal point for pilgrims for many generations and Murrisk is the village from which pilgrims begin their ascent. Behan undertook his own pilgrimage, which he admitted was more artistic than religious. From the summit of the mountain, Behan looked out on a landscape and seascape that captivated him. Features in the landscape such as the potato ridges and the empty shells of houses also recalled the impact of the Famine years. His sculpture would reflect the twin influence of land and sea.

In a television documentary about the making of the memorial, Behan described how he visited many famine sites in order to assemble a series of images that he could draw on later. His visit to the workhouse in Birr had a particular hold on him. While walking through the various sections, he was struck by the crowded conditions that must have prevailed in the workhouse during the Famine years. The confined spaces of the women's sleeping quarters along with the timber framed roof inspired the image of the coffin ship – 'the interior felt like and looked like the interior of a coffin ship'. The other feature in the landscape which had a particular resonance for him was the lazy bed – 'potato ridges built spade by spade, now lying under the grass inscribing the Famine into the very landscape. You learn to read the landscape, how it is marked by human habitation and how to incorporate that into your work'.[6]

As an artist Behan struggled in his efforts to come to terms with the scale of the disaster.

> Death is impersonal when it strikes in such great numbers. We struggle to find a single human signature in the midst of such devastation – some simple way of comprehending a large catastrophe. An artist's journey is a bit like that, trying to find the human scale in the suffering of a whole people. The image of the ship has deep ramifications throughout human history and human culture. As a symbol it is very much associated with the journey of life and the journey of death.[7]

The landscape around Clew Bay in County Mayo would remain uppermost in the artist's mind as he refined his image of the Famine ship. Behan regarded it as a place haunted by final journeys and absences. These overlapping themes would become a central concern in his work. The texture and colouring of the Famine ship would mirror the landscape of 'ridges, rivulets and bare rock'.

For famine victims, the ships that would take them away from Ireland proffered hope but also embodied the fear of the unknown. The stark image of the skeletal figures which make up the rigging of Behan's Famine ship reveals in no uncertain way the sad fate of the many who tried to leave the horror of the Famine behind them. Each art object, be it a painting or sculpture, presents its own interpretative challenge. They

Fig. 4 National Famine Memorial at Murrisk, County Mayo sculpted by John Behan and unveiled in 1997. The true witnesses to the horrors and suffering of the Famine are those who perished, a fact which is at the heart of Behan's sculpture. [Photos: Frank Coyne]

either provoke a response or not. It was while reading an account of the Irish Famine in Simon Schama's *A History of Britain* that the power of Behan's sculpture became more obvious to me:

> In Connemara on the Atlantic shore, it seems to have been the father's task to take their dead babies to the edge of the ocean to the ancient limbo spaces of water, land and sea; and dig little graves marked by

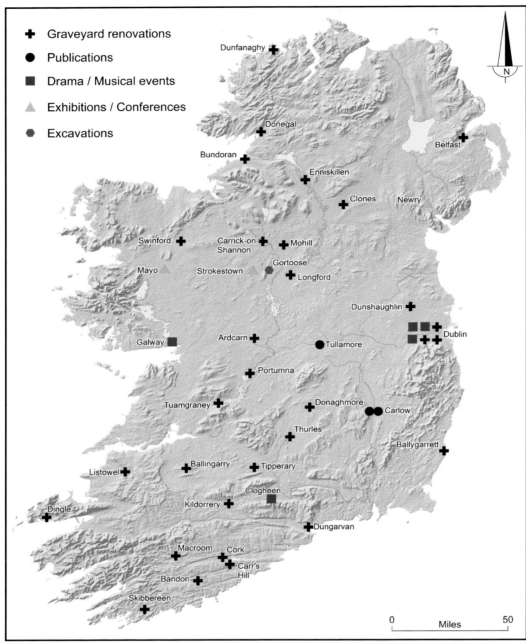

**Graveyard renovations**

**Publications**

**Drama / Musical events**

**Exhibitions / Conferences**

**Excavations**

Fig. 5 DISTRIBUTION OF FAMINE COMMEMORATION PROJECTS AND EVENTS, 1997. During 1997 the Irish Government's Famine commemoration committee allocated grants to fund a series of projects and events at local and national level. The range and scope of commemorative activities marked a fundamental shift in official and public attitudes towards an event that for too long had been cloaked in silence. [Source: Dáil Éireann, Volume 479, 14 May 1997]

tory and humanises it. It takes an imaginative approach, which evokes the horrors of the Famine in a very powerful and meaningful way.

**DIFFERENT WAYS OF SEEING**

Over three quarters of the one million people who fled Ireland during the Famine years made their way to the United States. It naturally follows that amongst Irish-Americans the Great Famine represents a substantial and significant communal memory. The institutionalization of that memory became a dominant theme from the mid-1990s onwards. Famine memorials have been built in cities such as Boston, Philadelphia and New York. While they may differ in their emphasis and approach, they nonetheless represent a desire to have the memory of the Famine marked in a very public way. The Boston memorial (Fig. 8), for example, is located at the corner of Washington and Scholl streets, near Downtown Crossing, close to the city's Freedom Trail which attracts millions of visitors annually while the New York Memorial is located close to Battery Park (see pp. 547–49).

The Boston memorial which was sculpted by Robert Shure was unveiled on 28 June 1998 when an estimated 7,000 people attended the dedication. The memorial narrative is predicated on sources such as John Mitchel, Lady Jane Wilde and William Carleton and the underlying message is one of the triumph of the Irish in the face of adversity, an oppressed people had not only escaped the hunger but also the callous treatment meted out to them by the British Government, and found freedoms in America that had been denied to them in their homeland. America was the haven, which allowed the emigrants not only to live but to also prosper. It is a narrative, which speaks more of success rather than failure, the American dream writ large. The *Boston Globe* editorial of 9 March 1998 commented:

a rough stone cut from the cliffs. Circles of thirty or forty of the wind-scoured, lichen-flecked stones, their jagged grey edges pointing this way that, stand by the roaring surf, the saddest little mausoleum in all of Irish history.[8]

The Famine ship memorial has been described as one of the most powerful commemorative symbols created during the one-hundred-and-fiftieth anniversary.[9] As O'Toole explains 'no art can do justice to the suffering of famine victims and any attempt to do so runs the risk of pathos. But what is too monstrous to be adequately described can be evoked'.[10] Behan's memorial defies stereotypes; it both illustrates his-

Beyond its particularly Irish dimension, the memorial

618

marks the beginning of the waves of nineteenth- and twentieth-century immigration that have made Boston the variegated place it is today. Thousands more would come: Italians, Jews, Greeks, Lithuanians, Chinese, Haitians, Dominicans, blacks from the American South and other ethnic groups, all seeking refuge from poverty and oppression. The triumph of the Irish is a parable of America.

The Famine, however devastating its consequences, marked the beginnings of the inexorable rise of the Catholic Irish in America. It could be argued that the emigrant experience is not really dealt with adequately in Shure's monument and to present that experience in such a positive light misrepresents the often tough and uncompromising conditions which the emigrants had to endure both on their journey to the New World and on their arrival. The monument seems more preoccupied with the constant striving forward rather than dealing with the tragic event itself.

Irish-America is not a monolith but is made up of many communities. What the Famine really means to the people who make up such communities is beyond the scope of this chapter. However if, as Paul Ricoeur suggests, cultures have founding events then the Famine represents such an event for a significant number of Irish Americans.[11]

Fig. 6 Rowan Gillespie's *Famine* on Custom House Quay, Dublin was also unveiled in 1997. Gillespie's intensely worked sculptural figures capture the despair and desolation of famine victims. The memorial's literalness in this case is a strength. The haunting figures speak of powerlessness in the face of a calamity which has shattered people's lives beyond imagination. [Photo: John Crowley]

For the many thousands who fled Ireland in the 'Hungry Forties' and in particular their descendants, the Famine marks the beginning of *their story*. It remains the touchstone of their identity as a people. The question of which version of the Famine becomes dominant in particular places at particular times is linked to the question of identity. The Famine as exile is very much the sustaining myth of Irish America. Myth in this context is not used in a pejorative sense but in the wider context of explaining 'how meaning is constructed out of a catastrophic event'.[12] The fact that a culture nurtures certain images of the Famine cannot be so lightly dismissed. It could be argued that criticisms of the Boston monument miss the point in not analysing more deeply the spaces and contexts in which the memorial is located. The dissonance that can often characterise debates about the meaning of the Famine in Ireland and the United States reflects in the end the very different needs of complex and diverse societies

## CONCLUSION: AESTHETICS AND POLITICS

The construction of public memorials to the Famine reveals a great deal not only about the aesthetics of memory but also significantly its politics. The poverty that prevailed in Dublin in the 1940s, for instance, can explain the rather muted official response to the one-hundredth anniversary of the Famine. A State commissioned Famine memorial did not materialise until 1967 and even then it was part of a trilogy of works by the sculptor Edward Delaney in which memorials to Wolfe Tone and Thomas Davis occupied the more open civic spaces.

Fig. 7  The pupils of Gaelscoil Dochtúir Uí Shúilleabháin, Skibbereen, stand around the mass grave at Abbeystrewery cemetery where between 8,000–10,000 Famine victims were buried. As part of the National Famine Commemoration in 2009, a minute's silence was observed in schools throughout the country in memory of the victims. [Photo: Denis Minihane]

The Famine memorial's comparative invisibility in a sense reflected the State's unease with this tragic event and its memorialisation.

This ambivalence stands in marked contrast to both the Irish Governments and indeed the wider public's response to the Famine in more recent decades. A rapidly changing political, socio-economic and cultural context provided a more favourable climate for the State and indeed the public to engage with the memory of the Famine. For example, the old certainties of Irish identity (nationalism and Catholicism) began to unravel and in such a climate there was no alternative but to construct 'new memories and new identities better suited to the complexities of a post-national era'.[13] The renewal in interest in the Great Famine and indeed in other historical events such as the Great War must be seen in the context of a rapidly changing Ireland.

John Behan's Famine ship invites the viewer to think and feel in unique ways about this tragic event. In that respect it is an important site in the production of new memories. It is clear that the memorial tries to bring people closer to the human realities of humiliation and despair which lie at the heart of the Famine story. Such despair and suffering has often been used and very often abused by those pushing a political agenda. Behan in a sense tries to unravel the different layers of meaning that have accumulated over time in his

efforts to present the visitor with a new way of seeing the Famine. In contrast the interpretation offered by the Boston memorial is rooted in a particular myth. The difference in approach reflects not only conflicting views of the Famine but also very complex and diverse identities. It is a clear manifestation of a much larger issue, the contested nature of Irishness that exists between those living in Ireland and the diaspora overseas.

Fig. 8  Robert Shure's Famine memorial in Boston. [Photo: A. Laburda]

# Famine memorial sites in County Cork

## John Crowley

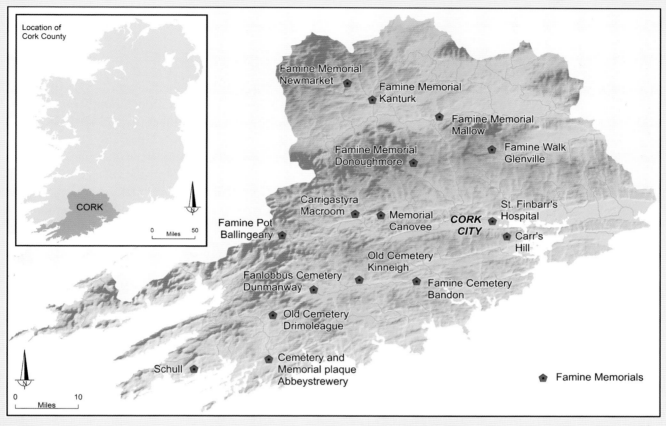

Fig. 1 FAMINE MEMORIAL SITES IN COUNTY CORK. The local commemoration of the Great Irish Famine is in many respects a very recent phenomenon. A small number of commemorative sites in County Cork – for example, those located in Skibbereen – have a more established history but a large number were unveiled to mark the 150th anniversary of the Famine (some of which are represented on this map). They are for the most part simple in design and emerged from the work of local committees, dedicated individuals and local history groups and societies.

Fig. 2 Archdeacon Robin Bantry-White speaking at an ecumenical ceremony in St Joseph's Cemetery, Tory Top Road, Cork City to mark National Famine Commemoration Day, 17 May 2009. Also in attendance was the Lord Mayor of Cork, Councillor Brian Bermingham, and Councillor Tom O'Driscoll. It is estimated that c.10,000 victims of famine were buried in St Joseph's in a plot donated by local Capuchin priest, Fr Theobald Mathew. [Photo: John Crowley]

Fig. 3 Unveiling and blessing of Kinneigh Famine memorial in 2009 by Fr Myles McSweeney. [Photo: Colum Cronin]

# 'Remembering, not forgetting', a commemorative composition

## Marian Ingoldsby

'Remembering, Not Forgetting' was composed in the autumn of 1995, for the one-hundred-and-fiftieth anniversary of the Irish Famine. The piece is of fourteen minutes' duration, composed for string quartet and uileann pipes. It was recorded in the Honan Chapel of University College, Cork, in December of that year, as an accompaniment to an exhibition of images of the Famine.

I drew my inspiration from a number of sources. I was initially shown some of the images in the form of slides, by Dr John Crowley of UCC's Geography Department. These included grotesque silhouettes of emaciated people dressed in rags, famine roads that struck me as particularly important, almost symbolic of lifeblood, and pictures of emigration. The collection of images conjured up an atmosphere of intense suffering, desolation, hunger and longing for resolution.

I selected the instruments for specific reasons. The plaintive tone of the uileann pipes, running with the credits, is quite haunting and suited to the aforementioned atmosphere. It is also tonal, the G major tonality contrasting greatly with the material played by the strings, the latter being dissonant, with deliberately unresolved harmonies, bitonality and angular individual lines. This angularity of line was suggested by several of the images shown to me. I did not have a sequence of events or pictures in mind, and this provided me with carte blanche in the sense that I could simply create my mood as I wished, unlike the film composer who must calculate at every moment.

In order to create an atmosphere, I used a melodic line consisting of semitones and bland intervals such as the fifth, which lends itself to the technique of droning. Such features appear in all string lines, with the additional gradual ascent to the high register, near to the midpoint of the piece, thus contributing to the general mood of unease, tension and suffering. I also tried to depict sadness through the use of range, low to high, and dissonance breaking through the tonal sections.

Drones were used both in dissonant and tonal sections. The uileann pipes enter on two occasions, with the intention of injecting an air of hope. I am reminded of the words of Emily Dickinson, "Hope is the thing with feathers – that perches in the soul –". Hope in this context is in the form of the tonality of G major.

In addition to the slides viewed, I found much inspiration in Helen Litton's book, *The Irish Famine: An Illustrated History*.[1] The contrast between the coloured

Fig. 1 *The Blind Piper* by Joseph Haverty (1794-1864), oil on canvas. [Source: National Gallery of Ireland]

Fig. 2 Part of the score of 'Remembering, not Forgetting', by Marian Ingoldsby.

and black-and-white images (lithographs) is quite striking, the latter capturing best the sadness and loneliness experienced by so many people who were forced to emigrate at the time.

The aforementioned climactic point, where the strings ascent the range, paves the way for the first entry of the uileann pipes, which is roughly at the centre point. Jerky counterpoints interrupt along the way, together with string tremolo effects played near the fingerboard, which provide the musical means of expressing the coldness, misery and bleakness of the black-and-white images of Famine victims. The melody played by the pipes is accompanied by simple string drones, this texture emerging after a low, lethargic cello solo. Between the two entries of the pipes, the tonal language changes dramatically, becoming intentionally tense and restless.

In general, the fourteen minutes of music represents states of tension, suffering, sadness and desolation, interspersed with moments of peacefulness and hope. While the atonality returns in the strings, I have used syncopation to move it on between uileann pipe entries, along with harmonies moving stealthily by semitone and tone shifts. These syncopated passages help to sustain the mood of hope, and lead towards a hopeful conclusion.

# The Big House and Famine memory: Strokestown Park House

*Terence Dooley*

In 1981, the elderly Olive Hales Pakenham Mahon prepared to leave her ancestral home at Strokestown Park for the last time, thus breaking a family link of 300 years. The grand neo-Palladian mansion, in part designed by Richard Castle, had been the focal point of the 27,000-acre estate granted to her ancestors in the seventeenth century. Outside the demesne walls, Thomas Mahon, 1st Baron Hartland, had constructed an impressive landlord-designed town during the boom of 1810–15, his primary ambition to create one of the widest streetscapes in Europe. It was an extravagant attempt to display his social, economic and new-found political status having been elevated to the peerage as a reward for his support of the Act of Union in 1800.

## MISMANAGEMENT AND DECLINE

However, as was so often the case with Irish landed families, the extravagance of one generation was often the downfall of another. The expansion of house, landscape and town had been dependent upon large-scale borrowing on the eve of economic depression that came with the ending of the Napoleonic Wars in 1815. Moreover, primogeniture did not take into consideration personality disorder, or the simple fact that not all eldest sons were born to be competent landlords or even to be fathers. The Hartland peerage ended abruptly in 1845 with the insanity of the 2nd Baron Hartland and his successor died childless. By the time the estate passed to Hartland's cousin, Major Denis Mahon, it had been horribly mismanaged by the Court of Chancery for ten years and huge debts had accrued, largely as a result of the accumulation of rental arrears to around £14,000.

Shortly after Mahon succeeded, the socio-economic situation deteriorated as potato blight and consequential

Fig. 1 Strokestown Park House by Sir John Thomas Selwin Ibbetson *c.* 1830. [Courtesy of Strokestown Park National Famine Museum]

famine ravaged the smallholder and cottier economy of the area. For many years, local lore perpetuated the myth that it was the callous treatment of his impoverished tenants that led to Mahon's murder in November 1847.[1] As with many such historical incidents, the circumstances were considerably more complex, but certainly the population decline of 88% of the estate's total during the Famine, the eviction of an estimated 3,000 people and, more particularly, the loss of life of hundreds of tenants on their way to America in so-called coffin ships (as high as 70% of those who left) perpetuated bitter local ancestral grievances.[2]

For decades after Mahon's murder, Strokestown Park lay unused and vacant. When his descendants did return, the Irish country house was very much in its twilight years, its decline hastened by a dramatic change in the socio-economic and political circumstances of landlords from the 1880s. Moreover, those who wanted to justify the redistribution of the vast estates, which had originally given country houses their *raison d'etre*, successfully demonised them as symbols of colonial oppression, licentiousness and sometimes debauchery.

## TRANSFER OF OWNERSHIP

Under various land acts, the ownership of the Strokestown estate was transferred to its occupying tenantry. The capital received from the sale, while significant, was diminished in the years which followed as the investment markets crumbled in the post-war decades. The house became unsustainable: the family could no longer afford the army of staff, including craftsmen retainers, to maintain it as they had done in the past and so the interior fabric fell into miserable and irreversible decay, the victim of various architectural diseases such as dry and wet rot. In a tragic parallel, Olive's personal life had also been blighted, most notably with the death of her young husband of five months, Captain Edward Stafford-King-Harman (1891–1914), killed on 6 November 1914 at Ypres. In just five months she had been married, become pregnant (a daughter would be born in early 1915) and made a widow by the Great War.

After independence, the prevailing political and economic climate made it inconceivable that the Government would acquire country houses for the cultural enrichment of the public or even, as political attitudes softened, invest in the preservation of all but a few. One politician (and former Cork IRA leader during the revolutionary period) who clearly articulated this in the Dáil was Sean Moylan. In 1944, as Minister for Lands, he condemned them as 'tombstones of a departed ascendancy' and remarked 'the sooner they go down the better. They are no use.' A decade later, on 3 November 1954, speaking in a Dáil debate on the National Monuments (Amendment) Bill, he declared: 'I do think the preservation of a few outstanding examples should be adequate. Many of the demands made concern buildings whose historical significance is that "lowlier rooftrees are sturdier for their fall" and I am not displaying any interest in those.'[3]

The historical significance of such attitudes was not lost on those who subsequently established the Famine Museum at Strokestown: Jim Callery later recalled that 'the attitude was to wipe them [country houses] off the face of the earth. There would be as little left of them as there was of the poor cottiers who were wiped out in the Famine and after it,' while Luke Dodd, the first museum administrator mused: 'the destruction of the Big House was an ideal means through which the Free State could symbolically be seen to break with the past.'[4] Throughout County Roscommon (and the country as a whole) great houses disappeared, some the victims of IRA activity during the revolutionary period 1920–23, others of the continued social and agrarian unrest that accompanied the revolution as agitators pressed for the compulsory acquisition and redistribution of estates, but most the victims of increased rates and taxation and especially depleted economic fortunes.[5]

It was only Olive's resilience that allowed her to retain Strokestown Park into the 1970s – even if living quarters contracted eventually to just one room that she could afford to heat. But former ascendancy families such as the Pakenham Mahons had long become non-entities, assigned to oblivion, in stark contrast to their socially prestigious ancestors. Moreover, by the 1970s, Olive's son, a serving British army officer, had no intentions of settling in Roscommon, and so, she had no option but to sell the house and its surrounding lands to a local garage proprietor, Jim Callery, whose company, Westward Group, had recently acquired the sole right to distribute Scania trucks in the Republic of Ireland. For years, the garage had operated out of premises on the Main Street, close to the triple-arch Gothic entrance to the park. It was not uncommon to see mechanical debris spilling untidily beyond its garage forecourt, much to the chagrin of Olive, and so a difficult relationship had traditionally existed between herself and Callery. He never made any secret of the fact that his reason for buying Strokestown Park had its roots in his entrepreneurial ambitions to expand his business rather that any recognition of the house as a significant part of Ireland's heritage.[6]

## A CHANGE OF ATTITUDE

However, at this point, developments took an ironic twist. Under the terms of the purchase agreement, Olive was allowed to reside at Strokestown Park for as long as she

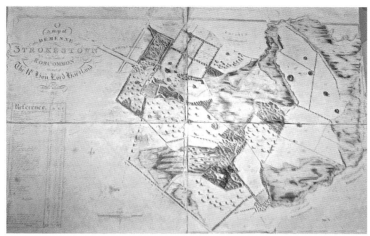

Fig. 2 Strokestown demesne as mapped by James Johnston in 1826.

wished. Jim Callery began to visit her on a regular basis and their relationship improved accordingly. On one occasion he got permission to wander through the house where he came upon a pile of estate records. One document changed his attitude towards the preservation of Strokestown Park; it was a petition from tenants of the townland of Cloonahee, written to the landlord during the Great Famine pleading with him for some form of relief: 'Our families are really and truly suffering in our presence and we cannot much longer withstand their cries for food. We have no food for them, our potatoes are rotten and we have no grain.' (Fig. 3) The emotive impact is understandable when one considers that Cloonahee was the townland in which Callery was born and reared; it is also a stark reminder of the value of preserving archives as a first step towards preserving the past and recreating the historical narratives in which the past is bound.

Callery realised how much of his own historical narrative and that of his direct ancestors was now in his possession and, as Christopher Ridgway, curator at Castle Howard in Yorkshire, concludes: 'he realised he had stumbled upon a cache of enormously important documents that had a public story to tell.'[7] Ridgway's interpretation of the documents having a *public* story to tell bears all the hallmarks of an eminent curator's intuition; the public story was as much a narrative of those looking in as those looking out from the big house. As a comprehensive collection of documents of various provenance and function they informed on so many aspects of the economic, social, political and cultural life of the estate community ranging from the landlord family to the destitute and impoverished who died of starvation and disease or who were cleared off the estate during the Famine and, just as pertinently, they offered valuable insights into who survived and why. The archive is now housed on loan to the OPW/NUIM Archive and Research Centre located on the top floor of Castletown House, which has been turned into a research centre under the auspices of the OPW and the Centre for the Study of the Historic Irish House and Estates at NUI Maynooth and

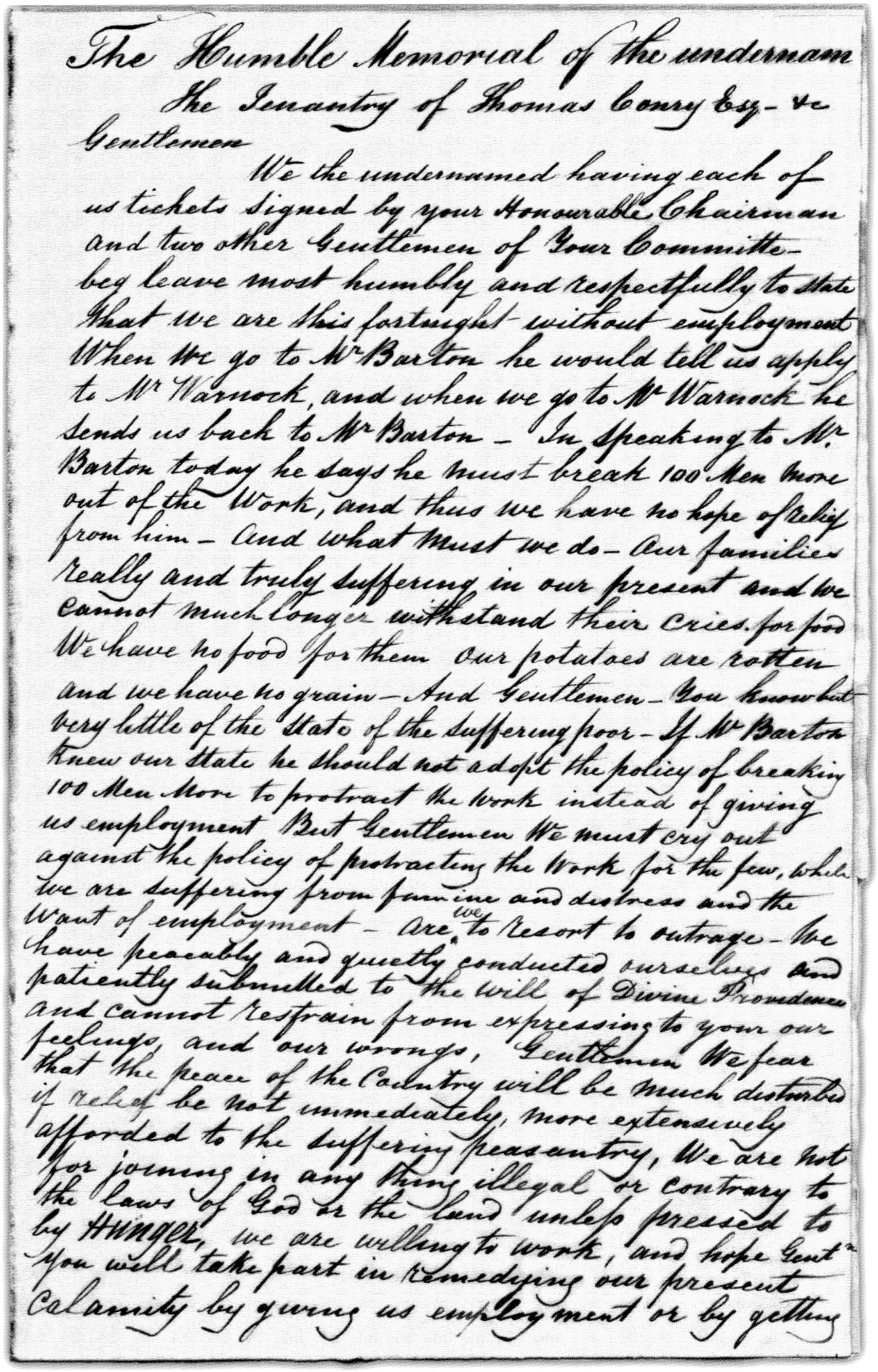
The Humble Memorial of the undernam
The Tenantry of Thomas Conry Esq – &c
Gentlemen
We the undernamed having each of
us tickets signed by your Honourable Chairman
and two other Gentlemen of Your Committe
beg leave most humbly and respectfully to state
that we are this fortnight without employment
When we go to Mr Barton he would tell us apply
to Mr Warnock, and when we go to Mr Warnock he
sends us back to Mr Barton – In Speaking to Mr
Barton today he says he must break 100 Men more
out of the Work, and thus we have no hope of Relief
from him – And what must we do – Our families
really and truly suffering in our present and we
cannot much longer withstand their cries for food
We have no food for them Our potatoes are rotten
and we have no grain – And Gentlemen – You know but
very little of the State of the suffering poor – If Mr Barton
knew our state he should not adopt the policy of breaking
100 Men More to protract the work instead of giving
us employment But Gentlemen We must cry out
against the policy of protracting the Work for the few, while
we are suffering from famine and distress and the
Want of employment – Are we to Resort to outrage – We
have peaceably and quietly conducted ourselves and
patiently submitted to the will of Divine Providence
and cannot restrain from expressing to your our
feelings, and our wrongs, Gentlemen We fear
that the peace of the Country will be much disturbed
if relief be not immediately, more extensively
afforded to the suffering peasantry, We are not
for joining in any thing illegal or contrary to
the laws of God or the land unless pressed to
by HUNGER, we are willing to work, and hope Gentn
you will take part in remedying our present
Calamity by giving us employment or by getting

Fig. 3 The petition sent on 22 August 1846 to Thomas Conry from the tenants of Cloonahee, Elphin, was found by Jim Callery in the Strokestown Park archives. It was, he claims, the single most important document in influencing him to save the house and establish the Famine Museum. [Courtesy of Strokestown Park National Famine Museum]

where they are being catalogued and conserved for the future use of researchers.

Strokestown Park was opened to the public in 1987 and the Famine Museum, under the curatorship of Luke Dodd, in 1994. The original cost of the project – purchase of house, lands and contents, preservation costs and the restoration of gardens – was estimated at £1.7 million with funding coming from a variety of sources, including Westward Garage Ltd., Saab Scania, Allied Irish Banks, Laragan Quarries, other private donations and £370,000, which was received from the European Regional Development Fund (in the Operational Programme for 1989–93).[8] However, the project, according to the Managing Director, Declan Jones, was 'by no stretch of the imagination a viable commercial undertaking'. From the Westward Group's financial perspective it remained a loss-maker, with the annual shortfall made up by Callery's company. In some respects, Callery was a victim of his own success. He was perceived as a private businessman indulging himself rather than as a philanthropist investing in a hugely important cultural project that had the possibility of becoming a tourist attraction of international status (an aspect perhaps not fully grasped by the wider local community) and the potential to build bridges not only to the past but also amongst traditionally polarised communities.

### FAMINE MUSEUM AND ITS CRITICS

From the outset the Famine Museum had its critics. Shortly after its opening in 1994 Terry Eagleton described it as 'a postmodern museum in a Palladian setting, bereft of all central narrative, skewing one image against another in a parody of conventional museum practice'.[9] In a more positive review of the exhibition experience Niall Ó Ciosáin rebuffed this pointing out that 'what strikes the visitor is precisely the clarity and power of narrative' and went on to powerfully invoke the idea that the exhibition 'describes poverty and starvation in precisely the place which did not suffer from them, with the implication that the luxury of the Big House depended on them'. Peter Gray, a leading expert on the Irish Famine, viewed the style of the museum as 'sober, didactic and educational without being oppressive'. (There was, of course, and there still is, some degree

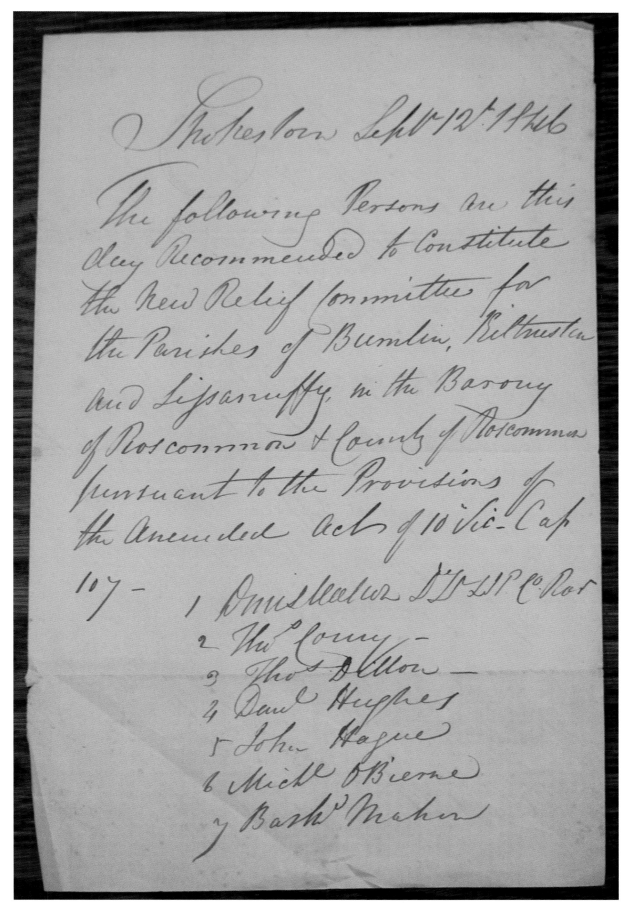

Fig. 4 Document dated 12 September 1846, listing the names of persons recommended to constitute the new Relief Committee for the parishes of Bumlin, Kiltrustan and Lissanuffy in the Barony of Roscommon, County Roscommon. It includes the name of landlord Denis Mahon. [Source: Strokestown Estate Archive, OPW–NUI Maynooth Archive and Research Centre at Castletown]

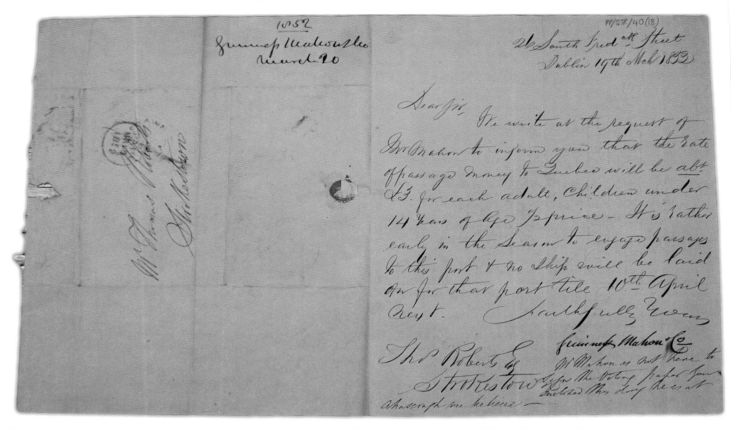

Fig. 5 Letter to Thomas Roberts from Guinness Mahon and Company, Solicitors and Land Agents, of 26 South Frederick Street, Dublin, addressing emigration arrangements for tenants from the Strokestown Estate (19 March 1852) stating ' . . . the rate of passage money to Quebec will be abt. £3 for each adult, children under 14 years of age ½ price – It is rather early in the Season to engage passages to this port & no ship will be laid on for that port till 10th April next'. [Source: Strokestown Estate Archive, OPW-NUI Maynooth Archive and Research Centre at Castletown PP/STR/40]

of fragmentation and looseness in terms of contextualisation and interpretation, but there are probably few exhibitions of this nature that can escape similar charges.) And it was largely inevitable that the juxtaposition of a traditional nationalist symbol of colonial decadence, grandeur and plenty (even at the height of Famine) with a Famine commemorative museum would lead to ambivalent attitudes. The late much-respected journalist and author, Nuala O'Faolain (d. 2008), not only captured this ambivalence but also revealed the almost cathartic effect that a visit there had for her personally. She had grown up to despise what houses such as Strokestown Park stood for: 'We cannot, or at least I cannot, look at the Big Houses without some degree of rage.' But then, after she had experienced a tour of the museum, she had to admit:

> We built those walls, we cleared those fields, and we meant no more to our masters than the people of Bangladesh mean to us now. But there's not much point in sulking about history. Better to embrace such legacies as we've got. Visiting Strokestown Park is some such tentative embrace.[10]

It is important to consider that the story of Strokestown Park and the National Famine Museum goes far beyond that of the Pakenham Mahon family in County Roscom-

mon. The history of the decline of the estate's owners, so graphically captured in the presentation of the house in a state of arrested decay reveals a more common Irish country house experience than that of houses meticulously restored in the economic boom of the later twentieth century. In world terms this physical symbol of former grandeur and extravagance sits uniquely alongside a National Famine Museum. The Big House is being forced, so to speak, to meet its own history and to explore its multifarious strands and aspects. In this respect the Strokestown experience continues to provide the visitor with a very different one to that available in most Irish (or English) country houses where tours are conventionally focused on the house's architecture and the material culture of the family. And then the exhibition goes beyond, ending with images of Famine in contemporary Africa, pointing to the potential for Strokestown to become an international focal point for a wider consideration of the experience of mass hunger and mass displacement and to take the debate beyond the realm of history right up to the present.

### A SITE OF MEMORY: TELLING THE STORY
In reading the aforementioned Cloonahee petition in total, it is difficult to reconcile the deference of 'humble and obedient servants' petitioning for relief, with the underlying anger that nothing is being done for their plight, an anger

that had potential, and eventually did, explode into anti-landlord violence. But in the presentation of the historical evidence in the museum, particularly that surrounding the murder of Denis Mahon, the paradoxes of what such historical records often ambiguously reveal and hide are rightly respected. Christopher Ridgway's point that when Jim Callery discovered the Cloonahee petition he realised that it had a *public* story to tell has already been made and, by extension, if Strokestown Park is to be a public memorial site to those who died, as well, indeed, to the death of the Protestant aristocratic way of life, it should not forget, as Niall Ó Ciosáin once put it, to 'listen more to those it is commemorating'.[11]

Today, Strokestown Park and the Irish National Famine Museum have survived because of the financial commitment of the Westward Group and a small but dedicated staff. However, it is unlikely that the Westward Group will be in a position to continue to finance the museum without some form of state assistance. The present economic downturn should not be a pretext to avoid providing this; there is already a growing realisation that tourism is central to the reinvigoration of the Irish economy. It would be timely to develop the museum to bring it to a world class level of presentation and to reach out to diverse audiences at home and abroad through multilingual provision, multimedia and interactive displays, internet access and so on, in order, amongst other things, to exploit its educational approach more extensively.

Strokestown is uniquely placed in terms of cultural and heritage cachet to become a significant tourist attraction and an international centre for Famine studies. If the local and national body politic and the wider community buys into this potential, the area's population may not be decimated yet again as young people emigrate in search of employment (in truth, no more voluntarily than they did just over 160 years ago.) It is worth considering the following piece written by the aforementioned Christopher Ridgway, keeping in mind his experience as curator of one of England's most important historic houses, Castle Howard:

> It is not unusual for historic houses to offer a range of attractions outdoors and indoors together with special displays, but the combination of these three elements at Strokestown presents a hugely rich potential for multiple, interlinked narratives, which could for example embrace ideas of consumption, production, deprivation, and sustainability, either in terms of yesteryear, today, or tomorrow. Indeed, given contemporary prognostications about global food shortages and climate change, it might be argued that these narratives, both historical and contemporary have never been more relevant. Strokestown has the potential to become *the most exciting house in Ireland* [my emphasis].[12]

Fig. 6  Strokestown Park House in 2011. Purchased by Jim Callery in the late 1970s, it is now opened to the public along with the adjoining National Famine Museum. It has been described by Christopher Ridgway, Curator of Castle Howard, as having the potential to be Ireland's 'most exciting house'. [Courtesy of Strokestown Park National Famine Museum]

# A Great Famine discovery of Viking gold:
## Vesnoy, Strokestown, County Roscommon

### John Sheehan

During the mid-nineteenth century a great number of archaeological artefacts were discovered in Ireland. The reasons for this are straightforward: this was the period when Ireland's population was at its highest, where the great majority of its people were rural and agricultural, and where agricultural practice in many parts of the country was dominated by the spade, increasing the chances of the discovery of artefacts. As a result of these factors, discoveries of more Viking-age gold and silver hoards were recorded during the 1840s – the decade of the Great Famine – than during any decade before or since, with the exception of the 1980s. One of these discoveries, a rare gold hoard, was made in 1849 at Vesnoy, on the Strokestown Demesne, County Roscommon.

In the years leading up to the Great Famine, much of the area around Strokestown was low-lying and prone to flooding. A small river, known as Strokestown River, which now forms the boundary between Vesnoy and Cloonradoon townlands, ran through Strokestown Demesne close to the late medieval ruins of Urney Church. It was diverted from its course in the 1780s to pass the Big House, for aesthetic reasons, and in 1845 Major Mahon installed a hydraulic pump on it to provide the house's water supplies.[1] The river, though small, was clearly viewed as an important component of the demesne's landscape.

One of the responsibilities of the Board of Works during the period of the Great Famine was to establish public

Fig. 1 View of Strokestown River, Strokestown Demesne, with part of the Big House visible in the distance. [Photo: John Sheehan]

Fig. 2 The Viking Age gold hoard from Vesnoy, Strokestown Demesne. Of late ninth-/tenth-century date, it was discovered during a Famine Relief drainage scheme in 1849. [Photo: John Sheehan]

works, as part of the Government's relief effort, by providing employment for the destitute poor. These works, employing large numbers of labourers, frequently took the form of arterial drainage schemes, as a result of which significant collections of antiquities were sometimes discovered.[2] Many of these finds were acquired by the Royal Irish Academy. One of these drainage schemes focused on the Strokestown River and the marshy land around it, and resulted in the 1849 discovery of the gold hoard at Vesnoy within the demesne.

Sir William Wilde records that the hoard was found

> lying just between the gravel and turf, at a depth of six feet under the surface, in the townland of Vesnoy, near the ruins of Urney Church, in making a new cut through the demesne of Strokestown, during the arterial drainage operations in the county Roscommon, in 1849, and was presented by the Earl of Clarendon, then Lord Lieutenant of Ireland.[3]

This is clearly the same find that is referred to in the Royal Irish Academy's *Museum Donation Book 1785–1856*: '25th June 1849 – Col. Jones exhibited by command of the Lord Lieutenant five gold rings found near Strokestown, Co Roscommon.' Referring to the presentation of the find to the Academy, a report in the *Ballina Chronicle* noted that 'Colonel Jones has lately presented to the Royal Irish Academy five antique gold rings, or bracelets, found in the Board of Works excavation at Strokestown, Roscommon'.[4] Jones

may be identified as Lt Col Harry D. Jones, Chairman of the Board of Works from 1845 to 1850, who was a member of the Relief Commission that was established in 1845. The Board of Works operated directly under the control of the Lord Lieutenant, explaining the Earl of Clarendon's association with the find. Unfortunately, the exact location of the hoard's findspot within the townland of Vesnoy was not recorded. It is clear, however, that it was either found in Strokestown River, on its banks or in the marshy area between Strokestown House and Urney Church.

The Strokestown hoard, now in the National Museum of Ireland's collections, comprises five penannular armrings. Four of these are of broad-band type while the fifth example is of rod type. Though unornamented, these armrings are gold versions of the common Hiberno–Scandinavian broad-band type which normally occur in silver. They were most probably produced in Viking Dublin and date to the later ninth and early tenth centuries.

Viking-age gold hoards are of rare occurrence in Ireland, from where large numbers of silver examples are on record. It has been observed that Viking Age gold finds in Scandinavia, Britain and Ireland are frequently associated with watery environments, such as bogs, marshes, rivers and the sea, and for this reason it has been suggested that they may represent ritual or votive deposits. It is equally plausible that treasures like this were concealed, for safety reasons, in periods of turmoil and stress. Whatever Viking Age reason motivated the deposition of the Strokestown Demesne hoard, it is at least known that its recovery was, indeed, during a period of distress.

# Mapping the Great Famine in Irish art

## Catherine Marshall

A community, political, religious, or whatever, is essentially a creation of human communications and it is only to be expected that the form of the communication will determine the character of the community.[1]

The Great Famine of 1845–52 was arguably the most defining moment in Irish history, with far-reaching influences on other cultures, communities and political systems. Yet discourse around it in Ireland and elsewhere has in many respects been restricted. If Adrian Hastings is correct that communities, however they define themselves, are created through human communication and formed by the character of that communication, then the Irish people, whether on the island of Ireland or scattered throughout the rest of the world, would appear to have lived until the mid-1990s, at least, in denial of an experience central to their collective history.

Cultural psychology tells us that the way we deal with trauma, the way we communicate it to ourselves and to others, is crucial to how we understand ourselves and to recovery in its aftermath. If that is so, there are serious issues to be addressed in relation to the silence surrounding the Famine from visual artists. Terry Eagleton, writing about the opening of the Famine Museum at Strokestown in 1994, noted that there had been up until then little exploration of the Famine by historians and 'a silence' about it in Irish literature. The modern period in Ireland, Eagleton said, had originated in a 'thoroughly traditional calamity' that had 'shattered space as well as time, unmaking the Irish nation and scattering it across the globe'.[2] In terms of visual art the silence has been deafening. There is truth in Eagleton's interpretation of the silence but the whole picture of Irish repression (to use a term from psychology) of the experience of the Famine is far more complex than he suggests.

In 2009, Fintan O'Toole described a proposal for a memorial to those who suffered child abuse in contemporary Ireland as the 'most difficult public art project in the history of the state'.[3] It must, he argued, be aimed both at 'those who can't forget and those who tried to hide it'. O'Toole particularly noted a dearth of responses 'however raw and immediate' from the artistic community, and went on to consider how the culture that enabled the abuse 'can conceive an artistic monument adequate to the task of both remembering and reminding'.[4] Revelations of clerical cover-ups of the abuse create a sense of fear and shame.

They also create awareness of why artistic responses were not immediately forthcoming.

### DISPLACEMENT AND THE LOSS OF IDENTITY

The Great Famine caused the death of a million people from hunger and fever and the loss of another million people through emigration. By the end of the century a further three million people had emigrated, while the pattern of life on the land all over Ireland, but especially along the western seaboard, had changed forever. Families were dislocated through death and migration. According to the psychologist Ciaran Benson the self is a locative system.[5] The noun 'I' derives its meaning from where and how the self is located in time and space. Displacement brings loss of identity, language and traditional culture and has a profound impact on the health of the self, which is reduced by any encroachments on those identifiers. By being removed from the places, communities and cultures that they knew over time, millions of Irish people were forced to find new identities. Benson argues that the tools necessary for rebuilding the self are to be found in creative engagement with the arts. It is precisely this channel for renewal that was most difficult for Irish people following the Famine.

A watercolour by the Irish artist, John James Barralet (1747–1815), *America Welcoming Irish Immigrants Ashore* (1796), offers the spectacle of a handsome Irish family disembarking from a boat, probably in Philadelphia, being graciously received by America.[6] American prosperity is suggested by the classical building into which the Irish family is being welcomed. It is balanced by the luggage being unloaded from the Irish boat, and the signs of Irish culture and industry (Irish harp, bales of linen, and a plough) surrounding the main image.

Cartoons of the Irish landing in America sixty years later, however, suggest a very different state of affairs. By the 1850s numerous images from the pages of *Harpers* and *Punch* show hostile, racist images of ignorant, impoverished and dirty Irish immigrants, clearly not welcome to their new destinations. The racist cartoons of Thomas Nast (1840–1902) and others have been well discussed elsewhere.[7] The differences in the earlier and later images can immediately be accounted for in the waves of ragged, starving, disease-ridden people who flooded into America during and following the Great Famine.

A further point must also be noted however. As the historian David Dickson has reminded us previous famines in

Fig. 1  Daniel Maclise, *The Marriage of the Princess Aoife of Leinster with Richard De Clare, Earl of Pembroke (Strongbow), 1854.* (Source:  National Gallery of Ireland).

Irish history were not accompanied by such hostility. He points to the monument erected on Killiney Hill, near Dalkey, County Dublin, following the famine of 1741, which, as Dickson notes, caused proportionally more loss of life than that of 1845. The inscription on the monument reads, 'Last year being hard with the poor walks about these hills and this were erected by John Mapas, June 1742.'[8] The problem about commemorating the Great Famine of 1845–52 was not famine alone but the way in which that particular famine was communicated to the community it most concerned and to the wider society to which they turned for assistance. Dominant economic discourse advocated the removal of impoverished tenants in 1845 to facilitate radical changes in the rural economy.

## ARTISTIC RESPONSES

To date, discussion surrounding images of the Famine has tended to focus on illustrations in *The Illustrated London News* and other journals. These illustrations were intended as visual records to accompany written texts about the terrible disasters unfolding in Ireland.[9] They were neither commissioned nor created as artworks, although they were clearly executed by artists, trained in the idealising, academic tradition. This chapter is concerned with those artworks that were conceived and executed as artistic responses to the Famine rather than its documentation. The absence is as important as the presence of visual art in this period. As Michael Baxandall has said, the Black Salons of 1906–10 provide the most important documentary evidence of Picasso's intentions, because of the omission of his name.[10] The reasons for the relative silence of visual artists, not just at the time of the Famine but right down to the present, have been outlined before,[11] but these need to be revised in the light of advances made in cultural psychology, Holocaust studies and current art practice, such as that of artist Walid Raad.[12] The task here is to begin to map the art works that have been produced and to see how they engage with the task of communicating the experience of collective trauma.

Walid Raad seeks to explore that which has not been documented about the turbulent history of the Lebanon, especially since 1975. He believes that such documentation is not possible but that its absence must be revealed. Using a variety of strategies Raad questions the veracity of human memory and the possibility of re-creating the original experience for posterity. Citing Jamal Toufic's *The Withdrawal of Tradition Past a Surpassing Disaster*, he looks at the failure of tradition to encompass trauma and the effect of over-sensitisation on those who experienced it. Fact and fiction become inextricable and Raad admits candidly, 'we have always urged our audience to treat our documents as "hysterical" in the sense that they are not based on any one person's actual memories but on "fantasies erected from the material of collective memories".' In acknowledging the 'hysterical' and the need to accept fictive accounts of trauma because of the truth they contain, Raad provides a new tool for looking at those artworks that do exist from the time of the Famine in Ireland. In looking at them, the obstacles in the way of expression – political oppression, the power of hostile critics and patrons, hidden censorship and the dependence of the artist on a market controlled by the dominant culture – must all be acknowledged.

If these factors influence artistic production in a global market now, they were even more relevant in the claustrophobic conditions governing art patronage in London in 1845. The commissioning of Irishman Daniel Maclise (1808–70) by Prince Albert to execute one of the frescoes in the Garden Pavilion at Buckingham Palace, followed by commissions for frescoes in the new Houses of Parliament in 1848 and 1849, during the height of the Famine should be set beside the attitudes of British governments to Ireland at that time. *The Marriage of Strongbow and Aoife* (Fig. 1) was one of the subjects nominated as a fresco for the Painted Chamber at Westminster. Maclise worked on his huge oil painting of this subject while the Famine raged at home in Ireland. A sketch for it was seen in his studio in 1849 but the completed picture was not shown until 1854, three years before Maclise was formally commissioned to paint two large frescoes (*The Meeting of Wellington and Blucher* and *The Death of Nelson*) in the Royal Gallery of the Houses of Parliament. The proposal to include *The Marriage of Strongbow and Aoife* in the decorative scheme of the new Parliament buildings was not pursued and the picture remained in the artist's possession until purchased by Sir Richard Wallace, and eventually donated to the National Gallery of Ireland in 1879, fifteen years after its completion. (Fig. 1)

### REPRESENTING TRAUMA UNDER A DIFFERENT GUISE

From the point of view of British and Irish history at the time, *The Marriage of Strongbow and Aoife* is of particular interest and can be read as a statement about the disastrous situation in contemporary Ireland, anticipating artists like Walid Raad by presenting the trauma under a different guise. The painting presents the unification of Ireland (Aoife) and England (Strongbow) as the sacrifice of beauty and culture to military power. The bride and her attendants are fair and open-faced, while the groom and his soldiers are dark, and inscrutable. The bodies of her dead and dying countrymen are piled high around her, punctuated by the figures of an ancient harpist and a keening woman, symbols of the culture that was currently being threatened by famine.

Strongbow stands, assertively, on a ruined cross, signalling his utter lack of respect for his bride's spirituality and shows no sympathy for her loss. Maclise, well-known for his attention to archaeological detail, has deliberately but inaccurately bedecked the bodies of the fallen Irish of 1170 with Bronze Age jewellery and artefacts. It is the death of Gaelic culture that Maclise presents here, although he would have

known that Gaelic culture was still an active force in Irish life in the mid-nineteenth century. The Famine, by destroying the communities where it was most alive, dealt that culture, especially the language, a particularly harsh and threatening blow. As a further indication of what English authority in Ireland might lead to, the figure of a warrior on the extreme bottom right of the picture grasps an axe, indicating the potential for armed resistance. Strongbow's contempt for Ireland in the painting is repeated in the statements of political leaders in Britain in the 1840s. Lord Clarendon, Lord Lieutenant of Ireland, wrote to Lord John Russell, the Prime Minister, saying: 'Esquimaux and New Zealanders are more thrifty and industrious than these people who deserve to be left to their fate instead of the hardworking people of England being taxed for their support, but can we do so? . . . We shall equally be blamed for keeping them alive or letting them die, and we have only to select between the censure of the Economists or the Philanthropists.'[13]

### ATTITUDES TOWARDS THE IRISH

While Maclise may not have been aware of Clarendon's letter, the historian W.E.H. Lecky (1838–1903) makes it clear that such attitudes to the Irish in Britain were widely known. He described, 'the ceaseless ridicule, the unwavering contempt, the studied depreciation of the Irish character and

Fig. 2  Erskine Nicol, *The Tenant; Castle Rackrent, 1860*, oil on canvas. [Source: Collection Brian Burns, Boston College Museum of Art]

Fig. 3 Lady Elizabeth Butler, *Listed for the Connaught Rangers*, 1878, oil on canvas [Source: Bury Art Gallery and Museum]

intellect habitual in the English newspapers'.[14] The conflation of the marriage of Strongbow and Aoife/Anglo–Irish unification with the death of Gaelic culture recurs in later graphic images, such as John Fergus O'Hea's (1838–1922) *Christmas 1884* (National Library of Ireland), when the figure of Erin rises from a tomb, inscribed 'Ireland Buried Here, 1171', brandishing a crucifix and wearing a Home Rule crown.[15] By locating the trauma of famine-ridden Ireland in the remote past Maclise found a temporal and spatial vehicle to express the dislocation that was central to contemporary experience.

Maclise's successful contemporary, William Mulready (1786–1853), suppressed knowledge of his Irish background, but was nonetheless ridiculed for his Irishness when he proposed a design for a new postal envelope in London in the 1840s. It is not surprising then, that few Irish artists attempted to represent the Famine. Virtually the only known contemporary painting to explicitly reference the subject was by the English artist G.F. Watts, although a number of others such as F.W. Topham who visited Ireland in 1844 and again in the 1860s and Florence Nightingale's cousin, Barbara L.S. Bodichon (1827–91), painted sympathetic scenes of Irish poverty. Among paintings by Irish artists, only *The Discovery of the Potato Blight* by Daniel McDonald (1821–53) and an eviction picture, *An Ejectment in Ireland (A Tear and a Prayer for Erin)*, by Robert George

Kelly (1822–1910) are mentioned in the lists of works shown at the Royal Hibernian Academy between 1845 and 1850. Kelly's sentimental eviction scene drew hostile attention in the House of Commons. In the charged political climate following the Famine and the failed Young Irelanders' rebellion of 1848, few Irish artists found it possible to parade their Irishness.

### AN OUTSIDER'S RESPONSE: THE SCOTTISH ARTIST, ERSKINE NICOL

In attempting to map the main landmarks in the representation of the Famine it is important to look at the most prolific painter of life among the Irish poor in the nineteenth century, the Scottish artist, Erskine Nicol (1825–1904). Nicol, who spent the years 1846–50 in Ireland and returned for several visits, could not be tainted with subversion if he painted Irish poverty, as a native artist was likely to be. Moreover, in generally presenting the Irish as well-fed, drunken, lazy, stupid and ignorant, Nicol offered an image of Irish life that was agreeable to his buyers in Britain, neither worthy of nor in genuine need of English philanthropy.

*The Tenant: Castle Rackrent* (Fig. 2) is one such picture. Seen from the landlord's position and that of a Government anxious to remove the tenants and alter the rural economy from smallholdings and a barter economy to ranching and a cash system, there is no evidence of traumatic dislocation.

Instead the threat to law and order posed by this formidable personage, involving the need for guns to protect the landlord, provides an argument to some to get rid of this tenant and others like him. The man's robust appearance makes the spill over of smallholdings into the bog on the estate map overhead, read more like Irish carelessness than hardship.

## THE DIASPORA

Terry Eagleton said the Famine unmade the Irish nation and scattered it all over the globe. One painting that combines eviction, poverty and the means to escape it is *Listed for the Connaught Rangers* (Fig. 3) by Lady Elizabeth Butler (1846–1933). The English artist Elizabeth Thompson married General Sir William Butler, an Irish soldier in the British Army. The picture was begun during her honeymoon visit to Kerry where she was much taken with the landscape and the Irish 'types' who inhabited it. In her diaries she noted her enthusiasm for her husband's plan to establish a regiment of Irish Guards as an alternative to mass emigration by young farmers driven from their land by English mismanagement.[16]

The lingering gaze of the young man on the left towards the remnants of a cottage from which he may have been evicted marks the point of rupture and brings ambiguity to the more confident swagger of his companion. It underlines a view held by Butler's husband and others, that the Irish made excellent soldiers abroad because they had nothing

Fig. 4 Sidney Nolan, *Captain Moses*, from The Wild Geese series, 1989, oil on canvas, 152 x 122 cms. [Source: Irish Museum of Modern Art]

left to lose. Although Butler was renowned as the greatest battle painter of the day in England this painting did not receive the favourable reviews she was accustomed to. Her only other Irish subject, *Evicted* (1890), was even less favourably received and did not sell.

## SYDNEY NOLAN'S *WILD GEESE* PAINTINGS

If Lady Butler's painting gives the reasons for emigration, a more searing group of pictures by the Australian artist, Sydney Nolan (1917–1992), painted over a century later suggests the degree of dislocation that the Famine set in train. Nolan, the grandson of Irish emigrants, was well-informed about his Irish heritage, which is referenced in his most famous work, the Ned Kelly pictures. He came to Ireland many times, and planned to rebuild the ruined cottage his grandfather had left near Mullaghmore in County Clare in the 1850s. Nolan announced his intention to donate fifty pictures to Ireland, one important picture from each year of his active life as a mature artist. The *Wild Geese* paintings (1989), which comprise a group of six large portrait heads painted in a highly expressionist style, form the first part of this intended donation. Sadly, Nolan died before his wishes were legalised and the remainder of the gift did not materialise.

However, the six *Wild Geese* pictures were painted expressly for Ireland. Together they make up the strongest visual statement about Irish emigration known. The title recalls those who left Ireland as soldiers after the failure of the Jacobite cause at the Battle of the Boyne, but the evidence from the pictures themselves indicates that it was a wider reading of Irish emigration that he had in mind. Although Nolan did not name the individual figures represented, one bearing the name *Captain Moses* (Fig. 4) purports to be a portrait of a certain Moses Nolan, who was hanged for recruiting Irishmen for the French armies in Dublin in 1720. The image is a self-portrait, indicating the artist's self-identification with his similarly named predecessor.

Another figure from this group of paintings who can be identified is James Joyce, whose emigration in 1904 led to the most in-depth re-creation of an abandoned birthplace in the history of Western literature. It is almost certain that Ernest Shackleton, the Irish explorer of the South Pole, which Nolan visited in the 1950s, and George Bernard Shaw are also included in the group while the two remaining figures have yet to be identified. All six, shorn of their obvious identifiers, accompanied by wretched-looking geese, stare starkly out of a garishly painted background, doomed to a life of exile.

## SWEEPING 'CONNAUGHT CLEAN'

At the height of the Famine, Lord Clarendon declared, 'I would sweep Connaught clean and turn in upon it new men and English money just as one would to Australia or any freshly discovered colony.'[17] The success of British policies to depopulate the countryside was unintentionally endorsed by successive governments in post-Independence

Fig. 5 Alanna O'Kelly, 2 x Still from the dvd film, *Sanctuary Wasteland*, 1994–98. [Source: Irish Museum of Modern Art]

Ireland which promoted the now sparsely populated west of Ireland, as depicted by painters such as Paul Henry (1876–1958), as a mecca for tourists. Henry's sanitised cottages nestle in the protection of the mountains, beckoning the descendants of those who fled them a century earlier with the promise that they will have them all to themselves. The memories of the earlier trauma have been wiped from the images as the Famine was also wiped from the discourse of officialdom in the new Ireland. When in 1945, exactly a century after the first occurrence of the potato blight, plans were proposed to hold an exhibition of painting and sculpture dedicated to an aspect of Irish history, the organisers shied away from holding a commemorative exhibition for Famine victims and opted instead to hold a Thomas Davis Memorial Exhibition, at the National College of Art a year later.

Denial of the suffering and the shame of the Famine and its aftermath was not challenged in visual art until the 1990s when Alanna O'Kelly (b. 1955) (Fig. 5) began a series of artworks dedicated to naming and mourning the pain, suffering and loss of the Famine years. O'Kelly rooted her work in the physical locations where some of the worst events had happened, drawing strength from the landscape, the remaining traces of lazy beds, abandoned houses and famine graves, gathering the placenames from which people had fled, reviving the old rituals of Gaelic Ireland, the keening and the laments. By imaginatively and creatively re-engaging with the places, both physical and imaginary, her work offered opportunities for Irish people to rediscover their traditions while acknowledging the sorrows encapsulated within them, and to begin to recover. If, as Ciaran Benson claims, 'art works to redefine experiential boundaries, and, in doing so, to assist expansions of self, including elaborations of collective self such as national identity,'[18] then the health and well-being of Irish people individually and collectively depend on artwork such as this.

# Sculpting Famine

## Annette Hennessy

I cannot remember when I first heard about the Famine. The thought of food is never too far from any child's mind so the idea of having nothing to eat was one of the worst things imaginable. I remember the illustrations in the history books at school, drawings of huge cauldrons in the workhouses. Every Monday we brought in a penny for the black babies, we saw scenes of Biafra on TV. I watched the 'Onedin Line' and thought of coffin ships. At this time in Ireland strange new foods were coming into the shops. When we ate sweet corn, my Dad said it was 'yellow meal', like the Indian meal they had in the Famine. He wouldn't eat it.

Coming up to the one-hundred-and-fiftieth anniversary there was a re-examination of the Famine with many new articles and books being published. I began to renew my interest and when the Sculptors' Society of Ireland advertised for applicants for the Famine Symposium, I applied. It was to be held in Skibbereen in association with the West Cork Arts Centre. I was familiar with West Cork and knew how badly Skibbereen in particular was affected.

In my artistic practice at that time I had been working in bronze using a lost wax casting process. I began to explore the possibilities of using wax itself as a material for sculpture. The first piece I exhibited was in the Triskel Arts Centre in Cork, as part of the 'Intermedia' exhibition, and was a collaboration with sound poet Sean O'Huigin. Two hundred small wax figures were suspended in the stairwell of the building accompanied by a soundtrack that consisted of layers and layers of voices. The effect was ethereal and more than the sum of its parts.

The figures were fragile but strong enough to withstand the duration of the exhibition. Being wax, they had no real permanence. The colour of the wax was important, as it was white (the colour of death) and, of course, there were religious associations – the use of candles in church, lighting candles in memory, etc. I proposed to adopt the same approach in placing the figures in the Skibbereen building that stood on the site of an auxiliary workhouse. The problem was how to address the theme without being obvious, trite, or mawkish. Moreover, while acknowledging and respecting the suffering and loss, I also wanted to refer to emigration.

Fig. 1a and 1b (right) *Famine* by Annette Hennessy, exhibited as part of the Skibbereen Sculpture Symposium, 1995.

As a figurative artist I try not to be too literal, but I used the powerful symbol of the boat to refer to both the spiritual journey taken by those who died and the actual journey taken by emigrants. I remember feeling nervous before we went into the old building. It was daunting enough to be setting foot on the site, which had once been the scene of such devastation. However, we were taken aback when we were met by piles of old fridges, freezers, old shop fittings and rubbish.

We spent the first few days manhandling decades of detritus and every so often you would hear the hiss of gas escaping from dead fridges. By the time we had cleared it out and before even starting to work we felt like we had paid our respects in some way. As an artist you are used to working alone and there is an added stress when you have to co-operate with others in a symposium situation. However, I was very happy that there were other people about in the building as I think most of us made sure we were never there alone.

During the symposium it was clear that there was a great deal of curiosity around the town and irrespective of what artwork we had done people were going to take the chance to come and see the building. Older people referred to it as the Dispensary. Most were aware of its existence, but had never been inside it. On the Open Day many people were visibly moved by what they saw and experienced in the building. Some time previously I had been told about a family that had lived up the town who were known as the 'donkey eaters' since Famine times. I was not told their name and it was obvious there were elements of secrecy and shame about the nickname. I felt more conscious than ever before of the long shadow cast by the Famine.

I was honoured to be invited to participate in the Famine Exhibition in University College Cork later that year. By then I had read more and talked more about the subject. Helen Comerford, a Kilkenny artist, told me she heard that before the Famine there had been more than forty named Irish cheeses. After the Famine all that knowledge and lore was gone and there were only a few different types being made. On the one hand there is such pity for the suffering and loss of life, and on the other, regret for the loss of generations and what might have been, the energy, experience and possibilities that left the country on those ships.

The realisation of the impact of the emigration caused me to alter the focus of the installation for the Boole Library. I worked with the words 'haemorrhage' and 'deluge' in my head. I cast a lot of different sizes of boat shapes and positioned them centrally under the suspended figures cascading from above but pointing outwards in all directions. When the exhibition travelled to Boston I remember meeting two elderly ladies who had left Ireland

in their youth and they had come into the city especially to see the exhibition. Half of my grandmother's siblings had emigrated at that time, too. They could never imagine the kind of country Ireland had become since they left. Many of the people who had come to the exhibition seemed to be from that generation.

In the intervening years I moved to north Antrim. The awareness of history, including that of the Famine, is infinitely complicated here. My children study the history of English kings and queens. But outside a few years ago a sign was erected pointing out a Famine graveyard. Up in the Glens I see lazy beds, deserted villages, and old wall-steads that tell their own story.

In our vegetable patch last year our potato crop was wiped out by blight and as I dug, the rotten stench turned my stomach – so I wonder if we do have a race memory and deep in our subconscious we are still marked by what took place over one hundred and sixty years ago?

# Literature and the Famine

## Chris Morash

Almost from the moment that the first blackened potato appeared in the summer of 1845, a body of Irish Famine writing in English began to appear. By the end of the nineteenth century, it had grown to at least fourteen novels, well over one hundred poems, and a small, but influential, number of plays – and that is only to stay safely within the bounds of unambiguously literary genres, without moving into the much larger catalogue of pamphlets, travel narratives, histories, journals, diaries, reports, letters and sermons which, when taken with an extensive oral tradition, form the full archive of Famine literature.

### GHASTLY INSPIRATION

While no work of literature ever exists in isolation from the culture that produced it, Famine literature is, by its nature, more than usually entangled in other forms of writing. For instance, the best-known Famine novel of the nineteenth

Fig. 1 *Portrait of novelist William Carleton* (1798–1869) by John Joseph Slattery, oil on canvas. [Source: © National Gallery of Ireland]

century, William Carleton's *The Black Prophet*, was first published serially in eight parts in the *Dublin University Magazine* from May to December, 1846. If we want to put this in a literary context, it means that by the time Carleton had reached his October 1846 instalment, Dickens' *Dombey and Son* had begun its serial publication in monthly parts. In that same October edition of the *Dublin University Magazine*, however, readers would have encountered an article on 'Irish Landlords'; only a few months later, the same magazine would publish one of the most important articles on the Famine, Isaac Butt's 'The Famine in the Land', which appeared in April 1847.[1] In other words, if we want to think about Carleton's novel as a piece of 'Famine literature', and to give equal weight to both words in that phrase ('Famine'/'literature'), it is useful to think of it as the product of the tension between these two contexts: the specific demands of the novel as a genre at a particular historical moment, and the wider discourse of the Famine as it emerged in the print media.

Read purely as a novel of its time, *The Black Prophet* has many conventional elements: an impressively nasty villain, a virtuous family and a hidden secret that threatens them. The form of the novel, however, is put under strain by the Famine setting (even though, if we are to be precise, the novel's opening lines make it clear that it is set 'twenty and odd years ago', later defined as 'the terrible realities of 1817'). To put it simply, there are moments at which the Famine threatens to overwhelm the narrative, so that it is almost as if foreground and background are reversed. For instance, after a vivid description of 'wild crowds, ragged, sickly, and wasted away to skin and bone, struggling for the dole of charity like so many hungry vultures', the authorial voice shifts tone – 'This, our readers will admit, was a most deplorable state of things . . . The misery which prevailed, as it had more than one source, so had it more than one aspect' – and proceeds to launch into an economic analysis of food scarcity, leaving behind the metaphorical language ('like so many hungry vultures') of the previous passage. Later, when Carleton begins to describe 'the ghastly impressions of famine' such as 'the children, . . . little living skeletons, wan and yellow, with a spirit of pain and suffering legible upon their fleshless but innocent features', he finds that he must go beyond editorialising, and quotes at length in a footnote from an eyewitness account of the 1817 famine, D.J. Corrigan's *On Fever and Famine as Cause and Effect in Ireland*.[2] In the end, the effect of *The Black*

*Prophet* is polyphonic, as economic, political, medical and theological voices erupt, and interrupt, the fictional narrator.

In this regard, *The Black Prophet* is not only the first Irish Famine novel; it is paradigmatic. For instance, Anthony Trollope's *Castle Richmond* (1860) uses its authorial interventions in a much more controlled way, but they are present nonetheless. Again, the main plot of *Castle Richmond* is not out of keeping with the rest of Trollope's *oeuvre* as a novelist; however, as its aristocratic protagonists unravel the intricacies of love and responsibility, they are constantly stumbling across the victims of the Famine, whether as figures in the landscape, or, in a couple of scenes, as glimpses into an almost hidden world that exists unseen in front of them. In one passage, the young protagonist, wrapped up in his own worries, happens across a cabin in which he sees a 'bundle of straw lying in a dark corner beyond the hearth', which turns out to be 'the body of a child, . . . stripped of every vestige of clothing'. As the novel moves

THE DAY AFTER THE EJECTMENT.

Fig. 2 After the ejectment, *The Illustrated London News*, 16 December 1848.

towards a conventional resolution of its romantic narrative, Trollope needs to find a comparable form of resolution in the world in which the novel is set, and so he concludes with an almost euphoric Malthusian vision of 'famine', 'pestilence' and 'exodus' as 'blessings coming from Omniscience and Omnipotence by which the black clouds were driven from the Irish firmament',[3] to clear away archaic social forms (much as the archaically irresponsible landlord is banished at the novel's end). In a similar attempt to find a larger narrative frame for the Famine, Mary Anne Sadlier's *New Lights: Or, Life in Galway* (1853), written for an emigrant readership in North America, reads the Famine as yet another instance of the religious steadfastness of the Catholic peasantry – a message that was clearly useful to reinforce for readers recently uprooted from their surround-

ings. It is the 'soupers', claims one of Sadlier's characters, who are the 'rale curse of the country. It's them that's worse than the Famine fifty times over.'[4] In both cases, there is a tacit recognition that the conventions of fiction are not, on their own, enough to contain the disruptive power of literary images of suffering.

### IMMEDIATE WITNESS

Famine poetry of the nineteenth century, on the other hand, tends to take the form of a much more immediate witness to suffering. Much of it dates from the period of the Famine itself, where it regularly appeared in weekly newspapers such as *The Nation*. 'It is a ghastly inspiration that Famine kindles', observed the paper's editors in March of 1846. 'Cypress and yew, and nightly-shrieking mandrake furnish the dismal coronals that our poets are gathering for us these days.'[5] If images of the dead and dying had the power to disrupt novels, the opposite was true in poetry, where there was a whole language of death that could all too easily domesticate the horror of what was taking place. For instance, the poem 'One of Many', that appeared in *The Irishman* in 1849 tries to signal in its title the scale of what was happening; however, the poem itself is trapped by the conventional poetic image of the poor, sickly child:

> I saw her, yes, and will never forget
> That face, on which sorrow's seal was set;
> 'Twas a pale-white hue, and her light blue eyes
> Were glazed like a dead-man's ere he dies.[6]

For the writer who wanted to evoke the sheer strangeness (and the scale) of what is taking place, then, there is a need to move beyond the simply describing suffering. So, one of the most powerful Famine poems is arguably James Clarence Mangan's 'Siberia', first published in *The Nation* on 18 April 1846. By not mentioning Ireland directly, and by using short lines, sharp rhymes, and relentless rhythm to create a desolate landscape of blank horror, the poem is an attempt to move beyond a sentimental poetic deathbed scene in which individual suffering overshadows the scale of the catastrophe:

> Blight and death alone.
> No summer shines.
> Night is interblent with Day.
> In Siberia's wastes alway
> The blood blackens, the heart pines.[7]

In the case of both of these poems, however, it could be argued that they only really achieve their full status as Famine poems in the context in which they were originally published, in the pages of a weekly newspaper. 'Siberia', for instance, shared the page in *The Nation* with a piece headed 'Extermination', about an eviction in Waterford, and a long piece from an American correspondent entitled 'The Distress in Ireland – Indian Corn'. Where *The Black Prophet* wove political and economic accounts of the Famine into its pages, these poems published in the weekly newspapers of the 1840s were able to stand on their own, for those other discourses were already present on the page.

Nineteenth-century playwrights, by contrast, approached the topic much later, largely because during the 1840s, the dominant theatrical form on the Irish stage was initially opera, and later a form of melodrama that was built around conciliatory endings (such as Dion Boucicault's *Colleen Bawn* of 1860). It was not until a more overtly politi-

cised form of Irish melodrama took shape that Hubert O'Grady's *The Famine* was first staged at the Queen's Theatre in Dublin on 26 April 1886. Appearing in the aftermath of the Ashbourne Land Purchase Act of 1885, O'Grady's play, with its tableaux of villains and virtuous peasants, draws on the conventions of earlier Irish plays, but leaves its audience in no doubt as to the larger historical narrative within which they should understand the Famine. 'If you will only look back to the years gone by', announces a character in the play's curtain line, 'you cannot but be convinced that all our trials and troubles can be traced to the great distress during *The Famine*'.[8] Only a few years later, however, W.B. Yeats began work on a very different kind of Famine play, and his *Countess Cathleen* (1892) is in some respects closer to Mangan's poetry, in which an almost sublime experience of suffering effectively allows the play's central character, the eponymous Countess, to glimpse a parallel spiritual reality. 'Leave me now,' she says to a starving peasant family, 'for I am desolate/I hear a whisper from beyond the thunder.'[9]

## TWENTIETH-CENTURY ATTEMPTS

In some respects, Yeats' play signals a shift in Famine literature in the twentieth century, and is the first of a series of attempts to write a (or perhaps even *the*) major work of Famine literature, a procession that would include Liam O'Flaherty's *Famine* (1937), Walter Macken's *The Stricken Land* (1962), Tom Murphy's play *Famine* (1968), and Joseph O'Connor's novel *Star of the Sea* (2003). At the same time, while the Famine has attracted some of the century's most accomplished literary figures, there has also been a steady stream of popular Famine writing across many genres, including horror fiction (Alan Ryan, *Cast a Cold Eye*, 1984), multi-generational historical fiction (Frances Sands, *Daughters of Hunger*, 2008), and children's books (Sionbhe Lally, *The Hungry Wind*, 1997). There was even a curious moment in the early 1990s when a book published as an eyewitness diary from the 1840s, attributed to Gerald Keegan, turned out to have been a forgotten late-nineteenth-century fictional tale.

Meanwhile, although not strictly dealing with the Famine as such, the Famine is nonetheless a presence (or perhaps 'trace' is a better word) in significant literary works such as Brian Friel's *Translations* (1980), which is set in 1839, but where the 'sweet smell' of potato crop failure is imagined just offstage. In a different way, it is the back story in historical novels such as Jane Urquhart's *Away* (1994), Margaret Atwood's *Alias Grace* (1996) and Joseph O'Connor's *Redemption Falls* (2008); in all three, the Famine acts as a kind of abyss of civilised life, a point of rupture, from which the characters escape early in the narrative, and struggle to re-establish a new kind of civility in an unfamiliar world. The same is true, although less explicit-

Fig. 3 *The Potato Gatherers* by George William ('AE') Russell 1867–1935. [Source: © National Museums Northern Ireland, Collection Armagh County Museum]

ly, in John B. Keane's play *The Field* (1965), where the Famine is a largely unspoken (but clearly understood) justification for murderous land-hunger of the central character, the Bull McCabe (a feature that was particularly evident in Jim Sheridan's 1990 film version).

As it has become apparent that the Famine may be a presence in a literary text even when it is not directly represented, the canon of Irish Famine literature has expanded. Of course, there had long been a self-evident example of this argument in Patrick Kavanagh's long poem, *The Great Hunger* (1942). Although clearly set in the Monaghan of the 1940s, the poem evokes the Famine in its title, and then develops this association, both in specific images, such as 'the potato-gatherers like mechanised scarecrows move / Along the side-fall of the hill,' and in its wider exploration of the small farmer's fearful, almost perverse attachment to the poor soil of a subsistence farm. With the example of *The Great*

*Hunger* before them as a way of understanding the Famine's place in Irish literature more as an historical force than as an object of representation, literary scholars have returned to the very core of the canon of Irish writing, where arguments have been made for traces of the Famine in such works as Bram Stoker's *Dracula*, J.M. Synge's *Playboy of the Western World*, and Samuel Beckett's *Endgame*. 'Did your seeds come up?' Hamm asks in *Endgame*. 'No,' Clov responds. 'They'll never sprout.'[10] And then, of course, there is that book that holds multitudes, James Joyce's *Ulysses*, for which there is a growing body of literature arguing that the Famine is a ghostly presence, not only in explicit references (such as the comparison of tobacco and the potato, the former 'a poisoner of the eye, ear, heart', the latter 'a killer of pestilence by absorption'), but also in its working through of ideas about fecundity, food, and the trauma of history.[11]

Fig. 4  The impact of evictions at Tullig, County Clare, as depicted in *The Illustrated London News*, 15 December 1849.

## INCONCEIVABLE REALITIES

As even this brief (and by no means comprehensive) glance through a century and a half of Irish Famine literature might suggest, the old cliché that the Famine was a silence in Irish writing is not really sustainable. Indeed, as the body of Irish Famine writing has grown in recent years, both as major new works such as *Star of the Sea* are written, and Famine traces become apparent in major canonical works, it may seem that it is becoming less and less possible to formulate any sort of useful generalizations about a body of writing that includes everything from a long satirical poem about estate management in the style of Pope (Samuel Ferguson's *Inheritor and Economist* of 1849), to a contemporary horror novel, in which a visiting American tourist is haunted by zombie-like spectres of the Famine dead (Alan Ryan's *Cast a Cold Eye*, 1984). Nonetheless, there are certain features of the Famine that produce a set of problems any writer must accommodate, regardless of the literary form or genre.

We can begin to think about the challenges posed by the Famine for any writer by turning to one of the earliest (although less known) Famine novels, William Carleton's *The Squanders of Castle Squander*, which first appeared in an abridged version in *The Illustrated London News* (the source of many of the most lasting visual images of the Famine), in January and May of 1852, before being published in two volumes in the magazine's Illustrated London Library later that year. Even before *The Black Prophet* had appeared in 1846, Carleton's reputation was founded on his position of being a writer who, as *The Nation* put it in 1847, had 'the frame and heart of an Irish peasant',[12] (although in later life Carleton was frequently at pains to present himself as an educated man of letters).[13] Given that it was the peasantry who suffered most directly when the potato crop failed, Carleton's place in the world of Irish letters, as the chronicler of peasant life, put him in a unique position of claiming to bear witness to the very epicentre of suffering. However, as we have seen with *The Black Prophet*, Carleton was by no means confident that his own authority as a peasant-writer was enough to convince his readers of the authenticity of his accounts of starvation, disease, and acute poverty. We get the first intimation of this in the footnotes to *The Black Prophet*, where he feels the need to corroborate his own fictional accounts of starvation and disease with a medical history. By the time he comes to write *The Squanders of Castle Squander*, this anxiety has grown to such proportions that it will spread, like some luxuriant weed, choking any semblance of a narrative structure. Even before that happens, however, the novel's authorial asides are increasingly peppered with observations on the sheer difficulty of writing about the Famine. Consider, for instance, this passage, in which a character driving through the Irish countryside witnesses an eviction:

> Dismay, wretchedness, desolation, despair, famine, and death were in all their most terrific aspects about and around us. This to be sure is a dreadful picture, even to him or her who may read it under the shelter of a comfortable roof, of when partaking of an abundant breakfast; but what must it not have been when witnessed on such a day as I have described, in all the horrors of its inconceivable reality as existing in a Christian land?[14]

The passage begins with a series of words that occur again and again in accounts of the Famine, whether in novels, newspapers or pamphlets: 'dismay, wretchedness, desolation, despair, famine and death'. Then, effectively acknowledging the inadequacy of this vocabulary, the next sentence opens up a gulf between the reader 'under the shelter of a comfortable roof . . . partaking of an abundant breakfast', and the world of the novel (and hence of the Famine), which constitutes an 'inconceivable reality'.

Carleton is far from unique in claiming that the Famine constitutes an 'inconceivable reality'. However, making this claim is not the same thing as saying that the Famine is, or should be, beyond the capacities of literature. Instead, treating the Famine as an 'inconceivable reality' becomes a literary trope in its own right; indeed, it becomes what is arguably the dominant trope of Irish Famine writing. As early as 1963, in a seminal essay, 'Hunger and Ideology', Stephen Marcus noted the similarity (at least in this regard) between accounts of the Irish Famine and accounts of the concentration camps at the end of World War II. 'Reality itself had grown so monstrous that human consciousness could scarcely conceive or apprehend it,' he writes, 'reality overwhelmed the human capacity to respond coherently to it.' Marcus goes on to identify the mid-nineteenth century, and the Famine in particular, as the moment at which 'an important modern truth' emerges: 'that however mad, wild, or grotesque art may seem to be, it can never touch or approach the madness of reality'.[15] In the years since Marcus' essay, this idea has informed one important line of commentary on Irish Famine literature, including Stuart McLean's 2004 study, *The Event and Its Terrors: Ireland, Famine, Modernity*, which begins by asking what is perhaps the key question in Famine writing: 'How does one give death its due?'[16]

What makes *The Squanders of Castle Squander* in some ways the paradigmatic piece of Irish Famine writing is the way in which it enacts the central problem of Famine writing *per se*: How does the writer conceive the inconceivable? We have already seen how a lyric poem that reduces the Famine to the suffering of a single individual does an injustice to the scale of suffering, or, at the very least, runs the risk of aestheticising hunger. The opposite problem, that of attempting to do justice to the scale of the event, runs the risk of tearing asunder the formal properties of literature itself – which is precisely what happens in *The Squanders of Castle Squander*. From the beginning of the second volume, the more conventional fictional characters are increasingly elbowed out of the way by a parade of grotesque figures, including an omnivorous bailiff named Greasy Pockets and a legless beggar named 'Bill-i-th'-bowl', who drags himself along the ground with his torso wedged into a bowl. As the characters from the first half of the novel (whose literary antecedents in Irish writing are recognisable from the work of Maria Edgeworth and Charles Lever), are hastily dispatched, even the grotesques give way to the sort of material that had been confined to the footnotes of *The Black Prophet*. By the final

chapter of *The Squanders of Castle Squander*, all pretence of writing a novel disappears, leaving a collage of essays in the *Dublin University Magazine*, extracts from political economists such as Hancock and Mill, his own earlier fiction, an account of the Great Exhibition of 1851, a bit of Defoe, and snippets from newspapers, concluding with a polemical attack on the Synod of Thurles, and rounding the whole thing off by reprinting the entire educational syllabus of Maynooth College for 1851.[17]

### LIMITS AND POSSIBILITIES OF REPRESENTATION

It might be tempting to say that *The Squanders of Castle Squander* is simply a failed novel (which, from one perspective, it is). However, just as the psychotic symptom may be read as a telltale sign of a condition that is not confined to psychosis, so too does the collapse of *The Squanders* tell us something about Famine writing as a whole. To say that the Famine constitutes an 'inconceivable reality' is not to say that it exists outside of literature, or outside of representation. It is to say, however, that the Famine challenges the limits and possibilities of literary representation, so that the subject of any Famine text is the search for an adequate form of representation. By the same token, the subject of any Famine text is the related (but by no means identical) search for an interpretative context in which death on a massive scale might make some kind of sense; more frequently than not, this leads the writer beyond the confines of the purely literary, into economics, politics or theology. When a novel like *The Black Prophet*, for instance, was published in the pages of the *Dublin University Magazine* in 1846, those other interpretative frameworks were present in the other articles in the magazine. Likewise, when Mangan's 'Siberia' appeared in the pages of *The Nation*, it was already in dialogue with other voices. Published in 1851, *The Squanders of Castle Squander* is among the first works to step into a post-Famine world, where the context is no longer immediately present; in doing so, it defined the problem for all subsequent Famine writing.

One of the most recent works of Irish Famine literature, Joseph O'Connor's *Star of the Sea* (2002), suggests that this problem has not diminished with time, nor is it likely to do so. O'Connor's novel weaves together elements from a range of nineteenth-century sources. Its basic narrative, centred around an aristocrat who must renounce a peasant girl he loves in order to save his estate, is essentially the plot from Gerald Griffin's novel *The Collegians* later reworked by Dion Boucicault as one of the most successful Irish plays of its time, *The Colleen Bawn* (1860). Working from this basic framework, O'Connor's novel weaves together a complex stylistic tapestry, mixing chapters presented as extracts from a ship's log with others that appear as parts of a memoir, or a novel of the period (with cameos from historical figures, including Dickens), all interspersed with illustrations

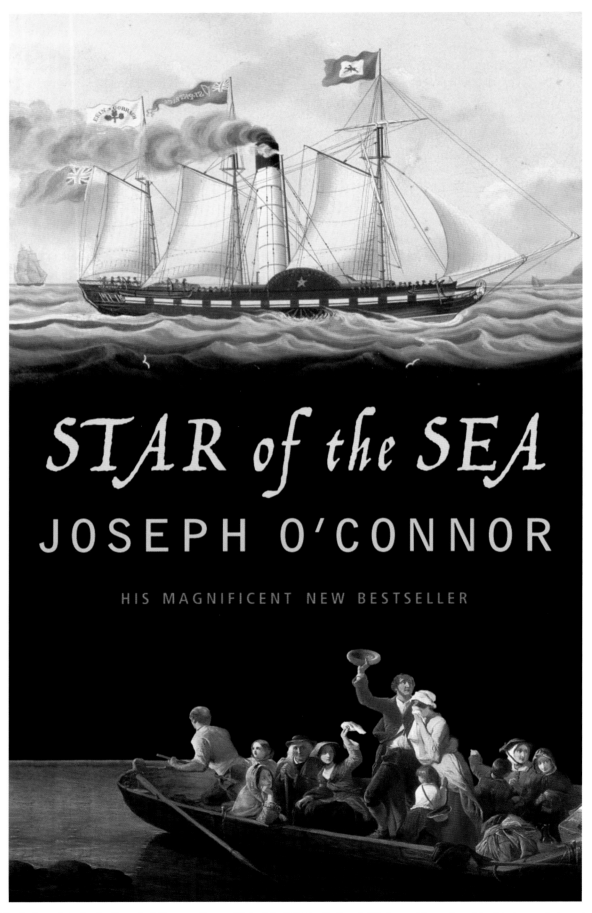

Fig. 5 *Star of the Sea* by Joseph O'Connor first published in 2002 by Secker & Warburg. [Reproduced by kind permission of The Random House Group Limited]

from nineteenth-century sources, such as *The Illustrated London News*, and as well as extracts (some real, some pastiche) from journals, poems and ballads of the 1840s. And yet, this is not to suggest that *Star of the Sea* is a failed novel, in the manner of *The Squanders of Castle Squander*; instead, it is a novel that has internalised the problem of the inadequacy of any single form of language to the suffering of the Famine, and has transformed this into its substance, aided by almost a century of artistic experimentation with the collage as a response to atrocity.

In the end, this may be the legacy of Famine literature to our understanding of the Famine. In some respects, the basic challenge in writing about the Famine may be compared to the challenge presented by mapping it: it is only on a large-scale map that the extent of what took place becomes visible; but the larger the scale, the more of the detail that constitutes lived experience is lost. If analyses of the Famine that read it in terms of long-term demographic, political or social change can often seem curiously myopic in their inability to account for the pain of an individual death, so too can a focus on the individual obscure the scale that made the events of the 1840s into something more than just another periodic crop failure. Famine literature is not simply about testifying to the reality – even the 'inconceivable reality' – of individual suffering. At its best, by acknowledging the inadequacy of any one form of discourse, literature makes us aware that if we are to glimpse the Famine at all, it is in the play of different languages, different discourses, so that the recognition of an 'inconceivable reality' is not an alibi for silence, but a reason for looking for new forms for bearing witness.

SECTION IX
HUNGER AND
FAMINE TODAY

Road relief scheme in Tigray,
northern Ethiopia. [Photo: Clare Keogh]

# The Great Famine and today's famines[1]

## Cormac Ó Gráda

During the Irish Famine sesquicentenary of the mid-1990s many Irish people were given to drawing analogies between the horrors endured by Irish Famine victims in the 1840s and the plight of the Third World poor in our own times. And, indeed, it was tempting to see a link between the generosity of ordinary Irish people towards the victims of disasters such as occurred in Biafra in the early 1970s, Ethiopia in the 1970s and 1980s, or Somalia in the 1990s, and Ireland's own sad past. This generosity must be set in perspective, however. The numbers suggest that we Irish in the 1990s really had little to crow about when it came to overseas development aid. Ireland then came close to being bottom in western Europe in terms of such aid as a percentage of GNP (though it must also be said that our performance these days is better).[2] What is distinctive about Irish overseas aid is the high share of non-governmental agencies, and the generous and spontaneous response of the public to Third World disasters. Nor, despite the seemingly endless run of demands, is that generosity showing signs of slackening; since 1995 Irish people have contributed several million pounds to relief in Rwanda, Malawi, Niger, and elsewhere, again mainly through non-governmental agencies.

Are we in some sense repaying the generosity of those who were good to Ireland in the 1840s – Irish expatriates, the Society of Friends, and the Catholic Church worldwide? Or are we somehow exorcising our own past, vicariously making amends for those who died for the lack of help at home long ago? The link was not lost on the creators of the Famine Museum at Strokestown, County Roscommon, one section of which is devoted to the problem of malnutrition and famine in the Third World. President Robinson reminded the large crowd invited to the opening of the Strokestown Museum in 1994 that 'the past gave Ireland a moral view-point and an historically informed compassion on some of the events happening now.'

### HISTORICAL LINKS

However, if we consider this historically, the link between the 1840s and today is not obvious or unbroken. The record suggests that the Irish Famine was relegated to being a slogan and a taboo for generations. It is curious that a tragedy which was marked so significantly during the 150th anniversary in 1995 was hardly commemorated at all in the 1940s, surely a far more appropriate anniversary than the 1990s. Indeed it might be argued that the more we have distanced ourselves from our own past and the more we have forgotten what really happened in the 1840s, the more generous we have become in the face of Third World disasters.

A more plausible historical link between history and Third World giving may be the Irish tradition of missionary activity far afield, particularly in sub-Saharan Africa. Such activity grew in tandem with the growing self-confidence of the Irish Church in the last century, particularly after the Famine. For generations ordinary Irish people respected missionaries and supported the missions, be it through buying *The Far East* and *The Word* or contributing to those collection boxes one still sees in retail outlets everywhere. Famine giving is arguably more in that tradition.[3] Historians have largely neglected Irish missionary endeavour, but for a century or more most Irish people (Catholic or Protestant) have had a close blood relation or a neighbour who ended up as a missionary in Africa or Asia. And to be honest, are not some of those ubiquitous billboard stereotypes of Third World children, smiling or crying, really the 'black babies' of old in another guise?

Surely if the sufferings of half-forgotten, wretched Irish Famine victims can inspire greater concern for the Third World today, then they may not have died entirely in vain. Yet history never quite repeats itself, and the contexts of Ireland's Famine and those modern African famines mentioned above are quite different. Superficially, of course, all famines are alike; contemporary accounts of *les années de misère* at the end of Louis XIV's reign and of Ireland's Great Hunger might well, *mutatis mutandis*, describe the horrors of Biafra or Ethiopia. But some of the differences are worth reflecting on.[4]

### COMPARISONS

First of all, today's famines, proportionately at least, are less murderous than the Great Famine. About one million people died directly as a result of the potato failures in the 1840s. By comparison, the official death toll in Bangladesh in 1974 was 26,000 out of a population of over 60 million. Even if the real cost in lives was considerably greater, the point of the comparison still stands. Another well-known famine of the 1970s, the Sahel Famine of 1973, killed perhaps 100,000 people in an area inhabited by 25 million. Again, in Ethiopia in 1972–74 about 200,000 are held to have died out of a population of 27 million. It is true that Stalin's Ukraine famine of the early 1930s, the Bengal famine of 1943, and the Great Chinese Famine (1958–61) during the Great Leap Forward killed far more people, but the reference populations were also proportionately greater. The excess mortality due to famine in Malawi in 2002 and Niger

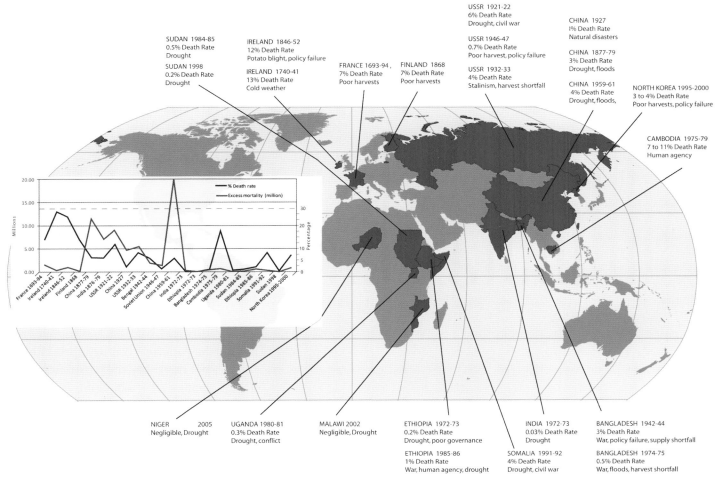

SUDAN 1984-85
0.5% Death Rate
Drought

SUDAN 1998
0.2% Death Rate
Drought

IRELAND 1846-52
12% Death Rate
Potato blight, policy failure

IRELAND 1740-41
13% Death Rate
Cold weather

FRANCE 1693-94 ,
7% Death Rate
Poor harvests

FINLAND 1868
7% Death Rate
Poor harvests

USSR 1921-22
6% Death Rate
Drought, civil war

USSR 1946-47
0.7% Death Rate
Poor harvest, policy failure

USSR 1932-33
4% Death Rate
Stalinism, harvest shortfall

CHINA 1927
1% Death Rate
Natural disasters

CHINA 1877-79
3% Death Rate
Drought, floods

CHINA 1959-61
4% Death Rate
Drought, floods,

NORTH KOREA 1995-2000
3 to 4% Death Rate
Poor harvests, policy failure

CAMBODIA 1975-79
7 to 11% Death Rate
Human agency

NIGER        2005
Negligible, Drought

UGANDA 1980-81
0.3% Death Rate
Drought, conflict

MALAWI 2002
Negligible, Drought

ETHIOPIA 1972-73
0.2% Death Rate
Drought, poor governance

ETHIOPIA 1985-86
1% Death Rate
War, human agency, drought

INDIA 1972-73
0.03% Death Rate
Drought

SOMALIA 1991-92
4% Death Rate
Drought, civil war

BANGLADESH 1942-44
3% Death Rate
War, policy failure, supply shortfall

BANGLADESH 1974-75
0.5% Death Rate
War, floods, harvest shortfall

Fig. 1a PERCENTAGE DEATH RATES AND ESTIMATED DEATH TOLLS FROM SELECTED FAMINES. [Adapted from Cormac Ó Gráda, *Famine: A Short History* (Princeton, New Jersey, 2009), pp. 23-24]

in 2005 was miniscule by comparison, far less than the annual death tolls from HIV/AIDS in those countries.[5] Ireland's Famine, then, was a 'great' Famine.

Secondly, unlike Biafra in the 1970s, or Somalia and the Sudan in the 1990s, Ireland faced no civil war or major unrest in the 1840s. Indeed, some contemporary observers spoke of a delusive calm in Ireland on the eve of the Famine. Faction-fighting and rural strife, so common in the 1820s and 1830s, had been quelled by an alliance of police and priests. Ordinary crime was also in decline.[6] Thus disrupted communications and military distractions were not a factor in Ireland during the Famine. The main road network was more than adequate, and bad weather in the guise of flooding or frost was no excuse for not getting relief to the people. Since the 1840s, improvements in transport, particularly the railway, have lessened the impact of local harvest failures in many parts of the world, notably in India. Yet even today, poor communications are also seen as exacerbating famine, giving rise to market fragmentation, as for example, in Bangladesh and in Wollo (in northeastern Ethiopia) in the 1970s.[7]

A third difference is that in today's famine-stricken areas, neighbouring regions or countries tend to be nearly

as poor as the region directly affected. We need think only of famine-afflicted Ethiopia or southern Sudan. But one of the remarkable things about the Irish Famine of the 1840s is its geographical setting: it occurred in the backyard of that prosperous region which Prince Albert would soon dub 'the workshop of the world'. This is not to overlook the harsh conditions faced by the British poor at the time.

Nor, fourthly, is the philosophical context the same today as in the 1840s. This is an important point. During the Irish Famine, the first editor of *The Economist*, James Wilson, answered Irish pleas for public assistance with the claim that 'it is no man's business to provide for another'. He asserted that official intervention would shift resources from the more to the less deserving, since 'if left to the natural law of distribution, those who deserved more would obtain it'. Wilson may have agonised in private about the inevitability of deaths in Ireland, but what really mattered is that in print the tone of *The Economist* was dogmatic and pitiless.

## 'DYING OF POLITICAL ECONOMY'

In the same vein, economist Nassau William Senior calmly defended policies that were reducing the Irish to starvation,

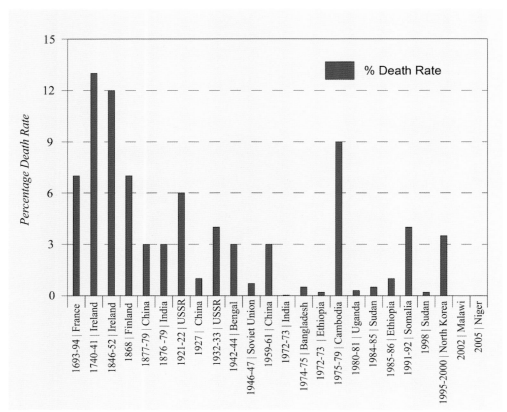

Fig. 1b  Proportion of famine-related deaths per total population for the countries depicted in Figure 1a. As can be seen from the graph Ireland experienced the greatest proportion of excess famine deaths both in 1740–41 and 1846–52. [Adapted from Cormac Ó Gráda, *Famine: A Short History* (Princeton, New Jersey, 2009), pp. 23–24]

remarking that they would provide 'illustrations valuable to a political economist'. Irish novelist Maria Edgeworth, by then an old woman, rightly accused people like Senior and Wilson of having 'a heart of iron – a nature from which the natural instinct of sympathy or pity have been destroyed'. They were not alone. Even the most Thatcherite of European politicians today would be deemed 'wet' if compared to some of those with power and influence in Westminster during the Famine. There is some truth, then, in John Mitchel's claim that in the 1840s 'Ireland died of political economy'.[8]

Still, it is important not to make nationalist hay out of this. Some of those who peddled this kind of ideology may also have heartily despised the Irish poor, and may have been religious bigots. But in the Netherlands in the 1840s, many died too. The attitude of government officials there towards their own starving poor was just as mean and doctrinaire as the attitude of Chancellor Charles Wood or Charles Trevelyan, the assistant secretary to the Treasury during the Famine years, towards the Irish. There it was a case of Dutchman against Dutchman.[9] Thus attitudes sometimes described as 'racist' were really as much about class as race. Nor should our rejection of dogmatism in the matter of relief blind us to the dangers of dependence on handouts outlasting the crisis itself – as, it is sometimes argued, happened in rural Ireland after the Famine.

While the attitude to relief is less harsh today, ideology

can still exacerbate crises or the risk of crises. For example, the structural adjustment package imposed on Somalia in the 1980s by the World Bank and the International Monetary Fund is held to have destabilised that country and weakened its resistance to crisis. Similarly, the insistence that Zimbabwe's grain marketing board balance its budget each year prompted the board to sell off its surplus in 1991, even though a food crisis threatened in 1992, a crisis averted only by record food imports. A recent study of a mild famine in the Malagasy Republic in the mid-1980s has made a similar point about the role of public policy in that instance.[10] But the damage inflicted by neo-liberal dogmatism in the twentieth century shrinks before that caused by the very different ideologies of Stalin and Mao which were responsible for the deaths of far greater numbers of the poor.[11]

If ideology can exacerbate famines, how can bureaucracy relieve them? History suggests that 'good' government can help avert famines. This seems to have happened in Kenya in 1984, when the timely importation of yellow maize, which was promptly distributed, averted a potential disaster. The maize, or 'yellow male' (echoes of Ireland), was sold mostly through ordinary market channels. The same has happened in Botswana. Again, in Bangladesh, following the famine in 1974, rapid intervention and food rationing by the government averted a repeat in 1979 and 1984. The ambitious public works programme set up in Maharashtra in India in the early 1970s is another well-known case in point. In these instances, the institutional infrastructure was there to begin with. The same could not be said of Ethiopia in the 1970s or the Sudan in the 1980s.[12] However, in this respect Ireland in the 1840s was at no disadvantage. The mandarins of Whitehall and Dublin Castle and their representatives were less corrupt and more sophisticated than most Third World bureaucracies today. In Ireland police monitoring and newspaper accounts of the second harvest failure in the summer of 1846 offered an 'early warning system' of looming disaster. The bureaucratic delays so often a feature of African administrators were hardly a constraint in the Irish context. In Ireland the problem was less institutional than ideological.

**ENTITLEMENTS**

It is often said of modern famines that they are less the

product of food shortages or poor harvests *per se* than a lack of purchasing power. In particular, Harvard economist Amartya Sen has pointed to famines in his native Bengal in the 1940s and in Ethiopia in the 1970s as products of a reduction in what he terms the 'entitlements' of the landless. Sen instances the Bengal famine as a 'boom' famine, brought on by war-time inflation and precautionary and speculative hoarding of foodstuffs. In Ethiopia in 1973, he argues, 'famine took place with no abnormal reduction in food output, and consumption of food per head at the height of the famine was fairly normal for Ethiopia as a whole'.[13] Such claims have not gone uncontested,[14] but they have some resonance for Ireland in the 1840s also. One of the most evocative images of the Irish Famine is of a people being left to starve while their corn was being shipped off under police and military protection to pay rents. Poverty in the midst of plenty, crudely put.

The Famine replicated and magnified graphically the hardships and exploitations at the heart of Irish society. However, this enduring, populist image of the Famine as starvation when there was enough food to go around over-simplifies. It ignores the sheer gravity of the potato failure, which produced a shortfall of one-third or so in calorie production three years in a row.[15] Dwelling on the exported grain ignored the reality that during the Famine grain exports were dwarfed by imports of cheaper grain, mainly maize. Moreover, the exported corn belonged not to the landless or near-landless masses, but Ireland's half a million farmers. Those farmers did not escape the crisis unscathed, but few of them perished; and they certainly would not have welcomed the lower prices that an export embargo would have brought in its train. Though generations of neglect and injustice may have produced conditions more likely to lead to Famine, this is not to deny that it was also a classic case of food shortage.

## EMIGRATION

Mass emigration is another legacy of the Great Famine, and one that also distinguished it from modern Third World famines. All famines induce people to move in search of food and in order to escape disease; there is much movement from rural areas into the towns. But a distinction must be made between local movements from more- to less-afflicted areas and permanent long-distance migration. For many of the Irish poor in the 1840s, unlike the Somali or Sudanese poor today, emigration provided a welcome safety valve. Estimates of Irish Famine-induced emigration can be only approximate for two reasons. First, the outflow was imperfectly enumerated at the time. Second, a significant share of the actual movement would have occurred in any case. Emigration during the early 1840s had been 50,000–100,000 a year. But Famine emigrants surely numbered half or more of those who emigrated between the mid-1840s and the early 1850s. The Famine emigration was

Fig. 2 *Hon. James Wilson* by Sir John Watson-Gordon, oil on canvas, 1858. [Source: © National Portrait Gallery] Wilson was the first editor of the *Economist* and was adamant that government intervention was not the answer to pleas of assistance from Ireland, boldly declaring that 'it is no man's business to provide for another'.

different to what had gone on before; probably the poorest of the poor died, lacking the funds and the knowledge to emigrate, while many of those who could scrape together the funds, or who were compensated for giving up their smallholdings, left.

Much has been written about the terrible conditions endured by these 'economic refugees' and the high mortality on 'coffin-ships'; indeed, half of those participating in a landlord-funded emigration scheme from the Strokestown estate, which surrounded the present museum, died in transit to the New World.[16] That was not the norm, however. Now, ignorance nearly always leads to exploitation, and it is hardly surprising that some desperate emigrants in Cove (Queenstown), Liverpool and elsewhere were cheated out of the little they had. But the fundamental comparative point to make here is that surely many of today's famine-stricken poor would give up every penny they have in return for manual jobs and poor accommodation in North America, Japan, or western Europe. The journey may have taken longer than it would today, but most of Ireland's 'boat people' eventually reached their destinations in North America or in Britain.

Perhaps it is because emigration was so important during and immediately after the Famine that Irish nationalists have had an ambiguous attitude towards emigration ever since. Yet reflecting on the alternative offered by Third World experience tells us that the Irish were 'lucky' to emigrate, and that many more would have died had this safety valve not existed.[17]

### FAMINE'S LONGEVITY

Another important feature of the Irish Famine, which of course makes it difficult to fit into any neat commemorative schedule, is that it was a very long drawn out affair. Beginning in the summer of 1846 with the second and near-total failure of the potato crop, Lord John Russell's Whig administration in Whitehall declared it to be 'over' in summer 1847. Responsibility for relieving those affected was then turned over to Ireland. But this was rather like adopting the strategy of Senator George Aiken of Vermont, who, on becoming fed up with the Vietnam War, is supposed to have exclaimed, 'let us declare victory, and get the hell out of there!', or words to that effect. The notion, it must be said, still has some resonance today. A recurring critique of the international aid community is that it 'goes in with emergency relief, declares early victory and leaves'.

The crisis sparked off in Ireland by the potato blight did not end in summer of 1847. Famine conditions lasted for a long time after, particularly in western counties such as Clare and Mayo. At the level of macro-economic indicators such as bank note circulation or company profits, the recovery took a long time to occur. The number of inmates in Ireland's bleak workhouses, a more immediate proxy for deprivation, remained high long after 1847. In 1852 they still numbered 166,821 or 2.6 per cent of the population; the total dropped to 129,401 in 1853 and 95,190 in 1854, and then fell off more gradually to 40,380 in 1859.

Because there was a population census in 1851, Irish historians are inclined to deal with the Famine as a five year block (1846–51). The ploy has its historical validity too. There is plenty of evidence, both statistical and narrative, for excess mortality in 1849 and 1850, and some would go so far as extend the Famine into the 1850s. The Great Famine therefore had more in common with the Pharaoh's seven lean years than the better-known famines of the 1980s and 1990s. Perhaps this meant that what is called today 'famine fatigue' was more of a problem in Ireland's case. This is implicit in the well-known efforts of the Society of Friends, who modified their relief strategies quite early on, exasperated at the unfeeling attitude of officialdom, and

Fig. 3 Ethiopia is one of a number of countries in the Horn of Africa which remain vulnerable to famine today. A severe drought and rising food costs resulted in a massive food crisis in 2008. Picture shows the difficulties of crowd control at a Government food distribution depot in Bedessa, southern Ethiopia. [Photo: Julien Behal/PA Wire]

Fig. 4 *Irish Emigrants* by John Joseph Barker (1824–1904), oil on canvas. [Source: © Victoria Art Gallery, Bath and North East Somerset Council/The Bridgeman Art Library]

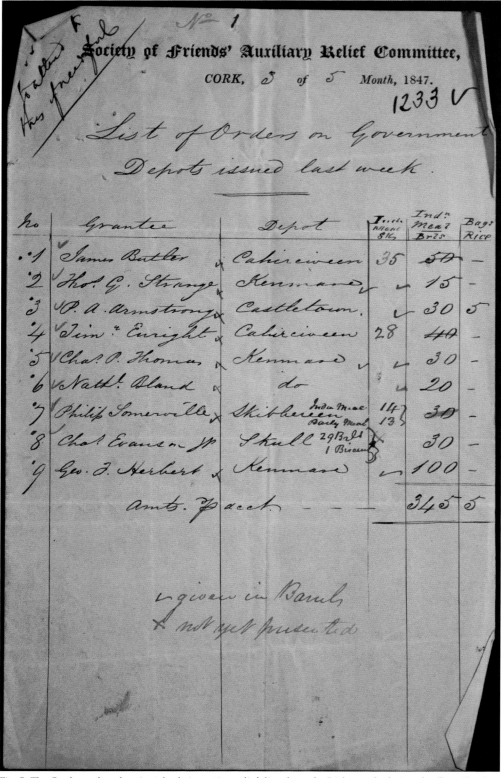

Fig. 5 The Quakers played a pivotal role in getting relief directly to the Irish people during the Great Famine. Growing frustration and impatience with the Government's response combined with fatigue meant that their heroic efforts would also diminish in time. [Source: Friends Historical Library]

argued that the Bengal famine of 1943 approximates the Irish experience in this respect, in that excess mortality also continued high for several years; however, this is contested by Tim Dyson and Arup Maharatna, who claim that excess mortality was confined to 1943 and 1944.[18]

Ireland's catastrophe was the product of three factors: a backward economy, bad luck, and the ideology briefly mentioned above. Those countless lazy beds that people carved out of wet, stony hillsides are a reminder that backwardness was compounded by land hunger. This raises the question, how poor was Ireland in the 1840s compared with, say, Ethiopia or Somalia today? Only the crudest answer is possible. However, we know that in the 1840s average income in Ireland was about two-fifths that of Great Britain, and that incomes in Britain have increased eight or tenfold in the meantime. Today, moreover, average incomes in Ethiopia are about 3% of Great Britain's, and in Somalia about 7%. Taken together, these numbers indicate that Irish living standards on the eve of the Great Famine lay somewhere between Ethiopia's and Somalia's today.

As for bad luck, traditional accounts explained the Famine as the inevitable product of over-population. However, the best recent analysis of the failure of the potato crop in 1845 deems it an ecological fluke, something (as Peter Solar has put it) 'far out of the range of actual or likely European experience'.[19] The Irish poor themselves, deeply religious and bewildered by what had hit them, were sometimes inclined to see the failure as God's revenge for earlier improvidence. In folk memory potatoes were particularly bountiful on the eve of the Famine, and in north Wexford, for example, 'people thought the blight was a visitation from God because of the careless way they treated the potatoes'. In the words of an east Cork song, *'ba mhaith é an práta, dob fhial is dob fhairsing é, chun é roinnt ar bhochtaibh Dé'*. Yet

refusing to heed government prodding to do more. It is also seen in the more modest efforts of local charities such as the Sick and Indigent Roomkeepers' Society in Dublin.

By contrast, the Finnish famine of the 1860s, another major catastrophe, lasted just one awful year. The latest verdict on the better-known Ukrainian famine of 1932–33 suggests that it too lasted a year at most. Amartya Sen has

Fig. 6 A mother weeps as her severely malnourished child is screened at Girarra Clinic southern Ethiopia in 2008. [Photo: Julien Behal/PA Wire]

those potatoes could not have been stored from one year to another in any case. It would be the stern historian indeed who would impose on an impoverished and largely illiterate people the degree of foresight needed to allow for three years of shortfall in succession.

## LOCAL MEMORY

In the 1930s, 1940s and 1950s, useful second-hand reminiscences of the Famine might still be had from old people throughout Ireland, particularly from Irish speakers in the worst-affected areas in the south and west. Unfortunately, not enough people, least of all historians, wanted to listen and record. Local memories are now much vaguer, and physical evidence of the Famine's ravages is scarce. The resulting amnesia has rid the Irish psyche of what was most troubling and traumatic about the 1840s: neighbours and relations being buried hurriedly and without ceremony, clearances and house-burnings, thieving on a massive scale, and strife about the scant food supply.[20] Modern reports of corruption and cruelty in famine areas in the Third World remind us what it must have been like in Ireland. Unless these horrors of the 1840s are given their due, a more tourism-

friendly, heroic, and sanitised version of that ugly chapter in Irish history is on the cards.

Finally, if the Irish attitudes to Third World famines are to be informed by our own Famine, what can the Third World tell us about the Great Famine? One message, perhaps, is that though aid can achieve much, how difficult it would have been to avoid all mortality in the 1840s. Yet the efficacy of the timely purchase and distribution of cheap food by the authorities is also a reminder that more could have been done along these lines for Ireland in late 1846 and early 1847 by buying up and re-distributing domestic stocks, before large quantities of grain could be obtained from abroad and processed for consumption. Another message is the amount of anti-social and often vicious behaviour which hardship provokes. Given the scenes of thieving and looting in Somalia and Rwanda depicted in the media, stories of robbers, cattle rustlers, and high death rates in bulging prisons in Ireland in the 1840s are hardly surprising. Finally, more recent famines are a reminder of the horrors endured by our own Irish poor in the 1840s, horrors sometimes downplayed in, or left out of, historical accounts.

# Food security, food poverty, food sovereignty: moving beyond labels to a world of change?

## Colin Sage

More than 920 million people in the developing world do not have enough to eat, and a further 34 million people in the industrialised countries and economies in transition also suffer from chronic food insecurity. Food insecurity is generally taken to mean a dietary intake of insufficient and appropriate food to meet the needs of growth, activity and the maintenance of good health. In addition to those suffering from chronic hunger, many millions more experience food insecurity on a seasonal or transitory basis. Prolonged periods of insufficient food intake results in protein-energy malnutrition with loss of body weight, reduced capacity to work and susceptibility to infectious, nutrient-depleting illnesses, such as gastro-intestinal infections, measles and malaria. Even mild undernourishment in children can lead to delayed or permanently stunted growth. There are almost 200 million children in the world displaying low height-for-age with almost half of the children of South Asia failing to reach the weights and heights considered to represent healthy growth.[1]

In a context where the world produces enough food for all, why has it proven so difficult to reduce the number of hungry and malnourished people in the world? And why, given the undertakings that were made at the 1996 World Food Summit to cut the number of malnourished people (then 840 million) by half by 2015, does that objective look increasingly unrealistic? Moreover, since that summit, the number of overweight and obese people has rapidly overtaken the number of hungry with the greatest proportion in developing countries. It might be argued, then, that malnourishment, meaning badly nourished, concerns both the underfed and overfed and raises profound questions about health, well-being and food security across the nutritional spectrum.

The purpose of this chapter, then, is to explore what we mean by food security and to ask whether it remains a sufficiently robust and useful concept. For it is apparent that contemporary economic uncertainties and increasingly complex, turbulent and unpredictable environmental futures not only make the goal of strengthening food security ever more vital, but highlight the need for fresh and critical thinking in ensuring that all people, especially the poorest, gain greater control in meeting their food needs. Ultimately, how we feed ourselves in the years to come will require a broader and more robust conceptualisation of food security than we have had hitherto. The notion of food sovereignty may make a valuable contribution to this thinking.

## FOOD SECURITY

It has been suggested that there are approximately 200 definitions and 450 indicators of food security[2] and this diversification of meaning reflects its wide interest as an object of study across a broad spectrum of academic disciplines (including the social, agricultural and nutrition sciences) and its application as a policy tool in various sectors of government. Although hitherto it had been largely confined to use in relation to the poorest countries, more recently food security has found its way into policy circles and documents concerned with food systems in countries of the North. Rising oil and food commodity prices have caused many countries that have long considered themselves highly food secure to take stock of their reliance upon global supply chains that deliver a high proportion of their food needs. Within the last couple of years food security has become closely tied to concerns over international land-leasing arrangements, climate change, freshwater depletion and 'peak oil'.

Food security first appeared at the 1974 World Food Conference where it was defined as: 'availability at all times of adequate world food supplies of basic foodstuffs . . . to sustain a steady expansion of food consumption . . . and to offset fluctuations in production and prices'.[3] The definition reflects the circumstances of the early-to-mid-1970s where drought across many major grain-producing regions of the world led to heavy demand on international grain markets. Famine stalked the Horn of Africa and the Sahel, as well as South Asia, and encouraged the popular view that food insecurity was both demographically induced ('overpopulation') and environmentally determined (caused by drought, flood or soil erosion).

The unfolding humanitarian disasters of the 1970s and 1980s, in which more than two million people died, did stimulate detailed analyses of the intersection of hunger, poverty, conflict, environmental degradation and the coping strategies of those affected. While detailed local-level studies revealed the limitations of overly deterministic causal relationships, they recognised that problematic long-term trends might combine with 'trigger' events (e.g. drought, armed conflict or economic crisis) to tip already stretched local societies into acute distress. Thus a local society vulnerable to seasonal food insecurity, marked by a hungry period before the next harvest, might be tipped into a situation of structural malnutrition and chronic food insecurity by such an event. Understanding the circumstances experienced by the most vulnerable was a particular feature of the analysis of Amartya Sen.

In his book *Poverty and Famines* (1981), Sen demonstrated that hunger and starvation are not an inevitable consequence of a decline in the *availability* of food but, rather, reflect the circumstances of people not being able to secure *access* to food. This can be explained, argues Sen, by understanding people's entitlement relations. On the basis of their initial endowments in land, other assets, and labour power, a person has entitlements to his own production, the sale of labour for wages or the exchange of products for other goods (e.g. food).[4] Under 'normal' conditions these entitlements provide the basis for survival. But new circumstances may unfavourably impact upon them, such as the occurrence of drought. Here, with the prolonged failure of rains and in the absence of irrigation, field crops simply shrivel and die. For local people who ordinarily earn wages by working in those fields and whose labour is no longer needed, at least until the return of the rains, their main entitlement to food (their wages) collapses and they become highly vulnerable to hunger. A similar predicament confronts those with a few livestock. In the absence of adequate grazing, animals weaken and their value drops. Meanwhile, under the law of supply and demand (exacerbated by the opportunism of intermediaries) grain prices soar, and the exchange rate of grain for animals deteriorates rapidly. This is a situation faced by all who must purchase their food needs and who experience a collapse in their entitlement relations.

Thus the 1980s witnessed a growing interest in household-level food security using livelihood- and gender-analysis to understand how vulnerable individuals and households cope with environmental, economic and political uncertainty, whether chronic or on seasonal, periodic or irregular time scales. Moreover, recognising the influence of external factors, such as economic shocks, on local food provisioning systems underlined the importance of appreciating the interconnections between the individual, local, regional, national and international levels. Initially, food security was concerned with basic foodstuffs, principally high calorie staples such as cereals and tubers, to resolve problems of protein-energy malnutrition. By the late 1980s, however, health and nutrition research had highlighted that nutritional well-being could not be assured from calorie consumption alone, with the role of disease better recognised as impairing the capacity of the body to absorb nutrients, as well as an improved understanding of micro-nutrients (e.g. iron, iodine) to human well-being.

By the time of the 1996 World Food Summit (WFS), the definition of food security had further evolved to reflect social and cultural influences over food preferences. Thus:

> Food security, at the individual, household, national, regional and global levels is achieved when all people, at all times, have physical and economic access to sufficient, safe and nutritious food to meet their dietary needs and food preferences for an active and healthy life.[5]

As part of this summit, heads of state agreed the Rome Declaration designed to achieve food security for all, and pledged an immediate target of 'reducing the number of undernourished people to half their present level no later than 2015'.[6] Yet, as we have seen, rather than moving toward the target of 400 million people, the ranks of the hungry have swelled from the 840 million. However, this is not from lack of hand wringing, as food security has increasingly come to be seen as part of a wider concern not just for human welfare but as a basic human right. In the WFS Plan of Action, a call was made for the implementation of Article 11 of the 1967 International Covenant on Economic, Social and Cultural Rights which affirms 'the right of everyone to an adequate standard of living for himself and his family, including adequate food, clothing and housing'. Yet while a specialist Right to Food unit now exists within the Food and Agriculture Organisation (FAO), more than 920 million people remain undernourished. This demonstrates a fundamental problem with food security: that despite the efforts to enshrine the human right to adequate food, there is no effective mechanism to ensure its fulfilment.

International human rights instruments are concerned primarily with the responsibilities of states to their own people, not to people elsewhere. The principle of national sovereignty, which underpins international law, generally restricts the intervention of foreign governments even when states may be failing to provide for and to protect their own citizens. Consequently, food security persists largely because of a failure of government at national level and a lack of international political will. This suggests that despite ongoing efforts to establish a legal right to food within international law, ultimately more immediate and practical solutions for strengthening food security are more likely to be found at local level.

## FOOD POVERTY

Despite a belief that most hungry people are located in the developing world, there is some awareness of food poverty in the most developed countries. Here, people's relationship to food is arguably more complex still: on low wages or welfare benefits, people lack sufficient money to buy appropriate food; yet they are surrounded by the thousands of products of the modern food system. Moreover, many of their fellow citizens are striving to reduce, rather than

Figs 1 One of the banners of the many farmers associations. represented by delegates at the Global Via Campesina conference in Mozambique in 2009. [Photo: Judith Hitchman]

increase, their calorie intake. Hunger and food insecurity are prevalent in the United States, with 11% of all households regarded as food insecure by the Department of Agriculture, with higher rates amongst African–American (22.4%) and Hispanic (17.9%) households.[7]

Food poverty can be considered a measure of both absolute and relative social deprivation. Absolute poverty means that people do not have enough money to pay rent, heat their living space ('fuel poverty'), buy clothes, afford transport and generally look after themselves, including buying sufficient food. Relative deprivation refers to circumstances where people lack the resources needed to enjoy the living conditions and amenities, and to access the types of diets that are customary, in the society to which they belong. Accordingly, food poverty can be linked to three proximate determinants.

The first relates to people having sufficient money to acquire an adequate quantity and quality of food; where shopping for food is driven by the need to maximise calories, and to achieve the sense of 'feeling filled' for every euro spent. The purchase of cheaper food may consequently be more affordable but is often the least healthy and may be a major determinant of obesity. Secondly, people may lack access to shops selling food at reasonable prices. With

many of the large chain supermarkets relocating to edge of town sites requiring access to a car, and with many low-income inner city communities marked by limited mobility, the term 'food deserts' has been used to describe the resulting loss of access to fresh, healthy and competitively priced food. A third aspect of food poverty concerns the ability of people to make appropriate purchasing choices and then to prepare that food in socially acceptable ways to deliver nourishment. For example, being trapped in a long-standing situation of food poverty frequently engenders a sense of disempowerment, a lack of interest in cooking and results in above-average consumption of ready-made food and snacks. Indeed, given that much of the urban landscape in the world today is dominated by symbols and signs for fast food and carbonated beverages, it is unsurprising that food poverty has also become linked to the issue of obesity and diet-related ill-health. While such outcomes should not be regarded as inevitable and also reflect the wider everyday geographies of people's lives such as living in environments that do not facilitate physical activity (access to outdoor recreation, green space, sense of security in the community), there is nevertheless clear evidence that social and economic deprivation is closely correlated with food poverty.[8]

While the existence of food poverty in wealthy, highly developed countries testifies to the failure of welfare policy and even to effective, socially inclusive national governance, its solution requires more than enhanced handouts. This is why food security has to be approached as an issue of social justice as well as a matter of human rights. For the Community Food Security Coalition in the United States food security is a condition in which 'all community residents obtain a safe, culturally-acceptable, nutritionally-adequate diet through a sustainable food system that maximises community self-reliance, social justice, and democratic decision-making'.[9] Such a definition demonstrates how the meaning of food security has evolved: from circumstances where an aggregate supply of calories at national or regional level was once sufficient guarantee that hunger was eliminated to a situation deeply entwined with human rights and the struggle of communities to define their own particular food needs. In this regard food sovereignty has emerged as an important notion.

## FOOD SOVEREIGNTY

Food sovereignty is most closely associated with civil society organisations (CSOs) and social movements engaged in the struggle against globalisation, but in recent years is a term that, if not quite mainstream in Washington, has certainly entered the vocabulary of agri-food policy analysts and advisors. It offers a counter-hegemonic perspective on food that is rooted in a rights-based framework that effectively insists upon food being treated as a basic human right.

It has been widely proclaimed and reaffirmed at meetings and fora held in parallel with events such as the World Food Summit of 1996 and its follow up in 2001, and a host of other gatherings around the world. Although it has become the widely adopted slogan of a broad-based and non-hierarchical movement, food sovereignty is most closely associated with the CSO La Via Campesina (meaning 'the peasant way' in Spanish), the International Peasant Movement (see Figs 1, 2 and 5).

Food sovereignty is largely formulated as an alternative policy proposition to liberalised industrial agriculture and is based upon a number of core assumptions. First, it attaches almost primordial significance to the family farm which itself is located within a community-based rural development model. Clearly this has to be underpinned by access to sufficient land to enable agrarian reform. (One of Via Campesina's core principles is that the landless and the marginalised should be given ownership and control of the land they work.) While enormous disparities in landholding do exist in many countries and agrarian reform might help to improve the efficient use of land, experiences of

reform in other countries have demonstrated that reallocation of land is no guarantee of food security (in the absence of tools, seeds, water, etc.). Increasingly there is a need to rethink land tenure institutions beyond individual property rights, with forms of common pool resources management offering a more collective solution while ensuring greater social inclusion and equity.

A second principle that emerges from a study of food sovereignty is the significance attached to sustainable methods of production, utilising indigenous biodiversity (seeds and livestock breeds) and reducing dependence upon agrichemicals. Here, much greater attention is placed upon utilising farmers' existing agricultural knowledge and locally adapted technologies. The term *agroecology* often features, as shorthand to denote a wide range of practices that have built upon tried and trusted indigenous methods and which operate in tandem with local resource constraints and possibilities. Interestingly, while critics of such an approach would argue that only the most modern technologies, led by the life sciences, can offer a future of greater food output, recent reports have tended to be much more cautious in

Fig. 2 A traditional part of Via Campesina meetings is the exchange of seeds. This action serves to maintain farmers' rights to freely exchange and sow traditional varieties of seed. It also expresses their opposition to the International Treaty on Plant Genetic Resources for Food and Agriculture (ITPGRFA); as well as their determination to fight against the multinational seed companies' efforts to monopolise the intellectual property of seeds. [Photo: Judith Hitchman]

Fig. 3 Preparing millet pancakes. At the Nyéléni centre, built for the first global food sovereignty forum in Mali in 2007, only local food is used for preparing meals. The centre is often used for training sessions. Local women from the village (Selingué) come to the centre to cook for trainees, which further increases local household income. Here they are preparing little millet and milk pancakes. [Photo: Judith Hitchman]

proclaiming the advantages of the latest seeds and higher levels of inputs. The recently published report of the International Assessment of Agricultural Knowledge, Science and Technology for Development (IAASTD 2009) makes interesting reading in this context, arguing for a rethinking of past policy assumptions in order to address the need for food and livelihood security under increasingly constrained environmental conditions.[10]

A third and final core principle of food sovereignty concerns its very proclamation of *sovereignty* in a globalised world. In this respect it appears as both defender of the nation-state, as constituting the sole legitimate authority to determine policies that affect its people; and critic of the globalisation project in general and its key agencies in particular. Since the introduction of structural adjustment programmes in the early 1980s by the International Monetary Fund and the World Bank, and further intensified by the foundation of the WTO in 1995, agriculture and food have been subject to powerful neo-liberal forces and a slew of international agreements, such as Trade Related Intellectu-

al Property Rights (TRIPS) and Technical Barriers to Trade (TBT) amongst many others, aimed at internationalising domestic food provisioning systems. As the proponents of food sovereignty argue:

> Global trade (rules) must not be afforded primacy over local and national developmental, social, environmental and cultural goals. Priority should be given to affordable, safe, healthy and good quality food, and to culturally appropriate subsistence production for domestic, sub-regional and regional markets.[11]

Food sovereignty, then, is not simply another definition of food security but provides a radical challenge to many of the existing assumptions about the way food and agricultural policies have and might continue to be developed. Its perspective is not that of the academy or of those in FAO headquarters in Rome, but of the rural poor, the hungry, and food insecure. As Windfuhr and Jonsén note, there is no

Fig. 4a and 4b (overleaf) Rice harvest in Selingué. Before food sovereignty was implemented in the village of Selingué, Mali, the farmers sold their own rice and purchased imported Asian rice – usually from Vietnam, and often old and of poor quality – for their own consumption. Since food sovereignty has been introduced, the farmers grow bananas as a cash crop, which they sell in Bamako, and now keep and eat their own rice, which makes them happy! Note the small Chinese winnowing machine which reduces the drudgery of some farming tasks. [Photos: Judith Hitchman]

of 1996. Indeed, such failure calls into question not only the effectiveness but the legitimacy of the existing institutional architecture of the world food system. Despite the High-Level Conferences on World Food Security, such as the one held in Rome in June 2008, and the formation of a High-Level Task Force on the Global Food Crisis chaired by the UN Secretary-General charged with catalysing urgent action (FAO 2008), it may be that food security needs rather less global leadership and more local-level action.[13] For, arguably, it is at the local level where the notion of food security is best grounded: how to achieve access to adequate food that is culturally and nutritionally appropriate throughout the year and from year to year, that provides for health and well-being.

Such an approach would embrace more publicly-funded, rather than privately-led, investment in agricultural research, where less emphasis would be placed on finding a magic bullet associated with gene technology, and more on building adaptive capacity, resilience-enhancing systems of production and locally appropriate technology portfolios. Finding ways to improve adaptation will be the key to building food and other dimensions of human security within a warmer, more crowded and more complex world.

one fully-fledged food sovereignty model with a set of policies available for governments to implement.[12] Yet, although there will be many vested interests deeply and violently opposed to much of what the notion represents, it is being developed by civil society organisations and social movements all over the world to improve the governance of food and agriculture and to address the core problems of hunger and food insecurity.

## MORE LOCAL-LEVEL ACTION

Food security has become inseparably linked to calls for social justice, human rights and community empowerment and, with the rise of the Via Campesina and other CSOs, with the demand for recovering food sovereignty. Such demands cannot be separated from the utter failure of the international community to meet the target of halving the number of hungry by 2015 set by the World Food Summit

This approach would necessarily rework understandings of food security, including those that are derived from specific local circumstances, and embark from a commitment for social justice, environmental sustainability and sound nutrition. It might be that food security would be facilitated by less, rather than more, globalisation. Indeed, such an approach might go further and argue for food sovereignty: effectively the right of local farmers to grow food for local consumers, rather than exclusively agri-commodities for export. Without retreating into autarchy, it might enshrine the basic principle that each country should endeavour to produce enough food to feed its own people. While this may seem like a radical set of measures, it is apparent that trade liberalization in food and agriculture has not delivered global food security to date, and that the diverse challenges ahead should be a cause to reflect upon a change of direction.

Figs 5  At all Via Campesina meetings, the banners of the many farmers associations are well represented. [Photo: Judith Hitchman]

# Images of famine: whose hunger?

## Luke Dodd

Since the Biafran famine in the 1960s, we have become accustomed to graphic images of such disasters in newspapers and on television screens. This coverage reached unprecedented levels with the Ethiopian famine in 1984–85; there is no question that the response it provoked put famine – especially in sub-Saharan Africa – on the global agenda and was responsible for successful aid campaigns. The reverberations are still being felt: Live 8, Make Poverty History and the British Government's campaign for debt relief and increased aid are unthinkable without it.

But while the effect on Western audiences of disturbing images from famines is not in doubt, questions surround the assumptions that inform many of them. Images are never innocent, and it is as naive to assume that a Western photographer might alight in Africa and take an image unfettered by his or her cultural baggage as it is to assume that an image, or series of images, can explain the complexities and problems of that huge continent with any degree of sophistication.

Many of the images used to raise public awareness and money play to, and indeed perpetuate, racial and sexual stereotypes. However noble the intention, do the abject and passive victims (invariably women and children) so beloved of photographers represent an extension of nineteenth-century colonialism – Africa as inferior, feminised, infantilised, the object of our charity? Furthermore, do they not work to reinforce a power relation between the West and Africa that, by prioritising aid, masks the gross inequities that keep a majority of the world's population in poverty?

Precisely for these reasons, many relief agencies have stopped using iconic images such as the lone, malnourished child with distended stomach or shots of a mother and child. Media organisations, however, have been slower to respond, and Live 8 recycled twenty-year-old Ethiopian images in its campaign a few years ago.

Photographs of starving victims operate within the recognisable canon of Christian iconography. The direct address, the concentration on one or two individuals, the supplicating look, the outstretched hand, the minimal settings are pictorial devices well known to any figurative artist from the late-medieval period onwards. Why is this method of picturing so dominant in our culture? Is there an alternative that is not so abstracted or aestheticised as to defeat the purpose?

If Biafra in the 1960s was the first mass-media famine, the Great Irish Famine (1845–50) was the first modern one: by the 1840s, Ireland had been completely plotted by means of a census and an ordnance survey, a level of bureaucratic infrastructure that meant it was the first famine to be tabulated. But although there were numerous photographic practitioners in Ireland at the time, no such images survive. The crisis was, however, covered in English publications such as *The Illustrated London News*, which used etchings. Despite the mass mortality (one million died), illustrations of victims are rare and tend to be

**BRIDGET O'DONNEL AND CHILDREN.**

Fig. 1 No photographs survive of the Great Irish Famine 1845–52 but illustrations such as that of Bridget O'Donnell and her children show a pictorially formal arrangement that has persisted into the twenty-first century. [Source: *The Illustrated London News*, 22 December, 1849]

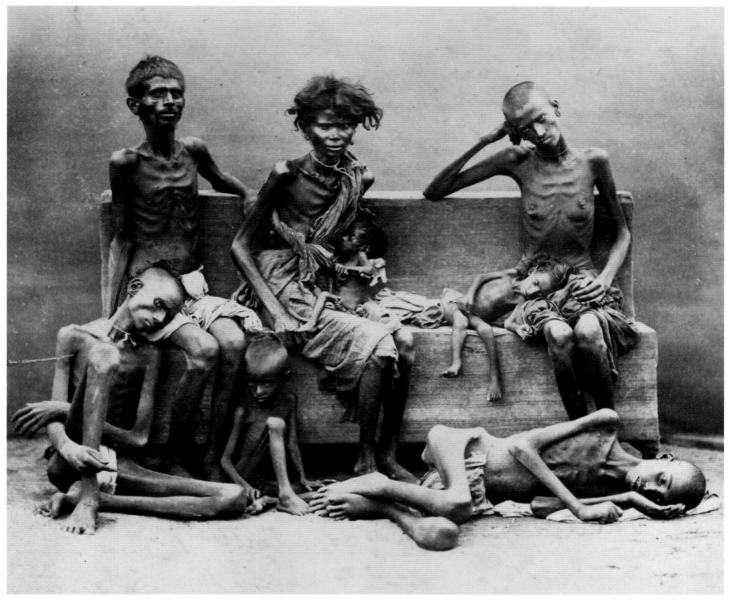

Fig. 2 Victims of the 1876 Madras famine posed by Captain Hooper as if for a Victorian family portrait. [Source: Sean Sexton]

sanitised and to use established conventions (tattered clothing, gaunt faces, lone figures, mothers and children, abject poses) rather than risk anything too graphic. The formal similarity of *Bridget O'Donnell and Children* (1849) to a large proportion of recent famine photography is shocking.

One of the earliest photographs to document victims is from the Madras famine of 1876–79 that killed around ten million people. Nothing is known of the photographer, Captain Hooper, although his title suggests he was part of the British military administration. The image is striking because it seems that the subjects were posed indoors: the figure to the right is too malnourished to sit and the figure on the floor to the left seems to be supported by a rope. It reveals extraordinary dispassion on the photographer's part, explained, perhaps, by the fact that until relatively recently famines were seen as natural occurrences; in other words, subject to the agency of God. There is no ambiguity

here. These images compromise the dignity of the subjects, and do little more than offer them up as fetish-like objects for a Western audience.

Is it possible to take a photograph that avoids exploitation while at the same time contributing to a debate about the wider political and economic (including aid) forces at work? The answer lies in our relationship to photography and the fallacious view that it is a transparent medium, an accurate representation of reality. Much is made of the work of Don McCullin and Sebastião Salgado as viable alternatives, usually citing their singular eye and the fact that both spend extended periods with their subjects, working on a series of images rather than trying to capture one shot that 'says it all'. I'm not so sure. Aestheticisation can introduce a certain distance and create a forum for debates about the fundamental nature of representation, but debates take a long time to filter down to the day-to-day workings of a busy newsdesk.

Fig. 3 Photographers scramble for the telling shot in Somalia, 1992. [Photo: Paul Lowe/Panos]

Things are changing, though – Paul Lowe's image of his fellow photojournalists' frenzied scramble to capture the iconic image of a lone, emaciated child in Somalia in 1992 (and the complicity of locals who know such images will bring aid) is a sign that a new generation is aware that a different way of picturing the poor, the dispossessed and the starving is part of a political debate about the West and its relationship to the rest of the planet.

# Fighting world hunger in the twenty-first century

*Connell Foley*

When we think of world hunger, many of us think of the extreme of famine. Famine is such an emotive word. It conjures up images of desolate, unproductive landscapes and skeletal bodies and death. Hunger is a word we are more comfortable with; we have nearly all experienced it at some time, the physical weakness we call hunger, but it is usually temporary and at one end of a continuum. Famine is at the other end. Nearly a billion people are estimated to experience hunger every day. For them, this is not a temporary feeling; it is a chronic state and they experience it for weeks and months on end. The consequences of going hungry for lengthy periods are many but are probably most significant for infants who become stunted and whose brain functions do not fully develop. Theirs is a future where their potential as human beings is already compromised. Blamelessly. Out of their control. Very often out of their parents' control.

While we know that hunger and probably very small scale famines are likely to continue, Cormac Ó Gráda's contention is that large-scale famines are less likely now than

several decades ago.[1] This is for a number of reasons: better famine early-warning systems; rising global income; the globalisation of and ease of access to information; more responsive humanitarian action from a diverse group of actors; the spread of various forms of accountability and relatively buoyant global agricultural production and productivity levels. However, there are also forces which threaten to increase the risk of large-scale famine: wild population growth, environmental degradation, uncontrolled changes from food crops to biofuels, climate change and the outbreak of major conflict over (most likely) natural resources.

The denouement of Peter Weir's film *The Year of Living Dangerously* (1982) sees the lone and ultimately failed protest by Billy Kwan, unfurling a banner from a hotel window as the autocratic head of state Sukarno is due to drive past.[2] The banner screams: 'Sukarno, feed your people.' This stereotype of the uncaring and distant head of state ignoring the voice of the poor resonates strongly with people. It also hints at the well-known assertion of Amartya

Fig. 1 A good annual yield of key staple crops is essential for food security. Here is a healthy wheat crop in Farkhar, Takhar Province, North East Afghanistan. [Photo: Connell Foley]

Sen that no substantial famine has occurred in a country with a relatively free press,[3] suggesting that good governance and democracy are key foundations to ensuring that hunger is known about, a primary need for response. The Right to Food is enshrined in the Convention on Economic, Social and Cultural Rights (1966) and UN agencies are now using human rights law to try to ensure that food security is achieved. Indeed, Article 11 of the International Covenant on Economic, Social and Cultural Rights states that:

> The fundamental right of everyone to be free from hunger, needs specific programmes:
> (a) To improve methods of production, conservation and distribution of food by making full use of technical and scientific knowledge, by disseminating knowledge of the principles of nutrition and by developing or reforming agrarian systems in such a way as to achieve the most efficient development and utilization of natural resources;
> (b) Taking into account the problems of both food-importing and food-exporting countries, to ensure an equitable distribution of world food supplies in relation to need.[4]

As late as 2009, Olivier De Schutter, the UN Special Rapporteur on the Right to Food, suggested that '[u]nless the right to food is placed at the very centre of the efforts of the international community to address the structural causes which have led to the global food crisis, we will repeat our mistakes.'[5]

CONCEPT OF HUNGER

While academics will argue about the definition and meaning of hunger, organisations like Concern understand it to mean: 'the discomfort, pain or weakness caused by the need for food. A condition in which people lack the required nutrients (protein, energy, vitamins and minerals) for fully productive, active and healthy lives.'[6] Institutions which deal with hunger on a daily basis aim for what is called 'food security'. The definition of food security that emerged from the 1996 World Food Summit was refined in 2001 to be: 'Food security [is] a situation that exists when all people, at all times, have physical, social and economic access to sufficient, safe and nutritious food that meets their dietary needs and food preferences for an active and healthy life.'[7]

The world's leaders in 1990 committed us all to the achievement of the Millennium Development Goals (MDGs) by 2015. The first MDG has two targets, the second of which is to halve the proportion of people who suffer from hunger (from 1990 to 2015) using two key indicators: a) the prevalence of underweight in children (under five years of age); and b) the proportion of population below minimum level of dietary energy consumption. While the percentage of undernourished people reduced from 1992 to 2006, in recent years the number of hungry people has been increasing, reaching over one billion in 2009 after a spike in global food prices. The UN Food and Agriculture Organisation (FAO) has estimated that this number will reduce due to supply rebalancing but with the growth in the world's population and changing food demands (of Indian and Chinese populations, in particular), it is unlikely that food security for the very poorest on the planet will be easily reached in the near future.[8]

DISTRIBUTION AND MONITORING OF GLOBAL HUNGER

The FAO produces an annual report called 'The State of Food Insecurity in the World' (SOFI), which is one monitoring mechanism for global hunger. It has been produced since the early 1990s. The outline of the report changes from year to year, but usually follows the following format: the first section looks at undernourishment across the world, reviewing trends in hunger at the global, regional and subregional levels. It also presents the FAO's most recent projections of undernourishment. The second section, 'Undernourishment in the regions', reviews the food security situation in each of the major developing regions and the transition countries. The third section, 'Towards the Summit commitments', summarises lessons from past experience in hunger reduction and presents the FAO's current thinking on how to accelerate progress towards meeting the agreed global targets.[9]

More recently, a Global Hunger Index (GHI) has been produced by the International Food Policy Research Institute (IFPRI) and now jointly with Concern Worldwide and the German non-governmental organisation (NGO) Welthungerhilfe. The GHI uses a simpler but robust multidimensional approach to measuring hunger. It combines three equally weighted indicators:

1. The proportion of undernourished as a percentage of the population (reflecting the share of the population with insufficient dietary energy intake).
2. The prevalence of underweight in children under the age of five (indicating the proportion of children suffering from low weight for their age).
3. The mortality rate of children under the age of five (partially reflecting the fatal synergy between inadequate dietary intake and unhealthy environments).[10]

Figure 2 shows the Global Hunger Index for 2011. It identifies the regions and countries where hunger is most severe and persistent, the index thirty and over being identified as 'extremely alarming' and twenty-five 'alarming'. Most of these are in Sub-Saharan Africa and the remainder are in Asia, mainly in South Asia. We should remember that these are not just statistics; they represent daily suffering for hundreds of millions of people.

It is important to note that the GHI looks only at the poorest and middle-income countries and excludes the developed world. It has to be acknowledged that hunger

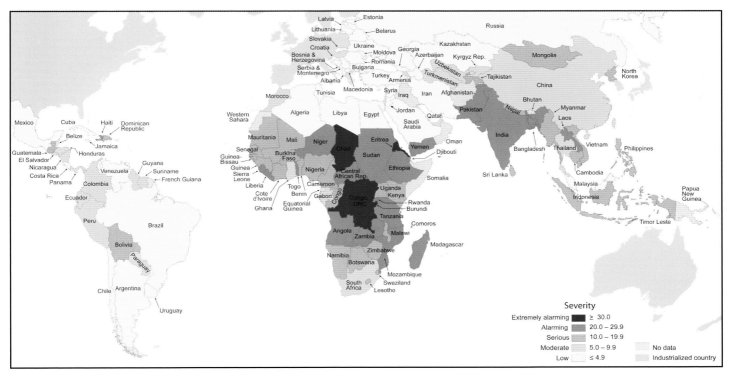

Fig. 2  THE 2011 GLOBAL HUNGER INDEX SCORES BY SEVERITY OF HUNGER. This map is based on data from the Food and Agriculture Organization of the United Nations, IFPRI, the Inter-agency Group for Child Mortality Estimation, MEASURE DHS (Demographic and Health Surveys), the United Nations Children's Fund, and the World Health Organization. The report from which this map comes can be found online at http://www.ifpri.org/publication/2011-global-hunger-index. [Adapted and reproduced with permission from the International Food Policy Research Institute (IFPRI) www.ifpri.org]

exists also in the developed world. Indeed, while most people think of developing countries when they think of extreme poverty (as opposed to hunger but closely associated with it), a recent report reveals that the majority of poor people now live in middle-income countries.[11] This study estimates that in 1990, about 93% of the world's poor people lived in developing or low-income countries. But by 2007–08, three-quarters of the world's approximately 1.3 billion poor people lived in middle-income countries (MICs) and only about a quarter of the world's poor – about 370 million people – live in the remaining thirty-nine low-income countries, which are largely in Sub-Saharan Africa. Given the GHI estimate of around a billion people going hungry each day, it is obvious that many of these are in middle-income countries, even if the severity level is moderate in China but alarming in India. While these reports track hunger on a global scale, there is a need not just to identify hunger once it is in place but to try to monitor indicators that will tell us where people will become hungry unless action is taken. This preventative monitoring is critical if we are to prevent hunger.

## MONITORING OF HUNGER NATIONALLY

There are many mechanisms in place in order to track possible hunger outbreaks or food insecurity at national level. These cover the three pillars of food security: food availability, food access and food utilisation. Food availability is tracked by many different agencies and actors, including UN agencies such as the FAO and the World Food Pro-

gramme (WFP) but also, very importantly, by national departments of agriculture or other national governmental bodies set up for such a purpose. At a country level, the inter-agency Food Insecurity and Vulnerability Information and Mapping Systems (FIVIMS) initiative supports networks of information system activities that gather and analyse relevant national and sub-national data that measure food insecurity and vulnerability. It looks at four dimensions of food security: food availability, food access, food utilisation and stability of access to food.

Another common mechanism to monitor food shortages is called the Famine Early Warning Systems Network (FEWS NET) which is a USAID-funded network of international partners to provide timely and rigorous early warning and vulnerability information on emerging and evolving food security issues. It supports national government partners to develop predictions of impending hunger by combining remote analyses of crop condition and agricultural production, often using satellite-based information, with on-the-ground monitoring – through household surveys and observation – of local socio-economic conditions.

So governments and development organisations use a variety of means to monitor food availability: remote-sensing of areas under cultivation; national database updates on land area under crops and expected yields; livestock levels; level of food exports; level of food imports and national-level secondary information alongside regular market and household surveys and other primary data collection and analysis. Other mechanisms used to predict food shortages

Fig. 3 The regular assessment of the availability and prices of different foods in local markets is essential. This market in Western Province in Zambia had lots of ground nuts and tomatoes but little else. Obviously, seasonality is taken into account during assessments. [Photo: Connell Foley]

in target populations include monitoring food prices in local markets and the sale of assets such as land, livestock and household furniture and goods.

Food access and food utilisation are not straightforward with the poorest people being the least able to access food, unless they are subsistence producers. Smallholder producers are very vulnerable to climatic hazards and depend hugely on rain-fed agriculture though irrigation can and does offer greater production security or allows greater frequency of cropping in a single year.

Traditionally NGOs have focused on the poorest and most vulnerable in society and access to available food is often a key component of this. Most NGOs focus on community- and household-level monitoring surveys of the availability of goods in local markets, the prices of a basic basket of food, household expenditure and household food consumption as well as specialised nutrition surveys. Quite often, NGOs have to advocate for a government response when they see localised hunger in what appears to be a stable national picture. Regular nutrition surveys as well as surveys examining what foods are available in local markets help in monitoring the use of foods.

## TREATMENT OF HUNGER TODAY

What happens when significant proportions of a population are hungry? Obviously the people need to be fed, but national governments and the international community often distinguish between two scenarios: a) large emergencies where there has been a catastrophic failure of crops and local production at regional or national level or where some major disaster has occurred, the consequences of which include people not having enough to eat; and b) chronic hunger in a population, often manifest in more frequent, usually seasonal, and more local inability to access food. (The latter will be dealt with in the next section.)

In the first case, large national or international humanitarian responses are required, usually precipitated by a call for help from a national government which is finding its own capacities over-stretched. In such cases, national government, key UN agencies, the Red Cross and Red Crescent societies and international NGOs work together to conduct needs analyses in the affected areas and then decide on how to manage food provision between them. The leading UN agency in food emergencies is the World Food Programme (WFP),[12] whose mandate is to eradicate hunger and malnutrition, with the ultimate goal of eliminating the need for food aid itself. Its core mandate has always been to save lives by feeding people in refugee and other emergency situations but its most recent strategic plan (2008–11) has seen a major shift from WFP as a food aid agency to WFP as a

672

food assistance agency. NGOs such as Concern have always been key implementing partners of WFP and are the agencies who actually distribute the food in a transparent and professional manner according to agreed international standards (e.g. the Sphere Standards).

The World Food Programme uses a standard ration in emergency or refugee situations that provides the required 2,100 kilocalories (kcal) of energy. The WFP food basket includes: a staple such as wheat flour or rice; lentils, chickpeas or other pulses; vegetable oil (fortified with vitamin A and D); sugar; and iodised salt. Often these are complemented with special blended foods, such as Corn Soya Blend, that have been fortified with important micronutrients.

Concern and Valid International made a major breakthrough,[13] initially in Malawi and Ethiopia, in terms of treating severely acutely malnourished children (under five) in the early years of this decade through the development of a model of community-based management of acute malnutrition (CMAM) (originally called community-based therapeutic care [CTC]). This innovation, adopted by the UN as a protocol in 2007, broke the limitations of therapeutic care which were that it was high cost, treated very few children for long periods of time and posed risk of cross-infection of other diseases.

## PREVENTION OF HUNGER TODAY
The main concern of governments, aid agencies and academics is to know and be able to effectively prevent hunger on a large scale. Concern believes that what is needed to combat global hunger is significant improvement in a number of key areas.

The kinds of interventions that Concern and similar implementing agencies manage to address in preventing hunger include the following:

### 1. Agriculture
Clearly, it is critical that at global, regional, national and local levels, there is enough food being produced by farmers or commercial food companies. While there is enough food available globally to feed the world's population, local availability is a serious issue. Therefore, increasing agricultural productivity is a common and necessary intervention, especially among smallholder and women farmers. The majority of poor households are still rural (70% on average in developing countries, though this is changing) and 80% of smallholder food production is achieved by women farmers. Typical programmes help poor farmers to access key inputs or services such as seeds, fertiliser, integrated pest management, water, agriculture extension or technical support. The programmes also look at promoting techniques that support multi-cropping or increasing the number of harvests per year (although increasingly they focus on sustainable models such as conservation or low-tillage agriculture) as a response to the difficulties brought about by climate change and by social vulnerabilities such as HIV.

Fig. 4 Concern staff setting out to distribute food aid using camels in Northern Eritrea. [Photo: Connell Foley]

Concern's Conservation Agriculture programme in Zimbabwe, for example, has shown the effectiveness of this model over traditional ones.[14]

*2. Natural resources management and responses to climate change*
Agricultural productivity is hugely dependent on natural resources and apart from agricultural practices which will conserve or positively manage the environment, there are other key interventions required to ensure that this fundamental resource is maximised and that the likelihood of natural disasters are reduced and their effects mitigated. One such intervention is watershed management. In Eritrea, for example, Concern found that the water table was sinking at close to one metre per year and that water availability for drinking and for agriculture was fast disappearing (see Fig. 5). In such desiccated, arid environments, vegetation cover is disappearing and flash flooding is common so that water does not percolate into the soil and regenerate it or the water table but instead flows away in torrential streams. Watershed management is about water and soil conservation (or, more poetically, 'making running water walk' and 'bringing the soil back to life'). Concern supported communities in two regions of Eritrea (Debub and Anseba) by providing cash-for-work to enable

them to build hill terraces (stone bunds along contour lines from the top of hills within the watershed) which trap the water, stopping it building up momentum and making it percolate into the soil. The result is not only less flash flooding but also soil build up behind bunds and re-vegetation along these contour lines. Obviously, reduced flash flooding also reduces various risks to communities and lowers vulnerability locally.

Another main thrust of natural resource management is more fair and equitable access to and decision-making over use of resources. Poor people are vulnerable to powerful people exploiting their local natural resources and community engagement in better governance processes for joint management of communal resources, e.g. joint forest management, is another key intervention facilitated by NGOs.

*3. Other income generation*
Reliance on staple crops is risky given the frequency of natural hazards such as drought. The other danger is that of poor nutrition from lack of dietary diversity, which should provide all the essential vitamins and micro-nutrients required for the optimum performance of the body and brain. It is notable how in many cultures, the word for 'to eat' is often linked to the dominant or staple crop. Some

Fig 5 The local community constructing stone terraces for watershed management at Habero Tselim, Anseba Zoba, Eritrea. The bunds are designed to make 'running water walk' and to 'bring the soil back to life'. [Photo: Connell Foley]

Fig. 6 A flash flood near Habero Tselim, Anseba Zoba, Eritrea. One of the purposes of watershed management is to prevent such flash flooding. [Photo: Connell Foley]

agri-ecological environments make the production of diverse crops difficult and this means that people have to buy in these essential vitamins and nutrients. This usually means that poor people have to earn income, either from the sale of surplus staple crops, from providing labour on the farms of wealthier farmers or from off-farm activities, such as part-time labouring, crafts, petty trade and the like. However, while such generating activities may generate income with which to buy food, where the family has sufficient staple crops, it is very often used to pay for health or education fees rather than to supplement the diet and this often does not have a major impact on improved nutrition.

The types of interventions implemented by government and NGOs to support income-generation are vocational training (skills training in trades), business planning and micro-finance (small scale loans and savings). Indeed, microfinance, associated with Mohammad Younis and the Grameen Bank in Bangladesh, has been seen globally as a successful intervention in terms of ensuring that poor people can access loans for small businesses and as a key stimulus for getting people out of extreme poverty. Obviously in urban areas where people do not grow their own food and where labour opportunities are more likely, it is these types of interventions that are most common.

## 4. Nutrition

Another improvement required is that of increased and more effective interventions to prevent undernutrition. This means ensuring that people can access food and utilise it correctly to be properly nourished. The types if interventions include all those listed in this section but also activities such as micronutrient supplementation (as extra foods or as sprinkles) as well as behaviour change in terms of proper cooking and use of foods. Based on findings in *The Lancet*,[15] Concern and IFPRI are jointly designing a new programme focused on what is called 'The Window of Opportunity', the time from conception to the first two years of age (-9 to 24 months) when proper nutrition is critical for the physical and cognitive development of the child. Interventions during this period are the only ones which will prevent stunting in children. The programme will focus on a number of key impact pathways, including: better agricultural productivity, kitchen gardens focused on dietary diversity, better understanding of diet needs, and changes in women's and men's behaviours related to food during this period.

## 5. Social protection and safety nets

These interventions refer to the provision of social protection to the destitute and those who cannot meet their basic

Fig. 7 Mothers and children attending a traditional supplementary feeding centre in Arotay, Anseba Zoba, Eritrea. Programmes designed to prevent undernutrition should see less need for responses like supplementary feeding or community therapeutic care. [Photo: Connell Foley]

needs. Social protection, the predictable and reliable funding for vulnerable segments of the population, is increasingly being adopted by governments in developing countries and good examples are Ethiopia's Productive Safety Net Programme and India's National Rural Employment Guarantee Act. During short-term crises, NGOs like Concern work with governments to provide temporary safety nets to populations at risk of hunger, especially in drought situations. This usually means unconditional cash transfers or, as is common in much of Latin America, conditional cash transfers where people are given welfare payments but have to adhere to conditions such as attendance at health clinics or at nutrition education sessions. Concern has run a number of very successful and innovative cash-transfer responses in Malawi, Kenya and Niger, combining regular market analyses, innovative community-based targeting, grievance procedures, gender analysis and disbursement technology such as mobile banks, mobile phones and smart cards.

## 6. Institutional development

Less obvious and probably less newsworthy in terms of showing immediate impact on hunger is work done on the enabling environment such as strengthening policies, institutions and processes for long-term, sustainable change. The

kinds of projects are capacity building of national and local government in terms of service delivery but also in governance, management and systems strengthening. Importantly, though one can consider institutional development from the viewpoint of the poor person and it is seen as a critical role of NGOs and other civil society actors to build the capacity of and empower poor people to have their voice heard with decision makers and government officials. People should be able to demand their rights but also be responsible for themselves commensurate with their capabilities.

In a globalised world where private companies have huge power, both in terms of wealth and revenue generation as well as providing employment opportunities, it is important that a society properly regulates and balances the power of different actors. In the case of food, it is important to listen to public officials responsible for the adequate availability of and access to food as well as to the agri-food businesses which play an important role in the development of the sector. It is also critical to listen to smallholder farmers and the consumers of food in order to ensure that their interests are not being sidelined. Generally, the balance of power tends to be with corporations and the greater national economic interest but this very often tilts the balance in favour of the middle-class consumers in urban areas and those with greater political influence and away from

676

the interests of the poor and producers. Where the independence of the judiciary is weak and where there is weak governance, this is especially true. It is therefore important to listen to people who are faced with problems accessing the key resources required to be productive. For marginal farmers, these include land, water, seeds, tools, fertilisers and other key ingredients. For the urban poor, these include education, vocational training and access to credit and to local markets. Processes have to be put in place and implemented seriously to hear these 'marginal voices' to ensure that food is shared equitably across society. A good example is the consultation with African farmers' organisations facilitated by IFAD and the Comprehensive Africa Agriculture Development Program (CAADP) of the African Union.[16]

## FIGHTING HUNGER: IRELAND'S ROLE

Ireland is playing a leading role in tackling global hunger today. Following the deliberations of the UN Hunger Task Force from 2002 to 2005, an Irish Hunger Task Force was set up to get the Irish Government to forge leadership on the issue.[17] The Irish Hunger Task Force report (2008) concluded that three priority areas can have the greatest impact in reducing, and ultimately eliminating, hunger:

• Increasing the productivity of smallholder, main-

ly women farmers in Africa;
• Implementing programmes focused on maternal and infant under-nutrition; and
• Ensuring real political commitment, at national and international levels, to give hunger the absolute priority it deserves.

Ireland is displaying a leadership role by putting its funds into hunger-focused programmes, with Irish Aid committing 20% of its budget to tackling hunger and the Hunger Task Force suggesting that other governments should follow suit. Ireland is also very supportive of African governments' commitments to increase public investment in agriculture by a minimum of 10% of their national budgets and to raise agricultural productivity by at least 6%. In September 2010, Ireland co-hosted with the US Government a special event at the MDG Summit to drive action on nutrition, especially undernutrition in the window of opportunity that occurs when a child is less than two.

Irish NGOs and research institutions continue to implement and research hunger-related issues all across the least-developed world and work closely with Irish Aid to contribute significantly to the achievement of the hunger target embedded in MDG 1. These achievements and commitments have been captured in the Irish Hunger Envoy's Report in November 2010.[18]

Fig. 8 Meeting with a farmers' group in Kholifa Mabang chiefdom, Tonkolili district, Sierra Leone. Listening to the voices of poor farmers is critical to understanding the obstacles they face in reducing hunger. [Photo: Connell Foley]

**IN THE END**
Connell Foley

But in the end there is also an emotional level at which each of us as human beings relates hunger in others that it is a scandal that such a basic need in a human being is not being met with such wealth in the world and the amount spent on so many things that people do not really need but this is the globalised world and market driven wealth creation and it is as if all hope of genuine equality is lost or being overlooked or as if the law will guarantee the rights of every individual in the same way when we know that this is just theory but the practice makes a nonsense of it so this scourge of many people having no energy because they have no food of their listlessness or their inability to maximise their innate potential continues and it continues because they sit in their shacks or houses far from the corridors of power far from the glare of the world's media because they are not a story that can sell knowing full well that if this such hunger was to happen in foxrock or mayfair or manhattan something would be done because it would be demanded and when we talk about political will being required to change this embedded inequity we talk about a tiny percentage of political will when what is needed is a large dose of committed leadership across the world and the ability to work to a common cause which has only been hinted at in the state-centred constituency feeding politics that dominates us and we each as individuals feels helpless to shape or change so in the end we come to the conclusion that this is really what is required to deliver the full realisation of true human rights as they were written and agreed not just some civil and political freedoms half way up maslow's hierarchy but those most basic needs required by every individual to at least live a life of dignity food water clean air energy or fuel and we come back to the basic elements of the cosmos earth air water, fire and how the poorest have always been ingenious at coping in the face of the adversity of nature and of man's inhumanity to woman and if you are a woman subsistence farmer in a remote part of the congo or niger and you have five extra mouths to feed because your brother died of hiv and you are looking at the sky you are looking at your land and you are calculating if there will be too little rain too late or too much so that your basic crop will be ruined and you do not know how you will feed your children or pay for some medicines but you get up every day and you do whatever you can gathering brush or working the land of others or selling yourself in whatever way you can because ...

*'If I gave up! If only I could give up! Before beginning, before beginning again! . . . You launch your voice, it dies away in the vault . . . You must go on . . . I can't go on . . . I'll go on.'*

– Samuel Beckett, *The Unnamable*

# Endnotes

INTRODUCTION

1. Cathal Póirtéir, *Famine Echoes* (Dublin, 1995), pp. 12-13.
2. Mary Daly, if in different ways, has drawn attention to some of these points and especially to the local individuals and groups who could have shown 'greater humanity and activity' and 'greater sympathy' during the Famine. See 'The operations of famine relief, 1845–47' in Cathal Póirtéir (ed.), *The Great Irish Famine* (Cork, 1995), pp. 123-134 and *The Famine in Ireland* (Dundalk, 1986).
3. Póirtéir, *Famine Echoes*, op. cit., p. 14 ; also Póirtéir, *Glórtha ón nGorta: Béaloideas na Gaeilge agus an Gorta Mór* (Dublin, 1996).
4. Cormac Ó Gráda, 'Cecil Woodham Smith agus Charles Trevelyan tar éis caoga blian', *Bliainiris* (forthcoming), pp. 9-10.
5. Quotation is from Cecil Woodham Smith's *The Great Hunger* (London, 1962) pp. 375-76.
6. Appearing originally and anonymously in the *Edinburgh Review*, vol. clxxv, January 1848, Charles Trevelyan's book was published in London in 1848.
7. Kevin Whelan, 'The revisionist debate in Ireland', *boundary*, 2 (31), 1, 2004, p. 201.
8. Published in Dublin in 1861, it first appeared in an American edition in 1860.
9. James Donnelly, 'The Great Famine: its interpreters, old and new' in *History Ireland*, 1, No. 3 (1993), pp. 27-33 and Cormac Ó Gráda, *Ireland: A New Economic History 1780–1939*, (Oxford, 1994), p. 176.
10. Published in Dublin in 1878. Further editions appeared – the third in 1902.
11. Originally published in Dublin in 1956. See R. D. Edwards and T. D. Williams (eds), *The Great Famine: Studies in Irish History* (Dublin, 1994; new edition with introduction and new bibliography by Cormac Ó Gráda). It should be noted that Theo Moody was initially involved as editor but soon withdrew from the project. See also 'Making famine history in Ireland in the 1940s and 1950s' in Cormac Ó Gráda, *Ireland's Great Famine: Interdisciplinary Perspectives* (Dublin, 2006), pp. 234-250.
12. Originally published by Hamish Hamilton (London) in 1962, *The Great Hunger* was published as a Four Square paperback edition in 1965 with a New English Library edition in 1970 and has been republished numerous times since.
13. Cormac Ó Gráda, *The Great Famine* (1994 [1956]), 'Introduction to New Edition', xx.
14. See Mary Daly, *The Famine in Ireland*, p. 138; review by R.F Foster, *Times Literary Supplement*, 13 February 1981, p. 15 and his 'We are all revisionists now', in *Irish Review*, 1, 1986, pp. 1-15. See also critical review by F.S.L. Lyons in *Irish Historical Studies*, vol xiv, no. 53, 1964, pp. 77-79.
15. See, for example, T.W. Freeman, *Pre-Famine Ireland: A Study in Historical Geography* (Manchester, 1957) and S.H. Cousens 'The restriction of population growth in pre-Famine Ireland' in *Proc. R.I.A.*, 64 (c), pp. 85-99 and his 'Regional death rates in Ireland during the Great Famine, for 1846 and 1851' in *Population Studies – A Journal of Demography*, 14(1), 1960, pp. 55-74.
16. Christine Kinealy, *A Death-Dealing Famine: The Great Hunger in Ireland* (London and Chicago, 1997), especially Chapter 1, 'The Great Hunger in Ireland: ideologies and interpretations', pp. 1-16; Cormac Ó Gráda, 'An Gorta Mór: The Great Famine 1845–50', Chapter 8 in *Ireland: A New Economic History 1780–1939* (Oxford, 1994), pp. 173-77; Kevin Whelan, 'The revisionist debate', pp. 194–205.
17. D. George Boyce, *Nationalism in Ireland* (London, 1982), p. 170.
18. First published by Allen Lane (London, 1988) and published by Penguin Books in 1989.
19. Cormac Ó Gráda, 'An Gorta Mór', pp. 173-177.
20. This viewpoint was strongly emphasised in Raymond Crotty's highly original *Irish Agricultural Production: Its Volume and Structure* (Cork, 1966), pp. 35-65; See also R.F. Foster, *Modern Ireland*, pp. 318-19.
21. First published by George Allen and Unwin in Boston.
22. Joel Mokyr, *Why Ireland Starved*, p. 291. Peter M. Solar, 'Why Ireland starved: a critical review of the econometric results', *Irish Economic and Social History*, XI (1984), pp. 101-06; P. L. McGregor, 'Demographic pressure and the Irish Famine: Malthus

after Mokyr', *Land Economics* 65[3] (1989), pp. 228-38. Mokyr's estimates of excess deaths were mapped in Liam Kennedy, Paul S. Ell, E.M. Crawford and L.A. Clarkson (eds), *Mapping the Great Irish Famine: A Survey of the Famine Decades* (Dublin, 1999), p. 37.
23. James S. Donnelly Jr., Chapters 14,15 and 16 in W.E. Vaughan (ed.), *A New History of Ireland under the Union 1801–70* (Oxford, 1989); and The Great Irish Potato Famine (Stroud, 2001).
24. Mary Daly, *Famine in Ireland*, pp. 110-11; R. F. Foster, *Modern Ireland*, p. 374. Vaughan's book was published in Dublin in 1994.
25. Tim P. O'Neill, 'Famine evictions', Chapter 2 in Carla King (ed.), *Famine, Land and Culture in Ireland* (Dublin, 2000), pp 29-70.
26. Christine Kinealy, *This Great Calamity: The Irish Famine 1845–52* (Dublin, 1994); see also her *A Death-Dealing Famine*.
27. See, for example, Cormac Ó Gráda's Ireland Before and After the Famine (Manchester, 1993); his *An Drochshaol: Béaloideas agus Amhráin* (Dublin, 1995) and *Black '47 and Beyond: The Great Irish Famine in History, Economy and Memory* (Princeton, N.J., 1999).
28. For a summary of many of these research questions, see Cormac Ó Gráda, 'Making Famine history in Ireland in 1995', in *Interdisciplinary Perspectives*, pp. 251-266, and his 'Ireland's Great Famine: an overview' in Cormac Ó Gráda, Richard Paping and Eric Vanhaute (eds), *When the Potato Failed: Causes and Effects of the Last European Subsistence Crisis 1845–1850* (Turanhout, 2007), pp. 43-58. With colleague Mary Daly and TCD historians David Dickson and David Fitzpatrick, he has also been a director of the National Famine Commemoration Research Project on Irish workhouses.
29. Peter Gray, *Famine, Land and Politics: British Governmental Irish Relief, 1845–50* (Dublin, 1999); the quotation is from his review in Field Day Review, 1, (2005), p. 265 of Robin Haines, *Charles Trevelyan and the Great Irish Famine* (Dublin, 2004).
30. Published by Notre Dame University, Indiana.
31. See stimulating commentaries in Terry Eagleton, *Heathcliff and The Great Hunger* (London, 1995); Christopher Morash, Writing the Irish Famine (Oxford, 1995) and Margaret Kelleher, *The Feminisation of Famine: Expressing the Inexpressible* (Cork, 1997).
32. Kevin O'Rourke, 'Did the Great Irish Famine matter?', Journal of Economic History, 5 (1991), pp. 1-22.
33. Maureen Gaffney, 'In two places at one time', *The Irish Times*, Weekend Supplement, 4 March, 1995.

## SECTION I: IRELAND BEFORE AND AFTER THE GREAT FAMINE

### THE STORY OF THE GREAT FAMINE: A GEOGRAPHICAL PERSPECTIVE

1. William J. Smyth, 'Introduction: Remembering the Great Irish Famine 1845–1851', *Journal of Economic Studies* 24.1/2 (1997), pp. 4–9. See also William J. Smyth, *Map-making, Landscapes and Memory: A Geography of Colonial and Early Modern Ireland, c.1530–1750* (Cork, 2006).
2. Terry Eagleton, *Heathcliff and the Great Hunger: Studies in Irish Culture* (London, 1995), p. 14.
3. Quoted in Eagleton, *Heathcliff*, p. 12.
4. Amartya Sen, *Identity and Violence: The Delusions of Destiny* (New York, 2006), p. 105. See also his 'Starvation and political economy: Famines, entitlement and alienation', address to the NYU/Ireland House conference on Famine and World Hunger, New York, May 1995. However, Ireland was not the only country to suffer such high famine loss.
5. Cormac Ó Gráda, 'An Gorta Mór: The Great Famine, 1845–50', in *Ireland: A New Economic History, 1780–1939* (Oxford, 1994), p. 180.
6. Joseph Lee, 'The Famine in history', in *Famine 150*, ed. Cormac Ó Gráda (Dublin, 1997), pp. 159–77.
7. Ó Gráda, 'An Gorta Mór', p. 173.

8. Joel Mokyr, *Why Ireland Starved: A Quantitative and Analytical History of the Irish Economy, 1800–1850* (London, 1983). See also his 'The deadly fungus: An econometric investigation into the short-term demographic impact of the Irish Famine', *Research in Population Economics* 2 (1980), pp. 238–39.

9. John O'Connor, *The Workhouses of Ireland: The Fate of Ireland's Poor* (Dublin, 1995), p. 120.

10. O'Connor, *Workhouses*, pp. 120–21.

11. Cathal Póirtéir, *Famine Echoes* (Dublin, 1995), p. 94.

12. Póirtéir, *Famine Echoes*, pp. 86–87.

13. Quoted in Cecil Woodham-Smith, *The Great Hunger* (London, 1968), pp. 157–58. Originally published in *The Times*, 24 December 1846.

14. See James S. Donnelly Jr, 'The administration of relief, 1846–7' and 'The Soup Kitchens', in *A New History of Ireland, V: Ireland under the Union, 1801–70*, ed. W.E. Vaughan (Oxford, 1989), pp. 275–310.

15. Póirtéir, *Famine Echoes*, pp. 244–59.

16. Ó Gráda, 'An Gorta Mór', pp. 186–87.

17. Reported in a host of local histories, such as Seamus Ó Riain, *Dunkerrin: A parish in Ely O Carroll* (Freshford, County Kilkenny, 1988), chapter 8; Daniel Grace, *The Great Famine in Nenagh Poor Law Union, County Tipperary* (Nenagh, 2000), pp. 37–40 and 184–87. See also regular reports in county newspapers for the Famine period, as in *The Tipperary Vindicator*.

18. Quoted in Woodham-Smith, *The Great Hunger*, p. 72, from an original letter sent by the Commissariat Officer at Waterford to Trevelyan on 24 April 1846.

19. Timothy W. Guinnane and Cormac Ó Gráda, *The Workhouse and Irish Famine Mortality*, Centre for Economic Research, U.C.D, 2000.

20. Ó Gráda, 'An Gorta Mór', p. 197. See also Peter Gray, *The Irish Famine* (London, 1995), pp. 64–68.

21. Kevin Whelan, 'The Green Atlantic in the eighteenth century', in *A New Imperial History: Culture, Identity and Modernity in Britain and Europe, 1660–1840*, ed. Kathleen Wilson (Cambridge, 2004), pp. 216–36. See also his *The Green Atlantic: Ireland in the Wider World in the Long Eighteenth Century* (Dublin, forthcoming).

22. F.S.L. Lyons, *Ireland since the Famine* (London, 1971), p. 19.

23. Cormac Ó Gráda, 'The Great Irish Famine: Winners and Losers', Working Paper WP 97/12, Department of Economics, U.C.D., 1997. See also Kevin O'Rourke, 'Did the Great Irish Famine matter?' *Journal of Economic History* 5 (1991), pp. 1–22.

MAPPING THE PEOPLE: THE GROWTH AND DISTRIBUTION OF THE POPULATION

1. Joseph Lee, 'On the accuracy of the pre-Famine Irish Censuses', in *Irish Population, Economy and Society*, ed. J.M. Goldstrom (Oxford, 1981), pp. 37–56.

2. G.S.L. Tucker, 'Irish fertility ratios before the Famine', *Economic History Review* 23 (1970), pp. 267–84.

3. The 1732 figures have been calculated from the Abstract of 1732 Census of Ireland, barony by barony (Ms. 1742) in Lambeth Palace Library. Where only county figures are available – as for County Londonderry and County Waterford – these are averaged across their constituent baronies. Family numbers have been subject to multipliers based on established average household size for each province for this period.

4. T. Jones Hughes, *Landholding, Society and Settlement in Nineteenth-Century Ireland: A Historical Geographer's Perspective* (Dublin, 2010), pp. 327–41.

5. See S.H. Cousens, 'The regional variation in emigration from Ireland between 1821 and 1841', *Transactions and Papers of the Institute of British Geographers* 37 (1965), pp. 15–30. See also his 'The restriction of population growth in pre-Famine Ireland', *Proceedings of the Royal Irish Academy* 64(c) (1966), pp. 85–99.

6. Kevin Whelan, 'Pre- and post-Famine landscape change', in *The Great Irish Famine*, ed. Cathal Póirtéir (Cork, 1995), p. 24.

7. Joel Mokyr and Cormac Ó Gráda, 'Poor and getting poorer? Irish living standards before the Famine', *Economic History Review* 51 (1988), pp. 209–35.

8. Cormac Ó Gráda, *Ireland before and after the Famine: Explorations in Economic History, 1800–1925* (Manchester, 1993), pp. 16–17.

9. E. Margaret Crawford, 'Food and famine', in *The Great Irish Famine*, ed. Póirtéir, pp. 60–74; Lawrence M. Geary, 'Famine, fever and the bloody flux', in *The Great Irish Famine*, ed. Póirtéir, pp. 74–85. See also Crawford's 'Dearth, diet and disease in Ireland, 1850: A case study of nutritional deficiency', *Medical History* 28 (1984), pp. 151–61.

1741 FAMINE

1. L.M. Cullen, 'The value of contemporary printed sources for Irish economic history in the eighteenth century', *Irish Historical Studies* 14 (1964), pp. 146–47, 152–53.

2. For analysis of the weather: John Post, *Food Shortage, Climatic Variability and Epidemic Disease in Preindustrial Europe: The Mortality Peak in the Early 1740s* (Ithaca, 1985), ch. 2; P.D. Jones and K.R. Briffa, 'Unusual climate in northwest Europe during the period 1730 to 1745 based on instrumental and documentary data', *Climatic Change* 79.3–4 (2006), 361–79.

3. Post, *Food Shortage*, pp. 22, 144–45, 178, 194–95, 225, 269–70.

4. Michael Drake, 'The Irish demographic crisis of 1740–41', in *Historical Studies VI*, ed. T.W. Moody (London, 1968), pp. 113, 118.

5. David Dickson, *Arctic Ireland: The Extraordinary Story of the Great Frost and Forgotten Famine of 1740–41* (Belfast, 1997), pp. 26–30, 34–35.

6. Dickson, *Arctic Ireland*, pp. 58–60, 67. For evidence of the light mortality in lowland

north Wicklow during the crisis, see Brian Gurrin, *A Century of Struggle in Delgany and Kilcoole . . . 1666–1779* (Dublin, 2000), pp. 34–40.

7. Dickson, *Arctic Ireland*, pp. 66–69.

THE POTATO: ROOT OF THE FAMINE

1. Wendell Berry, *The Gift of Good Land: Further Essays Cultural and Agricultural* (New York, 1981), pp. 20, 26, 27.

2. Lyndsay and Patrick Mikanowski, *Potato* (London: Grub Street, 2005), p. 14.

3. J. Feehan, G. O'Donovan, F. Renou-Wilson and D. Wilson, *The Bogs of Ireland: An Introduction to the Natural, Cultural and Industrial Heritage of Irish Peatlands*, rev. ed. (Dublin, 2008), pp. 37–72.

4. F.H.A. Aalen, K. Whelan and M. Stout, *Atlas of the Irish Rural Landscape* (Cork, 1997), pp. 88–89.

5. Asenath Nicholson, *Ireland's Welcome to the Stranger, or, an Excursion through Ireland in 1844 and 1845* (New York, 1847).

6. P.M. Austin Bourke, 'The extent of the potato crop in Ireland at the time of the Famine', *Journal of the Statistical and Social Inquiry Society of Ireland, 1959–1960*, reprinted as Appendix 6 in *Farming since the Famine: Irish Farm Statistics, 1847–1996* (Dublin, 1997), pp. 367–90.

7. W.D. Davidson, 'History of potato varieties', *Journal of the Department of Agriculture* (Ireland) 36.1 (1935), pp. 57–81.

8. J. O'Rourke, *The History of the Great Irish Famine of 1847, with Notices of Earlier Irish Famines* (Dublin, 1875), p. 559.

9. W.P. O'Brien, *The Great Famine in Ireland and a Retrospect of the Fifty Years 1845–1895* (London, 1896), p. 68.

BAUNREAGH, COUNTY LAOIS: THE FAILURE OF THE POTATO

1. John Feehan, *Farming in Ireland: History, Heritage and Environment* (Dublin, 2003), p. 263.

2. J. Feehan and G. O'Donovan, *The Bogs of Ireland: An Introduction to the Natural, Cultural and Industrial Heritage of Irish Peatlands* (Dublin, 1996), pp. 58–59.

3. William Steuart Trench, 'Report on reclaiming an extent of 112 Irish acres (equal to 181 English statute measure) of waste land, at Baunreigh, in the Queen's County, for which the Medal of the Society was awarded', *Reports and Transactions of the Royal Agricultural Improvement Society of Ireland* (1843), pp. 9–32.

4. John Feehan, *The Landscape of Slieve Bloom: A Study of Its Natural and Human Heritage* (Blackwater Press, 1979; reprinted,: Slieve Bloom Association, 2009), pp. 229–31.

5. William Steuart Trench, *Realities of Irish Life* (London, 1868), pp. 100–101.

DIET IN PRE-FAMINE IRELAND

1. For a comprehensive and detailed analysis of the pre-Famine diet, see L.A. Clarkson and E. Margaret Crawford, *Feast and Famine: Food and Nutrition in Ireland, 1500–1920* (Oxford, 2001), pp. 59–87.

2. Austin Bourke, '*The Visitation of God?' The Potato and the Great Irish Famine*, ed. Jacqueline Hill and Cormac Ó Gráda (Dublin, 1993), pp. 21, 42–43.

3. Angélique Day and Patrick McWilliams, eds, *Ordnance Survey Memoirs of Ireland, vol. 5: Parishes of County Tyrone, I* (Belfast, 1990), p. 141; Day and McWilliams, eds, *Ordnance Survey Memoirs of Ireland, vol. 1: Parishes of County Antrim, I* (Belfast, 1990), p. 9 (hereafter *OSM: County Antrim*).

4. Bourke, 'The Visitation of God?', p. 97.

5. *OSM: County Antrim, I*, pp. 9, 61; 'First report from his majesty's commissioners for inquiring into the condition of the poorer classes in Ireland', PP 1836 (369), XXXII, appendix (E).

6. T.C. Foster, *Letters on the Condition of the People of Ireland* (London, 1846), p. 111.

7. The ubiquity of herring is widely noted in contemporary accounts. See Clarkson and Crawford, *Feast and Famine*, pp. 59–87.

8. Mr and Mrs S.C. Hall, *Ireland: Its Scenery, Character, &c*, 3 vols (New York, 1843), vol. 1, p. 83.

9. Clarkson and Crawford, *Feast and Famine*, p. 73.

10. Clarkson and Crawford, *Feast and Famine*, p. 73. See also Bourke, 'The Visitation of God?', pp. 91–96.

11. H. Dutton, *Statistical Survey of the County of Clare, with Observations on the Means of Improvement* (Dublin, 1808), p. 43; H. Dutton, *A Statistical and Agricultural Survey of the County of Galway, with Observations on the Means of Improvement* (Dublin, 1824), p. 177.

12. T. Reid, *Travels in Ireland* (London, 1823), p. 204.

13. Michael McGrath, ed. and trans., *The Diary of Humphrey O'Sullivan*, 4 vols (London, 1928 [1936]), vol. 1, p. 197; William Tighe, *Statistical Observations Relative to the County of Kilkenny, Made in the Years 1800 and 1801* (Dublin, 1802), p. 490; OSM: County Antrim, I, p. 61.

14. *OSM: County Antrim, I*, pp. 9, 32.

15. Foster, *Letters on the Condition*, p. 106.

16. Reid, *Travels in Ireland*, pp. 204, 205.

17. Humphrey O'Sullivan makes reference to the hardship of July, calling it 'the waiting month', 'July of the Famine' and 'food scarce July'. See, for example, McGrath, *The Diary of Humphrey O'Sullivan*, vol. 2, pp. 303, 305.

18. Bourke, 'The Visitation of God?', p. 48.

19. See for example Henry D. Inglis, *Ireland in 1834: A Journey throughout Ireland, during the Spring, Summer, and Autumn of 1834, 2 vols* (London, 1835), vol. 1, p. 305; McGrath, *The Diary of Humphrey O'Sullivan*, vol. 2, pp. 299, 313; 'First report from his majesty's commissioners for inquiring into the condition of the poorer classes in Ireland', PP 1836 (369), XXXII, appendix (E).

20. See, for example, McGrath, *The Diary of Humphrey O'Sullivan*, vol. 2, p. 299.

21. McGrath, *The Diary of Humphrey O'Sullivan*, vol. 1, p. 51; vol. 2, pp. 181, 182, 185, 197, 303, 305.

22. McGrath, The Diary of Humphrey O'Sullivan, vol. 3, p. 151; Tighe, *Statistical Observations Relative to the County of Kilkenny*, p. 48.

23. Dutton, *Statistical Survey of the County of Clare*, p. 43, for example, lists 17 varieties.

24. Dutton, *Statistical Survey of the County of Clare*, p. 43.

25. Dutton, *Statistical Survey of the County of Clare*, p. 43; Dutton, *A Statistical and Agricultural Survey of the County of Galway*, p. 177; Tighe, *Statistical Observations Relative to the County of Kilkenny*, p. 480; for discussion of the regional distribution of varieties, see Bourke, 'The Visitation of God?', pp. 40–42.

26. Bourke, 'The Visitation of God?', pp. 40–42.

27. *OSM: County Antrim, I*, pp. 31–32.

28. Keith Lamb and Patrick Bowe, *A History of Gardening in Ireland* (Dublin, 1995), pp. 54–62.

29. Mary Forrest, 'Nurseries and nurserymen in Ireland from the early eighteenth to the early twenty-first century', *Studies in the History of Gardens and Designed Landscapes: An International Quarterly* 30.4 (2010), pp. 323–36.

30. Tighe, *Statistical Observations Relative to the County of Kilkenny*, p. 498.

## Section II: The Great Hunger

### The longue durée – imperial Britain and colonial Ireland

1. Mary Daly, 'The operation of Famine relief, 1845–57', in *The Great Irish Famine*, ed. Cathal Póirtéir (Cork, 1995), pp. 133–34. See also, Mary Daly, *The Famine in Ireland* (Dublin, 1986), pp. 93–95 and 113–14.

2. Compare accounts in E.R.R. Green, 'The Great Famine (1845–50)', in *The Course of Irish History*, ed. T.W. Moody and F.X. Martin (Cork, 1987), p. 273, and R.F. Foster, *Modern Ireland, 1600–1972* (London, 1988), pp. 325–28, with James Donnelly's essays on the Famine in *A New History of Ireland, V: Ireland under the Union, 1801–70*, ed. W.E. Vaughan (Oxford, 1993).

3. Christine Kinealy, *This Great Calamity: The Irish Famine, 1845–52* (Dublin, 1994), p. 49.

4. Charles Trevelyan's family originated from Cornwall. He began his career in India (1826–38) before becoming permanent head of the Treasury in London, where he was knighted in 1848 for his work in the Irish Famine. He helped to modernise the British civil service before serving again in India, first as governor of Madras and later as finance minister on the India Council. He died in 1886. (See also David Nally, below).

5. John Keating, *Irish Famine Facts* (Dublin, 1996), p. 38.

6. Keating, *Irish Famine Facts*, pp. 41–42.

7. Kinealy, *This Great Calamity*, pp. 116–17.

8. Keating, *Irish Famine Facts*, pp. 42–43.

9. Kinealy, *This Great Calamity*, pp. 205–10.

10. For example, the number on the Roscrea Union's outdoor relief list was reduced by half between August and October 1847 – but it climbed back again to August levels by December (Minutes, Roscrea Poor Law Union).

11. Peter Gray, 'Ideology and the Famine', in *The Great Irish Famine*, ed. Cathal Póirtéir (Cork, 1995), pp. 98–99.

12. The 'Gregory clause' as an amendment to the Poor Law Extension Bill was insisted on by the Conservatives in the House of Lords to guarantee their support for the bill. This may help explain the failure of the Irish MPs to oppose this infamous clause. See Gray 'Ideology', p. 98.

13. Quoted in Cecil Woodham-Smith, *The Great Hunger* (London, 1968), p. 104.

14. Kinealy, *This Great Calamity*, p. 102.

15. *Tipperary Vindicator*, 1 May 1847.

16. Kinealy, *This Great Calamity*, pp. 43–51 and 75–89.

17. Quoted in Woodham-Smith, *The Great Hunger*, p. 86.

18. Cormac Ó Gráda, 'An Gorta Mór: The Great Famine, 1845–50', in *Ireland: A New Economic History, 1780–1939* (Oxford, 1994), pp. 198–99.

19. Kinealy, *This Great Calamity*, pp. 282–85.

20. Woodham-Smith, *The Great Hunger*, pp. 70–71 and XX.

21. Quoted in Woodham-Smith, *The Great Hunger*, pp. 181–82.

22. Kinealy, *This Great Calamity*, p. 65 and 148–49.

23. Kinealy, *This Great Calamity*, pp. 205–10 and 229–50. See also Gray, *The Irish Famine*, pp. 58–68.

24. Woodham-Smith, *The Great Hunger*, p. 307.

25. Ó Gráda, 'An Gorta Mór', p. 197.

26. Ó Gráda, 'An Gorta Mór', p. 193.

27. Kinealy, *This Great Calamity*, pp. 254–62.

28. Quoted in Woodham-Smith, *The Great Hunger*, p. 378.

29. Quoted in Woodham-Smith, *The Great Hunger*, p. 314.

30. Quoted in Woodham-Smith, *The Great Hunger*, p. 379.

31. Quoted in Woodham-Smith, *The Great Hunger*, pp. 373–81.

32. Peter Gray, 'Ideology', pp. 102–3.

33. James S. Donnelly Jr, 'The administration of relief, 1846–7', in *A New History of Ireland, V: Ireland under the Union, 1801–70*, ed. W.E. Vaughan (Oxford, 1989), p. 285.

34. P.M. Austin Bourke, *The Visitation of God: The Potato and the Great Irish Famine* (Dublin, 1993). See also Gray, 'Ideology', pp. 91–93.

35. Gray, 'Ideology', pp. 98–99.

36. Gray, 'Ideology', pp. 99–100.

37. Amongst a number of commentaries on Irish morals (defective) and on the Irish character, it was Trevelyan's view 'that the Irish small-holder lives in a state of isolation – the type of which is to be sought for in the islands of the South Sea, rather than the great civilised communities of the ancient world' (quoted in Terry Eagleton, *Heathcliff and the Great Hunger: Studies in Irish Culture* [London, 1995], p. 55).

38. William J. Smyth, *Map-making, Landscapes and Memory: A Geography of Colonial and Early Modern Ireland, c.1530–1750* (Cork, 2006), pp. 21–53, 345–83 and 451–70.

39. Joel Mokyr, *Why Ireland Starved: A Quantitative and Analytical History of the Irish Economy, 1800–1850* (London, 1983), p. 29. See also William J. Smyth, 'Introduction: Remembering the Great Irish Famine 1845–1851', *Journal of Economic Studies* 24.1/2 (1997), pp. 6–7.

40. Jacinta Prunty, 'Military barracks and mapping in the nineteenth century: Sources and issues for Irish urban history', in *Surveying Ireland's Past: Multidisciplinary Essays in Honour of Anngret Simms*, ed. Howard B. Clarke, Jacinta Prunty and Mark Hennessy (Dublin, 2004), pp. 477–534.

41. Prunty, 'Military barracks', pp. 496–98 and 525–28.

42. See, for example, Des Cowman and Donald Brady, eds, *Teacht na bPrátaí Dubha: The Famine in Waterford, 1845–50* (Dublin, 1995), pp. 137–52 and 291–310; and Robert James Scally, *The End of Hidden Ireland: Rebellion, Famine and Emigration* (Oxford, 1995), pp. 95–104.

43. See Woodham-Smith, *The Great Hunger*, pp. 169 and 367–68.

44. Quoted in Woodham-Smith, *The Great Hunger*, p. 316.

45. Thomas Bartlett, 'The Academy of Warre': Military Affairs in Ireland, 30th O'Donnell Lecture (Dublin, 2002), pp. 9–18.

46. 'Returns relative to taxes, Great Britain and Ireland', H.C. (1854), pp. 18–25.

47. Prunty, 'Military barracks', pp. 498–99.

48. David Harvey, *The New Imperialism* (Oxford, 2003).

49. T. Jones Hughes, *Landholding, Society and Settlement in Nineteenth-Century Ireland: A Historical Geographer's Perspective* (Dublin, 2010), pp. 250–73 and 310–21.

50. Ó Gráda, 'An Gorta Mór', p. 180.

51. J. Barrington Moore, *The Social Origins of Dictatorship and Democracy* (Boston, 1966).

52. D.W. Meinig, 'Geographic analysis of imperial expansion', in *Period and Place: Research Methods in Historical Geography*, ed. Alan Baker and Mark Billinge (Cambridge, 1982), pp. 71–86.

53. Smyth, *Map-making, Landscapes and Memory*, pp. 442.

54. Bartlett, 'The Academy of Warre', p. 18. One Roscommon landlord argued that those who supported the repeal of the Corn Laws were 'seeking to excite the passions of the lower orders of England against our last and only resource, *after leaving Ireland nothing but agriculture*' (my italics) (quoted in Cormac Ó Gráda, *Ireland: A New Economic History, 1780–1939* [Oxford, 1994], p. 120).

55. David Nally, review of William J. Smyth, *Map-making, Landscapes and Memory*, H-Net Book Review (H-HistGeog), 2007 (online).

56. Kinealy, *This Great Calamity*, p. 4.

57. Patrick O'Connor, *Fairs and Markets in Ireland: A Cultural Geography* (Midleton, 2003), pp. 285–390.

58. Ó Gráda, *Ireland: A New Economic History*, pp. 69–75.

59. T.W. Freeman, *Pre-Famine Ireland: A Study in Historical Geography* (Manchester, 1957), pp. 37–50, especially p. 42.

60. Liz Young, 'Spaces for famine: A comparative geographical analysis of famine in Ireland and the Highlands in the 1840s', *Transactions of the Institute of British Geographers*, new series, 21 (1996), pp. 666–80.

61. Cormac Ó Gráda, *Ireland before and after the Famine: Explorations in Economic History, 1800–1923*, 2nd ed. (Manchester, 1993), p. 36. See also William J. Smyth, 'Introduction: Remembering', pp. 5–6.

62. Mokyr, *Why Ireland Starved*, pp. 248–52.

63. See, for example, the vast body of documentation available on the House of Commons Parliamentary Papers online. See also very useful 'Documents' section in Gray, *The Irish Famine*, pp. 130–83.

64. The quotation from Twistleton as regards the Statistical Department [of the Irish Poor Law Commission] who 'found themselves beaten by the Work' can be found in Woodham-Smith, *The Great Hunger*, p. 367.

65. Donnelly, 'The administration of relief, 1846–7', p. 306.

66. Gray, 'Ideology', pp. 102–3.

67. Mokyr, *Why Ireland Starved*, pp. 291–92. Mokyr continues by stating: 'There is no doubt that Britain could have saved Ireland. The British Treasury spent a total of £9.5 million on famine relief . . . A few years after the Famine, the British Government spent £69.3 million on an utterly futile venture in the Crimean. Half that sum spent

in Ireland in the critical years 1846–9 would have saved hundreds of thousands of lives . . . It is not unreasonable to surmise that had anything like the Famine occurred in England or Wales, the British Government would have overcome its theoretical scruples and would have come to the rescue of the starving at a much larger scale. Ireland was not considered part of the British community' (pp. x–x).

### THE COLONIAL DIMENSIONS OF THE GREAT IRISH FAMINE

1. M. Davis, *Late Victorian Holocausts: El Niño Famines and the Making of the Third World* (London, 2001), pp. 11–15.
2. C. Trevelyan, 'The Great Irish Famine', *The Times*, 29 June 1880.
3. C. Trevelyan, 'The threatened famine in Bengal', The Times, 27 November 1873.
4. A. Smith, *An Inquiry into the Nature and Causes of the Wealth of Nations*, 5th ed. ed. Edwin Cannon (London, 1904), bk 4, ch. 5. 44. See also R. Sheldon, 'Development, poverty and famines: The case of the British Empire', in *Empire, Development and Colonialism: The Past in the Present*, ed. M. Duffield and V. Hewitt (Woodbridge, Suffolk, 2009), pp. 74–87.
5. K. Polanyi, *The Great Transformation: The Political and Economic Origins of Our Times* (Boston, 2001), p. 141.
6. Trevelyan, 'The threatened famine'.
7. For striking exceptions, see J. Bender, 'The imperial politics of famine: The 1873–74 Bengal famine and Irish parliamentary nationalism', *Éire-Ireland* 42.1/2 (2007), pp. 132–56; C. Boylan, 'Victorian ideologies of improvement: Sir Charles Trevelyan in India and Ireland', in *Ireland and India: Colonies, Culture and Empire*, ed. Tadhg Foley and Maureen O'Connor (Dublin, 2007), pp. 167–78; L. Brennan, 'The Development of the Indian Famine Code' in *Famine a Geographical Phenomenon*, ed. B. Currey and G. Hugo (Dordrecht, 1984), pp. 91–112; P. Gray, 'Famine and land in Ireland and India, 1845–1880: James Caird and the political economy of hunger', *The History Journal* 49.1 (2006), pp. 193–215.
8. D. Nally, '"That Coming Storm": The Irish Poor Law, colonial biopolitics, and the Great Famine', *Annals of the Association of American Geographers* 98.3 (2008), pp. 714–41.
9. A. Rangasami, '"Failure of exchange entitlements" theory of famine: A response', *Economic and Political Weekly* 20.41/42 (1985), pp. 1747–52, 1797–1801.
10. J. Mitchel, *The History of Ireland: From the Treaty of Limerick to the Present Time* (Glasgow, 1869), vol. 2, p. 243.
11. T. Barnard, *The Kingdom of Ireland, 1641–1760* (New York: Palgrave Macmillan, 2004), pp. 25–32; P.J. Corish, *The Irish Catholic Experience: The Historical Survey* (Dublin: Gill and Macmillan, 1995), p. 12; R. Dudley Edwards and B. Hourican, *An Atlas of Irish History*, 3rd ed. (London, 2005), p. 163; C. Kinealy, *A Death-Dealing Famine: The Great Hunger in Ireland* (London, 1997), p. 18
12. W.J. Smyth, *Map-making, Landscapes and Memory: A Geography of Colonial and Early Modern Ireland, c.1530–1750* (Cork, 2006), pp. 377, 196.
13. 'Second report of the select committee on the state of disease, and condition of labouring poor in Ireland', Parliamentary Papers HC 1819 (409) viii, p. 457.
14. K. Marx, *Capital* (London, 1954), vol. 1, p. 657
15. W.T. Thornton, *Overpopulation and its Remedy; or An Enquiry into the Extent and Causes of the Distress among the Labouring Classes of the British Islands and the Means of Remedying It* (London, 1846), p. 94.
16. G. O'Brien, *The Economic History of Ireland from the Union to the Famine* (London, 1921), pp. 95–96.
17. R.H. Tawney, *Land and Labour in China* (Boston: Beacon Press, 1966), p. 77.
18. Anonymous, *Ireland in 1804*, ed. Seamus Grimes (Dublin, 1980), pp. 20, 36.
19. D.J. O'Donoghue, *Sir Walter Scott's Tour in Ireland in 1825* (Glasgow, 1905), p. 92.
20. G. Nicholls, *A History of the Irish Poor Laws* (New York, 1967 [1856]), p. 10.
21. N. Senior, Journals, *Conversations and Essays Relating to Ireland* (London, 1868), vol. 1, pp. 252–55; P. Gray, *Famine, Land and Politics: British Government and Irish Society, 1843–1859* (Dublin: Irish Academic Press, 1999), p. 56.
22. See N. Lebow, *White Britain and Black Ireland: The Influence of Stereotypes on Colonial Policy* (Philadelphia, 1976).
23. *The Times*, 31 December 1872.
24. G. Nicholls, *Poor Laws – Ireland: Three Reports by George Nicholls, Esq., to Her Majesty's Principal Secretary of State for the Home Department* (London, 1838), p. 16. As Lalor witheringly noted, 'The small landholdings are to be "consolidated" into large farmers, the small landholders "converted" into "independent labourers"; those labourers are, of course, to be paupers – those paupers to be supported by a Poor Law – that poor law is to be in your hands to manage and administer. Thus to be got rid of the surplus of population beyond what the landowners require' (J.F. Lalor, *Collected Writings* (1918), ed. L. Fogarty, introduction by J. Kelly, and preface by A. Griffith [Washington, DC, 1997], p. 22). See also, D. Lloyd, 'The political economy of the potato', *Nineteenth-Century Contexts* 29.2–3 (2007), pp. 311–35.
25. Nicholls, *A History of the Irish Poor Laws*, p. 168.
26. Nicholls, *Poor Laws – Ireland*, p. 167.
27. Nicholls, *Poor Laws – Ireland*, pp. 168–69.
28. G. Nicholls, *The Farmer's Guide: Compiled for the Use of the Small Farmers and Cotter Tenantry of Ireland* (Dublin, 1841), p. 1.
29. Nicholls, *The Farmer's Guide*, p. 167.
30. Nicholls, *The Farmer's Guide*, p. 181.

31. K. Whelan, 'The modern landscape: From plantation to the present', *Atlas of the Irish Rural Landscape*, ed. F.H.A. Aalen, K. Whelan and M. Stout (Cork, 1997), p. 69; T. Barnard, *Improving Ireland: Projectors, Prophets and Profiteers, 1641–1786* (Dublin, 2008), pp. 13–40.
32. Nicholls, *A History of the Irish Poor Laws*, p. 95.
33. Nicholls, *A History of the Irish Poor Laws*, p. 168.
34. These arguments are powerfully developed in Gray, *Famine, Land and Politics*.
35. R. Peel. *The Speeches of the Late Right Honourable Sir Robert Peel Delivered in the House of Commons, with an Explanatory Index, Volume IV, 1842–1850* (London, 1853), p. 599.
36. Senior, *Journals Conversations and Essays*, vol. 1, p. 180.
37. C. E. Trevelyan, *The Irish Crisis* (London, 1848), p. 65.
38. Anonymous, 'The working of the Irish Poor Law', *The Times*, 5 July 1849.
39. W. Gregory, *Sir William Gregory, K.C.M.G., Formerly Member of the Parliament and Sometime Governor of Ceylon* (London, 1894), p. 136.
40. P. Gray, 'Ideology and the Famine', in *The Great Irish Famine*, ed. C. Póirtéir (Dublin, 1995). p. 98.
41. I. Butt, *A Voice for Ireland: The Famine in the Land, What Has Been Done and What Is to Be Done* (Dublin, 1847), p. 21.
42. J. MacHale, *The Letters of the Most Reverend John MacHale, D.D., under Their Respective Signatures of Hierophilos; John, Bishop of Maronia; Bishop of Killala; and Archbishop of Tuam* (Dublin, 1847), p. 614.
43. Nicholls, *A History of the Irish Poor Laws*, p. 356–57.
44. J. Forbes, *Memorandums Made in Ireland in the Autumn of 1852* (London, 1853), vol. 1, pp. 297, 299–300.
45. Quoted in Gray, *Famine, Land and Politics*, p. 192.
46. Quoted in K. Whelan, 'Pre- and post-Famine landscape change', in *The Great Irish Famine*, ed. C. Póirtéir (Dublin, 1995), p. 29.
47. Trevelyan, *The Irish Crisis*, p. 1.
48. J.H. Ashworth, *The Rambles of an Englishman in the West; or, the Saxon in Ireland* (Boston, 1850), p. 221.
49. Quoted in Whelan, 'Pre- and post-Famine landscape change', p. 32.
50. Lalor, *Collected Writings*, p. 34.
51. H. Dorian, *The Outer Edge of Ulster: A Memoir of Social Life in Nineteenth-Century Ireland*, ed. B. Mac Suibhne and D. Dickson (Dublin, 2000 [1890]), pp. 237–38.
52. Dorian, *The Outer Edge of Ulster*, p. 252.
53. G.P. Scrope, *Some Notes of a Tour in England, Scotland & Ireland: Made with a View to the Inquiry Whether Our Labouring Population Be Really Redundant?: In Letters to the Editor of the Morning Chronicle* (London, 1849), p. 26.
54. Mitchel, *The Last Conquest of Ireland*, p. 66; Butt, *A Voice for Ireland*, p. 30.
55. I. Butt, *Land Tenure in Ireland: A Plea for the Celtic Race*, 3rd ed. (Dublin, 1866), p. 65. According to J.F. Lalor, the Irish people owed 'no obedience to laws enacted by another nation without our assent; nor respect to assumed rights of property which are starving and exterminating our people' (Lalor, *Collected Writings*, p. 85).
56. T. Pogge, *World Poverty and Human Rights* (Cambridge, 2002), pp. 23, 15.
57. E.M. Wood, *Empire of Capital* (London, Verso), 2003 p. 78.
58. L. Kennedy et al., eds, *Mapping the Great Irish Famine: A Survey of the Famine Decades* (Dublin, 1999), pp. 176–77.
59. Kennedy et al., eds, *Mapping the Great Irish Famine*, p. 162.
60. Senior, *Journals, Conversations and Essays, vol. 1*, pp. 256–57.
61. Whelan, 'The modern landscape', p. 68.
62. See D. Nally, *Human Encumbrances: Political Violence and the Great Irish Famine* (Notre Dame, 2011).

### BRITISH RELIEF MEASURES

1. Peter Gray, *Famine, Land and Politics: British Government and Irish Society, 1843–50* (Dublin, 1999), pp. 95–141.
2. Andrés Eiríksson, 'Food supply and food riots', in *Famine 150*, ed. C. Ó Gráda, (Dublin, 1997), pp. 67–93
3. S.J. Connolly, 'The Great Famine and Irish politics', in *The Great Irish Famine*, ed. Cathal Póirtéir (Cork, 1995), pp. 34–49.
4. Hansard, 3s, 88 (17 Aug. 1846), cols 766–99.
5. James Donnelly, *The Great Irish Potato Famine* (Stroud, Gloucestershire, Sutton, 2001), pp. 57–64.
6. See James S. Donnelly Jr, 'The administration of relief, 1846–7', in *A New History of Ireland, V: Ireland under the Union, 1801–70*, ed. W.E. Vaughan (Oxford, 1989), pp. 275–310.
7. Larry Geary, 'Famine, fever and bloody flux', in *The Great Irish Famine*, ed. Cathal Póirtéir (Cork, 1995), pp. 74–85.
8. Peter Gray, 'National humiliation and the great hunger: Fast and famine in 1847', in *Irish Historical Studies* 32 (2000) pp. 193–216; Christine Kinealy, 'Potatoes, providence and philanthropy: The role of private charity during the Irish famine', in *The Meaning of the Famine*, ed. Patrick O'Sullivan (London, 1997), pp. 140–171; Tim O'Neill, 'The charities and famine in mid-nineteenth century Ireland', in *Luxury and Austerity: Historical Studies XXI*, ed. J.R. Hill and C. Lennon (Dublin, 1999), pp. 137–59.
9. James S. Donnelly Jr, '"Irish property must pay for Irish poverty": British public opinion and the great Irish famine', in *Fearful Realities: New Perspectives on the Famine*,

ed. C. Morash and R. Hayes (Dublin, 1996).

10. Gray, *Famine, Land and Politics*, p. 288.

CHARLES TREVELYAN

1. See, for example, J.M. Hernon, 'A Victorian Cromwell: Sir Charles Trevelyan, the Famine and the age of improvement', *Éire-Ireland* 22 (1987), pp. 15–29.

2. Robin Haines, *Charles Trevelyan and the Great Irish Famine* (Dublin, 2004).

3. See Peter Gray, 'Ideology and the Famine', in *The Great Irish Famine*, ed. Cathal Póirtéir (Cork, 1995), pp. 86–103.

4. Peter Gray, *Famine, Land and Politics: British Government and Irish Society, 1843–50* (Dublin, 1999), p. 255

5. C.E. Trevelyan, *The Irish Crisis* (London, 1848), pp. 200–201.

THE OPERATION OF THE POOR LAW DURING THE FAMINE

1. 'Debate on Poor Laws (Ireland)', Hansard 33 (4 May 1836), cols 590–607. (Reports from Hansard are available online at: http://hansard.millbanksystems.com/ commons and http://hansard.millbanksystems.com/lords.)

2. Christine Kinealy, *A Disunited Kingdom? England, Ireland, Scotland and Wales, 1800–1949* (Cambridge, 1999 and 2007).

3. *Third Report of His Majesty's Commissioners for Inquiring into the Condition of the Poorer Classes in Ireland, with Appendix and Supplement*, 1836 (43) xxx, 1.

4. This point was made in the Queen's Speech at the opening of parliament in 1836. Quoted in 'Debate on Poor Laws (Ireland)'.

5. 1838 Poor Relief (Ireland Act), 1 & 2 Vict., *c*.56.

6. Lord Monteagle, 'Poor Law (Ireland)', Hansard 91 (26 March 1847), cols 418–88.

7. Medical Charities Act, 1851, 14 & 15 Vict., *c*.68.

8. Earl Grey, 'Poor Law (Ireland)', Hansard 91 (26 March 1847), cols 418–88.

9. Christine Kinealy, *This Great Calamity. The Irish Famine 1845 to 1852* (Dublin, 1994 and 2006), chapter 2.

10. Lord John Russell, 'Poor Relief (Ireland) Bill', Hansard 90 (12 March 1847), cols 1244–325.

11. Clarendon to Charles Wood, Clarendon's Letter Books, Bodleian Library, 12 July 1847.

12. Twistleton to Trevelyan, Treasury Papers, NAE, T.64.369 B/1, 14 December 1847.

13. Wood to Clarendon, Hickleton Papers (Papers of Charles Wood), A.4.181, 23 July 1847 (available on microform).

14. Marquis of Clanricarde to Clarendon, Clarendon Letter Books, 15 August 1847.

15. Clarendon to Lord Brougham, Clarendon Letter Books, 10 August 1847.

16. Clarendon to Wood, Clarendon Letter Books, 2 August 1847.

17. George Nicholls, *A History of the Irish Poor Law in Connexion with the Condition of the People* (London, 1856), p. 357.

18. Clarendon to Wood, Clarendon Letter Books, 12 August 1847.

19. Earl Grey, 'Poor Law (Ireland)', Hansard 91 (26 March 1847), cols 418–88.

20. Russell to Clarendon, Clarendon Letter Books, 15 August 1848.

21. Nicholls, *History of the Irish Poor Law*, pp. 356–59.

22. Evidence of Edward Twistleton, *Select Committee on the Irish Poor Law*, 1849, vol. 16, pp. 699–714.

23. Nicholls, *History of the Irish Poor Law*, p. 357.

QUEEN VICTORIA AND THE GREAT FAMINE

1. *The Times*, 4 January 1880.

2. *Cork Examiner*, 14 June 1995.

3. *An Phoblacht*, 15 May 2003.

4. *Freeman's Journal*, 5 July 1849.

5. *The Times*, 13 January and 19 October 1847.

6. Christine Kinealy, 'A right to march? The conflict at Dolly's Brae', in *Problems and Perspectives in Irish History since 1800*, ed. G. George Boyce and Roger Swift (Dublin, 2003).

7. *Liverpool Mercury*, 17 August 1849.

8. Victoria to Leopold, 6 August 1849, in Arthur Christopher Benson and Viscount Esher, eds, *The Letters of Queen Victoria: A Selection from Her Majesty's Correspondence between the Years 1837 and 1861*, 3 vols (London, 1907), vol. 2, pp. 224–25.

9. Victoria to Leopold, 11 August 1849, in Benson and Esher, eds, *The Letters of Queen Victoria*, p. 245.

10. *Banner of Ulster*, 3 and 14 August 1849.

11. John Mitchel, *Jail Journal, or Five years in British Prisons* (Glasgow, 1876), pp. 216 and 243.

12. Christine Kinealy, 'Famine Queen or Faerie Queen? Queen Victoria and Ireland', in *Politics and Power in Victorian Ireland*, ed. Roger Swift and Christine Kinealy (Dublin, 2006), p. 23.

13. James H. Murphy, *Abject Loyalty: Nationalism and Monarchy in Ireland during the Reign of Queen Victoria* (Washington, DC, 2001).

14. John Crowley, 'Constructing Famine memory: The role of monuments', in *Heritage, Memory and the Politics of Identity: New Perspectives on the Cultural Landscape*, ed. Niamh Moore and Yvonne Whelan (Hampshire, 2007), pp. 55–68.

15. *United Irishman*, 7 April 1900.

BURYING AND RESURRECTING THE PAST

1. According to James Murphy, 'Victoria owed her reputation as the "Famine Queen" principally to the later writings of the fervent nationalist Maud Gonne. In 1897 a funeral procession was organised in Dublin by Gonne to mark Victoria's diamond jubilee. The coffin bore the slogans "starved", "evicted" and "emigrated". An outdoor slide show was also planned for Rutland Street which depicted eviction scenes' (James Murphy, cited in Declan Kiberd, 'Emerald in the Crown', BBC Radio 4, 1 February 2001).

2. See John A. Murphy, *The College: A History of Queen's/University College Cork, 1844–1995* (Cork, 1999), pp. 232–38.

'THE LARGEST AMOUNT OF GOOD': QUAKER RELIEF EFFORTS

1. CRC, *Distress in Ireland*, 13 November 1846, Friends House Library, London (FHLL hereafter), Tract Box 99, 1–758. The full work in the famine was published as CRC, *Transactions of the Central Relief Committee of the Society of Friends during the Famine in Ireland in 1846 and 1847* (Dublin, 1852). The title is misleading as their relief continued into 1849.

2. See London Committee, *The Distress in Ireland*, 2 December 1846, FHLL, Tract Box 99, no number. Reports of W.F and W.E. Forster, Joseph Crossfield, Dr Bewley, Marcus Goodbody, James H. Tuke, George Alexander, William Todhunter, Richard Webb and Jonathan Pim are incorporated in the CRC and London Committee *Distress* reports and were widely circulated. W.F. Forster's report of his six-week investigation into the west and south of Ireland was printed and circulated in Ireland, Britain and North America. The report of CRC Secretary Jonathan Pim's investigative journey was also printed and circulated by the London Committee.

3. London Committee, *Address to Friends in North America*, FHL Dublin (FHLD) Room 4, Shelf J, Box 1–236.

4. Russell spent just under £9 million, or $45 million.

5. CRC, *Transactions*, p. 349.

6. The full breakdown of grants by province and county is given in Helen E. Hatton, *The Largest Amount of Good: Quaker Relief in Ireland, 1654–1921* (Montreal, 1993), appendix 1.

7. CRC Minute books, February 1847, Public Record Office of Ireland (PROI hereafter), 1A42–139. See also Cecil Woodham-Smith, *The Great Hunger: Ireland 1845–1849* (New York, 1962), p. 178.

8. CRC Ledger, PROI, 1A42–34.

9. CRC, *Distress in Ireland*, Sub-Committee for Clothing, FHLL, MS Box S-164. Also see London Committee, *An Appeal for Clothing for the Naked and Destitute Irish*, January 1847, PROI, 1A42–43 and London Committee, Minute Book, 2 June 1847, FHLL, MS Box S-164-18.

10. Ibid. See also CRC, *Transactions*, pp. 69–73 and Tuke Correspondence, FHLL, MS Box V-3.

11. CRC Minute Books, PROI, 1A42–141, Dr Edgar, 'Statement Respecting the Belfast Ladies Industrial Association for Connaught', December 1851.

12. RC, *Transactions*, pp. 67, 468–71.

13. J.H. Tuke, *A Visit to Connaught in the Autumn of 1847: A Letter Addressed to the Central Relief Committee of the Society of Friends* (London: Charles Gilpin, 1847). Extracts were also printed in CRC, *Transactions*, as was Richard Webb's second tour of Erris, pp. 208–11.

14. R. Barclay Fox, *Distress in Ireland: Narrative of R. Barclay Fox's Visit to Some Parts of the West of Ireland* (London 1847), and Hatton, *The Largest Amount of Good*, pp. 169–99.

15. See CRC, *Transactions*, pp. 384–90.

16. See CRC, *Transactions*, pp. 428–29, 431, 435. Also see PROI, 1A42–38 and 1A42–34, 1A42–139.

17. Todhunter Memoranda and Receipts, PROI, 1A42-37.

18. Rather than a multitude of individual library references, see 'Help the Men to Help Themselves', in Hatton, *The Largest Amount of Good*, pp. 200–22, for a full review of the fishing endeavours.

19. A tremendously long and hard-fought campaign sustained as the Quakers had done for the abolition of slavery, over years. See Hatton, *The Largest Amount of Good*, pp. 223–42.

'BORN ASTRIDE OF A GRAVE': THE GEOGRAPHY OF THE DEAD

1. E. Margaret Crawford, 'Food and famine', in *The Great Irish Famine*, ed. Cathal Póirtéir (Cork, 1995), pp. 60–74; Lawrence M. Geary, 'Famine, fever and the bloody flux' in the same volume, pp. 74–85. See also Crawford's 'Dearth, diet and disease in Ireland, 1850: A case study of nutritional deficiency', *Medical History* 28 (1984), pp. 151–61.

2. Samuel Beckett, *Waiting for Godot* (London, 1977).

3. See *Census of Ireland, 1851* (Dublin, 1856).

4. The Mokyr estimates were mapped in Liam Kennedy, Paul S. Ell, E.M. Crawford and L.A. Clarkson, eds, *Mapping the Great Irish Famine: A Survey of the Famine Decades* (Dublin, 1999), p. 37.

5. S.H. Cousens, 'Regional death rates in Ireland during the Great Famine, from 1846 to 1851', *Population Studies* 14 (1960), pp. 55–74. See also his 'Regional variation in mortality during the Great Irish Famine', *Proceedings of the Royal Irish Academy* 63(c)

(1963), pp. 127–49.

6. See *Census of Ireland, 1851, Part V: Tables of Deaths* (Dublin, 1856), vol. 2, pp. 29–51 and pp. 81–120. See also Phelim P. Boyle and Cormac Ó Gráda, 'Fertility trends, excess mortality and the Great Irish Famine', *Demography* 23.4 (1986), pp. 543–62.

7. Charles Trevelyan's *The Irish Crisis* (London, 1848) was written in the autumn of 1847.

8. Paul Krugman, *Irish Times*, 20/11/2010.

9. *Census of Ireland, 1851*, p. li.

10. Joel Mokyr, 'The deadly fungus: An econometric investigation into the short-term demographic impact of the Irish Famine', *Research in Population Economics* 2 (1980), p. 268. For details on civic district deaths, see *Census of Ireland, 1851*, pp. l–li.

SECTION III: THE WORKHOUSE

THE CREATION OF THE WORKHOUSE SYSTEM
1. John O'Connor, 'The Act of 1838', chapter 7 of his *The Workhouses of Ireland: The Fate of Ireland's poor* (Dublin, 1995), pp. 8–76.

2. As reported in 'Parliamentary Debates 1838', Hansard 40, col. 950.

3. Jeremy Bentham, *Management of the Poor* (Dublin, 1796); Nassau W. Senior, *Journals Relating to Ireland* (London, 1844); Edwin Chadwick, 'The new Poor Law', *Edinburgh Review* 63 (1836), pp. 487–537.

4. Christine Kinealy, *This Great Calamity: The Irish Famine, 1845–52* (Dublin, 1994), p. 23; see also Virginia Crossman, *The Poor Law in Ireland 1838–1948* (Dublin, 2006), pp. 3–18.

5. Felix Driver, *Power and Pauperism: The Workhouse System, 1834–1884* (Cambridge, 1993), p. 59.

6. Samuel Ferguson, 'Architecture in Ireland', *Dublin University Magazine* 29 (1847), pp. 693–708. Architect George Wilkinson, who designed the workhouses, was directed to make them 'uniform and cheap, durable and unattractive' (Kinealy, *The Great Calamity*, p. 25).

7. 'The English Bastile', *Social Science Review* 3 (1865), quoted in Driver, *Power and Pauperism*, p. 197.

8. Driver, *Power and Pauperism*, p. 20.

9. Driver, *Power and Pauperism*, p. 22.

10. O'Connor, *The Workhouses of Ireland*, chapter 10 (pp. 104–10) and chapter 12 (pp. 120–43); Crossman, *The Poor Law in Ireland*, pp. 38–59.

11. William J. Smyth, *Map-making, Landscapes and Memory: A Geography of Colonial and Early Modern Ireland, c.1530–1750* (Cork, 2006), chapter 10, pp. 345–83.

12. Kinealy, *This Great Calamity*, p. 23. The very able Thomas Aiskew Larcom came to Ireland to assist Thomas Colby with the six-inch Ordnance Survey of Ireland. He went on to supervise the social survey that is the 1841 Census, served on the Irish Famine Relief Commission and Board of Works before becoming Under-Secretary of State for Ireland.

13. Kevin Whelan, 'The Catholic parish, the Catholic chapel and village development in Ireland', *Irish Geography* 16 (1983), pp. 1–15.

14. O'Connor, *The Workhouses of Ireland*, p. 148.

15. *Census of Ireland, 1851, Part V: Tables of Deaths* (Dublin, 1856), vol. 2, p. 120.

CLASSIFY, CONFINE, DISCIPLINE AND PUNISH – THE ROSCREA UNION
1. The two main sources for this chapter are (i) the Roscrea Union Board of Guardians' Minute Books and (ii) letters from (and to) the Poor Law Commissioners and Local Government Board. The relevant minute books run from volume 3 (BG 141/A/3), covering the period February 1844 to January 1845, through volumes 4 to 15 (BG 141/A/15), covering the period April to November 1852. The relevant letter books run from volume 1 (BG 141/BC/1), covering the period 1839 to October 1844, through volumes 2 to volume 10 (BG 141/BC/10), which covers the period March 1852 to August 1852. These documents, in addition to all the other records for the County Tipperary unions, are held in the County Library in Thurles It is recognised that these particular records only allow a partial recovery of what actually happened in Roscrea Union in the Famine years. Close attention is also paid to newspaper accounts covering the Famine era in the region.

2. John O'Connor, *The Workhouses of Ireland: The Fate of Ireland's Poor* (Dublin, 1995), Appendix 13, pp. 259–64.

3. Cormac Ó Gráda, 'Yardsticks for workhouse management during the Great Famine' in *Poverty and Poor Law in Ireland*, ed. Victoria Crossman and Peter Gray (Dublin, 2010), p. 69–96. It should be noted that the joint TCD/UCD National Famine Project (under the direction of David Dickson and Cormac Ó Gráda) has produced important studies on the union workhouses of Ballina, Enniskillen, Ennistymon, Inishowen, the North Dublin Union and Parsonstown (Birr). There also have been other important workhouse studies of Ennis, Limerick, Lurgan-Portadown, Mullingar, Nenagh and Scariff, to name but some.

4. O'Connor, *Workhouses*, pp. 214–24 (Appendix 2: 'Barney's report on the execution of contracts for certain union workhouses in Ireland').

5. *Tipperary Vindicator*, 14 November 1846.

6. Ibid.

7. Ibid.

8. Minute Book, BG 141/A/6, spring 1847.

9. *Tipperary Vindicator*, 16 December 1846.

10. *Tipperary Vindicator*, 18 November 1846.

11. Ibid.

12. Ibid.

13. *Tipperary Vindicator*, 16 December 1846.

14. See the *Tipperary Vindicator*, 11 November 1846; 'State of the country', 21 November 1846; 12 December 1846; 9 January 1847.

15. *Tipperary Vindicator*, 12 December 1846.

16. *Tipperary Vindicator*, 21 November 1846.

17. Ibid.

18. *Tipperary Vindicator*, 25 November 1846.

19. Ibid.

20. *Tipperary Vindicator*, 13 January 1847; *Tipperary Vindicator*, 6 March 1847.

21. Ibid., 6 March 1847.

22. *Tipperary Vindicator*, 14 April 1847.

23. James Donnelly jnr, 'The administration of relief 1847–51' in *A New History of Ireland v: Ireland under the Union, 1801–70*, ed. W.E. Vaughan (Oxford, 1989), p. 315.

24. Letter Books, BG 141/BC/4, late March 1848. See also Séamus Ó Riain, *Dunkerrin: A Parish in Ely O Carroll: A History of Dunkerrin Parish from 1200 AD to the Present Day* (Freshford, County Kilkenny, 1988).

25. These figures have been compiled from O'Connor's, *Workhouses*, pp. 233–46 (Appendix 6: 'Statement showing the amount of workhouse accommodation in Ireland – 1st May 1847').

26. Letter Books, BG 141/BC/6, 2 August 1849.

27. *Census of Ireland in 1851* (Dublin, 1856), p. 1.

28. Letter Books, BG 141/BC/3, 17 June 1847.

29. Cathal Póirtéir, *Famine Echoes* (Dublin, 1995), p. 127

30. Distress (Ireland), *Supplementary Appendix to the Seventh and Last Report of the Relief Commissioners* (HCPP, London, 1848), pp. 18–21 (part II showing 'Proportion per cent to the population of persons relieved').

FAMINE AND WORKHOUSE CLOTHING
1. *House of Commons Parliamentary Papers, Papers Relating to the Relief of Distress, and State of Unions in Ireland* (HC PP), 4 January 1849, p. 143.

2. John O'Connor, *The Workhouses of Ireland: The Fate of Ireland's Poor* (Dublin: Anvil Books, 1995), p. 61.

3. O'Connor, *The Workhouses of Ireland*, p. 102.

4. Juliet Ash, *Dress Behind Bars: Prison Clothing as Criminality* (London: I.B. Tauris, 2010), p. 30.

5. HC PP, p. 128, 26 December 1848, Milford Union, Donegal.

6. Ash, *Dress Behind Bars*, p. 15.

7. HC PP, p. 113, 29 January 1849, Mayo.

8. HC PP, p. 109, 29 November 1848, Dublin. All the following quotations are taken from HCPP, London, 1849, pp. 104–157.

9. HC PP, p. 131, 19 December 1848.

10. Nellie Ó Cleirigh, *Hardship and High Living: Irish Women's Lives, 1808–1923* (Dublin, 2003), p. 75.

11. HC PP, p. 112, 18 December 1848, Mayo and Galway.

12. HC PP, p. 109, 29 November 1848, Dublin.

13. HC PP, p. 119, 20 December 1848, Oldcastle Union.

14. Ó Cleirigh, *Hardship and High Living*, p. 75.

15. O'Connor, *The Workhouses of Ireland*, p. 101.

16. *Official Catalogue of the Great Industrial Exhibition* (Dublin, 1853), p. 106.

17. Ash, *Dress Behind Bars*, p. 28.

18. O'Connor, *The Workhouses of Ireland*, p. 252.

19. O'Connor, *The Workhouses of Ireland*, p. 164.

20. 'Outfit for Each of the Emigrants' signed Lieutenant Henry . . . Emigration Officer, Custom House, Dublin, Roscrea Minute Book, December 13, 1848.

21. Roscrea Minute Book, December 13 1848, County Library, Thurles.

22. Elizabeth Ewing, *Women in Uniform: Their Costume through the Centuries* (London, 1975), p. 41.

23. Roscrea Minute Book, December 13, 1848.

24. Ash, *Dress Behind Bars*, p. 30.

25. O'Connor, *The Workhouses of Ireland*, p. 104.

THE CORK WORKHOUSE
1. *Gardener's Chronicle*, 13 September 1845, quoted in Helen Litton, *The Irish Famine: An Illustrated History* (Dublin, 1994), p. 17.

2. Joseph Burke, letter dated 12 November 1846, quoted in C. Tóibín and D. Ferriter, *The Irish Famine: A Documentary* (London, 2001), pp. 128.

3. Letter from Captain Martin to Cork Board of Guardians, 28 August, 1846, Cork Union Minute Book, BG/69/A5, Cork Archives Institute, Cork.

4. *Farmers' Gazette*, cited in the *Cork Examiner*, 20 September 1847.

5. Joseph Burke, letter dated 18 January 1847, quoted in Tóibín and Ferriter, *The Irish Famine*, pp. 129–30.

6. Canon John O'Rourke, *The Great Irish Famine* (Dublin: Veritas, 1989 [1874]), pp. 243–44.

7. Cooke T. and Scanlon M., 'On the workhouse system', in *Guide to the History of Cork* (Cork, 1985), p. 9.

8. Minute Book, BG/69/A5, March 1846, Cork Archives Institute, Cork.

9. Ibid., 28 February 1846.

10. Richard Dowden, Day Papers (1794–1861), U 140 C – incoming correspondence, Cork Archives Institute, Cork.

11. Cork Union Outgoing Letter Book, BG/69 /B1, 10 May 1848, Cork Archives Institute, Cork.

12. J. O'Connor, *The Workhouses of Ireland: The Fate of Ireland's Poor* (Dublin, 1995), p. 163.

13. *Cork Examiner*, 3 January 1849.

## ULSTER WORKHOUSES – IDEOLOGICAL GEOMETRY AND CONFLICT

1. Richard Whatley, *Third Report of the Royal Commission of Inquiry into the Conditions of the Poorer Classes in Ireland* (1836), p. 4.

2. George Nicholls, *Report of George Nicholls, Esq. to His Majesty's Principal Secretary of State for the Home Department, on the Poor Laws, Ireland* (London, 1837), pp. 11–12.

3. Nassau William Senior, *Poor Laws, Ireland: Confidential Letter from Nassau W. Senior, Esq. to His Majesty's Principal Secretary of State for the Home Department, on the 'Third Report from the Commissioners for Inquiring into the Condition of the Poor in Ireland, dated 14th April 1836* (London, 1837), pp. 4–12.

4. George Cornwall Lewis, *Remarks on the Third Report of the Irish Poor Inquiry Commissioners; Drawn up by the Desire of the Chancellor of the Exchequer, for the Purpose of Being Submitted to His Majesty's Government; with an Appendix and Supplementary remarks* (London, 1837), p. 21.

5. Nicholls, *Report of George Nicholls*, pp. 31–32, 17–19.

6. Jeremy Bentham, *Writings on the Poor Laws: 1748–1832*, ed. Michael Quinn, volume 1 of *The Collected Works of Jeremy Bentham* (Oxford, 2001).

7. *Fifth Annual Report of the Poor Law Commissioners: with Appendices, Presented to Parliament in Pursuance of the Act 1 & 2 VICT., Cap. 56* (May 1839), p. 32.

8. *Fifth Annual Report*, p. 32.

9. BG/38/1/8, pp. 183 and 217.

10. BG/20a/4, p. 204; BG/20a/5, p. 258.

11. BG/38/1/4, pp. 218–19.

12. BG/7a/2, p. 174.

13. BG/38/1/1, n.p.

14. BG/20a/1, p. 55.

15. BG/20a/2, p. 76.

16. Nicholls, *Report of George Nicholls*, p. 38

17. BG/7/a/4, p. 35.

18. BG/7/a/6, p. 358.

19. BG/7/a/6, p. 311.

20. BG/38/1/3, pp. 86–88, 97, 166.

21. BG/20/a/3, p. 265.

22. BG/38/1/4, pp. 215–16.

23. BG/20a/4, p. 183.

## LURGAN WORKHOUSE

1. All quotations in this case-study are taken from Gerard Mac Atasney, *This Dreadful Visitation: The Famine in Lurgan/Portadown* (Belfast, 1997).

## SECTION IV: POPULATION DECLINE AND SOCIAL TRANSFORMATIONS

## MORTALITY AND THE GREAT FAMINE

1. P.P. Boyle and Cormac Ó Gráda, 'Fertility trends, excess mortality and the Great Irish Famine', *Demography* 23 (1986), pp. 543–62; J. Mokyr, *Why Ireland Starved: A Quantitative and Analytical History of the Irish Economy, 1800–50*. 2nd ed. (London, 1985); Joel Mokyr and C. Ó Gráda, 'Famine disease and famine mortality: Lessons from the Great Irish Famine', *European Review of Economic History* 6.3 (2002), pp. 339–64.

2. Joseph Lee, 'On the accuracy of pre-famine censuses', in *Irish Population, Economy and Society*, ed. J.M. Goldstrom and L.A. Clarkson (Oxford, 1981), pp. 37–56.

3. Excellent recent studies of workhouse management during the Famine include Daniel Grace, *The Famine in Nenagh Poor Law Union* (Nenagh, 2000); Christine Kinealy, 'The response of the Poor Law to the Great Famine in County Galway', in *Galway: History and Society – Interdisciplinary Essays on the History of an Irish County*, ed. Gerard Moran and Raymond Gillespie (Dublin, 1996); Ciarán Ó Murchadha, *Sable Wings over the Sand: Ennis County Clare and Its Wider Community during the Great Famine* (Ennis, 1998); C. Ó Gráda, 'Yardsticks for workhouse management during the Great Famine', in *Poverty and the Poor Law in Ireland*, ed. Victoria Crossman and Peter Gray (Dublin, 2011); and Eva Ó Cathaoir, 'The Poor Law in County Wicklow', in *Wicklow: History & Society*, ed. Ken Hannigan and W. Nolan (Dublin, 1994).

4. 'The Census of Ireland for the year 1851, part V: Tables of Deaths, vol. 2', BPP (British Parliamentary Papers) 1856, XXX; Mokyr and Ó Gráda, 'Famine disease and famine mortality'.

5. Cormac Ó Gráda, *Black 47 and Beyond: The Great Irish Famine in History, Economy, and Memory* (Princeton, 1999), pp. 94–95.

6. Kate Macintyre, 'Famine and the female mortality advantage', in *Famine Demography*, ed. Tim Dyson and C. Ó Gráda (Oxford, 2002), pp. 240–60.

7. Patrick Hickey, 'Famine, mortality, and emigration: A profile of six parishes in the Poor Law Union of Skibbereen, 1846–7', in *Cork: History & Society*, ed. Patrick O'Flanagan and Cornelius Buttimer (Dublin, 1993), pp. 873–917.

8. Mokyr, *Why Ireland Starved*; P. McGregor, 'Demographic pressure and the Irish famine: Malthus after Mokyr', *Land Economics* 65 (1989), pp. 228–38 and Ó Gráda, *Black 47 and Beyond*.

9. Cormac Ó Gráda, 'School attendance and literacy before the Famine: A simple baronial analysis', University College Dublin Centre for Economic Research, Working Paper 10/22 (2010).

10. Desmond Norton, 'On landlord-assisted emigration from some Irish estates in the 1840s', *Agricultural History Review* 53.1 (2005), pp. 24–40; Desmond Norton, *Landlords, Tenants, Famine: The Business Records of an Irish Land Agency in the 1840s* (Dublin, 2006).

11. André, Charbonneau, Doris Drolet-Dubé, Sylvie Tremblay and Robert J. Grace, *A Register of Deceased Persons at Sea and on Grosse Île in 1847* (Ottawa, 1997); Peter Duffy, *The Killing of Major Denis Mahon: A Mystery of Old Ireland* (New York, 2007), pp. 123–35.

12. Tyler Anbinder, 'Moving beyond "rags to riches": The Emigrant Savings Bank and New York's Irish famine immigrants', forthcoming; C. Ó Gráda, *Ireland's Great Famine: Interdisciplinary Perspectives* (Dublin, 2006), pp. 143–74.

13. Frank Neal, *Black '47: Britain and the Famine Irish* (London, 1998); Ó Gráda, *Black 47 and Beyond*, pp. 111–13.

## 'VARIATIONS IN VULNERABILITY': UNDERSTANDING WHERE AND WHY THE PEOPLE DIED

1. Joel Mokyr, 'The deadly fungus: An econometric investigation into the short-term demographic impact of the Irish Famine', *Research in Population Economics* 2 (1980), pp. 238–39.

2. See T. Jones Hughes, 'Society and settlement in nineteenth-century Ireland' in his *Landholding, Society and Settlement in Nineteenth-Century Ireland: A Historical Geographer's Perspective* (Dublin, 2010), pp. 256–73.

3. See Cormac Ó Gráda, *Ireland's Great Famine: Interdisciplinary Perspectives* (Dublin, 2006), Table 1.1, p. 8.

4. For detailed reports on living conditions in the parishes of Caheragh, Kilgeever and Skull, see Cecil Woodham-Smith, *The Great Hunger* (London, 1968), pp. 177–78 and 308–9.

5. *Census of Ireland, 1841.* (Dublin, 1843), xiv.

6. Mokyr, 'The deadly fungus', p. 253.

7. Mokyr, 'The deadly fungus', p. 269.

8. Cormac Ó Gráda, *Ireland: A New Economic History, 1780–1939* (Oxford, 1994), p. 22.

9. S.H. Cousens, 'The restriction of population growth in pre-Famine Ireland', *Proceedings of the Royal Irish Academy* 64(c) (1966), pp. 85–99.

## MEDICAL RELIEF AND THE GREAT FAMINE

1. Joel Mokyr, *Why Ireland Starved: A Quantitative and Analytical History of the Irish Economy, 1800–1850*. 2nd ed. (London, 1985), pp. 263–68.

2. Robert Dirks, 'Famine and disease', in *The Cambridge World History of Human Disease* (Cambridge, 1993), pp. 160–61.

3. 'Disease (Ireland). Abstracts from representations made by medical superintendents of public institutions', British Parliamentary Papers (BPP hereafter) 1846 (120) XXXVII, p. 389.

4. 'Report from the select committee of the House of Lords on the laws relating to the destitute poor and into the operation of the medical charities in Ireland; together with the minutes of evidence taken before the said committee', BPP 1846 (694) XI, pt 1, pp. xxv–xxvi.

5. CSORP 1846 H 23498, National Archives of Ireland (NAI hereafter).

6. For an extended discussion on the pre-Famine medical charities network, see Laurence M. Geary, *Medicine and Charity in Ireland, 1718–1851* (Dublin, 2004); Ronald D. Cassell, *Medical Charities, Medical Politics: The Irish Dispensary System and the Poor Law, 1836–1872* (Woodbridge, Suffolk, and Rochester, NY, 1997).

7. 9 & 10 Vic., c.6, 'An act to make provision, until the first day of September one thousand eight hundred and forty-seven, for the treatment of poor persons afflicted with fever in Ireland', 24 March 1846.

8. CSORP 1846 H 6462, NAI; William MacArthur, 'Medical history of the famine', in *The Great Famine: Studies in Irish History, 1845–1852*, ed. R. Dudley Edwards and T. Desmond Williams (Dublin, 1956), pp. 289–90.

9. CSORP 1847 H 1704, NAI.

10. CSORP 1847 H 4789, NAI.

11. CSORP 1847 H 3420, NAI. See also Corrigan to the Lord Lieutenant, 24 February 1847, OP 1847/147, NAI.

12. 10 & 11 Vic., c.22, 'An act to amend, and continue until the first day of November one thousand eight hundred and forty-seven, and to the end of the then next session of parliament, an act for making provision for the treatment of poor persons afflicted

with fever in Ireland', 27 April 1847.

13. *Report of the Commissioners of Health, Ireland, on the Epidemics of 1846 to 1850* (Dublin, 1850), p. 26. This report was also published as a parliamentary paper under the same title, BPP 1852–53 (1562) XLI.

14. CSORP 1847 H 5560, 5622, 5970, 7784, 7867, NAI.

15. CSORP 1847 H 5970, NAI. See also MacArthur, 'Medical history of the famine', pp. 297–98.

16. *Report of the Commissioners of Health, Ireland, on the Epidemics of 1846 to 1850*, p. 58.

17. CSORP 1847 H 7888, NAI; see also, *Report of the Commissioners of Health, Ireland, on the Epidemics of 1846 to 1850*, pp. 45, 55–56; *Dublin Medical Press* (Hereafter *DMP*), 16 June 1847, pp. 380–81, 21 July, 4 August 1847, pp. 46, 77.

18. Robert James Graves, *A Letter Relative to the Proceedings of the Central Board of Health in Ireland* (Dublin, 1847), reprinted from *Dublin Quarterly Journal of Medical Science* (*DQJMS* hereafter), 4 (1847), pp. 513–44.

19. CSORP 1847 H 7888, NAI; see also, *Report of the Commissioners of Health, Ireland, on the Epidemics of 1846 to 1850*, pp. 45, 55–56.

20. See, for instance, *DMP*, 1 December 1847, pp. 345–46.

21. See, for instance, CSORP 1847 H 7794; 1847 H 8034, NAI; *DMP*, 15 December 1847, p. 373, 22 November 1848, pp. 330–32, 30 May 1849, p. 351, 6 June 1849, pp. 365–66.

22. See, for instance, CSORP 1847 H 5285, NAI; see also Central Board of Health to Cork board of guardians, 8 June 1848, CSORP 1848 H 5812, NAI.

23. *Report of the Commissioners of Health, Ireland, on the Epidemics of 1846 to 1850*, p. 4. For similar gender trends in admissions to and mortality in the country's fever hospitals generally, see 'The Census of Ireland for the year 1851, part V: Tables of deaths, vol. 1, containing the report, table of pestilences and analysis of the tables of deaths', BPP 1856 (2087–1) XXIX.261, pp. 371–81. For a discussion on fever morbidity and mortality in relation to gender, age and class, see E. Margaret Crawford, 'Typhus in nineteenth-century Ireland', in *Medicine, Disease and the State in Ireland, 1650–1940*, ed. Greta Jones and Elizabeth Malcolm (Cork, 1999), pp. 121–37, esp. pp. 124–29. See also MacArthur, 'Medical history of the famine', pp. 278–81; [W.R. Wilde], 'Report upon the recent epidemic fever in Ireland', *DQJMS* 7 (1849), pp. 64–126, 340–404, 8 (1849), pp. 1–86, 270–339.

24. CSORP 1847 H 3513, NAI.

25. 'Medical charities, Ireland. Second annual report of the commissioners for administering the laws for the relief of the poor in Ireland, under the medical charities act, 14 & 15 Vic. *c.*68', BPP 1854 (1759) XX.219, p. 13.

26. Hansard, 3s, 115 (1 April 1851), cols 895–900; 117 (25 June 1851), cols 1240–45; 118 (2, 24, 28 July 1851), cols 119–24, 1389–91, 1572–73.

27. From 1867 the Exchequer paid half of the salary of dispensary and workhouse medical officers, and half the cost of medicine and appliances. Such a development represented a considerable step on the road to a national health service, as opposed to one whose base was primarily local. 'Royal Commission on the Poor Laws and relief of distress. Report on Ireland', BPP 1909 (Cd. 4630) XXXVIII.1, p. 61.

28. 'An act to provide for the better distribution, support and management of medical charities in Ireland; and to amend an act of the eleventh year of her majesty, to provide for the execution of the laws for the relief of the poor in Ireland', 7 August 1851.

**'REPORT UPON THE RECENT EPIDEMIC FEVER IN IRELAND': THE EVIDENCE FROM CORK**

1. *Annual Report of the North Charitable Infirmary, of the City of Cork, Established in the Year 1750, under the 25th Act Geo. 11, from 5 January 1848 to 4 January 1849* (Cork, 1849), p. 4.

2. Leslie A. Clarkson and E. Margaret Crawford, eds, *Famine and Disease in Ireland*. 5 vols (London, 2005), vol. 2, p. 207.

3. [William Wilde], 'Report upon the recent epidemic fever in Ireland', *Dublin Quarterly Journal of Medical Science* 7 (1849), pp. 64–126, 340–404; 8 (1849), pp. 1–86, 270–339, esp. 7 (1849), pp. 64–68.

4. Ibid., 7 (1849), pp. 68–69, 71–72, 74–77, 79–82; 8 (1849), pp. 277–78.

5. For a similar account, see CSORP 1847 H 4327; CSORP 1847 H 4814, National Archives of Ireland, Lamprey to the Central Board of Health, 29 March 1847, the day after his arrival in Schull.

6. Compare with Daniel Donovan, 'Observations on the peculiar diseases to which the Famine of last year gave origin, and on the morbid effects of insufficient nourishment', *Dublin Medical Press*, 2 February, 1 March, 3 May 1848, pp. 67–68, 129–32, 275–78.

7. *Cork Constitution*, 7 February 1847, Traill to editor, 5 February.

8. *Dublin Quarterly Journal of Medical Science* 7 (1849), pp. 100–4.

9. Ibid., 8 (1849), pp. 278–89.

10. Ibid., pp. 270–77.

11. *Report of the Commissioners of Health, Ireland, on the Epidemics of 1846 to 1850* (Dublin, 1852), p. 12. This report was also published, under the same title, as a parliamentary paper (BPP 1852–53 [1562] XLI).

**EMIGRATION TO NORTH AMERICA IN THE ERA OF THE GREAT FAMINE, 1845–55**

1. Much of the information in this essay is based on Kerby A. Miller's *Emigrants and Exiles: Ireland and the Irish Exodus to North America* (New York, 1985), chapter 7 (here from p. 291); see the relevant citations, in that work, for specific sources. On the Famine Irish in the United States, also see David N. Doyle's 'The Irish as urban pioneers in the United States, 1850–1870', *Journal of American Ethnic History* 10.1–2 (Fall 1990-Winter 1991), pp. 36–59, and 'The re-making of Irish-America, 1845–80', in *A New History of Ireland VI: Ireland under the Union, II: 1871–1921*, ed. W.E. Vaughan (Oxford, 1996), pp. 725–63; as well as Cormac Ó Gráda's 'Irish emigration to the United States in the nineteenth century', in *America and Ireland, 1776–1976*, ed. David N. Doyle and Owen Dudley Edwards (Westport, Conn., 1980), pp. 93–104. The best overall survey of Irish–American history is Kevin Kenny's *The American Irish: A History* (Harlow, 2000); and on Irish emigration and settlement worldwide, see David Fitzpatrick, *Irish Emigration, 1801–1921* (Dublin, 1984); Patrick Fitzgerald and Brian Lambkin, *Migration in Irish History, 1607–2007* (Houndmills, Basingstoke, 2008); Eric Richards, *Britannia's Children: Emigration From England, Scotland, Wales and Ireland since 1600* (New York, 2004); and the essays in Andy Bielenberg, ed. *The Irish Diaspora* (Harlow, 2000). Also valuable is chapter 7 of James S. Donnelly Jr, *The Great Irish Potato Famine* (Phoenix Mill, Gloustershire, 2001), and many of the essays in Arthur Gribben, ed. *The Great Famine and the Irish Diaspora in America* (Amherst, Mass., 1999); Margaret M. Mulrooney, ed. *Fleeing the Famine: North America and Irish Refugees, 1845–1851* (Westport, Conn., 2003); and Patrick O'Sullivan, ed. *The Irish World Wide: History, Heritage, Identity*, 6 vols (Leicester, 1992–97), especially vol. 6, *The Meaning of the Famine*.

2. Miller, *Emigrants & Exiles*, pp. 291–92; Oliver MacDonagh, 'Irish Famine emigration to the United States', *Perspectives in American History* 10 (1976), pp. 410–11. On the Famine (and other Irish) emigrants in British North America, the best surveys are Cecil J. Houston and William J. Smyth, *Irish Emigration and Canadian Settlement: Patterns, Links, and Letters* (Toronto, 1990) and Mark G. McGowan and Bruce Elliott, 'Irish Catholics and Protestants', in *Encyclopedia of Ireland's Peoples*, ed. Paul R. Magocsi (Toronto, 1999); also useful in their breadth are Robert O'Driscoll and Lorna Reynolds, eds, *The Untold Story: The Irish in Canada*, 2 vols (Toronto, 1988); Thomas P. Power, ed. *The Irish in Atlantic Canada, 1780–1900* (Frederickton, N.B., 1991); and Peter M. Toner, ed. *Historical Essays on the Irish in New Brunswick: New Ireland Remembered* (Frederickton, N.B., 1988). On the travails of Famine voyages, especially in 1847 (but not exclusively; cholera ravaged many Irish emigrant ships in the early 1850s), see: Terry Coleman, *Going to America* (Garden City, N.Y., 1973); Edward Laxton, *The Famine Ships: The Irish Exodus to America, 1846–51* (London, 1996); and Donald McKay, *Flight from Famine: The Coming of the Irish to Canada* (Toronto, 1991).

3. Miller, *Emigrants & Exiles*, pp. 292–93. On evictions, see Tim P. O'Neill, 'Famine evictions', in *Famine, Land and Culture in Ireland*, ed. Carla King (Dublin, 2000), 29–70. The pathetic quotation is from a letter written by a Mrs Nolan, Clara Upper, County Kilkenny, to her son Patrick, in Providence, Rhode Island, in October 1850 (ms. in T2054/1, Public Record Office of Northern Ireland, Belfast). Arnold Schrier's pioneering work on emigrants' remittances (and much else) is in his *Ireland and the American Emigration, 1850–1900* (New York, 1970), p. 167.

4. Miller, *Emigrants & Exiles*, p. 293. The best work on pre-Famine Irish emigration remains William Forbes Adams, *Ireland and the Irish Emigration to the New World from 1815 to the Famine* (New Haven, Conn., 1932); but also see David N. Doyle, 'The Irish in North America, 1776–1845', in *A New History of Ireland, V: Ireland under the Union, I – 1801–1870*, ed. W.E. Vaughan (Oxford, 1989), pp. 682–725, as well as the later chapters in Doyle, *Ireland, Irishmen, and Revolutionary America* (Cork, 1981).

5. Miller, *Emigrants & Exiles*, pp. 293–95. On assisted Irish emigration during the Famine and generally, see Gerard Moran, *Sending Out Ireland's Poor: Assisted Emigration to North America in the Nineteenth Century* (Dublin, 2004).

6. Miller, *Emigrants & Exiles*, pp. 295–96.

7. Miller, *Emigrants & Exiles*, pp. 297–98. On the Irish language in America, see Thomas W. Ihde, ed. *The Irish Language in the United States: A Historical, Sociolinguistic, and Applied Linguistic Survey* (Westport, Conn., 1994).

8. On the motives of pre-Famine emigrants and the meanings of the oft-used term, 'independence', see Miller, *Emigrants & Exiles*, chapters 5–6; and Miller, *Ireland and Irish America: Culture, Class, and Transatlantic Migration* (Dublin, 2008), chapter 2.

9. Miller, *Emigrants & Exiles*, p. 298. Mary Rush's letter was originally published in the British Parliamentary Papers; for the full text and background information on her family in County Sligo and Quebec, see Miller, *Ireland & Irish America*, chapter 12. An outstanding, recently published collection of Famine letters, from County Kerry, is Sally Barber, ed. *The Prendergast Letters: Correspondence from Famine-Era Ireland, 1840–1850* (Amherst, Mass., 2006). On the Famine's impact on east Connacht, see Robert James Scally, *The End of Hidden Ireland: Rebellion, Famine, and Emigration* (New York, 1985).

10. Miller, *Emigrants & Exiles*, pp. 299–300. The quotations are from several letters written by Judith Phelan of Raheen, Queen's County, to her niece, Teresa Lawlor, in Memphis, Tenn., 23 May 1849 and 24 March 1850 (Teresa Lawlor Papers, California Historical Society, San Francisco). On Edmund Ronayne, see his quirky but fascinating memoir, *Ronayne's Reminiscences: A History of His Life and Renunciation of Romanism and Freemasonry* (Chicago, 1900); and on William Murphy, see Miller, *Ireland & Irish America*, chapter 10.

11. On the Famine Irish in the United States, generally, see Miller, *Emigrants & Exiles*, pp. 312–44; Doyle, 'The re-making of Irish-America, 1845–80'; and Kenny, *The American Irish*, chapter 3. Also relevant is Miller, *Ireland & Irish America*, chapter 11; as are

many of the valuable chapters in Kenny, ed. *New Directions in Irish-American History* (Madison, Wisc., 2003); Timothy J. Meagher, *The Columbia Guide to Irish American History* (New York, 2003), and J.J. Lee and Marion R. Casey, eds, *Making the Irish American: History and Heritage of the Irish in the United States* (New York, 2006), which also contains Miller's essay on the development of 'Scotch-Irish' ethnicity, 'Ulster Presbyterians and the "two traditions" in Ireland and America', pp. 255–71. On Irish women in America, generally, see Miller, *Ireland & Irish America*, chapter 13; but to the works of Hasia Diner, Janet Nolan, Patricia Kelleher, Rita Rhodes, and others, cited therein, should be added Margaret Lynch-Brennan, *The Irish Bridget: Irish Immigrant Women in Domestic Service in America, 1840–1930* (Syracuse, N.Y., 2009).

12. I wish to thank Professor David A. Wilson, of the University of Toronto, for commenting on my efforts (at New York University in 2002) to estimate the Famine emigrants' proportion of overall Irish Catholic settlers in nineteenth-century Canada. For a very different perspective on this matter, see Mark G. McGowan, *The Waning of the Green: Catholics, the Irish, and Identity in Toronto, 1887–1922* (Montreal, 1999), and especially his 2001 conference paper, 'A people's history?', since published as *Creating Canadian Historical Memory: The Case of the Famine Migration of 1847* (Ottawa, 2006).

Among Irish–Australians, Famine commemoration appears confined primarily to their nation's 'left-republican' tradition, although in sharp contrast to the Irish–Canadian experience, it appears likely that Famine-era Irish Catholic migrants to Australia and New Zealand comprised no more than 10–15% of all the Irish Catholics (including transported convicts) who debarked in the Antipodes during the 'long nineteenth century'. Indeed, Irish migration to New Zealand (of Protestants as well as Catholics) was overwhelmingly a post-Famine phenomenon. My thanks to Dr Malcolm Campbell, of the University of Auckland, for data on Irish migrants to Australasia. Valuable surveys of the Irish in Australia or New Zealand include: David Fitzpatrick, *Oceans of Consolation: Personal Accounts of Irish Migration to Australia* (Ithaca, N.Y., 1994); Lyndon Fraser, *A Distant Shore: Irish Migration and New Zealand Settlement* (Dunedin, N.Z., 2000); Chris McConville, *Croppies, Celts and Catholics: The Irish in Australia* (Melbourne, 1987); Patrick O'Farrell, *The Irish in Australia* (Kensington, N.S.W., 2001 ed.); Brad Patterson, ed. *The Irish in New Zealand: Historical Contexts & Perspectives* (Wellington, 2002); and Jock Phillips and Terry Hearn, *New Zealand Immigrants from England, Ireland and Scotland, 1800–1945* (Auckland, 2008). For interesting (and clashing) comparisons of Irish experiences in Australia and the U.S., see: Malcolm Campbell, *Ireland's New Worlds: Immigrants, Politics, and Society in the United States and Australia, 1815–1922* (Madison, Wisc., 2008), and David N. Doyle, 'The Irish in Australia and the United States: Some comparisons, 1800–1939', *Irish Economic and Social History* 16 (1989), pp. 73–94.

Recent surveys of the Famine (and other) Irish emigrants in Great Britain include: Brenda Collins, 'The Irish in Britain, 1780–1921', in *An Historical Geography of Ireland*, ed. B.J. Graham and L.J. Proudfoot (London, 1993), pp. 366–98; Graham Davis, *The Irish in Britain, 1815–1914* (Dublin, 1991); Liam Harte, *The Literature of the Irish in Britain* (Basingstoke, 2009); Donald M. MacRaild, *Irish Migrants in Modern Britain, 1750–1922* (New York, 1999) and *The Irish in Britain, 1815–1914* (Dundalk, 2006); Martin J. Mitchell, *The Irish in the West of Scotland, 1798–1848* (Edinburgh, 1998) and ed. *New Perspectives on the Irish in Scotland* (Edinburgh, 2008); Frank Neal, *Black '47: Britain and the Famine Irish* (Basingstoke, 1998); Paul O'Leary, *Immigration and Integration: The Irish in Wales, 1998–1922* (Cardiff, 2000); Roger Swift and Sheridan Gilley, eds, *The Irish in Britain, 1815–1939* (Savage, Md., 1989) and *The Irish in Victorian Britain: The Local Dimension* (Dublin, 1999); and David Fitzpatrick's essays in vols 5 (1989) and 6 (1996) of W.E. Vaughan, ed. *A New History of Ireland* (Oxford).

13. W.E.H. Lecky, cited in Miller, *Emigrants & Exiles*, p. 305.

14. Michael Flanagan, Napa, Calif., to John Flanagan, Tubbertoby, Clogherhead, County Louth, 14 April 1877 (courtesy of Peter and Mary Flanagan, Tubbertoby).

15. In general, the arguments in this and the following paragraphs are based on Miller, *Emigrants & Exiles*, pp. 300–12.

16. Oliver MacDonagh, 'Irish emigration to the United States of America and the British Colonies during the Famine', in *The Great Famine*, ed. Edwards and Williams, p. 329.

17. For the full text of this and other Famine songs, some of them in Irish (with translations), see Richard L. Wright, *Irish Emigrant Ballads and Songs* (Bowling Green, Ohio, 1975).

18. Most of the material in this section, on the Famine Irish in the United States, is derived from Miller, *Emigrants & Exiles*, pp. 312–44; see endnote 46, on pp. 620–21 of that work, for a list of books, articles and doctoral dissertations on the Irish in mid-nineteenth-century America, published prior to c.1983. To these should be added (in addition to works already cited above): Tyler Anbinder, *The Five Points: The 19th-Century New York City Neighborhood That Invented Tap Dance, Stole Elections, and Became the World's Most Notorious Slum* (New York, 2001); Ronald H. Bayor and Timothy J. Meagher, eds, *The New York Irish* (Baltimore, Md., 1996); Iver Bernstein, *The New York City Draft Riots* (New York, 1990); Susannah Ural Bruce, *The Harp and the Eagle: Irish-American Volunteers and the Union Army, 1861–1865* (New York, 2006); Dennis Clark, *Hibernia America: The Irish and Regional Cultures* (Westport, Conn., 1986); Michael C. Connolly ed. *They Change Their Sky: The Irish in Maine* (Bangor, Maine, 2004); Mary Lee Dunn, *Ballykilcline Rising: From Famine Ireland to Immigrant America* (Amherst, Mass., 2008); Joseph P. Ferrie, *Yankees Now: Immigrants in the Antebellum United States,*

*1840–1860* (New York, 1999); J. Matthew Gallman, *Receiving Erin's Children: Philadelphia, Liverpool, and the Irish Famine Migration, 1845–1855* (Chapel Hill, N.C., 2000); David T. Gleeson, *The Irish in the South, 1815–1877* (Chapel Hill, N.C., 2001); Michael A. Gordon, *The Orange Riots: Irish Political Violence in New York City, 1870 and 1871* (Ithaca, N.Y., 1993); Kevin Kenny, *Making Sense of the Molly Maguires* (New York, 1998); Lawrence J. McCaffrey et al., *The Irish in Chicago* (Urbana, Ill., 1987); Brian C. Mitchell, *The Paddy Camps: The Irish of Lowell, 1821–61* (Urbana, Ill., 1988); Scott Mulloy, *Irish Titan, Irish Toilers: Joseph Banigan and Nineteenth-Century New England Labor* (Durham, N.H., 2008); Margaret M. Mulrooney, *Black Powder, White Lace: The Du Pont Irish and Cultural Identity in Nineteenth-Century America* (Hanover, N.H., 2002); Richard B. Stott, *Workers in the Metropolis: Class, Ethnicity, and Youth in Antebellum New York City* (Ithaca, N.Y., 1990); Peter Way, *Common Labor: Workers and the Digging of North American Canals, 1780–1860* (New York, 1983); and Mark Wyman, *Immigrants in the Valley: Irish, Germans, and Americans in the Upper Mississippi Country, 1830–1860* (Chicago, 1984). Excellent also for the Famine emigrants in America, but much broader (chronologically and/or thematically) than most of the studies listed above, are: Daniel Cassidy, *How the Irish Invented Slang* (Oakland, Calif., 2007); Charles Fanning, *The Irish Voice in America: Irish-American Fiction from the 1760s to the 1980s* (Lexington, Ky., 1990); Robert R. Grimes, SJ, *How Shall We Sing in a Foreign Land? Music of Irish Catholic Immigrants in the Antebellum United States* (Notre Dame, Ind., 1996); John Duffy Ibsen, *Will the World Break Your Heart? Dimensions and Consequences of Irish-American Assimilation* (Hamden, Conn., 1990); Colleen McDannell, *The Christian Home in Victorian America, 1840–1900* (Bloomington, Ind., 1988); David Roediger, *The Wages of Whiteness: Race and the Making of the American Working Class* (London, 1991); and William H. A. Williams, *'Twas Only an Irishman's Dream: The Image of Ireland and the Irish in American Popular Song Lyrics, 1800–1920* (Urbana, Ill., 1996).

19. For example, see Ferrie, *Yankees Now*, p. 128 and *passim*, but also my review in *Labor History* 41.3 (2000), pp. 358–61.

20. Patrick Kieran Walsh, Cleveland, Ohio, letter to the *Cork Examiner*, issue of 11 June 1860.

21. Michael J. Adams, Sweet Springs, Va., letter to the *Cork Examiner*, issue of 10 August 1860. The classic work on anti-Irish and anti-Catholic prejudice in the U.S. is still Ray A. Billington, *The Protestant Crusade, 1800–1860* (New York, 1932), but see also L. Perry Curtis Jr, *Apes and Angels: The Irishman in Victorian Caricature* (Washington, D.C., 1997 rev. ed.); and Dale T. Knobel, *'America for the Americans': The Nativist Movement in the United States* (New York, 1996) and *Paddy and the Republic: Ethnicity and Nationality in Antebellum America* (Middletown, Conn., 1986).

22. Daniel Rowntree, Washington, D.C., to Laurence Rowntree, Dublin, 23 March 1852 (courtesy of Professor Emeritus Arnold Schrier, University of Cincinnati).

23. Patrick Kieran Walsh, *op cit.*

24. Important studies of Irish–American nationalism include: Thomas N. Brown, *Irish-American Nationalism, 1870–1890* (Philadelphia, 1966), which overstresses its bourgeois adherents and functions (in explaining Patrick Ford's and similar statements, for example); Eric Foner, 'Class, ethnicity, and radicalism in the Gilded Age: The Land League and Irish America', *Marxist Perspectives* 1 (1975); Matthew F. Jacobson, *Special Sorrows: The Diasporic Imagination of Irish, Polish, and Jewish Immigrants in the United States* (Cambridge, Mass., 1995); and Victor Walsh, '"A fanatic heart": The cause of Irish-American nationalism in Pittsburgh during the Gilded Age', *Journal of Social History* 15 (1981). My own interpretation is principally in *Emigrants & Exiles*, pp. 334–44, and in chapter 6 of *Ireland and Irish America*.

25. On Irish America in the late nineteenth and early twentieth centuries, see Miller, *Emigrants & Exiles*, pp. 492–555, and chapters 11–15 in Miller, *Ireland & Irish America*.

26. For example, William Jenkins, 'Deconstructing diasporas: Networks and identities among the Irish in Buffalo and Toronto, 1870–1919', in *Irish Migration, Networks and Ethnic Identities since 1750*, ed. Enda Delaney and Donald M. MacRaild (London, 2007), pp. 210–49, demonstrates how local and national social, political and legal circumstances could facilitate or smother Irish immigrant nationalism. Also instructive are Malcolm Campbell, 'John Redmond and the Irish National League in Australia and New Zealand, 1883', *History: The Journal of the Historical Association* (Oxford) 86 (2001), pp. 348–62, and Sean G. Brosnahan, 'The "Battle of the Borough" and the "Saige O Timaru,"' *New Zealand Journal of History* 28.1 (1994), pp. 41–59. Hence, although revisionists claim that relatively low levels of Irish nationalist activity and rhetoric in Canada, Australia and New Zealand signify high levels of Catholic Irish immigrant achievement and contentment, those societies' multifaceted 'colonial/imperial' contexts may have been at least equally important. By contrast, Irish-American nationalists would not face such concerted pressures until after U.S. entry into World War I inaugurated the 'special [U.S.–UK] relationship' and unleashed the new FBI and other official U.S. agencies against Irish nationalist activities, fund-raising, etc. Even then, however, Famine commemoration had become too integral to Irish-America's sense of ethnic identity to be displaced or submerged, although today its political implications may remain relevant in smaller circles than a century earlier; see, for instance, the recent collection of essays edited by Irish-American radical Tom Hayden, *Irish Hunger: Personal Reflections on the Legacy of the Famine* (Dubin: Wolfhound Press, 1997). In recent decades, this author's own experience is that, at Irish–American studies conferences and other 'polite' venues, the vengeful Fenian ballad, mentioned in the text, is normally 'revised' and tamed as 'Remember Skibbereen'.

## THE CITIES AND TOWNS OF IRELAND, 1841–1851
1. This chapter is wholly based on the data contained in the 1841 and 1851 Census.

### THE ROLES OF CITIES AND TOWNS DURING THE GREAT FAMINE
1. T.W. Freeman, *Pre-Famine Ireland: A Study in Historical Geography* (Manchester, 1957), p. 25.
2. David Dickson, 'The potato and Irish diet before the Great Famine', in *Famine 150*, ed. Cormac Ó Gráda (Dublin, 1997), p. 22
3. T. Jones Hughes, 'The origin and growth of towns in Ireland', chapter 11 in his *Landholding, Society and Settlement in Nineteenth-Century Ireland: A Historical Geographer's Perspective* (Dublin, 2010), pp. 240–47.
4. Freeman, *Pre-Famine Ireland*, p. 29.
5. Trevor McCavery, 'The Famine in County Down', in *The Famine in Ulster*, ed. Christine Kinealy and Trevor Parkhill (Belfast, 1997), pp. 98–99.
6. Eva Ó Cathaoir, 'The Poor Law in County Wicklow', chapter 13 in *Wicklow: History and Society*, ed. Ken Hannigan and William Nolan (Dublin, 1994), p. 504.
7. Freeman, *Pre-Famine Ireland*, p. 33.
8. Cormac Ó Gráda, *Ireland: A New Economic History, 1780–1939* (Oxford, 1994), pp. 97–98.
9. Quoted in Cecil Woodham-Smith, *The Great Hunger*, 2nd ed. (Sevenoaks, Kent, 1970), pp. 305–6.
10. All references to the conditions in towns in this paragraph are taken from the 'Records of the Scarcity Commission, March 1846', HC 1846 (201), pp. 1–29.
11. 'Correspondence relating to the measures adopted for the Relief of Distress in Ireland', Commissariat series, part I, HC 1847, pp. 279–285
12. Woodham-Smith, *The Great Hunger*, p. 104
13. Ibid., pp. 111, 119–21 and 175. See also local newspapers such as the *Waterford Mail*, which on 5 May 1847 reports of many people dying in Dungarvan and Abbeyside where by May 1847 'infected people [are] lying in the streets and lanes'.
14. 'Correspondence relating to the Measures Adopted for the Relief of the Distress in Ireland', Commissariat series, part II, HC 1847, pp. 72–74. See also "List of Donations", matching subscriptions raised by Relief Committees in Ireland, pp. 155–59, 185–86 and 224–25.
15. Ciarán Ó Murchadha, *Sable Wings over the Land: Ennis, County Clare and Its Wider Community during the Great Famine* (Ennis: CLASP Press, 1998), pp. 142–43.
16. William Fraher, 'The Dungarvan disturbances of 1846 and sequels', chapter 8 in *Teacht na bPrátaí Dubha: The Famine in Waterford, 1845–50*, ed. Des Cowman and Donald Brady (Dublin, 1995), pp. 139–44.
17. Ibid., p. 141.
18. Edmund O'Riordan, *Famine in the Valley* (Clogheen/Cahir, 1995), p. 48.
19. Eugene Broderick, 'The Famine in Waterford as reported in local newspapers', chapter 9 in *Teacht na bPrátaí Dubha: The Famine in Waterford, 1845–50*, ed. Des Cowman and Donald Brady (Dublin, 1995), pp. 162–63.
20. *Tipperary Vindicator*, 1 May 1847 and 19 May 1847.
21. Woodham-Smith, *The Great Hunger*, p. 121. See also pp. 87–88.
22. 'Abstract of returns furnished by the Marshal of Dublin . . . of pawn offices in Ireland, 1844–1847', in 'Papers relating to the relief of distress and state of unions of Ireland', HC 1849, pp. 104–57.
23. Ibid. 'Letter and circular of Commissioners' instructions to Poor Law inspectors, December 5, 1848', H.C. 1849, p. 109.
24. Christine Kinealy, *The Great Calamity: The Irish Famine, 1845–52* (Dublin, 1994), pp. 144–46.
25. Ibid., pp. 146–47 and 202. See also *The Great Hunger*, pp. 122, 132 and 160. Many local histories also deal with these themes: see, for example, Seamus Ó Riain, *Dunkerrin: A Parish in Elyocarroll* (Freshford: Willbrook, 1988), chapter 8; Daniel Grace, *The Great Famine in Nenagh Poor Law Union* (Nenagh, 2000), chapters 3 and 14, Murchadha, *Sable Wings over the Land*, pp. 89–101, 112–13, 142–43 and 171–74
26. Cormac Ó Gráda, chapter 8, 'The Great Famine' in his *New Economic History*, p. 202.
27. *Census of Ireland, 1851, Part V: Tables of Deaths* (Dublin, 1856), vol. 2, pp. 121–34.
28. Michael Martin, *Spike Island: Saints, Felons and Famine* (Dublin, 2010), pp. 65–77.
29. See Stephen A. Royle, 'Industrialisation, urbanisation and urban society in post-Famine Ireland, c.1850–1921', chapter 8 in *An Historical Geography of Ireland*, ed. B.J. Graham and L.J. Proudfoot (London, 1993), p. 288.
30. Thomas Carlyle, *Reminiscences of my Irish Journey in 1849* (London, 1882), p. 70.
31. Ibid., pp. 46–47.
32. Maurice Craig, *Dublin, 1660–1860* (Dublin, 1969), p. 309.
33. Mary Daly, *Dublin, the Deposed Capital: A Social and Economic History, 1860–1914* (Cork, 1984), p. 2.
34. Royle, 'Industrialisation', p. 270.
35. Ibid., p. 289.
36. T. Jones Hughes, 'Village and town in nineteenth-century Ireland', chapter 15 in his *Landholding, Society and Settlement in Nineteenth-Century Ireland*; see also his 'Origin and growth of towns in Ireland', chapter 11 in this book.

## THE IMPACT OF THE GREAT FAMINE ON SUBSISTENT WOMEN
1. G. Nicholls, *A History of the English Poor Law in Connection with the Legislation and Other Circumstances Affecting the Condition of the People* (London, 1856; rpt XXX: Augustus M. Kelley, 1969), p. 346
2. Nicholls, *A History of the Poor Law*, p. 331
3. Gerard J. Lyne, *The Lansdowne Estate in Kerry under W.S. Trench, 1849–72* (Dublin, 2001), pp. 553–555.
4. A.G.L. Shaw, *Convicts and the Colonies: A Study of Penal Transportation from Great Britain and Ireland to Australia and Other Parts of the British Empire* (London, 1966), p. 36.
5. Poor Law Minute Book, Killarney Poor Law Union, 1848.
6. Emigration. Papers relative to emigration to the Australian colonies. (In continuation of House of Commons Papers, no. 593, July 1849.) 1850 [1163] XL.29.
7. R.B. Madgwick, *Emigration into Eastern Australia, 1788–1851* (London, 1937), p. 221.

## THE LANDED CLASSES DURING THE GREAT IRISH FAMINE
1. Cathal Póirtéir, *Famine Echoes* (Dublin, 1995), p. 229.
2. J.S. Donnelly Jr, 'Mass eviction and the Irish Famine: The clearances revisited', in *The Great Irish Famine*, ed. C. Póirtéir (Dublin: Mercier Press); see also Andrés Eiriksson and Cormac Ó Gráda, *Irish Landlords and the Great Irish Famine*, UCD Centre for Economic Research, Working Paper Series, 1996, p. 162.
3. Cecil Woodham-Smith, *The Great Hunger: Ireland, 1845–1849* (London, 1991), p. 183.
4. Ciarán Ó Murchadha, 'The years of the Great Famine', in *Clare: History and Society – Interdisciplinary Essays on the History of an Irish County*, ed. M. Lynch and P. Nugent (Dublin, 2008), p. 257.
5. *Telegraph*, 14 July 1848.
6. J.S. Donnelly Jr, *The Great Irish Potato Famine* (Stroud: Sutton Publishers, 2001), p. 145–47.
7. *Clare Journal*, 22 August 1846.
8. *Limerick and Clare Examiner*, 29 August 1846; 7 April 1847.
9. *Clonmel Chronicle*, 4 April 1853; *Tipperary Free Press*, 16 April 1853; 21 May 1853.
10. Woodham-Smith, *The Great Hunger*, p. 364.
11. J.S. Donnelly Jr, 'Landlords and tenants', in *A New History of Ireland, V: Ireland under the Union 1801–70*, ed. W.E. Vaughan (Oxford, 1989), p. 346.
12. Edmund O'Riordan, *Famine in the Valley* (Clogheen/Cahir, 1995), pp. 51–52.
13. *Tipperary Free Press*, 23 December 1846.
14. Póirtéir, *Famine Echoes*, p. 207.
15. M. Larkin, *Mullinahone: Its Heritage and History* (Tipperary, 2002), p. 89–90.
16. B. Power, *Fermoy on the Blackwater* (Fermoy, 2009), p. 96–97.
17. Adrian Frazier, *George Moore 1852–1933* (New Haven and London, 2000), p. 8.
18. *Tipperary Free Press*, 14 January 1846.
19. *Tipperary Free Press*, 19 August 1846.
20. *Cork Examiner*, 1 January 1847.
21. *Tipperary Free Press*, 17 July 1847.
22. *Cork Examiner*, 23 February 1848.
23. *Freeman's Journal*, 1 February 1848.
24. *Cork Examiner*, 15 December 1848.
25. W.H. Wyndham-Quin, *The Fox Hound in County Limerick* (Dublin, 1919), pp. 9 and 97.
26. *Tipperary Free Press*, 12 January 1848.
27. *Cork Examiner*, 1 February 1847.
28. *Cork Examiner*, 6 December 1847.
29. *Tipperary Free Press*, 28 February 1846.
30. J. Welcome, *Irish Horse Racing: An Illustrated History* (Dublin 1982), p. 33.
31. S.J. Watson, *Between the Flags: A History of Irish Steeplechasing* (Dublin, 1969), p. 61.
32. *Cork Examiner*, 3 February 1847.
33. J.F. Maguire, *The Industrial Movement in Ireland, as Illustrated by the National Exhibition of 1852* (Cork, 1853).
34. John Mitchel, *The Last Conquest of Ireland (Perhaps)* (Glasgow, 1876), p. 219.

## 'TURNED OUT, THROWN DOWN': EVICTIONS IN DONOUGHMORE
1. Numbers remained unburied for over a fortnight, many were buried in ditches near their houses . . .' (see p.00).
2. The relevant records for these townlands are held in the National Archives of Ireland.
3. Ordnance Survey Name Books, Donoughmore parish, MSS at Ordnance Survey Office, Dublin.
4. Terence M. Dooley, *The Big House and the Landed Estates of Ireland: A Research Guide* (Dublin, 2007), p. 29. However, other studies suggest that close on twice that number of families wewe located.

## CONNACHT

### INTRODUCTION: THE PROVINCE OF CONNACHT AND THE GREAT FAMINE
1. *Census of Ireland, 1851, Part VI: General Report* (Dublin, 1856), Tables VI, XV.
2. This figure is based on the assumptions that the population of Ireland in the mid-

dle of the decade was *c*.8.6m and that Connacht's share was of the order of 18%.

3. *Census of Ireland*, *1851*, Tables I, IX.

4. Joel Mokyr, *Why Ireland Starved: A Quantitative and Analytical History of the Irish Economy, 1800–1850* (London, 1983), p. 28.

5. All the percentage calculations in this paragraph are derived from the *Census of Ireland*, *1851*, p. xii–xlvii.

6. Mokyr, *Why Ireland Starved*, p. 42.

7. E. Estyn Evans, *Irish Heritage: The Landscape, the People and Their Work* (Dundalk, 1942), pp. 58–62. See also his *Personality of Ireland*, 2nd ed. (Belfast, 1981).

8. Kevin Whelan, 'Pre- and post-Famine landscape change', in *The Great Irish Famine*, ed. Cathal Póirtéir (Cork, 1995), p. 24.

9. Liz Young, 'Spaces for famine: A comparative geographical analysis of famine in Ireland and the Highlands in the 1840s', *Transactions of the Institute of British Geographers*, new series, 21 (1996), pp. 666–80.

10. Cormac Ó Gráda alludes to the issue in 'An Gorta Mór: The Great Famine, 1845–50', Chapter 8 in his *Ireland: A New Economic History, 1780–1939* (Oxford, 1994), pp. 185–86.

11. Mokyr, *Why Ireland Starved*, p. 266, and S.H. Cousens, 'Regional death rates in Ireland during the Great Famine, from 1846 to 1851', *Population Studies* 14 (1960), p. 67.

12. *Census of Ireland*, *1851*, Tables VI, XV, which includes population data per county and city for both 1841 and 1851.

13. However, Liam Swords in *In Their Own Words: The Famine in North Connacht, 1845–49* (Dublin, 1999) recounts in great detail the experiences, words and reflections of eyewitnesses – priests, rectors, guardians, police and Poor Law inspectors – of the plight of the people during the Great Famine.

14. Quoted in Cecil Woodham-Smith, *The Great Hunger* (London, 1965), p. 200.

15. Woodham-Smith, *The Great Hunger*, p. 199.

16. *Census of Ireland*, *1851*, Tables XXXII, L.

17. Christine Kinealy, *This Great Calamity: The Irish Famine 1845–52* (Dublin, 1994), chapters 3, 4 and 5. See also Ivor Hamrock, comp. and ed., *The Famine in Mayo: A Portrait from Contemporary Sources, 1845–1850* (Castlebar, 1998), especially chapters 2, 7 and 8.

18. Christine Kinealy, 'The response of the Poor Law to the Great Famine in County Galway', in *Galway: History and Society – Interdisciplinary Essays on the History of an Irish County*, ed. Gerard Moran and Raymond Gillespie (Dublin, 1996), p. 381.

19. Kinealy, 'Response of the Poor Law', p. 390.

20. See Hamrock, *The Famine in Mayo*, especially chapter 3, 'Response of Landlords', pp. 27–30.

21. Ibid., p. 28.

22. Tim O'Neill, 'Famine evictions', in *Famine, Land and Culture in Ireland*, ed. Carla King (Dublin, 2000), pp. 29–70; see especially pp. 47–48. A list of 'clearances' by landlords, including the permanent eviction of 40 families or more, is provided for 1850–53 in Appendix I to this paper, pp. 59–61.

23. 'Ejectments Ireland: Return from the Courts of Queen's Bench, Common Pleas and Exchequer Ireland of the number of ejectments beginning with Hilary Term 1846 and ending with Hilary Term 1849', HC 1849, X, pp. 235–41; see also O'Neill 'Famine evictions', pp. 29–70.

24. 'Ejectments Ireland'.

25. Kinealy, 'Response of the Poor Law', p. 386.

26. Kinealy, 'Response of the Poor Law', p. 384; quotation is from Woodham-Smith, *The Great Hunger*, p. 154.

27. Quotation from Captain Pole of the Commissariat, December 1847, in Woodham-Smith, *The Great Hunger*, p. 325.

28. S.H. Cousens, 'The regional pattern of emigration during the Great Irish Famine, 1846–51', *Transactions and Papers of the Institute of British Geographers* 28 (1960), pp. 119–34, especially Figure 1, p. 121.

## CLIFDEN UNION, CONNEMARA, COUNTY GALWAY

1. Joseph Burke to Poor Law Commissioners, 22 July 1840, in Letter-Books of Joseph Burke, Assistant Poor Law Commissioner, 1838–55, Book 1839–40, no. 61, 'Formation of the Clifden Union', National Archives of Ireland.

2. Kathleen Villiers-Tuthill, *Patient Endurance: The Great Famine in Connemara*, rev. ed. (Galway, 2008), p. 11.

3. *The Dublin Almanac and General Register of Ireland* (Dublin, 1848).

4. Sir Randolph Routh to Charles Trevelyan, 31 July 1846, in 'Correspondence explanatory of the measures adopted by Her Majesty's Government for the relief of distress arising from the failure of the potato crop in Ireland', HC 1846 (735) XXXVII, pp. 338, 357; Villiers-Tuthill, *Patient Endurance*, pp. 49–51.

5. Commissioners to the Lords of the Treasury, 6 April 1847', in 'Reports of the Board of Public Works in Ireland, relating to measures adopted for the relief of distress in March, April and May 1847', HC 1847 (834) XVII, p. 6; Villiers-Tuthill, *Patient Endurance*, p. 63.

6. Villiers-Tuthill, *Patient Endurance*, pp. 62–63.

7. *First Annual Report of the Poor Law Commission*, (1848), HC 1847–48 (963) XXXIII, 377.

8. Villiers-Tuthill, *Patient Endurance*, pp. 118–30; Dominick Kerrigan to Chief Secretary, February 1848, Chief Secretary's Office Registered Papers, Distress Papers 1848,

National Archives of Ireland.

9. Deane to Poor Law Commissioners, 1 January 1848, in 'Papers relating to the proceedings for the relief of the distress and state of unions and workhouses in Ireland', fifth series, HC 1847–48 (919) LV

10. Villiers-Tuthill, *Patient Endurance*, pp. 112–16

## IN THE SHADOW OF SLIABH AN IARAINN

1. See Gerard Mac Atasney, *Leitrim and the Great Hunger: 'A Temporary Inconvenience'* (Carrick-on-Shannon: 1997), for all quotations discussed in this case-study.

## THE FAMINE IN COUNTY ROSCOMMON

1. 'The third report of the Commissioners appointed to enquire into the nature and extent of the several bogs in Ireland, and, the practicability of draining and cultivating them', HC 1813–14 (130), p. 16.

2. 'Population, Ireland: Census of the population, 1831', HC 1833 (23), p. 40; 'Report of the Commissioners appointed to take the Census of Ireland, for the year 1841', HC 1843 (504), p. 406.

3. 'Evidence taken before Her Majesty's Commissioners of Inquiry into the state of the law and practice in respect to the occupation of land in Ireland', part II, HC 1845 (616), p. 225–65, 324–79.

4. Ibid., pp. 258, 339, 359, 367.

5. A. Bourke, 'The extent of the potato crop in Ireland at the time of the Famine', *Journal of the Statistical and Social Inquiry Society of Ireland* 20.3 (1959/1960), vol. XX, part III, 1959/1960, pp. 1–35.

6. 'Returns of agricultural produce in Ireland, in the year 1847', HC 1847–48 (923), LVII.1. Potato cultivation for the county as a whole in 1847 was 11.5% of what it had been in 1844. In Roscommon it was 6.5%.

7. 'Evidence taken before Her Majesty's Commissioners of Inquiry into the state of the law and practice in respect to the occupation of land in Ireland', part II, HC 1845 (616), p. 336.

8. *The Nation*, 13 March 1847, p. 13.

9. 'Papers relating to proceedings for relief of distress, and state of unions and workhouses in Ireland', fifth series, HC 1847–48 (919), p. 265; *The Nation*, 26 February 1848, p. 5.

10. 'Papers relating to proceedings for relief of distress, and state of unions and workhouses in Ireland', sixth series, HC 1847–48 (955), pp. 401, 722, and eighth series, HC 1849 (1042), pp. 52, 56.

11. 'Correspondence explanatory of the measures adopted by Her Majesty's Government for the relief of distress arising from the failure of the potato crop in Ireland', HC 1846 (735), pp. 235–42; 'Correspondence from July, 1846, to January, 1847, relating to the measures adopted for the relief of the distress in Ireland', Commissariat series, HC 1847 (761), p. 251.

12. 'Correspondence explanatory of the measures adopted by Her Majesty's Government for the relief of distress arising from the failure of the potato crop in Ireland', HC 1846 (735), pp. 235–42; Of the 2,075 raised in Connaught between August and November 1846, only 3.2% came from Roscommon ('Correspondence from July, 1846, to January, 1847, relating to the measures adopted for the relief of the distress in Ireland', Commissariat series, HC 1847 [761], p. 251).

13. 'Correspondence from January to March, 1847, relating to the measures adopted for the relief of the distress in Ireland', Commissariat series, part II, HC 1847 (796), p. 27.

14. 'Correspondence from July, 1846, to January, 1847, relating to the measures adopted for the relief of the distress in Ireland', Board of Works series, HC 1847 (764), p. 456.

15. 'Correspondence from July, 1846, to January, 1847, relating to the measures adopted for the relief of the distress in Ireland', Commissariat series, part I, HC 1847 (761), pp. 44, 88–89.

16. Ibid., pp. 43, 59.

17. 'Correspondence from July, 1846, to January, 1847, relating to the measures adopted for the relief of the distress in Ireland', Commissariat series, HC 1847 (761), p. 450.

18. 'Distress (Ireland): Second report of the Relief Commissioners, constituted under the act 10th Vic., cap. 7', HC 1847 (819), p. 24; 'Distress (Ireland): Third report', HC 1847 (836), p. 30; 'Distress (Ireland): Fourth report', HC 1847 (859), p. 6; 'Distress (Ireland): Fifth report', HC 1847–48 (876), p. 10; 'Distress (Ireland): Sixth report', HC 1847–48 (876), p. 8.

19. 'Papers relating to proceedings for the relief of the distress, and state of the unions and workhouses, in Ireland', fourth series, HC 1847–48 (896), p. 113.

20. 'Papers relating to proceedings for relief of distress, and state of unions and workhouses in Ireland', sixth series, HC 1847–48 (955), p. 730.

21. 'Papers relating to proceedings for relief of distress, and state of unions and workhouses in Ireland', fifth series, HC 1847–48 (919), p. 204.

22. Ibid., p. 269.

23. 'Papers relating to proceedings for relief of distress, and state of unions and workhouses in Ireland', seventh series, HC 1847–48 (999), p. 84.

24. Throughout the autumn of 1846 Viscount Lorton had made several applications for corn depots to be established at constabulary barracks around the Boyle region, all of which were denied. 'Correspondence from July, 1846, to January, 1847, relating to the measures adopted for the relief of the distress in Ireland', Commissariat series, HC 1847 (761).

25. '[W]hat became of the outcasts was not known' (I. Weld, *Statistical Survey of County Roscommon* [Dublin, 1830], p. 250–51).
26. 'Papers relating to proceedings for relief of distress, and state of unions and workhouses in Ireland', sixth series, HC 1847–48 (955), p. 730.
27. 'Papers relating to proceedings for the relief of the distress, and state of unions and workhouses, in Ireland', eighth series, HC 1849 (1042), p. 53.
28. Ibid. p. 56.
29. 'Papers relating to proceedings for relief of distress, and state of unions and workhouses in Ireland', fifth series, HC 1847–48 (919), p. 204, 270.
30. 'Papers relating to proceedings for relief of distress, and state of unions and workhouses in Ireland', sixth series, HC 1847–48 (955), p. 755, 748, 757.
31. 'Papers relating to proceedings for relief of distress, and state of unions and workhouses in Ireland', sixth series, HC 1847–48 (955), p. 749.

BALLYKILCLINE, COUNTY ROSCOMMON
1. Ballykilcline is also unique in that three monographs have been written about it, two by historians: M.L. Dunn, *Ballykilcline Rising: From Famine Ireland to Immigrant America* (Massachusetts, 2008) and R.J. Scally, *The End of Hidden Ireland: Rebellion, Famine, and Emigration* (Oxford, 1995) and one by an historical archaeologist (C.E. Orser Jr, ed., *Unearthing Hidden Ireland: Historical Archaeology at Ballykilcline, County Roscommon* (Wordwell, 2006). Unless otherwise noted, the present information derives from these three sources. I would like to thank Mary Lee Dunn for her invaluable assistance with this account.
2. A. Coleman, *Riotous Roscommon: Social Unrest in the 1840s* (Dublin, 1999); M. Huggins, *Social Conflict in Pre-Famine Ireland: The Case of County Roscommon* (Dublin, 2007).
3. J. O'Donovan, *Letters Concerning Information Relative to the Antiquities of the County of Roscommon, Collected During the Progress of the Ordnance Survey in 1837*, vol. 2 (Bray, 1927); G. Knox, 'Letter to John Burke', Quit Rent Office Papers, C2, Cases and Opinions (2B.38.120), National Archives, Dublin.
4. The remarkable saga of the rent strike is detailed in House of Lords, *Lands of Ballykilcline, County Roscommon. Returns of Orders of the House of Lords, Dated 16th and 19th February 1847* (London, 1847).
5. S.J. Campbell, *The Great Irish Famine* (Strokestown, 1994), p. 42; G.J.P. Browne, 'The Mahon evictions', *Freeman's Journal*, 29 April 1848. An annotated copy in the Strokestown Park Papers suggests that some of Browne's information was in error. Nevertheless, the extent of the evictions was very real. E. Ellis, *Emigrants from Ireland, 1847–1852: State-Aided Emigration Schemes from Crown Estates in Ireland* (Baltimore, 1977), pp. 10–21.
6. C. Woodham-Smith, *The Great Hunger: Ireland, 1845–1849* (London, 1991), p. 325.
7. P. Duffy, *The Killing of Major Denis Mahon: A Mystery of Old Ireland* (New York, 2008); P. Vesey, *The Murder of Major Mahon, Roscommon, 1847* (Dublin, 2008).
8. R. Giffith, *Valuation of the Several Tenements Comprised in the Union of Strokestown, in the County of Roscommon* (Dublin, 1857).
9. C. Ó Gráda, *Black '47 and Beyond: The Great Irish Famine in History, Economy, and Memory.* (Princeton, 1999), p. 40.
10. The handwritten petition appears in the Pakenham-Mahon Papers and was housed in Strokestown Park House at the time of examination. Kincaid's comment was reproduced in *The Bonfire* [the newsletter of the Ballykilcline Society] 5.1 (2003), p. 1; L. Coyle, *A Parish History of Kilglass, Slatta, Ruskey,* (Boyle, 1994) p. 36. Dunn, *Ballykilcline Rising*, p. 33. Their collective history in the United States further makes the townland stand out as unique because in the late 1990s, several of their descendants joined together to create. The Ballykilcline Society. The members of the society are engaged in remembering their ancestors through genealogical research, fostering the local history of the Ballykilcline area, and holding reunions in Ireland, Canada and the United States.

LEINSTER

INTRODUCTION: THE PROVINCE OF LEINSTER AND THE GREAT FAMINE
1. *Census of Ireland, 1851, Part VI: General Report* (Dublin, 1856), pp. ix–liv.
2. Joel Mokyr, *Why Ireland Starved: A Quantitative and Analytical History of the Irish Economy, 1800–1850* (London, 1983), p. 26.
3. *Census of Ireland, 1851*, p. xxi.
4. *Census of Ireland, 1851*, p. xxiii.
5. See the subtitle of Seamus O'Brien's book, *Famine and Community in Mullingar Poor Law Union, 1845–49: Mud Cabins and Fat Bullocks* (Dublin, 1999).
6. 'Returns of agriculture produce, 1847', part II, H.P., Dublin, 1848.
7. Cormac Ó Gráda, *Ireland: A New Economic History, 1780–1939* (Oxford, 1994), p. 15.
8. See Timothy N. Guinnane and Cormac Ó Gráda, 'Mortality in the North Dublin Union during the Great Famine', in Cormac Ó Gráda, *Ireland's Great Famine: Interdisciplinary Perspectives* (Dublin, 2006).
9. Frank Corrigan, 'Dublin workhouses during the Great Famine', *Dublin Historical Record* 22.2 (1975), p. 64.
10. T.W. Freeman, *Pre-Famine Ireland: A Study in Historical Geography* (Manchester, 1957), pp. 176–82.

11. Freeman, *Pre-Famine Ireland*, pp. 41–43.
12. S.H. Cousens, 'The regional pattern of emigration during the Great Famine, 1846–51', *Transactions and Papers of the Institute of British Geographers* 28 (1960), pp. 119–34.
13. Freeman, *Pre-Famine Ireland*, pp. 168–72.
14. T. Jones Hughes, 'East Leinster in the mid-nineteenth century', in his *Landholding, Society and Settlement in Nineteenth-Century Ireland* (Dublin, 2010), p. 167.
15. See, for example, John Mannion's *The Peopling of Newfoundland: Essays in Historical Geography* (St. John's, 1977).
16. Hughes, 'East Leinster', p. 165.
17. Eva Ó Cathaoir, 'The Poor Law in County Wicklow', in *Wicklow: History and Society*, ed. Ken Hannigan and William Nolan (Dublin, pp. 503–80.
18. Ó Cathaoir, 'The Poor Law', p. 504.
19. Ó Cathaoir, 'The Poor Law', pp. 516–19.
20. Ó Cathaoir, 'The Poor Law', p. 544.
21. J.H. Martin, 'The social geography of mid-nineteenth century Dublin', in *Common Ground: Essays on the Historical Geography of Ireland*, ed. William J. Smyth and Kevin Whelan (Dublin, 1988), pp. 178–80.
22. Raymond J. Raymond, 'Dublin: The Great Famine, 1845–1860', *Dublin Historical Record* 30.4 (1978), Table 2, p. 104.
23. Martin, 'The social geography of Dublin', p. 184.
24. *Census of Ireland, 1851, Part V: Tables of Deaths* (Dublin, 1856), vol. 2, pp. 219–20.
25. Joel Mokyr, 'The deadly fungus: An econometric investigation into the short-term demographic impact of the Irish Famine', *Research in Population Economics* 2 (1980), pp. 248–49, and S.H. Cousens 'Regional death rates in Ireland during the Great Famine, from 1846 to 1851', *Population Studies* 14 (1960), pp. 55–74.

COUNTY MEATH DURING THE FAMINE
1. See Michael Herity, ed., *Ordnance Survey Letters Meath* (Dublin, 2001), p. 9.
2. Famine Relief Commission Papers (hereafter RLFC), series 3/1/511.
3. RLFC series 3/1/523.
4. RLFC series 3/1/910.
5. *Meath Herald*, 12 December 1846.
6. RLFC series 3/2/22/52.
7. 'Correspondence from January to March 1847 relating to the measures adopted for the relief of distress in Ireland', HC 1847 (797) LII, p. 256 (Extract from the journal of Captain Kennedy, inspecting officer, County Meath, for the week ending 6 February 1847).
8. RLFC series 3/2/22/2.
9. RLFC series 3/2/22/31.
10. *Meath Herald*, 8 May 1847.
11. RLFC series 3/2/22/20.
12. RLFC series 3/2/22/52.
13. Minute book, Dunshaughlin Board of Guardians, 23 October 1837, Meath County Library.
14. RLFC series 3/2/22/50.
15. Minute book, Kells Board of Guardians, 2 October 1847, Meath County Library.
16. *Meath Herald*, 18 March 1848.
17. *Meath Herald*, 18 March 1848.
18. 'Papers relating to proceedings for relief of distress, and state of unions and workhouses in Ireland', HC 1847–48 (956) XXIX, p. 128 (Mr Disney, Clifton Lodge to Poor Law Commissioners, 22 December 1847).
19. 'Papers relating to the proceedings for the relief of distress, and the state of the unions and workhouses in Ireland (eight series)', HC 1849 (1042) XLVIII, p. 64–65.
20. Ibid., p. 153.
21. Minute book, Kells Board of Guardians, 14 July 1849, Meath County Library.
22. *Meath Herald*, 3 October 1846.
23. Patterns of imports and exports from Drogheda port are discussed in Ned McHugh, 'Chapter 5: Exports and imports', *Journal of the County Louth Archaeological and Historical Society* 26.2 (2006), pp. 216–39.
24. 'Correspondence from January to March 1847 relating to the measures adopted for the relief of distress in Ireland', HC 1847 (797) LII, p. 256 (Extract from the journal of Captain Kennedy, inspecting officer, County Meath, for the week ending 6 February 1847).

BURYING THE FAMINE DEAD: KILKENNY UNION WORKHOUSE
1. H.D. Inglis, *Ireland in 1834: A Journey throughout Ireland, during the Spring, Summer, and Autumn of 1834*, 2 vols (London, 1835), vol. 1, pp. 98, 99.
2. W. Tighe, *Statistical Observations Relative to the County of Kilkenny Made in the Years 1800 & 1801* (Dublin, 1802), pp. 480–81.
3. C. Tóibín and D. Ferriter, *The Irish Famine: A Documentary* (London, 2001), p. 45.
4. *Kilkenny Journal*, 11 March 1848.
5. T. Patterson, 'Illegal outdoor relief in Kilkenny workhouse', *Old Kilkenny Review* 48 (1996), pp. 23–37
6. T. Patterson, 'Famine fever in Kilkenny', *Old Kilkenny Review* 49 (1997), pp. 74–88.
7. *Kilkenny Journal*, 17 April 1847.
8. *Kilkenny Journal*, 30 October 1847.

9. Minutes, Kilkenny Union Board of Guardians, March 1848, 267/8K, Local Studies, Kilkenny County Library, Kilkenny.

10. *Kilkenny Journal*, 25 August 1849.

11. *Kilkenny Journal*, 25 August 1849.

12. *Kilkenny Moderator*, 3 March 1851.

## 'KING'S COUNTY DURING THE GREAT FAMINE: POVERTY AND PLENTY'

1. *King's County Chronicle*, 17 October 1846. This newspaper as well as the *Leinster Express*, *The Times*, the Outrage Papers for King's County (National Archives of Ireland) and the papers of the Relief Commission (NAI) provide most of the primary source material from which this paper has been written.

2. William O'Connor Morris, *Memories and Thoughts of a Life* (London, 1895), pp. 128–29.

3. Joseph Grogan to Stewart and Kincaid, 16 October 1845 (Stewart & Kincaid Famine Archive, in private possession).

4. Brian Pey, ed., *Eglish and Drumcullen: A Parish in Firceall* (Birr, 2003), p. 111.

5. 'Commission of Public Works (Ireland), fourteenth report', HC 1847 [762], XVII, p. 457.

6. K.D.M. Snell, ed., *Letters from Ireland during the Famine of 1847* (Dublin, 1994), p. 171.

7. A.P.W. Malcomson, *The Calendar of the Rosse Papers* (Dublin, 2008).

8. Diary of John Plunkett Joly, 1843–48, National Library of Ireland, MS 17,035.

9. O'Connor Morris, *Memories*, p. 92.

10. 'Report on the inspection of the estate of Cloghan, King's County by the honourable Frederick Ponsonby for the Earl Fitzwilliam, June 1847', National Library of Ireland, MS 13,020.

## MUNSTER

## INTRODUCTION: THE PROVINCE OF MUNSTER AND THE GREAT FAMINE

1. All the percentage calculations in this paragraph are derived from the *Census of Ireland, 1851, Part VI: General Report* (Dublin, 1856), xii–xlvii.

2. T.W. Freeman, *Pre-Famine Ireland: A Study in Historical Geography* (Manchester, 1957), pp. 203–41.

3. Alwyn and Brinley Ress, *Celtic Heritage: Ancient Tradition in Ireland and Wales* (London, 1961), p. 201.

4. *Census of Ireland 1851*, xxii.

5. Joel Mokyr, *Why Ireland Starved: A Quantitative and Analytical History of the Irish Economy, 1800–1850* (London, 1983), p. 37.

6. *Census of Ireland, 1851*, xxxiii.

7. *Census of Ireland, 1851*, xxxi.

8. Freeman, *Pre-Famine Ireland*, p. 205.

9. T. Jones Hughes, *Landholding, Society and Settlement in Nineteenth Century Ireland: An Historical Geographer's Perspective* (Dublin, 2010), pp. 67–74.

10. Mokyr, *Why Ireland Starved*, p. 23.

11. *Census of Ireland 1851*. See, for example, significant percentage changes in number of deaths recorded for these counties in 1845 vis-à-vis those recorded from 1842 to 1844.

12. See Cecil Woodham-Smith, *The Great Hunger* (London, 1965), p. 119.

13. S.H. Cousens, 'The regional variation in mortality during the Great Irish Famine', *Proceedings of the Royal Irish Academy* 63(c) (1963), pp. 127–49.

14. *Census of Ireland, 1851, Part V: Tables of Deaths* (Dublin, 1856), vol. 2, pp. 361, 459, 583 and 653.

15. Data from Mr. John O'Connell, local historian in Donaghmore parish, County Cork.

16. S.H. Cousens, 'Regional death rates in Ireland during the Great Famine, from 1846 to 1851' *Population Studies* 14 (1960), pp. 64–66.

17. Karel Kiely, 'Poverty and famine in County Kildare', in *Kildare: History and Society*, ed. William Nolan and Thomas McGrath (Dublin, 2006), pp. 524–27.

18. Cousens, 'Regional death rates', pp. 69–70.

19. Ciarán Ó Murchadha, *Sable Wings over the Land: Ennis, County Clare and its Wider Community during the Great Famine* (Ennis, 1998), p. 148.

20. Ó Murchadha, *Sable Wings*, vi.

21. Ó Murchadha, *Sable Wings*, v.

22. 'Outrages (Ireland): Return of the number and description of outrages specially reported by the constabulary throughout Ireland in each of the years 1845 and 1846', HC 1847 (64), pp. 231–33.

23. Ibid., p. 233.

24. Ibid., p. 233.

25. 'Outrages (Ireland): Return of the outrages reported to the Royal Irish Constabulary Office from 1 January 1844 to 31 December 1880', HC 1881, especially p. 911. For other detailed examples, see Ó Murchadha, *Sable Wings*, pp. 89–101, 112–13, 142–43 and 171–74.

26. Andrés Eiríksson, 'Food supply and food riots', in *Famine 150: Commemorative Lectures*, ed. Cormac Ó Gráda (Dublin, 1997).

27. 'Appendix to report from the Select Committee on Outrages (Ireland)', HC 1852,

pp. 600–604. By 1849, the focus of protest had moved northwards – in areas now less affected by famine conditions – and centred on Counties Armagh, Louth and Monaghan.

28. 'Evictions (Ireland): Return by provinces and counties of the constabulary in each of the years from 1849 to 1880 inclusive', HC 1881, pp. 727–33.

29. James S. Donnelly Jr, 'Landlords and tenants', in *A New History of Ireland, V: Ireland under the Union 1801–70*, ed. W.E. Vaughan (Oxford, 1989), pp. 332–49.

30. 'Ejectments Ireland: Return from the courts of Queen's Bench, Common Pleas and Exchequeur Ireland of the number of ejectments, beginning with Hilary term 1846 and ending with Hilary term, 1849', HC 1849, X, pp. 235–41.

31. Ó Murchadha, *Sable Wings*, v; Woodham-Smith, *The Great Hunger*, pp. 317–21; *Tipperary Vindicator*, 24 April 1847.

32. Ó Murchadha, *Sable Wings*, p. 196.

33. Jack Burtchaell, 'An overview of the Famine in Waterford', in *Teacht na bPrátaí Dubha: The Famine in Waterford, 1845–1850*, ed. Des Cowman and Donald Brady (Dublin, 1995), p. 32.

34. Jack Burtchaell, 'The demographic impact of the Famine in County Waterford', in *Teacht na bPrátaí Dubha: The Famine in Waterford, 1845–1850*, ed. Des Cowman and Donald Brady (Dublin, 1995), pp. 274–75.

35. Kerby A. Miller, *Emigrants and Exiles: Ireland and the Irish Exodus to North America* (Oxford, 1985), p. 297.

## MORTALITY AND EMIGRATION IN SIX PARISHES IN THE UNION OF SKIBBEREEN, WEST CORK

1. Robert Traill came from Lisburn, County Antrim. He translated the works of the Jewish historian Josephus. Traill became rector of Schull in 1830. He had boasted that he 'waged war against Popery and its thousand forms of wickedness'. He is buried in Schull. One of his daughters married a John Synge and became the mother of J.M. Synge, the playwright (R. Skelton, *J.M. Synge and His World* (London, 1971), p. 9).

2. P. Hickey, *Famine in West Cork: The Mizen Peninsula, Land and People, 1800–1852* (Cork, 2002), pp. 141–88.

3. *Illustrated London News*, 13 and 20 February 1847.

4. W.S. Trench, *Realities of Irish Life* (London, 1868), p. 108.

5. R.C. Trench, *Letters and Memorials* (London, 1886), vol. 1, p. 889.

6. Hickey, *Famine in West Cork*, pp. 204–6.

7. Ibid, p. 211.

8. 'A return of deaths and emigrations in the western divisions of the Skibbereen Union, from 1 September 1846 to 12 September 1847', *Southern Reporter* 5 (October 1847).

9. D. Donovan, 'Observations on the peculiar disease to which the famine of last year gave origin and on the morbid effects of insufficient nourishment', *Dublin Medical Press* 29 (1848), p. 131.

10. Hickey, *Famine in West Cork*, p. 135.

11. W.R.W. Wilde, 'Report upon the recent epidemic fever in Ireland', *Dublin Journal of Medical Science* vol. 7 (1849), p. 101.

12. Hickey, *Famine in West Cork*, p. 209–92.

## FROM 'FAMINE ROADS' TO 'MANOR WALLS': THE FAMINE IN GLENVILLE, COUNTY CORK

1. Letter written on 1 March 1847 and subsequently published in the Cork Examiner.

2. Cork Examiner, 17 March 1847, cited in http://adminstaff.vassar.edu/sttaylor/FAMINE/Examiner/Archives/Mar1847.html

3. Ruth-Ann Harris and Donald M. Jacobs (eds.), The Search for Missing Friends: Irish Immigrant Advertisements Placed in the *Boston Pilot*, Volume 1 1831–50 (New England, 1989).

## THE FAMINE IN THE COUNTY TIPPERARY PARISH OF SHANRAHAN

1. William J. Smyth, 'Landholding changes, kinship networks and class transformation in rural Ireland: A case-study from County Tipperary', *Irish Geography* 16 (1983), pp. 16–35, especially pp. 17–24.

2. *Census of Ireland, 1841* (Dublin, 1843), pp. 228–29; *Census of Ireland, 1851, Part VI: General Report* (Dublin, 1856), pp. 332–433.

3. Ibid.

4. See John O'Connor, *The Workhouses of Ireland: the Fate of Ireland's Poor* (Dublin, 1995), p. 260.

5. *Census of Ireland, 1851, Part VI: General Report*, pp. 332–33.

6. William J. Smyth, 'Estate records and the making of the Irish landscape: An example from County Tipperary', *Irish Geography* 9 (1976), pp. 29–49.

7. *Census of Ireland, 1841*, p. 228.

8. Smyth, 'Estate records', pp. 29–31.

9. 'Manuscript of 1821 Census for Viscount Lismore's estate', originally held by the late Mr Tim Looney of Cahir, now in GPA Bolton Library, Cashel, County Tipperary.

10. Ibid.

11. Ibid.

12. Smyth, 'Estate records', pp. 29–39.

13. William J. Smyth, 'Nephews, dowries, sons and mothers: The geography of farm and marital transactions in eastern Ireland, c.1820–c.1970', in *Migration Mobility and*

*Modernisation*, ed. David J. Siddle (Liverpool, 2000), pp. 9–46, especially pp. 10–19. See also Abstract of Answers and Returns [County of Tipperary] under the Population Act of Ireland, 1821, pp. 206–7.

14. Edmund O'Riordan, *Famine in the Valley* (Clogheen/Cahir, 1995), p. 25.

15. Ibid., pp. 42–43.

16. Ibid., p. 42.

17. Ibid., pp. 45–46. See also p. 57.

18. Ibid., p. 47.

19. Ibid., p. 54.

20. Ibid., p. 55.

21. Ibid., p. 55.

22. Society of Friends, *Transactions of the Central Relief Committee of the Society of Friends during the Famine in Ireland in 1846 and 1847* (Dublin, 1852; rpt Dublin, 1996), p. 176.

23. Ibid., pp. 176–78. For an overview of work on the Society of Friends during the Famine, see Thomas P. O'Neill, 'The Society of Friends and the Great Famine', *Studies* 39.154 (1950), pp. 203–13.

24. Ibid., pp. 176–77.

25. Ibid., pp. 177–78. For a full report on the Society of Friends Auxiliary Committee at Clonmel, see pp. 36–37, 69, 49, 293, 300 and 439–40.

26. Smyth, 'Landholding changes', pp. 22–24.

27. *Tipperary Free Press*, January 1847. Quoted in O'Riordan, *Famine in the Valley*, pp. 55–56.

28. O'Riordan, *Famine in the Valley*, p. 56.

29. The annual round of gentry activities continued during these years with race meetings, hunting, cricket matches, dancing and house parties.

30. Early valuation six-inch maps formerly held in the Valuation Office, 6 Ely Place, Dublin 2, and now held in Valuation Office, Irish Life Building, Dublin 1.

31. Smyth, 'Landholding changes', pp. 25–35.

32. Housebooks of Griffith's Valuation, National Archives of Ireland.

33. Ibid.

34. Irish Folklore Commission, vol. 569, p. 15.

35. 'Copies of extracts of correspondence relating to the state of union workhouses in Ireland', HC 1847 (766), LV, p. 66, p. 84 and p. 105.

36. See O'Riordan, *Famine in the Valley*, which provides a detailed description and analysis of the origins and functions of Clogheen workhouse and union throughout the Famine years, pp. 22–38 and 66–74.

37. 'Distress (Ireland): Supplementary appendix to the seventh and last report of the Relief Commissioners', HC 1847–48 (956), XXIX, pp. 18–19 and p. 38.

38. O'Riordan, *Famine in the Valley*, pp. 68–70.

39. Ibid., p. 74.

40. Ibid., pp. 22–38, 66–74.

41. *Census of Ireland, 1851, Part V: Table of Deaths* (Dublin, 1856), pp. 96–97.

42. O'Riordan, *Famine in the Valley*, p. 74.

43. *Census of Ireland, 1851*; see also, O'Riordan, *Famine in the Valley*, pp. 76–78.

44. *Census of Ireland, 1841*, and *Census of Ireland, 1851*.

45. Ibid.

46. Ibid.

47. 1901 manuscript census for the parish of Shanrahan, National Archives of Ireland; available online at www.census.nationalarchives.ie.

48. The story of this emigrant death is told in O'Riordan, *Famine in the Valley*, p. 80.

49. Ibid., p. 80.

50. Smyth, 'Estate records', pp. 45–49. See also his 'Continuity and change in the territorial organisation of Irish rural communities', *Maynooth Review* 1.1 (1975), pp. 51–73.

## THE FAMINE IN THE DINGLE PENINSULA

1. 'First report of the Commissioners of inquiry into the state of the Irish fisheries; with the minutes of evidence and appendices', HC 1837 (77), XXII, 1, p. 125.

2. 'Report of the Commissioners appointed to take the Census of Ireland for the year 1841', HC 1843 (504), XXIV, 1, pp. 200–1; W.E. Vaughan and A.J. Fitzpatrick, eds, *Irish Historical Statistics: Population, 1821–1971* (Dublin, 1978), pp. 3, 9.

3. *Kerry Evening Post*, 19 Feb. 1846 (*KEP* hereafter).

4. DeMoleyns to Relief Commission, 25 May 1846 (National Archives of Ireland, Relief Commission, 11/2, Incoming Correspondence, Co. Kerry, 1846–47, 2-441–39 [Rel. comm., 11/2 hereafter]).

5. Rel. comm., 11/2, List of subscriptions to the Kerry relief committees. Kerry newspapers, Jan.-Aug. 1846.

6. *KEP* , 22 JULY 1846.

7. 'Correspondence from Jan. to Mar. 1847, relating to the measures adopted for the relief of distress in Ireland', Board of Works series, HC 1847 (797), LII, 1, p. 53.

8. *KEP*, 19 Dec. 1846.

9. *Kerry Examiner*, 20 Nov. 1846 (*KEx* hereafter).

10. *Tralee Chronicle*, 16 Jan. 1847 (*TC* hereafter).

11. *KEx*, 5 Mar. 1847.

12. *KEP*, 7 Nov. 1846; *TC*, 5 Dec. 1846.

13. Ibid., 3 Apr., 1847.

14. *TC*, 6 Mar. 1847.

15. *KEP*, Dec. 1846–Mar. 1847.

16. *KEP*, 24 Feb. 1847.

17. *KEP*, 1 Oct. 1847.

18. *KEP*, 17 July 1847.

19. Ms Rough Minutes of the Tralee Board of Guardians, 4 Dec. 1847; Kerry County Library, Tralee.

20. 'Accounts showing the total sum assessed in 'rate-in-aid' on each union in Ireland under the Act 12 Vic., c.24, with the amount paid by each union to the credit of the 'general rate-in-aid account' in Bank of Ireland and amount remaining to be paid; also showing the total sum appropriated to each union out of the 'general rate-in-aid account' down to 31 December 1851, and the amount unappropriated', HC 1852 (87), XLVI, 125, pp. 2–7.

21. Ms Minutes of the Dingle Board of Guardians, 19 Apr., 30 Aug. and 11 Sept. 1851.

22. Ibid., 21 June 1851.

These percentages are based on the 1851 Census returns.

23. Ms Minutes of the Dingle Board of Guardians, 23 June 1849, 31 May-26 July 1851; Kerry County Library, Tralee.

24. 'Papers relating to the proceedings for the relief of distress, and state of the unions and workhouses in Ireland', 6th series, Commissioners to Ross, 1 May 1848, HC, 1847–48 (955), LVI, 1, p. 167 (6th series hereafter).

25. 'Return of all notices served upon relieving officers of poor law districts in Ireland, by landlords and others, under the act of last session', 11 & 12 Vic., c.47, entitled, 'An act for the protection and relief of the destitute poor evicted from their dwellings', HC 1849 (517), XLIX, 279, pp. 2–35.

26. 6th series, Ross to Commissioners, 29 Feb. 1848, p. 161.

27. *The Census of Ireland for the Year 1851*, part 1, Munster, p. 214; *The Census of Ireland for the Year 1891*, part 1, Munster, p. 411. The real fall in Kerry's population may have been greater than 18.9% as it increased by 12% between 1831 and 1841 and, if this growth continued into the 1840s, the 1841 Census figures would not be an accurate reflection of its 1845 population. Corkaguiny's population, on the other hand, increased by just 0.3% in the ten years from 1831.

28. 'Fifth annual report of the Commissioners for administering the laws for the relief of the poor in Ireland, with appendices', app. B, HC 1851, XIV, pp. 204–6.

29. *KE*, 1 Oct. 1847.

## FAMINE RELIEF IN COVE AND THE GREAT ISLAND

1 *Slater's National Commercial Directory of Ireland 1846*, p. 224

2. Ibid.

3. *Cork Examiner*, 10 April 1846.

4. Ibid.

5. Ibid.

6. Ibid.

7. Ibid.

8. Minute Book of the Meetings of the Cove Famine Relief Committee, 9 April 1846 to 26 March 1847, p. 17, Cork Public Museum.

9. Letter from W.M. Drew, Honorary Secretary, Cove Famine Relief Committee, to the Secretary of the Poor Relief Commissioners, 22 April 1846, Minute Book, p. 26.

10. Letter from W.M. Drew, Honorary Secretary, Cove Famine Relief Committee, to the Secretary of the Poor Relief Commissioners, 24 May 1846, Minute Book, pp. 41–42.

11. Letter from Commissary-General, Cork, to Cove Famine Relief Committee, 8 June 1846, Minute Book, p. 44.

12. Minute Book, p. 5

13. The contribution of Lord Midleton to alleviating distress in the town was acknowledged by the relief committee at a meeting in February 1847 when he was thanked for 'his noble conduct in giving employment to hundreds of Labourers and Tradesmen in Cove for the last Three Years, with ample wages, as well as for his recent act of remitting generally 50%, and to his Poorer Tenants, 75% of his Rents'. Minute Book, p. 105. Much of the work had been provided on the construction of a quay which ran the length of Whitepoint, known locally as the Five-foot Way.

14. Letter from W.M. Drew, Honorary Secretary, Cove Famine Relief Committee, to the Secretary, Board of Works, 11 June 1846, Minute Book, p. 45.

15. Letter from W.M. Drew, Honorary Secretary, Cove Famine Relief Committee, to the Board of Works, 11 June 1846, Minute Book, p. 47.

16. Letter from W.M. Drew, Honorary Secretary, Cove Famine Relief Committee, to the Secretary, Board of Works, 31 October 1846, Minute Book, p. 74.

17. Letter from W.M. Drew, Honorary Secretary, Cove Famine Relief Committee, to James Smith Barry, 18 November 1846, Minute Book, p. 82.

18. Letter from W.E. Broughton, Captain, Royal Engineers, to the Cove Famine Relief Committee, 29 November 1846, Minute Book, p. 86.

19. Minute Book, p. 89.

20. 'Memorial of the Inhabitants of the Town of Cove to the Right Honourable Lord John Russell, First Lord of Her Majesty's Treasury', in 'Correspondence relating to the measures adopted for the relief of distress in Ireland', Board of Works series, part I, BPP 1847, Famine Ireland, vol. 6, p. 83.

21. 'Correspondence relating to the measures adopted for the relief of distress in Ire-

land', Board of Works series, part I, BPP 1847, Famine Ireland, vol. 6, p. 84.

22. Treasury Minute, 24 November 1846, 'Correspondence relating to the measures adopted for the relief of distress in Ireland', Board of Works series, part I, BPP 1847, Famine Ireland, vol. 6, p. 86.

23. Assistant Commissary-General Bishop to Sir R. Routh, 8 November 1846, 'Correspondence relating to the measures adopted for the relief of distress in Ireland', Board of Works series, part I, BPP 1847, Famine Ireland, vol. 6, p. 86.

24. Treasury Minute, 24 November 1846, 'Correspondence relating to the measures adopted for the relief of distress in Ireland', Board of Works series, part I, BPP 1847, Famine Ireland, vol. 6, p. 86.

25. Minute Book, p. 87.

26. Minute Book, p. 87.

27. Letter from W.M. Drew, Honorary Secretary, Cove Famine Relief Committee, to Sir Randolph Routh, Commissary-General, 31 January 1847, Famine Relief Commission Papers, 1845–47, NA RLFC3/2/6/11, Cork Public Museum.

28. Ibid.

29. Minute Book, p. 106.

30. Cork Examiner, 19 March 1847.

31. Letter from W.M. Drew, Honorary Secretary, Cove Famine Relief Committee, to the Secretary of the Poor Relief Commissioners, 21 April 1846, Minute Book, pp. 41–42.

## Visit of Queen Victoria to Cove, August 1849

1. J.D.A. Johnson, 'Queen Victoria's Visit to Cork', JCHAS 38 (1933), p. 104.

2. Cork Constitution, 4 August 1849.

3. James Coleman, Queenstown and the Places around Cork Harbour: A Handy Guide for the Tourist, Emigrant, or Casual Visitor (Cork: Guy and Company, 1893).

4. Cecil Woodham-Smith, The Great Hunger (London: Hamish Hamilton, 1962), p. 392.

5. The decision to change the name of the town to Queenstown followed a precedent set in 1821 when Dun Laoghaire was renamed Kingstown in honour of the visit of George IV. Following the establishment of the Irish Free State, Queenstown reverted to its original name, albeit the Irish language version of it, Cobh.

6. Cork Examiner, 25 July 1849.

7. Cork Examiner, 27 July 1849.

8. Ibid.

9. Ibid.

# Ulster

## Introduction: The Province of Ulster and the Great Famine

1. All comparative statistics in this paragraph are from Census of Ireland, 1851 (Dublin, 1856), pp. ix–xxxiii.

2. Joel Mokyr, Why Ireland Starved: A Quantitative and Analytical History of the Irish Economy, 1800–1850 (London, 1983).

3. See also Patrick Duffy, 'The Famine in County Monaghan', in The Famine in Ulster, ed. Christine Kinealy and Trevor Parkhill (Belfast, 1997), pp. 169–96.

4. Census of Ireland 1851.

5. Mokyr, Why Ireland Starved, p. 7.

6. Census of Ireland 1851, p. xxxiii.

7. M. Austin Bourke, 'The extent of the potato crop in Ireland at the time of the Famine', Journal of the Statistical and Social Inquiry Society of Ireland 20, part 3 (1959–60), pp. 1–35, especially p. 9.

8. See Christine Kinealy's introduction to The Famine in Ulster, ed. Christine Kinealy and Trevor Parkhill (Belfast, 1997), p. 14.

9. Ibid., p. 11–12.

10. Gerard Mac Atasney, 'The Famine in County Armagh', in The Famine in Ulster, ed. Christine Kinealy and Trevor Parkhill (Belfast, 1997), p. 35. Quotation taken from the Newry Telegraph, 6 March 1849.

11. Trevor McCavery, 'The Famine in County Down', in The Famine in Ulster, ed. Christine Kinealy and Trevor Parkhill (Belfast, 1997), pp. 98–99.

12. Ibid., pp. 124–25.

13. Ibid., pp. 104–7; see also E. Margaret Crawford, 'Fermanagh: Food, Famine and Fever', in Fermanagh: History and Society – Interdisciplinary Essays on the History of an Irish County, ed. Eileen M. Murphy and William J. Roulston (Dublin, 2004), pp. 267–86, and T.W. Freeman, Pre-Famine Ireland: A Study in Historical Geography (Manchester, 1957), especially pp. 269–307, for an overview of economic and social conditions in pre-Famine Ulster, especially with regard to the transition from domestic spinning and weaving to factory production.

14. Bourke, 'The extent of the potato crop', especially Tables 3 and 4, pp. 8–9; Margaret Crawford, 'Food and Famine: Diet in County Londonderry, 1820–1860', in Derry and Londonderry: History and Society, ed. Gerard O'Brien (Dublin, 1999), pp. 518–36.

15. Bourke, 'The extent of the potato crop', p. 8.

16. See also Duffy, 'The Famine in County Monaghan', pp. 169–98.

17. Anthony Begley and Soinbhe Lally, 'The Famine in County Donegal', in The Famine in Ulster, ed. Christine Kinealy and Trevor Parkhill (Belfast, 1997), p. 85.

18. Ibid., pp. 85–86.

19. For Ballyshannon, see Begley and Lally, 'The Famine in County Donegal', p. 91, and for Enniskillen, see Timothy W. Guinnane, Desmond McCabe and Cormac Ó Gráda, 'Agency and famine relief: Enniskillen workhouse during the Great Irish Famine', WP03/15, Centre for Economic Research Working Paper Series, Department of Economics, University College Dublin, 2004.

20. See Cecil Woodham-Smith, The Great Hunger (London, 1965), pp. 195–96.

21. Begley and Lally, 'The Famine in County Donegal', pp. 81–83; James Grant, 'The Great Famine in County Tyrone', in Tyrone: History and Society, ed. Charles Dillon and Henry Jefferies (Dublin, 2000), pp. 607–10.

22. Christine Kinealy, This Great Calamity: The Irish Famine, 1845–52 (Dublin, 1994), pp. 366–71, and James Grant, 'The Great Famine in County Tyrone', in Tyrone: History and Society, ed. Charles Dillon and Henry Jefferies (Dublin: Geography Publications, 2000), pp. 587–607.

23. Trevor McCavery, 'The Famine in County Down', p. 108.

24. Ibid., p. 107.

25. Cahal Dallat, 'The Famine in County Antrim', in The Famine in Ulster, ed. Christine Kinealy and Trevor Parkhill (Belfast, 1997), p. 26.

26. Mac Atasney, 'The Famine in County Armagh', p. 42. For other examples in the county, see James Grant, 'Some aspects of the Great Famine in County Armagh', in Armagh: History and Society, ed. J. Hughes and William Nolan (Dublin, 2001), pp. 809–50, especially pp. 813, 820–21 and 839.

27. Mac Atasney, 'The Famine in County Armagh', p. 53.

28. Dan Gallogly, 'The Famine in County Cavan', in The Famine in Ulster, ed. Christine Kinealy and Trevor Parkhill (Belfast, 1997), p. 65.

29. Begley and Lally, 'The Famine in County Donegal', art. cit., p. 89.

30. John Cunningham, 'The Famine in County Fermanagh', in The Famine in Ulster, ed. Christine Kinealy and Trevor Parkhill (Belfast, 1997), p. 135. For other examples see also E. Margaret Crawford, 'Fermanagh: Food, Famine and Fever', pp. 278 and 282.

31. McAtasney, 'Famine in Armagh', p. 52, Begley and Lally, 'Famine in Donegal', p. 119.

32. Begley and Lally, 'Famine in Donegal', p. 82 and McCavery 'Famine in Down', p. 123.

33. Begley and Lally, 'Famine in Donegal', p. 80.

34. Census of Ireland 1851, p. xxxvii.

35. Trevor Parkhill, 'The Famine in County Londonderry', in The Famine in Ulster, ed. Christine Kinealy and Trevor Parkhill (Belfast, 1997), p. 160.

36. 'Ejectments Ireland: Returns from the Courts of Queen's Bench, Common Pleas and Exchequer Ireland of the number of ejectments beginning with Hilary Term 1846 and ending with Hilary Term 1849', HC 1849, XLIX, pp. 235–43.

37. 'Evictions (Ireland): Return by provinces and counties of cases of evictions which had come to the knowledge of the constabulary in each of the years from 1849 to 1880 inclusive', HC 1881 (185), pp. 725–47.

38. Gallogly, 'The Famine in County Cavan', p. 72.

39. Begley and Lally, 'The Famine in County Donegal', p. 91.

40. S.H. Cousens, 'The regional pattern of emigration during the Great Irish Famine, 1846–51', Transactions and Papers of the Institute of British Geographers 28 (1960), pp. 119–34.

41. Gallogly, 'The Famine in County Cavan', pp. 71–75.

42. See, for example, S.H. Cousens, 'Regional death rates in Ireland during the Great Famine, from 1846 to 1851', Population Studies 14 (1960), pp. 55–74, especially p. 61, and Grant, 'Some aspects of the Great Famine in County Armagh', pp. 826–27 and especially Fig. 25.2 on p. 818.

43. McCavery, 'The Famine in County Down', p. 127. The original quotation is from the Newtownards Independent, 13 July 1872.

## The Great Famine and Religious Demography in Ulster

1. A much longer version of this essay, titled 'The Famine's Scars: William Murphy's Ulster and American Odyssey', was first published in Éire-Ireland 36.1-2 (Spring/Summer 2001), pp. 98–123, and was reprinted in Kevin Kenny, ed., New Directions in Irish–American History (Madison, Wis., 2003), pp. 36–60; in its final revision, it appears as chapter 10 of Kerby A. Miller, Ireland and Irish America: Culture, Class, and Transatlantic Migration (Dublin, 2008).

2. W.E. Vaughan and A.J. Fitzpatrick, eds, Irish Historical Statistics: Population, 1821–1971 (Dublin, 1978), pp. 15–16. Also see Liam Kennedy et al., Mapping the Great Irish Famine: A Survey of the Famine Decades (Dublin, 1999).

3. Joel Mokyr, Why Ireland Starved: A Quantitative and Analytical History of the Irish Economy, 1800–1850 (London, 1985), p. 267. Also see Cormac Ó Gráda, Ireland Before and After the Famine: Explorations in Economic History, 1800–1925 (Manchester, 1988), p. 87. Between 1841 and 1851, Counties Cavan and Monaghan lost 28.4% and 29.2% of their respective populations; see Vaughan and Fitzpatrick, Irish Historical Statistics, pp. 11, 13. In 1831 Cavan's and Monaghan's populations were 82% and 73% Catholic, respectively (calculated from the religious census data in the 'First report of the Commission of Public Instruction, Ireland', HC 1835, XXXIII).

4. On socio-economic developments in pre-Famine Ulster, especially in the northeastern counties, that generally stemmed the Famine's effects on the region, see the rele-

vant chapters of: Jonathan Bardon, *A History of Ulster* (Belfast, 1992); L.M. Cullen, *An Economic History of Ireland since 1660* (London, 1972), and ed., *The Formation of the Irish Economy* (Cork, 1969); and Liam Kennedy and Philip Ollerenshaw, eds, *An Economic History of Ulster, 1820–1939* (Manchester, 1985).

5. Calculated from the data in Vaughan and Fitzpatrick, *Irish Historical Statistics*, pp. 5–16.

6. Cormac Ó Gráda, *Black '47 and Beyond: The Great Irish Famine* (Princeton, NJ, 1999), p. 110.

7. David W. Miller, 'Irish Presbyterians and the Great Famine', in *Luxury and Austerity: Historical Studies XXI*, ed. J. Hill and C. Lennon (Dublin, 1999), p. 168, and Mokyr, *Why Ireland Starved*, p. 267. Also see Christine Kinealy, *This Great Calamity: The Irish Famine, 1845–52* (Dublin, 1994), pp. 233–34.

8. For the 1831 and 1834 religious censuses, see the 'First report of the Commission of Public Instruction, Ireland', HC 1835, XXXIII. In 1985–86 Miller and Kennedy of Queen's University, Belfast, embarked on a project to organise and compare the 1831–34 religious census figures with earlier and subsequent demographic data; for some preliminary results, see their 'The long retreat: Protestants, economy, and society, 1660–1926', in *Longford: Essays in County History*, ed. Raymond Gillespie and Gerard Moran (Dublin, 1991), pp. 31–61, and appendix 2, 'Irish migration and demography, 1659–1831', in Kerby A. Miller *et al.*, *Irish Immigrants in the Land of Canaan: Letters and Memoirs from Colonial and Revolutionary America, 1675–1815* (New York, 2003), pp. 656–78. More such publications, in collaboration with Dr Brian Gurrin of NUI-Maynooth, are forthcoming.

9. Christine Kinealy and Trevor Parkhill, eds., *The Famine in Ulster: The Regional Impact* (Belfast, 1997).

10. Ó Gráda, *Black '47 and Beyond*, p. 89.

11. Miller, 'Irish Presbyterians and the Great Famine', p. 168.

12. The parishes surveyed are: Ballycor (including Doagh Grange and Rashee), Ballynure, Carncastle (including Solar), Glenwhirry, Glynn, Inver, Killyglen Grange, Kilwaughter, Larne (not including its workhouse inhabitants in 1851) and Raloo; 1841–51 data in the 1841 and 1851 Irish Censuses, published in HC, 1843, XXIV, and HC, 1852–53, XCII (vol. 3, Ulster).

13. The Protestant proportions of the parishes' populations in 1831 were calculated from the 1831–34 religious censuses, in the 'First report of the Commission of Public Instruction, Ireland', HC, 1835, XXXIII.

14. The information about Kilwaughter parish, the Agnew estate and County Antrim contained in this and the following paragraphs was derived from the following sources: the 1831, 1841, and 1851 Irish Censuses, the 1831–34 Irish religious census, the Irish Poor Law reports of 1837–38, and the 1841 and 1851 Irish agricultural returns, all published in the *British Parliamentary Papers*; Samuel Lewis, *A Topographical Dictionary of Ireland*, vol. 2 (1837; rpt Baltimore, 1984); Angelique Day and Patrick McWilliams, eds., *Ordnance Survey Memoirs of Ireland, vol. 10: Parishes of County Antrim III, 1833, 1835, 1839–40: Larne and Island Magee* (Belfast, 1991), pp. 106–22; *Land Owners in Ireland: Return of Owners of Land of One Acre and Upwards in the Several Counties . . . in Ireland* (Dublin, 1876; rpt Baltimore, 1988); Classon Emmet Porter, *Congregational Memoirs of the Old Presbyterian Congregation of Larne and Kilwaughter* (orig. in *The Christian Unitarian* monthly, c.1864; rpt Larne, 1929); George Rutherford, comp., and R.S.J. Clarke, ed., *Old Families of Larne and District* (rpt Belfast, 2004); and Vaughan and Fitzpatrick, *Irish Historical Statistics*.

15. Day and McWilliams, *Ordnance Survey Memoirs*, p. 114. In 1831 the population of Kilwaughter parish included 1,476 Presbyterians, 484 Catholics, 25 members of the Church of Ireland and 31 other Protestant Dissenters.

16. On the Agnews' archaic paternalism, see Day and McWilliams, *Ordnance Survey Memoirs*, pp. 111–17. After the proprietor died in 1848, her heirs nullified her will's charitable bequest of £700 in Famine relief 'to the Poor of the Parish of Kilwaughter, without distinction of religion', and probably commenced wholesale evictions and clearances – as evidenced in the 1851 Census; see Porter, *Congregational Memoirs*, p. 91.

17. Between 1841 and 1851 the number of persons in Kilwaughter parish fell from 2,164 to 1,376. The total number of families in declined from 376 to 257; the number of families occupying third-class houses fell from 168 to 155, the number occupying fourth-class dwellings from 136 to 0, while the number of unoccupied houses more than doubled.

18. Between 1831 and 1861 the number of Presbyterians in Kilwaughter fell from 1,476 to 945. Meanwhile, the number of Catholics declined from 484 to 261 (-46%); the number of Anglicans in the parish increased from 25 to 58 (+132%); and the number of 'other Protestant Dissenters' rose from 31 to 35 (+13%). Nearly all of Kilwaughter's Catholics were concentrated in Mulloughsandall townland; their poverty is attested in Day and McWilliams, *Ordnance Survey Memoirs*, p. 114.

19. On Belfast, see: J.C. Beckett and R. Glasscock, eds., *Belfast: Origin and Growth of an Industrial City* (London, 1967), and W.A. Maguire, *Belfast* (Keele, 1993).

20. These and the following percentages are based on comparisons of data in the 1831 religious census (see n. 8) and in the official 1861 Irish Census in HC 1863, LIV (vol. 3, Ulster).

21. It is noteworthy that the Presbyterian proportion of Belfast's Protestant population also declined between 1831 and 1861 – from 57 to 53% – whereas the city's Anglican percentage fell from 40 to 37.5%, while 'other Protestants' increased their share of

Belfast's non-Catholic population from 3 to 9.5%. (In the same period, the Catholic proportion of the city's inhabitants rose slightly from 33 to 34%.)

In nine-county Ulster as a whole between 1831 and 1861, the 252% increase in the number of members of 'other Protestant' denominations – primarily of evangelical churches such as the Methodists and Baptists – is a complicating factor. However, it is likely that the actual increase was less dramatic, because in 1831 Methodists were often counted as members of the Church of Ireland, from which their separation was yet incomplete. In addition, there is no compelling reason to assume that in 1831–61 Presbyterians were more susceptible to the lure of conversion to Methodism or another evangelical sect than were Anglicans.

In the eighteenth century it was common for wealthy, ambitious, or upwardly-mobile Presbyterians to convert to the legally privileged Church of Ireland. If this trend continued during the nineteenth century (and Presbyterian clergy frequently lamented that it did), it would help explain the shifting balance between the two denominations. Also, conversion to Anglicanism by ordinary Presbyterians may have increased during times of unusual political or socioeconomic stress, as during the loyalist repressions of suspected United Irishmen in the 1790s. Did the Great Famine have similar effects? To our knowledge, no historians have investigated whether northern Presbyterians, as well as western Catholics, were subject to the blandishments of 'souperism'—and, if so, whether their susceptibility might have been a response to disproportionate Anglican/Orange influence—exerted by Ulster's landlords, clergy, magistrates and employers—over local relief distribution. Nevertheless, we believe that differential rates of out-migration were the principal reason why northern Presbyterians in 1831–61 suffered greater demographic decline than did Anglicans.

22. All figures calculated from the 1861, 1926, and 1961 data in Vaughan and Fitzpatrick, *Irish Historical Statistics*, pp. 4, 10–13, and 69–73.

23. See Miller *et al.*, *Irish Immigrants in the Land of Canaan*, appendix 2; and also chapter 8 in this volume.

24. On Irish Catholic responses to the Famine, generally, see Kerby A. Miller, *Emigrants and Exiles: Ireland and the Irish Exodus to North America* (New York, 1985), chapter 7; also see Miller, *Ireland and Irish* America, chapter 7.

25. John Kerr, New Orleans, to James Graham, Newpark, County Antrim, 29 January 1849 (MIC 144/1/13, Public Record Office of Northern Ireland, Belfast (PRONI hereafter); also see Kerr's letter of 26 November 1845, denouncing the Orange Order (MIC 144/1/7, PRONI), as well as the equally Irish-republican letters of Robert McElderry, a Presbyterian from Ballymoney, e.g. that of 12 May 1854, written from Lynchburg, Virginia (T2414/16, PRONI).

26. For analyses of these developments, see Miller, 'Forging "the Protestant way of life": Class conflict and the origins of unionist hegemony in early-nineteenth-century Ulster,' in *Transatlantic Perspectives on Ulster Presbyterianism: Religion, Politics and Identity*, ed. Mark G. Spencer and David A. Wilson (Dublin, 2006), since slightly revised and reprinted as chapter 8 in Miller, *Ireland and Irish America*; and Miller, '"Heirs of freedom" or "slaves to England"? Protestant society and unionist hegemony in nineteenth-century Ulster,' *Radical History Review* 104 (Spring 2009), pp. 17–40.

27. But see chapter 6 in Miller, *Ireland and Irish America*, where it is argued that the modern, formal expression of 'Scotch-Irish' identity first emerged in late-eighteenth-century America.

28. James Grant, 'The Great Famine and the Poor Law in Ulster: The rate-in-aid issue of 1849', *Irish Historical Studies* 105 (May 1990), pp. 35–36. Also on the rate-in-aid, see James S. Donnelly, Jr, 'The administration of relief, 1847–51', in *A New History of Ireland, V: Ireland Under the Union, I, 1801–70*, ed. W.E. Vaughan (Oxford, 1989), p. 328, Peter Gray, *Famine, Land and Politics: British Government and Irish Society, 1843–50* (Dublin, 1999), p. 317, and Kinealy, *This Great Calamity*, pp. 257–60.

29. E.g., see Bardon, *A History of Ulster*, p. 299, Grant, 'The Great Famine and the Poor Law in Ulster', pp. 36, 43, Kinealy, *This Great Calamity*, p. 259, and Kinealy and Parkhill, *The Famine in Ulster*, pp. 11–12, and Miller, 'Irish Presbyterians and the Great Famine', p. 174.

30. Grant, 'The Great Famine and the Poor Law in Ulster', pp. 31–33, Bardon, *A History of Ulster*, p. 287, and Kinealy and Parkhill, 'Introduction', *The Famine in Ulster*, pp. 11–12.

31. Kinealy, *This Great Calamity*, p. 218, and Cahal Dallat, 'The Famine in County Antrim', in *The Famine in Ulster: The Regional Impact*, ed. Christine Kinealy and Trevor Parkhill (Belfast, 1997), p. 28.

32. Miller, 'Irish Presbyterians and the Great Famine', pp. 167–75.

33. The slaughter at Dolly's Brae occurred on 12 July 1849, between Rathfriland and Castlewellan, County Down; no Orangemen were killed, seriously wounded, or arrested; at this time, the Orange Order was still predominantly Anglican, as were most Protestants in this part of County Down.

34. Alternatively, they could follow the logic of Ulster Protestant mythology, rooted in communal 'memories' of settler conflicts with Catholics, and blame their plight not on Protestant landlords and relief officials, but on fellow sufferers who were Irish 'papists'. Likewise, it is possible that unionist interpretations of the Famine heightened anti-Catholic and loyalist sentiments among Irish Protestant emigrants to America, just as the nationalist interpretation intensified Irish Catholics' animosities to the British Government and to Irish landlordism. In parts of mid- and outer Ulster, where

Protestant–Catholic competition for land was keen, such sentiments could be grounded in the realities of contemporary sectarian strife. However, the demographic data of 1766–1831 as well as of 1831–61 indicate that it was not Catholics but members of the Church of Ireland who were most likely to inherit Ulster from Presbyterians who, in proportion to their numbers, were most commonly subject to displacement before, during and after the Famine.

For an account and analysis of the physical and psychological travails of one Ulster Protestant 'victim' of the Great Famine, William Murphy, a poor orphan from Kilwaughter parish, County Antrim, see Miller, 'The Famine's Scars' (full citation in n. 1). Interestingly, in his letters from America, Murphy, a self-proclaimed 'rabid democrat', never blamed Irish 'papists' for his troubles, on either side of the Atlantic, or expressed other unionist shibboleths; perhaps life and death in Kilwaughter and then in Belfast's working-class slums, where his parents and most of his siblings died of poverty or disease, had inured him to facile notions of Protestant superiority and unionist entitlement.

## THE GREAT HUNGER IN BELFAST

1. *Banner of Ulster,* 15 February 1849 to Brian Walker, *Dancing to History's Tune: History, Myth and Politics in Ireland* (Belfast, 1996), p. 18.
2. R. Foster, *Oxford History of Ireland*, p. 167.
3. This includes Woodham-Smith, Ó Gráda and Donnelly.
4. *Newry Telegraph,* 6 March 1849.
5. Brenda Collins, 'The linen industry and emigration to Britain during the mid-nineteenth century', in *The Hungry Stream: Essays on Emigration and Famine*, ed. E. Margaret Crawford (Belfast, The Centre for Emigration Studies, Ulster-American Folk Park, and the Institute of Irish Studies, Queen's University, 1997), pp. 156–59.
6. Mr and Mrs S.C. Hall, *Ireland: Its Scenery, Character and History* (London, 1844 and 1984), p. 343.
7. *Belfast Newsletter*, 11 December 1846.
8. *Belfast Newsletter*, 20 November 1846; 11 December 1846.
9. *Belfast Newsletter*, 22 December 1846.
10. *Belfast Newsletter*, 8 January 1847.
11. *Belfast Newsletter*, 12 January 1847.
12. *Belfast Newsletter*, 22 January 1847. Henry Henderson to Sir Randolph Routh, 29 January 1847, Relief Commission Papers, 3/2/8/53, National Archives of Ireland.
13. *Belfast Newsletter*, 26 February 1847.
14. *Banner of Ulster*, 19 February 1847.
15. *Banner of Ulster*, 19 February 1847.
16. *Banner of Ulster*, 23 February 1847; *Belfast Newsletter*, 26 February 1847 and 5 March 1847.
17. *Banner of Ulster*, 19 March 1847.
18. *Banner of Ulster*, 16 April 1847 and 4 May 1847; *Belfast Newsletter,* 12 March 1847, 13 and 14 April 1847.
19. Public Record Office of Northern Ireland, Belfast (PRONI hereafter), Minutes of Belfast Board of Guardians (hereafter BG), BG7A/5, p. 60, 17 November 1846.
20. Ibid., p. 175, 26 January 1847.
21. Ibid., p. 228, 2 March 1847; p. 249, 9 March 1847. PRONI, Minutes of Belfast General Hospital, Mic 514/1/5, 27 February 1847; 6 March 1847; 8 March 1847.
22. PRONI, BG7/A/5, p. 278, 23 March 1847; pp. 298–301, 30 March 1847.
23. C. Kinealy and G. Mac Atasney, *The Hidden Famine: Hunger, Poverty and Sectarianism in Belfast* (London, 2000), pp. 87–88.
24. PRONI, BG7/A/5, p. 302, 25 March 1847; p. 345, 27 April 1847.
25. *Banner of Ulster* and *Belfast Newsletter*, 4 May 1847.
26. *Banner of Ulster* and *Belfast Newsletter*, 4 May 1847.
27. *Belfast Newsletter*, 7 May 1847; 25 May 1847; 28 May 1847; 8 June 1847.
28. *Banner of Ulster* and *Belfast Newsletter*, 16 July 1847.
29. *Belfast Newsletter*, 20 August 1847.
30. *Banner of Ulster*, 24 August 1847.
31. *Banner of Ulster*, 9 July 1847.
32. *Northern Whig*, 28 October 1847.
33. PRONI, BG7/A/8, p. 29, 13 December 1848.
34. Ibid.; BG7/A/7, p. 85, 12 April 1848; p. 113, 26 April 1848; pp. 124–26, 3 May 1848; p. 158, 24 May 1848; p. 186, 14 June 1848.
35. *Banner of Ulster*, 27 July 1849.
36. *Ninth Annual Report of the Poor Law Commissioners* (1856), Appendix B, pp. 92–93.
37. See the 1841 and 1851 Census of Ireland.
38. George Henry Bassett, *The Book of Antrim* (Dublin, 1888; rpt, 1989), p. 71.
39. Evidence of Edward Senior, 'Select Committee on Irish Poor Law', HC (1849) XVI, pp. 103–4; Warder, 6 January 1849, 7 March 1849.

## MAPPING THE FAMINE IN MONAGHAN

1. Shirley Papers, Public Record Office of Northern Ireland, Belfast (PRONI hereafter), 'Observations concerning the future letting and management of Estates in the County of Monaghan', A/4, p. 86.
2. Distress Papers, Box #1473, D.2010 (B. MacDonald, ed.), *Clogher Record* 17.2 (2001), p. 547.

3. Devon Commission, 1845, p. 923.
4. Trench's observations on the Shirley estate, PRONI, D.3531/5/55. see P.J. Duffy, 'Management problems on a large estate in mid-nineteenth-century Ireland', *Clogher Record* 16.1 (1997), pp. 101–22, especially p. 118.
5. Angelique Day and Patrick McWilliams, eds., *Ordnance Survey Memoirs: Counties of South Ulster*, vol. 40 (Belfast, 1998), p. 118.
6. Shirley petitions, PRONI, D.3531/P/Box 1.
7. Norman Steele, 'Observations on the future management of estates in the county' (1795), PRONI, D.3531/A/4, p. 86.
8. B. MacDonald, 'A time of desolation: Clones Poor Law Union, 1845–50', *Clogher Record* 17.1 (2000), p. 38.
9. Shirley Papers, PRONI, Correspondence, E.J. Shirley to E.P. Shirley, 31 August 1850, D.3531/C/2/1.
10. Carrickmacross Workhouse report, *Dundalk Democrat*, 8 Dec 1849, summarized in *Northern Standard*, 21 October 2004, p. 30.
11. Distress Papers, Box #1414, D.8819 (B. MacDonald, ed.), *Clogher Record* 17.2 (2001), p. 486.
12. Shirley Papers, PRONI, D.3531/P/Box 1. Most of the accounts refer to men employed over days without detailing the numbers of houses 'thrown down' – for example, 'men's wages executing ejectment decrees and pulling down the roofs of houses for 27th-28th August 1849: 10 men 2 days @ 1s-0 per day'.
13. P.J. Duffy, '"Disencumbering our crowded places": Theory and practice of estate emigration schemes in mid-nineteenth-century Ireland', in *To and From Ireland: Planned Migration Schemes, c.1600–2000*, ed. P.J. Duffy (Dublin, 2004), pp. 79–104, 84, 102.
14. Shirley Papers, PRONI, Improvement Books, D.3531/M/7/1-5.
15. Devon Commission, p. 884.
16. *Northern Standard*, 9 May 1846, quoted in MacDonald, 'A time of desolation', p. 23.
17. Distress Papers, Box #1407, D.4794 (B. MacDonald, ed.), *Clogher Record* 17.2 (2001), p. 417.
18. MacDonald, 'A time of desolation', p. 43.
19. Shirley Papers, PRONI, Correspondence, Charles Shirley to E.P. Shirley, 15 Dec 1849, D.3531/C/2/1.
20. Distress Papers, Box #1414, D.8819 (B. MacDonald, ed.), *Clogher Record* 17.2 (2001), p. 486.
21. *Northern Standard*, 9 May 1846, quoted in MacDonald, 'A time of desolation', p. 76.

## THE MANAGEMENT OF FAMINE IN DONEGAL IN THE HUNGRY FORTIES

1. J. Mac Laughlin, *Reimagining the Nation-State: The Contested Terrains of Nation-building* (London, 2001), pp. 135–45.
2. S. Clark, *The Social Origins of the Land War* (Princeton, 1979).
3. J. Mac Laughlin, 'Social class impact of the Famine in Donegal', in *Donegal: The Making of a Northern County*, ed. J. Mac Laughlin (Dublin, 2007), pp. 192–98.
4. *Londonderry Standard*, 15 January 1847.
5. Minutes of Board of Guardians, Glenties Union, 27 August 1846, County Library, Letterkenny.
6. Ibid.
7. Ibid, May 1842.
8. *Londonderry Standard*, 12 September 1846.
9. Ibid.
10. Minutes of Board of Guardians, Inishowen Union, 10 October 1843, County Library, Letterkenny.
11. J. Mac Laughlin, 'The evolution of modern demography and the debate on sustainable development', *Antipode* 31.3 (1999), pp. 324–32.
12. Minutes of Board of Guardians, Inishowen Union, 17 September 1847.
13. Minutes of Board of Guardians, Glenties Union, 7 December 1847.
14. Mac Laughlin, 'Social class impact of the Famine in Donegal', pp. 196–97.
15. Minutes of Board of Guardians, Inishowen Union, 20 August 1847.
16. Minutes of Board of Guardians, Glenties Union, 19 May 1847.
17. Minutes of Board of Guardians, Inishowen Union, June 1847.
18. Minutes of Board of Guardians, Inishowen Union, 12 May 1848.
19. Quoted in Mac Laughlin, Social class impact of the Famine in Donegal', p. 195.
20. Minutes of Board of Guardians, Inishowen Union, 19 March 1848.
21. Minutes of Board of Guardians, Inishowen Union, 10 January 1843.
22. Jim Mac Laughlin, 'Place, politics and culture in nation-building Ulster: Constructing nationalist hegemony in post-Famine Donegal', *Canadian Review of Studies in Nationalism* 20.1–2 (1993), pp. 34–46.

## SECTION V: WITNESSING THE FAMINE

### THE GREAT FAMINE IN GAELIC MANUSCRIPTS

1. Neil Buttimer, 'Literature: Gaelic literature in the nineteenth century, in James S. Donnelly, Jr., editor-in-chief, *Encyclopedia of Irish history and culture* (Farmington Hills, MI, 2004), pp. 399–401.
2. Roberto Casati and Achille C. Varzi (eds), *Events. International Research Library of Philosophy*, Vol. 15 (Aldershot, England and Brookfield, Vermont, 1999); Nicole Müller,

Agents in early Welsh and early Irish (Oxford, 1999).

3. William J. Smyth, *Map-making, landscapes and memory: a geography of colonial and early modern Ireland c. 1530–1750* (Cork, 2006), pp. 103–66.

4. Tadhg Ó Donnchadha (ed.), 'Cín Lae Ó Mealláin', *Analecta Hibernica*, No. 3 (September, 1931), pp. 1–61; the source of the diary itself, University College, Cork (UCC), Murphy Ms 3, is catalogued by Breandán Ó Conchúir, *Clár lámhscríbhinní Gaeilge Choláiste Ollscoile Chorcaí: Cnuasach Uí Mhurchú* (Baile Átha Cliath, 1999), pp. 8-9. Ill. 1 is reproduced from the document with the permission of Mr Crónán Ó Doibhlin, Boole Library, UCC, and with the assistance of Mr Tomás Tyner, Audio-Visual Media Services, UCC, whom I thank for also photographing Ill. 2. The spelling of extracts from the portion of the edition shown in Ill. 2 has been checked against the original

5. David Dickson, *Arctic Ireland: the extraordinary story of the great frost and forgotten famine of 1740–41* (Belfast, 1997).

6. Cornelius G. Buttimer, 'An Irish text on the "War of Jenkins' Ear"', *Celtica*, Vol. XX (1991), pp. 75-98, and Nessa O'Sullivan, 'Tadhg Ó Neachtain agus na nuachtáin', unpublished MA thesis (UCC, 1990).

7. Breandán Ó Conchúir, *Scríobhaithe Chorcaí 1700–1850* (Baile Átha Cliath, 1982), p. 23.

8. Proinsias Ó Drisceoil, *Seán Ó Dálaigh: éigse agus iomarbhá* (Corcaigh, 2007).

9. Liam P. Ó Murchú, *Cinnlae Amhlaoibh Uí Shúileabháin: reassessments*, Irish Texts Society Subsidiary Series, Vol. 14 (Dublin, 2004).

10. Cornelius G. Buttimer, 'Pláig fhollasach, pláigh choimhtheach: "Obvious plague, strange plague"', *Journal of the Cork Historical and Archaeological Society*, Vol. 102 (1997), pp. 41-68.

11. Liam Mac Mathúna, 'On the semantics of Irish words derived from IE *g ᵁher- "HOT"', *Celtica* Vol. XXI (1991), pp. 273-90.

12. For further consideration of the material, see Neil Buttimer, 'A stone on the cairn: the Great Famine in later Gaelic manuscripts' in Chris Morash and Richard Hayes (eds), *'Fearful realities': new perspectives on the Famine* (Dublin, 1996), pp. 93–109.

13. Noel Kissane, *The Irish Famine: a documentary history* (Dublin, 1995), p. 24.

14. Cornelius G. Buttimer, 'Catalogue of Irish manuscripts in the Boston Athenaeum',in Pádraig de Brún, Seán Ó Coileáin and Pádraig Ó Riain (eds), *Folia Gadelica: essays presented by former students to R. A. Breatnach, M.A., M.R.I.A.* (Cork, 1983), pp. 105-23.

15. L. Minc, 'Scarcity and survival: the role of oral tradition in mediating subsistence crises,' *Journal of Archaeological Anthropology*, Vol. V, Pt 1 (March, 1986), pp. 39-113.

16. Fionntán de Brún, 'Expressing the nineteenth century in Irish: the poetry of Aodh Mac Domhnaill (1802–1867)', *New Hibernia Review*, Vol. 15, No. 1 (Spring, 2011), pp. 81–106.

17. I am grateful to Ms Penelope Woods, Russell Library, National University of Ireland, Maynooth, for permission to cite this material.

18. Risteárd Ó Foghludha, *Pádraig Phiarais Cúndún 1777–1856* (Baile Átha Cliath, 1932).

19. Neil Buttimer, 'Comhfhreagras Corcaíoch', forthcoming.

20. James S. Donnelly, Jr, *Captain Rock: the Irish agrarian rebellion of 1821–1824* (Cork, 2009).

21. Mention of this dimension is largely absent, for instance, from Cormac Ó Gráda, 'New perspectives on the Irish Famine', *Bullán*, Vol. 3, No. 2 (1998), pp. 103-15, or from James S. Donnelly, Jr, *The Great Irish Potato Famine* (Sutton, 2002).

22. See Paul Bew, *Ireland: the politics of enmity 1789–2006* (Oxford, 2007), pp. 175-230.

23. For reflections on rejectionist tendencies, see Deborah Lipstadt, *Denying the Holocaust: the growing assault on truth and memory* (New York, 1993).

24. Raphael Lemkin, *Axis rule in occupied Europe: laws of occupation – analysis of government – proposals for redress* (Washington, D.C., 1944).

25. Amartya Sen, *Poverty and famines: an essay on entitlement and deprivation* (Oxford, 1981).

26. Ben Kiernan, *Blood and soil: a world history of genocide and extermination from Sparta to Darfur* (New Haven, 2007), pp. 169-212.

27. Thus, Joel Mokyr, on reviewing Morash and Hayes, *'Fearful realities'* (in *Victorian Studies*, Vol. 41, No. 2 (Winter 1998), pp. 319-21) invokes the term "hysteresis" (p. 320) when describing Irish economics after the Great Hunger. It may be worthwhile drawing attention to the word's wider usage in designating any system's dependence not only on its current environment but equally on that of its past as one searches for an appropriate terminology to capture post-Famine experience generally.

### THE ARTIST AS WITNESS: JAMES MAHONY

1. W.G. Strickland gives the date of Mahony's birth as 1810 (W.G. Strickland, *A Dictionary of Irish Artists* (Dublin, 1913), vol. 2, p. 88). Other suggestions are *c.*1816 (Rodney K. Engen, *Dictionary of Victorian Wood Engravers* [London, 1985], p. 173) and *c.*1800 (Anne Crookshank and the Knight of Glin, *Ireland's Painters, 1600–1940* [New Haven, CT, 2002], p. 203).

2. Margaret Crawford, 'The Great Irish Famine, 1845–9: Image versus reality', in *Ireland: Art into History*, ed. Raymond Gillespie and Brian P. Kennedy (Dublin, 1994), p. 77; Peter Murray, 'Representations of Ireland in the *Illustrated London News*', in *Whipping the Herring: Survival and Celebration in Nineteenth-Century Irish Art*, ed. P. Murray (Cork, 2006), p. 239.

3. M. Crawford, 'The Great Irish Famine', p. 77, Margarita Cappock, *The Depiction of*

*Ireland in the Illustrated London News, 1842–1900*, PhD, NCAD 1998, (unpublished) and P. Murray, 2006, ibid. p. 235–6

4. *Illustrated London News*, 13 February 1847.

5. *Illustrated London News*, 20 February 1847.

6. See J. Campbell, 'Separating Mahony and Mahoney', in Irish Arts Review, summer 2011, vol. 28, no. 2, p. 98–101.

7. NLI Ms. Notes 19,685 (A): file no. 21 (3).

8. Edwin de Bechtel, *Jacques Callot* (New York, 1955), cited by Ralph E. Shikes, *The Indignant Eye: The Artist as Social Critic in Prints and Drawings from the Fifteenth Century to Picasso* (Boston, 1969), p. 44.

9. Shikes, *The Indignant Eye*, p. 111.

10. Lorenz Eitner, *An Outline of 19th-Century European Painting* (New York, 1987), vol. 1, p. 67.

11. *Korea* by Peter Peri (1951), published in *Daily Worker*, 1 October 1952, and in James Hyman, *The Battle for Realism: Figurative Art in Britain during the Cold War, 1945–1960* (New Haven, CT, 2001), p. 117.

### ASENATH NICHOLSON'S IRISH JOURNEYS

1. Asenath Nicholson, *Lights and Shades of Ireland* (London, 1850), pp. iii–iv.

2. Nicholson, *Lights and Shades*, p. 244. See Maureen Murphy, 'Introduction', in Asenath Nicholson, *Annals of the Famine in Ireland*, ed. Maureen Murphy (Dublin, 1998), pp. 5–17.

3. Asenath Nicholson, *Ireland's Welcome to the Stranger* (London, 1847), pp. iii–iv.

4. Murphy, 'Introduction', p. 11.

5. Nicholson, *Ireland's Welcome*, pp. vi–vii.

6. Nicholson, *Ireland's Welcome*, p. iii.

7. Nicholson, *Ireland's Welcome*, p. 151.

8. Nicholson, *Ireland's Welcome*, p. 437.

9. Niall R. Branach, 'Edward Nangle and the Achill Island mission', *History Ireland* 8.3 (2000), pp. 35–38. See also Donnchadh Ó Corráin and Tomás O'Riordan, eds, *Ireland 1815–1870: Emancipation, Famine and Religion* (Dublin, 2011), p. 72.

10. Nicholson, *Ireland's Welcome*, pp. 437–38.

11. See Margaret Kelleher, *Feminisation of Famine: Expressions of the Inexpressible?* (Cork, 1997), pp. 74–86

12. Murphy, 'Introduction', p. 11.

13. Nicholson, *Lights and Shades*, p. 330.

14. Nicholson, *Lights and Shades*, p. 408.

15. Nicholson, *Lights and Shades*, p. 408.

16. Nicholson, *Lights and Shades*, pp. 216–17.

17. Nicholson, *Lights and Shades*, pp. 329–30.

18. Nicholson, *Lights and Shades*, p. 316.

19. Nicholson, *Lights and Shades*, p. 9.

20. Nicholson, *Ireland's Welcome*, p. 333.

### THOMAS CARLYLE AND FAMINE IRELAND

1. T. Carlyle, *Reminiscences of My Irish Journey* (London, 1882), p. 55.

2. S. Heffer, *Moral Desperado: A Life of Thomas Carlyle* (London, 1995), p. 274.

3. C. Pearl, *The Three Lives of Gavan Duffy* (Kensington, 1979), p. 43.

4. L. Geary, 'Charles Gavan Duffy, the Great Famine in Ireland and Famine memory in colonial Australia', *Australian Journal of Irish Studies* 7 (2007–8), p. 64.

5. See R.F. Foster, *Words Alone: Yeats and His Inheritances* (Oxford, 2011), pp. 81–85.

6. Heffer, *Moral Desperado*, p. 196.

7. Thomas Carlyle, "The Repeal of the Union", in *Rescued Essays of Thomas Carlyle*, ed. P. Newberry (London, 1882), p. 21.

8. Ibid., p. 40.

9. Carlyle, *Reminiscences*, p. 70.

10. Ibid., p. 84.

11. Ibid., p. 211.

12. Ibid., p. 107.

13. Ibid., p. 126.

14. Ibid., p. 136.

15. Thomas Carlyle, "Legislation for Ireland", in *Rescued Essays of Thomas Carlyle*, ed. P. Newberry (London, 1882), p. 60.

16. Geary, 'Charles Gavan Duffy', p. 52.

17. P. Gray, 'Famine relief policy in comparative perspective: Ireland, Scotland and northwestern Europe, 1845–49', *Éire-Ireland* 62 (1997), p. 108. See also, by the same author, *Famine, Land and Politics: British Government and Irish Society, 1843–50* (Dublin, 1999).

18. Carlyle, *Reminiscences*, p. 262.

19. J. Morrow, 'Thomas Carlyle, "Young Ireland" and the condition of Ireland question', *The Historical Journal* 51.3 (2008), p. 652. Carlyle's politics, beliefs and prejudices *vis-à-vis* Famine Ireland are also discussed in D. Nally, '"Eternity's Commissioner": Thomas Carlyle, the Great Irish Famine and the geopolitics of travel', *Journal of Historical Geography* 32 (2006), pp. 313–35.

20. Carlyle, *Reminiscences*, p. 206.

21.Ibid., p. 211.

## 'LE PAYS CLASSIQUE DE LA FAIM': FRANCE AND THE GREAT IRISH FAMINE

1. *Eloge funèbre de Daniel O'Connell prononcé à Notre-Dame de Paris le 10 février 1848 par Henri-Dominique Lacordaire* (Paris, 1848).

2. For instance, in the Eglise Saint-Roch and the Eglise Sainte-Clothilde.

3. *Circulaire au clergé du Diocèse de Montréal: Eveché de Montréal*, 19 February 1847.

4. J. Duval, *Histoire de l'émigration européenne, asiatique et africaine au XIXe siècle: Ses causes, ses caractères, ses effets* (Paris, 1862), p. 41.

5. Louis Blanc, *Lettres sur l'Angleterre* (Paris), 1866), vol. 2, p. 334.

6. Amédée Pichot, *L'Irlande* (Paris, 1850 ), vol. 1, pp. 226–27.

7. Edouard Déchy, *Voyage: Irlande en 1846 et 1847* (Paris, 1847), p. 114.

8. Charles Marchal, *Cri de misère* (Paris, 1848), p. 10–11.

9. Annie Keary, *L'Irlande il y a quarante ans*, trans. Mme de Witt (Paris, 1889), p. 289.

10. L'Abbé Alphonse Constant, *La voix de la famine* (Paris, 1846).

11. Amedée Pichot, *L'Irlande* (Paris, 1850), vol. 2, p. 308.

12. John Banim, *L'Anglo-Irlandais du dix-neuvième siècle* (Paris, 1829), vol. 1, p. 86.

13. *Dictionnaire encyclopédique des sciences médicales*, 4th series, vol. 1, 1877.

14. Aurèle Kervigan, *L'Angleterre telle qu'elle est ou seize ans d'observation . . .* (Paris, 1860), vol. 1, p. 343.

15. See Jean Canis, *Les massacres en Irlande* (Paris, 1881), p. 13.

16. C.R. Girard, *Les révélations de la Salette* (Grenoble, 1873), p. 25.

17. *Documents relatives à la Société de Saint-Vincent de Paul* (Paris, 1862), p. 10; see also the excellent and highly informative thesis by Máire Brighid Ní Chearbhaill, 'The Society of St Vincent de Paul in Dublin, 1926–1975', PhD thesis, National University of Ireland, Maynooth, 2008.

18. *Cork Examiner*, 28 February 1871.

19. *Cork Examiner*, 3 February 1871.

20. *Cork Examiner*, 27 February 1871.

21. *Cork Examiner*, 14 February 1871 .

22. *Cork Examiner*, 17 March 1871.

23. *Cork Examiner*, 12 January 1871.

## SECTION VI: THE SCATTERING

## EXODUS FROM IRELAND – PATTERNS OF EMIGRATION

1. S.H. Cousens, 'The regional pattern of emigration during the Great Irish Famine, 1846–51', *Transactions and Papers of the Institute of British Geographers* 28 (1960), pp. 119–34.

2. David Fitzpatrick, in *New History of Ireland, vol. IX: Maps, Genealogies, Lists* (Oxford, 1984), Map 14B, p. 620.

3. Cousens, 'The regional pattern of emigration', pp. 128–29.

4. For example, County Sligo had witnessed controversial 'sponsored' emigration of up to 2,000 persons from the estate of Lord Palmerston. McAdam Ferrie, a member of the Legislative Council of Canada, wrote a highly critical open letter to Britain's Colonial Secretary, Earl Grey, describing the terrible state of the starving paupers arriving in Quebec and complaining that they had been shipped off to 'this young and thinly populated country without regard to humanity or even to common decency'. For a full account, see Cecil Woodham-Smith, *The Great Hunger* (London, 1968), pp. 223–26.

5. Christine Kinealy, *The Great Calamity: The Irish Famine 1845–52* (Dublin, 1994), pp. 125–28.

6. See E. Estyn Evans, *The Personality of Ireland*, 2nd ed. (Belfast, 1981), which includes an appendix dealing with Lord George Hill's reports on living conditions in North Donegal on pp. 89–110.

7. 'Ejectments Ireland: Returns from the Courts of Queen's Bench, Common Pleas and Exchequer Ireland of the number of ejectments beginning with Hilary Term 1846 and ending with Hilary Term, 1849, both included', HC 1849, XLIX, pp. 235–43. See also James S. Donnelly Jr, 'Landlords and tenants', in *A New History of Ireland, V: Ireland under the Union 1801–70*, ed. W.E. Vaughan (Oxford, 1989), pp. 337–43, and his 'Mass eviction and the Irish Famine: The clearances revisited', in *The Great Irish Famine*, ed. C. Póirtéir (Dublin: Mercier Press), pp. 155–73. See also Tim P. O'Neill's chapter on 'Famine evictions' in *Famine, Land and Culture in Ireland*, ed. Carla King (Dublin, 2000), pp. 29–70, for a detailed assessment of the evidence on evictions.

8. Cousens, 'The regional pattern of emigration', p. 128.

9. Kerby A. Miller, *Migrants and Exiles: Ireland and the Irish Exodus to North America* (Oxford, 1985), pp. 291–92.

10. Miller, *Migrants and Exiles*, p. 292.

11. 'Extent and value of rateable property per Poor Law Union', HC 1844, XLII, pp. 495–96. See also 'Returns of agricultural produce in Ireland, in the year 1847', HC 1847–48 (923)'.

12. P.M. Austin Bourke, 'The agricultural statistics of the 1841 Census of Ireland: A Critical Review', *Economic History Review* 18 (1965), pp. 376–91.

13. *Census of Ireland, 1851, Part VI: General Report* (Dublin, 1856), p. lv.

14. 'Ejectments Ireland', pp. 235–41.

## LIVERPOOL AND THE GREAT IRISH FAMINE

1. J. Matthew Gallman, *Receiving Erin's Children: Philadelphia, Liverpool, and the Irish Famine Migration, 1845–1855* (Chapel Hill, 2000), p. 6. R. Lawton, 'Peopling the past', *Transactions of the Institute of British Geographers*, n.s., 12 (1987), p. 265.

2. Lawton, 'Peopling the past', p. 266.

3. *Illustrated London News*, 12 June 1847; see also F. Neal, Black '47: *Britain and the Famine Irish* (London, 1998), p. 61.

4. Gallman, *Receiving Erin's Children*, p. 91.

5. F. Neal, *Sectarian Violence: The Liverpool Experience, 1819–1914, an Aspect of Anglo-Irish History* (Manchester, 1988), p. 105.

6. F. Neal, *Black '47: Britain and the Famine Irish* (Liverpool, 1998), p. 137.

7. F. Neal, *Black '47: Britain and the Famine Irish*, adapted form Appendix 3, 4, p. 83.

8. Quoted in in Neal, *Sectarian Violence*, p. 109.

9. Neal, *Sectarian Violence*, p. 112.

10. Ibid., p. 110

11. Ibid, p. 112

12. R. Swift, 'Crime and the Irish in nineteenth-century Britain', in *The Irish in Britain, 1815–1939*, ed. R. Swift and S. Gilley (London, 1989), pp. 167–68.

13. Neal, *Black '47*, p. 61.

14. Ibid, adapted from Appendix 3.4, p. 83.

15. D. Beckingham, 'The Irish and the question of drunkenness: Catholic loyalty in nineteenth-century Liverpool', *Irish Geography* 42.2. (2009), p. 126; J. Belchem and D.M. MacRaild, 'Cosmopolitan Liverpool', in *Liverpool 800: Culture, Character and History*, ed. J. Belchem (Liverpool, 2006), pp. 311–91; Neal, *Black '47*, p. 137.

16. Neal, *Black '47*, p. 61; C.G. Pooley, 'Living in Liverpool: The modern city' in *Liverpool 800: Culture, Character and History*, ed. J. Belchem (Liverpool, 2006), pp. 187–88.

17. I.A. Glazier and M. Tepper, eds, *The Famine Immigrants: Lists of Irish Immigrants Arriving at the Port of New York, 1846–1851*, 7 vols (Baltimore, 1983–86), vol. 2, p. viii.

18. Glazier and Tepper, eds, *The Famine Immigrants*, vol. x, p. x.

19. Ira A. Glazier, Deirdre M. Mageean and Barnabus Okeke, 'Socio-demographic characteristics of Irish immigrants, 1846–1851', in *Maritime Aspects of Migration*, ed. Klaus Friedland (Cologne, 1989), pp. 243–78.

20. See Lawton, 'Peopling the past', pp. 259–83.

21. Beckingham, 'The Irish and the question of drunkenness', pp. 125–44.

## THE *FIDELIA*

1. Ira A., Glazier, P. Magdean, & B. Okebe, 'Socio-demographic characteristics of Irish immigrants, 1846–1851' in Friedland, Klaus ed. *Papers presented to a panel on Maritime Aspects of Migration*, 16th international Congress of Historical Sciences (Stuttgart, 1985); I. A. Glazier and M. Tepper eds., *The Famine Immigrants: Lists of Irish Immigrants Arriving at the Port of New York 1846–1851*, 7 vols. (Baltimore, 1983) pp. vii–ix. See also M. Gallman, *Receiving Erin's Children: Philadelphia, Liverpool, and the Irish Famine migration, 1845–1855* (Chapel Hill, North Carolina, 2000)

2. I. A. Glazier and M. Tepper eds, *The Famine Immigrants: Lists of Irish Immigrants Arriving at the Port of New York 1846–1851, Volumes 1–7* (Baltimore, 1983), pp. vii–ix.

3. Ibid., p. vii.

## IRISH FAMINE REFUGEES AND THE EMERGENCE OF GLASGOW CELTIC FOOTBALL CLUB

1. I. Maver, 'Glasgow flourishes: The story of a nation', *Scotland on Sunday*, 19 September 1999, supplement, pp. 18–21.

2. 'Ups and downs of a Clyde-built city', *The Sunday Mail*, Scotland's Story supplement, no. 32, 31 May 2000.

3. J.M. Bradley, *Ethnic and Religious Identity in Modern Scotland: Politics, Culture and Football* (Aldershot, 1995), p. 145. In 1755 the Government Commissioned Webster (previously Moderator of the General Assembly of the Church of Scotland) to obtain data for the first Census of Scotland.

4. The 1841 Census indicates that 126,000 people in Scotland (nearly 5% of the population) were Irish-born, a figure that included Scots–Irish Protestants from Ulster but excluded Irish offspring born in Scotland. For Handley, the latter would push the figure of migrants from the island of Ireland in Scotland to nearer 10% of the total population. Glasgow statistician James Cleland estimated that the total Catholic population of Glasgow in 1831 to be 26,965 and in 1836 to be 46,238. At this time most Catholics in Scotland lived in the city (J. Cleland, *The Former and Present State of Glasgow* [Glasgow, 1840].

5. J. Burrowes, *Irish: The Remarkable Saga of a Nation and a City* (Edinburgh, 2003), p. 15.

6. J.E. Handley, *The Irish in Scotland* (Glasgow, 1964). p. 182. This edition combines the author's *The Irish In Scotland, 1798–1845* (1943) and *The Irish in Modern Scotland* (1947).

7. Ibid.

8. F. Neal, *Black '47: Britain and the Famine Irish* (Basingstoke, 1997), p. 80.

9. Handley, *The Irish in Scotland*, p. 183.

10. Neal, *Black '47*, p. 89.

11. Ibid, p. 180.

12. Handley, *The Irish in Scotland*, p. 181.

13. Neal, *Black '47*, p. 160.

14. T.M. Devine, 'The Great Irish Famine and Scottish history', In *New Perspectives on the Irish in Scotland*, ed. M.J. Mitchell (Edinburgh, 2008) p. 27.

15. T. Gallagher, *Glasgow: The Uneasy Peace* (Manchester, 1987) p. 16.

16. J. McCaffrey, 'Roman Catholics in Scotland in the 19th and 20th centuries', *Records of the Scottish Church History Society* 21.2 (1983), pp. 275–300.

17. Only one Catholic Church was built in the Glasgow archdiocese (which covered much of the west-central population belt) prior to 1840 and four elsewhere. However, between 1841 until 1850 fifteen were built, including five in the city. During the period 1851–90 fifty were erected, including another nine within Glasgow's boundaries. 'Famine parishes' included St Alphonsus Calton (1846), St Mary Immaculate Pollockshaws (1846), St Patrick Anderston (1850), St Paul Shettleston (1850) and St Mungo Townhead (1850). Several others such as St Patricks' in Coatbridge, a frontier Irish town ten miles from Glasgow city centre, also emerged (1845), as did St John the Baptist in Port Glasgow to the west of the city in 1846. Information from *The Western Catholic Calendar*, published yearly by the Archdiocese of Glasgow (Glasgow, 2009).

18. B. Aspinwall, 'Children of the Dead End: The Formation of the Modern Archdiocese of Glasgow, 1815–1914', *The Innes Review* 43.2 (Autumn 1992), pp. 119–44.

19. B. Wilson, *Celtic: A Century with Honour* (Glasgow, 1988), pp. 10–17.

20. J.M. Bradley, ed., *Celtic Minded 3: Essays on Celtic Football Culture and Identity* (Argyll, 2009), p. 6.

### ARCHAEOLOGICAL EVIDENCE OF IRISH MIGRATION

1. D. Walker and M. Henderson, M. 'Smoking and health in London's East End in the first half of the 19th century', *Post-Medieval Archaeology* vol. 44, no. 1, pp. 209–22, (2010).

2. F. Neal, *Black '47: Britain and the Famine Irish* (London, 1988).

3. A. Miles, N. Powers, R. Wroe-Brown with D. Walker, *St Marylebone Church and Burial Ground: Excavations at St Marylebone Church of England School*. MoLAS Monograph 46 (2005).

4. S. Mays, 'The rise and fall of rickets in England', in P. Murphy and P. Wiltshire (eds) The Environmental Archaeology of Industry (Oxford, 2003), p. 149.

5. M. Brickley and R. Ives, The bioarchaeology of metabolic disease (Oxford, 2008)

6. C.A. Roberts and M. Cox, 2003, Health and Disease in Britain: from prehistory to the present day (Gloucestershire, 2000), p. 310.

### BLACK '47 AND TORONTO, CANADA

1. *Limerick Reporter*, 4 May 1847.

2. Library and Archives Canada (LAC), Colonial Office Papers 384/82, Colonial Land and Emigration Commission, Eighth General Report (June 1848), pp. 15–17, Reel 1746, frames 166–68. The United Province of Canada reported that 89,738 departed for its port (15,330 died en route, in quarantine or in hospital); New Brunswick reported 17,074 (with 2,115 dying); Halifax received 2,000; St John's received 993; and Prince Edward Island witnessed 536 arrivals. This provides a rough tally of 110,341 headed for what are now Canadian ports. By comparison, 119,000 Irish immigrants entered American ports in that same year. Donald H Akenson, *The Irish in Ontario* (Montreal and Kingston, 1984), pp. 29–32.

3. *The Globe* (Toronto), 19 August 1845, and Robert Morgan, *Early Cape Breton: From Founding to Famine, 1784–1851* (Sydney, 2000), pp. 136–52.

4. Marianna O'Gallagher and Rose Masson Dompierre, *Eyewitness: Grosse Île 1847* (Quebec, 1995), p. xx.

5. *Limerick Chronicle*, 22 May 1847.

6. LAC, Colonial Office Papers, 384/82, Colonial Land and Emigration Commission, Eighth General Report (June 1848), pp. 15–17.

7. Mark G. McGowan, *Death or Canada: The Irish Famine Migration to Toronto, 1847* (Toronto, 2009), p. 28.

8. British Parliamentary Papers, vol. 17, Sessions, 1847–48, Report of A.C. Buchanan, 31 March 1848, pp. 471–77.

9. This is suggested strongly in Robert Grace, 'Irish Immigration and Settlement in a Catholic City, 1842–1861', *Canadian Historical Review* 84 (June 2003), p. 240.

10. A good description of typhus is found in O'Gallagher and Dompierre, *Eyewitness*, p. 52.

11. O'Gallagher and Dompierre, *Eyewitness*, Table 8, p. 340.

12. LAC, Stephen De Vere Testimony, Select Committee, CO 384/79535; and Stephen De Vere to Earl Grey, 30 November 1847, in Arthur Doughty, ed., *The Elgin-Grey Papers, 1846–1852* (Ottawa, 1937), pp. 1341–42.

13. Colleen M. Towns, 'Relief and order: The public response to the 1847 Irish Famine migration to Upper Canada', MA thesis, Queen's University, Kingston, 1990, p. 35.

14. Nancy McMahon, 'Les Religieuses Hospitalières de St. Joseph and the typhus epidemic, Kingston, 1847–8', *Historical Studies* (Canadian Catholic Historical Association) 58 (1991), p. 54.

15. Towns, 'Relief and order', p. 47.

16. Hawke to A.C. Buchanan, 11 April 1847, Hawke Letterbook, Hawke Papers, RG 11-3, Archives of Ontario (hereafter Hawke Letterbook).

17. Hawke to J.E. Campbell, 29 June 1847, Hawke Letterbook.

18. Hawke to Buchanan, 15 July 1847, Hawke Letterbook.

19. Report of the Board of Health, 27 May 1847, Council Minutes, City of Toronto Archives.

20. *British Colonist*, 12 June 1847; Dominick Daly to W.H. Boulton (copy), 7 June 1847, Hawke Papers, RG 11-3, Archives of Ontario.

21. *The Globe* (Toronto), 5 August 1847.

22. James Young Diary, 13 August 1847, Archives of St James Cathedral Toronto.

23. *The Globe* (Toronto), 25 August 1847.

24. Hawke to Buchanan, 26 July 1847, Hawke Letterbook.

25. *The British Colonist*, 22 June 1847.

26. Ibid.

27. James T. Connor, *Doing Good: The Life of Toronto's General Hospital* (Toronto: University of Toronto Press, 200), p. 44.

28. *British Colonist*, 25 June 1847 and 23 July 1847.

29. *The Mirror*, 18 February 1848.

30. Hawke to Honourable W. Cayley, Inspector General, 23 November 1847, Hawke Letterbook; British Parliamentary Papers, Papers Relative to Emigration to the British Provinces in North America, no. 14, Copy of Dispatch from Earl of Elgin to Earl Grey, 17 March 1848; *The Mirror*, 26 November 1847.

31. Mark G. McGowan, *Michael Power: The Struggle to Build the Catholic Church on the Canadian Frontier* (Montreal and Kingston, 2005).

32. *The Mirror*, 22 September 1847.

33. *The Cross* (Halifax), 23 October 1847; *The Mirror*, 8 October 1847; and *Mélanges religieux*, 5 October 1847.

34. R.B. Sullivan to George Gurnett, 2 May 1848, Hawke Papers, RG 11-3, Archives of Ontario; Terrence O'Neil and Samuel G. Lynn to Samuel B. Harrison, Surrogate Court of York, 27 November 1851; *British Colonist*, 11 November 1851; Hawke to J.E. Sullivan, 9 November 1847, Hawke Letterbook.

35. McGowan, *Death or Canada*, p. 90; *British Colonist*, 31 July 1847 and 28 August 1847.

36. The story ran through issues of *The Mirror* in August and September 1847.

37. *The Mirror*, 10 September 1847; *The Patriot*, 17 August 1847; *British Colonist*, 20 August 1847; *Toronto Examiner*, 18 August 1847.

38. *The Globe* (Toronto), 28 July 1847; Andre Charbonneau and Doris Drolet-Dube, *A Register of the Deceased Persons at Sea and on Grosse Île in 1847* (Ottawa, 1997), pp. 60 and 99. Recently, historian Bruce Elliott has suggested that the Willis family may very well have been George and Sarah Willis, who emigrated from Offaly. Elliott found them in the database that formed the primary evidence for his *Irish Migrants in the Canadas: A New Approach* (Montreal and Kingston, 1988), email to the author, 29 May 2010.

39. Gilbert Tucker, 'Famine Immigration to Canada, 1847,' *American Historical Review* 36 (April 1933), p. 534.

40. Mark McGowan, *Creating Canadian Historical Memory: The Case of the Famine Migration of 1847* (Ottawa: Canadian Historical Association, Canada's Ethnic Group Series, No. 30).

### GROSSE ÎLE, QUEBEC

1. Marianna O'Gallagher and Rose Masson Dompierre, *Eyewitness: Grosse Île, 1847* (Quebec, 1995), p. xvii.

2. Susannah Moodie, 'A Visit to Grosse Île', chapter 1 of her *Roughing It in the Bush: or, Forest Life in Canada*, (1852).

3. O'Gallagher and Dompierre, *Eyewitness Grosse Île*, p. xviii.

4. O'Gallagher and Dompierre, *Eyewitness Grosse Île*, p. xx.

5. George Douglas to Rev. Armine W. Mountain (Quebec), 21 December 1846, citied in O'Gallagher and Dompierre, *Eyewitness Grosse Île*, pp. 7–8.

6. *Limerick Chronicle*, 29 May 1847.

7. *Morning Chronicle* (Quebec), 18 May 1847.

8. O'Gallagher and Dompierre, *Eyewitness Grosse Île*, Table 8, p. 352.

9. Andre Charbonneau and Andre Sevigny, *1847 Grosse Île: A Record of Daily Events* (Ottawa, 1997), p. 16.

10. O'Gallagher and Dompierre, *Eyewitness Grosse Île*, Table 8, p. 352; Gallery 7, National Famine Museum, Strokestown Park, County Roscommon; Stephen J. Campbell, *The Great Irish Famine: Words and Images from the Famine Museum, Strokestown Park, County Roscommon* (Strokestown, 1994), p. 48.(Ottawa, 2006), 11. Diane Lary 'Edward said: Orientalism and Occidentalism', vol. 17, no. 2, pp. 3–15.

11. Marianna O'Gallagher, *Grosse Île: Gateway to Canada, 1832–1837* (Quebec, 1984), pp. 117–43.

12. Peter Duffy, *The Killing of Denis Mahon: A Mystery of Old Ireland* (New York, 2007).

13. xiii'Examination of AC Buchanan,' 21 July 1847, as cited in O'Gallagher and Dompierre, *Eyewitness Grosse Île*, p. 201.

14. *Eyewitness*, 250.

15. Rev. E.A. Taschereau to Archbishop Joseph Signay, 3 June 1847, cited in O'Gallagher and Dompierre, *Eyewitness Grosse Île*, p. 84.

16. 'Report of AC Buchanan for 1848', Colonial Office Papers, vol. 384, Library and Archives Canada.

17. O'Gallagher, *Grosse Île*, p. 70.

18. Mark G. McGowan , *Creating Canadian Historical Memory: The Case of the Famine Migration of 1847*, Canada's Ethnic Group Series, no. 30 (Ottawa, 2006).

19. O'Gallagher, *Grosse Île*, p. 105.

### THE FAMINE AND NEW YORK CITY

1. New York State Commissioners of Emigration, *Annual Reports of the Commissioners of Emigration of the State of New York: From the Organization of the Commission, May 5,*

*1847, to 1860, Inclusive: Together with Tables and Reports, and Other Official Documents* (The Commission, 1861). Data for 1890 summarised in Table A.6 in R.H. Bayor and T.J. Meagher, *The New York Irish* (Baltimore, 1997), 558–59. I use the data from the 1861 report throughout this chapter for the total numbers of Irish immigrants to New York. For commentary on sources for nineteenth century Irish immigration, see C. Ó Gráda, 'A note on nineteenth-century Irish emigration statistics', *Population Studies* 29.1 (March 1975), pp. 143–49.

2. Paul A. Gilje, 'The development of an Irish–American community in New York before the Great Migration', in *The New York Irish*, ed. Ronald H. Bayor and Timothy J. Meagher (Baltimore, 1997); David N Doyle, 'The Irish in North America, 1776–1845,' in *A New History of Ireland, V: Ireland under the Union, 1801–1870*, ed. W.E. Vaughan (Oxford, 2009).

3. Ira Rosenwaike, *Population History of New York City* (Syracuse University Press, 1972).

4. Edwin G. Burrows and Mike Wallace, *Gotham: A History of New York City to 1898* (Oxford, 2000), pp. 544–45; Leo Hershkowitz, 'The Irish and the emerging city: Settlement to 1844,' in *The New York Irish*, ed. Ronald H. Bayor and Timothy J. Meagher (Baltimore, 1997).

5. Gilje, 'The development of an Irish–American community.'

6. Tyler Anbinder, *The Five Points: The 19th-Century New York City Neighborhood That Invented Tap Dance, Stole Elections, and Became the World's Most Notorious Slum* (New York, 2001); Burrows and Wallace, *Gotham*.

7. This quotation is from a description of Irish emigrants in 'Emigrants from Europe,' *New York Herald*, 14 June 1845. Even before famine immigration began in earnest, New Yorkers were used to describing Irish immigrants in terms of vast and almost unfathomable numbers.

8. Hasia R. Diner, '"The most Irish city in the Union": The era of the Great Migration, 1844–1877,' in *The New York Irish*, ed. Ronald H. Bayor and Timothy J. Meagher (Baltimore, 1997).

9. New York State Commissioners of Emigration, *Annual Reports*, p. 288.

10. Kerby A. Miller, *Emigrants and Exiles: Ireland and the Irish Exodus to North America* (New York, 1985), p. 296; calculated from the figures in New York State Commissioners of Emigration, *Annual Reports*.

11. Alan M. Kraut, *Silent Travelers: Germs, Genes and the 'Immigrant Menace'* (New York, 1994).

12. Alan M. Kraut, 'Plagues and prejudice,' in *Hives of Sickness: Public Health and Epidemics in New York City*, ed. David Rosner (New Brunswick, NJ, 1995).

13. New York State Commissioners of Emigration, *Annual Reports*, p. iv.

14. Friedrich Kapp, *Immigration, and the Commissioners of Emigration of the State of New York* (D. Taylor, 1870), p. 107.

15. Burrows and Wallace, *Gotham*, p. 508; Kapp, *Immigration, and the Commissioners*, pp. 126–29.

16. Burrows and Wallace, *Gotham*, p. 778.

17. For an example of an investigation of one of the worst private hospitals/almshouses, see Kapp, *Immigration, and the Commissioners*.

18. Bayor and Meagher, (eds) *The New York Irish*. Table 2, p. 110.

19. Tyler Anbinder, 'From Famine to Five Points: Lord Lansdowne's Irish tenants encounter North America's most notorious slum', *The American Historical Review* 107.2 (April 2002), pp. 351–87.

20. Diner, '"The most Irish city in the Union"'; Hasia R. Diner, *Erin's Daughters in America: Irish Immigrant Women in the Nineteenth Century* (Baltimore, 1983).

21. Helen E. Hatton, *The Largest Amount of Good: Quaker Relief in Ireland, 1654–1921* (Montreal, 1993); Christine Kinealy, *This Great Calamity: The Irish Famine, 1845–52* (Dublin, 1994), pp. 163–64.

22. Edward K. Spann, *The New Metropolis: New York City, 1840–1857* (New York: Columbia University Press, 1983); Diner, '"The Most Irish City in the Union"'.

23. Joseph P. Ferrie, *Yankees Now: Immigrants in the Antebellum United States, 1840–1860* (New York, 1999), chap. 6. While Roediger contends that non-African-American workers from a range of backgrounds employed a language of class to subvert non-white racial classification, Noel Ignatiev asserts that the Irish self-consciously sought the privileges of whiteness as a means of participating in American politics as American citizens, and of rejecting their 'Irishness' (David R. Roediger, *The Wages of Whiteness: Race and the Making of the American Working Class* [London & New York, 1999]; Noel Ignatiev, *How the Irish Became White* [New York, 1995]).

24. Diane Ravitch, *The Great School Wars: A History of the New York City Public Schools* (Baltimore, 2000).

25. C. Ó Gráda, 'The early history of Irish savings banks', WP08/04, Centre for Economic Research Working Paper Series, Department of Economics, University College Dublin, 2008; Marion R. Casey, 'Refractive history: Memory and the founders of the Emigrant Savings Bank,' in *Making the Irish American: History and Heritage of the Irish in the United States*, ed. J. Lee and Marion R. Casey (New York, 2006).

26. New York State Commissioners of Emigration, *Annual Reports*, Table A, Rosenwaike, *Population History of New York City*.

27. For discussions of post-Famine Irish immigration, see Miller, *Emigrants and Exiles*, p. 8; David Fitzpatrick, *Irish emigration 1801–1921* (Dublin, 1984). For post-Famine immigration to New York City, see Bayor and Meagher, *The New York Irish*, sec. III–V.

## THE GREAT FAMINE AND AUSTRALIA

1. Charles Bateson, *The Convict Ships* (Sydney, 1983), pp. 336–57; Robin Haines, *Life and Death in the Age of Sail* (Sydney, 2003), pp. 84, 113, 234 262.

2. Ruth Dudley Edwards, *An Atlas of Irish History* (London, 1973), p. 145; *The Macquarie Book of Events* (Macquarie University, NSW, 1983), pp. 63, 64; Thomas Keneally, *Australians: Origins to Eureka* (Sydney, 2009), pp. 503–4.

3. Patrick O'Farrell, *The Irish in Australia* (Sydney, 1986), pp. 25, 36; for Plunkett, see John N. Molony, *An Architect of Freedom* (Canberra, 1973) and *Australian Dictionary of Biography*, online edition (hereafter ADB), alphabetical listing for Plunkett; R. Therry, *Reminiscences of Thirty Years' Residence in New South Wales and Victoria* (London, 1863) and ADB; for Ned Ryan, see Niamh Brennan, 'The Ballagh Barracks "Rioters"', in *Exiles From Erin*, ed. Bob Reece (Dublin, 1991), pp. 64, 81–82; for Dan Deniehy, see Cyril Pearl, *Brilliant Dan Deniehy* (Melbourne, 1972) and ADB).

4. Thomas Keneally, *The Great Shame* (New York, 1998), pp. 280–81; John Molony, *The Eureka Stockade* (Melbourne, 2001), pp. 28–29.x

5. Haines, *Life and Death in the Age of Sail*, pp. 43–46; Keneally, *Australians*, pp. 346–47.

6. Mounteagle [*sic*] Papers, National Library of Ireland, 1 October 1846; Christine Kinealy, *A Death-Dealing Famine: The Great Hunger in Ireland* (London, 1997), pp. 122, 142.

7. Christopher O'Mahony and Valerie Thompson, *Poverty to Promise: The Monteagle Emigrants, 1838–58* (Sydney, 1994), pp. 97–98.

8. Oral evidence to author from Justice Terry Sheahan, New South Wales Land and Environment Court, August 1997.

9. O'Mahony and Thompson, *Poverty to Promise*, pp. 10, 13, 134.

10. Caroline Chisholm, *Emigration and Transportation Relatively Considered* (London, 1847); Trevor McClaughlin, *Barefoot and Pregnant? Irish Famine Orphans in Australia* (Melbourne, 1991), pp. 1–4.

11. McClaughlin, *Barefoot and Pregnant?*, pp. 3–23, *passim*; Richard Reid and Cheryl Mongan, *'A Decent Set of Girls': The Irish Famine Orphans of the* Thomas Arbuthnot (Yass, NSW, 1996), p. 98.

12. *Votes and Proceedings of the Legislative Council of New South Wales*, vol. 1, 1850, pp. 397, no. 271, 19 December 1848; McClaughlin, *Barefoot and Pregnant?*, pp. 21–23, *passim*; Reid and Mongan, *'A Decent Set of Girls'*, pp. 99–114, *passim*.

13. Bateson, *The Convict Ships*, pp. 368–69; Kinealy, *A Death-Dealing Famine*, p. 11; Sinead Curley, 'Clare Convicts before and after the Famine', in *Irish Convicts: The Origins of Convicts Transported to Australia*, ed. Bob Reece (Dublin, 1989), pp. 81–112, *passim*; G. Rudé, *Protest and Punishment* (Oxford, 1978), pp. 3–5, 34; L.L. Robson, *The Convict Settlers of Australia* (London, 1966), pp. 74–78.

14. Keneally, *Great Shame*, p. 181; Curley, 'Clare Convicts before and after the Famine', pp. 108–9.

15. Documents on Larkin and Shields, Ship's Indent, *Parmelia*, 4/7076; Ship's Indent *Whitby* 2/8282; Tickets of Leave and Pardons, 2/8208, 4/4163 etc., Archives Office of New South Wales; O'Farrell, *The Irish in Australia*, pp. 144, 171, 202–4, 221–40.

16. Charles Gavan Duffy, *Four Years of Irish History* (Sydney, 1883), pp. 7–12, 166–68, 553–55, 603–5, 641ff, 758–60; Richard Davis, *The Young Ireland Movement* (Dublin, 1987), pp. 37–81, 117–39, 147–55, 158–62; Blanche M. Touhill, *William Smith O'Brien and His Revolutionary Companions in Penal Exile* (Columbia, MO, 1981), pp. 1–27, *passim*.

17. Richard Davis, ed., *'To Solitude Confined': The Tasmanian Journal of William Smith O'Brien* (Sydney, 1995) from National Library of Ireland MS 3923 and MS 449; Touhill, *William Smith O'Brien*, pp. 56–59; T.J. Kiernan, *The Irish Exiles in Australia* (Melbourne, 1954), pp. 93–94.

18. T.J. Kiernan, *The Irish Exiles in Australia*, pp. 65, 70, 71, 94; Davis,'*To Solitude Confined*', pp. 39–40, 256; J.H. Cullen, *Young Ireland in Exile* (Dublin, 1928), pp. 118–24.

19. Keneally, *Great Shame*, pp. 241–48, 260–67, 320–27, 365–67, *passim*.

20. Davis,'*To Solitude Confined*', pp. 180, 407, 427

21. Touhill, *William Smith O'Brien*, pp. 182–210, *passim*.

22. Cyril Pearl, *The Three Lives of Gavan Duffy* (Sydney, 1979), pp. 163–230, *passim*; Keneally, *Great Shame*, pp. 284, 494–96, 582, 604.

23. Pearl, *Gavan Duffy*, p. 163–230.

24. Keneally, *Great Shame*, p. 284, 494–96, 582, 604.

## IRELAND AND MORETON BAY, 1848–52

1. *The Nation*, 8 December 1851.

2. Extensive work on the Irish orphan girls in Australia has been carried out by: Trevor McClaughlin, *Barefoot and Pregnant? Irish Famine Orphans in Australia*, vol. 1 (Melbourne: The Genealogical Society of Victoria, 1991); vol. 2 (2002); Richard Reid and Cheryl Mongan, *'A Decent Set of Girls': The Irish Famine Orphans of the* Thomas Arbuthnot, *1849–50* (Yass, NSW: Yass Heritage Project, 1996); Libby Connors, 'The politics of ethnicity: Irish Orphan Girls at Moreton Bay', in *Irish-Australian Studies: Papers delivered at the Seventh Irish-Australian Conference, July 1993*, ed. Rebecca Pelan (Sydney: Crossing Press, 1994), pp. 167–81; Libby Connors and Bernadette Turner, '"I cannot do any more": Resistance, respectability and ruin – recapturing the Irish Orphan Girls in the Moreton Bay districts', in *Irish Women in Colonial Australia*, ed. Trevor McClaughlin (St Leonards NSW: Allen & Unwin, 1998), pp. 105–22; Perry McIntyre and Joan Dwyer, 'Family history, "professional" history and academic history: Who

owes what to whom?', in *Descent* 29, pt 2 (1999), pp. 78–81. See also the website of the memorial established at Hyde Park Barracks, Sydney, where every year an oration is presented [www.irishfaminememorial.org].

3. Currently, 188 girls of nearly 4,000 despatched to Australia have been positively identified as Queensland residents. A few whose names are duplicated among the total group still defy precise allocation to specific colonies while yet others moved across borders during their lifetimes.

4. McClaughlin, *Barefoot and Pregnant?*, vol. 2, p. 147.

5. John Ward, 'Earl Henry Grey, 1802–1894', *Australian Dictionary of Biography*, vol. 1 (Melbourne: Melbourne University Press, 1966), p. 480.

6. 'Sir George Grey, 1799–1882', *Dictionary of National Biography*, vol. 23 (1891), pp. 183–84.

7. T.M. Devine, *Clanship to Crofters' War* (Manchester: Manchester University Press, 1994), p. 163. Trevelyan also was involved in the emigration of highlanders affected by famine to Australia.

8. Clarendon Papers, Box 80, 16 February 1849, quoted in Donal A. Kerr, '*A Nation of Beggars?' Priests, People and Politics in Famine Ireland, 1846–1852*, (Oxford: Clarendon Press, 1994), p. 197.

9. Elizabeth Rushen, *Single & Free: Female Migration to Australia, 1833–1837* (Kew, Vic.: Australian Scholarly Publishing, 2003).

10. R.B. Madgwick, *Immigration into Eastern Australia, 1788–1951* (Adelaide, SA: Sydney University Press, 1937/69), p. 193.

11. Trevelyan to Somerville, 25 January 1848, Trevelyan Papers, T64/368A, The National Archives, London.

12. Jennifer Harrison, 'A willing community: Origins of Irish immigration to Queensland', in *Brisbane: The Ethnic Presence since the 1850s*, Brisbane History Group Papers, No. 12 (1993), pp. 33–40. Both these ships carried Irish passengers who originated mainly in Armagh, Tipperary, Clare and Galway, the counties which were to feature so prominently in Queensland's nineteenth-century migration patterns.

13. Ignatius Murphy, *A People Starved: Life and Death in West Clare, 1845–1851* (Dublin: Irish Academic Press, 1996), pp. 12–13. W.E. Vaughan and A.J. Fitzpatrick, eds., *Irish Historical Statistics: Population, 1821–1971* (Dublin: Royal Irish Academy, 1978), p. 8, shows the population of County Clare in 1841 as 286,394 and in 1851 as 212,440, a decrease of over 25%.

14. *Illustrated London News*, 15 December 1849.

15. The situation in County Clare is described more fully in Jennifer Harrison, 'Old World famine, New World plenty: The career of Sir Arthur Edward Kennedy', *Familia: Ulster Genealogy Review* 15 (1999), pp. 68–86. 'Relating to proceedings for the relief of distress & the state of the unions and workhouses in Ireland, 1847–48', 11 February 1848, BPP, Famine Ireland 3, LVI, p. 790.

16. *Limerick Chronicle*, 10 November 1849.

17. *Illustrated London News*, 22 December 1849.

18. Richard Reid, 'The Great Famine – Australian Connections', in *Australian Commemoration of the Great Irish Famine*, ed. J. Ronayne and V. Noone (Melbourne: Victoria University, 1996), p. 29, refers to Kennedy's donation to the Mayo relief fund in 1880.

19. Walter Vandeleur, 18 years, arrived on the *Newcastle* at Brisbane on 14 November 1877, and was joined by Michael, 21, on the *Dunbar Castle* into Brisbane on 26 October 1880. Mathias Vandeleur, 25, James, 18, and Martin, 14, travelled together on the *Quetta*, which berthed on 6 April 1886. Then another Martin Vandeleur arrived on the *Tara* on 30 March 1892 (Queensland State Archives).

20. James Godkin, *The Land War in Ireland: A History for the Times* (New York, 1870).

21. Kerr, '*A Nation of Beggars?*', p. 198.

22. Richard Davis, *Revolutionary Imperialist: William Smith O'Brien, 1803–1864* (Sydney: Crossing Press, 1998), pp. 258–96; Robert Sloan, *William Smith O'Brien and the Young Ireland Rebellion of 1848* (Dublin: Four Courts Press, 2000), pp. 291–303.

23. Kevin O'Doherty was another who deliberately prefixed his name with the 'O' in deference to Daniel O'Connell.

24. Ross and Heather Patrick, *Exiles Undaunted: The Irish Rebels Kevin and Eva O'Doherty* (Brisbane: University of Queensland Press, 1989), pp. 3, 8, 109 and *passim*.

25. This figure represented approximately 25% of total immigration to Queensland. By 1881 the native-born outnumbered migrants. See Jennifer Harrison, 'The people of Queensland, 1859–1900: Where did the immigrants come from?', *Journal* (Royal Historical Society of Queensland)13.6 (1988), pp. 189–200.

26. Line 16 of Eavan Boland, 'That the Science of Cartography is Limited', Eavan Boland, *In a Time of Violence* (Manchester, 1994), p. 5.

## SECTION VII: LEGACY

### LAND REFORM IN POST-FAMINE IRELAND

1. *Census of Ireland, 1851, Parts I–VI* (Dublin, 1852–57); 'The Irish Census', review in *Irish Quarterly Review* vol. VI (December, 1858), p. 838. For quote from Trevelyan see *idem*.

2. John O'Donovan to Daniel MacCarthy, 19 February 1847, MS 132 (18), National Library of Ireland (NLI). For an incisive analysis of landlord reaction to the Famine, see Desmond Norton, *Landlord, Tenants, Famine: The business of an Irish Land Agency during the Famine* (Dublin, 2006). For the reaction of a specific landowner to post-

Famine reconstruction, see Gerard J. Lyne, *The Lansdowne Estate in Kerry under W.S. Trench, 1849–72* (Dublin, 2001).

3. John O'Donovan to Daniel MacCarthy, 1 April 1848, MS 132 (19), NLI.

4. Richard Davis, *The Young Ireland Movement* (Dublin, 1987); James S. Donnelly, *The Great Irish Potato Famine* (Stroud, Gloucestershire, 2002), chapters 8 and 9. John Mitchel's *Jail Journal* remains the most powerful indictment of British politics during the Famine.

5. 'The Irish Census', p. 836.

6. See Patrick O'Sullivan, ed. *The Irish Worldwide: History, Heritage and Identity*, 6 vols (London and New York, 1992–97), for a variety of perspectives on emigration.

7. James Fintan Lalor, 'X', *Irish Felon*, 24 June 1848. David N. Buckley, *James Fintan Lalor: Radical* (Cork, 1990), is an interesting biography. See also Tomás O Néill, *Fiontán O Leathlobhair* (Ath Cliath, 1962).

8. *Freeman's Journal*, 29 November 1880, quoting the *Guardian*.

9. 'The Irish Census', p. 842; James O'Shea, *Prince of Swindlers: John Sadleir, MP, 1813–56* (Dublin, 1999) has a fascinating account of the purchase of major estates under the Encumbered Estates Act by John Sadleir using bogus securities. Pádraig G. Lane, 'The Encumbered Estate's court and Galway land ownership, 1849–1858', in *Galway: History and Society*, ed. Gerard Moran and Raymond Gillespie (Dublin, 1996), pp. 375–419, is an important assessment of the regional impact of the legislation.

10. J.H. Whyte, *The Tenant League and Irish Politics in the Eighteen-fifties* (Dundalk, 1966).

11. *Freeman's Journal*, 15 October 1856.

12. Patrick Lavelle, *The Irish landlord since the Revolution* (Dublin, 1870).

13. W.E. Vaughan, *Sin, Sheep and Scotsmen: John Greig Adair and the Derryveagh Evictions* (Belfast, 1983).

14. Gerard Moran, 'William Scully and Ballycohey – a fresh look', *Tipperary Historical Society Journal* (1992), pp. 63–74.

15. E.R. Norman, *The Catholic Church and Irish Politics in the Eighteen-sixties* (Dundalk, 1969).

16. T.W. Moody, 'Fenianism, Home Rule and the Land War', in *The Course of Irish History*, ed. T.W. Moody and F.X. Martin, rev. and enlarged ed. (Cork, 1994), pp. 275–93.

17. For details of the various Land Acts and acreages transferred, see C.F. Kolbert and T. O'Brien, *Land Reform in Ireland: A Legal History of the Irish Land Problem and Its Settlement* (Cambridge, 1975); W.F. Bailey, 'Ireland since the Famine: A sketch of fifty years' economic and legislative changes', *Journal of the Statistical and Social Enquiry Society of Ireland*, vol. XI (1903), pp. 129–42; Joseph Johnston, *Irish Agriculture in Transition* (Dublin, 1951), pp. 1–12; D.A. Chart, 'Two centuries of Irish agriculture: A statistical retrospect, 1672–1905', *Journal of the Statistical and Social Inquiry Society of Ireland*, vol. XI (1903), pp. 163–74; Thomas O'Sullivan, 'Land policy in Ireland' in *Towards Modern Land Policies*, ed. Davis McEntire and Danilo Agnostini (Padua, 1970), pp. 123–61; William P. Coyne, ed. *Ireland: Industrial and Agricultural* (Dublin, 1901), especially 'Statistical survey of Irish agriculture in 1901', pp. 178–200. Table 1 is based on a combination of these sources.

18. *Return of Owners of Land of One Acre and Upwards in the Several Counties, Counties of Cities and Counties of Towns in Ireland, 1876* (reprint, Baltimore, Maryland, 1988). The editors of *The Times*, 7 January 1881, were so impressed by the findings that they produced a map of ownership in Ireland.

19. Tom Jones Hughes, 'The estate system of land ownership in nineteenth-century Ireland' in *The Shaping of Ireland: The Geographical Perspective*, ed. W. Nolan (Dublin, 1986), pp. 137–50.

20. For the economic and political contexts of land reform, see Cormac Ó Gráda, *Ireland: A New Economic History, 1780–1939* (Oxford, 1994); D. McCartney, 'From Parnell to Pearse, 1891–1921', in *The Course of Irish History*, ed. T.W. Moody and F.X. Martin, rev. and enlarged ed. (Cork, 1994), pp. 294–312; Paul Bew, *Land and the National Question in Ireland, 1858–1882* (Dublin, 1978); E.D. Steele, *Irish Land and British Politics: Tenant Right and Nationality* (Cambridge, 1973), W.E. Vaughan, *Landlords and Tenants in mid-Victorian Ireland* (Oxford, 1994).

21. Carla King, *Michael Davitt* (Dundalk, 1999), pp. 18–37; F.S.L. Lyons, *Charles Stewart Parnell* (London, 1977), p. 92 for reference to Westport speech.

22. Lyons, *Charles Stewart Parnell*, p. 134.

23. For vivid eyewitness accounts of the Boycott saga, see reports in the *Freeman's Journal*, 20–29 November 1880.

24. *Report from her majesty's commissioners of inquiry into the working of the landlord and tenant (Ireland) Act, 1870* (London, 1881).

25. Joseph Lee, *The Modernisation of Irish Society, 1848–1918* (Dublin, 1973), pp. 65–105, has an incisive analysis of the Land War.

26. Lawrence Geary, *The Plan of Campaign* (Cork, 1986). For Luggacurran, see *Freeman's Journal*, 23 March 1887.

27. D.G. Marnane, 'Fr. David Humphreys and New Tipperary' in *Tipperary: History and Society*, ed. T. McGrath and W. Nolan (Dublin, 1985), pp. 367–78.

28. Henry Norman, *A Chapter in the History of Irish Landlordism: Reprinted with Several Additional Chapters from the* Pall Mall Gazette *and Illustrated with Sketches from Instantaneous Photographs by the Author* (London, 1887); William O'Brien, *Christmas on the Galtees* (Dublin, 1878), was an immensely popular account of the great hardships faced by the tenants of Nathaniel Buckley; Mary Ryan, *The Clongorey Evictions* (Naas, 2001); see also the reproduction of the Lawrence photographs of eviction scenes on

the Vandeleur Estate, Kilrush, County Clare, in Noel Kissane, ed. *The Land War, 1879–1903* (Dublin, 1976).

29. Congested Districts Board Ireland, Inspector's local reports 1892–98 (known as the baseline reports). These were not published but bound in a large volume, two copies of which are known to be in existence. William Micks, *A History of the Congested Districts Board* (Dublin, 1925); W. Nolan, 'New farms and fields: Migration policies of state land agencies, 1891–1980' in *Common Ground: Essays on the Historical Geography of Ireland Presented to T. Jones Hughes*, ed. W.J. Smyth and K. Whelan (Cork, 1988), pp. 296–319; Ciara Breathnach, *The Congested Districts Board of Ireland, 1891–1923: Poverty and Development in the West of Ireland* (Dublin, 2005).

30. *The Irish Land Bill, 1903, Speech of the Rt. Hon., the O'Conor Don at the Irish Landowner's Convention, Dublin, on 24th April, 1903*, (London and Dublin, 1903), p. 12. For an evocative perspective on the final days of landlordism, see Mark Bence-Jones, *Twilight of the Ascendancy* (London, 1987); for a detailed study of the Irish Land Commission, see Terence Dooley, *The Land Question in Independent Ireland* (Dublin, 2004). For an excellent analysis of the travails of a grazier family in the early twentieth century, see Brendan Ó Cathaoir, 'Another Clare: Ranchers and moonlighters,' in *Clare: History and Society* (Dublin, 2008), pp. 359–423.

31. W.B. Yeats, 'Upon a House Shaken by the Land Agitation' in *The Green Helmet and Other Poems* (1910). Desmond McCabe, 'Sir William Gregory', *Dictionary of Irish Biography* (Cambridge, 2009), vol. 4, p. 260. The house at Coole Park was demolished in 1941.

32. The ballad 'Carden's Wild Domain' is attributed to Timothy Corcoran (1857–1928), who reputedly wrote it while serving as a Catholic priest in Dubuque, Iowa, U.S.A. 'Domain' is a variation of the word demesne, the parkland and home farm of the landlord from which tenants were excluded.

33. For farm statistics since the Famine, see Central Statistics Office, *Farming since the Famine: Irish Farm Statistics, 1847–1996* (Dublin, 1997). For the Catholic Church in post-Famine Ireland, see P.J. Corish, ed. *The History of Irish Catholicism* (Dublin, 1967–71) especially vol. 5, fascicules vii–x.

## LEGACY AND LOSS: THE GREAT SILENCE AND ITS AFTERMATH

1. In translation: Certainly, the Famine had an impact on Irish. But one could not suggest on that account that it was the primary reason for the loss of the language. Regarding the retreat of Irish, the Famine was but one of the influences. Seán de Fréine, 'An Gorta agus an Ghaeilge', in *Gnéithe den Ghorta*, ed. Cathal Póirtéir (Baile Átha Cliath, 1995), pp. 55–68.

2. Máiréad Nic Craith, *Malartú Teanga: An Ghaeilge i gCorcaigh sa Naoú hAois Déag* (Bremen, 1993).

3. Niall Ó Cíosáin, 'Gaelic culture and language shift' in *Nineteenth-Century Ireland: A Guide to Recent Research*, ed. Laurence M. Geary and Margaret Kelleher (Dublin, 2005). pp. 136–52.

4. Pierre Bourdieu, *Language and Symbolic Power* (Cambridge, 1991).

5. *Census of Ireland, 1851, Part IV: Report on Ages and Education* (London, 1855).

6. Nic Craith, *Malartú Teanga*.

7. Garrett FitzGerald, 'Estimates for baronies of minimum level of Irish-speaking amongst successive decennial cohorts: 1771–1781 to 1861–1871', *Proceedings of the Royal Irish Academy*, 84 C, No. 3 (1984), pp. 130, 118.

8. Claire Kramsch, *Language and Culture* (Oxford, 1998), p. 12.

9. Hans-Georg Gadamer, *Truth and Method* (London, 1975), p. 391.

10. George Steiner, *Errata: An Examined Life* (London, 1997), p. 87.

11. Rev. Patrick Dineen, *Foclóir Gaedhilge agus Béarla: An Irish-English Dictionary* (Dublin, 1927), p. 543.

12. Nuala Ní Dhomhnaill, *The Ten Minute Mermaid*, poems in Irish by Nuala Ní Dhomhnaill, translated by Paul Muldoon (Dublin, 2007 [1998]).

13. Adam Phillips, 'Like a mermaid out of water' (review of *The Fifty Minute Mermaid* by Nuala Ní Dhomhnaill, translated by Paul Muldoon), *The Observer*, 27 January 2008, available online at: http://www.guardian.co.uk/books/2008/jan/27/poetry.features (accessed 25 October 2011).

14. Homi Bhabha, *The Location of Culture* (London, 1994), p. 86.

15. Cf. Máiréad Nic Craith, *Plural Identities, Singular Narratives: The Case of Northern Ireland* (New York, 2002).

16. James Joyce, *A Portrait of the Artist as a Young Man* (London, 1977 [1916]), p. 172.

17. Steiner, *Errata*, p. 87.

18. Hugo Hamilton, *Sailor in the Wardrobe* (London, 2006), p. 55.

19. Brian Friel, *Translations* (London, 1981).

20. Gayatri Chakravorty Spivak, 'The Rani of Sirmur: An essay in reading the archives', *History and Theory* 24 (1985), p. 253.

21. Loreto Todd, *Green English: Ireland's Influence on the English Language* (Dublin, 1999), p. 23.

## FAMINE AND THE IRISH DIASPORA

1. See, for instance , G. Davis, 'The historiography of the Irish Famine' in *The Meaning of the Famine*, ed. P. O'Sullivan (London, 1997), pp. 15-39.

2. N. Ó Cíosáin, 'Approaching a Folklore Archive: The Irish Folklore Commission and the Memory of the Great Famine', *Folklore* 115(2), 2004, pp. 222-232.

3. R. Dudley Edwards and T. D. Williams, *The Great Famine: Studies in Irish History*

*1845–52* (Dublin, 1956).

4. C. Woodham-Smith, *The Great Hunger. Ireland 1845-49* (London, 1962).

5. John W. Warnock, *The Politics of Hunger* (New York, 1987), Michelle Burge McAlpin, *Subject to Famine* (Princeton, 1983) Jean Drèze and Amartya Sen, *Hunger and Public Action* (Oxford, 1991), Megan Vaughan, *The Story of an African Famine: Gender and Famine in Twentieth-Century Malawi* (Cambridge, 1987) all cite Woodham-Smith. See R. Lucking, 'The Famine World Wide: the Irish Famine and the development of famine policy and famine theory' in *The Meaning of the Famine*, ed. P. O'Sullivan, pp. 195-232.

6. Davis, op. cit, p. 15.

7. For a discussion of literature and famine, see M. Kelleher, 'Irish Famine in Literature' in *The Great Irish Famine*, ed. C. Póirtéir (Cork, 1995), pp. 232-247.

8. G. Bexar, 'John Mitchel's *The Last Conquest of Ireland (Perhaps)* and Liam O'Flaherty's Famine: A question of tone', *Nordic Journal of English Studies* 6(2), 2007, p. 77.

9. Ó Cíosáin, op.cit., p. 224.

10. Ó Cíosáin, op. cit., p. 225.

11. K. A. Miller, *Emigrants and Exiles: Ireland and the Irish Exile to North America* (Oxford, 1985).

12. J. King, 'Famine Diaries? Narratives about Emigration from Ireland to Lower Canada and Quebec, 1832–1853', Simon Fraser University: 142, unpublished MA thesis (1996).

13. Ó Cíosáin, op.cit., p. 228. See also C. Ó Gráda, *Black '47 and Beyond: the Great Irish Famine in History, Economy and Memory* (Princeton, 1999), p. 197.

14. See Bexar, op.cit.

15. D. H. Akenson, *Small Differences: Irish Catholics and Irish Protestants 1815-1922* (Montréal and Kingston, 1988), p. 145.

16. K. Marx, *The Eighteenth Brumaire of Louis Bonaparte* (New York, 1963).

17. D. Lowenthal, 'Fabricating Heritage', *History and Memory* 10(1), 1998, p. 20.

18. D. H. Akenson, *The Irish Diaspora: A Primer* (Toronto, 1993) p. 20.

19. Miller, op.cit., pp.193-279.

20. D. H. Akenson, *Small Differences: Irish Catholics and Irish Protestants 1815-1922* (Dublin, 1988), p. 183.

21. R. Dudley Edwards and B. Hourican , *An Atlas of Irish History* (Abingdon, 2005) p. 141.

22. K. Kenny, *The American Irish: A History* (Harlow, 2000), p. 97.

23. A. Charbonneau and A. Sévigny, *1847, Grosse-Île au fil des jours* (Ottawa, 1997), p. 24.

24. Miller, op. cit., p. 569.

25. F. Neal, 'The Famine Irish in England and Wales' in *The Meaning of the Famine*, ed. P. O'Sullivan. (London, 1997), pp. 56-80.

26. Neal, op.cit., p. 74.

27. Neal, op.cit., p. 76.

28. B. Elliott, *Irish Migrants in the Canadas: A new approach* (Kingston, 1988), pp. 231-243.

29. P. F. Maguire, *The Irish in America* (New York, 1880, 4th edition), chapter 9. I thank Jason King for pointing out that Maguire was the first to draw attention to the Irish orphans of Grosse Île.

30. M. O'Gallagher, 'The orphans of Grosse Île: Canada and the adoption of Irish Famine orphans, 1847-48' in *The Meaning of the Famine*, ed. P. O'Sullivan, pp. 81-111.

31. Irlandais O'Québec
http://www.musee-mccord.qc.ca/expositions/expositionsXSL.php?lang=2&expoId=55&page=accueil, accessed 23 |July 2011.

32. J.J. Lee and M. R. Casey, ed. *Making the Irish American: History and Heritage of the Irish in the United States* (New York, 2006), p. 22.

33. H. R. Diner, '"The Most Irish City in the Union": The Era of the Great Migration, 1844-1877' in *The New York Irish*, ed. R. H. Bayor and T. J. Meagher (Baltimore, 1996), pp. 87-106.

34. All data are taken from H. R. Diner, '"The Most Irish City in the Union": The Era of the Great Migration, 1844-1877' in Lee and Casey, op. cit., pp. 87-106.

35. Lee and Casey, op.cit., p. 22.

36. J. J. Lee, 'Millennial Reflections on Irish-American History', *Radharc* 1: 37, 2000.

37. E. O'Donnell, '"The Scattering Debris of the Irish Nation': The Famine Irish and New York City, 1845-1855" in *The Hungry Stream: Essays on Emigration and Famine* , ed. E. M. Ward, (Belfast, 1997), p. 52.

38. N. Ignatiev, *How the Irish became White* (New York, 1995).

39. D. N. Doyle, 'The Remaking of Irish America, 1845-1880' in Lee and Casey, op.cit., p. 215.

40. Akenson, *Small Differences*, p. 144.

41. D. N. Doyle, 'Cohesion and Diversity in the Irish Diaspora', *Irish Historical Studies* 39(123), 1999, p. 414.

42. Akenson, *The Irish Diaspora: A Primer*, p. 219.

43. T. Guinnane, *The Vanishing Irish* (Princeton N.J., 1997)

44. Government of Ireland Commission on Emigration and Other Population Problems: Reports. Health (Dublin, 1954).

45. Quoted in R. Gellately, 'Between Exploitation, Rescue and Annihilation: Reviewing Schindler's List', *Central European History* 26 (4), 1993, p. 475.

46. P. Nora, 'Reasons for the current upsurge in memory', Eurozine, 2002: http://www.eurozine.com/articles/2002-04-19-nora-en.html, accessed 2

January 2012.
47. Quote in T. Cole, *Images of the Holocaust: the Myth of the 'Shoah Business'* (London, 1999), p. 175.
48. C. Fogarty (1995) *The Mass Graves of Ireland.* http://www.irishholocaust.org/, accessed 20 April 2012.
49. L. Kennedy (undated), *The Great Irish Famine and the Holocaust:* http://www.qub.ac.uk/sites/irishhistorylive/IrishHistoryResources/ArticlesandLectures/TheGreatIrishFamineandtheHolocaust/, accessed 20 April 2012.
50. M. Robinson, 'Cherishing the Irish Diaspora: Address by Uachtarán na hÉireann Mary Robinson to a Joint Sitting of the Houses of the Oireachtas', 1995: http://www.oireachtas.ie/viewdoc.asp?fn=/documents/addresses/2Feb1995.htm, accessed 20 April 2012.

## SECTION VIII: REMEMBERING THE FAMINE

### [THE FOLKLORE OF THE FAMINE: *SEANCHAS AN DROCHSHAOIL*

1. Nicholás Tóibín, Rinn na nGael (CIC104); *Come West Along the Road, Treasures from the RTÉ TV Archives.*
2. Colm Ó Caodháin, *Amhráin ar an Sean-Nós*, RTÉ CD; Maighread Ní Dhomhnaill, *Celtic Christmas*, vol. 2 (Windham Hill Collection)
3. *Glórtha ón Ghorta*, Cathal Póirtéir (Baile Átha Cliath, 1996).
4. *Famine Echoes*, Cathal Póirtéir (Dublin, 1995).
5. Guy Beiner, *Remembering the Year of the French: Irish Folk History and Social Memory* (Madison, 2007), p. 83.
6. IFC 842:39–42.
7. Mary Daly, 'The State Papers of a forgotten and neglected people'; the National Folklore Collection and the writing of Irish history in *Béaloideas, The Journal of the Folklore of Ireland Society*, 78/2010, p. 65 and p. 78.
8. Gay Beiner, *Remembering the year of the French, Irish Folk History and Social Memory* (Wisconsin, 2007); Niall Ó Ciosáin, 'Famine memory and popular representation of scarcity', in Ian McBride ed., *History and Memory in Modern Ireland* (Cambridge, 2000); Cormac Ó Gráda, *Black '47 and Beyond. The Great Irish Famine in History, Economics, Economy and Memory* (Princeton, 1999); Cormac Ó Gráda, *An Drochshaol, Béaloideas agus Amhráin* (Baile Átha Cliath, 1994).

### SITES OF MEMORY

1. British Parliamentary Papers, Famine Ireland 3, Session 1847-48. P. 711; See Kieran Foley, 'The Great Famine in Iveragh' in J. Crowley and J. Sheehan (eds) The Iveragh Peninsula: A Cultural Atlas of the Ring of Kerry (Cork, 2009), pp. 217-223
2. Mary Daly, 'Why the Great Famine got forgotten in the dark 1940s', Sunday Tribune, 22 January 1995. See also K. C. Kearns, Ireland's Arctic Siege: The big freeze of 1947 (Dublin, 2011).
3. Declan Kiberd, Irish Classics (London, 2000), p. 651
4. Peter Gray and Kendrick Oliver, 'The memory of catastrophe', History Today, 51, 2, p. 12
5. Behan described his artistic journey in a documentary from the RTÉ True Lives series, entitled Famine Ship, first broadcast in 1999.
6. Ibid.
7. Ibid.
8. Simon Schama, A History of Britain III: The Fate of Empire 1776–2001 (London, 2001), p. 304.
9. Edna Longley, 'Northern Ireland: commemoration, elegy, forgetting' in I. McBride (ed), History and Memory in Modern Ireland (Cambridge, 2001).
10. Fintan O'Toole, Ex-Isle of Erin (Dublin, 1997), p. 10.
11. Paul Ricoeur in Richard Kearney, Visions of Europe (Dublin, 1992); See also Richard Kearney, 'Memory and forgetting in Irish culture' in H. Friberg, I. Gilsenan Nordin and L. Yding Pedersen, Recovering Memory: Irish Representations of Past and Present (Newcastle, 2007).
12. Richard Howells, The Myth of the Titanic (London, 1999), p. 4.
13. John R. Gillis, Commemorations: The Politics of National Identity (Princeton, 1994), p. 20.

### 'REMEMBERING, NOT FORGETTING', A COMMEMORATIVE COMPOSITION

1. Helen Litton, The Irish Famine: An Illustrated History (Dublin, 1994; second edition, 2004).

### THE BIG HOUSE AND FAMINE MEMORY

1. There have been a number of works published on his murder including: Anne Coleman, Riotous Roscommon: Social Unrest in the 1840s (Dublin, 1999); Peter Duffy, The Killing of Major Denis Mahon: A Mystery of Old Ireland (New York, 2007); Robert Scally, The End of Hidden Ireland: Rebellion, Famine and Emigration (Oxford, 1995); Patrick Vesey, The Murder of Major Mahon, Strokestown, County Roscommon, 1847 (Dublin, 2008).
2. For Strokestown see, Lorraine Pearsall, 'Strokestown Park and the making of the Famine Museum: An interview with Declan Jones', South Carolina Review 32.1 (Fall
1999), pp. 195–201; Nuala C. Johnson, 'Where geography and history meet: Heritage tourism and the big house in Ireland', Annals of the Association of American Geographers 86.3 (1996), pp. 551–66; Susan Hood, 'The Famine in the Strokestown Park House archive', The Irish Review, 17/18 (Winter 1995), pp. 109–17; see also, Stephen J. Campbell, The Great Irish Famine: Words and Images from the Famine Museum, Strokestown Park, County Roscommon (1994); and Strokestown Park House & Garden Visitors Book (n.d.).
3. Quoted in R.V. Comerford, 'Foreword', in The Irish Country House: Its Past, Present and Future, ed. Terence Dooley and Christopher Ridgway (Dublin, 2011).
4. Callery, quoted in Fintan O'Toole, 'Bleak House', Irish Times, 14 May 1994; Luke Dodd, 'Heritage and the "Big House": Whitewash for rural history' Irish Reporter 6 (9–11), p. 10.
5. For a study in the wider decline, see Terence Dooley, The Decline of the Big House in Ireland: A Study of Irish Landed Families 1860–1960 (Dublin, 2001).
6. O'Toole, 'Bleak House'; see also Irish Times, 20 September 1991.
7. Christopher Ridgway, 'Making and meaning in the historic house: New perspectives in England, Ireland, and Scotland', in The Irish Country House: Its Past, Present and Future, ed. Terence Dooley and Christopher Ridgway (Dublin, 2011).
8. Irish Times, 20 September 1991; O'Toole, 'Bleak House'; Pearsall, 'Strokestown Park'.
9. Terry Eagleton, 'Feeding off history', The Observer, 20 February 1994; Niall Ó Ciosáin, 'Hungry grass', Circa 68 (Summer 1994), p. 24; Peter Gray, 'Strokestown Famine Museum', History Ireland 2.2 (Summer 1994), p. 5.
10. Nuala O'Faolain, 'Preserving a house that divided us', Irish Times, 23 May 1988.
11. O Ciosáin, 'Hungry grass', p. 27.
12. Ridgway, 'Making and meaning in the historic house'.

### A GREAT FAMINE DISCOVERY OF VIKING GOLD: VESNOY, STROKESTOWN, COUNTY ROSCOMMON

1. C.J.T. Carson, Technology and the Big House in Ireland, c.1800 to c.1930 (New York, 2009), p. 21.
2. See, for instance, W.T. Mulvany, 'Collection of antiquities presented to the Royal Irish Academy on the part of the Commissioners of Public Works in Ireland', Proceedings of the Royal Irish Academy 5 (Appendix V), pp. xxxi–lxvi.
3. W.R. Wilde, A Descriptive Catalogue of the Antiquities of Gold in the Museum of the Royal Irish Academy (Dublin, 1862), pp. 51–52.
4. Ballina Chronicle, 4 July 1849.

### MAPPING THE GREAT FAMINE IN IRISH ART

1. Adrian Hastings, The Construction of Nationhood: Identity, Religion and Nationalism (Cambridge, 1997), p. 20.
2. Terry Eagleton, 'Feeding off history', The Observer Magazine, 20 February 1994.
3. Fintan O'Toole, 'Ministerial announcement of committee to look into memorial', Irish Times, 7 November 2009.
4. Ibid.
5. For a full discussion of this, see Ciaran Benson, The Cultural Psychology of Self: Place, Morality and Art in Human Worlds (London, 2001).
6. Reproduced in Anne Crookshank and the Knight of Glin, The Watercolours of Ireland: Works on Paper in Pencil, Pastel and Paint, c.1600–1914 (London, 1994) p. 57.
7. See L. Perry Curtis Jr, Apes and Angels: The Irishman in Victorian Caricature (Smithsonian, 2004); The Great Irish Famine, New Jersey Holocaust and Genocide Curriculum at Secondary Level (1996); Dennis Clark, 'Paddies, pigs and perils: The Irish in American cartoon depiction', Centre for Irish Studies (Philadelphia, n.d.) .
8. David Dickson, 'The other great Irish Famine', in The Great Irish Famine, ed. Cathal Póirtéir (Cork, 1995).
9. Margaret Crawford, 'The Great Irish Famine, 1845–9: Image versus reality', in Ireland: Art into History, ed. Raymond Gillespie and Brian P. Kennedy (Dublin, 1994); Niamh O'Sullivan, Aloysius O'Kelly: Art, Nation, Empire (Dublin, 2010), ch. 3; Curtis, Apes and Angels.
10. Michael Baxandall, Patterns of Intention: On the Historical Explanation of Pictures (New Haven, 1987).
11. Catherine Marshall, 'History and memorials: Fine art and the Great Famine in Ireland', in Visual, Material and Print Culture in Nineteenth-Century Ireland, ed. Ciara Breathnach and Catherine Lawless (Dublin, 2010).
12. Walid Raad, lecture delivered at the Oval Room, Rotunda, Parnell Street, Dublin, 19 November 2009, and The Raad Files, The Atlas Group Archive [www.theatlasgroup.org/].
13. Christine Kinealy, 'How politics fed the Famine', Natural History, January 1996, pp. 33–35.
14. W.E.H. Lecky, 'Leaders of public opinion in Ireland' [1861], in The Field Day Anthology of Irish Writing, ed. Seamus Deane (Derry, 1991), vol. 2, pp. 214–23.
15. Reproduced in L. Perry Curtis Jr, 'The Four Erins; Feminine images of Ireland, 1780–1900', Éire-Ireland 33.3/4 (1998/1999). p. 91.
16. Elizabeth Butler, From Sketch-book and Diary (London, 1909).
17. Kevin Whelan, 'Immoral Economy: Interpreting Erskine Nicol's The Tenant', in America's Eye: Irish Paintings from the Collection of Brian P. Burns, ed. Adele Dalsimer and Vera Kreilkamp (Boston, 1996), p. 59.
18. Benson, The Cultural Psychology of Self, p. 126.

## LITERATURE AND THE FAMINE

1. 'Irish landlords', *Dublin University Magazine* 28:4 (Oct. 1846), pp. 443–56; Isaac Butt, 'The famine in the land', *Dublin University Magazine* 29:4 (April 1846), pp. 501–40.
2. William Carleton, *The Black Prophet* (1847; rpt Shannon, 1972), pp. 1, 406, 188, 224, 226n.
3. Anthony Trollope, *Castle Richmond* (1860; New York, 1984), pp. 333, 438.
4. Mary Anne Sadlier, *New Lights: Or, Life in Galway* (??, 1853)
5. 'Answers to correspondents', *The Nation* (14 March 1846), p. 10.
6. Matthew Magrath, 'One of many', in *The Hungry Voice: Poetry of the Irish Famine*, ed. Chris Morash (1989; rpt Dublin, 2009), p. 62.
7. James Clarence Mangan, 'Siberia', in *The Hungry Voice*, p. 143.
8. Hubert O'Grady, *Famine* (ed. Stephen Watt), *The Journal of Irish Literature* 14.1 (1985), p. 49.
9. W.B. Yeats, *Collected Plays* (London, 1934), p. 33.
10. Julieann Ulin, '"Buried! Who would have buried her?": Famine "ghost graves" in Samuel Beckett's *Endgame*', in *Hungry Words: Images of the Famine in the Irish Canon*, ed. George Cusack and Sarah Goss (Dublin, 2006), p. 201. This collection also contains essays on traces of the Famine in *Dracula*, *Playboy of the Western World*, and *Ulysses*, among other texts.
11. James Joyce, *Ulysses* (New York, 1990), p. 478. See: Mary Lowe-Evans, *Crimes against Fecundity: Joyce and Population Control* (Syracuse, NY, 1989).
12. 'The Irish Peasantry', *The Nation* 3.44 (12 July 1845), p. 650.
13. Christopher Morash, *Writing the Irish Famine* (Oxford, 1995), pp. 155–62.
14. William Carleton, *The Squanders of Castle Squander* (London, 1852), vol. 2, pp. 92–93.
15. Steven Marcus, 'Hunger and Ideology', in *Representations: Essays on Literature and Society* (New York, 1975), pp. 10–11.
16. Stuart McLean, *The Event and Its Terrors: Ireland, Famine, Modernity* (Stanford, 2004), p. 1.
17. Carleton, *Squanders of Castle Squander*, vol. 2, pp. 271–311.

## SECTION IX: HUNGER AND FAMINE TODAY

### THE GREAT FAMINE AND TODAY'S FAMINES

1. This is a revised version of a chapter of the same title published in *The Great Irish Famine* ed. Cathal Póirtéir (Cork, 1995).
2. According to the OECD, Ireland's net official development assistance in 2007 as a percentage of Gross National Income (0.55%) placed it sixth out of the twenty-two members of that organisation's Development Assistance Committee (OECD Development Assistance Committee, *Aid Targets Slipping out of Reach?* [Paris, 2008], Annex A).
3. Edmund M. Hogan, *The Irish Missionary Movement: A Historical Survey, 1830–1980* (Dublin, 1990). Note also the remarks of the late Conor Cruise O'Brien in *To Katanga and Back* (London, 1965), p. 170.
4. C. Ó Gráda, *Famine: A Short History* (Princeton, 2009), ch. 2.
5. Amartya Sen, *Poverty and Famines: An Essay on Entitlement and Deprivation* (Oxford, 1981), pp. 86, 116, 134, 195–216; S.G. Wheatcroft and R.W. Davies, 'Population', in *The Economic Transformation of the Soviet Union, 1913–1945*, ed. R.W. Davies, M. Harrison and S.G. Wheatcroft (Cambridge, 1994) pp. 67–77; B. Ashton, K. Hill, A. Piazza and R. Zeitz, 'Famine in China, 1958–61', *Population and Development Review* 10.4 (1984), pp. 613–46. On Malawi and Niger see C. Ó Gráda, 'Famines past, famine's future', *Development & Change* 42.1 (2011).
6. Richard McMahon, 'A violent society? Homicide rates in Ireland, 1831–1850', *Irish Economic and Social History* 36 (2009), pp. 1–20.
7. Sen, *Poverty and Famines*, pp. 93–96; Stephen Devereux, *Theories of Famine* (London, 1993), pp. 95–97; W. Dando, *The Geography of Famine* (London, 1980), pp. 101–2.
8. The issue is discussed further in my own *Ireland Before and After the Famine* (Manchester, 1993), ch. 3, and *Ireland: A New Economic History, 1780–1939* (Oxford, 1994), ch. 8. See also Peter Gray, 'Punch and the Great Famine', *History Ireland* 1.2 (1993), pp. 26–33; R.D. Edwards, *The Pursuit of Reason: 'The Economist', 1843–1993* (London, 1993), ch. 4.
9. See M. Bergman, 'The potato blight in the Netherlands and its social consequences (1845–1847)', *International Review of Social History* 17.3 (1967), pp. 391–431; Richard Paping and Vincent Tassenaar, 'The consequences of the potato disease in the Netherlands, 1845–1860: A regional approach', in *When the Potato Failed: Causes and Effects of the Last European Subsistence Crisis, 1845–50*, ed. C. Ó Gráda, R. Paping, and E. Vanhaute (Turnhout, 2007), pp. 149–84.
10. Michel Garenne, Dominique Waltisperger, Pierre Cantrelle, and Osée Ralijoana, 'The demographic impact of a mild famine in an African city: The case of Antananarivo, 1985–87', in *Famine Demography: Perspectives from the Past and Present*, ed. Tim Dyson and C. Ó Gráda (Oxford, 2002), pp. 204–217.
11. Stephen G. Wheatcroft, 'Explaining the similarities between the Chinese and Soviet Leap famines," paper presented at the International Workshop on Famines of the Twentieth-Century, University of Melbourne, 8–11 June 2010; C. Ó Gráda, 'Great Leap into famine', *Population and Development Review* 37.1 (2011).
12. Devereux, *Theories of Famine*, pp. 133–47; information from Trócaire.
13. Sen, *Poverty and Famines*, chs. 6–7. See also Jean Drèze and Amartya Sen, *The Polit-*

*ical Economy of Hunger*, 3 vols (Oxford, 1991).
14. For discussion and references, see Devereux, *Theories of Famine*, pp. 76–81.
15. For an overview of the potato's importance and the shortfalls in 1845 and 1846, see Austin Bourke, *The Visitation of God? The Potato and the Irish Famine* (Dublin, 1993), chs. 4–8.
16. On emigration, the best single source remains Oliver MacDonagh, 'Irish emigration to the United States of America and the British colonies during the famine', in *The Great Famine: Studies in Irish History, 1845–52*, ed. R.D. Edwards and T.D. Williams, new edition (Dublin, 1994), pp. 319–90. See also, Desmond Norton, 'On landlord-assisted emigration from some Irish estates in the 1840s', *Agricultural History Review* 53.1 (2005), pp. 24–40; Robert Scally, *The End of Hidden Ireland: Rebellion, Famine, and Emigration* (New York, 1995). On Strokestown, see Stephen J. Campbell, *The Great Irish Famine: Words and Images from the Famine Museum, Strokestown Park, County Roscommon* (Strokestown, 1994), pp. 40–42; Peter Duffy, *The Killing of Major Denis Mahon* (New York, 2007).
17. This point is argued further in C. Ó Gráda and Kevin J. O'Rourke, 'Mass migration as disaster relief: Lessons from the Great Irish Famine', *European Review of Economic History* 1.1 (1997), pp. 3–25.
18. Sen, *Poverty and Famines*, p. 215; Tim Dyson and Arup Maharatna, 'Excess mortality during the Bengal famine: A re-evaluation', *Indian Economic and Social History* 28.3 (1991), pp. 281–97.
19. Peter Solar, 'The Great Famine was no ordinary subsistence crisis', in *Famine: The Irish Experience*, ed. E.M. Crawford (Edinburgh, 1989), p. 118.
20. For an overview, see C. Ó Gráda, *An Drochshaol: Béaloideas agus Amhráin* (Dublin, 1994); C. Ó Gráda, *Ireland's Great Famine: Interdisciplinary Perspectives* (Dublin, 2006), pp. 217–33.

### FOOD SECURITY, FOOD POVERTY, FOOD SOVEREIGNTY

1. Food and Agriculture Organization of the United Nations (hereafter FAO), *The State of Food Insecurity in the World 2008: High Food Prices and Food Security – Threats and Opportunities* (Rome, 2008); FAO, *World Agriculture: Towards 2030/2050. Interim Report: Prospects for Food, Nutrition, Agriculture and Major Commodity Groups* (Rome, 2006).
2. J. Hoddinott, *Operationalizing Household Food Security in Development Projects: An Introduction*, International Food Policy Research Institute Technical Guide No.1 (Washington, D.C., 1999).
3. E. Clay, *Food Security: A Status Review of the Literature*, research report (London, 1997).
4. A. Sen, *Poverty and Famines: An Essay on Entitlement and Deprivation* (Oxford, 1981).
5. FAO, *Report of the World Food Summit, 13–17 November 1996, Part One* (Rome, 1997).
6. FAO, *Report of the World Food Summit*, p. 83.
7. American Planning Association (APA), 'Policy guide on community and regional food planning' (2007), available online at: www.planning.org/policyguides.
8. W. Poortinga, 'Perceptions of the environment, physical activity, and obesity', *Social Science and Medicine* 63 (2006), pp. 2835–46.
9. M. Winne, 'Community food security: Promoting food security and building healthy food systems', Community Food Security Coalition (2008), p. 2, available online at: http://www.foodsecurity.org/PerspectivesOnCFS.pdf (accessed 25 October 2011).
10. International Assessment of Agricultural Knowledge, Science and Technology for Development (IAASTD), *Synthesis Report: A Synthesis of the Global and Sub-Global IAASTD Reports* (Washington, D.C., 2009).
11. Forum for New World Governance, 'Peoples' food sovereignty statement' (2010), available online at: http://www.world-governance.org (accessed 30 November 2010).
12. M. Windfuhr and J. Jonsén, *Food Sovereignty: Towards Democracy in Localized Food Systems* (Bourton-on-Dunsmore, Rugby, UK: ITDG Publishing, 2005).
13. FAO, *The State of Food Insecurity in the World 2008*.

### FIGHTING WORLD HUNGER IN THE TWENTY-FIRST CENTURY

1. C. Ó Gráda, *Famine: A Short History* (Princeton, 2009).
2. *The Year of Living Dangerously*, film directed by Peter Weir (Australia: McElroy & McElroy, Metro-Goldwyn-Mayer [MGM], 1982).
3. A. Sen, *Democracy as Freedom* (Oxford, 1999).
4. International Covenant on Economic, Social and Cultural Rights, adopted 16 December 1966, entered into force 3 January 1976, G.A. Res. 2200A (XXI), UN Doc. A/6316 (1966), 142 state parties.
5. O. De Schutter, 'The right to food: Fighting for adequate food in a global crisis", *Harvard International Review* 31 (Summer 2009) pp. 38–42.
6. Available online at: www.concern.net.
7. UN Food and Agriculture Organisation (FAO), *The State of Food Insecurity in the World 2001* (Rome, 2002). For the evolution of food security definitions, see: http://www.fao.org/docrep/ 005/y4671e/y4671e06.htm.
8. Available online at: www.fao.org.
9. Available online at: www.fao.org.
10. Global Hunger Index (2010), available online at: http://www.ifpri.org/publication/2010-global-hunger-index.
11. A. Sumner, *Global Poverty and the New Bottom Billion: What if Three-Quarters of the World's Poor Live in Middle-Income Countries?* (Sussex, 2010).

12. Available online at: www.wfp.org.

13. S. Collins, 'Changing the way we address severe malnutrition during famine', *The Lancet* 358 (2001), pp. 498–501.

14. P. Wagstaff and M. Harty, 'The impact of conservation agriculture on food security in three low veldt districts of Zimbabwe', *Trócaire Development Review* (2010), pp. 67–84.

15. *The Lancet*, 'Maternal and child undernutrition', special series (January 2008).

16. IFAD and ROPPA, "Farmers Speak Out: The Vision and Recommendations of Africa's Farmers' Organizations for the Comprehensive Africa Agriculture Development Program." International Food and Agricultural Development (Rome, 2010).

17. Irish Hunger Task Force (2008), available online at: http://www.irishaid.gov.ie/uploads/hunger_task_force.pdf.

18. Hunger Envoy Report (2010), available online at: http://www.irishaid.gov.ie/uploads/Hunger_Envoy_Report.pdf

19. S. Beckett, *The Unnamable* (New York, 1958)

# Index of Places

*Page references for counties and provinces refer to information about the county or province as a whole. References for specific towns are listed under the town name.*

Abbeyleix, County Laois 110, 123, 131, 140, 332, 496
Achill, County Mayo 187, 245, 282, 283, 284, 288, 290, 478–9
Adelaide, 554-5, 563
Aghadown, County Cork 195, 197, 474
Aghamore, County Mayo 187, 282, 286
Aghamullen, County Monaghan 13, 18, 443
Alice Springs, 554, 563
Allihies, County Cork 233
America *see United States*
Amsterdam, 31
Annaduff, County Leitrim 22, 194, 195, 282
Antrim, County 15, 49, 56, 146, 185, 187, 193, 194, 196, 200, 219, 269, 417, 418, 419, 421, 422, 423, 425, 426–9, 432, 460, 461, 497, 498, 500, 501, 502, 580, 639
Antrim town 89, 93, 129, 143, 162, 419
Aran Islands, County Galway 293
Ardee, County Louth 248, 329, 498
Ardmore, County Waterford 185
Arklow, County Wicklow 242, 248, 329
Armagh, County 13, 146, 185, 197, 200, 268, 417, 418, 419, 422, 423, 424, 425, 426, 429, 440, 449, 496, 498, 501, 502
Armagh town 228, 241, 245, 252, 253, 419, 420, 496, 553
Arthurstown, County Wexford 245, 326
Askeaton, County Limerick 244, 248, 466
Athboy, County Meath 250, 336, 338
Athlone, County Westmeath 108, 228, 241, 245, 251, 310, 311, 316
Athy, County Kildare 6, 94, 245, 326, 498
Australia 11, 97, 98, 148, 155, 214, 217, 263–4, 304, 396, 429, 489, 504, 550–67, 591, 592, 595

Bailieborough, County Cavan 93, 111
Ballina, County Mayo 51, 52, 57, 89, 91, 95, 104, 138, 240, 241, 245, 252, 253, 287, 288, 289, 290, 484, 500
Ballinamore, County Leitrim 298, 299, 300, 301, 302
Ballinasloe, County Galway 59, 138, 251, 153, 288
Ballincollig, County Cork 234, 237
Ballinrobe, County Mayo 89, 91, 95, 123, 138, 143, 147, 187, 245, 267, 290, 497
Ballintober, County Mayo 197, 282, 289, 290
Ballintober, County Roscommon 308, 311
Ballybunion, County Kerry 245

Ballycastle, County Antrim 111, 421
Ballydehob, County Cork 236, 372, 373, 374, 376, 378, 474
Ballyhaunis, County Mayo 145, 289
Ballyhean, County Mayo 197, 289
Ballykilcline, County Roscommon 314, 318–23
Ballymacarret, County Antrim 434, 436, 437
Ballymahon, County Longford 125
Ballymena, County Antrim 129, 241, 419, 496, 498
Ballymoe, County Roscommon 290, 308
Ballymoney, County Antrim 111, 422
Ballynakill, County Galway 13, 106, 185, 187, 290, 291, 292, 293, 294, 296, 564
Ballysakeery, County Mayo 195, 282, 289
Ballysheehan, County Tipperary 197, 361
Ballyshannon, County Donegal 110, 123, 138, 158, 159, 160–61, 162, 187, 300, 420–21, 422, 455, 500
Ballyvaughan, County Clare 125, 245, 367
Balrothery, County Dublin 250, 498
Baltimore, County Cork 245-7
Baltimore, USA, 216
Baltinglass, County Wicklow 93, 138, 242, 329
Baltyboys, County Wicklow 354-7
Banagher, County Offaly 235, 244, 245, 311, 350, 353
Banbridge, County Down 185, 422, 553
Bandon, County Cork 240, 241, 245, 498
Bangladesh 650, 651, 652, 675
Bangor, County Down 421
Bantry, County Cork 89, 91, 93, 165, 209, 210, 242, 245, 270, 360, 374, 378, 421, 497
Baunreagh, County Laois 38–40
Bawnboy, County Cavan 125, 161
Beara peninsula, County Cork 187, 233, 359
Belfast 20, 59, 89, 96–7, 110, 116, 143, 158, 159, 161, 162, 180, 181, 185, 189, 190, 228, 235, 240, 250, 252, 253, 254, 264, 270, 425, 426, 427–9, 430, 434–9, 496–7, 509, 514, 515, 525, 526, 553, 564
Belgium 30, 31, 68, 487
Belmullet, County Mayo 51, 104, 106, 125, 245, 286, 293, 371
Bengal 650, 653, 656
Biafra 638, 650, 651, 666
Binghamstown, County Mayo 250, 285
Birmingham, 396, 592
Birr, County Offaly 94, 111, 118–19, 123, 138, 241, 253, 255, 259, 350, 351, 352, 353, 496, 616–17
Blarney, County Cork 474
Blessington, County Wicklow 354
Bohermeen, County Meath 337, 339, 340
Borris, County Carlow 79

An Irish Aid-built road to Sinkata, Tigray, northern Ethiopia. [Photo: Clare Keogh]

Strokestown Sept 12th 1846

The following Persons are this day Recommended to Constitute the New Relief Committee for the Parishes of Bumlin, Kiltrustan and Lissonuffy in the Barony of Roscommon & County of Roscommon Pursuant to the Provisions of the Amended Acts of 10 Vic. Cap 107 —

1 Denis Mahon DL JP LtP Co Ros
2 The Coroner —
3 Thos Dillon —
4 David Hughes